T0344519

COMPUTATIONAL COMPLEXITY

This beginning graduate textbook describes both recent achievements and classical results of computational complexity theory. Requiring essentially no background apart from mathematical maturity, the book can be used as a reference for self-study for anyone interested in complexity, including physicists, mathematicians, and other scientists, as well as a textbook for a variety of courses and seminars. More than 300 exercises are included with a selected hint set.

The book starts with a broad introduction to the field and progresses to advanced results. Contents include definition of Turing machines and basic time and space complexity classes, probabilistic algorithms, interactive proofs, cryptography, quantum computation, lower bounds for concrete computational models (decision trees, communication complexity, constant depth, algebraic and monotone circuits, proof complexity), average-case complexity and hardness amplification, derandomization and pseudorandom constructions, and the PCP Theorem.

Sanjeev Arora is a professor in the department of computer science at Princeton University. He has done foundational work on probabilistically checkable proofs and approximability of **NP**-hard problems. He is the founding director of the Center for Computational Intractability, which is funded by the National Science Foundation.

Boaz Barak is an assistant professor in the department of computer science at Princeton University. He has done foundational work in computational complexity and cryptography, especially in developing "non-blackbox" techniques.

COMPUTATIONAL COMPLEXITY

A Modern Approach

SANJEEV ARORA
Princeton University

BOAZ BARAK
Princeton University

CAMBRIDGE
UNIVERSITY PRESS

CAMBRIDGE
UNIVERSITY PRESS

University Printing House, Cambridge CB2 8BS, United Kingdom

One Liberty Plaza, 20th Floor, New York, NY 10006, USA

477 Williamstown Road, Port Melbourne, VIC 3207, Australia

4843/24, 2nd Floor, Ansari Road, Daryaganj, Delhi - 110002, India

79 Anson Road, #06-04/06, Singapore 079906

Cambridge University Press is part of the University of Cambridge.

It furthers the University's mission by disseminating knowledge in the pursuit of education, learning and research at the highest international levels of excellence.

www.cambridge.org
Information on this title: www.cambridge.org/9780521424264

First published 2009
4th printing 2016

A catalogue record for this publication is available from the British Library

Library of Congress Cataloging in Publication data
Arora, Sanjeev.
  Computational complexity : a modern approach / Sanjeev Arora, Boaz Barak.
    p. cm.
  Includes bibliographical references and index.
  ISBN 978-0-521-42426-4 (hardback)
  1. Computational complexity. I. Barak, Boaz. II.Title.
  QA267.7.A76   2009
  511.3′52–dc22   2009002789

ISBN 978-0-521-42426-4 Hardback

To our wives—Silvia and Ravit

Contents

About this book

Computational complexity theory has developed rapidly in the past three decades. The list of surprising and fundamental results proved since 1990 alone could fill a book: These include new probabilistic definitions of classical complexity classes (**IP = PSPACE** and the **PCP** theorems) and their implications for the field of approximation algorithms, Shor's algorithm to factor integers using a quantum computer, an understanding of why current approaches to the famous **P** versus **NP** will not be successful, a theory of derandomization and pseudorandomness based upon computational hardness, and beautiful constructions of pseudorandom objects such as extractors and expanders.

This book aims to describe such recent achievements of complexity theory in the context of more classical results. It is intended to serve both as a textbook and as a reference for self-study. This means it must simultaneously cater to many audiences, and it is carefully designed with that goal in mind. We assume essentially no computational background and very minimal mathematical background, which we review in Appendix A. We have also provided a Web site for this book at http://www.cs.princeton.edu/theory/complexity with related auxiliary material, including detailed teaching plans for courses based on this book, a draft of all the book's chapters, and links to other online resources covering related topics. Throughout the book we explain the context in which a certain notion is useful, and *why* things are defined in a certain way. We also illustrate key definitions with examples. To keep the text flowing, we have tried to minimize bibliographic references, except when results have acquired standard names in the literature, or when we felt that providing some history on a particular result serves to illustrate its motivation or context. (Every chapter has a notes section that contains a fuller, though still brief, treatment of the relevant works.) When faced with a choice, we preferred to use simpler definitions and proofs over showing the most general or most optimized result.

The book is divided into three parts:

- *Part I: Basic complexity classes.* This part provides a broad introduction to the field. Starting from the definition of Turing machines and the basic notions of computability theory, it covers the basic time and space complexity classes and also includes a few more modern topics such as probabilistic algorithms, interactive proofs, cryptography, quantum computers, and the **PCP** Theorem and its applications.

- *Part II: Lower bounds on concrete computational models.* This part describes lower bounds on resources required to solve algorithmic tasks on concrete models such as circuits and decision trees. Such models may seem at first sight very different from Turing machines, but upon looking deeper, one finds interesting interconnections.
- *Part III: Advanced topics.* This part is largely devoted to developments since the late 1980s. It includes counting complexity, average case complexity, hardness amplification, derandomization and pseudorandomness, the proof of the **PCP** theorem, and natural proofs.

Almost every chapter in the book can be read in isolation (though Chapters 1, 2, and 7 must not be skipped). This is by design because the book is aimed at many classes of readers:

- *Physicists, mathematicians, and other scientists.* This group has become increasingly interested in computational complexity theory, especially because of high-profile results such as Shor's algorithm and the recent deterministic test for primality. This intellectually sophisticated group will be able to quickly read through Part I. Progressing on to Parts II and III, they can read individual chapters and find almost everything they need to understand current research.
- *Computer scientists who do not work in complexity theory per se.* They may use the book for self-study, reference, or to teach an undergraduate or graduate course in theory of computation or complexity theory.
- *Anyone—professors or students—who does research in complexity theory or plans to do so.* The coverage of recent results and advanced topics is detailed enough to prepare readers for research in complexity and related areas.

This book can be used as a textbook for several types of courses:

- *Undergraduate theory of computation.* Many computer science (CS) departments offer an undergraduate Theory of Computation course, using, say, Sipser's book [Sip96]. Our text could be used to supplement Sipser's book with coverage of some more modern topics, such as probabilistic algorithms, cryptography, and quantum computing. Undergraduate students may find these more exciting than traditional topics, such as automata theory and the finer distinctions of computability theory. The prerequisite mathematical background would be some comfort with mathematical proofs and discrete mathematics, as covered in the typical "discrete math" or "math for CS" courses currently offered in many CS departments.
- *Introduction to computational complexity for advanced undergrads or beginning grads.* The book can be used as a text for an introductory complexity course aimed at advanced undergraduate or graduate students in computer science (replacing books such as Papadimitriou's 1994 text [Pap94] that do not contain many recent results). Such a course would probably include many topics from Part I and then a sprinkling from Parts II and III and assume some background in algorithms and/or the theory of computation.
- *Graduate complexity course.* The book can serve as a text for a graduate complexity course that prepares graduate students for research in complexity theory or related areas like algorithms and machine learning. Such a course can use Part I to review basic material and then move on to the advanced topics of Parts II and III. The book contains far more material than can be taught in one term, and we provide on our Web site several alternative outlines for such a course.

- *Graduate seminars or advanced courses.* Individual chapters from Parts II and III can be used in seminars or advanced courses on various topics in complexity theory (e.g., derandomization, the PCP Theorem, lower bounds).

We provide several teaching plans and material for such courses on the book's Web site. If you use the book in your course, we'd love to hear about it and get your feedback. We ask that you do not publish solutions for the book's exercises on the Web though, so other people can use them as homework and exam questions as well.

As we finish this book, we are sorely aware of many more exciting results that we had to leave out. We hope the copious references to other texts will give the reader plenty of starting points for further explorations. We also plan to periodically update the book's Web site with pointers to newer results or expositions that may be of interest to our readers.

Above all, we hope that this book conveys our excitement about computational complexity and the insights it provides in a host of other disciplines.

Onward to **P** versus **NP**!

Acknowledgments

Our understanding of complexity theory was shaped through interactions with our colleagues, and we have learned a lot from far too many people to mention here. Boaz would like to especially thank two mentors—Oded Goldreich and Avi Wigderson—who introduced to him the world of theoretical computer science and still influence much of his thinking on this area.

We thank Luca Trevisan for coconceiving the book (8 years ago!) and helping to write the first drafts of a couple of chapters. Several colleagues have graciously agreed to review for us early drafts of parts of this book. These include Scott Aaronson, Noga Alon, Paul Beame, Irit Dinur, Venkatesan Guruswami, Jonathan Katz, Valentine Kavanets, Subhash Khot, Jiří Matoušek, Klaus Meer, Or Meir, Moni Naor, Alexandre Pinto, Alexander Razborov, Oded Regev, Omer Reingold, Ronen Shaltiel, Madhu Sudan, Amnon Ta-Shma, Iannis Tourlakis, Chris Umans, Salil Vadhan, Dieter van Melkebeek, Umesh Vazirani, and Joachim von zur Gathen. Special thanks to Jiří, Or, Alexandre, Dieter, and Iannis for giving us very detailed and useful comments on many chapters of this book.

We also thank many others who have sent notes on typos or bugs, provided comments that helped improve the presentations, or answered our questions on a particular proof or reference. These include Emre Akbas, Eric Allender, Djangir Babayev, Miroslav Balaz, Arnold Beckmann, Ido Ben-Eliezer, Siddharth Bhaskar, Goutam Biswas, Shreeshankar Bodas, Josh Bronson, Arkadev Chattopadhyay, Bernard Chazelle, Maurice Cochand, Nathan Collins, Tim Crabtree, Morten Dahl, Ronald de Wolf, Scott Diehl, Dave Doty, Alex Fabrikant, Michael Fairbank, Joan Feigenbaum, Lance Fortnow, Matthew Franklin, Rong Ge, Ali Ghodsi, Parikshit Gopalan, Vipul Goyal, Stephen Harris, Johan Håstad, Andre Hernich, Yaron Hirsch, Thomas Holenstein, Xiu Huichao, Moukarram Kabbash, Bart Kastermans, Joe Kilian, Tomer Kotek, Michal Koucy, Sebastian Kuhnert, Katrina LaCurts, Chang-Wook Lee, James Lee, John Lenz, Meena Mahajan, Mohammad Mahmoody-Ghidary, Shohei Matsuura, Mauro Mazzieri, John McCullough, Eric Miles, Shira Mitchell, Mohsen Momeni, Kamesh Munagala, Rolf Neidermeier, Robert Nowotniak, Taktin Oey, Toni Pitassi, Emily Pitler, Aaron Potechin, Manoj Prabhakaran, Yuri Pritykin, Anup Rao, Saikiran Rapaka, Nicola Rebagliati, Johan Richter, Ron Rivest, Sushant Sachdeva, Mohammad Sadeq Dousti, Rahul Santhanam, Cem Say, Robert Schweiker, Thomas

Schwentick, Joel Seiferas, Jonah Sherman, Amir Shpilka, Yael Snir, Nikhil Srivastava, Thomas Starbird, Jukka Suomela, Elad Tsur, Leslie Valiant, Vijay Vazirani, Suresh Venkatasubramanisn, Justin Vincent-Foglesong, Jirka Vomlel, Daniel Wichs, Avi Wigderson, Maier Willard, Roger Wolff, Jureg Wullschleger, Rui Xue, Jon Yard, Henry Yuen, Wu Zhanbin, and Yi Zhang. Thank you!

Doubtless this list is still missing some of the people who helped us with this project over the years—if you are one of them we are both grateful and sorry.

This book was typeset using LATEX, for which we're grateful to Donald Knuth and Leslie Lamport. Stephen Boyd and Lieven Vandenberghe kindly shared with us the LATEX macros of their book *Convex Optimization*.

Most of all, we'd like to thank our families—Silvia, Nia, and Rohan Arora and Ravit and Alma Barak.

Sanjeev would like to also thank his father, the original book author in his family.

Introduction

As long as a branch of science offers an abundance of problems, so long it is alive; a lack of problems foreshadows extinction or the cessation of independent development.

– David Hilbert, 1900

The subject of my talk is perhaps most directly indicated by simply asking two questions: first, is it harder to multiply than to add? and second, why? ... I (would like to) show that there is no algorithm for multiplication computationally as simple as that for addition, and this proves something of a stumbling block.

– Alan Cobham, 1964

The notion of *computation* has existed in some form for thousands of years, in contexts as varied as routine account keeping and astronomy. Here are three examples of tasks that we may wish to solve using computation:

- Given two integer numbers, compute their product.
- Given a set of n linear equations over n variables, find a solution, if it exists.
- Given a list of acquaintances and a list of all pairs among them who do not get along, find the largest set of acquaintances you can invite to a dinner party such that every two invitees get along with one another.

Throughout history people had a notion of a process of producing an output from a set of inputs in a finite number of steps, and they thought of "computation" as "a person writing numbers on a scratch pad following certain rules."

One of the important scientific advances in the first half of the twentieth century was that the notion of "computation" received a much more precise definition. From this definition, it quickly became clear that computation can happen in diverse physical and mathematical systems—Turing machines, lambda calculus, cellular automata, pointer machines, bouncing billiards balls, Conway's *Game of life*, and so on. Surprisingly, all these forms of computation are equivalent—in the sense that each model is capable of implementing all computations that we can conceive of on any other model (see Chapter 1). This realization quickly led to the invention of the standard *universal electronic computer*, a piece of hardware that is capable of executing all possible programs. The computer's rapid adoption in society in the subsequent decades brought computation into every aspect of modern life and made computational issues important in design, planning, engineering, scientific discovery, and many other human endeavors. Computer *algorithms*, which are methods of solving computational problems, became ubiquitous.

But computation is not "merely" a practical tool. It is also a major scientific concept. Generalizing from physical models such as cellular automata, scientists now view many natural phenomena as akin to computational processes. The understanding of reproduction in living things was triggered by the discovery of self-reproduction in computational machines. (In fact, a book by the physicist Schroedinger [Sch44] predicted the existence of a DNA-like substance in cells before Watson and Crick discovered it and was credited by Crick as an inspiration for that research.) Today, computational models underlie many research areas in biology and neuroscience. Several physics theories such as QED give a description of nature that is very reminiscent of computation, motivating some scientists to even suggest that the entire universe may be viewed as a giant computer (see Lloyd [Llo06]). In an interesting twist, such physical theories have been used in the past decade to design a model for *quantum computation*; see Chapter 10.

Computability versus complexity

After their success in defining computation, researchers focused on understanding what problems are *computable*. They showed that several interesting tasks are *inherently uncomputable*: No computer can solve them without going into infinite loops (i.e., never halting) on certain inputs. Though a beautiful topic, computability will not be our focus in this book. We discuss it briefly in Chapter 1 and refer the reader to standard texts [Sip96, HMU01, Koz97, Rog87] for more details. Instead, we focus on *computational complexity theory*, which focuses on issues of *computational efficiency*—quantifying the amount of computational resources required to solve a given task. In the next section, we describe at an informal level how one can quantify *efficiency*, and after that we discuss some of the issues that arise in connection with its study.

QUANTIFYING COMPUTATIONAL EFFICIENCY

To explain what we mean by *computational efficiency*, we use the three examples of computational tasks we mentioned earlier. We start with the task of multiplying two integers. Consider two different methods (or *algorithms*) to perform this task. The first is *repeated addition*: to compute $a \cdot b$, just add a to itself $b - 1$ times. The other is the *grade-school algorithm* illustrated in Figure I.1. Though the repeated addition algorithm is perhaps simpler than the grade-school algorithm, we somehow feel that

```
          5   7   7
          4   2   3
      ─────────────
      1   7   3   1
  1   1   5   4
2 3   0   8
─────────────────
2   4   4   0   7   1
```

Figure I.1. Grade-school algorithm for multiplication. Illustrated for computing $577 \cdot 423$.

the latter is *better*. Indeed, it is much more efficient. For example, multiplying 577 by 423 using repeated addition requires 422 additions, whereas doing it with the grade-school algorithm takes 3 multiplications of a number by a single digit and 3 additions.

We will quantify the efficiency of an algorithm by studying how its number of *basic operations* scales as we increase the *size* of the input. For this discussion, let the basic operations be addition and multiplication of single digits. (In other settings, we may wish to throw in division as a basic operation.) The *size* of the input is the number of digits in the numbers. The number of basic operations used to multiply two n-digit numbers (i.e., numbers between 10^{n-1} and 10^n) is at most $2n^2$ for the grade-school algorithm and at least $n10^{n-1}$ for repeated addition. Phrased this way, the huge difference between the two algorithms is apparent: Even for 11-digit numbers, a pocket calculator running the grade-school algorithm would beat the best current supercomputer running the repeated addition algorithm. For slightly larger numbers even a fifth grader with pen and paper would outperform a supercomputer. We see that *the efficiency of an algorithm is to a considerable extent much more important than the technology used to execute it.*

Surprisingly enough, there is an even faster algorithm for multiplication that uses the *Fast Fourier Transform*. It was only discovered some 40 years ago and multiplies two n-digit numbers using $cn \log n \log \log n$ operations, where c is some absolute constant independent of n; see Chapter 16. We call such an algorithm an $O(n \log n \log \log n)$-step algorithm: see our notational conventions below. As n grows, this number of operations is significantly smaller than n^2.

For the task of solving linear equations, the classic *Gaussian elimination* algorithm (named after Gauss but already known in some form to Chinese mathematicians of the first century) uses $O(n^3)$ basic arithmetic operations to solve n equations over n variables. In the late 1960s, Strassen found a more efficient algorithm that uses roughly $O(n^{2.81})$ operations, and the best current algorithm takes $O(n^{2.376})$ operations; see Chapter 16.

The dinner party task also has an interesting story. As in the case of multiplication, there is an obvious and simple inefficient algorithm: Try all possible subsets of the n people from the largest to the smallest, and stop when you find a subset that does not include any pair of guests who don't get along. This algorithm can take as much time as the number of subsets of a group of n people, which is 2^n. This is highly unpractical—an organizer of, say, a 70-person party, would need to plan it at least a thousand years in advance, even if she has a supercomputer at her disposal. Surprisingly, we still do not know of a significantly better algorithm for this task. In fact, as we will see in Chapter 2, we have reasons to suspect that no efficient algorithm *exists*, because this task turns out to be equivalent to the *independent set* computational problem, which, together with thousands of other important problems, is **NP**-complete. The famous "**P** versus **NP**" question (Chapter 2) asks whether or not any of these problems has an efficient algorithm.

PROVING NONEXISTENCE OF EFFICIENT ALGORITHMS

We have seen that sometimes computational tasks turn out to have nonintuitive algorithms that are more efficient than algorithms used for thousands of years. It would therefore be really interesting to prove for some computational tasks that the current algorithm is the *best*—in other words, no better algorithms exist. For instance, we could try to prove that the $O(n \log n \log \log n)$-step algorithm for multiplication cannot be improved upon (thus implying that multiplication is inherently more difficult than addition, which does have an $O(n)$-step algorithm). Or, we could try to prove that there is no algorithm for the dinner party task that takes fewer than $2^{n/10}$ steps. Trying to prove such results is a central goal of complexity theory.

How can we ever prove such a nonexistence result? There are infinitely many possible algorithms! So we have to *mathematically prove* that each one of them is less efficient that the known algorithm. This may be possible because computation is a mathematically precise notion. In fact, this kind of result (if proved) would fit into a long tradition of *impossibility results* in mathematics, such as the independence of Euclid's parallel postulate from the other basic axioms of geometry, or the impossibility of trisecting an arbitrary angle using a compass and straightedge. Such results count among the most interesting, fruitful, and surprising results in mathematics.

In complexity theory, we are still only rarely able to prove such nonexistence of algorithms. We do have important nonexistence results in some concrete computational models that are not as powerful as general computers, which are described in Part II of the book. Because we are still missing good results for general computers, one important source of progress in complexity theory is our stunning success in *interrelating* different complexity questions, and the rest of the book is filled with examples of these.

SOME INTERESTING QUESTIONS ABOUT COMPUTATIONAL EFFICIENCY

Now we give an overview of some important issues regarding computational complexity, all of which will be treated in greater detail in later chapters. An overview of mathematical background is given in Appendix A.

1. Computational tasks in a variety of disciplines such as the life sciences, social sciences, and operations research involve searching for a solution across a vast space of possibilities (e.g., the aforementioned tasks of solving linear equations and finding a maximal set of invitees to a dinner party). This is sometimes called *exhaustive search*, since the search *exhausts* all possibilities. Can this exhaustive search be replaced by a more *efficient* search algorithm?

   As we will see in Chapter 2, this is essentially the famous **P** vs. **NP** question, considered *the* central problem of complexity theory. Many interesting search problems are **NP**-complete, which means that if the famous conjecture **P** $\neq$ **NP** is true, then these problems do not have efficient algorithms; they are *inherently intractable*.

2. Can algorithms use randomness (i.e., coin tossing) to speed up computation?

   Chapter 7 introduces randomized computation and describes efficient *probabilistic algorithms* for certain tasks. But Chapters 19 and 20 show a surprising recent result giving strong evidence that randomness does *not* help speed up computation too much, in the sense that any probabilistic algorithm can be replaced with a *deterministic* algorithm (tossing no coins) that is almost as efficient.

3. Can hard problems become easier to solve if we allow the algorithms to err on a small number of inputs, or to only compute an *approximate* solution?

    Average-case complexity and *approximation algorithms* are studied in Chapters 11, 18, 19, and 22. These chapters also show fascinating connections between these questions, the power of randomness, different notions of mathematical proofs, and the theory of error correcting codes.

4. Can we derive any practical benefit from computationally hard problems? For example, can we use them to construct cryptographic protocols that are *unbreakable* (at least by any plausible adversary)?

    As described in Chapter 9, the security of digital cryptography is intimately related to the **P** vs. **NP** question (see Chapter 2) and average-case complexity (see Chapters 18).

5. Can we use the counterintuitive quantum mechanical properties of matter to build faster computers?

    Chapter 10 describes the fascinating notion of *quantum computers* that use quantum mechanics to speed up certain computations. Peter Shor has shown that, if ever built, quantum computers will be able to factor integers efficiently (thus breaking many current cryptosystems). However, currently there are many daunting obstacles to actually building such computers.

6. Do we need people to prove mathematical theorems, or can we generate mathematical proofs automatically? Can we check a mathematical proof without reading it completely? Do interactive proofs, involving a dialog between prover and verifier, have more power than standard "static" mathematical proofs?

    The notion of *proof*, central to mathematics, turns out to be central to computational complexity as well, and complexity has shed new light on the meaning of mathematical proofs. Whether mathematical proofs can be generated automatically turns out to depend on the **P** vs. **NP** question (see Chapter 2). Chapter 11 describes *probabilistically checkable proofs*. These are surprisingly robust mathematical proofs that can be checked simply by reading them in very few probabilistically chosen locations, in contrast to the traditional proofs that require line-by-line verification. Along similar lines we introduce the notion of *interactive proofs* in Chapter 8 and use them to derive some surprising results. Finally, *proof complexity*, a subfield of complexity studying the minimal proof length of various statements, is studied in Chapter 15.

At roughly 40 years, complexity theory is still an infant science, and many important results are less than 20 years old. We have few complete answers for any of these questions. In a surprising twist, computational complexity has also been used to prove some metamathematical theorems: They provide evidence of the difficulty of resolving some of the questions of . . . computational complexity; see Chapter 23.

We conclude with another quote from Hilbert's 1900 lecture:

> *Proofs of impossibility were effected by the ancients . . . [and] in later mathematics, the question as to the impossibility of certain solutions plays a preminent part. . . .*
>
> *In other sciences also one meets old problems which have been settled in a manner most satisfactory and most useful to science by the proof of their impossibility. . . . After seeking in vain for the construction of a perpetual motion machine, the relations were investigated which must subsist between the forces of nature if such a machine is to be impossible; and this inverted question led to the discovery of the law of the conservation of energy. . . .*

It is probably this important fact along with other philosophical reasons that gives rise to conviction . . . that every definite mathematical problem must necessarily be susceptible to an exact settlement, either in the form of an actual answer to the question asked, or by the proof of the impossibility of its solution and therewith the necessary failure of all attempts. . . . This conviction . . . is a powerful incentive to the worker. We hear within us the perpetual call: There is the problem. Seek its solution. You can find it by pure reason, for in mathematics there is no ignorance.

Notational conventions

We now specify some of the notations and conventions used throughout this book. We make use of some notions from discrete mathematics such as strings, sets, functions, tuples, and graphs. All of these are reviewed in Appendix A.

Standard notation

We let $\mathbb{Z} = \{0, \pm 1, \pm 2, \ldots\}$ denote the set of integers, and $\mathbb{N}$ denote the set of natural numbers (i.e., nonnegative integers). A number denoted by one of the letters i, j, k, ℓ, m, n is always assumed to be an integer. If $n \geq 1$, then $[n]$ denotes the set $\{1, \ldots, n\}$. For a real number x, we denote by $\lceil x \rceil$ the smallest $n \in \mathbb{Z}$ such that $n \geq x$ and by $\lfloor x \rfloor$ the largest $n \in \mathbb{Z}$ such that $n \leq x$. Whenever we use a real number in a context requiring an integer, the operator $\lceil \ \rceil$ is implied. We denote by $\log x$ the logarithm of x to the base 2. We say that a condition $P(n)$ holds for *sufficiently large n* if there exists some number N such that $P(n)$ holds for every $n > N$ (for example, $2^n > 100n^2$ for sufficiently large n). We use expressions such as $\sum_i f(i)$ (as opposed to, say, $\sum_{i=1}^n f(i)$) when the range of values i takes is obvious from the context. If u is a string or vector, then u_i denotes the value of the ith symbol/coordinate of u.

Strings

If S is a finite set then a *string* over the alphabet S is a finite ordered tuple of elements from S. In this book we will typically consider strings over the *binary* alphabet $\{0, 1\}$. For any integer $n \geq 0$, we denote by S^n the set of length-n strings over S (S^0 denotes the singleton consisting of the empty tuple). We denote by S^* the set of all strings (i.e., $S^* = \cup_{n \geq 0} S^n$). If x and y are strings, then we denote their concatenation (the tuple that contains first the elements of x and then the elements of y) by $x \circ y$ or sometimes simply xy. If x is a string and $k \geq 1$ is a natural number, then x^k denotes the concatenation of k copies of x. For example, 1^k denotes the string consisting of k ones. The length of a string x is denoted by $|x|$.

Additional notation

If S is a distribution then we use $x \in_R S$ to say that x is a random variable that is distributed according to S; if S is a set then this denotes that x is distributed uniformly over the members of S. We denote by U_n the uniform distribution over $\{0, 1\}^n$. For two length-n strings $x, y \in \{0, 1\}^n$, we denote by $x \odot y$ their dot product modulo 2; that is $x \odot y = \sum_i x_i y_i \pmod 2$. In contrast, the inner product of two n-dimensional real or complex vectors $\mathbf{u}, \mathbf{v}$ is denoted by $\langle \mathbf{u}, \mathbf{v} \rangle$ (see Section A.5.1). For any object x, we use $\llcorner x \lrcorner$ (not to be confused with the floor operator $\lfloor x \rfloor$) to denote the representation of x as a string (see Section 0.1).

0.1 REPRESENTING OBJECTS AS STRINGS

The basic computational task considered in this book is *computing a function*. In fact, we will typically restrict ourselves to functions whose inputs and outputs are finite *strings of bits* (i.e., members of $\{0, 1\}^*$).

Representation

Considering only functions that operate on bit strings is not a real restriction since simple encodings can be used to *represent* general objects—integers, pairs of integers, graphs, vectors, matrices, etc.—as strings of bits. For example, we can represent an integer as a string using the binary expansion (e.g., 34 is represented as 100010) and a graph as its adjacency matrix (i.e., an n vertex graph G is represented by an $n \times n$ 0/1-valued matrix A such that $A_{i,j} = 1$ iff the edge $\overline{ij}$ is present in G). We will typically avoid dealing explicitly with such low-level issues of representation and will use $\llcorner x \lrcorner$ to denote some canonical (and unspecified) binary representation of the object x. Often we will drop the symbols $\llcorner \lrcorner$ and simply use x to denote both the object and its representation.

Representing pairs and tuples

We use the notation $\langle x, y \rangle$ to denote the ordered pair consisting of x and y. A canonical representation for $\langle x, y \rangle$ can be easily obtained from the representations of x and y. For example, we can first encode $\langle x, y \rangle$ as the string $\llcorner x \lrcorner \# \llcorner y \lrcorner$ over the alphabet $\{0, 1, \#\}$ and then use the mapping $0 \mapsto 00, 1 \mapsto 11, \# \mapsto 01$ to convert this representation into a string of bits. To reduce notational clutter, instead of $\llcorner \langle x, y \rangle \lrcorner$ we use $\langle x, y \rangle$ to denote not only the pair consisting of x and y but also the representation of this pair as a binary string. Similarly, we use $\langle x, y, z \rangle$ to denote both the ordered triple consisting of x, y, z and its representation, and use similar notation for 4-tuples, 5-tuples, etc.

Computing functions with nonstring inputs or outputs

The idea of representation allows us to talk about computing functions whose inputs are not strings (e.g., functions that take natural numbers as inputs). In all these cases, we implicitly identify any function f whose domain and range are not strings with the function $g : \{0, 1\}^* \to \{0, 1\}^*$ that given a representation of an object x as input, outputs the representation of $f(x)$. Also, using the representation of pairs and tuples, we can also talk about computing functions that have more than one input or output.

0.2 DECISION PROBLEMS/LANGUAGES

An important special case of functions mapping strings to strings is the case of *Boolean* functions, whose output is a single bit. We identify such a function f with the subset $L_f = \{x : f(x) = 1\}$ of $\{0, 1\}^*$ and call such sets *languages* or *decision problems* (we use these terms interchangeably).[1] We identify the computational problem of computing f (i.e., given x compute $f(x)$) with the problem of deciding the language L_f (i.e., given x, decide whether $x \in L_f$).

EXAMPLE 0.1

By representing the possible invitees to a dinner party with the vertices of a graph having an edge between any two people who don't get along, the dinner party computational problem from the introduction becomes the problem of finding a maximum sized *independent set* (set of vertices without any common edges) in a given graph. The corresponding language is:

$$\mathsf{INDSET} = \{\langle G, k \rangle : \exists S \subseteq V(G) \text{ s.t. } |S| \geq k \text{ and } \forall u, v \in S, \overline{uv} \notin E(G)\}$$

An algorithm to solve this language will tell us, on input a graph G and a number k, whether there exists a conflict-free set of invitees, called an *independent set*, of size at least k. It is not immediately clear that such an algorithm can be used to actually find such a set, but we will see this is the case in Chapter 2. For now, let's take it on faith that this is a good formalization of this problem.

0.3 BIG-OH NOTATION

We will typically measure the computational efficiency of an algorithm as the number of a basic operations it performs as *a function of its input length*. That is, the efficiency of an algorithm can be captured by a function T from the set $\mathbb{N}$ of natural numbers to itself such that $T(n)$ is equal to the maximum number of basic operations that the algorithm performs on inputs of length n. However, this function T is sometimes overly dependant on the low-level details of our definition of a basic operation. For example, the addition algorithm will take about three times more operations if it uses addition of single digit *binary* (i.e., base 2) numbers as a basic operation, as opposed to *decimal* (i.e., base 10) numbers. To help us ignore these low-level details and focus on the big picture, the following well-known notation is very useful.

Definition 0.2 *(Big-Oh notation)* If f, g are two functions from $\mathbb{N}$ to $\mathbb{N}$, then we (1) say that $f = O(g)$ if there exists a constant c such that $f(n) \leq c \cdot g(n)$ for every sufficiently

---

[1] The word "language" is perhaps not an ideal choice to denote subsets of $\{0, 1\}^*$, but for historical reasons this is by now standard terminology.

large n, (2) say that $f = \Omega(g)$ if $g = O(f)$, (3) say that $f = \Theta(g)$ is $f = O(g)$ and $g = O(f)$, (4) say that $f = o(g)$ if for every $\epsilon > 0$, $f(n) \le \epsilon \cdot g(n)$ for every sufficiently large n, and (5) say that $f = \omega(g)$ if $g = o(f)$.

To emphasize the input parameter, we often write $f(n) = O(g(n))$ instead of $f = O(g)$, and use similar notation for $o, \Omega, \omega, \Theta$.

EXAMPLE 0.3

Here are some examples for use of big-Oh notation:

1. If $f(n) = 100n \log n$ and $g(n) = n^2$ then we have the relations $f = O(g), g = \Omega(f)$, $f = o(g), g = \omega(f)$.

2. If $f(n) = 100n^2 + 24n + 2 \log n$ and $g(n) = n^2$ then $f = O(g)$. We will often write this relation as $f(n) = O(n^2)$. Note that we also have the relation $g = O(f)$ and hence $f = \Theta(g)$ and $g = \Theta(f)$.

3. If $f(n) = \min\{n, 10^6\}$ and $g(n) = 1$ for every n then $f = O(g)$. We use the notation $f = O(1)$ to denote this. Similarly, if h is a function that tends to infinity with n (i.e., for every c it holds that $h(n) > c$ for n sufficiently large) then we write $h = \omega(1)$.

4. If $f(n) = 2^n$ then for every number $c \in \mathbb{N}$, if $g(n) = n^c$ then $g = o(f)$. We sometimes write this as $2^n = n^{\omega(1)}$. Similarly, we also write $h(n) = n^{O(1)}$ to denote the fact that h is bounded from above by some polynomial. That is, there exist a number $c > 0$ such that for sufficiently large n, $h(n) \le n^c$. We'll sometimes also also write $h(n) = \text{poly}(n)$ in this case.

For more examples and explanations, see any undergraduate algorithms text such as [DPV06, KT06, CLRS01] or Section 7.1 in Sipser's book [Sip96].

EXERCISES

0.1. For each of the following pairs of functions f, g determine whether $f = o(g), g = o(f)$ or $f = \Theta(g)$. If $f = o(g)$ then find the first number n such that $f(n) < g(n)$:
  (a) $f(n) = n^2, g(n) = 2n^2 + 100\sqrt{n}$.
  (b) $f(n) = n^{100}, g(n) = 2^{n/100}$.
  (c) $f(n) = n^{100}, g(n) = 2^{n^{1/100}}$.
  (d) $f(n) = \sqrt{n}, g(n) = 2^{\sqrt{\log n}}$.
  (e) $f(n) = n^{100}, g(n) = 2^{(\log n)^2}$.
  (f) $f(n) = 1000n, g(n) = n \log n$.

0.2. For each of the following recursively defined functions f, find a closed (nonrecursive) expression for a function g such that $f(n) = \Theta(g(n))$, and prove that this is the case. (*Note*: Below we only supply the recursive rule, you can assume that $f(1) = f(2) = \cdots = f(10) = 1$ and the recursive rule is applied for $n > 10$; in any case, regardless of how the base case is defined it won't make any difference to the answer. Can you see why?)
  (a) $f(n) = f(n-1) + 10$.
  (b) $f(n) = f(n-1) + n$.
  (c) $f(n) = 2f(n-1)$.

Figure 0.1. *Machine with Concrete* by Arthur Ganson. Reproduced with permission of the artist.

(d) $f(n) = f(n/2) + 10$.
(e) $f(n) = f(n/2) + n$.
(f) $f(n) = 2f(n/2) + n$.
(g) $f(n) = 3f(n/2)$.
(h) $f(n) = 2f(n/2) + O(n^2)$.
H531

0.3. The MIT museum contains a kinetic sculpture by Arthur Ganson called *Machine with Concrete* (see Figure 0.1). It consists of 13 gears connected to one another in a series such that each gear moves 50 times slower than the previous one. The fastest gear is constantly rotated by an engine at a rate of 212 rotations per minute. The slowest gear is fixed to a block of concrete and so apparently cannot move at all. Explain why this machine does not break apart.

PART ONE

BASIC COMPLEXITY CLASSES

CHAPTER 1

The computational model—and why it doesn't matter

The idea behind digital computers may be explained by saying that these machines are intended to carry out any operations which could be done by a human computer. The human computer is supposed to be following fixed rules; he has no authority to deviate from them in any detail. We may suppose that these rules are supplied in a book, which is altered whenever he is put on to a new job. He has also an unlimited supply of paper on which he does his calculations.

– Alan Turing, 1950

[Turing] has for the first time succeeded in giving an absolute definition of an interesting episte-mological notion, i.e., one not depending on the formalism chosen.

– Kurt Gödel, 1946

The problem of mathematically modeling computation may at first seem insur-mountable: Throughout history people have been solving computational tasks using a wide variety of methods, ranging from intuition and "eureka" moments to mechanical devices such as abacus or sliderules to modern computers. Besides that, other organisms and systems in nature are also faced with and solve computational tasks every day using a bewildering array of mechanisms. How can you find a simple mathematical model that captures all of these ways to compute? The problem is even further exacerbated since in this book we are interested in issues of *computational efficiency*. Here, at first glance, it seems that we have to be very careful about our choice of a computational model, since even a kid knows that whether or not a new video game program is "efficiently computable" depends upon his computer's hardware.

Surprisingly enough, it turns out there there is a simple mathematical model that suffices for studying many questions about computation and its efficiency—the *Turing machine*. It suffices to restrict attention to this single model since it seems able to *simulate* all physically realizable computational methods with little loss of efficiency. Thus the set of "efficiently solvable" computational tasks is at least as large for the Turing machine as for any other method of computation. (One possible exception is the quantum computer model described in Chapter 10, but we do not currently know if it is physically realizable.)

In this chapter, we formally define Turing machines and survey some of their basic properties. Section 1.1 sketches the model and its basic properties. That section also gives an overview of the results of Sections 1.2 through 1.5 for the casual readers who wish to skip the somewhat messy details of the model and go on to complexity theory, which begins with Section 1.6.

Since complexity theory is concerned with *computational efficiency*, Section 1.6 contains one of the most important definitions in this book: the definition of complexity class **P**, which aims to capture mathematically the set of all decision problems that can be efficiently solved. Section 1.6 also contains some discussion on whether or not the class **P** truly captures the informal notion of "efficient computation." The section also points out how throughout the book the definition of the Turing machine and the class **P** will be a starting point for definitions of many other models, including nondeterministic, probabilistic, and quantum Turing machines, Boolean circuits, parallel computers, decision trees, and communication games. Some of these models are introduced to study arguably realizable modes of physical computation, while others are mainly used to gain insights on Turing machine computations.

1.1 MODELING COMPUTATION: WHAT YOU REALLY NEED TO KNOW

Some tedious notation is unavoidable if one talks formally about Turing machines. We provide an intuitive overview of this material for casual readers who can then skip ahead to complexity questions, which begin with Section 1.6. Such a reader can always return to the skipped sections on the rare occasions in the rest of the book when we actually use details of the Turing machine model.

For thousands of years, the term "computation" was understood to mean application of mechanical rules to manipulate numbers, where the person/machine doing the manipulation is allowed a *scratch pad* on which to write the intermediate results. The Turing machine is a concrete embodiment of this intuitive notion. Section 1.2.1 shows that it can be also viewed as the equivalent of any modern programming language—albeit one with no built-in prohibition on its memory size.[1]

Here we describe this model informally along the lines of Turing's quote at the start of the chapter. Let f be a function that takes a string of bits (i.e., a member of the set $\{0, 1\}^*$) and outputs either 0 or 1. An *algorithm* for computing f is a set of mechanical rules, such that by following them we can compute $f(x)$ given any input $x \in \{0, 1\}^*$. The set of rules being followed is fixed (i.e., the same rules must work for all possible inputs) though each rule in this set may be applied arbitrarily many times. Each rule involves one or more of the following "elementary" operations:

1. Read a bit of the input.
2. Read a bit (or possibly a symbol from a slightly larger alphabet, say a digit in the set $\{0, \ldots, 9\}$) from the scratch pad or working space we allow the algorithm to use.

Based on the values read,

1. Write a bit/symbol to the scratch pad.
2. Either stop and output 0 or 1, or choose a new rule from the set that will be applied next.

---

[1] Though the assumption of a potentially infinite memory may seem unrealistic at first, in the complexity setting it is of no consequence since we will restrict our study to machines that use at most a finite number of computational steps and memory cells any given input (the number allowed will depend upon the input size).

Finally, the *running time* is the number of these basic operations performed. We measure it in asymptotic terms, so we say a machine runs in time $T(n)$ if it performs at most $T(n)$ basic operations time on inputs of length n.

The following are simple facts about this model.

1. The model is robust to almost any tweak in the definition such as changing the alphabet from $\{0, 1, \ldots, 9\}$ to $\{0, 1\}$, or allowing multiple scratchpads, and so on. The most basic version of the model can *simulate* the most complicated version with at most polynomial (actually quadratic) slowdown. Thus t steps on the complicated model can be simulated in $O(t^c)$ steps on the weaker model where c is a constant depending only on the two models. See Section 1.3.

2. An algorithm (i.e., a machine) can be represented as a bit string once we decide on some canonical encoding. Thus an algorithm/machine can be viewed as a possible *input* to another algorithm—this makes the boundary between *input, software,* and *hardware* very fluid. (As an aside, we note that this fluidity is the basis of a lot of computer technology.) We denote by M_α the machine whose representation as a bit string is α.

3. There is a *universal* Turing machine $\mathcal{U}$ that can *simulate* any other Turing machine given its bit representation. Given a pair of bit strings (x, α) as input, this machine simulates the behavior of M_α on input x. This simulation is very efficient: If the running time of M_α was $T(|x|)$, then the running time of $\mathcal{U}$ is $O(T(|x|) \log T(|x|))$. See Section 1.4.

4. The previous two facts can be used to easily prove the existence of functions that are not computable by any Turing machine; see Section 1.5. Uncomputability has an intimate connection to Gödel's famous Incompleteness Theorem; see Section 1.5.2.

1.2 THE TURING MACHINE

The *k-tape Turing machine* (TM) concretely realizes the above informal notion in the following way (see Figure 1.1).

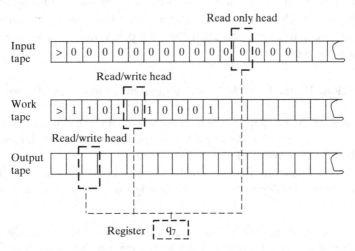

Figure 1.1. A snapshot of the execution of a three-tape Turing machine M with an input tape, a work tape, and an output tape.

Scratch pad

The scratch pad consists of k tapes. A *tape* is an infinite one-directional line of cells, each of which can hold a symbol from a finite set Γ called the *alphabet* of the machine. Each tape is equipped with a *tape head* that can potentially read or write symbols to the tape one cell at a time. The machine's computation is divided into discrete time steps, and the head can move left or right one cell in each step.

The first tape of the machine is designated as the *input* tape. The machine's head can only read symbols from that tape, not write them—a so-called read-only head. The $k - 1$ read-write tapes are called *work tapes*, and the last one of them is designated as the *output tape* of the machine, on which it writes its final answer before halting its computation.

There also are variants of Turing machines with *random access memory*,[2] but it turns out that their computational powers are equivalent to standard Turing machines (see Exercise 1.9).

Finite set of operations/rules

The machine has a finite set of *states*, denoted Q. The machine contains a "register" that can hold a single element of Q; this is the "state" of the machine at that instant. This state determines its action at the next computational step, which consists of the following: (1) read the symbols in the cells directly under the k heads; (2) for the $k - 1$ read-write tapes, replace each symbol with a new symbol (it has the option of not changing the tape by writing down the old symbol again); (3) change its register to contain another state from the finite set Q (it has the option not to change its state by choosing the old state again); and (4) move each head one cell to the left or to the right (or stay in place).

One can think of the Turing machine as a simplified modern computer, with the machine's tape corresponding to a computer's memory and the transition function and register corresponding to the computer's central processing unit (CPU). However, it's best to think of Turing machines as simply a formal way to describe algorithms. Even though algorithms are often best described by plain English text, it is sometimes useful to express them by such a formalism in order to argue about them mathematically. (Similarly, one needs to express an algorithm in a programming language in order to execute it on a computer.)

Formal definition. Formally, a TM M is described by a tuple (Γ, Q, δ) containing:

- A finite set Γ of the symbols that M's tapes can contain. We assume that Γ contains a designated "blank" symbol, denoted $\square$; a designated "start" symbol, denoted $\triangleright$; and the numbers 0 and 1. We call Γ the *alphabet* of M.
- A finite set Q of possible states M's register can be in. We assume that Q contains a designated start state, denoted q_{start}, and a designated halting state, denoted q_{halt}.

---

[2] *Random access* denotes the ability to access the ith symbol of the memory within a single step, without having to move a head all the way to the ith location. The name "random access" is somewhat unfortunate since this concept involves no notion of randomness—perhaps "indexed access" would have been better. However, "random access" is widely used, and so we follow this convention this book.

IF			THEN			
Input symbol read	Work/ output tape symbol read	Current state	Move input head	New work/ output tape symbol	Move work/ output tape	New state
⋮	⋮	⋮	⋮	⋮	⋮	⋮
a	b	q	Right $\longrightarrow$	b'	Left $\longleftarrow$	q'
⋮	⋮	⋮	⋮	⋮	⋮	⋮

Figure 1.2. The transition function of a two-tape TM (i.e., a TM with one input tape and one work/output tape).

- A function $\delta : Q \times \Gamma^k \to Q \times \Gamma^{k-1} \times \{L, S, R\}^k$, where $k \geq 2$, describing the rules M use in performing each step. This function is called the *transition function* of M (see Figure 1.2.)

If the machine is in state $q \in Q$ and $(\sigma_1, \sigma_2, \ldots, \sigma_k)$ are the symbols currently being read in the k tapes, and $\delta(q, (\sigma_1, \ldots, \sigma_k)) = (q', (\sigma'_2, \ldots, \sigma'_k), z)$ where $z \in \{L, S, R\}^k$, then at the next step the σ symbols in the last $k - 1$ tapes will be replaced by the σ' symbols, the machine will be in state q', and the k heads will move Left, Right, or Stay in place, as given by z. (If the machine tries to move left from the leftmost position of a tape then it will stay in place.)

All tapes except for the input are initialized in their first location to the *start* symbol ▷ and in all other locations to the *blank* symbol □. The input tape contains initially the start symbol ▷, a finite nonblank string x ("the input"), and the the blank symbol □ on the rest of its cells. All heads start at the left ends of the tapes and the machine is in the special starting state q_{start}. This is called the *start configuration* of M on input x. Each step of the computation is performed by applying the function δ as described previously. The special halting state q_{halt} has the property that once the machine is in q_{halt}, the transition function δ does not allow it to further modify the tape or change states. Clearly, if the machine enters q_{halt}, then it has *halted*. In complexity theory, we are typically only interested in machines that halt for every input in a finite number of steps.

EXAMPLE 1.1

Let PAL be the Boolean function defined as follows: for every $x \in \{0, 1\}^*$, PAL(x) is equal to 1 if x is a *palindrome* and equal to 0 otherwise. That is, PAL$(x) = 1$ if and only if x reads the same from left to right as from right to left (i.e., $x_1 x_2 \ldots x_n = x_n x_{n-1} \ldots x_1$). We now show a TM M that computes PAL within less than $3n$ steps.

Our TM M will use three tapes (input, work, and output) and the alphabet $\{\triangleright, \square, 0, 1\}$. It operates as follows:

1. Copy the input to the read-write work tape.
2. Move the input-tape head to the beginning of the input.
3. Move the input-tape head to the right while moving the work-tape head to the left. If at any moment the machine observes two different values, it halts and output 0.
4. Halt and output 1.

We now describe the machine more formally: The TM M uses five states denoted by $\{q_{\mathsf{start}}, q_{\mathsf{copy}}, q_{\mathsf{left}}, q_{\mathsf{test}}, q_{\mathsf{halt}}\}$. Its transition function is defined as follows:

1. On state q_{start}: Move the input-tape head to the right, and move the work-tape head to the right while writing the start symbol $\triangleright$; change the state to q_{copy}. (Unless we mention this explicitly, the function does not change the output tape's contents or head position.)
2. On state q_{copy}:
    - If the symbol read from the input tape is not the blank symbol $\square$, then move both the input-tape and work-tape heads to the right, writing the symbol from the input tape on the work tape; stay in the state q_{copy}.
    - If the symbol read from the input tape is the blank symbol $\square$, then move the input-tape head to the left, while keeping the work-tape head in the same place (and not writing anything); change the state to q_{left}.
3. On state q_{left}:
    - If the symbol read from the input tape is not the start symbol $\triangleright$, then move the input head to the left, keeping the work-tape head in the same place (and not writing anything); stay in the state q_{left}.
    - If the symbol read from the input tape is the start symbol $\triangleright$, then move the input tape to the right and the work-tape head to the left (not writing anything); change to the state q_{test}.
4. On state q_{test}:
    - If the symbol read from the input tape is the blank symbol $\square$ and the symbol read from the work-tape is the start symbol $\triangleright$, then write 1 on the output tape and change state to q_{halt}.
    - Otherwise, if the symbols read from the input tape and the work tape are not the same, then write 0 on the output tape and change state to q_{halt}.
    - Otherwise, if the symbols read from the input tape and the work tape are the same, then move the input-tape head to the right and the work-tape head to the left; stay in the state q_{test}.

Clearly, fully specifying a Turing machine is tedious and not always informative. Even though it is useful to work out one or two examples for yourself (see Exercise 1.1), in the rest of this book we avoid such overly detailed descriptions and specify TMs in a high-level fashion. For readers with some programming experience, Example 1.2 should convince them that they know (in principle at least) how to design a Turing machine for any computational task for which they know how to write computer programs.

1.2.1 The expressive power of Turing machines

At first sight, it may be unclear that Turing machines do indeed encapsulate our intuitive notion of computation. It may be useful to work through some simple examples, such as expressing the standard algorithms for addition and multiplication in terms of Turing machines computing the corresponding functions (see Exercise 1.1). Having done that, you may be ready for the next example; it outlines how you can translate a program in your favorite programming language into a Turing machine. (The reverse direction also holds: Most programming languages can simulate a Turing machine.)

EXAMPLE 1.2 (Simulating a general programming language using Turing machines)

(This example assumes some background in computing.)

We give a hand-wavy proof that for any program written in any of the familiar programming languages such as C or Java, there is an equivalent Turing machine. First, recall that programs in these programming languages can be translated (the technical term is *compiled*) into an equivalent *machine language* program. This is a sequence of instructions, each of one of a few simple types, for example, (a) read from memory into one of a finite number of registers, (b) write a register's contents to memory, (c) add the contents of two registers and store the result in a third, and (d) perform (c) but with other operations such as multiplication instead of addition. All these operations can be easily simulated by a Turing machine. The memory and registers can be implemented using the machine's tapes, while the instructions can be encoded by the machine's transition function. For example, it's not hard to design TM's that add or multiply two numbers. To simulate the computer's memory, a two-tape TM can use one tape for the simulated memory and the other tape to do binary-to-unary conversion that allows it, for a number i in binary representation, to read or modify the ith location of its first tape. We leave details to Exercise 1.8.

Exercise 1.10 asks you to give a more rigorous proof of such a simulation for a simple tailor-made programming language.

1.3 EFFICIENCY AND RUNNING TIME

Now we formalize the notion of running time. As every nontrivial computational task requires at least reading the entire input, we count the number of basic steps *as a function of the input length.*

Definition 1.3 *(Computing a function and running time)*
Let $f : \{0, 1\}^* \to \{0, 1\}^*$ and let $T : \mathbb{N} \to \mathbb{N}$ be some functions, and let M be a Turing machine. We say that *M computes f* if for every $x \in \{0, 1\}^*$, whenever M is initialized to the start configuration on input x, then it halts with $f(x)$ written on its output tape. We say *M computes f in $T(n)$-time*[4] if its computation on every input x requires at most $T(|x|)$ steps.

---

3   Formally we should write "T-time" instead of "$T(n)$-time," but we follow the convention of writing $T(n)$ to emphasize that T is applied to the input length.

EXAMPLE 1.4

It is easily checked that the Turing machine for palindrome recognition in Example 1.1 runs in $3n$ time.

Time-constructible functions

A function $T : \mathbb{N} \to \mathbb{N}$ is *time constructible* if $T(n) \geq n$ and there is a TM M that computes the function $x \mapsto \lfloor T(|x|) \rfloor$ in time $T(n)$. (As usual, $\lfloor T(|x|) \rfloor$ denotes the binary representation of the number $T(|x|)$.) Examples for time-constructible functions are n, $n \log n, n^2, 2^n$. Almost all functions encountered in this book will be time constructible, and we will restrict our attention to time bounds of this form. (Allowing time bounds that are not time constructible can lead to anomalous results.) The restriction $T(n) \geq n$ is to allow the algorithm time to read its input.

1.3.1 Robustness of our definition

Most of the specific details of our definition of Turing machines are quite arbitrary. It is a simple exercise to see that most changes to the definition do not yield a substantially different model, since our model can simulate any of these new models. In context of computational complexity, however, we have to verify not only that one model can simulate another, but also that it can do so efficiently. Now we state a few results of this type, which ultimately lead to the conclusion that the exact model is unimportant if we are willing to ignore polynomial factors in the running time. Variations on the model studied include restricting the alphabet Γ to be $\{0, 1, \square, \triangleright\}$, restricting the machine to have a single work tape, or allowing the tapes to be infinite in both directions. All results in this section are proved sketchily—completing these sketches into full proofs is a very good way to gain intuition on Turing machines, see Exercises 1.2, 1.3, and 1.4.

Claim 1.5 *For every $f : \{0, 1\}^* \to \{0, 1\}$ and time-constructible $T : \mathbb{N} \to \mathbb{N}$, if f is computable in time $T(n)$ by a TM M using alphabet Γ, then it is computable in time $4 \log |\Gamma| T(n)$ by a TM $\tilde{M}$ using the alphabet $\{0, 1, \square, \triangleright\}$.*   ◇

PROOF SKETCH: Let M be a TM with alphabet Γ, k tapes, and state set Q that computes the function f in $T(n)$ time. We describe an equivalent TM $\tilde{M}$ computing f with alphabet $\{0, 1, \square, \triangleright\}$, k tapes and a set Q' of states. The idea behind the transformation is simple: One can encode any member of Γ using $\log |\Gamma|$ bits.[5] Thus, each of $\tilde{M}$'s work tapes will simply encode one of M's tapes: For every cell in M's tape we will have $\log |\Gamma|$ cells in the corresponding tape of $\tilde{M}$ (see Figure 1.3).

To simulate one step of M, the machine $\tilde{M}$ will (1) use $\log |\Gamma|$ steps to read from each tape the $\log |\Gamma|$ bits encoding a symbol of Γ, (2) use its state register to store the symbols read, (3) use M's transition function to compute the symbols M writes and M's new state given this information, (4) store this information in its state register, and (5) use $\log |\Gamma|$ steps to write the encodings of these symbols on its tapes.

---

[5] Recall our conventions that log is taken to base 2, and noninteger numbers are rounded up when necessary.

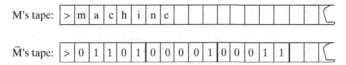

Figure 1.3. We can simulate a machine M using the alphabet $\{\triangleright, \square, \mathsf{a}, \mathsf{b}, \ldots, \mathsf{z}\}$ by a machine M' using $\{\triangleright, \square, 0, 1\}$ via encoding every tape cell of M using five cells of M'.

One can verify that this can be carried out if $\tilde{M}$ has access to registers that can store M's state, k symbols in Γ, and a counter from 1 to $\log |\Gamma|$. Thus, there is such a machine $\tilde{M}$ utilizing no more than $c|Q||\Gamma|^{k+1}$ states for some absolute constant c. (In general, we can always simulate several registers using one register with a larger state space. For example, we can simulate three registers taking values in the sets A, B and C, respectively, with one register taking a value in the set $A \times B \times C$, which is of size $|A||B||C|$.)

It is not hard to see that for every input $x \in \{0,1\}^n$, if on input x the TM M outputs $f(x)$ within $T(n)$ steps, then $\tilde{M}$ will output the same value within less than $4 \log |\Gamma| T(n)$ steps. ∎

Now we consider the effect of restricting the machine to use a *single tape*—one read-write tape that serves as input, work, and output tape (this is the standard computational model in many undergraduate texts such as [Sip96]). We show that going from multiple tapes to a single tape can at most square the running time. This quadratic increase is inherent for some languages, including the palindrome recognition considered in Example 1.1; see the chapter notes.

Claim 1.6 *Define a single-tape Turing machine to be a TM that has only one read-write tape, that is used as input, work, and output tape. For every $f : \{0,1\}^* \to \{0,1\}$ and time-constructible $T : \mathbb{N} \to \mathbb{N}$, if f is computable in time $T(n)$ by a TM M using k tapes, then it is computable in time $5kT(n)^2$ by a single-tape TM $\tilde{M}$.* ◇

PROOF SKETCH: Again the idea is simple: The TM $\tilde{M}$ encodes k tapes of M on a single tape by using locations $1, k+1, 2k+1, \ldots$ to encode the first tape, locations $2, k+2, 2k+2, \ldots$ to encode the second tape etc. (see Figure 1.4). For every symbol a in M's alphabet, $\tilde{M}$ will contain both the symbol a and the symbol $\hat{a}$. In the encoding of each tape, exactly one symbol will be of the "^ type," indicating that the corresponding head of M is positioned in that location (see Figure 1.4). $\tilde{M}$ will not touch the first $n+1$ locations of its tape (where the input is located) but rather start by taking $O(n^2)$ steps to copy the input bit by bit into the rest of the tape, while encoding it in the above way.

To simulate one step of M, the machine $\tilde{M}$ makes two sweeps of its work tape: First it sweeps the tape in the left-to-right direction and records to its register the k symbols that are marked by "^". Then $\tilde{M}$ uses M's transition function to determine the new state, symbols, and head movements and sweeps the tape back in the right-to-left direction to update the encoding accordingly. Clearly, $\tilde{M}$ will have the same output as M. Also, since on n-length inputs M never reaches more than location $T(n)$ of any of its tapes, $\tilde{M}$

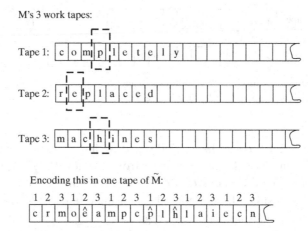

Figure 1.4. Simulating a machine M with three tapes using a machine $\tilde{M}$ with a single tape.

will never need to reach more than location $2n + kT(n) \leq (k+2)T(n)$ of its work tape, meaning that for each of the at most $T(n)$ steps of M, $\tilde{M}$ performs at most $5 \cdot k \cdot T(n)$ work (sweeping back and forth requires about $4 \cdot k \cdot T(n)$ steps, and some additional steps may be needed for updating head movement and book keeping). ■

Remark 1.7 *(Oblivious Turing machines)*
With a bit of care, one can ensure that the proof of Claim 1.6 yields a TM $\tilde{M}$ with the following property: Its head movements do not depend on the input but only depend on the input length. That is, every input $x \in \{0, 1\}^*$ and $i \in \mathbb{N}$, the location of each of M's heads at the ith step of execution on input x is only a function of $|x|$ and i. A machine with this property is called *oblivious*, and the fact that every TM can be simulated by an oblivious TM will simplify some proofs later on (see Exercises 1.5 and 1.6 and the proof of Theorem 2.10).

Claim 1.8 *Define a bidirectional TM to be a TM whose tapes are infinite in both directions. For every $f : \{0, 1\}^* \to \{0, 1\}^*$ and time-constructible $T : \mathbb{N} \to \mathbb{N}$, if f is computable in time $T(n)$ by a bidirectional TM M, then it is computable in time $4T(n)$ by a standard (unidirectional) TM $\tilde{M}$.*   ◇

PROOF SKETCH: The idea behind the proof is illustrated in Figure 1.5. If M uses alphabet Γ, then $\tilde{M}$ will use the alphabet Γ^2 (i.e., each symbol in $\tilde{M}$'s alphabet corresponds to a pair of symbols in M's alphabet). We encode a tape of M that is infinite in both direction using a standard (infinite in one direction) tape by "folding" it in an arbitrary location, with each location of $\tilde{M}$'s tape encoding two locations of M's tape. At first, $\tilde{M}$ will ignore the second symbol in the cell it reads and act according to M's transition function. However, if this transition function instructs $\tilde{M}$ to go "over the edge" of its tape, then instead it will start ignoring the first symbol in each cell and use only the second symbol. When it is in this mode, it will translate left movements into right movements and vice versa. If it needs to go over the edge again, then it will go back to reading the first symbol of each cell and translating movements normally. ■

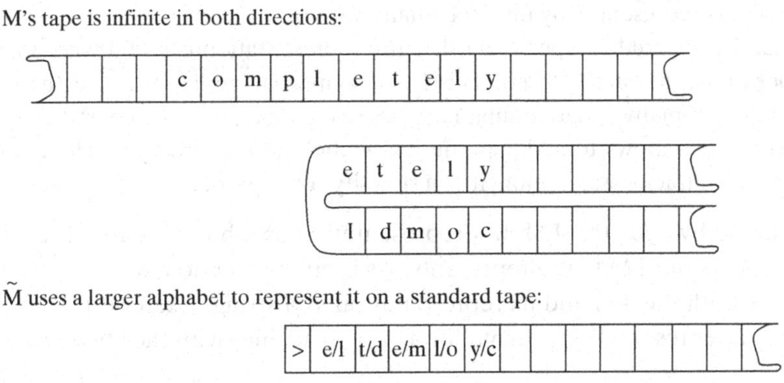

M's tape is infinite in both directions:

$\tilde{M}$ uses a larger alphabet to represent it on a standard tape:

Figure 1.5. To simulate a machine M with alphabet Γ that has tapes infinite in both directions, we use a machine $\tilde{M}$ with alphabet Γ^2 whose tapes encode the "folded" version of M's tapes.

Other changes that do not have a very significant effect include having two or three dimensional tapes, allowing the machine *random access* to its tape, and making the output tape *write only* (see Exercises 1.7 and 1.9; the texts [Sip96, HMU01] contain more examples). In particular none of these modifications will change the class **P** of polynomial-time computable decision problems defined in Section 1.6.

1.4 MACHINES AS STRINGS AND THE UNIVERSAL TURING MACHINE

It is almost obvious that we can represent a Turing machine as a string: Just write the description of the TM on paper, and encode this description as a sequence of zeros and ones. This string can be given as input to another TM. This simple observation is actually profound since it blurs the distinction between *software*, *hardware*, and *data*. Historically speaking, it motivated the invention of the *general-purpose* electronic computer, which is a single machine that can be adapted to any arbitrary task by loading it with an appropriate program (software).

Because we will use this notion of representing TMs as strings quite extensively, it may be worthwhile to spell out our representation a bit more concretely. Since the behavior of a Turing machine is determined by its transition function, we will use the list of all inputs and outputs of this function (which can be easily encoded as a string in $\{0, 1\}^*$) as the encoding of the Turing machine.[6] We will also find it convenient to assume that our representation scheme satisfies the following properties:

1. Every string in $\{0, 1\}^*$ represents *some* Turing machine.
   This is easy to ensure by mapping strings that are not valid encodings into some canonical trivial TM, such as the TM that immediately halts and outputs zero on any input.

---

[6] Note that the size of the alphabet, the number of tapes, and the size of the state space can be deduced from the transition function's table. We can also reorder the table to ensure that the special states q_{start}, q_{halt} are the first two states of the TM. Similarly, we may assume that the symbols $\triangleright, \square, 0, 1$ are the first four symbols of the machine's alphabet.

2. Every TM is represented by infinitely many strings.

    This can be ensured by specifying that the representation can end with an arbitrary number of 1s, that are ignored. This has a somewhat similar effect to the *comments* mechanism of many programming languages (e.g., the / ∗ ⋯ ∗ / construct in C, C++, and Java) that allows to add superfluous symbols to any program. Though this may seem like a nitpicky assumption, it will simplify some proofs.

We denote by $\llcorner M \lrcorner$ the TM M's representation as a binary string. If α is a string then M_α denotes the TM that α represents. As is our convention, we will also often use M to denote both the TM and its representation as a string. Exercise 1.11 asks you to fully specify a representation scheme for Turing machines with the above properties.

1.4.1 The universal Turing machine

Turing was the first to observe that general-purpose computers are possible, by showing a *universal* Turing machine that can *simulate* the execution of every other TM M given M's description as input. Of course, since we are so used to having a universal computer on our desktops or even in our pockets, today we take this notion for granted. But it is good to remember why it was once counterintuitive. The parameters of the universal TM are fixed—alphabet size, number of states, and number of tapes. The corresponding parameters for the machine being simulated could be much larger. The reason this is not a hurdle is, of course, the ability to use *encodings*. Even if the universal TM has a very simple alphabet, this suffices to represent the other machine's state and transition table on its tapes and then follow along in the computation step by step.

Now we state a computationally efficient version of Turing's construction due to Hennie and Stearns [HS66]. To give the essential idea we first prove a slightly relaxed variant where the term $T \log T$ below is replaced with T^2. But since the efficient version is needed a few times in the book, a full proof is also given at the end of the chapter (see Section 1.7).

> **Theorem 1.9** *(Efficient universal Turing machine)*
> *There exists a TM $\mathcal{U}$ such that for every $x, \alpha \in \{0, 1\}^*$, $\mathcal{U}(x, \alpha) = M_\alpha(x)$, where M_α denotes the TM represented by α.*
> *Moreover, if M_α halts on input x within T steps then $\mathcal{U}(x, \alpha)$ halts within $CT \log T$ steps, where C is a number independent of $|x|$ and depending only on M_α's alphabet size, number of tapes, and number of states.*

A common exercise in programming courses is to write an *interpreter* for a particular programming language using the same language. (An interpreter takes a program P as input and outputs the result of executing the program P.) Theorem 1.9 can be considered a variant of this exercise.

PROOF OF RELAXED VERSION OF THEOREM 1.9: Our universal TM $\mathcal{U}$ is given an input x, α, where α represents some TM M, and needs to output $M(x)$. A crucial observation is that we may assume that M (1) has a single work tape (in addition to the input and output tape) and (2) uses the alphabet $\{\triangleright, \square, 0, 1\}$. The reason is that $\mathcal{U}$ can transform a representation of every TM M into a representation of an equivalent TM $\tilde{M}$ that satisfies

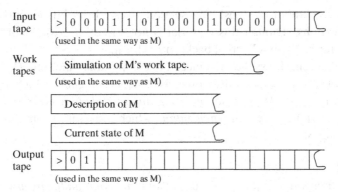

Figure 1.6. The universal TM $\mathcal{U}$ has in addition to the input and output tape, three work tapes. One work tape will have the same contents as the simulated machine M, another tape includes the description M (converted to an equivalent one-work-tape form), and another tape contains the current state of M.

these properties as shown in the proofs of Claims 1.5 and 1.6. Note that these transformations may introduce a quadratic slowdown (i.e., transform M from running in T time to running in $C'T^2$ time where C' depends on M's alphabet size and number of tapes).

The TM $\mathcal{U}$ uses the alphabet $\{\triangleright, \square, 0, 1\}$ and three work tapes in addition to its input and output tape (see Figure 1.6). $\mathcal{U}$ uses its input tape, output tape, and one of the work tapes in the same way M uses its three tapes. In addition, $\mathcal{U}$ will use its first extra work tape to store the table of values of M's transition function (after applying the transformations of Claims 1.5 and 1.6 as noted earlier), and its other extra work tape to store the current state of M. To simulate one computational step of M, $\mathcal{U}$ scans the table of M's transition function and the current state to find out the new state, symbols to be written and head movements, which it then executes. We see that each computational step of M is simulated using C steps of $\mathcal{U}$, where C is some number depending on the size of the transition function's table.

This high-level description can be turned into an exact specification of the TM $\mathcal{U}$, though we leave this to the reader. To work out the details, it may help to think first how to program these steps in your favorite programming language and then try to transform this into a description of a Turing machine. ■

Universal TM with time bound

It is sometimes useful to consider a variant of the universal TM $\mathcal{U}$ that gets a number T as an extra input (in addition to x and α), and outputs $M_\alpha(x)$ if and only if M_α halts on x within T steps (otherwise outputting some special failure symbol). By adding a time counter to $\mathcal{U}$, the proof of Theorem 1.9 can be easily modified to give such a universal TM. The time counter is used to keep track of the number of steps that the computation has taken so far.

1.5 UNCOMPUTABILITY: AN INTRODUCTION

It may seem "obvious" that every function can be computed, given sufficient time. However, this turns out to be false: There exist functions that cannot be computed

within any finite number of steps! This section gives a brief introduction to this fact
and its ramifications. Though this material is not strictly necessary for the study of
complexity, it forms the intellectual background for it.

The next theorem shows the existence of uncomputable functions. (In fact, it shows
the existence of such functions whose range is $\{0, 1\}$, i.e. *languages*; such uncomputable
functions with range $\{0, 1\}$ are also known as *undecidable languages*.) The theorem's
proof uses a technique called *diagonalization*, which is useful in complexity theory as
well; see Chapter 3.

Theorem 1.10
There exists a function $\mathsf{UC} : \{0, 1\}^* \to \{0, 1\}$ *that is not computable by any TM.*   ◇

PROOF: The function UC is defined as follows: For every $\alpha \in \{0, 1\}^*$, if $M_\alpha(\alpha) = 1$, then
$\mathsf{UC}(\alpha) = 0$; otherwise (if $M_\alpha(\alpha)$ outputs a different value or enters an infinite loop),
$\mathsf{UC}(\alpha) = 1$.

Suppose for the sake of contradiction that UC is computable and hence there exists
a TM M such that $M(\alpha) = \mathsf{UC}(\alpha)$ for every $\alpha \in \{0, 1\}^*$. Then, in particular, $M(\llcorner M \lrcorner) =
\mathsf{UC}(\llcorner M \lrcorner)$. But this is impossible: By the definition of UC,

$$\mathsf{UC}(\llcorner M \lrcorner) = 1 \Leftrightarrow M(\llcorner M \lrcorner) \neq 1$$

■

Figure 1.7 demonstrates why this proof technique is called *diagonalization*.

1.5.1 The Halting problem (first encounter with reductions)

The reader may well ask why should we care whether or not the function UC described
above is computable—who would want to compute such a contrived function anyway?

	0	1	00	01	10	11	...	α	...
0	01	1	*	0	1	0		$M_0(\alpha)$	
0	1	1	0	1	*	1		...	
00	*	0	0	0	1	*			
01	1	*	0	01	*	0			
...									
α	$M_\alpha(\alpha)$ ...							$M_\alpha(\alpha)$ 1-$M_\alpha(\alpha)$	
...									

Figure 1.7. Suppose we order all strings in lexicographic order, and write in a table the value of $M_\alpha(x)$ for all
strings α, x, where M_α denotes the TM represented by the string α and we use ⋆ to denote the case that $M_\alpha(x)$
is not a value in $\{0, 1\}$ or that M_α does not halt on input x. Then, function UC is defined by "negating" the
diagonal of this table. Since the rows of the table represent *all* TMs, we conclude that UC cannot be computed
by any TM.

We now show a more natural uncomputable function. The function HALT takes as input a pair $\langle \alpha, x \rangle$ and outputs 1 if and only if the TM M_α represented by α halts on input x within a finite number of steps. This is definitely a function we want to compute: Given a computer program and an input, we'd certainly like to know if the program is going to enter an infinite loop on this input. If computers could compute HALT, the task of designing bug-free software and hardware would become much easier. Unfortunately, we now show that computers cannot do this, even if they are allowed to run an arbitrarily long time.

Theorem 1.11
HALT *is not computable by any TM.*   ◇

PROOF: Suppose, for the sake of contradiction, that there was a TM M_{HALT} computing HALT. We will use M_{HALT} to show a TM M_{UC} computing UC, contradicting Theorem 1.10.

The TM M_{UC} is simple: On input α, M_{UC} runs $M_{HALT}(\alpha, \alpha)$. If the result is 0 (meaning that M_α does not halt on α), then M_{UC} outputs 1. Otherwise, M_{UC} uses the universal TM $\mathcal{U}$ to compute $b = M_\alpha(\alpha)$. If $b = 1$, then M_{UC} outputs 0; otherwise, it outputs 1.

Under the assumption that $M_{HALT}(\alpha, \alpha)$ outputs HALT(α, α) within a finite number of steps, the TM $M_{UC}(\alpha)$ will output UC(α). ∎

The proof technique employed to show Theorem 1.11 is called a *reduction*. We showed that computing UC is *reducible* to computing HALT—we showed that if there were a hypothetical algorithm for HALT then there would be one for UC. We will see many reductions in this book, often used (as is the case here) to show that a problem B is at least as hard as a problem A by showing an algorithm that could solve A given a procedure that solves B.

There are many other examples of interesting uncomputable (also known as *undecidable*) functions, see Exercise 1.12. There are even uncomputable functions whose formulation has seemingly nothing to do with Turing machines or algorithms. For example, the following problem cannot be solved in finite time by any TM: Given a set of polynomial equations with integer coefficients, find out whether these equations have an integer solution (i.e., whether there is an assignment of integers to the variables that satisfies the equations). This is known as the problem of solving Diophantine equations, and in 1900 Hilbert mentioned finding an algorithm for solving it (which he presumed to exist) as one of the top 23 open problems in mathematics. The chapter notes mention some good sources for more information on computability theory.

1.5.2 Gödel's Theorem

In the year 1900, David Hilbert, the preeminent mathematician of his time, proposed an ambitious agenda to base all of mathematics on solid axiomatic foundations, so that eventually all true statements would be rigorously proven. Mathematicians such as Russell, Whitehead, Zermelo, and Fraenkel, proposed axiomatic systems in the ensuing decades, but nobody was able to prove that their systems are simultaneously *complete* (i.e., prove all true mathematical statements) and *sound* (i.e., prove no false statements). In 1931, Kurt Gödel shocked the mathematical world by showing that this ongoing effort is doomed to fail—for every sound system S of axioms and rules of inference, there exist true number theoretic statements that cannot be proven in $\mathcal{S}$. Below we sketch a proof of this result. Note that we this discussion does not address Gödel's more powerful result, which says that any sufficiently powerful axiomatization of mathematics cannot prove its own consistency. Proving that is also not too hard given the ideas below.

Gödel's work directly motivated the work of Turing and Church on computability. Our presentation reverses this order: We use uncomputability to sketch a proof of Gödel's result. The main observation is the following: In any sufficiently powerful axiomatic system, for any input $\langle \alpha, x \rangle$ we can write a mathematical statement $\phi_{\langle \alpha, x \rangle}$ that is true iff $\mathsf{HALT}(\langle \alpha, x \rangle) = 1$. (A sketch of this construction appears below.) Now if the system is complete, it must prove at least one of $\phi_{\langle \alpha, x \rangle}$ or $\neg \phi_{\langle \alpha, x \rangle}$, and if it is sound, it cannot prove both. So if the system is both complete and sound, the following algorithm for the Halting problem is guaranteed to terminate in finite time for all inputs. "*Given input $\langle \alpha, x \rangle$, start enumerating all strings of finite length, and check for each generated string whether it represents a proof in the axiomatic system for either $\phi_{\langle \alpha, x \rangle}$ or $\neg \phi_{\langle \alpha, x \rangle}$. If one waits long enough, a proof of one of the two statements will appear in the enumeration, at which point the correct answer 1 or 0 is revealed, which you then output.*" (Note that this procedure implicitly uses the simple fact that proofs in axiomatic systems can be easily verified by a Turing machine, since each step in the proof has to follow mechanically from previous steps by applying the axioms.)

Now we sketch the construction of the desired statement $\phi_{\langle \alpha, x \rangle}$. Assume the axiomatic system has the ability to express statements about the natural number using the operators plus ($+$) and times ($\times$), equality and comparison relations ($=, >, <$), and logical operators such as AND ($\wedge$), OR ($\vee$), and NOT ($\neg$). The language also includes the quantifiers for-all ($\forall$) and exists ($\exists$) and the constant 1 (we can get any other constant c by adding 1 to itself c times). For example, the formal expression for "x divides y" will be $\mathsf{DIVIDES}(x, y) = \exists_k : y = x \times k$, and the expression for "y is prime" will be $\mathsf{PRIME}(y) = \forall_x (x=1) \vee (x=y) \vee \neg \mathsf{DIVIDES}(x, y)$ (where $\mathsf{DIVIDES}(x, y)$ is shorthand for the corresponding expression).

We can encode strings (and hence also Turing machines and their inputs and tapes) as numbers. Then one notes that a basic operation of the Turing machine only influences one (or a few, if the machine has mutiple tapes) of bits on its tape, which can be viewed as a simple arithmetic operation on the string/number representing the tape contents. With some work, one obtains an expression $\varphi_{\alpha, x}(t)$ that is true if and only if the TM M_α halts on input x within t steps. Hence, M_α halts on x if and only if $\exists_t \varphi_{\alpha, x}(t)$ is true, which is the desired mathematical statement. We leave the details as Exercise 1.13.

Note that this construction also implies, as first pointed out by Turing, that the set of true mathematical statements is undecidable, which showed that Hilbert's famous *Entscheidungsproblem* has no solution. (Hilbert had asked for a "mechanical procedure"—now interpreted as "algorithmic procedure"—for deciding truth of mathematical statements.)

1.6 THE CLASS P

A *complexity class* is a set of functions that can be computed within given resource bounds. We will now introduce our first complexity class. For reasons of technical convenience, throughout most of this book, we will pay special attention to Boolean functions, namely those that have only one bit of output. These functions define *decision problems* or *languages*. We say that a machine *decides* a language $L \subseteq \{0, 1\}^*$ if it computes the function $f_L : \{0, 1\}^* \rightarrow \{0, 1\}$, where $f_L(x) = 1 \Leftrightarrow x \in L$.

Definition 1.12 *(The class* **DTIME***)* Let $T : \mathbb{N} \rightarrow \mathbb{N}$ be some function. A language L is in **DTIME**$(T(n))$ iff there is a Turing machine that runs in time $c \cdot T(n)$ for some constant $c > 0$ and decides L.   ◇

The D in the notation **DTIME** refers to "deterministic." The Turing machine introduced in this chapter is more precisely called the *deterministic* Turing machine since for any given input x, the machine's computation can proceed in exactly one way. Later we will see other types of Turing machines, including nondeterministic and probabilistic TMs.

Now we try to make the notion of "efficient computation" precise. We equate this with *polynomial* running time, which means it is at most n^c for some constant $c > 0$. The following class captures this notion, where **P** stands for "polynomial."

Definition 1.13 *(The class* **P***)*
$\mathbf{P} = \cup_{c \geq 1}\mathbf{DTIME}(n^c)$.

Thus, we can phrase the question from the introduction as to whether the dinner party problem has an efficient algorithm as follows: *"Is* INDSET *in* **P***?"*, where INDSET is the language defined in Example 0.1.

EXAMPLE 1.14 *(Graph connectivity)*

In the *graph connectivity* problem, we are given a graph G and two vertices s, t in G. We have to decide if s is connected to t in G. This problem is in **P**. The algorithm that shows this uses *depth-first search*, a simple idea taught in undergraduate courses. The algorithm explored the graph edge-by-edge starting from s, marking visited edges. In subsequent edges, it also tries to explore all unvisited edges that are adjacent to previously visited edges. After at most $\binom{n}{2}$ steps, all edges are either visited or will never be visited.

See Exercise 1.14 for more examples of languages in **P**.

EXAMPLE 1.15

We give some examples to emphasize a couple of points about the definition of the class **P**. First, the class contains only decision problems. Thus we cannot say, for example, that "integer multiplication is in **P**." Instead, we may say that its decision version is in **P**, namely, the following language:

$$\big\{ \langle x, i \rangle : \text{The } i\text{th bit of } xy \text{ is equal to } 1 \big\}$$

Second, the running time is a function of the number of *bits* in the input. Consider the problem of solving a system of linear equations over the rational numbers. In other words, given a pair $\langle A, \mathbf{b} \rangle$ where A is an $m \times n$ rational matrix and $\mathbf{b}$ is an m dimensional rational vector, find out if there exists an n-dimensional vector $\mathbf{x}$ such that $A\mathbf{x} = \mathbf{b}$. The standard Gaussian elimination algorithm solves this problem in $O(n^3)$ *arithmetic operations*. But on a Turing machine, each arithmetic operation has to be done in the gradeschool fashion, bit by laborious bit. Thus, to prove that this decision problem is in **P**, we have to verify that Gaussian elimination (or some other algorithm for the problem) runs on a Turing machine in time that is polynomial in the number of bits required to represent $a_1, a_2, \ldots, a_n$. That is, in the case of Gaussian elimination, we need to verify that all the intermediate numbers involved in the computation can be represented by polynomially many bits. Fortunately, this does turn out to be the case (for a related result, see Exercise 2.3).

1.6.1 Why the model may not matter

We defined the classes of "computable" languages and **P** using Turing machines. Would they be different if we had used a different computational model? Would these classes be different for some advanced alien civilization, which has discovered computation but with a different computational model than the Turing machine?

We already encountered variations on the Turing machine model, and saw that the weakest one can simulate the strongest one with quadratic slow down. Thus *polynomial* time is the same on all these variants, as is the set of computable problems.

In the few decades after Church and Turing's work, many other models of computation were discovered, some quite bizarre. It was easily shown that the Turing machine can simulate all of them with at most polynomial slowdown. Thus, the analog of **P** on these models is no larger than that for the Turing machine.

Most scientists believe the **Church-Turing (CT) thesis**, which states that every physically realizable computation device—whether it's based on silicon, DNA, neurons or some other alien technology—can be simulated by a Turing machine. This implies that the set of *computable* problems would be no larger on any other computational model that on the Turing machine. (The CT thesis is not a theorem, merely a belief about the nature of the world as we currently understand it.)

However, when it comes to *efficiently* computable problems, the situation is less clear. The **strong form of the CT thesis** says that every physically realizable computation model can be simulated by a TM *with polynomial overhead* (in other words, t steps on the model can be simulated in t^c steps on the TM, where c is a constant that depends upon the model). If true, it implies that the class **P** defined by the aliens will be the same as ours. However, this strong form is somewhat controversial, in particular because of models such as *quantum computers* (see Chapter 10), which do not appear to be efficiently simulatable on TMs. However, it is still unclear if quantum computers can be physically realized.

1.6.2 On the philosophical importance of P

The class **P** is felt to capture the notion of decision problems with "feasible" decision procedures. Of course, one may argue whether **DTIME**(n^{100}) really represents "feasible" computation in the real world since n^{100} is prohibitively huge even for moderate values of n. However, in practice, whenever we show that a problem is in **P**, we usually find an n^3 or n^5 time algorithm (with reasonable constants), and not an n^{100} time algorithm. (It has also happened a few times that the first polynomial-time algorithm for a problem had high complexity, say n^{20}, but soon somebody simplified it to say an n^5 time algorithm.)

Note that the class **P** is useful only in a certain context. Turing machines are a crude model if one is designing algorithms that must run in a fraction of a second on the latest PC (in which case one must carefully account for fine details about the hardware). However, if the question is whether any subexponential algorithms exist for, say, the language INDSET of Example 0.1, then even an n^{20} time algorithm would be a fantastic breakthrough.

P is also a natural class from the viewpoint of a programmer. Suppose a programmer is asked to invent the definition of an "efficient" computation. Presumably, she would agree that a computation that runs in linear or quadratic time is efficient. Next, since programmers often write programs that call other programs (or subroutines), she might find it natural to consider a program efficient if it performs only efficient computations and calls subroutines that are efficient. The resulting notion of "efficient computations" obtained turns out to be exactly the class **P** [Cob64].

1.6.3 Criticisms of P and some efforts to address them

Now we address some possible criticisms of the definition of **P** and some related complexity classes that address these.

Worst-case exact computation is too strict. The definition of **P** only considers algorithms that compute the function on *every* possible input. Critics point out that not all possible inputs arise in practice, and our algorithms only need to be efficient on the types of inputs that do arise. This criticism is partly answered using *average-case complexity* and by defining an analog of **P** in that context; see Chapter 18. We also note that quantifying "real-life" distributions is tricky.

Similarly, in context of computing functions such as the size of the largest independent set in the graph, users are often willing to settle for *approximate* solutions. Chapters 11 and 22 contain a rigorous treatment of the complexity of approximation.

Other physically realizable models. We already mentioned the strong form of the Church-Turing thesis, which posits that the class **P** is not larger for any physically realizable computational model. However, some subtleties need discusssion.

(a) *Issue of precision.* TM's compute with discrete symbols, whereas physical quantities may be real numbers in $\mathbb{R}$. Thus one can conceive of computational models based upon physics phenomena that may be able to operate over real numbers. Because of the precision issue, a TM can only approximately simulate such computations. It seems though that TMs do not suffer from an inherent handicap (though a few researchers disagree). After all, real-life devices suffer from noise, and physical quantities can only be measured up to finite precision. Thus physical processes could not involve arbitrary precision, and the simulating TM can therefore simulate them using finite precision. Even so, in Chapter 16 we also consider a modification of the TM model that allows computations in $\mathbb{R}$ as a basic operation. The resulting complexity classes have fascinating connections with the standard classes.

(b) *Use of randomness.* The TM as defined is *deterministic.* If randomness exists in the world, one can conceive of computational models that use a source of random bits (i.e., coin tosses). Chapter 7 considers Turing machines that are allowed to also toss coins, and studies the complexity class **BPP**, which is the analog of **P** for those machines. However, we will see in Chapters 19 and 20 the intriguing possibility that randomized computation may be no more powerful than deterministic computation.

(c) *Use of quantum mechanics.* A more clever computational model might use some of the counterintuitive features of quantum mechanics. In Chapter 10, we define the complexity class **BQP**, which generalizes **P** in such a way. We will see problems in **BQP** that are currently not known to be in **P** (though there is no known proof that **BQP** $\neq$ **P**). However, it is not yet clear whether the quantum model is truly physically realizable. Also quantum computers currently seem able to efficiently solve only very few problems that are not known to be in **P**. Hence some insights gained from studying **P** may still apply to quantum computers.

(d) *Use of other exotic physics, such as string theory.* So far it seems that many such physical theories yield the same class **BQP**, though much remains to be understood.

Decision problems are too limited. Some computational problems are not easily expressed as decision problems. Indeed, we will introduce several classes in the book to capture tasks such as computing non-Boolean functions, solving search problems, approximating optimization problems, interaction, and more. Yet the framework of decision problems turn out to be surprisingly expressive, and we will often use it in this book.

1.6.4 Edmonds's quote

We conclude this section with a quote from Edmonds [Edm65], who in his celebrated paper on a polynomial-time algorithm for the maximum matching problem, explained the meaning of such a result as follows:

> *For practical purposes computational details are vital. However, my purpose is only to show as attractively as I can that there is an efficient algorithm. According to the dictionary, "efficient" means "adequate in operation or performance." This is roughly the meaning I want — in the sense that it is conceivable for maximum matching to have no efficient algorithm.*
>
> *There is an obvious finite algorithm, but that algorithm increases in difficulty exponentially with the size of the graph. It is by no means obvious whether or not there exists an algorithm whose difficulty increases only algebraically with the size of the graph.*
>
> *When the measure of problem-size is reasonable and when the sizes assume values arbitrarily large, an asymptotic estimate of . . . the order of difficulty of an algorithm is theoretically important. It cannot be rigged by making the algorithm artificially difficult for smaller sizes.*
>
> *One can find many classes of problems, besides maximum matching and its generalizations, which have algorithms of exponential order but seemingly none better. . . . For practical purposes the difference between algebraic and exponential order is often more crucial than the difference between finite and non-finite.*

It would be unfortunate for any rigid criterion to inhibit the practical development of algorithms which are either not known or known not to conform nicely to the criterion. Many of the best algorithmic idea known today would suffer by such theoretical pedantry. . . . However, if only to motivate the search for good, practical algorithms, it is important to realize that it is mathematically sensible even to question their existence. For one thing the task can then be described in terms of concrete conjectures.

1.7 PROOF OF THEOREM 1.9: UNIVERSAL SIMULATION IN $O(T \log T)$-TIME

We now show how to prove Theorem 1.9 as stated. That is, we show a universal TM $\mathcal{U}$ such that given an input x and a description of a TM M that halts on x within T steps, $\mathcal{U}$ outputs $M(x)$ within $O(T \log T)$ time (where the constants hidden in the O notation may depend on the parameters of the TM M being simulated).

The general structure of $\mathcal{U}$ will be as in Section 1.4.1. $\mathcal{U}$ will use its input and output tape in the same way M does and will also have extra work tapes to store M's transition table and current state and to encode the contents of M's work tapes. The main obstacle we need to overcome is that we cannot use Claim 1.6 to reduce the number of M's work tapes to one, since Claim 1.6 introduces too much overhead in the simulation. Therefore, we will show a different way to encode all of M's work tapes in a single tape of $\mathcal{U}$, which we call the *main* work tape of $\mathcal{U}$.

Let k be the number of tapes that M uses (apart from its input and output tapes) and Γ its alphabet. Following the proof of Claim 1.5, we may assume that $\mathcal{U}$ uses the alphabet Γ^k (as this can be simulated with a overhead depending only on $k, |\Gamma|$). Thus we can encode in each cell of $\mathcal{U}$'s main work tape k symbols of Γ, each corresponding to a symbol from one of M's tapes. This means that we can think of $\mathcal{U}$'s main work tape not as a single tape but rather as k *parallel tapes*; that is, we can think of $\mathcal{U}$ as having k tapes with the property that in each step all their read-write heads go in unison either one location to the left, one location to the right, or stay in place. While we can easily encode the contents of M's k work tapes in $\mathcal{U}$'s k parallel tapes, we still have to deal with the fact that M's k read-write heads can each move independently to the left or right, whereas $\mathcal{U}$'s parallel tapes are forced to move together. Paraphrasing the famous saying, our strategy to handle this is: *"If the head cannot go to the tape locations then the locations will go to the head."*

That is, since we can not move $\mathcal{U}$'s read-write head in different directions at once, we simply move the parallel tapes "under" the head. To simulate a single step of M, we shift all the nonblank symbols in each of these parallel tapes until the head's position in these parallel tapes corresponds to the heads' positions of M's k tapes. For example, if $k = 3$ and in some particular step M's transition function specifies the movements L, R, R, then $\mathcal{U}$ will shift all the nonblank entries of its first parallel tape one cell to the right, and shift the nonblank entries of its second and third tapes one cell to the left (see Figure 1.8). $\mathcal{U}$ can easily perform such shifts using an additional "scratch" work tape.

The approach above is still not good enough to get $O(T \log T)$-time simulation. The reason is that there may be as many as T nonblank symbols in each parallel tape, and so each shift operation may cost $\mathcal{U}$ as much as T operations per each step of M, resulting in $\Theta(T^2)$-time simulation. We will deal with this problem by encoding the information

M's 3 independent tapes:

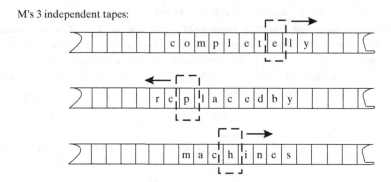

U's 3 parallel tapes (i.e., one tape encoding 3 tapes)

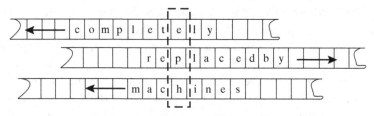

Figure 1.8. Packing k tapes of M into one tape of $\mathcal{U}$. We consider $\mathcal{U}$'s single work tape to be composed of k parallel tapes, whose heads move in unison, and hence we shift the contents of these tapes to simulate independent head movement.

on the tapes in a way that allows us to amortize the work of performing a shift. We will ensure that we do not need to move all the nonblank symbols of the tape in each shift operation. Specifically, we will encode the information in a way that allows half of the shift operations to be performed using $2c$ steps, for some constant c, a quarter of them using $4c$ steps, and more generally 2^{-i} fraction of the operations will take $2^i c$ steps, leading to simulation in roughly $cT \log T$ time (see below). (This kind of analysis is called *amortized analysis* and is widely used in algorithm design.)

Encoding M's tapes on $\mathcal{U}$'s tape

To allow more efficient shifts we encode the information using "buffer zones": Rather than having each of $\mathcal{U}$'s parallel tapes correspond exactly to a tape of M, we add a special kind of blank symbol $\boxtimes$ to the alphabet of $\mathcal{U}$'s parallel tapes with the semantics that this symbol is ignored in the simulation. For example, if the nonblank contents of M's tape are 010, then this can be encoded in the corresponding parallel tape of $\mathcal{U}$ not just by 010 but also by $0\boxtimes01$ or $0\boxtimes\boxtimes1\boxtimes0$ and so on.

For convenience, we think of $\mathcal{U}$'s parallel tapes as infinite in both the left and right directions (this can be easily simulated with minimal overhead: see Claim 1.8). Thus, we index their locations by $0, \pm1, \pm2, \ldots$. Normally we keep $\mathcal{U}$'s head on location 0 of these parallel tapes. We will only move it temporarily to perform a shift when, following our general approach, we simulate a left head movement by shifting the tape to the right and vice versa. At the end of the shift, we return the head to location 0.

We split each of $\mathcal{U}$'s parallel tapes into *zones* that we denote by $R_0, L_0, R_1, L_1, \ldots$ (we'll only need to go up to $R_{\log T}, L_{\log T}$). The cell at location 0 is not

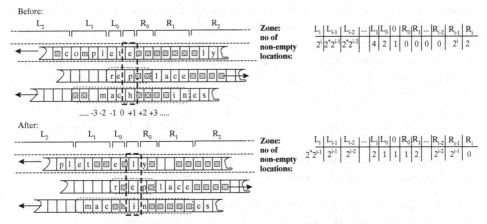

Figure 1.9. Performing a shift of the parallel tapes. The left shift of the first tape involves zones $R_0, L_0, R_1, L_1, R_2, L_2$, the right shift of the second tape involves only R_0, L_0, while the left shift of the third tape involves zones R_0, L_0, R_1, L_1. We maintain the invariant that each zone is either empty, half-full, or full and that the total number of nonempty cells in $R_i \cup L_i$ is $2 \cdot 2^i$. If before the left shift zones $L_0, \ldots, L_{i-1}$ were full and L_i was half-full (and so $R_0, \ldots, R_{i-1}$ were full and R_i half-full), then after the shift zones $R_0, L_0, \ldots, R_{i-1}, L_{i-1}$ will be half-full, L_i will be full and R_i will be empty.

at any zone. Zone R_0 contains the two cells immediately to the right of location C (i.e., locations $+1$ and $+2$), while Zone R_1 contains the four cells $+3, +4, +5, +6$. Generally, for every $i \geq 1$, Zone R_i contains the $2 \cdot 2^i$ cells that are to the right of Zone R_{i-1} (i.e., locations $[2^{i+1} - 1, \ldots, 2^{i+2} - 2]$). Similarly, Zone L_0 contains the two cells indexed by -1 and -2, and generally Zone L_i contains the cells $[-2^{i+2} + 2, \cdots, -2^{i+1} + 1]$. We shall always maintain the following invariants:

- Each of the zones is either *empty*, *full*, or *half-full* with non-⊠ symbols. That is, the number of symbols in zone R_i that are not ⊠ is either 0, 2^i, or $2 \cdot 2^i$ and the same holds for L_i. (We treat the ordinary □ symbol the same as any other symbol in Γ, and in particular a zone full of □'s is considered full.)
  We assume that initially all the zones are half-full. We can ensure this by filling half of each zone with ⊠ symbols in the first time we encounter it.
- The total number of non-⊠ symbols in $R_i \cup L_i$ is $2 \cdot 2^i$. That is, either R_i is empty and L_i is full, or R_i is full and L_i is empty, or they are both half-full.
- Location 0 always contains a non-⊠ symbol.

Performing a shift

The advantage in setting up these zones is that now when performing the shifts, we do not always have to move the entire tape, but we can restrict ourselves to only using some of the zones. We illustrate this by showing how $\mathcal{U}$ performs a left shift on the first of its parallel tapes (see also Figure 1.9):

1. $\mathcal{U}$ finds the smallest i_0 such that R_{i_0} is not empty. Note that this is also the smallest i_0 such that L_{i_0} is not full. We call this number i_0 the *index* of this particular shift.
2. $\mathcal{U}$ puts the leftmost non-⊠ symbol of R_{i_0} in position 0 and shifts the remaining leftmost $2^{i_0} - 1$ non-⊠ symbols from R_{i_0} into the zones $R_0, \ldots, R_{i_0-1}$ filling up exactly half the

symbols of each zone. Note that there is exactly room to perform this since all the zones $R_0, \ldots, R_{i_0-1}$ were empty and indeed $2^{i_0} - 1 = \sum_{j=0}^{i_0-1} 2^j$.

3. $\mathcal{U}$ performs the symmetric operation to the left of position 0. That is, for j starting from $i_0 - 1$ down to 0, $\mathcal{U}$ iteratively moves the $2 \cdot 2^j$ symbols from L_j to fill half the cells of L_{j+1}. Finally, $\mathcal{U}$ moves the symbol originally in position 0 (modified appropriately according to M's transition function) to L_0.

4. At the end of the shift, all of the zones $R_0, L_0, \ldots, R_{i_0-1}, L_{i_0-1}$ are half-full, R_{i_0} has 2^{i_0} fewer non-$\boxtimes$ symbols, and L_i has 2^i additional non-$\boxtimes$ symbols. Thus, our invariants are maintained.

5. The total cost of performing the shift is proportional to the total size of all the zones involved $R_0, L_0, \ldots, R_{i_0}, L_{i_0}$. That is, $O(\sum_{j=0}^{i_0} 2 \cdot 2^j) = O(2^{i_0})$ operations.

After performing a shift with index i the zones $L_0, R_0, \ldots, L_{i-1}, R_{i-1}$ are half-full, which means that it will take at least $2^i - 1$ left shifts before the zones $L_0, \ldots, L_{i-1}$ become empty or at least $2^i - 1$ right shifts before the zones $R_0, \ldots, R_{i-1}$ become empty. In any case, once we perform a shift with index i, the next $2^i - 1$ shifts of that particular parallel tape will all have index less than i. This means that for every one of the parallel tapes, at most a $1/2^i$ fraction of the total number of shifts have index i. Since we perform at most T shifts, and the highest possible index is $\log T$, the total work spent in shifting $\mathcal{U}$'s k parallel tapes in the course of simulating T steps of M is

$$O(k \cdot \sum_{i=1}^{\log T} \frac{T}{2^{i-1}} 2^i) = O(T \log T) . \ \blacksquare$$

WHAT HAVE WE LEARNED?

- There are many equivalent ways to mathematically model computational processes; we use the standard Turing machine formalization.
- Turing machines can be represented as strings. There is a *universal* TM that can simulate (with small overhead) any TM given its representation.
- There exist functions, such as the Halting problem, that cannot be computed by any TM regardless of its running time.
- The class **P** consists of all decision problems that are solvable by Turing machines in polynomial time. We say that problems in **P** are efficiently solvable.
- Low-level choices (number of tapes, alphabet size, etc..) in the definition of Turing machines are immaterial, as they will not change the definition of **P**.

CHAPTER NOTES AND HISTORY

Although certain algorithms have been studied for thousands of years, and some forms of computing devices were designed before the twentieth century (most notably Charles Babbage's difference and analytical engines in the mid 1800s), it seems fair to say that the foundations of modern computer science were only laid in the 1930s.

In 1931, Kurt Gödel shocked the mathematical world by showing that certain true statements about the natural numbers are *inherently unprovable*, thereby shattering an ambitious agenda set in 1900 by David Hilbert to base all of mathematics on solid axiomatic foundations. In 1936, Alonzo Church defined a model of computation called λ-calculus (which years later inspired the programming language LISP) and showed the existence of functions *inherently uncomputable* in this model [Chu36]. A few months later, Alan Turing independently introduced his Turing machines and showed functions inherently uncomputable by such machines [Tur36]. Turing also introduced the idea of the *universal* Turing machine that can be loaded with arbitrary programs. The two models turned out to be equivalent, but in the words of Church himself, Turing machines have "the advantage of making the identification with effectiveness in the ordinary (not explicitly defined) sense evident immediately." The anthology [Dav65] contains many seminal papers on computability. Part II of Sipser's book [Sip96] is a good gentle introduction to this theory, while the books [Rog87, HMU01, Koz97] go into a bit more depth. These books also cover *automata theory*, which is another area of the theory of computation not discussed in the current book. This book's Web site contains some additional links for information on both these topics.

During World War II, Turing designed mechanical code-breaking devices and played a key role in the effort to crack the German "Enigma" cipher, an achievement that had a decisive effect on the war's progress (see the biographies [Hod83, Lea05]).[7] After World War II, efforts to build electronic universal computers were undertaken in both sides of the Atlantic. A key figure in these efforts was John von Neumann, an extremely prolific scientist who was involved in everything from the Manhattan project to founding game theory in economics. To this day, essentially all digital computers follow the "von-Neumann architecture" he pioneered while working on the design of the EDVAC, one of the earliest digital computers [vN45].

As computers became more prevalent, the issue of efficiency in computation began to take center stage. Cobham [Cob64] defined the class **P** and suggested it may be a good formalization for efficient computation. A similar suggestion was made by Edmonds ([Edm65], see earlier quote) in the context of presenting a highly nontrivial polynomial-time algorithm for finding a maximum matching in general graphs. Hartmanis and Stearns [HS65] defined the class **DTIME**$(T(n))$ for every function T and proved the slightly relaxed version of Theorem 1.9 we showed in this chapter (the version we stated and prove below was given by Hennie and Stearns [HS66]). They also coined the name "computational complexity" and proved an interesting "speed-up theorem": If a function f is computable by a TM M in time $T(n)$ then for every constant $c \geq 1$, f is computable by a TM $\tilde{M}$ (possibly with larger state size and alphabet size than M) in time $T(n)/c$. This speed-up theorem is another justification for ignoring constant factors in the definition of **DTIME**$(T(n))$. Blum [Blu67] has given an axiomatic formalization of complexity theory that does not explicitly mention Turing machines.

We have omitted a discussion of some of the "bizarre conditions" that may occur when considering time bounds that are not time-constructible, especially "huge" time

---

[7] Unfortunately, Turing's wartime achievements were kept confidential during his lifetime, and so did not keep him from being forced by British courts to take hormones to "cure" his homosexuality, resulting in his suicide in 1954.

bounds (i.e., function $T(n)$ that are much larger than exponential in n). For example, there is a non-time-constructible function $T : \mathbb{N} \to \mathbb{N}$ such that every function computable in time $T(n)$ can also be computed in the much shorter time $\log T(n)$. However, we will not encounter non-time-constructible time bounds in this book.

The result that PAL requires $\Omega(n^2)$ steps to compute on TM's using a single read-write tape is from [Maa84], see also Exercise 13.3. We have stated that algorithms that take less than n steps are not very interesting as they do not even have time to read their input. This is true for the Turing machine model. However, if one allows *random access* to the input combined with *randomization* then many interesting computational tasks can actually be achieved in *sublinear* time. See [Fis04] for a survey of this line of research.

EXERCISES

1.1. Let f be the *addition* function that maps the representation of a pair of numbers x, y to the representation of the number $x + y$. Let g be the *multiplication* function that maps $\langle x, y \rangle$ to $\lfloor x \cdot y \rfloor$. Prove that both f and g are computable by writing down a full description (including the states, alphabet, and transition function) of the corresponding Turing machines.
H531

1.2. Complete the proof of Claim 1.5 by writing down explicitly the description of the machine $\tilde{M}$.

1.3. Complete the proof of Claim 1.6.

1.4. Complete the proof of Claim 1.8.

1.5. Define a TM M to be *oblivious* if its head movements do not depend on the input but only on the input length. That is, M is oblivious if for every input $x \in \{0, 1\}^*$ and $i \in \mathbb{N}$, the location of each of M's heads at the ith step of execution on input x is only a function of $|x|$ and i. Show that for every time-constructible $T: \mathbb{N} \to \mathbb{N}$, if $L \in \textbf{DTIME}(T(n))$, then there is an oblivious TM that decides L in time $O(T(n)^2)$. Furthermore, show that there is such a TM that uses only *two tapes*: one input tape and one work/output tape.
H531

1.6. Show that for every time-constructible $T: \mathbb{N} \to \mathbb{N}$, if $L \in \textbf{DTIME}(T(n))$, then there is an oblivious TM that decides L in time $O(T(n) \log T(n))$.
H531

1.7. Define a *two-dimensional* Turing machine to be a TM where each of its tapes is an infinite grid (and the machine can move not only Left and Right but also Up and Down). Show that for every (time-constructible) $T: \mathbb{N} \to \mathbb{N}$ and every Boolean function f, if g can be computed in time $T(n)$ using a two-dimensional TM then $f \in \textbf{DTIME}(T(n)^2)$.

1.8. Let LOOKUP denote the following function: on input a pair $\langle x, i \rangle$ (where x is a binary string and i is a natural number), LOOKUP outputs the ith bit of x or 0 if $|x| < i$. Prove that LOOKUP $\in \textbf{P}$.

1.9. Define a *RAM Turing machine* to be a Turing machine that has *random access memory*. We formalize this as follows: The machine has an infinite array A that is initialized to all blanks. It accesses this array as follows. One of the machine's work tapes is designated as the *address tape*. Also the machine has two special alphabet symbols denoted by R and W and an additional state we denote by q_{access}. Whenever the machine enters q_{access}, if its address tape contains $\llcorner i \lrcorner$R (where $\llcorner i \lrcorner$ denotes the binary representation of i) then the value $A[i]$ is written in the cell next to the R symbol. If its tape contains $\llcorner i \lrcorner$Wσ (where σ is some symbol in the machine's alphabet) then $A[i]$ is set to the value σ.

Show that if a Boolean function f is computable within time $T(n)$ (for some time-constructible T) by a RAM TM, then it is in **DTIME**$(T(n)^2)$.

1.10. Consider the following simple programming language. It has a single infinite array A of elements in $\{0, 1, \square\}$ (initialized to $\square$) and a single integer variable i. A program in this language contains a sequence of lines of the following form:

$$label : \text{If A[i] equals } \sigma \text{ then } cmds$$

where $\sigma \in \{0, 1, \square\}$ and *cmds* is a list of one or more of the following commands: (1) Set A[i] to τ where $\tau \in \{0, 1, \square\}$, (2) Goto *label*, (3) Increment i by one, (4) Decrement i by one, and (5) Output b and halt, where $b \in \{0, 1\}$. A program is executed on an input $x \in \{0, 1\}^n$ by placing the *i*th bit of x in A[i] and then running the program following the obvious semantics.

Prove that for every functions $f : \{0, 1\}^* \to \{0, 1\}$ and (time-constructible) $T : \mathbb{N} \to \mathbb{N}$, if f is computable in time $T(n)$ by a program in this language, then $f \in$ **DTIME**$(T(n))$.

1.11. Give a full specification of a representation scheme of Turing machines as binary string strings. That is, show a procedure that transforms any TM M (e.g., the TM computing the function PAL described in Example 1.1) into a binary string $\llcorner M \lrcorner$. It should be possible to recover M from $\llcorner M \lrcorner$, or at least recover a functionally equivalent TM (i.e., a TM $\tilde{M}$ computing the same function as M with the same running time).

1.12. A *partial* function from $\{0, 1\}^*$ to $\{0, 1\}^*$ is a function that is not necessarily defined on all its inputs. We say that a TM M computes a partial function f if for every x on which f is defined, $M(x) = f(x)$ and for every x on which f is not defined M gets into an infinite loop when executed on input x. If S is a set of partial functions, we define f_S to be the Boolean function that on input α outputs 1 iff M_α computes a partial function in S. *Rice's Theorem* says that for every nontrivial S (a set that is not the empty set nor the set of all partial functions computable by some Turing machine), the function f_S is not computable.

(a) Show that Rice's Theorem yields an alternative proof for Theorem 1.11 by showing that the function HALT is not computable.

(b) Prove Rice's Theorem.

H531

1.13. It is known that there is some constant C such that for every $i > C$ there is a prime larger than i^3 but smaller than $(i + 1)^3$ [Hoh30, Ing37]. For every $i \in \mathbb{N}$, let p_i denote the smallest prime between $(i + C)^3$ and $(i + C + 1)^3$. We say that a number n

encodes a string $x \in \{0,1\}^*$, if for every $i \in \{1, \ldots, |x|\}$, p_i divides n if and only if $x_i = 1$.[8]

(a) Show (using the operators described in Section 1.5.2) a logical expression $BIT(n,i)$ that is true if and only if p_i divides n.

(b) Show a logical expression $COMPARE(n,m,i,j)$ that is true if and only if the strings encoded by the numbers n and m agree between the ith and jth position.

(c) A *configuration* of a TM M is the contents of all its input tapes, its head location, and the state of its register. That is, it contains all the information about M at a particular moment in its execution. Show that such a configuration can be represented by a binary string. (You may assume that M is a single-tape TM as in Claim 1.6.)

(d) For a TM M and input $x \in \{0,1\}^*$, show an expression $INIT_{M,x}(n)$ that is true if and only if n encodes the initial configuration of M on input x.

(e) For a TM M show an expression $HALT_M(n)$ that is true if and only if n encodes a configuration of M after which M will halt its execution.

(f) For a TM M, show an expression $NEXT(n,m)$ that is true if and only if n,m encode configurations x,y of M such that y is the configuration that is obtained from x by a single computational step of M.

(g) For a TM M, show an expression $VALID_M(m,t)$ that is true if and only m a tuple of t configurations $x_1, \ldots, x_t$ such that x_{i+1} is the configuration obtained from x_i in one computational step of M.

(h) For a TM M and input $x \in \{0,1\}^*$, show an expression $HALT_{M,x}(t)$ that is true if and only if M halts on input x within t steps.

(i) Let $TRUE\text{-}EXP$ denote the function that on input (a string representation of) a number-theoretic statement φ (composed in the preceding formalism), outputs 1 if φ is true, and 0 if φ is false. Prove that $TRUE\text{-}EXP$ is uncomputable.

1.14. Prove that the following languages/decision problems on graphs are in **P**. (You may pick either the adjacency matrix or adjacency list representation for graphs; it will not make a difference. Can you see why?)

(a) $CONNECTED$—The set of all connected graphs. That is, $G \in CONNECTED$ if every pair of vertices u,v in G are connected by a path.

(b) $TRIANGLEFREE$—The set of all graphs that do not contain a triangle (i.e., a triplet u,v,w of connected distinct vertices).

(c) $BIPARTITE$—The set of all bipartite graphs. That is, $G \in BIPARTITE$ if the vertices of G can be partitioned to two sets A,B such that all edges in G are from a vertex in A to a vertex in B (there is no edge between two members of A or two members of B).

(d) $TREE$—The set of all trees. A graph is a *tree* if it is connected and contains no cycles. Equivalently, a graph G is a tree if every two distinct vertices u,v in G are connected by exactly one simple path (a path is simple if it has no repeated vertices).

1.15. Recall that normally we assume that numbers are represented as string using the *binary* basis. That is, a number n is represented by the sequence $x_0, x_1, \ldots, x_{\log n}$

---

[8] Technically speaking under this definition a number can encode more than one string. This will not be an issue, though we can avoid it by first encoding the string x as a $2|x|$ bit string y using the map $0 \mapsto 00, 1 \mapsto 11$ and then adding the sequence 01 at the end of y.

such that $n = \sum_{i=0}^{n} x_i 2^i$. However, we could have used other encoding schemes. If $n \in \mathbb{N}$ and $b \geq 2$, then *the representation of n in base b*, denoted by $\lfloor n \rfloor_b$ is obtained as follows: First, represent n as a sequence of digits in $\{0, \ldots, b - 1\}$, and then replace each digit $d \in \{0, \ldots, d - 1\}$ by its binary representation. The *unary* representation of n, denoted by $\lfloor n \rfloor$ unary is the string 1^n (i.e., a sequence of n ones).

(a) Show that choosing a different base of representation will make no difference to the class **P**. That is, show that for every subset S of the natural numbers, if we define $L_S^b = \{ \lfloor n \rfloor_b : n \in S \}$, then for every $b \geq 2$, $L_S^b \in \mathbf{P}$ iff $L_S^2 \in \mathbf{P}$.

(b) Show that choosing the unary representation may make a difference by showing that the following language is in **P**:

$$\text{UNARYFACTORING} = \{ \langle \lfloor n \rfloor \text{unary}, \lfloor \ell \rfloor \text{unary}, \lfloor k \rfloor \text{unary} \rangle : \text{there is a prime}$$

$$j \in (\ell, k) \text{ dividing } n \}$$

It is not known to be in **P** if we choose the binary representation (see Chapters 9 and 10). In Chapter 3 we will see that there is a problem that is *proven* to be in **P** when choosing the unary representation but not in **P** when using the binary representation.

CHAPTER 2

NP and NP completeness

[if $\phi(n) \approx Kn^2$]* then this would have consequences of the greatest magnitude. That is to say, it would clearly indicate that, despite the unsolvability of the [Hilbert] Entscheidungsproblem, the mental effort of the mathematician in the case of the yes-or-no questions would be completely replaced by machines.... [this] seems to me, however, within the realm of possibility.

— Kurt Gödel in a letter to John von Neumann, 1956

I conjecture that there is no good algorithm for the traveling salesman problem. My reasons are the same as for any mathematical conjecture: (1) It is a legitimate mathematical possibility, and (2) I do not know.

— Jack Edmonds, 1966

In this paper we give theorems that suggest, but do not imply, that these problems, as well as many others, will remain intractable perpetually.

— Richard Karp, 1972

If you have ever attempted a crossword puzzle, you know that it is much harder to solve it from scratch than to verify a solution provided by someone else. Likewise, solving a math homework problem by yourself is usually much harder than reading and understanding a solution provided by your instructor. The usual explanation for this difference of effort is that finding a solution to a crossword puzzle, or a math problem, requires *creative effort*. Verifying a solution is much easier since somebody else has already done the creative part.

This chapter studies the computational analog of the preceding phenomenon. In Section 2.1, we define a complexity class **NP** that aims to capture the set of problems whose solutions can be efficiently *verified*. By contrast, the class **P** of the previous chapter contains decision problems that can be efficiently *solved*. The famous **P** versus **NP** question asks whether or not the two classes are the same.

In Section 2.2, we introduce the important phenomenon of **NP**-*complete* problems, which are in a precise sense the "hardest problems" in **NP**. The number of real-life problems that are known to be **NP**-complete now runs into the thousands. Each of them has a polynomial algorithm if and only if **P** = **NP**. The study of **NP**-completeness

---

* In modern terminology, if SAT has a quadratic time algorithm

involves *reductions*, a basic notion used to relate the computational complexity of two different problems. This notion and its various siblings will often reappear in later chapters (e.g., in Chapters 7, 17, and 18). The framework of ideas introduced in this chapter motivates much of the rest of this book.

The implications of **P** = **NP** are mind-boggling. As already mentioned, **NP** problems seem to capture some aspects of "creativity" in problem solving, and such creativity could become accessible to computers if **P** = **NP**. For instance, in this case computers would be able to quickly find proofs for every true mathematical statement for which a proof exists. We survey this "**P** = **NP** Utopia" in Section 2.7.3. Resolving the **P** versus **NP** question is truly of great practical, scientific, and philosophical interest.

2.1 THE CLASS **NP**

Now we formalize the intuitive notion of *efficiently verifiable solutions* by defining a complexity class **NP**. In Chapter 1, we said that problems are "efficiently solvable" if they can be solved by a Turing machine in polynomial time. Thus, it is natural to say that solutions to the problem are "efficiently verifiable" if they can be verified in polynomial time. Since a Turing machine can only read one bit in a step, this means also that the presented solution has to be not too long—at most polynomial in the length of the input.

Definition 2.1 *(The class **NP**)*
A language $L \subseteq \{0, 1\}^*$ is in **NP** if there exists a polynomial $p : \mathbb{N} \to \mathbb{N}$ and a polynomial-time TM M (called the *verifier* for L) such that for every $x \in \{0, 1\}^*$,

$$x \in L \Leftrightarrow \exists u \in \{0, 1\}^{p(|x|)} \text{ s.t. } M(x, u) = 1$$

If $x \in L$ and $u \in \{0, 1\}^{p(|x|)}$ satisfy $M(x, u) = 1$, then we call u a *certificate* for x (with respect to the language L and machine M).

Some texts use the term *witness* instead of certificate. Clearly, $\mathbf{P} \subseteq \mathbf{NP}$ since the polynomial $p(|x|)$ is allowed to be 0 (in other words, u can be an empty string).

EXAMPLE 2.2 (INDSET ∈ **NP**)

To get a sense for the definition, we show that the INDSET language defined in Example 0.1 (about the "largest party you can throw") is in **NP**. Recall that this language contains all pairs $\langle G, k \rangle$ such that the graph G has a subgraph of at least k vertices with no edges between them (such a subgraph is called an *independent set*). Consider the following polynomial-time algorithm M: Given a pair $\langle G, k \rangle$ and a string $u \in \{0, 1\}^*$, output 1 if and only if u encodes a list of k vertices of G such that there is no edge between any two members of the list. Clearly, $\langle G, k \rangle$ is in INDSET if and only if there exists a string u such that $M(\langle G, k \rangle, u) = 1$ and hence INDSET is in **NP**. The list u of k vertices forming the independent set in G serves as the *certificate* that $\langle G, k \rangle$ is in INDSET. Note that if n is the number of vertices in G, then a list of k vertices can be encoded using $O(k \log n)$ bits, where n is the number of vertices in G. Thus, u is a string of at most $O(n \log n)$ bits, which is polynomial in the size of the representation of G.

EXAMPLE 2.3

Here are a few additional examples for decision problems in **NP** (see also Exercise 2.2):

Traveling salesperson: Given a set of n nodes, $\binom{n}{2}$ numbers $d_{i,j}$ denoting the distances between all pairs of nodes, and a number k, decide if there is a closed circuit (i.e., a "salesperson tour") that visits every node exactly once and has total length at most k. The certificate is the sequence of nodes in such a tour.

Subset sum: Given a list of n numbers $A_1, \ldots, A_n$ and a number T, decide if there is a subset of the numbers that sums up to T. The certificate is the list of members in such a subset.

Linear programming: Given a list of m linear inequalities with rational coefficients over n variables $u_1, \ldots, u_n$ (a linear inequality has the form $a_1 u_1 + a_2 u_2 + \cdots + a_n u_n \leq b$ for some coefficients $a_1, \ldots, a_n, b$), decide if there is an assignment of rational numbers to the variables $u_1, \ldots, u_n$ that satisfies all the inequalities. The certificate is the assignment (see Exercise 2.4).

0/1 integer programming: Given a list of m linear inequalities with rational coefficients over n variables $u_1, \ldots, u_m$, find out if there is an assignment of zeroes and ones to $u_1, \ldots, u_n$ satisfying all the inequalities. The certificate is the assignment.

Graph isomorphism: Given two $n \times n$ adjacency matrices M_1, M_2, decide if M_1 and M_2 define the same graph, up to renaming of vertices. The certificate is the permutation $\pi : [n] \to [n]$ such that M_2 is equal to M_1 after reordering M_1's indices according to π.

Composite numbers: Given a number N decide if N is a composite (i.e., non-prime) number. The certificate is the factorization of N.

Factoring: Given three numbers N, L, U decide if N has a prime factor p in the interval $[L, U]$. The certificate is the factor p.[1]

Connectivity: Given a graph G and two vertices s, t in G, decide if s is connected to t in G. The certificate is a path from s to t.

In the preceding list, the **connectivity**, **composite numbers**, and **linear programming** problems are known to be in **P**. For connectivity, this follows from the simple and well-known breadth-first search algorithm (see any algorithms text such as [KT06, CLRS01]). The composite numbers problem was only recently shown to be in **P** (see the beautiful algorithm of [AKS04]). For the linear programming problem, this is again highly nontrivial and follows from the Ellipsoid algorithm of Khachiyan [Kha79].

All the other problems in the list are not known to be in **P**, though we do not have any proof that they are not in **P**. The **Independent Set** (INDSET), **Traveling Salesperson**, **Subset Sum**, and **Integer Programming** problems are known to be **NP**-*complete*, which, as we will see in Section 2.2, implies that they are not in **P** unless **P** = **NP**. The **Graph Isomorphism** and **Factoring** problems are not known to be either in **P** nor **NP**-complete.

---

[1] There is a polynomial-time algorithm to check primality [AKS04]. We can also show that **Factoring** is in **NP** by using the primality certificate of Exercise 2.5.

2.1.1 Relation between NP and P

We have the following trivial relationships between **NP** and the classes **P** and **DTIME**$(T(n))$ of Chapter 1 (see Definitions 1.12 and 1.13).

Claim 2.4 *Let* **EXP** $= \bigcup_{c>1}$. *Then* **P** $\subseteq$ **NP** $\subseteq$ **EXP**. ◇

PROOF: (**P** $\subseteq$ **NP**): Suppose $L \in$ **P** is decided in polynomial-time by a TM N. Then $L \in$ **NP**, since we can take N as the machine M in Definition 2.1 and make $p(x)$ the zero polynomial (in other words, u is an empty string).

(**NP** $\subseteq$ **EXP**): If $L \in$ **NP** and $M, p()$ are as in Definition 2.1, then we can decide L in time $2^{O(p(n))}$ by enumerating all possible strings u and using M to check whether u is a valid certificate for the input x. The machine accepts iff such a u is ever found. Since $p(n) = O(n^c)$ for some $c > 1$, the number of choices for u is $2^{O(n^c)}$, and the running time of the machine is similar. ■

Currently, we do not know of any stronger relation between **NP** and deterministic time classes than the trivial ones stated in Claim 2.4. The question whether or not **P** = **NP** is considered *the* central open question of complexity theory and is also an important question in mathematics and science at large (see Section 2.7). Most researchers believe that **P** $\neq$ **NP** since years of effort have failed to yield efficient algorithms for **NP**-complete problems.

2.1.2 Nondeterministic Turing machines

The class **NP** can also be defined using a variant of Turing machines called *nondeterministic* Turing machines (abbreviated NDTM). In fact, this was the original definition, and the reason for the name **NP**, which stands for *nondeterministic polynomial time*. The only difference between an NDTM and a standard TM (as defined in Section 1.2) is that an NDTM has *two* transition functions δ_0 and δ_1, and a special state denoted by q_{accept}. When an NDTM M computes a function, we envision that at each computational step M makes an arbitrary choice as to which of its two transition functions to apply. For every input x, we say that $M(x) = 1$ if there *exists* some sequence of these choices (which we call the *nondeterministic choices* of M) that would make M reach q_{accept} on input x. Otherwise—if *every* sequence of choices makes M halt without reaching q_{accept}—then we say that $M(x) = 0$. We say that M runs in $T(n)$ time if for every input $x \in \{0, 1\}^*$ and every sequence of nondeterministic choices, M reaches either the halting state or q_{accept} within $T(|x|)$ steps.

Definition 2.5 For every function $T : \mathbb{N} \to \mathbb{N}$ and $L \subseteq \{0, 1\}^*$, we say that $L \in$ **NTIME**$(T(n))$ if there is a constant $c > 0$ and a $c \cdot T(n)$-time NDTM M such that for every $x \in \{0, 1\}^*, x \in L \Leftrightarrow M(x) = 1$. ◇

The next theorem gives an alternative characterization of **NP** as the set of languages computed by polynomial-time *nondeterministic* Turing machines.

Theorem 2.6 **NP** $= \bigcup_{c \in \mathbb{N}}$ **NTIME**(n^c). ◇

PROOF: The main idea is that the sequence of nondeterministic choices made by an accepting computation of an NDTM can be viewed as a certificate that the input is in the language, and vice versa.

Suppose $p : \mathbb{N} \to \mathbb{N}$ is a polynomial and L is decided by a NDTM N that runs in time $p(n)$. For every $x \in L$, there is a sequence of nondeterministic choices that makes N reach q_{accept} on input x. We can use this sequence as a *certificate* for x. This certificate has length $p(|x|)$ and can be verified in polynomial time by a *deterministic* machine, which simulates the action of N using these nondeterministic choices and verifies that it would have entered q_{accept} after using these nondeterministic choices. Thus, $L \in \mathbf{NP}$ according to Definition 2.1.

Conversely, if $L \in \mathbf{NP}$ according to Definition 2.1, then we describe a polynomial-time NDTM N that decides L. On input x, it uses the ability to make nondeterministic choices to write down a string u of length $p(|x|)$. (Concretely, this can be done by having transition δ_0 correspond to writing a 0 on the tape and transition δ_1 correspond to writing a 1.) Then it runs the deterministic verifier M of Definition 2.1 to verify that u is a valid certificate for x, and if so, enters q_{accept}. Clearly, N enters q_{accept} on x if and only if a valid certificate exists for x. Since $p(n) = O(n^c)$ for some $c > 1$, we conclude that $L \in \mathbf{NTIME}(n^c)$. ∎

As is the case with deterministic TMs, NDTMs can be easily represented as strings, and there exists a *universal* nondeterministic Turing machine (see Exercise 2.6). In fact, using nondeterminism, we can even make the simulation by a universal TM slightly more efficient.

One should note that, unlike standard TMs, NDTMs are not intended to model any physically realizable computation device.

2.2 REDUCIBILITY AND NP-COMPLETENESS

It turns out that the independent set problem is at least as hard as any other language in **NP**: If it has a polynomial-time algorithm then so do all the problems in **NP**. This fascinating property is called **NP**-*hardness*. Since most scientists conjecture that $\mathbf{NP} \neq \mathbf{P}$, the fact that a language is **NP**-hard can be viewed as evidence that it cannot be decided in polynomial time.

How can we prove that a language C is at least as hard as some other language B? The crucial tool we use is the notion of a *reduction* (see Figure 2.1).

Definition 2.7 *(Reductions,* **NP***-hardness and* **NP***-completeness)* A language $L \subseteq \{0, 1\}^*$ is *polynomial-time Karp reducible* to a language $L' \subseteq \{0, 1\}^*$ (sometimes shortened to just "polynomial-time reducible"), denoted by $L \leq_p L'$, if there is a polynomial-time computable function $f : \{0, 1\}^* \to \{0, 1\}^*$ such that for every $x \in \{0, 1\}^*$, $x \in L$ if and only if $f(x) \in L'$.

We say that L' is **NP**-*hard* if $L \leq_p L'$ for every $L \in \mathbf{NP}$. We say that L' is **NP**-*complete* if L' is **NP**-hard and $L' \in \mathbf{NP}$.

Some texts use the names "many-to-one reducibility" or "polynomial-time mapping reducibility" instead of "polynomial-time Karp reducibility."

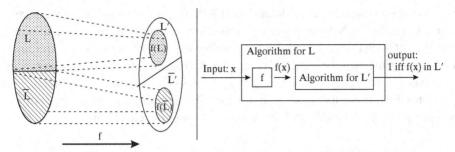

Figure 2.1. A Karp reduction from L to L' is a polynomial-time function f that maps strings in L to strings in L' and strings in $\bar{L} = \{0, 1\}^* \setminus L$ to strings in $\bar{L'}$. It can be used to transform a polynomial-time TM M' that decides L' into a polynomial-time TM M for L by setting $M(x) = M'(f(x))$.

The important (and easy to verify) property of polynomial-time reducibility is that if $L \leq_p L'$ and $L' \in \mathbf{P}$ then $L \in \mathbf{P}$—see Figure 2.1. This is why we say in this case that L' is *at least as hard* as L, as far as polynomial-time algorithms are concerned. Note that $\leq_p$ is a *relation* among languages, and part 1 of Theorem 2.8 shows that this relation is *transitive*. Later we will define other notions of reduction, and many will satisfy transitivity. Part 2 of the theorem suggests the reason for the term **NP**-hard—namely, an **NP**-hard languages is *at least as hard* as any other **NP** language. Part 3 similarly suggests the reason for the term **NP**-complete: to study the **P** versus **NP** question it suffices to study whether any **NP**-complete problem can be decided in polynomial time.

Theorem 2.8
1. *(Transitivity) If $L \leq_p L'$ and $L' \leq_p L''$, then $L \leq_p L''$.*
2. *If language L is **NP**-hard and $L \in \mathbf{P}$, then $\mathbf{P} = \mathbf{NP}$.*
3. *If language L is **NP**-complete, then $L \in \mathbf{P}$ if and only if $\mathbf{P} = \mathbf{NP}$.* ◇

PROOF: The main observation underlying all three parts is that if p, q are two functions that grow at most as n^c and n^d, respectively, then composition $p(q(n))$ grows as at most n^{cd}, which is also polynomial. We now prove part 1 and leave the others as simple exercises.

If f_1 is a polynomial-time reduction from L to L' and f_2 is a reduction from L' to L'', then the mapping $x \mapsto f_2(f_1(x))$ is a polynomial-time reduction from L to L'' since $f_2(f_1(x))$ takes polynomial time to compute given x. Finally, $f_2(f_1(x)) \in L''$ iff $f_1(x) \in L'$, which holds iff $x \in L$. ∎

Do **NP**-complete languages exist? In other words, does **NP** contain a single language that is as hard as any other language in the class? There is a simple example of such a language:

Theorem 2.9 *The following language is **NP**-complete:*

$$\mathsf{TMSAT} = \{\langle \alpha, x, 1^n, 1^t \rangle : \exists u \in \{0, 1\}^n \text{ s.t. } M_\alpha \text{ outputs } 1 \text{ on input } \langle x, u \rangle \text{ within } t \text{ steps}\}$$

where M_α denotes the (deterministic) TM represented by the string α.[2] ◇

---

[2] Recall that 1^k denotes the string consisting of k bits, each of them 1. Often in complexity theory we include the string 1^k in the input to allow a polynomial TM to run in time polynomial in k.

PROOF: Once you internalize the definition of **NP**, the proof of Theorem 2.9 is straight-forward. Let L be an **NP**-language. By Definition 2.1, there is a polynomial p and a verifier TM M such that $x \in L$ iff there is a string $u \in \{0, 1\}^{p(|x|)}$ satisfying $M(x, u) = 1$ and M runs in time $q(n)$ for some polynomial q. To reduce L to TMSAT, we simply map every string $x \in \{0, 1\}^*$ to the tuple $\langle \, \llcorner M \lrcorner, x, 1^{p(|x|)}, 1^{q(m)} \rangle$, where $m = |x| + p(|x|)$ and $\llcorner M \lrcorner$ denotes the representation of M as a string. This mapping can clearly be performed in polynomial time and by the definition of TMSAT and the choice of M,

$$\langle \, \llcorner M \lrcorner, x, 1^{p(|x|)}, 1^{q(m)} \rangle \in \mathsf{TMSAT} \Leftrightarrow$$

$$\exists_{u \in \{0,1\}^{p(|x|)}} \text{ s.t. } M(x, u) \text{ outputs 1 within } q(m) \text{ steps} \Leftrightarrow x \in L$$

■

TMSAT is not a very useful **NP**-complete problem since its definition is intimately tied to the notion of the Turing machine. Hence the fact that TMSAT is **NP**-complete does not provide much new insight. In Section 2.3, we show examples of more "natural" **NP**-complete problems.

2.3 THE COOK-LEVIN THEOREM: COMPUTATION IS LOCAL

Around 1971, Cook and Levin independently discovered the notion of **NP**-completeness and gave examples of combinatorial **NP**-complete problems whose definition seems to have nothing to do with Turing machines. Soon after, Karp showed that **NP**-completeness occurs widely and many problems of practical interest are **NP**-complete. To date, thousands of computational problems in a variety of disciplines have been shown to be **NP**-complete.

2.3.1 Boolean formulas, CNF, and SAT

Some of the simplest examples of **NP**-complete problems come from propositional logic. A *Boolean formula* over the variables $u_1, \ldots, u_n$ consists of the variables and the logical operators AND ($\wedge$), OR ($\vee$), and NOT ($\neg$). For example, $(u_1 \wedge u_2) \vee (u_2 \wedge u_3) \vee (u_3 \wedge u_1)$ is a Boolean formula. If φ is a Boolean formula over variables $u_1, \ldots, u_n$, and $z \in \{0, 1\}^n$, then $\varphi(z)$ denotes the value of φ when the variables of φ are assigned the values z (where we identify 1 with TRUE and 0 with FALSE). A formula φ is *satisfiable* if there exists some assignment z such that $\varphi(z)$ is TRUE. Otherwise, we say that φ is *unsatisfiable*.

The above formula $(u_1 \wedge u_2) \vee (u_2 \wedge u_3) \vee (u_3 \wedge u_1)$ is satisfiable, since the assignment $u_1 = 1, u_2 = 0, u_3 = 1$ satisfies it. In general, an assignement $u_1 = z_1, u_2 = z_2, u_3 = z_3$ satisfies the formula iff at least two of the z_i's are 1.

A Boolean formula over variables $u_1, \ldots, u_n$ is in *CNF form* (shorthand for *Conjunctive Normal Form*) if it is an AND of OR's of variables or their negations. For example, the following is a 3CNF formula: (here and elsewhere, $\bar{u}_i$ denotes $\neg u_i$)

$$(u_1 \vee \bar{u}_2 \vee u_3) \wedge (u_2 \vee \bar{u}_3 \vee u_4) \wedge (\bar{u}_1 \vee u_3 \vee \bar{u}_4)$$

More generally, a CNF formula has the form

$$\bigwedge_i \left(\bigvee_j v_{i_j} \right)$$

where each v_{i_j} is either a variable u_k or its negation $\bar{u}_k$. The terms v_{i_j} are called the *literals* of the formula and the terms $(\vee_j v_{i_j})$ are called its *clauses*. A kCNF is a CNF formula in which all clauses contain at most k literals. We denote by SAT the language of all satisfiable CNF formulae and by 3SAT the language of all satisfiable 3CNF formulae.[3]

2.3.2 The Cook-Levin Theorem

The following theorem provides us with our first natural **NP**-complete problems.

Theorem 2.10 (*Cook-Levin Theorem* [Coo71, Lev73])

1. SAT *is* **NP**-*complete.*
2. 3SAT *is* **NP**-*complete.*

We now prove Theorem 2.10 (an alternative proof, using the notion of *Boolean circuits*, is described in Section 6.1). Both SAT and 3SAT are clearly in **NP**, since a satisfying assignment can serve as the certificate that a formula is satisfiable. Thus we only need to prove that they are **NP**-hard. We do so by (a) proving that SAT is **NP**-hard and then (b) showing that SAT is polynomial-time Karp reducible to 3SAT. This implies that 3SAT is **NP**-hard by the transitivity of polynomial-time reductions. Part (a) is achieved by the following lemma.

Lemma 2.11 SAT *is* **NP**-*hard.* $\qquad \diamond$

To prove Lemma 2.11, we have to show how to reduce *every* **NP** language L to SAT. In other words, we need a polynomial-time transformation that turns any $x \in \{0, 1\}^*$ into a CNF formula φ_x such that $x \in L$ iff φ_x is satisfiable. Since we know nothing about the language L except that it is in **NP**, this reduction has to rely only upon the definition of computation and express it in some way using a Boolean formula.

2.3.3 Warmup: Expressiveness of Boolean formulas

As a warmup for the proof of Lemma 2.11, we show how to express various conditions using CNF formulae.

---

[3] Strictly speaking, a string representing a Boolean formula has to be *well-formed*: Strings such as $u_1 \wedge \wedge u_2$ do not represent any valid formula. As usual, we ignore this issue since it is easy to identify strings that are not well-formed and decide that such strings represent some fixed formula.

EXAMPLE 2.12 *(Expressing equality of strings)*

The formula $(x_1 \vee \overline{y_1}) \wedge (\overline{x_1} \vee y_1)$ is in CNF form. It is satisfied by only those values of x_1, y_1 that are equal. Thus, the formula

$$(x_1 \vee \overline{y_1}) \wedge (\overline{x_1} \vee y_1) \wedge \cdots \wedge (x_n \vee \overline{y_n}) \wedge (\overline{x_n} \vee y_n)$$

is satisfied by an assignment if and only if each x_i is assigned the same value as y_i.

Thus, though $=$ is not a standard Boolean operator like $\vee$ or $\wedge$, we will use it as a convenient shorthand since the formula $\phi_1 = \phi_2$ is equivalent to (in other words, has the same satisfying assignments as) $(\phi_1 \vee \overline{\phi_2}) \wedge (\overline{\phi_1} \vee \phi_2)$.

In fact, CNF formulae of exponential size can express *every* Boolean function, as shown by the following simple claim.

Claim 2.13 *(Universality of AND, OR, NOT)* *For every Boolean function* $f : \{0, 1\}^\ell \to \{0, 1\}$, *there is an ℓ-variable CNF formula* φ *of size* $\ell 2^\ell$ *such that* $\varphi(u) = f(u)$ *for every* $u \in \{0, 1\}^\ell$, *where the size of a CNF formula is defined to be the number of* $\wedge/\vee$ *symbols it contains.*   ◇

PROOF SKETCH: For every $v \in \{0, 1\}^\ell$, it is not hard to see that there exists a clause $C_v(z_1, z_2, \ldots, z_\ell)$ in ℓ variables such that $C_v(v) = 0$ and $C_v(u) = 1$ for every $u \neq v$. For example, if $v = \langle 1, 1, 0, 1 \rangle$, the corresponding clause is $\overline{z}_1 \vee \overline{z}_2 \vee z_3 \vee \overline{z}_4$.

We let φ be the AND of all the clauses C_v for v such that $f(v) = 0$. In other words,

$$\varphi = \bigwedge_{v : f(v) = 0} C_v(z_1, z_2, \ldots, z_\ell)$$

Note that φ has size at most $\ell 2^\ell$. For every u such that $f(u) = 0$ it holds that $C_u(u) = 0$ and hence $\varphi(u)$ is also equal to 0. On the other hand, if $f(u) = 1$, then $C_v(u) = 1$ for every v such that $f(v) = 0$ and hence $\varphi(u) = 1$. We get that for every u, $\varphi(u) = f(u)$. ∎

In this chapter, we will use Claim 2.13 only when the number of variables is some fixed constant.

2.3.4 Proof of Lemma 2.11

Let L be an **NP** language. By definition, there is polynomial time TM M such that for every $x \in \{0, 1\}^*$, $x \in L \Leftrightarrow M(x, u) = 1$ for some $u \in \{0, 1\}^{p(|x|)}$, where $p : \mathbb{N} \to \mathbb{N}$ is some polynomial. We show L is polynomial-time Karp reducible to SAT by describing a polynomial-time transformation $x \to \varphi_x$ from strings to CNF formulae such that $x \in L$ iff φ_x is satisfiable. Equivalently,

$$\varphi_x \in \mathsf{SAT} \text{ iff } \exists u \in \{0, 1\}^{p(|x|)} \text{ s.t. } M(x \circ u) = 1 \tag{2.1}$$

(where $\circ$ denotes concatenation).[4]

---

[4] Because the length $p(|x|)$ of the second input u is easily computable, we can represent the pair $\langle x, u \rangle$ simply by $x \circ u$, without a need to use a "marker symbol" between x and u.

How can we construct such a formula φ_x? The trivial idea is to use the transformation of Claim 2.13 on the Boolean function that maps $u \in \{0, 1\}^{p(|x|)}$ to $M(x, u)$. This would give a CNF formula ψ_x, such that $\psi_x(u) = M(x, u)$ for every $u \in \{0, 1\}^{p(|x|)}$. Thus a string u such that $M(x, u) = 1$ exists if and only if ψ_x is satisfiable. But this trivial idea is not useful for us, since the size of the formula ψ_x obtained from Claim 2.13 can be as large as $p(|x|)2^{p(|x|)}$. To get a smaller formula, we use the fact that M runs in polynomial time, and that each basic step of a Turing machine is highly *local* (in the sense that it examines and changes only a few bits of the machine's tapes). We express the correctness of these local steps using smaller Boolean formulae.

In the course of the proof, we will make the following simplifying assumptions about the TM M: (i) M only has two tapes—an input tape and a work/output tape—and (ii) M is an *oblivious* TM in the sense that its head movement does not depend on the contents of its tapes. That is, M's computation takes the same time for all inputs of size n, and for every i the location of M's heads at the ith step depends only on i and the length of the input.

We can make these assumptions without loss of generality because for every $T(n)$-time TM M there exists a two-tape oblivious TM $\tilde{M}$ computing the same function in $O(T(n)^2)$ time (see Remark 1.7 and Exercise 1.5).[5] Thus in particular, if L is in **NP**, then there exists a two-tape *oblivious* polynomial-time TM M and a polynomial p such that

$$x \in L \Leftrightarrow \exists u \in \{0, 1\}^{p(|x|)} \text{ s.t. } M(x \circ u) = 1 \tag{2.2}$$

Note that because M is oblivious, we can run it on the trivial input $(x, 0^{p(|x|)})$ to determine the precise head position of M during its computation on every other input of the same length. We will use this fact later on.

Denote by Q the set of M's possible states and by Γ its alphabet. The *snapshot* of M's execution on some input y at a particular step i is the triple $\langle a, b, q \rangle \in \Gamma \times \Gamma \times Q$ such that a, b are the symbols read by M's heads from the two tapes and q is the state M is in at the ith step (see Figure 2.2). Clearly the snapshot can be encoded as a binary string. Let c denote the length of this string, which is some constant depending upon $|Q|$ and $|\Gamma|$.

For every $y \in \{0, 1\}^*$, the snapshot of M's execution on input y at the ith step depends on (a) its state in the $(i - 1)$st step and (b) the contents of the current cells of its input and work tapes.

The insight at the heart of the proof concerns the following thought exercise. Suppose somebody were to claim the existence of some u satisfying $M(x \circ u) = 1$ and, as evidence, present you with the sequence of snapshots that arise from M's execution on $x \circ u$. How can you tell that the snapshots present a valid computation that was actually performed by M?

Clearly, it suffices to check that for each $i \leq T(n)$, the snapshot z_i is correct given the snapshots for the previous $i - 1$ steps. However, since the TM can only read/modify one bit at a time, to check the correctness of z_i it suffices to look at only *two* of the previous snapshots. Specifically, to check z_i we need to only look at the following: $z_{i-1}, y_{\mathsf{inputpos}(i)}, z_{\mathsf{prev}(i)}$ (see Figure 2.3). Here y is shorthand for $x \circ u$;

---

[5] In fact, with some more effort, we even simulate a nonoblivious $T(n)$-time TM by an oblivious TM running in $O(T(n) \log T(n))$-time; see Exercise 1.6. This oblivious machine may have more than two tapes, but the following proof below easily generalizes to this case.

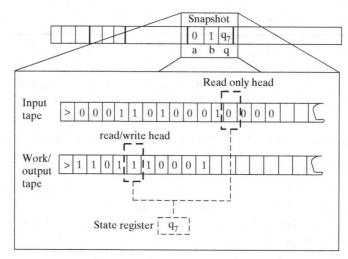

Figure 2.2. A snapshot of a TM contains the current state and symbols read by the TM at a particular step. If at the ith step M reads the symbols $0, 1$ from its tapes and is in the state q_7, then the snapshot of M at the ith step is $\langle 0, 1, q_7 \rangle$.

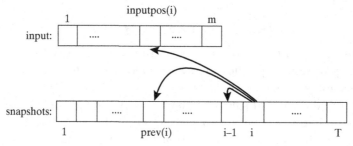

Figure 2.3. The snapshot of M at the ith step depends on its previous state (contained in the snapshot at the $(i-1)$st step), and the symbols read from the input tape, which is in position inputpos(i), and from the work tape, which was last written to in step prev(i).

inputpos(i) denotes the location of M's input tape head at the ith step (recall that the input tape is read-only, so it contains $x \circ u$ throughout the computation); and prev(i) is the last step before i when M's head was in the same cell on its work tape that it is on during step i.[6] The reason this small amount of information suffices to check the correctness of z_i is that the contents of the current cell have not been affected between step prev(i) and step i.

In fact, since M is a deterministic TM, for every triple of values to $z_{i-1}, y_{\text{inputpos}(i)}, z_{\text{prev}(i)}$, there is at most one value of z_i that is correct. Thus there is some function F (derived from M's transition function) that maps $\{0, 1\}^{2c+1}$ to $\{0, 1\}^c$ such that a correct z_i satisfies

$$z_i = F(z_{i-1}, z_{\text{prev}(i)}, y_{\text{inputpos}(i)}) \tag{2.3}$$

---

[6] If i is the first step that M visits a certain location, then we define prev$(i) = 1$.

Because M is oblivious, the values $\mathtt{inputpos}(i)$ and $\mathtt{prev}(i)$ do not depend on the particular input y. Also, as previously mentioned, these indices can be computed in polynomial-time by simulating M on a trivial input.

Now we turn the above thought exercise into a reduction. Recall that by (2.2), an input $x \in \{0, 1\}^n$ is in L if and only if $M(x \circ u) = 1$ for some $u \in \{0, 1\}^{p(n)}$. The previous discussion shows this latter condition occurs if and only if there exists a string $y \in \{0, 1\}^{n+p(n)}$ and a sequence of strings $z_1, \ldots, z_{T(n)} \in \{0, 1\}^c$ (where $T(n)$ is the number of steps M takes on inputs of length $n + p(n)$) satisfying the following four conditions:

1. The first n bits of y are equal to x.
2. The string z_1 encodes the initial snapshot of M. That is, z_1 encodes the triple $\langle \triangleright , \square, q_{\mathsf{start}} \rangle$ where $\triangleright$ is the start symbol of the input tape, $\square$ is the blank symbol, and q_{start} is the initial state of the TM M.
3. For every $i \in \{2, \ldots, T(n)\}$, $z_i = F(z_{i-1}, z_{\mathtt{inputpos}(i)}, z_{\mathtt{prev}(i)})$.
4. The last string $z_{T(n)}$ encodes a snapshot in which the machine halts and outputs 1.

The formula φ_x will take variables $y \in \{0, 1\}^{n+p(n)}$ and $z \in \{0, 1\}^{cT(n)}$ and will verify that y, z satisfy the AND of these four conditions. Thus $x \in L \Leftrightarrow \varphi_x \in \mathsf{SAT}$ and so all that remains is to show that we can express φ_x as a polynomial-sized CNF formula.

Condition 1 can be expressed as a CNF formula of size $4n$ (see Example 2.12). Conditions 2 and 4 each depend on c variables and hence by Claim 2.13 can be expressed by CNF formulae of size $c2^c$. Condition 3, which is an AND of $T(n)$ conditions each depending on at most $3c + 1$ variables, can be expressed as a CNF formula of size at most $T(n)(3c + 1)2^{3c+1}$. Hence the AND of all these conditions can be expressed as a CNF formula of size $d(n + T(n))$ where d is some constant depending only on M. Moreover, this CNF formula can be computed in time polynomial in the running time of M.

2.3.5 Reducing SAT to 3SAT

To complete the proof of Theorem 2.10, it suffices to prove the following lemma:

Lemma 2.14 SAT $\leq_p$ 3SAT.   ◇

PROOF: We give a transformation that maps each CNF formula φ into a 3CNF formula ψ such that ψ is satisfiable if and only if φ is. We demonstrate first the case that φ is a 4CNF. Let C be a clause of φ, say $C = u_1 \vee \overline{u}_2 \vee \overline{u}_3 \vee u_4$. We add a new variable z to the φ and replace C with the pair of clauses $C_1 = u_1 \vee \overline{u}_2 \vee z$ and $C_2 = \overline{u}_3 \vee u_4 \vee \overline{z}$. Clearly, if $u_1 \vee \overline{u}_2 \vee \overline{u}_3 \vee u_4$ is true, then there is an assignment to z that satisfies both $u_1 \vee \overline{u}_2 \vee z$ and $\overline{u}_3 \vee u_4 \vee \overline{z}$ and vice versa: If C is false, then no matter what value we assign to z either C_1 or C_2 will be false. The same idea can be applied to a general clause of size 4 and, in fact, can be used to change every clause C of size k (for $k > 3$) into an equivalent pair of clauses C_1 of size $k - 1$ and C_2 of size 3 that depend on the k variables of C and an additional auxiliary variable z. Applying this transformation repeatedly yields a polynomial-time transformation of a CNF formula φ into an equivalent 3CNF formula ψ. ∎

2.3.6 More thoughts on the Cook-Levin Theorem

The Cook-Levin Theorem is a good example of the power of abstraction. Even though the theorem holds regardless of whether our computational model is the C programming language or the Turing machine, it may have been considerably more difficult to discover in the former context.

The proof of the Cook-Levin Theorem actually yields a result that is a bit stronger than the theorem's statement:

1. We can reduce the size of the output formula φ_x if we use the efficient simulation of a standard TM by an oblivious TM (see Exercise 1.6), which manages to keep the simulation overhead logarithmic. Then for every $x \in \{0, 1\}^*$, the size of the formula φ_x (and the time to compute it) is $O(T \log T)$, where T is the number of steps the machine M takes on input x (see Exercise 2.12).

2. The reduction f from an **NP**-language L to SAT presented in Lemma 2.11 not only satisfied that $x \in L \Leftrightarrow f(x) \in$ SAT but actually the proof yields an efficient way to transform a certificate for x to a satisfying assignment for $f(x)$ and vice versa. We call a reduction with this property a *Levin* reduction. One can also modify the proof slightly (see Exercise 2.13) so that it actually supplies us with a one-to-one and onto map between the set of certificates for x and the set of satisfying assignments for $f(x)$, implying that they are of the same size. A reduction with this property is called *parsimonious*. Most of the known **NP**-complete problems (including all the ones mentioned in this chapter) have parsimonious Levin reductions from all the **NP** languages. As we will see later in Chapter 17, this fact is useful in studying the complexity of counting the *number* of certificates for an instance of an **NP** problem.

Why 3SAT?

The reader may wonder why the fact that 3SAT is **NP**-complete is so much more interesting than the fact that, say, the language TMSAT of Theorem 2.9 is **NP**-complete. One reason is that 3SAT is useful for proving the **NP**-completeness of other problems: It has very minimal combinatorial structure and thus is easy to use in reductions. Another reason is that propositional logic has had a central role in mathematical logic, which is why Cook and Levin were interested in 3SAT in the first place. A third reason is its practical importance: 3SAT is a simple example of *constraint satisfaction problems*, which are ubiquitous in many fields including artificial intelligence.

2.4 THE WEB OF REDUCTIONS

Cook and Levin had to show how *every* **NP** language can be reduced to SAT. To prove the **NP**-completeness of any other language L, we do not need to work as hard: by Theorem 2.8 it suffices to reduce SAT or 3SAT to L. Once we know that L is **NP**-complete, we can show that an **NP**-language L' is in fact **NP**-complete by reducing L to L'. This approach has been used to build a "web of reductions" and show that thousands of interesting languages are in fact **NP**-complete. We now show the **NP**-completeness of a few problems. More examples appear in the exercises (see Figure 2.4).

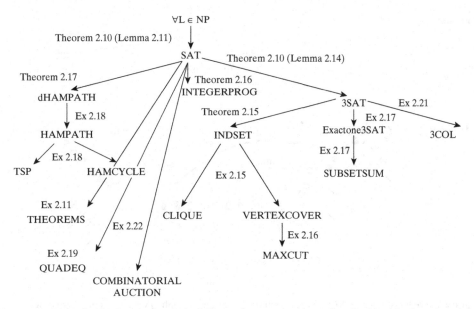

Figure 2.4. Web of reductions between the **NP**-completeness problems described in this chapter and the exercises. Thousands more are known.

Recall the problem of planning a dinner party where every pair of guests is on speaking terms, formalized in Example 0.1 as the language

$$\mathsf{INDSET} = \{\langle G, k\rangle : G \text{ has independent set of size } k\}$$

Theorem 2.15 INDSET *is* **NP**-*complete.*   ◇

PROOF: As shown in Example 2.2, INDSET is in **NP**, and so we only need to show that it is **NP**-hard, which we do by reducing $3\mathsf{SAT}$ to INDSET. Specifically, we will show how to transform in polynomial time every m-clause 3CNF formula φ into a $7m$-vertex graph G such that φ is satisfiable if and only if G has an independent set of size at least m.

The graph G is defined as follows (see Figure 2.5): We associate a cluster of 7 vertices in G with each clause of φ. The vertices in a cluster associated with a clause C correspond to the seven possible satisfying partial assignments to the three variables on which C depends (we call these *partial* assignments, since they only give values for some of the variables). For example, if C is $\overline{u_2} \vee \overline{u_5} \vee u_7$, then the seven vertices in the cluster associated with C correspond to all partial assignments of the form $u_1 = a, u_2 = b, u_3 = c$ for a binary vector $\langle a, b, c\rangle \neq \langle 1, 1, 0\rangle$. (If C depends on less than three variables, then we repeat one of the partial assignments and so some of the seven vertices will correspond to the same assignment.) We put an edge between two vertices of G if they correspond to *inconsistent* partial assignments. Two partial assignments are consistent if they give the same value to all the variables they share. For example, the assignment $u_2 = 0$, $u_{17} = 1$, $u_{26} = 1$ is inconsistent with the assignment $u_2 = 1$, $u_5 = 0$, $u_7 = 1$ because they share a variable (u_2) to which they give a different value. In addition, we put edges between every two vertices that are in the same cluster.

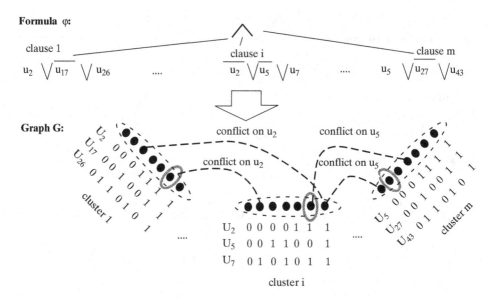

Figure 2.5. We transform a $3CNF$ formula φ with m clauses into a graph G with $7m$ vertices as follows: each clause C is associated with a cluster of 7 vertices corresponding to the 7 possible satisfying assignments to the variables C depends on. We put edges between any two vertices in the same cluster and any two vertices corresponding to *inconsistent* partial assignments. The graph G will have an independent set of size m if and only if φ was satisfiable. The figure above contains only a sample of the edges. The three circled vertices form an independent set.

Clearly, transforming φ into G can be done in polynomial time, and so all that remains to show is that φ is satisfiable iff G has an independent set of size m:

- Suppose that φ has a satisfying assignment u. Define a set S of m of G's vertices as follows: For every clause C of φ put in S the vertex in the cluster associated with C that corresponds to the restriction of u to the variables C depends on. Because we only choose vertices that correspond to restrictions of the assignment u, no two vertices of S correspond to inconsistent assignments and hence S is an independent set of size m.

- Suppose that G has an independent set S of size m. We will use S to construct a satisfying assignment u for φ. We define u as follows: For every $i \in [n]$, if there is a vertex in S whose partial assignment gives a value a to u_i, then set $u_i = a$; otherwise, set $u_i = 0$. This is well defined because S is an independent set, and hence each variable u_i can get at most a single value by assignments corresponding to vertices in S. On the other hand, because we put all the edges within each cluster, S can contain at most a single vertex in each cluster, and hence there is an element of S in every one of the m clusters. Thus, by our definition of u, it satisfies all of φ's clauses. ∎

We let $0/1$ IPROG be the set of satisfiable *0/1 Integer programs*, as defined in Example 2.3. That is, a set of linear inequalities with rational coefficients over variables $u_1, \ldots, u_n$ is in $0/1$ IPROG if there is an assignment of numbers in $\{0,1\}$ to $u_1, \ldots, u_n$ that satisfies it.

Theorem 2.16 $0/1$ IPROG *is* **NP***-complete.*   ◇

PROOF: $0/1$ IPROG is clearly in **NP** since the assignment can serve as the certificate. To reduce SAT to $0/1$ IPROG, note that every CNF formula can be easily expressed as

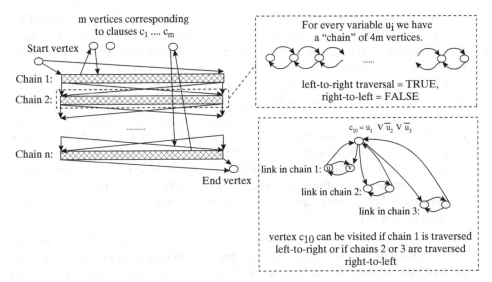

Figure 2.6. Reducing SAT to dHAMPATH. A formula φ with n variables and m clauses is mapped to a graph G that has m vertices corresponding to the clauses and n doubly linked chains, each of length $4m$, corresponding to the variables. Traversing a chain left to right corresponds to setting the variable to True, while traversing it right to left corresponds to setting it to False. Note that in the figure every Hamiltonian path that takes the edge from u to c_{10} must immediately take the edge from c_{10} to v, as otherwise it would get "stuck" the next time it visits v.

an integer program by expressing every clause as an inequality. For example, the clause $u_1 \vee \bar{u}_2 \vee \bar{u}_3$ can be expressed as $u_1 + (1 - u_2) + (1 - u_3) \geq 1$. ∎

A *Hamiltonian path* in a directed graph is a path that visits all vertices exactly once. Let dHAMPATH denote the set of all directed graphs that contain such a path.

Theorem 2.17 dHAMPATH *is* **NP**-*complete.*   ◇

PROOF: dHAMPATH is in **NP** since the ordered list of vertices in the path can serve as a certificate. To show that dHAMPATH is **NP**-hard, we show a way to map every CNF formula φ into a graph G such that φ is satisfiable if and only if G has a Hamiltonian path (i.e., a path that visits all of G's vertices exactly once).

The reduction is described in Figure 2.6. The graph G has (1) m vertices for each of φ's clauses $c_1,\ldots,c_m$, (2) a special starting vertex v_{start} and ending vertex v_{end}, and (3) n "chains" of $4m$ vertices corresponding to the n variables of φ. A chain is a set of vertices $v_1,\ldots,v_{4m}$ such that for every $i \in [4m-1]$, v_i and v_{i+1} are connected by two edges in both directions.

We put edges from the starting vertex v_{start} to the two extreme points of the first chain. We also put edges from the extreme points of the jth chain to the extreme points to the $(j+1)$th chain for every $j \in [n-1]$. We put an edge from the extreme points of the nth chain to the ending vertex v_{end}.

In addition to these edges, for every clause C of φ, we put edges between the chains corresponding to the variables appearing in C and the vertex v_C corresponding to C in the following way: If C contains the literal u_j, then we take two neighboring vertices v_i, v_{i+1} in the jth chain and put an edge from v_i to C and from C to v_{i+1}. If C contains the literal $\bar{u}_j$, then we connect these edges in the opposite direction (i.e., v_{i+1} to C and

C to v_i). When adding these edges, we never "reuse" a link v_i, v_{i+1} in a particular chain and always keep an unused link between every two used links. We can do this since every chain has $4m$ vertices, which is more than sufficient for this. We now prove that $\varphi \in \mathsf{SAT} \Leftrightarrow G \in \mathsf{dHAMPATH}$:

($\varphi \in \mathsf{SAT} \Rightarrow G \in \mathsf{dHAMPATH}$): Suppose that φ has a satisfying assignment $u_1, \ldots, u_n$. We will show a path that visits all the vertices of G. The path will start at v_{start}, travel through all the chains in order, and end at v_{end}. For starters, consider the path that travels the jth chain in left-to-right order if $u_j = 1$ and travels it in right-to-left order if $u_j = 0$. This path visits all the vertices except for those corresponding to clauses. Yet, if u is a satisfying assignment then the path can be easily modified to visit all the vertices corresponding to clauses: For each clause C, there is at least one literal that is true, and we can use one link on the chain corresponding to that literal to "skip" to the vertex v_C and continue on as before.

($G \in \mathsf{dHAMPATH} \Rightarrow \varphi \in \mathsf{SAT}$): Suppose that G has an Hamiltonian path P. We first note that the path P must start in v_{start} (as it has no incoming edges) and end at v_{end} (as it has no outgoing edges). Furthermore, we claim that P needs to traverse all the chains in order and, within each chain, traverse it either in left-to-right order or right-to-left order. This would be immediate if the path did not use the edges from a chain to the vertices corresponding to clauses. The claim holds because if a Hamiltonian path takes the edge $u \to w$, where u is on a chain and w corresponds to a clause, then it must at the next step take the edge $w \to v$, where v is the vertex adjacent to u in the link. Otherwise, the path will get stuck (i.e., will find every outgoing edge already taken) the next time it visits v; see Figure 2.1. Now, define an assignment $u_1, \ldots, u_n$ to φ as follows: $u_j = 1$ if P traverses the jth chain in left-to-right order, and $u_j = 0$ otherwise. It is not hard to see that because P visits all the vertices corresponding to clauses, $u_1, \ldots, u_n$ is a satisfying assignment for φ. ∎

In praise of reductions

Though originally invented as part of the theory of **NP**-completeness, the polynomial-time reduction (together with its first cousin, the randomized polynomial-time reduction defined in Section 7.6) has led to a rich understanding of complexity above and beyond **NP**-completeness. Much of complexity theory and cryptography today (thus, many chapters of this book) consists of using reductions to make connections between disparate complexity theoretic conjectures. Why do complexity theorists excel at reductions but not at actually proving lower bounds on Turing machines? Maybe human creativity is more adaptible to gadget-making and algorithm-design (after all, a reduction is merely an algorithm to transform one problem into another) than to proving lower bounds on Turing machines.

2.5 DECISION VERSUS SEARCH

We have chosen to define the notion of **NP** using Yes/No problems ("Is the given formula satisfiable?") as opposed to *search* problems ("Find a satisfying assignment to this formula if one exists"). Clearly, the search problem is harder than the corresponding decision problem, and so if $\mathbf{P} \neq \mathbf{NP}$, then neither one can be solved for an **NP**-complete problem. However, it turns out that for **NP**-complete problems they are equivalent in the sense that if the decision problem can be solved (and hence $\mathbf{P} = \mathbf{NP}$), then the search version of any $\mathbf{NP}$ problem can also be solved in polynomial time.

Theorem 2.18 *Suppose that* $\mathbf{P} = \mathbf{NP}$. *Then, for every* $\mathbf{NP}$ *language L and a verifier TM M for L (as per Definition 2.1), there is a polynomial-time TM B that on input* $x \in L$ *outputs a certificate for x (with respect to the language L and TM M).* ◇

PROOF: We need to show that if $\mathbf{P} = \mathbf{NP}$, then for every polynomial-time TM M and polynomial $p(n)$, there is a polynomial-time TM B with the following property: for every $x \in \{0,1\}^n$, if there is $u \in \{0,1\}^{p(n)}$ such that $M(x,u) = 1$ (i.e., a certificate that x is in the language verified by M) then $|B(x)| = p(n)$ and $M(x, B(x)) = 1$.

We start by showing the theorem for the case of SAT. In particular, we show that given an algorithm A that decides SAT, we can come up with an algorithm B that on input a satisfiable CNF formula φ with n variables, finds a satisfying assignment for φ using $2n + 1$ calls to A and some additional polynomial-time computation.

The algorithm B works as follows: We first use A to check that the input formula φ is satisfiable. If so, we first substitute $x_1 = 0$ and then $x_1 = 1$ in φ (this transformation, which simplifies and shortens the formula a little and leaves a formula with $n - 1$ variables, can certainly be done in polynomial time) and then use A to decide which of the two is satisfiable (at least one of them is). Say the first is satisfiable. Then we fix $x_1 = 0$ from now on and continue with the simplified formula. Continuing this way, we end up fixing all n variables while ensuring that each intermediate formula is satisfiable. Thus the final assignment to the variables satisfies φ.

To solve the search problem for an arbitrary $\mathbf{NP}$-language L, we use the fact that the reduction of Theorem 2.10 from L to SAT is actually a *Levin* reduction. This means that we have a polynomial-time computable function f such that not only $x \in L \Leftrightarrow f(x) \in$ SAT but actually we can map a satisfying assignment of $f(x)$ into a certificate for x. Therefore, we can use the algorithm above to come up with an assignment for $f(x)$ and then map it back into a certificate for x. ∎

The proof of Theorem 2.18 shows that SAT is *downward self-reducible*, which means that given an algorithm that solves SAT on inputs of length smaller than n we can solve SAT on inputs of length n. This property of SAT will be useful a few times in the rest of the book. Using the Cook-Levin reduction, one can show that all $\mathbf{NP}$-complete problems have a similar property.

2.6 coNP, EXP, AND NEXP

Now we define some additional complexity classes related to $\mathbf{P}$ and $\mathbf{NP}$.

2.6.1 coNP

If $L \subseteq \{0, 1\}^*$ is a language, then we denote by $\overline{L}$ the *complement* of L. That is, $\overline{L} = \{0, 1\}^* \setminus L$. We make the following definition:

Definition 2.19 $\mathbf{coNP} = \left\{ L : \overline{L} \in \mathbf{NP} \right\}.$ ◇

coNP is *not* the complement of the class **NP**. In fact, **coNP** and **NP** have a nonempty intersection, since every language in **P** is in **NP** ∩ **coNP** (see Exercise 2.23). The following is an example of a **coNP** language: $\overline{\text{SAT}} = \{\varphi : \varphi$ is not satisfiable$\}$. Students sometimes mistakenly convince themselves that $\overline{\text{SAT}}$ is in **NP**. They have the following polynomial time NDTM in mind: On input φ, the machine guesses an assignment. If this assignment does not satisfy φ then it accepts (i.e., goes into q_{accept} and halts), and if it does satisfy φ, then the machine halts without accepting. This NDTM does not do the job: indeed, it accepts every unsatisfiable φ, but in addition it also accepts many satisfiable formulae (i.e., every formula that has a single unsatisfying assignment). That is why pedagogically speaking we prefer the following definition of **coNP** (which is easily shown to be equivalent to the first, see Exercise 2.24).

Definition 2.20 (**coNP**, *alternative definition*) For every $L \subseteq \{0, 1\}^*$, we say that $L \in$ **coNP** if there exists a polynomial $p : \mathbb{N} \to \mathbb{N}$ and a polynomial-time TM M such that for every $x \in \{0, 1\}^*$,

$$x \in L \Leftrightarrow \forall u \in \{0, 1\}^{p(|x|)}, \ M(x, u) = 1 \qquad \diamond$$

Note the use of the "∀" quantifier in this definition where Definition 2.1 used ∃.

We can define **coNP**-completeness in analogy to **NP**-completeness: A language is **coNP**-complete if it is in **coNP** and every **coNP** language is polynomial-time Karp reducible to it.

EXAMPLE 2.21

The following language is **coNP**-complete:

$$\text{TAUTOLOGY} = \{\varphi : \ \varphi \text{ is a } tautology \text{—a Boolean formula}$$
$$\text{that is satisfied by every assignment}\}$$

It is clearly in **coNP** by Definition 2.20, and so all we have to show is that for every $L \in$ **coNP**, $L \leq_p$ TAUTOLOGY. But this is easy: Just modify the Cook-Levin reduction from $\overline{L}$ (which is in **NP**) to SAT. For every input $x \in \{0, 1\}^*$ that reduction produces a formula φ_x that is satisfiable iff $x \in \overline{L}$. Now consider the formula $\neg\varphi_x$. It is in TAUTOLOGY iff $x \in L$, and this completes the description of the reduction.

It's not hard to see that if **P** = **NP**, then **NP** = **coNP** = **P** (Exercise 2.25). Put in the contrapositive: If we can show that **NP** $\neq$ **coNP**, then we have shown **P** $\neq$ **NP**. Most researchers believe that **NP** $\neq$ **coNP**. The intuition is almost as strong as for the **P** versus **NP** question: It seems hard to believe that there is any short certificate for certifying that a given formula is a TAUTOLOGY, in other words, to certify that *every* assignment satisfies the formula.

2.6.2 **EXP and NEXP**

In Claim 2.4, we encountered the class **EXP** $= \cup_{c \geq 1} \text{DTIME}(2^{n^c})$, which is the exponential-time analog of **P**. The exponential-time analog of **NP** is the class **NEXP**, defined as $\cup_{c \geq 1} \text{NTIME}(2^{n^c})$.

As was seen earlier, because every problem in **NP** can be solved in exponential time by a brute force search for the certificate, $\mathbf{P} \subseteq \mathbf{NP} \subseteq \mathbf{EXP} \subseteq \mathbf{NEXP}$. Is there any point to studying classes involving exponential running times? The following simple result—providing merely a glimpse of the rich web of relations we will be establishing between disparate complexity questions—may be a partial answer.

Theorem 2.22 *If* **EXP** $\neq$ **NEXP**, *then* **P** $\neq$ **NP**.   ◇

PROOF: We prove the contrapositive: Assuming $\mathbf{P} = \mathbf{NP}$, we show $\mathbf{EXP} = \mathbf{NEXP}$. Suppose $L \in \mathbf{NTIME}(2^{n^c})$ and NDTM M decides it. We claim that then the language

$$L_{\mathrm{pad}} = \left\{ \langle x, 1^{2^{|x|^c}} \rangle : x \in L \right\} \tag{2.4}$$

is in **NP**. Here is an NDTM for L_{pad}: Given y, first check if there is a string z such that $y = \langle z, 1^{2^{|z|^c}} \rangle$. If not, output 0 (i.e., halt without going to the state q_{accept}). If y is of this form, then simulate M on z for $2^{|z|^c}$ steps and output its answer. Clearly, the running time is polynomial in $|y|$, and hence $L_{\mathrm{pad}} \in \mathbf{NP}$. Hence if $\mathbf{P} = \mathbf{NP}$, then L_{pad} is in **P**. But if L_{pad} is in **P** then L is in **EXP**: To determine whether an input x is in L, we just pad the input and decide whether it is in L_{pad} using the polynomial-time machine for L_{pad}. ∎

The *padding* technique used in this proof, whereby we transform a language by "padding" every string in a language with a string of (useless) symbols, is also used in several other results in complexity theory (see, e.g., Section 14.4.1). In many settings, it can be used to show that equalities between complexity classes "scale up"; that is, if two different types of resources solve the same problems within bound $T(n)$, then this also holds for functions T' larger than T. Viewed contrapositively, padding can be used to show that inequalities between complexity classes involving resource bound $T'(n)$ "scale down" to resource bound $T(n)$.

Like **P** and **NP**, many complexity classes studied in this book are contained in both **EXP** and **NEXP**.

2.7 MORE THOUGHTS ABOUT **P**, **NP**, AND ALL THAT

2.7.1 The philosophical importance of NP

At a totally abstract level, the **P** versus **NP** question may be viewed as a question about the power of nondeterminism in the Turing machine model. Similar questions have been completely answered for simpler models such as finite automata.

However, the certificate definition of **NP** also suggests that the **P** versus **NP** question captures a widespread phenomenon of some philosophical importance (and a source of great frustration): Recognizing the correctness of an answer is often much easier than coming up with the answer. Appreciating a Beethoven sonata is far easier than composing the sonata; verifying the solidity of a design for a suspension bridge is easier (to a civil engineer anyway!) than coming up with a good design; verifying the proof of a theorem is easier than coming up with a proof itself (a fact referred to in Gödel's letter quoted at the start of the chapter), and so forth. In such cases, coming up with the right answer seems to involve *exhaustive search* over an exponentially large set. The **P** versus **NP** question asks whether exhaustive search can be avoided in general. It seems obvious to most people—and the basis of many false proofs proposed by amateurs— that exhaustive search cannot be avoided. Unfortunately, turning this intuition into a proof has proved difficult.

2.7.2 **NP and mathematical proofs**

By definition, **NP** is the set of languages where membership has a short certificate. This is reminiscent of another familiar notion, that of a mathematical proof. As noticed in the past century, in principle all of mathematics can be axiomatized, so that proofs are merely formal manipulations of axioms. Thus the correctness of a proof is rather easy to verify—just check that each line follows from the previous lines by applying the axioms. In fact, for most known axiomatic systems (e.g., Peano arithmetic or Zermelo-Fraenkel Set Theory) this verification runs in time *polynomial* in the length of the proof. Thus the following problem is in **NP** for any of the usual axiomatic systems $\mathcal{A}$:

$$\text{THEOREMS} = \left\{ (\varphi, 1^n) : \varphi \text{ has a formal proof of length} \leq n \text{ in system } \mathcal{A} \right\}.$$

Gödel's quote from 1956 at the start of this chapter asks whether this problem can be solved in say quadratic time. He observes that this is a finite version of Hilbert's *Entscheidungsproblem*, which asked for an algorithmic decision procedure for checking whether a given mathematical statement has a proof (with no upper bound specified on the length of the proof). He points out that if THEOREMS can be solved in quadtratic time, then the undecidability of the *Entscheidungsproblem* would become less depressing, since we are usually only interested in theorems whose proof is not too long (say, fits in a few books).

Exercise 2.11 asks you to prove that THEOREMS is **NP**-complete. Hence the **P** versus **NP** question is a *rephrasing* of Gödel's question, which asks whether or not there is a algorithm that finds mathematical proofs in time polynomial in the length of the proof.

Of course, you know in your guts that finding correct math proofs is far harder than verifying their correctness. So presumably, you believe at an intuitive level that **P** $\neq$ **NP**.

2.7.3 **What if P = NP?**

If **P** = **NP**—specifically, if an **NP**-complete problem like 3SAT had a very efficient algorithm running in say $O(n^2)$ time—then the world would be mostly a computational Utopia. Mathematicians could be replaced by efficient theorem-discovering programs (a fact pointed out in Kurt Gödel's 1956 letter and recovered two decades later). In general, for every search problem whose answer can be efficiently verified (or has a short certificate of correctness), we will be able to find the correct answer or the short certificate in polynomial time. Artificial intelligence (AI) software would be perfect since we could easily do exhaustive searches in a large tree of possibilities. Inventors and engineers would be greatly aided by software packages that can design the perfect part or gizmo for the job at hand. Very large scale integration (VLSI) designers will be able to whip up optimum circuits, with minimum power requirements. Whenever a scientist has some experimental data, she would be able to automatically obtain the simplest theory (under any reasonable measure of simplicity we choose) that best explains these measurements; by the principle of Occam's Razor the simplest explanation is likely to be the right one.[7] Of course, in some cases, it took scientists centuries to come up with the simplest theories explaining the known data. This approach can be used to also approach nonscientific problems: One could find the simplest theory that explains, say, the list of books from the New York *Times*' bestseller list. (Of course even finding the right definition of "simplest" might require some breakthroughs in artificial intelligence and understanding natural language that themselves would use **NP**-algorithms.) All these applications will be a consequence of our study of the polynomial hierarchy in Chapter 5. (The problem of finding the smallest "theory" is closely related to problems like MIN-EQ-DNF studied in Chapter 5.)

Somewhat intriguingly, this Utopia would have no need for randomness. As we will later see, if **P** = **NP**, then randomized algorithms would buy essentially no efficiency gains over deterministic algorithms; see Chapter 7. (Philosophers should ponder this one.)

This Utopia would also come at one price: there would be no privacy in the digital domain. Any encryption scheme would have a trivial decoding algorithm. There would be no digital cash and no SSL, RSA, or PGP (see Chapter 9). We would just have to learn to get along better without these, folks.

This utopian world may seem ridiculous, but the fact that we can't rule it out shows how little we know about computation. Taking the half-full cup point of view, it shows how many wonderful things are still waiting to be discovered.

2.7.4 What if **NP** = co**NP**?

If **NP** = co**NP**, the consequences still seem dramatic. Mostly, they have to do with existence of short certificates for statements that do not seem to have any. To give an example, consider the **NP**-complete problem of finding whether or not a set of multivariate polynomials has a common root (see Exercise 2.20). In other words, it is **NP** complete to decide whether a system of equations of the following type has a solution:

$$f_1(x_1, \ldots, x_n) = 0$$
$$f_2(x_1, \ldots, x_n) = 0$$
$$\vdots$$
$$f_m(x_1, \ldots, x_n) = 0$$

where each f_i is a polynomial of degree at most 2.

If a solution exists, then that solution serves as a *certificate* to this effect (of course, we have to also show that the solution can be described using a polynomial number of

---

[7] Occam's Razor is a well-known principle in philosophy, but it has found new life in *machine learning*, a subfield of computer science. Valiant's Theory of the Learnable [Val84] gives mathematical basis for Occam's Razor. This theory is deeply influenced by computational complexity; an excellent treatment appears in the book of Kearns and Vazirani [KV94]. If **P** = **NP**, then many interesting problems in machine learning turn out to have polynomial-time algorithms.

bits, which we omit). The problem of deciding that the system does *not* have a solution is of course in **coNP**. Can we give a certificate to the effect that the system does *not* have a solution? Hilbert's Nullstellensatz Theorem seems to do that: It says that the system is infeasible iff there is a sequence of polynomials $g_1, g_2, \ldots, g_m$ such that $\sum_i f_i g_i = 1$, where 1 on the right-hand side denotes the constant polynomial 1.

What is happening? Does the Nullstellensatz prove **coNP** = **NP**? No, because the degrees of the g_is—and hence the number of bits used to represent them—could be exponential in n, m. (And it is simple to construct f_is for which this is necessary.)

However, if **NP** = **coNP** then there would be some *other* notion of a short certificate to the effect that the system is infeasible. The effect of such a result on mathematics could be even greater than the effect of Hilbert's Nullstellensatz. (The Nullstellensatz appears again in Chapters 15 and 16.)

2.7.5 Is there anything between NP and NP-complete?

NP-completeness has been an extremely useful and influential theory, since thousands of useful problems are known to be **NP**-complete (and hence they are presumably not in **P**). However, there remain a few interesting **NP** problems that are neither known to be in **P** nor known to be **NP**-complete. For such problems, it would be nice to have some other way to show that they are nevertheless difficult to solve, but we know of very few ways of quantifying this. Sometimes researchers turn the more famous problems of this type into bona fide classes of their own. Some examples are the problem of factoring integers (used in Chapter 9) or the so-called *unique games labeling problem* (Chapter 22). The complexity of these problems is related to those of many other problems. Similarly, Papadimitriou [Pap90] has defined numerous interesting classes between **P** and **NP** that capture the complexity of various interesting problems. The most important is **PPAD**, which captures the problem of finding *Nash Equilibria* in two-person games.

Sometimes we can show that some of these problems are unlikely to be **NP**-complete. We do this by showing that *if* the problem is **NP**-complete, then this violates some other conjecture (that we believe almost as much as **P** $\neq$ **NP**); we'll see such results for the *graph isomorphism* problem in Section 8.1.3.

Another interesting result in Section 3.3 called *Ladner's Theorem* shows that if **P** $\neq$ **NP**, then there exist problems that are neither in **P** nor **NP**-complete.

2.7.6 Coping with NP hardness

NP-complete problems turn up in a great many applications, from flight scheduling to genome sequencing. What do you do if the problem you need to solve turns out to be **NP**-complete? At the outset, the situation looks bleak: If **P** $\neq$ **NP**, then there simply does not *exist* an efficient algorithm to solve such a problem.[8] However, there may still be some hope: **NP**-completeness only means that (assuming **P** $\neq$ **NP**) the problem does

---

[8] Not however that sometimes simple changes in the problem statement can dramatically change its complexity. Therefore, modeling a practical situation with an abstract problem requires great care; one must take care not to unnecessarily model a simple setting with an **NP**-complete problem.

not have an algorithm that solves it *exactly* on *every* input. But for many applications, an *approximate* solution on *some* of the inputs might be good enough.

A case in point is the traveling salesperson problem (TSP), of computing: Given a list of pairwise distances between n cities, find the shortest route that travels through all of them. Assume that you are indeed in charge of coming up with travel plans for traveling salespeople that need to visit various cities around your country. Does the fact that TSP is **NP**-complete means that you are bound to do a hopelessly suboptimal job? This does not have to be the case.

First note that you do not need an algorithm that solves the problem on *all* possible lists of pairwise distances. We might model the inputs that actually arise in this case as follows: The n cities are points on a plane, and the distance between a pair of cities is the distance between the corresponding points (we are neglecting here the difference between travel distance and direct/arial distance). It is an easy exercise to verify that not all possible lists of pairwise distances can be generated in such a way. We call those that do *Euclidean* distances. Another observation is that computing the *exactly* optimal travel plan may not be so crucial. If you could always come up with a travel plan that is at most 1% longer than the optimal, this should be good enough.

It turns out that neither of these observations on its own is sufficient to make the problem tractable. The TSP problem is still **NP**-complete even for Euclidean distances. Also if $\mathbf{P} \neq \mathbf{NP}$, then TSP is hard to approximate within any constant factor. However, *combining* the two observations together actually helps: For every ϵ there is a $\text{poly}(n(\log n)^{O(1/\epsilon)})$-time algorithm that given Euclidean distances between n cities comes up with a tour that is at most a factor of $(1 + \epsilon)$ worse than the optimal tour [Aro96].

Thus, discovering that your problem is **NP**-complete should not be cause for immediate despair. Rather you should view this as indication that a more careful modeling of the problem is needed, letting the literature on complexity and algorithms guide you as to what features might make the problem more tractable. Alternatives to worst-case exact computation are explored in Chapters 18 and 11, which investigate *average-case complexity* and *approximation algorithms* respectively.

2.7.7 Finer explorations of time complexity

We have tended to focus the discussion in this chapter on the difference between polynomial and nonpolynomial time. Researchers have also explored finer issues about time complexity. For instance, consider a problem like INDSET. We believe that it cannot be solved in polynomial time. But what exactly is its complexity? Is it $n^{O(\log n)}$, or $2^{n^{0.2}}$ or $2^{n/10}$? Most researchers believe it is actually $2^{\Omega(n)}$. The intuitive feeling is that the trivial algorithm of enumerating all possible subsets is close to optimal.

It is useful to test this intuition when the size of the optimum independent set is at most k. The trivial algorithm of enumerating all k-size subsets of vertices takes $\binom{n}{k} \approx n^k$ time when $k \ll n$. (In fact, think of k as an arbitrarily large constant.) Can we do any better, say $2^k \text{poly}(n)$ time, or more generally $f(k)\text{poly}(n)$ time for some function f? The theory of *fixed parameter intractability* studies such questions. There is a large set of **NP** problems including INDSET that are *complete* in this respect, which means that one of them has a $f(k)\text{poly}(n)$ time algorithm iff all of them do. Needless to say, this notion of "completeness" is with respect to some special notion of reducibility; the book [FG06] is a good resource on this topic.

Similarly, one can wonder if there is an extension of **NP**-completeness that butresses the intuition that the true complexity of INDSET and many other **NP**-complete problems is $2^{\Omega(n)}$ rather than simply nonpolynomial. Impagliazzo, Paturi, and Zane [IPZ98] have such a theory, including a notion of *reducibility* tailored to studying this issue.

WHAT HAVE WE LEARNED?

- The class **NP** consists of all the languages for which membership can be certified to a polynomial-time algorithm. It contains many important problems not known to be in **P**. We can also define **NP** using nondeterministic Turing machines.
- **NP**-complete problems are the hardest problems in **NP**, in the sense that they have a polynomial-time algorithm if and only if $\mathbf{P} = \mathbf{NP}$. Many natural problems that seemingly have nothing to do with Turing machines turn out to be **NP**-complete. One such example is the language 3SAT of satisfiable Boolean formulae in 3*CNF* form.
- If $\mathbf{P} = \mathbf{NP}$, then for every search problem for which one can efficiently verify a given solution, one can also efficiently find such a solution from scratch.
- The class **coNP** is the set of complements of **NP**-languages. We believe that $\mathbf{coNP} \neq \mathbf{NP}$. This is a stronger assumption than $\mathbf{P} \neq \mathbf{NP}$.

CHAPTER NOTES AND HISTORY

Since the 1950s, Soviet scientists were aware of the undesirability of using exhaustive or brute force search, (which they called *perebor*,) for combinatorial problems, and asked the question of whether certain problems *inherently* require such search (see [Tra84] for a history). In the West, the first published description of this issue is by Edmonds [Edm65], in the paper quoted in the previous chapter. However, on both sides of the iron curtain, it took some time to realize the right way to formulate the problem and to arrive at the modern definition of the classes **NP** and **P**. Amazingly, in his 1956 letter to von Neumann we quoted earlier, Gödel essentially asks the question of **P** vs. **NP**, although there is no hint that he realized that one of the particular problems he mentions is **NP**-complete. Unfortunately, von Neumann was very sick at the time, and as far as we know, no further research was done by either on them on this problem, and the letter was only discovered in the 1980s.

In 1971, Cook published his seminal paper defining the notion of **NP**-completeness and showing that SAT is **NP** complete [Coo71]. Soon afterwards, Karp [Kar72] showed that 21 important problems are in fact **NP**-complete, generating tremendous interest in this notion. Meanwhile, in the USSR, Levin independently defined **NP**-completeness (although he focused on search problems) and showed that a variant of SAT is **NP**-complete. Levin's paper [Lev73] was published in 1973, but he had been giving talks on his results since 1971; also in those days there was essentially zero communication between eastern and western scientists. Trakktenbrot's survey [Tra84] describes Levin's discovery and also gives an accurate translation of Levin's paper. See Sipser's survey [Sip92] for more on the history of **P** and **NP** and a full translation of Gödel's remarkable letter.

The book by Garey and Johnson [GJ79] and the web site [CK00] contain many more examples of **NP** complete problems. Some such problems have been studied well before the invention of computers: The traveling salesperson problem has been studied in the nineteenth century (see [LLKS85]). Also, a recently discovered letter by Gauss to Schumacher shows that Gauss was thinking about methods to solve the famous *Euclidean Steiner Tree* problem—today known to be **NP**-hard—in the early nineteenth century. See also Wigderson's survey [Wig06] for more on the relations between **NP** and mathematics.

Aaronson [Aar05] surveys various attempts to solve **NP** complete problems via "nontraditional" computing devices.

Even if **NP** $\neq$ **P**, this does not necessarily mean that all of the utopian applications mentioned in Section 2.7.3 are automatically ruled out. It may be that, say, 3SAT is hard to solve in the worst case on every input but actually very easy on the average, See Chapter 18 for a more detailed study of *average-case* complexity. Also, Impagliazzo [Imp95b] has an excellent survey on this topic.

An intriguing possibility is that it is simply impossible to resolve the **P** vs. **NP** question using the accepted axioms of mathematics: This has turned out to be the case with some other questions such as Cantor's "Continuum Hypothesis." Aaronson's survey [Aar03] explores this possibility.

Alon and Kilian (in personal communication) showed that in the definition of the language **Factoring** in Example 2.3, the condition that the factor p is prime is necessary to capture the factoring problem, since without this condition this language is **NP**-complete (for reasons having nothing to do with the hardness of factoring integers).

EXERCISES

2.1. Prove that allowing the certificate to be of size at *most* $p(|x|)$ (rather than equal to $p(|x|)$) in Definition 2.1 makes no difference. That is, show that for every polynomial-time Turing machine M and polynomial $p : \mathbb{N} \to \mathbb{N}$, the language

$$\{x : \exists u \text{ s.t. } |u| \leq p(|x|) \text{ and } M(x, u) = 1\}$$

is in **NP**.

2.2. Prove that the following languages are in **NP**:

Two coloring: 2COL $= \{G : $ graph G has a coloring with two colors$\}$, where a coloring of G with c colors is an assignment of a number in $[c]$ to each vertex such that no adjacent vertices get the same number.

Three coloring: 3COL $= \{G : $ graph G has a coloring with three colors$\}$.

Connectivity: CONNECTED $= \{G : G$ is a connected graph$\}$.

Which ones of them are in **P**?

H531

2.3. Let LINEQ denote the set of satisfiable rational linear equations. That is, LINEQ consists of the set of all pairs $\langle A, \mathbf{b} \rangle$ where A is an $m \times n$ rational matrix and $\mathbf{b}$ is an m dimensional rational vector, such that $A\mathbf{x} = \mathbf{b}$ for some n-dimensional vector $\mathbf{x}$. Prove that LINEQ is in **NP** (the key is to prove that if there exists such a vector $\mathbf{x}$, then there exists an $\mathbf{x}$ whose coefficients can be represented using a number of bits that is polynomial in the representation of $A,\mathbf{b}$). (Note that LINEQ is actually in **P**: Can you show this?)

H531

2.4. Show that the $\mathsf{Linear}\ \mathsf{Programming}$ problem from Example 2.3 is in **NP**. (Again, this problem is actually in **P**, though by a highly nontrivial algorithm [Kha79].)

H531

2.5. [Pra75] Let $\mathsf{PRIMES} = \left\{ \lfloor n \rfloor : n \text{ is prime} \right\}$. Show that $\mathsf{PRIMES} \in$ **NP**. You can use the following fact: A number n is prime iff for every prime factor q of $n-1$, there exists a number $a \in \{2, \dots, n-1\}$ satisfying $a^{n-1} = 1 \pmod{n}$ but $a^{(n-1)/q} \neq 1 \pmod{n}$.

H531

2.6. Prove the existence of a *nondeterministic universal TM* (analogously to the deterministic universal TM of Theorem 1.9). That is, prove that there exists a representation scheme of NDTMs, and an NDTM $\mathcal{NU}$ such that for every string α, and input x, $\mathcal{NU}(x, \alpha) = M_\alpha(x)$.

(a) Prove that there exists a universal NDTM $\mathcal{NU}$ such that if M_α halts on x within T steps, then $\mathcal{NU}$ halts on x, α within $CT \log T$ steps (where C is a constant depending only on the machine represented by α).

(b) Prove that there is such a universal NDTM that runs on these inputs for at most Ct steps.

H532

2.7. Prove Parts 2 and 3 of Theorem 2.8.

2.8. Let HALT be the Halting language defined in Theorem 1.11. Show that HALT is **NP**-hard. Is it **NP**-complete?

2.9. We have defined a relation $\leq_p$ among languages. We noted that it is *reflexive* (i.e., $L \leq_p L$ for all languages L) and *transitive* (i.e., if $L \leq_p L'$ and $L' \leq_p L''$ then $L' \leq_p L''$). Show that it is not *symmetric*, namely, $L \leq_p L'$ need not imply $L' \leq_p L$.

2.10. Suppose $L_1, L_2 \in$ **NP**. Then is $L_1 \cup L_2$ in **NP**? What about $L_1 \cap L_2$?

2.11. Mathematics can be axiomatized using for example the *Zermelo-Frankel* system, which has a finite description. Argue at a high level that the following language is **NP**-complete. (You don't need to know anything about ZF.)

$$\left\{ \langle \varphi, 1^n \rangle : \text{math statement } \varphi \text{ has a proof of size at most } n \text{ in the ZF system} \right\}$$

The question of whether this language is in **P** is essentially the question asked by Gödel in the chapter's initial quote.

H532

2.12. Show that for every time-constructible $T : \mathbb{N} \to \mathbb{N}$, if $L \in$ **NTIME**$(T(n))$, we can give a polynomial-time Karp reduction from L to $3\mathsf{SAT}$ that transforms instances of size n into 3CNF formulae of size $O(T(n)\log T(n))$. Can you make this reduction also run in $O(T(n)\operatorname{poly}(\log T(n)))$?

2.13. Recall that a reduction f from an **NP**-language L to an **NP**-languages L' is *parsimonious* if the number of certificates of f is equal to the number of certificates of $f(x)$.

(a) Prove that the reduction from every **NP**-language L to SAT presented in the proof of Lemma 2.11 can be made parsimonious.

H532

(b) Show a parsimonious reduction from SAT to 3SAT.

2.14. Cook [Coo71] used a somewhat different notion of reduction: A language L is *polynomial-time Cook reducible* to a language L' if there is a polynomial time TM M that, given an *oracle* for deciding L', can decide L. An oracle for L' is a magical extra tape given to M, such that whenever M writes a string on this tape and goes into a special "invocation" state, then the string—in a single step!—gets overwritten by 1 or 0 depending upon whether the string is or is not in L'; see Section 3.4 for a more precise definition.

Show that the notion of cook reducibility is transitive and that 3SAT is Cook-reducible to TAUTOLOGY.

2.15. In the CLIQUE problem, we are given an undirected graph G and an integer K and have to decide whether there is a subset S of at least K vertices such that every two distinct vertices $u, v \in S$ have an edge between them (such a subset is called a *clique* of G). In the VERTEX COVER problem, we are given an undirected graph G and an integer K and have to decide whether there is a subset S of at most K vertices such that for every edge $\overline{ij}$ of G, at least one of i or j is in S (such a subset is called a *vertex cover* of G). Prove that both these problems are **NP**-complete.

H532

2.16. In the MAX CUT problem, we are given an undirected graph G and an integer K and have to decide whether there is a subset of vertices S such that there are at least K edges that have one endpoint in S and one endpoint in $\overline{S}$. Prove that this problem is **NP**-complete.

2.17. In the Exactly One 3SAT problem, we are given a 3CNF formula φ and need to decide if there exists a satisfying assignment u for φ such that every clause of φ has exactly one TRUE literal. In the SUBSET SUM problem, we are given a list of n numbers $A_1, \ldots, A_n$ and a number T and need to decide whether there exists a subset $S \subseteq [n]$ such that $\sum_{i \in S} A_i = T$ (the problem size is the sum of all the bit representations of all numbers). Prove that both Exactly One3SAT and SUBSET SUM are **NP**-complete.

H532

2.18. Prove that the language HAMPATH of *undirected* graphs with Hamiltonian paths is **NP**-complete. Prove that the language TSP described in Example 2.3 is **NP**-complete. Prove that the language HAMCYCLE of undirected graphs that contain Hamiltonian cycle (a simple cycle involving all the vertices) is **NP**-complete.

2.19. Let QUADEQ be the language of all satisfiable sets of *quadratic equations* over 0/1 variables (a quadratic equations over $u_1, \ldots, u_n$ has the form $\sum_{i,j \in [n]} a_{i,j} u_i u_j = b$) where addition is modulo 2. Show that QUADEQ is **NP**-complete.

H532

2.20. Let REALQUADEQ be the language of all satisfiable sets of quadratic equations over *real* variables. Show that REALQUADEQ is **NP**-complete.

H532

2.21. Prove that 3COL (see Exercise 2.2) is **NP**-complete.

H532

2.22. In a typical auction of n items, the auctioneer will sell the ith item to the person that gave it the highest bid. However, sometimes the items sold are related to one another (e.g., think of lots of land that may be adjacent to one another) and so people may be willing to pay a high price to get, say, the three items $\{2, 5, 17\}$, but only if they get all of them together. In this case, deciding what to sell to whom might not be an easy task. The COMBINATORIAL AUCTION problem is to decide, given numbers n, k, and a list of pairs $\{\langle S_i, x_i \rangle\}_{i=1}^{m}$ where S_i is a subset of $[n]$ and x_i is an integer, whether there exist disjoint sets $S_{i_1}, \ldots, S_{i_\ell}$ such that $\sum_{j=1}^{\ell} x_{i_j} \geq k$. That is, if x_i is the amount a bidder is willing to pay for the set S_i, then the problem is to decide if the auctioneer can sell items and get a revenue of at least k, under the obvious condition that he can't sell the same item twice. Prove that COMBINATORIAL AUCTION is **NP**-complete.

H532

2.23. Prove that $\mathbf{P} \subseteq \mathbf{NP} \cap \mathbf{coNP}$.

2.24. Prove that Definitions 2.19 and 2.20 do indeed define the same class **coNP**.

2.25. Prove that if $\mathbf{P} = \mathbf{NP}$, then $\mathbf{NP} = \mathbf{coNP}$.

2.26. Show that $\mathbf{NP} = \mathbf{coNP}$ iff 3SAT and TAUTOLOGY are polynomial-time reducible to one another.

2.27. Give a definition of **NEXP** without using NDTMs, analogous to Definition 2.1 of the class **NP**, and prove that the two definitions are equivalent.

2.28. We say that a language is **NEXP**-complete if it is in **NEXP** and every language in **NEXP** is polynomial-time reducible to it. Describe a **NEXP**-complete language L. Prove that if $L \in \mathbf{EXP}$ then $\mathbf{NEXP} = \mathbf{EXP}$.

2.29. Suppose $L_1, L_2 \in \mathbf{NP} \cap \mathbf{coNP}$. Then show that $L_1 \oplus L_2$ is in $\mathbf{NP} \cap \mathbf{coNP}$, where $L_1 \oplus L_2 = \{x : x \text{ is in exactly one of } L_1, L_2\}$.

2.30. (Berman's Theorem 1978) A language is called *unary* if every string in it is of the form 1^i (the string of i ones) for some $i > 0$. Show that if there exists an **NP**-complete unary language then $\mathbf{P} = \mathbf{NP}$. (See Exercise 6.9 for a strengthening of this result.)

H532

2.31. Define the language UNARY SUBSET SUM to be the variant of the SUBSET SUM problem of Exercise 2.17 where all numbers are represented by the *unary* representation (i.e., the number k is represented as 1^k). Show that UNARY SUBSET SUM is in **P**.

H532

2.32. Prove that if every *unary* **NP**-language is in **P** then $\mathbf{EXP} = \mathbf{NEXP}$. (A language L is unary iff it is a subset of $\{1\}^*$, see Exercise 2.30.)

2.33. Let $\Sigma_2 \mathsf{SAT}$ denote the following decision problem: Given a quantified formula ψ of the form

$$\psi = \exists_{x \in \{0,1\}^n} \forall_{y \in \{0,1\}^m} \text{ s.t. } \varphi(x,y) = 1$$

where φ is a CNF formula, decide whether ψ is true. That is, decide whether there exists an x such that for every y, $\varphi(x,y)$ is true. Prove that if $\mathbf{P} = \mathbf{NP}$, then $\Sigma_2 \mathsf{SAT}$ is in $\mathbf{P}$.

2.34. Suppose that you are given a graph G and a number K and are told that either (i) the smallest vertex cover (see Exercise 2.15) of G is of size at most K or (ii) it is of size at least $3K$. Show a polynomial-time algorithm that can distinguish between these two cases. Can you do it with a smaller constant than 3? Since VERTEX COVER is $\mathbf{NP}$-hard, why does this algorithm not show that $\mathbf{P} = \mathbf{NP}$?

CHAPTER 3

Diagonalization

> [T]he relativized **P** =?**NP** question has a positive answer for some oracles and a negative answer for other oracles. We feel that this is further evidence of the difficulty of the **P** =?**NP** question.
>
> – Baker, Gill, Solovay [BGS75]

A basic goal of complexity theory is to prove that certain complexity classes (e.g., **P** and **NP**) are not the same. To do so, we need to exhibit a machine in one class that differs from every machine in the other class in the sense that their answers are different on at least one input. This chapter describes *diagonalization*—essentially the only general technique known for constructing such a machine.

We already encountered diagonalization in Section 1.5, where it was used to show the existence of uncomputable functions. Here it will be used in more clever ways. We first use diagonalization in Sections 3.1 and 3.2 to prove *hierarchy theorems*, which show that giving Turing machines more computational resources allows them to solve a strictly larger number of problems. We then use diagonalization in Section 3.3 to show a fascinating theorem of Ladner: If **P** ≠ **NP**, then there exist problems that are neither **NP**-complete nor in **P**.

Though diagonalization led to some of these early successes of complexity theory, researchers concluded in the 1970s that diagonalization alone may not resolve **P** versus **NP** and other interesting questions; Section 3.4 describes their reasoning. Interestingly, these limits of diagonalization are proved using diagonalization itself.

The results on limitations of diagonalization caused this technique to go out of favor for many years, and other approaches such as circuit lower bounds became more popular (see Chapter 14 for an introduction). But now those other approaches are also stuck, whereas some recent results use diagonalization as a key component (see Section 20.4 for an example). Hence future complexity theorists should master this simple idea before going on to anything fancier!

Machines as strings and the universal TM

The one common tool used in all diagonalization proofs is the representation of TMs by strings. We recall some salient aspects of this representation as mentioned in Section 1.4. First, it is *effective* in the sense that there is a *universal* TM that, given any string x, can simulate the machine represented by x with a small (i.e., at most logarithmic) overhead.

Second, every string $x \in \{0, 1\}^*$ represents some TM (denoted by M_x), and every TM is represented by infinitely many strings. (This may appear nitpicky but it simplifies proofs.) Finally, throughout the chapter, we use the notation M_i, where $i \in \mathbb{N}$, for the machine represented by the string that is the binary expansion of the number i (without the leading 1).

3.1 TIME HIERARCHY THEOREM

The Time Hierarchy Theorem shows that allowing Turing machines more computation time strictly increases the set of languages that they can decide. Recall that for a function $f : \mathbb{N} \to \mathbb{N}$, **DTIME**$(f(n))$ is the set of languages decided by a TM running in time $O(f(n))$. As usual, we restrict attention to time-constructible functions f, which means that the mapping $x \mapsto f(|x|)$ can be computed in $O(f(n))$ time (see Sections 1.3 and 1.6).

Theorem 3.1 *Time Hierarchy Theorem* [HS65]
If f, g are time-constructible functions satisfying $f(n) \log f(n) = o(g(n))$, then

$$\text{DTIME}(f(n)) \subsetneq \text{DTIME}(g(n)) \tag{3.1}$$

PROOF: To showcase the essential idea of the proof of Theorem 3.1 with minimal notation, we prove the simpler statement **DTIME**$(n) \subsetneq$ **DTIME**$(n^{1.5})$.

Consider the following Turing machine D: "*On input x, run for $|x|^{1.4}$ steps the Universal TM $\mathcal{U}$ of Theorem 1.9 to simulate the execution of M_x on x. If $\mathcal{U}$ outputs some bit $b \in \{0, 1\}$ in this time, then output the opposite answer (i.e., output $1 - b$). Else output 0.*" Here M_x is the machine represented by the string x.

By definition, D halts within $n^{1.4}$ steps and hence the language L decided by D is in **DTIME**$(n^{1.5})$. We claim that $L \notin$ **DTIME**(n). For contradiction's sake, assume that there is some TM M and constant c such that TM M, given any input $x \in \{0, 1\}^*$, halts within $c|x|$ steps and outputs $D(x)$.

The time to simulate M by the universal Turing machine $\mathcal{U}$ on every input x is at most $c'c|x| \log |x|$ for some number c' that depends on the alphabet size and number of tapes and states of M but is independent of $|x|$. There is some number n_0 such that $n^{1.4} > c'cn \log n$ for every $n \geq n_0$. Let x be a string representing the machine M whose length is at least n_0 (such a string exists since M is represented by infinitely many strings). Then, $D(x)$ will obtain the output $b = M(x)$ within $|x|^{1.4}$ steps, but by definition of D, we have $D(x) = 1 - b \neq M(x)$. Thus we have derived a contradiction.

The proof Theorem 3.1 for general f, g is similar and uses the observation that the slowdown in simulating a machine using $\mathcal{U}$ is at most logarithmic. ■

3.2 NONDETERMINISTIC TIME HIERARCHY THEOREM

The following is the hierarchy theorem for *non-deterministic* Turing machines.

Theorem 3.2 *Nondeterministic Time Hierarchy Theorem* [Coo72]
If f, g are time constructible functions satisfying $f(n + 1) = o(g(n))$, then

$$\text{NTIME}(f(n)) \subsetneq \text{NTIME}(g(n)) \tag{3.2}$$

PROOF: Again, we just showcase the main idea by proving $\mathbf{NTIME}(n) \subsetneq \mathbf{NTIME}(n^{1.5})$. The first instinct is to duplicate the proof of Theorem 3.1, since there is a universal TM for nondeterministic computation as well (see Exercise 2.6). However, this alone does not suffice because the definition of the new machine D requires the ability to "flip the answer," in other words, to efficiently compute, given the description of an NDTM M and an input x, the value $1 - M(x)$. It is not obvious how to do this using the universal nondeterministic machine, since as we saw earlier in our discussion of the conjecture $\mathbf{NP} \neq \mathbf{coNP}$ (Section 2.6.1), it is unclear how a nondeterministic machine can just "flip the answer." Specifically, we do not expect that that the complement of an $\mathbf{NTIME}(n)$ language will be in $\mathbf{NTIME}(n^{1.5})$. Now of course, the complement of every $\mathbf{NTIME}(n)$ language is trivially decidable in *exponential* time (even deterministically) by examining all the possibilities for the machine's nondeterministic choices, but on first sight this seems to be completely irrelevant to proving $\mathbf{NTIME}(n) \subsetneq \mathbf{NTIME}(n^{1.5})$. Surprisingly, this trivial exponential simulation of a nondeterministic machine does suffice to establish a hierarchy theorem.

The key idea will be *lazy diagonalization*, so named because the new machine D is in no hurry to diagonalize and only ensures that it flips the answer of each linear-time NDTM M_i in only one string out of a sufficiently large (exponentially large) set of strings.

Define the function $f : \mathbb{N} \to \mathbb{N}$ as follows: $f(1) = 2$ and $f(i+1) = 2^{f(i)^{1.2}}$. Given n, it's not hard to find in $O(n^{1.5})$ time the number i such that n is sandwiched between $f(i)$ and $f(i+1)$. Our diagonalizing machine D will try to flip the answer of M_i on *some* input in the set $\{1^n : f(i) < n \leq f(i+1)\}$. D is defined as follows:

> "On input x, if $x \notin 1^*$, reject. If $x = 1^n$, then compute i such that $f(i) < n \leq f(i+1)$ and
> 1. If $f(i) < n < f(i+1)$ then simulate M_i on input 1^{n+1} using nondeterminism in $n^{1.1}$ time and output its answer. (If M_i has not halted in this time, then halt and accept.)
> 2. If $n = f(i+1)$, accept 1^n iff M_i rejects $1^{f(i)+1}$ in $(f(i)+1)^{1.1}$ time."

Part 2 requires going through all possible $2^{(f(i)+1)^{1.1}}$ branches of M_i on input $1^{f(i)+1}$, but that is fine since the input size $f(i + 1)$ is $2^{f(i)^{1.2}}$. Hence the NDTM D runs in $O(n^{1.5})$ time.

Let L be the language decided by D. We claim that $L \notin \mathbf{NTIME}(n)$. Indeed, suppose for the sake of contradiction that L is decided by an NDTM M running in cn steps (for some constant c). Since each NDTM is represented by infinitely many strings, we can find i large enough such that $M = M_i$ and on inputs of length $n \geq f(i)$, M_i can be simulated in less than $n^{1.1}$ steps. This means that the two steps in the description of D ensure, respectively, that

$$\text{If } f(i) < n < f(i+1), \quad \text{then } D(1^n) = M_i(1^{n+1}) \tag{3.3}$$

$$\text{whereas} \quad D(1^{f(i+1)}) \neq M_i(1^{f(i)+1}) \tag{3.4}$$

By our assumption M_i and D agree on all inputs 1^n for n in the semi-open interval $(f(i), f(i+1)]$. Together with (3.3), this implies that $D(1^{f(i+1)}) = M_i(1^{f(i)+1})$, contradicting (3.4). (See Figure 3.1.) ∎

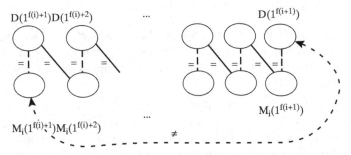

Figure 3.1. The values of D and M_i on inputs 1^n for $n \in (f(i), f(i+1)]$. Full lines denote equality by the design of D, dashed lines denote equality by the assumption that $D(x) = M_i(x)$ for every x, and the dashed arrow denotes inequality by the design of D. Combining all these relations leads to a contradiction.

3.3 LADNER'S THEOREM: EXISTENCE OF **NP**-INTERMEDIATE PROBLEMS

One of the striking aspects of **NP**-completeness is that a surprisingly large number of **NP** problems—including some that were studied for many decades—turned out to be **NP**-complete. This phenomenon suggests a bold conjecture: Every problem in **NP** is either in **P**- or **NP**-complete. If **P** = **NP**, then the conjecture is trivially true but uninteresting. In this section, we show that if (as widely believed) **P** $\neq$ **NP**, then this conjecture is false—there is a language $L \in \textbf{NP} \backslash \textbf{P}$ that is not **NP**-complete. A feature of the proof is an interesting and Gödelian definition of a language SAT_H which "encodes" the difficulty of solving itself.

> **Theorem 3.3** *("NP intermediate" languages* [Lad75])
> *Suppose that* **P** $\neq$ **NP**. *Then there exists a language* $L \in \textbf{NP} \backslash \textbf{P}$ *that is not* **NP**-*complete.*

PROOF: For every function $H : \mathbb{N} \to \mathbb{N}$, we define the language SAT_H to contain all length-n satisfiable formulae that are padded with $n^{H(n)}$ 1's; that is, $\mathrm{SAT}_H = \left\{ \psi 01^{n^{H(n)}} : \psi \in \mathrm{SAT} \text{ and } n = |\psi| \right\}$.
We now define a function $H : \mathbb{N} \to \mathbb{N}$ as follows:

> $H(n)$ is the smallest number $i < \log \log n$ such that for every $x \in \{0, 1\}^*$ with $|x| \leq \log n$, M_i outputs $\mathrm{SAT}_H(x)$ within $i|x|^i$ steps.[1] If there is no such number i then $H(n) = \log \log n$.

H is well defined since $H(n)$ determines membership in SAT_H of strings whose length is greater than n, and the definition of $H(n)$ only relies upon checking the status of strings of length at most $\log n$. In fact, the definition of H directly implies an $O(n^3)$-time recursive algorithm that computes $H(n)$ from n (see Exercise 3.6).[2] We defined H in this way to ensure the following claim.

Claim $\mathrm{SAT}_H \in \textbf{P}$ *iff* $H(n) = O(1)$ *(i.e., there's some C such that $H(n) \leq C$ for every n). Moreover, if* $\mathrm{SAT}_H \notin \textbf{P}$ *then $H(n)$ tends to infinity with n.*

---

[1] Recall that M_i is the machine represented by the binary expansion of i, and $\mathrm{SAT}_H(x)$ is equal to 1 iff $x \in \mathrm{SAT}_H$.

[2] "Recursive algorithm" is a term borrowed from standard programming practice, where one calls a program "recursive" if it has the ability to call itself on some other input.

PROOF OF CLAIM:

$(\text{SAT}_H \in \mathbf{P} \Rightarrow H(n) = O(1))$: Suppose there is a machine M solving SAT_H in at most cn^c steps. Since M is represented by infinitely many strings, there is a number $i > c$ such that $M = M_i$. The definition of $H(n)$ implies that for $n > 2^{2^i}$, $H(n) \le i$. Thus $H(n) = O(1)$.

$(H(n) = O(1) \Rightarrow \text{SAT}_H \in \mathbf{P})$: If $H(n) = O(1)$ then H can take only one of finitely many values, and hence there exists an i such that $H(n) = i$ for infinitely many n's. But this implies that the TM M_i solves SAT_H in in^i-time: for otherwise, if there was an input x on which M_i fails to output the right answer within this bound, then for every $n > 2^{|x|}$ we would have $H(n) \ne i$. Note that this holds even if we only assumed that there's some constant C such that $H(n) \le C$ for infinitely many n's, hence proving the "moreover" part of the claim.

Using this claim we can show that if $\mathbf{P} \ne \mathbf{NP}$ then SAT_H is neither in $\mathbf{P}$ nor $\mathbf{NP}$ complete:

- Suppose that $\text{SAT}_H \in \mathbf{P}$. Then by the claim, $H(n) \le C$ for some constant C, implying that SAT_H is simply SAT padded with at most a polynomial (namely, n^C) number of 1's. But then a polynomial-time algorithm for SAT_H can be used to solve SAT in polynomial time, implying that $\mathbf{P} = \mathbf{NP}$!
- Suppose that SAT_H is $\mathbf{NP}$-complete. This means that there is a reduction f from SAT to SAT_H that runs in time $O(n^i)$ for some constant i. Since we already concluded SAT_H is not in $\mathbf{P}$, the claim above implies that $H(n)$ tends to infinity. Since the reduction works in $O(n^i)$ time only, for large enough n it must map SAT instances of size n to SAT_H instances of size smaller than $n^{H(n)}$. Thus for large enough formulae φ, the reduction f must map it to a string of the type $\psi 01^{H(|\psi|)}$ where ψ is smaller by some fixed polynomial factor, say, smaller than $\sqrt[3]{n}$. But the existence of such a reduction yields a simple polynomial-time recursive algorithm for SAT, contradicting the assumption $\mathbf{P} \ne \mathbf{NP}$! (Completing the details is left as Exercise 3.6.)

∎

Though the theorem shows the existence of some non-$\mathbf{NP}$-complete language in $\mathbf{NP} \setminus \mathbf{P}$ if $\mathbf{NP} \ne \mathbf{P}$, this language seems somewhat contrived, and the proof has not been strengthened to yield a more natural language. In fact, there are remarkably few candidates for such languages, since the status of most natural languages has been resolved thanks to clever algorithms or reductions. Two interesting exceptions are the *Factoring* and *Graph isomorphism* languages (see Example 2.3). No polynomial-time algorithm is currently known for these languages, and there is strong evidence that they are not $\mathbf{NP}$ complete (see Chapter 8).

3.4 ORACLE MACHINES AND THE LIMITS OF DIAGONALIZATION

Quantifying the limits of diagonalization is not easy. Certainly, the diagonalization in Sections 3.2 and 3.3 seems more clever than the one in Section 3.1 or the one that proves the undecidability of the halting problem in Section 1.5.

For concreteness, let us say that "diagonalization" is any technique that relies solely upon the following properties of Turing machines:

I   The existence of an effective representation of Turing machines by strings.
II The ability of one TM to simulate any another without much overhead in running time or space.

Any argument that only uses these facts is treating machines as *black boxes*: The machine's internal workings do not matter. We now show a general way to define variants of Turing machines called *oracle Turing machines* that still satisfy these two properties. However, one way of defining the variant results in TMs for which $\mathbf{P} = \mathbf{NP}$, whereas another way results in TMs for which $\mathbf{P} \neq \mathbf{NP}$. We conclude that to resolve $\mathbf{P}$ versus $\mathbf{NP}$ we need to use some other property in addition to **I** and **II**.

Oracle machines are TMs that are given access to a black box or "oracle" that can magically solve the decision problem for some language $O \subseteq \{0, 1\}^*$. The machine has a special *oracle tape* on which it can write a string $q \in \{0, 1\}^*$ and in one step gets an answer to a query of the form "Is q in O?" This can be repeated arbitrarily often with different queries. If O is a difficult language (say, which cannot be decided in polynomial time, or even undecidable), then this oracle gives an added power to the TM.

Definition 3.4 (*Oracle Turing machines*) An *oracle* Turing machine is a TM M that has a special read-write tape we call M's *oracle tape* and three special states $q_{query}, q_{yes}, q_{no}$. To execute M, we specify in addition to the input a language $O \subseteq \{0, 1\}^*$ that is used as the *oracle* for M. Whenever during the execution M enters the state q_{query}, the machine moves into the state q_{yes} if $q \in O$ and q_{no} if $q \notin O$, where q denotes the contents of the special oracle tape. Note that, regardless of the choice of O, a membership query to O counts only as a single computational step. If M is an oracle machine, $O \subseteq \{0, 1\}^*$ a language, and $x \in \{0, 1\}^*$, then we denote the output of M on input x and with oracle O by $M^O(x)$.

Nondeterministic oracle TMs are defined similarly.   ◇

Definition 3.5 For every $O \subseteq \{0, 1\}^*$, $\mathbf{P}^O$ is the set containing every language that can be decided by a polynomial-time deterministic TMs with oracle access to O and $\mathbf{NP}^O$ is the set of every language that can be decided by a polynomial-time nondeterministic TM with oracle access to O.   ◇

EXAMPLE 3.6

To illustrate the definition of oracle TMs, we show the following simple facts:
1. Let $\overline{SAT}$ denote the language of *unsatisfiable* formulae. Then $\overline{SAT} \in \mathbf{P}^{SAT}$.
   Indeed, given oracle access to SAT, to decide whether a formula φ is in $\overline{SAT}$, a polynomial-time oracle TM can ask its oracle if $\varphi \in SAT$, and then gives the opposite answer as its output.
2. Let $O \in \mathbf{P}$. Then $\mathbf{P}^O = \mathbf{P}$.
   Indeed, allowing an oracle can only help compute more languages and so $\mathbf{P} \subseteq \mathbf{P}^O$. If $O \in \mathbf{P}$, then it is redundant as an oracle, since we can transform any polynomial-time

oracle TM using O into a standard TM (no oracle) by simply replacing each oracle call with the computation of O. Thus $\mathbf{P}^O \subseteq \mathbf{P}$.

3. Let EXPCOM be the following language

$$\{\langle M, x, 1^n \rangle : M \text{ outputs 1 on } x \text{ within } 2^n \text{ steps}\}$$

Then $\mathbf{P}^{\mathsf{EXPCOM}} = \mathbf{NP}^{\mathsf{EXPCOM}} = \mathbf{EXP}$. (Recall that $\mathbf{EXP} = \cup_c \mathbf{DTIME}(2^{n^c})$.) Clearly, an oracle to EXPCOM allows one to perform an exponential-time computation at the cost of one call, and so $\mathbf{EXP} \subseteq \mathbf{P}^{\mathsf{EXPCOM}}$. On the other hand, if M is a nondeterministic polynomial-time oracle TM, we can simulate its execution with a EXPCOM oracle in exponential time: Such time suffices both to enumerate all of M's nondeterministic choices and to answer the EXPCOM oracle queries. Thus $\mathbf{EXP} \subseteq \mathbf{P}^{\mathsf{EXPCOM}} \subseteq \mathbf{NP}^{\mathsf{EXPCOM}} \subseteq \mathbf{EXP}$.

The key fact about oracle TMs is that *regardless of what the oracle O is*, the set of all TM's with access to O satisfy Properties **I** and **II**. The reason is that we can represent TMs with oracle O as strings, and use this representation to simulate such TMs using a universal TM (that itself also has access to O). Thus any result about TMs or complexity classes that uses only **I** and **II** also holds for the set of all TMs with oracle O. Such results are called *relativizing* results. Many results in this book (and in particular Theorems 3.1, 3.2 and 3.3) are of this type.

The next theorem implies that whichever of $\mathbf{P} = \mathbf{NP}$ or $\mathbf{P} \neq \mathbf{NP}$ is true; it cannot be a relativizing result.

Theorem 3.7 *(Baker, Gill, Solovay [BGS75])*
There exist oracles A, B such that $\mathbf{P}^A = \mathbf{NP}^A$ and $\mathbf{P}^B \neq \mathbf{NP}^B$.

PROOF: We set A to be the language EXPCOM of Example 3.6, implying that $\mathbf{P}^A = \mathbf{NP}^A = \mathbf{EXP}$.

For any language B, let U_B be the unary language

$$U_B = \left\{ 1^n : \text{some string of length } n \text{ is in } B \right\}$$

For every oracle B, the language U_B is clearly in $\mathbf{NP}^B$, since a nondeterministic TM can make a nondeterministic guess for the string $x \in \{0, 1\}^n$ such that $x \in B$. We now construct an oracle B such that $U_B \notin \mathbf{P}^B$, implying that $\mathbf{P}^B \neq \mathbf{NP}^B$.

Construction of B

For every i, we let M_i be the oracle TM represented by the binary expansion of i. We construct B in stages, where stage i ensures that M_i^B does not decide U_B in $2^n/10$ time. Initially we let B be empty and gradually add strings to it. Each stage determines the status of a finite number of strings (i.e., whether or not these strings will ultimately be in B).

Stage i: So far, we have declared whether or not a finite number of strings are in B. Choose n large enough so that it exceeds the length of any such string, and run M_i on input 1^n for $2^n/10$ steps. Whenever M_i queries the oracle about strings whose status has been determined, we answer consistently. When M_i queries strings whose status is undetermined, we declare that the string is not in B. After letting M_i finish computing on

1^n, we now wish to ensure that the answer of M_i on 1^n (whatever it was) is incorrect. The main point is that we have only decided the fate of at most $2^n/10$ strings in $\{0, 1\}^n$, and all of them were decided to be not in B. So if M_i accepts 1^n, we declare that all remaining strings of length n are also not in B, thus ensuring $1^n \notin U_B$. Conversely, if M_i rejects 1^n, we pick any string x of length n that M_i has not queried (such a string exists because M_i made at most $2^n/10$ queries) and declare that x is in B, thus ensuring $1^n \in B_u$. In either case, the answer of M_i is incorrect. Since every polynomial $p(n)$ is smaller than $2^n/10$ for large enough n, and every TM M is represented by infinitely many strings, our construction will ensure that M does not decide U_B. Thus we have shown U_B is not in $\mathbf{P}^B$ (and in fact the same proof shows it is not in $\mathbf{DTIME}^B(f(n))$ for every $f(n) = o(2^n)$). ∎

Let us now answer our original question: Can diagonalization or any simulation method resolve $\mathbf{P}$ vs $\mathbf{NP}$? Answer: Possibly, but it has to use some fact about TMs that does not hold in presence of oracles (i.e., a *nonrelativizing* fact). Even though many results in complexity relativize, there are some notable exceptions such as $\mathbf{IP} = \mathbf{PSPACE}$ (see Chapter 8) and the $\mathbf{PCP}$ Theorem (see Chapter 11). Of course, we still don't know how to use these nonrelativizing techniques to solve the $\mathbf{P}$ vs. $\mathbf{NP}$ question!

Remark 3.8 Oracle TMs are useful in many other places in complexity theory. For instance, they crop up in Theorem 5.12 and in Chapter 17. In the latter setting, the oracle provided to the TM is not merely a language (i.e., Boolean function) but a general function $f : \{0, 1\}^* \to \{0, 1\}^*$. Generally an oracle TM is a useful abstraction of an algorithm that uses another function as a black-box subroutine, without caring how it is implemented.

3.4.1 Logical independence versus relativization

The notion of relativization was inspired by *independence results* in mathematical logic, which showed that certain natural mathematical statements cannot be proved or disproved in a particular system of axioms. Two well-known examples are the independence of Euclid's fifth postulate from the first four (which led to discovery of noneuclidean geometries) and the independence of the Continuum Hypothesis from Zermelo–Fraenkel Set Theory.

Since relativization results show that the statement $\mathbf{P} = \mathbf{NP}$ can neither be proved nor disproved using "known techniques," they can also be viewed as independence results. However, they do not have the same feeling of preciseness as, say, the result about the independence of the Continuum Hypothesis, since the notion of "known techniques" is left vague.

An article of Arora, Impagliazzo and Vazirani [AIV93] tries to clarify this issue. It gives an axiomatic system analogous to Cobham's axiomatic characterization of $\mathbf{P}$ from 1964, and this axiomatic system is shown to imply exactly those statements about $\mathbf{P}$ that relativize. Thus a nonrelativizing statement is one that is not provable in this axiomatic system.

The question then arises: How can we extend this axiomatic system to allow it to prove nonrelativizing results? One idea is to add every nonrelativizing result as a new axiom whenever it gets discovered. A more conservative approach would be to find a *single* nonrelativizing fact that implies all known nonrelativizing results. Surprisingly, this can be done: This single nonrelativizing fact is essentially the Cook-Levin Theorem encountered in Chapter 2. The proof of the Cook-Levin Theorem uses the fact that computation is *local* (i.e., the fact that each basic step of a Turing machine only examines and modifies a constant number of tape locations). The article [AIV93] describes a few ways to formalize the fact that computation is local, and all of these seem to (a) not relativize (see Exercise 3.7), (b) imply all known nonrelativizing results in the axiomatic setting, and (c) make the axiomatic system strong enough so that if **P** versus **NP** is provable at all, then similarly interesting statements can be proved in the axiomatic system.

Of course, knowing that the local checkability of computation is going to be key for resolving **P** versus **NP** does not give much insight into how to actually resolve this problem—no more than the insight that the basic axioms for arithmetic give into how to prove Fermat's Last Theorem.

WHAT HAVE WE LEARNED?

- Diagonalization uses the representation of Turing machines as strings to separate complexity classes.
- We can use it to show that giving a TM more of the same type of resource (time, nondeterminism, space) allows it to solve more problems and to show that, assuming **NP** $\neq$ **P**, **NP** has problems neither in **P**- nor **NP**-complete.
- Results proven solely using diagonalization *relativize* in the sense that they hold also for TMs with oracle access to O, for every oracle $O \subseteq \{0, 1\}^*$. We can use this to show the limitations of such methods. In particular, relativizing methods alone cannot resolve the **P** vs. **NP** question.

CHAPTER NOTES AND HISTORY

Georg Cantor invented diagonalization in the nineteenth century to show that the set of real numbers is uncountable. Kurt Gödel used a similar technique in his proof of the *Incompleteness Theorem*. Computer science undergraduates often encounter diagonalization when they are taught the undecidabilty of the *Halting Problem*.

The time hierarchy theorem is from Hartmanis and Stearns's pioneering paper [HS65]. The nondeterministic Time Hierarchy Theorem is from Cook [Coo72], though the simple proof given here is essentially from [Zak83]. A similar proof works for other complexity classes such as the levels of the polynomial hierarchy discussed in the next chapter. Ladner's Theorem is from [Lad75], but the proof here is from an unpublished manuscript by Impagliazzo. We only proved a simple form of Ladner's Theorem. The full theorem exhibits an infinite hierarchy of classes between **P** and **NP** assuming **P** $\neq$ **NP**, in the sense that each class is contained in the higher class, but no class is polynomial-time reducible to a problem in a lower class. The notion of relativizations of the **P** versus **NP** question is from Baker, Gill, and Solovay [BGS75].

The notion of oracle Turing machines can be used to study interrelationships of complexity classes. In fact, Cook [Coo71] defined **NP**-completeness using oracle machines.

A subfield of complexity theory called *structural complexity* has carried out a detailed study of oracle machines and classes defined using them; see the book of Hemaspaandra and Ogihara [HO02] for more on this topic.

The relativitization results of Baker, Gill, and Solovay focused interest on circuit lower bounds as a way to separate complexity classes, an effort that also stalled a decade later. Chapter 23 formalizes why known proof techniques ("natural proofs") may not suffice to prove interesting circuit lower bounds.

The term *superiority* introduced in the exercises does not appear in the literature per se, but it is related to concepts such as *immunity* and *almost everywhere complexity*, which have been studied.

EXERCISES

3.1. Show that the following language is undecidable:

$$\left\{ \llcorner M \lrcorner : M \text{ is a machine that runs in } 100n^2 + 200 \text{ time} \right\}$$

3.2. Show that $\mathbf{SPACE}(n) \neq \mathbf{NP}$. (Note that we do not know if either class is contained in the other.)

3.3. Show that there is a language $B \in \mathbf{EXP}$ such that $\mathbf{NP}^B \neq \mathbf{P}^B$.

3.4. Say that a class C_1 is *superior to* a class C_2 if there is a machine M_1 in class C_1 such that for every machine M_2 in class C_2 and every large enough n, there is an input of size between n and n^2 on which M_1 and M_2 answer differently.
   (a) Is $\mathbf{DTIME}(n^{1.1})$ superior to $\mathbf{DTIME}(n)$?
   (b) Why does our proof of the Nondeterministic Hierarchy Theorem not prove that $\mathbf{NTIME}(n^{1.1})$ superior to $\mathbf{NTIME}(n)$?

3.5. Show that there exists a function that is not time-constructible.

3.6. **(a)** Prove that the function H defined in the proof of Theorem 3.3 is computable in polynomial time.
   H532
   (b) Let SAT_H be defined as in the proof of Theorem 3.3 for a polynomial-time computable function $H : \mathbb{N} \rightarrow \mathbb{N}$ such that $\lim_{n \to \infty} H(n) = \infty$. Prove that if SAT_H is **NP**-complete, then SAT is in **P**.
   H532

3.7. Show that there is an oracle A and a language $L \in \mathbf{NP}^A$ such that L is not polynomial-time reducible to $3\mathsf{SAT}$ even when the machine computing the reduction is allowed access to A.

3.8. Suppose we pick a random unary language B in the following way: For every n with probability $1/2$, B has no strings of length n, and with probability $1/2$, it has a single random string x of length n. Prove that with high probability $\mathbf{P}^B \neq \mathbf{NP}^B$. (To give an answer that is formally correct, you may need to know elementary measure theory.)

3.9. Suppose we pick a random language C by choosing every string to be in C independently with probability $1/2$. Prove that with high probability $\mathbf{P}^C \neq \mathbf{NP}^C$.

CHAPTER 4

Space complexity

[Our] construction ... also suggests that what makes "games" harder than "puzzles" [e.g., **NP**-complete problems] is the fact that the initiative ["the move"] can shift back and forth between the players.

– Shimon Even and Robert Tarjan, 1976

In this chapter we study the *memory requirements* of computational tasks. To do this we define *space-bounded computation,* which places limits on the number of tape cells a TM can use during its computation. We define both deterministic and nondeterministic versions of such machines and study complexity classes of problems solvable by such machines. In Sections 4.2.1 and 4.3.2, we show some surprising relations between these variants.

As in the case of **NP**, we define a notion of *complete* problems for these classes, and identify concrete and interesting problems that are *complete* for space-bounded classes. It turns out that for polynomial space bounds, the complete problems involve finding winning strategies in two-player games with perfect information such as Chess and Go (see Section 4.2.2). As pointed out in Even and Tarjan's quote at the beginning of the chapter, our current understanding is that computing such strategies is inherently different from (and possibly more difficult than) solving **NP** problems such as SAT.

We also study computations that run in *sublinear* space—in other words, the input is much larger than the algorithm's work space. This notion is both useful and interesting, so we define the class **L** corresponding to computations using logarithmic space in Section 4.1.2 and study its *nondeterministic* variant in Section 4.3.

4.1 DEFINITION OF SPACE-BOUNDED COMPUTATION

The formal definition of deterministic and non-deterministic space bounded computation is as follows (see also Figure 4.1).

Definition 4.1 *(Space-bounded computation)*
Let $S : \mathbb{N} \to \mathbb{N}$ and $L \subseteq \{0, 1\}^*$. We say that $L \in \mathbf{SPACE}(s(n))$ if there is a constant c and a TM M deciding L such at most $c \cdot s(n)$ locations on M's work tapes (excluding

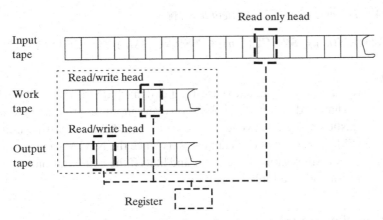

Figure 4.1. Space bounded computation. Only cells used in the read-write tapes count toward the space bound.

the input tape) are ever visited by M's head during its computation on every input of length n.

Similarly, we say that $L \in \mathbf{NSPACE}(s(n))$ if there is an NDTM M deciding L that never uses more than $c \cdot s(n)$ nonblank tape locations on length n inputs, regardless of its nondeterministic choices.

Actually, none of the machines in this chapter will use their output tapes, so the space bound should be thought of as applying only to the work tape. Analogously to time complexity, we will restrict our attention to space bounds $S : \mathbb{N} \to \mathbb{N}$ that are *space-constructible* by which we mean that there is a TM that computes $S(|x|)$ in $O(S(|x|))$ space given x as input. Intuitively, if S is space-constructible, then the machine "knows" the space bound it is operating under. This is a very mild restriction since all functions of interest, including $\log n$, n, and 2^n, are space-constructible.

Since the TM's work tapes are separated from its input tape, it makes sense to consider space-bounded machines that use space less than the input length, namely, $S(n) < n$. This is in contrast to time-bounded computation, where $\mathbf{DTIME}(T(n))$ for $T(n) < n$ does not make much sense since the TM does not have enough time to read the entire input. We will require however that $S(n) > \log n$ since the work tape has length n, and we would like the machine to at least be able to "remember" the index of the cell of the input tape that it is currently reading.

$\mathbf{DTIME}(S(n)) \subseteq \mathbf{SPACE}(S(n))$ since a TM can access only one tape cell per step. But a $\mathbf{SPACE}(S(n))$ machine can run for much longer than $S(n)$ steps, since space can be *reused*: A cell on the work tape can be overwritten an arbitrary number of times. In fact, a space $S(n)$ machine can easily run for as much as $2^{\Omega(S(n))}$ steps— think for example of the machine that uses its work tape of size $S(n)$ to maintain a counter that it increments from 1 to $2^{S(n)-1}$. The next theorem (whose proof appears in Section 4.1.1) shows that this is tight in the sense that any languages in $\mathbf{SPACE}(S(n))$ (and even $\mathbf{NSPACE}(S(n))$) is in $\mathbf{DTIME}(2^{O(S(n))})$. Surprisingly enough, up to logarithmic terms, this theorem contains the only relationships we know between the power of space-bounded and time-bounded computation. Improving this would be a major result.

Theorem 4.2 *For every space constructible $S : \mathbb{N} \rightarrow \mathbb{N}$,*

$$\mathbf{DTIME}(S(n)) \subseteq \mathbf{SPACE}(S(n)) \subseteq \mathbf{NSPACE}(S(n)) \subseteq \mathbf{DTIME}(2^{O(S(n))}) \qquad \diamond$$

Remark 4.3

Some texts define a nondeterministic space-bounded machine with the aditional restriction that it has to halt and produce an answer on every input regardless of the sequence of nondeterministic choices. However, if we focus on $\mathbf{NSPACE}(S(n))$ where $S(n)$ is space-constructible, this restriction is unnecessary since the NDTM can be easily modified to always halt: It simply keeps a counter and halts if the computation runs for more than $2^{cS(n)}$ steps for some suitable constant c.

4.1.1 Configuration graphs

To prove Theorem 4.2, we use the notion of a *configuration graph* of a Turing machine. This notion will also be quite useful for us later in this chapter and the rest of the book. Let M be a (deterministic or nondeterministic) TM. A *configuration* of a TM M consists of the contents of all nonblank entries of M's tapes, along with its state and head position, at a particular point in its execution. For every space $S(n)$ TM M and input $x \in \{0, 1\}^*$, the *configuration graph of M on input x*, denoted $G_{M,x}$, is a directed graph whose nodes correspond to all possible configurations of M where the input contains the value x and the work tapes have at most $S(|x|)$ nonblank cells. The graph has a directed edge from a configuration C to a configuration C' if C' can be reached from C in one step according to M's transition function (see Figure 4.2). If M is deterministic, then the graph has out-degree one, and if M is nondeterministic, then the graph has out-degree at most two. By modifying M to erase all its work tapes before halting, we can assume that there is only a single configuration C_{accept} on which M halts and outputs 1. This means that M accepts the input x iff there exists a directed path in $G_{M,x}$ from C_{start} to C_{accept}. We will use the following claim about configuration graphs, where part 2 will be used only in a subsequent section.

Claim 4.4 *Let $G_{M,x}$ be the configuration graph of a space-$S(n)$ machine M on some input x of length n. Then,*

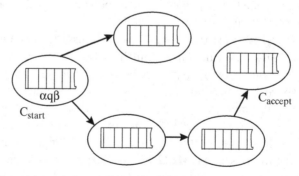

Figure 4.2. The configuration graph $G_{M,x}$ is the graph of all configurations of M's execution on x where there is an edge from a configuration C to a configuration C' if C' can be obtained from C in one step. It has out-degree one if M is deterministic and out-degree at most two if M is nondeterministic.

1. *Every vertex in $G_{M,x}$ can be described using $cS(n)$ bits for some constant c (depending on M's alphabet size and number of tapes) and in particular, $G_{M,x}$ has at most $2^{cS(n)}$ nodes.*
2. *There is an $O(S(n))$-size CNF formula $\varphi_{M,x}$ such that for every two strings C, C', $\varphi_{M,x}(C, C') = 1$ if and only if C and C' encode two neighboring configuration in $G_{M,x}$.* ◇

PROOF SKETCH: Part 1 follows from observing that a configuration is completely described by giving the contents of all work tapes, the position of the head, and the state the TM is in (see Section 1.2). We can encode a configuration by first encoding the snapshot (i.e., state and current symbol read by all tapes) and then encoding in sequence the nonblank contents of all the work tapes, inserting special "marker" symbols to denote the locations of the heads.

Part 2 follows using similar ideas as in the proof of the Cook-Levin Theorem (Theorem 2.10). There we showed that deciding whether two configurations are neighboring can be expressed as the AND of many checks, each depending on only a constant number of bits, and such checks can be expressed by constant-sized CNF formulas by Claim 2.13. The number of variables is proportional to the workspace. ∎

Now we can prove Theorem 4.2.

PROOF OF THEOREM 4.2: Clearly **DTIME**$(S(n)) \subseteq$ **SPACE**$(S(n)) \subseteq$ **NSPACE**$(S(n))$, and so we just need to show **NSPACE**$(S(n)) \subseteq$ **DTIME**$(2^{O(S(n))})$. By enumerating over all possible configurations, we can construct the graph $G_{M,x}$ in $2^{O(S(n))}$-time and check whether C_{start} is connected to C_{accept} in $G_{M,x}$ using the standard (linear in the size of the graph) breadth-first search algorithm for connectivity (e.g., see [CLRS01]). ∎

4.1.2 Some space complexity classes

The following complexity classes will be of particular interest:

Definition 4.5

$$\textbf{PSPACE} = \cup_{c>0}\textbf{SPACE}(n^c)$$

$$\textbf{NPSPACE} = \cup_{c>0}\textbf{NSPACE}(n^c)$$

$$\textbf{L} = \textbf{SPACE}(\log n)$$

$$\textbf{NL} = \textbf{NSPACE}(\log n) \qquad\qquad ◇$$

We can think of **PSPACE** and **NPSPACE** as the space analogs of the time complexity classes **P** and **NP**, respectively. Since time bounds shorter than the input length don't make much sense, there are no time analogs for **L** and **NL**.

EXAMPLE 4.6

We show how $3\text{SAT} \in$ **PSPACE** by describing a TM that decides 3SAT in linear space (that is, $O(n)$ space, where n is the size of the 3SAT instance). The machine just uses the linear space to cycle through all 2^k assignments in order, where k is the number of variables. Note that once an assignment has been checked it can be erased from the work tape, and the work tape can then be reused to check the next assignment. A similar idea of cycling through all potential certificates applies to any **NP** language, so in fact **NP** ⊆ **PSPACE**.

EXAMPLE 4.7

Using the grade school method for arithmetic and the fact that a logspace machine has enough space to keep a counter up to n, it is easily checked that the following languages are in **L**:

$$\text{EVEN} = \{x : x \text{ has an even number of 1s}\}$$

$$\text{MULT} = \{(\llcorner n \lrcorner, \llcorner m \lrcorner, \llcorner nm \lrcorner) : n \in \mathbb{N}\}$$

It seems difficult to conceive of any complicated computations apart from elementary arithmetic that use only $O(\log n)$ space. Nevertheless, we cannot currently even rule out that $3\text{SAT} \in \mathbf{L}$; in other words, it is open whether **NP** $\neq$ **L** (see Exercise 4.6). Space-bounded computations with space $S(n) \ll n$ seem relevant to computational problems such as *web crawling*. The world wide web may be viewed crudely as a directed graph, whose nodes are webpages and edges are hyperlinks. Web crawlers seek to explore this graph for all kinds of information. The following problem PATH is natural in this context:

$$\text{PATH} = \big\{\langle G, s, t \rangle : G \text{ is a directed graph in which there is a path from } s \text{ to } t\big\} \quad (4.1)$$

We show that PATH $\in$ **NL**. Note that if there is a path from s to t, then there is one of length at most n. Thus a nondeterministic machine can take a "nondeterministic walk" starting at s, always maintaining the index of the vertex it is at, and using nondeterminism to select a neighbor of this vertex to go to next. The machine accepts iff the walk ends at t in at most n steps, where n is the number of nodes. If the nondeterministic walk has run for n steps already and t has not been encountered, the machine rejects. The work tape only needs to hold $O(\log n)$ bits of information at any step, namely, the number of steps that the walk has run for, and the identity of the current vertex.

Is PATH in **L** as well? This is an open problem, which, as we will shortly see, is equivalent to whether or not **L** = **NL**. That is, PATH captures the "essence" of **NL** just as 3SAT captures the "essence" of **NP**. Formally, we will show that PATH is **NL**-complete. A recent surprising result shows that the restriction of PATH to *undirected* graphs is in **L**; see Chapters 7 and 20.

4.1.3 Space Hierarchy Theorem

Analogously to time-bounded classes, there is also a hierarchy theorem for space-bounded computation.

Theorem 4.8 *(Space Hierarchy Theorem* [SHL65]*)*
If f, g are space-constructible functions satisfying $f(n) = o(g(n))$, then

$$\mathbf{SPACE}(f(n)) \subsetneq \mathbf{SPACE}(g(n)) \quad (4.2)$$

The proof is completely analogous to the proof of the Time Hierarchy Theorem (Theorem 3.1) except that one can have a universal TM using only a constant factor of space overhead, and hence we don't need the logarithmic term of Theorem 3.1. We leave the proof of Theorem 4.8 as Exercise 4.1.

4.2 PSPACE COMPLETENESS

As already indicated, we do not know if $\mathbf{P} = \mathbf{PSPACE}$, though we strongly believe that the answer is NO. Indeed, since $\mathbf{NP} \subseteq \mathbf{PSPACE}$, $\mathbf{P} = \mathbf{PSPACE}$ implies $\mathbf{P} = \mathbf{NP}$. Recall that we denote $L \leq_p L'$ if L is polynomial-time reducible to L' (see Definition 2.7). We now present some complete problems for **PSPACE** reduction. (Do you see why the latter notion would be uninteresting?).

Definition 4.9 A language L' is **PSPACE**-*hard* if for every $L \in \mathbf{PSPACE}$, $L \leq_p L'$. If in addition $L' \in \mathbf{PSPACE}$ then L' is **PSPACE**-*complete.*   ◇

Using our observations about polynomial-time reductions from Chapter 2, we see that if any **PSPACE**-complete language is in **P** then so is every other language in **PSPACE**. Using the contrapositive, if $\mathbf{PSPACE} \neq \mathbf{P}$ then a **PSPACE**-complete language is not in **P**. Thus intuitively speaking, a **PSPACE**-complete language is the "most difficult" problem of **PSPACE**. The following language can be easily shown to be **PSPACE**-complete (see Exercise 4.2):

$$\mathsf{SPACE\,TMSAT} = \left\{ \langle M, w, 1^n \rangle : \mathrm{DTM}\ M\ \mathrm{accepts}\ w\ \mathrm{in\ space}\ n \right\} \tag{4.3}$$

Now we show another **PSPACE**-complete problem that is more interesting. It uses the following notion.

Definition 4.10 (*Quantified Boolean Formula*) A *quantified Boolean formula* (QBF) is a formula of the form $Q_1 x_1 Q_2 x_2 \cdots Q_n x_n \varphi(x_1, x_2, \ldots, x_n)$ where each Q_i is one of the two quantifiers $\forall$ or $\exists$, $x_1, \ldots, x_n$ range over $\{0, 1\}$, and φ is a plain (unquantified) Boolean formula. The quantifiers $\forall$ and $\exists$ have their standard meaning of "for all" and "exists."

The previous definition restricts attention to quantified Boolean formulae in *prenex normal form* (i.e., all quantifiers appear all the way to the left). One can also consider quantified Boolean formulae where the quantifiers can appear elsewhere in the formula. However, we can transform every quantified formula into an equivalent formula in prenex form in polynomial time using identities such as $\neg \forall x \phi(x) = \exists x \neg \phi(x)$ and $\psi \vee \exists x \varphi(x) = \exists x\ \psi \vee \varphi(x)$ where ψ does not contain x. Unlike in the case of the SAT and 3SAT problems, we do not require that the inner unquantified formula φ is in CNF or 3CNF form. However this choice is also not important, since using auxiliary variables in a similar way to the proof of the Cook-Levin Theorem, we can in polynomial time transform a general quantified Boolean formula to an equivalent formula where the inner unquantified formula is in 3CNF form.

Since all the variables of a QBF are bound by some quantifier, the QBF is always either *true* or *false*, something that is best illustrated with an example.

EXAMPLE 4.11

Consider the formula $\forall x \exists y \, (x \wedge y) \vee (\overline{x} \wedge \overline{y})$ where $\forall$ and $\exists$ quantify over the universe $\{0, 1\}$. Some reflection shows that this is saying "for every $x \in \{0, 1\}$ there is a $y \in \{0, 1\}$ that is equal to x," which we can also informally represent as $\forall x \exists y (x = y)$. This formula is *true*. (The symbols $=$ and $\neq$ are not logical symbols per se, but are used as informal shorthand to make the formula more readable; see also Example 2.12.) However, switching the second quantifier to $\forall$ gives $\forall x \forall y \, (x \wedge y) \vee (\overline{x} \wedge \overline{y})$, which is *false*.

EXAMPLE 4.12

Recall that the SAT problem is to decide, given a Boolean formula φ that has n free variables $x_1, \ldots, x_n$, whether or not φ has a satisfying assignment $x_1, \ldots, x_n \in \{0, 1\}^n$ such that $\varphi(x_1, \ldots, x_n)$ is true. An equivalent way to phrase this problem is to ask whether the *quantified* Boolean formula $\psi = \exists x_1, \ldots, x_n \varphi(x_1, \ldots, x_n)$ is true. You should also verify that the *negation* of the formula $Q_1 x_1 \cdots Q_n x_n \varphi(x_1, x_2, \ldots, x_n)$ is the same as $Q'_1 x_1 \cdots Q'_n x_n \neg \varphi(x_1, x_2, \ldots, x_n)$, where Q'_i is $\exists$ if Q_i was $\forall$ and vice versa. The switch of $\exists$ to $\forall$ in case of SAT gives instances of TAUTOLOGY, the **coNP**-complete language we encountered in Chapter 2.

We define the language TQBF to be the set of quantified Boolean formulae that are true.

Theorem 4.13 *([SM73])*
TQBF *is* **PSPACE**-*complete.*

PROOF: First we show that TQBF $\in$ **PSPACE**. Let

$$\psi = Q_1 x_1 Q_2 x_2 \ldots Q_n x_n \varphi(x_1, x_2, \ldots, x_n) \tag{4.4}$$

be a quantified Boolean formula with n variables, where we denote the size of φ by m. We show a simple recursive algorithm A that can decide the truth of ψ in $O(n + m)$ space. We will solve the slightly more general case where, in addition to variables and their negations, φ may also include the constants 0 (i.e., "false") and 1 (i.e., "true"). If $n = 0$ (there are no variables) then the formula contains only constants and can be evaluated in $O(m)$ time and space, and so we assume $n > 0$. For $b \in \{0, 1\}$, denote by $\psi_{\lceil x_1 = b}$ the modification of ψ where the first quantifier Q_1 is dropped and all occurrences of x_1 are replaced with the constant b. Algorithm A will work as follows: if $Q_1 = \exists$ then output 1 iff *at least one* of $A(\psi_{\lceil x_1 = 0})$ and $A(\psi_{\lceil x_1 = 1})$ outputs 1. If $Q_1 = \forall$ then output 1 iff *both* $A(\psi_{\lceil x_1 = 0})$ and $A(\psi_{\lceil x_1 = 1})$ output 1. By the definition of $\exists$ and $\forall$, it is clear that A does indeed return the correct answer on any formula ψ.

Let $s_{n,m}$ denote the space A uses on formulas with n variables and description size m. The crucial point is—and here we use the fact that space can be *reused*—that both recursive computations $A(\psi_{\lceil x_1 = 0})$ and $A(\psi_{\lceil x_1 = 1})$ can run in the same space. Specifically, after computing $A(\psi_{\lceil x_1 = 0})$, the algorithm A needs to retain only the single bit of output from that computation and can *reuse* the rest of the space for the computation of $A(\psi_{\lceil x_1=1})$. Thus assuming that A uses $O(m)$ space to write $\psi_{\lceil x_1=b}$ for its recursive calls, we'll get that $s_{n,m} = s_{n-1,m} + O(m)$ yielding $s_{n,m} = O(n \cdot m)$.[1]

We now show that $L \leq_p \mathsf{TQBF}$ for every $L \in \mathbf{PSPACE}$. Let M be a machine that decides L in $S(n)$ space and let $x \in \{0, 1\}^n$. We show how to construct a quantified Boolean formula of size $O(S(n)^2)$ that is true iff M accepts x. Let $m = O(S(n))$ denote the number of bits needed to encode a configuration of M on length n inputs. By Claim 4.4, there is a Boolean formula $\varphi_{M,x}$ such that for every two strings $C, C' \in \{0, 1\}^m$, $\varphi_M(C, C') = 1$ iff C and C' encode two adjacent configurations in the configuration graph $G_{M,x}$. We will use $\varphi_{M,x}$ to come up with a polynomial-sized quantified Boolean formula ψ that has polynomially many variables bound by quantifiers and two unquantified variables such that for every $C, C' \in \{0, 1\}^m$, $\psi(C, C')$ is true iff C has a directed path to C' in $G_{M,x}$. By plugging in the values C_{start} and C_{accept} to ψ we get a quantified Boolean formula that is true iff M accepts x.

We define the formula ψ inductively. We let $\psi_i(C, C')$ be true if and only if there is a path of length at most 2^i from C to C' in $G_{M,x}$. Note that $\psi = \psi_m$ and $\psi_0 = \varphi_{M,x}$. The crucial observation is that there is a path of length at most 2^i from C to C' if and only if there is a configuration C'' with a path of length at most 2^{i-1} from C to C'' and a path of length at most 2^{i-1} from C'' to C'. This suggest defining ψ_i as follows: $\psi_i(C, C') = \exists C'' \ \psi_{i-1}(C, C'') \wedge \psi_{i-1}(C'', C')$.

However, this definition is not good, since ψ_i's size is at least twice the size of ψ_{i-1}, and so a simple induction shows that ψ_m has size about 2^m, which is way too large. Instead, we use additional quantified variables to save on description size, using the following more succinct definition for $\psi_i(C, C')$:

$$\exists C'' \forall D^1 \forall D^2 \big((D^1 = C \wedge D^2 = C'') \vee (D^1 = C'' \wedge D^2 = C') \big) \Rightarrow \psi_{i-1}(D^1, D^2)$$

(Here, as in Example 4.11, $=$ and $\Rightarrow$ are simply used as a convenient shorthand and can be replaced by appropriate combinations of the standard Boolean operations.) Note that $size(\psi_i) \leq size(\psi_{i-1}) + O(m)$ and hence $size(\psi_m) \leq O(m^2)$. We leave it to the reader to verify that the two definitions of ψ_i are indeed logically equivalent. As noted previously, we can convert the final formula to prenex form in polynomial time. ∎

4.2.1 Savitch's Theorem

The astute reader may notice that because the proof of Theorem 4.13 uses the notion of a configuration graph and does not require this graph to have out-degree one, it actually yields a stronger statement: That TQBF is not just hard for **PSPACE** but in fact even for **NPSPACE**! Since $\mathsf{TQBF} \in \mathbf{PSPACE}$, this implies that **PSPACE** = **NSPACE**, which

---

[1] This analysis suffices to show that TQBF is in **PSPACE**, but A can actually be made to use linear space, specifically, $O(m + n)$. The reason is that A is always invoked on restrictions of the same formula ψ. So it can keep a global partial assignment array that for each variable x_i will contain either $0, 1$ or 'q' (if it's quantified and not assigned any value). A will use this global space for its operation, where in each call it will find the first quantified variable, set it to 0 and make the recursive call, then set it to 1 and make the recursive call, and then set it back to 'q'. We see that A's space usage is given by the equation $s_{n,m} = s_{n-1,m} + O(1)$, which resolves to $O(n + m)$.

is quite surprising since our intuition is that the corresponding classes for time (**P** and **NP**) are different. In fact, using the same ideas, one can obtain the following theorem:

Theorem 4.14 *(Savitch's Theorem* [Sav70]*)*
For any space-constructible $S : \mathbb{N} \to \mathbb{N}$ *with* $S(n) \geq \log n$, **NSPACE**$(S(n)) \subseteq$ **SPACE**$(S(n)^2)$.

PROOF: The proof closely follows the proof of Theorem 4.13. Let $L \in$ **NSPACE**$(S(n))$ be a language decided by a TM M such that for every $x \in \{0, 1\}^n$, the configuration graph $G = G_{M,x}$ has at most $M = 2^{O(S(n))}$ vertices, and determining whether $x \in L$ is equivalent to determining whether C_{accept} can be reached from C_{start} in this graph. We describe a recursive procedure REACH?(u, v, i) that returns "YES" if there is a path from u to v of length at most 2^i and "NO" otherwise. Again, the main observation is that there is a path from u to v of length at most 2^i iff there's a vertex z with an at most 2^{i-1} long path from u to z and at most 2^{i-1} long path from z to v. Hence on inputs u, v, i, REACH? will enumerate over all vertices z (at a cost of $O(\log M)$ space) and output "YES" if it finds one z such that REACH?$(u, z, i-1) = $ "YES" and REACH?$(z, v, i-1) = $ "YES". Once again, although the algorithm makes n recursive invocations it can *reuse* the space in each of these invocations. Thus, if we let $s_{M,i}$ be the space complexity of REACH?(u, v, i) on an M-vertex graph, then $s_{M,i} = s_{M,i-1} + O(\log M)$ and thus $s_{M,\log M} = O(\log^2 M) = O(S(n)^2)$. Since C_{accept} is reachable from C_{start} iff it can be reached via a path of length at most M, this concludes the proof. ∎

We remark that the running time of the algorithm obtained from the proof of Theorem 4.14 can be as high as $2^{\Omega(s(n)^2)}$, which is in contrast to the upper bound of $2^{O(s(n))}$ (for an entirely different algorithm) given in Theorem 4.2.

4.2.2 The essence of PSPACE: Optimum strategies for game playing

Recall that the central feature of **NP**-complete problems is that a yes answer has a short certificate (see Definition 2.1). The analogous concept for **PSPACE**-complete problems seems to be that of a winning strategy for a two-player game with perfect information. A good example of such a game is Chess: Two players alternately make moves, and the moves are made on a board visible to both, hence the term *perfect information*. What does it mean for a player to have a "winning strategy"? The first player has a winning strategy iff there is a first move for player 1 such that for every possible first move of player 2 there is a second move of player 1 such that … (and so on) such that at the end player 1 wins. Deciding whether or not the first player has a winning strategy seems to require searching the tree of all possible moves. This is reminiscent of **NP**, for which we also seem to require exponential search. But the crucial difference is the lack of a short "certificate" for the statement "Player 1 has a winning strategy," since the only certificate we can think of is the winning strategy itself, which, as noticed, requires exponentially many bits to even *describe*. Thus we seem to be dealing with a fundamentally different phenomenon than the one captured by **NP**.

The interplay of existential and universal quantifiers in the description of the the winning strategy motivates us to invent the following game.

EXAMPLE 4.15 *(The QBF game)*

The "board" for the QBF game is a Boolean formula φ whose free variables are $x_1, x_2, \ldots, x_{2n}$. The two players alternately make moves, which involve picking values for $x_1, x_2, \ldots,$ in order. Thus player 1 will pick values for the odd-numbered variables $x_1, x_3, x_5, \ldots$ (in that order), and player 2 will pick values for the even-numbered variables $x_2, x_4, x_6, \ldots$. We say player 1 wins iff at the end $\varphi(x_1, x_2, \ldots, x_{2n})$ is true.

In order for player 1 to have a *winning strategy* he must have a way to win for all possible sequences of moves by player 2, namely, if

$$\exists x_1 \forall x_2 \exists x_3 \forall x_4 \cdots \forall x_{2n} \varphi(x_1, x_2, \ldots, x_{2n}),$$

which is just saying that this quantified Boolean formula is true.

Thus deciding whether player 1 has a winning strategy for a given board in the QBF game is **PSPACE**-complete.

At this point, the reader is probably thinking of familiar games such as Chess, Go, and Checkers and wondering whether complexity theory may help differentiate between them—for example, to justify the common intuition that Go is more difficult than Chess. Unfortunately, formalizing these issues in terms of asymptotic complexity (i.e., using an infinite language) is tricky because these are finite games, and as far as the existence of a winning strategy is concerned, there are at most three choices: Player 1 has a winning strategy, Player 2 does, or neither does (they can play to a draw). However, one can study generalizations of these games to an $n \times n$ board where n is arbitrarily large—this may involve stretching the rules of the game since the definition of chess is tailored to an 8×8 board. After generalizing this way, one gets an infinite sequence of game situations, and then one can show that for most common games, including chess, determining which player has a winning strategy in the $n \times n$ version is **PSPACE**-complete (see [Pap94] or [GJ79]). Thus if **NP** $\neq$ **PSPACE**, then there is no short certificate for exhibiting that either player in such games has a winning strategy.

Proving **PSPACE**-completeness of games may seem like a frivolous pursuit, but similar ideas lead to **PSPACE**-completeness of some practical problems. Usually, these problems involve repeated moves by an agent who faces an adversary with unlimited computational power. For instance, many computational problems of robotics involve a robot navigating in a changing environment. If we wish to be pessimistic about the environment, then its moves may be viewed as the moves of an adversary. With this assumption, solving many problems of robotics is **PSPACE**-complete. Some researchers feel that the assumption that the environment is adversarial is unduly pessimistic. Unfortunately, even assuming a benign or "indifferent" environment still leaves us with a **PSPACE**-complete problem; see the reference to *Games against nature* in the chapter notes.

4.3 **NL** COMPLETENESS

Now we consider problems that form the "essence" of nondeterministic logarithmic space computation, in other words, problems that are *complete* for **NL**. What kind of reduction should we use? When choosing the type of reduction to define completeness for a complexity class, we must keep in mind the complexity phenomenon we seek to understand. In this case, the complexity question is whether or not **NL** = **L**. We cannot use the polynomial-time reduction since **L** ⊆ **NL** ⊆ **P** (see Exercise 4.3). The reduction should not be more powerful than the weaker class, which is **L**. For this reason we use *logspace* reductions, which, as the name implies, are computed by a deterministic TM running in logarithmic space. To define these, we must tackle the tricky issue that a logspace machine might not even have the memory to write down its output. The way out is to require that the reduction should be able to compute any desired bit of the output in logarithmic space. In other words, the reduction f is *implicitly computable* in logarithmic space, in the sense that there is an $O(\log|x|)$-space machine that on input $\langle x, i \rangle$ outputs $f(x)_i$ provided that $i \leq |f(x)|$.

Definition 4.16 *(logspace reduction and **NL**-completeness)*
A function $f : \{0, 1\}^* \to \{0, 1\}^*$ is *implicitly logspace computable*, if f is polynomially bounded (i.e., there's some c such that $|f(x)| \leq |x|^c$ for every $x \in \{0, 1\}^*$) and the languages $L_f = \{\langle x, i \rangle \mid f(x)_i = 1\}$ and $L_f' = \{\langle x, i \rangle \mid i \leq |f(x)|\}$ are in **L**.

A language B is *logspace reducible* to language C, denoted $B \leq_l C$, if there is a function $f : \{0, 1\}^* \to \{0, 1\}^*$ that is implicitly logspace computable and $x \in B$ iff $f(x) \in C$ for every $x \in \{0, 1\}^*$.

We say that C is **NL**-*complete* if it is in **NL** and for every $B \in$ **NL**, $B \leq_l C$.

Another way (used by several texts) to think of logspace reductions is to imagine that the reduction is given a separate "write-once" output tape, on which it can either write a bit or move to the right but never move left or read the bits it wrote down previously. The two notions are easily proved to be equivalent (see Exercise 4.8).

The next lemma shows that logspace reducibility satisfies the usual properties one expects. It also implies that an **NL**-complete language is in **L** iff **NL** =**L**.

Lemma 4.17

1. *If $B \leq_l C$ and $C \leq_l D$ then $B \leq_l D$.*
2. *If $B \leq_l C$ and $C \in$ **L** then $B \in$ **L**.*   ◇

PROOF: We prove that if f, g are two functions that are logspace implicitly computable, then so is the function h where $h(x) = g(f(x))$. Then part 1 of the Lemma follows by letting f be the reduction from B to C and g be the reduction from C to D. Part 2 follows by letting f be the reduction from B to C and g be the characteristic function of C (i.e., $g(y) = 1$ iff $y \in C$).

Let M_f, M_g be the logspace machines that compute the mappings $x, i \mapsto f(x)_i$ and $y, j \mapsto g(y)_j$ respectively. We construct a machine M_h that given input x, j with $j \leq |g(f(x))|$, outputs $g(f(x))_j$. Machine M_h will pretend that it has an additional (fictitious) input tape on which $f(x)$ is written, and it is merely simulating M_g on this input (see Figure 4.3). Of course, the true input tape has x, j written on it. To maintain its fiction, M_h always maintains on its work tape the index, say i, of the cell on the fictitious tape that M_g is currently reading; this requires only $\log |f(x)|$ space. To compute

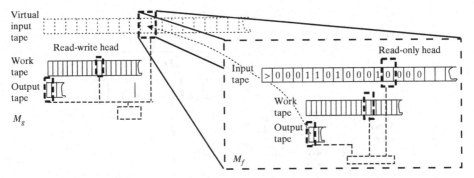

Figure 4.3. Composition of two implicitly logspace computable functions f, g. The machine M_g uses calls to f to implement a "virtual input tape." The overall space used is the space of M_f + the space of $M_g + O(\log|f(x)|)$ $= O(\log|x|)$.

for one step, M_g needs to know the contents of this cell, in other words, $f(x)|_i$. At this point M_h temporarily suspends its simulation of M_g (copying the contents of M_g's work tape to a safe place on its own work tape) and invokes M_f on inputs x, i to get $f(x)|_i$. Then it resumes its simulation of M_g using this bit. The total space M_h uses is $O(\log|g(f(x))|+s(|x|)+s'(|f(x)|))$. Since $|f(x)| \leq poly(x)$, this expression is $O(\log|x|)$. ∎

Now we exhibit an **NL**-complete language. Recall from Section 4.1.2 the language PATH of triples $\langle G, s, t \rangle$ such that vertex t can be reached from s in the directed graph G. We have the following result.

Theorem 4.18
PATH *is* **NL**-*complete.*

PROOF: We have already seen that PATH is in **NL**. Let L be any language in **NL** and M be a machine that decides it in space $O(\log n)$. We describe a logspace implicitly computable function f that reduces L to PATH. For any input x of size n, $f(x)$ will be the configuration graph $G_{M,x}$ whose nodes are all possible $2^{O(\log n)}$ configurations of the machine on input x, along with the start configuration C_{start} and the accepting configuration C_{acc}. In this graph there is a path from C_{start} to C_{acc} iff M accepts x. The graph is represented as usual by an *adjacency matrix* that contain 1 in the $\langle C, C' \rangle$th position (i.e., in the Cth row and C'th column if we identify the configurations with numbers between 0 and $2^{O(\log n)}$) iff there's an edge C from C' in $G_{M,x}$. To finish the proof, we need to show that this adjacency matrix can be computed by a logspace reduction, in other words, to describe a logspace machine that can compute any desired bit in it. This is easy since given $\langle C, C' \rangle$ a deterministic machine can in space $O(|C| + |C'|) = O(\log|x|)$ examine C, C' and check whether C' is one of the (at most two) configurations that can follow C according to the transition function of M. ∎

4.3.1 Certificate definition of NL: Read-once certificates

In Chapter 2, we saw an alternative definition of **NP** that replaced nondeterminism with the notion of a *certificate* of membership. Now try to define the class **NL** using

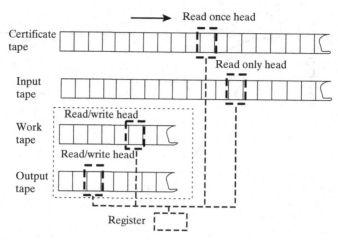

Figure 4.4. Certificate view of **NL**. The certificate for input x is placed on a special read-once tape on which the machine's head can never move to the left.

certificates instead of nondeterministic TMs. We need to address one tricky issue: A certificate may be polynomially long, so a logspace machine may not have the space to store it. Thus the certificate-based definition of **NL** assumes that the certificate is provided to the logspace machine on a separate tape that is "*read once*," meaning that the machine's head on the tape can only sweep the tape from left to right once, and thus never read the same bit of the certificate twice. Specifically, at each step, the machine's head on that tape can either stay in place or move to the right. It is easily seen that the following is an alternative definition of **NL** (see also Figure 4.4), since read-once access to bits in a certificate is just an alternative way to view nondeterministic choices during a computation.

Definition 4.19 (**NL**-*alternative definition*) A language L is in **NL** if there exists a deterministic TM M (called the *verifier*) with an additional special read-once input tape, and a polynomial $p : \mathbb{N} \to \mathbb{N}$ such that for every $x \in \{0, 1\}^*$,

$$x \in L \Leftrightarrow \exists u \in \{0, 1\}^{p(|x|)} \text{ s.t. } M(x, u) = 1$$

where by $M(x, u)$ we denote the output of M where x is placed on its input tape and u is placed on its special read-once tape, and M uses at most $O(\log |x|)$ space on its read-write tapes for every input x.   ◇

In the above scenario, what if we remove the read-once restriction and allow the TM's head to move back and forth on the certificate, and read each bit multiple times? Surprisingly, this changes the class from **NL** to **NP**; see Exercise 4.7.

4.3.2 NL = coNL

Analogously to **coNP**, we define **coNL** as the set of languages that are *complements* of **NL** languages. A simple example for a **coNL** language is $\overline{\text{PATH}}$, the complement of the PATH language. A decision procedure for this language must accept the tuple

$\langle G, s, t \rangle$ when there is no path from s to t in the graph. It is easy see that $\overline{\text{PATH}}$ is not only in **coNL** but is in fact **coNL**-complete, which means that every **coNL** language is logspace reducible to it. Unlike in the case of PATH, there is no natural certificate for the *nonexistence* of a path from s to t; thus it seemed "obvious" to researchers that $\overline{\text{PATH}} \notin \textbf{NL}$. The discovery of the following theorem in the 1980s proved them wrong.

Theorem 4.20 *(Immerman-Szelepcsényi Theorem* [Imm88, Sze87]*)*
$\overline{\text{PATH}} \in \textbf{NL}$.

PROOF: By the certificate-based definition of **NL** from Section 4.3.1, it suffices to show an $O(\log n)$-space verification algorithm (or "verifier" for short) A such that for every n-vertex graph G and vertices s and t, there exists a polynomial certificate u such that $A(\langle G, s, t \rangle, u) = 1$ if and only if t is not reachable from s in G. Here A has only read-once access to u. Below, for simplicity, we identify G's vertices with the numbers $\{1, \ldots, n\}$.

It is best to approach the rest of the proof from the mindset of the person trying to design the certificate. Once we describe the certificate, it will be easy to see that it can be checked by a logspace verifier with read-once access.

Let C_i be the set of vertices that are reachable from s in G within at most i steps. We will use the simple fact that membership in C_i is easily certified. For every $i \in [n]$ and vertex v, the following is a certificate that v is in C_i: the sequence of vertices $v_0, v_1, \ldots, v_k$ along the path from s to v, where $k \le i$. Note that the certificate is indeed of size at most polynomial in n. The algorithm can check the certificate using read-once access by verifying that (1) $v_0 = s$; (2) for $j > 0$, there is an edge from v_{j-1} to v_j; (3) $v_k = v$; and (4) (using simple counting) that the path ends within at most i steps.

Now we use the fact that membership in C_i is certifiable to design two more sophisticated types of certificates.

1. A certificate that a vertex v is not in C_i, assuming the verifier has already been told (i.e., convinced about) the size of C_i.
2. A certificate that $|C_i| = c$ for some number c, assuming the algorithm has already been convinced about the size of C_{i-1}.

Since $C_0 = \{s\}$ (and the verifier knows this), we can provide the second kind of certificate to the verifier iteratively to convince it of the sizes of the sets $C_1, \ldots, C_n$. Finally, since C_n is just the set of all vertices reachable from s, and the verifier has been convinced of $|C_n|$, we can use the first kind of certificate to convince the verifier $t \notin C_n$.

Certifying that v is not in C_i, given $|C_i|$. The certificate is simply the list of certificates to the effect that u is in C_i for every $u \in C_i$ sorted in ascending order of vertices (recall that the vertices are numbers in $[n]$). The verifier checks that (1) each certificate is valid, (2) the vertex u for which a certificate is given is indeed larger than the previous vertex, (3) no certificate is provided for v, and (4) the total number of certificates provided is exactly $|C_i|$. If $v \notin C_i$, then the verifier will accept the above certificate, but if $v \in C_i$ there will not exist $|C_i|$ certificates that vertices $u_1 < u_2 < \cdots < u_{|C_i|}$ are in C_i where $u_j \ne v$ for every j.

Certifying that v is not in C_i, given $|C_{i-1}|$. Before showing how we certify that $|C_i| = c$ given $|C_{i-1}|$, we show how to certify that $v \notin C_i$ with this information. This is very similar to the above procedure: the certificate is the list of $|C_{i-1}|$ certificates to the effect that $u \in C_{i-1}$ for every $u \in C_{i-1}$ in ascending order. The algorithm checks everything as before except that in step (3) it verifies that no certificate is given for v *or for a neighbor of v*. Since $v \in C_i$ if and only if there exists $u \in C_{i-1}$ such that $u = v$ or u is a neighbor of v in G, the procedure will not accept a false certificate by the same reasons as above.

Certifying that $|C_i| = c$ given $|C_{i-1}|$. We have already described how to give, for any vertex v, certificates to the effect that $v \in C_i$ or $v \notin C_i$ (whichever is true). The certificate that $|C_i| = c$ will consist of n certificates for each of the vertices 1 to n in ascending order. For every vertex u, there will be an appropriate certificate depending on whether $u \in C_i$ or not. The verifier will verify all the certificates and count the vertices that have been certified to be in C_i. If this count is equal to c, the verifier accepts. ∎

Using the notion of the configuration graph we can modify the proof of Theorem 4.20 to prove the following (see Exercise 4.11).

Corollary 4.21 *For every space constructible $S(n) > \log n$,* **NSPACE**$(S(n)) =$ **coNSPACE**$(S(n))$.   ◇

Our understanding of space-bounded complexity
The following is our understanding of the relations between the various space-bounded and time-bounded complexity classes:

$$\mathbf{L} \subseteq \mathbf{NL} \subseteq \mathbf{P} \subseteq \mathbf{NP} \subseteq \mathbf{PSPACE} \subseteq \mathbf{EXP}$$

Since the hierarchy theorems imply that $\mathbf{L} \subsetneq \mathbf{PSPACE}$ and $\mathbf{P} \subsetneq \mathbf{EXP}$, we know that at least some of these inclusions are strict, but we don't know which ones. In fact, most researchers believe all of the inclusions are strict.

WHAT HAVE WE LEARNED?

- Turning machines can be used to model memory usage as well as computation time.
- **PSPACE**, the class of languages that can be decided in polynomial space contains both **P** and **NP**, and is believed to be a strict superset of both. It has a complete problem TQBF that is a natural generalization of SAT, and captures the complexity of finding an optimal strategy in games such as chess.
- Storage space is often more precious than time, and hence low-space classes such as **L** and **NL** are of great interest.
- Certain results from time complexity, such as Hierarchy theorems, do carry over to space complexity. But sometimes space complexity has a very different behavior: non-deterministic space is closed under complement, and we can simulate non-deterministic space deterministically with only quadratic overhead. Analogous statements for time complexity are believed to be false, as we believe that $\mathbf{NP} \neq \mathbf{coNP}$ and $\mathbf{NP} \neq \mathbf{P}$.

CHAPTER NOTES AND HISTORY

The concept of space complexity had already been explored in the 1960s; in particular, the Space Hierarchy Theorem of Stearns, Hartnmanis, and Lewis [SHL65] and Savitch's Theorem [Sav70] predate the Cook-Levin Theorem. Stockmeyer and Meyer [SM73] proved the **PSPACE**-completeness of TQBF soon after Cook's paper appeared. A few years later Even and Tarjan pointed out the connection to game playing and proved the **PSPACE**-completeness of a game called Generalized Hex. Papadimitriou's book [Pap94] gives a detailed account of **PSPACE**-completeness. He also shows **PSPACE**-completeness of several *Games against nature* first defined in [Pap85]. Unlike the TQBF game, where one player is *Existential* and the other *Universal*, here the second player chooses moves randomly. The intention is to model games played against nature—where "nature" could mean not just weather, for example, but also large systems such as the stock market that are presumably "indifferent" to the fate of individuals. Papadimitriou describes an alternative characterization **PSPACE** using such games. A stronger result, namely, a characterization of **PSPACE** using interactive proofs, will be described in Chapter 8.

The trivial bound **DTIME**$(S(n)) \subseteq$ **SPACE**$(S(n))$ of Theorem 4.2 was improved by Hopcroft, Paul, and Valiant [HPV75] to **DTIME**$(S(n)) \subseteq$ **SPACE**$(S(n)/\log S(n))$.

Immerman's proof of Theorem 4.20 is part of a larger subarea of complexity theory called *descriptive complexity*, which gives new and *machineless* characterizations of complexity classes using the language of mathematical logic. See his book [Imm99] for a survey of this field.

EXERCISES

4.1. Prove the existence of a universal TM for space-bounded computation (analogously to the deterministic universal TM of Theorem 1.9). That is, prove that there exists a TM SU such that for every string α, and input x, if the TM M_α represented by α halts on x before using t cells of its work tapes, then $SU(\alpha, t, x) = M_\alpha(x)$, and, moreover, SU uses at most Ct cells of its work tapes, where C is a constant depending only on M_α. (Despite the fact that the bound here is better than the bound of Theorem 1.9, the proof of this statement is actually easier than the proof of Theorem 1.9.) Use this to prove Theorem 4.8.

4.2. Prove that the language SPACETM of (4.3) is **PSPACE**-complete.

4.3. Prove that every language L that is not the empty set or $\{0, 1\}^*$ is complete for **NL** under polynomial-time Karp reductions.

4.4. Show that the following language is **NL**-complete:

$$\left\{ \llcorner G \lrcorner : G \text{ is a strongly connected digraph} \right\}$$

4.5. Show that 2SAT is in **NL**.

4.6. Suppose we define **NP**-completeness using logspace reductions instead of polynomial-time reductions. Show (using the proof of the Cook-Levin Theorem) that SAT and 3SAT continue to be **NP**-complete under this new definition. Conclude that SAT $\in$ **L** iff **NP** = **L**.

H533

4.7. Prove that in the certificate definition of **NL** (Section 4.3.1) if we allow the verifier machine to move its head back and forth on the certificate, then the class being defined changes to **NP**.

H533

4.8. Define a function $f : \{0, 1\}^* \to \{0, 1\}^*$ to be write-once logspace computable if it can be computed by an $O(\log n)$-space TM M whose output tape is "write-once" in the sense that, in each step, M can either keep its head in the same position on that tape or write to it a symbol and move one location to the right. The used cells of the output tape are not counted against M's space bound.

Prove that f is write-once logspace computable if and only if it is implicitly logspace computable in the sense of Definition 4.16.

4.9. Show that TQBF is complete for **PSPACE** also under logspace reductions.

4.10. Show that in every finite two-person game with perfect information (by *finite* we mean that there is an a priori upper bound n on the number of moves after which the game is over and one of the two players is declared the victor—there are no draws) one of the two players has a winning strategy.

4.11. Prove Corollary 4.21.

4.12. Define **polyL** to be $\cup_{c>0}$**SPACE**$(\log^c n)$. Steve's Class SC (named in honor of Steve Cook) is defined to be the set of languages that can be decided by deterministic machines that run in polynomial time and $\log^c n$ space for some $c > 0$.

It is an open problem whether PATH $\in$ SC. Why does Savitch's Theorem not resolve this question?

Is SC the same as **polyL** $\cap$ **P**?

CHAPTER 5   The polynomial hierarchy and alternations

[S]ynthesizing circuits is exceedingly difficulty. It is even more difficult to show that a circuit found in this way is the *most* economical one to realize a function. The difficulty springs from the large number of essentially different networks available.

– Claude Shannon, 1949

We have already encountered some ways of "capturing" the essence of families of computational problems by showing that they are complete for some natural complexity class. This chapter continues this process by studying another family of natural problems (including one mentioned in Shannon's quote at the begginning of this chapter) whose essence is not captured by nondeterminism alone. The correct complexity class that captures these problems is the *polynomial hierarchy*, denoted **PH**, which is a generalization of **P**, **NP** and **coNP**. It consists of an infinite number of subclasses (called levels) each of which is important in its own right. These subclasses are conjectured to be distinct, and this conjecture is a stronger form of **P** $\neq$ **NP**. This conjecture tends to crop up (sometimes unexpectedly) in many complexity theoretic investigations, including in Chapters 6, 7, and 17 of this book.

In this chapter we provide three equivalent definitions of the polynomial hierarchy:

1. In Section 5.2 we define the polynomial hierarchy as the set of languages defined via polynomial-time predicates combined with a constant number of alternating forall ($\forall$) and exists ($\exists$) quantifiers, generalizing the definitions of **NP** and **coNP** from Chapter 2.
2. In Section 5.3 we show an equivalent characterization of the polynomial hierarchy using *alternating* Turing machines, that are a generalization of nondeterministic Turing machines defined in Section 2.1.2.
3. In Section 5.5 we show the polynomial hierarchy can also be defined using *oracle* Turing machines (Section 3.4).

A fourth characterization using uniform families of circuits will be given in Chapter 6. In Section 5.4, we use the different characterizations of the polynomial hierarchy to show an interesting result: SAT cannot be solved using simultaneously linear time and logarithmic space. This represents a frontier of current approaches to **P** versus **NP**.

5.1 THE CLASS Σ_2^p

To motivate the study of **PH**, we focus on some computational problems that seem to not be captured by **NP**-completeness.

As warmup, let's recall the following **NP** problem INDSET (see Example 2.2), for which we *do* have a short certificate of membership:

$$\mathsf{INDSET} = \big\{ \langle G, k \rangle : \text{graph } G \text{ has an independent set of size} \geq k \big\}$$

Consider a slight modification to this problem, namely, determining the largest independent set in a graph (phrased as a decision problem):

$$\mathsf{EXACT\ INDSET} = \big\{ \langle G, k \rangle : \text{the largest independent set in } G \text{ has size exactly } k \big\}$$

Now there seems to be no short certificate for membership: $\langle G, k \rangle \in \mathsf{EXACT\ INDSET}$ iff *there exists* an independent set of size k in G and *every other* independent set has size at most k.

Similarly, consider the problem referred to in Shannon's quote, namely, to determine the smallest Boolean formulas equivalent to a given formula. For convenience, we state it as a decision problem.

$$\mathsf{MIN\text{-}EQ\text{-}DNF} = \big\{ \langle \varphi, k \rangle : \exists \mathsf{DNF} \text{ formula } \psi \text{ of size} \leq k$$
$$\text{that is equivalent to the DNF formula } \varphi \big\}$$

where a DNF formula is a Boolean formula that is an OR of ANDs and we say that two formulas are equivalent if they agree on all possible assignments. The complement of this language is refered to in Shannon's quote, except Shannon is interested more generally in small circuits rather than just DNF formulas.

$$\overline{\mathsf{MIN\text{-}EQ\text{-}DNF}} = \big\{ \langle \varphi, k \rangle : \forall \mathsf{DNF} \text{ formula } \psi \text{ of size} \leq k$$
$$\exists \text{ assignment } u \text{ s.t. } \varphi(u) \neq \psi(u) \big\}$$

Again, there is no obvious notion of a certificate of membership for MIN-EQ-DNF. Thus to capture languages such as EXACT INDSET and MIN-EQ-DNF, we seem to need to allow not only a single "exists" quantifier (as in Definition 2.1 of **NP**) or "for all" quantifier (as in Definition 2.20 of **coNP**) but a combination of both quantifiers. This motivates the following definition.

Definition 5.1 The class Σ_2^p is the set of all languages L for which there exists a polynomial-time TM M and a polynomial q such that

$$x \in L \Leftrightarrow \exists u \in \{0, 1\}^{q(|x|)} \, \forall v \in \{0, 1\}^{q(|x|)} \, M(x, u, v) = 1$$

for every $x \in \{0, 1\}^*$.   ◇

Note that Σ_2^p contains both the classes **NP** and **coNP**.

EXAMPLE 5.2

The language EXACT INDSET above is in Σ_2^p, since, as we noted previously, a pair $\langle G, k \rangle$ is in EXACT INDSET iff *there exists* a size-k subset S of G's vertices such that *for every* S' that is a $(K + 1)$-sized subset, S is an independent set in G and S' is not an independent set in G. (Exercise 5.9 shows a finer placement of EXACT INDSET.)

The language MIN-EQ-DNF is also in Σ_2^p, since a pair $\langle \varphi, k \rangle$ is in MIN-EQ-DNF iff *there exists* a DNF formula ψ such that *for every* assignment u, $\varphi(u) = \psi(u)$. It is known to be Σ_2^p-complete [Uma98].

5.2 THE POLYNOMIAL HIERARCHY

The definition of the polynomial hierarchy generalizes those of **NP**, **coNP**, and Σ_2^p. This class consists of every language that can be defined via a combination of a polynomial-time computable predicate and a constant number of $\forall/\exists$ quantifiers.

Definition 5.3 *(Polynomial hierarchy)*
For $i \geq 1$, a language L is in Σ_i^p if there exists a polynomial-time TM M and a polynomial q such that

$$x \in L \Leftrightarrow \exists u_1 \in \{0, 1\}^{q(|x|)} \forall u_2 \in \{0, 1\}^{q(|x|)} \cdots Q_i u_i \in \{0, 1\}^{q(|x|)} M(x, u_1, \ldots, u_i) = 1$$

where Q_i denotes $\forall$ or $\exists$ depending on whether i is even or odd, respectively.

The *polynomial hierarchy* is the set $\mathbf{PH} = \cup_i \Sigma_i^p$.

Note that $\Sigma_1^p = \mathbf{NP}$. For every i, define $\Pi_i^p = \mathbf{co}\Sigma_i^p = \left\{ \overline{L} : L \in \Sigma_i^p \right\}$. Thus $\Pi_1^p = \mathbf{coNP}$. Also, for every i, note that $\Sigma_i^p \subseteq \Pi_{i+1}^p \subseteq \Sigma_{i+2}^p$, and hence $\mathbf{PH} = \cup_{i>0} \Pi_i^p$.

5.2.1 Properties of the polynomial hierarchy

We believe that $\mathbf{P} \neq \mathbf{NP}$ and $\mathbf{NP} \neq \mathbf{coNP}$. An appealing generalization of these conjectures is that for every i, Σ_i^p is strictly contained in Σ_{i+1}^p. This conjecture is used often in complexity theory. It is often stated as *"the polynomial hierarchy does not collapse,"* where the polynomial hierarchy is said to collapse if there is some i such that $\Sigma_i^p = \Sigma_{i+1}^p$. As we will see below, this would imply $\Sigma_i^p = \cup_{j \geq 1} \Sigma_j^p = \mathbf{PH}$. In this case, we say that the polynomial hierarchy *collapses to the ith level*. The smaller i is, the weaker—and hence more believable—it is to conjecture that $\mathbf{PH}$ does not collapse to the ith level.

Theorem 5.4

1. *For every $i \geq 1$, if $\Sigma_i^p = \Pi_i^p$ then $\mathbf{PH} = \Sigma_i^p$; that is, the hierarchy collapses to the ith level.*
2. *If $\mathbf{P} = \mathbf{NP}$ then $\mathbf{PH} = \mathbf{P}$; that is, the hierarchy collapses to $\mathbf{P}$.*

PROOF: We do the second part; the first part is similar and is left as Exercise 5.12. Assuming $\mathbf{P} = \mathbf{NP}$, we prove by induction on i that $\Sigma_i^p, \Pi_i^p \subseteq \mathbf{P}$. Clearly this is true for $i = 1$ by assumption since $\Sigma_1^p = \mathbf{NP}$ and $\Pi_1^p = \mathbf{coNP}$. We assume it is true for $i - 1$ and prove that $\Sigma_i^p \subseteq \mathbf{P}$. Since Π_i^p consists of complements of languages in Σ_i^p and $\mathbf{P}$ is closed under under complementation, it would also then follow that $\Pi_i^p \subseteq \mathbf{P}$.

Let $L \in \Sigma_i^p$. By definition, there is a polynomial-time Turing machine M and a polynomial q such that

$$x \in L \Leftrightarrow \exists u_1 \in \{0, 1\}^{q(|x|)} \, \forall u_2 \in \{0, 1\}^{q(|x|)} \cdots Q_i u_i \in \{0, 1\}^{q(|x|)} \, M(x, u_1, \ldots, u_i) = 1 \tag{5.1}$$

where Q_i is $\exists/\forall$ as in Definition 5.3. Define the language L' as follows:

$$\langle x, u_1 \rangle \in L' \Leftrightarrow \forall u_2 \in \{0, 1\}^{q(|x|)} \cdots Q_i u_i \in \{0, 1\}^{q(|x|)} \, M(x, u_1, u_2, \ldots, u_i) = 1$$

Clearly, $L' \in \Pi_{i-1}^p$ and so under our assumption L' is in $\mathbf{P}$. This implies that there is a polynomial-time TM M' computing L'. Plugging M' in (5.1), we get

$$x \in L \Leftrightarrow \exists u_1 \in \{0, 1\}^{q(|x|)} \, M'(x, u_1) = 1.$$

But this means $L \in \mathbf{NP}$ and hence under our assumption that $\mathbf{P} = \mathbf{NP}$, $L \in \mathbf{P}$. ∎

5.2.2 Complete problems for levels of PH

Recall that a language B *reduces* to a language C via a polynomial-time Karp reduction, denoted by $B \leq_p C$, if there is a polynomial-time computable function $f : \{0, 1\}^* \rightarrow \{0, 1\}^*$ such that $x \in B \Leftrightarrow f(x) \in C$ for every x (see Definition 2.7). We say that a language L is Σ_i^p-*complete* if $L \in \Sigma_i^p$ and for every $L' \in \Sigma_i^p$, $L' \leq_p L$. We define Π_i^p-completeness and $\mathbf{PH}$-completeness in the same way. In this section, we show that for every $i \in \mathbb{N}$, both Σ_i^p and Π_i^p have complete problems. By contrast, the polynomial hierarchy itself is believed not to have a complete problem, as is shown by the following simple claim.

Claim 5.5 *If there exists a language L that is $\mathbf{PH}$-complete, then there exists an i such that $\mathbf{PH} = \Sigma_i^p$ (and hence the hierarchy collapses to its ith level.)*   ◇

PROOF SKETCH: Since $L \in \mathbf{PH} = \cup_i \Sigma_i^p$, there exists i such that $L \in \Sigma_i^p$. Since L is $\mathbf{PH}$-complete, we can reduce every language of $\mathbf{PH}$ to L. But every language that is polynomial-time reducible to a language in Σ_i^p is itself in Σ_i^p and so we have shown $\mathbf{PH} \subseteq \Sigma_i^p$. ∎

It is not hard to see that just like $\mathbf{NP}$ and $\mathbf{coNP}$, $\mathbf{PH}$ is also contained in $\mathbf{PSPACE}$. A simple corollary of Claim 5.5 is that unless the polynomial hierarchy collapses, $\mathbf{PH} \neq \mathbf{PSPACE}$. Indeed, otherwise the $\mathbf{PSPACE}$-complete problem TQBF defined in Section 4.2 would be $\mathbf{PH}$-complete.

EXAMPLE 5.6 (Complete problems for different levels)

For every $i \geq 1$, the class $\mathbf{\Sigma}_i^p$ has the following complete problem involving quantified Boolean expression of the following type with a limited number of alternations:

$$\Sigma_i \mathsf{SAT} = \exists u_1 \forall u_2 \exists \cdots Q_i u_i \; \varphi(u_1, u_2, \ldots, u_i) = 1 \tag{5.2}$$

where φ is a Boolean formula not necessarily in CNF form (though the form does not make any difference), each u_i is a vector of Boolean variables, and Q_i is $\forall$ or $\exists$ depending on whether i is even or odd respectively. Notice that for every i, $\Sigma_i \mathsf{SAT}$ is a special case of the TQBF problem of Section 4.2. Exercise 5.1 asks you to prove that $\Sigma_i \mathsf{SAT}$ is indeed $\mathbf{\Sigma}_i^p$-complete. One can similarly define a problem $\Pi_i \mathsf{SAT}$ that is $\mathbf{\Pi}_i^p$-complete.

In the $\mathsf{SUCCINCT \; SET \; COVER}$ problem we are given a collection $S = \{\varphi_1, \varphi_2, \ldots, \varphi_m\}$ of 3-DNF formulas on n variables, and an integer k. We need to determine whether there *exists* a subset $S' \subseteq \{1, 2, \ldots, m\}$ of size at most k for which $\vee_{i \in S'} \varphi_i$ is a tautology (i.e., evaluates to 1 for *every* assignment to the variables). By its definition it's clear that $\mathsf{SUCCINCT \; SET \; COVER}$ is in $\mathbf{\Sigma}_2^p$. Umans showed that it is $\mathbf{\Sigma}_2^p$-complete [Uma98].

5.3 ALTERNATING TURING MACHINES

Alternating Turing machines (ATMs) are generalizations of nondeterministic Turing machines. Recall that even though NDTMs are not a realistic computational model, studying them helps us to focus on a natural computational phenomenon, namely, the apparent difference between *guessing* an answer and *verifying* it. ATMs plays a similar role for certain languages for which there is no obvious short *certificate* for membership and, hence, that cannot be characterized using nondeterminism alone.

Alternating TMs are similar to NDTMs in the sense that they have *two* transition functions that they can choose from each step, but they also have the additional feature that every internal state except q_{accept} and q_{halt} is labeled with either $\exists$ or $\forall$. Similar to the NDTM, an ATM can evolve at every step in two possible ways. Recall that a non-deterministic TM accepts its input if there *exists* some sequence of choices that leads it to the state q_{accept}. In an ATM, this existential quantifier over each choice is replaced with the appropriate quantifier according to the labels at each state. The name "alternating" refers to the fact that the machine can *alternate* between states labeled with $\exists$ and $\forall$.

Definition 5.7 *(Alternating time)*
For every $T : \mathbb{N} \to \mathbb{N}$, we say that an alternating TM M runs in $T(n)$-time if for every input $x \in \{0, 1\}^*$ and for every possible sequence of transition function choices, M halts after at most $T(|x|)$ steps.

We say that a language L is in **ATIME**$(T(n))$ if there is a constant c and a $c \cdot T(n)$-time ATM M such that for every $x \in \{0, 1\}^*$, M *accepts* x iff $x \in L$. The definition of accepting an input is as follows:

Recall that $G_{M,x}$ denotes the directed acyclic *configuration graph* of M on input x, where there is an edge from a configuration C to configuration C' iff C' can be obtained from C

by one step of M's transition function (see Section 4.1.1). We label some of the vertices in this graph by "ACCEPT" by repeatedly applying the following rules until they cannot be applied anymore:

The configuration C_{accept} where the machine is in q_{accept} is labeled "ACCEPT".

If a configuration C is in a state labeled $\exists$ and there is an edge from C to a configuration C' labeled "ACCEPT", then we label C "ACCEPT".

If a configuration C is in a state labeled $\forall$ and both the configurations C', C'' reachable from it in one step are labeled "ACCEPT" then we label C "ACCEPT".

We say that M *accepts* x if at the end of this process the starting configuration C_{start} is labeled "ACCEPT".

We will also be interested in alternating TM's that are restricted to a fixed number of alternations.

Definition 5.8 For every $i \in \mathbb{N}$, we define $\Sigma_i\mathbf{TIME}(T(n))$ (resp. $\Pi_i\mathbf{TIME}(T(n))$) to be the set of languages accepted by a $T(n)$-time ATM M whose initial state is labeled "$\exists$" (resp. "$\forall$") and on which every input and on every (directed) path from the starting configuration in the configuration graph, M can alternate at most $i-1$ times from states with one label to states with the other label.   ⋄

Proving the following claim is left as Exercise 5.2.

Claim 5.9 *For every $i \in \mathbb{N}$, $\Sigma_i^p = \cup_c \Sigma_i\mathbf{TIME}(n^c)$ and $\Pi_i^p = \cup_c \Pi_i\mathbf{TIME}(n^c)$.*   ⋄

5.3.1 Unlimited number of alternations

Definition 5.8 for **PH** restricted attention to ATMs whose number of alternations is some fixed constant i independent of the input size. But let us now go back to considering polynomial-time alternating Turing machines with no a priori bound on the number of quantifiers. Letting $\mathbf{AP} = \cup_c \mathbf{ATIME}(n^c)$, we have the following theorem.

Theorem 5.10 AP = PSPACE.

PROOF SKETCH: **PSPACE** $\subseteq$ **AP** follows since TQBF is trivially in **AP** (just "guess" values for each existentially quantified variable using an $\exists$ state and for universally quantified variables using a $\forall$ state, and do a deterministic polynomial-time computation at the end), and every **PSPACE** language reduces to TQBF. To show that **AP** $\subseteq$ **PSPACE**, we can use a recursive procedure similar to the one used to show that TQBF $\in$ **PSPACE** (see Exercise 5.5). ■

Similarly, one can consider alternating Turing machines that run in polynomial space. The class of languages accepted by such machines is called **APSPACE**, and Exercise 5.7 asks you to prove that **APSPACE = EXP**. Similarly, the set of languages accepted by alternating logspace machines is equal to **P**.

5.4 TIME VERSUS ALTERNATIONS: TIME-SPACE TRADEOFFS FOR SAT

Despite the fact that SAT is widely believed to require exponential (or at least super-polynomial) time to solve, and to require linear (or at least super-logarithmic) space, we currently have no way to prove these conjectures. In fact, as far as we know, SAT may have both a linear time algorithm and a logarithmic space one. But we can rule out at least the most trivial algorithm: One that runs *simultaneously* in linear time and logarithmic space. In fact, we can prove the following stronger theorem.

Theorem 5.11 *(Time/space tradeoff for* SAT*[For97a, FLvMV00])*
For every two functions $S, T : \mathbb{N} \to \mathbb{N}$, *define* **TISP**$(T(n), S(n))$ *to be the set of languages decided by a TM M that on every input x takes at most* $O(T(|x|))$ *steps and uses at most* $O(S(|x|))$ *cells of its read-write tapes. Then,* SAT $\notin$ **TISP**$(n^{1.1}, n^{0.1})$.

Most texts define the class **TISP**$(T(n), S(n))$ with respect to TMs with RAM memory (i.e., TMs that have random access to their tapes; such machines can be defined similarly to oracle TM's in Section 3.4). Theorem 5.11 and its proof carry over for that model as well. We also note that stronger results are known for both models (see Exercise 5.6 and the chapter notes).

PROOF: We will show that

$$\textbf{NTIME}(n) \nsubseteq \textbf{TISP}(n^{1.2}, n^{0.2}). \tag{5.3}$$

This implies the result for SAT by following the ideas of the proof of the Cook-Levin Theorem (Theorem 2.10), since a careful analysis of that proof yields a reduction from the task of deciding membership in an **NTIME**$(T(n))$-language to the task of deciding whether an $O(T(n) \log T(n))$-sized formula is satisfiable, where every output bit of this reduction can be computed in polylogarithmic time and space. (See Exercise 4.6; also the proof of Theorem 6.15 later in the book uses a similar analysis.) Hence, if SAT $\in$ **TISP**$(n^{1.1}, n^{0.1})$ then **NTIME**$(n) \subseteq$ **TISP**$(n^{1.1}$ polylog$(n), n^{0.1}$ polylog$(n))$. Our main step in proving (5.3) is the following claim, showing how to replace time with alternations:

Claim 5.11.1 **TISP**$(n^{12}, n^2) \subseteq \Sigma_2$**TIME**$(n^8)$.   ◇

PROOF OF CLAIM 5.11.1: The proof is similar to the proofs of Savitch's Theorem and the **PSPACE**-completeness of TQBF (Theorems 4.14 and 4.13). Suppose that L is decided by a machine M using n^{12} time and n^2 space. For every $x \in \{0, 1\}^*$, consider the configuration graph $G_{M,x}$ of M on input x. Each configuration in this graph can be described by a string of length $O(n^2)$ and x is in L if and only if there is a path of length n^{12} in this graph from the starting configuration C_{start} to an accepting configuration. There is such a path if and only if there *exist* n^6 configurations $C_1, \ldots, C_{n^6}$ (requiring a total of $O(n^8)$ bits to specify) such that if we let $C_0 = C_{start}$ then C_{n^6} is accepting and *for every* $i \in [n^6]$ the configuration C_i is computed from C_{i-1} within n^6 steps. Because the latter condition can be verified in, say, $O(n^7)$ time, we get an $O(n^8)$-time Σ_2-TM for deciding membership in L. ∎

Our next step will show that, under the assumption that (5.3) does not hold (and hence $\mathbf{NTIME}(n) \subseteq \mathbf{TISP}(n^{1.2}, n^{0.2}) \subseteq \mathbf{DTIME}(n^{1.2})$), we can replace alternations with time.

Claim 5.11.2 *Suppose that* $\mathbf{NTIME}(n) \subseteq \mathbf{DTIME}(n^{1.2})$. *Then* $\mathbf{\Sigma}_2\mathbf{TIME}(n^8) \subseteq \mathbf{NTIME}(n^{9.6})$. $\diamond$

PROOF OF CLAIM 5.11.2: Using the equivalence between alternating time and the polynomial hierarchy (see Claim 5.9), L is in $\mathbf{\Sigma}_2\mathbf{TIME}(n^8)$ if and only if there is an TM M such that

$$x \in L \Leftrightarrow \exists u \in \{0, 1\}^{c|x|^8} \, \forall v \in \{0, 1\}^{d|x|^8} \, M(x, u, v) = 1$$

for some constants c, d, where M runs in time $O(|x|^8)$. Yet if $\mathbf{NTIME}(n) \subseteq \mathbf{DTIME}(n^{1.2})$, then by a simple padding argument (à la the proof of Theorem 2.22) we have a deterministic algorithm D that on inputs x, u with $|x| = n$ and $|u| = cn^8$ runs in time $O((n^8)^{1.2}) = O(n^{9.6})$-time and returns 1 if and only if there exists some $v \in \{0, 1\}^{dn^8}$ such that $M(x, u, v) = 0$. Thus

$$x \in L \Leftrightarrow \exists u \in \{0, 1\}^{c|x|^8} \, D(x, u) = 0 \,.$$

implying that $L \in \mathbf{NTIME}(n^{9.6})$ ■

Together, Claims 5.11.1 and 5.11.2 show that the assumption that $\mathbf{NTIME}(n) \subseteq \mathbf{TISP}(n^{1.2}, n^{0.2})$ leads to contradiction: The assumption plus a simple padding argument implies that $\mathbf{NTIME}(n^{10}) \subseteq \mathbf{TISP}(n^{12}, n^2)$, which by Claim 5.11.1 implies that $\mathbf{NTIME}(n^{10}) \subseteq \mathbf{\Sigma}_2\mathbf{TIME}(n^8)$. But together with Claim 5.11.2, this implies that $\mathbf{NTIME}(n^{10}) \subseteq \mathbf{NTIME}(n^{9.6})$, contradicting the nondeterministic Time Hierarchy Theorem (Theorem 3.2). ■

5.5 DEFINING THE HIERARCHY VIA ORACLE MACHINES

Recall the definition of *oracle machines* from Section 3.4. These are machines with access to a special tape they can use to make queries of the form "is $q \in O$" for some language O. For every $O \subseteq \{0, 1\}^*$, oracle TM M and input x, we denote by $M^O(x)$ the output of M on x with access to O as an oracle. We have the following characterization of the polynomial hierarchy.

Theorem 5.12 *For every* $i \geq 2$, $\mathbf{\Sigma}_i^p = \mathbf{NP}^{\mathbf{\Sigma}_{i-1}\mathsf{SAT}}$, *where the latter class denotes the set of languages decided by polynomial-time NDTMs with access to the oracle* $\mathbf{\Sigma}_{i-1}\mathsf{SAT}$. $\diamond$

PROOF: We showcase the proof idea by showing that $\mathbf{\Sigma}_2^p = \mathbf{NP}^{\mathsf{SAT}}$. Suppose that $L \in \mathbf{\Sigma}_2^p$. Then, there is a polynomial-time TM M and a polynomial q such that

$$x \in L \Leftrightarrow \exists u_1 \in \{0, 1\}^{q(|x|)} \, \forall u_2 \in \{0, 1\}^{q(|x|)} \, M(x, u_1, u_2) = 1$$

Yet for every fixed u_1 and x, the statement "for every u_2, $M(x, u_1, u_2) = 1$" is the negation of an $\mathbf{NP}$-statement and hence its truth can be determined using an oracle for

SAT. Thus there is a simple NDTM N that given oracle access for SAT can decide L: On input x, nondeterministically guess u_1 and use the oracle to decide if $\forall u_2 M(x, u_1, u_2) = 1$. We see that $x \in L$ iff there exists a choice u_1 that makes N accept.

On the other hand, suppose that L is decidable by a polynomial-time NDTM N with oracle access to SAT. Notice, N could make polynomially many queries from the SAT oracle, and every query could depend upon all preceding queries. At first sight this seems to give N more power than a Σ_2^p machine, which, as we saw earlier, has the capability to nondeterministically make a *single* query to a **coNP** language. The main idea in replacing N by an equivalent Σ_2^p machine is to nondeterministically guess all future queries *as well as the* SAT *oracle's answers* and then to make a single **coNP** query whose answer verifies that all this guessing was correct.

More precisely, x is in L if and only if there exists a sequence of nondeterministic choices and correct oracle answers that makes N accept x. That is, there is a sequence of choices $c_1, \ldots, c_m \in \{0, 1\}$ and answers to oracle queries $a_1, \ldots, a_k \in \{0, 1\}$ such that on input x, if the machine N uses the choices $c_1, \ldots, c_m$ in its execution and receives a_i as the answer to its ith query, then (1) M reaches the accepting state q_{accept}, and (2) all the answers are correct. Let φ_i denote the ith query that M makes to its oracle when executing on x using choices $c_1, \ldots, c_m$ and receiving answers $a_1, \ldots, a_k$. Then, the condition (2) can be phrased as follows: if $a_i = 1$, then there exists an assignment u_i such that $\varphi_i(u_i) = 1$, and if $a_i = 0$, then for every assignment v_i, $\varphi_i(v_i) = 0$. Thus, we have that

$$x \in L \Leftrightarrow \exists c_1, \ldots, c_m, a_1, \ldots, a_k, u_1, \ldots, u_k \forall v_1, \ldots, v_k \text{ such that}$$

$$N \text{ accepts } x \text{ using choices } c_1, \ldots, c_m \text{ and answers } a_1, \ldots, a_k \text{ AND}$$

$$\forall i \in [k] \text{ if } a_i = 1 \text{ then } \varphi_i(u_i) = 1 \text{ AND}$$

$$\forall i \in [k] \text{ if } a_i = 0 \text{ then } \varphi_i(v_i) = 0$$

implying that $L \in \Sigma_2^p$. ∎

Because having oracle access to a complete language for a class allows us to solve every language in that class, some texts use the class name instead of the complete language in the notation for the oracle, and so denote the class $\Sigma_2^p = \mathbf{NP}^{\text{SAT}}$ by $\mathbf{NP}^{\mathbf{NP}}$, the class Σ_3^p by $\mathbf{NP}^{\mathbf{NP}^{\mathbf{NP}}}$, and so on.

WHAT HAVE WE LEARNED?

- The polynomial hierarchy is the set of languages that can be defined via a constant number of alternating quantifiers. It also has equivalent definitions via alternating TMs and oracle TMs. It contains several natural problems that are not known (or believed) to be in **NP**.
- We conjecture that the hierarchy does not collapse in the sense that each of its levels is distinct from the previous ones.
- We can use the concept of alternations to prove that SAT cannot be solved simultaneously in linear time and sublinear space.

CHAPTER NOTES AND HISTORY

In his seminal paper, Karp [Kar72] mentions that "a polynomial-bounded version of Kleene's Arithmetic Hierarchy becomes trivial if $\mathbf{P} = \mathbf{NP}$," a result that seems to foreshadow Theorem 5.4. The definition and careful study of the polynomial hierarchy were initiated by Meyer and Stockmeyer [MS72], who also proved that if $\Sigma_i^p = \Pi_i^p$, then $\mathbf{PH} = \Sigma_i^p$ and showed the completeness of $\Sigma_i\mathsf{SAT}$ for the ith level of the hierarchy.

The class **DP** mentioned in Exercise 5.9 was defined by Papadimitriou and Yannakakis [PY82], who used it to characterize the complexity of identifying the facets of a polytope.

Our knowledge of complete problems for various levels of **PH** is not as rich as it is for **NP**. See Schaefer and Umans's surveys [SU02a, SU02b] for a list of some interesting examples. The SUCCINCT SET-COVER problem is from Umans [Uma98].

A time-space lower bound for satisfiability was first proved by Fortnow [For97a] and later improved by [FLvMV00, Wil05, DvM05], with the current record set by Williams [Wil07] who showed that SAT is not in $\mathbf{TISP}(n^c, n^{0(1)})$ for any $c < 2\cos(\pi/7) = 1.801$. All these works are inspired by a proof technique in Kannan's 1983 paper [Kan83].

EXERCISES

5.1. Show that the language $\Sigma_i\mathsf{SAT}$ of (5.2) is complete for Σ_i^p under polynomial-time reductions.

H533

5.2. Prove Claim 5.9.

5.3. Show that if 3SAT is polynomial-time reducible to $\overline{\mathsf{3SAT}}$, then $\mathbf{PH} = \mathbf{NP}$.

5.4. Show that the definition of **PH** using ATMs coincides with our other definitions.

5.5. Prove Theorem 5.10.

5.6. Adapt the proof of Theorem 5.11 to show that SAT $\notin \mathbf{TISP}(n^c, n^d)$ for every constants c, d such that $c(c + d) < 2$.

5.7. Show that $\mathbf{APSPACE} = \mathbf{EXP}$.

H533

5.8. Complete the proof of Theorem 5.12 using the sketch given there.

5.9. The class **DP** is defined as the set of languages L for which there are two languages $L_1 \in \mathbf{NP}, L_2 \in \mathbf{coNP}$ such that $L = L_1 \cap L_2$. (Do not confuse **DP** with $\mathbf{NP} \cap \mathbf{coNP}$, which may seem superficially similar.) Show that

   (a) EXACT INDSET $\in \Pi_2^p$.

   (b) EXACT INDSET $\in \mathbf{DP}$.

   (c) Every language in **DP** is polynomial-time reducible to EXACT INDSET.

5.10. Suppose A is some language such that $\mathbf{P}^A = \mathbf{NP}^A$. Then show that $\mathbf{PH}^A \subseteq \mathbf{P}^A$ (in other words, the proof of Theorem 5.4 *relativizes*).

5.11. Show that SUCCINCT SET-COVER $\in \Sigma_2^p$.

5.12. Prove the first part of Theorem 5.4: For every i, if $\Sigma_i^p = \Pi_i^p$, then the polynomial hierarchy collapses to the ith level.

5.13. [Sch96] This problem studies the Vapnik-Chervonenkis (VC) dimension, an important concept in machine learning theory. If $\mathcal{S} = \{S_1, S_2, \ldots, S_m\}$ is a collection of subsets of a finite set U, the *VC dimension* of $\mathcal{S}$, denoted $VC(\mathcal{S})$, is the size of the largest set $X \subseteq U$ such that for every $X' \subseteq X$, there is an i for which $S_i \cap X = X'$. (We say that X is *shattered* by $\mathcal{S}$.)

A Boolean circuit C succinctly represents collection $\mathcal{S}$ if S_i consists of exactly those elements $x \in U$ for which $C(i, x) = 1$. Finally,

$$\text{VC-DIMENSION} = \{\langle C, k\rangle : C \text{ represents a collection } \mathcal{S} \text{ s.t. } VC(\mathcal{S}) \geq k\}$$

(a) Show that VC-DIMENSION $\in \Sigma_3^p$.
(b) Show that VC-DIMENSION is Σ_3^p-complete.
H533

CHAPTER 6

Boolean circuits

One might imagine that $\mathbf{P} \neq \mathbf{NP}$, but SAT is tractable in the following sense: for every ℓ there is a very short program that runs in time ℓ^2 and correctly treats all instances of size ℓ.

– Karp and Lipton, 1982

This chapter investigates a model of computation called the *Boolean circuit*, which is a generalization of Boolean formulas and a simplified model of the silicon chips used to make modern computers. It is a natural model for *nonuniform* computation, which crops up often in complexity theory (e.g., see Chapters 19 and 20). In contrast to the standard (or *uniform*) TM model where the same TM is used on all the infinitely many input sizes, a nonuniform model allows a different algorithm to be used for each input size. Thus Karp and Lipton's quote above refers to the possibility that there could be a small and efficient silicon chip that is tailor-made to solve every 3SAT problem on say, $100,000$ variables. The existence of such chips is not ruled out even if $\mathbf{P} \neq \mathbf{NP}$. As the reader might now have guessed, in this chapter we give evidence that such efficient chip solvers for 3SAT are unlikely to exist, at least as the number of variables in the 3*CNF* formula starts to get large.

Another motivation for studying Boolean circuits is that they seem mathematically simpler than Turing machines. Hence proving *lower bounds* might be easier for circuits than for Turing machines. In fact, circuit lower bounds could in principle let us prove $\mathbf{P} \neq \mathbf{NP}$, as we see in Section 6.1. Since the late 1970s, researchers have tried to prove circuit lower bounds. Chapter 14 will describe the partial successes of this effort and Chapter 23 describes where and why it is stuck.

In Section 6.1, we define Boolean circuits and the class $\mathbf{P}_{/poly}$ of languages computed by polynomial-sized circuits. We also show that $\mathbf{P}_{/poly}$ contains the class $\mathbf{P}$ of languages computed by polynomial-time Turing machines and use them to give an alternative proof of the Cook-Levin Theorem (Theorem 2.10). In Section 6.2, we study *uniformly generated* circuit families and show that such families give rise to an alternative characterization of $\mathbf{P}$. Going in the reverse direction, we show in Section 6.3, a characterization of $\mathbf{P}_{/poly}$ using Turing machines that "take advice." In Section 6.4, we study the Karp-Lipton result alluded to above, namely, if the polynomial hierarchy $\mathbf{PH}$ (defined in Chapter 5) does not collapse, then $\mathbf{NP} \not\subseteq \mathbf{P}_{/poly}$. Of course, proving (unconditionally) that $\mathbf{NP} \not\subseteq \mathbf{P}_{/poly}$ is difficult since that would imply $\mathbf{NP} \neq \mathbf{P}$. However, it is even an open problem to find a function in **NEXP** that is not in $\mathbf{P}_{/poly}$! The one thing we do know is that *almost all* Boolean functions require exponential-sized circuits; see Section 6.5. In Section 6.6, we give yet another characterization of the polynomial hierarchy, this time using exponential-sized uniformly generated circuits of constant depth. Finally in Section 6.7.1 we study some interesting subclasses of $\mathbf{P}_{/poly}$ such as **NC** and **AC** and show their relation to parallel computing. We introduce **P**-*completeness* as a way to study whether or not a computational problem has efficient parallel algorithms.

6.1 BOOLEAN CIRCUITS AND $\mathbf{P}_{/POLY}$

A Boolean circuit is a procedural diagram showing how to derive an output from a binary input string by applying a sequence of basic Boolean operations OR ($\vee$), AND ($\wedge$), and NOT ($\neg$) on the input bits. For example, Figure 6.1 shows a circuit computing the XOR function on two bits. Now we give the formal definition. For convenience, we assume the circuit produces 1 bit of output; it is trivial to generalize the definition to circuits with more than one bit of output, though we typically will not need this generalization.

Definition 6.1 *(Boolean circuits)* For every $n \in \mathbb{N}$, an *n-input, single-output Boolean circuit* is a directed acyclic graph with *n sources* (vertices with no incoming edges) and one *sink* (vertex with no outgoing edges). All nonsource vertices are called *gates* and are labeled with one of $\vee$, $\wedge$ or $\neg$ (i.e., the logical operations OR, AND, and NOT). The vertices labeled with $\vee$ and $\wedge$ have fan-in (i.e., number of incoming edges) equal to 2 and the vertices labeled with $\neg$ have fan-in 1. The *size* of C, denoted by $|C|$, is the number of vertices in it.

If C is a Boolean circuit, and $x \in \{0, 1\}^n$ is some input, then the *output* of C on x, denoted by $C(x)$, is defined in the natural way. More formally, for every vertex v of C, we give it a value $\mathtt{val}(v)$ as follows: If v is the ith input vertex then $\mathtt{val}(v) = x_i$ and otherwise $\mathtt{val}(v)$ is defined recursively by applying v's logical operation on the values of the vertices connected to v. The output $C(x)$ is the value of the output vertex.

Though this definition restricts fan-in to 2, this is essentially without loss of generality since a $\vee$ or $\wedge$ gate with fan-in f can be easily repaced with a subcircuit consisting

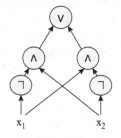

Figure 6.1. A circuit C computing the XOR function (i.e., $C(x_1, x_2) = 1$ iff $x_1 \neq x_2$).

of $f-1$ gates of fan-in 2. However, fan-in will become important again in Section 6.7.1 when we study circuits with restricted *depth*. Note also that the Boolean formulas studied in earlier chapters are circuits where the fan-out (i.e., number of outgoing edges) of each vertex is 1. The advantage of fan-out 2 over fan-out 1 is that it allows an intermediate value inside the circuit to be reused many times. (Note that fan-out 2 can be used to trivially implement arbitrary fan-out.)

One motivation for this definition is that it models the silicon chips used in modern computers.[1] Thus if we show that a certain task can be solved by a small Boolean circuit, then it can be implemented efficiently on a silicon chip.

As usual, we use asymptotic analysis to study the complexity of deciding a language by circuits.

Definition 6.2 *(Circuit families and language recognition)* Let $T : \mathbb{N} \to \mathbb{N}$ be a function. A $T(n)$-*size circuit family* is a sequence $\{C_n\}_{n \in \mathbb{N}}$ of Boolean circuits, where C_n has n inputs and a single output, and its size $|C_n| \le T(n)$ for every n.

We say that a language L is in $\mathbf{SIZE}(T(n))$ if there exists a $T(n)$-size circuit family $\{C_n\}_{n \in \mathbb{N}}$ such that for every $x \in \{0, 1\}^n$, $x \in L \Leftrightarrow C_n(x) = 1$.   ◇

EXAMPLE 6.3

The language $\{1^n : n \in \mathbb{Z}\}$ can be decided by a linear-sized circuit family. The circuit is simply a tree of AND gates that computes the AND of all input bits. The language $\{< m, n, m+n > : m, n \in \mathbb{Z}\}$ also has linear-sized circuits that implement the grade-school algorithm for addition. Recall that this algorithm adds two numbers bit by bit. Addition of two bits is done by a circuit of $O(1)$ size; this produces a carry bit that is used as input for the addition of the bits in the next position.

Since a CNF formula is a special type of a circuit, Claim 2.13 shows that every function f from $\{0, 1\}^n$ to $\{0, 1\}$ can be computed by a Boolean circuit size $n2^n$. In fact, Exercise 6.1 shows that size $O(2^n/n)$ also suffices. Therefore, interesting complexity classes arise when we consider "small" circuits such as the following case:

Definition 6.5 *(The class $\mathbf{P}_{/\mathrm{poly}}$)* $\mathbf{P}_{/\mathrm{poly}}$ is the class of languages that are decidable by polynomial-sized circuit families. That is, $\mathbf{P}_{/\mathrm{poly}} = \cup_c \mathbf{SIZE}(n^c)$.

Of course, one can make the same kind of objections to the practicality of $\mathbf{P}_{/\mathrm{poly}}$ as for $\mathbf{P}$: namely, in what sense is a circuit family of size n^{100} practical, even though it has polynomial size. This was answered to some extent in Section 1.6.2. Another answer is that, as complexity theorists, we hope (eventually) to show that languages such as SAT are not in $\mathbf{P}_{/\mathrm{poly}}$. Thus the result will only be stronger if we allow even such large circuits in the definition of $\mathbf{P}_{/\mathrm{poly}}$.

---

[1] Actually, the circuits in silicon chips are not acyclic and use cycles to implement memory. However, any computation that runs on a silicon chip with C gates and finishes in time T can be performed by a Boolean circuit of size $O(C \cdot T)$.

NOTE 6.4 *(Straight-line programs)*

Instead of modeling Boolean circuits as labeled graphs, we can also model them a *straight-line programs*. A program P is *straight-line* if it contains no branching or loop operations (such as if or goto), and hence P's running time is bounded by the number of instructions it contains.

The equivalence between Boolean circuits and straight-line programs is fairly general and holds (up to polynomial factors) for essentially any reasonable programming language. However it is most obviously demonstrated using straight-line programs with *Boolean operations*. A *Boolean straight-line program* of length T with input variables $x_1, x_2, \ldots, x_n \in \{0, 1\}$ is a sequence of T statements of the form $y_i = z_{i_1} \ OP \ z_{i_2}$ for $i = 1, 2, \ldots, T$ where OP is either $\vee$ or $\wedge$ and each z_{i_1}, z_{i_2} is either an input variable, or the negation of an input variable, or y_j for $j < i$. For every setting of values to the input variables, the straight-line computation consists of executing these simple statements in order, thereby finding values for $y_1, y_2, \ldots, y_T$. The *output* of the computation is the value of y_T.

It is straightforward to show that a function f on n bits can be computed by an S-line straight-line program of this form if and only if it can be computed by an S-sized Boolean circuit (see Exercise 6.2). As an example, we write a straight-line program in input variables x_1, x_2 that is equivalent to the circuit in Figure 6.1.

$$y_1 = \neg x_1;$$

$$y_2 = \neg x_2;$$

$$y_3 = y_1 \wedge x_2;$$

$$y_4 = x_1 \wedge y_2;$$

$$y_5 y_3 \vee y_4$$

6.1.1 Relation between $\mathbf{P}_{/poly}$ and $\mathbf{P}$

What is the relation between $\mathbf{P}_{/poly}$ and $\mathbf{P}$? First we show $\mathbf{P} \subseteq \mathbf{P}_{/poly}$.

Theorem 6.6
$\mathbf{P} \subseteq \mathbf{P}_{/poly}$.

PROOF: The proof is very similar to the proof of the Cook-Levin Theorem (Theorem 2.10). In fact Theorem 6.6 can be used to give an alternative proof to the Cook-Levin Theorem.

Recall that by Remark 1.7 we can simulate every time $O(T(n))$ TM M by an *oblivious* TM $\tilde{M}$ (whose head movement is independent of its input) running in time $O(T(n)^2)$ (or even $O(T(n) \log T(n))$ time if we are more careful). Thus it suffices to show that for every oblivious $T(n)$-time TM M, there exists an $O(T(n))$-sized circuit family $\{C_n\}_{n \in \mathbb{N}}$ such that $C_n(x) = M(x)$ for every $x \in \{0, 1\}^n$.

Let M be such an oblivious TM, let $x \in \{0, 1\}^*$ be some input for M and define the *transcript* of M's execution on x to be the sequence $z_1, \ldots, z_{T(n)}$ of *snapshots* (the machine's state and symbols read by all heads) of the execution at each step in time. We can encode each such snapshot z_i by a constant-sized binary string, and furthermore, we can compute the string z_i based on the input x, the previous snapshot z_{i-1} and the snapshots $z_{i_1}, \ldots, z_{i_k}$, where z_{i_j} denotes the last step that M's jth head was in the same position as it is in the ith step.[2] Because these are only a constant number of strings of constant length, this means that we can compute z_i from these previous snapshots using a constant-sized circuit.

The composition of all these constant-sized circuits gives rise to a circuit that computes from the input x the snapshot $z_{T(n)}$ of the last step of $\tilde{M}$'s execution on x. There is a simple constant-sized circuit that, given $z_{T(n)}$ outputs 1 if and only if $z_{T(n)}$ is an accepting snapshot (in which M outputs 1 and halts). Thus there is an $O(T(n))$-sized circuit C_n such that $C_n(x) = M(x)$ for every $x \in \{0, 1\}^n$. ■

Remark 6.7 The proof of Theorem 6.6 actually gives a stronger result than its statement: The circuit is not only of polynomial size but can also be computed in polynomial time, and even in logarithmic space. One only needs to observe that it's possible to simulate every TM M by an oblivious TM $\tilde{M}$ such that the function that maps n, i to the $\tilde{M}$'s position on n-length inputs in the ith tape can be computed in logarithmic space.

The inclusion $\mathbf{P} \subseteq \mathbf{P}_{/poly}$ is proper. For instance, there are unary languages that are undecidable and hence are not in $\mathbf{P}$ (or for that matter in $\mathbf{EXP}$), whereas every unary language is in $\mathbf{P}_{/poly}$.

Claim 6.8 *Let* $L \subseteq \{0, 1\}^*$ *be a unary language (i.e.,* $L \subseteq \{1^n : n \in \mathbb{N}\}$*). Then,* $L \in \mathbf{P}_{/poly}$. ◇

PROOF: We describe a circuit family of linear size. If $1^n \in L$, then the circuit for inputs of size n is the circuit from Example 6.3, and otherwise it is the circuit that always outputs 0. ■

And here is a unary language that is undecidable. It is just the unary version of the halting problem (see Section 1.5.1).

$\mathsf{UHALT} = \{1^n : n\text{'s binary expansion encodes a pair } \langle M, x \rangle \text{ such that } M \text{ halts on input } x\}$

6.1.2 Circuit satisfiability and an alternative proof of the Cook-Levin Theorem

Boolean circuits can be used to provide an alternative proof for the Cook-Levin Theorem (Theorem 2.10) using the following language.

Definition 6.9 (*Circuit satisfiability or* CKT-SAT) The language CKT-SAT consists of all (strings representing) circuits that produce a single bit of output and that have a

---

[2] Because M is oblivious, the indices $i_1, \ldots, i_k$ depend only on i and not on the actual input x.

satisfying assignment. That is, a string representing an n-input circuit C is in CKT-SAT iff there exists $u \in \{0, 1\}^n$ such that $C(u) = 1$.

CKT-SAT is clearly in **NP** because the satisfying assignment can serve as the certificate. The Cook-Levin Theorem follows immediately from the next two lemmas.

Lemma 6.10 CKT-SAT *is* **NP**-*hard.* ◇

PROOF: If $L \in$ **NP** then there is a polynomial-time TM M and a polynomial p such that $x \in L$ iff $M(x, u) = 1$ for some $u \in \{0, 1\}^{p(|x|)}$. But the proof of Theorem 6.6 yields a polynomial-time transformation from M, x to a circuit C such that $M(x, u) = C(u)$ for every $u \in \{0, 1\}^{\text{poly}(|x|)}$. Thus, x is in L iff $C \in$ CKT-SAT. ∎

Lemma 6.11 CKT-SAT $\leq_p$ 3SAT. ◇

PROOF: If C is a circuit, we map it to a 3CNF formula φ as follows: For every node v_i of C, we will have a corresponding variable z_i in φ. If the node v_i is an AND of the nodes v_j and v_k, then we add to φ clauses that are equivalent to the condition "$z_i = (z_j \wedge z_k)$". That is, we add the clauses

$$(\overline{z}_i \vee \overline{z}_j \vee z_k) \wedge (\overline{z}_i \vee z_j \vee \overline{z}_k) \wedge (\overline{z}_i \vee z_j \vee z_k) \wedge (z_i \vee \overline{z}_j \vee \overline{z}_k)$$

Similarly, if v_i is an OR of v_j and v_k, then we add clauses equivalent to "$z_i = (z_j \vee z_k)$", and if v_i is the NOT of v_j, then we add the clauses $(z_i \vee z_j) \wedge (\overline{z}_i \vee \overline{z}_j)$. Finally, if v_i is the output node of C, then we add the clause (z_i) to φ (i.e., we add the clause that is true iff z_i is true). It is not hard to see that the formula φ is satisfiable if and only if the circuit C is. Clearly, the reduction also runs in time polynomial in the input size. ∎

6.2 UNIFORMLY GENERATED CIRCUITS

The class **P**/poly fits rather awkwardly in the complexity world since it contains even undecidable languages such as the language UHALT defined in Section 6.1.1. The root of the problem is that for a language L to be in **P**/poly, it suffices that a circuit family for L *exists* even if we have no way of actually constructing the circuits. Thus it may be fruitful to try to restrict attention to circuits that can actually be built, say using a fairly efficient Turing machine.

Definition 6.12 (**P**-*uniform circuit families*) A circuit family $\{C_n\}$ is **P**-*uniform* if there is a polynomial-time TM that on input 1^n outputs the description of the circuit C_n. ◇

However, restricting circuits to be **P**-uniform "collapses". **P**/poly to the class **P**.

Theorem 6.13 *A language L is computable by a* **P**-*uniform circuit family iff $L \in$* **P**. ◇

PROOF SKETCH: If L is computable by a circuit family $\{C_n\}$ that is generated by a polynomial-time TM M, then we can come up with a polynomial-time TM $\tilde{M}$ for L

as follows: On input x, the TM $\tilde{M}$ will run $M(1^{|x|})$ to obtain the circuit $C_{|x|}$ which it will then evaluate on the input x.

The other direction is obtained by following closely the proof of Theorem 6.6 and noting that it actually yields a **P**-uniform circuit family for any $L \in \mathbf{P}$. ∎

6.2.1 Logspace-uniform families

We can impose an even stricter notion of uniformity: generation by logspace machines. Recall that a function $f : \{0, 1\}^* \to \{0, 1\}^*$ is *implicitly logspace computable* if the mapping $x, i \mapsto f(x)_i$ can be computed in logarithmic space; see Definition 4.16.

Definition 6.14 *(logspace-uniform circuit families)* A circuit family $\{C_n\}$ is *logspace-uniform* if there is an implicitly logspace computable function mapping 1^n to the description of the circuit C_n. ◇

Since logspace computations run in polynomial time, logspace-uniform circuits are also **P**-uniform. We note that Definition 6.14 is robust to variations in how we represent circuits using strings. A concrete way is to represent a circuit of size S by the $S \times S$ adjacency matrix of its underlying directed graph and an array of size S that provides the labels (gate type) of each vertex. Identifying the vertices with numbers in $[S]$, we let the first n vertices be the input vertices and the last vertex be the output vertex. In other words, the family $\{C_n\}$ is logspace-uniform if and only if the following functions are computable in $O(\log n)$ space:

- $\mathsf{SIZE}(n)$ returns the size S (in binary representation) of the circuit C_n.
- $\mathsf{TYPE}(n, i)$, where $i \in [m]$, returns the label of the ith vertex of C_n. That is it returns one of $\{\vee, \wedge, \neg, NONE\}$.
- $\mathsf{EDGE}(n, i, j)$ returns 1 if there is a directed edge in C_n from the ith vertex to the jth vertex.

Note that both the inputs and the outputs of these functions can be encoded using a logarithmic (in $|C_n|$) number of bits. Exercise 6.10 asks you to prove that the class of languages decided by such circuits does not change if we use the adjacency list (as opposed to matrix) representation. A closer scrutiny of the proof of Theorem 6.6 shows that it implies the following theorem (see Exercise 6.4).

Theorem 6.15 *A language has logspace-uniform circuits of polynomial size iff it is in **P**.* ◇

6.3 TURING MACHINES THAT TAKE ADVICE

We can define $\mathbf{P}_{/\mathbf{poly}}$ in an equivalent way using Turing machines that "take advice." Such a machine has, for each n, an *advice string* α_n, which it is allowed to use in its computation whenever the input has size n.

Definition 6.16 Let $T, a : \mathbb{N} \to \mathbb{N}$ be functions. The class of *languages decidable by time-$T(n)$ TMs with $a(n)$ bits of advice*, denoted $\mathbf{DTIME}(T(n))/a(n)$, contains every L

such that there exists a sequence $\{\alpha_n\}_{n \in \mathbb{N}}$ of strings with $\alpha_n \in \{0, 1\}^{a(n)}$ and a TM M satisfying

$$M(x, \alpha_n) = 1 \Leftrightarrow x \in L$$

for every $x \in \{0, 1\}^n$, where on input (x, α_n) the machine M runs for at most $O(T(n))$ steps. ◇

EXAMPLE 6.17

Every unary language can be be decided by a polynomial time Turing machine with 1 bit of advice. The advice string for inputs of length n is the single bit indicating whether or not 1^n is in the language. In particular, this is true of the language UHALT defined in Section 6.1.1.

Turing machines with advice yield the following characterization of **P**/poly.

Theorem 6.18 (*Polynomial-time TM's with advice decide* **P**/poly)
$$\mathbf{P}_{/poly} = \cup_{c,d} \mathbf{DTIME}(n^c)/n^d$$

PROOF: If $L \in \mathbf{P}_{/poly}$, then it's computable by a polynomial-sized circuit family $\{C_n\}$. We can just use the description of C_n as an advice string on inputs of size n, where the TM is simply the polynomial-time TM M that on input a string x and a string representing an n-input circuit C outputs $C(x)$.

Conversely, if L is decidable by a polynomial-time Turing machine M with access to an advice family $\{\alpha_n\}_{n \in \mathbb{N}}$ of size $a(n)$ for some polynomial a, then we can use the construction of Theorem 6.6 to construct for every n a polynomial-sized circuit D_n such that on every $x \in \{0, 1\}^n, \alpha \in \{0, 1\}^{a(n)}, D_n(x, \alpha) = M(x, \alpha)$. We let the circuit C_n be the polynomial circuit that given x computes the value $D_n(x, \alpha_n)$. That is, C_n is equal to the circuit D_n with the string α_n "hard-wired" as its second input. (By hard-wiring an input into a circuit, we mean taking a circuit C with two inputs $x \in \{0, 1\}^n, y \in \{0, 1\}^m$ and fixing the inputs corresponding to y. This gives the circuit C_y that for every x returns $C(x, y)$. It is easy to do so while ensuring that the size of C_y is not greater than the size of C. This simple idea is often used in complexity theory.) ∎

6.4 P/POLY AND NP

Karp and Lipton formalized the question of whether or not SAT has small circuits as: Is SAT in **P**/poly? They showed that the answer is "NO" if the polynomial hierarchy does not collapse.

Theorem 6.19 (*Karp-Lipton Theorem* [KL80])
If **NP** $\subseteq$ **P**/poly, *then* **PH** $= \Sigma_2^p$.

PROOF: By Theorem 5.4, to show **PH** $= \Sigma_2^p$, it suffices to show that $\Pi_2^p \subseteq \Sigma_2^p$ and in particular it suffices to show that Σ_2^p contains the Π_2^p-complete language Π_2SAT consisting of all true formulas of the form

$$\forall u \in \{0, 1\}^n \, \exists v \in \{0, 1\}^n \, \varphi(u, v) = 1 \qquad (6.1)$$

where φ is an unquantified Boolean formula.

If $\mathbf{NP} \subseteq \mathbf{P}_{/\text{poly}}$, then there *exists* a polynomial p and a $p(n)$-sized circuit family $\{C_n\}_{n \in \mathbb{N}}$ such that for every Boolean formula φ and $u \in \{0, 1\}^n$, $C_n(\varphi, u) = 1$ if and only if there exists $v \in \{0, 1\}^n$ such that $\varphi(u, v) = 1$. Thus the circuit solves the *decision problem* for SAT. However, our algorithm of Theorem 2.18 converts any decision algorithm for SAT into an algorithm that actually outputs a satisfying assignment whenever one exists. Thinking of this algorithm as a circuit, we obtain from the family $\{C_n\}$ a $q(n)$-sized circuit family $\{C'_n\}_{n \in \mathbb{N}}$, where $q(\cdot)$ is a polynomial, such that for every such formula φ and $u \in \{0, 1\}^n$, if there is a string $v \in \{0, 1\}^n$ such that $\varphi(u, v) = 1$, then $C'_n(\varphi, u)$ outputs such a string v. (Note: We did not formally define circuits with more than one bit of output, but it is an obvious generalization of Definition 6.1.)

Of course, the assumption $\mathbf{NP} \subseteq \mathbf{P}_{/\text{poly}}$ only implies the *existence* of such circuits. The main idea of Karp-Lipton is that this circuit can be "guessed" using $\exists$ quantification. Since the circuit outputs a satisfying assignment if one exists, this answer can be checked directly. Formally, since C'_n can be described using $10q(n)^2$ bits, if (6.1) holds then the following quantified formula is true:

$$\exists w \in \{0, 1\}^{10q(n)^2} \, \forall u \in \{0, 1\}^n \text{ s.t. } w \text{ describes a circuit } C' \text{ and } \varphi(u, C'(\varphi, u)) = 1 \quad (6.2)$$

Furthermore, if (6.1) is false, then for some u, *no* v exists such that $\varphi(u, v) = 1$, and hence (6.2) is false as well. Thus (6.2) holds if and only if (6.1) does! Finally, since evaluating a circuit on an input can be done deterministically in polynomial time, the truth of (6.2) can be verified in Σ_2^p. ∎

Similarly, the following theorem shows that $\mathbf{P}_{/\text{poly}}$ is unlikely to contain $\mathbf{EXP}$.

Theorem 6.20 *(Meyer's Theorem [KL80])*
If $\mathbf{EXP} \subseteq \mathbf{P}_{/\text{poly}}$ *then* $\mathbf{EXP} = \Sigma_2^p$.

PROOF SKETCH: Let $L \in \mathbf{EXP}$. Then L is computable by an $2^{p(n)}$-time-oblivious TM M, where p is some polynomial. Let $x \in \{0, 1\}^n$ be some input string. For every $i \in [2^{p(n)}]$, we denote by z_i the encoding of the ith snapshot of M's execution on input x (see the proof of Theorem 6.6). If M has k tapes, then $x \in L$ if and only if for every $k + 1$ indices $i, i_1, \ldots, i_k$, the snapshots $z_i, z_{i_1}, \ldots, z_{i_k}$ satisfy some easily checkable criteria: If z_i is the last snapshot, then it should encode M outputting 1, and if $i_1, \ldots, i_k$ are the last indices where M's heads were in the same locations as in i, then the values read in z_i should be consistent with the input and the values written in $z_{i_1}, \ldots, z_{i_k}$. (Note that these indices can be represented in polynomial time.) But if $\mathbf{EXP} \subseteq \mathbf{P}_{/\text{poly}}$, then there is a $q(n)$-sized circuit C (for some polynomial q) that computes z_i from i. Now the main point is that the correctness of the transcript implicitly computed by this circuit can be expressed as a $\mathbf{coNP}$ predicate (namely, one that checks that the transcript satisfies all local criteria). Hence, $x \in L$ iff the following condition is true

$$\exists C \in \{0, 1\}^{q(n)} \, \forall i, i_1, \ldots, i_k \in \{0, 1\}^{p(n)} \, T(x, C(i), C(i_1), \ldots, C(i_k)) = 1$$

where T is some polynomial-time TM checking these conditions. This implies that $L \in \Sigma_2^p$. ∎

Theorem 6.20 implies that if $\mathbf{P} = \mathbf{NP}$, then $\mathbf{EXP} \not\subseteq \mathbf{P}_{/\text{poly}}$. Indeed, by Theorem 5.4, if $\mathbf{P} = \mathbf{NP}$, then $\mathbf{P} = \Sigma_2^p$, and so if $\mathbf{EXP} \subseteq \mathbf{P}_{/\text{poly}}$, we'd get $\mathbf{P} = \mathbf{EXP}$, contradicting the Time Hierarchy Theorem (Theorem 3.1). Thus upper bounds (in this case, $\mathbf{NP} \subseteq \mathbf{P}$) can potentially be used to prove circuit lower bounds.

6.5 CIRCUIT LOWER BOUNDS

Since $\mathbf{P} \subseteq \mathbf{P}_{/\text{poly}}$, if we ever prove $\mathbf{NP} \not\subseteq \mathbf{P}_{/\text{poly}}$, then we will have shown $\mathbf{P} \neq \mathbf{NP}$. The Karp-Lipton Theorem gives evidence that $\mathbf{NP} \not\subseteq \mathbf{P}_{/\text{poly}}$. Can we resolve $\mathbf{P}$ versus $\mathbf{NP}$ by proving $\mathbf{NP} \not\subseteq \mathbf{P}_{/\text{poly}}$? There is reason to invest hope in this approach as opposed to proving direct lower bounds on Turing machines. By representing computation using circuits, we seem to actually peer into the guts of it rather than treating it as a black box. Thus we may be able to get around the limitations of relativizing methods shown in Chapter 3. Indeed, it is easy to show that *some* functions do require very large circuits to compute.

Theorem 6.21 (*Existence of hard functions* [Sha49a])
For every $n > 1$, there exists a function $f : \{0, 1\}^n \to \{0, 1\}$ that cannot be computed by a circuit C of size $2^n/(10n)$.

PROOF: The proof uses a simple counting argument:

- The number of functions from $\{0, 1\}^n$ to $\{0, 1\}$ is 2^{2^n}.
- Since every circuit of size at most S can be represented as a string of $9 \cdot S \log S$ bits (e.g., using the adjacency list representation), the number of such circuits is at most $2^{9S \log S}$.

Setting $S = 2^n/(10n)$, we see that the number of circuits of size S is at most $2^{9S \log S} \leq 2^{2^n 9n/10n} < 2^{2^n}$. Hence the number of functions computed by such circuits is smaller than 2^{2^n}, implying that there exists a function that is not computed by circuits of that size. We note that using a more careful calculation, one can obtain a bound of $(1-\epsilon)2^n/n$ for every $\epsilon > 0$ and even $2^n(1 + \log n/n - O(1/n))$ (see [FM05]). ∎

There is another way to phrase this proof. Suppose that we pick a function $f : \{0, 1\}^n \to \{0, 1\}$ at random by picking for every one of the 2^n possible inputs $x \in \{0, 1\}^n$ the value $f(x)$ in $\{0, 1\}$ uniformly and independently. Then, for every fixed circuit C and input x, the probability that $C(x) = f(x)$ is $1/2$, and since these choices are independent, the probability that C computes f (i.e., $C(x) = f(x)$ for *every* $x \in \{0, 1\}^n$) is 2^{-2^n}. Since there are at most $2^{0.92^n}$ circuits of size at most $2^n/(10n)$, we can apply the union bound (see Section A.2) to conclude that the probability that *there exists* such a circuit C computing f is at most

$$\frac{2^{0.92^n}}{2^{2^n}} = 2^{-0.1 \cdot 2^n}$$

a number that tends very fast to zero as n grows. In particular, since this number is smaller than one, it implies that there exists a function f that is not computed by any circuit of size at most $2^n/(10n)$. This proof technique (showing an object with a particular property exists by showing a random object satisfies this property with nonzero probability) is called the *probabilistic method*, and it is widely used in theoretical computer science and combinatorics (e.g., see Chapters 13, 19, and 21 of this book). Note that it yields a stronger result than Theorem 6.21: Not only does there exist a hard function (not computable by $2^n/(10n)$-sized circuits), but in fact the *vast majority* of the functions from $\{0, 1\}^n$ to $\{0, 1\}$ are hard. This gives hope that we should be able to find one such function that also happens to lie in **NP**, thus proving **NP** $\not\subseteq$ **P**$_{/poly}$. Sadly, such hopes have not yet come to pass. After two decades, the best circuit size lower bound for an **NP** language is only $(5 - o(1))n$ [ILMR05]. (However, see Exercise 6.5 for a better lower bound for a language in **PH**.) On the positive side, we have had notable success in proving lower bounds for more restricted circuit models, as we will see in Chapter 14.

6.6 NONUNIFORM HIERARCHY THEOREM

Just like time-bounded Turing machines (deterministic or nondeterministic), and space bounded machines, Boolean circuits also have a hierarchy theorem. That is, larger circuits can compute strictly more functions than smaller ones:

Theorem 6.22 *(Nonuniform Hierarchy Theorem)*
For every functions $T, T' : \mathbb{N} \to \mathbb{N}$ with $2^n/n > T'(n) > 10T(n) > n$,

$$\mathbf{SIZE}(T(n)) \subsetneq \mathbf{SIZE}(T'(n))$$

PROOF: Interestingly, the diagonalization methods of Chapter 3 do not seem to apply in this setting; nevertheless, we are able to prove Theorem 6.22 using the counting argument of Theorem 6.21. To show the idea, we prove that $\mathbf{SIZE}(n) \subsetneq \mathbf{SIZE}(n^2)$.

By Theorem 6.21, for every ℓ, there is a function $f : \{0, 1\}^\ell \to \{0, 1\}$ that is not computable by $2^\ell/(10\ell)$-sized circuits. On the other hand, by Claim 2.13, every function from $\{0, 1\}^\ell$ to $\{0, 1\}$ is computable by a $2^\ell 10\ell$-sized circuit (see also Exercise 6.1 for a tighter bound).

Therefore, if we set $\ell = 1.1 \log n$ and let $g : \{0, 1\}^n \to \{0, 1\}$ be the function that applies f on the first ℓ bits of its input, then

$$g \in \mathbf{SIZE}(2^\ell 10\ell) = \mathbf{SIZE}(11n^{1.1} \log n) \subseteq \mathbf{SIZE}(n^2)$$

$$g \notin \mathbf{SIZE}(2^\ell/(10\ell)) = \mathbf{SIZE}(n^{1.1}/(11 \log n)) \supseteq \mathbf{SIZE}(n)$$

■

6.7 FINER GRADATIONS AMONG CIRCUIT CLASSES

This section introduces some subclasses of **P**$_{/poly}$, which are interesting for two reasons. First, separating **NP** from these subclasses may give insight into how to separate **NP** from **P**$_{/poly}$. Second, these subclasses correspond to interesting computational models in their own right.

Perhaps the most interesting connection is to *massively parallel computers*, which we will now briefly describe. (A detailed understanding is not necessary as the validity of Theorem 6.27 does not depend upon it.) In a parallel computer, one uses simple off-the-shelf microprocessors and links them using an *interconnection network* that allows them to send messages to each other. Usual interconnection networks such as the *hypercube* allows linking n processors such that interprocessor communication is possible—assuming some upper bounds on the total load on the network—in $O(\log n)$ steps. The processors compute in lock-step (for instance, to the ticks of a global clock) and are assumed to do a small amount of computation in each step, say an operation on $O(\log n)$ bits. Thus each processor has enough memory to remember its own address in the interconnection network and to write down the address of any other processor, and thus send messages to it.

We will say that a computational problem has an *efficient parallel algorithm* if it can be solved for inputs of size n using a parallel computer with $n^{O(1)}$ processors in time $\log^{O(1)} n$.

EXAMPLE 6.23

Given two n bit numbers x, y, we wish to compute $x + y$ fast in parallel. The grade-school algorithm proceeds from the least significant bit and maintains a *carry bit*.

The most significant bit is computed only after n steps. This algorithm does not take advantage of parallelism. A better algorithm called *carry lookahead* assigns each bit position to a separate processor and then uses interprocessor communication to propagate carry bits. It takes $O(n)$ processors and $O(\log n)$ time.

There are also efficient parallel algorithms for integer multiplication and division. (The latter is quite nonintuitive and unlike the grade-school algorithm!)

Many matrix computations can be done efficiently in parallel: These include computing the product, rank, determinant, and inverse. (See exercises and chapter notes.)

Some graph theoretic algorithms such as shortest paths and minimum spanning tree also have fast parallel implementations.

However well-known polynomial-time problems such as maximum flows and linear programming are not known to have any good parallel implementations and are conjectured not to have any; see our discussion of **P**-completeness in Section 6.7.2.

6.7.1 The classes NC and AC

Now we relate parallel computation to circuits. The *depth* of a circuit is the length of the longest directed path from an input node to the output node.

Definition 6.24 (*The class* NC) For every d, a language L is in $\mathbf{NC}^d$ if L can be decided by a family of circuits $\{C_n\}$ where C_n has poly(n) size and depth $O(\log^d n)$. The class **NC** is $\cup_{i \geq 1} \mathbf{NC}^i$.   ◇

One can also define *uniform* **NC**, by requiring the circuits to be logspace-uniform. A related class is the following.

Definition 6.25 *(AC)* The class $\mathbf{AC}^i$ is defined similarly to $\mathbf{NC}^i$ except gates are allowed to have unbounded fan-in (i.e., the OR and AND gates can be applied to more than two bits). The class $\mathbf{AC}$ is $\cup_{i \geq 0} \mathbf{AC}^i$.   ◇

Since unbounded (but $\text{poly}(n)$) fan-in can be simulated using a tree of ORs/ANDs of depth $O(\log n)$, $\mathbf{NC}^i \subseteq \mathbf{AC}^i \subseteq \mathbf{NC}^{i+1}$. The inclusion is known to be strict for $i = 0$, as we will see in Chapter 14. Note that $\mathbf{NC}^0$ is extremely limited since the circuit's output depends upon a constant number of input bits, but $\mathbf{AC}^0$ does not suffer from this limitation.

EXAMPLE 6.26

The language PARITY $= \{x : x$ has an odd number of 1s$\}$ is in $\mathbf{NC}^1$. The circuit computing it has the form of a binary tree. The answer appears at the root; the left subtree computes the parity of the first $|x|/2$ bits, and the right subtree computes the parity of the remaining bits. The gate at the top computes the parity of these two bits. Clearly, unwrapping the recursion implicit in our description gives a circuit of depth $O(\log n)$. It is also logspace-uniform.

   In Chapter 14, we will show that PARITY is not in $\mathbf{AC}^0$.

It turns out that $\mathbf{NC}$ characterizes the languages with efficient parallel algorithms:

Theorem 6.27 *(NC and parallel algorithms)*
A language has efficient parallel algorithms iff it is in $\mathbf{NC}$.

PROOF SKETCH: Suppose a language $L \in \mathbf{NC}$ and is decidable by a circuit family $\{C_n\}$ where C_n has size $N = O(n^c)$ and depth $D = O(\log^d n)$. Take a general-purpose parallel computer with N nodes and configure it to decide L as follows. Compute a description of C_n and allocate the role of each circuit node to a distinct processor. Each processor, after computing the output at its assigned node, sends the resulting bit to every other circuit node that needs it. Assuming the interconnection network delivers all messages in $O(\log N)$ time, the total running time is $O(\log^{d+1} N)$. (Note that if the circuit is nonuniform, so is this parallel algorithm. On the other hand, if the circuit is logspace-uniform, then so is the parallel algorithm.)

   The reverse direction is similar, with the circuit having $N \cdot D$ nodes arranged in D layers, and the ith node in the tth layer performs the computation of processor i at time t. The role of the interconnection network is played by the circuit wires. ∎

6.7.2 P-completeness

A major open question is whether every polynomial-time algorithm has an efficient parallel implementation, or in other words, whether $\mathbf{P} = \mathbf{NC}$. We believe that the answer is NO (though we are currently even unable to separate $\mathbf{PH}$ from $\mathbf{NC}^1$). This motivates the theory of **P**-*completeness*, which can be used to study which problems are likely to be efficiently parallelizable (i.e., are in $\mathbf{NC}$) and which are not.

Definition 6.28 A language is **P**-*complete* if it is in **P** and every language in **P** is logspace-reducible to it (as per Definition 4.16). ◇

The following theorem is left for the reader as Exercise 6.15.

Theorem 6.29 *If language L is* **P**-*complete then*

1. $L \in$ **NC** *iff* **P** = **NC**.
2. $L \in$ **L** *iff* **P** = **L**. *(Where* **L** *is the set of languages decidable in logarithmic space; see Definition 4.5.)* ◇

The following is a fairly natural **P**-complete language.

Theorem 6.30 *Let* CIRCUIT-EVAL *denote the language consisting of all pairs* $\langle C, x \rangle$ *where C is an n-input single-output circuit and* $x \in \{0, 1\}^n$ *is such that* $C(x) = 1$. *Then* CIRCUIT-EVAL *is* **P**-*complete.* ◇

PROOF SKETCH: The language is clearly in **P**. A logspace-reduction from any other language in **P** to this language is implicit in the proof of Theorem 6.15. ∎

6.8 CIRCUITS OF EXPONENTIAL SIZE

As noted, every language has circuits of size $O(2^n/n)$. But actually finding these circuits may be difficult—sometimes even undecidable. If we place a uniformity condition on the circuits, that is, require them to be efficiently computable, then the circuit complexity of some languages could exceed 2^n. In fact it is possible to give alternative definitions of some familiar complexity classes, analogous to the definition of **P** in Theorem 6.15.

Definition 6.31 *(DC-Uniform)* Let $\{C_n\}_{n \geq 1}$ be a circuit family. We say that it is a *Direct Connect uniform* (DC uniform) family if there is a polynomial-time algorithm that, given $\langle n, i \rangle$, can compute in polynomial time the ith bit of (the adjacency matrix representation of) the circuit C_n. More precisely, a family $\{C_n\}_{n \in \mathbb{N}}$ is DC uniform iff the functions SIZE, TYPE, and EDGE defined in Section 6.2.1 are computable in polynomial time.

Note that the circuits may have exponential size, but they have a succinct representation in terms of a TM, which can systematically generate any required vertex of the circuit in polynomial time. Now we give a (yet another) characterization of the class **PH**, this time as languages computable by uniform circuit families of bounded depth.

Theorem 6.32 $L \in PH$ *iff L can be computed by a DC uniform circuit family* $\{C_n\}$ *that satisfies the following conditions*

1   *that uses AND, OR, NOT gates.*
2   *that has size* $2^{n^{O(1)}}$ *and constant depth.*
3   *its gates can have unbounded (exponential) fan-in.*

4   *its NOT gates appear only at the input level (i.e., they are only applied directly to the input
     and not to the result of any other gate).*   ◇

We leave proving Theorem 6.32 as Exercise 6.17. If we drop the restriction that the
circuits have constant depth, then we obtain exactly **EXP** (see Exercise 6.18).

WHAT HAVE WE LEARNED?

- Boolean circuits can be used as an alternative computational model to TMs. The
  class $\mathbf{P_{/poly}}$ of languages decidable by polynomial-sized circuits is a strict superset of
  P but does not contain **NP** unless the hierarchy collapses.
- Almost every function from $\{0, 1\}^n$ to $\{0, 1\}$ requires exponential-sized circuits.
  Finding even one function in **NP** with this property would show that $\mathbf{P} \neq \mathbf{NP}$.
- The class **NC** of languages decidable by (uniformly constructible) circuits with
  polylogarithmic depth and polynomial size corresponds to computational tasks that
  can be efficiently parallelized.

CHAPTER NOTES AND HISTORY

Circuits have been studied in electrical engineering since the 1940s, at a time when
gates were implemented using vacuum tube devices. Shannon's seminal paper [Sha49a]
stated the problem of finding the smallest circuit implementing a Boolean function,
and showed that the circuit complexity of the hardest Boolean function on n bits is
$\Theta(2^n/n)$. Such topics are studied in fields called "switching theory" or "Logic Synthesis." Savage [Sav72] makes some of the first connections between Turing machine
computations and circuits and describes the tight relationship between circuits and
straight-line programs.

The class $\mathbf{P_{/poly}}$ and its characterization as the set of languages computed by
polynomial-time TM's with polynomial advice (Theorem 6.18) is due to Karp and Lipton [KL80]. They also give a more general definition that can be used to define the
class $\mathcal{C}/a(n)$ for every complexity class $\mathcal{C}$ and function $a : N \to \mathbb{N}$. However, we do not
use this definition in this book since it does not seem to capture the intuitive notion of
advice for classes such as $\mathbf{NP} \cap \mathbf{coNP}$, **BPP**, and others.

Karp and Lipton [KL80] originally proved Theorem 6.19 with the weaker conclu-
sion $\mathbf{PH} = \Sigma_3^p$; they attribute the stronger version given here to Sipser. They also state
Theorem 6.20 and attribute it to A. Meyer.

NC stands for "Nick's Class," defined first by Nick Pippenger and named by Steve
Cook in his honor. However, the "A" in **AC** stands not for a person but for "alternations." The class of **NC** algorithms as well as many related issues in parallel computation
are discussed in the text by Leighton [Lei91].

Boppana and Sipser give an excellent survey of the knowledge on circuits lower
bounds circa 1989 [BS90]. Fortunately (or unfortunately) this survey is still fairly
representative of the state of the art. See also Chapter 14.

EXERCISES

6.1. In this exercise, we'll prove Shannon's result that every function $f : \{0, 1\}^n \to \{0, 1\}$ can be computed by a circuit of size $O(2^n/n)$. (This bound was improved by Lupanov ([Lup58], see also [Weg87, FM05]) to $\frac{2^n}{n}(1 + o(1))$, where $o(1)$ is a term that tends to zero with n.)

   (a) Prove that every such f can be computed by a circuit of size less than $10 \cdot 2^n$.

   H533

   (b) Improve this bound to show that any such function f can be computed by a circuit of size less than $1000 \cdot 2^n/n$.

6.2. Prove that for every $f : \{0, 1\}^n \to \{0, 1\}$ and $S \in \mathbb{N}$, f can be computed by a Boolean circuit of size S if and only if f can be computed by an S-line program of the type described in Example 6.4.

6.3. Describe a *decidable* language in $\mathbf{P}_{/\mathbf{poly}}$ that is not in $\mathbf{P}$.

6.4. Prove Theorem 6.15.

6.5. [Kannan [Kan81]] Show for every $k > 0$ that $\mathbf{PH}$ contains languages whose circuit complexity is $\Omega(n^k)$.

   H533

6.6. Solve question 6.5 with $\mathbf{PH}$ replaced by Σ_2^p (if your solution didn't already do this).

6.7. (Upper Bounds Can Imply Lower Bounds) Show that if $\mathbf{P} = \mathbf{NP}$, then there is a language in $\mathbf{EXP}$ that requires circuits of size $2^n/n$.

   H533

6.8. A language $L \subseteq \{0, 1\}^*$ is sparse if there is a polynomial p such that $|L \cap \{0, 1\}^n| \leq p(n)$ for every $n \in \mathbb{N}$. Show that every sparse language is in $\mathbf{P}_{/\mathbf{poly}}$.

6.9. (Mahaney's Theorem [Mah80]) Show that if a sparse language is $\mathbf{NP}$-complete, then $\mathbf{P} = \mathbf{NP}$. (This is a strengthening of Exercise 2.30 of Chapter 2.)

   H533

6.10. Show a logspace implicitly computable function f that maps any n-vertex graph in adjacency matrix representation into the same graph in adjacency list representation. You can think of the adjacency list representation of an n-vertex graph as a sequence of n strings of size $O(n \log n)$ each, where the ith string contains the list of neighbors of the ith vertex in the graph (and is padded with zeros if necessary).

6.11. (*Open Problem*) Suppose we make a stronger assumption than $\mathbf{NP} \subseteq \mathbf{P}_{/\mathbf{poly}}$: every language in $\mathbf{NP}$ has linear size circuits. Can we show something stronger than $\mathbf{PH} = \Sigma_2^p$?

6.12. **(a)** Describe an $\mathbf{NC}$ circuit for the problem of computing the product of two given $n \times n$ matrices A, B over a finite field $\mathbb{F}$ of size at most polynomial in n.

   H533

   (b) Describe an $\mathbf{NC}$ circuit for computing, given an $n \times n$ matrix, the matrix A^n over a finite field $\mathbb{F}$ of size at most polynomial in n.

   H533

   (c) Conclude that the PATH problem (and hence every $\mathbf{NL}$ language) is in $\mathbf{NC}$.

6.13. A *formula* is a circuit in which every node (except the input nodes) has out-degree 1. Show that a language is computable by polynomial-size formulas iff it is in nonuniform $\mathbf{NC}^1$, where this denotes the variant of $\mathbf{NC}^1$ dropping requirements that the circuits are generated by logspace algorithms.
H533

6.14. Show that $\mathbf{NC}^1 \subseteq \mathbf{L}$. Conclude that $\mathbf{PSPACE} \neq \mathbf{NC}^1$.

6.15. Prove Theorem 6.29. That is, prove that if L is $\mathbf{P}$-complete then $L \in \mathbf{NC}$ (resp. $\mathbf{L}$) iff $\mathbf{P} = \mathbf{NC}$ (resp. $\mathbf{L}$).

6.16. (Csansky's Algorithm [Csa76]: requires some linear algebra) Show that the problem

$$\{< M, k >: \ M \text{ is a matrix with determinant } k\}$$

is in $\mathbf{NC}$. (M has integer entries, and you can assume without loss of generality that the underlying field is $\mathbb{C}$.)
H533

6.17. Prove Theorem 6.32 (that $\mathbf{PH}$ is the set of languages with constant-depth DC uniform circuits).

6.18. Show that $\mathbf{EXP}$ is exactly the set of languages with DC uniform circuits of size 2^{n^c}, where c is some constant (c may depend upon the language).

6.19. Show that if linear programming has a fast parallel algorithm, then $\mathbf{P} = \mathbf{NC}$.
H533

CHAPTER 7

Randomized computation

Why should we fear, when chance rules everything, And foresight of the future there is none;
'Tis best to live at random, as one can.

– Sophocles, Oedipus Rex

We present here the motivation and a general description of a method dealing with a class of problems in mathematical physics. The method is, essentially, a statistical approach to the study of differential equations.

– N. Metropolis and S. Ulam, "The Monte Carlo Method," 1949

We do not assume anything about the distribution of the instances of the problem to be solved. Instead we incorporate randomization into the algorithm itself... It may seem at first surprising that employing randomization leads to efficient algorithms. This claim is substantiated by two examples. The first has to do with finding the nearest pair in a set of n points in $\mathbb{R}^k$. The second example is an extremely efficient algorithm for determining whether a number is prime.

– Michael Rabin, 1976

So far, we used the Turing machine (as defined in Chapter 1) as our standard model of computation. But there is one aspect of reality this model does not seem to capture: the ability to make *random choices* during the computation. (Most programming languages provide a built-in *random number generator* for this.) Scientists and philosophers may still debate if true randomness exists in the world, but it definitely seems that when tossing a coin (or measuring the results of other physical experiments) we get an outcome that is sufficiently random and unpredictable for all practical purposes. Thus it makes sense to consider algorithms (and Turing machines) that can toss a coin—in other words, use a source of random bits. A moment's reflection suggests that such algorithms have been implicitly studied for a long time. Think for instance of basic procedures in classical statistics such as an opinion poll—it tries to estimate facts about a large population by taking a small random sample of the population. Similarly, randomization is also a natural tool for simulating real-world systems that are themselves probabilistic, such as nuclear fission or the stock market. Statistical ideas have also been long used in study of differential equations; see the quote by Metropolis and Ulam at the beginning of the chapter. They named such algorithms *Monte Carlo methods* after the famous European gambling resort.

In the last few decades, randomization was also used to give simpler or more efficient algorithms for many problems—in areas ranging from number theory to network routing—that on the face of it have nothing to do with probability. We will see some examples in this chapter. We will not address the issue of the *quality* of random number generators in this chapter, defering that discussion to Chapters 9, 20, and 21.

As complexity theorists, our main interest in this chapter is to understand the power of Turing machines that can toss random coins. We give a mathematical model for *probabilistic computation* and define in Section 7.1 the complexity class **BPP** that aims to capture the set of decision problems efficiently solvable by probabilistic algorithms.[1] Section 7.2 gives a few examples of nontrivial probabilistic algorithms, demonstrating that randomization may give added power to the algorithm designer. In fact, since random number generators are ubiquitous (leaving aside for the moment the question of how good they are), the class **BPP** (and its sister classes **RP, coRP**, and **ZPP**) is arguably as important as **P** in capturing the notion of "efficient computation." The preceding examples suggest that **P** is a proper subset of **BPP**, though somewhat surprisingly, there are reasons to believe that actually **BPP** may be the same as **P**; see Chapter 20.

Our definition of a probabilistic algorithm will allow it to output a wrong answer with some small probability. At first sight, the reader might be concerned that these errors could make such algorithms impractical. However, in Section 7.4 we show how to reduce the probability of error to a minuscule quantity.

This chapter also studies the relationship between **BPP** and classes studied in earlier chapters such as $\mathbf{P}_{/poly}$ and **PH**.

Many of the notions studied in the previous chapters can be extended to the probabilistic setting. For example, in Sections 7.6 and 7.7 we will describe randomized reductions and probabilistic logspace algorithms. These are probabilistic analogs of reductions and logspace algorithms studied in Chapters 2 and 4.

The role of randomness in complexity theory extends far beyond a study of randomized algorithms and classes such as **BPP**. Entire areas such as cryptography (see Chapter 9) and interactive and probabilistically checkable proofs (see Chapters 8 and 11) rely on randomness in an essential way, sometimes to prove results whose statement seemingly did not involve randomness in any way. Thus this chapter lays the groundwork for many later chapters of the book.

Throughout this chapter and the rest of the book, we will use some notions from elementary probability on finite sample spaces; see Appendix A for a quick review.

7.1 PROBABILISTIC TURING MACHINES

A randomized algorithm is an algorithm that may involve random choices such as initializing a variable with an integer chosen at random from some range. In practice randomized algorithms are implemented using a *random number generator*. In fact, it turns out (see Exercise 7.1) that it suffices to have a random number generator that generates *random bits*—they produce the bit 0 with probability 1/2 and bit 1 with probability 1/2. We will often describe such generators as tossing *fair coins*.

---

[1] **BPP** stands for bounded-error probabilistic polynomial-time; see chapter notes.

Just as we used standard Turing machines in Chapter 1 to model deterministic (i.e., nonprobabilistic) algorithms, to model randomized algorithms we use probabilistic Turing machines (PTMs).

Definition 7.1 A *probabilistic Turing machine* (PTM) is a Turing machine with two transition functions δ_0, δ_1. To execute a PTM M on an input x, we choose in each step with probability $1/2$ to apply the transition function δ_0 and with probability $1/2$ to apply δ_1. This choice is made independently of all previous choices.

The machine only outputs 1 ("Accept") or 0 ("Reject"). We denote by $M(x)$ the random variable corresponding to the value M writes at the end of this process. For a function $T : \mathbb{N} \to \mathbb{N}$, we say that M runs in $T(n)$-time if for any input x, M halts on x within $T(|x|)$ steps regardless of the random choices it makes.

Recall from Section 2.1.2 that a nondeterministic TM is also a TM with two transition functions. Thus a PTM is syntactically similar. The difference is in how we interpret the working of the TM. In a PTM, each transitition is taken with probability $1/2$, so a computation that runs for time t gives rise to 2^t *branches* in the graph of all computations, each of which is taken with probability $1/2^t$. Thus $\Pr[M(x) = 1]$ is simply the *fraction* of branches that end with M outputting a 1. The main difference between an NDTM and a PTM lies in how we interpret the graph of all possible computations: An NDTM is said to *accept* the input if there *exists* a branch that outputs 1, whereas in the case of a PTM we consider the *fraction* of branches for which this happens. On a conceptual level, PTMs and NDTMs are very different, as PTMs, like deterministic TMs and unlike NDTMs, are intended to model realistic computation devices.

The following class **BPP** aims to capture efficient probabilistic computation. Below, for a language $L \subseteq \{0, 1\}^*$ and $x \in \{0, 1\}^*$, we define $L(x) = 1$ if $x \in L$ and $L(x) = 0$ otherwise.

Definition 7.2 *(The classes **BPTIME** and **BPP**)* For $T : \mathbb{N} \to \mathbb{N}$ and $L \subseteq \{0, 1\}^*$ we say that a PTM M decides L in time $T(n)$ if for every $x \in \{0, 1\}^*$, M halts in $T(|x|)$ steps regardless of its random choices, and $\Pr[M(x) = L(x)] \geq 2/3$.

We let **BPTIME**$(T(n))$ be the class of languages decided by PTMs in $O(T(n))$ time and define **BPP** $= \cup_c$**BPTIME**(n^c).

Note that the PTM in the previous definition satisfies a very strong "excluded middle" property: For every input, it either accepts it with probability at least $2/3$ or rejects it with probability at least $2/3$. This property makes Definition 7.2 quite *robust*, as we will see in Section 7.4. For instance, we will see that the constant $2/3$ is arbitrary in the sense that it can be replaced with any other constant greater than half without changing the classes **BPTIME**$(T(n))$ and **BPP**. We can also make other modifications such as allowing "unfair" coins (that output "Heads" with probability different than $1/2$) or allowing the machine to run in *expected* polynomial-time.

While Definition 7.2 allows the PTM M on input x to output a value different from $L(x)$ (i.e., output the wrong answer) with positive probability, this probability is only over the random choices that M makes in the computation. In particular, for *every* input

x, $M(x)$ will output the right value $L(x)$ with probability at least $2/3$. Thus **BPP**, like **P**, is still a class capturing complexity on *worst-case* inputs.

Since a deterministic TM is a special case of a PTM (where both transition functions are equal), the class **BPP** clearly contains **P**. To study the relationship of **BPP** with other classes, it will be helpful to have the following alternative definition.

An alternative definition As we did with **NP**, we can define **BPP** using deterministic TMs where the sequence of "coin tosses" needed for every step are provided to the TM as an additional input.

> **Definition 7.3** (**BPP**, *alternative definition*) A language L is in **BPP** if there exists a polynomial-time TM M and a polynomial $p : \mathbb{N} \to \mathbb{N}$ such that for every $x \in \{0, 1\}^*$, $\Pr_{r \in_R \{0,1\}^{p(|x|)}}[M(x, r) = L(x)] \geq 2/3$.

From this definition it is clear that **BPP** $\subseteq$ **EXP** since in time $2^{\text{poly}(n)}$ it is possible to enumerate all the possible random choices of a polynomial-time PTM. Currently researchers only know that **BPP** is sandwiched between **P** and **EXP** but are even unable to show that **BPP** is a proper subset of **NEXP**.

A central open question of complexity theory is whether or not **BPP** = **P**. Based on previous chapters, the reader would probably guess that complexity theorists believe that **BPP** $\neq$ **P**. Not true! Many complexity theorists actually believe that **BPP** = **P**, in other words, there is a way to transform *every* probabilistic algorithm to a deterministic algorithm (one that does not toss any coins) while incurring only a polynomial slowdown. The reasons for this surprising belief are described in Chapters 19 and 20.

7.2 SOME EXAMPLES OF PTMS

The following examples demonstrate how randomness can be a useful tool in computation. We will see many more examples in the rest of this book.

7.2.1 Finding a median

A *median* of a set of numbers $\{a_1, \ldots, a_n\}$ is any number x such that at least $\lfloor \frac{n}{2} \rfloor$ of the a_i's are smaller or equal to x and at least $\lfloor \frac{n}{2} \rfloor$ of them are larger or equal to x. Finding a median of a given set of number is useful in many calculations. One simple way to do so is to sort the numbers and then output the $\lfloor \frac{n}{2} \rfloor$ smallest of them, but this takes $O(n \log n)$ time.[2] We now show a simple probabilistic algorithm to find the median in $O(n)$ time. There are known linear time deterministic algorithms for this problem, but the following probabilistic algorithm is still the simplest and most practical known.

Our algorithm will actually solve a more general problem: finding the kth smallest number in the set for every k. It works as follows.

---

[2] We are assuming here that we can perform basic operations on each number at unit cost. To account for such operations, this bound and the bound below needs to include an additional multiplicative factor of k, where k is the number of bits needed to represent each of the a_i's.

ALGORITHM FINDKTHELEMENT($k, a_1, \ldots, a_n$):

1.   Pick a random $i \in [n]$ and let $x = a_i$.
2.   Scan the list $\{a_1, \ldots, a_n\}$ and count the number m of a_i's such that $a_i \leq x$.
3.   If $m = k$, then output x.
4.   Otherwise, if $m > k$, then copy to a new list L all elements such that $a_i \leq x$ and run
     FINDKTHELEMENT(k, L).
5.   Otherwise (if $m < k$) copy to a new list H all elements such that $a_i > x$ and run
     FINDKTHELEMENT($k - m, H$).

FINDKTHELEMENT($k, a_1, \ldots, a_n$) clearly outputs the kth smallest element and so the only issue is analyzing its running time. Intuitively, we expect that in each recursive call the number of elements will shrink by at least $n/10$ (since in the worst case, where $k = n/2$, we expect to get a new list with roughly $\frac{3}{4}n$ elements). Thus, if $T(n)$ is the running time of the algorithm, then it is given by the formula $T(n) = O(n) + T(\frac{9}{10}n)$ which implies $T(n) = O(n)$. We now prove this formally.

Claim 7.4 *For every input $k, a_1, \ldots, a_n$ to FINDKTHELEMENT, let $T(k, a_1, \ldots, a_n)$ be the expected number of steps the algorithm takes on this input. Let $T(n)$ be the maximum of $T(k, a_1, \ldots, a_n)$ over all length n inputs. Then $T(n) = O(n)$.*

PROOF: All nonrecursive operations of the algorithm can be executed in a linear number of steps: say cn for some constant c. We'll prove by induction that $T(n) \leq 10cn$. Indeed, fix some input $k, a_1, \ldots, a_n$. For every $j \in [n]$ we choose x to be the jth smallest element of $a_1, \ldots, a_n$ with probability $\frac{1}{n}$, and then we perform either at most $T(j)$ steps (if $j > k$) or $T(n - j)$ steps (if $j < k$). Thus we can see that

$$T(k, a_1, \ldots, a_n) \leq cn + \frac{1}{n}\left(\sum_{j>k} T(j) + \sum_{j<k} T(n-j)\right)$$

Plugging in our inductive assumption that $T(j) \leq 10cj$ for $j < n$, we get

$$T(k, a_1, \ldots, a_n) \leq cn + \frac{10c}{n}\left(\sum_{j>k} j + \sum_{j<k}(n-j)\right) \leq cn + \frac{10c}{n}\left(\sum_{j>k} j + kn - \sum_{j<k} j\right)$$

Using the fact that $\sum_{j>k} j \leq \frac{n(n-k)}{2}$ and $\sum_{j<k} j \geq \frac{k^2}{2}(1 - o(1)) \geq \frac{k^2}{2.5}$ (for large enough k) we get

$$T(k, a_1, \ldots, a_n) \leq cn + \frac{10c}{n}\left(\frac{n(n-k)}{2} + kn - \frac{k^2}{2.5}\right) = cn + \frac{10c}{n}\left(\frac{n^2}{2} + \frac{kn}{2} - \frac{k^2}{2.5}\right)$$

$$\leq cn + \frac{10c}{n}\frac{9n^2}{10} = 10cn$$

where the one before last inequality can be shown by considering separately the case $k < n/2$ and the case $k \geq n/2$. ∎

7.2.2 Probabilistic Primality Testing

In *primality testing*, we are given an integer N and wish to determine whether or not it is prime. Algorithms for primality testing were sought after even before the advent of computers, as mathematicians needed them to test various conjectures[3]. Ideally, we want efficient algorithms that run in time polynomial in the size of N's representation, in other words, poly$(\log N)$ time. For centuries mathematicians knew of no such efficient algorithms for this problem.[4] Then in the 1970's efficient probabilistic algorithms for primality testing were discovered, giving one of the first demonstrations of the power of probabilistic algorithms. We note that in a very recent breakthrough, Agrawal, Kayal, and Saxena [AKS04] gave a *deterministic* polynomial-time algorithm for primality testing.

Formally, primality testing consists of checking membership in the following language

$$\mathsf{PRIMES} = \left\{ \llcorner N \lrcorner : N \text{ is a prime number} \right\}$$

We now sketch an algorithm showing that PRIMES is in **BPP** (and in fact in **coRP**; see Section 7.3). For every number N, and $A \in [N-1]$, define

$$QR_N(A) = \begin{cases} 0 & gcd(A, N) \neq 1 \\ +1 & \begin{array}{l} A \text{ is a } \textit{quadratic residue} \text{ modulo } N \\ \text{That is, } A = B^2 (\bmod N) \text{ for some } B \text{ with } gcd(B, N) = 1 \end{array} \\ -1 & \text{Otherwise} \end{cases}$$

We use the following facts, all of which can be proven using elementary number theory (e.g., see [Sho05]):

- For every odd prime N and $A \in [N-1]$, $QR_N(A) = A^{(N-1)/2} \pmod{N}$.
- For every odd N, A define the *Jacobi symbol* $(\frac{N}{A})$ as $\prod_{i=1}^{k} QR_{P_i}(A)$ where $P_1, \ldots, P_k$ are all the (not necessarily distinct) prime factors of N (i.e., $N = \prod_{i=1}^{k} P_i$). Then, the Jacobi symbol is computable in time $O(\log A \cdot \log N)$.
- For every odd composite N, among all $A \in [N-1]$ such that $gcd(N, A) = 1$, at most *half* of the A's satisfy $(\frac{N}{A}) = A^{(N-1)/2} \pmod{N}$.

Together these facts imply a simple algorithm for testing primality of N (which we can assume without loss of generality is odd). *Choose a random* $1 \leq A < N$. *If* $gcd(N, A) > 1$ *or* $(\frac{N}{A}) \neq A^{(N-1)/2} \pmod{N}$ *then output "composite"; otherwise, output "prime."* This algorithm will always output "prime" if N is prime, but if N is composite, it will output "composite" with probability at least $1/2$. Of course, this probability can be amplified by repeating the test a constant number of times.

---

[3] An interesting anecdote is that Gauss, even though he was a very fast human computer himself, used the help of a human supercomputer—an autistic person who excelled at fast calculations—to do primality testing.

[4] In fact, in his letter to von Neumann quoted in Chapter 2, Gödel explicitly mentioned this problem as an example for an interesting problem in **NP** not known to be efficiently solvable.

Curiously, the *search* problem corresponding to primality testing—finding the factorization of a given composite number N—seems very different and much more difficult. The conjectured hardness of this problem underlies many current cryptosystems, though as we'll see in Chapter 10, it can be solved efficiently in the model of *quantum computers*.

7.2.3 Polynomial identity testing

We now describe a polynomial-time probabilistic algorithm for a problem that has no known efficient deterministic algorithm. The problem is the following: we are given a polynomial with integer coefficients in an implicit form, and we want to decide whether this polynomial is in fact identically zero. We assume we get the polynomial in the form of an *algebraic circuit*. This is analogous to the notion of a Boolean circuit, but instead of the operators $\wedge, \vee$, and $\neg$, we have the operators $+$, $-$, and $\times$ (see also Section 16.1.3). Formally, an n-variable algebraic circuit is a directed acyclic graph with the sources labeled by a variable name from the set $x_1, \ldots, x_n$, and each nonsource node having in-degree two is labeled by an operator from the set $\{+, -, \times\}$. There is a single sink in the graph, which we call the *output* node. The algebraic circuit defines a polynomial from $\mathbb{Z}^n$ to $\mathbb{Z}$ by placing the inputs on the sources and computing the value of each node using the appropriate operator.[5] A simple induction shows that the circuit computes a function $f(x_1, x_2, \ldots, x_n)$ of the inputs that can be described by a multivariate polynomial in $x_1, x_2, \ldots, x_n$. We define ZEROP to be the set of algebraic circuits that compute the identically zero polynomial. Determining membership in ZEROP is also called *polynomial identity testing* since we can reduce the problem of deciding whether two circuits C, C' compute the same polynomial to ZEROP by constructing the circuit D such that $D(x_1, \ldots, x_n) = C(x_1, \ldots, x_n) - C'(x_1, \ldots, x_n)$. The polynomial identity testing problem plays an important role in complexity theory; see for instance Chapters 8, 11, and 20.

The ZEROP problem is nontrivial because a very compact circuit can represent polynomials with a large number of terms. For instance, the polynomial $\prod_i (1 + x_i)$ can be computed using a circuit of size $2n$ but has 2^n terms if we open all parentheses. Surprisingly, there is in fact a simple and efficient probabilistic algorithm for testing membership in ZEROP. At the heart of this algorithm is the following fact, often known as the Schwartz-Zippel Lemma, whose proof appears in Appendix A (see Lemma A.36).

Lemma 7.5 *Let $p(x_1, x_2, \ldots, x_m)$ be a nonzero polynomial of total degree[6] at most d. Let S be a finite set of integers. Then, if $a_1, a_2, \ldots, a_m$ are randomly chosen with replacement from S, then*

$$\Pr[p(a_1, a_2, \ldots, a_m) \neq 0] \geq 1 - \frac{d}{|S|}$$

---

[5] We can also allow the circuit to contain constants such as $0, 1$ and other numbers, but this does not make much difference in this context.

[6] The total degree of a monomial $x_1^{e_1} \cdot x_2^{e_2} \cdots x_n^{e_m}$ is equal to $e_1 + \cdots + e_m$. The total degree of a polynomial is the largest total degree of its monomials.

A size m circuit C contains at most m multiplications and so defines a polynomial of degree at most 2^m. This suggests the following simple probabilistic algorithm: Choose n numbers $x_1, \ldots, x_n$ from 1 to $10 \cdot 2^m$ (this requires $O(n \cdot m)$ random bits), evaluate the circuit C on $x_1, \ldots, x_n$ to obtain an output y and then accept if $y = 0$, and reject otherwise. Clearly if $C \in \mathsf{ZEROP}$, then we always accept. By Lemma 7.5, if $C \notin \mathsf{ZEROP}$, then we will reject with probability at least $9/10$.

However, there is a problem with this algorithm. Since the degree of the polynomial represented by the circuit can be as high as 2^m, the output y and other intermediate values arising in the computation may be as large as $(10 \cdot 2^m)^{2^m}$—a value that requires exponentially many bits just to write down!

We solve this problem using a technique called *fingerprinting*. The idea is to perform the evaluation of C on $x_1, \ldots, x_n$ modulo a number k that is chosen at random in $[2^{2m}]$. Thus instead of computing $y = C(x_1, \ldots, x_n)$, we compute the value $y \pmod{k}$. Clearly, if $y = 0$, then $y \pmod{k}$ is also equal to 0. On the other hand, we claim that if $y \neq 0$, then with probability at least $\delta = \frac{1}{4m}$, k does not divide y—this suffices because we can repeat this procedure $O(1/\delta)$ times and accept only if the output is zero in all these repetitions. Indeed, assume that $y \neq 0$, and let $\mathcal{B} = \{p_1, \ldots, p_\ell\}$ denote the set of distinct prime factors of y. It is sufficient to show that with probability at least δ, the number k will be a prime number not in $\mathcal{B}$. Yet, by the Prime Number Theorem, for sufficiently large m, the number of primes in $[2^{2m}]$ is at least $\frac{2^{2m}}{2m}$. Since y can have at most $\log y \leq 5m2^m = o(\frac{2^{2m}}{2m})$ prime factors, for sufficiently large m, the number of k's in $[2^{2m}]$ such that k is prime and is not in $\mathcal{B}$ is at least $\frac{2^{2m}}{4m}$, meaning that a random k will have this property with probability at least $\frac{1}{4m} = \delta$.

7.2.4 Testing for perfect matching in a bipartite graph

Let $G = (V, E)$ be a bipartite graph with two equal parts. That is, $V = V_1 \cup V_2$, where V_1, V_2 are disjoint and of equal size, and $E \subseteq V_1 \times V_2$. A *perfect matching* in G is a subset of edges $E' \subseteq E$ such that every vertex appears exactly once in E'. Alternatively, setting $n = |V_1| = |V_2|$ and identifying both these sets with the set $[n]$, we may think of E' as a permutation $\sigma : [n] \to [n]$ mapping every $i \in [n]$ to the unique $j \in [n]$ such that $\overline{ij} \in E'$. Several deterministic algorithms are known for detecting if a perfect matching exists in a given graph. Here we describe a very simple randomized algorithm (due to Lovász) using the Schwartz-Zippel Lemma.

For a $2n$-vertex bipartite graph $G = (V, E)$ as earlier, let X be an $n \times n$ matrix of real variables whose $(i, j)^{\text{th}}$ entry $X_{i,j}$ is equal to the variable $x_{i,j}$ if the edge $\overline{ij}$ is in E and equal to 0 otherwise. Recall that the determinant of a matrix A is defined as follows:

$$\det(A) = \sum_{\sigma \in S_n} (-1)^{sgn(\sigma)} \prod_{i=1}^{n} A_{i,\sigma(i)}$$

where S_n is the set of all permutations of $[n]$ and $sgn(\sigma)$ is the parity of the number of transposed pairs in σ (i.e., pairs $\langle i, j \rangle$ such that $i < j$ but $\sigma(i) > \sigma(j)$); see Section A.5. Thus $\det(X)$ is a degree n polynomial in the variables $\{x_{i,j}\}_{\overline{ij} \in E}$ that has a monomial for every perfect matching that exists in the graph. In other words, G has a perfect matching if and only if $\det(X)$ is not the identically zero polynomial. Now, even though $\det(X)$ may have exponentially many monomials, for every setting of values to the $x_{i,j}$ variables $\det(X)$ can be efficiently evaluated using the well-known algorithm for computing determinants.

This leads, in conjunction with Lemma 7.5, to Lovász's randomized algorithm: Pick random values for $x_{i,j}$'s from $[2n]$, substitute them in X, and compute the determinant. If the determinant is nonzero, output "accept" else output "reject." Besides its simplicity, this algorithm also has an advantage that it has an efficient parallel implementation (using the **NC** algorithm for computing determinants; see Exercise 6.16).

7.3 ONE-SIDED AND "ZERO-SIDED" ERROR: **RP, coRP, ZPP**

The class **BPP** captures what we call probabilistic algorithms with *two-sided* error. That is, it allows an algorithm for a language L to output (with some small probability) both 0 when $x \in L$ and 1 when $x \notin L$. However, many probabilistic algorithms have the property of *one-sided* error. For example, if $x \notin L$, they will *never* output 1, although they may output 0 when $x \in L$. This type of behavior is captured by the class **RP** which we now define.

Definition 7.6 RTIME$(T(n))$ contains every language L for which there is a probabilistic TM M running in $T(n)$ time such that

$$x \in L \Rightarrow \Pr[M(x) = 1] \geq \frac{2}{3}$$

$$x \notin L \Rightarrow \Pr[(x) = 0] = 0$$

We define **RP** $= \cup_{c>0}$**RTIME**(n^c). $\qquad\qquad\qquad\qquad\diamond$

Note that **RP** $\subseteq$ **NP**, since every accepting branch is a "certificate" that the input is in the language. In contrast, we do not know if **BPP** $\subseteq$ **NP**. The class **coRP** $= \{L \mid \overline{L} \in$ **RP**$\}$ captures one-sided error algorithms with the error in the "other direction" (i.e., may output 1 when $x \notin L$ but will never output 0 if $x \in L$).

"Zero-sided" error. For a PTM M, and input x, we define the random variable $T_{M,x}$ to be the running time of M on input x. That is, $\Pr[T_{M,x} = T] = p$ if with probability p over the random choices of M on input x, it will halt within T steps. We say that M has *expected running time* $T(n)$ if the expectation $E[T_{M,x}]$ is at most $T(|x|)$ for every $x \in \{0, 1\}^*$. We now define PTMs that never err (also called "zero error" machines).

Definition 7.7 The class **ZTIME**$(T(n))$ contains all the languages L for which there is a machine M that runs in an expected-time $O(T(n))$ such that for every input x, whenever M halts on x, the output $M(x)$ it produces is exactly $L(x)$.

We define **ZPP** $= \cup_{c>0}$**ZTIME**(n^c). $\qquad\qquad\qquad\qquad\diamond$

The next theorem ought to be slightly surprising, since the corresponding question for nondeterminism (i.e., whether or not $\mathbf{P} = \mathbf{NP} \cap \mathbf{coNP}$) is open.

Theorem 7.8   ZPP = RP $\cap$ coRP.   ◇

We leave the proof of this theorem to the reader (see Exercise 7.6). To summarize, we have the following relations between the probabilistic complexity classes:

$$\mathbf{ZPP} = \mathbf{RP} \cap \mathbf{coRP}$$

$$\mathbf{RP} \subseteq \mathbf{BPP}$$

$$\mathbf{coRP} \subseteq \mathbf{BPP}$$

7.4 THE ROBUSTNESS OF OUR DEFINITIONS

When we defined **P** and **NP**, we argued that our definitions are robust and are likely to be the same for an alien studying the same concepts in a faraway galaxy. Now we address similar issues for probabilistic computation.

7.4.1 Role of precise constants: Error reduction

The choice of the constant $2/3$ seemed pretty arbitrary. We now show that we can replace $2/3$ with any constant larger than $1/2$ and in fact even with $1/2 + n^{-c}$ for a constant $c > 0$.

Lemma 7.9 *For $c > 0$, let $\mathbf{BPP}_{1/2+n^{-c}}$ denote the class of languages L for which there is a polynomial-time PTM M satisfying $\Pr[M(x) = L(x)] \geq 1/2 + |x|^{-c}$ for every $x \in \{0, 1\}^*$. Then $\mathbf{BPP}_{1/2+n^{-c}} = \mathbf{BPP}$.*

Since clearly $\mathbf{BPP} \subseteq \mathbf{BPP}_{1/2+n^{-c}}$, to prove this lemma we need to show that we can transform a machine with success probability $1/2 + n^{-c}$ into a machine with success probability $2/3$. We do this by proving a much stronger result: we transform such a machine into a machine with success probability exponentially close to one!

> **Theorem 7.10** *(Error reduction for **BPP**)*
>
> *Let $L \subseteq \{0, 1\}^*$ be a language and suppose that there exists a polynomial-time PTM M such that for every $x \in \{0, 1\}^*$, $\Pr[M(x) = L(x)] \geq \frac{1}{2} + |x|^{-c}$.*
>
> *Then for every constant $d > 0$ there exists a polynomial-time PTM M' such that for every $x \in \{0, 1\}^*$, $\Pr[M'(x) = L(x)] \geq 1 - 2^{-|x|^d}$.*

PROOF: The machine M' simply does the following: *for every input $x \in \{0, 1\}^*$, run $M(x)$ for $k = 8|x|^{2c+d}$ times obtaining k outputs $y_1, \ldots, y_k \in \{0, 1\}$. If the majority of these outputs is 1, then output 1; otherwise, output 0.*

To analyze this machine, define for every $i \in [k]$ the random variable X_i to equal 1 if $y_i = L(x)$ and to equal 0 otherwise. Note that $X_1, \ldots, X_k$ are independent Boolean random variables with $\mathrm{E}[X_i] = \Pr[X_i = 1] \geq p$ for $p = 1/2 + |x|^{-c}$. The Chernoff bound (see Corollary A.15) implies that for δ sufficiently small:

$$\Pr\left[|\sum_{i=1}^{k} X_i - pk| > \delta pk\right] < e^{-\frac{\delta^2}{4}pk}$$

In our case $p = 1/2 + |x|^{-c}$ and setting $\delta = |x|^{-c}/2$ guarantees that if $\sum_{i=1}^{k} X_i \geq pk - \delta pk$ then we will output the right answer. Hence, the probability we output a wrong answer is bounded by

$$e^{-\frac{1}{4|x|^{2c}}\frac{1}{2}8|x|^{2c+d}} \leq 2^{-|x|^d} \quad \blacksquare$$

A similar (and even easier to prove) result holds for the one-sided error classes **RP** and **coRP**; see Exercise 7.4. In that case, we can even change the constant $2/3$ to values smaller than $1/2$.

These error reduction results imply that we can take a probabilistic algorithm that succeeds with quite modest probability and transform it into an algorithm that succeeds with overwhelming probability. In fact, even for moderate values of n, an error probability that is of the order of 2^{-n} is so small that for all practical purposes, probabilistic algorithms are just as good as deterministic algorithms.

Randomness-efficient repetitions

The proof of Theorem 7.10 uses $O(k)$ independent repetitions to transform an algorithm with success probability $2/3$ into an algorithm with success probability $1 - 2^{-k}$. Thus, if the original used m random coins, then the new algorithm will use $O(km)$ coins. Surprisingly, we can do better: There is a transformation that only uses $O(m + k)$ random coins to achieve the same error reduction. This transformation will be described in Chapter 21 (Section 21.2.5).

7.4.2 Expected running time versus worst-case running time

When defining **RTIME**$(T(n))$ and **BPTIME**$(T(n))$, we required the machine to halt in $T(n)$ time regardless of its random choices. We could have used *expected* running time instead, as in the definition of **ZPP** (Definition 7.7). It turns out this yields an equivalent definition: We can transform a PTM M whose expected running time is $T(n)$ to a PTM M' that always halts after at most $100T(n)$ steps by simply adding a counter and halting with an arbitrary output after too many steps have gone by. By Markov's inequality (see Lemma A.7), the probability that M runs for more than $100T(n)$ steps is at most $1/100$, and so this will change the acceptance probability by at most $1/100$.

7.4.3 Allowing more general random choices than a fair random coin

One could conceive of real-life computers that have a "coin" that comes up heads with probability ρ that is not $1/2$. We call such a coin a ρ-coin. Indeed it is conceivable that for a random source based upon quantum mechanics, ρ is an irrational number, such as $1/e$. Could such a coin give probabilistic algorithms new power? The following claim shows that it will not, at least if ρ is efficiently computable. (The exercises show that if ρ is not efficiently computable, then a ρ-coin can indeed provide additional power.)

NOTE 7.11 *(The Chernoff bound and statistical estimation)*
The Chernoff bound is extensively used (sometimes under different names) in many areas of computer science and other sciences. A typical scenario is the following: There is a universe $\mathcal{U}$ of objects, a fraction μ of them have a certain property, and we wish to estimate μ. For example, in the proof of Theorem 7.10, the universe was the set of 2^m possible coin tosses of some probabilistic algorithm, and we wanted to know how many of them make the algorithm accept its input. As another example, $\mathcal{U}$ can be the set of all the citizens of the United States, and we wish to find out how many of them own a dog.

A natural approach for computing the fraction μ is to *sample n* members of the universe independently at random, find out the number k of the sample's members that have the property, and then guess that μ is k/n. Of course, a guess based upon a small sample is unlikely to produce the exact answer. For instance, the true fraction of dog owners may be 10%, but in a sample of size say 1000, we may find that only 99 (i.e., 9.9%) people are dog owners. So we set our goal only to *estimate* the true fraction μ up to an *error* of $\pm\epsilon$ for some $\epsilon > 0$. Despite allowing ourselves this error margin, we may get really unlucky, and our sample may turn out to be really unrepresentative (e.g., there is a nonzero probability that the entire sample of 1000 consists of dog owners). So we allow a small *probability of failure* δ that our estimate will not lie in the interval $[\mu - \epsilon, \mu + \epsilon]$. The natural question is *how many samples do we need in order to estimate μ up to an error of $\pm\epsilon$ with probability at least* $1 - \delta$? The Chernoff bound tells us that (considering μ as a constant) this number is $O(\log(1/\delta)/\epsilon^2)$.

Setting $\rho = \log(1/\delta)$, this implies that the probability that k is $\rho\sqrt{n}$ far from μn decays *exponentially* with ρ. That is, this probability has the famous "bell curve" shape:

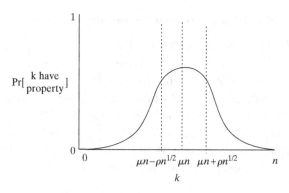

We will use this exponential decay phenomena many times in this book. See for instance the proof of Theorem 7.14, showing that **BPP** $\subseteq$ **P$_{/\text{poly}}$**.

Lemma 7.12 *A coin with* $\Pr[Heads] = \rho$ *can be simulated by a PTM in expected time* $O(1)$ *provided the ith bit of ρ is computable in* $\text{poly}(i)$ *time.* $\diamond$

PROOF: Let the binary expansion of ρ be $0.p_1p_2p_3\ldots$. The PTM generates a sequence of random bits $b_1, b_2, \ldots$, one by one, where b_i is generated at step i. If $b_i < p_i$, then the machine outputs "heads" and stops; if $b_i > p_i$, the machine outputs "tails" and halts; otherwise, the machine goes to step $i + 1$. Clearly, the machine reaches step $i + 1$ iff $b_j = p_j$ for all $j \leq i$, which happens with probability $1/2^i$. Thus the probability of "heads" is $\sum_i p_i \frac{1}{2^i}$, which is exactly ρ. Furthermore, the expected running time is $\sum_i i^c \cdot \frac{1}{2^i}$. For every constant c, this infinite sum is bounded by another constant (see Exercise 7.2). ∎

Conversely, probabilistic algorithms that only have access to ρ-coins do not have less power than standard probabilistic algorithms:

Lemma 7.13 *von-Neumann* [vN51] *A coin with* $\Pr[Heads] = 1/2$ *can be simulated by a probabilistic TM with access to a stream of ρ-biased coins in expected time* $O(\frac{1}{\rho(1-\rho)})$. ◇

PROOF: We construct a TM M that given the ability to toss ρ-coins, outputs a $1/2$-coin. The machine M tosses pairs of coins until the first time it gets a pair containing two different results (i.e., "Heads-Tails" or "Tails-Heads"). Then, if the first of these two results is "Heads" it outputs "Heads" and otherwise it outputs "Tails."

The probability that a pair of coins comes up "Head-Tails" is $\rho(1 - \rho)$, while the probability it comes up "Tails-Heads" is $(1 - \rho)\rho = \rho(1 - \rho)$. Hence, in each step M halts with probability $2\rho(1 - \rho)$, and conditioned on M halting in a particular step, the outputs "Heads" and "Tails" are equiprobable (i.e., M's output is a fair coin). Note that we did not need to know ρ to run this simulation. ∎

Weak random sources.   Physicists (and philosophers) are still not completely certain that randomness exists in the world, and even if it does, it is not clear that our computers have access to an endless stream of independent coins. Conceivably, it may be the case that we only have access to a source of *imperfect* randomness that, although somewhat unpredictable, does not consist of independent coins. In Chapter 21, we show how to use such imperfect sources to run probabilistic algorithms that were designed assuming perfect randomness.

7.5 RELATIONSHIP BETWEEN **BPP** AND OTHER CLASSES

Below we will show that **BPP** $\subseteq$ **P**$_{/poly}$. Thus **P** $\subseteq$ **BPP** $\subseteq$ **P**$_{/poly}$. Furthermore, we show that **BPP** $\subseteq \Sigma_2^p \cap \Pi_2^p$ and so if **NP** = **P**, then **BPP** = **P**. Of course, since we do not believe **P** = **NP**, this still leaves open the possibility that **P** $\neq$ **BPP**. However, as mentioned above (and will be elaborated in Chapters 19 and 20), we can show that if certain plausible complexity-theoretic conjectures are true, then **BPP** = **P**. Thus we suspect that **BPP** is the same as **P** and hence (by the Time Hierarchy Theorem) **BPP** is a proper subset of, say, **DTIME**$(n^{\log n})$. Yet currently researchers are not even able to show that **BPP** is a proper subset of **NEXP**.

7.5.1 **BPP** $\subseteq$ **P**$_{/poly}$

Now we show that all **BPP** languages have polynomial sized circuits. Together with Theorem 6.19 this shows that unless the polynomial-hierarchy collapses, 3SAT cannot be solved in probabilistic polynomial time.

Theorem 7.14 [Adl78]

BPP $\subseteq$ **P**$_{/poly}$.

PROOF: Suppose $L \in$ **BPP**, then by the alternative definition of **BPP** and the error reduction procedure of Theorem 7.10, there exists a TM M that on inputs of size n uses m random bits and such that for every $x \in \{0, 1\}^n$, $\Pr_r[M(x,r) \neq L(x)] \leq 2^{-n-1}$. Say that a string $r \in \{0, 1\}^m$ is *bad* for an input $x \in \{0, 1\}^n$ if $M(x,r) \neq L(x)$ and otherwise call r *good* for x. For every x, at most $\frac{2^m}{2^{n+1}}$ strings r are bad for x. Adding over all $x \in \{0, 1\}^n$, there are at most $2^n \cdot \frac{2^m}{2^{n+1}} = 2^m/2$ strings r that are bad for *some* x. In particular, there exists a string $r_0 \in \{0, 1\}^m$ that is good for *every* $x \in \{0, 1\}^n$. We can hardwire such a string r_0 to obtain a circuit C (of size at most quadratic in the running time of M) that on input x outputs $M(x, r_0)$. The circuit C will satisfy $C(x) = L(x)$ for every $x \in \{0, 1\}^n$. $\blacksquare$

7.5.2 BPP is in PH

At first glance, **BPP** seems to have nothing to do with the polynomial hierarchy, so the next theorem is somewhat surprising.

Theorem 7.15 *(Sipser-Gács Theorem)*

BPP $\subseteq \Sigma_2^p \cap \Pi_2^p$.

PROOF: It is enough to prove that **BPP** $\subseteq \Sigma_2^p$ because **BPP** is closed under complementation (i.e., **BPP** = **coBPP**).

Suppose $L \in$ **BPP**. Then by the alternative definition of **BPP** and the error reduction procedure of Theorem 7.10 there exists a polynomial-time deterministic TM M for L that on inputs of length n uses $m = \text{poly}(n)$ random bits and satisfies

$$x \in L \Rightarrow \Pr_r[M(x,r) \text{ accepts }] \geq 1 - 2^{-n}$$

$$x \notin L \Rightarrow \Pr_r[M(x,r) \text{ accepts }] \leq 2^{-n}$$

For $x \in \{0, 1\}^n$, let S_x denote the set of r's for which M accepts the input pair $\langle x, r \rangle$. Then either $|S_x| \geq (1 - 2^{-n})2^m$ or $|S_x| \leq 2^{-n}2^m$, depending on whether or not $x \in L$. We will show how to check, using two quantifiers, which of the two cases is true.

Figure 7.1. There are only two possible sizes for the set of r's such that $M(x,r) = $ Accept: Either this set is almost all of $\{0, 1\}^m$, or it is a tiny fraction of $\{0, 1\}^m$. In the former case, a few random "shifts" of this set are quite likely to cover all of $\{0, 1\}^m$. In the latter case, the set's size is so small that a few shifts cannot cover $\{0, 1\}^m$.

For a set $S \subseteq \{0, 1\}^m$ and string $u \in \{0, 1\}^m$, we denote by $S + u$ the "shift" of the set S by u: $S + u = \{x + u : x \in S\}$ where $+$ denotes vector addition modulo 2 (i.e., bitwise XOR). Let $k = \lceil \frac{m}{n} \rceil + 1$. Theorem 7.15 is implied by the following two claims (see Figure 7.1).

Claim 1: For every set $S \subseteq \{0, 1\}^m$ with $|S| \leq 2^{m-n}$ and every k vectors $u_1, \ldots, u_k$, $\cup_{i=1}^{k}(S + u_i) \neq \{0, 1\}^m$.

PROOF: Since $|S + u_i| = |S|$, by the union bound we have $|\cup_{i=1}^{k}(S + u_i)| \leq k|S| < 2^m$ (for sufficiently large n). ∎

Claim 2: For every set $S \subseteq \{0, 1\}^m$ with $|S| \geq (1 - 2^{-n})2^m$, there exist $u_1, \ldots, u_k$ such that $\cup_{i=1}^{k}(S + u_i) = \{0, 1\}^m$.

PROOF: This follows from the probabilistic method: We claim that if $u_1, \ldots, u_k$ are chosen independently at random, then $\Pr[\cup_{i=1}^{k}(S + u_i) = \{0, 1\}^m] > 0$. Indeed, for $r \in \{0, 1\}^m$, let B_r denote the "bad event" that r is not in $\cup_{i=1}^{k}(S + u_i)$. It suffices to prove that $\Pr[\exists_{r \in \{0,1\}^m} B_r] < 1$, which will follow by the union bound if we can show for every r that $\Pr[B_r] < 2^{-m}$. But $B_r = \cap_{i \in [k]} B_r^i$ where B_r^i is the event that $r \notin S + u_i$, or, equivalently, that $r + u_i \notin S$ (using the fact that modulo 2, $a + b = c \Leftrightarrow a = c + b$). Yet, $r + u_i$ is a uniform element in $\{0, 1\}^m$, and so it will be in S with probability at least $1 - 2^{-n}$. Furthermore, the events B_r^i are independent for different i's implying that $\Pr[B_r] = \Pr[B_r^i]^k \leq 2^{-nk} < 2^{-m}$. ∎

Together Claims 1 and 2 show that $x \in L$ if and only if the following statement is true:

$$\exists u_1, \ldots, u_k \in \{0, 1\}^m \ \forall r \in \{0, 1\}^m \ \ r \in \cup_{i=1}^{k}(S_x + u_i)$$

or, equivalently,

$$\exists u_1, \ldots, u_k \in \{0, 1\}^m \ \forall r \in \{0, 1\}^m \ \bigvee_{i=1}^{k} M(x, r \oplus u_i) \text{ accepts}$$

which represents a Σ_2^p computation since k is $\text{poly}(n)$. Hence we have shown $L \in \Sigma_2$. ∎

7.5.3 Hierarchy theorems and complete problems?

The reader may have wondered if **BPP** has complete problems, or if probabilistic computation has hierarchy theorems. Now we discuss this.

Complete problems for BPP?

Though a very natural class, **BPP** behaves differently in some ways from other classes we have seen. For example, we know of no complete languages for **BPP**. One reason for this difficulty is that the defining property of **BPTIME** machines is *semantic*, namely, that they accept every input string either with probability at least 2/3 or with probability at most 1/3. Testing whether a given TM M has this property is undecidable. By contrast, the defining property of an NDTM is *syntactic*: Given a string, it is easy to determine if it is a valid encoding of an NDTM. Complete problems seem easier to find for syntactically defined classes than for semantically defined ones. For example, consider the following natural attempt at a **BPP**-complete language: Define L to contain all tuples $\langle M, x, 1^t \rangle$ such that on input x, M outputs 1 within t steps with probability at least $2/3$. The language L is indeed **BPP**-hard but is not known to be in **BPP** since for $\langle M, x, 1^t \rangle \notin L$ we could have $\Pr[M(x) = 1] = 1/2$ (say), which is greater than $1/3$. In fact, we will see in Chapter 17 that this language is **#P**-complete and hence unlikely to be in any level of the polynomial hierarchy unless the hierarchy collapses. However if, as believed, **BPP** = **P**, then **BPP** does have a complete problem (since **P** does).

Does BPTIME have a hierarchy theorem?

Is every problem in $\mathbf{BPTIME}(n^2)$ also in $\mathbf{BPTIME}(n)$? One would imagine not, and this seems like the kind of result we should be able to prove using the diagonalization techniques of Chapter 3. However currently we are even unable to show that, say, $\mathbf{BPTIME}(n) \neq \mathbf{BPTIME}(n^{(\log n)^{10}})$. The standard diagonalization techniques fail, again apparently because the defining property of **BPTIME** machines is semantic. However, recently there has been some progress on obtaining hierarchy theorems for some closely related classes (see the chapter notes).

7.6 RANDOMIZED REDUCTIONS

Since we have defined randomized algorithms, it also makes sense to define a notion of randomized reduction between two languages. This proves useful in some complexity settings (e.g., see Chapters 8 and 17).

Definition 7.16 Language B reduces to language C under a randomized polynomial time reduction, denoted $B \leq_r C$, if there is a probabilistic TM M such that for every $x \in \{0, 1\}^*$, $\Pr[B(M(x)) = C(x)] \geq 2/3$. $\diamond$

Although not transitive, this notion of reduction is useful in the sense that if $C \in$ **BPP** and $B \leq_r C$, then $B \in$ **BPP**. This observation also alerts us to the possibility that we could have defined **NP**-completeness using randomized reductions instead of deterministic reductions, since arguably **BPP** is as good as **P** as a formalization of the notion of efficient computation. Recall that the Cook-Levin Theorem shows that **NP** may be defined as the set $\{L : L \leq_p 3\mathsf{SAT}\}$. In the previous definition, if we replace "deterministic polynomial-time reduction" with "randomized reduction" then we obtain a somewhat different class.

Definition 7.17 $\mathbf{BP \cdot NP} = \{L : L \leq_r 3\mathsf{SAT}\}$.

We explore the properties of $\mathbf{BP \cdot NP}$ in the exercises, including whether or not it is likely that $\overline{3\mathsf{SAT}} \in \mathbf{BP \cdot NP}$.

One interesting application of randomized reductions will be shown in Chapter 17, where we present a (variant of a) randomized reduction from $3\mathsf{SAT}$ to solving a special case of $3\mathsf{SAT}$ where we are guaranteed that the formula is either unsatisfiable or has a *single unique* satisfying assignment.

7.7 RANDOMIZED SPACE-BOUNDED COMPUTATION

We can extend the definition of space-bounded computation from Chapter 4 to the probabilistic setting, saying that a PTM uses space $S(n)$ if in any branch of its computation on a length n input, the number of work-tape cells that are ever nonblank is at most $O(S(n))$. The most interesting case is when the work tape has $O(\log n)$ size. The classes **BPL** and **RL** are the two-sided error and one-sided error probabilistic analogs of the class **L** defined in Chapter 4.

> **Definition 7.18** (*The classes* **BPL** *and* **RL**) A language L is in **BPL** if there is an $O(\log n)$-space probabilistic TM M such that $\Pr[M(x) = L(x)] \geq 2/3$.
> A language L is in **RL** if there is an $O(\log n)$-space probabilistic TM M such that if $x \in L$ then $\Pr[M(x) = 1] \geq 2/3$ and if $x \notin L$ then $\Pr[M(x) = 1] = 0$.

The reader can verify that the error reduction procedure described in Chapter 7 can be implemented with only logarithmic space overhead. Hence, also in these definitions the choice of the precise constant is not significant. We note that **RL** $\subseteq$ **NL**, and thus **RL** $\subseteq$ **P**. The exercises ask you to show that **BPL** $\subseteq$ **P** as well.

One famous **RL**-algorithm is the algorithm for solving UPATH, the restriction of the **NL**-complete PATH problem (see Chapter 4) to undirected graphs. That is, given an n-vertex undirected graph G and two vertices s and t, determine whether s is connected to t in G.

Theorem 7.19 *([AKL$^+$79])* UPATH $\in$ **RL**.

The algorithm for UPATH is actually very simple: Take a random walk of length $\ell = 100n^4$ starting from s. That is, initialize the variable v to the vertex s and in each step choose a random neighbor u of v, and set $v \leftarrow u$. Accept iff the walk reaches t within ℓ steps. This is a logspace algorithm since it only needs to store a counter, the index of the current vertex, and some scratch space to compute the next neighbor in the walk. Clearly, if s is not connected to t, then the algorithm will never accept. It can be shown that if s is connected to t then the expected number of steps it takes for a walk from s to hit t is at most $10n^4$ and hence our algorithm will accept with probability at least $3/4$. We leave the analysis as Exercise 7.11. Chapter 21 introduces some general tools for the analysis of random walks on graphs, from which this bound (and better ones) easily follow.[7] In Chapter 21 (Section 21.4) we show a recent *deterministic* logspace algorithm for the same problem.

More generally, we do know some nontrivial relations between probabilistic and deterministic logspace computation. It is known that **BPL** (and hence also **RL**) is contained in $\mathbf{SPACE}(\log^{3/2} n)$. See Section 21.6 and the chapter notes of Chapter 21 for more on this topic.

---

[7] The best bound known on the expected number of steps for a walk from s to visit all the vertices connected to s in an n-vertex graph is $\frac{4}{27}n^3 + o(n^3)$ [Fei95] and this is tight, as can be shown by analyzing the random walk on the "lollipop graph," consisting of a path of length $n/3$ connected to a clique of length $2n/3$.

WHAT HAVE WE LEARNED?

- The class **BPP** consists of languages that can be solved by a probabilistic polynomial-time algorithm. The probability is only over the algorithm's coins and not the choice of input. It is arguably a better formalization of efficient computation than **P**.
- **RP**, **coRP**, and **ZPP** are subclasses of **BPP** corresponding to probabilistic algorithms with one-sided and zero-sided error.
- Using repetition, we can considerably amplify the success probability of probabilistic algorithms.
- We only know that $\mathbf{P} \subseteq \mathbf{BPP} \subseteq \mathbf{EXP}$, but we suspect that $\mathbf{BPP} = \mathbf{P}$.
- **BPP** is a subset of both $\mathbf{P}_{/poly}$ and **PH**. In particular, the latter implies that if $\mathbf{NP} = \mathbf{P}$, then $\mathbf{BPP} = \mathbf{P}$.
- Randomness is used in complexity theory in many contexts beyond **BPP**. Two examples are randomized reductions and randomized logspace algorithms, but we will see many more later.

CHAPTER NOTES AND HISTORY

Early researchers realized the power of randomization since their computations—e.g., for design of nuclear weapons—used probabilistic tools such as Monte Carlo simulations. Turing machines were defined by De Leeuw et al. [dLMSS56]. The definitions of **BPP** (bounded-error probabilistic polynomial-time), **RP** (randomized polynomial-time) and **ZPP** (zero-error probabilistic polynomial-time) are from Gill [Gil77]. The reason **BPP** is not called simply **PP** (i.e., "probabilistic-time") is that Gill gave the name **PP** to a much more powerful class in [Gil74] (see Chapter 17).

The algorithm used to show PRIMES is in **coRP** is due to Solovay and Strassen [SS77]. Another primality test from the same era is due to Rabin [Rab80]. Over the years, many better primality tests were proposed. In a recent breakthrough, Agrawal, Kayal, and Saxena finally proved that PRIMES $\in$ **P** [AKS04]. Both the probabilistic and deterministic primality testing algorithms are described in Shoup's book [Sho05]. The fingerprinting technique used in the polynomial identity-testing algorithm is by Karp and Rabin [KR81]. Lovász's randomized **NC** algorithm [Lov79] for deciding the *existence* of perfect matchings is unsatisfying in the sense that when it outputs "Accept," it gives no clue how to find a matching! Subsequent probabilistic **NC** algorithms can find a perfect matching as well; see [KUW85, MVV87]. Readers interested in randomized algorithms are referred to the books by Mitzenmacher and Upfal [MU05] and Motwani and Raghavan [MR95].

$\mathbf{BPP} \subseteq \mathbf{P}_{/poly}$ (Theorem 7.14) is from Adelman [Adl78]. $\mathbf{BPP} \subseteq \mathbf{PH}$ is due to Sipser [Sip83], and the stronger form $\mathbf{BPP} \subseteq \Sigma_2^p \cap \Pi_2^p$ (Theorem 7.15) is due to P. Gács. The proof we presented is due to Lautemann [Lau83]. Recent work shows that **BPP** is contained in classes that are seemingly weaker than $\Sigma_2^p \cap \Pi_2^p$ [Can96, RS95].

Even though a hierarchy theorem for **BPP** seems beyond our reach, there has been some success in showing hierarchy theorems for the seemingly related class **BPP**/1 (i.e., **BPP** with a single bit of nonuniform advice) [Bar02, FS04, GST04]. We note that the problematic issues with both existence of complete problems and of hierarchy theorems do not occur in the generalization of **BPP** to *promise problems*, or equivalently to Boolean functions that may be defined only on a subset of $\{0, 1\}^*$.

The notation **BP · NP** defined in Section 7.6 can be generalized to arbitrary complexity classes other than **NP**, see Lecture G of [Koz06]. Under this generalization, **BP · P = BPP**.

Chapter 21 contains a much more through treatment of random walks, covering both the randomness-efficient error reduction procedure mentioned in Section 7.4.1 and analysis of the logspace connectivity algorithm sketched in Section 7.7.

EXERCISES

7.1. Show that one can efficiently simulate choosing a random number from 1 to N using coin tosses. That is, show that for every N and $\delta > 0$ there is a probabilistic algorithm A running in $\text{poly}(\log N \log(1/\delta))$-time with output in $\{1, \ldots, N, ?\}$ such that (1) conditioned on not outputting $?$, A's output is uniformly distributed in $[N]$ and (2) the probability that A outputs $?$ is at most δ.

7.2. Show that for every $c > 0$, the infinite sum $\sum_{i \geq 1} \frac{i^c}{2^i}$ is bounded by some constant (depending on c). That is, prove that for every $c > 0$ there is D such that for every $n \geq 1$, $\sum_{i=1}^{n} \frac{i^c}{2^i} \leq D$.

7.3. Show, given the numbers $\langle a, n, p \rangle$ (in binary representation), how to compute a^n (mod p) in polynomial time.
H534

7.4. (Error Reduction for **RP**) Let $L \subseteq \{0, 1\}^*$ be such that there exists a polynomial-time PTM M satisfying for every $x \in \{0, 1\}^*$: (1) If $x \in L$, then $\Pr[M(x) = 1)] \geq n^{-c}$ and (2) if $x \notin L$, then $\Pr[M(x) = 1] = 0$.
Prove that for every $d > 0$ there exists a polynomial-time PTM M' such that for every $x \in \{0, 1\}^*$, **(1)** if $x \in L$ then $\Pr[M'(x) = 1] \geq 1 - 2^{-n^d}$ and **(2)** if $x \notin L$ then $\Pr[M'(x) = 1] = 0$.
H534

7.5. Let us study to what extent Lemma 7.12 truly needs the assumption that ρ is efficiently computable. Describe a real number ρ such that given a random coin that comes up "Heads" with probability ρ, a Turing machine can decide an undecidable language in polynomial time.
H534

7.6. **(a)** Prove that a language L is in **ZPP** iff there exists a polynomial-time PTM M with outputs in $\{0, 1, ?\}$ such that for every $x \in \{0, 1\}^*$, with probability 1, $M(x) \in \{L(x), ?\}$ and $\Pr[M(x) = ?] \leq 1/2$.
(b) Prove Theorem 7.8: Show that **ZPP = RP ∩ coRP**.

7.7. A nondeterministic circuit has two inputs x, y. We say that C accepts x iff there exists y such that $C(x, y) = 1$. The size of the circuit is measured as a function of $|x|$. Let **NP**/*poly* be the languages that are decided by polynomial size nondeterministic circuits. Show that **BP · NP** $\subseteq$ **NP**/*poly*.

7.8. Show that if $\overline{\text{3SAT}} \in \mathbf{BP} \cdot \mathbf{NP}$, then $\mathbf{PH}$ collapses to Σ_3^p. (Thus it is unlikely that $\overline{\text{3SAT}} \leq_r \text{3SAT}$.)

H534

7.9. Show that $\mathbf{BPL} \subseteq \mathbf{P}$.

H534

7.10. Show that the random walk idea for solving connectivity does not work for directed graphs. In other words, describe a directed graph on n vertices and a starting point s such that the expected time to reach t is $\Omega(2^n)$, even though there is a directed path from s to t.

7.11. (UPATH $\in \mathbf{RL}$ worked out) Let G be an n vertex graph where all vertices have the same degree.

    (a) We say that a distribution $\mathbf{p}$ over the vertices of G (where $\mathbf{p}_i$ denotes the probability that vertex i is picked by $\mathbf{p}$) is *stationary* if when we choose a vertex i according to $\mathbf{p}$ and take a random step from i (i.e., move to a random neighbor j or i), then the resulting distribution is $\mathbf{p}$. Prove that the uniform distribution on G's vertices is stationary.

    (b) For $\mathbf{p}$ a distribution over the vertices of G, let $\Delta(\mathbf{p}) = \max_i\{\mathbf{p}_i - 1/n\}$. For every k, denote by $\mathbf{p}^k$ the distribution obtained by choosing a vertex i at random from $\mathbf{p}$ and taking k random steps on G. Prove that if G is connected and non-bipratite, then there exists k such that $\Delta(\mathbf{p}^k) \leq (1 - n^{-10n})\Delta(\mathbf{p})$. Conclude that:

        (a) The uniform distribution is the only stationary distribution for G.

        (b) For every pair of vertices u, v of G, if we take a sufficiently long random walk starting from u, then the expected fraction of times we hit the vertex v is roughly $1/n$. That is, show that for sufficiently large N, the expected number of times an N-step walk from u hits v will be at least $N/(2n)$.

    (c) For a vertex u in G, denote by E_u the expected number of steps it takes for a random walk starting from u to reach back u. Show that $E_u \leq 10n$.

H534

    (d) For every two vertices u, v denote by $E_{u,v}$ the expected number of steps it takes for a random walk starting from u to reach v. Show that if u and v are connected by a path of length at most k then $E_{u,v} \leq 100kn^2$. Conclude that for every s and t that are connected in a graph G, the probability that an $1000n^3$ random walk from s does not hit t is at most $1/10$.

H534

    (e) Let G be an n-vertex graph that is not necessarily regular (i.e., each vertex may have different degree). Let G' be the graph obtained by adding a sufficient number of parallel self-loops to each vertex to make G regular. Prove that if a k-step random walk in G from a vertex s hits a vertex t with probability at least 0.9, then a $10n^2k$-step random walk in G' from s will hit t with probability at least $1/2$.

CHAPTER 8

Interactive proofs

What is intuitively required from a theorem-proving procedure? First, that it is possible to "prove" a true theorem. Second, that it is impossible to "prove" a false theorem. Third, that communicating the proof should be efficient, in the following sense. It does not matter how long must the prover compute during the proving process, but it is essential that the computation required from the verifier is easy.

– Goldwasser, Micali, and Rackoff, 1985

The standard notion of a mathematical proof is closely related to the certificate definition of **NP**. To prove that a statement is true one provides a sequence of symbols on a piece of paper, and the verifier checks that they represent a valid proof/certificate. A valid proof/certificate exists only for true statements. However, people often use a more general way to convince one another of the validity of statements: they *interact* with one another, where the person verifying the proof (called *verifier* from now on) asks the person providing it (called *prover* from now on) for a series of explanations before he is convinced.

It seems natural to try to understand the power of such interactive proofs from the complexity-theoretic perspective. For example, can one prove in a succinct way that a given formula is *not* satisfiable? This problem is **coNP**-complete, and hence is believed to not have a polynomial-sized proof in the traditional sense. The surprising fact is that it does have succinct proofs when the verifier is allowed to interact with the prover (Section 8.3), and in fact so does TQBF and every other problem in **PSPACE**. (We note that these succinct interactive proofs require that the verifier be randomized, and this is crucial; see Section 8.1.) Such facts alone make the study of interactive proofs very important. Furthermore, study of interactive proofs yields new insights into other issues—cryptographic protocols (see Remark 8.8 and Section 9.4); limits on the power of approximation algorithms (Section 8.5); program checking (Section 8.6); and evidence that some famous problems like *graph isomorphism* (see Section 8.1.3) and *approximate shortest lattice vector* (see chapter notes) are *not* **NP**-complete.

8.1 INTERACTIVE PROOFS: SOME VARIATIONS

As mentioned, interactive proofs introduce *interaction* into the basic **NP** scenario. Instead of the prover sending a written proof to the verifier, the verifier conducts an interrogation of the prover, repeatedly asking questions and listening to the prover's responses. At the end, the verifier decides whether or not to accept the input. Of course, the message of each party at any point in the interaction can depend upon messages sent and received so far. The prover is assumed to be an all-powerful machine (see the notes following Definition 8.3), though, as we will see, it suffices to assume it is a **PSPACE** machine; see the remark after Definition 8.6.

We have several further choices to make in completing the definition: (a) Is the prover deterministic or probabilistic? (b) Is the verifier deterministic or probabilistic? (c) If we allow probabilistic machines, how do we define "accept" and "reject"? We saw in Chapter 7 several choices for this depending upon the type of error allowed (one-sided versus two-sided).

Let us explore the effect of some of these choices.

8.1.1 Warmup: Interactive proofs with deterministic verifier and prover

First, we consider interactive proofs with deterministic verifier and prover.

EXAMPLE 8.1

Let us consider a trivial example of such an interactive proof for membership in 3SAT. Proceeding clause by clause, the verifier asks the prover to announce the values for the literals in the clause. The verifier keeps a record of these answers, and accepts at the end if all clauses were indeed satisfied, and the prover never announced conflicting values for a variable.

Thus both verifier and prover are deterministic.

Of course, in this case we may well ask what the point of interaction is, as the prover could just announce values of all clauses in the very first round, and then take a nap from then on. In fact, we will soon see this is a subcase of a more general phenomenon: Interactive proofs with deterministic verifiers never need to last more than a single round.

First, let us clarify the word "interaction" in Example 8.1. By this we mean that the verifier and prover are two deterministic functions that at each round of interaction compute the next question/response as a function of the input and the questions and responses of the previous rounds.

Definition 8.2 (*Interaction of deterministic functions*) Let $f, g : \{0, 1\}^* \rightarrow \{0, 1\}^*$ be functions and $k \geq 0$ be an integer (allowed to depend upon the input size). A *k-round interaction* of f and g on input $x \in \{0, 1\}^*$, denoted by $\langle f, g \rangle(x)$ is the sequence of strings

$a_1, \ldots, a_k \in \{0, 1\}^*$ defined as follows:

$$a_1 = f(x)$$
$$a_2 = g(x, a_1)$$
$$\ldots \tag{8.1}$$
$$a_{2i+1} = f(x, a_1, \ldots, a_{2i}) \qquad \text{for } 2i < k$$
$$a_{2i+2} = g(x, a_1, \ldots, a_{2i+1}) \qquad \text{for } 2i + 1 < k$$

The *output* of f at the end of the interaction denoted $\mathsf{out}_f \langle f, g \rangle(x)$ is defined to be $f(x, a_1, \ldots, a_k)$; we assume this output is in $\{0, 1\}$.   ◇

Definition 8.3 (*Deterministic proof systems*) We say that a language L has a *k-round deterministic interactive proof system* if there's a deterministic TM V that on input $x, a_1, \ldots, a_i$ runs in time polynomial in $|x|$, and can have a k-round interaction with any function P such that

(Completeness) $x \in L \Rightarrow \exists P : \{0, 1\}^* \to \{0, 1\}^* \ \mathsf{out}_V \langle V, P \rangle(x) = 1$

(Soundness) $x \notin L \Rightarrow \forall P : \{0, 1\}^* \to \{0, 1\}^* \ \mathsf{out}_V \langle V, P \rangle(x) = 0$

The class **dIP** contains all languages with a $k(n)$-round deterministic interactive proof system where $k(n)$ is polynomial in n.   ◇

Notice, this definition places no limits on the computational power of the prover P; this makes intuitive sense, since a false assertion should *not* be provable, no matter how clever the prover. Note also that because we place no such limits, it does not matter that we allow the prover in the completeness and soundness conditions to depend on x (see also Exercise 8.2).

As hinted in Example 8.1, **dIP** actually is a class we know well.

Lemma 8.4 dIP = NP.   ◇

PROOF: Trivially, every **NP** language has a one-round deterministic proof system and thus is in **dIP**. Now we prove that if $L \in$ **dIP** then $L \in$ **NP**. If V is the verifier for L, then a certificate that an input is in L is just a transcript $(a_1, a_2, \ldots, a_k)$ causing the verifier V to accept. To verify this transcript, one checks that indeed $V(x) = a_1$, $V(x, a_1, a_2) = a_3, \ldots$, and $V(x, a_1, \ldots, a_k) = 1$. If $x \in L$ then such a transcript exists. Conversely, if such a transcript $(a_1, \ldots, a_k)$ exists then we can define a prover function P to satisfy $P(x, a_1) = a_2$, $P(x, a_1, a_2, a_3) = a_4$, and so on. This deterministic prover satisfies $\mathsf{out}_V \langle V, P \rangle(x) = 1$, which implies $x \in L$. ∎

8.1.2 The class IP: Probabilistic verifier

The message of Section 8.1.1 is that in order for interaction to provide any benefit, we need to let the verifier be *probabilistic*. This means that the verifier's questions will be computed using a probabilistic algorithm. Furthermore, the verifier will be allowed to come to a wrong conclusion (e.g., accept a proof for a wrong statement) with some small probability. As in the case of probabilistic algorithms, this probability is over the choice of the verifier's coins, and we require the verifier to reject proofs for a wrong statement with good probability *regardless* of the strategy the prover uses. Allowing this combination of interaction and randomization has a huge effect: As we will see in Section 8.3, the set of languages that have such interactive proof systems jumps from **NP** to **PSPACE**.

EXAMPLE 8.5

As an intuitive example for the power of combining randomization and interaction, consider the following scenario: Marla has one red sock and one yellow sock, but her friend Arthur, who is color-blind, does not believe her that the socks have different colors. How can she convince him that this is really the case?

Here is a way to do so. Marla gives both socks to Arthur, tells him which sock is yellow and which one is red, and Arthur holds the red sock in his right hand and the yellow sock in his left hand. Then Marla turns her back to Arthur and he tosses a coin. If the coin comes up "heads" then Arthur keeps the socks as they are; otherwise, he switches them between his left and right hands. He then asks Marla to guess whether he switched the socks or not. Of course Marla can easily do so by seeing whether the red sock is still in Arthur's right hand or not. But if the socks were identical then she would not have been able to guess the answer with probability better than $1/2$. Thus if Marla manages to answer correctly in all of, say, 100 repetitions of this game, then Arthur can indeed be convinced that the socks have different colors.

The principle behind this "interactive proof system" actually underlies the systems for graph nonisomorphism and quadratic nonresiduosity that we will see later in this chapter (Section 8.1.3 and Example 8.9). In the sock example, the verifier, being color-blind, has less power (i.e., fewer capabilities) than the prover. In general interactive proofs, the verifier—being polynomial-time—also has less computational power than the prover.

Now we give a precise definition of an interactive proof with a *probabilistic* verifier. To extend Definition 8.2 to model an interaction between f and g where f is probabilistic, we add an additional m-bit input r to the function f in (8.1), that is, $a_1 = f(x, r)$, $a_3 = f(x, r, a_1, a_2)$, and so on. However, the function g is evaluated only on the a_i's and does not get r as an additional input. (This models the fact that the prover cannot "see" the verifier's coins but only his messages; for this reason, this is called the *private coins* model for interactive proofs, as opposed to the *public coins* model of Section 8.2.) The interaction $\langle f, g \rangle(x)$ is now a random variable over $r \in_R \{0, 1\}^m$. Similarly the output $\text{out}_f \langle f, g \rangle(x)$ is also a random variable.

Definition 8.6 *(Probabilistic verifiers and the class **IP**)* For an integer $k \geq 1$ (that may depend on the input length), we say that a language L is in **IP**$[k]$ if there is a probabilistic polynomial-time Turing machine V that can have a k-round interaction with a function $P: \{0, 1\}^* \rightarrow \{0, 1\}^*$ such that

(Completeness) $x \in L \Rightarrow \exists P \Pr[\text{out}_V \langle V, P \rangle(x) = 1] \geq 2/3$ (8.2)

(Soundness) $x \notin L \Rightarrow \forall P \Pr[\text{out}_V \langle V, P \rangle(x) = 1] \leq 1/3$ (8.3)

where all probabilities are over the choice of r.
We define $\mathbf{IP} = \cup_{c \geq 1} \mathbf{IP}[n^c]$.

Now we study the robustness of this definition. First we show that the probabilities $2/3$ and $1/3$ in Definition 8.6 can be made arbitrarily close to 1 and 0, respectively, by using the same boosting technique we used for **BPP** (see Section 7.4.1).

Lemma 8.7 *The class* **IP** *defined in Definition 8.6 is unchanged if we replace the completeness parameter $2/3$ by $1 - 2^{-n^s}$ and the soundness parameter $1/3$ by 2^{-n^s} for any fixed constant $s > 0$.*   ◇

PROOF: The verifier repeats the entire protocol over and over again, say m times, and accepts at the end iff more than $1/2$ the runs resulted in an accept. If $x \in L$, then a prover that can make the verifier accept with probability $2/3$ in each repetition will at the end succeed with probability $1 - 2^{-\Omega(m)}$ by the Chernoff bound (Theorem A.14). If $x \notin L$, we have to argue that every prover strategy will fail with high probability. We claim that that the prover can succeed in each repetition of the protocol with probability only $1/3$—irrespective of what happened in earlier rounds. The reason is that even though the prover's responses in this repetition may depend arbitrarily on its responses in the earlier repetitions, since the expression in (8.3) holds for all provers, it holds in particular for the prover that knows the questions of earlier rounds.

Thus Chernoff bounds again imply that the probability that the prover succeed in a majority of the repetitions only with probability $2^{-\Omega(m)}$. Choosing $m = O(n^s)$ completes the proof. ∎

We now make several assertions about the class **IP**. Exercise 8.1 asks you to prove some of them.

1. Allowing the prover to be probabilistic, that is, allowing the answer function a_i to depend upon some random string used by the prover (and unknown to the verifier), does not change the class **IP**. The reason is that for any language L, if a probabilistic prover P can make a verifier V accept with some probability, then averaging implies that there is a deterministic prover that makes V accept with the same probability.
2. Since the prover can use an arbitrary function, it can in principle use unbounded computational power or even compute undecidable functions. However, we can show that given any verifier V, we can compute the optimum prover (which, given x, maximizes the verifier's acceptance probability) using poly($|x|$) space (and hence also $2^{\text{poly}(|x|)}$ time). Thus $\mathbf{IP} \subseteq \mathbf{PSPACE}$.
3. Replacing the constant $2/3$ with 1 in the completeness requirement (8.2) does not change the class **IP**. This is a nontrivial fact. It was originally proved in a complicated way but today can be proved using our characterization of **IP** in Section 8.3.
4. By contrast, replacing the constant $1/3$ with 0 in the soundness condition (8.3) is equivalent to having a deterministic verifier and hence reduces the class **IP** to **NP**.

5. *Private Coins:* Thus far the prover functions do not depend upon the verifier's random strings, only on the messages/questions the verifier sends. In other words, the verifier's random string is *private*. Often these are called *private coin* interactive proofs. In Section 8.2 we also consider the model of *public-coin* proofs (also known as *Arthur-Merlin* proofs) where all the verifier's questions are simply obtained by tossing coins and revealing them to the prover.

6. The proof of Lemma 8.7 sequentially repeats the basic protocol m times and takes the majority answer. In fact, using a more complicated proof, it can be shown that we can decrease the probability without increasing the number of rounds using *parallel repetition*, where the prover and verifier will run m executions of the protocol in parallel (i.e., by asking all m questions in one go). The proof of this fact is easier for the case of *public-coin* protocols.

8.1.3 Interactive proof for graph nonisomorphism

We present another example of a language in **IP** that is not known to be in **NP**. The usual ways of representing graphs—adjacency lists, adjacency matrices—involve labeling each vertex with a unique number. We say two graphs G_1 and G_2 are *isomorphic* if they are the same up to a renumbering of vertices; in other words, if there is a permutation π of the labels of the nodes of G_1 such that $\pi(G_1) = G_2$, where $\pi(G_1)$ is the labeled graph obtained by applying π on its vertex labels. The graphs in Figure 8.1, for example, are isomorphic with $\pi = (12)(3654)$. (This is the permutation in which 1 and 2 are mapped to each other, 3 to 6, 6 to 5, 5 to 4, and 4 to 1.) If G_1 and G_2 are isomorphic, we write $G_1 \cong G_2$. The GI problem is the following: given two graphs G_1, G_2 decide if they are isomorphic.

Clearly GI $\in$ **NP**, since a certificate is simply the description of the permutation π. The graph isomorphism problem is important in a variety of fields and has a rich history (see [Hof82]). It is open whether GI is **NP**-complete, and, along with the factoring problem, it is the most famous **NP**-problem that is not known to be either in **P** or **NP**-complete. In Section 8.2.4, we show that that GI is not **NP**-complete unless the polynomial hierarchy collapses. The first step of this proof will be an interactive proof for the complement of GI: the problem GNI of deciding whether two given graphs are *not* isomorphic.

Protocol: *Private-coin* Graph Nonisomorphism

> *V:* Pick $i \in \{1, 2\}$ uniformly randomly. Randomly permute the vertices of G_i to get a new graph H. Send H to P.
>
> *P:* Identify which of G_1, G_2 was used to produce H. Let G_j be that graph. Send j to V.
>
> *V:* Accept if $i = j$; reject otherwise.

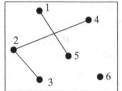 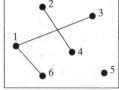

Figure 8.1. Two isomorphic graphs.

To see that Definition 8.6 is satisfied by the protocol, note that if $G_1 \not\cong G_2$ then there exists a prover such that $\Pr[V \text{ accepts}] = 1$ because if the graphs are nonisomorphic, an all-powerful prover can certainly tell which one of the two is isomorphic to H. On the other hand, if $G_1 \cong G_2$, the best any prover can do is to randomly guess because a random permutation of G_1 looks exactly like a random permutation of G_2. Thus in this case for every prover, $\Pr[V \text{ accepts}] \leq 1/2$. This probability can be reduced to 1/3 by sequential or parallel repetition.

Remark 8.8 (Zero-knowledge proofs)
Now we briefly touch upon *zero-knowledge proofs*, a topic related to interactive proofs that underlies a huge research effort in cryptography. Roughly speaking, a *zero-knowledge proof* system for membership in a language is an interactive proof protocol where the verifier is convinced at the end that the input x is in the language, but learns *nothing else*. How can we quantify that the verifier learns nothing else? We do this by showing that the verifier could have produced the transcript of the protocol in polynomial time with no help from the prover. We will see in Section 9.4 that the above protocol for graph nonisomorphism is zero-knowledge.

One can see why such a concept might be useful in cryptography. It raises the possibility of parties being able to prove things to each other without revealing any secrets (e.g., to prove that you hold the password without revealing the password itself). This was one of the original motivations for the invention of the notion of interactive proofs. Section 9.4 of contains a formal definition and some examples of zero-knowledge protocols. (That section does not depend on the other material of Chapter 9 and hence can be read in isolation from that chapter.)

EXAMPLE 8.9 (*Quadratic nonresiduosity*)

Here is another example for an interactive proof for a language not known to be in **NP**. We say that a number a is a *quadratic residue* mod$p$ if there is another number b such that $a \equiv b^2 \pmod{p}$. Such a b is called the *square root* of a (mod p). Clearly, $-b$ is another square root, and there are no other square roots since the equation $x^2 - a$ has at most two solutions over $\mathrm{GF}(p)$.

The language of pairs (a, p) where p is a prime and a is a quadratic residue mod p is in **NP**, since a square root constitutes a membership proof. Of course, the fact that p is a prime also has a short membership proof, and indeed primality can be tested in polynomial time; see Chapter 2.

In contrast, the language QNR of pairs (a, p) such that p is a prime and a is *not* a quadratic residue modulo p has no natural short membership proof and is not known to be in **NP**. But it does have a simple interactive proof if the verifier is probabilistic.

The verifier takes a random number r mod p and a random bit $b \in \{0, 1\}$ (kept secret from the prover). If $b = 0$ she sends the prover r^2 mod p and if $b = 1$ she sends ar^2 mod p. She asks the prover to guess what b was and accepts iff the prover guesses correctly.

If a is a quadratic residue, then the distribution of ar^2 and r^2 are identical; both are random elements of the group of quadratic residues modulo p. (To see this, note that every quadratic residue a' can be written as as^2 where s is a square root of a/a'.) Thus the prover has probability at most 1/2 of guessing b.

On the other hand, if a is a nonresidue, then the distributions ar^2 and r^2 are completely distinct: The first is a random nonresidue modulo p, and the second is a random quadratic residue modulo p. An all-powerful prover can tell them apart, and thus guess b with probability 1. Thus it can make the verifier accept with probability 1.

8.2 PUBLIC COINS AND **AM**

Our proof system for graph nonisormorphism and nonresiduosity seemed to crucially rely on the verifier's access to a source of *private random coins* that are not seen by the prover. Allowing the prover full access to the verifier's random string leads to the model of *interactive proofs with public coins*.

Definition 8.10 *(AM, MA)* For every k the complexity class **AM**[k] is defined as the subset of **IP**[k] (see Definition 8.6) obtained when we restrict the verifier's messages to be random bits, and not allowing it to use any other random bits that are not contained in these messages.

An interactive proof where the verifier has this form is called a *public coin* proof, sometimes also known as an *Arthur-Merlin* proof.[1]　　　　　　　　　　　　　　　　　　　◇

We denote by **AM** the class **AM**[2].[2] That is, **AM** is the class of languages with an interactive proof that consist of the verifier sending a random string, and the prover responding with a message, where the verifier's decision is obtained by applying a deterministic polynomial-time function to the transcript. The class **MA** denotes the class of languages with a two-round public-coin interactive proof with the prover sending the first message. That is, $L \in$ **MA** if there's a proof system for L that consists of the prover first sending a message, and then the verifier tossing coins and computing its decision by doing a deterministic polynomial-time computation involving the input, the prover's message and the coins.

Remark 8.11
We mention some properties of the class **AM**[k]:

1. Note that even in a public-coins proof, the prover doesn't get to see immediately all of the verifier's random coins, but rather they are revealed to the prover iteratively message by message. That is, an **AM**[k]-proof is an **IP**[k]-proof where the verifier's random tape r consists of $\lceil k/2 \rceil$ strings $r_1, \ldots, r_{\lceil k/2 \rceil}$, his ith message is simply the string

---

[1]　According to an old legend, Arthur was a great king of medieval England and Merlin was his court magician. Babai [Bab85] used the name "Arthur-Merlin" for this model by drawing an analogy between the prover's infinite power and Merlin's magic. While Merlin cannot predict the coins that Arthur will toss in the future, Arthur has no way of hiding from Merlin's magic the results of the coins he tossed in the past.

[2]　Note that **AM** = **AM**[2] while **IP** = **IP**[poly]. Although this is indeed somewhat inconsistent, it is the standard notation used in the literature. Some sources denote the class **AM**[3] by **AMA**, the class **AM**[4] by **AMAM**, and so on.

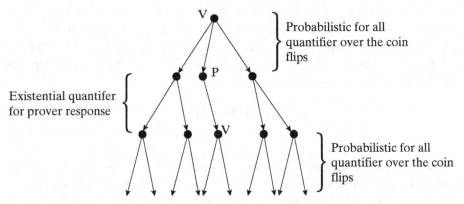

Figure 8.2. AM[k] looks like $\prod_k^p$, with the ∀ quantifier replaced by probabilistic choice.

r_i, and the decision whether to accept or reject is obtained by applying a deterministic polynomial-time computable function to the transcript.

2. **AM**[2] = **BP** · **NP** where **BP** · **NP** is the class in Definition 7.17. In particular it follows that **AM**[2] $\subseteq$ Σ_3^p. (See Exercise 8.3.)

3. For constants $k \geq 2$ we have **AM**[k] = **AM**[2] (Exercise 8.7). This "collapse" is somewhat surprising because **AM**[k] at first glance seems similar to **PH** with the ∀ quantifiers changed to "probabilistic ∀" quantifiers, where *most* of the branches lead to acceptance. See Figure 8.2.

4. It is an open problem whether there is any nice characterization of **AM**[$\sigma(n)$], where $\sigma(n)$ is a suitably slowly growing function of n, such as $\log \log n$.

8.2.1 Simulating private coins

Clearly for every k, **AM**[k] $\subseteq$ **IP**[k]. The interactive proof for GNI seemed to crucially depend upon the fact that P cannot see the random bits of V. If P knew those bits, P would know i and so could trivially always guess correctly. Thus it may seem that allowing the verifier to keep its coins private adds significant power to interactive proofs, and so the following result should be quite surprising:

Theorem 8.12 *(Goldwasser-Sipser* [GS87])
For every $k : \mathbb{N} \to \mathbb{N}$ with $k(n)$ computable in poly(n),

$$\mathbf{IP}[k] \subseteq \mathbf{AM}[k+2]$$

We sketch the proof of Theorem 8.12 in Section 8.12 after proving the next Theorem, which concerns the subcase of GNI.

Theorem 8.13 GNI $\in$ **AM**[2].   ◇

The proof of Theorem 8.13 is a good example of how nontrivial interactive proofs can be designed by recasting the problem. The key idea is to look at graph nonisomorphism in a different, more quantitative, way. Consider the following set of labeled graphs $S = \{H : H \cong G_1 \text{ or } H \cong G_2\}$. Note that it is easy to certify that a graph H is a member of S, by providing the permutation mapping either G_1 or G_2 to H. An n vertex graph G has at most $n!$ equivalent graphs. For simplicity assume first that both G_1 and G_2 have each exactly $n!$ equivalent graphs. The size of S differs by a factor 2 depending upon whether or not G_1 is isomorphic to G_2.

$$\text{if } G_1 \not\cong G_2 \text{ then } |S| = 2n! \tag{8.4}$$

$$\text{if } G_1 \cong G_2 \text{ then } |S| = n! \tag{8.5}$$

Now consider the general case where G_1 or G_2 may have less than $n!$ equivalent graphs. An n-vertex graph G has less than $n!$ equivalent graphs iff it has a nontrivial *automorphism*, which is a permutation π that is not the identity permutation and yet $\pi(G) = G$. Let $aut(G)$ denote the set of automorphisms of graph G. We change the definition of S to

$$S = \{(H, \pi) : H \cong G_1 \text{ or } H \cong G_2 \text{ and } \pi \in aut(H)\}$$

Using the fact that $aut(G)$ is a subgroup, one can verify that S satisfies (8.4) and (8.5). Also, membership in this set is easy to certify.

Thus to convince the verifier that $G_1 \not\cong G_2$, the prover has to convince the verifier that case (8.4) holds rather than (8.5). This is done by using a *set lower bound protocol*.

8.2.2 Set lower bound protocol

Suppose there is a set S known to both prover and verifier, such that membership in S is easily certifiable, in the sense that given some string x that happens to be in S, the prover—using its superior computational power—can provide the verifier a certificate to this effect. (To put it more formally, S is in **BP·NP**.) The *set lower bound protocol* is a public-coins protocol that allows the prover to *certify* the approximate size of S. Note that the prover—using its superior computational power—can certainly compute and announce $|S|$. The question is how to convince the verifier that this answer is correct, or even approximately correct. Suppose the prover's claimed value for $|S|$ is K. The protocol below has the property that if the true value of $|S|$ is indeed at least K, then the prover can cause the verifier to accept with high probability, whereas if the true value of $|S|$ is at most $K/2$ (the prover's answer is grossly on the high side), then the verifier will reject with high probability, no matter what the prover does. This protocol is called the *set lower bound protocol* and it clearly suffices to complete the proof of Theorem 8.13.

Tool: Pairwise independent hash functions
The main tool in the set lower bound protocol is a *pairwise independent hash function collection*, which has also found numerous other applications in complexity theory and computer science (see Note 8.16).

Definition 8.14 (*Pairwise independent hash functions*) Let $\mathcal{H}_{n,k}$ be a collection of functions from $\{0, 1\}^n$ to $\{0, 1\}^k$. We say that $\mathcal{H}_{n,k}$ is *pairwise independent* if for every $x, x' \in \{0, 1\}^n$ with $x \neq x'$ and for every $y, y' \in \{0, 1\}^k$, $\Pr_{h \in_R \mathcal{H}_{n,k}}[h(x) = y \wedge h(x') = y'] = 2^{-2k}$.   ◇

An equivalent formulation is that for every two distinct but fixed strings $x, x' \in \{0, 1\}^n$, when we choose h at random from $\mathcal{H}_{n,k}$, then the random variable $\langle h(x), h(x') \rangle$ is distributed according to the uniform distribution on $\{0, 1\}^k \times \{0, 1\}^k$.

We can identify the elements of $\{0, 1\}^n$ with the *finite field* $GF(2^n)$ containing 2^n elements (see Section A.4). Recall that the addition (+) and multiplication (·) operations in this field are efficiently computable and satisfy the usual commutative and distributive laws, every element x has an additive inverse (denoted by $-x$) and, if nonzero, a multiplicative inverse (denoted by x^{-1}). The following theorem provides a construction of a family of *efficiently computable* pairwise independent hash functions (see also Exercise 8.4 for a different construction).

Theorem 8.15 (*Efficient pairwise independent hash functions*) *For every n, define the collection $\mathcal{H}_{n,n}$ to be $\{h_{a,b}\}_{a,b \in GF(2^n)}$ where for every $a, b \in GF(2^n)$, the function $h_{a,b} : GF(2^n) \to GF(2^n)$ maps x to $ax + b$. Then, $\mathcal{H}_{n,n}$ is a collection of pairwise independent hash functions.* ◇

Theorem 8.15 implies the existence of an efficiently computable family of pairwise independent hash functions $\mathcal{H}_{n,k}$ for every n, k: if $k > n$ we can use the collection $\mathcal{H}_{k,k}$ and extend n bit inputs to k bits by padding with zeros. If $k < n$, then we can use the collection $\mathcal{H}_{n,n}$ and reduce n bit outputs to k bits by truncating the last $n - k$ bits.

PROOF: For every $x \neq x' \in GF(2^n)$ and $y, y' \in GF(2^n)$, $h_{a,b}(x) = y$ and $h_{a,b}(x') = y'$ iff a, b satisfy the equations:

$$a \cdot x + b = y$$
$$a \cdot x' + b = y'$$

These equations imply that $a = (y - y')(x - x')^{-1}$; this is well-defined because $x - x' \neq 0$. Since $b = y - a \cdot x$, the pair $\langle a, b \rangle$ is completely determined by these equations, and so the probability that this happens over the choice of a, b is exactly one over the number of possible pairs, which indeed equals $\frac{1}{2^{2n}}$. ■

The lower-bound protocol
The lower-bound protocol is as follows.

Protocol: Goldwasser-Sipser Set Lower Bound Protocol

Conditions: $S \subseteq \{0, 1\}^m$ is a set such that membership in S can be certified. Both parties know a number K. The prover's goal is to convince the verifier that $|S| \geq K$ and the verifier should reject with good probability if $|S| \leq \frac{K}{2}$. Let k be an integer such that $2^{k-2} < K \leq 2^{k-1}$.

V: Randomly pick a function $h : \{0, 1\}^m \to \{0, 1\}^k$ from a pairwise independent hash function collection $\mathcal{H}_{m,k}$. Pick $y \in_R \{0, 1\}^k$. Send h, y to prover.

P: Try to find an $x \in S$ such that $h(x) = y$. Send such an x to V, together with a certificate that $x \in S$.

V's output: If $h(x) = y$ and the certificate validates that $x \in S$ then accept; otherwise reject.

NOTE 8.16 *(The Hashing paradigm* [CW77]*)*

In many computer programs, hash functions are used to create a *hash table*. The goal is to store a set $S \subseteq \{0, 1\}^n$ so as to be able to efficiently answer *membership queries*, which ask whether or not a given element x is in S. The set S could change dynamically (i.e., elements may be added or deleted), but its size is guaranteed to be much smaller than 2^n, the number of all possible elements.

To create a hash table of size 2^k, we pick a hash function h mapping $\{0, 1\}^n$ to $\{0, 1\}^k$ and store $x \in S$ at location $h(x)$. If we ever need to later determine whether or not x is in S, we just compute $h(x)$ and go look for x at this location in the hash table. Notice, if $h(x) = h(y)$, then both x, y are stored in the same location; this is called a *collision*. Such collisions can be dealt with, but at a cost to efficiency, and hence we want to minimize them by choosing a sufficiently "random" hash function.

Instead of using a fixed hash function, it makes sense to use a random function from a *hash function collection*, such as the collection in Theorem 8.15. This will guarantee that that most elements of $\{0, 1\}^k$ have roughly $|S|2^{-k}$ preimages in S (which is the expected number if h were a completely random function). In particular, if S has size roughly 2^k, then we expect the mapping to be one-to-one or almost one-to-one, and so the expected number of collisions is small. Therefore, the image of S under h should look like this:

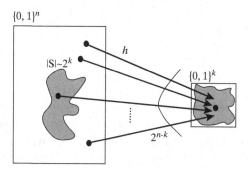

Hash tables are a preferred solution in many cases because of the ease with which they handle sets that change dynamically. The foregoing analysis of the expectation continues to apply so long as the size of S remains less than 2^k and the hash function is picked from a collection using random bits that are *independent* of the set S.

In theoretical computer science, hash functions have found a variety of uses. One example is Lemma 17.19, which shows that if the collection is pairwise independent and $S \subseteq \{0, 1\}^n$ has size roughly 2^k, then with good probability the value 0^k will have exactly one preimage in S. Another example is the *Leftover Hash Lemma* (Lemma 21.26) that shows that if S is larger than 2^k then a random element of S is mapped by h almost perfectly to a random element of $\{0, 1\}^k$.

Pairwise independent hash functions are but one example of a hash function collection. Once can study other collections featuring various tradeoffs between efficiency and uniformity of output, including almost pairwise independence, k-wise independence, ϵ-biased, and more. See the survey by Luby and Wigderson [LW06].

Clearly, the prover (being all powerful) can make the verifier accept iff h, y happen to be such that an $x \in S$ exists satisfying $h(x) = y$. The following claim shows that, for $p^* = K/2^k$, there is a gap of $\frac{3}{4}p^*$ versus $p^*/2$ in the probability of this happening in the two cases we are interested in ($|S| \geq K$ versus $|S| < K/2$). While the claim is stated only for $|S| \leq K$, note that clearly a larger set only increases the probability that the prover can make the verifier accept.

Claim 8.16.1 *Let $S \subseteq \{0, 1\}^m$ satisfy $|S| \leq \frac{2^k}{2}$. Then, for $p = |S|/2^k$*

$$p \geq \Pr_{h \in_R \mathcal{H}_{m,k}, y \in_R \{0,1\}^k} [\exists_{x \in S} : h(x) = y] \geq \frac{3p}{4} - \frac{p}{2^k}. \qquad \diamond$$

PROOF: The upper bound on the probability follows trivially by noticing that the set $h(S)$ of y's with preimages in S has size that is at most $|S|$. We now prove the lower bound. In fact, we show the stronger statement that

$$\Pr_{h \in_R \mathcal{H}_{m,k}} [\exists_{x \in S} h(x) = y] \geq \frac{3}{4}p$$

for *every* $y \in \{0, 1\}^k$. Indeed, for every $x \in S$ define E_x as the event that $h(x) = y$. Then, $\Pr[\exists x \in S : h(x) = y] = \Pr[\vee_{x \in S} E_x]$. By the inclusion-exclusion principle (Corollary A.2), this is at least

$$\sum_{x \in S} \Pr[E_x] - \frac{1}{2} \sum_{x \neq x' \in S} \Pr[E_x \cap E_{x'}]$$

However, by pairwise independence of the hash functions, if $x \neq x'$, then $\Pr[E_x] = 2^{-k}$ and $\Pr[E_x \cap E_{x'}] = 2^{-2k}$ and so (up to the low order term $|S|/2^{2k}$) this probability is at least

$$\frac{|S|}{2^k} - \frac{1}{2}\frac{|S|^2}{2^{2k}} = \frac{|S|}{2^k}\left(1 - \frac{|S|}{2^{k+1}}\right) \geq \frac{3}{4}p \quad \blacksquare$$

Proving Theorem 8.13
The public-coin interactive proof system for GNI consists of the verifier and prover running several iterations of the set lower bound protocol for the set S as defined above, where the verifier accepts iff the fraction of accepting iterations is at least $5p^*/8$ (note that $p^* = K/2^k$ can be easily computed by the verifier). Using the Chernoff bound (Theorem A.14), it can be easily seen that a constant number of iterations will suffice to ensure completeness probability at least $2/3$ and soundness error at most $1/3$.

Finally, the number of rounds stays at 2 because the verifier can do all iterations in *parallel*: Pick several choices of h, y and send them all to the prover at once. It is easily checked that the above analysis of the probability of the prover's success is unaffected even if the prover is asked many questions in parallel. $\blacksquare$

Remark 8.17
Note that, unlike the private-coins protocol for GNI, the public-coins protocol of Theorem 8.13 does not have perfect completeness (i.e., the completeness parameter is not 1), since the set lower bound protocol does not satisfy this property. However, we can construct a public-coins set lower bound protocol with completeness parameter 1

(see Exercise 8.5), thus implying a perfectly complete public-coins proof for GNI. This can be generalized to show that every private-coins proof system (even one not satisfying perfect completeness) can be transformed into a perfectly complete public-coins system with a similar number of rounds.

8.2.3 Sketch of proof of Theorem 8.12

Our transformation of the private-coins protocol for GNI into a public-coins protocol suggests how to do such a transformation for every other private-coins protocol. The idea is that the public-coin prover demonstrates to the public-coin verifier an approximate lower bound on the size of the set of random strings which would have made the private-coin verifier accept in the original protocol.

Think how our public-coins protocol for GNI relates to the private-coin protocol of Section 8.1.3. The set S roughly corresponds to the set of possible messages sent by the verifier in the protocol, where the verifier's message is a random element in S. If the two graphs are isomorphic, then the verifier's message completely hides its choice of a random $i \in_R \{1, 2\}$, whereas if they're not, then the message distribution completely reveals it (at least to a prover that has unbounded computation time). Thus roughly speaking in the former case the mapping from the verifier's coins to the message is 2-to-1, whereas in the latter case it is 1-to-1, resulting in a set that is twice as large. In fact we can think of the public-coin prover as convincing the verifier that the private-coin verifier would have accepted with large probability. The idea behind the proof of $\mathbf{IP}[k] \subseteq \mathbf{AM}[k+2]$ is similar, but one has to proceed in a round-by-round fashion, and the prover has to prove to the verifier that certain messages are quite likely to be sent by the verifier—in other words, the set of random strings that make the verifier send these messages in the private-coin protocol is quite large.

8.2.4 Can GI be NP-complete?

As mentioned earlier, it is an open problem if GI is **NP**-complete. We now prove that if GI is **NP**-complete, then the polynomial hierarchy collapses.

Theorem 8.18 ([BHZ87]) *If* GI *is* **NP**-*complete, then* $\Sigma_2 = \Pi_2$.   ◇

PROOF: We show that under this condition, $\Sigma_2 \subseteq \Pi_2$; this will imply $\Sigma_2 = \Pi_2$ because $\Sigma_2 = \mathbf{co}\Pi_2$.

If GI is **NP**-complete, then GNI is **coNP**-complete, which implies that there exists a function f such that for every n variable formula φ, $\forall_y \varphi(y)$ holds iff $f(\varphi) \in$ GNI. Consider an arbitrary Σ_2 SAT formula

$$\psi = \exists_{x \in \{0,1\}^n} \forall_{y \in \{0,1\}^n} \varphi(x, y)$$

The formula ψ is equivalent to

$$\exists_{x \in \{0,1\}^n} g(x) \in \text{GNI}$$

where $g(x) = f(\varphi_{\restriction x})$, and $\varphi_{\restriction x}$ is the formula obtained from $\varphi(x, y)$ by fixing x.

Using Remark 8.17 and the comments of Section 8.11, GNI has a two-round **AM** proof with perfect completeness[3] and (after appropriate amplification) soundness error less than 2^{-n}. Let V be the verifier algorithm for this proof system, and denote by m the length of the verifier's random tape and by m' the length of the prover's message. We claim that ψ is true if and only if

$$\forall_{r\in\{0,1\}^m}\exists_{x\in\{0,1\}^n}\exists_{a\in\{0,1\}^{m'}}(V(g(x),r,a)=1) \tag{8.6}$$

Indeed, if ψ is true, then perfect completeness clearly implies (8.6). If on the other hand ψ is false, this means that

$$\forall_{x\in\{0,1\}^n}g(x)\notin \mathsf{GNI}$$

Now, using the fact that the soundness error of the interactive proof is less than 2^{-n} and the number of x's is 2^n, we conclude (by the "probabilistic method basic principle") that there exists a *single* string $r \in \{0,1\}^m$ such that for every $x \in \{0,1\}^n$, the prover in the **AM** proof for GNI has no response a that will cause the verifier to accept $g(x)$ if the verifier's first message is r. In other words,

$$\exists_{r\in\{0,1\}^m}\forall_{x\in\{0,1\}^n}\forall_{a\in\{0,1\}^{m'}}(V(g(x),r,a)=0)$$

which is exactly the negation of (8.6). Since deciding the truth of (8.6) is in $\mathbf{\Pi}_2$ (as it is a statement of the form $\forall x\exists y P(x,y)$ for some polynomial-time computable predicate P), we have shown $\mathbf{\Sigma}_2 \subseteq \mathbf{\Pi}_2$. ∎

8.3 IP = PSPACE

It was an open question for a while to characterize **IP**, the set of languages that have interactive proofs. All we knew was that $\mathbf{NP} \subseteq \mathbf{IP} \subseteq \mathbf{PSPACE}$, and there was evidence (e.g., the protocols for quadratic nonresiduosity and GNI) that the first containment is proper. Most researchers felt that the second containment would also be proper. They reasoned as follows. We know that interaction alone does not give us any languages outside **NP** (Section 8.1.1). We also suspect (see Chapter 7) that randomization alone does not add significant power to computation—researchers even suspect that $\mathbf{BPP} = \mathbf{P}$, based upon evidence described in Chapter 20. So how much more power could the *combination* of randomization and interaction provide? "Not much," the evidence up to 1990 seemed to suggest. For any fixed k, **IP**$[k]$ collapses to the class $\mathbf{AM} = \mathbf{AM}[2]$, which equals $\mathbf{BP} \cdot \mathbf{NP}$ as mentioned in Remark 8.11, and $\mathbf{BP} \cdot \mathbf{NP}$ seems not "much different" from **NP**.[4] Finally, there were simply no protocols known that required k to be superconstant, so $\mathbf{IP} = \mathbf{IP}[\text{poly}(n)]$ did not seem much bigger than $\mathbf{IP}[O(1)]$. The following result from 1990, giving a surprising characterization of **IP**, shows that this intuition was drastically wrong.

---

[3] It is possible to do the rest of this proof without relying on perfect completeness; we leave the details to the interested reader.

[4] In fact, under plausible complexity conjectures, $\mathbf{AM} = \mathbf{NP}$, see Exercise 20.7.

Theorem 8.19 ([LFKN90, Sha90])
IP = PSPACE.

By our earlier remarks, we only need to show the nontrivial direction **PSPACE** $\subseteq$ **IP**, and for this it suffices to show $\mathsf{TQBF} \in \mathbf{IP}[poly(n)]$ because every $L \in$ **PSPACE** is polytime reducible to TQBF. We describe a protocol for TQBF that uses public coins and also has the property that if the input is in TQBF, then there is a prover that makes the verifier accept with probability 1.

Rather than tackle the job of designing a protocol for TQBF right away, let us first think about how to design one for $\overline{3\mathsf{SAT}}$. How can the prover convince the verifier than a given 3CNF formula has no satisfying assignment? We show how to prove something even more general: The prover can prove to the verifier that the *number* of satisfying assignments is exactly K for some number K. That is, we give an interactive proof for membership in the following language.

Definition 8.20 ($\#\mathsf{SAT}_D$)

$\#\mathsf{SAT}_\mathrm{D} = \big\{ \langle \phi, K \rangle : \phi$ is a $3CNF$ formula and it has exactly K satisfying assignments$\big\}$

$\diamond$

This clearly contains $\overline{SAT}$ as a special case (when $K = 0$). In Chapter 17 we will see that $\#\mathsf{SAT}_\mathrm{D}$ is a complete problem for a powerful class called **#P**.

Note that the *set lower bound* protocol of Section 8.2.2 can tackle an approximation version of this problem, namely, prove the value of K within a factor 2 (or any other constant factor). The protocol takes only two rounds. By contrast, our protocol for $\#\mathsf{SAT}_\mathrm{D}$ will use n rounds. The idea of *arithmetization* introduced in this protocol will also prove useful in our protocol for TQBF.

8.3.1 Arithmetization

The key idea will be to take an algebraic view of Boolean formulas by representing them as polynomials. Note that $0, 1$ can be thought of both as truth values and as elements of some finite field $\mathbb{F}$. Thus $x_i \wedge x_j$ is true iff $x_i \cdot x_j = 1$ in the field, and $\neg x_i$ is true iff $1 - x_i = 1$.

Arithmetization refers to the following trick. Given any 3CNF formula $\varphi(x_1, x_2, \ldots, x_n)$ with m clauses and n variables, we introduce field variables $X_1, X_2, \ldots, X_n$. For any clause of size 3, we can write an equivalent degree 3 polynomial, as in the following example:

$$x_i \vee \overline{x_j} \vee x_k \longleftrightarrow X_i(1 - X_j)X_k$$

Let us denote the polynomial for the jth clause by $p_j(X_1, X_2, \ldots, X_n)$, where the notation allows the polynomial to depend on all n variables even though, as is clear in the previous example, each p_j only depends upon at most three variables. For every $0, 1$ assignment to $X_1, X_2, \ldots, X_n$, we have $p_j(X_1, X_2, \ldots, X_n) = 1$ if the assignment satisfies the clause and $p_j(X_1, X_2, \ldots, X_n) = 0$ otherwise.

Multiplying these polynomials, we obtain a multivariate polynomial $P_\varphi(X_1, X_2, \ldots, X_n) = \prod_{j \leq m} p_j(X_1, \ldots, X_n)$ that evaluates to 1 on satisfying assignments and to 0 for unsatisfying assignments. This polynomial has degree at most $3m$. We represent such a polynomial as a product of all the above degree 3 polynomials without opening up the parenthesis, and so $P_\varphi(X_1, X_2, \ldots, X_n)$ has a representation of size $O(m)$. This conversion of φ to P_φ is called *arithmetization*. Once we have written such a polynomial, nothing stops us from substituting arbitrary values from the field $\mathbb{F}$ instead of just $0, 1$ and evaluating the polynomial. As we will see, this gives the verifier unexpected power over the prover.

8.3.2 Interactive protocol for $\#SAT_D$

Now we prove the following result.

Theorem 8.21 $\#SAT_D \in \mathbf{IP}$.   ◇

PROOF: Given input $\langle \phi, K \rangle$, where ϕ is a 3CNF formula of n variables and m clauses, we construct P_ϕ by arithmetization, as in Section 8.3.1. The number of satisfying assignments $\#\phi$ of ϕ satisfies

$$\#\phi = \sum_{b_1 \in \{0,1\}} \sum_{b_2 \in \{0,1\}} \cdots \sum_{b_n \in \{0,1\}} P_\phi(b_1, \ldots, b_n) \tag{8.7}$$

The prover's claim is that this sum is exactly K, and from now on, we can forget about the formula and concentrate only on this claim about the polynomial P_ϕ.

To start, the prover sends to the verifier a prime p in the interval $(2^n, 2^{2n}]$. The verifier can check that p is prime using a probabilistic or deterministic primality testing algorithm. All computations described here are done in the field $\mathbb{F} = \mathbb{F}_p$ of integers modulo p. Note that since the sum in (8.7) is between 0 and 2^n, this equation is true over the integers iff it is true modulo p. Thus, from now on we consider (8.7) as an equation in the field $\mathbb{F}_p$. We'll prove the theorem by showing a general protocol, *Sumcheck*, for verifying equations such as (8.7).

Sumcheck protocol

Given a degree d polynomial $g(X_1, \ldots, X_n)$, an integer K, and a prime p, we show how the prover can provide an interactive proof for the claim

$$K = \sum_{b_1 \in \{0,1\}} \sum_{b_2 \in \{0,1\}} \cdots \sum_{b_n \in \{0,1\}} g(X_1, \ldots, X_n) \tag{8.8}$$

where all computations are modulo p. To execute the protocol the only property of g that the verifier needs is that it has a poly(n) size representation and thus for any assignment of values for the variables from the field GF(p), say $X_1 = b_1, X_2 = b_2, \ldots, X_n = b_n$, the verifier can evaluate $g(b_1, b_2, \ldots, b_n)$ in polynomial time. As noted earlier, this property is satisfied by $g = P_\phi$.

For each sequence of values $b_2, b_3, \ldots, b_n$ to $X_2, X_3, \ldots, X_n$, note that $g(X_1, b_2, b_3, \ldots, b_n)$ is a univariate degree d polynomial in the variable X_1. Thus the following is also a univariate degree d polynomial:

$$h(X_1) = \sum_{b_2 \in \{0,1\}} \cdots \sum_{b_n \in \{0,1\}} g(X_1, b_2, \ldots, b_n) \tag{8.9}$$

If Claim (8.8) is true, then we must have $h(0) + h(1) = K$.

Consider the following protocol.

Protocol: Sumcheck Protocol to Check Claim (8.8)

V: If $n = 1$, check that $g(1) + g(0) = K$. If so accept; otherwise reject. If $n \geq 2$, ask P to send $h(X_1)$ as defined in (8.9).

P: Sends some polynomial $s(X_1)$ (if the prover is not "cheating," then we'll have $s(X_1) = h(X_1)$).

V: Reject if $s(0) + s(1) \neq K$; otherwise pick a random number a in $GF(p)$. Recursively use the same protocol to check that

$$s(a) = \sum_{b_2 \in \{0,1\}} \cdots \sum_{b_n \in \{0,1\}} g(a, b_2, \ldots j, b_n)$$

Claim *If (8.8) is false, then V rejects with probability at least $(1 - \frac{d}{p})^n$.*

The claim implies the theorem since if (8.8) is true, then the prover can make the V accept with probability 1, and with our choice of p, the $(1 - \frac{d}{p})^n$ is roughly $1 - dn/p$ and is very close to 1.

PROOF OF CLAIM: Assume that (8.8) is false. We prove the claim by induction on n. For $n = 1$, V simply evaluates $g(0), g(1)$ and rejects with probability 1 if their sum is not K. Assume the hypothesis is true for degree d polynomials in $n - 1$ variables.

In the first round, the prover P is supposed to return the polynomial h. If it indeed returns h, then since $h(0) + h(1) \neq K$ by assumption, V will immediately reject (i.e., with probability 1). So assume that the prover returns some $s(X_1)$ different from $h(X_1)$. Since the degree d nonzero polynomial $s(X_1) - h(X_1)$ has at most d roots, there are at most d values a such that $s(a) = h(a)$. Thus when V picks a random a,

$$\Pr_a[s(a) \neq h(a)] \geq 1 - \frac{d}{p} \tag{8.10}$$

If $s(a) \neq h(a)$, then the prover is left with an incorrect claim to prove in the recursive step. By the induction hypothesis, the prover fails to prove this false claim with probability at least $\geq \left(1 - \frac{d}{p}\right)^{n-1}$ Thus we have

$$\Pr[V \text{ rejects}] \geq \left(1 - \frac{d}{p}\right) \cdot \left(1 - \frac{d}{p}\right)^{n-1} = \left(1 - \frac{d}{p}\right)^n \tag{8.11}$$

This completes the proof of the claim and hence of Theorem 8.21. ∎

8.3.3 Protocol for TQBF: proof of Theorem 8.19

We use a very similar idea to obtain a protocol for TQBF. Given a quantified Boolean formula $\Psi = \forall x_1 \exists x_2 \forall x_3 \cdots \exists x_n \phi(x_1, \ldots, x_n)$, we use arithmetization to construct the polynomial P_ϕ. Thus $\Psi \in$ TQBF if and only if

$$\prod_{b_1 \in \{0,1\}} \sum_{b_2 \in \{0,1\}} \prod_{b_3 \in \{0,1\}} \cdots \sum_{b_n \in \{0,1\}} P_\phi(b_1, \ldots, b_n) \neq 0 \tag{8.12}$$

A first thought is that we could use the same protocol as in the $\#SAT_D$ case, except since the first variable x_1 is quantified with $\forall$, we check that $s(0) \cdot s(1) = K$, and do something analogous for all other variables that are quantified with $\forall$. There is nothing basically wrong with this apart from the running time. Multiplying polynomials, unlike addition, increases the degree. If we define $h(X_1)$ analogously as in (8.9) by making X_1 a free variable in (8.12), then its degree may be as high as 2^n. This polynomial may have 2^n coefficients and so cannot be transmitted to a polynomial-time verifier.

The solution is to observe that the claimed statement (8.12) only uses $\{0, 1\}$ values and for $x \in \{0, 1\}$, $x^k = x$ for all $k \geq 1$. Thus in principle we can convert any polynomial $p(X_1, \ldots, X_n)$ into a *multilinear* polynomial $q(X_1, \ldots, X_n)$ (i.e., the degree of $q(\cdot)$ in any variable X_i is at most one) that agrees with $p(\cdot)$ on all $X_1, \ldots, X_n \in \{0, 1\}$. Specifically, we define a *linearization* operator on polynomials where for any polynomial $p(\cdot)$ let $L_{X_i}(p)$ (or $L_i(p)$ for short) be the polynomial defined as follows:

$$L_{X_i}(p)(X_1, \ldots, X_n) = X_i \cdot p(X_1, \ldots, X_{i-1}, 1, X_{i+1}, \ldots, X_n)$$
$$+ (1 - X_i) \cdot p(X_1, \ldots, X_{i-1}, 0, X_{i+1}, \ldots, X_n) \tag{8.13}$$

Thus $L_i(p)$ is linear in X_i and agrees with $p(\cdot)$ whenever $X_i \in \{0, 1\}$. So $L_1(L_2(\cdots (L_n(p) \cdots)$ is a multilinear polynomial agreeing with $p(\cdot)$ on all values in $\{0, 1\}$.

We will also think of $\forall x_i$ and $\exists x_i$ as operators on polynomials where

$$\forall_{X_i} p(X_1, X_2, \ldots, X_n) = p(X_1, \ldots, X_{i-1}, 0, X_{i+1}, \ldots, X_n)$$
$$\cdot p(X_1, \ldots, X_{i-1}, 1, X_{i+1}, \ldots, X_n) \tag{8.14}$$

$$\exists_{X_i} p(X_1, X_2, \ldots, X_n) = p(X_1, \ldots, X_{i-1}, 0, X_{i+1}, \ldots, X_n)$$
$$+ p(X_1, \ldots, X_{i-1}, 1, X_{i+1}, \ldots, X_n) \tag{8.15}$$

Thus the claim (8.12) may be rephrased as follows: If we apply the sequence of operators $\forall_{X_1} \exists_{X_2} \forall_{X_3} \cdots \exists_{X_n}$ (where $\exists_{X_n}$ is applied first and $\forall_{X_1}$ is applied last) on the polynomial $P_\phi(X_1, \ldots, X_n)$, then we get a nonzero value K.

As observed, since this claim only concerns values taken when variables are in $\{0, 1\}$, it is unaffected if we sprinkle in any arbitrary sequence of the linearization operators in between. We will sprinkle in linearization operators so that the intermediate polynomials arising in our sum check protocol all have low degree. Specifically, we use the expression

$$\forall_{X_1} L_1 \exists_{X_2} L_1 L_2 \forall_{X_3} L_1 L_2 L_3 \cdots \exists_{X_n} L_1 L_2 L_3 \cdots L_n P_\phi(X_1, \ldots, X_n)$$

The size of the expression is $O(1 + 2 + 3 + \cdots + n) = O(n^2)$.

Now we give an inductive description of the protocol. Suppose for some polynomial $g(X_1, \ldots, X_k)$ the prover has the ability to convince the verifier that $g(a_1, a_2, \ldots, a_k) = C$ with probability 1 for any $a_1, a_2, \ldots, a_k, C$ when this is true and probability less than ϵ when it is false. Let $U(X_1, X_2, \ldots, X_l)$ be any polynomial on l variables obtained as

$$U(X_1, X_2, \ldots, X_l) = \mathcal{O}g(X_1, \ldots, X_k)$$

where $\mathcal{O}$ is either $\exists_{X_i}$, or $\forall_{X_i}$ or L_{X_i} for some variable. (Thus l is $k - 1$ in the first two cases and k in the third.) Let d be an upper bound (known to the verifier) on the degree of U with respect to x_i. (In our case, $d \leq 3m$.) We show how the prover can convince the verifier that $U(a_1, a_2, \ldots, a_l) = C'$ with probability 1 for any $a_1, a_2, \ldots, a_k, C'$ for which it is true and with probability at most $\epsilon + d/p$ when it is false.

By renaming variables if necessary, assume $i = 1$. The verifier's check is as follows.

Case 1: $\mathcal{O} = \exists_{X_1}$. The prover provides a degree d polynomial $s(X_1)$ that is supposed to be $g(X_1, a_2, \ldots, a_k)$.

Verifier checks if $s(0) + s(1) = C'$. If not, it rejects. If yes, it picks a random value $a \in \mathbb{F}_p$ and asks prover to prove $s(a) = g(a, a_2, \ldots, a_k)$.

Case 2: $O = \forall_{X_1}$. Same as above but use $s(0) \cdot s(1)$ instead of $s(0) + s(1)$.

Case 3: $O = L_{X_1}$. Prover wishes to prove that $U(a_1, a_2, \ldots, a_k) = C'$. Prover provides a degree d polynomial $s(X_1)$ that is supposed to be $g(X_1, a_2, \ldots, a_k)$.

Verifier checks if $a_1 s(0) + (1 - a_1)s(1) = C'$. If not, it rejects. If yes, it picks random $a \in \mathbb{F}_p$ and asks prover to prove $s(a) = g(a, a_2, \ldots, a_k)$.

The proof of correctness follows as in case of $\#SAT_D$, by using the observation that if $s(X_1)$ is not the right polynomial, then with probability $1 - d/p$ the prover is still stuck with proving an incorrect statement at the next round. ∎

An alternative proof of Theorem 8.19 is outlined in Exercise 8.8.

8.4 THE POWER OF THE PROVER

A curious feature of many known interactive proof systems is that in order to prove membership in language L, the prover needs to do more powerful computation than just deciding membership in L. We give some examples.

1. The public-coin system for graph nonisomorphism in Theorem 8.13 requires the prover to produce, for some randomly chosen hash function h and a random element y in the range of h, a graph H such that $h(H)$ is isomorphic to either G_1 or G_2 and $h(x) = y$. This seems harder than just solving graph nonisomorphism (though we do not know of any proof that it is).

2. The interactive proof for $\overline{3SAT}$, a language in **coNP**, requires the prover to at the very least be able to compute $\#SAT_D$, which is not known to be computable in polynomial time even if we have an oracle for $\overline{3SAT}$. In fact we see in Chapter 17 that the ability to compute $\#SAT_D$ is **#P**-complete, which implies $\mathbf{PH} \subseteq \mathbf{P}^{\#SAT_D}$.

In both cases, it is an open problem whether the protocol can be redesigned to use a weaker prover. By contrast, the protocol for TQBF is different from the previous protocols in that the prover requires no more computational power than the ability to compute TQBF—the reason is that, as mentioned, the prover's replies can be computed in **PSPACE**, which reduces to TQBF. This observation underlies the following result, which is in the same spirit as the Karp-Lipton results described in Chapter 6, except the conclusion is stronger since **MA** is contained in Σ_2 (indeed, **MA**-proof system for L with perfect completeness trivially implies that $L \in \Sigma_2$). See also Lemma 20.18 in Chapter 20 for a related result.

Theorem 8.22 *If* **PSPACE** $\subseteq$ **P$_{/poly}$** *then* **PSPACE** = **MA**.   ◇

PROOF: If **PSPACE** $\subseteq$ **P$_{/poly}$**, then the prover in our TQBF protocol can be replaced by a circuit of polynomial size. Merlin (the prover) can just give this circuit to Arthur (the verifier) in Round 1, and Arthur then runs the interactive proof using this "prover." No more interaction is needed. Note that there is no need for Arthur to put blind trust in Merlin's circuit, since the correctness proof of the TQBF protocol shows that if the formula is not true, then *no* prover can make Arthur accept with high probability. ∎

8.5 MULTIPROVER INTERACTIVE PROOFS (MIP)

It is also possible to define interactive proofs that involve more than one prover. The important assumption is that the provers do not communicate with each other *during the protocol*. They may communicate *before* the protocol starts and, in particular, agree upon a shared strategy for answering questions. The analogy often given is that of the police interrogating two suspects in separate rooms. The suspects may be accomplices who have decided upon a common story to tell the police, but since they are interrogated separately, they may inadvertently reveal an inconsistency in the story.

The set of languages with multiprover interactive provers is called **MIP**. The formal definition is analogous to Definition 8.6. We assume there are two provers (allowing polynomially many provers does not change the class; see Exercise 8.12), and in each round the verifier sends a query to each of them—the two queries need not be the same. Each prover sends a response in each round.

Clearly, **IP** $\subseteq$ **MIP** since the verifier can always simply ignore one prover. However, it turns out that **MIP** is probably strictly larger than **IP** (unless **PSPACE** = **NEXP**). That is, we have the following theorem.

Theorem 8.23 *(*[BFL90]*)* **NEXP** = **MIP**.   ◇

We will say more about this theorem in Chapter 11, as well as a related class called **PCP**. Intuitively, one reason why two provers are more useful than one is that the second prover can be used to force *nonadaptivity*. That is, consider the interactive proof as an "interrogation" where the verifier asks questions and gets back answers from the prover. If the verifier wants to ensure that the answer of a prover to the question q is a function only of q and does not depend on the previous questions the prover heard, the prover can ask the second prover the question q and accept only if both answers agree with one another. This technique was used to show that multiprover interactive proofs can be used to implement (and in fact are equivalent to) a model of a "probabilistically checkable proof in the sky." In this model, we go back to an **NP**-like notion of a proof as a static string, but this string may be huge and so is best thought of as a huge table, consisting of the prover's answers to all the possible verifier's questions. The verifier checks the proof by looking at only a few entries in this table that are chosen randomly from some distribution. If we let the class **PCP**$[r, q]$ be the set of languages that can be proven using a table of size 2^r and q queries to this table then Theorem 8.23 can be restated as follows:

Theorem 8.24 *(Theorem 8.23, restated)* **NEXP** = **PCP**[poly, poly] = $\cup_c$**PCP**$[n^c, n^c]$. ◇

It turns out Theorem 8.23 can be scaled down to to obtain **NP** = **PCP**[polylog, polylog]. In fact (with a lot of work) the following has been shown; see Chapter 11.

Theorem 8.25 *(The **PCP** Theorem, [AS92, ALM+92])* **NP** = **PCP**$[O(\log n), O(1)]$. ◇

This theorem, which is described in Chapter 11 and proven in Chapter 22, has had many applications in complexity, and in particular establishes that for many **NP**-complete optimization problems, obtaining an *approximately optimal* solution is as hard as coming up with the optimal solution itself. Thus, it seems that complexity theory has come full circle with interactive proofs: By starting with **NP** and adding interaction, randomization, and multiple provers to it, we get to classes as high as **NEXP**, and then end up with new and fundamental insights about the class **NP**.

8.6 PROGRAM CHECKING

The discovery of the interactive protocol for $\#\text{SAT}_D$ was triggered by a research area called *program checking*, sometimes also called *instance checking*. Blum and Kannan initiated this area motivated by the observation that even though program verification— deciding whether or not a given program solves a certain computational task on all inputs—is undecidable, in many situations it would suffice to have a weaker guarantee of the program's "correctness" on an input-by-input basis. This is encapsulated in the notion of a *program checker*. A checker for a program P is another program that may run P as a subroutine. Whenever P is run on an input, C's job is to detect if P's answer is incorrect ("buggy") on that particular input. To do this, the checker may also compute P's answer on some other inputs. Formally, the checker C is a TM that expects to have the code of another program, which it uses as a black box. We denote by C^P the result of running C when it is provided P as a subroutine.

Definition 8.26 Let T be a computational task. A *checker* for T is a probabilistic polynomial-time TM C that, given any program P that is a claimed program for T and any input x, has the following behavior:

1. If P is a correct program for T (i.e., $\forall y\ P(y) = T(y)$), then $P[C^P$ accepts $P(x)] \geq \frac{2}{3}$.
2. If $P(x) \neq T(x)$, then $P[C^P$ accepts $P(x)] < \frac{1}{3}$.   ◇

Note that checkers don't certify the correctness of a program. Furthermore, even in the case that P is correct on x (i.e., $P(x) = C(x)$) but the program P is not correct on inputs other than x, the output of the checker is allowed to be arbitrary.

Surprisingly, for many problems, checking seems easier than actually computing the problem. Blum and Kannan suggested that one should build such checkers into the software for these problems; the overhead introduced by the checker would be negligible and the program would be able to automatically check its work.

EXAMPLE 8.27 (Checker for graph nonisomorphism)

The input for the problem of graph nonisomorphism is a pair of labeled graphs $\langle G_1, G_2 \rangle$, and the problem is to decide whether $G_1 \cong G_2$. As noted, we do not know of an efficient algorithm for this problem. But it has an efficient checker.

There are two types of inputs depending upon whether or not the program claims $G_1 \cong G_2$. If it claims that $G_1 \cong G_2$ then one can change the graph little by little and use the program to actually obtain a permutation π mapping G_1 to G_2 (or if this fails, finds a bug in the program; see Exercise 8.11). We now show how to check the claim that $G_1 \not\cong G_2$ using our earlier interactive proof of graph nonisomorphism.

Recall the IP for graph nonisomorphism:

- In case prover admits $G_1 \not\cong G_2$, repeat k times:
- Choose $i \in_R \{1, 2\}$. Permute G_i randomly into H.
- Ask the prover whether G_1, H are isomorphic and check to see if the answer is consistent with the earlier answer.

Given a computer program P that supposedly computes graph isomorphism, how would we check its correctness? The program checking approach suggests we use an IP while regarding the program as the prover. Let C be a program that performs the above protocol using as prover the claimed program P.

Theorem 8.28 *If P is a correct program for graph nonisomorphism, then C outputs "correct" always. Otherwise, if $P(G_1, G_2)$ is incorrect then $P[C$ outputs "correct"$] \leq 2^{-k}$. Moreover, C runs in polynomial time.* ◇

8.6.1 Languages that have checkers

Whenever a language L has an interactive proof system where the prover can be implemented using oracle access to L, this implies that L has a checker. Thus the following theorem is a fairly straightforward consequence of the interactive proofs we have seen.

Theorem 8.29 *The problems Graph Isomorphism* (GI), $\#SAT_D$ *and True Quantified Boolean Formulas* (TQBF) *have checkers.* ◇

Similarly, it can be shown [Rub90] that problems that are random self-reducible and downward self-reducible also have checkers. (For a definition of downward self-reducibility, see Exercise 8.9.)

Using the fact that **P**-complete languages are reducible to each other via **NC**-reductions (in fact, even via the weaker logspace reductions), it suffices to show a checker in **NC** for one **P**-complete language (as was shown by Blum and Kannan) to obtain the following interesting fact.

Theorem 8.30 *For any **P**-complete language, there exists a program checker in **NC**.* ◇

Since we believe that **P**-complete languages cannot be computed in **NC**, this provides additional evidence that checking is easier than actual computation.

Blum and Kannan actually provide a precise characterization of languages that have checkers using interactive proofs, but it is omitted here because it is technical.

8.6.2 Random self-reducibility and the permanent

Most checkers are designed by observing that the output of the program at x should be related to its output at some other points. The simplest such relationship, which holds for many interesting problems, is random self-reducibility.

Roughly speaking, a problem is *random-self-reducible* if solving the problem on any input x can be reduced to solving the problem on a sequence of random inputs $y_1, y_2, \ldots,$ where each y_i is uniformly distributed among all inputs. (The correct definition is more general and technical, but this vague one will suffice here.) This property is important in understanding the average-case complexity of problems, an angle that is addressed further in Theorem 8.33 and Section 19.4.

EXAMPLE 8.31

Suppose a function $f : \mathrm{GF}(2)^n \to \mathrm{GF}(2)$ is linear; that is, there exist coefficients $a_1, a_2, \ldots, a_n$ such that $f(x_1, x_2, \ldots, x_n) = \sum_i a_i x_i$.

Then for any $\mathbf{x}, \mathbf{y} \in \mathrm{GF}(2)^n$ we have $f(\mathbf{x}) + f(\mathbf{y}) = f(\mathbf{x} + \mathbf{y})$. This fact can be used to show that computing f is *random-self-reducible*. If we want to compute $f(\mathbf{x})$ where x is aribitrary, it suffices to pick a random $\mathbf{y}$ and compute $f(\mathbf{y})$ and $f(\mathbf{x} + \mathbf{y})$, and both $\mathbf{y}$ and $\mathbf{x} + \mathbf{y}$ are random vectors (though not independently distributed) in $\mathrm{GF}(2)^n$ (Aside: This simple observation will appear later in a different context in the linearity test of Chapter 11.)

Example 8.31 may appear trivial, but in fact some very nontrivial problems are also random-self-reducible. The *permanent* of a matrix is superficially similar to the determinant and is defined as follows.

Definition 8.32 Let $A \in F^{n \times n}$ be a matrix over the field F. The permanent of A is

$$\mathrm{perm}(A) = \sum_{\sigma \in S_n} \prod_{i=1}^{n} a_{i,\sigma(i)} \qquad (8.16)$$

◇

The problem of calculating the permanent is clearly in **PSPACE**. In Chapter 17 we will see that computing the permanent is **#P**-complete, which means that it is essentially equivalent to $\#SAT_D$. In particular, if the permanent can be computed in polynomial time then $\mathbf{P} = \mathbf{NP}$. Here we show that the permanent is random-self-reducible. The main observation used is that if we think of $perm(A)$ as a function of n^2 variables (denoting the entries of the matrix A), then by (8.16) this function is a polynomial of degree n.

Theorem 8.33 *(Lipton [Lip91]) There is a randomized algorithm that, given an oracle that can compute the permanent on $1 - \frac{1}{3n}$ fraction of the inputs in $\mathbb{F}^{n \times n}$ (where the finite field $\mathbb{F}$ has size $> 3n$), can compute the permanent on all inputs correctly with high probability.* ◇

PROOF: Let A be some input matrix. Pick a random matrix $R \in_R \mathbb{F}^{n \times n}$ and let $B(x) = A + x \cdot R$ for a variable x. Notice that

- $perm(B(x))$ is a degree n univariate polynomial.
- For any fixed $a \neq 0$, $B(a)$ is a random matrix, and hence the probability that the oracle computes $perm(B(a))$ correctly is at least $1 - \frac{1}{3n}$.

Now the algorithm for computing the permanent of A is straightforward. Fix any $n + 1$ distinct points $a_1, a_2, \ldots, a_{n+1}$ in the field and query the oracle on all matrices $\{B(a_i) | 1 \leq i \leq n + 1\}$. According to the union bound, with probability of at least $1 - \frac{n+1}{n} \approx \frac{2}{3}$, the oracle will compute the permanent correctly on all matrices. Recall the fact (see Theorem A.35) that given $n + 1$ (point, value) pairs $\{(a_i, b_i) | i \in [n + 1]\}$, there exists a unique degree n polynomial p that satisfies $\forall i \; p(a_i) = b_i$. Therefore, given that the values $B(a_i)$ are correct, the algorithm can interpolate the polynomial $B(x)$ and compute $B(0) = perm(A)$. ∎

The hypothesis of Theorem 8.33 can be weakened so that the oracle only needs to compute the permanent correctly on a fraction of $\frac{1}{2} + \varepsilon$ for any constant $\varepsilon > 0$ of the inputs. This uses a stronger interpolation theorem; see Section 19.6.

8.7 INTERACTIVE PROOF FOR THE PERMANENT

Although the existence of an interactive proof for the Permanent follows from that for $\#SAT$ and $TQBF$, we describe a specialized protocol as well. This is both for historical context (this protocol was discovered before the other two protocols) and also because this protocol may be helpful for further research.

The protocol will use the random-self-reducibility of the permanent and downward self-reducibility, a property encountered in Chapter 2 in the context of SAT (see also Exercise 8.9). In the case of permanent, this is the observation that

$$perm(A) = \sum_{i=1}^{n} a_{1i} perm(A_{1,i})$$

where $A_{1,i}$ is a $(n - 1) \times (n - 1)$ submatrix of A obtained by removing the first row and ith column of A (recall that the analogous formula for the determinant uses alternating signs). Thus computing the $n \times n$ permanent reduces to computing n permanents of $(n - 1) \times (n - 1)$ matrices.

For ease of notation, we assume the field $\mathbb{F}$ is equal to $GF(p)$ for some prime $p > n$, and so $1, 2, \ldots, n \in \mathbb{F}$, and reserve a_{ij} for the (i, j)th element of the matrix. For every $n \times n$ matrix A, and $i \in [n]$, we define $D_A(i)$ to be the $(n - 1) \times (n - 1)$ matrix $A_{1,i}$. If $x \in \mathbb{F} \setminus [n]$; then we define $D_A(x)$ in the unique way such that for every $j, k \in [n-1]$, the function $(D_A(x))_{j,k}$ is a univariate polynomial of degree at most n. Note that since the permanent of an $(n - 1) \times (n - 1)$ matrix is a degree-$(n - 1)$ polynomial in the entries of the matrix, $\mathrm{perm}(D_A(x))$ is a univariate polynomial of degree at most $(n - 1)n < n^2$.

8.7.1 The protocol

We now show an interactive proof for the permanent. Specifically, define L_{perm} to contain all tuples $\langle A, p, k \rangle$ such that $p > n^4$ is prime, A is an $n \times n$ matrix over $GF(p)$, and $\mathrm{perm}(A) = k$. We prove the following theorem.

Theorem 8.34 $L_{\mathrm{perm}} \in \mathbf{IP}$.   ◇

PROOF: The proof is by induction—we assume that we have an interactive proof for matrices up to size $(n - 1)$, and show a proof for $n \times n$ matrices. That is, we assume inductively that for each $(n - 1) \times (n - 1)$ matrix B, the prover can make the verifier accept the claim $\mathrm{perm}(B) = k'$ with probability 1 if it is true and with probability at most ϵ if it is false. (Clearly, in the base case when $n - 1 = 1$, the permanent computation is trivial for the verifier and hence $\epsilon = 0$ in the base case.) Then we show that for every $n \times n$ matrix A the prover can make the verifier accept the claim $\mathrm{perm}(A) = k$ with probability 1 if it is true and with probability at most $\epsilon + (n - 1)^2/p$ if it is false. The following simple exchange shows this.

- *Round 1:* Prover sends to verifier a polynomial $g(x)$ of degree $(n - 1)^2$, which is supposedly $\mathrm{perm}(D_A(x))$.
- *Round 2:* Verifier checks whether: $k = \sum_{i=1}^{m} a_{1,i} g(i)$. If not, it rejects at once. Otherwise, the verifier picks a random element of the field $b \in_R \mathbb{F}_p$ and asks the prover to prove that $g(b) = \mathrm{perm}(D_A(b))$. Notice, $D_A(b)$ is an $(n - 2) \times (n - 2)$ matrix over $\mathbb{F}_p$, and so now use the inductive hypothesis to design a protocol for this verification.

Now we analyze this protocol. If $\mathrm{perm}(A) = k$, then an all-powerful prover can provide $\mathrm{perm}(D_A(x))$ and thus by the inductive hypothesis make the verifier accept with probability 1.

On the other hand, suppose that $\mathrm{perm}(A) \neq k$. If in the first round, the polynomial $g(x)$ sent is the correct polynomial $\mathrm{perm}(D_A(x))$, then

$$\sum_{i=1}^{m} a_{1,i} g(i) = \mathrm{perm}(A) \neq k$$

and the verifier would immediately reject. Hence we only need to consider a prover that sends $g(x) \neq \mathrm{perm}(D_A(x))$. Since two polynomials of degree $(n - 1)^2$ can only agree for less than $(n - 1)^2$ values of x, the chance that the randomly chosen $b \in \mathbb{F}_p$ is one of them is at most $(n - 1)^2/p$. if b is not one of these values, then the prover is stuck with proving an incorrect claim, which by the inductive hypothesis he can prove with conditional probability at most ϵ. This finishes the proof of correctness.

Unwrapping the inductive claim, we see that the probability that the prover can convince this verifier about an incorrect value of the permanent of an $n \times n$ matrix is at most

$$\frac{(n-1)^2}{p} + \frac{(n-2)^2}{p} + \cdots + \frac{1}{p} \leq \frac{n^3}{p}$$

which is much smaller than $1/3$ for our choice of p. $\blacksquare$

WHAT HAVE WE LEARNED?

- An *interactive proof* is a generalization of mathematical proofs in which the prover and polynomial-time probabilistic verifier interact.
- Allowing randomization and interaction seems to add significantly more power to proof system: The class **IP** of languages provable by a polynomial-time interactive proofs is equal to **PSPACE**.
- All languages provable by a *constant round* proof system are in the class **AM**; that is, they have a proof system consisting of the the verifier sending a single random string to the prover, and the prover responding with a single message.
- Interactive proofs have surprising connections to cryptography, approximation algorithms (rather, their nonexistence), and program checking.

CHAPTER NOTES AND HISTORY

Interactive proofs were defined in 1985 by Goldwasser, Micali, and Rackoff [GMR85] for cryptographic applications and (independently, and using the public-coin definition) by Babai [Bab85]; see also Babai and Moran [BM88]. The private-coins interactive proof for graph non-isomorphism was given by Goldreich, Micali, and Wigderson [GMW87]. Simulations of private coins by public coins (Theorem 8.12) were given by Goldwasser and Sipser [GS87] (see [Gol08, Appendix A] for a good exposition of the full proof). It was influenced by earlier results such as **BPP** $\subseteq$ **PH** (Section 7.5.2) and the fact that one can approximate $\#\mathsf{SAT}_\mathsf{D}$ in $\mathbf{P}^{\Sigma_2^p}$. *Multiprover* interactive proofs were defined by Ben-Or et al. [BOGKW88] for the purposes of obtaining zero-knowledge proof systems for **NP** (see also Section 9.4) without any cryptographic assumptions.

The general feeling at the time was that interactive proofs are only a "slight" extension of **NP** and that not even $\overline{\mathsf{3SAT}}$ has interactive proofs. For example, Fortnow and Sipser [FS88] conjectured that this is the case and even showed an oracle O relative to which $\mathbf{coNP}^O \not\subseteq \mathbf{IP}^O$ (thus in the terminology of Section 3.4, **IP** = **PSPACE** is a *nonrelativizing* theorem).

The result that **IP** = **PSPACE** was a big surprise, and the story of its discovery is very interesting. In the late 1980s, Blum and Kannan [BK95] introduced the notion of program checking. Around the same time, Beaver and Feigenbaum [BF90] and Lipton [Lip91] published papers appeared that fleshed out the notion of random-self-reducibility and the connection to checking. Inspired by some of these developments,

Nisan proved in December 1989 that the permanent problem (hence also $\#SAT_D$) has *multiprover* interactive proofs. He announced his proof in an email to several colleagues and then left on vacation to South America. This email motivated a flurry of activity in research groups around the world. Lund, Fortnow, and Karloff showed that $\#SAT_D$ is in **IP** (they added Nisan as a coauthor and the final paper is [LFKN90]). Then Shamir showed that **IP** =**PSPACE** [Sha90] and Babai, Fortnow, and Lund [BFL90] showed **MIP** = **NEXP**. This story—as well as subsequent developments such as the **PCP** Theorem—is described in Babai's entertaining surveys [Bab90, Bab94]. See also the chapter notes to Chapter 11.

The proof of **IP** = **PSPACE** using the linearization operator is due to Shen [She92]. The question about the power of the prover is related to the complexity of decision versus search, as explored by Bellare and Goldwasser [BG94]; see also Vadhan [Vad00]. Theorem 8.30 has been generalized to languages within **NC** by Goldwasser et al. [GGH+07].

The result that approximating the shortest vector to within a $\sqrt{n/\log n}$ is in **AM**[2] and hence probably not **NP**-hard (as mentioned in the introduction) is due to Goldreich and Goldwasser [GG98]. Aharonov and Regev [AR04] proved that approximating this problem to within $\sqrt{n}$ is in **NP** ∩ **coNP**.

EXERCISES

8.1. Prove the assertions about IP made in Section 8.1. That is, prove:

    (a) Let **IP'** denote the class obtained by allowing the prover to be probabilistic in Definition 8.6. That is, the prover's strategy can be chosen at random from some distribution on functions. Prove that **IP'** = **IP**.

    (b) Prove that **IP** ⊆ **PSPACE**.

    (c) Let **IP'** denote the class obtained by changing the constant 2/3 in (8.2) to 1. Prove that **IP'** = **IP**.

    H534

    (d) Let **IP'** denote the class obtained by changing the constant 1/3 in (8.3) to 0. Prove that **IP'** = **NP**.

8.2. Let **IP'** denote the class obtained by requiring in the completeness condition (8.2) that there exists a single prover P for every $x \in L$ (rather than for every $x \in L$ there is a prover). Prove that **IP'** = **IP**.

8.3. Show that **AM**[2] = **BP** · **NP**.

8.4. Let $k \leq n$. Prove that the following family $\mathcal{H}_{n,k}$ is a collection of pairwise independent functions from $\{0, 1\}^n$ to $\{0, 1\}^k$: Identify $\{0, 1\}$ with the field GF(2). For every $k \times n$ matrix A with entries in GF(2), and $\mathbf{b} \in GF(2)^k$, $\mathcal{H}_{n,k}$ contains the function $h_{A,\mathbf{b}} :$ $GF(2)^n \rightarrow GF(2)^k$ defined as $h_{A,\mathbf{b}}(x) = Ax + \mathbf{b}$.

8.5. Prove that there exists a perfectly complete **AM**[$O(1)$] protocol for proving a lower bound on set size.

    H534

8.6. Prove that for every **AM**[2] protocol for a language L, if the prover and the verifier repeat the protocol k times in parallel (verifier runs k independent random strings for each message) and the verifier accepts only if all k copies accept, then the probability that the verifier accepts $x \notin L$ is at most $(1/3)^k$. (Note that you *cannot* assume the prover is acting independently in each execution.) Can you generalize your proof for every k?

8.7. (Babai-Moran [BM88]) Prove that for every constant $k \geq 2$, **AM**$[k+1] \subseteq$ **AM**$[k]$.
H534

8.8. In this exercise we explore an alternative way to generalize the proof that **coNP** $\subseteq$ **IP** to show that **IP** = **PSPACE**.

    (a) Suppose that φ is a QBF formula (not necessarily in prenex form) satisfying the following property: If $x_1, \ldots, x_n$ are φ's variable sorted according to their order of appearance, then every variable x_i there is at most a single universal quantifier involving x_j (for $j > i$) appearing before the last occurrence of x_i in φ. Show that, in this case, when we run the sumcheck protocol of Section 8.3.2 with the modification that we use the check $s(0) \cdot s(1) = K$ for product operations, the prover only needs to send polynomials of degree $O(n)$.
H534

    (b) Show that we can transform every size n QBF formula ψ into a logically equivalent size $O(n^2)$ formula φ with the above property.
H534

8.9. Define a language L to be *downward-self-reducible* if there's a polynomial-time algorithm R that for any n and $x \in \{0, 1\}^n$, $R^{L_{n-1}}(x) = L(x)$ where by L_k we denote an oracle that solves L on inputs of size at most k. Prove that if L is downward-self-reducible, then $L \in$ **PSPACE**.

8.10. Complete the proof in Example 8.27 and show that graph isomorphism has a checker. Specifically, you have to show that if the program claims that $G_1 \cong G_2$, then we can do some further investigation (including calling the programs on other inputs) and with high probability conclude that either (a) the program was right on this input or (b) the program is wrong on *some* input and hence is not a correct program for graph isomorphism.

8.11. Show that **MIP** $\subseteq$ **NEXP**.

8.12. Show that if we redefine multiprover interactive proofs to allow, instead of two provers, as many as $m(n) = \text{poly}(n)$ provers on inputs of size n, then the class **MIP** is unchanged.
H535

CHAPTER 9

Cryptography

Human ingenuity cannot concoct a cipher which human ingenuity cannot resolve.

– E. A. Poe, 1841

In designing a good cipher ... it is not enough merely to be sure none of the standard methods of cryptanalysis work—we must be sure that no method whatever will break the system easily. This, in fact, has been the weakness of many systems. ... The problem of good cipher design is essentially one of finding difficult problems, subject to certain other conditions. This is a rather unusual situation, since one is ordinarily seeking the simple and easily soluble problems in a field.

– C. Shannon [Sha49b]

While the **NP** complete problems show promise for cryptographic use, current understanding of their difficulty includes only worst case analysis. For cryptographic purposes, typical computational costs must be considered.

– W. Diffie and M. Hellman [DH76]

Cryptography is much older than computational complexity. Ever since people began to write, they invented methods for "secret writing" that would be difficult to decipher for others. But the numerous methods of *encryption* or "secret writing" devised over the years all had one common characteristic—sooner or later they were broken. But everything changed in 1970s, when, thanks to the works of several researchers, *modern cryptography* was born, whereby computational complexity was used to argue about the security of the encryption schemes. In retrospect, this connection seems like a natural one, since the codebreaker has bounded computational resources (even if she has computers at her disposal) and therefore to ensure security one should try to ensure that the codebreaking problem is computationally difficult.

Another notable difference between modern cryptography and the older notion is that the security of encryption no longer relies upon the the encryption technique being kept secret. In modern cryptography, the encryption technique itself is well-known; nevertheless, it is hard to break. Furthermore modern cryptography is about much more than encryption and involves design of schemes for secure computation in a variety of settings. The security of all these schemes is proven by means of reductions similar (but not identical) to those used in the theory of **NP**-completeness.

This new focus on building cryptosystems from basic problems via reductions enabled modern cryptography to achieve two seemingly contradictory goals. On the one hand, these new schemes are much more secure—systems such as the RSA encryption [RSA78] have withstood more attacks by talented mathematicians assisted with state-of-the-art computers than every previous encryption in history. On the other hand, their security requirements are much more stringent—we require the schemes to remain secure even when the encryption key is known to the attacker (i.e., *public key* encryption), and even when the attacker gets access to encryptions and decryptions of text of her choice (so-called *chosen plaintext* and *chosen ciphertext* attacks). Moreover, modern cryptography provides schemes that go much beyond simple encryption—tools such as digital signatures, zero knowledge proofs, electronic voting and auctions, and more. All of these are shown to be secure against *every* polynomial-time attack, and not just attacks we can think of today, as long as the underlying computational problem is indeed hard.

Research on modern cryptography led to significant insights that had impact and applications in complexity theory and beyond. One is the notion of *pseudorandomness*. Philosophers and scientists have struggled for years to quantify when a bit string is "random enough." Cryptography's answer to this question is that it suffices if this string is drawn from a distribution that "looks random" to all *efficient* (i.e., polynomial-time) observers (see Section 9.2.3). This notion is crucial for the construction of many cryptographic schemes, but it is also extremely useful in other areas where random bits are needed. For example, cryptographic pseudorandom generators can be used to reduce the randomness requirements of *probabilistic algorithms* such as the ones we saw in Chapter 7; see also Chapter 20. Another new insight is the notion of *simulation*. A natural question in cryptography is how one can demonstrate that an attacker cannot learn *anything* about some secret information from observing the behavior of parties holding this information. Cryptography's answer is to show that the attacker's observations can be *simulated* without any access to the secret information. This is epitomized in the notion of *zero knowledge proofs* covered in Section 9.4, and used in many other cryptographic applications.

We start the chapter in Section 9.1 with Shannon's definition of *perfectly secret* encryption and the limitations of such systems. These limitations lead us to consider encryptions that are only secure against polynomial-time eavesdroppers—we construct these in Section 9.2 using *pseudorandom generators*. Then, in Section 9.2.3, we show how these generators can be constructed from seemingly weaker assumptions. In Section 9.4, we describe *zero knowledge proofs*, a fascinating concept that has had deep implications for cryptography and complexity alike. Finally, in Section 9.5 we sketch how these concepts can be used to achieve security in a variety of settings. Cryptography is a huge topic, and so naturally this chapter covers only a tiny sliver of it; the chapter notes contain some excellent choices for further reading. Cryptography is intimately related to other notions studied in this book such as *average-case complexity*, *hardness amplifications*, and *derandomization*; see chapters 18, 19, and 20.

9.1 PERFECT SECRECY AND ITS LIMITATIONS

The fundamental task of cryptography is *encryption*. In this section, we describe this task at a high level and discuss what it could possibly mean for encryption to be *secure*.

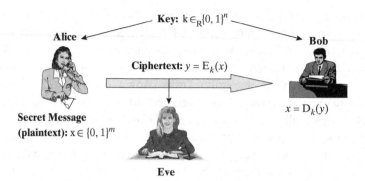

Figure 9.1. In a private key encryption, Alice and Bob share a secret key k chosen at random. To send a plaintext message x to Bob, Alice sends $y = \mathsf{E}_k(x)$ where $\mathsf{E}(\cdot)$ is the *encryption* function that takes a key k and plaintext x to compute the ciphertext y. Bob can decode x by running the decryption algorithm D on inputs k, y.

We introduce a simple idea for encryption called the *one time pad* which is shown to provide such security, but also shown to suffer from serious limitations.

The basic setting is described in Figure 9.1—Alice wants to send a secret message x (known as the *plaintext*) to Bob, but her adversary Eve is eavesdropping on the communication channel between Alice and Bob. Thus Alice will "scramble" the plaintext x using an *encryption algorithm* E to obtain a *ciphertext* y, which she sends to Bob. Presumably it will be hard or even impossible for Eve to decode the plaintext x from the ciphertext y, but Bob will be able to do so using the *decryption algorithm* D.

Of course, Bob is seeing the same information that Eve is, so in order to do something that Eve cannot, Bob has to know something that Eve doesn't. In the simple setting of private key encryption, we assume that Alice and Bob share some secret string k (known as the *key*) that is chosen at random. (Presumably, Alice and Bob met beforehand and agreed on the key k.)

Thus, the encryption scheme is composed of a pair of algorithms (E, D) each taking a key and a message (where we write the key input as a subscript), such that for every key k and plaintext x

$$\mathsf{D}_k(\mathsf{E}_k(x)) = x \tag{9.1}$$

The condition (9.1) says nothing about the *security* of the scheme and could be satisfied by the trivial "encryption" that just outputs the plaintext message. It turns out that defining security is quite subtle. A first attempt at a definition might be to say that a scheme is secure if Eve cannot compute x from $\mathsf{E}_k(x)$, but this may not be sufficient because this does not rule out the possibility of Eve computing some *partial information* on x. For example, if Eve knows that the plaintext is either the message "buy" or "sell", then it will be enough for her to learn only the first character of the message, even if she can't recover it completely. Shannon gave the following definition of secure private key encryption that ensures Eve does not learn *anything* about the plaintext from the ciphertext:

Definition 9.1 *(Perfect secrecy)* Let (E, D) be an encryption scheme for messages of length m and with a key of length n satisfying (9.1). We say that (E, D) is *perfectly secret* if for every pair of messages $x, x' \in \{0, 1\}^m$, the distributions $E_{U_n}(x)$ and $E_{U_n}(x')$ are identical.[1]   ◇

In a perfectly secret encryption, the ciphertext that Eve sees always has the same distribution, regardless of the plaintext, and so Eve gets absolutely no information on the plaintext. It might seem like a condition so strong that it's impossible to satisfy, but in fact there's a very simple perfectly secret encryption scheme. In the *one-time pad* scheme, to encrypt a message $x \in \{0, 1\}^n$ we choose a random key $k \in_R \{0, 1\}^n$ and encrypt x by simply sending $x \oplus k$ ($\oplus$ denotes bitwise XOR—vector addition modulo 2). The receiver can recover the message x from $y = x \oplus k$ by XORing y once again with k. It's not hard to see that the ciphertext is distributed uniformly regardless of the plaintext message encrypted, and hence the one-time pad is perfectly secret (see Exercise 9.1).

Of course, as the name suggests, a "one-time pad" must never be reused on another message. If two messages x, x' are encoded using the same pad k, this gives Eve both $k \oplus x$ and $k \oplus x'$, allowing her to compute $(k \oplus x) \oplus (k \oplus x') = x \oplus x'$, which is some nontrivial information about the messages. In fact, one can show (see Exercise 9.2) that no perfectly secret encryption scheme can use a key size shorter than the message size!

9.2 COMPUTATIONAL SECURITY, ONE-WAY FUNCTIONS, AND PSEUDORANDOM GENERATORS

Though a one-time pad does provide perfect secrecy, it fails utterly as a practical solution to today's applications where one wishes to securely exchange megabytes or even gigabytes of information. Our discussion above implies that perfect secrecy would require private keys that are as long as the messages, and it is unclear such huge keys can be securely exchanged among users. Ideally we want to keep the shared secret key fairly small, say a few hundred bits long. Obviously, to allow this, we must relax the perfect secrecy condition somehow. As stated in the introduction, the main idea will be to design encryption schemes that are secure only against eavesdroppers that are *efficient* (i.e., run in polynomial-time). However, the next lemma shows that even with this restriction on the eavesdropper, achieving perfect secrecy is impossible with small key sizes if $\mathbf{P} = \mathbf{NP}$. Hence assuming $\mathbf{P} \neq \mathbf{NP}$ will be *necessary* for proceeding any further. In fact we will rely on assumptions stronger than $\mathbf{P} \neq \mathbf{NP}$—specifically, the assumption that a *one-way function exists*. It is an important research problem to weaken the assumption (ideally to just $\mathbf{P} \neq \mathbf{NP}$) under which cryptographic schemes can be proven secure.

Lemma 9.2 *Suppose that* $\mathbf{P} = \mathbf{NP}$. *Let* (E, D) *be any polynomial-time computable encryption scheme satisfying (9.1) with key shorter than the message. Then, there is a polynomial-time algorithm A such that for every input length m, there is a pair of messages* $x_0, x_1 \in \{0, 1\}^m$ *satisfying:*

$$\Pr_{\substack{b \in_R \{0,1\} \\ k \in_R \{0,1\}^n}} [A(E_k(x_b)) = b] \geq 3/4 \tag{9.2}$$

where $n < m$ *denotes the key length for messages of length m.*   ◇

---

[1] Recall that U_n denotes the uniform distribution over $\{0, 1\}^n$.

Such an algorithm breaks the security of the encryption scheme since, as demonstrated by the "buy"/"sell" example of Section 9.1, a minimal requirement from an encryption is that Eve cannot tell which one of two random messages was encrypted with probability much better than $1/2$.

PROOF OF LEMMA 9.2: Let (E, D) be an encryption for messages of length m and with key length $n < m$ as in the lemma's statement. Let $S \subseteq \{0, 1\}^*$ denote the support of $E_{U_n}(0^m)$. Note that $y \in S$ if and only if $y = E_k(0^m)$ for some k; hence if $\mathbf{P} = \mathbf{NP}$, then membership in S can be efficiently verified. Our algorithm A will be very simple—on input y, it outputs 0 if $y \in S$, and 1 otherwise. We claim that setting $x_0 = 0^m$, there exists some $x_1 \in \{0, 1\}^m$ such that (9.2) holds.

Indeed, for every message x, let D_x denote the distribution $E_{U_n}(x)$. By the definition of A and the fact that $x_0 = 0^m$, $\Pr[A(D_{x_0}) = 0] = 1$. Because

$$\Pr_{\substack{b \in_R \{0,1\} \\ k \in_R \{0,1\}^n}}[A(E_k(x_b)) = b] = \frac{1}{2} \Pr[A(D_{x_0}) = 0] + \frac{1}{2} \Pr[A(D_{x_1}) = 1]$$

$$= \frac{1}{2} + \frac{1}{2} \Pr[A(D_{x_1}) = 1]$$

it suffices to show that there's some $x_1 \in \{0, 1\}^m$ such that $\Pr[A(D_{x_1}) = 1] \geq 1/2$. In other words, it suffices to show that $\Pr[D_{x_1} \in S] \leq 1/2$ for some $x_1 \in \{0, 1\}^m$.

Suppose otherwise that $\Pr[D_x \in S] > 1/2$ for every $x \in \{0, 1\}^m$. Define $S(x, k)$ to be 1 if $E_k(x) \in S$ and to be 0 otherwise, and let $T = E_{x \in_R \{0,1\}^m, k \in_R \{0,1\}^n}[S(x, k)]$. Then under our assumption, $T > 1/2$. But reversing the order of expectations, we see that

$$T = \underset{k \in \{0,1\}^n}{E}[\underset{x \in \{0,1\}^m}{E}[S(x, k)]] \leq 1/2$$

where the last inequality follows from the fact that for every fixed key k, the map $x \mapsto E_k(x)$ is one-to-one and hence at most $2^n \leq 2^m/2$ of the x's can be mapped under it to a set S of size $\leq 2^n$. Thus we obtained a contradiction to the assumption that $\Pr[D_x \in S] > 1/2$ for every $x \in \{0, 1\}^m$. ∎

Before proceeding further, we make a simple definition that will greatly simplify notation throughout this chapter.

Definition 9.3 (*Negligible functions*) A function $\epsilon : \mathbb{N} \to [0, 1]$ is called *negligible* if $\epsilon(n) = n^{-\omega(1)}$ (i.e., for every c and sufficiently large n, $\epsilon(n) < n^{-c}$).

Because negligible functions tend to zero very fast as their input grows, events that happen with negligible probability can be safely ignored in most practical and theoretical settings.

9.2.1 One way functions: Definition and some examples

The above discussion suggests that complexity-theoretic conjectures are necessary to prove the security of encryption schemes. Now we introduce an object that is useful not only in this context but also many others in cryptography. This is a *one-way function*—a function that is easy to compute but hard to invert for a polynomial-time algorithm.

Definition 9.4 *(One-way functions)* A polynomial-time computable function $f: \{0, 1\}^* \to \{0, 1\}^*$ is a *one-way function* if for every probabilistic polynomial-time algorithm A there is a negligible function $\epsilon : \mathbb{N} \to [0, 1]$ such that for every n,

$$\Pr_{\substack{x \in_R \{0,1\}^n \\ y=f(x)}} [A(y) = x' \text{ s.t. } f(x') = y] < \epsilon(n)$$

Conjecture 9.5 There exists a one-way function.

Exercise 9.5 asks you to show that Conjecture 9.5 implies that $\mathbf{P} \neq \mathbf{NP}$. Most researchers believe Conjecture 9.5 is true because there are several examples for functions that no one has yet been able to invert. Now we describe some of these examples.

Multiplication: Simple multiplication turns out to be hard to invert. That is, the function that treats its input $x \in \{0, 1\}^n$ as describing two $n/2$-bit numbers A and B and outputs $A \cdot B$ is believed to be one way. Inverting this function is known as the *integer factorization problem*. Of course, it's easy to factor a number N using at most N (or even only $\sqrt{N}$) trial divisions. But since N is represented by $\log N$ bits, this trivial algorithm is actually an exponential-time algorithm. At the moment, no polynomial (i.e., polylog(N)) time algorithm is known for this problem, and the best factoring algorithm runs in time $2^{O(\log^{1/3} N \sqrt{\log \log N})}$ [LLMP90].[2]

A more standard implementation of a one-way function based on factoring is the following. Treat the input $x \in \{0, 1\}^n$ as a random speed that is used to generate two random $n^{1/3}$-bit primes P and Q. (We can do so by generating random numbers and testing their primality using the algorithm described in Chapter 7.) Then output $P \cdot Q$.

Factoring integers has captured the attention of mathematicians for at least two millennia, way before the invention of computers. Yet no efficient factorization algorithm was found, leading to the conjecture that no such algorithm exists. Then this function is indeed one-way, though this conjecture is obviously much stronger than the conjecture that $\mathbf{P} \neq \mathbf{NP}$ or the conjecture that *some* one-way function exists.

RSA and Rabin functions: (These examples require a bit of number theory; see Section A.3 for a quick review.) The *RSA function*[3] is another very popular candidate for a one-way function. We assume that for every input length n there is an n-bit composite integer N that was generated in some way, and some number e that is coprime to $\varphi(N) = |\mathbb{Z}_N^*|$ where $\mathbb{Z}_N^*$ is the multiplicative group of numbers coprime to N. (Typically N would be generated as a product of two $n/2$-long primes; e is often set to be simply 3.) The function $RSA_{N,e}$ treats its input as a number X in $\mathbb{Z}_N^*$ and outputs X^e (mod N).[4] It can be shown that because e is coprime to $\varphi(N)$, this function is one-to-one on Z_N^*.

---

[2] If A and B are chosen randomly, then it's not hard to find *some* prime factor of $A \cdot B$, since $A \cdot B$ will have a small prime factor with high probability. But finding all the prime factors or even finding any representation of $A \cdot B$ as the multiplication of two numbers each no larger than $2^{n/2}$ can be shown to be equivalent (up to polynomial factor) to factoring the product of two random primes.

[3] RSA are the initials of this function's discoverers—Rivest, Shamir, and Adleman; see the chapter notes.

[4] We can map the input to $\mathbb{Z}_N^*$ by simply reducing the input modulo N—the probability (over the choice of the input) that the result will not be coprime to N is negligible.

A related candidate one-way function is the *Rabin function* that given a number N that is the product of two odd primes P, Q such that $P, Q = 1 \pmod 4$, maps $X \in QR_N$ into $X^2 \pmod N$, where QR_N is the set of *quadratic residues* modulo N (an element $X \in \mathbb{Z}_N^*$ is a quadratic residue modulo N if $X = W^2 \pmod N$ for some $W \in \mathbb{Z}_N^*$). Again, it can be shown that this function is one-to-one on QR_N.

While both the RSA function and the Rabin function are believed to be hard to invert, inverting them is actually easy if one knows the factorization of N. In the case of the RSA function, the factorization can be used to compute $\varphi(N)$ and from that the number d such that $d = e^{-1} \pmod{\varphi(N)}$. It's not hard to verify that the function Y^d $\pmod N$ is the inverse of the function $X^e \pmod N$. In the case of the Rabin function, if we know the factorization, then we can use the Chinese Remainder Theorem to reduce the problem of taking a square root modulo N to taking square roots modulo the prime factors of N, which can be done in polynomial time. Because these functions are conjectured to be hard to invert but become easy to invert once you know certain information (i.e., N's factorization), they are known as *trapdoor* one-way functions and are crucial to obtaining *public key* cryptography. It it known that inverting Rabin's function is in fact *computationally equivalent* to factoring N (see Exercise 9.7). No such equivalence is known for the RSA function.

Levin's universal one-way function: There is a function $f_\mathcal{U}$ that has a curious property: if any one-way function exists, *some* one-way function f, then $f_\mathcal{U}$ is also a one-way function. For this reason, the function $f_\mathcal{U}$ is called a *universal* one-way function. It is defined as follows: Treat the input as a list $x_1, \ldots, x_{\log n}$ of $n/\log n$ bit long strings. Output $M_1^{n^2}(x_1), \ldots, M_{\log n}^{n^2}(x_n)$ where M_i denotes the ith Turing machine according to some canonical representation, and we define $M^t(x)$ to be the output of the Turing machine M on input x if M uses at most t computational steps on input x. If M uses more than t computational steps on x, then we define $M^t(x)$ to be the all-zeroes string $0^{|x|}$. Exercise 9.6 asks you to prove the universality of $f_\mathcal{U}$.

There are also examples of candidate one-way functions that have nothing to do with number theory (e.g., one-way functions arising from block ciphers such as the AES [DR02] which work by repeatedly scrambling bits of the input in some way).

9.2.2 Encryption from one-way functions

Now we show that one-way functions can be used to design secure encryption schemes with keys much shorter than the message length.

Theorem 9.6 *(Encryption from one-way function)*
Suppose that one-way functions exist. Then for every $c \in \mathbb{N}$ there exists a computationally secure encryption scheme (E, D) using n-length keys for n^c-length messages.

Of course to make sense of Theorem 9.6, we need to define the term "computationally secure." The idea is to follow the intuition that a secure encryption should not reveal any partial information about the plaintext to a polynomial-time eavesdropper, but due to some subtleties, the actual definition is somewhat cumbersome. Thus, for the sake of presentation, we'll use a simpler relaxed definition that an encryption is "computationally secure" if any individual bit of the plaintext chosen at random cannot be guessed by the eavesdropper with probability nonnegligibly higher than $1/2$. That is, we say that a scheme (E, D) using length n keys for length m messages is computationally secure if for every probabilistic polynomial-time A, there's a negligible function $\epsilon : \mathbb{N} \to [0, 1]$ such that

$$\Pr_{\substack{k \in_R \{0,1\}^n \\ x \in_R \{0,1\}^m}} [A(E_k(x)) = (i, b) \text{ s.t. } x_i = b] \leq 1/2 + \epsilon(n) \qquad (9.3)$$

The full-fledged, stronger notion of computational security (whose standard name is *semantic security*) is developed in Exercise 9.9, where it is also shown that Theorem 9.6 holds also for this stronger notion.

9.2.3 Pseudorandom generators

Recall the one-time pad idea of Section 9.1, whose sole limitation was the need for a shared random string whose length is the same as the combined length of all the messages that need to be transmitted. The main idea in the proof of Theorem 9.6 is to show how to take a small random key of length n and stretch it to a much larger string of length m that is still "random enough" that it provides security against polynomial-time eavesdroppers when used as a one-time pad. This stretching of the random string uses a tool called a *pseudorandom generator*, which has applications even beyond cryptography.

EXAMPLE 9.7

What is a random-enough string? Scientists have struggled with this question before. Here is Kolmogorov's definition: *A string of length n is random if no Turing machine whose description length is $< 0.99n$ (say) outputs this string when started on an empty tape.* This definition is the "right" definition in some philosophical and technical sense (which we will not get into here) but is not very useful in the complexity setting because checking if a string is random according to this definition is undecidable.

Statisticians have also attempted definitions that boil down to checking if the string has the "right number" of patterns that one would expect by the laws of statistics (e.g., the number of times 11100 appears as a substring). (See [Knu73] for a comprehensive discussion.) It turns out that such definitions are too weak in the cryptographic setting: One can find a distribution that passes these statistical tests but still will be completely insecure if used to generate the pad for the one-time pad encryption scheme.

Cryptography's answer to the question posed in Example 9.7 is simple and satisfying. First, instead of trying to describe what it means for a single string to be "random-looking," we focus on distributions on strings. Second, instead of focusing on individual tester algorithms as the statisticians did, we say that the distribution has to "look" like the uniformly random distribution to *every* polynomial-time algorithm. Such a distribution is called *pseudorandom*. The distinguisher algorithm is given a sample string that is drawn from either the uniform distribution or the unknown distribution. The algorithm outputs "1" or "0" depending upon whether or not this string looks random to it. (An example of such an algorithm is the statistics-based tester of

Example 9.7.) The distribution is said to be *pseudorandom* if the probability that the polynomial-time algorithm outputs 1 is essentially the same on the two distributions, *regardless* of which algorithm is used.[5]

Definition 9.8 *(Secure pseudorandom generators)* Let $G : \{0, 1\}^* \to \{0, 1\}^*$ be a polynomial-time computable function. Let $\ell : \mathbb{N} \to \mathbb{N}$ be a polynomial-time computable function such that $\ell(n) > n$ for every n. We say that G is a *secure pseudorandom generator of stretch* $\ell(n)$, if $|G(x)| = \ell(|x|)$ for every $x \in \{0, 1\}^*$ and for every probabilistic polynomial-time A, there exists a negligible function $\epsilon : \mathbb{N} \to [0, 1]$ such that

$$\left| \Pr[A(G(U_n)) = 1] - \Pr[A(U_{\ell(n)}) = 1] \right| < \epsilon(n)$$

for every $n \in \mathbb{N}$.

Theorem 9.9 *(Pseudorandom generators from one-way functions [HILL99]* *If one-way functions exist, then for every $c \in \mathbb{N}$, there exists a secure pseudorandom generator with stretch $\ell(n) = n^c$.*

Definition 9.8 states that it's infeasible for polynomial-time adversaries to distinguish between a completely random string of length $\ell(n)$ and a string that was generated by applying the generator G to a much shorter random string of length n. Thus, it's not hard to verify that Theorem 9.9 implies Theorem 9.6: If we modify the one-time pad encryption to generate its n^c-length random key by applying a secure pseudorandom generator with stretch n^c to a shorter key of length n, then a polynomial-time eavesdropper would not be able to tell the difference. To see this, assume there is an adversary A that can predict a bit of the plaintext with probability noticeably larger than $1/2$, thus violating the computational security requirement (9.3). Then because such prediction is impossible when the key is truly random (see Exercise 9.3), A can be used to distinguish between a pseudorandom and truly random key, thus contradicting the security of the generator as per Definition 9.8. ∎

9.3 PSEUDORANDOM GENERATORS FROM ONE-WAY PERMUTATIONS

We will prove only the special case of Theorem 9.9 when the one-way function is a permutation.

Lemma 9.10 *Suppose that there exists a one-way function $f : \{0, 1\}^* \to \{0, 1\}^*$ such that f is one-to-one for every $x \in \{0, 1\}^*$, $|f(x)| = |x|$. Then, for every $c \in \mathbb{N}$, there exists a secure pseudorandom generator with stretch n^c.* ◇

The proof of Lemma 9.10 does demonstrate some of the ideas behind the proof of the more general Theorem 9.9. Moreover, these ideas, including the *hybrid argument*

---

[5] Note that this definition is reminiscent of a "blind test": For instance, we say that an artificial sweetner is "sugar-like" if the *typical* consumer cannot tell the difference between it and sugar in a blind-test. However, the definition of a pseudorandom distribution is more stringent since the distribution has to fool *all* distinguisher algorithms. The analogous notion for a sweetner would require it to taste like sugar to *every* human.

and the *Goldreich-Levin Theorem*, are of independent interest and have found several applications in other areas of computer science.

9.3.1 Unpredictability implies pseudorandomness

To prove Lemma 9.10, it will be useful to have the following alternative characterization of pseudorandom generators. Historically, this definition was the original definition proposed for the notion of *pseudorandom generator*. It is a weaker notion and hence easier to achieve by explicit constructions. Yao's proof that it is equivalent to Definition 9.8 was a major discovery.

Let $G : \{0, 1\}^* \to \{0, 1\}^*$ be a polynomial-time computable function with stretch $\ell(n)$ (i.e., $|G(x)| = \ell(|x|)$ for every $x \in \{0, 1\}^*$). We call G *unpredictable* if for every probabilistic polynomial-time B, there is a negligible function $\epsilon : \mathbb{N} \to [0, 1]$ such that

$$\Pr_{\substack{x \in_R \{0,1\}^n \\ y = G(x) \\ i \in_R [\ell(n)]}} [B(1^n, y_1, \ldots, y_{i-1}) = y_i] \leq 1/2 + \epsilon(n) \tag{9.4}$$

In other words, predicting the ith bit given the first $i - 1$ bits (where i is a randomly chosen index) is difficult for every polynomial-time algorithm.

Clearly, if G is a pseudorandom generator then it is also unpredictable. Indeed, if $y_1, \ldots, y_{\ell(n)}$ were uniformly chosen bits then it would be impossible to predict y_i given $y_1, \ldots, y_{i-1}$, and hence if such a predictor exists when $y = G(x)$ for a random x, then the predictor can distinguish between the distribution $U_{\ell(n)}$ and $G(U_n)$. Interestingly, the converse direction also holds.

Theorem 9.11 *(Unpredictability implies pseudorandomness* [Yao82a]*)*
Let $\ell : \mathbb{N} \to \mathbb{N}$ *be some polynomial-time computable function, and* $G : \{0, 1\}^* \to \{0, 1\}^*$ *be a polynomial-time computable function such that* $|G(x)| = \ell(|x|)$ *for every* $x \in \{0, 1\}^*$. *If* G *is unpredictable, then it is a secure pseudorandom generator. Moreover, for every probabilistic polynomial-time algorithm* A, *there exists a probabilistic polynomial-time* B *such that for every* $n \in \mathbb{N}$ *and* $\epsilon > 0$, *if* $\Pr[A(G(U_n)) = 1] - \Pr[A(U_{\ell(n)}) = 1] \geq \epsilon$, *then*

$$\Pr_{\substack{x \in_R \{0,1\}^n \\ y = G(x) \\ i \in_R [\ell(n)]}} [B(1^n, y_1, \ldots, y_{i-1}) = y_i] \geq 1/2 + \epsilon/\ell(n)$$

PROOF: First, note that the main result does follow from the "moreover" part. Indeed, suppose that G is not a pseudorandom generator and hence there is some algorithm A and constant c such that

$$\left| \Pr[A(G(U_n)) = 1] - \Pr[A(U_{\ell(n)}) = 1] \right| \geq n^{-c} \tag{9.5}$$

for infinitely many n's. Then we can ensure (perhaps by changing A to the algorithm $1 - A$ that flips the one-bit answer of A), that for infinitely many n's, (9.5) holds without the absolute value. For every such n, we'll get a predictor B that succeeds with probability $1/2 + n^{-c}/\ell(n)$, contradicting the unpredictability property.

We turn now to proving this "moreover" part. Let A be some probabilistic polynomial-time algorithm that is supposedly more likely to output 1 on inputs from the distribution $G(U_n)$ than on inputs from $U_{\ell(n)}$. Our predictor algorithm B will be quite simple: On input 1^n, $i \in [\ell(n)]$ and $y_1, \ldots, y_{i-1}$, Algorithm B will choose $z_i, \ldots, z_{\ell(n)}$ independently at random, and compute $a = A(y_1, \ldots, y_{i-1}, z_i, \ldots, z_{\ell(n)})$. If $a = 1$ then B surmises its guess for z_i is correct and outputs z_i; otherwise it outputs $1 - z_i$.

Let $n \in \mathbb{N}$ and $\ell = \ell(n)$ and suppose that $\Pr[A(G(U_n)) = 1] - \Pr[A(U_{\ell(n)}) = 1] \geq \epsilon$. We'll show that

$$\Pr_{\substack{x \in_R \{0,1\}^n \\ y=G(x) \\ i \in_R [\ell]}} [B(1^n, y_1, \ldots, y_{i-1}) = y_i] \geq 1/2 + \epsilon/\ell \tag{9.6}$$

To analyze B's performance, we define the following ℓ distributions $\mathcal{D}_0, \ldots, \mathcal{D}_\ell$ over $\{0, 1\}^\ell$. (This technique is called the *hybrid argument*.) For every i, the distribution $\mathcal{D}_i$ is obtained as follows: choose $x \in_R \{0, 1\}^n$ and let $y = G(x)$, output $y_1, \ldots, y_i, z_{i+1}, \ldots, z_\ell$, where $z_{i+1}, \ldots, z_\ell$ are chosen independently at random in $\{0, 1\}$. Note that $\mathcal{D}_0 = U_\ell$ while $\mathcal{D}_\ell = G(U_n)$. For every $i \in \{0, .., \ell\}$, define $p_i = \Pr[A(\mathcal{D}_i) = 1]$. Note that $p_\ell - p_0 \geq \epsilon$. Thus writing

$$p_\ell - p_0 = (p_\ell - p_{\ell-1}) + (p_{\ell-1} - p_{\ell-2}) + \cdots + (p_1 - p_0)$$

we get that $\sum_{i=1}^{\ell}(p_i - p_{i-1}) \geq \epsilon$ or in other words, $\mathrm{E}_{i \in [\ell]}[p_i - p_{i-1}] \geq \epsilon/\ell$. We will prove (9.6) by showing that for every i,

$$\Pr_{\substack{x \in_R \{0,1\}^n \\ y=G(x)}} [B(1^n, y_1, \ldots, y_{i-1}) = y_i] \geq 1/2 + (p_i - p_{i-1})$$

Recall that B makes a guess z_i for y_i and invokes A to obtain a value a, and then outputs z_i if $a = 1$ and $1 - z_i$ otherwise. Thus B predicts y_i correctly if either $a = 1$ and $y_i = z_i$ or $a \neq 1$ and $y_i = 1 - z_i$, meaning that the probability this event happens is

$$1/2 \Pr[a = 1 | z_i = y_i] + 1/2(1 - \Pr[a = 1 | z_i = 1 - y_i]) \tag{9.7}$$

Yet, one can verify that conditioned on $z_i = y_i$, B invokes A with the distribution $\mathcal{D}_i$, meaning that $\Pr[a = 1 | z_i = y_i] = p_i$. On the other hand, if we don't condition on z_i, then the distribution B invokes A is equal to $\mathcal{D}_{i-1}$. Hence,

$$p_{i-1} = \Pr[a = 1] = 1/2 \Pr[a = 1 | z_i = y_i] + 1/2 \Pr[a = 1 | z_i = 1 - y_i]$$

$$= 1/2 p_i + 1/2 \Pr[a = 1 | z_i = 1 - y_i]$$

Plugging this into (9.7), we get that B predicts y_i with probability $1/2 + p_i - p_{i-1}$. ∎

9.3.2 Proof of Lemma 9.10: The Goldreich-Levin Theorem

Let f be some one-way permutation. To prove Lemma 9.10, we need to use f to come up with a pseudorandom generator with arbitrarily large polynomial stretch $\ell(n)$. It turns out that the crucial step is obtaining a pseudorandom generator that extends its input by one bit (i.e., has stretch $\ell(n) = n + 1$). This is achieved by the following theorem.

Theorem 9.12 *(Goldreich-Levin Theorem* [GL89]*)*
Suppose that $f : \{0, 1\}^* \to \{0, 1\}$ *is a one-way function such that* f *is one-to-one and* $|f(x)| = |x|$ *for every* $x \in \{0, 1\}^*$. *Then, for every probabilistic polynomial-time algorithm* A *there is a negligible function* $\epsilon : \mathbb{N} \to [0, 1]$ *such that*

$$\Pr_{x, r \in_R \{0,1\}^n} [A(f(x), r) = x \odot r] \leq 1/2 + \epsilon(n)$$

where $x \odot r$ *is defined to be* $\sum_{i=1}^{n} x_i r_i$ (mod 2).

Theorem 9.12 immediately implies that the function $G(x, r) = f(x), r, x \odot r$ is a secure pseudorandom generator that extends its input by one bit (mapping $2n$ bits into $2n + 1$ bits). Indeed, otherwise by Theorem 9.11 there would be a predictor B for this function. But because f is a permutation over $\{0, 1\}^n$, the first $2n$ bits of $G(U_{2n})$ are completely random and independent and, hence, cannot be predicted from their predecessors with probability better than $1/2$. This means that a predictor for this function would have to succeed at predicting the $(2n + 1)$th bit from the previous $2n$ bits with probability noticeably larger than $1/2$, which exactly amounts to violating Theorem 9.12.

PROOF OF THEOREM 9.12: Suppose, for the sake of contradiction, that there is some probabilistic polynomial-time algorithm A that violates the theorem's statement. We'll use A to show a probabilistic polynomial-time algorithm B that inverts the permutation f, which contradicts the assumption that it is one way. Specifically, we will show that if for some n,

$$\Pr_{x, r \in_R \{0, 1\}^n} [A(f(x), r) = x \odot r] \geq 1/2 + \epsilon \tag{9.8}$$

then B will run in $O(n^2/\epsilon^2)$ time and invert the one-way permutation f on inputs of length n with probability at least $\Omega(\epsilon)$. This means that if A's success probability is more than $1/2 + n^{-c}$ for some constant c and infinitely many n's, then B runs in polynomial-time and inverts the one-way permutation with probability at least $\Omega(n^{-c})$ for infinitely many n's.

Let n, ϵ be such that (9.8) holds. Then by a simple averaging argument, for at least an $\epsilon/2$ fraction of the x's, the probability over r that $A(f(x), r) = x \odot r$ is at least $1/2 + \epsilon/2$. We'll call such x's *good* and show an algorithm B that with high probability inverts $f(x)$ for every good x.

To restate the scenario here (and point out its connection to the program checking idea introduced in Chapter 8, which came later historically speaking) is that we are given a "black box" that computes an unknown linear function $x \mapsto x \odot r$ for at least $1/2 + \epsilon/2$ fraction of r's, and we have to give an efficient algorithm that reconstructs x in time polynomial in $|x|$ and $1/\epsilon$.

As a warm-up, note that if $\Pr_r[A(f(x), r) = x \odot r] = 1$, for all r, then it is easy to recover x from $f(x)$: just run $A(f(x), e^1), \ldots, A(f(x), e^n)$ where e^i is the string whose ith coordinate is equal to one and all the other coordinates are zero. Clearly, $x \odot e^i$ is the ith bit of x, and hence by making these n calls to A we can recover x completely. Of course, this idea breaks down if $\Pr_r[A(f(x), r) = x \odot r]$ is less than 1. Below, we first describe a simpler reconstruction algorithm that works when this probability is 0.9. The more general algorithm extends this simpler algorithm.

Recovery for success probability 0.9

Now suppose that for an $\Omega(\epsilon)$ fraction of x's, we had $\Pr_r[A(f(x), r) = x \odot r] \geq 0.9$. For such an x, we cannot trust that $A(f(x), e^i) = x \odot e^i$, since it may be that $e^1, \ldots, e^n$ are among the $2^n/10$ strings r on which A answers incorrectly. Still, there is a simple way to bypass this problem: If we choose $r \in_R \{0, 1\}^n$, then the string $r \oplus e^i$ is also uniformly distributed. Hence by the union bound, the probability that the algorithm A answers incorrectly on either string is

$$\Pr_r[A(f(x), r) \neq x \odot r \text{ or } A(f(x), r \oplus e^i) \neq x \odot (r \oplus e^i)] \leq 0.2$$

But $x \odot (r \oplus e^i) = (x \odot r) \oplus (x \odot e^i)$, which means that if we choose r at random, and compute $z = A(f(x), r)$ and $z' = A(f(x), r \odot e^i)$, then $z \oplus z'$ will be equal to the ith bit of x with probability at least 0.8. To obtain *every* bit of x, we amplify this probability to $1 - 1/(10n)$ by taking majorities. Specifically, we use the following algorithm.

Algorithm B

1. Choose $r^1, \ldots, r^m$ independently at random from $\{0, 1\}^n$ (we'll specify m shortly).
2. For every $i \in [n]$:
    *   Compute the values $z_1 = A(f(x), r^1), z_1' = A(f(x), r^1 \odot e^i), \ldots, z_m = A(f(x), r^m), z_m' = A(f(x), r^m \oplus e^i)$.
    *   Guess that x_i is the majority value among $\{z_j \oplus z_j'\}_{j \in [m]}$.

We claim that if $m = 200n$, then for every $i \in [n]$, the majority value will be correct with probability at least $1 - 1/(10n)$ (and hence B will recover *every* bit of x with probability at least 0.9). To prove the claim, we define the random variable Z_j to be 1 if both $A(f(x), r^j) = x \odot r^j$ and $A(f(x), r^j \oplus e^i) = x \odot (r^j \oplus e^i)$; otherwise $Z_j = 0$. Note that the variables $Z_1, \ldots, Z_m$ are independent and by our previous discussion $E[Z_j] \geq 0.8$ for every j. It suffices to show that with probability $1 - 1/(10n)$, more than $m/2$ of the Z_j's are equal to 1. In other words, letting $Z = Z_1 + \cdots + Z_m$, it suffices to show that $\Pr[Z \leq m/2] \leq 1/(10n)$. But, since $E[Z] = \sum_j E[Z_j] \geq 0.8m$, all we need to do is bound $\Pr[|Z - E[Z]| \geq 0.3m]$. By Chebychev's Inequality (Lemma A.12),[6]

$$\Pr\left[|Z - E[Z]| \geq k\sqrt{\text{Var}(Z)}\right] \leq 1/k^2$$

In our case, because the Z_j's are independent 0/1 random variables, $\text{Var}(Z) = \sum_{j=1}^m \text{Var}(Z_j)$ and $\text{Var}(Z_j) \leq 1$ for every j, implying that

$$\Pr[|Z - E[Z]| \geq 0.3m] \leq \frac{1}{(0.3\sqrt{m})^2}$$

which is smaller than $1/(10n)$ by our choice of $m = 200n$.

---

[6] We could have gotten an even better bound using the Chernoff Inequality, but this analysis is easier to extend to the general case of lower success probability.

Recovery for success probability $1/2 + \epsilon/2$

The above analysis crucially used the unrealistic assumption that for many x's, $A(f(x), r)$ is correct with probability at least 0.9 over r. It's not hard to see that once this probability falls below 0.75, that analysis breaks down, since we no longer get any meaningful information by applying the union bound on the events $A(f(x), r) = x \odot r$ and $A(f(x), r \oplus e^i) = x \odot (r \oplus e^i)$. Unfortunately, in general our only guarantee is that if x is good, then this probability is at least $1/2 + \epsilon/2$ (which could be much smaller than 0.75). The crucial insight needed to extend the proof is that all of the above analysis would still carry over even if the strings $r^1, \dots, r^m$ are only chosen to be *pairwise independent* as opposed to fully independent. Indeed, the only place where we used independence is to argue that the random variables $Z_1, \dots, Z_m$ satisfy $\text{Var}(\sum_j Z_j) = \sum_j \text{Var}(Z_j)$, and this condition holds also for pairwise independent random variables (see Claim A.13).

We'll now show how to pick $r^1, \dots, r^m$ in a pairwise indpendent fashion in such a way that we "know" each $x \odot r^i$ already. This may seem ridiculous since x is unknown, and indeed the catch is that we can do it only thanks to some exhaustive guessing, to be made clear soon. Set k such that $m \leq 2^k - 1$ and do as follows:

1. Choose k strings $s^1, \dots, s^k$ independently at random from $\{0, 1\}^n$.
2. For every $j \in [m]$, we associate a unique nonempty set $T_j \subseteq [k]$ with j in some canonical fashion and define $r^j = \sum_{t \in T_j} s^t \pmod{2}$. That is, r^j is the bitwise XOR of all the strings among $s^1, \dots, s^k$ that belong to the jth set.

It can be shown that the strings $r^1, \dots, r^m$ are pairwise independent (see Exercise 8.4). Moreover, for every $x \in \{0, 1\}^n$, $x \odot r^j = \sum_{t \in T_j} x \odot s^t$. This means that if we know the k values $x \odot s^1, \dots, x \odot s^k$ then we can deduce the m values $x \odot r^1, \dots, x \odot r^m$. This is where exhaustive guessing comes in. Since $2^k = O(m)$, we can enumerate over *all possible guesses* for $x \odot s^1, \dots, x \odot s^k$ in polynomial time. This leads us to the following algorithm B' to invert $f(\cdot)$.

Algorithm B'

Input: $y \in \{0, 1\}^n$, where $y = f(x)$ for an unknown x.

We assume that x is "good" and hence $\Pr_r[A(f(x), r) = x \odot r] \geq 1/2 + \epsilon/2$. (We don't care how B performs on x's that are not good.)

Operation: Let $m = 200n/\epsilon^2$ and k be the smallest such that $m \leq 2^k - 1$. Choose $s^1, \dots, s^k$ independently at random in $\{0, 1\}^k$, and define $r^1, \dots, r^m$ as previously. For every string $w \in \{0, 1\}^k$, do the following:

- Run the algorithm B under the assumption that $x \odot s^t = w_t$ for every $t \in [k]$. That is, for every $i \in [n]$, we compute our guess z_j for $x \odot r^j$ by setting $z_j = \sum_{t \in T_j} w_t$. We compute the guess z'_j for $x \odot (r_j \oplus e^i)$ as before by setting $z'_j = A(y, r^j \oplus e^i)$.
- As before, for every $i \in [n]$, our guess for x_i is the majority value among $\{z_j \oplus z'_j\}_{j \in [m]}$.
- We test whether our guess for $x = x_1, \dots, x_n$ satisfies $f(x) = y$. If so, we halt and output x.

The analysis is almost identical to the previous case. In one of the 2^k iterations, we will guess the correct values $w_1, \ldots, w_k$ for $x \odot s^1, \ldots, x \odot s^k$. We'll show that in this particular iteration, for every $i \in [n]$ Algorithm B' guesses x_i correctly with probability at least $1 - 1/(10n)$. Indeed, fix some $i \in [n]$ and define the random variables $Z_1, \ldots, Z_m$ as we did before: Z_j is a 0/1 variable that equals 1 if both $z_j = x \odot r^j$ and $z'_j = x \odot (r^j \oplus e^i)$. In the iteration where we chose the right values $w_1, \ldots, w_k$, it always holds that $z_j = x \odot r^j$ and hence Z_j depends only on the second event, which happens with probability at least $1/2 + \epsilon/2$. Thus all that is needed is to show that for $m = 100n/\epsilon^2$, if $Z_1, \ldots, Z_m$ are pairwise independent 0/1 random variables, where $E[Z_j] \geq 1/2 + \epsilon/2$ for every j, then $\Pr[\sum_j Z_j \leq m/2] \leq 1/(10n)$. But this follows immediately from Chebychev's inequality. ∎

Getting arbitrarily large stretch

Theorem 9.12 provides us with a secure pseudorandom generator of stretch $\ell(n) = n+1$, but to complete the proof of Lemma 9.10 (and to obtain useful encryption schemes with short keys) we need to show a generator with arbitrarily large polynomial stretch. This is achieved by the following theorem.

Theorem 9.13 *If f is a one-way permutation and $c \in \mathbb{N}$, then the function G that maps $x, r \in \{0, 1\}^n$ to $r, f^\ell(x) \odot r, f^{\ell-1}(x) \odot r, \ldots, f^1(x) \odot r$, where $\ell = n^c$ is a secure pseudorandom generator of stretch $\ell(2n) = n + n^c$. (f^i denotes the function obtained by applying the function f repeatedly to the input n times.)*   ◇

PROOF: By Yao's Theorem (Theorem 9.11), it suffices to show that individual bits of f are hard to predict. For contradiction's sake, assume there is a PPT machine A such that when $x, r \in \{0, 1\}^n$ and $i \in \{1, \ldots, N\}$ are randomly chosen,

$$\Pr[A \text{ predicts } f^i(x) \odot r \text{ given } (r, f^\ell(x) \odot r, f^{N-1}(x) \odot r, \ldots, f^{i+1}(x) \odot r)] \geq \frac{1}{2} + \epsilon$$

We will show a probabilistic polynomial-time algorithm B that on such n's will predict $x \odot r$ from $f(x), r$ with probability at least $1/2 + \epsilon$. Thus if A has nonnegligible success, then B violates Theorem 9.12.

Algorithm B is given r and y such that $y = f(x)$ for some x. It will then pick $i \in \{1, \ldots, N\}$ randomly, and compute the values $f^{\ell-i}(y), \ldots, f(y)$ and output $a = A(r, f^{\ell-i-1}(y) \odot r, \ldots, f(y) \odot r, y \odot r)$. Because f is a permutation, this is exactly the same distribution obtained where we choose $x' \in_R \{0, 1\}^n$ and set $x = f^i(x')$, and hence A will predict $f^i(x') \odot r$ with probability $1/2 + \epsilon$, meaning that B predicts $x \odot r$ with the same probability. ∎

9.4 ZERO KNOWLEDGE

Normally we think of a proof as presenting the evidence that some statement is true, and hence typically after carefully reading and verifying a proof for some statement, you learn much more than the mere fact that the statement is true. But does it have to be this way? For example, suppose that you figured out how to schedule all of the flights of some airline in a way that saves them millions of dollars. You want to *prove* to the airline that there exists such a schedule, without actually *revealing* the schedule to them (at least not before you receive your well-deserved payment). Is this possible?

A similar scenario arises in the context of authentication—suppose a company has a sensitive building, that only a select group of employees is allowed to enter. One way to enforce this is to choose two random prime numbers P and Q and reveal these numbers to the selected employees, while revealing $N = P \cdot Q$ to the guard outside the building. The guard will be instructed to let inside only a person demonstrating knowledge of N's factorization. But is it possible to demonstrate such knowledge without revealing the factorization?

It turns out this is in fact possible to do, using the notion of *zero knowledge proof.* Zero knowledge proofs are interactive probabilistic proof systems, just like the systems we encountered in Chapter 8. However, in addition to the *completeness* property (prover can convince the verifier to accept with high probability) and *soundness* property (verifier will reject false statements with high probability), we require an additional *zero knowledge* property, that roughly speaking, requires that the verifier does not learn anything from the interaction apart from the fact that the statement is true. That is, zero knowledge requires that *whatever the verifier learns after participating in a proof for a statement x, she could have computed by herself, without participating in any interaction.* Below we give the formal definition for zero knowledge proofs of **NP** languages. (One can define zero knowledge also for languages outside **NP**, but the zero knowledge condition makes it already highly nontrivial and very useful to obtain such proof systems even for languages in **NP**.)

Definition 9.14 *(Zero knowledge proofs)* Let L be an **NP**-language, and let M be a polynomial time Turing machine such that $x \in L \Leftrightarrow \exists_{u \in \{0,1\}^{p(|x|)}}$ s.t. $M(x,y) = 1$ where $p()$ is a polynomial.

A pair P, V of interactive probabilistic polynomial-time algorithms is called a *zero knowledge proof* for L, if the following three condition hold:

Completeness: For every $x \in L$ and u a certificate for this fact (i.e., $M(x,u) = 1$), $\Pr[\mathsf{out}_V \langle P(x,u), V(x) \rangle] \geq 2/3$, where $\langle P(x,u), V(x) \rangle$ denotes the interaction of P and V where P gets x, u as input and V gets x as input, and $\mathsf{out}_V I$ denotes the output of V at the end of the interaction I.

Soundness: If $x \notin L$, then for *every* strategy P^* and input u, $\Pr[\mathsf{out}_V \langle P^*(x,u), V(x) \rangle] \leq 1/3$. (The strategy P^* needs not run in polynomial time.)

Perfect Zero Knowledge: For every probabilistic polynomial-time interactive strategy V^*, there exists an expected probabilistic polynomial-time (stand-alone) algorithm S^* such that for every $x \in L$ and u a certificate for this fact,

$$\mathsf{out}_{V^*} \langle P(x,u), V^*(x) \rangle \equiv S^*(x) \tag{9.9}$$

(That is, these two random variables are identically distributed even though S does not have access to any certificate for x.) This algorithm S^* is called the *simulator* for V^*, as it simulates the outcome of V^*'s interaction with the prover.

The zero knowledge condition means that the verifier cannot learn anything new from the interaction, even if she does not follow the protocol but rather uses some other strategy V^*. The reason is that she could have learned the same thing by just running the stand-alone algorithm S^* on the publicly known input x. The perfect zero knowledge condition can be relaxed by requiring that the distributions in (9.9) have small *statistical distance* (see Section A.2.6) or are *computationally indistinguishable* (see Exercise 9.17). The resulting notions are called respectively *statistical zero knowledge* and *computational zero knowledge* and are central to cryptography and complexity theory. The class of languages with statistical zero knowledge proofs, known as **SZK**, has some fascinating properties and is believed to lie strictly between **P** and **NP** (see [Vad99] for an excellent survey). In contrast, it is known ([GMW86], see also [BCC86]) that if one-way functions exist then *every* **NP** language has a computational zero knowledge proof, and this result has significant applications in the design of cryptographic protocols (see the chapter notes).

The idea of using *simulation* to demonstrate security is also central to many aspects of cryptography. Aside from zero knowledge, it is used in the definition of semantic security for encryptions (see Exercise 9.9), secure multiparty computation (Section 9.5.4), and many other settings. In all these cases, security is defined as the condition that an attacker cannot learn or do anything that she could not have done in an idealized and "obviously secure" setting (e.g., in encryption in the ideal setting the attacker doesn't see even the ciphertext, while in zero knowledge in the ideal setting there is no interaction with the prover).

EXAMPLE 9.15

We show a perfect zero knowledge proof for the language GI of graph isomorphism. The language GI is in **NP** and has a trivial proof satisfying completeness and soundness— send the isomorphism to the verifier. But that proof is not known to be zero knowledge, since we do not know of a polynomial-time algorithm that can find the isomorphism between two given isomorphic graphs.

Zero-knowledge proof for graph isomorphism:

Public input: A pair of graphs G_0, G_1 on n vertices. (For concreteness, assume they are represented by their adjacency matrices.)

Prover's private input: A permutation $\pi : [n] \to [n]$ such that $G_1 = \pi(G_0)$, where $\pi(G)$ denotes the graph obtained by transforming the vertex i into $\pi(i)$ (or equivalently, applying the permutation π to the rows and columns of G's adjacency matrix).

Prover's first message: Prover chooses a random permutation $\pi_1 : [n] \to [n]$ and sends to the verifier the adjacency matrix of $\pi_1(G_1)$.

Verifier's message: Verifier chooses $b \in_R \{0, 1\}$ and sends b to the prover.

Prover's last message: If $b = 1$, the prover sends π_1 to the verifier. If $b = 0$, the prover sends $\pi_1 \circ \pi$ (i.e., the permutation mapping n to $\pi_1(\pi(n))$) to the verifier.

Verifier's check: Letting H denote the graph received in the first message and π the permutation received in the last message, the verifier accepts if and only if $H = \pi(G_b)$.

Clearly, if both the prover and verifier follow the protocol, then the verifier will accept with probability one. For soundness, we claim that if G_0 and G_1 are *not* isomorphic, then the verifier will reject with probability at least $1/2$ (this can be reduced further by repetition). Indeed, in that case regardless of the prover's strategy, the graph H that he sends in his first message cannot be isomorphic to both G_0 and G_1, and there has to exist $b \in \{0, 1\}$ such that H is not isomorphic to G_b. But the verifier will choose this value b with probability $1/2$, and then the prover will not be able to find a permutation π such that $H = \pi(G_b)$, and hence the verifier will reject.

Let V^* be some verifier strategy. To show the zero knowledge condition, we use the following simulator S^*: On input a pair of graphs G_0, G_1, the simulator S^* chooses $b' \in_R \{0, 1\}$, a random permutation π on $[n]$ and computes $H = \pi(G_{b'})$. It then feeds H to the verifier V^* to obtain its message $b \in \{0, 1\}$. If $b = b'$ then S^* sends π to V^* and outputs whatever V^* outputs. Otherwise (if $b \neq b'$) the simulator S^* restarts from the beginning.

The crucial observation is that S^*'s first message is distributed in exactly the same way as the prover's first message—a random graph that is isomorphic to G_0 and G_1. This also means that H reveals nothing about the choice of b', and hence the probability that $b' = b$ is $1/2$. If this happens, then the messages H and π that V^* sees are distributed identically to the distribution of messages that it gets in a real interaction with the prover. Because S^* succeeds in getting $b' = b$ with probability $1/2$, the probability it needs k iterations is 2^{-k}, which means that its expected running time is $T(n) \sum_{k=1}^{\infty} 2^{-k} = O(T(n))$, where $T(n)$ denotes the running time of V^*. Thus, S^* runs in expected probabilistic polynomial-time.[7]

This is a family of functions each of which is efficiently computable and has a polynomial-sized representation (and thus is far from being random). Nevertheless, the typical function in this family is indistinguishable from a random function to every computationally limited observer who only has the ability to observe the output of the function on any desired inputs of her choosing.

9.5 SOME APPLICATIONS

Now we give some applications of the ideas introduced in the chapter.

9.5.1 Pseudorandom functions and their applications

Pseudorandom functions are a natural generalization of pseudorandom generators. This is of course reminiscent of the definition of a pseudorandom generator, whose output also has to pass a "blind test" versus a truly random string. The difference here is that the object being talked about is a function, whose truth table has exponential size. The distinguishing algorithm (which runs in polynomial time) only has the ability to ask for the value of the function at any inputs of its choosing.

Definition 9.16 Let $\{f_k\}_{k \in \{0,1\}^*}$ be a family of functions such that $f_k : \{0, 1\}^{|k|} \to \{0, 1\}^{|k|}$ for every $k \in \{0, 1\}^*$, and there is a polynomial-time algorithm that computes $f_k(x)$ given $k \in \{0, 1\}^*, x \in \{0, 1\}^{|k|}$. We say that the family is *pseudorandom* if for every probabilistic polynomial-time oracle[8] Turing machine A there is a negligible function

---

[7] In Chapter 18 we will see a stricter notion of expected probabilistic polynomial-time (see Definition 18.4). This simulator satisfies this stricter notion as well.

[8] See Section 3.4 for the definition of oracle Turing machines.

$\epsilon : \mathbb{N} \to [0,1]$ such that

$$\left| \Pr_{k \in_R \{0,1\}^n}[A^{f_k(\cdot)}(1^n) = 1] - \Pr_{g \in_R \mathcal{F}_n}[A^g(1^n) = 1] \right| < \epsilon(n)$$

for every n, where $\mathcal{F}_n$ denotes the set of all functions from $\{0,1\}^n$ to $\{0,1\}^n$.   ◇

One can verify that if $\{f_k\}$ is a pseudorandom function family, then for every poly-nomial $\ell(n)$, the function G that maps $k \in \{0,1\}^n$ to $f_k(1), \dots, f_k(\ell(n))$ (where we use some canonical encoding of the numbers $1, \dots, \ell(n)$ as strings in $\{0,1\}^n$) is a secure pseudorandom generator. Thus pseudorandom functions imply the existence of secure pseudorandom generators of arbitrary polynomial stretch. It turns out that the converse is true as well.

Theorem 9.17 *([GGM84]) Suppose that there exists a secure pseudorandom generator G with stretch $\ell(n) = 2n$. Then there exists a pseudorandom function family.*   ◇

PROOF: Let G be a secure pseudorandom generator as in the theorems statement map-ping length-n strings to length-$2n$ strings. For every $x \in \{0,1\}^n$, we denote by $G_0(x)$ the first n bits of $G(x)$, and by $G_1(x)$ the last n bits of $G(x)$. For every $k \in \{0,1\}^n$ we will define the function $f_k(\cdot)$ as follows:

$$f_k(x) = G_{k_n}(G_{k_{n-1}}(\cdots(G_{k_1}(x))\cdots)) \tag{9.10}$$

for every $x \in \{0,1\}^n$. Note that $f_k(x)$ can be computed by making n invocations of G, and hence clearly runs in polynomial time. Another way to view f_k is given in Figure 9.2— think of a full depth n binary tree whose root is labeled by k, and where we label the two children of a vertex labeled by y with the values $G_0(y)$ and $G_1(y)$ respectively. Then

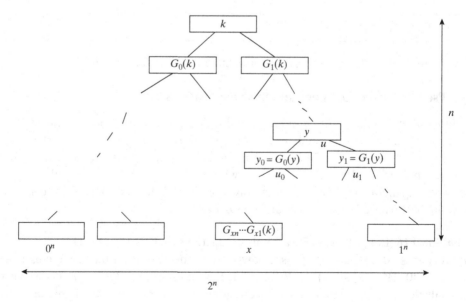

Figure 9.2. The pseudorandom function $f_k(x)$ outputs the label of the xth node in a depth n binary tree where the root is labeled by k, and the children u_0, u_1 of every node u labeled y are labeled by $G_0(y)$ and $G_1(y)$.

$f_k(x)$ denotes the label of the xth leaf of this tree. Of course, actually writing the tree down would take exponential time and space, but as is shown by (9.10), we can compute the label of each leaf in polynomial time by following the length n path from the root to this leaf.

Why is this function family pseudorandom? We'll show this by transforming a T-time algorithm A that distinguishes between f_{U_n} and a random function with bias ϵ into a $\text{poly}(n)T$-time algorithm B that distinguishes between U_{2n} and $G(U_n)$ with bias $\epsilon/(nT)$.

Assume without loss of generality that A makes exactly T queries to its oracle (we can ensure that by adding superfluous queries). Now, we can implement an oracle $\mathcal{O}$ to f_{U_n} in the following way: The oracle $\mathcal{O}$ will label vertices of the depth n full binary tree as needed. Initially, only the root is labeled by a random string k. Whenever, a query of A requires the oracle to label the children u_0, u_1 of a vertex v labeled by y, the oracle will invoke G on y to obtain $y_0 = G_0(y)$ and $y_1 = G_1(y)$ and then label u_0, u_1 with y_0, y_1, respectively, and delete the label y of u. Note that indeed, once u_0 and u_1 are labeled, we have no further need for the label of u. Following the definition of f_k, the oracle $\mathcal{O}$ answers a query x with the label of the xth vertex. Note that $\mathcal{O}$ invokes the generator G at most Tn times. By adding superfluous invocations, we can assume $\mathcal{O}$ invokes the generator exactly Tn times.

Now we use a hybrid argument for every $i \in \{0, \ldots, Tn\}$, define the oracle $\mathcal{O}_i$ as follows: The oracle $\mathcal{O}_i$ follows the operation of $\mathcal{O}$, but for the first i invocations of G, instead of the labels y_0, y_1 of the children of a node labeled y by setting $y_0 = G_0(y)$ and $y_1 = G_1(y)$, the oracle $\mathcal{O}_i$ chooses both y_0 and y_1 independently at random from $\{0, 1\}^n$. Note that $\mathcal{O}_0$ is the same as the oracle $\mathcal{O}$ to f_{U_n}, but $\mathcal{O}_{nT}$ is an oracle to a completely random function. Let $p_i = \Pr[A^{\mathcal{O}_i}(1^n) = 1]$. Then, as in the proof of Theorem 9.11, we may assume $p_{Tn} - p_0 \geq \epsilon$ and deduce that $\mathrm{E}_{i \in_R [Tn]}[p_i - p_{i-1}] \geq \epsilon/(Tn)$. Our algorithm B to distinguish U_{2n} from $G(U_n)$ will do as follows: On input $y \in \{0, 1\}^{2n}$, choose $i \in_R [Tn]$ and execute A with access to the oracle $\mathcal{O}_{i-1}$, using random values for the first $i - 1$ invocations of G. Then, in the ith invocation use the value y instead of the result of invoking G. In all the rest of the invocations B runs G as usual and at the end outputs what A outputs. One can verify that for every choice of i, if the input y is distributed as U_{2n}, then B's output is distributed as $A^{\mathcal{O}_i}(1^n)$, while if it is distributed according to $G(U_n)$, B's output is distributed as $A^{\mathcal{O}_{i-1}}(1^n)$. $\blacksquare$

A pseudorandom function family is a way to turn a random string $k \in \{0, 1\}^n$ into an implicit description of an exponentially larger "random looking" string, namely, the table of all values of the function f_k. This has proved a powerful primitive in cryptography. For example, while we discussed encryption schemes for a single message, in practice we often want to encrypt many messages with the same key. Pseudorandom functions allow Alice and Bob to share an "exponentially large one-time pad." That is, Alice and Bob can share a key k $\{0, 1\}^n$ of a pseudorandom function, and whenever she wants to encrypt a message $x \in \{0, 1\}^n$ for Bob, Alice will choose $r \in_R \{0, 1\}^n$, and send $(r, f_k(r) \oplus x)$. Bob can find x since he knows the key k, but for an adversary that does not know the key, it looks as if Alice sent two random strings (as long as she doesn't choose the same string r to encrypt two different messages, but this can only happen with exponentially small probability). Pseudorandom functions are also used for *message authentication codes*. If Alice and Bob share a key k of a pseudorandom function, then when Alice sends a message x to Bob, she can append the value $f_k(x)$ to this message. Bob can verify that the pair (x, y) he receives satisfies $y = f_k(x)$. An adversary Eve that controls the communication line between Alice and Bob cannot change the message x to x' without being detected, since the probability that Eve can predict the value of $f_k(x')$ is negligible (after all, a random function is unpredictable). Furthermore, pseudorandom function generators have also figured in a very interesting explanation of why current lower bound techniques have been unable to separate **P** from **NP**; see Chapter 23.

9.5.2 Derandomization

The existence of pseudorandom generators implies subexponential deterministic algorithms for **BPP**: This is usually referred to as *derandomization* of **BPP**. That is, if $L \in$ **BPP** then for every $\epsilon > 0$ there is a 2^{n^ϵ}-time deterministic algorithm A such that for every sampleable distribution of inputs $\{X_n\}$ where $X_n \in \{0, 1\}^n$, $\Pr[A(X_n) = L(X_n)] > 0.99$. (Note that the randomness is only over the choice of the inputs—the algorithm A is deterministic.) The algorithm A works by simply reducing the randomness requirement of the probabilistic algorithm for L to n^ϵ using a pseudorandom generator, and then enumerating over all the possible inputs for the pseudorandom generator. We will see stronger derandomization results for **BPP** in Chapter 20.

9.5.3 Tossing coins over the phone and bit commitment

How can two parties A and B toss a fair random coin over the phone? (Many cryptographic protocols require this basic primitive.) If only one of them actually tosses a coin, there is nothing to prevent him from lying about the result. The following fix suggests itself: Both players toss a coin and they take the XOR as the shared coin. Even if B does not trust A to use a fair coin, he knows that as long as his bit is random, the XOR is also random. Unfortunately, this idea also does not work because the player who reveals his bit first is at a disadvantage: The other player could just "adjust" his answer to get the desired final coin toss.

This problem is addressed by the following scheme, which assumes that A and B are polynomial-time Turing machines that cannot invert one-way permutations. First, A chooses two strings x_A and r_A of length n and sends a message $(f_n(x_A), r_A)$, where f_n is a one-way permutation. Now B selects a random bit b and sends it to A. Then A reveals x_A, and they agree to use the XOR of b and $(x_A \odot r_A)$ as their coin toss. Note that B can verify that x_A is the same as in the first message by applying f_n; therefore, A cannot change her mind after learning B's bit. (For this reason, we say that A's first message is a cryptographic *commitment* to the bit $x_A \odot r_A$.) On the other hand, by Theorem 9.12, B cannot predict $x_A \odot r_A$ from A's first message, and so cannot bias her bit according to the choice of $x_A \odot r_A$.

9.5.4 Secure multiparty computations

This concerns a vast generalization of the setting in Section 9.5.3. There are k parties and the ith party holds a string $x_i \in \{0, 1\}^n$. They wish to compute $f(x_1, x_2, \ldots, x_k)$ where $f : \{0, 1\}^{nk} \to \{0, 1\}$ is a polynomial-time computable function known to all of them.

(The setting in Section 9.5.3 is a subcase whereby each x_i is a bit—randomly chosen as it happens—and f is XOR.) Clearly, the parties can just exchange their inputs (suitably encrypted if need be so that unauthorized eavesdroppers learn nothing) and then each of them can compute f on his or her own. However, this leads to all of them knowing each other's input, which may not be desirable in many situations. For instance, we may wish to compute statistics (such as the average) on the combination of several medical databases that are held by different hospitals. Strict privacy and nondisclosure laws may forbid hospitals from sharing information about individual patients. (The original example Yao gave in introducing the problem was of k people who wish to compute the average of their salaries without revealing their salaries to each other.)

We say that a multiparty protocol for computing f is *secure* if at the end no party learns anything new apart from the value of $f(x_1, x_2, \ldots, x_k)$. The formal definition is inspired by the definition of zero knowledge and says that whatever a party or a coalition of parties learn during the protocol can be simulated in an ideal setting where they only get to send their inputs to some trusted authority that computes f on these inputs and broadcasts the result. Amazingly, there are protocols to achieve this task securely for every number of parties and for every polynomial-time computable f—see the chapter notes.[9]

9.5.5 Lower bounds for machine learning

In *machine learning* the goal is to learn a succinct function $f : \{0, 1\}^n \to \{0, 1\}$ from a sequence of type $(x_1, f(x_1)), (x_2, f(x_2)), \ldots$, where the x_i's are randomly chosen inputs. Clearly, this is impossible in general since a random function has no succinct description. But suppose f has a succinct description (e.g., as a small circuit). Can we learn f in that case?

The existence of pseudorandom functions implies that even though a function may be polynomial-time computable, there is no way to learn it from examples in polynomial time. In fact it is possible to extend this impossibility result to more restricted function families such as $\mathbf{NC}^1$ (see Kearns and Valiant [KV89]).

WHAT HAVE WE LEARNED?

- Cryptography is an age-old endeavor. Many systems of secret writing were invented in the past, but all were broken. Since the mid 1970s, modern cryptosystems were invented whose security follows from the hardness of certain simple-to-state computational problems. Many of these modern systems have not been broken.
- Information-theoretic secure encryption ensures that even a computationally unbounded eavesdropper gets no information on the plaintext from the encrypted ciphertext. This can be achieved by a one-time pad, though it (inherently) requires a prohibitively large secret key.

---

[9] Returning to our medical database example, we see that the hospitals can indeed compute statistics on their combined databases without revealing any information to each other—at least any information that can be extracted feasibly. It is unclear if current privacy laws allow hospitals to perform such secure multiparty protocols using patient data—this is an example of the law lagging behind scientific progress.

- A more practical version of a one-time pad is based on *pseudorandom generators*, which are used to stretch a small truly random string to a much longer string that "looks random" to computationally bounded adversaries.
- *One-way functions* are functions mapping strings to strings that are easy to compute but difficult to invert on the average input. Many candidates are known, but lacking complexity lower bounds we cannot yet *prove* that these are truly one-way.
- One-way functions exist if and only if pseudorandom generators exist. The "only if" direction is easy, but the "if" direction requires more work. In this chapter we saw how to create a pseudorandom generator from a special type of a one-way function called a *one-way permutation*.
- Modern cryptography is about much more than just secure encryption. Many protocols have been designed for securely performing more sophisticated tasks such as coin tossing, voting, auctions, and much more. *Zero knowledge proofs* play an important part in achieving such results.
- *Pseudorandom functions* can be thought of as a pseudorandom generator with "exponential stretch." They have many cryptographic applications, and we'll also see a fascinating complexity application in Chapter 23.

CHAPTER NOTES AND HISTORY

We have chosen to model potential eavesdroppers, and hence also potential inverting algorithms for the one-way functions as probabilistic polynomial-time Turing machines. An equally justifiable choice is to model these as *polynomial-sized circuits* or, equivalently, probabilistic polynomial-time Turing machines that can have some input-length dependent polynomial-sized constants "hardwired" into them as advice. All the results of this chapter hold for this choice as well, and in fact some proofs and definitions become slightly simpler. We chose to use uniform Turing machines to avoid making this chapter dependant on Chapter 6.

Goldreich's book [Gol04] is a good source for much of the material of this chapter (and more than that), while the undergraduate text [KL07] is a gentler introduction for the basics. For more coverage of recent topics, especially in applied cryptography, see Boneh and Shoup's upcoming book [BS08]. For more on computational number theory, see the books of Shoup [Sho05] and Bach and Shallit [BS96].

Kahn's book [Kah96] is an excellent source for the fascinating history of cryptography over the ages. Up until the mid 20th century, this history followed Edgar Alan Poe's quote in the chapter's start—every cipher designed and widely used was ultimately broken. Shannon [Sha49b] was the first to rigorously study the security of encryptions. He showed the results presented in Section 9.1, giving the first formal definition of security and showing that it's necessary and sufficient to have the key as large as the message to satisfy the definition. Shannon realized that computational difficulty is the way to bypass this bound, though he did not suggest a concrete approach. This is not surprising since the mathematical study of efficient computation (i.e., algorithm design and complexity theory) only really began in the 1960s, and with this study came the understanding of the dichotomy between polynomial time and exponential time.

Around 1974, Diffie and Hellman and independently Merkle began to question the age-old notion that secure communication requires sharing a secret key in advance. This resulted in the groundbreaking paper of Diffie and Hellman [DH76] that put forward the notion of *public key cryptography*. This paper also suggested the first implementation of this notion—what is known today as the *Diffie-Hellman key exchange* protocol, which also immediately yields a public key encryption scheme known today as El-Gamal encryption. But, to fully realize their agenda of both confidential and authenticated communication without sharing secret keys, Diffie and Hellman needed *trapdoor permutations*, which they conjectured to exist but did not have a concrete implementation for.[10] The first construction for such trapdoor permutations was given by Rivest, Shamir, and Adleman [RSA78]. The resulting encryption and signature schemes were quite efficient and are still the most widely used such schemes today. Rivest et al. conjectured that the security of their trapdoor permutation is equivalent to the factoring problem, though they were not able to prove it (and no proof has been found in the years since). Rabin [Rab79] later showed a trapdoor permutation that is in fact equivalent to the factoring problem.

Interestingly, similar developments also took place within the closed world of the intelligence community and in fact somewhat before the works of [DH76, RSA78], although this only came to light more than 20 years later [Ell99]. In 1970, James Ellis of the British intelligence agency GCHQ also realized that it might be possible to have secure encryption without sharing secret keys. No one in the agency had found a possible implementation for this idea until in 1973, Clifford Cocks suggested to use a trapdoor permutation that is a close variant of the RSA trapdoor permutation, and a few months later Malcolm Williamson discovered what we know today as the Diffie-Hellman key exchange. (Other concepts such as digital signatures, Rabin's trapdoor permutations, and public key encryption from the codes/lattices seem not to have been anticipated in the intelligence community.) Perhaps it is not very surprising that these developments happened in GCHQ before their discovery in the open literature, since between Shannon's work and the publication of [DH76], cryptography was hardly studied outside of the intelligence community.

Despite the well-justified excitement they generated, the security achieved by the RSA and Diffie-Hellman schemes on their own was not fully satisfactory and did not match the kind of security that Shannon showed the one-time pad can achieve in the sense of not revealing even partial information about the message. Goldwasser and Micali [GM82] showed how such strong security can be achieved in a paper that was the basis and inspiration for many of the works that followed achieving strong notions of security for encryption and other tasks. Another milestone was reached by Goldwasser, Micali, and Rivest [GMR84], who gave strong security definitions for digital signatures and showed how these can be realized under the assumption that integer factorization is hard.

Pseudorandom generators were used in practice since the early days of computing. Shamir [Sha81] was the first to explicitly connect intractability to pseudorandomness,

---

[10] Diffie and Hellman actually used the name "public key encryption" for the concept today known as trapdoor permutations. Indeed, trapdoor permutations can be thought of as a variant of public key encryptions with a deterministic (i.e., not probabilistic) encryption function. But following the work [GM82], we know that the use of probabilistic encryption is both essential for strong security and useful to get encryption without using trapdoor permutations (as is the case in the Diffie-Hellman/El-Gamal encryption scheme).

by showing that if the RSA function is one-way, then there exists a generator that can be proven to satisfy a certain weak pseudorandomness property (block unpredictability). Blum and Micali [BM82] defined the stronger notion of next bit unpredictability and showed a factoring-based generator satisfying it. Yao [Yao82a] defined the even stronger definition of pseudorandomness as fooling all polynomial-time tests (Definition 9.8) and proved that this notion is *equivalent* to next-bit unpredictability (Theorem 9.11). In the same work Yao also proved (using a different proof than the one we presented) Lemma 9.10, constructing a pseudorandom generator from any one-way permutation. The Goldreich-Levin theorem was proven in [GL89], though we presented an unpublished proof due to Rackoff. Theorem 9.9 (pseudorandom generators from one-way functions) and its very technical proof is by Håstad, Impagliazzo, Luby, and Levin [HILL99] (the relevant conference publications are a decade older). The construction of pseudorandom functions in Section 9.5.1 is due to Goldreich, Goldwasser, and Micali [GGM84].

Zero knowledge proofs were invented by Goldwasser, Micali, and Rackoff [GMR85], who also showed a zero knowledge proof for problem of quadratic residuosity (see also Example 8.9). Goldreich, Micali, and Wigderson [GMW86] showed that if one-way functions exist, then there is a computational zero knowledge proof system for every language in **NP**. The zero knowledge protocol for graph isomorphism of Example 9.15 is also from the same paper. Independently, Brassard, Chaum, and Crépeau [BCC86] gave a perfect zero knowledge argument for **NP** (where the soundness condition is computational, and the zero knowledge condition is with respect to unbounded adversaries), under a specific hardness assumption.

Yao [Yao82b] suggested the first protocol for realizing securely *any* two party functionality, as described in Section 9.5.4, but his protocol only worked for passive (also known as "eavesdropping" or "honest but curious") adversaries. Goldreich, Micali, and Wigderson [GMW87] extended this result for every number of parties and also showed how to use zero knowledge proofs to achieve security also against *active* attacks, a paradigm that has been used many times since.

Some early cryptosystems were designed using the SUBSET SUM problem, but many of those were broken by the early 1980s. In the last few years, interest in such problems—and also the related problems of computing approximate solutions to the shortest and nearest lattice vector problems—has revived, thanks to a one-way function described in Ajtai [Ajt96], and a public-key cryptosystem described in Ajtai and Dwork [AD97] (and improved on since then by other researchers). These constructions are secure on *most* instances if and only if they are secure on *worst-case* instances. (The idea used is a variant of random self-reducibility.) Oded Regev's survey [Reg06] as well as his lecture notes (available from his home page) are a good source for more information on this fascinating topic (see also the older book [MG02]). The hope is that such ideas could eventually be used to base cryptography on *worst-case* type conjectures such as $\mathbf{P} \neq \mathbf{NP}$ or $\mathbf{NP} \cap \mathbf{coNP} \not\subseteq \mathbf{BPP}$, but there are still some significant obstacles to achieving this.

Much research has been devoted to exploring the exact notions of security that one needs for various cryptographic tasks. For instance, the notion of semantic security (see Section 9.2.2 and Exercise 9.9) may seem quite strong, but it turns out that for most applications it does not suffice, and we need the stronger notion of *chosen ciphertext security* [RS91, DDN91]. See the Boneh-Shoup book [BS08] for more on this topic. Zero knowledge proofs play a central role in achieving security in such settings.

EXERCISES

9.1. Prove that the one-time pad encryption is perfectly secret as per Definition 9.1.

9.2. Prove that if (E, D) is a scheme satisfying (9.1) with message-size m and key-size $n < m$, then there exist two messages $x, x' \in \{0, 1\}^m$ such that $E_{U_n}(x)$ is not the same distribution as $E_{U_n}(x')$.

H535

9.3. Prove that in the one-time pad encryption, no eavesdropper can guess any bit of the plaintext with probability better than $1/2$. That is, prove that for every function A, if (E, D) denotes the one-time pad encryption then

$$\Pr_{\substack{k \in_R \{0,1\}^n \\ x \in_R \{0,1\}^n}} [A(E_k(x)) = (i, b) \text{ s.t. } x_i = b] \le 1/2$$

Thus, the one-time pad satisfies in a strong way the condition (9.3) of computational security.

9.4. Exercise 9.2 and Lemma 9.2 show that for security against unbounded time adversaries (or efficient time if $\mathbf{P} = \mathbf{NP}$) we need key as large as the message. But they actually make an implicit subtle assumption: The encryption process is *deterministic*. In a *probabilistic encryption scheme*, the encryption function E may be probabilistic; that is, given a message x and a key k, the value $E_k(x)$ is not fixed but is distributed according to some distribution $Y_{x,k}$. Of course, because the decryption function is only given the key k and not the internal randomness used by E, we modify the requirement (9.1) to require $D_k(y) = x$ for *every* y in the support of $E_k(x)$. Prove that even a probabilistic encryption scheme cannot have a key that's significantly shorter than the message. That is, show that for every probabilistic encryption scheme (D, E) using n-length keys and $n + 10$-length messages, there exist two messages $x_0, x_1 \in \{0, 1\}^{n+10}$ and function A such that

$$\Pr_{\substack{b \in_R \{0,1\} \\ k \in_R \{0,1\}^n}} [A(E_k(x_b)) = b] \ge 9/10 \tag{9.11}$$

Furthermore, prove that if $\mathbf{P} = \mathbf{NP}$, then this function A can be computed in polynomial time.

H535

9.5. Show that if $\mathbf{P} = \mathbf{NP}$, then one-way functions do not exist.

9.6. (a) Show that if there exists a one-way function f, then there exists a one-way function g that is computable in n^2 time.

H535

   (b) Show that if there exists a one-way function f then the function $f_{\mathcal{U}}$ described in Section 9.2.1 is one way.

9.7. Prove that if there's a polylog(M) algorithm to invert the Rabin function $f_M(X) = X^2$ (mod M) of Section 9.2.1 on a $1/$ polylog(M) fraction of its inputs, then we can factor M in polylog(M) time.

H535

9.8. Let $\{(p_n, g_n)\}_{n\in\mathbb{N}}$ be some sequence of pairs of n-bit numbers such that p_n is prime and g_n is a generator of the group $\mathbb{Z}_{p_n}^*$, and there is a deterministic polynomial-time algorithm such that $S(1^n) = (p_n, g_n)$ for every $n \in \mathbb{N}$.

   Suppose A is an algorithm with running time $t(n)$ that on input g_n^x (mod p_n) manages to find x for $\delta(n)$ fraction of $x \in \{0, \ldots, p_n - 1\}$. Prove that for every $\epsilon > 0$, there is a randomized algorithm A' with running time $O(\frac{1}{\delta \log 1/\epsilon}(t(n) + \text{poly}(n)))$ such that for *every* $x \in \{0, \ldots, p_n - 1\}$, $\Pr[A'(g_n^x \text{ (mod } p_n)) = x] \geq 1 - \epsilon$. This property is known as the *self reducibility* of the discrete logarithm problem.

H535

9.9. We say that a sequence of random variables $\{X_n\}_{n\in\mathbb{N}}$ where $X_n \in \{0, 1\}^{m(n)}$ for some polynomial $m(\cdot)$ is *sampleable* if there's a probabilistic polynomial-time algorithm D such that X_n is equal to the distribution $D(1^n)$ for every n. Let (E, D) be an encryption scheme such that for every n, (E, D) uses length n keys to encrypt length $m(n)$ messages for some polynomial $m(\cdot)$. We say that (E, D) is *semantically secure*, if for every sampleable sequence $\{X_n\}$ (where $X_n \in \{0, 1\}^{m(n)}$, every polynomial-time computable function $f : \{0, 1\}^* \to \{0, 1\}$, and every probabilistic polynomial-time algorithm A, there exists negligible function $\epsilon : \mathbb{N} \to [0, 1]$ and a probabilistic polynomial-time algorithm B such that

$$\Pr_{\substack{k \in_R \{0,1\}^n \\ x \in_R X_n}} [A(\mathsf{E}_k(x)) = f(x)] \leq \Pr_{x \in_R X_n} [B(1^n) = f(x)] + \epsilon(n).$$

That is A cannot compute $f(x)$ given an encryption of x better than just guessing it using the knowledge of the distribution X_n.

(a) Prove that if (E, D) is semantically secure, then it also satisfies the condition of "computational security" of Section 9.2.2.

(b) Prove that if G is a pseudorandom generator mapping $\{0, 1\}^n$ to $\{0, 1\}^m$, then the encryption $\mathsf{E}_k(x) = x \oplus G(k)$, $\mathsf{D}_k(y) = y \oplus G(k)$ is semantically secure.

H535

(c) Prove that semantic security is equivalent to its special case where for every n, X_n is the uniform distribution over a pair of strings x_0^n, x_1^n and f is the function that maps x_0^n to 0 and x_1^n to 1 for every n.

H535

9.10. Show that if there exists a secure pseudorandom generator with stretch $\ell(n) = n+1$, then for every c there exists a pseudorandom generator with stretch $\ell(n) = n^c$.

H535

9.11. Show that if f is a one-way permutation then so is f^k (namely, $f(f(f(\cdots (f(x)))))$ where f is applied k times) where $k = n^c$ for some fixed $c > 0$.

9.12. Assuming one-way functions exist, show that the result of Exercise 9.11 fails for one-way functions. That is, design a one-way function f where f^{n^c} is not one-way for some constant c.

9.13. Suppose $x \in \{0, 1\}^m$ is an unknown vector. Let $r^1, \ldots, r^m \in \{0, 1\}^m$ be randomly chosen, and $x \odot r_i$ revealed to us for all $i = 1, 2, \ldots, m$. Describe a deterministic algorithm to reconstruct x from this information and show that the probability (over the choice of the r^i's) that it works at least $1/4$. This shows that if $r^1, \ldots, r^m$ are fully independent then we cannot guess $x \odot r^1, \ldots, x \odot r^m$ with probability much better than 2^{-m} (and hence it was crucial to move to a merely pairwise independent collection of vectors in the proof of Theorem 9.12).

H535

9.14. Suppose somebody holds an unknown n-bit vector a. Whenever you present a randomly chosen subset of indices $S \subseteq \{1, \ldots, n\}$, then with probability at least $1/2 + \epsilon$, she tells you the parity of all the bits in a indexed by S. Describe a guessing strategy that allows you to guess a (an n bit string!) with probability at least $(\frac{\epsilon}{n})^c$ for some constant $c > 0$.

9.15. Say that two sequences $\{X_n\}, \{Y_n\}$ of random variables, where $X_n, Y_n \in \{0, 1\}^{m(n)}$ for some polynomial $m(n)$, are *computationally indistinguishable* if for every probabilistic polynomial-time A there exists a negligible function $\epsilon : \mathbb{N} \to [0, 1]$ such that

$$\left| \Pr[A(X_n) = 1] - \Pr[A(Y_n) = 1] \right| < \epsilon(n)$$

for every n. Prove that:

(a) If $f : \{0, 1\}^* \to \{0, 1\}^*$ is a polynomial-time computable function and $\{X_n\}, \{Y_n\}$ are computationally indistinguishable, then so are the sequences $\{f(X_n)\}, \{f(Y_n)\}$.

(b) A polynomial-time computable function G with stretch $\ell(n)$ is a secure pseudorandom generator if and only if the sequences $\{U_{\ell(n)}\}$ and $\{G(U_n)\}$ are computationally indistinguishable.

(c) An encryption scheme (E, D) with $\ell(n)$-length messages for n-length keys is semantically secure if and only if for every pair of probabilistic polynomial time algorithms X_0, X_1, where $|X_0(1^n)| = |X_1(1^n)| = \ell(n)$, the sequences $\{\mathsf{E}_{U_n}(X_0(1^n))\}$ and $\{\mathsf{E}_{U_n}(X_1(1^n))\}$ are computationally indistinguishable.

9.16. Suppose that one-way permutations exist. Prove that there exists a pair of polynomially sampleable computationally indistinguishable distributions $\{G_n\}$ and $\{H_n\}$ over n-vertex graphs such that for every n, G_n and H_n are n-vertex graphs, and $\Pr[G_n \text{ is 3-colorable}] = 1$ but $\Pr[H_n \text{ is 3-colorable}] = 0$. (A graph G is 3-colorable if G's vertices can be colored in one of three colors so that no two neighboring vertices have the same color, see Exercise 2.2).

H535

9.17. Say that a language L has a *computational zero knowledge* proof if it satisfies the relaxation of Definition 9.14 where condition (9.9) is replaced by the condition that $\{\mathsf{out}_{v^*}\langle P(X_n, U_n), V^*(X_n)\rangle\}$ and $\{S^*(X_n)\}$ are computationally indistinguishable for every sampleable distribution (X_n, U_n) such that $|X_n| = n$ and $\Pr[M(X_n, U_n) = 1] = 1$,

(a) Prove that if there exists a computational zero knowledge proof for some language L that is **NP**-complete via a Levin reduction (Section 2.3.6), then there exists a computational zero knowledge proof for every $L \in \mathbf{NP}$.

(b) Prove that the following protocol (due to Blum [Blu87]) is a computational zero knowledge proof system with completeness 1 and soundness error $1/2$ for the language of Hamiltonian circuits:[11]

Common input Graph G on n vertices.

Prover's private input A Hamiltonian cycle C in the graph.

Prover's first message Choose a random permutation π on the vertices of G, and let M be the adjacency matrix of G with its rows and columns permuted according to π. For every $i, j \in [n]$, choose $x^{i,j}, r^{i,j} \in_R \{0, 1\}^n$ and send to the verifier $f(x^{i,j}), r^{i,j}, (x^{i,j} \odot r^{i,j}) \oplus M_{i,j}$.

Verifier's message Verifier chooses $b \in_R \{0, 1\}$ and sends b to prover.

Prover's last message If $b = 0$, the prover sends to the verifier all randomness used in the first message. That is, the prover reveals the permutation π, the matrix M, and reveals $x_{i,j}$ for every $i, j \in [n]$. If $b = 1$, the prover computes C', which is the permuted version of the cycle C (i.e., C' contains $(\pi(i), \pi(j))$ for every edge $\overline{ij} \in C$). It then sends C' to the verifier and reveals only the randomness corresponding to these edges. That is, for every $(i, j) \in C'$ it sends $x_{i,j}$ to the verifier.

Verifier's check If $b = 0$, the verifier checks that the prover's information is consistent with its first message—that M is the permuted adjacency matrix of G according to π, and that the values $x_{i,j}$ are consistent with $M_{i,j}$ and the values $y_{i,j}$ that the prover sent in its first message. If $b = 1$, then the verifier checks that C' is indeed a Hamiltonian cycle, and that the values the prover sent are consistent with its first message and with $M_{i,j} = 1$ for every $(i, j) \in C'$. The verifier accepts if and only if these checks succeed.

---

[11] The soundness error can be reduced by repetition.

CHAPTER 10

Quantum computation

Turning to quantum mechanics...secret, secret, close the doors! we always have had a great deal of difficulty in understanding the world view that quantum mechanics represents.... It has not yet become obvious to me that there's no real problem. I cannot define the real problem, therefore I suspect there's no real problem, but I'm not sure there's no real problem. So that's why I like to investigate things.

– Richard Feynman, 1964

The only difference between a probabilistic classical world and the equations of the quantum world is that somehow or other it appears as if the probabilities would have to go negative.

– Richard Feynman, in "Simulating Physics with Computers," 1982

Our first result is the existence of an efficient universal quantum Turing machine in Deutsch's model.... We give the first formal evidence that quantum Turing machines violate the modern complexity theoretic formulation of the Church Turing thesis. We show the existence of a problem relative to an oracle that can be solved in polynomial time on a quantum Turing machine but require super polynomial time on a bounded error probabilistic Turing machine.

– E. Bernstein and U. Vazirani, "Quantum Complexity Theory," 1997

Quantum computing is a new computational model that may be physically realizable and may provide an exponential advantage over "classical" computational models such as probabilistic and deterministic Turing machines. In this chapter we survey the basic principles of quantum computation and some of the important algorithms in this model.

One important reason to study quantum computers is that they pose a serious challenge to the *strong Church-Turing thesis* (see Section 1.6.3), which stipulates that every physically reasonable computation device can be simulated by a Turing machine with at most polynomial slowdown. As we will see in Section 10.6, there is a polynomial-time algorithm for quantum computers to factor integers, whereas despite much effort, no such algorithm is known for deterministic or probabilistic Turing machines. If in fact there is no efficient classical algorithm to factor integers (and indeed society currently relies on this conjecture since it underlies the presumed security of cryptographic schemes such as RSA) *and* if quantum computers are physically realizable, then the strong Church-Turing thesis is wrong. Physicists are also interested in quantum computers because studying them may shed light on quantum mechanics, a Theory that, despite its great success in predicting experiments, is still not fully understood.

Very little physics is needed to understand the central results of quantum computing. One basic fact is that the physical parameters (energy, momentum, spin, etc.) of an elementary particle such as an electron are *quantized* and can only take values in a discrete set. Second, contrary to our basic intuition, the value of a physical parameter of a particle (including location, energy, etc.) at any moment in time is not a single number. Rather the parameter has a kind of *probability wave* associated with it, involving a "smearing" or "superposition" over all possible values. The parameter only achieves a definite value when it is *measured* by an observer, at which point we say that the probability wave *collapses* to a single value.

This smearing of a parameter value until it is observed may seem analogous to philosophical musings such as "if a tree falls in a forest with no one present to hear it, does it make a sound?" But these probability waves are very real, and their interaction and mutual interference creates experimentally measurable effects. Furthermore, according to quantum mechanics, the probability waves are associated not just with single particles, but also with any collection of particles (such as humans!). This interaction of probability waves corresponding to collections of particles is key to the power of quantum computing and underlies the apparent exponential speedup provided by this model on certain problems. At the same time, it is simplistic to describe quantum computing—as many popular science authors do—as a "vastly parallel" computer. This "vast parallelism" is tightly regulated by the laws of quantum mechanics, which currently seems to allow exponential speedups only for a few well-structured problems.

The chapter is organized as follows. In Section 10.1 we describe the two-slit experiment, one of many experiments that illustrate the smearing/interference effects of quantum mechanics. In Section 10.2 we formalize a simple quantum system called "qubit" (short for "quantum bit") that is the fundamental unit of quantum computing. We describe operations that can be performed on systems of one or few qubits and illustrate them in Section 10.2.1 using the famous EPR paradox, an experiment that serves to demonstrate (and verify) the counterintuitive nature of quantum mechanics. Then in Section 10.3 we define the n-qubit *quantum register*, and operations (including computations) that can be performed on such registers. We define *quantum circuits* and the class **BQP**, which is the quantum analog of **BPP**. The three ensuing sections describe three basic algorithms known for quantum computers, due to Grover, Simon, and Shor, respectively. Several important topics in quantum computing, including lower bounds, quantum cryptography and quantum error correction, are not covered in this chapter; see the chapter notes for links to further reading.

This chapter utilizes some basic facts of linear algebra and the space $\mathbb{C}^n$. These are reviewed in Appendix A; see also Section 10.3.1.

10.1 QUANTUM WEIRDNESS: THE TWO-SLIT EXPERIMENT

Now we describe an experiment, called the *two-slit experiment*, that illustrates the fact that basic physical properties of an elementary particle are "smeared."

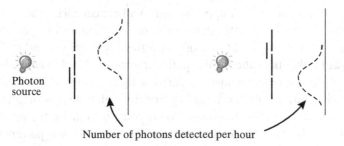

Number of photons detected per hour

Figure 10.1. In the two-slit experiment an photon source is placed between a wall with two slits and a detector array. When one slit is covered then, as expected, the number of photon detected is largest directly behind the open slit.

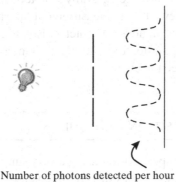

Number of photons detected per hour

Figure 10.2. When both slits are open in the two-slit experiment, the number of photons detected at each position is *not* the sum of numbers when either slit is opened. There are even positions that are hit when each slit is open on its own, but are *not* hit when both slits are open.

Suppose that, as in Figure 10.1, a source that fires photons one by one (say, at the rate of one photon per second) is placed in front of a wall containing two tiny slits. Beyond the wall, we place an array of detectors that light up whenever a photon hits them. We measure the number of times each detector lights up during an hour. When we cover one of the slits, we would expect that the detectors that are directly behind the open slit will receive the largest number of hits, and as Figure 10.1 shows, this is indeed the case. When both slits are uncovered, we expect that the number of times each detector is hit is the sum of the number of times it is hit when the first slit is open and the number of times it is hit when the second slit is open. In particular, uncovering both slits should only *increase* the number of times each location is hit.

Surprisingly, this is not what happens. The pattern of hits exhibits the "interference" phenomena depicted in Figure 10.2. In particular, at several detectors the total hit rate is *lower* when both slits are open as compared to when a single slit is open. This defies explanation if photons behave as particles or "little balls."

According to quantum mechanics, it is wrong to think of a photon as a little ball that can either go through the first slit or the second (i.e., has a definite property). Rather, somehow the photon instantaneously explores all possible paths to the detectors through all open slits. Some paths are taken with positive "amplitude" and some with negative "amplitude" (see the quote from Feynman at the start of the chapter) and two paths arriving at a detector with opposite signs will cancel each other. The end result is that the distribution of hit rates depends upon the number of open slits, since the photon "finds out" how many slits are open via this exploration of all possible paths.

You might be skeptical about this "path exploration," and to check if it is actually going on, you place a detector at each slit that lights up whenever a photon passes through that slit. Thus if a photon is really going through both slits simultaneously, you hope to detect it at both slits. However, when you try to make the photon reveal its quantum nature this way, the quantum nature (i.e., interference pattern) disappears! The hit rates now observed exactly correspond to what they would be if photons were little balls: the sum of the hits when each slit is open. The explanation is that, as stated earlier, *observing* an object "collapses" its distribution of possibilities and so changes the result of the experiment.[1] One moral to draw from this is that quantum computers, if they are ever built, will have to be carefully isolated from external influences and noise, since noise may be viewed as a "measurement" performed by the environment on the system. Of course, we can never completely isolate the system, which means we have to make quantum computation tolerant of a little noise. This seems to be possible under some noise models; see the chapter notes.

10.2 QUANTUM SUPERPOSITION AND QUBITS

Now we describe quantum superposition using a very simple quantum system called a *qubit*, which lays the groundwork for our formal development of quantum computing in the next section. As a helpful example for readers who are new to quantum mechanics, we also describe the famous EPR paradox, though understanding it is not strictly necessary to understand the rest of the chapter.

Classical computation involves manipulation of storage elements with finite memory: the tape cell of a Turing machine, or a bit in case of a Boolean circuit. The analogous unit of storage in quantum computing is a *qubit*. We can think of it as an elementary particle that can be in two basic states (which could correspond to values of energy, or spin or some other physical parameter), which we denote by zero and one. However, unlike a classical bit, this particle can be simultaneously in both basic states. Thus the state of a qubit at any time is called a *superposition* of these basic states. Formally, we denote the basic states by $|0\rangle$ and $|1\rangle$ and generally allow a qubit to be in any state of the form $\alpha_0 |0\rangle + \alpha_1 |1\rangle$, where α_0, α_1 are called *amplitudes* and are complex numbers satisfying $|\alpha_0|^2 + |\alpha_1|^2 = 1$.[2] If isolated from outside influences, the qubit stays in this superposition, until it is observed by an observer. When the qubit is observed, with probability $|\alpha_0|^2$, it is revealed to be in state zero (i.e., $|0\rangle$) and with probability $|\alpha_1|^2$ it is revealed to be in state one (i.e., $|1\rangle$). After observation the amplitude wave *collapses*, and the values of the amplitudes are irretrievably lost.

---

[1]   Of course, it is unclear why humans or detectors placed by humans serve to "collapse" the probability wave, and inanimate objects such as slits do not. This is one of the puzzles of quantum mechanics, see the chapter notes.

[2]   We note that in quantum mechanics the above is known as a *pure* quantum state, see also the remarks following Definition 10.9.

In this section we restrict attention to the case where the amplitudes are real (though possibly negative) numbers. The power and "weirdness" of quantum computing is already exhibited in this case (see also Exercise 10.5).

Analogously, a system of two qubits can exist in four basic states $|00\rangle, |01\rangle, |10\rangle, |11\rangle$ and the state of a two-qubit system at any time is described by a superposition of the type

$$\alpha_{00} |00\rangle + \alpha_{01} |01\rangle + \alpha_{10} |10\rangle + \alpha_{11} |11\rangle$$

where $\sum_{b_1, b_2} |\alpha_{b_1 b_2}|^2 = 1$. When this system is observed, its state is revealed to be $|b_1 b_2\rangle$ with probability $|\alpha_{b_1 b_2}|^2$.

We will sometimes denote the state $|xy\rangle$ as $|x\rangle |y\rangle$. Readers who are mystified by the $|\cdot\rangle$ notation (which unfortunately is inescapable due to long tradition) may wish to look at Note 10.1 for a more geometric description.

NOTE 10.1 *(The Geometry of Quantum States)*

It is often helpful to think of quantum states geometrically as vectors. For example, in case of the single qubit system (with real amplitudes), the two basic states can be visualized as two orthogonal unit vectors $|0\rangle$ and $|1\rangle$ in $\mathbb{R}^2$ (say, $|0\rangle = (1, 0)$ and $|1\rangle = (0, 1)$). The state of the system, which we denoted by $\alpha_0 |0\rangle + \alpha_1 |1\rangle$, can be interpreted as a vector that is the sum of α_0 times the first vector and α_1 times the second. Since α_0, α_1 are real numbers satisfying $\alpha_0^2 + \alpha_1^2 = 1$, there is a unique angle $\theta \in [0, 2\pi)$ such that $\alpha_0 = \cos \theta, \alpha_1 = \sin \theta$. Thus we can think of the system state as $\cos \theta |0\rangle + \sin \theta |1\rangle$; that is, it is a unit vector that makes an angle θ with the $|0\rangle$ vector and an angle $\pi/2 - \theta$ with the $|1\rangle$ vector. When measured, the system's state is revealed to be $|0\rangle$ with probability $\cos^2 \theta$ and $|1\rangle$ with probability $\sin^2 \theta$.

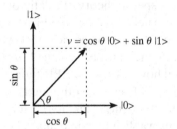

Although it's harder to visualize states with complex coefficients or more than one qubit, geometric intuition can still be useful when reasoning about such states.

EXAMPLE 10.2

The following are two legitimate state vectors for a one-qubit quantum system: $\frac{1}{\sqrt{2}} |0\rangle + \frac{1}{\sqrt{2}} |1\rangle$ and $\frac{1}{\sqrt{2}} |0\rangle - \frac{1}{\sqrt{2}} |1\rangle$. Even though in both cases, if the qubit is measured, it will contain either 0 or 1 with probability 1/2, these are considered distinct states. We will see that it is possible to differentiate between them using quantum operations.

Because states are always unit vectors, we often drop the normalization factor and so, say, use $|0\rangle - |1\rangle$ to denote the state $\frac{1}{\sqrt{2}}|0\rangle - \frac{1}{\sqrt{2}}|1\rangle$.

We call the state where all coefficients are equal the *uniform* state. For example, the uniform state for a two-qubit system is

$$|00\rangle + |01\rangle + |10\rangle + |11\rangle$$

(where we dropped the normalization factor of $\frac{1}{2}$). Using our earlier notation of $|x\rangle |y\rangle$ for $|xy\rangle$ (an operation that is easily checked to respect the distributive law), so we can also write the uniform state of a two-qubit system as

$$(|0\rangle + |1\rangle)(|0\rangle + |1\rangle)$$

which shows that this state just consists of two one-qubit systems in uniform state.

To manipulate the state of a qubit, we have to use a *quantum operation*, which is a function that maps the current state to the new state. In this section, we will only use operations on single qubits. Quantum mechanics allows only *unitary* operations, which are linear operations that preserve the invariant $|\alpha_0|^2 + |\alpha_1|^2 = 1$. In the case of single qubit operations with real coefficients, this means that the allowed operations involve either a *reflection* of the state vector about a fixed vector in $\mathbb{R}^2$ or a *rotation* of the state vector by some angle $\theta \in [0, 2\pi)$.

10.2.1 EPR paradox

The EPR paradox, named after its proposers, Einstein, Podosky, and Rosen [EPR35] was a thought experiment that shows that quantum mechanics allows systems in two far corners of the universe to instantaneously coordinate their actions, seemingly contradicting the axiom of Einstein's special theory of relativity that nothing in the universe can travel faster than light. Einstein, who despite his status as a founder of quantum theory (with his 1905 paper on the photoelectric effect) was never quite comfortable with it, felt that quantum mechanics must be modified to remove such paradoxes.

In 1964 John Bell showed how to turn the EPR thought experiment into an *actual* experiment. Two systems far away from each other in the universe have a shared quantum state (actually, a two-qubit system). This shared state allows them to coordinate their actions in a way that is provably impossible in a "classical" system.

Since then Bell's experiment has been repeated in a variety of settings, always with the same result: The predictions of quantum mechanics are correct, contrary to Einstein's intuition. Today, the EPR paradox is not considered a paradox, since the systems involved do not *transmit* information faster than the speed of light—they merely act upon information that was already shared, albeit in the form of a quantum superposition. Now we describe a version (due to Clauser et al. [CHSH69]) of Bell's experiment:

The parity game

We start by describing a game that seems to involve no quantum mechanics at all. Two players Alice and Bob are isolated from each other. The experimenter asks them to participate in the following guessing game.

1. The experimenter chooses two random bits $x, y \in_R \{0, 1\}$.
2. He presents x to Alice and y to Bob.
3. Alice and Bob respond with bits a, b, respectively.
4. Alice and Bob win if and only if $a \oplus b = x \wedge y$, where $\oplus$ denotes the XOR operation (addition modulo 2).

Note that the players' isolation from each other can be ensured using the special theory of relativity. The players are separated by a light year (say), each accompanied by an assistant of the experimenter. At a designated time, the experimenter's assistants toss their independent random coins to create x and y, present them to Alice and Bob respectively, receive their answers, and transmit everything to the experimenter at a central location. Alice and Bob, being separated by a light year, cannot exchange any information between the time they received x, y and before they gave their answers.

It is easy for Alice and Bob to ensure that they win with probability at least $3/4$ (e.g., by always sending $a = b = 0$). Now we show that this is the best they can do, which seems intuitive since the setup forbids them from *coordinating* their responses. Thus a *strategy* for the players is a pair of functions $f, g : \{0, 1\} \to \{0, 1\}$ such that the players' answers a, b are computed only as functions of the information they see, namely, $a = f(x)$ and $b = g(y)$. A *probabilistic strategy* is a distribution on strategies.

Theorem 10.3 ([Bel64, CHSH69]) *In the previous scenario, no (deterministic or probabilistic) strategy used by Alice and Bob can cause them to win with probability more than $3/4$.* ◇

PROOF: Assume for the sake of contradiction that there is a (possibly probabilistic) strategy that causes them to win with probability more than $3/4$. By a standard averaging argument there is a fixed choice of the players' randomness that succeeds with at least the same probability, and hence we may assume without loss of generality that the players' strategy is deterministic.

The function $f : \{0, 1\} \to \{0, 1\}$ that Alice uses can be one of only four possible functions: It can be either the constant function zero or one, the function $f(x) = x$ or the function $f(x) = 1 - x$. We analyze the case that $f(x) = x$; the other cases are similar. Now Alice's response a is merely x, so the players win iff $b = (x \wedge y) \oplus x$. On input y, Bob needs to find b that makes them win. If $y = 1$, then $x \wedge y = x$, and hence choosing $b = 0$ will ensure Alice and Bob win with probability 1. However, if $y = 0$, then $(x \wedge y) \oplus x = x$, and since Bob does not know x, the probability that his output b is equal to x is at most $1/2$. Thus the total probability of a win is at most $3/4$. ∎

The parity game with sharing of quantum information

Now we show that if Alice and Bob can share a two-qubit system (which they created in a certain state, and split between them before they they were taken a light year apart), then they can circumvent Theorem 10.3 and win the parity game with probability better than $3/4$ using the following strategy:

1. Before the game begins, Alice and Bob prepare a two-qubit system in the state $|00\rangle +$ $|11\rangle$, which we will call the *EPR state*.

2. Alice and Bob split the qubits: Alice takes the first qubit, and Bob takes the second qubit. Note that quantum mechanics does not require the individual bits of a two-qubit quantum system to be physically close to one another. It is important that Alice and Bob have not *measured* these qubits yet.
3. Alice receives the qubit x from the experimenter, and if $x = 1$, then she applies a rotation by $\pi/8$ (22.5 degrees) operation to her qubit. Since the operation involves only her qubit, she can perform it even with no input from Bob. (The semantics of performing a single qubit operation on a multiple-qubit system follow the natural intuition, but see Section 10.3.3 for a formal description.)
4. Bob receives the qubit y from the experimenter, and if $y = 1$ he applies a rotation by by $-\pi/8$ (-22.5 degrees) operation to his qubit.
5. Both Alice and Bob measure their respective qubits and output the values obtained as their answers a and b.

Note that the order in which Alice and Bob perform their rotations and measurements does not matter: It can be shown that all orders yield exactly the same distribution (e.g., see Exercise 10.6). While splitting a two-qubit system and applying unitary transformations to the different parts may sound far fetched, this experiment had been performed several times in practice, verifying the following prediction of quantum mechanics:

Theorem 10.4
With the above strategy, Alice and Bob win with probability at least 0.8.   ◇

PROOF: Recall that Alice and Bob win the game if they output a different answer when $x = y = 1$ and the same answer otherwise. The intuition behind the proof is that unless $x = y = 1$, the states of the two qubits will be "close" to one another (with the angle between being at most $\pi/8 = 22.5$), and in the other case the states will be "far" (having angle $\pi/4$ or 45). Specifically we will show that (denoting by a Alice's output and by b Bob's):

1. If $x = y = 0$, then $a = b$ with probability 1.
2. If $x \neq y$, then $a = b$ with probability $\cos^2(\pi/8) \geq 0.85$
3. If $x = y = 1$, then $a = b$ with probability $1/2$.

Implying that the overall acceptance probability is at least $\frac{1}{4} \cdot 1 + \frac{1}{2} \cdot 0.85 + \frac{1}{4} \cdot \frac{1}{2} = 0.8$.

In the case (1) both Alice and Bob perform no operation on their qubits, and so when measured it will be either in the state $|00\rangle$ or $|11\rangle$, both resulting in Alice and Bob's outputs being equal. To analyze case (2), it suffices to consider the case that $x = 0, y = 1$ (the other case is symmetrical). In this case Alice applies no transformation to her qubit, and Bob rotates his qubit in a $-\pi/8$ angle. Imagine that Alice first measures her qubit, and then Bob makes his rotation and measurements (this is OK as the order of measurements does not change the outcome). With probability $1/2$, Alice will get the value 0, and Bob's qubit will collapse to the state $|0\rangle$ rotated by a $-\pi/8$ angle, meaning that Bob will obtain the value 0 with probability $\cos^2(\pi/8)$ when measuring. Similarly, if Alice gets the value 1, then Bob will also output 1 with $\cos^2(\pi/8)$ probability.

To analyze case (3), we just use direct computation. In this case, after both rotations are performed, the two-qubit system has the state

$$(\cos(\pi/8)|0\rangle + \sin(\pi/8)|1\rangle)(\cos(\pi/8)|0\rangle - \sin(\pi/8)|1\rangle)$$

$$+ (-\sin(\pi/8)|0\rangle + \cos(\pi/8)|1\rangle)(\sin(\pi/8)|0\rangle + \cos(\pi/8)|1\rangle)$$

$$= \left(\cos^2(\pi/8) - \sin^2(\pi/8)\right)|00\rangle - 2\sin(\pi/8)\cos(\pi/8)|01\rangle$$

$$+ 2\sin(\pi/8)\cos(\pi/8)|10\rangle + \left(\cos^2(\pi/8) - \sin^2(\pi/8)\right)|11\rangle.$$

But since

$$\cos^2(\pi/8) - \sin^2(\pi/8) = \cos(\pi/4) = \tfrac{1}{\sqrt{2}} = \sin(\pi/4) = 2\sin(\pi/8)\cos(\pi/8)$$

all coefficients in this state have the same absolute value; hence, when measured, the two-qubit system will yield either one of the four values $00, 01, 10$ and 11 with equal probability $1/4$. ■

The constant 0.8 can be somewhat improved upon; see Exercise 10.1. Also, there are known games with more dramatic differences in success probabilities between the classical and quantum cases. In an interesting twist, in recent years the ideas behind EPR's and Bell's experiments have been used for a practical goal: encryption schemes whose security depends only on the principles of quantum mechanics, rather than any unproven conjectures such as $\mathbf{P} \neq \mathbf{NP}$ (see chapter notes).

10.3 DEFINITION OF QUANTUM COMPUTATION AND BQP

In this section we describe quantum operations, which lead to the definition of quantum gates, quantum computation, and **BQP**, the class of languages with efficient quantum decision algorithms.

10.3.1 Some necessary linear algebra

We use in this chapter several elementary facts and notations involving the space $\mathbb{C}^M$. These are reviewed in Section A.5, but here is a quick reminder:

- If $z = a + ib$ is a complex number (where $i = \sqrt{-1}$), then $\bar{z} = a - ib$ denotes the *complex conjugate* of z. Note that $z\bar{z} = a^2 + b^2 = |z|^2$.
- The *inner product* of two vectors $\mathbf{u}, \mathbf{v} \in \mathbb{C}^m$, denoted by $\langle \mathbf{u}, \mathbf{v} \rangle$, is equal to $\sum_{x \in [M]} \mathbf{u}_x \bar{\mathbf{v}}_x$.[3]
- The *norm* of a vector $\mathbf{u}$, denoted by $\|\mathbf{u}\|_2$, is equal to $\sqrt{\langle \mathbf{u}, \mathbf{u} \rangle} = \sqrt{\sum_{x \in [M]} |\mathbf{u}_x|^2}$.
- If $\langle \mathbf{u}, \mathbf{v} \rangle = 0$ we say that $\mathbf{u}$ and $\mathbf{v}$ are *orthogonal*.
- A set $\{\mathbf{v}^i\}_{i \in [M]}$ of vectors in $\mathbb{C}^M$ is an *orthonormal basis* of $\mathbb{C}^M$ if for every $i, j \in [M]$, $\langle \mathbf{v}^i, \mathbf{v}^j \rangle$ is equal to 1 if $i = j$ and equal to 0 if $i \neq j$.

---

[3] Some quantum computing texts use $\sum_{x \in [M]} \bar{\mathbf{u}}_x \mathbf{v}_x$ instead.

- If A is an $M \times M$ matrix, then A^* denotes the *conjugate transpose* of A. That is, $A^*_{x,y} = \overline{A}_{y,x}$ for every $x, y \in [M]$.
- An $M \times M$ matrix A is *unitary* if $AA^* = I$, where I is the $M \times M$ identity matrix.

Note that if z is a *real* number (i.e., z has no imaginary component), then $\overline{z} = z$. Hence, if all vectors and matrices involved are real then the inner product is equal to the standard inner product of $\mathbb{R}^n$ and the conjugate transpose operation is equal to the standard transpose operation. Also, for real vectors $\mathbf{u}, \mathbf{v}$, $\langle \mathbf{u}, \mathbf{v} \rangle = \cos\theta \|\mathbf{u}\|_2 \|\mathbf{v}\|_2$, where θ is the angle between the $\mathbf{u}$ and $\mathbf{v}$.

The next claim (left as Exercise 10.2) summarizes properties of unitary matrices.

Claim 10.5 *For every $M \times M$ complex matrix A, the following conditions are equivalent:*

1. *A is unitary (i.e., $AA^* = I$).*
2. *For every vector $\mathbf{v} \in \mathbb{C}^M$, $\|A\mathbf{v}\|_2 = \|\mathbf{v}\|_2$.*
3. *For every orthonormal basis $\{\mathbf{v}^i\}_{i \in [M]}$ of $\mathbb{C}^M$, the set $\{A\mathbf{v}^i\}_{i \in [M]}$ is an orthonormal basis of $\mathbb{C}^M$.*
4. *The columns of A form an orthonormal basis of $\mathbb{C}^M$.*
5. *The rows of A form an orthonormal basis of $\mathbb{C}^M$.*

10.3.2 The quantum register and its state vector

In a standard digital computer, we implement a bit of memory by a physical object that has two states: the ON or 1 state and the OFF or 0 state. By taking m such objects together we have an *m-bit register* whose state can be described by a string in $\{0, 1\}^m$. A *quantum register* is composed of m qubits, and its state is a *superposition* of all 2^m basic states (the "probability wave" alluded to in Section 10.1): a vector $\mathbf{v} = \langle \mathbf{v}_{0^m}, \mathbf{v}_{0^{m-1}1}, \ldots, \mathbf{v}_{1^m} \rangle \in \mathbb{C}^{2^m}$, where $\sum_x |\mathbf{v}_x|^2 = 1$. According to quantum mechanics, when *measuring* the register (i.e., reading its value), we will obtain the value x with probability $|\mathbf{v}_x|^2$, and furthermore this operation will *collapse* the state of the register to the vector $|x\rangle$ (in other words, the coefficients corresponding to the basic states $|y\rangle$ for $y \neq x$ will become 0). In principle such a quantum register can be implemented by any collection of m objects that can have ON and OFF states, although in practice there are significant challenges for such an implementation.

10.3.3 Quantum operations

Now we define operations allowed by quantum mechanics.

Definition 10.6 *(Quantum operation)* A *quantum operation* for an m-qubit register is a function $F: \mathbb{C}^{2^m} \to \mathbb{C}^{2^m}$ that maps its previous state to the new state and satisfies the following conditions:

   Linearity: F is a linear function. That is, for every $\mathbf{v} \in \mathbb{C}^{2^n}$, $F(\mathbf{v}) = \sum_x \mathbf{v}_x F(|x\rangle)$.

   Norm preservation: F maps unit vectors to unit vectors. That is, for every $\mathbf{v}$ with $\|\mathbf{v}\|_2 = 1$, $\|F(\mathbf{v})\|_2 = 1$.

The second condition (norm preservation) is quite natural given that only unit vectors can describe states. The linearity condition is imposed by the theory of quantum mechanics. Together, these two conditions imply that every quantum operation F can be described by a $2^m \times 2^m$ *unitary* matrix. The following is immediate.

Lemma 10.7 (Composition of quantum operations) *If A_1, A_2 are matrices representing any quantum operations, then their composition (i.e., applying A_1 followed by applying A_2) is also a quantum operation whose matrix is $A_2 A_1$.* ◇

In particular, since $A_1 A_1^* = I$, every quantum operation has a corresponding "inverse" operation that cancels it. (Quantum computation is "reversible.")

Since quantum operations are linear, it suffices to describe their behavior on any linear basis for the space $\mathbb{C}^{2^m}$, and so we often specify quantum operations by the way they map the standard basis. However, not every classical operation is unitary, so designing quantum operations requires care.

10.3.4 Some examples of quantum operations

Here are some examples of quantum operations.

Flipping qubits. If we wish to "flip" the first qubit in an m-qubit register, (i.e., apply the NOT operation on the first qubit), then this can be done as a quantum operation that maps the basis state $|b, x\rangle$ for $b \in \{0, 1\}, x \in \{0, 1\}^{m-1}$ to the basis state $|1 - b, x\rangle$. The matrix of this operation is a permutation on the standard basis, and permutation matrices are always unitary. **Important note on notation:** This example involved an operation on the first qubit, so the remaining qubits in x are unaffected and unnecessarily cluttering the notation. From now on, whenever we describe operations on only a subset of qubits, we will often drop the unaffected qubits from the notation. Thus the NOT operation can be described as $|0\rangle \mapsto |1\rangle$ and $|1\rangle \mapsto |0\rangle$.

Reordering qubits. If we wish to exchange the values of two qubits, the following operation (again, unitary since it is a permutation of basic states) suffices: $|01\rangle \mapsto |10\rangle$ and $|10\rangle \mapsto |01\rangle$, with $|00\rangle$ and $|11\rangle$ being mapped to themselves. This operation is described by the following $2^2 \times 2^2$ matrix (where we index the rows and columns according to lexicographical order $|00\rangle, |01\rangle, |10\rangle, |11\rangle$):

$$\begin{pmatrix} 1 & 0 & 0 & 0 \\ 0 & 0 & 1 & 0 \\ 0 & 1 & 0 & 0 \\ 0 & 0 & 0 & 1 \end{pmatrix}$$

Note that by combining such operations we can arbitrarily reorder the qubits of an m-qubit register.

Copying qubits. Now suppose we wish to copy the first qubit into the second. Proceeding naively, we might try the following: both $|10\rangle$ and $|11\rangle$ map to $|11\rangle$, whereas both $|00\rangle$ and $|01\rangle$ map to $|00\rangle$. However, this is not a reversible operation and hence not unitary! In fact, the so-called *no cloning theorem* rules out any quantum operation that copies qubits; see the Chapter notes. However, while designing quantum algorithms it usually suffices to copy a qubit in "write once" fashion, by keeping around a supply of fresh qubits in a predetermined state, say $|0\rangle$, and only writing them over once. Now the operation $|xy\rangle \mapsto |x(x \oplus y)\rangle$ provides the effect of copying the first qubit, assuming the algorithm designer takes care to apply it only where the second qubit is a fresh (i.e., unused) qubit in state $|0\rangle$, and thus the operation never encounters the states $|01\rangle, |11\rangle$. Since this operation negates the second qubit y if and only if x is in the state $|1\rangle$, it is known as the *controlled NOT* (or CNOT for short) operation in the literature.

Rotation on single qubit. Thinking of the phase of a qubit as a two-dimensional vector as in Note 10.2, we may wish to apply a rotation to this state vector by an angle θ. This corresponds to the operation $|0\rangle \mapsto \cos\theta\,|0\rangle + \sin\theta\,|1\rangle$, and $|1\rangle \mapsto -\sin\theta\,|0\rangle + \cos\theta\,|1\rangle$, described by the matrix $\left(\begin{smallmatrix} \cos\theta & -\sin\theta \\ \sin\theta & \cos\theta \end{smallmatrix}\right)$, which is unitary. Note that when $\theta = \pi$ (i.e., 180) this amounts to flipping the sign of the state vector (i.e., the map $\mathbf{v} \mapsto -\mathbf{v}$).

AND of two bits. Now consider the classical AND operation, concretely, the operation that replaces the first qubit of the register by the AND of the first two bits. One would try to think of this as a linear operation $|b_1 b_2\rangle \mapsto |b_1 \wedge b_2\rangle\,|b_2\rangle$ for $b_1, b_2 \in \{0, 1\}$. But this is unfortunately not reversible and hence not unitary.

However, there is a different way to achieve the effect of an AND operation. This uses a "reversible AND," which uses an additional scratchpad in the form of a fresh qubit b_3. The operation is $|b_1\rangle\,|b_2\rangle\,|b_3\rangle \mapsto |b_1\rangle\,|b_2\rangle\,|b_3 \oplus (b_1 \wedge b_2)\rangle$ for all $b_1, b_2, b_3 \in \{0, 1\}$. This operation is unitary (in fact, permutation matrix) and thus a valid quantum operation, described by the following matrix

$$\begin{pmatrix} 1 & 0 & 0 & 0 & 0 & 0 & 0 & 0 \\ 0 & 1 & 0 & 0 & 0 & 0 & 0 & 0 \\ 0 & 0 & 1 & 0 & 0 & 0 & 0 & 0 \\ 0 & 0 & 0 & 1 & 0 & 0 & 0 & 0 \\ 0 & 0 & 0 & 0 & 1 & 0 & 0 & 0 \\ 0 & 0 & 0 & 0 & 0 & 1 & 0 & 0 \\ 0 & 0 & 0 & 0 & 0 & 0 & 0 & 1 \\ 0 & 0 & 0 & 0 & 0 & 0 & 1 & 0 \end{pmatrix}$$

As before, the algorithm designer will only apply this operation when b_3 is a fresh qubit in state $|0\rangle$. This operation is also known in quantum computing as the *Toffoli gate*. One can similarly obtain a "reversible OR" quantum operation. Together, the reversible OR and AND gates are key to showing that quantum computers can simulate ordinary Turing machines (see Section 10.3.7).

The Hadamard operation. The *Hadamard* gate is the single qubit operation that (up to normalization) maps $|0\rangle$ to $|0\rangle + |1\rangle$ and $|1\rangle$ to $|0\rangle - |1\rangle$. More succinctly the state $|b\rangle$ is mapped to $|0\rangle + (-1)^b\,|1\rangle$. The corresponding matrix is $\frac{1}{\sqrt{2}}\left(\begin{smallmatrix} 1 & 1 \\ 1 & -1 \end{smallmatrix}\right)$.

Note that if we apply a Hadamard gate to every qubit of an m-qubit register, then for every $x \in \{0, 1\}^m$ the state $|x\rangle$ is mapped to

$$(|0\rangle + (-1)^{x_1}\,|1\rangle)(|0\rangle + (-1)^{k_2}\,|1\rangle)\cdots(|0\rangle + (-1)^{x_m}\,|1\rangle)$$

$$= \sum_{y\in\{0,1\}^m} \left(\prod_{i\,:\,y_i=1}(-1)^{x_i}\right)|y\rangle = \sum_{y\in\{0,1\}^m} -1^{x\odot y}\,|y\rangle \quad (10.1)$$

where $x \odot y$ denotes the dot product modulo 2 of x and y. The unitary matrix corresponding to this operation is the $2^m \times 2^m$ matrix whose $(x,y)^{\text{th}}$ entry is $\frac{-1^{x \odot y}}{\sqrt{2^n}}$ (identifying $[2^m]$ with $\{0,1\}^m$). This operation plays a key role in quantum algorithms.[4]

10.3.5 Quantum computation and BQP

Even though the rules of quantum mechanics allow an arbitrary unitary matrix operation to be applied on the current state of a qantum register, not all such operations can be feasibly implemented. However, highly "local" operations—those that act on only a finite number of qubits—could perhaps be implemented. We thus define these as *elementary steps* in quantum computation.

Definition 10.8 *(Elementary quantum operations or quantum gates)* A quantum operation is called *elementary*, or sometimes a *quantum gate*, if it acts on three or less qubits of the register.[5] ◇

Note that an elementary operation on an m-qubit register can be specified by three indices in $[m]$ and an 8×8 unitary matrix. For example, if U is any 8×8 unitary matrix that has to be applied to the qubits numbered $2,3,4$, then this can be viewed as an elementary quantum operation $F : \mathbb{C}^{2^m} \to \mathbb{C}^{2^m}$ that maps the basis state $|x_1 x_2 \ldots x_m\rangle$ to the state $|x_1\rangle (U |x_2 x_3 x_4\rangle) |x_5 \ldots x_m\rangle$ for all $x_1, x_2, \ldots, x_m \in \{0,1\}$.

Now we can define quantum computation: It is a sequence of elementary operations applied to a quantum register.

Definition 10.9 *(Quantum computation and the class **BQP**)* Let $f : \{0,1\}^* \to \{0,1\}$ and $T : \mathbb{N} \to \mathbb{N}$ be some functions. We say that f is *computable in quantum $T(n)$-time* if there is a polynomial-time classical TM that on input $(1^n, 1^{T(n)})$ for any $n \in \mathbb{N}$ outputs the descriptions of quantum gates $F_1, \ldots, F_T$ such that for every $x \in \{0,1\}^n$, we can compute $f(x)$ by the following process with probability at least $2/3$:

1. Initialize an m qubit quantum register to the state $|x0^{n-m}\rangle$ (i.e., x padded with zeroes), where $m \leq T(n)$.
2. Apply one after the other $T(n)$ elementary quantum operations $F_1, \ldots, F_T$ to the register.
3. Measure the register and let Y denote the obtained value. (That is, if $\mathbf{v}$ is the final state of the register, then Y is a random variable that takes the value y with probability $|\mathbf{v}_y|^2$ for every $y \in \{0,1\}^m$.)
4. Output Y_1.

A Boolean function $f : \{0,1\}^* \to \{0,1\}$ is in **BQP** if there is some polynomial $p : \mathbb{N} \to \mathbb{N}$ such that f is computable in quantum $p(n)$-time.

---

[4] We will encounter this matrix again in Chapters 11 and 19 where we describe the *Walsh-Hadamard* error correcting code. (Though there will describe it as a 0/1 matrix over GF(2) rather than ±1 matrix over $\mathbb{C}$.)

[5] The constant three is arbitrary in the sense that replacing it with every constant greater or equal to two would lead to an equivalently powerful model.

Some remarks are in order:

1. This definition easily generalizes to functions with more than one bit of output.
2. Elementary operations are represented by 8×8 matrices of complex numbers, which a classical TM cannot write per se. However, it suffices for the TM to write the most significant $O(\log T(n))$ bits of the complex number; see Exercise 10.8.
3. It can be shown that the set of elementary operations or gates (which is an infinite set) can be reduced without loss of generality to two *universal operations*; see Section 10.3.8
4. Readers familiar with quantum mechanics or quantum computing may notice that our definition of quantum computation disallows several features that are allowed by quantum mechanics, such as *mixed* states that involve both quantum superposition and probability and measurement in different bases than the standard basis. However, none of these features adds to the computing power of quantum computers. Another feature that we do not explicitly allow is performing partial measurements of some of the qubits in the course of the computation. Exercise 10.7 shows that such partial measurements can always be eliminated without much loss of efficiency, though it will sometime be convenient for us to describe our algorithms as using them.

Quantum versus probabilistic computation

At this point the reader may think that the quantum model "obviously" gives exponential speedup as the states of registers are described by 2^m-dimensional vectors and operations are described by $2^m \times 2^m$ matrices. However, this is not the case. One can describe even ordinary probabilistic computation in a similar way: We can think of the state of a classical m-bit register as a 2^m-dimensional vector whose xth coordinate denotes the probability that the register contains the string x, and considers probabilistic operations as linear stochastic maps from $\mathbb{R}^{2^m}$ to $\mathbb{R}^{2^m}$; see Exercise 10.4. The added power of quantum computing seems to derive from the fact that here we allow vectors to have *negative* coefficients (recall Feynman's quote from the start of the chapter), and the norm that is preserved at each step is the Euclidean (i.e., ℓ_2) norm rather than the sum (i.e., ℓ_1) norm (see also Exercise 10.5). Note also that classical computation, whether deterministic or probabilistic, is a subcase of quantum computation, as we see in Section 10.3.7.

10.3.6 Quantum circuits

Definition 10.9 is reminiscent of the the definition of classical *straight-line* programs, which as we saw in Chapter 6 is an equivalent model to Boolean circuits (see Note 6.4). Similarly, one can define quantum computation and **BQP** also in terms of *quantum circuits* (in fact, this is the definition appearing in most texts). Quantum circuits are similar to Boolean circuits: These are directed acyclic graphs with sources (vertices with in-degree zero) denoting the inputs, sinks (vertices with out-degree zero) denoting the outputs and internal nodes denoting the gates. One difference is that this time the gates are labeled not by the operations AND,OR and NOT but by 2×2, 4×4 or 8×8 unitary matrices. Another difference is that (since copying is not allowed) the out-degree of gates and even inputs cannot be arbitrarily large but rather the out-degree of each input vertex is one, and the in-degree and out-degree of each gate are equal (and are at most 3). We also allow special "workspace" or "scratchpad" inputs that are initialized to the state $|0\rangle$.

Such circuits are often described in the literature using diagrams such as the one below, depicting a circuit that on input $|q_0\rangle |q_1\rangle$ first applies the Hadamard operation on $|q_0\rangle$ and then applies the mapping $|q_0 q_1\rangle \mapsto |q_0(q_0 \oplus q_1)\rangle$:

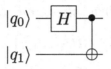

10.3.7 Classical computation as a subcase of quantum computation

In Section 10.3.3, we saw quantum implementations of the classical NOT and AND operations. More generally, we can efficiently simulate any classical computation using quantum operations.

Lemma 10.10 *(Boolean circuits as a subcase of quantum circuits) If $f:\{0, 1\}^n \to \{0, 1\}^m$ is computable by a Boolean circuit of size S then there is a sequence of $2S+m+n$ quantum operations computing the mapping $|x\rangle |0^{2m+S}\rangle \mapsto |x\rangle |f(x)\rangle |0^{S+m}\rangle$.* ◇

PROOF: Replace each Boolean gate (AND, OR, NOT) by its quantum analog as already outlined. The resulting computation maps $|x\rangle |0^{2m}\rangle |0^S\rangle \mapsto |x\rangle |f(x)0^m\rangle |z\rangle$, where z is the string of values taken by the internal wires in the Boolean circuit (these correspond to scratchpad memory used by the quantum operations at the gates) and the string 0^m consists of qubits unused so far. Now copy $f(x)$ onto the string 0^m using m operations of the form $|bc\rangle \mapsto |b(b \oplus c)\rangle$. Then run the operations corresponding to the Boolean operations in reverse (applying the inverse of each operation). This erases the original copy of $f(x)$ as well as $|z\rangle$ and leaves behind clean bits in state $|0\rangle$, together with one copy of $f(x)$. ∎

Since a classical Turing machine computation running in $T(n)$ steps has an equivalent Boolean circuit of size $O(T(n) \log T(n))$ it also follows that $\mathbf{P} \subseteq \mathbf{BQP}$. Using the Hadamard operation that maps $|0\rangle$ to $|0\rangle + |1\rangle$ we can get a qubit that when measured gives $|0\rangle$ with probability $1/2$ and $|1\rangle$ with probability $1/2$, simulating a coin toss. Thus the following corollary is immediate.

Corollary 10.11 $\mathbf{BPP} \subseteq \mathbf{BQP}$.   ◇

10.3.8 Universal operations

Allowing every three-qubit quantum operation as "elementary" seems problematic since this set is infinite. By contrast, classical Boolean circuits only need the gates

AND, OR and NOT. Fortunately, a similar result holds for quantum computation. The following theorem (whose proof we omit) shows that there is a set of few operations that suffice to construct any quantum operation:

Theorem 10.12 *(Universal basis for quantum operations* [Deu89, Kit97]*)*
For every $D \geq 3$ and $\epsilon > 0$, there is $\ell \leq 100(D \log 1/\epsilon)^3$ such that the following is true. Every $D \times D$ unitary matrix U can be approximated as a product of unitary matrices $U_1, \ldots, U_\ell$ in the sense that its $(i,j)$the entry for each $i,j \leq D$ satisfies

$$\left| U_{i,j} - (U_\ell \cdots U_1)_{i,j} \right| < \epsilon$$

and each U_r corresponds to applying either the Hadamard gate $\frac{1}{\sqrt{2}}\left(\begin{smallmatrix} 1 & 1 \\ 1 & -1 \end{smallmatrix}\right)$, the Toffoli gate $|abc\rangle \mapsto |ab(c \oplus a \wedge b)\rangle)$, or the phase shift gate $\left(\begin{smallmatrix} 1 & 0 \\ 0 & i \end{smallmatrix}\right)$, on at most three qubits.

It can be shown that such ϵ-approximation for, say, $\epsilon < \frac{1}{10T}$ suffices for simulating any T-time quantum computation (see Exercise 10.8), and hence we can replace any computation using T arbitrary elementary matrices by a computation using only one of the above three gates. Other universal gates are also known, and in particular Shi [Shi03] showed that for, the purpose of quantum computation, the Hadamard and Toffoli gates alone suffice (this uses the fact that complex numbers are not necessary for quantum computation, see Exercise 10.5).

One corollary of Theorem 10.12 is that three-qubit gates can be used to simulate k-qubit gates for every constant $k > 3$ (albeit at a cost exponential in k since it is represented by $2^k \times 2^k$ matrix). This means that when designing quantum algorithms, we can consider every k-qubit gate as elementary as long as k is smaller than some absolute constant. We can use this fact to obtain a quantum analog of the "i f *cond* then" construct of classical programming languages. That is, given a T step quantum circuit for an n-qubit quantum operation U, then we can compute the quantum operation *Controlled-U* in $O(T)$ steps, where Controlled-U maps a vector $|x_1 \ldots x_n x_{n+1}\rangle$ to $|U(x_1 \ldots x_n)x_{n+1}\rangle$ if $x_{n+1} = 1$ and to itself otherwise. The reason is that we can transform every elementary operation F in the computation of U to the analogous "Controlled-F" operation. Since the "Controlled-F" operation depends on at most four qubits, it too can be considered elementary.

10.4 GROVER'S SEARCH ALGORITHM

We now describe Grover's algorithm, one of the basic and quite useful algorithms for quantum computers. This section can be read independently of Sections 10.5 and 10.6, which describe Simon's and Shor's algorithms, and so the reader who is anxious to see the integer factorization algorithm can skip ahead to Section 10.5.

Consider the **NP**-complete problem SAT of finding, given an n-variable Boolean formula φ, whether there exists an assignment $a \in \{0, 1\}^n$ such that $\varphi(a) = 1$. Using "classical" deterministic or probabilistic TM's, we do not know how to solve this problem better than the trivial $poly(n)2^n$-time algorithm.[6] Grover's algorithm solves SAT in $poly(n)2^{n/2}$-time on a quantum computer. This is a significant improvement over the classical case, even if it falls way short of showing that $\mathbf{NP} \subseteq \mathbf{BQP}$. In fact, Grover's algorithm solves an even more general problem, namely, satisfiability of a circuit with n inputs.

Theorem 10.13 *(Grover's algorithm [Gro96])*
There is a quantum algorithm that given as input every polynomial-time computable function $f : \{0, 1\}^n \rightarrow \{0, 1\}$ (i.e., represented as a circuit computing f) finds in $poly(n)2^{n/2}$ time a string a such that $f(a) = 1$ (if such a string exists).

Grover's algorithm is best described geometrically. We assume that the function f has a *single* satisfying assignment a. (The techniques described in Section 17.4.1 allow us to reduce the general problem to this case.) Consider an n-qubit register, and let $\mathbf{u}$ denote the *uniform state vector* of this register. That is, $\mathbf{u} = \frac{1}{2^{n/2}} \sum_{x \in \{0,1\}^n} |x\rangle$. The angle between $\mathbf{u}$ and the basis state $|a\rangle$ is equal to the inverse cosine of their inner product $\langle \mathbf{u}, |a\rangle \rangle = \frac{1}{2^{n/2}}$. Since this is a positive number, this angle is smaller than $\pi/2$ (90), and hence we denote it by $\pi/2 - \theta$, where $\sin \theta = \frac{1}{2^{n/2}}$ and hence (using the inequality $\theta \geq \sin \theta$ for $\theta > 0$), $\theta \geq 2^{-n/2}$.

The algorithm starts with the state $\mathbf{u}$, and at each step it gets nearer the state $|a\rangle$. If its current state makes an angle $\pi/2 - \alpha$ with $|a\rangle$, then at the end of the step it makes an angle $\pi/2 - \alpha - 2\theta$. Thus, in $O(1/\theta) = O(2^{n/2})$ steps, it will get to a state $\mathbf{v}$ whose inner product with $|a\rangle$ is larger than, say, $1/2$, implying that a measurement of the register will yield a with probability at least $1/4$.

The main idea is that to rotate a vector $\mathbf{w}$ toward the unknown vector $|a\rangle$ by an angle of θ, it suffices to take two *reflections* around the vector $\mathbf{u}$ and the vector $\mathbf{e} = \sum_{x \neq a} |a\rangle$ (the latter is the vector orthogonal to $|a\rangle$ on the plane spanned by $\mathbf{u}$ and $|a\rangle$). See Figure 10.3 for a "proof by picture."

To complete the algorithm's description, we need to show how we can perform the reflections around the vectors $\mathbf{u}$ and $\mathbf{e}$. That is, we need to show how we can in polynomial time transform a state $\mathbf{w}$ of the register into the state that is $\mathbf{w}$'s reflection around $\mathbf{u}$ (respectively, $\mathbf{e}$). In fact, we will not work with an n-qubit register but with an m-qubit register for m that is polynomial in n. However, the extra qubits will only serve as "scratch workspace" and will always contain zero except during intermediate computations (thanks to the "cleanup" idea of the proof of Lemma 10.10), and hence can be safely ignored.

Reflecting around e

Recall that to reflect a vector $\mathbf{w}$ around a vector $\mathbf{v}$, we express $\mathbf{w}$ as $\alpha\mathbf{v} + \mathbf{v}^\perp$ (where $\mathbf{v}^\perp$ is orthogonal to $\mathbf{v}$) and output $\alpha\mathbf{v} - \mathbf{v}^\perp$. Thus the reflection of $\mathbf{w}$ around $\mathbf{e}$ is equal to $\sum_{x \neq a} \mathbf{w}_x |x\rangle - \mathbf{w}_a |a\rangle$. Yet, it is easy to perform this transformation.

---

[6] There are slightly better algorithms for special cases such as 3SAT.

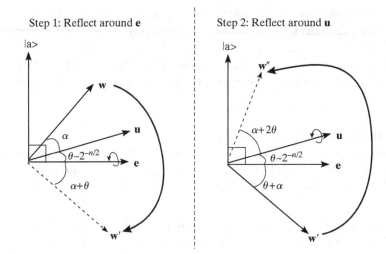

Figure 10.3. We transform a vector **w** in the plane spanned by $|a\rangle$ and **u** into a vector **w''** that is 2θ radians close to $|a\rangle$ by performing two reflections. First, we reflect around $\mathbf{e} = \sum_{x \neq a} |x\rangle$ (the vector orthogonal to $|a\rangle$ on this plane), and then we reflect around **u**. If the original angle between **w** and $|a\rangle$ was $\pi/2 - \theta - \alpha$, then the new angle will be $\pi/2 - \theta - \alpha - 2\theta$. We can restrict our attention to the plane spanned by **u** and $|a\rangle$ as the reflections leave all vectors orthogonal to this plane fixed.

1. Since f is computable in polynomial time, we can compute the transformation $|x\sigma\rangle \mapsto$ $|x(\sigma \oplus f(x))\rangle$ in polynomial time (this notation ignores the extra workspace that may be needed, but this won't make any difference). This transformation maps $|x0\rangle$ to $|x0\rangle$ for $x \neq a$ and $|a0\rangle$ to $|a1\rangle$.
2. Then, we apply the elementary transformation (known as a Z gate) $|0\rangle \mapsto |0\rangle$, $|1\rangle \mapsto$ $-|1\rangle$ on the qubit σ. This maps $|x0\rangle$ to $|x0\rangle$ for $x \neq a$ and maps $|a1\rangle$ to $-|a1\rangle$.
3. Then, we apply the transformation $|x\sigma\rangle \mapsto |x(\sigma \oplus f(x))\rangle$ again, mapping $|x0\rangle$ to $|x0\rangle$ for $x \neq a$ and maps $|a1\rangle$ to $|a0\rangle$.

The final result is that the vector $|x0\rangle$ is mapped to itself for $x \neq a$, but $|a0\rangle$ is mapped to $-|a0\rangle$. Ignoring the last qubit, this is exactly a reflection around $|a\rangle$.

Reflecting around u

To reflect around **u**, we first apply the Hadamard operation to each qubit, mapping **u** to $|0\rangle$. Then, we reflect around $|0\rangle$ (this can be done in the same way as reflecting around $|a\rangle$, just using the function $g : \{0, 1\}^n \to \{0, 1\}$ that outputs 1 iff its input is all zeroes instead of f). Then, we apply the Hadamard operation again, mapping $|0\rangle$ back to **u**.

Together these operations allow us to take a vector in the plane spanned by $|a\rangle$ and **u** and rotate it 2θ radians closer to $|a\rangle$. Thus if we start with the vector **u**, we will only need to repeat them $O(1/\theta) = O(2^{n/2})$ times to obtain a vector that, when measured, yields $|a\rangle$ with constant probability.

This completes the proof of Theorem 10.13. For the sake of completeness, Figure 10.4 contains the full description of Grover's algorithm. ∎

Operation	State (neglecting normalizing factors)
Goal: Given a polynomial-time computable $f : \{0, 1\}^n \to \{0, 1\}$ with a unique $a \in \{0, 1\}^n$ such that $f(a) = 1$, find a. **Quantum register:** We use an $n + 1 + m$-qubit register, where m is large enough so we can compute the transformation $\lvert x\sigma 0^m \rangle \mapsto \lvert x(\sigma \oplus f(x))0^m \rangle$.	

Operation	State (neglecting normalizing factors)
	Initial state: $\lvert 0^{n+m+1} \rangle$
Apply Hadamard operation to first n qubits.	$\mathbf{u} \lvert 0^{m+1} \rangle$ (where $\mathbf{u}$ denotes $\sum_{x\in\{0,1\}^n} \lvert x\rangle$)
For $i = 1, \ldots, 2^{n/2}$ do:	$\mathbf{v}^i \lvert 0^{m+1} \rangle$ We let $\mathbf{v}^1 = \mathbf{u}$ and maintain the invariant that $\langle \mathbf{v}^i, \lvert a\rangle\rangle = \sin(i\theta)$, where $\theta \sim 2^{-n/2}$ is such that $\langle \mathbf{u}, \lvert a\rangle\rangle = \sin(\theta)$
Step 1: *Reflect around* $\mathbf{e} = \sum_{x\neq a} \lvert x\rangle$:	
1.1 Compute $\lvert x\sigma 0^m\rangle \mapsto \lvert x(\sigma \oplus f(x))0^m\rangle$	$\sum_{x\neq a} \mathbf{v}_x^i \lvert x\rangle \lvert 0^{m+1}\rangle + \mathbf{v}_a^i \lvert a\rangle \lvert 10^m\rangle$
1.2 If $\sigma = 1$ then multiply vector by -1, otherwise do not do anything.	$\sum_{x\neq a} \mathbf{v}_x^i \lvert x\rangle \lvert 0^{m+1}\rangle - \mathbf{v}_a^i \lvert a\rangle \lvert 10^m\rangle$
1.3 Compute $\lvert x\sigma 0^m\rangle \mapsto \lvert x(\sigma \oplus f(x))0^m\rangle$.	$\mathbf{w}^i \lvert 0^{m+1}\rangle = \sum_{x\neq a} \mathbf{v}_x^i \lvert x\rangle \lvert 0^{m+1}\rangle - \mathbf{v}_a^i \lvert a\rangle \lvert 00^m\rangle$. ($\mathbf{w}^i$ is $\mathbf{v}^i$ reflected around $\sum_{x\neq a} \lvert x\rangle$.)
Step 2: *Reflect around* $\mathbf{u}$:	
2.1 Apply Hadamard operation to first n qubits.	$\langle \mathbf{w}^i, \mathbf{u}\rangle \lvert 0^n\rangle \lvert 0^{m+1}\rangle + \sum_{x\neq 0^n} \alpha_x \lvert x\rangle \lvert 0^{m+1}\rangle$, for some coefficients α_x's (given by $\alpha_x = \sum_z (-1)^{x\odot z} \mathbf{w}_z^i \lvert z\rangle$).
2.2 Reflect around $\lvert 0\rangle$:	
2.2.1 If first n-qubits are all zero, then flip $n + 1$st qubit.	$\langle \mathbf{w}^i, \mathbf{u}\rangle \lvert 0^n\rangle \lvert 10^m\rangle + \sum_{x\neq 0^n} \alpha_x \lvert x\rangle \lvert 0^{m+1}\rangle$
2.2.2 If $n + 1$st qubit is 1, then multiply by -1.	$-\langle \mathbf{w}^i, \mathbf{u}\rangle \lvert 0^n\rangle \lvert 10^m\rangle + \sum_{x\neq 0^n} \alpha_x \lvert x\rangle \lvert 0^{m+1}\rangle$
2.2.3 If first n-qubits are all zero, then flip $n + 1$st qubit.	$-\langle \mathbf{w}^i, \mathbf{u}\rangle \lvert 0^n\rangle \lvert 0^{m+1}\rangle + \sum_{x\neq 0^n} \alpha_x \lvert x\rangle \lvert 0^{m+1}\rangle$
2.3 Apply Hadamard operation to first n qubits.	$\mathbf{v}^{i+1} \lvert 0^{m+1}\rangle$ (where $\mathbf{v}^{i+1}$ is $\mathbf{w}^i$ reflected around $\mathbf{u}$)
Measure register and let a' be the obtained value in the first n qubits. If $f(a') = 1$ then output a'. Otherwise, repeat.	

Figure 10.4. Grover's search algorithm.

10.5 SIMON'S ALGORITHM

Although beautiful, Grover's algorithm still has a significant drawback: it is merely quadratically faster than the best known classical algorithm for the same problem. In contrast, in this section we show *Simon's algorithm* that is a polynomial-time quantum algorithm solving a problem for which the best known classical algorithm takes *exponential* time.

Simon's problem

Given: A polynomial-size classical circuit for a function $f : \{0, 1\}^n \to \{0, 1\}^n$ such that there exists $a \in \{0, 1\}^n$ satisfying $f(x) = f(y)$ iff $x = y \oplus a$ for every $x, y \in \{0, 1\}^n$.
Goal: Find this string a (which is called the "period" of f).

Theorem 10.14 *(Simon's algorithm* [Sim94])
There is a polynomial-time quantum algorithm for Simon's problem.

Two natural questions are (1) why is this problem interesting? and (2) why do we believe it is hard to solve for classical computers? The best answer to (1) is that, as we will see in Section 10.6, a generalization of Simon's problem turns out to be crucial in the quantum polynomial-time algorithm for the famous *integer factorization* problem. Regarding (2), of course we do not know for certain that this problem does not have a classical polynomial-time algorithm (in particular, if **P** = **NP** then there obviously exists such an algorithm). However, some intuition why it may be hard can be gleaned from the following *black box* model: Suppose that you are given access to a black box (or oracle) that on input $x \in \{0, 1\}^n$ returns the value $f(x)$. Would you be able to learn a by making at most a subexponential number of queries to the black box? It is not hard to see that if a is chosen at random from $\{0, 1\}^n$ and f is chosen at random subject to the condition that $f(x) = f(y)$ iff $x = y \oplus a$, then no classical algorithm can successfully recover a with reasonable probability using significantly less than $2^{n/2}$ queries to the black box. Indeed, an algorithm using fewer queries is very likely to never get the same answer to two distinct queries, in which case it gets no information about the value of a.

10.5.1 Proof of Theorem 10.14

Simon's algorithm is actually quite simple. It uses a register of $2n + m$ qubits, where m is the number of workspace bits needed to compute f. (Below we will ignore the last m qubits of the register, since they will be always set to all zeroes except in intermediate steps of f's computation.) The algorithm first uses n Hadamard operations to set the first n qubits to the uniform state and then apply the operation $|xz\rangle \mapsto |x(z \oplus f(x))\rangle$ to the register, resulting (up to normalization) in the state

$$\sum_{x \in \{0,1\}^n} |x\rangle |f(x)\rangle = \sum_{x \in \{0,1\}^n} (|x\rangle + |x \oplus a\rangle) |f(x)\rangle. \qquad (10.2)$$

We then *measure* the second n bits of the register, collapsing its state to

$$|xf(x)\rangle + |(x \oplus a)f(x)\rangle \qquad (10.3)$$

for some string x (that is chosen uniformly from $\{0, 1\}^n$). You might think that we're done as the state (10.3) clearly encodes a; however, we cannot directly learn a from this state: If we measure the first n bits we will get with probability $1/2$ the value x and with probability $1/2$ the value $x \oplus a$. Even though a can be deduced from these two values

---

Goal: Given a polynomial-time computable $f : \{0,1\}^n \mapsto \{0,1\}^n$ such that there is some $a \in \{0,1\}^n$ satisfying $f(x) = f(y)$ iff $y = x \oplus a$ for every $x, y \in \{0,1\}^n$, find a.

Quantum register: We use an $2n + m$-qubit register, where m is large enough so we can compute the transformation $|xz0^m\rangle \mapsto |x(z+f(x))0^m\rangle$. (Below we ignore the least m qubits of the register as they will always contain 0^m except in intermediate computations of f.)

Operation	State (neglecting normalizing factors)
	Initial state: $|0^{2n}\rangle$
Apply Hadamard operation to first n qubits.	$\sum_x |x0^n\rangle$
Compute $|xz\rangle \mapsto |x(y \oplus f(x))\rangle$.	$\sum_x |xf(x)\rangle = \sum_x(|x\rangle + |x \oplus a\rangle)|f(x)\rangle$
Measure second n bits of register.	$(|x\rangle + |x \oplus a\rangle)|f(x)\rangle$
Apply Hadamard to first n bits.	$\left(\sum_y(-1)^{x \odot y}(1 + (-1)^{a \odot y})|y\rangle\right)|f(x)\rangle$
	$= 2\sum_{y:a \odot y = 0}(-1)^{x \odot y}|y\rangle|f(x)\rangle$
Measure first n qubits of register to obtain a value y such that $y \odot a = 0$. Repeat until we get a sufficient number of linearly independent equations on a.	

Figure 10.5. Simon's algorithm.

combined, each one of them on its own yields no information about a. (This point is well worth some contemplation as it underlies the subtleties involved in quantum computation and demonstrates why a quantum algorithm is *not* generally equivalent to performing exponentially many classical computation in parallel.)

However, consider now what happens if we perform another n Hadamard operations on the first n bits. Since this maps x to the vector $\sum_y(-1)^{x \odot y}|y\rangle$, the new state of the first n bits will be

$$\sum_y\left((-1)^{x \odot y} + (-1)^{(x \oplus a) \odot y}\right)|y\rangle = \sum_y\left((-1)^{x \odot y} + (-1)^{x \odot y}(-1)^{a \odot y}\right)|y\rangle \quad (10.4)$$

For every $y \in \{0,1\}^m$, the yth coefficient in the state (10.4) is nonzero if and only if if and only if $a \odot y = 0$, and in fact if measured, the state (10.4) yields a uniform $y \in \{0,1\}^n$ satisfying $a \odot y = 0$.

Repeating the entire process k times, we get k uniform strings $y_1, \ldots, y_k$ satisfying $y \odot a = 0$ or in other words, k *linear equations* (over the field GF(2)) on the variables $a_1, \ldots, a_n$. It can be easily shown that if, say, $k \geq 2n$ then with high probability there will be $n - 1$ linearly independent equations among these (see Exercise 10.9), and hence we will be able to retrieve a from these equations using Gaussian elimination. This completes the proof of Theorem 10.14. For completeness, a full description of Simon's algorithm can be found in Figure 10.5. ∎

10.6 SHOR'S ALGORITHM: INTEGER FACTORIZATION USING QUANTUM COMPUTERS

The *integer factorization* problem is to find, given an integer N, the set of all *prime factors* of N (i.e., prime numbers that divide N). By a polynomial-time algorithm for this problem, we mean an algorithm that runs in time polynomial in the description of N

(i.e., poly($\log(N)$) time). Although people have thought about factorization for at least 2,000 years, we still do not know of a polynomial-time algorithm for it: The best classical algorithm takes roughly $2^{(\log N)^{1/3}}$ steps to factor N [LLMP90]. In fact, the presumed difficulty of this problem underlies many popular encryption schemes (such as RSA, see Section 9.2.1). Therefore, it was quite a surprise when in 1994 Peter Shor showed the following result, which is now the most famous algorithm for quantum computers, and the strongest evidence that **BQP** may contain problems outside of **BPP**.

Theorem 10.15 *Shor's algorithm: Factoring in* **BQP** *[Sho97]*
There is a quantum algorithm that given a number N, runs in time poly($\log(N)$) *and outputs the prime factorization of N.*

Shor's ideas in nutshell

The algorithm uses the following observations. First, since N has at most $\log N$ factors, it clearly suffices to show how to find a *single* factor of N in poly($\log N$) time because we can then repeat the algorithm with N divided by that factor, and thus find all factors. Second, it is a well-known fact that in order to find a single factor, it suffices to be able to find the *order* of a random number A (mod N), in other words, the smallest r such that $A^r \equiv 1$ (mod N). This is detailed in Section 10.6.4, but the idea is that with good probability, the order r of A will be even and furthermore $A^{r/2} - 1$ will have a nontrivial common factor with N, which we can find using a GCD (greatest common divisor) computation. Third, the mapping $A \mapsto A^x$ (mod N) is computable in poly($\log N$) time even on classical TMs (and so in particular by quantum algorithms) using *fast exponentiation*; see Exercise 10.10.

Using these observations we can come up with a simple polylog(N)-time quantum algorithm that transforms a quantum register initialized to all zeros into the state that is the uniform superposition of all states of the type $|x\rangle$, where $x \leq N$ and satisfies $A^x \equiv y_0$ (mod N) for some randomly chosen $y_0 \leq N - 1$. By elementary number theory, the set of such x's form an *arithmetic progression* of the type $x_0 + ri$ for $i = 1, 2, \ldots$ where $A^{x_0} \equiv y_0$ (mod N) and r is the order of A.

By now the problem is beginning to look quite a bit like Simon's problem, since we have created a quantum state involving a strong periodicity (namely, an arithmetic progression) and we are interested in determining its period. In engineering and mathematics, a classical tool for detecting periods is the Fourier transform (see Section 10.6.1). In the next section, we describe the *Quantum Fourier Transform (QFT)*, which allows us to detect periods in a quantum state. This is a quantum algorithm that takes a register from some arbitrary state $f \in \mathbb{C}^M$ into a state whose vector is the Fourier transform $\hat{f}$ of f. The QFT takes only $O(\log^2 M)$ elementary steps and is thus very efficient. Note that we cannot say that this algorithm "computes" the Fourier transform, since the transform is stored in the amplitudes of the state, and as mentioned earlier, quantum mechanics give no way to "read out" the amplitudes per se. The only way to get information from a quantum state is by *measuring* it, which yields a single basis state with probability that is related to its amplitude. This is hardly representative of the entire Fourier transform vector, but sometimes (as is the case in Shor's algorithm) this is enough to get highly nontrivial information, which we do not know how to obtain using classical (nonquantum) computers.

10.6.1 The Fourier transform over $\mathbb{Z}_M$

We now define the *Fourier transform over* $\mathbb{Z}_M$ (the group of integers in $\{0, \ldots, M-1\}$ with addition modulo M). We give a definition that is specialized to the current context. For more discussion on the Fourier transform, a tool that has found numerous uses in complexity theory, see Chapter 22.

Definition 10.16 For every vector $f \in \mathbb{C}^M$, the *Fourier transform of* f is the vector $\hat{f}$ where the xth coordinate of $\hat{f}$ is[7]

$$\hat{f}(x) = \frac{1}{\sqrt{M}} \sum_{y \in \mathbb{Z}_M} f(x)\omega^{xy}$$

where $\omega = e^{2\pi i/M}$. ◇

The Fourier transform is simply a representation of f in the *Fourier basis* $\{\chi_x\}_{x \in \mathbb{Z}_M}$, where χ_x is the vector/function whose yth coordinate is $\frac{1}{\sqrt{M}\omega^{xy}}$. The inner product of any two vectors χ_x, χ_z in this basis is equal to

$$\langle \chi_x, \chi_z \rangle = \frac{1}{M} \sum_{y \in \mathbb{Z}_M} \omega^{xy} \overline{\omega^{zy}} = \frac{1}{M} \sum_{y \in \mathbb{Z}_M} \omega^{(x-z)y}$$

But if $x = z$ then $\omega^{(x-z)} = 1$ and hence this sum is equal to 1. On the other hand, if $x \neq z$, then this sum is equal to $\frac{1}{M} \frac{1-\omega^{(x-y)M}}{1-\omega^{x-y}} = \frac{1}{M} \frac{1-1}{1-\omega^{x-y}} = 0$ using the formula for the sum of a geometric series. In other words, this is an *orthonormal* basis which means that the Fourier transform map $f \mapsto \hat{f}$ is a *unitary* operation.

What is so special about the Fourier basis? For one thing, if we identify vectors in $\mathbb{C}^M$ with functions mapping $\mathbb{Z}_M$ to $\mathbb{C}$, then it's easy to see that every function χ in the Fourier basis is a *homomorphism* from $\mathbb{Z}_M$ to $\mathbb{C}$ in the sense that $\chi(y+z) = \chi(y)\chi(z)$ for every $y, z \in \mathbb{Z}_M$. Also, every function χ is *periodic* in the sense that there exists $r \in \mathbb{Z}_M$ such that $\chi(y+r) = \chi(z)$ for every $y \in \mathbb{Z}_M$ (indeed if $\chi(y) = \omega^{xy}$ then we can take r to be ℓ/x where ℓ is the least common multiple of x and M). Thus, intuitively, if a function $f : \mathbb{Z}_M \to \mathbb{C}$ is itself periodic (or roughly periodic), then when representing f in the Fourier basis, the coefficients of basis vectors with periods agreeing with the period of f should be large, and so we might be able to discover f's period from this representation. This does turn out to be the case, and is a crucial point in Shor's algorithm.

Fast Fourier transform

Denote by FT_M the operation that maps every vector $f \in \mathbb{C}^M$ to its Fourier transform $\hat{f}$. The operation FT_M is represented by an $M \times M$ matrix whose (x, y)th entry is ω^{xy}. The trivial algorithm to compute it takes M^2 operations. The famous *fast Fourier transform* (FFT) algorithm computes the Fourier transform in $O(M \log M)$ operations. We now sketch the idea behind this classical algorithm because the same idea will be used in the *quantum* Fourier transform algorithm described in Section 10.6.2.

---

[7]   In the context of Fourier transform it is customary and convenient to denote the xth coordinate of a vector f by $f(x)$ rather than f_x.

Note that

$$\hat{f}(x) = \frac{1}{\sqrt{M}} \sum_{y \in \mathbb{Z}_M} f(y)\omega^{xy}$$

$$= \frac{1}{\sqrt{M}} \sum_{y \in \mathbb{Z}_M, y \text{ even}} f(y)\omega^{-2x(y/2)} + \omega^x \frac{1}{\sqrt{M}} \sum_{y \in \mathbb{Z}_M, y \text{ odd}} f(y)\omega^{2x(y-1)/2}$$

Now since ω^2 is an $M/2$th root of unity and $\omega^{M/2} = -1$, letting W be the $M/2 \times M/2$ diagonal matrix with diagonal entries $\omega^0, \ldots, \omega^{M/2-1}$, we get that

$$FT_M(f)_{low} = FT_{M/2}(f_{even}) + W \, FT_{M/2}(f_{odd}) \tag{10.5}$$

$$FT_M(f)_{high} = FT_{M/2}(f_{even}) - W \, FT_{M/2}(f_{odd}) \tag{10.6}$$

where for an M-dimensional vector $\mathbf{v}$, we denote by $\mathbf{v}_{even}$ (resp. $\mathbf{v}_{odd}$) the $M/2$-dimensional vector obtained by restricting $\mathbf{v}$ to the coordinates whose indices have least significant bit equal to 0 (resp. 1) and by $\mathbf{v}_{low}$ (resp. $\mathbf{v}_{high}$) the restriction of $\mathbf{v}$ to coordinates with most significant bit 0 (resp. 1).

Equations (10.5) and (10.6) are the crux of the divide-and-conquer idea of the FFT algorithm, since they allow to replace a size-M problem with two size-$M/2$ subproblems, leading to a recursive time bound of the form $T(M) = 2T(M/2) + O(M)$ which solves to $T(M) = O(M \log M)$.

10.6.2 Quantum fourier transform over $\mathbb{Z}_M$

The *quantum Fourier transform* is an algorithm to change the state of a quantum register from $f \in \mathbb{C}^M$ to its Fourier transform $\hat{f}$.

> **Lemma 10.17** *(Quantum Fourier transform [BV93])*
> *For every m and $M = 2^m$ there is a quantum algorithm that uses $O(m^2)$ elementary quantum operations and transforms a quantum register in state $f = \sum_{x \in \mathbb{Z}_m} f(x) \, |x\rangle$ into the state $\hat{f} = \sum_{x \in \mathbb{Z}_M} \hat{f}(x) \, |x\rangle$, where $\hat{f}(x) = \frac{1}{\sqrt{M}} \sum_{y \in \mathbb{Z}_m} \omega^{xy} f(x)$.*

PROOF: The crux of the algorithm is Equations (10.5) and (10.6), which allow the problem of computing FT_M, the problem of size M, to be split into two identical subproblems of size $M/2$ involving computation of $FT_{M/2}$, which can be carried out recursively using the same elementary operations. (Aside: Not every divide-and-conquer classical algorithm can be implemented as a fast quantum algorithm; we are really using the structure of the problem here.)

The transformation W on $m-1$ qubits can be defined by $|x\rangle \mapsto \omega^x = \omega^{\sum_{i=0}^{m-2} 2^i x_i}$ (where x_i is the ith qubit of x). It can be easily seen to be the result of applying for every $i \in \{0, \ldots, m-2\}$ the following elementary operation on the ith qubit of the register: $|0\rangle \mapsto |0\rangle$ and $|1\rangle \mapsto \omega^{2^i} |1\rangle$.

The final state is equal to $\hat{f}$ by (10.5) and (10.6). (We leave verifying this and the running time to Exercise 10.14.) ∎

Quantum Fourier Transform FT_M	
Initial state: $f = \sum_{x \in \mathbb{Z}_M} f(x) \lvert x \rangle$	
Final state: $\hat{f} = \sum_{x \in \mathbb{Z}_M} \hat{f}(x) \lvert x \rangle$.	
Operation	**State** (neglecting normalizing factors)
	$f = \sum_{x \in \mathbb{Z}_M} f(x) \lvert x \rangle$
Recursively run $FT_{M/2}$ on $m-1$ most significant qubits.	$(FT_{M/2} f_{even}) \lvert 0 \rangle + (FT_{M/2} f_{odd}) \lvert 1 \rangle$
If LSB is 1 then compute W on $m-1$ most significant qubits (see below).	$(FT_{M/2} f_{even}) \lvert 0 \rangle + (W FT_{M/2} f_{odd}) \lvert 1 \rangle$
Apply Hadmard gate H to least significant qubit.	$(FT_{M/2} f_{even})(\lvert 0 \rangle + \lvert 1 \rangle) + (W FT_{M/2} f_{odd})(\lvert 0 \rangle - \lvert 1 \rangle)$ $= (FT_{M/2} f_{even} + W FT_{M/2} f_{odd}) \lvert 0 \rangle$ $+ (FT_{M/2} f_{even} - W FT_{M/2} f_{odd}) \lvert 1 \rangle$
Move LSB to the most significant position.	$\lvert 0 \rangle (FT_{M/2} f_{even} + W FT_{M/2} f_{odd})$ $+ \lvert 1 \rangle (FT_{M/2} f_{even} - W FT_{M/2} f_{odd}) = \hat{f}$

10.6.3 Shor's order-finding algorithm

We now present the central step in Shor's factoring algorithm: a quantum polynomial-time algorithm to find the *order* of an integer A modulo an integer N.

Lemma 10.18 *There is a polynomial-time quantum algorithm that on input A, N (represented in binary) finds the smallest r such that $A^r = 1$ (mod N).*   ◇

PROOF: Let $m = \lceil 5 \log M \rceil$ and let $M = 2^m$. Our register will consist of $m + \text{polylog}(N)$ qubits. Note that the function $x \mapsto A^x$ (mod N) can be computed in $\text{polylog}(N)$ time (see Exercise 10.10), and so we will assume that we can compute the map $\lvert x \rangle \lvert y \rangle \mapsto \lvert x \rangle \lvert y \oplus \lfloor A^x \ (\text{mod } N) \rfloor \rangle$ (where $\lfloor X \rfloor$ denotes the representation of the number $X \in \{0, \ldots, N-1\}$ as a binary string of length $\log N$).[8] Now we describe the order-finding algorithm. It uses a tool of elementary number theory called *continued fractions* which allows us to approximate (using a classical algorithm) an arbitrary real number α with a rational number p/q, where there is a prescribed upper bound on q (see Section 10.6.5). In the analysis, it will suffice to show that this algorithm outputs the order r with probability at least $\Omega(1/\log N)$ (we can always amplify the algorithm's success by running it several times and taking the smallest output).

Analysis: the case that $r \mid M$
We start by analyzing the algorithm in the case that $M = rc$ for some integer c. Though very unrealistic (remember that M is a power of 2!), this case gives the intuition why Fourier transforms are useful for detecting periods.

CLAIM: *In this case the value x measured will be equal to ac for a random $a \in \{0, \ldots, r-1\}$.*

The claim concludes the proof since it implies that $x/M = a/r$ where a is random integer less than r. Now for every r, at least $\Omega(r/\log r)$ of the numbers in $[r-1]$ are

---

[8] To compute this map, we may need to extend the register by some additional $\text{polylog}(N)$ many qubits, but we can ignore them as they will always be equal to zero except in intermediate computations.

Order finding algorithm

Goal: Given numbers N and $A < N$ such that $gcd(A, N) = 1$, find the smallest r such that $A^r = 1 \pmod{N}$.

Quantum register: We use an $m + \text{polylog}(N)$-qubit register, where $m = \lceil 5 \log N \rceil$. Below we treat the first m bits of the register as encoding a number in $\mathbb{Z}_M$.

Operation	State *(including* normalizing factors)
Apply Fourier transform to the first m bits.	$\frac{1}{\sqrt{M}} \sum_{x \in \mathbb{Z}_M} |x\rangle) \, |0^n\rangle$
Compute the transformation $|x\rangle |y\rangle \mapsto$ $|x\rangle |y \oplus (A^x \pmod{N})\rangle$.	$\frac{1}{\sqrt{M}} \sum_{x \in \mathbb{Z}_M} |x\rangle |A^x \pmod{N}\rangle$
Measure the second register to get a value y_0.	$\frac{1}{\sqrt{K}} \sum_{\ell=0}^{K-1} |x_0 + \ell r\rangle |y_0\rangle$ where x_0 is the smallest number such that $A^{x_0} = y_0 \pmod{N}$ and $K = \lfloor (M - 1 - x_0)/r \rfloor$.
Apply the Fourier transform to the first register.	$\frac{1}{\sqrt{M}\sqrt{K}} \left(\sum_{x \in \mathbb{Z}_n} \sum_{\ell=0}^{K-1} \omega^{(x_0 + \ell r)x} |x\rangle \right) |y_0\rangle$

Measure the first register to obtain a number $x \in \mathbb{Z}_M$. Find a rational approximation a/b with a, b coprime and $b \le N$ that approximates the number $\frac{x}{M}$ within $1/(10M)$ accuracy (see Section 10.6.5). If this approximation satisfies $A^b = 1 \pmod{N}$ then output b.

---

coprime to r. Indeed, the prime number theorem (see Section A.3) says that there at least this many primes in this interval, and since r has at most $\log r$ prime factors, all but $\log r$ of these primes are co-prime to r. Thus when the algorithm computes a rational approximation for x/M, the denominator it will find will indeed be r.

To prove the claim, we compute for every $x \in \mathbb{Z}_M$ the absolute value of $|x\rangle$'s coefficient before the measurement. Up to some normalization factor this is

$$\left| \sum_{\ell=0}^{c-1} \omega^{(x_0 + \ell r)x} \right| = \left| \omega^{x_0 c' c} \right| \left| \sum_{\ell=0}^{c-1} \omega^{r \ell x} \right| = 1 \cdot \left| \sum_{\ell=0}^{c-1} \omega^{r \ell x} \right| \tag{10.7}$$

If c does not divide x, then ω^r is a cth root of unity, so $\sum_{\ell=0}^{c-1} w^{r \ell x} = 0$ by the formula for sums of geometric progressions. Thus, such a number x would be measured with zero probability. But if $x = cj$ then $\omega^{r \ell x} = w^{rcj\ell} = \omega^{Mj} = 1$, and hence the amplitudes of all such x's are equal for all $j \in \{0, 2, \ldots, r - 1\}$.

The general case

In the general case, where r does not necessarily divide M, we will not be able to show that the measured value x satisfies $M | xr$. However, we will show that with $\Omega(1/\log r)$ probability, (1) xr will be "almost divisible" by M in the sense that $0 \le xr \pmod{M} < r/10$ and (2) $\lfloor xr/M \rfloor$ is coprime to r. Condition (1) implies that $|xr - cM| < r/10$ for $c = \lfloor xr/M \rfloor$. Dividing by rM gives $\left| \frac{x}{M} - \frac{c}{r} \right| < \frac{1}{10M}$. Therefore, $\frac{c}{r}$ is a rational number with denominator at most N that approximates $\frac{x}{M}$ to within $1/(10M) < 1/(4N^4)$. It is not hard to see that such an approximation is unique (Exercise 10.11) and hence in this case the algorithm will come up with c/r and output the denominator r (see Section 10.6.5).

Thus all that is left is to prove the next two lemmas. The first shows that there are $\Omega(r/\log r)$ values of x that satisfy the above two conditions and the second shows that each is measured with probability $\Omega((1/\sqrt{r})^2) = \Omega(1/r)$.

Lemma 10.19 *There exist $\Omega(r/\log r)$ values $x \in \mathbb{Z}_M$ such that*
1. $0 < xr \pmod{M} < r/10.$
2. $\lfloor xr/M \rfloor$ *and* r *are coprime.*   ◇

Lemma 10.20 *If x satisfies $0 < xr \pmod{M} < r/10$ then, before the measurement in the final step of the order-finding algorithm, the coefficient of $|x\rangle$ is at least $\Omega(\frac{1}{\sqrt{r}})$.*   ◇

PROOF OF LEMMA 10.19: We prove the lemma for the case that r is coprime to M, leaving the general case as Exercise 10.15. In this case, the map $x \mapsto rx \pmod{M}$ is a permutation of $\mathbb{Z}_M^*$. There are at least $\Omega(r/\log r)$ numbers in $[1 \ldots r/10]$ that are coprime to r (take primes in this range that are not one of r's at most $\log r$ prime factors) and hence $\Omega(r/\log r)$ numbers x such that $rx \pmod{M} = xr - \lfloor xr/M \rfloor M$ is in $[1 \ldots r/10]$ and coprime to r. But this means that $\lfloor rx/M \rfloor$ can not have a nontrivial shared factor with r, as otherwise this factor would be shared with $rx \pmod{M}$ as well. ∎

PROOF OF LEMMA 10.20: Let x be such that $0 < xr \pmod{M} < r/10$. The absolute value of $|x\rangle$'s coefficient in the state before the measurement is

$$\frac{1}{\sqrt{K}\sqrt{M}} \left| \sum_{\ell=0}^{K-1} \omega^{\ell rx} \right| \tag{10.8}$$

where $K = \lfloor (M - x_0 - 1)/r \rfloor$. Note that $\frac{M}{2r} < K < \frac{M}{r}$ since $x_0 < N \ll M$.

Setting $\beta = \omega^{rx}$ (note that since $M \nmid rx$, $\beta \neq 1$) and using the formula for the sum of a geometric series, this is at least

$$\frac{\sqrt{r}}{2M} \left| \frac{1 - \beta^{\lceil M/r \rceil}}{1-\beta} \right| = \frac{\sqrt{r}}{2M} \frac{\sin(\theta \lceil M/r \rceil/2)}{\sin(\theta/2)} \tag{10.9}$$

where $\theta = \frac{rx \pmod{M}}{M}$ is the angle such that $\beta = e^{i\theta}$ (see Figure 10.6 for a proof by picture of the last equality). Under our assumptions $\lceil M/r \rceil \theta < 1/10$; hence

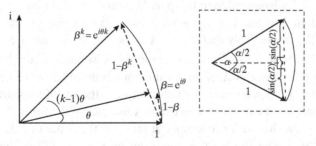

Figure 10.6. A complex number $z = a + ib$ can be thought of as the two-dimensional vector (a, b) of length $|z| = \sqrt{a^2 + b^2}$. The number $\beta = e^{i\theta}$ corresponds to a unit vector of angle θ from the x-axis. For any such β, if k is not too large (say $k < 1/\theta$), then by elementary geometric considerations $\frac{|1-\beta^k|}{|1-\beta|} = \frac{2\sin(\theta/2)}{2\sin(k\theta/2)}$. We use here the fact (proved in the dotted box above) that in a unit cycle, the chord corresponding to an angle α is of length $2\sin(\alpha/2)$.

(using the fact that $\sin\alpha \sim \alpha$ for small angles α), the coefficient of x is at least $\frac{\sqrt{r}}{4M}\lceil M/r\rceil \geq \frac{1}{8\sqrt{r}}$. ∎

This completes the proof of Lemma 10.18. ∎

10.6.4 Reducing factoring to order finding

The reduction of the factoring problem to the order-finding problem is classical (in particular, predates quantum computing) and follows from the following two lemmas.

Lemma 10.21 *For every nonprime N that is not a prime power, the probability that a random X in the set $\mathbb{Z}_N^* = \{X \in [N-1] : \gcd(X,N) = 1\}$ has an even order r and furthermore, $X^{r/2} \neq -1 \pmod N$ is at least $1/4$.*   ◇

Lemma 10.22 *For every N and Y, if $Y^2 = 1 \pmod N$ but $Y \pmod N \notin \{+1, -1\}$, then $\gcd(Y-1, N) \notin 1, N$.*   ◇

Together, Lemmas 10.21 and 10.22 show that, given a composite N that is not a prime power, if we choose A at random in $[N-1]$, then with good probability either $\gcd(A, N)$ or $\gcd(A^{r/2} - 1, N)$ will yield a nontrivial factor F of N. We can then use recursion to find the prime factors of F and N/F respectively, leading to a polylog(N) time factorization algorithm. (Note that if N is a prime power then it is easy to find its factorization by simply going over all $\ell \in [\log N]$ and trying the ℓth root of N.) Thus to prove Theorem 10.15 all that is left is to prove Lemmas 10.21 and 10.22. The proofs rely on some basic facts from number theory; see Section A.3 for a quick review.

PROOF OF LEMMA 10.22: Under our assumptions, N divides $Y^2 - 1 = (Y-1)(Y+1)$ but does not divide neither $Y-1$ or $Y+1$. But this means that $\gcd(Y-1, N) > 1$ since if $Y-1$ and N were coprime, then since N divides $(Y-1)(Y+1)$, it would have to divide $Y+1$ (Exercise 10.12). Since $Y-1 < N$, obviously $\gcd(Y-1, N) < N$ and hence we're done. ∎

PROOF OF LEMMA 10.21: We prove the lemma for the case $N = PQ$ for primes P, Q: The proof can be suitably generalized for every N. Now, by the Chinese Remainder Theorem, every $X \in \mathbb{Z}_N^*$ is isomorphic to the pair $\langle X \pmod P, X \pmod Q\rangle$. In particular, choosing a random number $X \in \mathbb{Z}_N^*$ is equivalent to choosing two random numbers Y, Z in $\mathbb{Z}_P^*$ and $\mathbb{Z}_Q^*$ respectively and setting X to be the unique number corresponding to the pair $\langle Y, Z\rangle$. Now for every k, $X^k \pmod N$ is isomorphic to $\langle Y^k \pmod P, Z^k \pmod Q\rangle$ and so the *order* of X is the least common multiple of the orders of Y and Z modulo P and Q, respectively. We will complete the proof by showing that with probability at least $1/2$, the order of Y is even: A number of the form $2^k c$ for $k \geq 1$ and c odd. We then show that with probability at least $1/2$, the order of Z has the form $2^\ell d$ for d odd and $\ell \neq k$. This implies that the order of X is $r = 2^{\max\{k,\ell\}}lcm(c, d)$ (where lcm denotes the least common multiple), which means that $X^{r/2}$ will be equal to 1 in at least one coordinate. Since $-1 \pmod N$ is isomorphic to the tuple $\langle -1, -1\rangle$, this means that $X^{r/2} \neq -1 \pmod P$.

Thus all that is left is to prove the following:

- Y has even order with probability at least $1/2$.

Indeed, the set of numbers in $\mathbb{Z}_P^*$ with odd order is a *subgroup* of $\mathbb{Z}_P^*$: if Y, Y' have odd orders r, r', respectively, then $(YY')^{rr'} = 1 \pmod{P}$, which means that the order of YY' divides the odd number rr'. Yet -1 has even order, implying that this is a *proper* subgroup of $\mathbb{Z}_P^*$, taking at most $1/2$ of $\mathbb{Z}_P^*$.

- There is a number ℓ_0 such that with probability exactly $1/2$, the order of of a random $Z \in \mathbb{Z}_Q^*$ is a number of the form $2^\ell c$ for $\ell \leq \ell_0$. (This implies that for every fixed k, the probability that the order has the form $2^k d$ is at most $1/2$.)

  For every ℓ, define G_ℓ to be the subset of $\mathbb{Z}_Q^*$ whose order modulo Q is of the form $2^j c$ where $j \leq \ell$ and c is odd. It can be verified that for every ℓ, G_ℓ is a subgroup of $G_{\ell+1}$; furthermore, because modulo a prime P, the mapping $x \mapsto x^2 \pmod{P}$ is two-to-one and maps $G_{\ell+1}$ into G_ℓ (Exercise 10.13), $|G_\ell| \geq |G_{\ell+1}|/2$. It follows that if we take ℓ_0 to be the largest such that G_{ℓ_0} is a proper subgroup of $\mathbb{Z}_P^*$, then $|G_{\ell_0}| = |Z_P^*|/2$. ∎

10.6.5 Rational approximation of real numbers

In many settings, including Shor's algorithm, we are given a real number in the form of a program that can compute its first t bits in $\text{poly}(t)$ time. We are interested in finding a close approximation to this real number of the form a/b, where there is a prescribed upper bound on b. Continued fractions is a tool in number theory that is useful for this.

A *continued fraction* is a number of the following form:

$$a_0 + \cfrac{1}{a_1 + \cfrac{1}{a_2 + \cfrac{1}{a_3 + \dots}}}$$

for a_0 a non-negative integer and $a_1, a_2, \dots$ positive integers.

Given a real number $\alpha > 0$, we can find its representation as an *infinite* fraction as follows: Split α into the integer part $\lfloor \alpha \rfloor$ and fractional part $\alpha - \lfloor \alpha \rfloor$, find recursively the representation R of $1/(\alpha - \lfloor \alpha \rfloor)$, and then write

$$\alpha = \lfloor \alpha \rfloor + \frac{1}{R}$$

If we continue this process for n steps, we get a rational number, denoted by $[a_0, a_1, \dots, a_n]$, which can be represented as $\frac{p_n}{q_n}$ with p_n, q_n coprime. The following facts can be proven using induction:

- $p_0 = a_0, q_0 = 1$ and for every $n > 1$, $p_n = a_n p_{n-1} + p_{n-2}$, $q_n = a_n q_{n-1} + q_{n-2}$
- $\frac{p_n}{q_n} - \frac{p_{n-1}}{q_{n-1}} = \frac{(-1)^{n-1}}{q_n q_{n-1}}$

Furthermore, it is known that

$$\left| \frac{p_n}{q_n} - \alpha \right| < \frac{1}{q_n q_{n+1}} \tag{10.10}$$

which implies that $\frac{p_n}{q_n}$ is the *closest* rational number to α with denominator at most q_n. It also means that if α is extremely close to a rational number, say, $\left| \alpha - \frac{a}{b} \right| < \frac{1}{4b^4}$ for some coprime a, b, then we can find a, b by iterating the continued fraction algorithm for $\text{polylog}(b)$ steps. Indeed, let q_n be the first denominator such that $q_{n+1} \geq b$. If $q_{n+1} > 2b^2$ then (10.10) implies that $\left| \frac{p_n}{q_n} - \alpha \right| < \frac{1}{2b^2}$. But this means that $\frac{p_n}{q_n} = \frac{a}{b}$ since there is at most one rational number of denominator at most b that is so close to α. On the other hand, if $q_{n+1} \leq 2b^2$, then since $\frac{p_{n+1}}{q_{n+1}}$ is closer to α than $\frac{a}{b}$, $\left| \frac{p_{n+1}}{q_{n+1}} - \alpha \right| < \frac{1}{4b^4}$, again meaning that $\frac{p_{n+1}}{q_{n+1}} = \frac{a}{b}$. It's not hard to verify that $q_n \geq 2^{n/2}$, implying that p_n and q_n can be computed in polylog(q_n) time.

10.7 BQP AND CLASSICAL COMPLEXITY CLASSES

What is the relation between **BQP** and the classes we already encountered such as **P**, **BPP** and **NP**? This is very much an open questions. It not hard to show that quantum computers are at least not infinitely powerful compared to classical algorithms.

Theorem 10.23 **BQP** $\subseteq$ **PSPACE**.

PROOF SKETCH: To simulate a T-step quantum computation on an m qubit register, we need to come up with a procedure `Coeff` that for every $i \in [T]$ and $x \in \{0, 1\}^m$, the xth coefficient (up to some accuracy) of the register's state in the ith execution. We can compute `Coeff` on inputs x, i using at most eight recursive calls to `Coeff` on inputs $x', i - 1$ (for the at most eight strings that agree with x on the three bits that the F_i's operation reads and modifies). Since we can reuse the space used by the recursive operations, if we let $S(i)$ denote the space needed to compute `Coeff`(x, i) then $S(i) \leq S(i-1) + O(\ell)$ (where ℓ is the number of bits used to store each coefficient).

To compute, say, the probability that if measured after the final step the first qubit of the register is equal to 1, just compute the sum of `Coeff`(x, T) for every $x \in \{0, 1\}^n$. Again, by reusing the space of each computation this can be done using polynomial space. ∎

In Exercise 17.7 later in the book, you are asked to improve Theorem 10.23 to show that **BQP** $\subseteq$ **P$^{\#P}$** (where **#P** is the counting version of **NP** described in Chapter 17). One can even show **BQP** $\subseteq$ **PP** [ADH97] (see Definition 17.6). But these are essentially the best bounds we know on **BQP**.

Does **BQP** = **BPP**? The main reason to believe this is false is the polynomial-time quantum algorithm for integer factorization, whereas no similar algorithm is believed to exist for probabilistic computation. Although this is not as strong as the evidence for, say **NP** $\not\subseteq$ **BPP** (after all **NP** contains thousands of well-studied problems that have resisted efficient algorithms), the factorization problem is one of the oldest and most well-studied computational problems, and the fact that we still know no efficient algorithm for it makes the conjecture that none exists appealing. Also note that unlike other famous problems for which we eventually found efficient algorithms (e.g., linear programming [Kha79] and primality testing [AKS04]), we do not even have a heuristic algorithm that is conjectured to work (even without proof) or experimentally works on, say, numbers that are product of two random large primes.

What is the relation between **BQP** and **NP**? It seems that quantum computers only offer a quadratic speedup (using Grover's search) on **NP**-complete problems. There are also oracle results showing that **NP** problems require exponential time on quantum computers [BBBV97]. So most researchers believe that **NP** $\not\subseteq$ **BPP**. On the other hand, there is a problem in **BQP** (the Recursive Fourier Sampling or RFS problem [BV93]) that is not known to be in the polynomial-hierarchy, let alone in **NP**. Thus it seems that **BQP** and **NP** may be incomparable classes.

10.7.1 Quantum analogs of NP and AM

Can we define an analog of **NP** in the quantum computing world? The class **NP** was defined using the notion of a certificate that is checked by a deterministic polynomial-time (classical) TM. However, quantum computation includes probabilistic classical computation as a subcase. Therefore the correct classical model to look at is the one where the certificate is verified by a polynomial-time randomized algorithm, namely, **MA** (see Definition 8.10). Thus the quantum analog of **NP** is denoted by **QMA**. More generally, one can define *quantum interactive proofs*, which generalize the definition of **AM**[k]. These turn out to be surprisingly powerful. Three-round quantum interactive proofs suffice to capture **PSPACE**, as shown by Watrous [Wat03]. If the same were true of classical interactive proofs, then **PH** would collapse.

A "Quantum Cook-Levin Theorem" was proven by Kitaev (unpublished, see Umesh Vazirani's lecture notes, which are linked from this book's Web site). This shows that a quantum analog of 3SAT, called Q5SAT, is *complete* for **QMA**. In this problem are given m elementary quantum operations $H_1, H_2, \ldots, H_m$ on an n-bit quantum register. Each operation acts upon only 5 bits of the register (and hence is represented by a $2^5 \times 2^5$ matrix, which implicitly defines a $2^n \times 2^n$ matrix). Let H be the $2^n \times 2^n$ matrix $\sum_j H_j$. We are promised that either all eigenvalues of H are $\geq b$ or there is an eigenvalue of H that is $\leq a$ where $0 \leq a \leq b \leq 1$ and $b - a$ is at least $1/n^c$ where c is a constant. We have to determine which case holds.

The reader could try to prove this completeness result as an exercise. As a warmup, first show how to reduce 3SAT to Q5SAT.

WHAT HAVE WE LEARNED?

- Quantum mechanics leads to counterintuitive behavior, whereby systems of n particles can simultaneously exist in a superposition of 2^n states.
- A quantum computer consists of a register of n *qubits* on which we can apply *quantum operations*, which can be described by $2^n \times 2^n$ unitary matrices. An elementary quantum operation can affect up to three of these qubits and is represented by an 8×8 matrix.
- Grover's algorithm allows us to solve n-variable instances of SAT in $2^{n/2}$ time. It also extends to finding a satisfying assignment of an n-input (classical) circuit.
- Simon's and Shor's algorithms use the fact that a quantum computer can efficiently compute a *Fourier transform* of the state vector, to obtain *exponential speedups* over the best known algorithms for classical computers (i.e., Turing machines). Fourier transforms can be used to detect *periodic* behavior in the state vector.
- Shor's algorithm factors n-bit integers in poly(n) time on a quantum computer. This challenges the strong Church-Turing thesis, since many believe that such an algorithm does not exist for classical computers.
- One can study quantum analogs of many other classical computational models, such as decision trees, communication protocols, interactive proofs, and so on.
- It is still an open question whether quantum computers can be built. This is an active area of research, and theoretical work suggests that there is no inherent obstacle.

CHAPTER NOTES AND HISTORY

Since a quantum computer is reversible (Lemma 10.7), an important precursor of quantum computing was a field called *reversible computing* [Ben87], which seeks to find thermodynamic limits to the speed of classical computers. Toffoli's gate was invented in that context.

In 1982, Feynman [Fey82] pointed out that there seems to be no efficient simulation of quantum mechanics on classical Turing machines, and suggested that building quantum computers might allow us to run such simulations. (In fact, this still might be their most important application if they are ever built.) He also raised the possibility that quantum TMs may have more computational power than classical TMs. In 1985 Deutsch [Deu85] formally defined a quantum Turing machine, though in retrospect his definition is unsatisfactory. Better definitions then appeared in Deutsch-Josza [DJ92] and Bernstein-Vazirani [BV93]. The latter paper was the first to demonstrate the existence of a universal quantum TM that can simulate all other quantum TMs with only polynomial slowdown. Yao [Yao93] generalized these results to quantum circuits, and our definition of quantum computation follows Yao. (The Bernstein-Vazirani quantum TM model is known to be less noise-tolerant than the circuit model, and thus less likely to be realized.) Deutsch [Deu89] showed that a certain three-qubit gate is *universal* for quantum circuits, while Solovay (unpublished manuscript, 1995) and, independently, Kitaev [Kit97] showed that universal gates can approximate every unitary matrix with precision exponentially small in the number of gates, yielding Theorem 10.12 (though we stated it with a particular universal basis mentioned in the book [NC00]).

Bernstein and Vazirani also introduced the quantum algorithm for computing the Fourier transform and gave evidence that it provides superpolynomial speedups over classical algorithms. The papers of Simon and Shor gave further evidence along these lines, and in particular Shor's paper caught the imagination of the scientific world, as well as of governments worldwide (who now feared for the security of their cryptosystems).

Quantum computation has a fascinating connection with cryptography. On the one hand, if quantum computers are ever built, then Shor's algorithm and various generalizations thereof could be used to completely break the security of RSA and all other factoring or discrete-log-based cryptosystems. On the other hand, it turns out that using quantum mechanics and the ideas underlying the EPR/Bell "paradox," it is possible to have *unconditionally secure* public key cryptography, a concept known as *quantum key distribution* [BB84] and more generally as *quantum cryptography*. That is, these cryptosystem are secure against even computationally unbounded adversaries. In fact, constructing these systems does not require the full-fledged power of quantum computers, and prototype implementations already exist. Still, there are very significant engineering challenges and issues that can compromise the real-world applicability and security of these systems. One should note however that even if quantum computers are built, it may very well be possible to still have conventional computational cryptography that is resistant even to polynomial-time quantum algorithms. For example, as far as we know, quantum computers can at best invert one-way functions (Definition 9.4) quadratically faster than classical algorithms (using Grover's search). Thus, most researchers believe that *private key cryptography* (including even digital signatures!) will be just as resistant against quantum computers as it is against "classical" Turing machines. Even for public key cryptography, there are (few) candidates systems that are based on problems not known to have efficient quantum algorithms. Perhaps the most promising direction is basing such schemes on certain problems on *integer lattices* (see the notes for Chapter 9).

Grover's and Simon's algorithms actually operate in a more general model known as the *quantum black-box* model, in which an algorithm is given black-box access to an oracle computing the unitary transformation $|x\rangle |y\rangle \mapsto |x\rangle |y \oplus f(x)\rangle$ for some function f and tries to discover properties of f. There have been interesting upper bounds and lower bounds on the power of such algorithms. In particular, we know that Grover's Algorithm is optimal in this model [BBBV97]. We also have several other "Grover-like" algorithms in this model; see the survey [Amb04]. One can view Grover's algorithm as evaluating an OR over $N = 2^n$-variables. Thus a natural question is whether it can be generalized into more general formulas; a particularly interesting special case is AND-OR trees (i.e., OR of ANDs of ORs ...) that arise in various applications such game strategies. This was question was open for a while, and in particular we didn't know if quantum algorithms can beat the best randomized algorithm for the full binary balanced AND-OR tree, which needs to look at $O(N^{\log(\frac{1+\sqrt{33}}{4})}) = O(N^{0.753\cdots})$ variables [Sni81, SW86]. In a recent breakthrough, Farhi, Goldstone, and Gutmann [FGG07] showed an $O(N^{1/2+o(1)})$-time quantum algorithm for this problem, a result that was generalized by Ambainis et al [ACR+07] to hold for all AND-OR trees.

Research on quantum computing has generated some interesting insights on both "classical" computational complexity, and "noncomputational" physics. A good example for a result of the first kind is the paper of Aharonov and Regev [AR04], which uses quantum insights to show a classical computational complexity result (that a $\sqrt{n}$-approximation of the lattice shortest vector problem is in **coNP**). Examples for the results of the second kind include the works on quantum error correction (see below) and results on adiabatic computation [AvDK+04, AGIK07, vDMV01], that clarified this model and refuted some of the physicists' initial intuitions about it.

The chapter did not discuss the issue of *quantum error correction*, which tackles the following important issue: How can we run a quantum algorithm when at every possible step there is a probability of noise interfering with the computation? The issue is undoubtedly crucial, since an implementation of Shor's Algorithms for interesting values of N requires hundreds of thousands of particles to stay in quantum superposition for large-ish periods of time. Thus far it is an open question whether this is practically achievable. Physicists' original intuition was that noise and decoherence will make quantum computing impractical; one obstacle cited was the *No-Cloning Theorem* [WZ82], which seems to rule out use of classical error-correction ideas in quantum computing. However, Shor's followup paper on *quantum error correction* [Sho95] contradicted this intuition and spurred much additional work. Aharonov and Benor showed that under reasonable noise models, so long as the probability of noise at a single step is lower than some constant threshold, one can perform arbitrarily long computations and get the correct answer with high probability; see the articles by Preskill [Pre97, Pre98]. Unfortunately, current estimates of the true noise rate in physical systems are higher than this threshold.

In fact it is unclear what the correct model of noise should be; this question is related to the issue of what is the reality underlying the quantum description of the world. Though the theory has had fantastic success in predicting experimental results (which perhaps is *the* criteria by which a physical theory is judged), some physicists are understandably uncomfortable with the description of nature as maintaining a huge array of possible states, and changing its behavior when it is observed. The popular science book [Bru04] contains a good (even if a bit biased) review of physicists' and philosophers' attempts at providing more palatable descriptions that still manage to predict experiments.

On a more technical level, while no one doubts that quantum effects exist at microscopic scales, scientists question why they do not manifest themselves at the macrosopic level (or at least not to human consciousness). Physicist Penrose [Pen90] has gone so far as to make a (highly controversial) suggestion about a link between human consciousness and the collapse of the probability wave. A *Scientific American* article by Yam [Yam97] describes various other explanations that have been advanced over the years, including *decoherence* (which uses quantum theory to explain the absence of macroscopic quantum effects) and *hidden variable theories* (which restore a deterministic order to world). No single explanation seems to please all researchers.

Finally, we note that since qubits are such a simple example of a quantum system, there is a growing movement to teach introductory quantum mechanics using qubits and quantum computing rather than, say, the standard model of the hydrogen atom or electron-in-a-box. This is an interesting example of how the computational worldview (as opposed to computation in the sense of number-crunching) is seeping into the sciences.

For details of these and many other topics in quantum computing and information, see the books by Kitaev, Shen, and Vyalyi [KVS02] and Nielsen and Chuang [NC00]. Some excellent lecture notes and surveys can be found on the home pages of Umesh Vazirani and Scott Aaronson. Aaronson's Scientific American article [Aar08] provides an excellent popular-science exposition of the field.

EXERCISES

10.1. Show a quantum strategy that enables Alice and Bob to win the parity game of Theorems 10.3 and 10.4 with probability 0.85.

10.2. Prove Claim 10.5.

H535

10.3. For each one of the following operations: Hadamard, NOT, controlled-NOT, rotation by $\pi/4$, and Toffoli, write down the 8×8 matrix that describes the mapping induced by applying this operation on the first qubits of a three-qubit register.

10.4. Define a linear function $F : \mathbb{R}^{2^m} \to \mathbb{R}^{2^m}$ to be an *elementary probabilistic operation* if it satisfies the following conditions:

- F is *stochastic*: that is, for every $\mathbf{v} \in \mathbb{R}_m$ such that $\sum_x \mathbf{v}_x = 1$, $\sum_x (A\mathbf{v})_x = 1$.
- F depends on at most three bits. That is, there is a linear function $G : \mathbb{R}^{2^3} \to \mathbb{R}^{2^3}$ and three coordinates $i < j < k \in [m]$ such that for every vector of

the form $|x_1 x_2 \cdots x_m\rangle$,

$$F|x_1 \cdots x_m\rangle$$
$$= \sum_{a,b,c \in \{0,1\}} (G|x_i x_j x_k\rangle)_{abc} |x_1 \ldots x_{i-1} a x_{i+1} \ldots x_{j-1} b x_{j+1} \ldots x_{k-1} c x_{k+1} \ldots x_m\rangle$$

Let $f : \{0, 1\}^* \to \{0, 1\}$ and $T : \mathbb{N} \to \mathbb{N}$ be some functions. We say that f is *computable in probabilistic $T(n)$-time* if for every $n \in \mathbb{N}$ and $x \in \{0, 1\}^n$, $f(x)$ can be computed by the following process:

(a) Initialize an m-bit register to the state $|x0^{n-m}\rangle$ (i.e., x padded with zeroes), where $m \leq T(n)$.

(b) Apply one after the other $T(n)$ elementary operations $F_1, \ldots, F_T$ to the register (where we require that there is a polynomial-time TM that on input $1^n, 1^{T(n)}$ outputs the descriptions of $F_1, \ldots, F_T$).

(c) Measure the register and let Y denote the obtained value. (That is, if $\mathbf{v}$ is the final state of the register, then Y is a random variable that takes the value y with probability $\mathbf{v}_y$ for every $y \in \{0, 1\}^n$.)

We require that the first bit of Y is equal to $f(x)$ with probability at least $2/3$.

Prove that a function $f : \{0, 1\}^* \to \{0, 1\}$ is computable in $p(n)$-probabilistic $p(n)$-time per the above definition for some polynomial p iff $f \in \mathbf{BPP}$.

10.5. Prove that if $f \in \mathbf{BQP}$ then f has a quantum polynomial-time algorithm in which all of the matrices are real—contain no numbers of the form $a + ib$ for $b \neq 0$. (This exercise can be thought of as showing that the power of quantum mechanics as opposed to classical probabilistic computation comes from the fact that we allow negative numbers in state representations, and not from the fact that we allow complex numbers.)

H535

10.6. Suppose that a two-qubit quantum register is in an arbitrary state $\mathbf{v}$. Show that the following three experiments will yield the same probability of output:

(a) Measure the register and output the result.

(b) First measure the first qubit and output it, then measure the second qubit and output it.

(c) First measure the second qubit and output it, then measure the first qubit and output it.

10.7. Suppose that f is computed in T time by a quantum algorithm that uses a partial measurements in the middle of the computation, and then proceeds differently according to the result of that measurement. Show that f is computable by $O(T)$ elementary operations.

10.8. Show that in a quantum computation that runs for T steps, we can replace each gate with any other gate (i.e., 8×8 matrix), which is the same in the $10 \log T$ most significant bits. Show that the amplitudes in the resulting final states are the same in the first T bits.

10.9. Prove that if for some $a \in \{0, 1\}^n$, the strings $y_1, \ldots, y_{n-1}$ are chosen uniformly at random from $\{0, 1\}^n$ subject to $y_i \odot a = 0$ for every $i \in [n-1]$, then with probability at least $1/10$, there exists no nonzero string $a' \neq a$ such that $y_i \odot a' = 0$ for every $i \in [n-1]$. (In other words, the vectors $y_1, \ldots, y_{n-1}$ are linearly independent.)

10.10. Prove that given $A, x \in \{0, \ldots, M-1\}$, we can compute (using a classical TM!) A^x (mod M) in time polynomial in $\log M$.

H535

10.11. Prove that for every $\alpha < 1$, there is at most a single rational number a/b such that $b < N$ and $|\alpha - a/b| < 1/(2N^2)$.

10.12. Prove that if A, B are numbers such that N and A are coprime but N divides AB, then N divides B.

H535

10.13. Complete the proof of Lemma 10.21:
  (a) Prove that for every prime P, the map $x \mapsto x^2$ (mod P) is two-to-one on $\mathbb{Z}_P^*$.
  (b) Prove that if X's order modulo P is of the form $2^j c$ for some $j \geq 1$ and odd c, then the order of X^2 is of the form $2^{j-1} c'$ for odd c'.
  (c) Complete the proof of Lemma 10.21 for an arbitrary composite N that is not a prime power.

10.14. Prove Lemma 10.17.

10.15. Complete the proof of Lemma 10.19 for the case that r and M are not coprime. That is, prove that also in this case there exist at least $\Omega(r/\log r)$ values x's such that $0 \leq rx$ (mod M) $\leq r/2$ and $\lceil M/x \rceil$ and r are coprime.

H535

10.16. (Uses Knowledge of Continued Fractions) Suppose $j, r \leq N$ are mutually coprime and unknown to us. Show that if we know the first $2 \log N$ bits of j/r then we can recover j, r in polynomial time.

CHAPTER 11

PCP theorem and hardness of approximation: An introduction

[M]ost problem reductions do not create or preserve such gaps.... To create such a gap in the generic reduction (cf. Cook)... also seems doubtful. The intuitive reason is that computation is an inherently unstable, non-robust mathematical object, in the the sense that it can be turned from non-accepting to accepting by changes that would be insignificant in any reasonable metric.
– Papadimitriou and Yannakakis [PY88]

The contribution of this paper is two-fold. First, a connection is shown between approximating the size of the largest clique in a graph and multiprover interactive proofs. Second, an efficient multiprover interactive proof for NP languages is constructed, where the verifier uses very few random bits and communication bits.
– Feige, Goldwasser, Lovász, Safra, and Szegedy [FGL^{+}91]

We give a new characterization of **NP**: it contains exactly those languages L for which membership proofs can be verified probabilistically in polynomial time using logarithmic number of random bits, and by reading a sub logarithmic number of bits from the proof.
– Arora and Safra [AS92]

This chapter describes the **PCP** Theorem, a surprising discovery of complexity theory, with many implications to algorithm design. Since the discovery of **NP**-completeness in 1972 researchers had mulled over the issue of whether we can efficiently compute *approximate* solutions to **NP**-hard optimization problems. They failed to design such approximation algorithms for most problems (see Section 11.1 for an introduction to approximation algorithms). They then tried to show that computing approximate solutions is also hard, but apart from a few isolated successes this effort also stalled. Researchers slowly began to realize that the Cook-Levin-Karp-style reductions do not suffice to prove any limits on approximation algorithms (see the quote at the beginning of the chapters from an influential Papadimitriou-Yannakakis paper that appeared a few years before the discoveries described in this chapter). The **PCP** Theorem, discovered in 1992, gave a new definition of **NP** and provided a new starting point for reductions. It was considered very surprising at the time (see the note at the end of Section 11.2.2).

As we discuss in Section 11.2, there are two ways to view the **PCP** theorem. One view of the **PCP** Theorem is that it constructs *locally testable proof systems*: The

PCP Theorem gives a way to transform every mathematical proof into a form that is checkable by only looking at very few (probabilistically chosen) symbols of the proof. (The acronym "PCP" stands for *Probabilistically Checkable Proofs*.) Another view of the **PCP** Theorem is that it is a result about *hardness of approximation*: The **PCP** theorem shows that for many **NP**-complete optimization problems, computing an *approximate* solution is as hard as computing the exact solution (and hence cannot be done efficiently unless **P = NP**). We show the equivalence of these two views in Section 11.3.

In Section 11.4 we demonstrate the usefulness of the **PCP** Theorem by using it to derive a very strong hardness of approximation result for the INDSET and MIN-VERTEX-COVER problems.

Although only one result is known as *the* **PCP** Theorem (Theorem 11.5), several related "**PCP** theorems" have been discovered, differing in various setting of parameters. In this chapter we prove such a theorem (Theorem 11.19 in Section 11.5) giving a weaker—but still useful—result than the full-fledged **PCP** Theorem. Another motivation for showing Theorem 11.19 is that it will play a part in the proof of the **PCP** Theorem, which appears in full in Chapter 22.

The various **PCP** theorems have revolutionized our understanding of the approximability of **NP**-hard problems. Chapter 22 will surveys several of these theorems.

11.1 MOTIVATION: APPROXIMATE SOLUTIONS TO **NP**-HARD OPTIMIZATION PROBLEMS

As mentioned in Chapter 2, one of the main motivations for the theory of **NP**-completeness was to understand the computational complexity of computing optimum solutions to combinatorial problems such as TSP or INDSET. Since **P ≠ NP** implies that thousands of **NP**-hard optimization problems do not have efficient algorithms, attention then focused on whether or not they have efficient *approximation algorithms*. In many practical settings, obtaining an approximate solution to a problem may be almost as good as solving it exactly and could be a lot easier. Researchers are therefore interested in finding the best possible approximation algorithms for **NP**-hard optimization problems. For instance, it would be good to understand whether or not we could approximate interesting **NP**-problems within an arbitrary precision: If we could, then **P ≠ NP** would not be such a a big deal in practice. Many researchers suspected that there are inherent limits to approximation, and proving such limits was the main motivation behind the discovery of the **PCP** theorem.

In this section we illustrate the notion of approximation algorithms with an example. Let MAX-3SAT be the problem of finding, given a 3CNF Boolean formula φ as input, an assignment that maximizes the number of satisfied clauses. This problem is of course **NP**-hard, because the corresponding decision problem, 3SAT, is **NP**-complete. We define an approximation algorithm for MAX-3SAT in the following way.

Definition 11.1 (*Approximation of* MAX-3SAT) For every 3CNF formula φ, the *value* of φ, denoted by $\mathrm{val}(\varphi)$, is the maximum fraction of clauses that can be satisfied by any assignment to φ's variables. In particular, φ is satisfiable iff $\mathrm{val}(\varphi) = 1$.

For every $\rho \leq 1$, an algorithm A is a ρ-*approximation* algorithm for MAX-3SAT if for every 3CNF formula φ with m clauses, $A(\varphi)$ outputs an assignment satisfying at least $\rho \cdot \mathsf{val}(\varphi)m$ of φ's clauses.

Now we give two simple examples of approximation algorithms; see the Chapter notes for references to more nontrivial algorithms.

EXAMPLE 11.2 (1/2-*Approximation for* MAX-3SAT)

We describe a polynomial-time algorithm that computes a 1/2-approximation for MAX-3SAT. The algorithm assigns values to the variables one by one in a greedy fashion, whereby the ith variable is assigned the value that results in satisfying at least 1/2 the clauses in which it appears. Any clause that gets satisfied is removed and not considered in assigning values to the remaining variables. Clearly, the final assignment will satisfy at least 1/2 of all clauses, which is certainly at least half of the maximum that the optimum assignment could satisfy.

Using semidefinite programming one can also design a polynomial-time $(7/8 - \epsilon)$-approximation algorithm for every $\epsilon > 0$ (see chapter notes). Obtaining such a ratio is trivial if we restrict ourselves to 3*CNF* formulae with three distinct variables in each clause. Then a random assignment has probability 7/8 to satisfy each clause. Linearity of expectations (Claim A.3) implies that a random assignment is expected to satisfy a 7/8 fraction of the clauses. This observation can be turned into a simple probabilistic or even deterministic 7/8-approximation algorithm (see Exercise 11.3).

For a few problems, one can even design $(1-\epsilon)$-approximation algorithms for *every* $\epsilon > 0$. Exercise 11.12 asks you to show this for the **NP**-complete *knapsack* problem.

EXAMPLE 11.3 (1/2-*Approximation for* MIN-VERTEX-COVER)

The decision problem VERTEX-COVER was introduced in Example 2.15 in Chapter 2. The optimization version is MIN-VERTEX-COVER, in which we are given a graph and wish to determine the size of the minimum vertex cover (which, recall, is a set of vertices such that every graph edge contains one these vertices). For $\rho \leq 1$, a ρ-approximation algorithm for MIN-VERTEX-COVER is an algorithm that on input a graph G outputs a vertex cover whose size is at most $1/\rho$ times the size of the minimum vertex cover.[1] We now show a 1/2-approximation algorithm for MIN-VERTEX-COVER:

Start with $S \leftarrow \emptyset$. Pick any edge in the graph e_1, and add both its endpoints to S. Delete these two vertices from the graph as well as all edges adjacent to them. Iterate this process, picking edges $e_2, e_3, \ldots$ and adding their endpoints to S until the graph becomes empty.

Clearly, the set S at the end is such that every graph edge has an endpoint in S. Thus S is a vertex cover. Furthermore, the sequence of edges $e_1, e_2, \ldots$ used to build up S are pairwise disjoint; in other words, they form a *matching*. The cardinality of S is twice the number of edges in this matching. Furthermore, the minimum vertex cover must by

---

[1] Many texts call such an algorithm a $1/\rho$-*approximation algorithm* instead.

definition include at least one endpoint of each matching edge. Thus the cardinality of S is at most twice the cardinality of the minimum vertex cover.

11.2 TWO VIEWS OF THE **PCP** THEOREM

The **PCP** Theorem can be viewed in two alternative ways, and internalizing both these ways is crucial to understanding both the theorem and its proof. One view of this theorem is that it talks about new, extremely robust proof systems. The other is that it talks about approximating combinatorial optimization problems.

11.2.1 **PCP Theorem and locally testable proofs**

The first view of the **PCP** Theorem (and the reason for its name) is as providing a new kind of proof systems. Suppose someone wants to convince you that a Boolean formula is satisfiable. He could present the usual certificate, namely, a satisfying assignment, which you could then check by substituting back into the formula. However, doing this requires reading the entire certificate. The **PCP** Theorem shows an interesting alternative: This person can easily rewrite his certificate so you can verify it by probabilistically selecting a constant number of locations—as low as 3 bits—to examine in it. Furthermore, this probabilistic verification has the following properties: (1) A correct certificate will never fail to convince you (i.e., no choice of your random coins will make you reject it) and (2) if the formula is unsatisfiable, then you are guaranteed to reject *every claimed certificate* with high probability.

Of course, since Boolean satisfiability is **NP**-complete, every other **NP** language can be deterministically and efficiently reduced to it. Thus the **PCP** Theorem applies to every **NP** language. We mention one counterintuitive consequence. Let $\mathcal{A}$ be any one of the usual axiomatic systems of mathematics for which proofs can be verified by a deterministic TM in time that is polynomial in the length of the proof. Recall the following language is in **NP**:

$$L = \left\{ \langle \varphi, 1^n \rangle : \varphi \text{ has a proof in } \mathcal{A} \text{ of length } \leq n \right\}$$

The **PCP** Theorem asserts that L has probabilistically checkable certificates. Such certificate can be viewed as an alternative notion of "proof" for mathematical statements that is just as valid as the usual notion. However, unlike standard mathematical proofs, where every line of the proof has to be checked to verify its validity, this new notion guarantees that proofs are probabilistically checkable by examining only a constant number of bits in them.[2]

We now make a more formal definition. Recall that a language L is in **NP** if there is a poly-time Turing machine V ("verifier") that, given input x, checks certificates (or

---

[2] One newspaper article about the discovery of the **PCP** Theorem carried the headline "New shortcut found for long math proofs!"

membership proofs) to the effect that $x \in L$ (see Definition 2.1). In other words,

$$x \in L \Rightarrow \exists \pi \quad \text{s.t. } V^{\pi}(x) = 1$$
$$x \notin L \Rightarrow \forall \pi \quad V^{\pi}(x) = 0$$

where V^{π} denotes "a verifier with access to certificate π."

The class **PCP** is a generalization of this notion, with the following changes. First, the verifier is probabilistic. Second, the verifier has *random access* to the proof string Π. This means that each bit of the proof string can be independently *queried* by the verifier via a special *address tape*: If the verifier desires say the ith bit in the proof string, it writes i on the address tape and then receives the bit $\pi[i]$.[3] The definition of **PCP** treats *queries* to the proof as a precious resource to be used sparingly. Note also that since the address size is *logarithmic* in the proof size, this model in principle allows a polynomial-time verifier to check membership proofs of exponential size.

Verifiers can be *adaptive* or *nonadaptive*. A nonadaptive verifier selects its queries based only on its input and random tape. In other words, no query depends upon the responses to any of the prior queries. By contrast, an adaptive verifier can rely upon bits it has already queried in π to select its next queries. We restrict verifiers to be *nonadaptive*, since most **PCP** Theorems can be proved using nonadaptive verifiers, but Exercise 11.2 explores the power of adaptive queries.

Definition 11.4 *(PCP verifier)* Let L be a language and $q, r : \mathbb{N} \to \mathbb{N}$. We say that L has an $(r(n), q(n))$-**PCP** *verifier* if there's a polynomial-time probabilistic algorithm V satisfying:

> *Efficiency:* On input a string $x \in \{0, 1\}^n$ and given random access to a string $\pi \in \{0, 1\}^*$ of length at most $q(n)2^{r(n)}$ (which we call the *proof*), V uses at most $r(n)$ random coins and makes at most $q(n)$ nonadaptive queries to locations of π (see Figure 11.1). Then it outputs "1"(for "accept") or "0" (for "reject"). We let $V^{\pi}(x)$ denote the random variable representing V's output on input x and with random access to π.

> *Completeness:* If $x \in L$, then there exists a proof $\pi \in \{0, 1\}^*$ such that $\Pr[V^{\pi}(x) = 1] = 1$. We call this string π the *correct proof* for x.

> *Soundness:* If $x \notin L$ then for every proof $\pi \in \{0, 1\}^*$, $\Pr[V^{\pi}(x) = 1] \leq 1/2$.

We say that a language L is in **PCP**$(r(n), q(n))$ if there are some constants $c, d > 0$ such that L has a $(c \cdot r(n), d \cdot q(n))$-**PCP** verifier.

The **PCP** Theorem says that every **NP** language has a highly efficient **PCP** verifier.

Theorem 11.5 *(The **PCP** Theorem* [AS92, ALM$^+$92]*)* **NP** = **PCP**$(\log n, 1)$.

---

[3] For a precise formalization, see Exercise 1.9 discussing RAM Turing machines or Section 5.5 discussing oracle Turing machines.

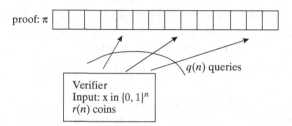

Figure 11.1. A **PCP** verifier for a language L gets an input x and has random access to a string π. If $x \in L$, then there exists a string π that makes the verifier accepts, while if $x \notin L$, then the verifier rejects *every* proof π with probability at least 1/2.

Remark 11.6 Some notes are in order:

1. The soundness condition stipulates that if $x \notin L$ then the verifier has to reject *every* proof with probability at least 1/2. Establishing this is the most difficult part of the proof.

2. The restriction that proofs checkable by an (r, q)-verifier are of length at most $q2^r$ is inconsequential, since such a verifier can look on at most this number of locations with nonzero probability over all 2^r choices for its random string.

3. Note that $\mathbf{PCP}(r(n), q(n)) \subseteq \mathbf{NTIME}(2^{O(r(n))} q(n))$ since a nondeterministic machine could guess the proof in $2^{O(r(n))} q(n)$ time and verify it deterministically by running the verifier for all $2^{O(r(n))}$ possible choices of its random coin tosses. If the verifier accepts for all these possible coin tosses, then the nondeterministic machine accepts.

    As a special case, $\mathbf{PCP}(\log n, 1) \subseteq \mathbf{NTIME}(2^{O(\log n)}) = \mathbf{NP}$: this is the trivial direction of the **PCP** Theorem.

4. The statement of the **PCP** Theorem allows verifiers for different **NP** languages to use a different number of query bits (so long as this number is constant). However, since every **NP** language is polynomial-time reducible to SAT, all these numbers can be upper bounded by a universal constant, namely, the number of query bits required by a verifier for SAT.

5. The constant 1/2 in the soundness requirement of Definition 11.4 is arbitrary, in the sense that changing it to any other positive constant smaller than 1 will not change the class of languages defined. Indeed, a **PCP** verifier with soundness 1/2 that uses r coins and makes q queries can be converted into a **PCP** verifier using cr coins and cq queries with soundness 2^{-c} by just repeating its execution c times (see Exercise 11.1).

EXAMPLE 11.7

To get a better sense for what a **PCP** proof system looks like, we sketch two nontrivial **PCP** systems:

1. The language GNI of pairs of nonisomorphic graphs is in $\mathbf{PCP}(poly(n), 1)$. Say the input for GNI is $\langle G_0, G_1 \rangle$, where G_0, G_1 have both n nodes. The verifier expects π to contain, for each labeled graph H with n nodes, a bit $\pi[H] \in \{0, 1\}$ corresponding to whether $H \equiv G_0$ or $H \equiv G_1$ ($\pi[H]$ can be arbitrary if neither case holds). In other words, π is an (exponentially long) array of bits indexed by the (adjacency matrix representations of) all possible n-vertex graphs.

The verifier picks $b \in \{0, 1\}$ at random and a random permutation. She applies the permutation to the vertices of G_b to obtain an isomorphic graph, H. She queries the corresponding bit of π and accepts iff the bit is b.

If $G_0 \not\equiv G_1$, then clearly a proof π that makes the verifier accept with probability 1 can be constructed. If $G_1 \equiv G_2$, then the probability that any π makes the verifier accept is at most $1/2$.

2. The protocols in Chapter 8 can be used (see Exercise 11.7) to show that the *permanent* has **PCP** proof system with polynomial randomness and queries. Once again, the length of the proof will be exponential.

In fact, both of these results are a special case of the following theorem.

Theorem 11.8 *(Scaled-up* **PCP***,* [BFLS91, ALM$^+$92, AS92]*)* **PCP**$(\text{poly}(n), 1) = $ **NEXP**

Above we use **PCP**$(\text{poly}(n), 1)$ to denote the class $\cup_{c \geq 1}$**PCP**$(n^c, 1)$. Theorem 11.8 can be thought of as a "scaled-up" version of the **PCP** Theorem. We omit the proof, which uses similar techniques to the original proof of the **PCP** Theorem and Theorem 8.19 (**IP** = **PSPACE**). $\diamond$

11.2.2 **PCP** and hardness of approximation

Another view of the **PCP** Theorem is that it shows that for many **NP** optimization problems, computing *approximate* solutions is no easier than computing exact solutions.

For concreteness, we focus for now on MAX-3SAT. Until 1992, we did not know whether or not MAX-3SAT has a polynomial-time ρ-approximation algorithm for *every* $\rho < 1$. It turns out that the **PCP** Theorem means that the answer is NO (unless **P** = **NP**). The reason is that it can be equivalently stated as follows.

Theorem 11.9 *(**PCP** Theorem: Hardness of approximation view) There exists $\rho < 1$ such that for every $L \in$ **NP** there is a polynomial-time function f mapping strings to (representations of) 3CNF formulas such that*

$$x \in L \Rightarrow \text{val}(f(x)) = 1 \tag{11.1}$$

$$x \notin L \Rightarrow \text{val}(f(x)) < \rho \tag{11.2}$$

This immediately implies the following corollary.

Corollary 11.10 *There exists some constant $\rho < 1$ such that if there is a polynomial-time ρ-approximation algorithm for MAX-3SAT then* **P** = **NP**. $\diamond$

Indeed, Theorem 11.9 shows for every $L \in$ **NP**, a way to convert a ρ-approximation algorithm A for MAX-3SAT into an algorithm deciding L, since (11.1) and (11.2) together imply that $x \in L$ iff $A(f(x))$ yields an assignment satisfying at least a ρ fraction of $f(x)$'s clauses.

Later, in Chapter 22, we show a stronger **PCP** Theorem by Håstad, which implies that for every $\epsilon > 0$, if there is a polynomial-time $(7/8 + \epsilon)$-approximation algorithm for MAX-3SAT, then **P** = **NP**. Hence the approximation algorithm for this problem mentioned in Example 11.2 is very likely *optimal*. The **PCP** Theorem (and the other **PCP** theorems that followed it) imply a host of such *hardness of approximation* results for many important problems, often showing that known approximation algorithms are optimal unless **P = NP**.

Why doesn't the Cook-Levin reduction suffice to prove Theorem 11.9?

The first idea one would try to prove Theorem 11.9 is the reduction from any **NP** language to 3SAT in the Cook-Levin Theorem (Theorem 2.10). Unfortunately, it doesn't yield such an *f* because it does not satisfy property (11.2): Exercise 11.11 asks you to show that one can always satisfy almost all of the clauses in the formulae produced by the reduction. (This is what Papadimitriou and Yannakakis referred to in their quote at the start of this chapter.) Hence $\text{val}(\cdot)$ is almost 1 for these formulas, whereas Theorem 11.9 requires that $\text{val}(\cdot) < \rho$ in one case.

11.3 EQUIVALENCE OF THE TWO VIEWS

We now show the equivalence of the "proof view" and the "hardness of approximation view" of the **PCP** Theorem. That is, we show that Theorem 11.5 is equivalent to Theorem 11.9. To do so we introduce the notion of *constraint satisfaction problems* (CSP). This is a generalization of 3SAT that turns up in many applications and also plays an important role in the proof of the **PCP** Theorem. A CSP problem generalizes 3SAT by allowing clauses of arbitrary form (instead of just OR of literals), including those depending upon more than 3 variables.

Definition 11.11 *(Constraint satisfaction problems (CSP))* If q is a natural number, then a qCSP instance φ is a collection of functions $\varphi_1, \ldots, \varphi_m$ (called *constraints*) from $\{0, 1\}^n$ to $\{0, 1\}$ such that each function φ_i depends on at most q of its input locations. That is, for every $i \in [m]$ there exist $j_1, \ldots, j_q \in [n]$ and $f : \{0, 1\}^q \to \{0, 1\}$ such that $\varphi_i(\mathbf{u}) = f(u_{j_1}, \ldots, u_{j_q})$ for every $\mathbf{u} \in \{0, 1\}^n$.

We say that an *assignment* $\mathbf{u} \in \{0, 1\}^n$ *satisfies* constraint φ_i if $\varphi_i(\mathbf{u}) = 1$. The fraction of constraints satisfied by $\mathbf{u}$ is $\frac{\sum_{i=1}^m \varphi_i(\mathbf{u})}{m}$, and we let $\text{val}(\varphi)$ denote the maximum of this value over all $\mathbf{u} \in \{0, 1\}^n$. We say that φ is *satisfiable* if $\text{val}(\varphi) = 1$. We call q the *arity* of φ.

EXAMPLE 11.12

3SAT is the subcase of qCSP where $q = 3$, and the constraints are OR's of the involved literals.

Notes

1. We define the *size* of a qCSP-instance φ to be m, the number of constraints it has. Because variables not used by any constraints are redundant, we always assume $n \le qm$. Note that a qCSP instance over n variables with m constraints can be described using $O(mq \log n2^q))$ bits. (In all cases we are interested in, q will be a constant independent of n, m.)

2. The simple greedy approximation algorithm for $3\mathsf{SAT}$ can be generalized for the $\mathsf{MAX}\,q\mathsf{CSP}$ problem of maximizing the number of satisfied constraints in a given $q\mathsf{CSP}$ instance. For any $q\mathsf{CSP}$ instance φ with m constraints, this algorithm will output an assignment satisfying $\frac{\mathsf{val}(\varphi)}{2^q}m$ constraints.

11.3.1 Equivalence of Theorems 11.5 and 11.9

We now show the equivalence of the two formulations of the **PCP** Theorem (Theorems 11.5 and 11.9) by showing that they are both equivalent to the **NP**-hardness of a certain gap version of $q\mathsf{CSP}$.

Definition 11.13 *(Gap* CSP*)* For every $q \in \mathbb{N}, \rho \leq 1$, define $\rho\text{-}\mathsf{GAP}q\mathsf{CSP}$ to be the problem of determining for a given $q\mathsf{CSP}$-instance φ whether (1) $\mathsf{val}(\varphi) = 1$ (in which case we say φ is a YES instance of $\rho\text{-}\mathsf{GAP}q\mathsf{CSP}$) or (2) $\mathsf{val}(\varphi) < \rho$ (in which case we say φ is a NO instance of $\rho\text{-}\mathsf{GAP}q\mathsf{CSP}$).

We say that $\rho\text{-}\mathsf{GAP}q\mathsf{CSP}$ is **NP**-hard for every language **L** in **NP** if there is a polynomial-time function f mapping strings to (representations of) $q\mathsf{CSP}$ instances satisfying:

Completeness: $x \in L \Rightarrow \mathsf{val}(f(x)) = 1.$

Soundness: $x \notin L \Rightarrow \mathsf{val}(f(x)) < \rho.$

Theorem 11.14 *There exist constants* $q \in \mathbb{N}$, $\rho \in (0,1)$ *such that* $\rho\text{-}\mathsf{GAP}q\mathsf{CSP}$ *is* **NP**-*hard.*   ◇

We now show that Theorems 11.5, 11.9, and 11.14 are all equivalent to one another.

Theorem 11.5 implies Theorem 11.14

Assume that $\mathbf{NP} \subseteq \mathbf{PCP}(\log n, 1)$. We will show that $1/2\text{-}\mathsf{GAP}q\mathsf{CSP}$ is **NP**-hard for some constant q. It is enough to reduce a single **NP**-complete language such as $3\mathsf{SAT}$ to $1/2\text{-}\mathsf{GAP}q\mathsf{CSP}$ for some constant q. Under our assumption, $3\mathsf{SAT}$ has a **PCP** system in which the verifier V makes a constant number of queries, which we denote by q, and uses $c \log n$ random coins for some constant c. Given every input x and $r \in \{0, 1\}^{c \log n}$, define $V_{x,r}$ to be the function that on input a proof π outputs 1 if the verifier will accept the proof π on input x and coins r. Note that $V_{x,r}$ depends on at most q locations. Thus for every $x \in \{0, 1\}^n$, the collection $\varphi = \{V_{x,r}\}_{r \in \{0,1\}^{c \log n}}$ is a polynomial-sized $q\mathsf{CSP}$ instance. Furthermore, since V runs in polynomial-time, the transformation of x to φ can also be carried out in polynomial-time. By the completeness and soundness of the **PCP** system, if $x \in 3\mathsf{SAT}$, then φ will satisfy $\mathsf{val}(\varphi) = 1$, while if $x \notin 3\mathsf{SAT}$, then φ will satisfy $\mathsf{val}(\varphi) \leq 1/2$. ∎

Theorem 11.14 implies Theorem 11.5

Suppose that $\rho\text{-}\mathsf{GAP}q\mathsf{CSP}$ is **NP**-hard for some constants $q, \rho < 1$. Then this easily translates into a **PCP** system with q queries, ρ soundness, and logarithmic randomness for any language L: Given an input x, the verifier will run the reduction $f(x)$ to obtain a $q\mathsf{CSP}$ instance $\varphi = \{\varphi_i\}_{i=1}^m$. It will expect the proof π to be an assignment to the variables of φ, which it will verify by choosing a random $i \in [m]$ and checking that φ_i is satisfied (by making q queries). Clearly, if $x \in L$, then the verifier will accept with probability 1,

Table 11.1. Two views of the **PCP** Theorem.

Proof view		Hardness of approximation view
PCP verifier (V)	$\longleftrightarrow$	CSP instance (φ)
PCP proof (π)	$\longleftrightarrow$	Assignment to variables ($\mathbf{u}$)
Length of proof	$\longleftrightarrow$	Number of variables (n)
Number of queries (q)	$\longleftrightarrow$	Arity of constraints (q)
Number of random bits (r)	$\longleftrightarrow$	Logarithm of number of constraints ($\log m$)
Soundness parameter (typically $1/2$)	$\longleftrightarrow$	Maximum of $\mathsf{val}(\varphi)$ for a NO instance
Theorem 11.5 (**NP** $\subseteq$ **PCP**$(\log n, 1)$)	$\longleftrightarrow$	Theorem 11.14 (ρ-$\mathsf{GAP}q\mathsf{CSP}$ is **NP**-hard),
		Theorem 11.9 ($\mathsf{MAX\text{-}3SAT}$ is **NP**-hard to ρ-approximate)

while if $x \notin L$, it will accept with probability at most ρ. The soundness can be boosted to $1/2$ at the expense of a constant factor in the randomness and number of queries (see Exercise 11.1). ∎

Theorem 11.9 is equivalent to Theorem 11.14

Since $3CNF$ formulas are a special case of $3\mathsf{CSP}$ instances, Theorem 11.9 implies Theorem 11.14. We now show the other direction.

Let $\epsilon > 0$ and $q \in \mathbb{N}$ be such that by Theorem 11.14, $(1 - \epsilon)$-$\mathsf{GAP}q\mathsf{CSP}$ is **NP**-hard. Let φ be a $q\mathsf{CSP}$ instance over n variables with m constraints. Each constraint φ_i of φ can be expressed as an AND of at most 2^q clauses, where each clause is the OR of at most q variables or their negations. Let φ' denote the collection of at most $m2^q$ clauses corresponding to all the constraints of φ. If φ is a YES instance of $(1 - \epsilon)$-$\mathsf{GAP}q\mathsf{CSP}$ (i.e., it is satisfiable), then there exists an assignment satisfying all the clauses of φ'. If φ is a NO instance of $(1 - \epsilon)$-$\mathsf{GAP}q\mathsf{CSP}$, then every assignment violates at least an ϵ fraction of the constraints of φ and hence violates at least an $\frac{\epsilon}{2^q}$ fraction of the constraints of φ'. We can use the Cook-Levin technique of Chapter 2 (Theorem 2.10), to transform any clause C on q variables $u_1, \ldots, u_q$ to a set $C_1, \ldots, C_q$ of clauses over the variables $u_1, \ldots, u_q$ and additional auxiliary variables $y_1, \ldots, y_q$ such that (1) each clause C_i is the OR of at most three variables or their negations, (2) if $u_1, \ldots, u_q$ satisfy C then there is an assignment to $y_1, \ldots, y_q$ such that $u_1, \ldots, u_q, y_1, \ldots, y_q$ simultaneously satisfy $C_1, \ldots, C_q$, and (3) if $u_1, \ldots, u_q$ does not satisfy C then for every assignment to $y_1, \ldots, y_q$, there is some clause C_i that is not satisfied by $u_1, \ldots, u_q, y_1, \ldots, y_q$.

Let φ'' denote the collection of at most $qm2^q$ clauses over the $n + qm2^g$ variables obtained in this way from φ'. Note that φ'' is a $3\mathsf{SAT}$ formula. Our reduction will map φ to φ''. Completeness holds since if φ were satisfiable, then so would be φ' and hence also φ''. Soundness holds since if every assignment violates at least an ϵ fraction of the constraints of φ, then every assignment violates at least an $\frac{\epsilon}{2^q}$ fraction of the constraints of φ', and so every assignment violates at least an $\frac{\epsilon}{q2^q}$ fraction of the constraints of φ'' ∎

11.3.2 Review of the two views of the PCP Theorem

It is worthwhile to review this very useful equivalence between the "proof view" and the "hardness of approximation view" of the **PCP** Theorem, as outlined in Table 11.1.

11.4 HARDNESS OF APPROXIMATION FOR VERTEX COVER AND INDEPENDENT SET

The **PCP** Theorem implies hardness of approximation results for many more problems than just 3SAT and CSP. As an example we show a hardness of approximation result for the maximum independent set (MAX-INDSET) problem we encountered in Chapter 2 (Example 2.2) and for the MIN-VERTEX-COVER problem encountered in Example 11.3. Note that the inapproximability result for MAX-INDSET is stronger than the result for MIN-VERTEX-COVER since it rules out ρ-approximation for every $\rho < 1$.

Theorem 11.15 *There is some* $\gamma < 1$ *such that computing a* γ-*approximation to* MIN-VERTEX-COVER *is* **NP**-*hard. For every* $\rho < 1$, *computing a* ρ-*approximation to* INDSET *is* **NP**-*hard.*   ◇

Since a vertex cover is a set of vertices touching all edges of the graph, its complement is an an independent set. Thus the two problems are trivially equivalent with respect to exact solution: The largest independent set is simply the complement of the smallest vertex cover. However, this does not imply that they are equivalent with respect to approximation. Denoting the size of the minimum vertex cover by VC and the size of the largest independent set by IS, we see that $VC = n - IS$. Thus a ρ-approximation for INDSET would produce an independent set of size $\rho \cdot IS$, and if we wish to use this to compute an approximation to MIN-VERTEX-COVER, then we obtain a vertex cover of size $n - \rho \cdot IS$. This yields an approximation ratio of $\frac{n-IS}{n-\rho IS}$ for MIN-VERTEX-COVER, which could be arbitrarily small if IS is close to n. In fact, Theorem 11.15 shows that if **P** $\neq$ **NP**, then the approximability of the two problems is inherently different: We already saw that MIN-VERTEX-COVER has a polynomial-time 1/2-approximation algorithm (Example 2.2) whereas if **P** $\neq$ **NP**, then INDSET does not have a ρ-approximation algorithm for *every* $\rho < 1$.

We first show using the **PCP** Theorem that there is some constant $\rho < 1$ such that both problems cannot be ρ-approximated in polynomial-time (unless **P** = **NP**). We then show how to "amplify" the approximation gap and make ρ as small as desired in case of INDSET.

Lemma 11.16 *There exist a polynomial-time computable transformation f from 3CNF formulas to graphs such that for every 3CNF formula* φ, $f(\varphi)$ *is an n-vertex graph whose largest independent set has size* $\mathsf{val}(\varphi)\frac{n}{7}$.   ◇

PROOF SKETCH: We apply the "normal" **NP**-completeness reduction for INDSET (see proof of Theorem 2.15) on this 3CNF formula, and observe that it satisfies the desired property. We leave verifying the details as Exercise 11.5. ∎

The following corollary is immediate.

Corollary 11.17 *If* **P** $\neq$ **NP**, *then there are some constants* $\rho < 1, \rho' < 1$ *such that the problem* INDSET *cannot be* ρ-*approximated in polynomial time and* MIN-VERTEX-COVER *cannot be* ρ'-*approximated.*   ◇

PROOF: Let L be any **NP** language. Theorem 11.9 implies that the decision problem for L can be reduced to approximating MAX-3SAT. Specifically, the reduction produces a 3CNF formula φ that is either satisfiable or satisfies $\mathsf{val}(\varphi) < \rho$, where $\rho < 1$ is some constant. Then we can apply the reduction of Lemma 11.16 on this 3CNF formula and conclude that a ρ-approximation to INDSET would allow us to do a ρ-approximation to MAX-3SAT on φ. Thus it follows that ρ-approximation to INDSET is **NP**-hard.

The result for MIN-VERTEX-COVER follows from the observation that the minimum vertex cover in the graph resulting from the reduction of the previous paragraph has size $n - \mathsf{val}(\varphi)\frac{n}{7}$. It follows that if MIN-VERTEX-COVER had a ρ'-approximation for $\rho' = 6/(7 - \rho)$, then it would allow us to find a vertex cover of size $\frac{1}{\rho'}(n - \frac{n}{7})$ in the case $\mathsf{val}(\varphi) = 1$, and this size is at most $n - \rho n/7$. Thus we conclude that such an approximation would allow us to distinguish the cases $\mathsf{val}(\varphi) = 1$ and $\mathsf{val}(\varphi) < \rho$, which by Theorem 11.9 is **NP**-hard. ∎

To complete the proof of Theorem 11.15, we need to amplify this approximation gap for INDSET. Such amplification is possible for many combinatorial problems thanks to a certain "self-improvement" property. In case of INDSET, a simple self-improvement is possible using a *graph product*.

PROOF: (Of Theorem 11.15) For any n-vertex graph G, define G^k to be a graph on $\binom{n}{k}$ vertices whose vertices correspond to all subsets of vertices of G of size k Two subsets S_1, S_2 are adjacent if $S_1 \cup S_2$ is an independent set in G. It is easily checked that the largest independent of G^k corresponds to all k-size subsets of the largest independent set in G and therefore has size $\binom{\mathrm{IS}}{k}$, where IS is the size of the largest independent set in G. Thus if we take the graph produced by the reduction of Corollary 11.17 and take its k-wise product, then the ratio of the size of the largest independent set in the two cases is $\binom{\mathrm{IS}}{k}/\binom{\rho \cdot \mathrm{IS}}{k}$ which is approximately a factor ρ^k. Choosing k large enough, ρ^k can be made smaller than any desired constant. The running time of the reduction becomes n^k, which is polynomial for every fixed k. ∎

Remark 11.18 *(Levin Reductions)*

In Chapter 2, we defined L' to be **NP**-hard if every $L \in$ **NP** reduces to L'. The reduction was a polynomial-time function f such that $x \in L \Leftrightarrow f(x) \in L'$. In all cases, we proved that $x \in L \Rightarrow f(x) \in L'$ by showing a way to map a *certificate* for the fact that $x \in L$ to a certificate for the fact that $x' \in L'$. Although the definition of a Karp reduction does not require that this mapping between certificates is efficient, this was often the case. Similarly we proved that $f(x) \in L' \Rightarrow x \in L$ by showing a way to map a certificate for the fact that $x' \in L'$ to a certificate for the fact that $x \in L$. Again the proofs typically yield an efficient way to compute this mapping. We call reductions with these properties Levin reductions (see the proof of Theorem 2.18). It is worthwhile to observe that the **PCP** reductions of this chapter also satisfy this property. For example, the proof of Theorem 11.16 actually yields a way not just to map, say, a CNF formula φ into a graph G such that φ is satisfiable iff G has a "large" independent set, but actually shows how to efficiently map a satisfying assignment for φ into a large independent set in G and a not-too-small independent set in G into a satisfying assignment for φ. This will become clear from our proof of the **PCP** Theorem in Chapter 22.

We now prove a weaker version of the **PCP** Theorem, showing that every **NP** statement has an exponentially long proof that can be locally tested by only looking at a constant number of bits. In addition to giving a taste of how one proves **PCP** theorems, techniques from this section will be used in the proof of the full-fledged **PCP** Theorem in Chapter 22.

Theorem 11.19 (*Exponential-sized* **PCP** *system for* **NP** [ALM+92]) **NP** ⊆ **PCP**(poly(n), 1).

We prove this theorem by designing an appropriate verifier for an **NP**-complete language. The verifier expects the proof to contain an encoded version of the usual certificate. The verifier checks such an encoded certificate by simple probabilistic tests.

11.5.1 Tool: Linearity testing and the Walsh-Hadamard code

We use the *Walsh-Hadamard code* (see also Section 19.2.2, though the treatment here is self-contained). It is a way to encode bit strings of length n by *linear functions* in n variables over GF(2). The encoding function $\mathsf{WH} : \{0, 1\}^* \to \{0, 1\}^*$ maps a string $\mathbf{u} \in \{0, 1\}^n$ to the truth table of the function $\mathbf{x} \mapsto \mathbf{u} \odot \mathbf{x}$, where for $\mathbf{x}, \mathbf{y} \in \{0, 1\}^n$ we define $\mathbf{x} \odot \mathbf{y} = \sum_{i=1}^n x_i y_i \pmod{2}$. Note that this is a very inefficient encoding method: An n-bit string $\mathbf{u} \in \{0, 1\}^n$ is encoded using $|\mathsf{WH}(\mathbf{u})| = 2^n$ bits. If $f \in \{0, 1\}^{2^n}$ is equal to $\mathsf{WH}(\mathbf{u})$ for some $\mathbf{u}$, then we say that f is a *Walsh-Hadamard codeword*. Such a string $f \in \{0, 1\}^{2^n}$ can also be viewed as a function from $\{0, 1\}^n$ to $\{0, 1\}$.

Below, we repeatedly use the following fact (see Claim A.31).

RANDOM SUBSUM PRINCIPLE: *If* $\mathbf{u} \neq \mathbf{v}$ *then for* 1/2 *the choices of* $\mathbf{x}$, $\mathbf{u} \odot \mathbf{x} \neq \mathbf{v} \odot \mathbf{x}$.

The random subsum principle implies that the Walsh-Hadamard code is an error-correcting code with minimum distance 1/2, by which we mean that for every $\mathbf{u} \neq \mathbf{v} \in \{0, 1\}^n$, the encodings $\mathsf{WH}(\mathbf{u})$ and $\mathsf{WH}(\mathbf{v})$ differ in at least half the bits. Now we talk about local tests for the Walsh-Hadamard code (i.e., tests making only $O(1)$ queries).

Local testing of Walsh-Hadamard code

Suppose we are given access to a function $f : \{0, 1\}^n \to \{0, 1\}$ and want to *test* whether or not f is actually a codeword of Walsh-Hadamard. Since the Walsh-Hadamard code-words are precisely the set of all *linear* functions from $\{0, 1\}^n$ to $\{0, 1\}$, we can test f by checking that

$$f(\mathbf{x} + \mathbf{y}) = f(\mathbf{x}) + f(\mathbf{y}) \tag{11.3}$$

for all the 2^{2n} pairs $\mathbf{x}, \mathbf{y} \in \{0, 1\}^n$ (where "+" on the left side of (11.3) denotes vector addition over GF(2)^n and on the right side denotes addition over GF(2)). This test works by definition, but it involves reading all 2^n values of f.

Can we test f by reading only a *constant* number of its values? The natural test is to choose $\mathbf{x}, \mathbf{y}$ at random and verify (11.3). Clearly, even such a local test accepts a linear function with probability 1. However, now we can no longer guarantee that every function that is not linear is rejected with high probability! For example, if f is very close to being a linear function, meaning that f is obtained by modifying a linear function on a very small fraction of its inputs, then such a *local* test will encounter the nonlinear part with very low probability, and thus not be able to distinguish f from a linear function. So we set our goal less ambitiously: a test that on one hand accepts every linear function, and on the other hand rejects with high probability every function that is *far from linear*. The natural test suffices for this job.

Definition 11.20 Let $\rho \in [0,1]$. We say that $f, g : \{0,1\}^n \to \{0,1\}$ are *ρ-close* if $\Pr_{\mathbf{x} \in_R \{0,1\}^n}[f(\mathbf{x}) = g(\mathbf{x})] \geq \rho$. We say that f is *ρ-close to a linear function* if there exists a linear function g such that f and g are ρ-close.   ◇

Theorem 11.21 *(Linearity Testing [BLR90]) Let $f : \{0,1\}^n \to \{0,1\}$ be such that*

$$\Pr_{\mathbf{x},\mathbf{y} \in_R \{0,1\}^n}[f(\mathbf{x}+\mathbf{y}) = f(\mathbf{x})+f(\mathbf{y})] \geq \rho$$

for some $\rho > 1/2$. Then f is ρ-close to a linear function.   ◇

We defer the proof of Theorem 11.21 to Section 22.5 of Chapter 22. For every $\delta \in (0, 1/2)$, we can obtain a linearity test that rejects with probability at least $1/2$ every function that is not $(1-\delta)$-close to a linear function, by testing Condition (11.3) repeatedly $O(1/\delta)$ times with independent randomness. We call such a test a *$(1-\delta)$-linearity test*.

Local decoding of Walsh-Hadamard code

Suppose that for $\delta < \frac{1}{4}$ the function $f : \{0,1\}^n \to \{0,1\}$ is $(1-\delta)$-close to some linear function $\tilde{f}$. Because every two linear functions differ on half of their inputs, the function $\tilde{f}$ is uniquely determined by f. Suppose we are given $\mathbf{x} \in \{0,1\}^n$ and random access to f. Can we obtain the value $\tilde{f}(\mathbf{x})$ using only a constant number of queries? The naive answer is that since most $\mathbf{x}$'s satisfy $f(\mathbf{x}) = \tilde{f}(\mathbf{x})$, we should be able to learn $\tilde{f}(\mathbf{x})$ with good probability by making only the single query $\mathbf{x}$ to f. The problem is that $\mathbf{x}$ could very well be one of the places where f and $\tilde{f}$ differ. Fortunately, there is still a simple way to learn $\tilde{f}(\mathbf{x})$ while making only two queries to f:

1. Choose $\mathbf{x}' \in_R \{0,1\}^n$.
2. Set $\mathbf{x}'' = \mathbf{x} + \mathbf{x}'$.
3. Let $\mathbf{y}' = f(\mathbf{x}')$ and $\mathbf{y}'' = f(\mathbf{x}'')$.
4. Output $\mathbf{y}' + \mathbf{y}''$.

Since both $\mathbf{x}'$ and $\mathbf{x}''$ are individually uniformly distributed (even though they are dependent), by the union bound with probability at least $1 - 2\delta$ we have $\mathbf{y}' = \tilde{f}(\mathbf{x}')$ and $\mathbf{y}'' = \tilde{f}(\mathbf{x}'')$. Yet by the linearity of $\tilde{f}$, $\tilde{f}(\mathbf{x}) = \tilde{f}(\mathbf{x}' + \mathbf{x}'') = \tilde{f}(\mathbf{x}') + \tilde{f}(\mathbf{x}'')$, and hence with at least $1 - 2\delta$ probability, $\tilde{f}(\mathbf{x}) = \mathbf{y}' + \mathbf{y}''$. (We use here the fact that over GF(2), $a + b = a - b$.) This technique is called *local decoding* of the Walsh-Hadamard code since it allows to recover any bit of the correct codeword (the linear function $\tilde{f}$) from a corrupted version (the function f) while making only a constant number of queries. It is also known as *self correction* of the Walsh-Hadamard code.

Figure 11.2. The **PCP** proof that a set of quadratic equations is satisfiable consists of $\mathrm{WH}(u)$ and $\mathrm{WH}(u \otimes u)$ for some vector u. The verifier first checks that the proof is close to having this form and then uses the local decoder of the Walsh-Hadamard code to ensure that u is a solution for the quadratic equation instance. The dotted areas represent corrupted coordinates.

11.5.2 Proof of Theorem 11.19

We will show a $(\mathrm{poly}(n), 1)$-verifier proof system for a particular **NP**-complete language L. The result that **NP** $\subseteq$ **PCP**$(\mathrm{poly}(n), 1)$ follows since every **NP** language is reducible to L. The **NP**-complete language L we use is QUADEQ, the language of systems of quadratic equations over $\mathrm{GF}(2) = \{0, 1\}$ that are satisfiable.

EXAMPLE 11.22

The following is an instance of QUADEQ over the variables $u_1, \ldots, u_5$:

$$u_1 u_2 + u_3 u_4 + u_1 u_5 = 1$$

$$u_2 u_3 + u_1 u_4 = 0$$

$$u_1 u_4 + u_3 u_5 + u_3 u_4 = 1$$

This instance is satisfiable since the all-1 assignment satisfies all the equations.

QUADEQ is **NP**-complete, as can be checked by reducing from the **NP**-complete language $\mathsf{CKT\text{-}SAT}$ of satisfiable Boolean circuits (see Section 6.1.2). The idea is to have a variable represent the value of each wire in the circuit (including the input wires) and to express AND and OR using the equivalent quadratic polynomial: $x \vee y = 1$ iff $(1 - x)(1 - y) = 0$, and so on. Details are left as Exercise 11.15.

Since $u_i = (u_i)^2$ in $\mathrm{GF}(2)$, we can assume the equations do not contain terms of the form u_i (i.e., all terms are of degree exactly two). Hence m quadratic equations over the variables $u_1, \ldots, u_n$ can be described by an $m \times n^2$ matrix A and an m-dimensional vector $\mathbf{b}$ (both over $\mathrm{GF}(2)$). Indeed, the problem QUADEQ can be phrased as the task, given such $A, \mathbf{b}$, of finding an n^2-dimensional vector U satisfying (1) $AU = \mathbf{b}$ and (2) U is the *tensor product* $\mathbf{u} \otimes \mathbf{u}$ of some n-dimensional vector $\mathbf{u}$.[4]

The PCP verifier

We now describe the **PCP** system for QUADEQ (see Figure 11.2). Let $A, \mathbf{b}$ be an instance of QUADEQ and suppose that $A, \mathbf{b}$ is satisfiable by an assignment $\mathbf{u} \in \{0, 1\}^n$. The verifier V gets access to a proof $\pi \in \{0, 1\}^{2^n + 2^{n^2}}$, which we interpret as a pair of functions $f : \{0, 1\}^n \to \{0, 1\}$ and $g : \{0, 1\}^{n^2} \to \{0, 1\}$. In the correct **PCP** proof π for A, b, the

---

[4] If $\mathbf{x}, \mathbf{y}$ are two n-dimensional vectors then their *tensor product*, denoted $\mathbf{x} \otimes \mathbf{y}$, is the n^2-dimensional vector (or $n \times n$ matrix) whose $\langle i, j \rangle$th entry is $x_i y_j$ (identifying $[n^2]$ with $[n] \times [n]$ in some canonical way). See also Section 21.3.3.

function f will be the Walsh-Hadamard encoding for $\mathbf{u}$, and the function g will be the Walsh-Hadamard encoding for $\mathbf{u} \otimes \mathbf{u}$. That is, we will design the **PCP** verifier V in a way ensuring that it accepts proofs of this form with probability one, hence satisfying the completeness condition. The analysis repeatedly uses the random subsum principle.

Step 1: Check that f, g are linear functions. As already noted, this isn't something that the verifier can check per se using local tests. Instead, the verifier performs a 0.999-linearity test on both f, g, and rejects the proof at once if either test fails.

Thus, if either of f, g is not 0.999-close to a linear function, then V rejects with high probability. Therefore for the rest of the procedure we can assume that there exist two linear functions $\tilde{f} : \{0, 1\}^n \to \{0, 1\}$ and $\tilde{g} : \{0, 1\}^{n^2} \to \{0, 1\}$ such that $\tilde{f}$ is 0.999-close to f, and $\tilde{g}$ is 0.999-close to g. (Note: In a correct proof, the tests succeed with probability 1 and $\tilde{f} = f$ and $\tilde{g} = g$.)

In fact, we will assume that for Steps 2 and 3, the verifier can query $\tilde{f}, \tilde{g}$ at any desired point. The reason is that local decoding allows the verifier to recover any desired value of $\tilde{f}, \tilde{g}$ with good probability, and Steps 2 and 3 will only use a small (less than 20) number of queries to $\tilde{f}, \tilde{g}$. Thus with high probability (say > 0.9) local decoding will succeed on all these queries.

> NOTATION: To simplify notation and in the rest of the procedure we use f, g for $\tilde{f}, \tilde{g}$ respectively. (This is OK since as argued previously, V can query $\tilde{f}, \tilde{g}$ at will.) In particular we assume both f and g are linear, and thus they must encode some strings $\mathbf{u} \in \{0, 1\}^n$ and $\mathbf{w} \in \{0, 1\}^{n^2}$. In other words, f, g are the functions given by $f(\mathbf{r}) = \mathbf{u} \odot \mathbf{r}$ and $g(\mathbf{z}) = \mathbf{w} \odot \mathbf{z}$.

Step 2: Verify that g encodes $\mathbf{u} \otimes \mathbf{u}$, where $\mathbf{u} \in \{0, 1\}^n$ is the string encoded by f. The verifier does the following test ten times using independent random bits: "Choose $\mathbf{r}, \mathbf{r}'$ independently at random from $\{0, 1\}^n$, and if $f(\mathbf{r})f(\mathbf{r}') \neq g(\mathbf{r} \otimes \mathbf{r}')$ then halt and reject."

In a correct proof, $\mathbf{w} = \mathbf{u} \otimes \mathbf{u}$, so

$$f(\mathbf{r})f(\mathbf{r}') = \left(\sum_{i \in [n]} u_i r_i\right)\left(\sum_{j \in [n]} u_j r'_j\right) = \sum_{i,j \in [n]} u_i u_j r_i r'_j = (\mathbf{u} \otimes \mathbf{u}) \odot (\mathbf{r} \otimes \mathbf{r}'),$$

which in the correct proof is equal to $g(\mathbf{r} \otimes \mathbf{r}')$. Thus Step 2 never rejects a correct proof.

Suppose now that, unlike the case of the correct proof, $\mathbf{w} \neq \mathbf{u} \otimes \mathbf{u}$. We claim that in each of the ten trials V will halt and reject with probability at least $\frac{1}{4}$. (Thus the probability of rejecting in at least one trial is at least $1 - (3/4)^{10} > 0.9$.) Indeed, let W be an $n \times n$ matrix with the same entries as $\mathbf{w}$, let U be the $n \times n$ matrix such that $U_{i,j} = u_i u_j$, and think of $\mathbf{r}$ as a row vector and $\mathbf{r}'$ as a column vector. In this notation,

$$g(\mathbf{r} \otimes \mathbf{r}') = \mathbf{w} \odot (\mathbf{r} \otimes \mathbf{r}') = \sum_{i,j \in [n]} w_{i,j} r_i r'_j = \mathbf{r} W \mathbf{r}'$$

$$f(\mathbf{r})f(\mathbf{r}') = (\mathbf{u} \odot \mathbf{r})(\mathbf{u} \odot \mathbf{r}') = (\sum_{i=1}^{n} u_i r_i)(\sum_{j=1}^{n} u_j r'_j) = \sum_{i,j \in [n]} u_i u_j r_i r'_j = \mathbf{r} U \mathbf{r}'$$

And V rejects if $\mathbf{r} W \mathbf{r}' \neq \mathbf{r} U \mathbf{r}'$. The random subsum principle implies that if $W \neq U$ then at least $1/2$ of all $\mathbf{r}$ satisfy $\mathbf{r} W \neq \mathbf{r} U$. Applying the random subsum principle for each such $\mathbf{r}$, we conclude that at least $1/2$ the $\mathbf{r}'$ satisfy $\mathbf{r}W\mathbf{r}' \neq \mathbf{r}U\mathbf{r}'$. We conclude that the trial rejects for at least $1/4$ of all pairs $\mathbf{r}, \mathbf{r}'$.

Step 3: Verify that g encodes a satisfying assignment. Using all that has been verified about f, g in the previous two steps, it is easy to check that any particular equation, say the kth equation of the input, is satisfied by $\mathbf{u}$, namely,

$$\sum_{i,j} A_{k,(i,j)} u_i u_j = b_k \qquad (11.4)$$

Denoting by $\mathbf{z}$ the n^2 dimensional vector $(A_{k,(i,j)})$ (where i, j vary over $[1 \ldots n]$), we see that the left-hand side is nothing but $g(\mathbf{z})$. Since the verifier knows $A_{k,(i,j)}$ and b_k, it simply queries g at $\mathbf{z}$ and checks that $g(\mathbf{z}) = b_k$.

The drawback of this idea is that in order to check that $\mathbf{u}$ satisfies the entire system, the verifier needs to make a query to g for each $k = 1, 2, \ldots, m$, whereas the number of queries is required to be independent of m. Luckily, we can use the random subsum principle again! The verifier takes a random subset of the equations and computes their sum mod 2. (In other words, for $k = 1, 2, \ldots, m$ multiply the equation in (11.4) by a random bit and take the sum.) This sum is a new quadratic equation, and the random subsum principle implies that if $\mathbf{u}$ does not satisfy even one equation in the original system, then with probability at least $1/2$ it will not satisfy this new equation. The verifier checks that $\mathbf{u}$ satisfies this new equation.

Overall, we get a verifier V such that (1) if $A, \mathbf{b}$ is satisfiable then V accepts the correct proof with probability 1 and (2) if $A, \mathbf{b}$ is not satisfiable then V accepts every proof with probability at most 0.8. The probability of accepting a proof for a false statement can be reduced to $1/2$ by simple repetition, completing the proof of Theorem 11.19. ∎

WHAT HAVE WE LEARNED?

- Computing approximate solutions to **NP**-hard problems is an important research endeavor. The classical Cook-Levin-Karp reductions did not rule out the existence of approximation algorithms for many interesting **NP**-hard problem.
- Nontrivial approximation algorithms can be designed for many **NP**-hard problems.
- The **PCP** Theorem gives a new probabilistic characterization of **NP**, and also shows that the MAX-3SAT problem cannot be approximated within arbitrary accuracy if **P** $\neq$ **NP**. In fact, these two results are equivalent to one another.
- There are many other **PCP** theorems with different choices of parameters. In this chapter we saw a simple one where the verifier uses poly(n) random bits and examines only $O(1)$ bits in the proof.
- Proofs of **PCP** theorems involve some interesting way to encode a satisfying assignment to a boolean formula. This is accompanied by procedures that can efficiently check any string that is claimed to be such an encoding. In this chapter we saw a proof using the Hadamard code (that just consists of linear functions over GF(2)).

CHAPTER NOTES AND HISTORY

The notion of approximation algorithms predates the discovery of **NP**-completeness; for instance Graham's 1966 paper [Gra66] already gives an approximation algorithm for a scheduling problem that was later proven **NP**-complete. Shortly after the discovery of **NP**-completeness, Johnson [Joh74] formalized the issue of computing approximate solutions, gave some easy approximation algorithms (such as the 1/2-approximation for MAX-SAT) for a variety of problems and posed the question of whether better algorithms exist. Over the next 20 years, although a few results were proven regarding the hardness of computing approximate solutions (such as for general TSP in Sahni and Gonzalez [SG76]) and a few approximation algorithms were designed, it became increasingly obvious that we were lacking serious techniques for proving the hardness of approximation. The main difficulty seemed to be that there were no obvious interreducibilies among problems that preserved approximability. The paper by Papadimitriou and Yannakakis [PY88] showed such interreducibilities among a large set of problems they called MAX-SNP, and showed further that $\mathsf{MAX\text{-}3SAT}$ is *complete* for this class. This made $\mathsf{MAX\text{-}3SAT}$ an attractive problem to study both from the point of view of algorithm design and for proving hardness results.

Soon after this work, seemingly unrelated developments occurred in the study of interactive proofs, some of which we studied in Chapter 8. The most relevant for the topic of this chapter was the result of Babai, Fortnow and Lund [BFL90] that **MIP = NEXP**, which was soon made to apply to **NP** in the paper of Babai, Fortnow, Levin, and Szegedy [BFLS91]. After this, there were a sequence of swift developments. In 1991 came a stunning result by Feige, Goldwasser, Lovasz, Safra, and Szegedy [FGL$^+$91] which showed that if SAT does not have subexponential time algorithms, then the INDSET problem cannot be approximated within a factor $2^{\log^{1-\epsilon} n}$ for any $\epsilon > 0$. This was the first paper to connect hardness of approximation with **PCP**-like theorems, though at the time many researchers felt (especially because the result did not prove **NP**-completeness per se) that this was the "wrong approach" and the result would ultimately be reproven with no mention of interactive proofs. (Intriguingly, Dinur's Gap Amplification Lemma in Chapter 22 brings us closer to that dream.) However, a year later Arora and Safra [AS92] further refined the ideas of [BFL90] (and introduced the idea of verifier composition) to prove that approximating INDSET is actually **NP**-complete. They also proved a surprising new characterization of **NP** in terms of **PCP**, namely, **NP = PCP**$(\log n, \sqrt{\log n})$. At that point it became clear that if the query parameter could be sublogarithmic, it might well be made a constant! The subsequent paper of Arora, Lund, Motwani, Sudan, and Szegedy [ALM$^+$92] took this next step (in the process introducing the constant-bit verifier of Section 11.5, as well as other ideas) to prove **NP = PCP**$(\log n, 1)$, which they showed also implied the **NP**-hardness of approximating $\mathsf{MAX\text{-}3SAT}$. Since then many other **PCP** theorems have been proven, as surveyed in Chapter 22. (Note that in this chapter we derived the hardness result for INDSET from the result for $\mathsf{MAX\text{-}3SAT}$, even though historically the former happened first.)

The overall idea in the AS-ALMSS proof of the **PCP** Theorem (as indeed the one in the proof of **MIP = NEXP**) is similar to the proof of Theorem 11.19. In fact Theorem 11.19 is the only part of the original proof that still survives in our writeup; the rest of the proof in Chapter 22 is a more recent proof due to Dinur. However, in addition to using encodings based upon the Walsh-Hadamard code, the AS-ALMSS proof also used encodings based upon low-degree multivariate polynomials. These have associated procedures analogous to the linearity test and local decoding, though the proofs of correctness are a fair bit harder. The proof also drew intuition from the topic of self-testing and self-correcting programs [BLR90, RS92].

The PCP Theorem led to a flurry of results about hardness of approximation. See Trevisan [Tre05] for a recent survey and Arora-Lund [AL95] for an older one.

The PCP Theorem, as well as its cousin, **MIP = NEXP**, does not relativize [FRS88].

In this chapter we only talked about some very trivial approximation algorithms, which are not very representative of the state of the art. See Hochbaum [Hoc97] and Vazirani [Vaz01] for a good survey of the many ingenious approximation algorithms that have been developed.

EXERCISES

11.1. Prove that for every two functions $r, q : \mathbb{N} \rightarrow \mathbb{N}$ and constant $s < 1$, changing the constant in the soundness condition in Definition 11.4 from $1/2$ to s will not change the class **PCP**(r, q).

11.2. Prove that any language L that has a **PCP**-verifier using r coins and q *adaptive* queries also has a standard (i.e., nonadaptive) verifier using r coins and 2^q queries.

11.3. Give a probabilistic polynomial-time algorithm that given a 3CNF formula φ with exactly three distinct variables in each clause, outputs an assignment satisfying at least a $7/8$ fraction of φ's clauses.
H536

11.4. Give a *deterministic* polynomial-time algorithm with the same approximation guarantee as in Exercise 11.3.
H536

11.5. Prove Lemma 11.16.

11.6. Prove that **PCP**$(0, \log n) = $ **P**. Prove that **PCP**$(0, \text{poly}(n)) = $ **NP**.

11.7. Let L be the language of pairs $\langle A, k \rangle$ such that A is a 0/1 matrix and $k \in \mathbb{Z}$ satisfying $\text{perm}(A) = k$ (see Section 8.6.2). Prove that L is in **PCP**$(\text{poly}(n), \text{poly}(n))$.

11.8. ([AS92]) Show that if $\text{SAT} \in \text{\textbf{PCP}}(r(n), 1)$ for $r(n) = o(\log n)$ then **P** = **NP**. This shows that the PCP Theorem is probably optimal up to constant factors.
H536

11.9. (A simple PCP Theorem using logspace verifiers) Using the fact that a correct tableau can be verified in logspace, we saw the following exact characterization of **NP**:

$$\textbf{NP} = \{L : \text{there is a logspace machine } M \text{ s.t } x \in L \text{ iff } \exists y : M \text{ accepts } (x, y).\}$$

Note that M has two-way access to y. Let L-PCP$(r(n))$ be the class of languages whose membership proofs can be probabilistically checked by a logspace machine that uses $O(r(n))$ random bits but makes only one pass over the proof. (To use the terminology from above, it has two-way access to x but one-way access to y.) As in the PCP setting, "probabilistic checking of membership proofs" means that for $x \in L$ there is a proof y that the machine accepts with probability 1 and if not, the machine rejects with probability at least $1/2$. Show that $\mathbf{NP} = L\text{-PCP}(\log n)$. Don't assume the PCP Theorem!

H536

(This simple PCP Theorem is implicit in Lipton [Lip90]. The suggested proof is due to van Melkebeek.)

11.10. Suppose we define $J\text{-}PCP(r(n))$ similarly to $L\text{-}PCP(r(n))$, except the verifier is only allowed to read $O(r(n))$ successive bits in the membership proof. (It can decide which bits to read.) Then show that $J\text{-}PCP(\log n) \subseteq \mathbf{L}$.

11.11. This question explores why the reduction used to prove the Cook-Levin Theorem (Section 2.3) does not suffice to prove the hardness of approximation MAX-3SAT. Recall that for every **NP** language L, we defined a reduction f such that if a string $x \in L$, then $f(x) \in 3\text{SAT}$. Prove that there is a $x \notin L$ such that $f(x)$ is a 3SAT formula with m constraints having an assignment satisfying more than $m(1 - o(1))$ of them, where $o(1)$ denotes a function that tends to 0 with $|x|$.

H536

11.12. Show a poly$(n, 1/\epsilon)$-time $(1+\epsilon)$-approximation algorithm for the knapsack problem. That is, show an algorithm that given $n+1$ numbers $a_1, \ldots, a_n \in \mathbb{N}$ (each represented by at most n bits) and $k \in [n]$, finds a set $S \subseteq [n]$ with $|S| \le k$ such that $\sum_{i \in S} a_i \ge \frac{\mathrm{opt}}{1+\epsilon}$ where

$$\mathrm{opt} = \max_{S \subseteq [n], |S| \le k} \sum_{i \in S} a_i$$

H536

11.13. Show a polynomial-time algorithm that given a satisfiable 2CSP-instance φ (over binary alphabet) finds a satisfying assignment for φ.

11.14. Show a *deterministic* poly$(n, 2^q)$-time algorithm that given a $q\text{CSP}$-instance φ (over binary alphabet) with m clauses outputs an assignment satisfying $m/2^q$ of these assignment.

H536

11.15. Prove that QUADEQ is **NP**-complete.

H536

11.16. Consider the following problem: Given a system of linear equations in n with coefficients that are rational numbers, determine the largest subset of equations that are simultaneously satisfiable. Show that there is a constant $\rho < 1$ such that approximating the size of this subset is **NP**-hard.

H536

11.17. Prove the assertion in the previous question when the equations are over GF(2) and each equation involves only three variables each.

LOWER BOUNDS FOR CONCRETE COMPUTATIONAL MODELS

CHAPTER 12 Decision trees

Let no one say that taking action is hard ... the hardest thing in the world is making a decision.
– Franz Grillparzer (1791–1872)

Currently, resolving many of the basic questions on the power of Turing machines seems out of reach. Thus it makes sense to study simpler, more limited computing devices as a way to get some insight into the elusive notion of efficient computation. Moreover, such limited computational models often arise naturally in a variety of applications, even outside computer science, and hence studying their properties is inherently worthwhile.

Perhaps the simplest such model is that of *decision trees*. Here the "complexity" measure for a Boolean function f is the number of bits we need to examine in an input x in order to compute $f(x)$. This chapter surveys the basic results and open questions regarding decision trees. Section 12.1 defines decision trees and decision tree complexity. We also define nondeterministic and probabilistic versions of decision trees just as we did for Turing machines; these are described in Sections 12.2 and 12.3, respectively. Section 12.4 contains some techniques for proving *lower bounds* on decision trees. We also present Yao's *Min Max Lemma* (see Note 12.8), which is useful for proving lower bounds for randomized decision tree complexity and, more generally, lower bounds for randomized complexity in other computational models.

12.1 DECISION TREES AND DECISION TREE COMPLEXITY

Let $f : \{0, 1\}^n \to \{0, 1\}$ be some function. A *decision tree* for f is a tree for which each internal node is labeled with some x_i, and has two outgoing edges, labeled 0 and 1. Each tree leaf is labeled with an output value 0 or 1. The computation on input $x = x_1 x_2 \ldots x_n$ proceeds at each node by inspecting the input bit x_i indicated by the node's label. If $x_i = 1$ the computation continues in the subtree reached by taking the 1-edge. The 0-edge is taken if the bit is 0. Thus input x follows a path through the tree. The output value at the leaf is $f(x)$. For example, Figure 12.1 describes a decision tree for the majority function.

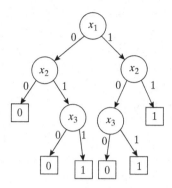

Figure 12.1. A decision tree for computing the majority function $Maj(x_1, x_2, x_3)$ on three bits. That is, the output is 1 if at least two of the input bits are 1, and otherwise the output is 0.

Decision trees often arise in a medical setting, as a compact way to describe how to reach a diagnosis from data of symptoms and test results. They are also used in operations research (to describe algorithms to make business decisions) and machine learning (where the goal is to discover such trees by looking at many examples). However, our focus is to use decision trees as a simple computational model for which we are able to prove some nontrivial lower bounds.

The decision tree complexity of a function is the number of bits examined by the most efficient decision tree on the worst case input to that tree. That is, we make the following definition.

Definition 12.1 *(Decision tree complexity)* The cost of tree t on input x, denoted by $cost(t, x)$, is the number of bits of x examined by t.

The *decision tree complexity* of a function f, is defined as

$$D(f) = \min_{t \in T_f} \max_{x \in \{0,1\}^n} cost(t, x)$$

where T_f denotes the set of all decision trees that compute f.

Since every Boolean function f on $\{0, 1\}$ can be computed by the full binary tree of depth n (and 2^n vertices), $D(f) \le n$ for every $f : \{0, 1\}^n \to \{0, 1\}$. We'll be interested in finding out for various interesting functions whether this trivial bound is the best possible or they have more efficient decision trees.

EXAMPLE 12.2

Here are some examples for the decision tree complexity of some particular functions:
   OR Function: Let $f(x_1, x_2, \ldots, x_n) = \bigvee_{i=1}^{n} x_i$. In this case we can show that there is no decision tree with smaller depth than the trivial bound of n. To do that we use an *adversary argument.* Let t be some decision tree solving f. We think of an execution of t, where some adversary answers t's questions on the value of every input bit. The adversary will always respond that x_i equals 0 for the first $n - 1$ queries. Thus the decision tree will be "in suspense" until the value of the nth bit is revealed,

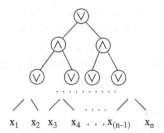

Figure 12.2. A circuit computing the AND-OR function. The circuit has k layers of alternating gates, where $n = 2^k$.

whose value will determine whether or not the OR of the bits is 1 or 0. Thus $D(f)$ is n. (To state this argument another way, we have shown that if the tree asks at most $n - 1$ questions on every branch, then there are two inputs x, x' that follow the same path from root to leaf and yet $f(x) = 0$ whereas $f(x') = 1$. Thus the tree must have answered incorrectly on one of x and x').

Graph connectivity: Suppose that we are given an m-vertex graph G as input, represented as a binary string of length $n = \binom{m}{2}$ binary string, with the eth coordinate equal to 1 if the edge e is in G, and equal to 0 otherwise. We would like to know how many bits of the adjacency matrix a decision tree algorithm might have to inspect to determine whether or not G is connected (i.e., every two points are connected by a path of edges). Once again, we show that it's not possible to beat the trivial $\binom{m}{2}$ bound.

We again give an adversary argument. The adversary constructs a graph, edge by edge, as it responds to the algorithm's queries. At each step, the answers to the preceding queries defines a *partial graph* such that it can be extended to both a *connected* and *disconnected* graph using the edges that have not been queried so far. Thus the algorithm (i.e., decision tree) is in "suspense" until every single possible edge has been queried.

For every query of an edge e made by the tree, our adversary will answer 0 (i.e., that the edge is not present), unless such an answer forces the current partial graph to become disconnected, in which case it answers 1. An easy induction shows that this strategy ensures that the current partial graph is a "forest" (i.e., consists of trees that are vertex-disjoint), and furthermore this forest does not turn into a connected graph until the very last edge gets queried. Thus the algorithm remains "in suspense" as long as it didn't query all possible $\binom{m}{2}$ edges.

AND-OR Function For every k, we define f_k to be the following function taking inputs of length $n = 2^k$:

$$f_k(x_1, \ldots, x_n) = \begin{cases} f_{k-1}(x_1, \ldots, x_{2^{k-1}}) \wedge f_{k-1}(x_{2^{k-1}}, \ldots, x_{2^k+1}) & \text{if } k \text{ is even} \\ f_{k-1}(x_1, \ldots, x_{2^{k-1}}) \vee f_{k-1}(x_{2^{k-1}}, \ldots, x_{2^k+1}) & \text{if } k > 1 \text{ and is odd} \\ x_i & \text{if } k = 1 \end{cases}$$

The AND-OR function f_k can be computed by a circuit of depth k (see Figure 12.2). By contrast, its decision tree complexity is 2^k (see Exercise 12.2).

Address function Suppose that $n = k + 2^k$ and let f be the function that maps $x_1, \ldots, x_k, y_1, \ldots, y_{2^k}$ to the input y_x. That is, the function treats the first $k \sim \log n$

bits as an index to an array specified by the last $n - k$ bits. Clearly, this function has a decision tree of depth $k + 1$ (examine the first k bits, and use that to find out which bit to examine among the last $n - k$ bits), and hence $D(f) \le \log n + 1$. On the other hand, Exercise 12.1 implies that $D(f) \ge \Omega(\log n)$.

12.2 CERTIFICATE COMPLEXITY

We now introduce the notion of *certificate complexity*. This can be viewed as the non-deterministic version of decision tree complexity, analogous to the relation between non-deterministic and deterministic Turing machine (see Chapter 2).

Definition 12.3 *(Certificate complexity)* Let $f : \{0, 1\}^n \to \{0, 1\}$ and $x \in \{0, 1\}^n$. A *0-certificate* for x is a subset $S \subseteq \{0, 1\}^n$, such that $f(x') = 0$ for every x' such that $x'|_S = x|_S$ (where $x|_S$ denotes the substring of x in the coordinates in S). Similarly, if $f(x) = 1$ then a *1-certificate* for x is a subset $S \subseteq \{0, 1\}^n$ such that $f(x') = 1$ for every x' satisfying $x|_S = x'|_S$.

The *certificate complexity* of f is defined as the minimum k such that every string x has a $f(x)$-certificate of size at most k. (Note that a string cannot have both a 0-certificate and a 1-certificate.)

If f has a decision tree t of depth k, then $C(f) \le k$, since the set of locations examined by t on input x serves as an $f(x)$-certificate for x. Thus, $C(f) \le D(f)$. But sometimes $C(f)$ can be strictly smaller than $D(f)$:

EXAMPLE 12.4

We study the certificate complexity of some of the functions described in Example 12.2.
Graph connectivity: Let f be the graph connectivity function. Recall that for an m-vertex graph, the decision tree complexity of f is $D(f) = \binom{m}{2} = \frac{m(m-1)}{2}$. A 1-certificate for a graph G is a set of edges whose existence in G implies that it is connected. Thus every connected m-vertex graph G has a 1-certificate of size $m - 1$—any spanning tree for G. A 0-certificate for G is a set of edges whose non-existence forces G to be disconnected—a cut. Since the number of edges in a cut is maximized when its two sides are equal, every m-vertex graph has a 0-certificate of size at most $(m/2)^2 = m^2/4$. On the other hand, for some graphs (e.g., the graph consisting of two disjoint cliques of size $n/2$) do not have smaller 0-certificate. Thus $C(f) = m^2/4$.

AND-OR function Let f_k be the AND-OR function on $n = 2^k$-length inputs. Recall that $D(f) = 2^k$. We show that $C(f) \le 2^{\lceil k/2 \rceil}$, which roughly equals $\sqrt{n}$. Recall that f_k is defined using a circuit of k layers. Each layer contains only OR-gates or only AND-gates, and the layers have alternative gate types. The bottom layer receives the bits of input x as input and the single top layer gate outputs the answer $f_k(x)$. If $f(x) = 1$, we can construct a 1-certificate as follows. For every AND-gate in the tree of gates we have to prove that both its children evaluate to 1, whereas for every OR-gate we only need to prove that *some* child evaluates to 1. Thus the 1-certificate is a subtree in which the AND-gates have two children but the OR gates only have one each. This mean that the subtree only needs to involve $2^{\lceil k/2 \rceil}$ input bits. If $f(x) = 0$, a similar argument applies, but the role of OR-gates and AND-gates, and values 1 and 0 are reversed.

Recall that in Chapter 2 (Definition 2.1) we defined **NP** to be the class of functions f for which an efficient Turing machine can be convinced that $f(x) = 1$ via a short certificate. Similarly, we can think of 1-certificates as a way to convince a decision tree that $f(x) = 1$, and hence we have the following analogies

$$\text{low decision tree complexity} \leftrightarrow \quad \textbf{P}$$

$$\text{low 1-certificate complexity} \leftrightarrow \quad \textbf{NP}$$

$$\text{low 0-certificate complexity} \leftrightarrow \quad \textbf{coNP}$$

Thus, the following result should be quite surprising, since it shows that, unlike what is believed to hold for Turing machines, in the decision tree world "**P** = **NP** ∩ **coNP**".

Theorem 12.5 *For function f, $D(f) \leq C(f)^2$.*   ◇

PROOF: Let $f : \{0, 1\}^n \to \{0, 1\}$ be some function satisfying $C(f) = k$. For every $x \in \{0, 1\}^n$, denote by S_x the k-sized subset of $[n]$ that is the $f(x)$-certificate for x. The rest of the proof relies on the observation that every 1-certificate must intersect every 0-certificate, since otherwise there exists a single input string that contains both certificates, which is impossible.

The following decision tree algorithm determines the value of f in at most k^2 queries. It maintains a set $\mathcal{X}$ consisting of all inputs that are consistent with the replies to queries so far.

Initially $\mathcal{X} = \{0, 1\}^n$. If there is some $b \in \{0, 1\}$ such that $f(x) = b$ for every $x \in \mathcal{X}$, then halt and output b. Otherwise choose any $x_0 \in \mathcal{X}$ such that $f(x_0) = 0$ and query all the bits in S_{x_0} that have not been queried so far. Remove from $\mathcal{X}$ every string $x' \in \{0, 1\}$ that is not consistent with the answers to the queries. Repeat until f has the same value on all remaining strings in $\mathcal{X}$.

Because every input x has some certificate proving the correct answer $f(x)$, this algorithm will eventually output the correct answer for every input. Furthermore, each time it queries the bits in a 0-certificate, all 1-certificates effectively shrink by at least one since, as noted, each 1-certificate must intersect each 0-certificate. (Of course, the 1-certificate could be completely eliminated if the answer to some query is inconsistent with it. The same elimination could also happen to a 0-certificate.) Thus in k iterations of this step, all 1-certificates must shrink to 0, which means that all remaining strings in $\mathcal{X}$ only have 0-certificates and hence the algorithm can answer 0. Since each iteration queries at most k bits, we conclude that the algorithm finishes after making at most k^2 queries. ∎

12.3 RANDOMIZED DECISION TREES

As in the case of Turing machines, we can define a *randomized* analog of decision trees. In a randomized decision tree, the choice of which input location to query is determined probabilistically. An equivalent, somewhat more convenient description is that a randomized decision tree is a probability distribution over deterministic decision trees. We will consider randomized trees that always output the right answer but use randomization to possibly speed up their expected cost (this is analogous to the class **ZPP** of Section 7.3).

Definition 12.6 *(Randomized decision trees)* For every function f, let $\mathcal{P}_f$ denote the set of probability distributions over decision trees that compute f. The *randomized tree complexity* of f is defined as

$$R(f) = \min_{P \in \mathcal{P}_f} \max_{x \in \{0,1\}^n} \mathop{E}_{t \in_R P} [cost(t,x)] \tag{12.1}$$

The randomized decision tree complexity thus expresses how well the best possible probability distribution of trees will do against the worst possible input. Obviously, $R(f) \leq D(f)$—a deterministic tree is just a special case of such a probability distribution. It's also not hard to verify that $R(f) \geq C(f)$, because for every input $x \in \{0, 1\}^n$, every tree t deciding f yields an $f(x)$-certificate of x of size $cost(t,x)$. Thus the expectation in (12.1) is bounded below by the size of the smallest certificate for x. (This is analogous to the fact that **ZPP** $\subseteq$ **NP** $\cap$ **coNP**.)

EXAMPLE 12.7

Consider the majority function, $f = Maj(x_1, x_2, x_3)$. It is straightforward to see that $D(f) = 3$. We show that $R(f) \leq 8/3$. We'll use a randomized decision tree that picks a random permutation of x_1, x_2, x_3 and makes its queries by this order, stopping when it got two identical answers. If all of x's bits are the same, then this tree will always stop after two queries. If two bits are the same and the third is different, say $x_1 = 1$ and $x_2 = x_3 = 0$, then the algorithm will make two queries if it orders x_1 last, which happens with probability $1/3$. Otherwise it makes three queries. Thus the expected cost is $2 \cdot 1/3 + 3 2/3 = 8/3$. Later in Example 12.9, we'll see that in fact $R(f) = 8/3$.

12.4 SOME TECHNIQUES FOR PROVING DECISION TREE LOWER BOUNDS

We've seen the adversary method for showing lower bounds on deterministic decision tree complexity, but it does not always seem useful, especially when considering certificate complexity and randomized decision tree complexity. We now discuss some more sophisticated techniques for showing such lower bounds. These techniques have also found other uses in complexity theory and beyond.

12.4.1 Lower Bounds on Randomized Complexity

Randomized decision trees are complicated creatures—distributions over decision trees—and hence are harder to argue about than deterministic decision trees. Fortunately, Yao had shown that we can prove lower bounds on randomized trees by reasoning about deterministic trees. Specifically, Yao's Min-Max Lemma (see Note 12.8) shows that for every function f we can lower bound $R(f)$ by k if we can find a distribution $\mathcal{D}$ over the inputs $\{0, 1\}^n$ for which we prove that $E_{x \in_R \mathcal{D}}[cost(t,x)] \geq k$ (in words, the *average* cost of t on an input drawn according to distribution $\mathcal{D}$ is at least k) for every deterministic decision tree for f. In other words, rather than arguing about distributions on trees and specific inputs, we can instead argue about distributions on inputs and specific trees.

NOTE 12.8 *(Yao's Min-Max Lemma)*

Yao's Min-Max Lemma is used in a variety of settings to prove lower bounds on randomized algorithms. Let $\mathcal{X}$ be a finite set of inputs and $\mathcal{A}$ be a finite set of deterministic algorithms that solve some computational problem f on these inputs. For $x \in \mathcal{X}$ and $A \in \mathcal{A}$, we denote by $cost(A,x)$ the *cost* incurred by algorithm A on input x (the cost could be running time, decision tree complexity, etc.). A *randomized algorithm* can be viewed as a probability distribution $\mathcal{R}$ on $\mathcal{A}$. The *cost* of $\mathcal{R}$ on input x, denoted by $cost(\mathcal{R},x)$, is $E_{A \in_R \mathcal{R}}[cost(A,x)]$. The *randomized complexity* of the problem is

$$\min_{\mathcal{R}} \max_{x \in \mathcal{X}} cost(\mathcal{R},x) \qquad (12.2)$$

Let $\mathcal{D}$ be a distribution on inputs. For any deterministic algorithm A, the cost incurred by it on $\mathcal{D}$, denoted $cost(A, \mathcal{D})$, is $E_{x \in_R \mathcal{D}}[cost(A,x)]$. The *distributional complexity* of the problem is

$$\max_{\mathcal{D}} \min_{A \in \mathcal{A}} cost(A, \mathcal{D}) \qquad (12.3)$$

Yao's Lemma says that the two quantities (12.2) and (12.3) are equal. It is easily derived from von Neumann's Min-Max Theorem for zero-sum games (see Note 19.1.2). The switch of quantifiers featured in Yao's Lemma is typically useful for lower bounding randomized complexity. To do so, one defines (using some insight and some luck) a suitable distribution $\mathcal{D}$ on the inputs for some function f. Then one proves that *every* deterministic algorithm for f incurs high cost, say C, on this distribution. By Yao's Lemma, it follows that the randomized complexity then is at least C.

EXAMPLE 12.9

We return to considering the function f that is the majority of three bits, and we seek to find a lower bound on $R(f)$. Consider a distribution over inputs such that inputs in which all three bits match, namely 000 and 111, occur with probability 0. All other inputs occur with probability 1/6. For any decision tree, that is, for any order in which the three bits are examined, there is exactly a 1/3 probability that the first two bits examined will be the same value, and thus there is a 1/3 probability that the cost is 2. There is then a 2/3 probability that the cost is 3. Thus for every decision tree for majority, the overall expected cost for this distribution is 8/3. This implies by Yao's Lemma that $R(f) \geq 8/3$. Combining with Example 12.7 we conclude $R(f) = 8/3$.

12.4.2 Sensitivity

The *sensitivity* of a function is another method that allows us to prove lower bounds on decision tree complexity.

Definition 12.10 *(Sensitivity and Block Sensitivity)* If $f : \{0, 1\}^n \to \{0, 1\}$ is a function and $x \in \{0, 1\}^n$, then the *sensitivity of f on x*, denoted $s_x(f)$, is the number of bit positions i such that $f(x) \neq f(x^i)$, where x^i is x with its ith bit flipped. The *sensitivity* of f, denoted by $s(f)$, is $\max_x \{s_x(f)\}$.

The *block sensitivity of f on x*, denoted $bs_x(f)$, is the maximum number b such that there are disjoint blocks of bit positions $B_1, B_2, \ldots, B_b$ such that $f(x) \neq f(x^{B_i})$ where x^{B_i} is x with all its bits flipped in block B_i. The *block sensitivity* of f denoted $bs(f)$ is $\max_x \{bs_x(f)\}$. $\diamond$

Clearly $s(f) \leq bs(f)$. It is conjectured that there is a constant c such that $bs(f) = O(s(f)^c)$ for all f but this is wide open (though it is known that it must hold that $c \geq 2$). It's not hard to show that both the sensitivity and block sensitivity of f lower bound its deterministic decision tree complexity:

Lemma 12.11 *For any function, $s(f) \leq bs(f) \leq D(f)$.* $\diamond$

PROOF: Let x be such that $bs_x(f) = bs(f) = s$ for some s and $B_1, \ldots, B_s$ be the corresponding blocks. For every decision tree t for f, when given b as input t has to query at least one coordinate in each of the blocks B_i for $i \in [s]$ in order to distinguish between x and x^{B_i}. ∎

On the other hand, the sensitivity squared also upper bounds the certificate complexity of f:

Theorem 12.12 $C(f) \leq s(f)bs(f)$. $\diamond$

PROOF: For any input $x \in \{0, 1\}^n$ we describe a certificate for x of size $s(f)bs(f)$. This certificate for an input x is obtained by considering the largest number of disjoint blocks of variables $B_1, B_2, \ldots, B_b$ that achieve $b = bs_x(f) \leq bs(f)$. We'll take each B_i to be of minimal size – if $f(x) \neq f(x^{B'_i})$ for some strict subset B'_i of B_i, then we'll use B'_i instead. This means that setting $x' = x^{B_i}, f(x') \neq f(x^{ij})$ for every $j \in B_i$, implying that $|B_i| \leq s(f)$ for every $i \in [b]$. Thus the certificate size is at most $s(f)bs(f)$.

We claim that setting these variables according to x constitutes a certificate for x. Suppose not, and let x' be an input such that $f(x') \neq f(x)$ but x' is consistent with the above certificate. Let B_{b+1} denote the variables that need to be flipped to make x equal x'. That is, $x' = x^{B_{b+1}}$. Then B_{b+1} must be disjoint from $B_1, B_2, \ldots, B_b$, which contradicts $b = bs_x(f)$. ∎

Table 12.1. Summary of notions introduced in this chapter and relations between them. We only proved that $D(f) \leq bs(f)^4$, but the stronger relation $D(f) \leq bs(f)^3$ is known [BBC$^+$98].

$D(f)$	Deterministic decision tree complexity (corresponds to **P**)
$R(f)$	Randomized decision tree complexity (corresponds to **ZPP**)
$C(f)$	Certificate complexity (corresponds to **NP** ∩ **coNP**)
$s(f)$	Sensitivity of f (maximum number of bits that flip $f(x)$)
$bs(f)$	Block sensitivity of f (maximum number of blocks that flip $f(x)$)
$deg(f)$	Degree of multilinear polynomial for f

$$C(f) \leq R(f) \leq D(f) \leq C(f)^2$$
$$s(f) \leq bs(f) \leq D(f) \leq bs(f)^3$$
$$C(f) \leq s(f)bs(f)$$
$$bs(f) \leq 2deg(f)$$
$$D(f) \leq deg(f)^2 bs(f) \leq 2deg(f)^4$$

12.4.3 The degree method

Recent work on decision tree lower bounds has used *polynomial representations* of Boolean functions. Recall that a multilinear polynomial is a polynomial whose degree in each variable is 1.

Definition 12.13 An n-variate polynomial $p(x_1, x_2, \ldots, x_n)$ over the reals *represents* f: $\{0, 1\}^n \to \{0, 1\}$ if $p(x) = f(x)$ for all $x \in \{0, 1\}^n$.

The *degree* of f, denoted $deg(f)$, is the degree of the multilinear polynomial that represents f. (Exercise 12.7 asks you to show that the multilinear polynomial representation is unique, so $deg(f)$ is well-defined.)

EXAMPLE 12.14

The AND of n variables $x_1, x_2, \ldots, x_n$ is represented by the multilinear polynomial $\prod_{i=1}^{n} x_i$ and OR is represented by $1 - \prod_{i=1}^{n}(1 - x_i)$.

The degree of AND and OR is n, and so is their decision tree complexity. In fact, $deg(f) \leq D(f)$ for very function f (see Exercise 12.7). A rough inequality in the other direction is also known, though we omit the proof.

Theorem 12.15

1. $bs(f) \leq 2 \cdot deg(f)$.
2. $D(f) \leq deg(f)^2 bs(f)$. ◇

Table 12.1 contains summary of the various complexity measures introduced in this chapter.

WHAT HAVE WE LEARNED?

- The decision tree complexity of a function f is the number of input bits that need to be examined to determine f's value. There are randomized and nondeterministic variants of this notion.
- Unlike what we believe to hold in the Turing machine model, all notions of decision tree complexity (deterministic, randomized, and nondeterministic) are polynomially related to one another.
- Yao's Min-Max Lemma reduces the task of proving worst-case bounds on probabilistic algorithms to proving average-case bounds for deterministic algorithms.
- Other techniques to prove lower bounds on decision trees include the adversary method, sensitivity and block sensitivity, and the degree method.

CHAPTER NOTES AND HISTORY

Decision trees have been used to encode decisions in medicine and operations research since the early days of computing. Pollack [Pol65] describes an algorithm to transform decision trees into a computer program, minimizing either the total program size or the running time (i.e., decision tree complexity). Garey[Gar72] formally defined decision trees and gave some algorithms to evaluate them, while Hyafil and Rivest proved an early **NP**-completeness result for the task of finding an optimal decision tree for a classification problem [HR76].

Buhrman and de Wolf [BdW02] give a good survey of decision tree complexity. The result that the decision tree complexity of connectivity and many other problems is $\binom{n}{2}$ has motivated the following conjecture (attributed variously to Anderaa, Karp, and Rosenberg): *Every nonconstant monotone graph property f on m-vertex graphs satisfies $D(f) = \binom{m}{2}$*. Here "monotone" means that adding edges to the graph cannot make it go from having the property to not having the property (e.g., connectivity). "Graph property" means that the property does not depend upon the vertex indices (e.g., conditions such as connectivity, having a k-clique etc., are graph properties while the condition that vertex 1 and vertex 2 have an edge between them is not). This conjecture was shown to be true by Rivest and Vuillemin [RV76] if m is a prime power, but in general it's only known to hold up to a constant factor [KSS83]; the proof uses topology and is excellently described in Du and Ko [DK00]. Another conjecture is that even the randomized decision tree complexity of monotone graph properties is $\Omega(n^2)$ but here the best lower bound is close to $n^{4/3}$ [Yao87, Kin88, Haj90]. See [LY02] for a survey on these conjectures and the progress so far.

The notion of sensitivity was defined by Cook, Dwork and Reischuk [CDR86], while the notion of Block sensitivity was defined by Nisan [Nis89], who also proved Theorem 12.12. In both cases the motivation was to prove lower bounds for parallel random access machines.

Part 1 of Theorem 12.15 is due to Nisan and Szegedi [NS92]. Part 2 is due to Nisan and Smolensky (unpublished), see [BdW02] for a proof.

The polynomial method for decision tree lower bounds is surveyed in [BdW02]. The method can be used to lower bound randomized decision tree complexity (and, more recently, *quantum* decision tree complexity) but then one needs to consider polynomials that *approximately* represent the function.

EXERCISES

12.1. Suppose f is any function that depends on all its bits; in other words, for each bit position i there is an input x such that $f(x) \neq f(x^i)$ (where x^i denotes the string obtained by flipping x's ith bit). Show that $s(f) = \Omega(\log n)$.

H536

12.2. For every $k \in \mathbb{N}$, let f_k be the AND-OR function on strings of length 2^k (see Example 12.2). Prove that $D(f_k) = 2^k$.

H536

12.3. Let f be a function on $n = k^2$ variables that is the AND of k OR's, each of disjoint k variables. Prove that $s(f) = bs(f) = C(f) = \sqrt{n}, deg(f) = D(f) = n, R(f) \geq \Omega(n)$.

12.4. Let f be a function on $n = k^2$ variables that is the OR of k applications of $g : \{0, 1\}^k \to \{0, 1\}$, each on a disjoint block of k variables, where $g(x_1, \ldots, x_k) = 1$ if there exists $i \in [k - 1]$ such that $x_i = x_{i=1} = 1$ and $x_j = 0$ for all $j \neq i$. Prove that $s(f) = \sqrt{n}$ and $bs(f) = n/2$.

12.5. Show that for every $f : \{0, 1\}^n \to \{0, 1\}$, there exists a unique multilinear polynomial that represents f.

12.6. Find the multilinear representation of the PARITY of n variables.

12.7. Show that $deg(f) \leq D(f)$.

CHAPTER 13

Communication complexity

In this paper we have studied the information exchange needed, when two processors cooperate to compute Boolean-valued functions.

– Andrew Yao, 1979

Communication complexity concerns the following scenario. There are two players with unlimited computational power, each of whom holds an n bit input, say x and y. Neither knows the other's input, and they wish to collaboratively compute $f(x, y)$ where the function $f: \{0, 1\}^n \times \{0, 1\}^n \to \{0, 1\}$ is known to both. Furthermore, they had foreseen this situation (e.g., one of the parties could be a spacecraft and the other could be the base station on earth), so they had already—before they knew their inputs x, y—agreed upon a protocol for communication.[1] The *cost* of this protocol is the *number of bits communicated* by the players for the *worst-case* choice of inputs x, y.

Researchers have studied many modifications of this basic scenario, including randomized protocols, nondeterministic protocols, and average-case protocols. Furthermore, lower bounds on communication complexity have uses in a variety of areas, including lower bounds for parallel and VLSI computation, circuit lower bounds, polyhedral theory, data structure lower bounds, and more. Communication complexity has been one of the most successful models studied in complexity, as it strikes the elusive balance of being simple enough so that we can actually prove strong lower bounds, but general enough so we can obtain important applications of these lower bounds.

In this chapter we give only a very rudimentary introduction to this area. In Section 13.1 we provide the basic definition of two-party deterministic communication complexity. In Section 13.2 we survey some of the techniques used to prove *lower bounds* for the communication complexity of various functions, using the equality function (i.e., $f(x, y) = 1$ iff $x = y$) as a running example. In Section 13.3 we define *multiparty* communication complexity and show a lower bound for the generalized inner product function. Section 13.4 contains a brief survey of other models studied, including probabilistic and

---

[1] Do not confuse this situation with *information theory*, where an algorithm is given messages that have to be transmitted over a noisy channel, and the goal is to transmit them robustly while minimizing the amount of communication. In communication complexity the channel is not noisy and the players determine what messages to send.

nondeterministic communication complexity. The chapter notes mention some of the many applications of communication complexity.

13.1 DEFINITION OF TWO-PARTY COMMUNICATION COMPLEXITY

Now we formalize the informal description of communication complexity given above.

> **Definition 13.1** *(Two-party communication complexity)* Let $f : \{0, 1\}^{2n} \to \{0, 1\}$ be a function. A *t-round two-party protocol* Π *for computing f* is a sequence of t functions $P_1, \ldots, P_t : \{0, 1\}^* \to \{0, 1\}^*$. An execution of Π on inputs x, y involves the following: Player 1 computes $p_1 = P_1(x)$ and sends p_1 to Player 2, Player 2 computes $p_2 = P_2(y, p_1)$ and sends p_2 to Player 1, and so on. Generally, at the ith round, if i is odd, then Player 1 computes $p_i = P_i(x, p_1, \ldots, p_{i-1})$ and sends p_i to Player 2, and similarly if i is even then Player 2 computes $p_i = P_i(y, p_1, \ldots, p_{i-1})$ and sends p_i to Player 1.
>
> The protocol Π is valid if for every pair of inputs x, y, the last message sent (i.e., the message p_t) is equal to the value $f(x, y)$. The *communication complexity* of Π is the maximum number of bits communicated (i.e., maximum of $|p_1| + \ldots + |p_t|$) over all inputs $x, y \in \{0, 1\}^n$. The *communication complexity* of f, denoted by $C(f)$ is the minimum communication complexity over all valid protocols Π for f.

For every function, $C(f) \leq n+1$ since the trivial protocol is for first player to communicate his entire input, whereupon the second player computes $f(x, y)$ and communicates that single bit to the first. Can they manage with less communication?

EXAMPLE 13.2 *(Parity)*

Suppose the function $f(x, y)$ is the *parity* of all the bits in x, y. Then $C(f) = 2$. Clearly, $C(f) \geq 2$ since the function depends nontrivially on each input, so each player must transmit at least one bit. The fact that $C(f) \leq 2$ is demonstrated by the following protocol: Player 1 sends the parity a of the bits in x and Player 2 sends a XOR'd with the parity of the bits in y.

EXAMPLE 13.3 *(Halting Problem)*

Consider the function $H : \{0, 1\}^n \times \{0, 1\}^n \to \{0, 1\}$ defined as follows. If $x = 1^n$ and $y = code(M)$ for some Turing machine M such that M halts on x, then $H(x, y) = 1$ and otherwise $H(x, y) = 0$. The communication complexity of this is at most 2; first player sends a bit indicating whether or not his input is 1^n. The second player then determines the answer and sends it to the first player. This example emphasizes that the players have unbounded computational power, including ability to solve the Halting Problem.

Sometimes students ask whether a player can communicate by not saying anything? (After all, they have three options in each round: send a 0, or 1, or not send anything.)

We can regard such protocols as having one additional bit of communication, and analyze them analogously.

13.2 LOWER BOUND METHODS

Now we discuss methods for proving lower bounds on communication complexity. As a running example in this chapter, we will use the equality function:

$$EQ(x, y) = \begin{cases} 1 & \text{if } x = y \\ 0 & \text{otherwise} \end{cases}$$

It turns out that almost no improvement is possible over the trivial $n + 1$ bit communication protocol for this function.

Theorem 13.4 *Equality has linear communication complexity*
$C(EQ) \geq n.$

We will prove Theorem 13.4 by several methods below.

13.2.1 The fooling set method

The first proof of Theorem 13.4 uses an idea called *fooling sets*. For any communication protocol for any function, suppose x, x' are any two different n-bit strings such that the communication pattern (i.e., sequence of bits transmitted) is the same on the input pairs (x, x) and (x', x'). Then we claim that the players' final answer must be the same on all four input-pairs $(x, x), (x, x'), (x', x), (x', x')$. This is shown by an easy induction. If player 1 communicates a bit in the first round, then by hypothesis this bit is the same whether his input is x or x'. If player 2 communicates in the second round, then his bit must also be the same on both inputs x and x' since he receives the same bit from player 1. And so on. We conclude that at the end, the players' answer on (x, x) must agree with their answer on (x, x').

To show $C(EQ) \geq n$ it suffices to note that if a protocol exists whose complexity is at most $n - 1$, then there are only 2^{n-1} possible communication patterns. But there are 2^n choices for input pairs of the form (x, x), and so by the pigeonhole principle, there exist two distinct pairs (x, x) and (x', x') on which the communication pattern is the same. But then the protocol must be incorrect, since $EQ(x, x') = 0 \neq EQ(x, x)$. This completes the proof. This argument can be easily generalized as follows (Exercise 13.1).

Lemma 13.5 *Say that a function $f : \{0, 1\}^n \times \{0, 1\}^n \to \{0, 1\}$ has a size M fooling set if there is an M-sized subset $S \subseteq \{0, 1\}^n \times \{0, 1\}^n$ and a value $b \in \{0, 1\}$ such that (1) for every $\langle x, y \rangle \in S$, $f(x, y) = b$ and (2) for every distinct $\langle x, y \rangle, \langle x', y' \rangle \in S$, either $f(x, y') \neq b$ or $f(x', y) \neq b$.*
If f has a size-M fooling set then $C(f) \geq \log M.$ ◇

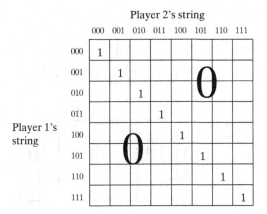

Figure 13.1. Matrix $M(f)$ for the equality function when the inputs to the players have 3 bits. The numbers in the matrix are values of f.

EXAMPLE 13.6 *(Disjointness)*

Let x, y be interpreted as characteristic vectors of subsets of $\{1, 2, \ldots, n\}$. Let $\mathrm{DISJ}(x, y) = 1$ if these two subsets are disjoint; otherwise $\mathrm{DISJ}(x, y) = 0$. As a corollary of Lemma 13.5 we obtain that $C(\mathrm{DISJ}) \geq n$ since the following 2^n pairs constitute a fooling set:

$$S = \left\{ (A, \overline{A}) : A \subseteq \{1, 2, \ldots, n\} \right\}$$

13.2.2 The tiling method

The tiling method for lower bounds takes a more global view of the function f. Consider the matrix of f, denoted $M(f)$, which is a $2^n \times 2^n$ matrix whose (x, y)th entry is the value $f(x, y)$ (see Figure 13.1.) We visualize the communication protocol in terms of this matrix.

A *combinatorial rectangle* (or just rectangle for short) in the matrix M is a submatrix of M that corresponds to entries in $A \times B$ where $A \subseteq \{0, 1\}^n$, $B \subseteq \{0, 1\}^n$. We say that $A \times B$ is *monochromatic* if for all x in A and y in B, $M_{x,y}$ is the same. If the protocol begins with the first player sending a bit, then $M(f)$ partitions into two rectangles of the type $A_0 \times \{0, 1\}^n$, $A_1 \times \{0, 1\}^n$, where A_b is the subset of the input for which the first player communicates the bit b. Notice, $A_0 \cup A_1 = \{0, 1\}^n$. If the next bit is sent by the second player, then each of the two rectangles above is further partitioned into two smaller rectangles depending upon what this bit was. Finally, if the total number of bits communicated is k then the matrix gets partitioned into 2^k rectangles. Note that each rectangle in the partition corresponds to a subset of input pairs for which the communication pattern thus far has been identical. (See Figure 13.2 for an example.) When the protocol stops, the value of f is determined by the sequence of bits sent by the two players, and thus must be the same for all pairs x, y in that rectangle. Thus the set of all communication patterns must lead to a partition of the matrix into *monochromatic* rectangles.

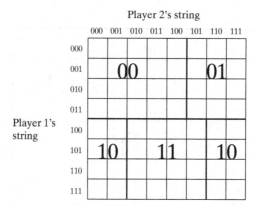

Figure 13.2. Two-way communication matrix after two steps. The large number labels are the concatenation of the bit sent by the first player with the bit sent by the second player.

Definition 13.7 A monochromatic tiling of $M(f)$ is a partition of $M(f)$ into disjoint monochromatic rectangles. We denote by $\chi(f)$ the minimum number of rectangles in any monochromatic tiling of $M(f)$.   ◇

We have the following connection to communication complexity.

Theorem 13.8 *(Tiling and communication complexity [AUY83])*
$\log_2 \chi(f) \leq C(f) \leq 16(\log_2 \chi(f))^2.$

PROOF: The first inequality follows from our above discussion, namely, if f has communication complexity k then it has a monochromatic tiling with at most 2^k rectangles. The second inequality is left as Exercise 13.5. ∎

The following observation shows that for every function f whose communication complexity can be lower bounded using the fooling set method, the communication complexity can also be lower bounded by the tiling method. Hence the latter method subsumes the former.

Lemma 13.9 *If f has a fooling set with m pairs, then $\chi(f) \geq m$.*   ◇

PROOF: If (x_1, y_1) and (x_2, y_2) are two of the pairs in the fooling set, then they cannot be in a monochromatic rectangle since not all of $(x_1, y_1), (x_2, y_2), (x_1, y_2), (x_2, y_1)$ have the same f value. ∎

13.2.3 The rank method

Now we introduce an algebraic method to lower bound $\chi(f)$ (and hence the communication complexity of f). Recall the notion of *rank* of a square matrix: The size of the largest subset of rows that are linearly independent. The following lemma (left as Exercise 13.6) gives an equivalent characterization of the rank.

Lemma 13.10 *The rank of an $n \times n$ matrix M over a field $\mathbb{F}$, denoted by rank(M), is the minimum value of ℓ such that M can be expressed as*

$$M = \sum_{i=1}^{\ell} B_i$$

where each B_i is an $n \times n$ matrix of rank 1.   ◇

Note that $0, 1$ are elements of every field, so we can compute the rank of a binary matrix over any field we like. The choice of field can be crucial; see Exercise 13.10.

Observing that every monochromatic rectangle can be viewed (by filling out entries outside the rectangle with 0's) as a matrix of rank at most 1, we obtain the following theorem.

Theorem 13.11 *For every function f, $\chi(f) \geq rank(M(f))$.*   ◇

EXAMPLE 13.12

The matrix for the equality function is simply the identity matrix, and hence rank($M(Eq)$) $= 2^n$. Thus, $C(EQ) \geq \log \chi(EQ) \geq n$, yielding another proof of Theorem 13.4.

13.2.4 The discrepancy method

For this method it is convenient to transform f into a ± 1-valued function by using the map $b \mapsto (-1)^b$ (i.e., $0 \mapsto +1, 1 \mapsto -1$). Thus $M(f)$ will also be a ± 1 matrix. We defined the *discrepancy* of a rectangle $A \times B$ in a $2^n \times 2^n$ matrix M to be

$$\frac{1}{2^{2n}} \left| \sum_{x \in A, y \in B} M_{x,y} \right|$$

The *discrepancy* of the matrix $M(f)$, denoted by Disc(f), is the maximum discrepancy among all rectangles. The following easy lemma relates it to $\chi(f)$.

Lemma 13.13 $\chi(f) \geq \dfrac{1}{Disc(f)}.$ ◇

PROOF: If $\chi(f) \leq K$, then there exists a monochromatic rectangle having at least $2^{2n}/K$ entries. Such a rectangle will have discrepancy at least $1/K$. ∎

Lemma 13.13 can be very loose. For the equality function, the discrepancy is at least $1 - 2^{-n}$ (namely, the discrepancy of the entire matrix), which would only give a lower bound of 2 for $\chi(f)$. However, $\chi(f)$ is at least 2^n, as already noted.

Now we describe a method to upper bound the discrepancy using *eigenvalues*.

Lemma 13.14 (*Eigenvalue Bound*) *For any symmetric real matrix M, the discrepancy of a rectangle $A \times B$ is at most $\lambda_{max}(M)\sqrt{|A||B|}/2^{2n}$, where $\lambda_{max}(M)$ is the magnitude of the largest eigenvalue of M.* $\diamond$

PROOF: The proof uses the fact that for all unit vectors x, y, $x^T M y \le \lambda_{max}(M)|<x,y>|$. Let $\mathbf{1}_S \in \mathbb{R}^{2^n}$ denote the characteristic vectors of a subset $S \subseteq \{0, 1\}^n$ (i.e., the xth coordinate of $\mathbf{1}_S$ is equal to 1 if $x \in S$ and to 0 otherwise). Note $\|\mathbf{1}_S\|_2 = \sqrt{\sum_{x \in S} 1^2} = \sqrt{|S|}$. Note also that for every $A, B \subseteq \{0, 1\}^n$, $\sum_{x \in A, y \in B} M_{x,y} = \mathbf{1}_A^\dagger M \mathbf{1}_B$.

The discrepancy of the rectangle $A \times B$ is

$$\frac{1}{2^{2n}} \mathbf{1}_A^\dagger M \mathbf{1}_B \le \frac{1}{2^{2n}} \lambda_{max}(M) \left| \mathbf{1}_A^\dagger \mathbf{1}_B \right| \le \frac{1}{2^{2n}} \lambda_{max}(M) \sqrt{|A||B|}$$

where the last inequality uses Cauchy-Schwarz. ∎

EXAMPLE 13.15

The *mod 2 inner product* function defined as $f(x, y) = x \odot y = \sum_i x_i y_i \pmod 2$ has been encountered a few times in this book. To bound its discrepancy, let N be the ± 1 matrix corresponding to f (i.e., $M_{x,y} = (-1)^{x \odot y}$). It is easily checked that every two distinct rows (columns) of N are orthogonal, every row has ℓ_2 norm $2^{n/2}$, and that $N^T = N$. Thus we conclude that $N^2 = 2^n I$ where I is the unit matrix. Hence every eigenvalue is either $+2^{n/2}$ or $-2^{n/2}$, and thus Lemma 13.14 implies that the discrepancy of a rectangle $A \times B$ is at most $2^{-3n/2} \sqrt{|A||B|}$ and the overall discrepancy is at most $2^{-n/2}$ (since $|A|, |B| \le 2^n$).

13.2.5 A technique for upper bounding the discrepancy

We describe an upper bound technique for the discrepancy that will later be useful also in the multiparty setting (Section 13.3). As in Section 13.2.4, we assume that f is a ± 1-valued function. We define the following quantity.

Definition 13.16 $\mathcal{E}(f) = E_{a_1, a_2, b_1, b_2} \left[\prod_{i=1,2} \prod_{j=1,2} f(a_i, b_j) \right]$. $\diamond$

Note that $\mathcal{E}(f)$ can be computed, like the rank, in time that is polynomial in the size of the matrix $M(f)$. By contrast, the definition of discrepancy involves a maximization over all possible subsets A, B, and a naive algorithm for computing it would take time exponential in the size of $M(f)$. (Indeed, the discrepancy is **NP**-hard to compute exactly, though it can be approximated efficiently – see the chapter notes.) The following lemma relates these two quantities.

Lemma 13.17

$$Disc(f) \le \mathcal{E}(f)^{1/4}.$$

PROOF: We need to show that for every rectangle $A \times B$,

$$\mathcal{E}(f) \geq \left(\frac{1}{2^{2n}} \left| \sum_{a \in A, b \in B} f(a,b) \right| \right)^4$$

Let g, h the characteristic functions of A and B, respectively. (That is $g(a)$ equals 1 if $a \in A$ and 0 otherwise; $h(b)$ equals 1 if $b \in B$ and 0 otherwise.) Then, the right-hand side is simply $\left(E_{a,b \in \{0,1\}^n}[f(a,b)g(a)h(b)] \right)^4$. But

$$\mathcal{E}(f) = \underset{a_1,a_2}{E} \left[\underset{b_1,b_2}{E} \left[\prod_{i=1,2} \prod_{j=1,2} f(a_i, b_j) \right] \right]$$

$$= \underset{a_1,a_2}{E} \left[\left(\underset{b}{E}[f(a_1,b)f(a_2,b)] \right)^2 \right]$$

$$\geq \underset{a_1,a_2}{E} \left[g(a_1)^2 g(a_2)^2 \left(\underset{b}{E}[f(a_1,b)f(a_2,b)] \right)^2 \right] \qquad \text{(using } g(a) \leq 1\text{)}$$

$$= \underset{a_1,a_2}{E} \left[\left(\underset{b}{E}[f(a_1,b)g(a_1)f(a_2,b)g(a_2)] \right)^2 \right]$$

$$\geq \left(\underset{a_1,a_2}{E} \left[\underset{b}{E}[f(a_1,b)g(a_1)f(a_2,b)g(a_2)] \right] \right)^2 \qquad \text{(using } E[X^2] \geq E[X]^2\text{)}$$

$$= \left(\underset{b}{E} \left[\left(\underset{a}{E}[f(a,b)g(a)] \right)^2 \right] \right)^2$$

$$\geq \left(\underset{a,b}{E}[f(a,b)g(a)h(b)] \right)^4 \qquad \text{(repeating previous steps)}$$

$$\geq (\text{Disc}(f))^4.$$

∎

Exercise 13.12 asks you to derive a lower bound for the inner product function using this technique. We will see another example in Section 13.3.

13.2.6 Comparison of the lower bound methods

The tiling argument is the strongest lower bound technique, since bounds on rank, discrepancy, and fooling sets imply a bound on $\chi(f)$, and hence can never prove better lower bounds than the tiling argument. Also, as implied by Theorem 13.10, $\log \chi(f)$ characterizes the communication complexity of f up to a polynomial factor. The rank and fooling set methods are incomparable, meaning that each can be stronger than the other for some function. However, if we ignore constant factors, the rank method is always at least as strong as the fooling set method (see Exercise 13.8). Also, we can separate the power of these lower bound arguments. For instance, we know functions for which a polynomial gap exists between $\log \chi(f)$ and $\log \text{rank}(M(f))$. However, the following conjecture (we only state one form of it) says that rank is in fact optimal up to a polynomial factor.

Conjecture 13.18 (*Log rank conjecture*) There is a constant $c > 1$ such that $C(f) = O(\log(\text{rank}(M(f)))^c)$ for all f and all input sizes n, where rank is taken over the reals.

Of course, the difficult part of this conjecture is to show that low rank implies a low-complexity protocol for f. Though we are still far from proving this, Nisan and Wigderson have shown that at least low rank implies low value of $1/\text{Disc}(f)$.

Theorem 13.19 (*[NW94]*) $1/\text{Disc}(f) = O(\text{rank}(f)^{3/2})$.   ◇

13.3 MULTIPARTY COMMUNICATION COMPLEXITY

There is more than one way to generalize communication complexity to a multiplayer setting. The most interesting model turns out to be the "number on the forehead" model: Each player has a string on his head that everybody else can see but he cannot. That is, there are k players and k strings $x_1, \ldots, x_k$, and Player i gets all the strings *except* for x_i. The players are interested in computing a value $f(x_1, x_2, \ldots, x_k)$ where $f : (\{0, 1\}^n)^k \to \{0, 1\}$ is some fixed function. As in the two-player case, the k players have an agreed-upon protocol for communication (which was decided before they were given their strings), and all their communication is posted on a "public blackboard" that all of them can see (the protocol also determines the order in which the players write on the blackboard). The last message sent should be the value $f(x_1, \ldots, x_k)$ of the function on the inputs. By analogy with the two-player case, we denote by $C_k(f)$ the number of bits that must be exchanged by the best protocol. Note that it is at most $n + 1$, since it suffices for any $j \neq i$ to write x_i on the blackboard, at which point the ith player knows all k strings and can determine and publish $f(x_1, \ldots, x_k)$.

EXAMPLE 13.20

Consider computing the function

$$f(x_1, x_2, x_3) = \bigoplus_{i=1}^{n} \text{maj}(x_{1i}, x_{2i}, x_{3i})$$

in the three-party model where x_1, x_2, x_3 are n bit strings. The communication complexity of this function is 3: Each player counts the number of i's such that she can determine the majority of x_{1i}, x_{2i}, x_{3i} by examining the bits available to her. She writes the parity of this number on the blackboard, and the final answer is the parity of the players' bits. This protocol is correct because the majority for each row is known by either one or three players, and both are odd numbers.

EXAMPLE 13.21 (*Generalized Inner Product*)

The *generalized inner product function* $GIP_{k,n}$ maps nk bits to 1 bit as follows

$$f(x_1, \ldots, x_k) = \bigoplus_{i=1}^{n} \bigwedge_{j=1}^{k} x_{ji} \tag{13.1}$$

Notice, for $k = 2$ this reduces to the mod 2 inner product of Example 13.15.

For the two-player model we introduced the notion of a monochromatic rectangle in order to prove lower bounds. Specifically, a communication protocol can be viewed as a way of partitioning the matrix $M(f)$: If the protocol exchanges c bits, then the matrix is partitioned into 2^c rectangles, all of which must be monochromatic if the protocol is valid.

The corresponding notion in the k-party case is a cylinder intersection. A *cylinder in dimension i* is a subset S of the inputs such that if $(x_1, \ldots, x_k) \in S$ then $(x_1, \ldots, x_{i-1}, x_i', x_{i+1}, \ldots, x_k) \in S$ for all x_i' also. A *cylinder intersection* is $\cap_{i=1}^{k} T_i$ where T_i is a cylinder in dimension i. Since player i's communication does not depend upon x_i, it can be viewed as partitioning the set of inputs according to cylinders in dimension i. Thus we conclude that at the end of the protocol, the cube $\{0,1\}^{nk}$ is partitioned using cylinder intersections, and if the protocol communicates c bits, then the partition consists of at most 2^c monochromatic cylinder intersections. Thus we have proved the following lemma.

Lemma 13.22 *If every partition of $M(f)$ into monochromatic cylinder intersections requires at least R cylinder intersections, then the k-party communication complexity is at least $\lceil \log_2 R \rceil$, where $M(f)$ is the k-dimensional table whose $(x_1, \ldots, x_k)$th entry is $f(x_1, \ldots, x_k)$.* ◇

Discrepancy-based lower bound

In this section, we will assume as in our earlier discussion of discrepancy that the range of the function f is $\{-1, 1\}$. We define the *k-party discrepancy* of f by analogy to the 2-party case

$$\text{Disc}(f) = \frac{1}{2^{nk}} \max_{T} \left| \sum_{(a_1, a_2, \ldots, a_k) \in T} f(a_1, a_2, \ldots, a_k) \right|$$

where T ranges over all cylinder intersections.

To upper bound the discrepancy we introduce the k-party analog of $\mathcal{E}(f)$. Let a *(k, n)-cube* be (multi) subset D of $\{0,1\}^{nk}$ of 2^k points of the form $\{a_1, a_1'\} \times \{a_2, a_2'\} \times \cdots \times \{a_k, a_k'\}$, where each $a_i, a_i' \in \{0,1\}^n$. We define

$$\mathcal{E}(f) = \mathop{\mathbf{E}}_{\substack{D \\ (k,n)\text{ cube}}} \left[\prod_{\mathbf{a} \in D} f(\mathbf{a}) \right]$$

Notice that the definition of $\mathcal{E}(f)$ for the two-party case is recovered when $k = 2$. The next lemma is also an easy generalization.

Lemma 13.23 $\text{Disc}(f) \leq (\mathcal{E}(f))^{1/2^k}$.

The proof is analogous to the proof of Lemma 13.17 and is left as Exercise 13.14. The only difference is that we need to repeat the basic step of that proof k times instead of two times.

Now we can prove a lower bound for the Generalized Inner Product (GIP) function. Note that since we changed the range to $\{-1, 1\}$, this function is now defined as

$$GIP_{k,n}(x_1, x_2, \ldots, x_k) = (-1)^{\sum_{i \leq n} \prod_{j \leq k} x_{ji}} \tag{13.2}$$

(this definition can omit calculations modulo 2 since $(-1)^m = (-1)^{m \pmod 2}$ for every m).

Theorem 13.24 *(Lower bound for generalized inner product)*
The function $GIP_{k,n}$ has k-party communication complexity $\Omega(n/4^k)$.

PROOF: By Lemma 13.23 it suffices to upper bound $\mathcal{E}(GIP_{k,n})$. Using (13.2) we see that for every k,n,

$$GIP_{k,n}(x_1,\ldots,x_k) = \prod_{i=1}^{n} GIP_{k,1}(x_{1,i},\ldots,x_{k,i})$$

where we define $GIP_{k,1}(x_1,\ldots,x_k) = (-1)^{\prod_{j\leq k} x_i}$. Thus

$$\mathcal{E}(GIP_{k,n}) = \mathop{\mathbf{E}}_{\substack{D \\ (k,n)\text{-cube}}} [\prod_{\mathbf{a}\in D} \prod_{i=1}^{n} GIP_{k,1}(\mathbf{a}_i)]$$

where for a vector $\mathbf{a} = (a_1,\ldots,a_k)$ in $(\{0,1\}^n)^k$, $\mathbf{a}_i$ denotes the k bit string $a_{1,i},\ldots,a_{k,i}$. But because each coordinate is chosen independently, the right hand side is equal to

$$\prod_{i=1}^{n} \mathop{\mathbf{E}}_{\substack{C \\ (k,1)\text{ cube}}} [\prod_{\mathbf{a}\in C} GIP_{k,1}(\mathbf{a})] = \mathcal{E}(GIP_{k,1})^n$$

But $\mathcal{E}(GIP_{k,1}) \leq 1 - 2^{-k}$. Indeed a random $(k,1)$-cube $C = \{a_1,a_1'\} \times \cdots \times \{a_k,a_k'\}$ has probability 2^{-k} to satisfy the event E that for every i the pair (a_i,a_i') is either $(0,1)$ or $(0,1)$. But since $GIP_{k,1}(\mathbf{a}) = -1$ if and only if $\mathbf{a}$ is the all ones vector, if E happens then there is exactly one k-bit vector $\mathbf{a}$ in C such that $GIP_{k,1}(\mathbf{a}) = -1$ and for all other vectors $\mathbf{b} \in C$, $GIP_{k,1}(\mathbf{b}) = 1$. Hence if E happens, then $\prod_{\mathbf{a}\in C} GIP_{k,1}(\mathbf{a}) = -1$, and since this product is always at most 1,

$$\mathcal{E}(GIP_{k,1}) = \mathop{\mathbf{E}}_{\substack{C \\ (k,1)\text{ cube}}} [\prod_{\mathbf{a}\in C} GIP_{k,1}(\mathbf{a})] \leq 2^{-k} \cdot -1 + (1 - 2^{-k}) \cdot 1 \leq 1 - 2^{-k}$$

Hence $\mathcal{E}(GIP_{k,n}) \leq (1 - 2^{-k})^n \leq e^{-n/2^k} = 2^{-\Omega(n/2^k)}$. Thus $\mathrm{Disc}(GIP_{k,n}) \leq 2^{-\Omega(n/4^k)}$, implying that the k-party communication complexity of $GIP_{k,n}$ is $\Omega(n/4^k)$. $\blacksquare$

At the moment, we do not know of any explicit function f for which $C_k(f) \geq n2^{-o(k)}$ and in particular have no nontrivial lower bound for computing explicit functions $f : (\{0,1\}^n)^k \to \{0,1\}$ for $k \geq \log n$. Such a result could be useful to obtain new circuit lower bounds; see Section 14.5.1.

13.4 OVERVIEW OF OTHER COMMUNICATION MODELS

We outline some of the alternative settings in which communication complexity has been studied.

Randomized protocols: One can consider *randomized* protocols for jointly computing the value of a function. In such protocols, all players have access to a shared random string r, which they use in determining their actions. We define $R(f)$ to be the *expected* number of bits communicated by the players. It turns out that randomization can some-times make a significant difference. For example, the equality function has a randomized communication protocol with $O(\log n)$ complexity (see Exercise 13.15). Nevertheless, there are techniques to prove lower bounds for such protocols as well.

Nondeterministic protocols: One can also define *nondeterministic communication complexity* analogously to the definition of the class **NP**. In a non-deterministic protocol, the players are both provided an additional third input z ("nondeterministic guess") of some length m that may depend on x, y. Apart from this guess, the protocol is deter-ministic. We require that $f(x, y) = 1$ iff there exists a string z that makes the players output 1, and the cost of the protocol is m plus the number of bits communicated. As in other settings, nondeterminism can make a significant difference. For example, both the *inequality* and *intersection* functions (i.e., the negations of the functions EQ and the function DISJ of Example 13.6) are easily shown to have logarithmic nondeterministic communication complexity. Analogously to the definition of **coNP**, one can define the co-nondeterministic communication complexity of f to be the nondeterministic commu-nication complexity of the function $g(x, y) = 1 - f(x, y)$. Interestingly, it can be shown that if f has nondeterministic communication complexity k and co-nondeterministic communication complexity ℓ, then $C(f) \leq 10k\ell$, hence implying that in the communi-cation complexity world the intersection of the classes corresponding to **NP** and **coNP** is equal to the class corresponding to **P**. In contrast, we believe that $\mathbf{P} \neq \mathbf{NP} \cap \mathbf{coNP}$.

Average case protocols: Just as we can study average-case complexity in the Turing machine model, we can study communication complexity when the inputs are chosen from a distribution $\mathcal{D}$. This is defined as

$$C_{\mathcal{D}}(f) = \min_{\mathcal{P}\text{protocol for } f} \mathop{\mathrm{E}}_{(x,y)\in_R \mathcal{D}} [\text{Number of bits exchanged by } \mathcal{P} \text{ on } x, y]$$

Computing a non-Boolean function: Here the function's output is not just $\{0, 1\}$ but an m-bit number for some m. We discuss one example in the exercises.

Asymmetric communication: In this model the "cost" of communication is asymmetric: There is some B such that it costs the first player B times as much to transmit a bit than it does the second player. The goal is to minimize the total cost.

Computing a relation: One can consider protocols that aim to hit a relation rather than computing a function. That is, we have a relation $R \subseteq \{0, 1\}^n \times \{0, 1\}^n \times \{1, 2, \ldots, m\}$ and given $x, y \in \{0, 1\}^n$ the players seek to agree on any $b \in \{1, 2, \ldots, m\}$ such that $(x, y, b) \in R$. See Exercise 13.16.

These and many other settings are discussed in [KN97].

WHAT HAVE WE LEARNED?

- The *communication complexity* of a two input function f is the number of bits that a player holding x and a player holding y need to exchange to compute $f(x, y)$.
- Methods to lower bound the communication complexity of specific functions include the fooling set, tiling, rank, and discrepancy methods. Using these methods we have several examples of explicit functions on two n-bit inputs whose communication complexity is at least n.

- The *multiparty communication complexity* of a k-input function f is the number of bits that k parties need to exchange to compute f where the ith player has all the inputs *except* the ith input. The best known lower bound of the k-party communication complexity of an explicit function is of the form $n/2^{-\Omega(k)}$.
- Other models of communication complexity studies include probabilistic, nondeterministic, and average-case communication complexity, and the communication complexity of computing relations.

CHAPTER NOTES AND HISTORY

This chapter barely scratched the surface of this self-contained miniworld within complexity theory; an excellent and detailed treatment can be found in the book by Kushilevitz and Nisan [KN97] (though it does not contain some of the newer results).

Communication complexity was first defined by Yao [Yao79]. Other early papers that founded the field were Papadimitriou and Sipser [PS82], Mehlhorn and Schmidt [MS82] (who introduced the rank lower bound), and Aho, Ullman and Yannakakis [AUY83].

We briefly discussed parallel computation in Chapter 6. Yao [Yao79] invented communication complexity as a way to lower bound the running time of parallel computers for certain tasks. The idea is that the input is distributed among many processors, and if we partition these processors into two halves, we may lower bound the computation time by considering the amount of communication that must necessarily happen between the two halves. A similar idea is used to prove time-space lower bounds for VLSI circuits. For instance, in a VLSI chip that is an $m \times m$ grid, if the communication complexity for a function is greater than c, then the time required to compute it is at least c/m.

Communication complexity is also useful in time-space lower bounds for Turing machines (see Exercise 13.4), and circuit lower bounds (see Chapter 14).

Data structures such as heaps, sorted arrays, and lists are basic objects in algorithm design. Often, algorithm designers wish to determine if the data structure they have designed is the best possible. Communication complexity lower bounds can be used to establish such results; see [KN97]. *Streaming algorithms*, in which an algorithm can only make one pass on a very large input, is another area where communication complexity bounds imply various optimality and impossibility results. Alon, Matias, and Szegedy [AMS96] were the first to use communication complexity as a tool for proving lower bounds on streaming algorithms. Ever since, there has been extensive research on both the application of communication complexity to lower bound problems in stream algorithms, as well as in the development of new tools for communication complexity inspired by the need to tighten existing gaps in streaming problems like frequency estimation (see e.g., [CSWY01, BYJKS02]).

Yannakakis [Yan88] has shown how to use communication complexity lower bounds to prove lower bounds on the size of polytopes representing **NP**-complete problems. Solving the open problem mentioned in Exercise 13.13 would prove a lower bound for the polytope representing vertex cover.

Theorem 13.24 is due to Babai, Nisan and Szegedy, though our proof follows Raz's simplification [Raz00] of Chung's proof [Chu90].

Computing the discrepancy (also known as the *cut norm*) of a given real matrix, and even approximating it to an arbitrarily small constant is **NP**-hard. But it can be approximated using semidefinite programming within some constant factor K_G; see Alon and Naor [AN04]. (K_G is a number between 1.5 and 1.8 that is known as *Grothendieck's constant*; determining its exact value is a major open problem.) The notion of discrepancy is known as *regularity* in the context of the famous *Szemerédi regularity lemma* [Sze76]. In that context the parameter $\mathcal{E}(f)$ is analogous to the fraction of four-cycles in a given bipartite graph, which is again related to the regularity of the graph. Multiparty discrepancy is related to the hypergraph regularity lemma, and the parameter $\mathcal{E}(f)$ was used by Gowers [Gow07] in his proof of his lemma. A closely related group-theoretic parameter (sometimes known as Gowers's norm or Gowers's uniformity) was used by Gowers [Gow01] in his proof of the quantitatively improved version of Szemerédi's Theorem guaranteeing the existence of large arithmetic progression in dense sets. The book by Tau and Vu [TV06] contains an excellent exposition of these topics.

Lovasz and Saks [LS88] have observed that the log rank conjecture is related to a conjecture in discrete mathematics concerning chromatic number and rank of the adjacency matrix. The original log rank conjecture was that $C(f) = O(\log \operatorname{rank}(M(f)))$ but this was disproved by Raz and Spieker [RS93]. A comparison of rank and fooling set arguments appears in the paper by Dietzfelbinger, Hromkovic, and Schnitger [DHS94].

In general, the complexity of computing $C(f)$ and $C_k(f)$ is not understood, and this may have some connection to why it is difficult in practice for us to prove lower bounds on these quantities. It is also intriguing that the lower bounds that we do prove involve quantities such as rank that are computable in polynomial time given $M(f)$. (This is an instance of the more widespread phenomenon of *natural proofs* encountered in Chapter 23.) In this regard, it is interesting to note that the *Discrepancy* parameter is **NP**-hard to compute but can be approximated within a constant multiplicative factor in the two-player setting by a polynomial-time algorithm [AN04]. By contrast, computing the discrepancy in the three-player setting seems very hard (though no hardness results seem to appear anywhere); this may perhaps explain why lower bounds are so difficult in the multiplayer setting.

One relatively recent area not mentioned in this chapter is *quantum* communication complexity, where the parties may exchange quantum states with one another, see [Bra04]. Interestingly, some techniques developed in this setting [She07] were used to obtain new $\Omega(n^{1/(k-1)}/2^{2^k})$ lower bounds on the k-party communication complexity of the *disjointness* function [LS07, CA08], thus leading to a strong separation of nondeterministic and deterministic k-party communication complexity.

EXERCISES

13.1. Prove Lemma 13.5.

13.2. Prove that for every set $S \subseteq \{(x,x) : x \in \{0, 1\}^n\}$ and any communication protocol Π that correctly computes the equality function on n-bit inputs, there exists a pair of inputs in S on which Π uses at least $\log |S|$ bits.

13.3. Prove that a single tape TM (one whose input tape is also its read-write work tape) takes at least $O(n^2)$ to decide the language of *palindromes* PAL $= \{x_n \cdots x_1 x_1 \cdots x_n : x_1, \ldots, x_n \in \{0, 1\}^n, n \in \mathbb{N}\}$ of Example 1.1.

H537

13.4. If $S(n) \leq n$, show that a space $S(n)$ TM takes at least $\Omega(n^2/S(n))$ steps to decide the language $\{x\#x : x \in \{0, 1\}^*\}$.

H537

13.5. Prove the second inequality of Theorem 13.8. That is, prove that for every $f : \{0, 1\}^n \times \{0, 1\}^n \to \{0, 1\}$, $C(f) = O(\log^2 \chi(f))$.

H537

13.6. Prove Lemma 13.10.

H537

13.7. Show that for almost all functions $f : \{0, 1\}^n \times \{0, 1\}^n \to \{0, 1\}$ the rank of $M(f)$ over GF(2) is n, whereas the size of the largest fooling set is less than $3 \log n$. This shows that the rank lower bound can be exponentially better than the fooling set lower bound.

13.8. For two $n \times n$ matrices A, B, define its *tensor product* $A \otimes B$ as the $n^2 \times n^2$ matrix whose entries are indexed by 4-tuples from $[n]$. Show that the rank of $A \otimes B$ (over any field) is the product of the ranks of A and B.

Use this fact to show that if a function f has a fooling set of size S then the rank method can be used to give a lower bound of at least $1/2 \lceil \log S \rceil$ on the communication complexity. This shows that the rank method is never much worse than the fooling set method.

13.9. Show that if M is 0/1 real matrix, and M' is the ± 1 matrix obtained by applying the transformation $a \mapsto (-1)^a$ to the entries of M, then $\text{rank}(M) - 1 \leq \text{rank}(M') \leq \text{rank}(M) + 1$.

H537

13.10. Consider x, y as vectors over $GF(2)^n$, and let $f(x, y)$ be their inner product mod 2. Prove using the rank method that the communication complexity is n.

H537

13.11. Let $f : \{0, 1\}^n \times \{0, 1\}^n \to \{0, 1\}$ be such that all rows of $M(f)$ are distinct. Show that $C(f) \geq \log n$.

H537

13.12. Prove that $\mathcal{E}(IP) \leq 2^{-n}$, where IP is the inner product function. Derive a lower bound for the communication complexity of IP.

H537

13.13. For any graph G with n vertices, consider the following communication problem. Player 1 receives a clique C in G, and player 2 receives an independent set I. They have to communicate in order to determine $|C \cap I|$. (Note that this number is either 0 or 1.) Prove an $O(\log^2 n)$ upper bound on the communication complexity.

Can you improve your upper bound or prove a lower bound better than $\Omega(\log n)$? (Open question)

13.14. Prove Lemma 13.23.

13.15. Prove that the randomized communication complexity of the equality function (i.e., $R(EQ)$) is at most $O(\log n)$. (Note that a randomized communication protocol is allowed to output the wrong answer with probability at most $1/3$.)

H537

13.16. (Karchmer-Wigderson games [KW88]) Consider the following problem about computing a relation. Associate the following communication problem with any function $f:\{0,1\}^n \to \{0,1\}$. Player 1 gets any input x such that $f(x) = 0$, and player 2 gets any input y such that $f(y) = 1$. They have to communicate to determine a bit position i such that $x_i \neq y_i$. Show that the communication complexity of this problem is *exactly* the minimum depth of any circuit that computes f. (The maximum fan-in of each gate is 2.)

H537

13.17. Use Exercise 13.16 to show that computing the parity of n bits requires depth at least $2 \log n$.

13.18. Show that the following computational problem is in **EXP**: Given the matrix $M(f)$ of a Boolean function, and a number K, decide if $C(f) \leq K$.

(Open since Yao [Yao79].) Can you show this problem is complete for some complexity class?

13.19. ([AMS96]) A space-$S(n)$ *streaming algorithm* is a space-$S(n)$ TM M that makes only one sweep of its input. This setup naturally occurs in many applications. Prove that there is no space-$o(n)$ streaming algorithm that solves the following problem: Given a sequence $x_1, \ldots, x_m$ in $[n]$, compute the frequency of the *most frequent element* – $\max_{x \in [n]} |\{i : x_i = x\}|$. Can you show that one cannot even *approximate* this problem to within a $3/4$ factor in $o(n)$?

H537

CHAPTER 14

Circuit lower bounds:
Complexity theory's Waterloo

In Chapter 2 we saw that if there is any **NP** language that cannot be computed by polynomial-sized circuits, then **NP** $\neq$ **P**. Thus proving circuit lower bounds is a potential approach for proving **NP** $\neq$ **P**. Furthermore, there is a reason to hope that this is a viable approach, since the Karp-Lipton Theorem (Theorem 6.19) shows that if the polynomial hierarchy **PH** does not collapse, then there *exists* an **NP** language that does not have polynomial size circuits.

In the 1970s and 1980s, many researchers came to believe that proving circuit lower bounds represented the best route to resolving **P** versus **NP**, since circuits seem easier to reason about than Turing machines. The success in this endeavor was mixed.

Progress on general circuits has been almost nonexistent: a lower bound of n is trivial for any function that depends on all its input bits. We are unable to prove even a superlinear circuit lower bound for any **NP** problem—the best we can do after years of effort is $5n - o(n)$.

To make life (comparatively) easier, researchers focused on restricted circuit classes, and were successful in proving some good lower bounds. We prove some of the major results of this area, specifically, for bounded depth circuits (Section 14.1), bounded depth circuits with "counting" gates (Section 14.2), and monotone circuits (Section 14.3). In all these results we have a notion of "progress" of the computation. We show that small circuits simply cannot achieve the amount of progress necessary to compute the output from the inputs.

In Section 14.4 we indicate the questions at the frontier of circuit lower bound research, where we are currently stuck. A researcher starting work on this area may wish to focus on one of the open questions described there. Later in Chapter 23 we'll explain some of the inherent obstacles that need to be overcome to make further progress.

14.1 AC⁰ AND HÅSTAD'S SWITCHING LEMMA

As we saw in Chapter 6, $\mathbf{AC}^0$ is the class of languages computable by circuit families of constant depth, polynomial size, and whose gates have unbounded fan-in. (We need to allow the fan-in in the circuit to be unbounded since otherwise the output cannot receive information from all input bits.)

We saw in Chapter 2 (Claim 2.13) that every Boolean function can be computed by a circuit of depth 2 and exponential size—that is, a CNF (or DNF) formula. When students study digital logic design they learn how to do "circuit minimization" using Karnaugh maps, and the circuits talked about in that context are depth 2 circuits. Indeed, it is easy to show (using for example the Karnaugh map technique) that the minimum DNF or CNF representing even very simple functions (such as the parity function described below) has to be of exponential size. However, those techniques do not seem to generalize to even depth 3 circuits, not to mention the class AC^0 of (arbitrarily large) constant depth circuits of polynomial size that we encountered in Section 6.7.1.

The burning question in the late 1970s was whether problems like Clique and TSP have AC^0 circuits. In 1981, Furst, Saxe, and Sipser and, independently, Ajtai showed that they do not. In fact their lower bound applied to a much simpler function.

Theorem 14.1 *([FSS81, Ajt83])*
Let $\oplus$ be the parity function. That is, for every $x \in \{0, 1\}^n$, $\oplus(x_1, \ldots, x_n) = \sum_{i=1}^{n} x_i$ (mod 2). Then $\oplus \notin$ AC^0.

The main tool in the proof of Theorem 14.1 is the concept of *random restrictions*. Let f be a function computable by a depth d circuit of polynomial size and suppose that we choose at random a vast majority (i.e., $n - n^\epsilon$ for some constant $\epsilon > 0$ depending on d) of the input variables and fix each such variable to be either 0 or 1 at random. We'll prove that with positive probability, the function f subject to this restriction is *constant* (i.e., it is either always zero or always one). Since the parity function cannot be made a constant by fixing values to a subset of the variables, it follows that it cannot be computed by a constant depth polynomial-sized circuit.

14.1.1 Håstad's Switching Lemma

As in Section 2.3, we define a k-CNF to be a Boolean formula that is an AND of OR's where each OR involves at most k variables. Similarly, a k-DNF is an OR of AND's where each AND involves at most k variables. If f is a function on n variables and ρ is a partial assignment (also known as a *restriction*) to the variables of f, then we denote by $f|_\rho$ the restriction of f under ρ. That is, $f|_\rho$ takes an assignment τ to the variables not assigned by ρ as input, and outputs f applied to ρ and τ. Now we prove the main lemma about how a circuit simplifies under a random restriction.

Lemma 14.2 *(Håstad's Switching Lemma [Hås86]) Suppose f is expressible as a k-DNF, and let ρ denote a random restriction that assigns random values to t randomly selected input bits. Then for every $s \geq 2$.*

$$\Pr_{\rho}[f|_\rho \text{ is not expressible as } s\text{-CNF}] \leq \left(\frac{(n-t)k^{10}}{n} \right)^{s/2} \qquad (14.1)$$

where $f|_\rho$ denotes the function f restricted to the partial assignment ρ.

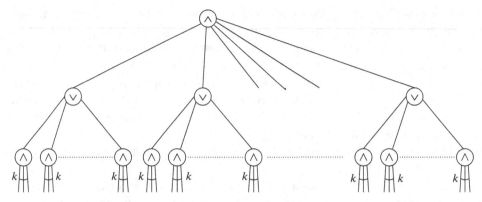

Figure 14.1. Circuit before Håstad switching transformation.

We defer the proof of Lemma 14.2 to Section 14.1.2. We'll typically use this lemma with k, s constants and $t \approx n - \sqrt{n}$ in which case the guaranteed bound on the probability will be n^{-c} for some constant c. Note that by applying Lemma 14.2 to the function $\neg f$, we can get the same result with the terms DNF and CNF interchanged.

Proving Theorem 14.1 from Lemma 14.2

Now we show how Håstad's Lemma implies that parity is not in $\mathbf{AC}^0$. We start with any $\mathbf{AC}^0$ circuit and assume that the circuit has been simplified as follows (these simplifications are straightforward to do and are left as Exercises 14.1 and 14.2): (a) All fan-outs are 1; the circuit is a tree. (b) All not gates are at the input level of the circuit; equivalently, the circuit has $2n$ input wires, with the last n of them being the negations of the first n. (c) The $\vee$ and $\wedge$ gates alternate (i.e., at each level of the tree there are either only $\vee$ gates or only $\wedge$ gates). (d) The bottom level has $\wedge$ gates of fan-in 1.

Let n^b denote an upper bound on the number of gates in the circuit with the above properties. We randomly restrict more and more variables, where each step with high probability will reduce the depth of the circuit by 1 and will keep the bottom level at a constant fan-in. Specifically, letting n_i stand for the number of unrestricted variables after step i, we restrict $n_i - \sqrt{n_i}$ variables at step $i + 1$. Since $n_0 = n$, we have $n_i = n^{1/2^i}$. Let $k_i = 10b2^i$. We'll show that with high probability, after the ith restriction, we're left with a depth-$(d-i)$ circuit with at most k_i fan-in in the bottom level. Indeed, suppose that the bottom level contains $\wedge$ gates and the level above it contains $\vee$ gates. The function each such $\vee$ gate computes is a k_i-DNF and hence by Lemma 14.2, with probability $1 - \left(\frac{k_i^{10}}{n^{1/2^{i+1}}} \right)^{k_{i+1}/2}$, which is at least $1 - 1/(10n^b)$ for large enough n, the function such a gate computes after the $(i+1)$th iteration will be expressible as a k_{i+1}-CNF. Since the top gate of a CNF formula is $\wedge$, we can merge those $\wedge$ gates with the $\wedge$ gate above them, reducing the depth of the circuit by one (see Figures 14.1 and 14.2). The symmetric reasoning applies in the case the bottom level consists of $\vee$ gates–in this case we use the lemma to transform the k_i-CNF of the level above it into a k_{i+1}-DNF. Note that we apply the lemma at most once per each of the at most n^b gates of the original circuit. By the union bound, with probability $9/10$, if we continue this process for $d - 2$ steps, we'll get a depth two circuit with fan-in $k = k_{d-2}$ at bottom level. That is, either a

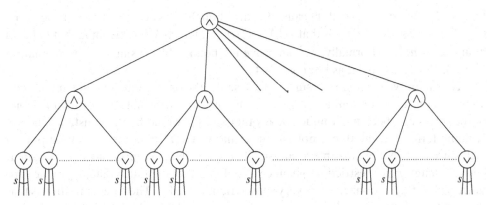

Figure 14.2. Circuit after Håstad switching transformation. Notice that the new layer of ∧ gates can be collapsed with the single ∧ parent gate, to reduce the number of levels by one.

k-CNF or k-DNF formula. But such a formula can be made constant by fixing at most k of the variables (e.g., in a DNF ensuring that the first clause has value 1). Since the parity function is not constant under any restriction of less than n variables, this proves Theorem 14.1. ∎

14.1.2 Proof of the Switching Lemma (Lemma 14.2)

Now we prove the Switching Lemma. The original proof was more complicated; this one is due to Razborov.

We need a few definitions. Let a *min-term* of a function f be a partial assignment to f's variables that makes f output 1 *irrespective of the assignments to the remaining variables.* Thus every term in a k-DNF formula for f yields a size-k min-term of f. A *max-term* is a partial assignment to f's variables that makes f output 0 regardless of the other variables. Thus every clause in a k-CNF formula for f yields a size-k max-term of f. We will assume throughout that min-terms (respectively max-terms) are minimal, in the sense that no assignment to a proper subset of the term's variables would make the function 1 (respectively, 0). Thus a function that is *not* expressible as an s-CNF must have at least one max-term of length $s + 1$ (see Exercise 14.3).

If π and ρ are restrictions on disjoint sets of variables, then we denote by $\pi\rho$ their union (i.e., if π assigns values to variables in S and ρ assigns values to variables in T then $\pi\rho$ assigns value to variables in $S \cup T$ according to either π or ρ, respectively).

Let R_t denote the set of all restrictions of t variables, where $t \geq n/2$. Note that $|R_t| = \binom{n}{t}2^t$. Denote by B the set of *bad restrictions*–those $\rho \in R_t$ for which $f|_\rho$ is *not* expressible as an s-CNF. To prove the lemma we need to show that B is small, which we do by showing a one-to-one mapping from it to the cartesian product of the set R_{t+s} of restrictions to $(t+s)$ variables and $\{0, 1\}^\ell$ for some $\ell = O(s \log k)$. This cartesian product has size $\binom{n}{t+s}2^{t+s}2^{O(s \log k)} = \binom{n}{t+s}2^t k^{O(s)}$. Hence the probability $|B|/|R_t|$ of picking a bad restriction is bounded by

$$\frac{\binom{n}{t+s}2^t k^{O(s)}}{\binom{n}{t}2^t} = \frac{\binom{n}{t+s}k^{O(s)}}{\binom{n}{t}} \tag{14.2}$$

Intuitively, this ratio is small because k, s are thought of as constants and hence for t that is very close to n, it holds that $\binom{n}{t+s} \approx \binom{n}{t}/n^s$ and $n^s \gg k^{O(s)}$, meaning that (14.2) is bounded by $n^{-\Omega(s)}$. Formally, we can prove the bound (14.1) using the approximation $\binom{n}{a} \approx (ne/a)^a$; we leave it as Exercise 14.4.

Thus to prove the lemma it suffices to describe the one-to-one mapping mentioned above. Let us reason about a restriction ρ that is bad for the k-DNF formula f. None of the terms of f becomes 1 under ρ, as otherwise $f|_\rho$ would be the constant function 1. Some terms become 0, but not all, since that would also fix the overall output. In fact, since $f|_\rho$ is not expressible as an s-CNF, it has some max-term, say π, of length at least s. That is, π is a restriction of some variables not set by ρ such that $f|_{\rho\pi}$ is the sero function but $f|_{\rho\pi'}$ is nonzero for every substriction π' of π. The rough intuition is that the one-to-one mapping will map ρ to $\rho\sigma$, where σ is a suitably defined assignment to π's variables, and hence $\rho\sigma$ restricts at least $t + s$ variables.

Order the terms of f in some arbitrary order $t_1, t_2, \ldots$, and within the terms, order the variables in some arbitrary order. By definition, $\rho\pi$ is a restriction that sets f to 0, and thus sets all terms of f to 0. We split π into $m \le s$ substrictions $\pi_1, \pi_2, \ldots \pi_m$ as follows. Assume we have already found $\pi_1, \pi_2, \ldots, \pi_{i-1}$ such that $\pi_1\pi_2 \cdots \pi_{i-1} \ne \pi$. Let t_{l_i} be the *first* term in our ordering of terms that is not set to 0 under $\rho\pi_1\pi_2 \cdots \pi_{i-1}$. Such a term must exist since π is a max-term, and $\pi_1\pi_2 \cdots \pi_{i-1}$ being a proper subset of it cannot be a max-term. Let Y_i be the variables of t_{l_i} that are set by π but are not set by $\rho\pi_1 \cdots \pi_{i-1}$. Since π sets the term t_{l_i} to 0, Y_i cannot be empty. We define π_i to be the restriction that coincides with π on Y_i (and hence sets t_{l_i} to 0). We define σ_i to be the restriction of Y_i that keeps t_{l_i} from being 0 (such a restriction must exist since otherwise t_{l_i} would be 0). This process continues until the first time where defining π_m as above would mean that $\pi_1, \ldots, \pi_m$ (and hence also $\sigma_1, \sigma_2, \ldots, \sigma_m$) together assign at least s variables. If necessary, we trim π_m in some arbitrary way (i.e., make it assign values to fewer variables) so that these restrictions together assign exactly s variables.

Our mapping will map ρ to $(\rho\sigma_1\sigma_2 \ldots \sigma_m, c)$ where c is an $O(s \log k)$ length string defined below. To show that the mapping is one-to-one, we need to show how to invert it uniquely. This is harder than it looks since a priori there is no way to identify ρ from $\rho\sigma_1\sigma_2 \ldots \sigma_m$. Indeed the purpose of the auxiliary information in c is to help us do precisely that, as described next.

Suppose we are given the assignment $\rho\sigma_1\sigma_2 \ldots \sigma_m$. We can plug this assignment into f and then infer which term serves as t_{l_1}: It is the first one to that is not fixed to 0. (It is the first term not fixed to 0 by ρ, this property is maintained by σ_1, and $\sigma_2, \ldots, \sigma_m$ do not assign values to variables in the term t_{l_1}.) Let s_1 be the number of variables in π_1. The string c will contain the number s_1, the indices in t_{l_1} of the variables in π_1, and the values that π_1 assigns to these variables. Note once we know t_{l_1} this information is sufficient to reconstruct π_1. Moreover, since each term has at most k variables, we only need $O(s_1 \log k)$ bits to store this information. Having reconstructed π_1, we can change the restriction $\rho\sigma_1\sigma_2 \cdots \sigma_m$ to $\rho\pi_1\sigma_2 \cdots \sigma_m$ and work out which term is t_2: it is once again the first nonzero term under the new restriction (note that π_1 sets t_{l_1} to 0). The next $O(s_2 \log k)$ bits of c will give us the assignment π_2 (where s_2 is the number of variables in π_2). We continue this process until we have processed all m terms and figured out what $\pi_1, \ldots, \pi_m$ are. Now we can "undo" them to reconstruct ρ, thus demonstrating

that the mapping is one-to-one. The total length of auxiliary information required is
$O((s_1 + s_2 + \cdots + s_m)\log k) = O(s\log k)$. ∎

14.2 CIRCUITS WITH "COUNTERS": ACC

After the $\mathbf{AC}^0$ lower bounds of the previous section were proved, researchers were
inspired to extend them to more general classes of circuits. The simplest extension
seemed to be to allow gates other than $\vee$ and $\wedge$ in the circuit, while continuing to insist
that the depth stays $O(1)$. A simple example of such a gate is the parity gate, which
computes the parity of its input bits. Clearly, an $\mathbf{AC}^0$ circuit provided with even a single
parity gate can compute the parity function. But are there still other explicit functions
that it cannot compute? Razborov proved the first lower bound for such circuits using
his *Method of Approximations*. Smolensky later extended this work and clarified this
method for the circuit class considered here.

Definition 14.3 (ACC0) For any integer m, the MOD_m gate outputs 0 if the sum of its
inputs is 0 modulo m, and 1 otherwise.

For integers $m_1, m_2, \ldots, m_k > 1$ we say a language L is in $\mathbf{ACC0}(m_1, m_2, \ldots, m_k)$
if there exists a circuit family $\{C_n\}$ with constant depth and polynomial size (and
unbounded fan-in) consisting of $\wedge$, $\vee$, $\neg$, and $MOD_{m_1}, \ldots, MOD_{m_k}$ gates accepting L.

The class $\mathbf{ACC0}$ contains every language that is in $\mathbf{ACC0}(m_1, m_2, \ldots, m_k)$ for some
$k \geq 0$ and $m_1, m_2, \ldots, m_k > 1$.   ◇

Good lower bounds are known only when the circuit has one kind of modular gate.

Theorem 14.4 (*Razborov-Smolensky* [Razb87, Smo87])
For distinct primes p and q, the function MOD_p is not in $\mathbf{ACC0}(q)$.

We exhibit the main idea of this result by proving that the parity function cannot
be computed by an $\mathbf{ACC0}(3)$ circuit.

PROOF: The proof proceeds in two steps.

Step 1. In the first step, we show (using induction on h) that for any depth h MOD_3
circuit on n inputs and size S, there is a polynomial of degree $(2l)^h$, which agrees with
the circuit on $1 - S/2^l$ fraction of the inputs. If our circuit C has depth d, then we set
$2l = n^{1/2d}$ to obtain a degree $\sqrt{n}$ polynomial that agrees with C on $1 - S/2^{n^{1/2d}/2}$ fraction
of inputs.

Step 2 We show that no polynomial of degree $\sqrt{n}$ agrees with MOD_2 on more than
49/50 fraction of inputs.

Together, the two steps imply that $S > 2^{n^{1/2d}/2}/50$ for any depth d circuit computing
MOD_2, thus proving the theorem. Now we give details.

Step 1. Consider a node v in the circuit at a depth h. (If v is an input node, then we say it has depth 0.) If $g(x_1, \ldots, x_n)$ is the function computed at the node v, then we desire a polynomial $\tilde{g}(x_1, \ldots, x_n)$ over GF(3) with degree $(2l)^h$, such that $g(x_1, \ldots, x_n) = \tilde{g}(x_1, \ldots, x_n)$ for "most" $x_1, \ldots, x_n \in \{0, 1\}$. We will also ensure that on every input in $\{0, 1\}^n \subseteq GF(3)$, polynomial $\tilde{g}$ takes a value in $\{0, 1\}$. This is without loss of generality since we can just square the polynomial. (Recall that the elements of $GF(3)$ are $0, -1, 1$ and $0^2 = 0$, $1^2 = 1$ and $(-1)^2 = 1$.)

We construct the approximating polynomial by induction. When $h = 0$ the "gate" is an input wire x_i, which is exactly represented by the degree 1 polynomial x_i. Suppose we have constructed approximators for all nodes up to height $h - 1$ and g is a gate at height h.

1. If g is a NOT gate, then $g = \neg f_1$ for some other gate f_1 that is at height $h - 1$ or less. The inductive hypothesis gives an approximator $\tilde{f}_1$ for f_1. Then we use $\tilde{g} = 1 - \tilde{f}_1$ as the approximator polynomial for g; this has the same degree as $\tilde{f}_1$. Whenever $\tilde{f}_1(x) = f_1(x)$ then $\tilde{g}(x) = g(x)$, so we introduced no new error.

2. If g is a MOD_3 gate with inputs $f_1, f_2, \ldots, f_k$, we use the approximation $\tilde{g} = (\sum_{i=0}^{k} \tilde{f}_i)^2$. The degree increases to at most $2 \times (2l)^{h-1} < (2l)^h$. Since $0^2 = 0$ and $(-1)^2 = 1$, we introduced no new error.

3. If g is an AND or an OR gate, we need to be more careful. We give the solution for OR; De Morgan's law allows AND gates to be handled similarly. Suppose $g = \vee_{i=0}^{k} f_i$. The naive approach would be to replace g with the polynomial $1 - \prod_{i=0}^{k}(1 - \tilde{f}_i)$. Unfortunately, this multiplies the degree by k, the fan-in of the gate, which could greatly exceed $2l$. The correct solution involves introducing some error. If $g = \vee_{i=0}^{k} f_i$, then on input x, $g(x) = 1$ if and only if at least one of the f_i's outputs 1 on x. Furthermore, by the *random subsum principle* (see Claim A.31) if there is some i such that $f_i(x) = 1$, then the sum (over GF(3)) of a random subset of $\{f_i(x)\}$ is nonzero with probability at least $1/2$.

    Randomly pick l subsets $T_1, \ldots, T_l$ of $\{1, \ldots, k\}$. Compute the l polynomials $(\sum_{j \in T_1} \tilde{f}_j)^2, \ldots, (\sum_{j \in T_l} \tilde{f}_j)^2$, each of which has degree at most twice than that of the largest input polynomial. Compute the OR of these l terms using the naive approach. We get a polynomial of degree at most $2l \times (2l)^{h-1} = (2l)^h$. For any x, the probability over the choice of subsets that this polynomial differs from $OR(\tilde{f}_1, \ldots, \tilde{f}_k)$ is at most $\frac{1}{2^l}$. So, by the probabilistic method, there *exists* a choice for the l subsets such that the probability over the choice of x that this polynomial differs from $OR(\tilde{f}_1, \cdots, \tilde{f}_k)$ is at most $\frac{1}{2^l}$. We use this choice of the subsets to construct the approximator.

Applying the above procedure for each gate gives an approximator for the output gate of degree $(2l)^d$ where d is depth of the entire circuit. Each operation of replacing a gate by its approximator polynomial introduces error on at most $1/2^l$ fraction of all inputs, so the overall fraction of erroneous inputs for the approximator is at most $S/2^l$. (Note that errors at different gates may affect each other. Error introduced at one gate may be canceled out by errors at another gate higher up. Thus, we are being pessimistic in applying the union bound to *upper bound* the probability that any of the approximator polynomials anywhere in the circuit miscomputes.)

Step 2. Suppose that a polynomial f agrees with the MOD_2 function for all inputs in a set $G' \subseteq \{0, 1\}^n$. If the degree of f is bounded by $\sqrt{n}$, then we show that $|G'| < (\frac{49}{50})2^n$.

Consider the change of variables $y_i = 1 + x_i \pmod{3}$. (Thus $0 \to 1$ and $1 \to -1$.) This changes the input domain from $\{0, 1\}$ to $\{\pm 1\}^n$. Under this transformation f is some other polynomial, say $g(y_1, y_2, \ldots, y_n)$, which still has degree $\sqrt{n}$. The set G' is transformed to a subset G of $\{\pm 1\}^n$ of the same size on which g and the (transformed version) of MOD_2 agree.

But it's not hard to see that MOD_2 is transformed to the function $\prod_{i=1}^{n} y_i$. Thus $g(y_1, y_2, \ldots, y_n)$, a degree $\sqrt{n}$ polynomial, agrees with $\Pi_{i=1}^n y_i$ on G. This is decidedly odd, and we show that any such G must be small. Specifically, let F_G be the set of all functions $S : G \to \{0, 1, -1\}$. Clearly, $|F_G| = 3^{|G|}$, and we will show $|F_G| \le 3^{\left(\frac{49}{50}\right)2^n}$, whence Step 2 follows.

Lemma 14.5 *For every $S \in F_G$, there exists a polynomial g_S, which is a sum of monomials $a_I \prod_{i \in I} y_i$ where $|I| \le \frac{n}{2} + \sqrt{n}$ such that $g_S(x) = S(x)$ for all $x \in G$.* $\diamond$

PROOF: Let $\hat{S} : GF(3)^n \to GF(3)$ be any function which agrees with S on G. Then $\hat{S}$ can be written as a polynomial in the variables y_i. However, we are only interested in its values on $(y_1, y_2, \ldots, y_n) \in \{-1, 1\}^n$, when $y_i^2 = 1$ and so every monomial $\Pi_{i \in I} y_i^{r_i}$ has, without loss of generality, $r_i \le 1$. Thus $\hat{S}$ is a polynomial of degree at most n. Now consider any of its monomial terms $\Pi_{i \in I} y_i$ of degree $|I| > n/2$. We can rewrite it as

$$\Pi_{i \in I} y_i = \Pi_{i=1}^n y_i \Pi_{i \in \bar{I}} y_i \tag{14.3}$$

which takes the same values as $g(y_1, y_2, \ldots, y_n) \Pi_{i \in \bar{I}} y_i$ over G. Thus every monomial in $\hat{S}$ can be replaced with a monomial with degree at most $\frac{n}{2} + \sqrt{n}$. ∎

To conclude, we bound the number of possible polynomials g_S as in Lemma 14.5. This number is at most 3 to the power of the number of possible monomials. But the number of possible such monomials is

$$\left|\{I \subset [n] : |I| \le n/2 + \sqrt{n}\}\right| = \sum_{i=0}^{n/2+\sqrt{n}} \binom{n}{i}$$

Using bounds on the tail of the binomial distribution (or direct calculation) it can be shown that this is less than $\frac{49}{50} 2^n$. ∎

14.3 LOWER BOUNDS FOR MONOTONE CIRCUITS

A Boolean circuit is *monotone* if it contains only AND and OR gates, and no NOT gates. Such a circuit can only compute monotone functions, defined as follows.

Definition 14.6 *For $x, y \in \{0, 1\}^n$, we denote $x \preccurlyeq y$ if every bit that is 1 in x is also 1 in y. A function $f : \{0, 1\}^n \to \{0, 1\}$ is monotone if $f(x) \le f(y)$ for every $x \preccurlyeq y$.* $\diamond$

An alternative characterization is that f is *monotone* if for every input x, changing a bit in x from 0 to 1 cannot change the value of the function from 1 to 0.

It is easy to check that every monotone circuit computes a monotone function, and every monotone function can be computed by a (sufficiently large) monotone circuit. CLIQUE is a monotone function since adding an edge to the graph cannot destroy any clique that existed in it. It is therefore natural to try to show that CLIQUE cannot be computed by polynomial-size monotone circuits. Razborov was first to prove such a result. This was soon improved by Andreev and further improved by Alon and Boppana, who proved the following theorem.

Theorem 14.7 *(Monotone-circuit lower bound for* CLIQUE*[Razb85a, And85, AB87])*
Denote by $\text{CLIQUE}_{k,n} : \{0, 1\}^{\binom{n}{2}} \to \{0, 1\}$ *be the function that on input an adjacency matrix of an n-vertex graph G outputs 1 iff G contains a k-vertex clique.*
There exists some constant $\epsilon > 0$ such that for every $k \leq n^{1/4}$, there's no monotone circuit of size less than $2^{\epsilon\sqrt{k}}$ that computes $\text{CLIQUE}_{k,n}$.

Of course, we believe that Theorem 14.7 holds (at least roughly) for *nonmonotone* circuits as well (i.e., that **NP** $\not\subseteq$ **P$_{/\text{poly}}$**). In fact, one of the original hopes behind considering monotone circuits was that there is some connection between monotone and nonmonotone circuit complexity. One plausible conjecture was that for *every* monotone function f, the monotone circuit complexity of f is polynomially related to its general (nonmonotone) circuit complexity. Alas, this conjecture was refuted by Razborov [Razb85b], and in fact the gap between the two complexities is now known to be exponential [Tar88].

14.3.1 Proving Theorem 14.7

Clique indicators

To get some intuition as to why this theorem might be true, let's show that $\text{CLIQUE}_{k,n}$ cannot be computed (or even approximated) by subexponential monotone circuits of a very special form. For every $S \subseteq [n]$, let $\mathbf{C}_S$ denote the function on $\{0, 1\}^{\binom{n}{2}}$ that outputs 1 on a graph G iff the set S is a clique in G. We call $\mathbf{C}_S$ the *clique indicator* of S. Note that $\text{CLIQUE}_{k,n} = \bigvee_{S \subseteq [n], |S|=k} \mathbf{C}_S$. We'll now prove that $\text{CLIQUE}_{k,n}$ can't be computed by an OR of less than $n^{\sqrt{k}/20}$ clique indicators.

Let $\mathcal{Y}$ be the following distribution on n-vertex graphs: Choose a set $K \subseteq [n]$ with $|K| = k$ at random, and output the graph that has a clique on K and no other edges. Let $\mathcal{N}$ be the following distribution on n-vertex graphs: Choose a function $c : [n] \to [k - 1]$ at random, and place an edge between u and v iff $c(u) \neq c(v)$. With probability one, $\text{CLIQUE}_{n,k}(\mathcal{Y}) = 1$ and $\text{CLIQUE}_{n,k}(\mathcal{N}) = 0$. The fact that $\text{CLIQUE}_{n,k}$ requires an OR of at least $n^{\sqrt{k}/20}$ clique indicators follows immediately from the following lemma.

Lemma 14.8 *Let n be sufficiently large, $k \leq n^{1/4}$ and $S \subseteq [n]$. Then either $\Pr[\mathbf{C}_S(\mathcal{N}) = 1] \geq 0.99$ or $\Pr[\mathbf{C}_S(\mathcal{Y}) = 1] \leq n^{-\sqrt{k}/20}$* ◇

PROOF: Let $\ell = \sqrt{k - 1}/10$. If $|S| \leq \ell$, then by the birthday bound (see Example A.4) we expect a random $f : S \to [k - 1]$ to have less than 0.01 collisions, and hence by

Markov's inequality the probability that f is one to one is at least 0.99. This implies that $\Pr[C_S(\mathcal{N}) = 1] \geq 0.99$.

If $|S| > \ell$, then $\Pr[C_S(\mathcal{Y}) = 1]$ is equal to the probability that $S \subseteq K$ for a random $K \subseteq [n]$ of size k. This probability is equal to $\binom{n-\ell}{k-\ell}/\binom{n}{k}$ which, by the formula for the binomial coefficients, is less than $\left(\frac{2k}{n}\right)^{\ell} \leq n^{-0.7\ell} < n^{-\sqrt{k}/20}$ (for sufficiently large n). ∎

Approximation by clique indicators

Together with Lemma 14.8, the following lemma implies Theorem 14.7.

Lemma 14.9 *Let C be a monotone circuit of size $s < 2^{\sqrt{k}/2}$. Then, there exist sets $S_1, \ldots, S_m$ with $m \leq n^{\sqrt{k}/20}$ such that*

$$\Pr_{G \in_R \mathcal{Y}}[\bigvee_i C_{S_i}(G) \geq C(G)] > 0.9 \tag{14.4}$$

$$\Pr_{G \in_R \mathcal{N}}[\bigvee_i C_{S_i}(G) \leq C(G)] > 0.9 \tag{14.5}$$

◇

PROOF: Set $\ell = \sqrt{k}/10, p = 10\sqrt{k} \log n$ and $m = (p-1)^{\ell}\ell!$. Note that $m \ll n^{\sqrt{k}/20}$. We can think of the circuit C as a sequence of s monotone functions $f_1, \ldots, f_s$ from $\{0, 1\}^{\binom{n}{2}}$ to $\{0, 1\}$, where each function f_k is either the AND or OR of two functions $f_{k'}, f_{k''}$ for $k', k'' < k$ or is the value of an input variable $x_{u,v}$ for $u, v \in [n]$ (i.e., $f_k = C_{\{u,v\}}$). The function that C computes is f_s. We'll show a sequence of functions $\tilde{f}_1, \ldots, \tilde{f}_s$ such that each function $\tilde{f}_k$ is (1) an OR of at most m clique indicators $C_{S_1}, \ldots, C_{S_m}$ with $|S_i| \leq \ell$ and (2) $\tilde{f}_k$ approximates f_k, in the sense that the two agree with good probabiity on inputs drawn from the distributions $\mathcal{Y}$ and $\mathcal{N}$. (Thus conditions (14.4) and (14.5) are a special case of this notion of approximation.) We call any function $\tilde{f}_k$ satisfying (1) an (ℓ, m)-*function*.

We construct the functions $\tilde{f}_1, \ldots, \tilde{f}_s$ by induction. For $1 \leq k \leq s$, if f_k is an input variable, then we let $\tilde{f}_k = f_k$. If $f_k = f_{k'} \vee f_{k''}$, then we let $\tilde{f}_{k'} \sqcup \tilde{f}_{k''}$, and if $f_k = f_{k'} \wedge f_{k''}$, then we let $\tilde{f}_{k'} \sqcap \tilde{f}_{k''}$, where the operations $\sqcup, \sqcap$ will be defined below. We'll prove that for every $f, g : \{0, 1\}^{\binom{n}{2}} \to \{0, 1\}$ **(a)** if f and g are (m, ℓ)-functions, then so is $f \sqcup g$ (resp. $f \sqcap g$) and **(b)** $\Pr_{G \in_R \mathcal{Y}}[f \sqcup g\ (G) < f \vee g\ (G)] < 1/(10s)$ (resp. $\Pr_{G \in_R \mathcal{Y}}[f \sqcap g\ (G) < f \wedge g\ (G)] < 1/(10s)$) and $\Pr_{G \in_R \mathcal{N}}[f \sqcup g\ (G) > f \vee g\ (G)] < 1/(10s)$ (resp. $\Pr_{G \in_R \mathcal{Y}}[f \sqcap g\ (G) < f \wedge g\ (G)] < 1/(10s)$). The lemma will then follow by using the union bound that with probability ≥ 0.9 the equations of Condition (b) hold for all $\tilde{f}_1, \ldots, \tilde{f}_s$. We'll now describe the two operations $\sqcup, \sqcap$. Condition (a) will follow from the definition of the operations, while Condition (b) will require a proof.

The operation f ⊔ g

Let f, g be two (m, ℓ)-functions; that is, $f = \bigvee_{i=1}^m C_{S_i}$ and $g = \bigvee_{j=1}^m C_{T_j}$ (if f or g is the OR of less than m clique indicators we can add duplicate sets to make the number m). Consider the function $h = C_{Z_1} \vee \cdots \vee C_{Z_{2m}}$ where $Z_i = S_i$ and $Z_{m+j} = T_j$ for $1 \leq i, j \leq m$. The function h is not an (m, ℓ)-function since it is the OR of $2m$ clique indicators. We make it into an (m, ℓ)-function in the following way: As long as there are more than m distinct sets, find p subsets $Z_{i_1}, \ldots, Z_{i_p}$ that are in a *sunflower* formation. That is, there exists a set $Z \subseteq [n]$ such that for every $1 \leq j, j' \leq p$, $Z_{i_j} \cap Z_{i_{j'}} = Z$. (The name "sunflower" comes from viewing the sets $Z_{i_1} \setminus Z, \ldots, Z_{i_p} \setminus Z$ as the petals of a sunflower with center Z.) Replace the functions $C_{Z_{i_1}}, \ldots, C_{Z_{i_p}}$ in the function h with the function C_Z. Once we obtain an (m, ℓ)-function h', we define $f \sqcup g$ to be h'. We won't get stuck because of the following lemma (whose proof we defer).

Lemma 14.10 *Sunflower Lemma [ER60]* *Let $\mathcal{Z}$ be a collection of distinct sets each of cardinality at most ℓ. If $|\mathcal{Z}| > (p-1)^{\ell} \ell!$ then there exist p sets $Z_1, \ldots, Z_p \in \mathcal{Z}$ and a set Z such that $Z_i \cap Z_j = Z$ for every $1 \leq i, j \leq p$.* ◇

The operation $f \sqcap g$

Let f, g be two (m, ℓ)-functions; that is, $f = \bigvee_{i=1}^{m} C_{S_i}$ and $g = \bigvee_{j=1}^{m} C_{T_j}$. Let h be the function $\bigvee_{1 \leq i, j \leq m} C_{S_i \cup T_j}$. We perform the following steps on h: (1) Discard any function C_Z for $|Z| > \ell$. (2) Reduce the number of functions to m by applying the Sunflower Lemma as above.

Proving Condition (b)

To complete the proof of the lemma, we prove the following four equations:

- $\Pr_{G \in_R \mathcal{Y}}[f \sqcup g\,(G) < f \vee g\,(G)] < 1/(10s)$

  If $Z \subseteq Z_1, \ldots, Z_p$ then for every i, $C_{Z_i}(G)$ implies that $C_Z(G)$ and hence the operation $f \sqcup g$ can't introduce any "false negatives."

- $\Pr_{G \in_R \mathcal{N}}[f \sqcup g\,(G) > f \vee g\,(G)] < 1/(10s)$.

  We can introduce a "false positive" on a graph G only if when we replace the clique indicators for a sunflower $Z_1, \ldots, Z_p$ with the clique indicator for the common intersection Z, it is the case that $C_Z(G)$ holds even though $C_{Z_i}(G)$ is false for every i. Recall that we choose $G \in_R \mathcal{N}$ by choosing a random function $c : [n] \to [k-1]$ and adding an edge for every two vertices u, v with $c(u) \neq c(v)$. Thus, we get a false positive if c is one-to-one on Z (we denote this event by B) but *not* one-to-one on Z_i for every $1 \leq i \leq p$ (we denote these events by $A_1, \ldots, A_p$). We'll show that the intersection of B and $A_1, \ldots, A_p$ happens with probability at most 2^{-p}, which (by the choice of p) is less than $1/(10m^2 s)$. Since we apply the reduction step at most m times, the equation will follow.

  For every i, $\Pr[A_i | B] < 1/2$. Indeed, since $|Z_i| = \ell < \sqrt{k-1}/10$, the birthday bound says that $\Pr[A_i] < 1/2$ and conditioning on having no collisions in Z only makes this event less likely. Conditioned on B, the events $A_1, \ldots, A_p$ are independent, since they depend on the values of c on disjoint sets, and hence $\Pr[A_1 \wedge \cdots \wedge A_p \wedge B] \leq \Pr[A_1 \wedge \cdots \wedge A_p | B] = \prod_{i=1}^{p} \Pr[A_p | B] \leq 2^{-p}$.

- $\Pr_{G \in_R \mathcal{Y}}[f \sqcap g\,(G) < f \wedge g\,(G)] < 1/(10s)$

  By the distributive law $f \wedge g = \bigvee_{i,j}(C_{S_i} \wedge C_{T_j})$. A graph G in the support of $\mathcal{Y}$ consists of a clique over some set K. For such a graph $C_{S_i} \wedge C_{T_j}$ holds iff $S_i, T_j \subseteq K$, and thus $C_{S_i} \wedge C_{T_j}$ holds iff $C_{S_i \cup T_j}$ holds. We can introduce a false negative when we discard functions of the form C_Z for $|Z| > \ell$, but by Lemma 14.8, for such sets Z, $\Pr[C_Z(\mathcal{Y}) = 1] < n^{-\sqrt{k}/20} < 1/(10sm^2)$. The equation follows since we discard at most m^2 such sets.

- $\Pr_{G \in_R \mathcal{N}}[f \sqcap g\,(G) > f \wedge g\,(G)] < 1/(10s)$

  Since $C_{S \cup T}$ implies both C_S and C_T, we can't introduce false positives by moving from $f \wedge g$ to $\bigvee_{i,j} C_{S_i \cup T_j}$. We can't introduce false positives by discarding functions from the

OR. Thus, the only place where we can introduce false positives is where we replace the clique indicators of a sunflower with the clique indicator of the common intersection. We bound this probability in the same way as this was done for the $\sqcup$ operator. ∎

Proof of the Sunflower Lemma (Lemma 14.10)
The proof is by induction on ℓ. The case $\ell = 1$ is trivial since distinct sets of size 1 must be disjoint (hence forming a sunflower with center $Z = \emptyset$). For $\ell > 1$ let $\mathcal{M}$ be a maximal subcollection of $\mathcal{Z}$ containing only disjoint sets. We can assume that $|\mathcal{M}| < p$ since otherwise $\mathcal{M}$ is already a sufficiently large sunflower. Because of $\mathcal{M}$'s maximality for every $Z \in \mathcal{Z}$, there exists $x \in \cup\mathcal{M} = \cup_{M \in \mathcal{M}}M$ such that $x \in Z$. Since $|\cup\mathcal{M}| \le (p-1)\ell$, by averaging, there's an $x \in \cup\mathcal{M}$ that appears in at least a $\frac{1}{\ell(p-1)}$ fraction of the sets in $\mathcal{Z}$. Let $Z_1, \ldots, Z_t$ be the sets containing x, and note that $t > (p-1)^{\ell-1}(\ell-1)!$. Thus, by induction there are p sets among the $(\ell-1)$-sized sets $Z_1 \setminus \{x\}, \ldots, Z_t \setminus \{x\}$ that form a sunflower, adding back x we get the desired sunflower among the original sets. Note that the statement (and proof) assume nothing about the size of the universe the sets in $\mathcal{Z}$ live in. ∎

14.4 CIRCUIT COMPLEXITY: THE FRONTIER

Now we sketch the "frontier" of circuit lower bounds, namely, the dividing line between what we can prove and what we cannot. Along the way we re-encounter multiparty communication, since it may prove useful for proving some new circuit lower bounds.

14.4.1 Circuit lower bounds using diagonalization

We already mentioned that the best lower bound on circuit size for an **NP** problem is $5n - o(n)$. For **PH** better lower bounds are known: Exercises 6.5 and 6.6 asked you to show using diagonalization that for every $k > 0$, some language in **PH** (in fact in Σ_2^p) requires circuits of size $\Omega(n^k)$. One imagines that classes "higher up" than **PH** should have even harder languages. Thus a natural open question is:

Frontier 1: Does **NEXP** have languages that require super-polynomial size circuits?

If we go a little above **NEXP**, we can actually prove a super-polynomial lower bound: We know that $\mathbf{MA_{EXP}} \not\subseteq \mathbf{P_{/poly}}$ where $\mathbf{MA_{EXP}}$ is the set of languages accepted by a one-round proof system with an all powerful prover and an exponential time *probabilistic* verifier. (This is the exponential time analog of the class **MA** defined in Section 8.2.) This follows from the fact that if $\mathbf{MA_{EXP}} \subseteq \mathbf{P_{/poly}}$ then in particular $\mathbf{PSPACE} \subseteq \mathbf{P_{/poly}}$. However, by $\mathbf{IP} = \mathbf{PSPACE}$ (Theorem 8.19) in this case $\mathbf{PSPACE} = \mathbf{MA}$ (the prover can send in one round the circuit for computing the prover strategy in the interactive proof). By simple padding this implies that $\mathbf{MA_{EXP}}$ equals the class of languages in *exponential space*, which can be directly shown to not contain $\mathbf{P_{/poly}}$ using diagonalization. Interestingly, this lower bound does not relativize—there is an oracle under which $\mathbf{MA_{NEXP}} \subseteq \mathbf{P_{/poly}}$ [BFT98]. (The result that $\mathbf{IP} = \mathbf{PSPACE}$ used in the proof also does not relativize.)

14.4.2 Status of ACC versus P

The result that PARITY is not in **AC0** separates **NC1** from **AC0**. The next logical step would be to separate **ACC0** from **NC1**. Less ambitiously, we would like to show even a function in **P** or **NP** that is not in **ACC0**.

The Razborov-Smolensky method seems to fail when we allow the circuit even two types of modular gates, say MOD_2 and MOD_3. In fact if we allow the bounded depth circuit modular gates that do arithmetic mod q, when q is not a prime – a prime power, to be exact – we reach the limits of our knowledge. (The exercises ask you to figure out why the proof of Theorem 14.4 does not seem to apply when the modulus is a composite number.) To give one example, it is consistent with current knowledge that the CLIQUE function can be computed by linear size circuits of constant depth consisting entirely of MOD_6 gates. The problem seems to be that low-degree polynomials modulo m where m is composite are surprisingly expressive [BBR92].

Frontier 2:   Show CLIQUE is not in **ACC0(6)**.

Or even less ambitiously:

Frontier 2.1:   Exhibit a language in **NEXP** that is not in **ACC0(6)**.

It is worth noting that thus far we are talking about *nonuniform* circuits (to which Theorem 14.4 also applies). Stronger lower bounds are known for uniform circuits: Allender and Gore [AG94] have shown that a decision version of the Permanent (and hence the Permanent itself) requires exponential size "Dlogtime-uniform" **ACC0** circuits. (A circuit family $\{C_n\}$ is *Dlogtime uniform* if there exists a deterministic Turing machine M that given a number n and a pair of gates g, h determines in $O(\log n)$ time what types of gates g and h are and whether g is h's parent in C_n.)

But going back to nonuniform **ACC0**, we wish to mention an alternative representation of **ACC0** circuits that may be useful in further lower bounds. A *symmetric* gate is a gate whose output depends only on the number of inputs that are 1. For example, majority and mod gates are symmetric. Yao has shown that **ACC0** circuits can be simplified to give an equivalent depth 2 circuits with a symmetric gate at the output (Figure 14.3). Beigel and Tarui subsequently improved Yao's result.

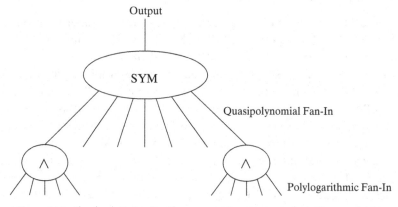

Figure 14.3. The depth 2 circuit with a symmetric output gate from Theorem 14.11.

Theorem 14.11 *([Yao90, BT91]) If $f \in$ **ACC0**, then f can be computed by a depth 2 circuit C with a symmetric gate with quasipolynomial (i.e., $2^{\log^k n}$) fan-in at the output level and $\wedge$ gates that has polylogarithmic fan-in at the input level.* $\diamond$

We will revisit this theorem in Section 14.5.1.

14.4.3 Linear circuits with logarithmic depth

When we restrict circuits to have bounded fan-in we necessarily need to allow them to have nonconstant (in fact, $\Omega(\log n)$) depth to allow the output to depend on all bits of the input. With this in mind, the simplest interesting circuit class seems to be the class of bounded fan-in circuits having $O(n)$ size and $O(\log n)$ depth.

Frontier 3: Find an explicit n-bit Boolean function that cannot be computed by circuits of $O(n)$ size and $O(\log n)$ depth.

Subfrontier: Find such a function that is not Boolean and maps $\{0, 1\}^n$ to $\{0, 1\}^n$.

(Note that by counting one can easily show that *some* function on n bits requires super-polynomial size circuits and hence bounded fan-in circuits with more than logarithmic depth; see the exercises in Chapter 6. Hence we want to show this for an explicit function (e.g., CLIQUE).)

Valiant thought about this problem in the 1970s. His initial candidates for lower bounds boiled down to showing that a certain graph called a *superconcentrator* needed to have superlinear size. He failed to prove this and instead ended up proving that such superconcentrators do exist! However a side product of Valiant's investigations was the following important lemma concerning depth-reduction for such circuits.

Lemma 14.12 *([Val75a]) In any directed acyclic graph with m edges and depth d, there is a set S of $km/\lceil \log d \rceil$ edges whose removal leaves the graph with depth at most $d/2^{k-1}$.* $\diamond$

PROOF SKETCH: Sort the graphs into d levels such that if $\overrightarrow{uv}$ is an edge, then u is at a lower level than v. Letting $\ell = \lceil \log d \rceil$, we can use the binary basis to represent every level as an ℓ-bit string. We label each edge $\overrightarrow{uv}$ with the number $i \in [\ell]$ such that i is the most significant bit in which the levels of u and v differ. We let I be the k "least popular" labels, and let S be the set of edges that are labeled with a number in I. Clearly, $|S| \le km/\ell$. Moreover, it can be shown that every path longer than $2^{\ell-k} \le d/2^{k-1}$ must contain more than $\ell - k$ distinct labels (and hence an edge in S). We leave completing this proof as Exercise 14.10. ∎

This lemma can be applied as follows. Suppose we have an $O(n)$-size circuit C of depth $c \log n$ with n inputs $\{x_1, \ldots, x_n\}$ and n outputs $\{y_1, \ldots, y_n\}$, and suppose $2^k \sim c/\epsilon$ where $\epsilon > 0$ is arbitrarily small. One can find $O(n/\log \log n)$ edges in C whose removal results in a circuit with depth at most $\epsilon \log n$. But then, since C has *bounded* fan-in, we must have that each output y_i is connected to at most $2^{\epsilon \log n} = n^\epsilon$ inputs. So each output y_i in C is completely determined by n^ϵ inputs and the values of the removed wires. So the removed wires somehow allowed some kind of "compression" of the truth tables of

$y_1, y_2, \ldots, y_n$. We do not expect this to be the case for any reasonably complex function. Surprisingly, no one has been able to exhibit an explicit function for which this is not the case.

14.4.4 Branching programs

Just as circuits are used to investigate time requirements of Turing machines, *branching programs* are used to as a combinatorial tool to investigate space complexity. A *branching program* on n input variables $x_1, x_2, \ldots, x_n$ is a directed acyclic graph all of whose nodes of nonzero out-degree are labeled with a variable x_i. It has two nodes of out-degree zero that are labeled with an output value, ACCEPT or REJECT. The edges are labeled by 0 or 1. One of the nodes is designated the start node. A setting of the input variables determines a way to walk on the directed graph from the start node to an output node. At any step, if the current node has label x_i, then we take an edge going out of the node whose label agrees with the value of x_i. The branching program is *deterministic* if every nonoutput node has exactly one 0 edge and one 1 edge leaving it. Otherwise it is *nondeterministic*. The *size* of the branching program is the number of nodes in it. The branching program complexity of a language is defined analogously with circuit complexity. Sometimes one may also require the branching program to be *leveled*, whereby nodes are arranged into a sequence of levels with edges going only from one level to the next. Then the *width* is the size of the largest level.

Theorem 14.13 *If $S(n) \geq \log n$ and $L \in$ **SPACE**$(S(n))$, then L has branching program complexity at most $c^{S(n)}$ for some constant $c > 1$.*

PROOF: Essentially mimics our proof of Theorem 4.2 that **SPACE**$(S(n)) \subseteq$ **DTIME**$(2^{O(S(n))})$. The nodes of the branching program correspond to the configurations of the space-bounded TM, and it is labeled with variable x_i if the configuration shows the TM reading the ith bit in the input at that step. ∎

A similar result holds for NDTMs and nondeterministic branching program complexity.

Frontier 4: Describe a problem in **P** (or even **NP**) that requires branching programs of size greater than $n^{1+\epsilon}$ for some constant $\epsilon > 0$.

There is some evidence that branching programs are more powerful than one may imagine. For instance, branching programs of constant width (reminiscent of a TM with $O(1)$ bits of memory) seem inherently weak. Thus the next result is unexpected.

Theorem 14.14 *(Barrington [Bar86]) A language has polynomial size, width five branching programs iff it is in **NC**1.*   ◇

14.5 APPROACHES USING COMMUNICATION COMPLEXITY

Here we outline a concrete approach (rather, a setting) in which better lower bounds may lead to a resolution of some of the questions above. It relates to generalizations of

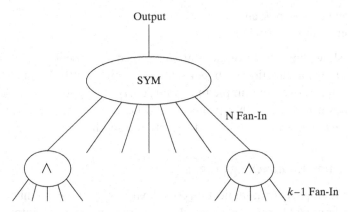

Figure 14.4. If f is computed by the above circuit, then f has a k-party protocol of complexity $k\log N$.

communication complexity introduced earlier. Mostly we will use *multiparty communication complexity* (in the "number on the forehead model" defined in Section 13.3), though Section 14.5.4 will use *communication complexity of a relation*.

14.5.1 Connection to ACC0 circuits

Suppose $f(x_1, \ldots, x_n)$ has a depth-2 circuit with a symmetric gate with fan-in N at the output and $\wedge$ gates with fan-in $k - 1$ at the input level (see Figure 14.4). Razborov and Wigderson [RW93] observed that in this case f's k-party communication complexity is at most $k \log N$. To see this, first partition the $\wedge$ gates amongst the players. Each bit is not known to exactly one player, so the input bits of each $\wedge$ gate are known to at least one player; assign the gate to such a player with the lowest index. Players then broadcast how many of their gates output 1. Since this number has at most $\log N$ bits, the claim follows.

Our hope is to employ this connection with communication complexity in conjunction with Theorem 14.11 to obtain lower bounds on **ACC0** circuits. For example, note that by Theorem 13.24, there is an explicit n-bit function requiring $\Omega(n/4^k)$ k-party communication complexity, and hence this function cannot by computed by a polynomial (or even quasipolynomial) depth-2 circuit as above with bottom fan-in $k - 1 < \log n/4$. However, this is not enough to obtain a lower bound on **ACC0** circuits since we need to show that k is not polylogarithmic to employ Theorem 14.11. But a k-party communication complexity lower bound of $\Omega(n/\text{poly}(k))$ for say the CLIQUE function would close Frontier 2.

14.5.2 Connection to linear size logarithmic depth circuits

Suppose that $f : \{0,1\}^n \times \{0,1\}^{\log n} \to \{0,1\}^n$ has bounded fan-in circuits of linear size and logarithmic depth. If $f(x,j,i)$ denotes the ith bit of $f(x,j)$, then Valiant's Lemma implies that $f(x,j,i)$ has a simultaneous 3-party protocol—that is, a protocol where all parties speak only once and write simultaneously on the blackboard (i.e., nonadaptively)—where

- (x,j) player sends $O(n/\log\log n)$ bits;

- (x, i) player sends n^ϵ bits; and
- (i, j) player sends $O(\log n)$ bits.

So, if we can show that a function does not have such a protocol, then we would have a lower bound for the function on linear size logarithmic depth circuits with bounded fan-in. For example, even the simple function $f(x, j, i) = x_{j \oplus i}$, where $j \oplus i$ is the bitwise XOR, not known to have such a protocol, and hence may not be computable by a bounded fan-in circuit of linear size and logarithmic depth.

14.5.3 Connection to branching programs

The notion of multiparty communication complexity (at least the "number on the forehead" model discussed here) was invented by Chandra, Furst, and Lipton [CFL83] for proving lower bounds on branching programs, especially the constant-width branching programs discussed in Section 14.4.4.

14.5.4 Karchmer-Wigderson communication games and depth lower bounds

The result that PARITY is not in **AC**0 separates **NC**1 from **AC**0. The next step would be to separate **NC**2 from **NC**1. (Of course, ignoring for the moment the issue of separating **ACC**0 from **NC**1.) Karchmer and Wigderson described how communication complexity can be used to prove lower bounds on the minimum depth required to compute a function. They showed the following result about monotone circuits, whose proof we omit.

Theorem 14.15 ([KW88]) *Detecting whether a graph has a perfect matching is impossible for monotone circuits of bounded fan-in and depth $O(\log n)$.*   ⋄

However, we do describe the basic *Karchmer-Wigderson* game used to prove the above result, since it is relevant for nonmonotone circuits as well. For a function $f : \{0, 1\}^n \to \{0, 1\}$ this game is defined as follows.

There are two players, **ZERO** *and* **ONE**. *Player* **ZERO** *receives an input x such that* $f(x) = 0$ *and Player* **ONE** *receives an input y such that* $f(y) = 1$. *They communicate bits to each other, until they can agree on an* $i \in \{1, 2, \ldots, n\}$ *such that* $x_i \neq y_i$.

The mechanism of communication is defined similarly as in Chapter 13; there is a protocol that the players agree on in advance before receiving the input. Note that the key difference from the scenario in Chapter 13 is that the final answer is not a single bit; furthermore, the final answer is not unique (the number of acceptable answers is equal to the number of bits that x, y differ on). Sometimes this is described as *computing a relation*. The relation in this case consists of all triples (x, y, i) such that $f(x) = 0, f(y) = 1$ and $x_i \neq y_i$.

We define $C_{KW}(f)$ as the communication complexity of the above game; namely, the maximum over all $x \in f^{-1}(0), y \in f^{-1}(1)$ of the number of bits exchanged in computing an answer for x, y. The next theorem shows that this parameter has a suprising alternative characterization. It assumes that circuits don't have NOT gates and instead the NOT gates are pushed down to the inputs using DeMorgan's law. (In other words, the inputs may be viewed as $x_1, x_2, \ldots, x_n, \overline{x_1}, \overline{x_2}, \ldots, \overline{x_n}$.) Furthermore, AND and OR gates have fan-in 2. (None of these assumptions is crucial and affects the theorem only marginally.)

Theorem 14.16 ([KW88]) $C_{KW}(f)$ *is exactly the minimum depth among all circuits that compute* f. $\diamond$

PROOF: First, we show that if there is a circuit C of depth K that computes f then $C_{KW}(f) \leq K$. Each player has a copy of C, and evaluates this circuit on the input given to him. Of course, it evaluates to 0 for Player **ZERO** and to 1 for Player **ONE**. Suppose that the top gate is an OR. Then for Player **ONE** at least one of the two incoming wires to this gate must be 1, and so in the first round, Player **ONE** sends one bit communicating which of these wires it was. Note that this wire is 0 for Player **ZERO**. In the next round the players focus on the gate that produced the value on this wire. (If the top gate is an AND on the other hand, then in the first round Player **ZERO** speaks, conveying which of the two incoming wires was 0. This wire will be 1 for Player **ONE**.) This goes on and the players go deeper down the circuit, always maintaining the invariant that the current gate has value 1 for Player **ONE** and 0 for Player **ZERO**. Finally, after at most K steps, they arrive at an input bit. According to the invariant being maintained, this bit must be 1 for Player **ONE** and 0 for Player **ZERO**. Thus they both know an index i that is a valid answer.

For the reverse direction, we have to show that if $C_{KW}(f) = K$, then there is a circuit of depth at most K that computes f. We prove a more general result. For any two disjoint nonempty subsets $A \subseteq f^{-1}(0)$ and $B \subseteq f^{-1}(1)$, let $C_{KW}(A, B)$ be the communication complexity of the Karchmer-Wigderson game when x always lies in A and y in B. We show that there is a circuit of depth $C_{KW}(A, B)$ that outputs 0 on every input from A and 1 on every input from B. Such a circuit is called a *distinguisher* for sets A, B. The proof is by induction on $K = C_{KW}(A, B)$. The base case $K = 0$ is trivial since this means that the players do not have to communicate at all to agree on an answer, say i. Hence $x_i \neq y_i$ for all $x \in A, y \in B$, which implies that either (a) $x_i = 0$ for every $x \in A$ and $y_i = 1$ for every $y \in B$ or (b) $x_i = 1$ for every $x \in A$ and $y_i = 0$ for every $y \in B$. In case (a) we can use the depth 0 circuit x_i, and in case (b) we can use the circuit $\overline{x_i}$ to distinguish A, B.

For the inductive step, suppose $C_{KW}(A, B) = K$, and at the first round Player **ZERO** speaks. Then A is the disjoint union of two sets A_0, A_1 where A_b is the set of inputs in A for which Player **ZERO** sends bit b. Then $C_{KW}(A_b, B) \leq K - 1$ for each b, and the inductive hypothesis gives a circuit C_b of depth at most $K - 1$ that distinguishes A_b, B. We claim that $C_0 \wedge C_1$ distinguishes A, B (note that it has depth at most K). The reason is that $C_0(y) = C_1(y) = 1$ for every $y \in B$, whereas for every $x \in A$, $C_0(x) \wedge C_1(x) = 0$ since if $x \in A_b$ then $C_b(x) = 0$. $\blacksquare$

Thus we have the following frontier.

Frontier 5: Show that some function f in **P** (or even **NEXP**!) has $C_{KW}(f) = \Omega(\log n \log \log n)$.

Karchmer, Raz, and Wigderson [KRW95] describe a candidate function that may work. It uses the fact that a function on k bits has a truth table of size 2^k, and that most functions on k bits are hard (e.g., require circuit size $\Omega(2^k/k)$, circuit depth $\Omega(k)$, etc.). They define the function by assuming that part of the n-bit input encodes a very hard function, and this hard function is applied to the remaining input in a "tree" fashion.

For any function $g : \{0,1\}^k \to \{0,1\}$ and $s \geq 1$ define $g^{\circ s} : \{0,1\}^{k^s} \to \{0,1\}$ as follows. If $s = 1$ then $g^{\circ s} = g$. Otherwise express the input $x \in \{0,1\}^{k^s}$ as $x_1 x_2 x_3 \cdots x_k$ where each $x_i \in \{0,1\}^{k^{s-1}}$ and define

$$g^{\circ s}(x_1 x_2 \cdots x_k) = g(g^{\circ(s-1)}(x_1) g^{\circ(s-1)}(x_2) \cdots g^{\circ(s-1)}(x_k))$$

Clearly, if g can be computed in depth d then $g^{\circ s}$ can be computed in depth sd. But, it seems hard to reduce the depth beyond that for an arbitrary choice of the function g.

Now we describe the KRW candidate function $f : \{0,1\}^n \to \{0,1\}$. Let $k = \lfloor \log \frac{n}{2} \rfloor$ and s be the largest integer such that $k^s \leq n/2$ (thus $s = \Theta(\frac{\log n}{\log \log n})$.) For any n-bit input x, let g_x be the function whose truth table is the first 2^k bits of x. Let $x|_2$ be the string of the last k^s bits of x. Then

$$f(x) = g_x^{\circ s}(x|_2)$$

According to our earlier intuition, when the first 2^k bits of x represent a really hard function – as they must for many choices of the input – then $g_x^{\circ s}(x|_2)$ should require depth $\Omega(sk) = \Omega(\frac{\log^2 n}{\log \log n})$. Of course, proving this seems difficult.

This type of complexity questions, whereby we are asking whether s instances of a problem are s times as hard as a single instance, are called *direct sum* questions. Similar questions have been studied in a variety of computational models, and sometimes counterintuitive results have been proven for them. One example is that by a counting argument there exists an $n \times n$ matrix A over $\{0,1\}$, such that the smallest circuit computing the linear function $v \mapsto Av$ for $v \in \{0,1\}^n$ is of size $\Omega(n^2)$. However, computing this function on n independent instances $v_1, \ldots, v_n$ can be done significantly faster than n^3 steps using fast matrix multiplication [Str69] (the current record is roughly $O(n^{2.38})$ [CW90]).

WHAT HAVE WE LEARNED?

- While we believe many explicit functions have *exponential* circuit complexity, there is no known *super-linear* lower bound for any such function.
- By contrast, there are some highly nontrivial lower bounds for *restricted* classes of circuits such as constant-depth and monotone circuits.
- There are several exciting frontiers in circuit complexity, progress on which could give us significant new insights on the power of computation.

CHAPTER NOTES AND HISTORY

Shannon defined circuit complexity, including monotone circuit complexity, in 1949. The topic was studied in Russia since the 1950s. (See Trakhtenbrot [Tra84] for some references.) Savage [Sav72] was the first to observe the close relationship between time required to decide a language on a TM and its circuit complexity and to suggest circuit lower bounds as a way to separate complexity classes. A burst of results in the 1980s, such as the separation of **P** from **AC0** [FSS81, Ajt83] and Razborov's separation of monotone **NP** from monotone $\mathbf{P}_{/\text{poly}}$ [Razb85a] raised hopes that a resolution of **P** versus **NP** might be near. These hopes were dashed by Razborov himself [Razb89] when he showed that his method of approximations was unlikely to apply to nonmonotone circuits. Later Razborov and Rudich [RR94] formalized what they called *natural proofs* to show that all lines of attack considered up to that point were unlikely to work. (See Chapter 23.)

Our presentation in Sections 14.2 and 14.3 closely follows that in Boppana and Sipser's excellent survey of circuit complexity [BS90], which is still useful and current 15 years later. (It omits discussion of lower bounds on algebraic circuits; see [Raz04] for a recent result.)

Håstad's switching lemma [Hås86] is a stronger form of results from [FSS81, Ajt83, Yao85]. The Razborov-Smolensky method of using approximator polynomials is from [Razb87], strengthened in [Smo87]. Valiant's observations about superlinear circuit lower bounds are from a 1975 paper [Val75b] and an unpublished manuscript – lack of progress on this basic problem gets more embarrassing by the day!.

The $5n - o(n)$ lower bound on general circuits is by Iwama and Morizumi, improving on a previous $4.5n - o(n)$ by Lachish and Raz; the full version of both results is [ILMR05].

Barrington's theorem is a good example of how researchers' intuition about circuits can sometimes be grossly incorrect. His theorem can be seen as a surprisingly simple way to compute **NC1** functions and has proved very influential in cryptography research (e.g., see [GMW87, Kil88, AIK04]).

EXERCISES

14.1. Suppose that f is computable by an $\mathbf{AC}^0$ circuit C of depth d and size S. Prove that f is computable by an $\mathbf{AC}^0$ circuit C' of size $< 10S$ and depth d that does not contain NOT gates but instead has n additional inputs that are negations of the original n inputs.

H537

14.2. Suppose that f is computable by an $\mathbf{AC}^0$ circuit C of depth d and size S. Prove that f is computable by an $\mathbf{AC}^0$ circuit C' of size $< (10S)^d$ and depth d where each gate has fan-out 1.

14.3. Prove that if all the max-terms of a Boolean function f are of size at most s then f is expressible as an s-CNF.

H538

14.4. Prove that for $t > n/2$, $\binom{n}{t+k} \leq \binom{n}{t}\left(\frac{e(n-t)}{n}\right)^k$. Use this to complete the proof of Lemma 14.2 (Section 14.1.2).

H538

14.5. Show that $\mathbf{ACC0} \subseteq \mathbf{NC1}$.

14.6. Identify reasons why the Razborov-Smolensky method does not work when the circuit has MOD m gates, where m is a composite number.

14.7. Show that representing the OR of n variables $x_1, x_2, \ldots, x_n$ exactly with a polynomial over $GF(q)$ where q is prime requires degree exactly n.

14.8. The Karchmer-Wigderson game can be used to prove *upper bounds*, and not just lower bounds. Show using this game that PARITY and MAJORITY are in **NC**1.

14.9. Show that for every constant c, if a language is computed by a polynomial-size branching program of width c then it is in **NC**1.

14.10. Complete the full proof of Valiant's Lemma (Lemma 14.12).

H538

CHAPTER 15

Proof complexity

Surprisingly, the proof complexity of the pigeonhole principles essentially depends on the number of pigeons.

– Alexander Razborov, 2001

In defining **NP** we sought to capture the phenomenon whereby if certain statements (such as "this Boolean formula is satisfiable") are true, then there is a short certificate to this effect. Furthermore, we introduced the conjecture **NP** $\neq$ **coNP** according to which certain types of statements (such as "this Boolean formula is *not* satisfiable") do not have short certificates in general. In this chapter we are interested in investigating this phenomenon more carefully, especially in settings where the existence of a short certificate is not obvious.

We start in Section 15.1 with some motivating examples. In Section 15.2 we formalize the notion of a *proof system* using a very simple example, propositional proofs. We also prove exponential lower bounds for the resolution proof system using two methods that serve as simple examples of important techniques in proof complexity. Section 15.3 surveys some other proof systems that have been studied and lower bounds known for them. Finally, Section 15.4 presents some metamathematical ruminations about whether proof complexity can shed some light on the difficulty of resolving **P** versus **NP**. There is a related, equally interesting question of *finding* short certificates assuming they exist, which we will mostly ignore except in the chapter notes.

15.1 SOME EXAMPLES

We start with a few examples, many of which were studied before the notion of computational complexity arose. Consider the following computational tasks:

1. **Infeasibility of systems of linear inequalities**. You are given a system

$$\langle \mathbf{a}_1, \mathbf{x} \rangle \leq b_1$$
$$\langle \mathbf{a}_2, \mathbf{x} \rangle \leq b_2$$
$$\vdots$$
$$\langle \mathbf{a}_m, \mathbf{x} \rangle \leq b_m$$

where $\mathbf{a}_i \in \mathbb{R}^n$ and $b_i \in \mathbb{R}$ for every i. Certify that there is no nonnegative vector $\mathbf{x} \in \mathbb{R}^n$ satisfying this system.

2. **Infeasibility of systems of linear inequalities over the integers.** The same setting as above, but with each $\mathbf{a}_i \in \mathbb{Z}^n$ and $b_i \in \mathbb{Z}$, and the solution $\mathbf{x}$ also has to be in $\mathbb{Z}^n$.

3. **Infeasibility of systems of polynomial equations.** Given a system of polynomials $g_1(x_1, x_2, \ldots, x_n), g_2(x_1, x_2, \ldots, x_n), \ldots, g_m(x_1, x_2, \ldots, x_n)$ with real coefficients, certify that the system $g_i(x_1, \ldots, x_n) = 0 \; \forall i = 1, 2, \ldots, m$ has no common solution.

4. **Contradictions.** Given a Boolean formula φ in n variables, certify that it has no satisfying assignment.

5. **Nontrivial words in a finitely presented group.** We are given a group over finite set S (meaning every group element is a *word* of the form $s_1^{\rho_1} s_2^{\rho_2} \cdots s_n^{\rho_n}$ where n is any positive integer and each ρ_i is an integer, possibly negative). The group is implicitly described by means of a finite set of *relations* of the type $s_1^{\rho_1} s_2^{\rho_2} \cdots s_n^{\rho_n} = e$ where each $s_i \in S$, $\rho_i \in \mathbb{Z}$, and $e \in S$ is some designated *identity* element. These relations imply that given a word w, it is nontrivial to know whether it simplifies to e by repeatedly applying the relations. If a word can be simplified to e, then this has a finite proof, namely, the sequence of relations that need to be applied during the simplification. We are interested in the problem where, given a word w, we have to certify that it is not equal to e (i.e., is nontrivial).

In each of the above examples, there seems to be no obvious short certificate. But sometimes such intuition can lead us astray. For instance, an old result called Farkas's Lemma (see Note 19.1.2) implies that there is indeed a short certificate for the first problem: The system is infeasible if and only if there is a combination of the inequalities that leads to a clear contradiction, in other words a $\mathbf{y} \in \mathbb{R}^m$ such that $\sum_{i=1}^n y_i \mathbf{a}_i$ is nonnegative but $\sum_i y_i b_i < 0$. The "size" of such a certificate $\mathbf{y}$ is small—it can be represented using a number of bits that is polynomial in the number of bits used to represent the inputs a_i's and b_i's.

The next three problems are **coNP**-hard (and the word problem is undecidable in general and **coNP**-hard for specific groups; see chapter notes); therefore, if **NP** $\neq$ **coNP**, we do not expect short proofs for them. Nevertheless, it is interesting to study the length of the shortest proof for *specific* instances of the problem. For instance, certifying unsatisfiability (or the computationally equivalent problem of certifying *tautologyhood*, see Example 2.21) is a natural problem that arises in fields such as artificial intelligence and formal verification of computer systems and circuits, and there we are interested in the tautologyhood of a single, carefully constructed instance. In fact, in our meta-mathematical musings in Section 15.4 you can read about a single formula (or family of formulas) related to the **P** versus **NP** question that we complexity theorists suspect is a tautology but whose tautologyhood seems difficult to prove. Similarly, in algebraic geometry, one may be interested in understanding the behavior of a single system of equations.

We note that there are languages/decision problems that are *unconditionally proven* not to have short certificates, namely languages outside of **coNP** (such languages can be shown to exist by diagonalization arguments à la Chapter 3). Also, a famous language that does not have any finite certificate at all is the language of true statements on the natural numbers in first-order logic (this is the famous Gödel's incompleteness theorem, see also Section 1.5.2).

15.2 PROPOSITIONAL CALCULUS AND RESOLUTION

Propositional logic formalizes simple modes of reasoning that have been used in philosophy for two millennia. The basic object of study is the Boolean formula, and an important task is to verify that a given formula is a tautology (i.e., evaluates to TRUE on every assignment). For convenience, we study the complement problem of verifying that the formula is a *contradiction*, namely, has no satisfying assignment. We also study this only for CNF formulas as we know how to reduce the general case to it. Specifically, to verify that a general Boolean formula ψ is a tautology, it suffices to use our reduction from Chapter 2 to transform $\neg\psi$ into an equivalent CNF formula (with additional new variables) and verify that this new formula is a contradiction.

Now we describe a simple procedure called *resolution* that tries to produce a proof that a given formula is a contradiction. Let φ be a CNF formula on the variables $x_1, x_2, \ldots, x_n$. Denote by $C_1, \ldots, C_m$ the clauses of φ. For $j = m+1, m+2, \ldots$, the resolution procedure derives a new clause C_j that is implied by the previous clauses $C_1, \ldots, C_{j-1}$ using the following rule: Suppose that there is a variable x_i and clauses C, D such that both the clause $x_i \vee C$ and $\neg x_i \vee D$ have been derived before (i.e., are in $\{C_1, \ldots, C_{j-1}\}$) then $C_j = C \vee D$. Note that the procedure may have many possible choices for C_j (the proof will be the sequence of choices). The procedure ends when it had derived an obvious contradiction: namely both the clause x_i and $\neg x_i$ for some variable x_i. The *resolution refutation* for φ is a sequence of clauses $C_1, \ldots, C_T$ containing such an obvious contradiction where $C_1, \ldots, C_m$ are φ's clauses and for $j > i$, C_j is derived from $C_1, \ldots, C_{j-1}$ using the above rule. Clearly, every clause we derive is in fact logically implied by the previous ones, and hence resolution is a *sound* proof system: There exists a resolution refutation for φ only if $\neg\varphi$ is a tautology. It is also not to hard to show that resolution is *complete*: If $\neg\varphi$ is a tautology, then there exists a resolution refutation for φ of length $2^{O(n)}$ (see Exercise 15.1). The question is whether there are formulas that require such long refutations, or perhaps every unsatisfiable formula has a polynomial-sized refutation? Since Boolean unsatisfiability is **coNP**-complete and we believe that $\mathbf{NP} \neq \mathbf{coNP}$, we believe that the answer is NO. Below we prove unconditionally that the answer is No.

15.2.1 Lower bounds using the bottleneck method

We describe Haken's *bottleneck* technique [Hak85] for proving lower bounds for resolution. We will also encounter a version of the *restriction* idea used earlier in Chapter 6 in context of circuit lower bounds.

The tautology considered here is elementary yet basic to mathematics: the *pigeonhole principle*. Colloquially, it says that if you put m pigeons into n holes, where $m > n$, then at least one hole must contain more than one pigeon. Mathematically, it asserts that there is no one-to-one and onto mapping from a set of size m to a set of size n. Though obvious, this principle underlies many nontrivial facts in mathematics such as the famous *Minkowski Convex Body Theorem*. (See chapter notes.) Thus it is plausible that a simple proof system like resolution would have trouble proving it succinctly, and this is what we will show.

The propositional version of the pigeonhole principle consists of the class of tautologies $\{\neg\mathrm{PHP}_n^m : m > n\}$ where $\neg\mathrm{PHP}_n^m$ is the following CNF formula. For integers $i \leq m, j \leq n$ it has a variable P_{ij}, which is supposed to be assigned "true" if pigeon i is assigned to hole j. It has $m + \binom{m}{2}n \leq m^3$ clauses, which are, (i) $P_{i,1} \vee P_{i,2} \vee \cdots \vee P_{i,n}$ for each $i \leq m$; this says that the ith pigeon is assigned to some hole. (ii) $\neg P_{ik} \vee \neg P_{j,k}$ for each $i, j \leq m, k \leq n$; this says that the kth hole does not get both the ith pigeon and the jth pigeon. Thus the entire ensemble of this type of clauses says that no hole gets more than 1 pigeon.

Theorem 15.1 *For any $n \geq 2$, every resolution refutation of $\neg PHP_{n-1}^n$ has size at least $2^{n/20}$.* $\diamond$

We will think of "testing" a resolution refutation by assigning values to the variables. A correct refutation proof shows that no assignment can satisfy all the given set of clauses. We will allow refutations that only show that a certain subset of assignments cannot satisfy all the given clauses. In other words, when we substitute any assignment from this subset, the refutation correctly derives a contradiction. Of course, the refutation may not correctly derive a contradiction for other assignments, so this is a *relaxation* of the notion of resolution refutation. However, any lower bound for this relaxed notion will also apply to the general notion.

The set of assignments used to test the proof will correspond to mappings that map $n-1$ pigeons to $n-1$ holes in a one-to-one manner and leave the nth pigeon unassigned. In other words, the set of variable P_{ij}'s that are assigned true constitute a matching of size $n - 1$. There are $n!$ such assignments. If the index of the sole unassigned pigeon is k we call such an assignment k-*critical*.

Restricting attention to these test assignments simplifies notation since it allows us to make all clauses in the refutation *monotone* (i.e., with no occurence of negated variables). For each clause C in the resolution proof we produce a *monotonized* clause by replacing each negated variable $\neg P_{ij}$ by $\vee_{l \neq i} P_{lj}$. It is easily checked that after this transformation the new clause is satisfied by exactly the same set of test assignments as the original clause. The next lemma (proved a little later) shows that monotonized refutations must always have a large clause.

Lemma 15.2 *Every monotonized resolution refutation of $\neg PHP_{n-1}^n$ must contain a clause with at least $2n^2/9$ variables.* $\diamond$

With this lemma in hand, we can prove Theorem 15.1 as follows. Say that a clause in the monotonized refutation is *large* if it has at least $n^2/10$ variables. Let L be the number of large clauses; the lemma shows that $L \geq 1$. We define a *restriction* to some of the variables that greatly reduces the number of large clauses. Averaging shows that there exists a variable P_{ij} that occurs in $1/10$th of the large clauses. Define a restriction such that $P_{ij} = 1$ and $P_{i,j'} = 0$ for $j' \neq j$ and $P_{i',j} = 0$ for $i' \neq i$. This sets all monotonized clauses containing P_{ij} to true, which means they can be removed from the resolution proof, leaving at most $9/10L$ large clauses. Furthermore, one pigeon and one hole have been removed from contention by the restriction, so we now have a monotonized resolution proof for $\neg PHP_{n-2}^{n-1}$. Repeating the above step $t = \log_{10/9} L$ times, we obtain a monotonized resolution proof for $\neg\text{PHP}^{n-t}_{n-1-t}$ that has no large clauses. The proof of Theorem 15.1 follows by noticing that if $L < 2^{n/20}$, then $t < n/3$, and so we have a monotonized refutation of $\neg\text{PHP}^{n-t}_{n-t-1}$ with no clauses larger than $n^2/10$, which is less than $2(n-t)^2/9$, and hence this contradicts Lemma 15.2.

Thus to finish we prove Lemma 15.2.

PROOF: (or Lemma 15.2) For each clause C in the monotonized refutation, let

$$witness(C) = \{i \; : \; \text{there is an } i\text{-critical assignment } \alpha \text{ falsifying } C\}$$

The *complexity* of a clause, $\text{comp}(C)$ is $|witness(C)|$. Whenever resolution is used to derive clause C from two previous clauses C', C'' then $\text{comp}(C) \leq \text{comp}(C')+\text{comp}(C'')$ since every assignment that falsifies C must falsify at least one of C', C''. Thus if C is the *first* clause in the refutation whose complexity is $> n/3$, then $n/3 < \text{comp}(C) < 2n/3$. We show that such a C is large.

Specifically, we show that if $\text{comp}(C) = t$, then it contains at least $t(n-t)$ distinct literals, which finishes the proof since $t(n-t) > 2n^2/9$.

Fix any $i \in witness(C)$ and any i-critical assignment α that falsifies C. For each $j \notin witness(C)$, consider the j-critical assignment α' obtained by replacing i by j; that is, if α mapped pigeon j to hole l, then α' leaves j unassigned and maps pigeon i to l. Since $j \notin witness(C)$, this j-critical assignment must satisfy C, and so we conclude that C contains variable $P_{i,l}$. By running over all $n-t$ values of $j \notin witness(C)$ and using the same α, we conclude that C contains $n-t$ distinct variables of the type $P_{i,l}$. Repeating the argument for all $i \in witness(C)$ we conclude that C contains at least $t(n-t)$ variables. ∎

15.2.2 Interpolation theorems and exponential lower bounds for resolution

This section describes a different lower bound technique for resolution that uses an interesting idea called the *Interpolation Theorem*, which plays a role in several results in proof complexity. The lower bound is also interesting because it uses the lower bound for monotone circuits presented in Chapter 14.

First we state the classical (and folklore) version of the Interpolation Theorem.

Theorem 15.3 (*Classical Interpolation Theorem*)
Let φ be a Boolean formula over the variables $x_1, \ldots, x_n, z_1, \ldots, z_k$ and ψ be a Boolean formula over the variables $y_1, \ldots, y_m, z_1, \ldots, z_k$ (i.e., the only shared variables are $z_1, \ldots, z_k$). Then $\varphi(\mathbf{x}, \mathbf{z}) \vee \psi(\mathbf{y}, \mathbf{z})$ is a tautology if and only if there is a Boolean function $I : \{0, 1\}^k \rightarrow \{0, 1\}$ such that

$$(\varphi(\mathbf{x}, \mathbf{z}) \vee I(\mathbf{z})) \wedge (\psi(\mathbf{y}, \mathbf{z}) \vee \neg I(\mathbf{z})) \tag{15.1}$$

is a tautology.

PROOF: It's easy to see that (15.1) is a tautology if and only if for every fixed assignment $\mathbf{c}$ to the $\mathbf{z}$ variables, either $\varphi(\mathbf{x}, \mathbf{c})$ is a tautology or $\psi(\mathbf{y}, \mathbf{c})$ is a tautology. Hence if (15.1) is a tautology, then $\varphi(\mathbf{x}, \mathbf{z}) \vee \psi(\mathbf{y}, \mathbf{z})$ is true for every assignment to the $\mathbf{x}, \mathbf{y}, \mathbf{z}$ variables.

On the other hand, suppose that there exists some c such that neither $\varphi(\mathbf{x}, \mathbf{c})$ nor $\psi(\mathbf{y}, \mathbf{c})$ are tautologies. Then this means that there are assignments $\mathbf{a}$ to the $\mathbf{x}$ variables, $\mathbf{b}$ to the $\mathbf{y}$ variables such that both $\varphi(\mathbf{a}, \mathbf{c})$ and $\psi(\mathbf{b}, \mathbf{c})$ are false. ∎

We will be interested in a quantitative version of this interpolation theorem that upper bounds the computational complexity of $I(\cdot)$ as a function of the size of the smallest resolution refutation.

Theorem 15.4 *(Feasible Interpolation Theorem)*
In the setting of Theorem 15.3, if $\neg\big(\varphi(\mathbf{x}, \mathbf{z}) \vee \psi(\mathbf{y}, \mathbf{z})\big)$ *has a resolution refutation of size S, then a function I satisfying the conditions of Theorem 15.3 can be computed by a circuit of size $O(S^2)$.*
Furthermore, if the variables of $\mathbf{z}$ appear only positively in ψ then the above circuit is monotone (i.e., contains no negation gates). Similarly, if the variables of $\mathbf{z}$ appear only negatively in φ then the above circuit is monotone.

PROOF: To prove Theorem 15.4 we need to show how, given a length S resolution refutation for $\neg(\varphi(\mathbf{x}, \mathbf{z}) \vee \psi(\mathbf{y}, \mathbf{z}))$ and an assignment $\mathbf{c}$ to the $\mathbf{z}$ variables, we can find in $O(S^2)$ time a value $I(\mathbf{c}) \in \{0, 1\}$ such that if $I(\mathbf{c}) = 0$ then $\varphi(\mathbf{x}, \mathbf{c})$ is a tautology and if $I(\mathbf{c}) = 1$, then $\psi(\mathbf{y}, \mathbf{c})$ is a tautology. (We know such a value $I(\mathbf{c})$ exists by Theorem 15.3.)

We show, given $\mathbf{C}$, how to compute $I(\mathbf{c})$ by transforming the size S refutation of $\neg(\varphi(\mathbf{x}, \mathbf{z}) \vee \psi(\mathbf{y}, \mathbf{z}))$ to a refutation of either $\neg\varphi(\mathbf{x}, \mathbf{c})$ or a refutation of $\neg\psi(\mathbf{y}, \mathbf{c})$ in $O(S^2)$ time. To do so, we "strip" the clauses of $\mathbf{z}$ variables. That is, we will transform the resolution refutation $C_1, \ldots, C_S$ of $\neg(\varphi(\mathbf{x}, \mathbf{z}) \vee \psi(\mathbf{y}, \mathbf{z}))$ into a valid resolution refutation $\tilde{C}_1, \ldots, \tilde{C}_S$ of $\neg(\varphi(\mathbf{x}, \mathbf{c}) \vee \psi(\mathbf{y}, \mathbf{c}))$ where each clause $\tilde{C}_i$ contains either only $\mathbf{x}$ variables (i.e., is an $\mathbf{x}$-clause) or only $\mathbf{y}$ variables (is a $\mathbf{y}$-clause). But since at the end we derive either a contradiction of the form x_i and $\neg x_i$ or a contradiction of the form y_i and $\neg y_i$ it follows that we have proven that one of these formulae is a contradiction.

We do this transformation step by step. Suppose that clauses $C_1, \ldots, C_{j-1}$ were "stripped" of the $\mathbf{z}$ variables to obtain $\tilde{C}_1, \ldots, \tilde{C}_{j-1}$, and furthermore each clause $\tilde{C}_j$ contains either only $\mathbf{x}$-variables or only $\mathbf{y}$-variables, and we now want to "strip" the clause C_j. It is of the form $C \vee D$ where the clauses $C' = w \vee C$ and $D' = \neg w \vee D$ were derived before for some variable w. By induction we have already obtained "stripped" versions $\tilde{C}$ and $\tilde{D}$ of the clauses C', D'. If $\tilde{C}$ and $\tilde{D}$ are both $\mathbf{x}$-clauses then w must be an $\mathbf{x}$-variable contained in both,[1] and we proceed with the usual resolution rule. The case that $\tilde{C}$ and $\tilde{D}$ are both $\mathbf{y}$-clauses is treated similarly. If $\tilde{C}$ is a $\mathbf{x}$-clause and $\tilde{D}$ is a $\mathbf{y}$-clause, then w must be a $\mathbf{z}$-variable, in which case we can just plug in its value according to $\mathbf{c}$, and so if $w = 0$, we simply set $\tilde{C}_j = \tilde{C}$, and if $w = 1$, we set $\tilde{C}_j = \tilde{D}$. We think of the last step in the refutation as containing the empty clause (the one obtained by using the resolution rule on two clauses containing a variable w and its negation $\neg w$). Since the clause $\tilde{C}_j$ is implied by C_j for every j, the last step in the stripped version contains the empty clause as well, implying that the new resolution proof also ends with an obvious contradiction.

---

[1] We maintain the invariant that we never remove an $\mathbf{x}$-variable from an $\mathbf{x}$-clause or a $\mathbf{y}$-variable from a $\mathbf{y}$-clause.

We leave the "furthermore" part as Exercise 15.2. However, note that it makes sense since if the $\mathbf{z}$ variables appear only positively in ψ then changing any of them from zero to one is only more likely to make ψ a tautology and hence change $I(\mathbf{c})$ from zero to one. Similar reasoning applies if the $\mathbf{z}$ variables only appear negatively in φ. ∎

We are now ready to prove a lower bound on resolution.

Theorem 15.5 *(Exponential resolution lower bound)*
There is a constant ϵ such that if for every $n \in \mathbb{N}$, we let $\varphi_n, \psi_n : \{0, 1\}^{O(n^2)} \to \{0, 1\}$ be the following Boolean functions:

- $\varphi_n(\mathbf{x}, \mathbf{z}) = \text{TRUE}$ *iff the string $\mathbf{x}$ represents a clique of size $n^{1/4}$ in the graph represented by $\mathbf{z}$*
- $\psi_n(\mathbf{y}, \mathbf{z}) = \text{TRUE}$ *iff the string $\mathbf{y}$ represents a proper $n^{1/4} - 1$ coloring for the graph represented by $\mathbf{z}$*

Then, the smallest resolution refutation for $\varphi_n(\mathbf{x}, \mathbf{z}) \wedge \psi_n(\mathbf{y}, \mathbf{z})$ has size at least $2^{\epsilon n^{1/8}}$.

Note that because a graph with a k-clique has no $k - 1$ coloring, the formula $\varphi_n(\mathbf{x}, \mathbf{z}) \wedge \psi_n(\mathbf{y}, \mathbf{z})$ is indeed unsatisfiable. Also, it is not hard to express both φ_n and ψ_n as $O(n^2)$-sized CNFs such that φ_n contains the $\mathbf{z}$ variables positively and ψ_n contains them negatively (Exercise 15.3).

Theorem 15.5 follows immediately from Theorem 15.4 and the proof of Theorem 14.7 that gave an exponential lower bound for the monotone circuit complexity of the clique function. This is because that proof actually showed that for $k < n^{1/4}$, there is no $2^{o(\sqrt{k})}$-sized monotone circuit that distinguishes between graphs having a k-clique and graphs whose chromatic number is at most $k - 1$. ∎

15.3 OTHER PROOF SYSTEMS: A TOUR D'HORIZON

Now we briefly explain some other proof systems that have been considered. Several of these are related to the computational problems we mentioned in Section 15.1.

Cutting planes
This proof system addresses the problem of certifying infeasibility of a set of linear inequalities with integer coefficients and variables. As mentioned in the introduction, this problem is **coNP**-complete. For instance, given any 3CNF formula φ we can represent it by such a set so that the formula is a contradiction iff this set is infeasible. To do so, for each Boolean variable x_i in φ put an integer variable X_i satisfying $0 \leq X_i \leq 1$ (in other words, $X_i \in \{0, 1\}$). For a clause $x_i \vee x_j \vee x_k$ write a linear inequality $X_i + X_j + X_k \geq 1$. (If any variable x_i appears negated in the clause, use $1 - X_i$ in the corresponding inequality.)

The cutting planes proof system, given an infeasible set of linear inequalities with integer variables and coefficients, produces a proof of infeasibility by deriving the inequality $0 \geq 1$ in a finite number of steps. It produces a sequence of inequalities $l_1 \geq 0, l_2 \geq 0, \dots, l_T \geq 0$ where the rth inequality is either (a) an inequality appearing in the linear system, (b) $\alpha l_u + \beta l_v \geq 0$ where α, β are nonnegative integers and $u, v < r$, or (c) is derived from some l_u for $u < r$ using the following rule: if l_u has the form

$$\sum_{i=1}^{n} a_i x_i - b \geq 0$$

where the numbers $a_1, a_2, \ldots, a_n$ have a greatest common divisor D that is at least 2 (i.e., is nontrivial), then the new inequality is

$$\sum_{i=1}^{n} \frac{a_i}{D} x_i - \lceil \frac{b}{D} \rceil \geq 0$$

(The interesting case is when D does *not* divide b, and hence $\lceil b/D \rceil$ is different from b/D.) There is a feasible interpolation theorem for cutting planes, and it has been used to prove exponential lower bounds in [BPR97, Pud97].

Nullstellensatz and polynomial calculus

These concern infeasibility of sets of equations defined by polynomials. Note that we can also represent infeasibility of 3SAT by such equations. For each variable x_i in the 3CNF formula, have a variable X_i and an equation $X_i^2 - X_i = 0$, thus ensuring that every solution satisfies $X_i \in \{0, 1\}$. We can then transform each clause to a degree-3 equation. For example the clause $x_i \vee x_j \vee \bar{x}_k$ is transformed to the equation $(1 - X_i)(1 - X_j)X_k = 0$.

Hilbert's Nullstellensatz is a basic result in algebra that gives an exact criterion for infeasibility: A set of equations $p_1(X_1, \ldots, X_n) = 0, p_2(X_1, X_2, \ldots, X_n) = 0, \ldots, p_m(X_1, \ldots, X_m) = 0$ in a field $\mathbb{F}$ is infeasible iff there exist polynomials $g_1, g_2, \ldots, g_m$ such that

$$\sum_i g_i(X_1, \ldots, X_n) p_i(X_1, \ldots, X_n) = 1 \tag{15.2}$$

Notice, these g_i's (if they exist) prove that there can be no assignment of $X_1, \ldots, X_n$ that satisfies all the p_i's, since plugging in any such assignment into (15.2) would lead to the contradiction $0 = 1$. Thus the nontrivial part of Hilbert's Theorem is the fact that such g_i's exist for every infeasible set. (Note that in general the g_i's may have coefficients in some extension field, but in this particular case where the set of polynomials includes $X_i(X_i - 1)$ for all i the solution if any must be 0/1 and then g_i's also must have coefficients in the field.)

Now we define the Nullstellensatz proof system. The axioms are the p_i's and the proof of infeasibility is a sequence of g_i's that satisfy (15.2). Hilbert's Theorem shows that this proof system is sound and complete. We assume that all polynomials are written out explicitly with all coefficients, and the *size* of the proof is the number of bits required to write these coefficients.

Polynomial calculus is similar, except the g_i's can be computed using a straight-line computation instead of being explicitly written out with all coefficients. (Recall that every polynomial can be computed by a straight-line program.) Concretely, a refutation in polynomial calculus is a finite sequence of polynomials $f_1, f_2, \ldots, f_T$ such that each f_r is either (a) one of the input polynomials p_i, (b) $\alpha f_u + \beta f_v$ where α, β are constants and

$u, v < r$, or (c) $x_i f_u$ where x_i is a variable and $u < r$. The *size* of the refutation is T and the *degree* is the maximum degree of any f_u.

Exponential lower bounds for the above two proof systems are proved by proving a lower bound of $n^{\Omega(1)}$ on the *degree*; such lower bounds were first proven in [BCE+95].

Frege and Extended Frege

The *Frege* proof system is a general system of reasoning in predicate calculus using a finite set of axiom schemes and inference rules. Resolution is a special case, where all formulas used in the proof are clauses (i.e., disjunctions). An intermediate family is *bounded depth Frege*, where all formulas used in the proof have bounded depth. Ajtai [Ajt88] gave the first lower bounds for bounded depth Frege systems using a clever restriction argument inspired by the restriction argument for **AC**0 that is described in Chapter 14.

Extended Frege is a variant whereby the proof is allowed to introduce new variables $y_1, y_2, \ldots$ and at any step declare that $y_i = \psi$ for some formula ψ. The advantage of this is that now we can use y_i as a bona-fide variable in rules such as resolution, potentially saving a lot of steps. (In general, allowing a proof system to introduce new variables can greatly add to its power.)

No lower bounds are known for Frege and Extended Frege systems, and it is known that existing techniques such as interpolation theorems will likely not work (assuming reasonable complexity assumptions such as "RSA cryptosystem is secure").

15.4 METAMATHEMATICAL MUSINGS

Several researchers suspect that the **P** versus **NP** question may be independent of the axioms of mathematics. Even if it is not independent, it sure seems difficult to prove for us. Could this question can be a source of tautologies that are difficult to prove in concrete proof systems?

For instance, consider resolution and Frege-like systems for certifying tautologies. We can try to consider the minimum proof size required for a concrete propositional formula that says "SAT instances of size n cannot be solved by circuits of size n^{100}." This formula (first defined in [Razb98]) has $O(n^{100})$ variables denoted **Z** and has the form

$$\mathbf{Z} \text{ is an encoding of an } n\text{-input circuit of size } n^{100}$$

$$\Rightarrow \text{circuit } \mathbf{Z} \text{ does not compute SAT} \tag{15.3}$$

Note that the conclusion part of (15.3) is an OR over all 2^n inputs of size n and it says that the value computed by circuit **Z** on one of these inputs is not the true value of SAT. Thus such a formula has size $2^{O(n)}$, and *we think* it is a tautology for large enough n. The trivial proof of tautologyhood has size $2^{O(n^{100})}$, however, which is *super-polynomial* in the size of the formula. Can we show that the proof complexity of this formula is super-polynomial for resolution and Frege systems? Razborov [Razb98] showed a super-polynomial lower bound for polynomial calculus. He also proposed a different encoding of the above formula for which even resolution lower bounds seemed difficult.

Raz showed that this formula is either not a tautology or requires resolution proofs of super-polynomial size [Razb01, Razb03a, Razb04a]. But similar lower bounds for much stronger systems, say Frege, have not been obtained.

Independence from weak theories of arithmetic

Most results in mathematics can be derived using popular axiomatic systems such as Zermelo-Fraenkel (with axiom of choice) or Peano arithmetic. But many results in combinatorics, since they have a more finitary character, do not seem to require the full power of these axiomatic systems. Instead, one can use weaker axiomatic systems such as the PV system of Cook [Coo75] or the "bounded arithmetic" hierarchy S_i^1 of Buss [Bus90]. Researchers who wish to prove the independence of **P** versus **NP** from say Peano arithmetic should perhaps first try to prove independence from such weaker theories. There are deep connections between these theories and the Extended Frege proof system, and lower bounds for the "circuit lower bound formulae" for Extended Frege will imply such independence (see the survey [Razb04b]).

WHAT HAVE WE LEARNED?

- Proof complexity aims at proving lower bounds on proof size for tautological formulae in various proof systems.
- If **NP** $\neq$ **coNP**, then for every complete proof and efficiently verifiable proof system there should exist tautological formulas that do not have polynomial-sized proofs.
- For some proof systems, such as Resolution, Polynomial Calculus, and Cutting Plane, there are known exponential lower bounds on proof sizes of various tautologies. However, no super-polynomial lower bounds are known for the Frege and Extended Frege proof systems.

CHAPTER NOTES AND HISTORY

Since proof systems are "nondeterministic," there is in general no obvious algorithm to produce a short proof (if one exists). Nevertheless, heuristic algorithms exist for producing short proofs for many of these systems, and these heuristics are extremely important in practice. In fact, in most cases, the definition of the proof system was inspired by the corresponding heuristic algorithm. Thus proof size lower bounds for all these proof systems prove lower bounds on *running times* of the corresponding heuristic algorithm.

For instance, the definition of resolution is inspired by the Davis-Putnam heuristic [DP60], which inspired a slew of other heuristics such as "resolve the two clauses that produces the smallest resolvent." Haken [Hak85] gave the first super-polynomial lower bounds on the running time of such heuristics; see also [Urq87, CS88] for extensions of this work.

Similarly, the definition of the cutting plane proof system by Chvatal [Chv73] was inspired by Gomory's cutting plane method [Gom63], an important heuristic in commercial software for integer programming.

Cook and Reckhow were the first to suggest the importance of proof sizes in complexity theory, and to start the research program in proof complexity. The word problem for finitely presented groups was articulated by mathematician Dehn in the early twentieth century, who gave algorithms for it in many interesting groups. Novikov showed in 1955 that the problem is undecidable in general. Recent work shows that the word problem is in **NP**-complete for some groups [SBR02], implying that the problem of deciding that a given word is *not* trivial is **coNP**-complete. See the book [BMMS00] for a survey.

The Feasible Interpolation Theorem and its use in lower bounds was developed in the string of papers [Kra94, Razb95, BPR97, Kra97, Pud97].

The polynomial calculus is related to algorithms for solving systems of polynomial equations by computing Groebner bases.

The pigeonhole principle is a source of hard-to-prove tautologies for several weak proof systems including resolution and the polynomial calculus. However, it has a polynomial sized proof in the Frege system.

See the book by Krajicek [Kra95] for an introduction to proof complexity and bounded arithmetic.

EXERCISES

15.1. Prove that if φ is an unsatisfiable CNF formula on n variables, then there exists a $2^{O(n)}$-length resolution refutation for φ.

H538

15.2. Complete the proof of Theorem 15.4 by showing:
 (a) If ψ contains the $\mathbf{z}$ variables only positively (without negations) then the algorithm for computing $I(\mathbf{c})$ can be implemented by an $O(S^2)$-sized monotone circuit.

H538

 (b) If φ contains the $\mathbf{z}$ variables only negatively (always with negations), then the algorithm for computing $I(\mathbf{c})$ can be implemented by an $O(S^2)$-sized monotone circuit.

H538

15.3. Show that both the functions φ_n and ψ_n described in the statement of Theorem 15.5 can be expressed by CNF formulas of size $O(n^2)$. Furthermore, show that the formula φ_n contains the $\mathbf{z}$ variables only positively and the formula ψ_n contains them only negatively.

15.4. Prove that the cutting plane proof system is sound and complete.

H538

15.5. Write down the tautology described in words in (15.3).

15.6. Write down a tautology expressing the pigeonhole principle mentioned in the chapter notes.

H538

CHAPTER 16

Algebraic computation models

Is Horner's rule optimal for the evaluation of a polynomial?

– Ostrowski (1954)

The Turing machine model captures computations on bits (equivalently, integers), but many natural and useful algorithms are most naturally described as operating on uncountable sets such as the real numbers $\mathbb{R}$ or complex numbers $\mathbb{C}$. A simple example is *Newton's method* for finding roots of a given real-valued function f. It iteratively produces a sequence of candidate solutions $x_0, x_1, x_2, \ldots, \in \mathbb{R}$ where $x_{i+1} = x_i - f(x_i)/f'(x_i)$. Under appropriate conditions this sequence can be shown to converge to a root of f. Likewise, a wide variety of algorithms in numerical analysis, signal processing, computational geometry, robotics, and symbolic algebra typically assume that a basic computational step involves an operation $(+, \times, /)$ in some arbitrary field $\mathbb{F}$. Such algorithms are studied in a field called *computer algebra* [vzGG99].

One could defensibly argue that allowing arbitrary field operations in an algorithm is unrealistic (at least for fields such as $\mathbb{R}$) since real-life computers can only do arithmetic using finite precision. Indeed, in practice, algorithms like Newton's method have to be carefully implemented within the constraints imposed by finite precision arithmetic. In this chapter though, we take a different approach and study models which do allow arithmetic operations on real numbers (or numbers from fields other than $\mathbb{R}$). Such an idealized model may not be directly implementable but it provides a useful approximation to the asymptotic behavior as computers are allowed to use more and more precision in their computations. Furthermore, from the perspective of lower bounds, one can hope that techniques from well-developed areas of mathematics such as algebraic geometry and topology may prove handy. As we've seen in Chapter 14, so far we have not been able to prove strong lower bounds for Boolean circuits.

EXAMPLE 16.1 *(Pitfalls awaiting designers of such models)*

Devising a meaningful, well-behaved model of algebraic computation is not an easy task: Allowing (arbitrary precision) arithmetic on real numbers as a basic step can quickly lead to unrealistically strong models. For instance, with n iterations of the basic operation $x \leftarrow x^2$ one can compute 2^{2^n}, a number with 2^n bits. In fact, Shamir has shown how to factor any integer N in poly($\log N$) time on any model that allows arithmetic (including the mod operation) with arbitrary precision (see Exercise 16.10) whereas factoring is a notoriously hard problem for classical TMs.

Furthermore, a real number can encode infinite amount of information. For example, a single real number is enough to encode the answer to every instance of SAT (or any other language, in general). Thus, we have to be careful in defining a model that allows even a single hardwired real number in its programs. By contrast, we can easily allow a normal Turing machine to have any constant number of integers built into its program.

The usual way to avoid such pitfalls is to restrict the algorithm's ability to access individual bits. Alternatively, when the goal is proving nontrivial lower bounds, it is OK to consider unrealistically powerful models. After all, lower bounds for unrealistically powerful models will apply to more realistic (and hence, weaker) models as well.

This chapter is a sketchy introduction to algebraic complexity. It introduces three algebraic computation models: algebraic circuits, algebraic computation trees, and algebraic Turing machines. The algebraic TM is closely related to the standard Turing machine model and allows us to study the issues such as decidability and complexity for inputs over arbitrary fields just we did them earlier for inputs over $\{0, 1\}$. We introduce an undecidable problem (namely, deciding membership in the Mandelbrot set) and an **NP**-complete problem (decision version of Hilbert's Nullstellensatz) in this model. In general, there seems to be a close connection between algebraic complexity and complexity in the Turing machine world; see Section 16.1.4.

Throughout this chapter, we will consider algorithms that get as input a tuple of numbers over a field or a ring $\mathbb{F}$ (typically $\mathbb{R}$ or $\mathbb{C}$). The input $(x_1, x_2, \ldots, x_n) \in \mathbb{F}^n$ is said to have size n. A *language* over a field/ring $\mathbb{F}$ is a subset of $\cup_{n \geq 1} \mathbb{F}^n$.

16.1 ALGEBRAIC STRAIGHT-LINE PROGRAMS AND ALGEBRAIC CIRCUITS

In this section we define two simple models of algebraic computation, which turn out to be equivalent. Different authors sometimes prefer one model over the other for reasons of taste or ease of notation. We will also define analogs of **P** and **NP** for these models and survey the known results, including notions of reductions and completeness for these classes.

16.1.1 Algebraic straight-line programs

An *algebraic straight-line program* over field $\mathbb{F}$ (or more generally, $\mathbb{F}$ could be a ring) is defined by analogy with Boolean straight line programs (see Note 6.4). It is reminiscent of a fragment of a standard programming language like C or C++, but it has only simple "assignment" statements; no looping or conditional (e.g., **if-then-else**) statements. The formal definition follows.

Definition 16.2 *(Algebraic straight-line program over $\mathbb{F}$)* An *algebraic straight line program* of length T with *input variables* $x_1, x_2, \ldots, x_n \in \mathbb{F}$ and *built-in constants* $c_1, c_2, \ldots, c_k \in \mathbb{F}$ is a sequence of T statements of the form $y_i = z_{i_1} \; OP \; z_{i_2}$ for

$i = 1, 2, \ldots, T$ where OP is one of the field operations $+$ or $\times$ and each of z_{i_1}, z_{i_2} is either an input variable, or a built-in constant, or y_j for $j < i$. For every setting of values to the input variables, the straight-line computation consists of executing these simple statements in order, finding values for $y_1, y_2, \ldots, y_T$. The *output* of the computation is the value of y_T. We can analogously define straight-line programs with multiple outputs.

EXAMPLE 16.3 *(Polynomial Evaluation)*

For any $a \in \mathbb{F}$ the function $\sum_i a^i x_i$ is computable by a straight-line program of length at most $3n - 2$. We provide the program with a single built-in constant, namely, a. The inputs are $x_1, x_2, \ldots, x_n$. (These inputs are being thought of as the coefficients of a degree $n - 1$ polynomial, which is being evaluated at the constant a.) Then computing $a, a^2, a^3, \ldots, a^n$ takes $n - 1$ steps. Multiplying a^i with x_i for $i = 1, 2, \ldots, n$ takes another n steps. Accumulating the sum $\sum_i a^i x_i$ takes another $n - 1$ steps.

As is clear, the model defined above is *nonuniform*, since a different straight-line program could be used for each input length. As usual, we are interested in asymptotic complexity, that is, the length (as a function of n) of the shortest family of algebraic straight-line programs that compute a family of functions $\{f_n\}$ where f_n is a function of n variables. Exercise 16.1 asks you to show that straight-line programs over GF(2) are essentially equivalent to Boolean circuits, and the same is true for circuits over any finite field. Thus, the case when $\mathbb{F}$ is infinite is usually of greatest interest.

Recall that the *degree* of a multivariate polynomial $p(x_1, \ldots, x_n)$ is defined to be the maximum degree among all its monomials, where the degree of the monomial $c \prod_i x_i^{d_i}$ is $\sum_i d_i$. As the following lemma shows, every straight-line program computes a multivariate polynomial of degree related to its length.

Lemma 16.4 *The output of a straight-line program of length T with variables $x_1, x_2, \ldots, x_n$ is a polynomial $p(x_1, x_2, \ldots, x_n)$ of degree at most 2^T.* ◇

PROOF: Follows by an easy induction. Each input variable x_i is a polynomial of degree 1, and every step either adds two previous polynomials or multiplies them. The degree of the product of two polynomials is at most the sum of their degrees. Hence the degree can at most double at each of the T steps. ∎

What if we allow the division operator $\div$ as a standard operation in a straight-line program? Since there is no way for the program to *test* a value for being nonzero, it could divide by 0 and then the output could be undefined. Another subtlety is that even division by a nonzero polynomial $p(x)$ could lead to undefined result if x is a root of p. Nevertheless, if we consider the formal object being computed, it is well-defined: The next lemma shows that this formal object is a *rational function*, that is, a function of the type $f(x_1, x_2, \ldots, x_n)/g(x_1, \ldots, x_n)$ where f, g are polynomials. The *degree* of the rational function f/g is the sum of degrees of f and g. We omit the (easy) proof.

Lemma 16.5 *If $\div$ (only by nonzero polynomials and scalars) is allowed as an elementary operation, then for every straight-line program Π of size t there exists a rational function r of degree at most 2^T that agrees with Π on every input value on which Π is defined.* $\diamond$

Strassen [Str73] gave a general method to transform programs that use division into programs that do not use this operator and have similar size, see also Remark 16.8.

16.1.2 Examples

Here are some examples of interesting functions that are computable by polynomial length algebraic straight-line programs.

Polynomial multiplication Given $(a_0, a_1, \ldots, a_n)$ and $(b_0, b_1, \ldots, b_n)$ compute the product of the polynomials $\sum_i a_i x^i$ and $\sum_j b_j x^j$, in other words the vector $(c_0, c_1, \ldots, c_{2n-1})$ where $c_k = \sum_{i+j=k} a_i b_j$. Using the ideas of Example 16.3, one obtains a trivial algorithm with straight line complexity $O(n^2)$. Using the fast Fourier transform (next example), this can be improved to $O(n \log n)$ for fields that have a primitive mth root of unity, where m is the smallest power of 2 greater than $2n$. The idea is to evaluate the polynomials at m points using the FFT, multiply these values, and use *interpolation* (inverse FFT) to recover the c_i's. A similar approach also works for all fields but with slightly higher $O(n \log n \log \log n)$ run time (Schoenhage and Strassen [SS71]).

Fast Fourier Transform The *discrete Fourier transform* of a vector $\mathbf{x} = (\mathbf{x}_0, \mathbf{x}_1, \ldots, \mathbf{x}_{n-1}) \in \mathbb{C}^n$ is the vector $M \cdot \mathbf{x}$, where M is the $n \times n$ matrix whose (i,j)th entry is ω^{ij} where ω is a primitive nth root of 1 (i.e., a complex number satisfying $\omega^n = 1$ and not satisfying $\omega^r \neq 1$ for any nonzero $r < n$). See Section 10.6.1. The trivial idea for a straight-line program is to do something like polynomial evaluation (the first example above) for each row of M where ω is a built-in constant; this would give a straight-line program of length $O(n^2)$. Surprisingly, one can do much better: There is a program of length $O(n \log n)$ to compute the discrete Fourier transform using the famous *fast Fourier transform* algorithm due to Cooley and Tukey [CT65] outlined in Section 10.6.1. It is not known if this algorithm is optimal, though Morgenstern [Mor73] has shown that it is optimal in a more restricted model where the only "built in" constants are 0, 1. Some extensions of this result are also known, see [Cha94].

Matrix Multiplication The *matrix multiplication* problem is to compute, given two $n \times n$ matrices $X = (X_{i,j})$ and $Y = (Y_{i,j})$, their product, which is the $n \times n$ matrix Z such that

$$Z_{i,j} = \sum_{k=1}^{n} X_{i,k} Y_{k,j} \qquad (16.1)$$

The equation (16.1) yields an straight-line program for this problem of size $O(n^3)$. (As mentioned above, the definition of straight-line programs can be easily generalized to handle multiple outputs.) It may seem "obvious" that this is the best one can do, as each of the n^2 outputs requires n operation to compute. However, starting with the work of Strassen in 1969 [Str69], a series of surprising new algorithms have been discovered with complexity $O(n^\omega)$ for $\omega < 3$ (see Exercise 16.4). The current record is $\omega \sim 2.376..$ [CW90]. It is known that the complexity of matric multiplication is equivalent to several other linear algebra problems (see the survey [vzG88]). Raz [Raz02] has proven that in the model where the only built-in constants are $0, 1$, straight-line programs for matrix multiplication must have size at least $\Omega(n^2 \log n)$.

Determinant The *determinant* of an $n \times n$ matrix $X = (X_{i,j})$ is defined as

$$\det(X) = \sum_{\sigma \in S_n} (-1)^{sgn(\sigma)} \prod_{i=1}^{n} X_{i,\sigma(i)}$$

where S_n is the set of all $n!$ permutations on $\{1, 2, \ldots, n\}$ and $sgn(\sigma)$ is the parity of the number of transposed pairs in σ (i.e., pairs $\langle i, j \rangle$ with $i > j$ but $\sigma(i) < \sigma(j)$). The determinant can be computed using the familiar Gaussian elimination algorithm, but in fact there are improved algorithms (see Exercise 16.6) that also have low *depth* (as defined below in Section 16.1.3).

The determinant function is a good illustration of how the polynomial defining a function may have exponentially many terms—in this case $n!$—but nevertheless be computable by a polynomial length straight-line program. The status of lower bounds for algebraic straight line programs is very bad, as the reader probably expects by now. We do know that computing the middle symmetric polynomial requires $\Omega(n \log n)$ operations but do not know of any better bounds for any *explicit* polynomial [BCS97].

16.1.3 Algebraic circuits

An *algebraic circuit* over a field $\mathbb{F}$ is defined by analogy with a Boolean circuit (see Chapter 6). It consists of a directed acyclic graph. The leaves are called *input nodes* and labeled $x_1, x_2, \ldots, x_n$; these take values in $\mathbb{F}$ rather than being Boolean variables. We also allow the circuit to have k additional special input nodes that are labeled with arbitrary constants $c_1, \ldots, x_k$ from the field. Each internal node, called a *gate*, is labeled with one of the arithmetic operations $\{+, \times\}$ rather than with the Boolean operations $\vee, \wedge, \neg$ used in Boolean circuits. We consider only circuits with a single output node and with the in-degree of each gate being 2. The *size* of the circuit is the number of gates in it. The *depth* of the circuit is the length of the longest path from input to output in it. One can also consider algebraic circuits that allow division ($\div$) at the gates. An *algebraic formula* is a circuit where each gate has out-degree equal to 1.

To evaluate a circuit, we perform each gate's operation by applying it on the numbers present on the incoming wires (= edges), and then passing this output to all its outgoing wires. The output of the circuit is the number present on the wire of its output node at the end of this process. The next lemma (left as an easy Exercise 16.7) shows that this model is equivalent to algebraic straight-line programs.

Lemma 16.6 *Let $f : \mathbb{F}^n \rightarrow \mathbb{F}$ be some function. If f has an algebraic straight line program of size S, then it has an algebraic circuit of size $3S$. If f is computable by an algebraic circuit of size S then it is computable by an algebraic straight line program of length S. Moreover, if the circuit is a formula, then the equivalent straight-line program is used once (i.e., every variable y_i that is not an input occurs on the right-hand side of an assignment only once).*   ◇

Note that the equivalence is only up to a small constant factor (3) because in a circuit we don't allow parallel edges and hence the operation $x \mapsto x^2$ will require first copying x by adding to it zero.

16.1.4 Analogs of P, NP for algebraic circuits

There are functions that are conjectured to require super-polynomial or even exponential algebraic circuit complexity. The *permanent* (see Sections 8.6.2 and 17.3.1) is one such function. For an $n \times n$ matrix X, the permanent of X is defined as

$$\mathsf{perm}(X) = \sum_{\sigma \in S_n} \prod_{i=1}^{n} X_{i,\sigma(i)}$$

At first sight seems the permanent seems very similar to the determinant. However, unlike the determinant that has a polynomial-time algorithm (and also a polynomial length algebraic straight-line program), the permanent is conjectured to not have such an algorithm. (As shown in Chapter 17, the permanent is **#P**-complete, which in particular means that it does not have a polynomial-time algorithm unless $\mathbf{P} = \mathbf{NP}$.)

Valiant [Val79a] defined analogs of **P** and **NP** for algebraic circuits, as well as as a notion of reducibility. The determinant and permanent functions turn out to play a vital role in this theory, since they are *complete* problems for the following important classes.

Definition 16.7 (AlgP$_{/\mathrm{poly}}$, AlgNP$_{/\mathrm{poly}}$)
Let $\mathbb{F}$ be a field, we say that a family of polynomials $\{p_n\}_{n \in \mathbb{N}}$ (where p_n takes n variables over $\mathbb{F}$) has *polynomially-bounded degree* if there is a constant c such that for every n the degree of p_n is at most cn^c.
The class **AlgP$_{/\mathrm{poly}}$** (or **AlgP$_{/\mathrm{poly}}^{\mathbb{F}}$** when we wish to emphasize the underlying field) contains all polynomially bounded degree families of polynomials that are computable by algebraic circuits (using no $\div$) of polynomial size and polynomial degree.
The class **AlgNP$_{/\mathrm{poly}}$** is the class of polynomially bounded degree families $\{p_n\}$ that are definable as

$$p_n(x_1, x_2, \ldots, x_n) = \sum_{e \in \{0,1\}^{m-n}} g_m(x_1, x_2, \ldots, x_n, e_{n+1}, \ldots, e_m)$$

where $g_m \in$ **AlgP$_{/\mathrm{poly}}$** and m is polynomial in n.

Many texts use the names **VP** and **VNP** for the classes **AlgP$_{/\mathrm{poly}}$** and **AlgNP$_{/\mathrm{poly}}$**, where V stands for Valiant, who defined these classes and proved several fundamental results of their properties. We chose to use the notation **AlgP$_{/\mathrm{poly}}$, AlgNP$_{/\mathrm{poly}}$** to emphasize the nonuniformity of these classes.

Remark 16.8
Disallowing the $\div$ operation in the definition of **AlgP$_{/\mathrm{poly}}$** may seem like a strong restriction, but Strassen [Str73] has shown that for infinite fields, the class **AlgP$_{/\mathrm{poly}}$**

is unchanged whether or not $\div$ is allowed. Similarly, the class $\mathbf{AlgNP}_{/\mathrm{poly}}$ is unchanged if we require g_m to have polynomial *formula* size in addition to being in $\mathbf{AlgP}_{/\mathrm{poly}}$ [Val79a].

EXAMPLE 16.9

To illustrate the definition of $\mathbf{AlgNP}_{/\mathrm{poly}}$ we show that permanent is in $\mathbf{AlgNP}_{/\mathrm{poly}}$. A permutation on $[n]$ will be represented by an $n \times n$ *permutation matrix* whose each entry is $0/1$ and whose each row/column contains exactly one 1. The crux of the proof is to express the condition that values to some n^2 variables form a permutation.

For any set of n variables $c_1, c_2, \ldots, c_n$ let the polynomial $\mathtt{Exactly\text{-}one}$ be such that for any $0/1$ assignment to the c_i's this polynomial is 1 if exactly one of c_i's is 1, and zero otherwise.

$$\mathtt{Exactly\text{-}one}(c_1, c_2, \ldots, c_n) = \sum_{i \leq n} c_i \prod_{j \neq i} (1 - c_j)$$

Now define a polynomial $\mathtt{Is\text{-}permutation}$ with n^2 binary variables σ_{ij} for $1 \leq i, j \leq n$ that verifies that each row and column contains exactly one 1.

$$\mathtt{Is\text{-}permutation}(\sigma)$$
$$= \prod_i \mathtt{Exactly\text{-}one}(\sigma_{i1}, \sigma_{i2}, \ldots, \sigma_{in}) \mathtt{Exactly\text{-}one}(\sigma_{1i}, \sigma_{2i}, \ldots, \sigma_{ni}).$$

Finally, let $\mathtt{Permpoly}$ be a polynomial of n^2 variables σ_{ij} for $1 \leq i, j \leq n$ and n^2 variables X_{ij} for $1 \leq i, j \leq n$ defined as

$$\mathtt{Permpoly}(\sigma, \mathbf{X}) = \mathtt{Is\text{-}permutation}(\sigma) \prod_i \left(\sum_j X_{ij} \sigma_{ij} \right)$$

Clearly, $\mathtt{Permpoly} \in \mathbf{AlgP}_{/\mathrm{poly}}$. Finally, the permanent of $\mathbf{X}$ can be written as

$$\sum_{\sigma \in \{0,1\}^{n^2}} \mathtt{Permpoly}(\sigma, \mathbf{X})$$

we have shown that the permanent function is in $\mathbf{AlgNP}_{/\mathrm{poly}}$.

The definition of $\mathbf{AlgNP}_{/\mathrm{poly}}$ is somewhat unexpected and merits some discussion. Valiant was motivated by the view that $+$ is the algebraic analog of the Boolean OR. Recall that a language A is in $\mathbf{NP}$ if there is a language $B \in \mathbf{P}$ such that $x \in A \Leftrightarrow \exists e$ s.t. $(x, e) \in B$. Thus the definition of $\mathbf{NP}$ involves $\exists_{e \in \{0,1\}^{m-n}}$, which is equivalent to an OR, viz., $\bigvee_{e \in \{0,1\}^{m-n}}$. The algebraic analog is the operation $\sum_{e \in \{0,1\}^{m-n}}$, and this is the defining feature of $\mathbf{AlgNP}_{/\mathrm{poly}}$. Note that this makes $\mathbf{AlgNP}_{/\mathrm{poly}}$ closer to $\#\mathbf{P}$ in spirit than to $\mathbf{NP}$.

Now we arrive at a key notion: reduction between algebraic problems that preserve algebraic circuit complexity. As usual, we want a reduction f from problem A to problem B to satisfy the property that an efficient algorithm (i.e., polynomial-length straight-line program or polynomial size circuit) for B should give us an efficient algorithm for A.

Some thought suggests that it suffices to let the reduction be an arbitrary polynomially bounded degree family that is computable by a polynomial-length straight-line program. The definition suggested by Valiant is much stricter: It requires the reduction to be an extremely trivial "change of variables." Obviously, the stricter the definition of reduction, the harder it is to prove completeness results. So the fact that such a simple reduction suffices here is surprising. (Of course, if we think about most classical **NP**-completeness results from the 1970s, they also involve simple local transformations using gadgets, instead of arbitrary polynomial-time transformations.)

Definition 16.10 *(Projection reduction)* A function $f(x_1, \ldots, x_n)$ is a *projection* of a function $g(y_1, y_2, \ldots, y_m)$ if there is a mapping σ from $\{y_1, y_2, \ldots, y_m\}$ to $\{0, 1, x_1, x_2, \ldots, x_n\}$ such that $f(x_1, x_2, \ldots, x_n) = g(\sigma(y_1), \sigma(y_2), \ldots, \sigma(y_m))$.

We say that f is *projection-reducible* to g if f is a projection of g. ◇

EXAMPLE 16.11

The function $f(x_1, x_2) = x_1 + x_2$ is projection reducible to $g(y_1, y_2, y_3) = y_1^2 y_3 + y_2$ since $f(x_1, x_2) = g(1, x_1, x_2)$.

One way to think of a projection reduction is that if we had a silicon chip for computing g then we could convert it to a chip for f by appropriately hardwiring its input wires, feeding either some x_i or 0 or 1 into each input wire. The next theorem shows that a chip for the determinant or permanent would be fairly "universal" in that it can be made to compute large families of other functions. Its proof uses clever gadget constructions and is omitted here.

Theorem 16.12 *(Completeness of determinant and permanent [Val79a])*
For every field $\mathbb{F}$ and every polynomial family on n variables that is computable by an algebraic formula of size u is projection reducible to the determinant function (over the same field) on $u + 2$ variables.

For every field except those that have characteristic 2, every polynomial family in $\mathbf{AlgNP}_{/poly}$ *is projection reducible to the permanent function (over the same field) with polynomially more variables.*

Moreover, it was shown by Valiant et al. [VSBR81] that every function in $\mathbf{AlgP}_{/poly}$ has an algebraic formula of size $2^{O(\log^2 n)}$ (see also Exercise 16.6). Thus separating $\mathbf{AlgP}_{/poly}$ and $\mathbf{AlgNP}_{/poly}$ will follow from the following purely mathematical conjecture that makes no mention of computation.

Conjecture 16.13 *(Valiant)* For every field that does not have characteristic 2, the $n \times n$ permanent cannot be obtained as a projection of the $m \times m$ determinant where $m = 2^{O(\log^2 n)}$.

Conjecture 16.13 is a striking example of the close connection between computational complexity and interesting questions in pure mathematics. Another intriguing fact is that it is necessary to show $\mathbf{AlgP}_{/poly} \neq \mathbf{AlgNP}_{/poly}$ before one can show $\mathbf{P} \neq \mathbf{NP}$ (see chapter notes).

16.2 ALGEBRAIC COMPUTATION TREES

Now we move to a more powerful computational model, the algebraic computation tree. This can be defined for computations over an arbitrary ring (see the comments after Definition 16.15), but for simplicity we define it for for computations on real-valued inputs. This model augments the straight-line program model (with $\div$) with the ability to do conditional branches based upon whether or not a variable y_v is greater than 0. Depending upon the result of this comparison, the computation proceeds in one of two distinct directions. Thus the overall structure is a binary tree rather than a straight line (as the name suggests). The ability to branch based upon a variable value is somewhat reminiscent of a Boolean decision tree of Chapter 12, but here the variables (indeed, also the input) are real numbers instead of bits.

Formally, the model can be used to solve *decision problems* on real inputs; it computes a Boolean-valued function $f : \mathbb{R}^n \to \{0, 1\}$ (i.e., a language).

EXAMPLE 16.14 *(Some decision problems)*

The following examples illustrate some of the languages (over real numbers) whose complexity we might want to study.

Element Distinctness Given n numbers $x_1, x_2, \ldots, x_n$, determine whether they are all distinct. This is equivalent to the question whether $\prod_{i \neq j}(x_i - x_j) \neq 0$.

Real-valued subset sum Given a list of n real numbers $x_1, \ldots, x_n$, determine whether there is a subset $S \subseteq [n]$ such that $\sum_{i \in S} x_i = 1$.

As motivation for the definition of the model, consider the trivial algorithm for Element Distinctness: sort the numbers in $O(n \log n)$ steps and then check in another $O(n)$ steps if any two adjacent numbers in the sorted order are the same. Is this trivial algorithm actually optimal, or can we solve the problem in $o(n \log n)$ steps? The answer must clearly depend on the computational model we allow. The *algebraic computation tree* model studied in this section is powerful enough to implement known algorithms for the problem. As we will see in Section 16.2.1 below, it turns out that in this model the above trivial algorithm for Element Distinctness is optimal up to constant factors.

Recall that comparison-based sorting algorithms only ask questions of the type "Is $x_i > x_j$?", which is the same as asking whether $x_i - x_j > 0$. The left-hand side term of this last inequality is a linear function. We can imagine other algorithms that may use more complicated functions. In *Algebraic Computation Trees*, we allow (a) the ability to use any rational function and (b) the introduction of new variables together with the ability to do arithmetic on them and ask questions about them. The *cost* is the number of arithmetic operations and branching steps on the worst case input.

Definition 16.15 *(Algebraic Computation Tree over* $\mathbb{R}$*)* An *algebraic computation tree* is a way to represent a function $f : \mathbb{R}^n \to \{0, 1\}$ by showing how to compute $f(x_1, x_2, \ldots, x_n)$ for any input vector $(x_1, x_2, \ldots, x_n)$. It is a binary tree where each of the nodes is of one of the following types:

- Leaf labeled "Accept" or "Reject".
- Computation node v labeled with y_v, where $y_v = y_u$ OP y_w and y_u, y_w are either one of $\{x_1, x_2, \ldots, x_n\}$ or the labels of ancestor nodes and the operator OP is in $\{+, -, \times, \div, \sqrt{\ }\}$.
- Branch node with out-degree 2. The branch that is taken depends on the evaluation of some condition of the type $y_u = 0$ or $y_u \geq 0$ or $y_u \leq 0$ where y_u is either one of $\{x_1, x_2, \ldots, x_n\}$ or the labels of an ancestor node in the tree.

The computation on any input $(x_1, x_2, \ldots, x_n)$ follows a single path from the root to a leaf, evaluating functions at internal nodes (including branch nodes) in the obvious way, until it reaches a leaf. It reaches a leaf marked "Accept" iff $f(x_1, x_2, \ldots, x_n) = 1$. The complexity of the computation on the path is measured using the following costs (which reflect real-life costs to some degree):

- $+, -$ are free.
- $\times, \div, \sqrt{\ }$ and branch nodes are charged unit cost.

The *depth* of the tree is the maximum cost of any path in it.

This definition allows $\sqrt{\ }$ as an elementary operation, which may not make sense for all fields (such as the rational numbers). The notion of algebraic computation tree extends to arbitrary ordered fields by omitting the $\sqrt{\ }$ as an operation. The notion also extends to fields that are not ordered by only allowing decision nodes that have a two-way branch based upon whether or not a variable is $= 0$.

A fragment of an algebraic computation tree is shown in Figure 16.1.

Definition 16.16 *(Algebraic computation tree complexity)* Let $f : \mathbb{R}^n \to \{0, 1\}$. The *algebraic computation tree complexity* of f is

$$AC(f) = \min_{\substack{\text{computation} \\ \text{tree } T \text{ for } f}} \{\text{depth of } T\}$$

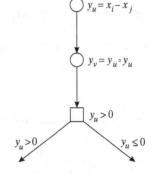

Figure 16.1. An algebraic computation tree.

The algebraic computation tree model is much more powerful than a real-life programming language. The reason is that a tree of depth d could have 2^d nodes, so a depth d algebraic computation tree would yield (in the worst case) only a classical algorithm with a description of size 2^d. This is why the following theorem (whose proof we omit) does not imply an efficient algorithm for the **NP**-complete subset sum problem:

Theorem 16.17 *(Meyer auf der Heide [adH88]) The real-number version of* SUBSET SUM *can be solved using an algebraic computation tree of depth $O(n^5)$.*   ◇

This theorem suggests that algebraic computation trees are best used to investigate lower bounds such as $n \log n$ or n^2 rather than something more ambitious like a super-polynomial lower bound for the real-number version of SUBSET SUM.

16.2.1 The topological method for lower bounds

To prove lower bounds for the minimum cost of an algebraic computation tree algorithm for a function f, we will use the *topology* of the sets $f^{-1}(1)$ and $f^{-1}(0)$, specifically, the number of connected components.

Definition 16.18 *(Connected components)* A set $S \subseteq \mathbb{R}^n$ is *connected* if for all $\mathbf{x}, \mathbf{y} \in S$ there is path p from $\mathbf{x}$ to $\mathbf{y}$ that lies entirely in S (in other words, a continuous function mapping $[0, 1] \subseteq \mathbb{R}$ to $\mathbb{R}^n$ such that $f(0) = \mathbf{x}, f(1) = \mathbf{y}$, and $f(t) \in S$ for all $t \in [0, 1]$). A *connected component* of $W \subseteq \mathbb{R}^n$ is a connected subset of W that is not a proper subset of any other connected subset of W. We let $\#(W)$ denote the number of connected components of W.   ◇

The following theorem relates the number of connected components to the algebraic computation tree complexity.

Theorem 16.19 *(Topological lower bound on algebraic tree complexity [BO83])*
For every $f : \mathbb{R}^n \to \{0, 1\}$,

$$AC(f) = \Omega\Big(\log\left(\max\left\{\#(f^{-1}(1)), \#(\mathbb{R}^n \setminus f^{-1}(1))\right\}\right) - n\Big)$$

Before proving this theorem, let us first use it to prove the promised lower bound for Element Distinctness. This bound follow directly from the following theorem, since $\log n! = \Omega(n \log n)$.

Theorem 16.20 *Let $W = \{(x_1, \ldots, x_n) \mid \prod_{i \neq j} (x_i - x_j) \neq 0\}$. Then,*

$$\#(W) \geq n!$$ ◇

PROOF: For each permutation σ let

$$W_\sigma = \{(x_1, \ldots, x_n) \mid x_{\sigma(1)} < x_{\sigma(2)} < \ldots < x_{\sigma(n)}\}$$

That is, let W_σ be the set of n-tuples $(x_1, \ldots, x_n)$, which respect the (strict) order given by σ. Note that $W_\sigma \subseteq W$ for all σ. It suffices to prove for all $\sigma' \neq \sigma$ that the sets W_σ and $W_{\sigma'}$ are not connected.

For any two distinct permutations σ and σ', there exist two distinct i, j with $1 \leq i, j \leq n$, such that $\sigma^{-1}(i) < \sigma^{-1}(j)$ but $\sigma'^{-1}(i) > \sigma'^{-1}(j)$. Thus, in W_σ we have $X_j - X_i > 0$, while in $W_{\sigma'}$ we have $X_i - X_j > 0$. Consider any path from W_σ to $W_{\sigma'}$. Since $X_j - X_i$ has different signs at the endpoints, the intermediate value principle says that somewhere along the path this term must become 0. That point can belong in neither W_σ nor $W_{\sigma'}$, so Definition 16.18 then implies that W_σ and $W_{\sigma'}$ cannot be connected. ∎

Now we turn to the proof of Theorem 16.19. This theorem is proved in two steps. First, we try to identify the property of functions with algebraic computation tree complexity: They can be defined as solution sets of a "few" systems of equations.

Lemma 16.21 *If $f : \mathbb{R}^n \to \{0, 1\}$ has a decision tree of depth d then $f^{-1}(1)$ (and also $f^{-1}(0)$) is a union of at most 2^d sets $C_1, C_2, \ldots, \subseteq \mathbb{R}^n$ where C_i can be described as follows: There is a system of up to d equations of the form*

$$p_{i_r}(y_1, \ldots, y_d, x_1, \ldots, x_n) \bowtie 0$$

where p_{i_r} for $r \leq d$ is a degree 2 polynomial, $\bowtie$ is in $\{\leq, \geq, =, \neq\}$, and $y_1, \ldots, y_d$ are new variables. Then C_i is the set of $(x_1, x_2, \ldots, x_n)$ for which there are some $y_1, y_2, \ldots, y_d$ such that $(y_1, \ldots, y_d, x_1, \ldots, x_n)$ is a solution to the above system. Additionally, we may assume without loss of generality (at the cost of doubling the number of y_i's) that there are no $\neq$ constraints in this system of equations. ◇

PROOF: The tree has 2^d leaves, so it suffices to associate a set C_i with each leaf, which is the set of $(x_1, x_2, \ldots, x_n)$ that end up at that leaf. Associate a variable $y_1, y_2, \ldots, y_d$ with the (at most) d computation or branching nodes appearing along the path from root to this leaf. For each computation node, we associate an equation with it in the obvious way (see Figure 16.2). For example, if the node computes $y_v = y_u \div y_w$, then it implies

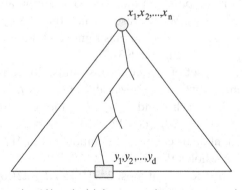

Figure 16.2. A computation path p of length d defines a set of constraints over the n input variables x_i and d additional variables y_j, which correspond to the nodes on p.

the constraint $y_v y_w - y_u = 0$. For each branch node, we associate an obvious inequality. Thus any $(x_1, x_2, \ldots, x_n)$ that end up at the leaf is a vector for which there exist values of $y_1, y_2, \ldots$, such that the combined vector is a solution to this system of d equations and inequalities.

To replace the "$\neq$" constraints with "$=$" constraints we take a constraint like

$$p_i(y_1, \ldots, y_m) \neq 0$$

introduce a new variable z_i and impose the constraint

$$q_i(y_1, \ldots, y_m, z_i) \equiv 1 - z_i p_i(y_1, \ldots, y_m) = 0$$

(This transformation, called Rabinovitch's trick, holds for all fields.) Notice, the maximum degree of the constraint remains 2 because the trick is used only for the branch $y_u \neq 0$ which is converted to $1 - z_v y_u = 0$.

Similarly, the constraint $p_i(y_1, \ldots, y_m) > 0$ is handled by introducing a new variable z_i and imposing the constraint $p_i(y_1, \ldots, y_m) = z_i^2$. ∎

We find Rabinovitch's trick useful also in Section 16.3.2 where we prove a completeness result for Hilbert's Nullstellensatz.

Now to prove lower bounds on $AC(W)$ via the topological argument, we need some result about the number of connected components of the set of solutions to an algebraic system. The following is a central result in mathematics.

Theorem 16.22 *(Consequence of Milnor-Thom Theorem)* *If $S \subseteq \mathbb{R}^n$ is defined by degree d constraints with m equalities and h inequalities then*

$$\#(S) \leq d(2d-1)^{n+h-1} \qquad \diamond$$

Note that the above upper bound is independent of m. Now we can prove Ben-Or's Theorem.

PROOF OF THEOREM 16.19: Suppose that the depth of a computation tree for W is d, so that there are at most 2^d leaves. We will use the fact that if $S \subseteq \mathbb{R}^n$ and $S|_k$ is the set of points in S with their last $n - k$ coordinates removed (i.e., projection on the first k coordinates) then $\#(S|_k) \leq \#(S)$ (Figure 16.3).

For every leaf there is a set of degree 2 constraints. So, consider a leaf ℓ and the corresponding constraints C_ℓ, which are in variables $y_1, \ldots, y_d, x_1, \ldots, x_n$. Let $W_\ell \subseteq \mathbb{R}^n$ be the subset of inputs that reach ℓ and $S_\ell \subseteq \mathbb{R}^{n+d}$ the set of points that satisfy the constraints C_ℓ. Note that $W_\ell = C_\ell|_n$ (i.e., W_ℓ is the projection of C_ℓ onto the first n coordinates). So, the number of connected components in W_ℓ is upperbounded by $\#(C_\ell)$. By Theorem 16.22 it holds that $\#(C_\ell) \leq 2 \cdot 3^{n+d-1} \leq 3^{n+d}$. Therefore the total number of connected components is at most $2^d 3^{n+d}$, so $d \geq \Omega(\log(\#(W))) - O(n)$. By repeating the same argument for $\mathbb{R}^n - W$ we have that $d \geq \Omega(\log(\#(\mathbb{R}^n - W))) - O(n)$. ∎

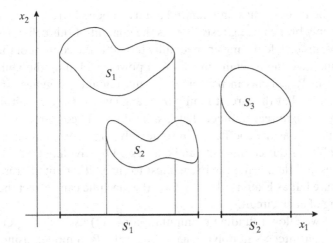

Figure 16.3. Projection can merge but not add connected components.

16.3 THE BLUM-SHUB-SMALE MODEL

The models for algebraic complexity introduced so far were *nonuniform*. Now we introduce a *uniform* model due to Blum, Shub, and Smale [BSS89]. This involves Turing machines that compute over some arbitrary field or ring $\mathbb{F}$ (e.g., $\mathbb{F} = \mathbb{R}, \mathbb{C}, GF(2)$); the input is a string in $\mathbb{F}^n$ for $n \geq 1$ and the output is Accept/Reject. Each cell can hold an element of $\mathbb{F}$, and, initially, all but a finite number of cells are "blank." Thus the model is a generalization of the standard Turing machine model with bit operations, which can be seen as operating over the field $GF(2)$; see Exercise 16.9. The machine has a finite set of internal states. Each state belongs to one of the following three categories:

- *Shift state:* Move the head to the left or to the right of the current position.
- *Branch state:* If the content of the current cell is a, then goto state q_1 else goto state q_2.
- *Computation state:* This state has a hard-wired function f associated with it. When the machine is in this state, it reads the contents of the current cell, say $a \in \mathbb{F} \cup \{\text{blank}\}$, and replaces it with a new value $f(a)$. If $\mathbb{F}$ is a ring, f is a polynomial over $\mathbb{F}$, whereas if $\mathbb{F}$ is a field, then we allow f to be any rational function of the form g/h where g, h are polynomials and h is nonzero. In either case, f is represented using a constant number of elements of $\mathbb{F}$. These can be viewed as "hard-wired" constants for the machine.

Note that in our standard model of the TM, the computation and branch operations can be executed in the same step, whereas here they have to be performed separately. This is purely for notational ease. But, now in order to branch, the machine has to be able to "remember" the value it just read one step ago. For this reason the machine has a single "register" onto which it can copy the contents of the cell currently under the head, and whose value can be used in the next step.

Like other models for algebraic complexity we have studied, the BSS model seems more powerful than real-world computers. For instance, by repeating the operation $x \leftarrow x^2$, the BSS machine can compute and store in one cell (without overflow) the number x^{2^n} in n steps.

However, the machine has only limited ability to benefit from such computations because it can only branch using tests like "Is the content of this cell equal to a?" The slight variant of this test, featuring an inequality test—"Is the content of the cell greater than a?"—would give the machine much more power, including the ability to decide every language in $\mathbf{P}_{/poly}$ (thus in particular, an undecidable language) in polynomial time. The reason is that the circuit family of a language in $\mathbf{P}_{/poly}$ circuit family can be represented by a *single* real number that is a hard-wired "constant" into the Turing machine (specifically, as the coefficient of some polynomial $p(x)$ belonging to a state). The individual bits of this coefficient can be accessed by dividing by 2 an appropriate number of times and then using the branch test to check if the number is greater than 0. (The details are left as Exercise 16.12.) Thus the machine can extract the polynomial length encoding of each circuit.

Similarly, if we allow rounding (computation of $\lfloor x \rfloor$) as a basic operation then it is possible to factor integers in polynomial time on the BSS model, using the ideas of Shamir mentioned earlier (see Exercise 16.10).

Note also that the BSS model is closely related to a more classical model: algebraic circuits with "branch" gates and a "uniformity" condition (so the circuits for different input sizes have to be constructible by some conventional Turing machine). This is analogous to the connection between conventional TMs and uniform boolean circuits shown in Chapter 6.

16.3.1 Complexity classes over the complex numbers

It is now time to define some complexity classes related to the BSS model. For simplicity we restrict attention to machines over the field $\mathbb{C}$. As usual, the complexity of these Turing machines is defined with respect to the input size (i.e., number of cells occupied by the input). The following complexity classes correspond to $\mathbf{P}$ and $\mathbf{NP}$ over $\mathbb{C}$.

Definition 16.23 $(\mathbf{P}_{\mathbb{C}}, \mathbf{NP}_{\mathbb{C}})$ $\mathbf{P}_{\mathbb{C}}$ contains every language over $\mathbb{C}$ that can be decided by a BSS Turing machine over $\mathbb{C}$ in polynomial time. A language L is said to be in $\mathbf{NP}_{\mathbb{C}}$ if there exists a language $L_0 \in \mathbf{P}_{\mathbb{C}}$ and a number $d > 0$, such that an input x is in L iff there exists a string $(y_1, \ldots, y_{n^d})$ in $\mathbb{C}^{n^d}$ such that (x, y) is in L_0.   ◇

It is also interesting to study the complexity of standard languages (i.e., whose inputs are bit strings) with respect to this model. Thus we make the following definition:

$$0\text{-}1\text{-}\mathbf{NP}_{\mathbb{C}} = \{L \cap \{0, 1\}^* \mid L \in \mathbf{NP}_{\mathbb{C}}\}$$

Note that the input for a $0\text{-}1\text{-}\mathbf{NP}_{\mathbb{C}}$ machine is binary but the nondeterministic "witness" may consist of complex numbers. Trivially, $\mathbf{NP}$ is a subset of $0\text{-}1\text{-}\mathbf{NP}_{\mathbb{C}}$. The reason is that even though the "witness" for the BSS machine consists of a string of complex numbers, the machine can first check if they are all 0 or 1 using equality checks. Having verified that the witness is actually a Boolean string, the machine continues as a normal Turing machine to verify it.

Is $0\text{-}1\text{-}\mathbf{NP}_{\mathbb{C}}$ much larger than $\mathbf{NP}$? We know that that $0\text{-}1\text{-}\mathbf{NP}_{\mathbb{C}} \subseteq \mathbf{PSPACE}$. In 1997 Koiran [Koi97] proved that if one assumes the Riemann hypothesis, then $0\text{-}1\text{-}\mathbf{NP}_{\mathbb{C}} \subseteq \mathbf{AM}$. As shown in Chapter 20 (see Exercise 20.7), under reasonable assumptions $\mathbf{AM} = \mathbf{NP}$ so Koiran's result suggests that it's likely that $0\text{-}1\text{-}\mathbf{NP}_{\mathbb{C}} = \mathbf{NP}$.

16.3.2 Complete problems and Hilbert's Nullstellensatz

The language $\mathbf{HN}_{\mathbb{C}}$ is defined as the decision version of Hilbert's Nullstellensatz over $\mathbb{C}$. (We encountered this principle in Section 2.7, and it also appears in Section 15.3.) The input consists of m polynomials $p_1, p_2, \ldots, p_m$ of degree d over $x_1, \ldots, x_n$. The output is "yes" iff the polynomials have a common root $a_1, \ldots, a_n$. Note that this problem is general enough to encode SAT, since we can represent each clause by a polynomial of degree 3:

$$x \vee y \vee z \leftrightarrow (1-x)(1-y)(1-z) = 0$$

Next we use this fact to prove that the language $0\text{-}1\text{-}\mathbf{HN}_{\mathbb{C}}$ (where the polynomials have 0-1 coefficients) is complete for $0\text{-}1\text{-}\mathbf{NP}_{\mathbb{C}}$.

Theorem 16.24 ([BSS89]) $0\text{-}1\text{-}\mathbf{HN}_{\mathbb{C}}$ *is complete for* $0\text{-}1\text{-}\mathbf{NP}_{\mathbb{C}}$. ◇

PROOF SKETCH: It is straightforward to verify that $0\text{-}1\text{-}\mathbf{HN}_{\mathbb{C}}$ is in $0\text{-}1\text{-}\mathbf{NP}_{\mathbb{C}}$. To prove the hardness part we imitate the proof of the Cook-Levin Theorem (Theorem 2.10). Recall that there we reduced every **NP**-computation into an AND of many *local* tests, each depending on only a constant number of variables. Here, we do the same, reasoning as in the case of algebraic computation trees (see Lemma 16.21) that we can express these local checks with polynomial constraints of bounded degree. The computation states $c \leftarrow q(a,b)/r(a,b)$ are easily handled by setting $p(c) \equiv q(a,b) - cr(a,b)$. For the branch states $p(a,b) \neq 0$ we can use Rabinovitch's trick to convert them to equality checks $q(a,b,z) = 0$. Thus the degree of our constraints depends upon the degree of the polynomials hard-wired into the machine. Also, the polynomial constraints use real coefficients (involving real numbers hard-wired into the machine). Converting these polynomial constraints to use only 0 and 1 as coefficients requires work. The idea is to show that the real numbers hard-wired into the machine have no effect since the input is a binary string. We omit this argument here. ■

16.3.3 Decidability Questions: Mandelbrot Set

Since the Blum-Shub-Smale model is more powerful than the ordinary Turing machine, it makes sense to also revisit decidability questions. In this section we mention an interesting undecidable problem for this model: membership problem for the *Mandelbrot set*, a famous fractal. The chapter notes mention one motivation for studying such questions, connected to Roger Penrose's claim that artificial intelligence is impossible.

Definition 16.25 *(Mandelbrot set decision problem)* Let $P_C(Z) = Z^2 + C$. Then, the Mandelbrot set is defined as

$$\mathcal{M} = \{ C \in \mathbb{C} \mid \text{the sequence } P_C(0), P_C(P_C(0)), P_C(P_C(P_C(0)))\ldots \text{ is bounded} \}$$

◇

Note that the complement of $\mathcal{M}$ is recognizable if we allow inequality constraints. This is because the sequence is unbounded iff some number $P_C^k(0)$ has complex magnitude greater than 2 for some k (exercise!), and this can be detected in finite time. However, detecting that $P_C^k(0)$ is bounded for every k seems harder. Indeed, we have the following theorem.

Theorem 16.26 $\mathcal{M}$ *is undecidable by a machine over* $\mathbb{C}$.   ◇

PROOF SKETCH: The proof uses some mathematical tools that are beyond the scope of this book and hence we only give a rough sketch here. The proof uses the topology of the Mandelbrot set and the notion of *Hausdorff* dimension. A *ball* of radius r in a metric space is a set of the form $B(x_0, r) = \{y : \text{dist}(x_0, y) < r\}$. Very roughly speaking, the Hausdorff dimension of a space is d if as $r \to 0$, then the minimum number of balls of radius r required to cover a set grows as $1/r^d$ as r goes to 0.

Let $\mathcal{N}$ be any TM over the complex numbers that supposedly decides this set. Consider T steps of the computation of this TM. Reasoning as in Theorem 16.24 and in our theorems about algebraic computation trees, we conclude (see also Exercise 16.11) that the sets of inputs accepted in T steps is a finite union of semialgebraic sets (i.e., sets defined using solutions to a system of polynomial equations). Hence the language accepted by $\mathcal{N}$ is a countable union of semialgebraic sets, which is known to imply that its Hausdorff dimension is 1. But it is known that the Mandelbrot set has Hausdorff dimension 2, hence $\mathcal{M}$ cannot decide it. ∎

WHAT HAVE WE LEARNED?

- It is possible to study computational complexity in more algebraic settings where a basic operation is over a field or ring. We saw analogs of Boolean circuits, straight-line programs, decision trees, and Turing machines.
- One can define *complete* problems in some algebraic complexity classes and even study decidability.
- Proving lower bounds for algebraic computation trees involves interesting topological methods involving the number of connected components in the set of solutions to a system of polynomial equations.
- There are interesting connections between algebraic complexity and the notions of complexity used in the rest of the book. Two examples: (a) Valiant's result that the permanent is complete for **AlgNP$_{/\text{poly}}$**; (b) complexity classes defined using the BSS model of TMs using complex-valued inputs have connections to standard complexity classes.

CHAPTER NOTES AND HISTORY

It is natural to consider the minimum number of arithmetic operations required to produce a desired output from the input. The first formalization of this question appears to be by A. Scholz in 1937 [Sch37], roughly contemporaneous with Turing's work on undecidability. The notion of a straight-line program goes back to Ostrowski's [Ost54] investigation of the optimality of Horner's rule for evaluating a polynomial. The formal definitions of the straight-line program and algebraic computation tree models first appear in Strassen [Str72] and Rabin [Rab72], respectively, though Rabin restricted attention to linear functions instead of general polynomials. The work of Strassen in the 1960s and 1970s did much to establish algebraic complexity theory. Volume 2 of Knuth's book from 1969 [Knu69] gives a nice survey of the state of knowledge at that time. Algebraic computation trees attracted attention in computational geometry, where three-way branching on a linear function can be interpreted as the query that asks wheter a point $x \in \mathbb{R}^n$ is on the hyperplane defined by the linear function, or to the left/right of it.

The classes $\mathbf{AlgP}_{/poly}$ and $\mathbf{AlgNP}_{/poly}$ were defined by Valiant [Val79a], though he used the term "$\mathbf{P}$-definable" for $\mathbf{AlgNP}_{/poly}$ and $\mathbf{AlgP}$ for $\mathbf{AlgP}_{/poly}$. Later works also used the names $\mathbf{VNP}$ and $\mathbf{VP}$ for these classes. The theory was fleshed out by Skyum and Valiant [SV85], who also gave an extension of Valiant's theory of completeness via projections to the standard $\mathbf{NP}$ class. This extension relies on the observation that the Cook-Levin reduction itself is a projection reduction. One interesting consequence of this extended theory is that it shows $\mathbf{AlgP}_{/poly}? = \mathbf{AlgNP}_{/poly}$ must necessarily be resolved before resolving $\mathbf{P}? = \mathbf{NP}$.

The $\mathbf{NC}$ algorithm for computing the determinant mentioned in Section 16.1.4 is due to Csanky [Csa76]. It works for fields of characteristic 0. Many generalizations of this algorithm exist. The fact that determinant has algebraic formulas of size $2^{poly(\log n)}$ is due to Valiant et al. [VSBR81]. In fact, they show a general transformation of any algebraic circuit of size S computing a polynomial f to a circuit computing f of depth $O(\log S \log \deg(f))$. (The depth of a circuit is, as usual, the length of longest path from input to output in the graph.)

The problem of proving lower bounds on algebraic computation trees has a long history, and Ben-Or's theorem (Theorem 16.19) falls somewhere in the middle of it. More recent work by Bjorner et al. [BLY92] and Yao [Yao94] shows how to prove lower bounds for cases where the $\#(W)$ parameter is small. These rely on other topological parameters associated with the set, such as Betti numbers.

A general reference on algebraic complexity (including algorithms and lower bounds) is the 1997 book by Bürgisser et al. [BCS97]. A good modern survey of computer algebra is the book by von zur Gathen and Gerhad [vzGG99].

One important topic not covered in the chapter is Strassen's lower bound technique for algebraic circuits based upon the notion of *degree* of an algebraic variety. It leads to optimal $\Omega(n \log n)$ lower bounds for several problems. A related topic is the famous Baur-Strassen Lemma, which shows that one can compute the partial derivatives of f in the same resources required to compute f. See [BCS97] for details on both.

The best survey of results on the BSS model is the book by Blum et al. [BCSS97]. The question of decidability of the Mandelbrot fractal set is from Roger Penrose's controversial criticism of artificial intelligence [Pen89]. The full story of this debate is long, but in a nutshell, one of the issues Roger Penrose raised was that humans have an intuitive grasp of many things that seem beyond the capabilities of the Turing machine model. He mentioned computation over $\mathbb{R}$ – exemplified by our definition of the Mandelbrot set – as an example. He suggested that such mathematical objects are beyond the purview of computer science – he suggested that one cannot talk about the decidability of such sets. The BSS work shows that actually such questions can be easily studied using simple variations of the TM model. A careful evaluation of the BSS model appears in a recent survey of Braverman and Cook [BC06], who point out some of its conceptual limitations and propose modeling real computations using a bit-based model (i.e., closer to the standard TM).

EXERCISES

16.1. Show for every finite field $\mathbb{F}$ there is a constant c such that for every Boolean function $f : \{0, 1\}^n \rightarrow \{0, 1\}$ with Boolean circuit complexity S, the size of the smallest algebraic circuit over $\mathbb{F}$ that computes S is between S/c and $c \cdot S$.

16.2. Sketch the $O(n \log n)$ size straight-line program for the fast Fourier transform.

16.3. Sketch an algorithm for multiplying two degree n univariate polynomials with complex coefficients in $O(n \log n)$ operations ($+$ and $\times$) over the complex numbers.

16.4. ([Str69])
   (a) Prove that for every $\omega > 2$, if there *exists* $k \in \mathbb{N}$ and an algebraic straight-line program Π_k that computes the matrix multiplication of $k \times k$ matrices using at most k^ω multiplication gates, then for *every* $n \in \mathbb{N}$ there is an algebraic straight-line program of size $O(n^\omega)$ that computes matrix multiplication for $n \times n$ matrices.
   H538
   (b) Prove that there exists an algebraic straight-line program that uses seven multiplication gates and computes the matrix multiplication of 2×2 matrices. Conclude that there is an algebraic straight-line program of size $O(n^{2.81})$ for multiplying $n \times n$ matrices.
   H538

16.5. Prove that any function that can be computed by an algebraic circuit of depth d can be computed by an algebraic *formula* of size $O(2^d)$.

16.6. ([Berch]) In this exercise we show a small depth polynomial-size algebraic circuit for the determinant. Such a circuit can also be obtained by following the Gaussian elimination and using Stassen's [Str73] technique of eliminating division operations.
   (a) Show that there is an $O(n^3)$-size algebraic circuit of $O(\log n)$ depth to multiply two $n \times n$ matrices.
   (b) Show that for every $i \in [n]$ there is an $O(n^3)$-size algebraic circuit of depth $O(\log^2 n)$ that computes M^i for any $n \times n$ matrix M.
   (c) Recall that for a matrix A, the characteristic polynomial p_A is defined as $p_A(x) = \det(A - xI)$, prove that if $A = \begin{smallmatrix} A_{1,1} & \mathbf{r} \\ \mathbf{c} & M \end{smallmatrix}$, (where M is an $(n-1) \times (n-1)$ matrix, $\mathbf{r}$ is an $(n-1)$-dimensional row vector, $\mathbf{c}$ is an $(n-1)$-dimensonal column vector) then $p_A = Cp_M$ (treating p, q as column vectors ordered from highest to lowest coefficient), where C is the following $(n-1) \times n$ matrix:

$$C_{i,j} = \begin{cases} 0 & i < j \\ 1 & i = j \\ -A_{1,1} & i = j+1 \\ -\mathbf{r}M^{i-j-2}\mathbf{c} & i \geq j+2 \end{cases}$$

H538

(d) Prove that the determinant can be computed by an algebraic circuit of size poly(n) and depth $O(\log^2 n)$. (By making various optimizations the size of the circuit can be made as small as $O(n^{\omega+1+\epsilon})$ for every constant $\epsilon > 0$, where ω is the number such that there is an $O(n^\omega)$-sized $O(\log n)$ depth algebraic circuit for matrix multiplication.)

16.7. Prove Lemma 16.6.

16.8. Suppose we are interested in the problem of computing the number of Hamilton cycles in graphs. Model this as an algebraic computational problem and show that this function is in **AlgNP**$_{/\text{poly}}$.

H538

16.9. Show that the BSS model over the field GF(2) is equivalent to the standard TM model.

16.10. (Shamir [Sha79]) Show that any computational model that allows arithmetic (including "mod" or integer division) on arbitrarily large numbers can factor any given integer n in poly($\log n$) time.

H539

16.11. Show that if a function $f : \mathbb{R}^n \to \{0, 1\}$ can be computed in time T on algebraic TM then it has an algebraic computation tree of depth $O(T)$.

16.12. Prove that if we give the BSS model (over $\mathbb{R}$) the power to test "$a > 0$?" with arbitrary precision, then all of **P**$_{/\text{poly}}$ can be decided in polynomial time.

H539

PART THREE ADVANCED TOPICS

CHAPTER 17 Complexity of counting

It is an empirical fact that for many combinatorial problems the detection of the existence of a solution is easy, yet no computationally efficient method is known for counting their number ... for a variety of problems this phenomenon can be explained.

– L. Valiant, 1979

The class **NP** captures the difficulty of finding *certificates*. However, in many contexts, one is interested not just in a single certificate but actually in counting the *number* of certificates. This chapter studies **#P** (pronounced "sharp p"), a complexity class that captures this notion.

Counting problems arise in diverse fields such as statistical estimation, statistical physics, network design, and economics, often in situations having to do with estimations of probability. Counting problems are also studied in a field of mathematics called *enumerative combinatorics*, which tries to obtain closed-form mathematical expressions for counting problems. To give an example, in 1847 Kirchoff showed how the resistance of a network can be determined by counting the number of *spanning trees* in it, for which he gave a formula involving a simple determinant computation. Results in this chapter will show that for many other natural counting problems, such efficiently computable expressions are unlikely to exist.

In Section 17.1 we give an informal introduction to counting problems and how they arise in statistical estimation. We also encounter an interesting phenomenon: A counting problem can be difficult even though the corresponding decision problem is easy.

Then in Section 17.2 we initiate a formal study of counting problems by defining the class **#P**. The quintessential problem in this class is #SAT, the problem of counting the number of satisfying assignments to a Boolean formula. We then introduce **#P**-completeness and prove the **#P**-completeness of an important problem, computing the *permanent* of a 0, 1 matrix.

We then consider whether **#P** is related to the concepts we have studied before. Section 17.4 shows a surprising result of Toda: an oracle for #SAT can be used to solve every problem in **PH** in polynomial time. The proof involves an interesting probabilistic argument, even though the statement of the theorem involves no probabilities.

17.1 EXAMPLES OF COUNTING PROBLEMS

In counting problems the output is a *number* rather than just $0, 1$ as in a decision problem. Counting analogs of the usual decision problems are of great interest in complexity theory. We list a couple of examples.

- #CYCLE is the problem of computing, given a directed graph G, the number of simple cycles in G. (A simple cycle is one that does not visit any vertex twice.) The corresponding decision problem of deciding if the graph has a cycle is trivial and can be solved in linear time.
- #SAT is the problem of computing, given a Boolean formula ϕ, the number of satisfying assignments for ϕ. Here of course, the corresponding decision problem is **NP**-complete, so presumably the counting problem is even harder.

17.1.1 Counting problems and probability estimation

Counting problems often arise in situations where we have to do estimations of probability.

EXAMPLE 17.1

In the GraphReliability problem we are given a directed graph on n nodes. Suppose we are told that each node can fail with probability $1/2$ and want to compute the probability that node 1 has a path to n.

A moment's thought shows that under this simple node failure model, the remaining graph is uniformly chosen at random from all induced subgraphs of the original graph. Thus the correct answer is

$$\frac{1}{2^n} (\text{number of subgraphs in which node 1 has a path to } n)$$

Again, it is trivial to determine the *existence* of a path from 1 to n.

EXAMPLE 17.2 *(Maximum likelihood estimation in Bayes Nets)*

Suppose some data is generated by a probabilistic process but some of the data points are missing. This setting is considered in a variety of fields including machine learning and economics. In *maximum likelihood estimation* we try to come up with the most likely value of the missing data points.

A simple model of data generation is *Bayes Net*, and we restrict attention to a particularly simple example of a Bayes Net. There are n *hidden* variables $x_1, \ldots, x_n \in \{0, 1\}$, whose values are picked be nature by tossing n fair random coins independently. These values are *hidden* from us. The values actually available to us are m *visible* random variables $y_1, y_2, \ldots, y_n$, each of which is an OR of up to 3 hidden variables or their negations. We observe that all of $y_1, y_2, \ldots, y_n$ are 1. We now have to estimate the a posteriori probabilty that x_1 is 1.

Of course, a complexity theorist can immediately realize that an OR of three literals is a $3CNF$ clause, and thus recast the problem as follows: We are given a $3CNF$ Boolean formula with n variables and m clauses. What is the fraction of satisfying assignments that have $x_1 = 1$? This problem turns out to be equivalent to #SAT (see Exercise 17.1 and also the chapter notes).

EXAMPLE 17.3 *(Estimation problems in statistical physics)*

One of the most intensively studied models in statistical physics is the *Ising model*, introduced in the 1920s by Lenz and Ising to study ferromagnetism. An instance of the model is given by a set of *n sites*, a set of *interaction energies* V_{ij} for each unordered pair of sites i, j, a *magnetic field intensity B*, and an *inverse temperature β*. A *configuration* of the system defined by these parameters is one of 2^n possible assignments σ of ± 1 spins to each site. The *energy* of a configuration σ is given by the *Hamilton $H(\sigma)$* defined by

$$H(\sigma) = -\sum_{\{i,j\}} V_{ij}\sigma_i\sigma_j - B\sum_k \sigma_k. \tag{17.1}$$

The interesting part of this sum is the first term, consisting of a contribution from pairs of sites. The importance of this expression comes from the *Gibbs distribution*, according to which the probability that the system is in configuration σ is proportional $\exp(-\beta H(\sigma))$. This implies that the probability of configuration σ is $1/Z \times \exp(-\beta H(\sigma))$, where the normalizing factor Z, called the *partition function* of the system, is

$$Z = \sum_{\sigma \in \{1,1\}^n} \exp(-\beta H(\sigma))$$

Computing the partition function exactly also turns out to be equivalent to #SAT (see chapter notes).

17.1.2 Counting can be harder than decision

What is the complexity of #SAT and #CYCLE? Clearly, if #SAT has a polynomial-time algorithm, then SAT $\in$ **P** and so **P** = **NP**. How about #CYCLE? The corresponding decision problem—given a directed graph decide if it has a cycle—can be solved in linear time by breadth-first-search. The next theorem suggests that the counting problem may be much harder.

Theorem 17.4 *If #CYCLE has a polynomial-time algorithm, then* **P** = **NP**. ◇

PROOF: We show that if #CYCLE can be computed in polynomial time, then Ham $\in$ **P**, where Ham is the **NP**-complete problem of deciding whether or not a given digraph has a Hamiltonian cycle (i.e., a simple cycle that visits all the vertices in the graph). Given a graph G with n vertices, we construct a graph G' such that G has a Hamiltonian cycle iff G' has at least n^{n^2} cycles.

To obtain G', replace each edge (u, v) in G by the gadget shown in Figure 17.1. The gadget has $m = n \log n$ levels. It is an acyclic digraph, so cycles in G' correspond to

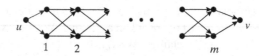

Figure 17.1. Reducing Ham to #CYCLE: by replacing every edge in G with the above gadget to obtain G', every simple cycle of length ℓ in G becomes $(2^m)^\ell$ simple cycles in G'.

cycles in G. Furthermore, there are 2^m directed paths from u to v in the gadget, so a simple cycle of length ℓ in G yields $(2^m)^\ell$ simple cycles in G'.

Notice, if G has a Hamiltonian cycle, then G' has at least $(2^m)^n > n^{n^2}$ cycles. If G has no Hamiltonian cycle, then the longest cycle in G has length at most $n - 1$. The number of cycles is bounded above by n^{n-1}. So G' can have at most $(2^m)^{n-1} \times n^{n-1} < n^{n^2}$ cycles. ■

17.2 THE CLASS #P

We now try to capture the above counting problems using the complexity class **#P**. Note that it contains functions whose output is a natural number, and not just 0/1.

Definition 17.5 (#P) A function $f : \{0, 1\}^* \to \mathbb{N}$ is in **#P** if there exists a polynomial $p : \mathbb{N} \to \mathbb{N}$ and a polynomial-time TM M such that for every $x \in \{0, 1\}^*$:

$$f(x) = \left| \left\{ y \in \{0, 1\}^{p(|x|)} : M(x,y) = 1 \right\} \right|.$$

Of course, the definition implies that $f(x)$ can be expressed using poly($|x|$) bits.

As in the case of **NP**, we can also define **#P** using nondeterministic TMs. That is, **#P** consists of all functions f such that $f(x)$ is equal to the number of paths from the initial configuration to an accepting configuration (in brief, "accepting paths") in the *configuration graph* $G_{M,x}$ of a polynomial-time NDTM M on input x (see Section 4.1.1). Clearly, all the counting problems in Section 17.1 fall in this class.

The big open question regarding **#P** is whether all problems in this class are efficiently solvable. We define **FP** to be the set of functions from $\{0, 1\}^*$ to $\{0, 1\}^*$ (equivalently, from $\{0, 1\}^*$ to $\mathbb{N}$) computable by a deterministic polynomial-time Turing machine, is the analog of efficiently computable functions (i.e., the analog of **P** for functions with more than one bit of output). Then the question is whether **#P** = **FP**. Since computing the number of certificates is at least as hard as finding out whether a certificate exists, if **#P** = **FP**, then **NP** = **P**. We do not know whether the other direction also holds: whether **NP** = **P** implies that **#P** = **FP**. We do know that if **PSPACE** = **P**, then **#P** = **FP**, since counting the number of certificates can be done in polynomial space.

17.2.1 The class PP: Decision-problem analog for #P

Similar to the case of search problems, even when studying counting complexity, we can often restrict our attention to *decision problems*. The following is one such problem.

Definition 17.6 (**PP**) A language L is in **PP** if there exists a polynomial-time TM M and a polynomial $p : \mathbb{N} \to \mathbb{N}$ such that for every $x \in \{0, 1\}^*$,

$$x \in L \Leftrightarrow \left| \left\{ u \in \{0, 1\}^{p(|x|)} : M(x, u) = 1 \right\} \right| \geq \frac{1}{2} \cdot 2^{p(|x|)} \qquad \diamond$$

That is, for x to be in L it does not need just one certificate (as is the case in **NP** – see Definition 2.1) but rather a *majority* of certificates.

Lemma 17.7 **PP** = **P** $\Leftrightarrow$ **#P** = **FP**. $\diamond$

PROOF: The nontrivial direction is that if **PP** = **P**, then **#P** = **FP**. Let f be a function in **#P**. Then there is some polynomial-time TM M such that for every input x, $f(x)$ is the number $\#_M(x)$ of strings $u \in \{0, 1\}^m$ such that $M(x, u) = 1$, where m is some polynomial in $|x|$ that is the length of certificates that M takes.

For every two TM's M_0, M_1 taking m-bit certificates, denote in this proof by "$M_0 + M_1$" the TM M' that takes $n + 1$ bit certificate where $M'(x, bu) = M_b(x, u)$. Then $\#_{M_0+M_1}(x) = \#_{M_0}(x) + \#_{M_1}(x)$. Also, for $N \in \{0 \ldots 2^m\}$, we denote by M_N the TM that on input x, u outputs 1 iff the string u, when considered as a number, is smaller than N. Clearly $\#_{M_N}(x) = N$. If **PP** = **P** then we can determine in polynomial-time if

$$\#_{M_N+M}(x) = N + \#_M(x) \geq 2^m \tag{17.2}$$

Thus to compute $\#_M(x)$ we can use binary search to find the smallest N that satisfies (17.2), which will equal $2^m - \#_M(x)$. ■

Intuitively speaking, **PP** corresponds to computing the most significant bit of functions in **#P**: if the range is $[0, N - 1]$, we have to decide whether the function value is $\geq N/2$. One can also consider decision problems corresponding to the *least* significant bit; this is called $\oplus$**P** (see Definition 17.15).

Another related class is **BPP** (see Chapter 7), where we are guaranteed that the fraction of accepting paths of an NDTM is either $\geq 2/3$ or $\leq 1/3$ and have to determine which is true. But **PP** seems very different from **BPP** because the fraction of accepting paths in the two cases could be $\geq 1/2$ or $\leq 1/2 - \exp(-n)$, and the lack of a "gap" between the two cases means that random sampling would require $\exp(n)$ trials to distuinguish between them. (By contrast, the sampling problem for **BPP** is easy, and we even think it can be replaced by a deterministic algorithm; see Chapter 20.)

17.3 #P COMPLETENESS

Now we define **#P**-completeness. Loosely speaking, a function f is **#P**-complete if it is in **#P**, and a polynomial-time algorithm for f implies that **#P** = **FP**. To formally define **#P**-completeness, we use the notion of *oracle* TMs, as defined in Section 3.4. Recall that a TM M has *oracle access* to a language $O \subseteq \{0, 1\}^*$ if it can make queries of the form "Is $q \in O$?" in one computational step. We generalize this to non-Boolean functions by saying that M has oracle access to a function $f : \{0, 1\}^* \to \{0, 1\}^*$, if it is given access to the language $O = \{\langle x, i \rangle : f(x)_i = 1\}$. We use the same notation for functions mapping $\{0, 1\}^*$ to $\mathbb{N}$, identifying numbers with their binary representation as strings. For a function $f : \{0, 1\}^* \rightarrow \{0, 1\}^*$, we define $\mathbf{FP}^f$ to be the set of functions that are computable by polynomial-time TMs that have oracle access to a function f.

Definition 17.8 A function f is **#P**-*complete* if it is in **#P** and every $g \in$ **#P** is in $\mathbf{FP}^f$. $\diamond$

If $f \in \mathbf{FP}$ then $\mathbf{FP}^f = \mathbf{FP}$. Thus the following is immediate.

Proposition 17.9 *If f is* **#P**-*complete and $f \in$ **FP**, then* **FP** = **#P**. $\diamond$

Counting versions of many **NP**-complete languages such as $3\mathsf{SAT}$, Ham, and CLIQUE naturally lead to **#P**-complete problems. We demonstrate this with $\#\mathsf{SAT}$.

Theorem 17.10 $\#\mathsf{SAT}$ *is* **#P**-*complete.* $\diamond$

PROOF: Consider the Cook-Levin reduction from any L in **NP** to SAT we saw in Section 2.3. This is a polynomial-time computable function $f : \{0, 1\}^* \rightarrow \{0, 1\}^*$ such that for every $x \in \{0, 1\}^*$, $x \in L \Leftrightarrow f(x) \in \mathsf{SAT}$. However, the proof that the reduction works actually gave us more information than that. In Section 2.3.6 we saw that it provides a *Levin reduction*, by which we mean the proof showed a way to transform a *certificate* that x is in L into a certificate (i.e., satisfying assignment) showing that $f(x) \in \mathsf{SAT}$, and also vice versa (transforming a satisfying assignment for $f(x)$ into a witness that $x \in L$).

In fact, for the reduction in question, this mapping from the certificates of x to the assignments of $f(x)$ is one-to-one and onto (i.e., a bijection). Thus the number of satisfying assignments for $f(x)$ is equal to the number of certificates for x. Such reductions are called *parsimonious*. (More generally, the definition of a parsimonius reduction allows the witness mapping to be k-to-1 or 1-to-k, so the number of witnesses for the two problems are still the same up to scaling by k. ∎

As shown below, there are **#P**-complete problems for which the corresponding decision problems are in fact in **P**.

17.3.1 Permanent and Valiant's Theorem

Now we study another problem. The *permanent* of an $n \times n$ matrix A is defined as

$$\mathsf{perm}(A) = \sum_{\sigma \in S_n} \prod_{i=1}^{n} A_{i,\sigma(i)} \qquad (17.3)$$

where S_n denotes the set of all permutations of n elements. Recall that the expression for the determinant is similar

$$\det(A) = \sum_{\sigma \in S_n} sgn(\sigma) \prod_{i=1}^{n} A_{i,\sigma(i)}$$

except for an additional "sign" term (see Section A5). This similarity does not translate into computational equivalence: The determinant can be computed in polynomial-time, whereas computing the permanent seems much harder, as we see below. (For another perspective on the hardness of the permanent, see Chapter 16.)

The permanent function can also be interpreted combinatorially. First, suppose the matrix A has each entry in $\{0,1\}$. Then it may be viewed as the adjacency matrix of a bipartite graph $G(X, Y, E)$, with $X = \{x_1, \ldots, x_n\}$, $Y = \{y_1, \ldots, y_n\}$ and $\{x_i, y_j\} \in E$ iff $A_{i,j} = 1$. For each permutation σ the term $\prod_{i=1}^{n} A_{i,\sigma(i)}$ is 1 iff σ is a *perfect matching* (which is a set of n edges such that every node is in exactly one edge). Thus if A is a $0,1$ matrix, then $\mathrm{perm}(A)$ is simply the number of perfect matchings in the corresponding graph G. Note that the whether or not a perfect matching *exists* can be determined in polynomial-time. In particular, computing $\mathrm{perm}(A)$ is in **#P**. If A is a $\{-1,0,1\}$ matrix, then $\mathrm{perm}(A) = \left| \{\sigma : \prod_{i=1}^{n} A_{i,\sigma(i)} = 1\} \right| - \left| \{\sigma : \prod_{i=1}^{n} A_{i,\sigma(i)} = -1\} \right|$. Thus one can make two calls to a $\#$SAT oracle to compute $\mathrm{perm}(A)$. Finally, if A has general integer entries (possibly negative) the combinatorial view of $\mathrm{perm}(A)$ is as follows. Consider matrix A as the the adjacency matrix of a weighted n-node complete digraph with self loops and 0 edge weights allowed. Associate with each permutation σ a *cycle cover*, which is a subgraph on the same set of vertices but only a subset of the original edges, where each node has in-degree and out-degree 1. Such a subgraph must decompose into disjoint cycles. The *weight* of the cycle cover is the product of the weights of the edges in it. Then $\mathrm{perm}(A)$ is equal to the sum of weights of all possible cycle covers. Using this observation one can show that computing the permanent is in **FP**$^{\#\mathsf{SAT}}$ (see Exercise 17.2).

The next theorem came as a surprise to researchers in the 1970s, since it implies that if $\mathrm{perm} \in$ **FP**, then **P** = **NP**. Thus, unless **P** = **NP**, computing the permanent is much more difficult then computing the determinant.

Theorem 17.11 *(Valiant's Theorem* [Val79b]*)*
perm *for* $0,1$ *matrices is* **#P**-*complete.*

Theorem 17.11 involves very clever gadget constructions. As warmup, we introduce a simple idea.

Convention: In drawings of gadgets in the rest of the chapter, the underlying graph is a complete digraph, but edges that are missing from the figure have weight 0 and hence can be ignored while considering cycle covers. Unmarked edges have weight $+1$. We will also sometimes allow *parallel edges* (with possibly different weights) from a node to another node. This is not allowed per se in the definition of permanent, where there is a single edge of weight $A_{i,j}$ from i to j. But since we are describing reductions, we have the freedom to later replace each parallel edge of weight w by a path of length 2 whose two edges of weight 1 and w. This just requires adding a new node (not connected to anything else) in the middle of each parallel edge.

EXAMPLE 17.12

Consider the graph in Figure 17.2. Even without knowing what the subgraph G' is, we show that the permanent of the whole graph is 0. For each cycle cover in G' of weight

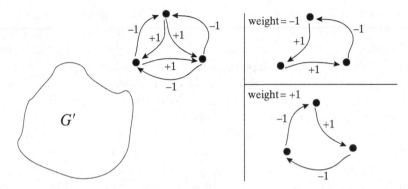

Figure 17.2. The above graph G consists of two vertex-disjoint subgraphs, one called G' and the other is the "gadget" shown. The gadget has only two cycle covers of nonzero weight, namely, weight -1 and 1. Hence the total weight of cycle covers of G is zero regardless of the choice of G', since for every cycle cover of weight w in G', there exist two covers of weight $+w$ and $-w$ in the graph G.

w there are exactly two cycle covers for the three nodes, one with weight $+w$ and one with weight $-w$. Any nonzero weight cycle cover of the whole graph is composed of a cycle cover for G' and one of these two cycle covers. Thus the sum of the weights of all cycle covers of G is 0.

PROOF OF VALIANT'S THEOREM (THEOREM 17.11): We reduce the **#P**-complete problem #3SAT to perm. Given a Boolean $3CNF$ formula ϕ with n variables and m clauses, first we shall show how to construct an integer matrix, or equivalently, a weighted digraph G', with some negative entries such that $\mathrm{perm}(G') = 4^{3m} \cdot (\#\phi)$, where $\#\phi$ stands for the number of satisfying assignments of ϕ. Later we shall show how to to get a digraph G with weights $0, 1$ from G' such that knowing $\mathrm{perm}(G)$ allows us to compute $\mathrm{perm}(G')$.

The main idea is that our construction will result in two kinds of cycle covers in the digraph G': those that correspond to satisfying assignments of ϕ (we will make this precise) and those that don't. Using reasoning similar to that used in Example 17.12, we will use negative weights to ensure that the contribution of the cycle covers that do not correspond to satisfying assignments cancels out. On the other hand, we will show that each satisfying assignment contributes 4^{3m} to $\mathrm{perm}(G')$, and so $\mathrm{perm}(G') = 4^{3m} \cdot (\#\phi)$.

To construct G' from ϕ, we combine three kinds of gadgets shown in Figure 17.3. There is a variable gadget for each variable, a clause gadget for each clause, and a way to connect them using gadgets called *XOR* gadgets. All are shown in Figure 17.3.

XOR gadget. Suppose we have a weighted digraph H and wish to ensure for some pair of edges $\overrightarrow{u\,u'}$ and $\overrightarrow{v\,v'}$, *exactly one* of these edges is present in any cycle cover that counts towards the final sum. To do so, we can construct a new digraph H' in which this pair of edges is replaced by the XOR gadget of Figure 17.3.

Every cycle cover of H of weight w that uses exactly one of the edges $\overrightarrow{u\,u'}$ and $\overrightarrow{v\,v'}$ is mapped to a set of cycle covers in H' whose total weight is $4w$ (i.e., the set of covers that enter the gadget at u and exit at u' or enter it at v and exit at v'), while all the other cycle covers of H' have total weight 0 (this uses reasoning similar to Example 17.12, see Exercise 17.3).

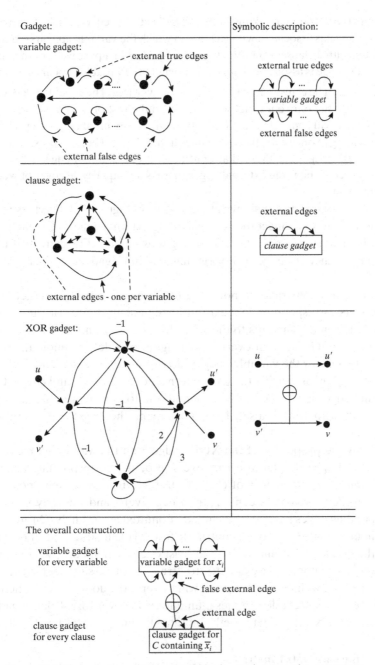

Figure 17.3. The gadgets used in the proof of Valiant's Theorem (Theorem 17.11).

Variable gadget. The variable gadget has both *internal edges* (that are not involved with any other part of the graph) and *external edges* (that will be connected via XOR gadgets to other edges of the graph). We partition the external edges to "true" edges and "false" edges. The variable gadget has only two possible cycle covers, corresponding to an assignment of 0 or 1 to that variable. Assigning 1 corresponds to using cycle taking all the "true" external edges, and covering all other vertices with self loops. Similarly, assigning 0 correspond to taking all the "false" external edges. Each external edge of a variable gadget is associated with a clause in which the variable appears—a true edge is associated with a clause where the variables appears in a positive (non-negated) form, while a false edge is associated with a clause where the variable appears in negated form.

Clause gadget. The clause gadget consists of four vertices. The edges labeled with "external edge" are the only ones that will connect to the rest of the graph. Specifically, the external edge will connect via a XOR gadget with an external edge of a variable gadget corresponding to one of the three variables in the clause. The only possible cycle covers of the clause gadget are those that omit at least one external edge. Also for a given proper subset of the three external edges there is a unique cycle cover of weight 1 that contains them.

The overall construction is shown at the bottom of Figure 17.3. If a clause C contains the variable x, then we connect the corresponding external edge of C's gadget with the corresponding (true) external edge of x's gadget using the XOR gadget (if C contains the negation of x, then the edge corresponding to X in x's gadget will be a false external edge).

To analyze this construction, note that because each variable gadget has exactly two cycle covers corresponding to the 0 and 1 assignments, there is a one-to-one correspondence between assignments to the variables $x_1, \ldots, x_n$ and the cycle covers of the variable gadgets of G'. Now for every such assignment $\mathbf{x}$, let $C_\mathbf{x}$ denote the set of cycle covers in G' that cover the variable gadgets according to the assignment $\mathbf{x}$. That is, we cover variable x_i's gadget using the true external edges if $x_i = 1$ and cover it using the false external edges if $x_i = 0$. Let $w(\mathbf{x})$ denote the total weight of assignments in $C_\mathbf{x}$. It suffices to show that if $\mathbf{x}$ is a satisfying assignment, then $w(\mathbf{x}) = 4^{3m}$, and if $\mathbf{x}$ is not satisfying, then $w(\mathbf{x}) = 0$.

Indeed, by the properties of the XOR gadget and the way we connected clauses and variables, if $x_i = 1$ then in cycle covers in $C_\mathbf{x}$ the corresponding external edge has to be *omitted* in the gadget of every clause in which x_i appears positively, and has to be *included* for clauses containing x_i negatively, and similarly if $x_i = 0$ then the corresponding edges have to be included or omitted accordingly. (More accurately, covers without this property do not contribute toward the final sum.) But because every cover for the clause gadget has to omit at least one external edge, we see that unless every clause has a literal that evaluates to "true" in the assignment $\mathbf{x}$ (i.e., unless $\mathbf{x}$ satisfies ϕ) the total weight of covers in $C_\mathbf{x}$ will be zero. If $\mathbf{x}$ does satisfy φ, then this total weight will be 4^{3m} (since $\mathbf{x}$ determines a unique cycle cover for all clause gadgets that passes through the XOR gadget exactly $3m$ times). Thus $\mathrm{perm}(G') = 4^{3m}(\#\phi)$.

Reducing to the case of 0,1 matrices

This transformation goes in two steps. First we create a graph G'' with edge weights in $\{-1, 0, 1\}$ and the same permanent as G'. Then we remove negative weights to create a graph G whose permanent contains enough information to compute $\mathrm{perm}(G') = \mathrm{perm}(G'')$. The transformations may blow up the number of vertices by a factor $O(nL^2 \log n)$, where L is the number of *bits* required to describe all the weights in G'.

Notice that an edge whose weight is a power of 2, say 2^k, can be replaced by a path (consisting of new nodes not connected to anything else) of k edges, each of weight 2. Similarly, an edge whose weight is $2^k + 2^{k'}$ can be replaced by two parallel paths of weight 2^k and $2^{k'}$ respectively. Combining these observations, we can replace an edge whose weight is not a power of 2 by a set of parallel paths determined by its binary expansion; the total number of nodes in these paths is quadratic in the number of bits required to represent the original weight. This gives a graph G'' with weights in $\{-1, 0, 1\}$ and at most $O(L^2)$ new vertices.

To get rid of the negative weights, we use modular arithmetic. The permanent of an n-vertex graph with edge weights in $\{\pm 1\}$ is a number x in $[-n!, +n!]$ and hence it suffices to compute this permanent modulo $2^m + 1$ where $m = n^2$. But $-1 \equiv 2^m \pmod{2^m + 1}$, so the permanent modulo $2^m + 1$ is unchanged if we replace all weight -1 edges with edges of weight 2^m. Such edges can be replaced by an unweighted subgraph of size $O(m) = O(n \log n)$ as before. Thus we obtain a graph G with all weights $0, 1$ and whose permanent can be used to compute the original permanent (specifically, by taking the remainder modulo $2^m + 1$). The number of new vertices is at most $O(nL^2 \log n)$. ∎

17.3.2 Approximate solutions to #P problems

Since computing exact solutions to **#P**-complete problems is presumably difficult, a natural question is whether we can *approximate* the number of certificates in the sense of the following definition.

Definition 17.13 Let $f : \{0, 1\}^* \to \mathbb{N}$ and $\alpha < 1$. An algorithm A is an α-*approximation* for f if for every x, $\alpha f(x) \le A(x) \le f(x)/\alpha$.   ◇

Not all **#P** problems behave identically with respect to this notion. Approximating certain problems within any constant factor $\alpha > 0$ is **NP**-hard (see Exercise 17.4). For other problems such as 0/1 permanent, there is a *fully polynomial randomized approximation scheme* (FPRAS), which is an algorithm that, for any ϵ, δ, computes a $(1-\epsilon)$-approximation to the function with probability $1-\delta$ (in other words, the algorithm is allowed to give an incorrect answer with probability δ) in time $\text{poly}(n, \log 1/\delta, \log 1/\epsilon)$. Such approximation of counting problems is sufficient for many applications, in particular those where counting is needed to obtain estimates for the probabilities of certain events (e.g., see our discussion of the graph reliability problem in Example 17.1). Interestingly, if $\mathbf{P} = \mathbf{NP}$, then *every* **#P** problem has an FPRAS (and in fact an FPTAS: i.e., a *deterministic* polynomial-time approximation scheme); see Exercise 17.5.

Now we explain the basic idea behind the approximation algorithm for the permanent—as well as other similar algorithms for a host of **#P**-complete problems. This is only a sketch; the chapter notes contain additional references.

One result that underlies these algorithms is due to Jerrum, Valiant and Vazirani [JVV86]. It shows that under fairly general conditions there is a close connection (in the sense the two are interreducible in polynomial time) between

1. Having an approximate formula for the size of a set S and
2. Having an efficient algorithm for generating a uniform random (or approximately uniform) element of S

The basic idea is a counting version of the *downward self-reducibility* idea we saw in Chapter 2.

Suppose we are trying to use sampling to do approximate counting and S is a subset of $\{0, 1\}^n$. Let $S = S_0 \cup S_1$ where S_b is the subset of strings in S whose first bit is 1. By sampling a few random elements of S we can estimate $p_1 = |S_1| / |S|$ up to some reasonabable accuracy. Then we fix the first bit of the string and use our algorithm recursively to estimate $|S_1|$ and multiply it by our estimate of $1/p_1$ to obtain an estimate $|S|$.

To produce a random sample from S using approximate counting, one again proceeds in a bit-by-bit fashion and reverses the above argument. First we estimate $|S_1|$, $|S|$ and use their ratio to estimate p_1. Produce a bit b by tossing a random coin with bias p_1 (i.e., if the coin comes up heads make the bit 1 else make it 0). Then make b the first bit of the sample and recursively use the same algorithm to produce a sample from S_b.

The main point is that to do approximate counting it suffices to draw a random sample from S. All the algorithms try to sample from S using the *Markov Chain Monte Carlo* method. One defines a connected d-uniform digraph on S and does a random walk on this graph. Since the graph is d-regular for some d, the stationary distribution of the walk is uniform on S. Under appropriate conditions on the expansion of the graph (establishing which is usually the meat of the argument) the walk "mixes," and the sample becomes close to uniform.

17.4 TODA'S THEOREM: $\mathbf{PH} \subseteq \mathbf{P}^{\#SAT}$

An important open question in the 1980s concerned the relative power of the polynomial-hierarchy $\mathbf{PH}$ and the class of counting problems $\#\mathbf{P}$. Both are natural generalizations of $\mathbf{NP}$, but it seemed that their features—alternation and the ability to count certificates, respectively—are not directly comparable to each other. Thus it came as big surprise when in 1989 Toda showed the following theorem.

Theorem 17.14 *(Toda's Theorem* [Tod91]*)*
$\mathbf{PH} \subseteq \mathbf{P}^{\#SAT}$.

That is, we can solve any problem in the polynomial hierarchy given an oracle to a $\#\mathbf{P}$-complete problem.

Note that we already know, even without Toda's Theorem, that if $\#\mathbf{P} = \mathbf{FP}$ then $\mathbf{NP} = \mathbf{P}$ and so $\mathbf{PH} = \mathbf{P}$. However, this does not imply that any problem in $\mathbf{PH}$ can be computed in polynomial-time using an oracle to $\#SAT$. For example, one implication of Toda's Theorem is that a *subexponential* (i.e., $2^{n^{o(1)}}$-time) algorithm for $\#SAT$ will imply such an algorithm for any problem in $\mathbf{PH}$. Such an implication is not known to hold from a $2^{n^{o(1)}}$-time algorithm for SAT.

To prove Toda's Theorem, we first consider formulas with an *odd* number of satisfying assignments. The following is the underlying complexity class.

Definition 17.15 A language L is in the class $\oplus\mathbf{P}$ (pronounced "parity P") iff there is a polynomial time NTM M such that $x \in L$ iff the number of accepting paths of M on input x is odd.   ⋄

As in the proof of Theorem 17.10, the fact that the standard **NP**-completeness reduction is parsimonious implies the following problem $\oplus SAT$ is $\oplus\mathbf{P}$-complete (under many-to-one Karp reductions).

Definition 17.16 *($\oplus$ quantifier and $\oplus SAT$)* Define the quantifier $\oplus$ as follows: For every Boolean formula φ on n variables $\bigoplus_{x\in\{0,1\}^n} \varphi(x)$ is true if the number of x's such that $\varphi(x)$ is true is odd.[a] The language $\oplus SAT$ consists of all the true quantified Boolean formula of the form $\bigoplus_{x\in\{0,1\}^n} \varphi(x)$ where φ is an unquantified Boolean formula (not necessarily in CNF form).

---

[a] Note that if we identify true with 1 and 0 with false, then $\bigoplus_{x\in\{0,1\}^n} \varphi(x) = \sum_{x\in\{0,1\}^n} \varphi(x) \pmod 2$. Also note that $\bigoplus_{x\in\{0,1\}^n} \varphi(x) = \bigoplus_{x_1\in\{0,1\}} \cdots \bigoplus_{x_n\in\{0,1\}} \varphi(x_1,\ldots,x_n)$.

$\oplus\mathbf{P}$ can be considered as the class of decision problems corresponding to the least significant bit of a **#P**-problem. One imagines that therefore it is not too powerful. For instance, it is even unclear whether we can reduce **NP** to this class. The first half of Toda's proof shows, surprisingly, a *randomized* reduction from **PH** to $\oplus SAT$. The second half is going to be a clever "derandomization" of this reduction, and is given in Section 17.4.4.

Lemma 17.17 *(Randomized reduction from **PH** to $\oplus SAT$) Let $c \in \mathbb{N}$ be some constant. There exists a probabilistic polynomial-time algorithm A that given a parameter m and any quantified Boolean formula ψ of size n with with c levels of alternations, runs in* $poly(n,m)$ *times and satisfies*

$$\psi \text{ is true} \Rightarrow \Pr[A(\psi) \in \oplus SAT] \geq 1 - 2^{-m}$$

$$\psi \text{ is false} \Rightarrow \Pr[A(\psi) \in \oplus SAT] \leq 2^{-m}$$

Of course, to reduce **PH** to $\oplus SAT$ we better first figure out how to reduce **NP** to $\oplus SAT$, which is already unclear. This will involve a detour into Boolean formulas with unique satisfying assignments.

17.4.1 A detour: Boolean satisfiability with unique solutions

Suppose somebody gives us a Boolean formula and promises us that it has either no satisfying assignment, or a unique satisfying assignment. Such formulas arise if we encode some classic math problems using satisfiability (see, e.g., the number-theoretic DISCRETE LOG problem in Chapter 9 that is the basis of some encryption schemes). Let $USAT$ be the language of Boolean formulas that have a unique satisfying assignment. Is it still difficult to decide satisfiability of such special instances (in other words, to answer "yes" if the formula is in $USAT$ and "no" if the formula is in $\overline{SAT}$, and an arbitrary answer in every other case)? The next result of Valiant and Vazirani shows that if we had a polynomial-time algorithm for this problem, then **NP** = **RP**. This was a surprise to most researchers in the 1980s.

Theorem 17.18 *(Valiant-Vazirani Theorem* [VV86])
There exists a probabilistic polynomial-time algorithm f such that for every n-variable Boolean formula φ

$$\varphi \in \mathsf{SAT} \Rightarrow \Pr[f(\varphi) \in \mathsf{USAT}] \geq \frac{1}{8n}$$

$$\varphi \notin \mathsf{SAT} \Rightarrow \Pr[f(\varphi) \in \mathsf{SAT}] = 0$$

We emphasize that the conclusion in the second part is not just that $f(\varphi) \notin \mathsf{USAT}$ but in fact $f(\varphi) \notin \mathsf{SAT}$.

The proof of Theorem 17.18 uses the following lemma on pairwise independent hash functions, which were introduced in Section 8.2.2.

Lemma 17.19 *(Valiant-Vazirani Lemma) Let $\mathcal{H}_{n,k}$ be a pairwise independent hash function collection from $\{0, 1\}^n$ to $\{0, 1\}^k$ and $S \subseteq \{0, 1\}^n$ such that $2^{k-2} \leq |S| \leq 2^{k-1}$. Then*

$$\Pr_{h \in_R \mathcal{H}_{n,k}} [\text{there is a unique } x \in S \text{ satisfying } h(x) = 0^k] \geq \frac{1}{8}$$

$\diamond$

PROOF: For every $x \in S$, let $p = 2^{-k}$ be the probability that $h(x) = 0^k$ when $h \in_R \mathcal{H}_{n,k}$. Note that for every $x \neq x'$, $\Pr[h(x)=0^k \wedge h(x')=0^k] = p^2$. Let N be the random variable denoting the number of $x \in S$ satisfying $h(x) = 0^k$. Note that $E[N] = |S|p \in [\frac{1}{4}, \frac{1}{2}]$. By the inclusion-exclusion principle

$$\Pr[N \geq 1] \geq \sum_{x \in S} \Pr[h(x)=0^k] - \sum_{x<x' \in S} \Pr[h(x)=0^k \wedge h(x')=0^k] = |S|p - \binom{|S|}{2}p^2$$

and by the union bound we get that $\Pr[N \geq 2] \leq \binom{|S|}{2}p^2$. Thus

$$\Pr[N = 1] = \Pr[N \geq 1] - \Pr[N \geq 2] \geq |S|p - 2\binom{|S|}{2}p^2 \geq |S|p - |S|^2p^2 \geq \frac{1}{8}$$

where the last inequality is obtained using the fact that $\frac{1}{4} \leq |S|p \leq \frac{1}{2}$. ∎

Now we prove Theorem 17.18.

PROOF OF THEOREM 17.18: Given a formula φ on n variables, choose k at random from $\{2,\ldots,n+1\}$ and a random hash function $h \in_R \mathcal{H}_{n,k}$. Consider the statement

$$\exists_{x \in \{0,1\}^n} \varphi(x) \wedge (h(x) = 0^k) \tag{17.4}$$

If φ is unsatisfiable, then (17.4) is false since no x satisfies $\varphi(x)$. If φ is satisfiable, then with probability at least $1/8n$ there exists a unique assignment x satisfying (17.4). After all if S is the set of satisfying assignments of φ, then with probability $1/n$, k satisfies $2^{k-2} \leq |S| \leq 2^{k-1}$, conditioned on which, with probability $1/8$, there is a unique x such that $\varphi(x) \wedge h(x) = 0^n$.

The idea of the preceding paragraph is implemented as follows. The reduction consists of using the Cook-Levin transformation to express the (deterministic) computation inside the $\exists^u$ sign in (17.4). Write a formula τ on variables $x \in \{0, 1\}^n, y \in \{0, 1\}^m$

(for $m = \text{poly}(n)$) such that $h(x) = 0$ if and only if there exists a *unique* y such that $\tau(x, y) = 1$. Here the y variables come from the need to represent a TM's computation in the Cook-Levin reduction.[1] The output Boolean formula is

$$\psi = \varphi(x) \wedge \tau(x, y)$$

where x, y are the variables. ∎

17.4.2 Properties of $\bigoplus$ and proof of Lemma 17.17 for NP, coNP

In Lemma 17.17 the reduction is allowed to fail only with extremely low probability 2^{-m}, where m is arbitrary. If we are willing to settle for a much higher failure probability, then the Valiant-Vazirani lemma trivially implies a reduction from **NP** to $\oplus$SAT. Specifically, in the conclusion of Theorem 17.18 the formula has a unique satisfying assignment in the first case, and 1 is an odd number. In the second case of the conclusion the formula has no satisfying assignment, and 0 is an even number. Thus the following is a trivial corollary of Theorem 17.18.

Corollary 17.20 (*Consequence of Valiant-Vazirani*) *There exists a probabilistic polynomial-time algorithm A such that for every n-variable Boolean formula* φ

$$\varphi \in \text{SAT} \Rightarrow \Pr[A(\varphi) \in \oplus\text{SAT}] \geq \tfrac{1}{8n}$$
$$\varphi \notin \text{SAT} \Rightarrow \Pr[A(\varphi) \in \oplus\text{SAT}] = 0 \qquad \diamond$$

It is an open problem to boost the probability of $1/8n$ in the Valiant-Vazirani reduction to USAT (Theorem 17.18) to even a constant, say $1/2$. However, such a boosting is indeed possible for $\oplus$SAT, since it turns out to be much more expressive than USAT. Let us examine some facts about the $\bigoplus$ quantifier.

For a Boolean formula φ on n variables, let $\#(\varphi)$ denote the number of satisfying assignments of φ. Given two formulas φ, ψ on variables $x \in \{0, 1\}^n$, $y \in \{0, 1\}^m$, we can construct in polynomial-time an $n + m$ variable formula $\varphi \cdot \psi$ and a $(\max\{n, m\} + 1)$-variable formula $\varphi + \psi$ such that $\#(\varphi \cdot \psi) = \#(\varphi)\#(\psi)$ and $\#(\varphi + \psi) = \#(\varphi) + \#(\psi)$. Indeed, take $(\varphi \cdot \psi)(x, y) = \varphi(x) \wedge \varphi(y)$ and $(\varphi + \psi)(z) = \big((z_0 = 0) \wedge \varphi(z_1, \ldots, z_n)\big) \vee \big((z_0 = 1) \wedge (z_{m+1} = 0) \wedge \cdots \wedge (z_n = 0) \wedge \psi(z_1, \ldots, z_m)\big)$, where we are assuming $m < n$. For a formula φ, we use the notation $\varphi + 1$ to denote the formula $\varphi + \psi$ where ψ is some canonical formula with a single satisfying assignment.

Since the product of numbers is even iff one of the numbers is even, and since adding one to a number flips the parity, for every two formulas φ, ψ as above

$$\Big(\bigoplus_x \varphi(x)\Big) \wedge \Big(\bigoplus_y \psi(y)\Big) \Leftrightarrow \bigoplus_{x,y} (\varphi \cdot \psi)(x, y) \tag{17.5}$$

$$\neg \bigoplus_x \varphi(x) \Leftrightarrow \bigoplus_{x,z} (\varphi + 1)(x, z) \tag{17.6}$$

---

[1] For some implementations of hash functions, such as the one described in Exercise 8.4, one can construct such a formula directly without using the y variables or going through the Cook-Levin reduction.

$$\left(\bigoplus_x \varphi(x)\right) \vee \left(\bigoplus_y \psi(y)\right) \Leftrightarrow \bigoplus_{x,y,z}((\varphi + 1) \cdot (\psi + 1) + 1)(x, y, z) \qquad (17.7)$$

The meaning of the observation in (17.6) is that $\oplus\mathbf{P}$ is closed under complementation, namely, for any φ we can write another formula ψ in polynomial time such that $\neg \bigoplus_x \varphi(x)$ is equivalent to $\bigoplus_y \psi(y)$. The meaning of observations in (17.5) and (17.7) is that a polynomial number of ANDs and ORs of $\oplus$SAT instances can also be converted in polynomial time to a single $\oplus$SAT instance that is equivalent.

Now we prove Lemma 17.17 for $\mathbf{NP}$ and $\mathbf{coNP}$ (i.e., when the formula φ has a single $\forall$ or $\exists$ quantifier). In fact it suffices to give a reduction from just $\mathbf{NP}$. Since $\oplus\mathbf{P}$ is closed under complementation, that same reduction will be a probabilistic reduction of $\mathbf{coNP}$ to $\overline{\oplus\mathbf{P}}$, and hence to $\oplus\mathbf{P}$.

PROOF: (Lemma 17.17; when φ has only $\exists$ quantifier) Suppose φ is a Boolean formula (i.e., a quantified formula with one $\exists$ quantifier). The idea for reducing it to $\oplus$SAT is the obvious one: Run the reduction of Corollary 17.20 $R = O(mn)$ times, each time producing a $\oplus$ formula. The final formula is the OR of these formulas. If the original formula was satisfiable, then this new formula is true with probability at least $1 - (1 - 1/8n)^R = 1 - 2^{-m}$, and if the original formula was not satisfiable, this new formula is never true. Finally, apply the observation in (17.7) R times to turn this new formula into a single $\oplus$ formula, while possibly blowing up the formula's size by a polynomial factor. ∎

17.4.3 Proof of Lemma 17.17: General case

The proof of the general case involves an induction on c, the number of quantifier alternations in φ. The base case $c = 1$ (i.e., $\mathbf{NP}$ or $\mathbf{coNP}$) was already proved. To prove the general case, we need a more abstract version of the Valiant-Vazirani Lemma, where we observe that the reduction never looks at what formula it is working with, so this formula could be an arbitrary Boolean function. (Using terminology from Chapter 3, the Valiant-Vazirani Lemma *relativizes*.)

Lemma 17.21 *(Valiant-Vazirani, oblivious version) There is a probabilistic polynomial-time procedure that, given input 1^n, produces a Boolean formula $\tau(x, y)$ where x is a vector of n Boolean variables and y is also a vector of Boolean variables, such that for any Boolean function $\beta : \{0, 1\}^n \to \{0, 1\}$,*

$$\exists_{x_1} \beta(x_1) \Rightarrow \Pr[\bigoplus_{x_1, y} \tau(x_1, y) \wedge (\beta(x_1) = 1)] \geq \frac{1}{8n} \qquad (17.8)$$

$$\neg\exists_{x_1} \beta(x_1) \Rightarrow \Pr[\bigoplus_{x_1, y} \tau(x_1, y) \wedge (\beta(x_1) = 1)] = 0. \qquad (17.9)$$

◇

Now we can prove Lemma 17.17.

PROOF: (Lemma 17.17) Let φ have c quantifier alternations. As observed in Section 17.4.2, $\oplus$SAT is closed under complementation, so we may assume wlog that the first quantifier is an $\exists$. Thus

$$\varphi = \exists_{x_1} \psi(x_1)$$

where $\psi(x_1)$ is a quantified Boolean formula with at most $c-1$ quantifier alternations, in which the variables in x_1 are free. Suppose x_1 consists of n Boolean variables. By the inductive hypothesis, there is a randomized reduction such that for each value of x_1 it produces a $\oplus SAT$ formula $\beta(x_1) = \oplus_z \rho(z, x_1)$ that is equivalent to the formula $\psi(x_1)$ with probability at least $1 - 2^{-(m+2)}$. Now imagine running the reduction of Lemma 17.21 $K = O(mn)$ times with independent random bits, and let $\tau_1(x_1, y), \tau_2(x_1, y), \ldots, \tau_K(x_1, y)$ be the Boolean formulas produced. Consider the formula

$$\alpha = \bigvee_{j=1}^{K} (\oplus_{x_1, y} \tau_j(x_1, y) \wedge \beta(x_1)).$$

If $\exists_{x_1} \beta(x_1)$ is true, then according to Lemma 17.21, $\Pr[\alpha \text{ is true}] \geq 1 - (1 - 1/8n)^K = 1 - 2^{-O(m)}$. Conversely if $\exists_{x_1} \beta(x_1)$ is false, then $\Pr[\alpha \text{ is true}] = 0$.

To finish, note that since the inductive hypothesis implies $\beta(x_1)$ is a $\oplus SAT$ instance, we can convert α also into a $\oplus SAT$ instance (with polynomial blowup in size) by using the transformations of Section 17.4.2. The two sources of error are (a) the conversion of $\psi(x_1)$ into an equivalent $\oplus SAT$ instance, which by the inductive hypothesis fails with probability $2^{-(m+2)}$, and (b) the Valiant-Vazirani error when we replace $\exists_{x_1}$ to construct α as above, which also has failure probability $2^{-(m+2)}$. Thus the overall error probability is $2 \times 2^{-(m+2)}$, which is less than 2^{-m}. ∎

17.4.4 Step 2: Making the reduction deterministic

Now we derandomize the randomized reduction of Lemma 17.17 to complete the proof of Toda's Theorem (Theorem 17.14). The following deterministic reduction will be the key tool.

Lemma 17.22 *There is a (deterministic) polynomial-time transformation T that, for every formula Boolean α formula $\beta = T(\alpha, 1^\ell)$ is such that*

$$\alpha \in \oplus SAT \Rightarrow \#(\beta) = -1 \pmod{2^{\ell+1}}$$

$$\alpha \notin \oplus SAT \Rightarrow \#(\beta) = 0 \pmod{2^{\ell+1}}$$

$\diamond$

PROOF: Recall that for every pair of formulas φ, τ we defined formulas $\varphi + \tau$ and $\varphi \cdot \tau$ satisfying $\#(\varphi + \tau) = \#(\varphi) + \#(\tau)$ and $\#(\varphi \cdot \tau) = \#(\varphi)\#(\tau)$, and note that these formulas are of size at most a constant factor larger than φ, τ. Consider the formula $4\tau^3 + 3\tau^4$ (where τ^3 for example is shorthand for $\tau \cdot (\tau \cdot \tau)$). One can easily check that

$$\#(\tau) = -1 \pmod{2^{2^i}} \Rightarrow \#(4\tau^3 + 3\tau^4) = -1 \pmod{2^{2^{i+1}}} \tag{17.10}$$

$$\#(\tau) = 0 \pmod{2^{2^i}} \Rightarrow \#(4\tau^3 + 3\tau^4) = 0 \pmod{2}^{2^{i+1}} \tag{17.11}$$

Let $\psi_0 = \alpha$ and $\psi_{i+1} = 4\psi_i^3 + 3\psi_i^4$. Let $\beta = \psi_{\lceil \log(\ell+1) \rceil}$. Repeated use of equations (17.10) and (17.11) shows that if $\#(\psi)$ is odd, then $\#(\beta) = -1 \pmod{2^{\ell+1}}$ and if $\#(\psi)$ is even, then $\#(\beta) = 0 \pmod{2^{\ell+1}}$. Also, the size of β is only $\exp(O(\log \ell))$ times larger than size of α, so the reduction runs in time polynomial in the input length. ∎

PROOF OF THEOREM 17.14 USING LEMMAS 17.17 AND 17.22.: Let f be the reduction in Lemma 17.17 obtained by setting the parameter $m = 2$. Since it is a randomized reduction, we may think of it as a deterministic function taking two inputs, the quantified formula ψ and the random string r. Let R be the number of bits in the random string. Then let T be the reduction in Lemma 17.22 obtained by setting $\ell = R + 2$, and which therefore runs in $\text{poly}(R, |f(\psi)|)$ time.

Consider the combined reduction $T \circ f$ (i.e., apply f followed by T) as a deterministic function applied to the input φ, r, and focus on the value of the following sum modulo $2^{\ell+1}$:

$$\sum_{r \in \{0,1\}^R} \#(T \circ f(\psi, r)) \tag{17.12}$$

If ψ is true, then at least $3/4$ of the terms are -1 modulo $2^{\ell+1}$ and the remaining terms are 0 modulo $2^{\ell+1}$. Thus the sum modulo $2^{\ell+1}$ lies between -2^R and $-\lceil 3/4 \times 2^R \rceil$ in this case.

If ψ is false on the other hand, then at least $3/4$ of the terms are 0 modulo $2^{\ell+1}$ and the remaining terms are -1 modulo $2^{\ell+1}$. Thus the sum modulo $2^{\ell+1}$ is between $-\lceil \frac{1}{4} \times 2^R \rceil$ and 0 in this case.

Since $2^{\ell+1} > 2^{R+2}$, these two ranges are disjoint. So if we can somehow evaluate the expression in (17.12) using a query to a $\#$SAT oracle, we can tell which of the two ranges its value lies in, and hence determine if ψ is true.

But it is straightforward to come up with such a query for the $\#$SAT oracle using the Cook-Levin construction to express the deterministic computation represented by $T \circ f$. Specifically, denote the vector of variables of the Boolean formula $T \circ f(\varphi, r)$ by y. We write a Boolean formula $\Gamma(r, y, z)$ that is 1 for an assignment (r, y, z) iff y is a satisfying assignment $T \circ F(\varphi, r)$. Such a formula can be written by applying the Cook-Levin construction on the circuit that first computes $T \circ f(\varphi, r)$ (where φ is "hard-wired" into the circuit), and then substitutes the assignment y into this formula. The variables z correspond to values of inner wires of this circuit, and since the circuit is deterministic, its value is uniquely determined given y, r.

Hence $\#(\Gamma(r, y, z)) \bmod 2^{\ell+1}$ is exactly (17.12), and so the query for the $\#$SAT oracle is to ask for $\#(\Gamma)$. ∎

17.5 OPEN PROBLEMS

- What is the exact power of $\oplus$SAT and #SAT ?
- What is the average case complexity of $n \times n$ permanent modulo small prime, say 3 or 5 ? Note that for a prime $p > n$, random self-reducibility of permanent implies that if permanent is hard to compute on the worst case for randomized algorithms, then it is hard to compute on $1 - O(n/p)$ fraction of inputs (i.e., it is hard to compute on average; see Theorem 8.33).

WHAT HAVE WE LEARNED?

- The class **#P** consists of functions that count the number of certificates for a given instance. If $\mathbf{P} \neq \mathbf{NP}$, then it is not solvable in polynomial time.
- Counting analogs of many natural **NP**-complete problems are **#P**-complete, but there are also **#P**-complete counting problems for which the corresponding decision problem is in **P**. For example the problem perm of finding the permanent of a matrix – equivalent to counting the number of perfect matchings in a graph – is **#P**-complete, whereas deciding whether a graph has a perfect matching is in **P**.
- Surprisingly, counting is more powerful than alternating quantifiers: We can solve every problem in the polynomial hierarchy using an oracle to a **#P**-complete problem.
- The classes **PP** and ⊕**P** contain the decision problems that correspond to the most significant and least significant bits (respectively) of a **#P** function. The class **PP** is as powerful as **#P** itself, in the sense that if **PP** = **P** then **#P** = **FP**. We do not know if this holds for ⊕**P** but we do know that every language in **PH** randomly reduces to ⊕**P**.

CHAPTER NOTES AND HISTORY

The definition of **#P** as well as several interesting examples of **#P** problems appeared in Valiant's seminal paper [Val79c]. The **#P**-completeness of the permanent is from his other paper [Val79b]. The **#P**-completeness of computing the partition function of the Ising model (Example 17.3) is due to Jerrum and Sinclair [JS90], where an FPRAS for the problem is also given. The **#P**-completeness of Bayes Net max likelihood estimation (Example 17.2) first appears in Roth [Rot93]. Dagum and Luby [DL93] have shown that even approximating the probabilities is **NP**-hard. Welsh's book [Wel93] shows the rich mathematical structure of the class **#P** and the mathematical problems (involving knot theory, graph colorings, and tilings) it captures.

For an introduction to FPRAS's for computing approximations to many counting problems, see the relevant chapter in Vazirani [Vaz01] (an excellent resource on approximation algorithms in general) and the survey article by Jerrum and Sinclair [Hoc97]. The FPRAS for the permanent problem is due to Jerrum, Sinclair, and Vigoda [JSV01].

Toda's Theorem is proved in [Tod91]. This result had a very beneficial effect on complexity theory because it showed the power of using arithmetic arguments in reasoning about complexity classes (a theme developed further in Chapters 8 and 11).

In addition to classes covered in this chapter such as **#P** and ⊕**P**, many other complexity classes also involve some notion of counting. See the survey by Fortnow [For97b].

EXERCISES

17.1. Show that the problem of Example 17.2 is indeed equivalent to #SAT and hence **#P**-complete.

17.2. Show that computing the permanent for matrices with integer entries is in $\mathbf{FP}^{\#SAT}$.

17.3. Complete the analysis of the XOR gadget in the proof of Theorem 17.11. Let G be any weighted graph containing a pair of edges $\overrightarrow{uu'}$ and $\overrightarrow{vv'}$, and let G' be the graph obtained by replacing these edges with the XOR gadget. Prove that every cycle cover of G of weight w that uses exactly one of the edges $\overrightarrow{uu'}$ is mapped to a set of cycle covers in G' whose total weight is $4w$, and all the other cycle covers of G' have total weight 0.

17.4. Show that if there is a polynomial-time algorithm that approximates $\#\mathsf{CYCLE}$ within a factor $1/2$, then $\mathbf{P} = \mathbf{NP}$.

17.5. Show that if $\mathbf{NP} = \mathbf{P}$, then for every $f \in \#\mathbf{P}$ there is a randomized polynomial-time algorithm that approximates f within a factor of $1/2$. Can you show the same for a factor of $1 - \epsilon$ for arbitrarily small constant $\epsilon > 0$? Can you make these algorithms *deterministic*?

    Note that we do not know whether $\mathbf{P} = \mathbf{NP}$ implies that exact computation of functions in $\#\mathbf{P}$ can be done in polynomial time.

H539

17.6. Show that for every language in $\mathbf{AC}^0$ there is a depth three circuit of $n^{\mathrm{poly}(\log n)}$ size that decides it on $1 - 1/\mathrm{poly}(n)$ fraction of inputs and looks as follows: It has a single $\oplus$ gate at the top, and the other gates are $\vee, \wedge$ of fan-in at most $\mathrm{poly}(\log n)$.

H539

17.7. Improve Theorem 10.23 to show that $\mathbf{BQP} \subseteq \mathbf{P}^{\#\mathbf{P}}$.

H539

CHAPTER 18

Average case complexity: Levin's theory

There is a large gap between a problem not being easy and the same problem being difficult.
– Russell Impagalizzo, 1995

So far we only studied the complexity of algorithms that solve computational task on *every* possible input; that is, *worst-case* complexity. With few exceptions (such as Chapter 9) most complexity classes we defined also concerned worst-case complexity; **NP**-completeness being a canonical example.

One frequent objection to this whole framework is that practitioners are only interested in instances of the problem that arise "in practice," and the worst-case behavior of algorithms may never be encountered. Of course, it is not always easy to quantify what these real-life instances are. Algorithm designers have tried to formalize this in various ways and to design efficient algorithm that work for "many" or "most" of these instances—this body of work is known variously as *average-case analysis* or *analysis of algorithms*. It has been discovered that several **NP**-hard problems are actually quite easy on the "average" graph, depending upon how one formulates "average". One way to formalize an average graph is that it is generated *randomly*. The simplest model of generating an n-vertex random graph is to toss an unbiased coin for each of the $\binom{n}{2}$ potential edges to decide whether or not to include it in the graph. This method ends up generating each n-vertex graph with probability $2^{-\binom{n}{2}}$. (If each edge is picked with probability p instead of $1/2$, the resulting distribution is called $G(n, p)$, also well-studied.) On such random graphs, many **NP**-complete problems are easy. 3-COLOR can be solved in linear time with high probability. CLIQUE and INDSET can be solved in $n^{2 \log n}$ time, which is only a little more than polynomial and much less than $2^{\epsilon n}$, the running time of the best algorithms on worst-case instances. And yet, our study of one-way functions in Chapter 9 also suggests that not all **NP** problems are easy on random instances.

The question arises whether we can come up with a theory analogous to **NP**-completeness for average-case complexity, and to identify problems that are "hardest" or "complete" with respect to some appropriate notion of reducibility. This chapter surveys such a theory due to L. Levin (the same person involved in the Cook-Levin Theorem). For simplicity we restrict our study to decision problems.

The first goal in this theory is to make precise what we mean by "average" instances of a problem. This is done by assuming that inputs are drawn from a specific *distribution*. But then the question arises: What is the class of distributions that arise "in practice"? Levin makes a daring suggestion: We allow any distribution from which we can draw samples in polynomial time (**P**-samplable distribution). Levin's reasoning was that the "real-life" instances must be produced by the actions of the world around us. If we believe in the strong form of the Church-Turing Thesis (Section 1.6.1), then the world can be simulated on a Turing machine, and it is fair to assume that the "computation" that produced our instance was not very complicated (i.e., efficient). Hence we can assume the time to produce the instance was polynomial in the instance size. See Section 18.2 for details.

Thus an "average-case problem" consists of a decision problem together with a distribution on inputs that is poly-time samplable. Then the question arises how one should define an "efficient algorithm" for such an average-case problem—in other words, the analog of the class **P**. This turns out to be slightly subtle, and we give the precise definition of the class distP in Section 18.1. In Section 18.3 we try to define an analog of **NP**-completeness for average-case complexity. This has some subtleties, especially the notion of "reduction" needed. We define the class distNP—the average-case analog of **NP**—a corresponding notion of distNP-completeness and show that there exist a few problems that are distNP complete. However, unlike the case of **NP** completeness, we do not have a rich variety of natural problems that have been proven distNP complete.

Finding out the true average case complexity of **NP** problems is one of complexity theory's most important goals. In Section 18.4 we examine our current knowledge in this area, and how it connects to the broader study of complexity.

18.1 DISTRIBUTIONAL PROBLEMS AND distP

The average-case complexity of a problem is only well-defined with respect to a particular *distribution* on inputs. We now make this more precise.

Definition 18.1 *(Distributional problem)* A *distributional problem* is a pair $\langle L, \mathcal{D} \rangle$ where $L \subseteq \{0, 1\}^*$ is a language, and $\mathcal{D} = \{\mathcal{D}_n\}$ is a sequence of distributions, with $\mathcal{D}_n$ being a distribution over $\{0, 1\}^n$.

EXAMPLE 18.2

Here are some examples for distributional problems.

Planted clique Let $G_{n,p}$ be the distribution over n-vertex graph where each edge is chosen to appear in the graph independently with probability p. This distribution is clearly **P**-computable. The most common case is $p = 2$, in which case every graph in $G_{n,p}$ has equal probability and we call a graph drawn from this distribution a "random graph."

Let $k : \mathbb{N} \to \mathbb{N}$ be some function such that $k(n) \leq n$. A naive way to give an average-case analog of the CLIQUE problem would be to decide whether a random graph has a $k(n)$-clique. However, it turns out this problem is not so difficult, since with very high probability the clique number of a random graph is equal to an easily computable value (roughly equal to $2\log n$) [BE76, Mat76].[1]

Thus, the "right" average-case analog of the $k(n)$-clique problem uses the following distribution $\mathcal{D}_n$. With probability $1/2$ output a random n-vertex graph, and with probability $1/2$ choose a random $k(n)$-sized subset S of the vertices and output a random graph conditioned on S being a clique in the graph. The problem is to decide whether the given graph has a clique of size at least $k(n)$. Note that for $k(n) \gg 2\log n$, the probability that a random graph has such a clique is very small. Using spectral methods, it is known how to solve this problem efficiently for $k(n) \sim \sqrt{n}$ [Kuc95, AKS98]. But for, say $k(n) = n^{0.49}$ the problem is wide open.

Random $3\,\mathrm{SAT}$ A random 3CNF formula on n vertices and m clauses can be obtained by choosing each clause as the OR of three random literals. Clearly, the larger the number m of clauses, the less likely the formula is to be satisfiable. If can be easily shown that there exists constant $c_1 < c_2$ such that if the number of clauses m is less than $c_1 n$, then the formula will be satisfiable with very high probability, and if $m > c_2 n$, then it will be unsatisfiable with very high probability (e.g., $c_1 = 1, c_2 = 8$ will do). In fact, Friedgut [Fri99] showed that there is a function $f(n)$ (where $c_1 n \le f(n) \le c_2(n)$ for every n) such that for every $\epsilon > 0$, if the number of clauses m is smaller than $(1 - \epsilon)f(n)$, then the formula will be satisfiable with high probability, and if this number is larger than $(1 + \epsilon)f(n)$, then it will be unsatisfiable with high probability. It is believed that $f(n) = c^* n$ for some constant $c^* \sim 4.26$. For m that is very close to this value, the problem of determining satisfiability of a random n-variable m-clause 3CNF formula seems hard. In fact, because in this chapter we require average-case algorithms to *always* output the correct answer (see Definition 18.4), the problem remains hard for much larger value m. At the moment no expected polynomial-time algorithm is known even in the case of $m = n^{1.1}$, despite the fact that such a formula will be unsatisfiable with overwhelming probability (some partial progress was made in [GK01, FO04, FKO06]).

Decoding a random linear code Let A be an $m \times n$ matrix over GF(2), where $m > n$ (say, $m = 10n$). The *decoding* problem of A is to find, given a vector $\mathbf{z} \in \mathrm{GF}(2)^m$, the closest vector $\mathbf{y}$ to $\mathbf{z}$ such that $\mathbf{y}$ is in the image of A (i.e., $\mathbf{y} = A\mathbf{x}$ for some $\mathbf{x} \in \mathrm{GF}(2)^n$). (This is motivated by considering A as the generating matrix for an *error correcting code*; see also Section 19.2.) There are efficient algorithms to do this for matrices A of various special forms, but for a random matrix A no efficient algorithm is known. This problem is also known as the problem of *learning parity with noise*.

The decoding problem is of course a search problem. Fix $\epsilon > 0$ to some constant. The following analogous decision problem $(L, \mathcal{D}_n)$ is not known to be in distP. We let (a) L contain all pairs $\langle A, \mathbf{y} \rangle$ such that $\mathbf{y}$ is within Hamming distance at most ϵm to a vector in A's image and (b) the distribution $\mathcal{D}_n$ outputs with probability $1/2$ a random $m \times n$ matrix A and a random vector $\mathbf{y} \in_R \mathrm{GF}(2)^m$, and with probability

---

[1] For infinitely many n's, with probability $1 - o(1)$, the clique number of a random n-vertex graph will be equal to $g(n)$ where $g(n) = \lfloor 2(\log n - \log\log n + \log(e) + 1) \rfloor$. For every n with probability $1 - o(1)$, this number will be in the set $\{g(n) - 1, g(n), g(n) + 1\}$. See also Exercise 18.2.

1/2, a random $m \times n$ matrix A, and $\mathbf{y} = A\mathbf{x} + \mathbf{e}$ where $\mathbf{x}$ is chosen at random in $GF(2)^n$ and $\mathbf{e}$ is a random vector in $GF(2)^m$ having exactly $\lfloor cm \rfloor$ entries equal to 1.

Both problems are related to the *subset sum* problem and problems on discrete lattices in $\mathbb{R}^n$ that have proven useful in cryptography; see the notes to Chapter 9.

Our next step is to define the class distP – the average-case analog of **P** – that aims to capture the set of distributional problems $\langle L, \mathcal{D} \rangle$ that are efficiently solvable.[2] For every algorithm A and input x, let $\mathtt{time}_A(x)$ denote the number of steps A takes on input x. A natural candidate definition is to say that $\langle L, \mathcal{D} \rangle$ is solvable in polynomial-time on the average if there is an algorithm A such that $A(x) = L(x)$ for every x and a polynomial p such that for every n, $E_{x \in_R \mathcal{D}_n}[\mathtt{time}_A(x)] \leq p(n)$.

Unfortunately, it turns out that this definition is not robust in the following sense: If we change the model of computation to a different model with quadratic slow down (for example, change from multiple tape Turing machines to one-tape Turing machines), then a polynomial-time algorithm can suddenly turn into an exponential-time algorithm, as demonstrated by the following simple claim.

Claim 18.3 *There is an algorithm A such that for every n we have $E_{x \in_R \{0,1\}^n}[\mathtt{time}_A(x)] \leq n + 1$ but $E_{x \in_R \{0,1\}^n}[\mathtt{time}_A^2(x)] \geq 2^n$.*   ◇

PROOF: Consider an algorithm A that halts in n steps on every input except for the all-zeros input, on which it runs for 2^n steps. The expected running time of A is $(1 - 2^{-n})n + 2^{-n}2^n \leq n + 1$. On the other hand, if we square the running time, then the expectation becomes $(1 - 2^{-n})n^2 + 2^{-n}2^{2n} \geq 2^n$. ∎

This motivates the following definition.

Definition 18.4 *(Polynomial on average and* distP*)* A distributional problem $\langle L, \mathcal{D} \rangle$ is in distP if there is an algorithm A for L and constants C and $\epsilon > 0$ such that for every n

$$\mathop{E}_{x \in_R \mathcal{D}_n}\left[\frac{\mathtt{time}_A(x)^\epsilon}{n}\right] \leq C \tag{18.1}$$

Notice that $\mathbf{P} \subseteq$ distP: If a language can be decided deterministically by an algorithm A in time $O(|x|^c)$, then $\mathtt{time}_A(x)^{1/c} = O(|x|)$ and the expectation in (18.1) is bounded by a constant regardless of the distribution. Second, the definition is robust to changes in computational models: if the running times get squared, we just multiply c by 2, and the expectation in (18.1) is again bounded.

Another feature of this definition is that there is a high probability that the algorithm runs in polynomial time. Indeed, by Markov's inequality, (18.1) implies that for every $K > 1$, $\Pr[\frac{\mathtt{time}_A(x)^\epsilon}{n} \geq KC] = \Pr[\mathtt{time}_A(x) \geq (KCn)^{1/\epsilon}]$ is at most $1/K$.

---

[2] In this chapter we restrict ourselves to deterministic algorithms, although the theory extends naturally to probabilistic algorithms, yielding average-case analogs of classes such as **BPP, RP, coRP**, and **ZPP**.

Finally, we note that the definition is robust to minor changes. For instance, for every $d > 0$, the following condition is equivalent to (18.1): There exist ϵ, C such that

$$\mathop{E}_{x \in_R \mathcal{D}_n} \left[\frac{\text{time}_A(x)^\epsilon}{n^d} \right] \leq C \tag{18.2}$$

see Exercise 18.6.

18.2 FORMALIZATION OF "REAL-LIFE DISTRIBUTIONS"

Real-life problem instances arise out of the world around us (images that have to be understood, a building that has to be navigated by a robot, etc.), and the world does not spend a lot of time tailoring instances to be hard for our algorithm – arguably, the world is indifferent to our algorithm. One may formalize this indifference in terms of computational ease, by hypothesizing that the instances are produced by an efficient algorithm (see also the discussion of Section 1.6.3). We can formalize this in two ways.

*Polynomial time computable (or **P**-computable) distributions.* Such distributions have an associated deterministic polynomial time machine that, given input $x \in \{0, 1\}^n$, can compute the *cumulative probability* $\mu_{\mathcal{D}_n}(x)$, where

$$\mu_{\mathcal{D}_n}(x) = \sum_{y \in \{0,1\}^n : y \leq x} \Pr_{\mathcal{D}_n}[y]$$

Here $\Pr_{\mathcal{D}_n}[y]$ denotes the probability assigned to string y and $y \leq x$ means y either precedes x in lexicographic order or is equal to x.

Denoting the lexicographic predecessor of x by $x - 1$, we have

$$\Pr_{\mathcal{D}_n}[x] = \mu_{\mathcal{D}_n}(x) - \mu_{\mathcal{D}_n}(x - 1)$$

which shows that if $\mu_{\mathcal{D}_n}$ is computable in polynomial time, then so is $\Pr_{\mathcal{D}_n}[x]$. The converse is known to be false if $\mathbf{P} \neq \mathbf{NP}$ (Exercise 18.3). The uniform distribution is **P**-computable as are many other distributions that are defined using explicit formulas.

*Polynomial time samplable (or **P**-samplable) distributions.* These distributions have an associated probabilistic polynomial time machine that can produce samples from the distribution. Specifically, we say that $\mathcal{D} = \{\mathcal{D}_n\}$ is **P**-samplable if there is a polynomial p and a probabilistic $p(n)$-time algorithm S such that for every n, the random variables $A(1^n)$ and $\mathcal{D}_n$ are identically distributed.

If a distribution is **P**-computable then it is **P**-samplable, but the converse is not true if $\mathbf{P} \neq \mathbf{P}^{\#\mathbf{P}}$ (see Exercises 18.4 and 18.5). In this chapter we mostly restrict attention to **P**-computable distributions, but the theory can be extended to **P**-samplable distributions; see Section 18.3.2.

18.3 distnp AND ITS COMPLETE PROBLEMS

The following complexity class is at the heart of our study of average case complexity; it is the average-case analog of **NP**.

Definition 18.5 *(The class* distNP*)* A distributional problem $\langle L, \mathcal{D} \rangle$ is in distNP if $L \in$ **NP** and $\mathcal{D}$ is **P**-computable.

We now define reduction between distributional problems.

Definition 18.6 *(Average-case reduction)* We say that a distributional problem $\langle L, \mathcal{D} \rangle$ *average-case reduces* to a distributional problem $\langle L', \mathcal{D}' \rangle$, denoted by $\langle L, \mathcal{D} \rangle \leq_p \langle L', \mathcal{D}' \rangle$, if there is a polynomial-time computable f and polynomials $p, q : \mathbb{N} \to \mathbb{N}$ satisfying

1. *(Correctness)* For every $x \in \{0, 1\}^*$, $x \in L \Leftrightarrow f(x) \in L'$
2. *(Length regularity)* For every $x \in \{0, 1\}^*$, $|f(x)| = p(|x|)$
3. *(Domination)* For every $n \in \mathbb{N}$ and $y \in \{0, 1\}^{p(n)}$, $\Pr[y = f(\mathcal{D}_n)] \leq q(n) \Pr[y = \mathcal{D}'_{p(n)}]$

The first condition is the standard reduction condition, ensuring that a decision algorithm for L' easily converts into a decision algorithm for L. The second condition is technical, and is used to simplify the definition and to show that the reducibility relation is transitive (see Exercise 18.7). We now motivate the third condition, which says that $\mathcal{D}'$ "dominates" (up to a polynomial factor) the distribution $f(\mathcal{D})$ obtained by applying f on $\mathcal{D}$. Realize that the goal of the definition is to ensure that "if $\langle L, \mathcal{D} \rangle$ is hard, then so is $\langle L', \mathcal{D}' \rangle$," or equivalently, the contrapositive "if $\langle L', \mathcal{D}' \rangle$ is easy, then so is $\langle L, \mathcal{D} \rangle$." Thus if an algorithm A' is efficient for problem $(L', \mathcal{D}')$, then it would be nice if the "obvious" algorithm for the problem $(L, \mathcal{D})$ worked: Namely, on input x obtained from the distribution $\mathcal{D}$, compute $y = f(x)$ and run algorithm A' on y. A priori, this does not work since one cannot rule out the possibility that A' is very slow on some input that is unlikely to be sampled according to distribution $\mathcal{D}'$ but that has a high probability of showing up as $f(x)$ when we sample x according to $\mathcal{D}$. The domination condition rules out this possibility.

Theorem 18.7 *If* $\langle L, \mathcal{D} \rangle \leq_p \langle L', \mathcal{D}' \rangle$ *and* $\langle L', \mathcal{D}' \rangle \in$ distP *then* $\langle L, \mathcal{D} \rangle \in$ distP.   ◇

PROOF: Suppose that A' is a polynomial-time algorithm for $\langle L', \mathcal{D}' \rangle$. That is, there are constants $C, \epsilon > 0$ such that for every m

$$\mathrm{E}[\frac{\mathrm{time}_{A'}(\mathcal{D}'_m)^\epsilon}{m}] \leq C \tag{18.3}$$

Let f be the reduction from $\langle L, \mathcal{D} \rangle$ to $\langle L', \mathcal{D}' \rangle$ and let A be the "obvious" algorithm for deciding L: Given input x it computes $f(x)$ and then outputs $A'(f(x))$. Since A decides L, all that is left to show is that A runs in time-polynomial on the average with respect to the distribution $\mathcal{D}$.

For simplicity, assume that for every x, $|f(x)| = |x|^d$ and that computing f on length n inputs is faster than the running time of A' on length n^d inputs and hence $\mathrm{time}_A(x) \leq 2\mathrm{time}_{A'}(f(x))$. (The proof easily extends when we drop these assumptions.) We prove the lemma by showing that

$$\mathrm{E}[\frac{(\frac{1}{2}\mathrm{time}_A(\mathcal{D})^\epsilon)}{q(n)n^d}] \leq C$$

where q denotes the polynomial occurring in the domination condition. By Exercise 18.6, this suffices to show that $\langle L, \mathcal{D} \rangle \in \text{dist}\mathbf{P}$.

Indeed, by the definition of A and our assumptions,

$$\text{E}[\frac{(\frac{1}{2}\text{time}_A(\mathcal{D}_n))^\epsilon}{q(n)n^d}] \leq \sum_{y \in \{0,1\}^{n^d}} \Pr[y = f(\mathcal{D}_n)]\frac{\text{time}_{A'}(y)^\epsilon}{q(n)n^d}$$

$$\leq \sum_{y \in \{0,1\}^{n^d}} \Pr[y = \mathcal{D}'_{n^d}]\frac{\text{time}_{A'}(y)^\epsilon}{n^d} \text{ (by domination)}$$

$$= \text{E}[\frac{\text{time}_{A'}(\mathcal{D}'_{n^d})^\epsilon}{n^d}] \leq C \text{ by (18.3)} \blacksquare$$

18.3.1 A complete problem for distNP

Of course, Theorem 18.7 is useful only if we can find reductions between interesting problems. Now we show that this is the case: We exhibit a problem (albeit an artificial one) that is complete for distNP. We say that $\langle L', \mathcal{D}' \rangle$ is distNP-*complete* if $\langle L', \mathcal{D}' \rangle$ is in distNP and $\langle L, \mathcal{D} \rangle \leq_p \langle L', \mathcal{D}' \rangle$ for every $\langle L, \mathcal{D} \rangle \in \text{dist}\mathbf{NP}$. We have the following theorem.

Theorem 18.8 *(Existence of a* distNP-*complete problem* [Lev86]) *Let U contain all tuples* $\langle M, x, 1^t \rangle$ *where there exists a string* $y \in \{0, 1\}^\ell$ *such that the nondeterministic TM M outputs 1 on input x within t steps.*

For every n, we let $\mathcal{U}_n$ *be the following distribution on length n tuples* $\langle M, x, 1^t \rangle$: *the string representing M is chosen at random from all strings of length at most* $\log n$, *t is chosen at random in the set* $\{0, \dots, n - |M|\}$ *and x is chosen at random from* $\{0, 1\}^{n-t-|M|}$. *This distribution is polynomial-time computable (Exercise 18.8).*[3]

Then, $\langle U, \mathcal{U} \rangle$ *is* distNP-*complete.*

The problem U is of course **NP**-complete via a trivial reduction: Given a language L decidable by a $p(n)$-time NDTM M, we can reduce L to U by mapping the string x into the tuple $\langle M, x, 1^t \rangle$. However, this reduction does not necessarily work as an *average-case* reduction, since it may not satisfy the domination condition. The problem is that we need to reduce *every* distributional problem $\langle L, \mathcal{D} \rangle$ to $\langle U, \mathcal{U} \rangle$ and will run into trouble if $\mathcal{D}$ has any "peaks," namely inputs x of length n that are obtained with significantly higher than 2^{-n} probability in $\mathcal{D}$, whereas the output of the reduction is a predetermined string $\langle M, x, 1^t \rangle$ whose probability in $\mathcal{U}_n$ is no more than 2^{-n}.

The obstacle is surmounted using the following lemma, which shows that for polynomial-time computable distributions, we can apply a simple transformation on the inputs such that the resulting distribution has no "peaks."

---

[3] Strictly speaking, the inputs might be represented by a few more than n bits to account for separators and the like, but these details can be easily taken care of and are ignored below.

Lemma 18.9 *(Peak elimination) Let $\mathcal{D} = \{\mathcal{D}_n\}$ be a **P**-computable distribution. Then there is a polynomial-time computable function $g : \{0, 1\}^* \to \{0, 1\}^*$ such that*

1. *g is one-to-one: $g(x) = g(z)$ iff $x = z$.*
2. *For every $x \in \{0, 1\}^*$, $|g(x)| \leq |x| + 1$.*
3. *For every string $y \in \{0, 1\}^m$, $\Pr[y = g(\mathcal{D}_m)] \leq 2^{-m+1}$.* $\diamond$

PROOF: For any string $x \in \{0, 1\}^n$, define $h(x)$ to be the largest common prefix of the binary representations of $\mu_{\mathcal{D}_n}(x)$ and $\mu_{\mathcal{D}_n}(x - 1)$. Note that if $\Pr_{\mathcal{D}_n}[x] \geq 2^{-k}$, then since $\mu_{\mathcal{D}_n}(x) - \mu_{\mathcal{D}_n}(x-1) = \Pr_{\mathcal{D}_n}(x)$, the values $\mu_{\mathcal{D}_n}(x)$ and $\mu_{\mathcal{D}_n}(x-1)$ must differ somewhere in the first k bits, implying that $|h(x)| \leq k$. Note also that because $\mathcal{D}$ is **P**-samplable, the function h is computable in polynomial-time. Furthermore, h is one-to-one because only two binary strings s_1 and s_2 can have the longest common prefix z; a third string s_3 sharing z as a prefix must have a longer prefix with either s_1 or s_2.

Now define for every $x \in \{0, 1\}^n$

$$g(x) = \begin{cases} 0x & \text{if } \Pr_{\mathcal{D}_n}[x] \leq 2^{-n} \\ 1h(x) & \text{otherwise} \end{cases}$$

Clearly, g is one-to-one and satisfies $|g(x)| \leq |x| + 1$. We now show that $\Pr[y = g(\mathcal{D}_n)] \leq 2^{-n}$ for every $y \in \{0, 1\}^{n+1}$. If y is not $g(x)$ for any x, this is trivially true since $\Pr_{g \circ \mathcal{D}}(y) = 0$. If $y = 0x$, where $\Pr_{\mathcal{D}}(x) \leq 2^{-|x|}$, then $\Pr_{g \circ \mathcal{D}}(y) \leq 2^{-|y|+1}$ and we also have nothing to prove. Finally, if $y = g(x) = 1h(x)$ where $\Pr_{\mathcal{D}}(x) > 2^{-|x|}$, then as already noted, $|h(x)| \leq \log 1 / \Pr_{\mathcal{D}}(x)$ and so $\Pr_{g \circ \mathcal{D}}(y) = \Pr_{\mathcal{D}}(x) \leq 2^{-|y|+1}$. $\blacksquare$

Now we are ready to prove Theorem 18.8.

PROOF OF THEOREM 18.8: Let $\langle L, \mathcal{D} \rangle$ be in dist**NP** and let M be the polynoimal-time nondeterministic TM M accepting L. Define the following NDTM M': On input y, guess x such that $y = g(x)$ (where g is the function obtained by Lemma 18.9) and execute $M(x)$. Let p be the polynomial running time of M'.

To reduce $\langle L, \mathcal{D} \rangle$ to $\langle U, \mathcal{U} \rangle$, we simply map every string x into the tuple $\langle M', g(x), 1^k \rangle$ where $k = p(n) + \log n + n - |M'| - |g(x)|$ (we may assume that for sufficiently large n, the description length $|M'|$ of M is at most $\log n$). This reduction obviously satisfies the length regularity requirement. Also, because the function g is one-to-one, it satisfies the correctness condition as well. Hence, all that is left is to show the domination condition.

Indeed by Lemma 18.9, the probability that a length m tuple $\langle M', y, 1^t \rangle$ is obtained by the reduction is at most $2^{-|y|+1}$. Yet this tuple is obtained with probability at least $2^{-\log m} 2^{-|y|} \frac{1}{m}$ by $\mathcal{U}_m$, and hence the domination condition is satisfied. $\blacksquare$

The proof relies crucially on the fact that every TM can be described by a string of constant size (i.e., independent of the input length). In fact, the proof leads to an efficiency loss that is exponential in this constant. Since this constant may be quite large for typical **NP** languages, this would be a consideration in practice.

18.3.2 **P-samplable distributions**

Arguably some distributions arising in nature could be samplable even if they are not computable. Define samp**NP** to be the set of distributional problems $\langle L, \mathcal{D} \rangle$ such that $L \in$ **NP** and $\mathcal{D}$ is **P**-samplable, and say that $\langle L', \mathcal{D}' \rangle$ is samp**NP**-complete if $\langle L', \mathcal{D}' \rangle \in$ samp**NP** and $\langle L, \mathcal{D} \rangle \leq_p \langle L', \mathcal{D}' \rangle$ for every $\langle L, \mathcal{D} \rangle \in$ samp**NP**. Fortunately, we can transform results such as Theorem 18.8 to samp**NP**-completeness via the following result.

Theorem 18.10 *([IL90]) If $\langle L, \mathcal{D} \rangle$ is* dist**NP**-*complete, then it is also* samp**NP**-*complete.* ◇

The (omitted) proof uses techniques from derandomization, and specifically the leftover hash lemma (Lemma 21.26).

18.4 PHILOSOPHICAL AND PRACTICAL IMPLICATIONS

The reader has seen many complexity classes and conjectures by now, so it may be useful to consider all possible scenarios for the world of complexity. Impagliazzo [Imp95b] has partitioned these scenarios nicely under highly memorable names. At the moment, we do not know which of the scenarios is true (i.e., which of the following worlds is the one we live in):

Algorithmica: Algorithmica is the world where **P** = **NP** or its moral equivalent (e.g., **NP** ⊆ **BPP**). To be more concrete, let's define Algorithmica as the world where there exists a simple and magical linear time algorithm for the SAT problem. As discussed in Section 2.7.3, this world is a computational utopia. We would be able to automate various tasks that currently require significant creativity: engineering, programming, mathematics, and perhaps even writing, composing, and painting. On the other hand, this algorithm could also be used to break cryptographic schemes, and hence almost all of the cryptographic applications currently used will disappear.

Heuristica: Heuristica is the world where **P** ≠ **NP** and yet dist**NP**, samp**NP** ⊆ dist**P**. That is, we have an efficient and magical algorithm that "almost" solves every **NP** problem. There may exist inputs on which it fails or runs for a long time, but it's hard to find such inputs, and we almost never encounter them in real life. In some respects, Heuristica is very similar to Algorithmica – after all, it seems hard to distinguish between the two if we can't find an input on which the magical algorithm fails! Indeed, many applications of **NP** = **P** still hold in this world, including solving **NP**-optimization problems, coming up with short mathematical proofs, and breaking cryptographic schemes. However, some applications might not hold. In particular, even though we know that if **P** = **NP**, then the polynomial hierarchy **PH** collapses to **P** (see Theorem 5.4), we don't have an analogous result for average case complexity.

Pessiland: Pessiland is the world where dist**NP** and samp**NP** are *not* in dist**P**, but still there do not exist any one-way functions (see Chapter 9). Impagliazzo called this world Pessiland because in some sense it is the worst-possible world. On the one hand, we don't have any of the exciting algorithmic wonders of Algorithmica and Heuristica, but on the other hand, we don't have most of cryptography either. (Recall from Chapter 9 that one-way functions are known to be essential to most cryptographic applications.)

Minicrypt: Minicrypt is the world where one-way functions exist (and hence `dist`**NP** $\not\subseteq$ `dist`**P**; see Exercise 18.10), but all the *highly structured* problems in **NP** such as integer factoring are solvable in polynomial-time. More formally, this is the world where although one-way functions exist, there are no public key encryption schemes or key exchange protocols. Although many cryptographic applications (private key encryption, pseudorandom generators and functions, digital signatures) are achievable using only one-way functions, there are several important and exciting ones (public key encryption, secure multiparty computation) that are not known to be achievable using such functions.

Cryptomania: Cryptomania is the world where the problem of factoring large integers (or some other highly structured problem such as discrete log and shortest lattice vector) is exponentially hard on the average case. Most researchers believe this is the world we live in. While we don't have general-purpose algorithms in this world and have to resort to heuristics, approximations, creativity, and hard work to solve many important computational tasks, we do seem to have a host of exciting cryptographic applications. These include the ability of two parties to communicate secretly without prior sharing of keys (public key encryption, currently widely used to enable online commerce) and even more sophisticated cryptographic applications such secure online auction and voting schemes and more.

Strictly speaking, Impagliazzo has left out some intermediate scenarios, which we lump into "Weirdland." Say, where the complexity of SAT is a not linear or quadratic but a very large polynomial like n^{100} or a very slow growing superpolynomial function like $n^{\log n}$. Or where the complexity of problems like SAT shifts wildly for different input sizes so that it is feasible for some input sizes and infeasible for others. But, qualitatively speaking, the above five scenarios are the main possibilities for the average-case hardness of **NP**. Narrowing this list down is in some sense *the* central task of computational complexity.

WHAT HAVE WE LEARNED?

- Average case complexity is defined with respect to a particular distribution on the inputs. The same problem might be easy with one distribution and hard with another.
- The class `dist`**P** is the average case analog of the class **P** and models distributional problems with efficient algorithms.
- The average-case analog of **NP** is either `dist`**NP** or `samp`**NP**, depending on whether we pick **P**-computable or **P**-samplable distributions as our model of "real-life" distributions. The distributional problem $\langle U, \mathcal{U} \rangle$ of Theorem 18.8 is complete for both classes.
- Like the **P** vs. **NP** question, the average-case hardness of **NP** is still open. At the moment, we do not even know any nontrivial relation between the two questions. For example, we do not know if **NP** $\not\subseteq$ **P** implies that `dist`**NP** $\not\subseteq$ `dist`**P**.

CHAPTER NOTES AND HISTORY

One of the most natural distributions over inputs is the distribution of *random graphs*. Study of such graphs started with a 1959 paper of Erdos and Renyi [ER59]; a good survey of this vast area is the text by Bollobas [Bol01]. Analysis of average-case behavior of algorithms is also known as *probabilistic analysis of algorithms*; see the survey by Reed [FR98]. Spielman and Teng [ST01] introduced *smoothed analysis of algorithms* – a notion that lies between worst-case analysis and probabilistic analysis, for which it would be fascinating to have an analog of the theory of **NP**-completeness.

Levin outlined his theory and Theorem 18.8 in [Lev86]. His formalization is more general than the one in this chapter. For instance, almost all the algorithms occurring in his version of the theory (e.g., the algorithm that computes a **P**-computable distribution or the one that computes a reduction) are allowed to be randomized.

The extension of Levin's theorem to **P**-samplable distributions is from Impagliazzo and Levin [IL90]. Many basic facts about Levin's theory, such as the effect of changing the assumptions, or the interrelationship among assumptions such as **P**-samplability and **P**-computability, are discussed in Ben-David et al. [BDCGL89]; see the survey by Goldreich [Gol97]. Johnson's survey [Joh84] of average-case complexity is old (it appeared around the time of Levin's original paper) but still highly readable. One of the goals in this area has been to prove the average-case completeness of "natural" **NP** problems. A recent paper of Livne [Liv06] gives the strongest such result (where the problems are "natural," though the distributions are not).

EXERCISES

18.1. Describe an algorithm that decides three-colorability on the uniform distribution of graphs (each edge is chosen with probability $1/2$) in expected polynomial-time.
H539

18.2. Describe an algorithm that solves the CLIQUE problem on the distribution $\langle G, k \rangle$ where G is a uniformly chosen n-vertex graph and k is chosen at random from $[n]$ in $n^{2\log n}$ expected time.
H539

18.3. Show that if $\mathbf{P} \neq \mathbf{NP}$, then there is a family $\mathcal{D} = \{\mathcal{D}_n\}$ of distributions on n-bit strings such that for every $x \in \{0, 1\}^n$, there is an algorithm to compute $\Pr[\mathcal{D}_n = x]$ but $\mathcal{D}$ is not **P**-computable.

18.4. Show that if a distribution is **P**-computable, then it is **P**-samplable.

18.5. Show that if $\mathbf{P}^{\#\mathbf{P}} \neq \mathbf{P}$, then there is a polynomial time-sampleable distribution that is not polynomial time-computable.
H539

18.6. Show that if an algorithm satisfies (18.2) then it satisfies (18.1), with possibly different constants ϵ, C.
H539

18.7. Show that the notion of reducibility defined in this chapter is transitive. In other words, if $\langle L_1, \mathcal{D}_1 \rangle \leq_p \langle L_2, \mathcal{D}_2 \rangle$ and $\langle L_2, \mathcal{D}_2 \rangle \leq_p \langle L_3, \mathcal{D}_3 \rangle$, then $\langle L_1, \mathcal{D}_1 \rangle \leq_p \langle L_3, \mathcal{D}_3 \rangle$.

18.8. Show that the distribution $\mathcal{U}$ of Theorem 18.8 is **P**-computable.

18.9. Show that the function g defined in Lemma 18.9 (Peak Elimination) is efficiently invertible in the following sense: If $y = g(x)$, then given y we can reconstruct x in $|x|^{O(1)}$ time.

18.10. Show that if one-way functions exist, then $\mathsf{dist}\mathbf{NP} \nsubseteq \mathsf{dist}\mathbf{P}$.

CHAPTER 19   Hardness amplification and error-correcting codes

> Core: the heart of something, the center both literal and figurative.
>   – Columbia Guide to Standard American English, 1993

Complexity theory studies the *computational hardness* of functions. In this chapter we are interested in functions that are hard to compute on the "average" instance, continuing a topic that played an important role in Chapters 9 and 18 and will do so again in Chapter 20. The special focus in this chapter is on techniques for *amplifying* hardness, which is useful in a host of contexts. In *cryptography* (see Chapter 9), hard functions are necessary to achieve secure encryption schemes of nontrivial key size. Many conjectured hard functions like factoring are only hard on a few instances, not all. Thus these functions do not suffice for some cryptographic applications, but via hardness amplification we can turn them into functions that do suffice. Another powerful application will be shown in Chapter 20—derandomization of the class **BPP** under worst-case complexity theoretic assumptions. Figure 19.1 contains a schematic view of this chapter's sections and the way their results are related to that result. In addition to their applications in complexity theory, the ideas covered in this chapter have had other uses, including new constructions of error-correcting codes and new algorithms in machine learning.

For simplicity we study hardness amplification in context of Boolean functions though this notion can apply to functions that are not Boolean-valued. Section 19.1 introduces the first technique for hardness amplification, namely, *Yao's XOR Lemma*. It allows us to turn weakly hard functions into strongly hard functions. Roughly speaking, a Boolean function f is said to be *weakly hard* if every moderate-sized circuit fails to compute it on some nonnegligible fraction of inputs, say 0.01 fraction. The function is *strongly hard* if every moderate-sized circuit fails to compute it on almost *half* the inputs, say $1/2 - \epsilon$ fraction of inputs. (Note that every Boolean function can be computed correctly on at least half the inputs by a trivial circuit, namely one that always outputs 1 or always outputs 0.) The section describes a way to transform every function using a simple XOR construction that does not greatly increase the complexity of computing it but has the property that if the function we started with was weakly hard, then it becomes strongly hard. This construction is very useful in cryptographic applications, as mentioned in Chapter 9. The construction involves identifying the "hard core" of a function, which is intriguing.

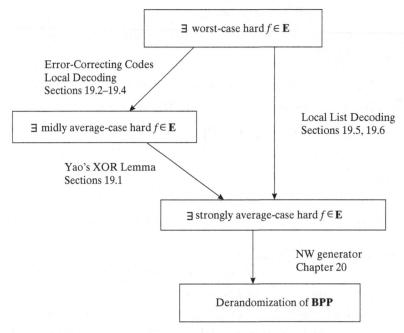

Figure 19.1. Organization of Chapter 19.

We then turn our attention to a different technique for hardness amplification that produces strongly hard functions starting with functions that are merely guaranteed to be hard in the *worst case*. This is highly nontrivial as there is often quite a difference between the worst-case and average-case complexity of computational problems. (For example, although finding the smallest factor of a given integer seems difficult in general, it's trivial to do for half the integers—namely, the even ones.) The main tool we use is *error-correcting codes*. We review the basic definition and constructions in Sections 19.2 and 19.3, while Section 19.4 covers *local decoding*, which is the main notion needed to apply error-correcting codes in our setting. As a result we obtain a way to transform every function f that is hard in the worst case into a function $\hat{f}$ that is mildly hard in the average case.

Combining the transformation of Section 19.4 with Yao's XOR Lemma of Section 19.1, we are able to get functions that are extremely hard on the average case from functions that are only hard on the worst case. Alas, quantitatively speaking the above transformation is not optimal, in the sense that even if the original function was worst-case hard for exponential-sized (i.e., size $2^{\Omega(n)}$) circuits, we are only able to guarantee that the transformed function will only be hard in the average case for subexponential sized (i.e., size $2^{n^{\Omega(1)}}$) circuits. In Sections 19.5 and 19.6 we show a stronger result that transforms in one fell swoop a function f that is hard on the worst case to a function $\hat{f}$ that is *extremely hard* on the average case. This transformation uses error-correcting codes in a more sophisticated way, via an independently interesting notion called *list decoding*. List decoding is covered in Section 19.5, while Section 19.6 describes *local list decoding*, which is the extension of list decoding needed for our purposes.

Readers who are familiar with the theory of error-correcting codes can skim through Sections 19.2 and 19.3 in a first reading (pausing to remind themselves of the Reed-Solomon and Reed-Muller codes in Definitions 19.10 and 19.12 and their associated decoding algorithms) and go on to Section 19.4.

19.1 MILD TO STRONG HARDNESS: YAO'S XOR LEMMA

Yao's XOR Lemma transforms a function that has "mild" average-case hardness to a function that has strong average-case hardness. The transformation is actually quite simple and natural, but its analysis is somewhat involved (yet, in our opinion, beautiful). To state the lemma, we need to define precisely the meaning of worst-case hardness and average-case hardness of a function.

Definition 19.1 (*Average-case and worst-case hardness*) For $f : \{0, 1\}^n \to \{0, 1\}$ and $\rho \in [0, 1]$ we define the ρ-*average case hardness of* f, denoted $H^\rho_{\text{avg}}(f)$, to be the largest S such that for every circuit C of size at most S, $\Pr_{x \in_R \{0,1\}^n}[C(x) = f(x)] < \rho$. For an infinite $f : \{0, 1\}^* \to \{0, 1\}$, we let $H^\rho_{\text{avg}}(f)(n)$ denote $H^\rho_{\text{avg}}(f_n)$ where f_n is the restriction of f to $\{0, 1\}^n$.

We define the *worst-case hardness* of f, denoted $H_{\text{wrs}}(f)$, to equal $H^1_{\text{avg}}(f)$ and define the *average-case hardness of* f, denoted $H_{\text{avg}}(f)$, to equal $\max \left\{ S : H^{1/2+1/S}_{\text{avg}}(f) \geq S \right\}$. That is, $H_{\text{avg}}(f)$ is the largest number S such that $\Pr_{x \in_R \{0,1\}^n}[C(x) = f(x)] < 1/2 + 1/S$ for every Boolean circuit C on n inputs with size at most S.

Note that for every function $f : \{0, 1\}^n \to \{0, 1\}$, $H_{\text{avg}}(f) \leq H_{\text{wrs}}(f) \leq O(2^n/n)$ (see Exercise 6.1). This definition of average-case hardness is tailored to the application of derandomization and, in particular, only deals with the uniform distribution over the inputs. See Chapter 18 for a more general treatment of average-case complexity. We can now state Yao's lemma.

Theorem 19.2 (*Yao's XOR Lemma* [Yao82a])
For every $f : \{0, 1\}^n \to \{0, 1\}$, $\delta > 0$ *and* $k \in \mathbb{N}$, *if* $\epsilon > 2(1 - \delta)^k$ *then*

$$H^{1/2+\epsilon}_{\text{avg}}(f^{\oplus k}) \geq \frac{\epsilon^2}{400n} H^{1-\delta}_{\text{avg}}(f)$$

where $f^{\oplus k} : \{0, 1\}^{nk} \to \{0, 1\}$ *is defined by* $f^{\oplus k}(x_1, \dots, x_k) = \sum_{i=1}^k f(x_i) \pmod 2$.

Yao's Lemma says that if small circuits cannot compute f with probability better than $1 - \delta$, then somewhat smaller circuits cannot compute $f^{\oplus k}$ with probability better than $1/2 + 2(1 - \delta)^k$. Intuitively, it makes sense that if you can only compute f on a $1 - \delta$ fraction of the inputs, then given a random k tuple $x_1, \dots, x_k$, unless all of these k inputs fall into this "good set" of inputs (which happens with probability $(1 - \delta)^k$), you will have to guess the answer to $\sum_{i=1}^k f(x_i) \pmod 2$ at random and be successful with probability at most $1/2$; see also Exercise 19.1. But making this intuition into a proof takes some effort. The main step is the following beautiful result of Impagliazzo.

Lemma 19.3 *(Impagliazzo's Hardcore Lemma* [Imp95a]*) Say that a distribution H over* $\{0, 1\}^n$ *has density* δ *if for every* $x \in \{0, 1\}^*$, $\Pr[H = x] \leq 1/(\delta 2^n)$. *For every* $\delta > 0, f :$ $\{0, 1\}^n \rightarrow \{0, 1\}$, *and* $\epsilon > 0$, *if* $\mathsf{H}_{\mathsf{avg}}^{1-\delta}(f) \geq S$, *then there exists a density-*δ *distribution* H *such that for every circuit* C *of size at most* $\frac{\epsilon^2 S}{100n}$,

$$\Pr_{x \in_R H}[C(x) = f(x)] \leq 1/2 + \epsilon \qquad \qquad \diamond$$

A priori, one can think that a function f that is hard to compute by small circuits with probability $1 - \delta$ could have two possible forms: (a) the hardness is sort of "spread" all over the inputs (different circuits make mistakes on different inputs), and the function is roughly $1 - \delta$-hard on every significant set of inputs or (b) there is a subset H of roughly a δ fraction of the inputs such that on H the function is *extremely hard* (cannot be computed better than $\frac{1}{2} + \epsilon$ for some tiny ϵ) and on the rest of the inputs the function may be even very easy. Such a set may be thought of as lying at the core of the hardness of f and is sometimes called the *hardcore set*. Impagliazzo's Lemma shows that actually *every* hard function has the form (b). (While the lemma talks about distributions and not sets, it is possible to transform it into a result on sets, see Exercise 19.2.)

19.1.1 Proof of Yao's XOR Lemma using Impagliazzo's Hardcore Lemma

We now show how to use Impagliazzo's Hardcore Lemma (Lemma 19.3) to prove Yao's XOR Lemma (Theorem 19.2). Let $f : \{0, 1\}^n \rightarrow \{0, 1\}$ be a function such that $\mathsf{H}_{\mathsf{avg}}^{1-\delta}(f) \geq S$, let $k \in \mathbb{N}$, and suppose, toward a contradiction, that there is a circuit C of size $S' = \frac{\epsilon^2}{400n} S$ such that

$$\Pr_{(x_1,\ldots,x_k) \in_R U_n^k}\left[C(x_1, \ldots, x_k) = \sum_{i=1}^{k} f(x_i) \pmod 2\right] \geq 1/2 + \epsilon \qquad (19.1)$$

where $\epsilon > 2(1 - \delta)^k$. We will first prove the lemma for the case $k = 2$ and then indicate how the proof can be generalized for every k.

Let H be the hardcore density-δ distribution obtained from Lemma 19.3, on which every S'-sized circuit fails to compute f with probability better than $1/2 + \epsilon/2$. We can think of the process of picking a uniform element in $\{0, 1\}^n$ as follows: First toss a biased coin that comes up "Heads" with probability δ. Then, if the coin came up "Heads" then pick a random element according to H, and if it came up "Tails" pick an element according to the distribution G, which is the "complement" of H. Namely, G is defined by setting $\Pr[G = x] = (2^{-n} - \delta \Pr[H = x])/(1-\delta)$. (Exercise 19.3 asks you to verify that G is indeed a distribution and that this process does indeed yield a uniform element.) We shorthand this and write

$$U_n = (1 - \delta)G + \delta H \qquad (19.2)$$

If we consider the distribution $(U_n)^2$ of picking *two independent* random strings and concatenating them, then by (19.2) we can write

$$(U_n)^2 = (1 - \delta)^2 G^2 + (1 - \delta)\delta GH + \delta(1 - \delta)HG + \delta^2 H^2 \qquad (19.3)$$

where we use G^2 to denote the concatenation of two independent copies of G, GH to denote the concatenation of a string chosen from G and a string chosen independently from H, and so on.

Now for every distribution $\mathcal{D}$ over $\{0, 1\}^{2n}$, let $P_\mathcal{D}$ be the probability of the event of the left-hand side of (19.1). That is, $P_\mathcal{D}$ is the probability that $C(x_1, x_2) = f(x_1) + f(x_2)$ (mod 2) where x_1, x_2 are chosen from $\mathcal{D}$. Combining (19.1) and (19.3) we get

$$1/2 + \epsilon \leq P_{(U_n)^2} = (1 - \delta)^2 P_{G^2} + (1 - \delta)\delta P_{GH} + \delta(1 - \delta)P_{HG} + \delta^2 P_{H^2} \qquad (19.4)$$

But since $\epsilon > 2(1 - \delta)^2$ and $P_{G^2} \leq 1$, (19.4) implies

$$1/2 + \frac{\epsilon}{2} \leq (1 - \delta)\delta P_{GH} + \delta(1 - \delta)P_{HG} + \delta^2 P_{H^2} \qquad (19.5)$$

Since the coefficients on the right-hand side of (19.5) sum up to less than 1, the averaging principle implies that at least one of these probabilities must be larger than the left-hand side. For example, assume that $P_{HG} \geq 1/2 + \epsilon/2$ (the other cases are symmetrical). This means that

$$\Pr_{x_1 \in_R H, x_2 \in_R G}[C(x_1, x_2) = f(x_1) + f(x_2) \quad (\text{mod } 2)] > 1/2 + \frac{\epsilon}{2}$$

Thus by the averaging principle, there exists a fixed string x_2 such that

$$\Pr_{x_1 \in_R H}[C(x_1, x_2) = f(x_1) + f(x_2) \quad (\text{mod } 2)] > 1/2 + \frac{\epsilon}{2}$$

or, equivalently,

$$\Pr_{x_1 \in_R H}[C(x_1, x_2) + f(x_2) \quad (\text{mod } 2) = f(x_1)] > 1/2 + \frac{\epsilon}{2}$$

But this means that we have an S'-sized circuit D (the circuit computing the mapping $x_1 \mapsto C(x_1, x_2) + f(x_2)$ (mod 2)) that computes f on inputs chosen from H with probability better than $1/2 + \epsilon/2$, contradicting the fact that H is hardcore!

This completes the proof for the case $k = 2$. The proof for general k follows along the same lines, using the equation

$$(U_n)^k = (1 - \delta)^k G^k + (1 - \delta)^{k-1}\delta G^{k-1}H + \cdots + \delta^k H^k$$

in place of (19.3); we leave verifying the details to the reader as Exercise 19.4. ∎

19.1.2 Proof of Impagliazzo's Lemma

We now turn to proving Impagliazzo's Hardcore Lemma (Lemma 19.3). Let f be a function with $H_{\text{avg}}^{1-\delta}(f) \geq S$ and let $\epsilon > 0$. To prove the lemma we need to show a density

δ distribution H on which *every* circuit C of size $S' = \frac{\epsilon^2 S}{100n}$ cannot compute f with probability better than $1/2 + \epsilon$.

Let's think of this task as a game between two players named *Russell* and *Noam*. Noam wants to compute the function f, and Russell wants Noam to fail. The game proceeds as follows: Russell first chooses a δ-density distribution H, and then Noam chooses a circuit C of size at most S'. At the game's conclusion, Russell pays Noam v dollars, where $v = \Pr_{x \in_R H}[C(x) = f(x)]$. Assume toward a contradiction that the lemma is false, and hence for every δ-density distribution H chosen by Russell, Noam can find an S'-sized circuit C on which $\Pr_{x \in_R H}[C(x) = f(x)] \geq 1/2 + \epsilon$.

Now this game is a zero-sum game, and so we can use von Neumann's *Min-Max Theorem* (see Note 19.1.2) that says that if we allow *randomized* (also known as mixed) strategies, then Noam can achieve the same value even if he plays first. By randomized strategies we mean that Noam and Russell can also select arbitrary distributions over their choices. In Russell's case this makes no difference as a distribution over density-δ distributions is still a density-δ distribution.[1] However in Noam's case we need to allow him to choose a *distribution* $\mathcal{C}$ over S'-sized circuits. Our assumption, combined with the min-max theorem, means that there exists such a distribution $\mathcal{C}$ satisfying

$$\Pr_{C \in_R \mathcal{C}, x \in_R H}[C(x) = f(x)] \geq 1/2 + \epsilon \tag{19.6}$$

for *every* δ-density H.

Call a string $x \in \{0, 1\}^n$ "bad" if $\Pr_{C \in_R \mathcal{C}}[C(x) = f(x)] < 1/2 + \epsilon$ and call x "good" otherwise. There are less than $\delta 2^n$ bad x's. Indeed, otherwise we could let H be the uniform distribution over the bad x's and it would violate (19.6). Now let us choose a circuit C as follows: Set $t = 50n/\epsilon^2$, pick $C_1, \dots, C_t$ independently from $\mathcal{C}$, and define $C(x)$ to equal the majority of $C_1(x), \dots, C_t(x)$ for every $x \in \{0, 1\}^n$. Note that the size of C is $tS' < S$. We claim that if we choose the circuit C in this way, then for every good $x \in \{0, 1\}^n, \Pr[C(x) \neq f(x)] < 2^{-n}$. Indeed, this follows by applying the Chernoff bound (see Corollary A.15). Since there are at most 2^n good x's, we can apply the union bound to deduce that there exists a size S circuit C such that $C(x) = f(x)$ for *every* good x. But since there are less than $\delta 2^n$ bad x's, this implies that $\Pr_{x \in_R U_n}[C(x) = f(x)] > 1 - \delta$, contradicting the assumption that $\mathsf{H}^{1-\delta}_{\mathsf{avg}}(f) \geq S$.

Taken in the contrapositive, Lemma 19.3 implies that if for every significant chunk of the inputs there is some circuit that computes f with on this chunk with some advantage over $1/2$, then there is a single circuit that computes f good probability over all inputs. In machine learning, such a result (transforming a way to weakly predict some function into a way to strongly predict it) is called *boosting* of learning methods. Although the proof we presented here is nonconstructive, Impagliazzo's original proof was constructive and was used to obtain a boosting algorithm yielding some new results in machine learning, see [KS99].

---

[1] In fact, the set of density δ distributions can be viewed as the set of distributions over $\delta 2^n$-flat distributions, where a distribution is K-flat if it is uniform over a set of size K (see Exercise 19.7). This fact means that we can think of the game as finite and so use the Min-Max Theorem in the form it is stated in Note 19.4.

NOTE 19.4 *(The Min-Max Theorem)*

A *zero-sum game* is, as the name implies, a game between two parties in which whatever one party loses is won by the other party. It is modeled by an $m \times n$ matrix $A = (a_{i,j})$ of real numbers. The game consists of only two moves. One party, called the *minimizer* or *column player*, chooses an index $j \in [n]$, while the other party, called the *maximizer* or *row player*, chooses an index $i \in [m]$. The *outcome* is that the column player has to pay $a_{i,j}$ units of money to the row player (if $a_{i,j}$ is negative, then the row player pays the column player $|a_{i,j}|$ units). Clearly, the *order* in which players make their moves is important. The Min-Max Theorem says that, surprisingly, if we allow the players randomized strategies, then the order of play is immaterial.

By *randomized* (also known as *mixed*) strategies, we mean that the column player chooses a *distribution* over the columns; that is, a vector $\mathbf{p} \in [0,1]^n$ with $\sum_{i=1}^{n} p_i = 1$. Similarly, the row player chooses a distribution $\mathbf{q}$ over the rows. The amount paid is the expectation of $a_{i,j}$ for j chosen from $\mathbf{p}$ and i chosen from $\mathbf{q}$. If we think of $\mathbf{p}$ as a column vector and $\mathbf{q}$ as a row vector then this is equal to $\mathbf{q}A\mathbf{p}$. The Min-Max Theorem says that

$$\min_{\substack{\mathbf{p}\in[0,1]^n \\ \Sigma_i p_i=1}} \max_{\substack{\mathbf{q}\in[0,1]^m \\ \Sigma_i q_i=1}} \mathbf{q}A\mathbf{p} = \max_{\substack{\mathbf{q}\in[0,1]^m \\ \Sigma_i q_i=1}} \min_{\substack{\mathbf{p}\in[0,1]^n \\ \Sigma_i p_i=1}} \mathbf{q}A\mathbf{p} \qquad (19.7)$$

As discussed in Exercise 19.6, the Min-Max Theorem can be proven using the following result, known as the *Separating Hyperplane Theorem*: If C and D are disjoint convex subsets of $\mathbb{R}^m$, then there is a hyperplane that separates them. (A subset $C \subseteq \mathbb{R}^m$ is *convex* if whenever it contains a pair of points $\mathbf{x}, \mathbf{y}$, it contains the line segment $\{\alpha\mathbf{x} + (1 - \alpha)\mathbf{y} : 0 \le \alpha \le 1\}$ with $\mathbf{x}$ and $\mathbf{y}$ as its endpoints.) We ask you to prove (a relaxed variant of) the separating hyperplane theorem in Exercise 19.5 but here is a "proof by picture" for the two-dimensional case.

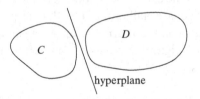

19.2 TOOL: ERROR-CORRECTING CODES

Our next goal will be to construct average-case hard functions using functions that are only worst-case hard. Our main tool will be *error-correcting codes*. An error-correcting code maps strings into slightly larger strings in a way that "amplifies differences" in the sense that every two distinct strings (even if they differ by just one bit) get mapped into two strings that are "very far" from one another. The formal definition follows.

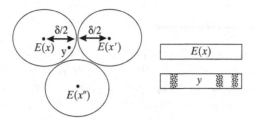

Figure 19.2. In a δ-distance error-correcting code, $\Delta(E(x), E(x')) \geq \delta$ for every $x \neq x'$. We can recover x from every string y in which less than $\delta/2$ coordinates were corrupted (i.e., $\Delta(y, E(x)) < \delta/2$) since the $\delta/2$-radius balls around every codeword are disjoint. The dotted areas represent corrupted coordinates.

Definition 19.5 *(Error-correcting codes)* For $x, y \in \{0, 1\}^m$, the *fractional Hamming distance* of x and y, denoted $\Delta(x, y)$, is equal to $\frac{1}{m} |\{i : x_i \neq y_i\}|$.

For every $\delta \in [0, 1]$, a function $E : \{0, 1\}^n \to \{0, 1\}^m$ is an *error-correcting code (ECC) with distance* δ, if for every $x \neq y \in \{0, 1\}^n$, $\Delta(E(x), E(y)) \geq \delta$. We call the set $Im(E) = \{E(x) : x \in \{0, 1\}^n\}$ the set of *codewords* of E.

Note that some texts define an error-correcting code not as a function $E : \{0, 1\}^n \to \{0, 1\}^m$ but rather as a 2^n-sized subset of $\{0, 1\}^m$ (corresponding to $Im(E)$ in our notation). Error-correcting codes have had a vast number of practical and theoretical applications in computer science and engineering, but their motivation stems from the following simple application: Suppose that Alice wants to transmit a string $x \in \{0, 1\}^m$ to Bob, but her channel of communication to Bob is *noisy* and every string y she sends might be corrupted in as many as 10% of its coordinates. That is, her only guarantee is that Bob would receive a string y' satisfying $\Delta(y, y') \leq 0.1$. Alice can perform this task using an error-correcting code $E : \{0, 1\}^n \to \{0, 1\}^m$ of distance $\delta > 0.2$. The idea is that she sends to Bob $y = E(x)$ and Bob receives a string y' satisfying $\Delta(y, y') \leq 0.1$. Since $\Delta(y, E(w)) > 0.2$ for every $w \neq x$, it follows that y is the unique codeword of E that is of distance at most 0.1 from y', and so Bob can find y and from it find x such that $E(x) = y$ (see Figure 19.2). One can see from this example that we'd want codes with as large a distance δ as possible, as small output length m as possible, and of course we'd like both Alice and Bob to be able to carry the encoding and decoding efficiently. The following lemma shows that, ignoring issues of computational efficiency, pretty good error-correcting codes exist.

Lemma 19.6 *(Gilbert-Varshamov Bound) For every $\delta < 1/2$ and sufficiently large n, there exists a function $E : \{0, 1\}^n \to \{0, 1\}^{n/(1-H(\delta))}$ that is an error-correcting code with distance δ, where $H(\delta) = \delta \log(1/\delta) + (1 - \delta) \log(1/(1 - \delta))$.*[2]   ◇

PROOF: We prove a slightly weaker statement: the existence of a δ-distance ECC $E : \{0, 1\}^n \to \{0, 1\}^m$ where $m = 2n/(1 - H(\delta))$ instead of $m = n/(1 - H(\delta))$. To do so, we simply choose E at random. That is, we choose 2^n random strings $y_1, y_2, \ldots, y_{2^n} \in \{0, 1\}^m$ and E maps the input $x \in \{0, 1\}^n$ (which we can identify with a number in $[2^n]$) to the string y_x.

---

[2] $H(\delta)$ is called the *Shannon entropy function*. It is not hard to see that $H(1/2) = 1, H(0) = 0$, and $H(\delta) \in (0, 1)$ for every $\delta \in (0, 1/2)$.

It suffices to show that the probability that for some $i < j$ with $i, j \in [2^n]$, $\Delta(y_i, y_j) < \delta$ is less than 1. But for every string y_i, the number of strings that are of distance at most δ to it is $\binom{m}{\lceil \delta m \rceil}$, which is less than $0.99 \cdot 2^{H(\delta)m}$ for m sufficiently large (see Appendix A), and so for every $j > i$, the probability that y_j falls in this ball is bounded by $0.99 \cdot 2^{H(\delta)m}/2^m$. Since there are at most 2^{2n} such pairs i, j, we only need to show that $0.99 \cdot 2^{2n} \frac{2^{H(\delta)m}}{2^m} < 1$, which is indeed the case for our choice of m. By a slightly more clever argument, we can prove the lemma as stated; see Exercise 19.9. It turns out that as δ tends to zero, there do exist codes with smaller values of m than $n/(1 - H(\delta))$, but it is not known whether or not Lemma 19.6 is optimal for δ tending to $1/2$. ∎

Why half?

Lemma 19.6 only provides codes of distance δ for $\delta < 1/2$, and you might wonder whether this is inherent or perhaps codes of even greater distance exist. It turns out we can have codes of distance $1/2$, but only if we allow m to be exponentially larger than n (i.e., $m \geq 2^{n-1}$). For every $\delta > 1/2$, if n is sufficiently large then there is no ECC $E : \{0, 1\}^n \to \{0, 1\}^m$ that has distance δ, no matter how large m is. Both these bounds are explored in Exercise 19.10.

NOTE 19.7 *(High-dimensional geometry)*

While we are normally used to geometry in two or three dimensions, we can get some intuition on error-correcting codes by considering the geometry of *high-dimensional spaces*. Perhaps the strongest effect of high dimension is the following: Compare the volume of the cube with all sides 1 and the ball of radius $1/4$. In one dimension, the ratio between these volumes is $1/(1/2) = 2$, in two dimensions it is $1/(\pi/4^2) = 16/\pi$, while in three dimensions it is $1/(4/3\pi/4^3) = 48/\pi$. As the number of dimension grows, this ratio grows exponentially in the number of dimensions. (The volume of a ball of radius r in m dimensions is roughly $\frac{\pi^{m/2}}{\lfloor m/2 \rfloor!} r^m$.) Similarly for any two radii $r_1 > r_2$, the volume of the m-dimension ball of radius r_1 is exponentially larger than the volume of the r_2-radius ball.

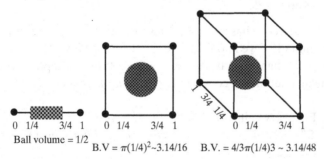

Ball volume = 1/2

B.V $= \pi(1/4)^2 \sim 3.14/16$ B.V. $= 4/3\pi(1/4)3 \sim 3.14/48$

This intuition lies behind the existence of an error-correcting code with, say, distance $1/4$ mapping n bit strings into $m = 5n$ bit strings. We can have $2^{m/5}$ codewords that are all of distance at least $1/4$ from one another because, also in the discrete setting, the volume (i.e., number of points contained) of the radius-$1/4$ ball is exponentially smaller than the volume of the cube $\{0, 1\}^n$. Therefore, we can "pack" $2^{m/5}$ such balls within the cube.

19.2.1 Explicit codes

The mere existence of an error-correcting code is not sufficient for most applications: We need to be able to actually compute them. For this we need to show an *explicit function* $E : \{0, 1\}^n \to \{0, 1\}^m$ that is an error-correcting code satisfying the following properties:

> *Efficient encoding* There is a poly(m) time algorithm to compute $E(x)$ from x.
>
> *Efficient decoding* There is a polynomial-time algorithm to compute x from every y such that $\Delta(y, E(x)) < \rho$ for some ρ. For this to be possible, the number ρ must be less than $\delta/2$, where δ is the distance of E; see Exercise 19.11.

We now describe some explicit functions that are error correcting codes.

19.2.2 Walsh-Hadamard code

For two strings $x, y \in \{0, 1\}^n$, we define $x \odot y = \sum_{i=1}^{n} x_i y_i \pmod 2$. The *Walsh-Hadamard code* is the function $\mathsf{WH} : \{0, 1\}^n \to \{0, 1\}^{2^n}$ that maps every string $x \in \{0, 1\}^n$ into the string $z \in \{0, 1\}^{2^n}$ satisfying $z_y = x \odot y$ for every $y \in \{0, 1\}^n$ (where z_y denotes the yth coordinate of z, identifying $\{0, 1\}^n$ with $[2^n]$ in some canonical way).

Claim 19.8 *The function* WH *is an error correcting code of distance* $1/2$.   ◇

PROOF: First, note that WH is a linear function. That is, $\mathsf{WH}(x+y) = \mathsf{WH}(x) + \mathsf{WH}(y)$, where $x+y$ denotes the componentwise addition of x and y modulo 2 (i.e., bitwise XOR). Thus, for every $x \neq y \in \{0, 1\}^n$, the number of 1's in the string $\mathsf{WH}(x) + \mathsf{WH}(y) = \mathsf{WH}(x + y)$ is equal to the number of coordinates on which $\mathsf{WH}(x)$ and $\mathsf{WH}(y)$ differ. Thus, it suffices to show that for every $w \neq 0^n$, at least half of the coordinates in $\mathsf{WH}(w)$ are 1. Yet this follows from the random subsum principle (Claim A.31) that says that the probability that $w \odot y = 1$ for $y \in_R \{0, 1\}^n$ is exactly $1/2$. ∎

19.2.3 Reed-Solomon code

The Walsh-Hadamard code has a serious drawback: Its output size is exponential in the input size. By Lemma 19.6 we know that we can do much better (at least if we're willing to tolerate a distance slightly smaller than $1/2$). To get toward explicit codes with better output, we'll make a detour via codes with *nonbinary* alphabet.

Definition 19.9 For every finite set Σ and $x, y \in \Sigma^m$, we define $\Delta(x, y) = \frac{1}{m} |\{i : x_i \neq y_i\}|$. We say that $E : \Sigma^n \to \Sigma^m$ is an *error-correcting code with distance* δ *over alphabet* Σ if for every $x \neq y \in \Sigma^n$, $\Delta(E(x), E(y)) \geq \delta$.   ◇

Allowing a larger alphabet makes the problem of constructing codes easier. For example, every ECC with distance δ over the binary ($\{0, 1\}$) alphabet automatically implies an ECC with the same distance over the alphabet $\{0, 1, 2, 3\}$: Just encode strings over $\{0, 1, 2, 3\}$ as strings over $\{0, 1\}$ in the obvious way. However, the other direction does not work: If we take an ECC over $\{0, 1, 2, 3\}$ and transform it into a code over

{0, 1} in the natural way, the distance might grow from δ to 2δ (see Exercise 19.12). The Reed-Solomon code is a construction of an error-correcting code that can use as its alphabet any sufficiently large field $\mathbb{F}$.

Definition 19.10 *(Reed-Solomon Code)* Let $\mathbb{F}$ be a field and n, m numbers satisfying $n \leq m \leq |\mathbb{F}|$. The *Reed-Solomon code* from $\mathbb{F}^n$ to $\mathbb{F}^m$ is the function $\mathsf{RS} : \mathbb{F}^n \to \mathbb{F}^m$ that on input $a_0, \ldots, a_{n-1} \in \mathbb{F}^n$ outputs the string $z_0, \ldots, z_{m-1}$ where $z_j = \sum_{i=0}^{n-1} a_i f_j^i$, and f_j denotes the jth element of $\mathbb{F}$ under some ordering. $\diamond$

Note that an equivalent way of defining the Reed Solomon code is that it takes as input a description of the $n - 1$ degree polynomial $A(x) = \sum_{i=1}^{n-1} a_i x^i$ and outputs the evaluation of A on the points $f_0, \ldots, f_{m-1}$.

Lemma 19.11 *The Reed-Solomon code* $\mathsf{RS} : \mathbb{F}^n \to \mathbb{F}^m$ *has distance* $1 - \frac{n}{m}$. $\diamond$

PROOF: As in the case of Walsh-Hadamard code, the function RS is also linear in the sense that $\mathsf{RS}(a + b) = \mathsf{RS}(a) + \mathsf{RS}(b)$ (where addition is taken to be componentwise addition in $\mathbb{F}$). Thus as before we only need to show that for every $a \neq 0^n$, $\mathsf{RS}(a)$ has at most n coordinates that are zero. But follows immediately from the fact that a nonzero $n - 1$ degree polynomial has at most n roots (see Appendix A). ∎

19.2.4 Reed-Muller codes

Both the Walsh-Hadamard and and the Reed-Solomon codes are special cases of the following family of codes known as Reed-Muller codes.

Definition 19.12 *(Reed-Muller Codes)* Let $\mathbb{F}$ be a finite field, and let ℓ, d be numbers with $d < |\mathbb{F}|$. The *Reed-Muller code* with parameters $\mathbb{F}, \ell, d$ is the function $\mathsf{RM} : \mathbb{F}^{\binom{\ell+d}{d}} \to \mathbb{F}^{|\mathbb{F}|^\ell}$ that maps every ℓ-variable polynomial P over $\mathbb{F}$ of total degree d to the values of P on all the inputs in $\mathbb{F}^\ell$.

That is, the input is a polynomial of the form

$$P(x_1, \ldots, x_\ell) = \sum_{i_1 + \cdots + i_\ell \leq d} c_{i_1, \ldots, i_\ell} x_1^{i_1} x_2^{i_2} \cdots x_\ell^{i_\ell}$$

specified by the vector of $\binom{\ell+d}{d}$ coefficients $\{c_{i_1, \ldots, i_\ell}\}$ and the output is the sequence $\{P(x_1, \ldots, x_\ell)\}$ for every $x_1, \ldots, x_\ell \in \mathbb{F}$. $\diamond$

Setting $\ell = 1$ one obtains the Reed-Solomon code (for $m = |\mathbb{F}|$), while setting $d = 1$ and $\mathbb{F} = \mathrm{GF}(2)$ one obtains a slight variant of the Walsh-Hadamard code (i.e., the code that maps every $x \in \{0, 1\}^n$ into a $2 \cdot 2^n$ long string z satisfying $z_{y,a} = x \odot y + a$ (mod 2) for every $y \in \{0, 1\}^n$, $a \in \{0, 1\}$). The Schwartz-Zippel Lemma (Lemma A.36) shows that the Reed-Muller code is an ECC with distance $1 - d/|\mathbb{F}|$. Note that this implies the previously stated bounds for the Walsh-Hadamard and Reed-Solomon codes.

19.2.5 Concatenated codes

The Walsh-Hadamard code has the drawback of exponential-sized output, and the Reed-Solomon code has the drawback of a nonbinary alphabet. We now show we can combine them both to obtain a code without either of these drawbacks.

Definition 19.13 If RS is the Reed-Solomon code mapping $\mathbb{F}^n$ to $\mathbb{F}^m$ (for some $n, m, \mathbb{F}$) and WH is the Walsh-Hadamard code mapping $\{0, 1\}^{\log |\mathbb{F}|}$ to $\{0, 1\}^{2^{\log |\mathbb{F}|}} = \{0, 1\}^{|\mathbb{F}|}$, then the code WH $\circ$ RS maps $\{0, 1\}^{n \log |\mathbb{F}|}$ to $\{0, 1\}^{m|\mathbb{F}|}$ in the following way:

1. View RS as a code from $\{0, 1\}^{n \log |\mathbb{F}|}$ to $\mathbb{F}^m$ and WH as a code from $\mathbb{F}$ to $\{0, 1\}^{|\mathbb{F}|}$ using the canonical representation of elements in $\mathbb{F}$ as strings in $\{0, 1\}^{\log |\mathbb{F}|}$.
2. For every input $x \in \{0, 1\}^{n \log |\mathbb{F}|}$, WH $\circ$ RS(x) is equal to WH$(\text{RS}(x)_1), \ldots, \text{WH}(\text{RS}(x)_m)$ where RS$(x)_i$ denotes the ith symbol of RS(x).

Note that the code WH $\circ$ RS can be computed in time polynomial in n, m and $|\mathbb{F}|$. We now analyze its distance.

Claim 19.14 *Let $\delta_1 = 1 - n/m$ be the distance of* RS *and $\delta_2 = 1/2$ be the distance of* WH. *Then* WH $\circ$ RS *is an ECC of distance $\delta_1 \delta_2$.* ◇

PROOF: Let x, y be two distinct strings in $\{0, 1\}^{\log |\mathbb{F}| n}$. If we set $x' = \text{RS}(x')$ and $y' = \text{RS}(y')$ then $\Delta(x', y') \geq \delta_1$. If we let x'' (resp. y'') to be the binary string obtained by applying WH to each of these blocks, then whenever two blocks are distinct, the corresponding encoding will have distance δ_2, and so $\delta(x'', y'') \geq \delta_1 \delta_2$. ∎

Because for every $k \in \mathbb{N}$, there exists a finite field $|\mathbb{F}|$ of size in $[k, 2k]$ (e.g., take a prime in $[k, 2k]$ or a power of two), we can use this construction to obtain, for every n, a polynomial-time computable ECC $E : \{0, 1\}^n \to \{0, 1\}^{20n^2}$ of distance 0.4.

Both Definition 19.13 and Lemma 19.14 easily generalize for codes other than Reed-Solomon and Hadamard. Thus, for every two ECC's $E_1 : \{0, 1\}^n \to \Sigma^m$ and $E_2 : \Sigma \to \{0, 1\}^k$, their concatenation $E_2 \circ E_1$ is a code from $\{0, 1\}^n$ to $\{0, 1\}^{mk}$ that has distance at least $\delta_1 \delta_2$ where δ_1 (resp. δ_2) is the distance of E_1 (resp. E_2), see Figure 19.3. In particular, using a different binary code than WH, it is known how to use concatenation

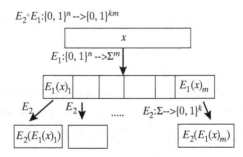

Figure 19.3. If E_1, E_2 are ECC's such that $E_1 : \{0, 1\}^n \to \Sigma^m$ and $E_2 : \sigma \to \{0, 1\}^k$, then the concatenated code $E : \{0, 1\}^n \to \{0, 1\}^{nk}$ maps x into the sequence of blocks $E_2(E_1(x)_1), \ldots, E_2(E_1(x)_m)$.

to obtain a polynomial-time computable ECC $E : \{0, 1\}^n \rightarrow \{0, 1\}^m$ of constant distance $\delta > 0$ such that $m = O(n)$; see Exercise 19.18.

19.3 EFFICIENT DECODING

To actually use an error-correcting code to store and retrieve information, we need a way to efficiently *decode* a message x from its encoding $E(x)$ even if this encoding has been corrupted in some fraction ρ of its coordinates. We now show how to do this for the Reed-Solomon code and for concatenated codes.

19.3.1 Decoding Reed-Solomon

Recall that the Reed-Solomon treats its input as describing a polynomial and outputs the values of this polynomial on m inputs. We know (see Theorem A.35) that a univariate degree d polynomial can be interpolated from any $d + 1$ values. Here we consider a *robust* version of this procedure, whereby we wish to recover the polynomial from m values of which ρm are "faulty" or "noisy."

Theorem 19.15 (*Unique decoding for Reed-Solomon* [BW86])
There is a polynomial-time algorithm that given a list $(a_1, b_1), \ldots, (a_m, b_m)$ of pairs of elements of a finite field $\mathbb{F}$ such that there is a d-degree polynomial $G : \mathbb{F} \rightarrow \mathbb{F}$ satisfying $G(a_i) = b_i$ for t of the numbers $i \in [m]$, with $t > \frac{m}{2} + \frac{d}{2}$, recovers G.

Since Reed-Solomon is an ECC with distance $1 - \frac{d}{m}$, Theorem 19.15 means that we can efficiently recover the correct polynomial from a version corrupted in ρ places as long as ρ is smaller than half the distance. This is optimal in the sense that once the fraction of errors is larger than half the distance, we are no longer guaranteed the existence of a unique solution.

PROOF OF THEOREM 19.15: As a warmup, we start by considering the case that the number of errors is very small. (This setting is still sufficiently strong for many applications.)

Randomized interpolation: The case of $t \geq (1 - \frac{1}{2(d+1)})m$. Assume that t is quite large: $t > (1 - \frac{1}{2(d+1)})m$. In this case, we can just select $d + 1$ pairs $(x_1, y_1), \ldots, (x_{d+1}, y_{d+1})$ at random from the set $\{(a_i, b_i)\}$ and use standard polynomial interpolation to compute the unique a d-degree polynomial P such that $P(x_j) = y_j$ for all $j \in [d + 1]$. We then check whether P agrees with at least t pairs of the entire sequence, and if so, we output P (otherwise we try again). By the union bound, the probability that $x_j \neq G(y_j)$ for one of the $d + 1$ chosen pairs is at most $(d + 1)\frac{m-t}{t} \leq 1/2$, and hence with probability at least $1/2$ it will be the case that $P = G$.

Berlekamp-Welch Procedure: The case of $t \geq \frac{m}{2} + \frac{d}{2} + 1$. We now prove Theorem 19.15 using a procedure known as the *Berlekamp-Welch decoding*. For simplicity of notations, we assume that $m = 4d$ and $t = 3d$. However, the proof generalizes to any parameters m, d, t satisfying $t > \frac{m}{2} + \frac{d}{2}$; see Exercise 19.13. Thus, we assume that there exists a

d-degree polynomial G such that

$$G(a_i) = b_i \text{ for at least } 3d \text{ of } i\text{'s in } [m] = [4d] \tag{19.8}$$

We will use the following decoding procedure:

1. Find a degree $2d$ polynomial $C(x)$ and a degree-d nonzero polynomial $E(x)$ such that

$$C(a_i) = b_i E(a_i) \text{ for every } i \in [m] \tag{19.9}$$

This can be done by considering (19.9) as a set of $4d$ linear equations with the unknowns being the $2d + 1$ coefficients of $C(x)$ and the $d + 1$ coefficients of E. These equations have a solution with nonzero $E(x)$ since one can define $E(x)$ to a nonzero polynomial that is equal to zero on every a_i such that $G(a_i) \neq b_i$ (under our assumption (19.8) there are at most d such places).[3]

2. Divide C by E: Get a polynomial P such that $C(x) = E(x)P(x)$ (we will show that E divides C without remainder). Output P.
   We know by (19.8) and (19.9) that $C(x) = G(x)E(x)$ for at least $3d$ values, meaning that $C(x) - G(x)E(x)$ is a degree $2d$ polynomial with at least $3d$ roots. This means that this polynomial is identically zero (i.e., $C(x) = G(x)E(x)$ for every $x \in \mathbb{F}$). Thus it does indeed hold that $G = C/E$.

∎

19.3.2 Decoding concatenated codes

Decoding concatenated codes can be achieved through the natural algorithm. Recall that if $E_1 : \{0, 1\}^n \to \Sigma^m$ and $E_2 : \Sigma \to \{0, 1\}^k$ are two ECC's, then $E_2 \circ E_1$ maps every string $x \in \{0, 1\}^n$ to the string $E_2(E_1(x)_1) \cdots E_2(E_1(x)_n)$. Suppose that we have a decoder for E_1 (resp. E_2) that can handle ρ_1 (resp. ρ_2) errors. Then, we have a decoder for $E_2 \circ E_1$ that can handle $\rho_2\rho_1$ errors. The decoder, given a string $y \in \{0, 1\}^{mk}$ composed of m blocks $y_1, \ldots, y_m \in \{0, 1\}^k$, first decodes each block y_i to a symbol z_i in Σ, and then uses the decoder of E_1 to decode $z_1, \ldots, z_m$. The decoder can indeed handle $\rho_1\rho_2$ errors since if $\Delta(y, E_2 \circ E_1(x)) \leq \rho_1\rho_2$, then at most ρ_1 of the blocks of y have distance at least ρ_2 from the corresponding block of $E_2 \circ E_1(x)$.

19.4 LOCAL DECODING AND HARDNESS AMPLIFICATION

We now show the connection between error-correcting codes and hardness amplification. The idea is actually quite simple (see also Figure 19.4). A function $f : \{0, 1\}^n \to \{0, 1\}$ can be viewed as a binary string of length $N = 2^n$. Suppose we encode f to a string $\hat{f} \in \{0, 1\}^M$ using an ECC mapping $\{0, 1\}^N$ to $\{0, 1\}^M$ with distance larger than, say, 0.2. Then we can view $\hat{f}$ as a function from $\{0, 1\}^{\log M}$ to $\{0, 1\}$ and at least in principle it should be possible to recover f from a corrupted version of $\hat{f}$ where, say, at most 10% of the locations have been modified. In other words, if it is possible to compute $\hat{f}$

---

[3] One can efficiently find such a solution by trying to solve the equations after adding to them an equation of the form $E_j = e_j$ where E_j is the jth coefficient of $E(x)$ and e_j is a nonzero element of $\mathbb{F}$. The number of such possible equations is polynomial, and at least one of them will result in a satisfiable set of equations.

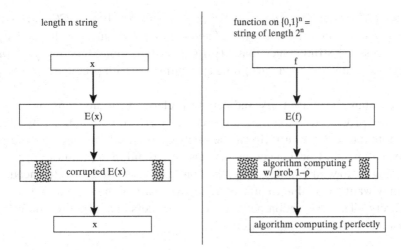

Figure 19.4. An ECC allows us to map a string x to $E(x)$ such as x can be reconstructed from a corrupted version of $E(x)$. The idea is to treat a function $f : \{0, 1\}^n \to \{0, 1\}$ as a string in $\{0, 1\}^{2^n}$, encode it using an ECC to a function $\hat{f}$. Intuitively, $\hat{f}$ should be hard on the average case if f was hard on the worst case, since an algorithm to solve $\hat{f}$ with probability $1 - \rho$ could be transformed (using the ECC's decoding algorithm) to an algorithm computing f on every input.

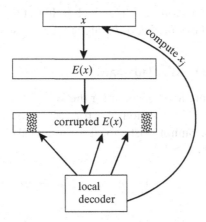

Figure 19.5. A local decoder gets access to a corrupted version of $E(x)$ and an index i and computes from it x_i (with high probability).

with probability at least 0.9, then it should be possible to compute f exactly. Taking the contrapositive this means that if f is hard to compute in the worst case, then $\hat{f}$ is hard to compute in the average case!

To make this idea work we need to show we can transform every circuit that correctly computes many bits of $\hat{f}$ into a circuit that correctly computes all the bits of f. This is formalized using a *local decoder* (see Figure 19.5), which is a decoding algorithm that given *random access* to a (possibly corrupted) codeword y' close to $E(x)$ can compute any any desired bit of the original input x. Since we are interested in the circuits that could be of size as small as poly(n) – in other words, *polylogarithmic* in $N = 2^n$ – this must also be the running time of the local decoder.

Definition 19.16 *(Local decoder)* Let $E : \{0, 1\}^n \to \{0, 1\}^m$ be an ECC and let ρ and q be some numbers. A *local decoder for E handling ρ errors* is an algorithm D that, given random access to a string y such that $\Delta(y, E(x)) < \rho$ for some (unknown) $x \in [n]$, and an index $j \in \mathbb{N}$, runs for polylog(m) time and outputs x_j with probability at least $2/3$.

The constant $2/3$ is arbitrary and can be replaced with any constant larger than $1/2$, since the probability of getting a correct answer can be amplified by repetition. We also note that Definition 19.16 can be easily generalized for codes with larger (i.e., nonbinary) alphabet. Local decoding may also be useful in applications of ECCs that have nothing to do with hardness amplification (e.g., if we use ECC's to encode a huge file, we may want to be able to efficiently recover part of the file without decoding it in its entirety). The connection between local decoders and hardness amplification is encapsulated in the following theorem.

Theorem 19.17 *(Hardness amplification from local decoding)*
Suppose that there exists an ECC with polynomial-time encoding algorithm and a local decoding algorithm handling ρ errors. Suppose also that there is $f \in \mathbf{E}$ with $\mathsf{H}_{\mathsf{wrs}}(f)(n) \geq S(n)$ for some function $S : \mathbb{N} \to \mathbb{N}$ satisfying $S(n) \geq n$. Then, there exists $\epsilon > 0$ and $\hat{f} \in \mathbf{E}$ with $\mathsf{H}_{\mathsf{avg}}^{1-\rho}(\hat{f})(n) \geq S(\epsilon n)^\epsilon$.

We leave the proof of Theorem 19.17, which follows the ideas described above, as Exercise 19.14. We now show *local decoder* algorithms for several explicit codes.

19.4.1 Local decoder for Walsh-Hadamard

The following is a two-query local decoder for the Walsh-Hadamard code that handles ρ errors for every $\rho < 1/4$. This fraction of errors we handle is best possible, as it can be easily shown that there cannot exist a local (or nonlocal) decoder for a binary code handling ρ errors for every $\rho \geq 1/4$.

Theorem 19.18 *For every $\rho < 1/4$, the walsh-Hadamard code has a local decoder handling ρ errors.*   ◇

PROOF: Theorem 19.18 is proven by the following algorithm:

WALSH-HADAMARD LOCAL DECODER for $\rho < 1/4$.

> *Input:* $j \in [n]$, random access to a function $f : \{0, 1\}^n \to \{0, 1\}$ such that $\Pr_y[g(y) \neq x \odot y] \leq \rho$ for some $\rho < 1/4$ and $x \in \{0, 1\}^n$.
>
> *Output:* A bit $b \in \{0, 1\}$. *(Our goal: $x_j = b$.)*
>
> *Operation:* Let e^j be the vector in $\{0, 1\}^n$ that is equal to 0 in all the coordinates except for the jth and equal to 1 on the jth coordinate. The algorithm chooses $y \in_R \{0, 1\}^n$ and outputs $f(y) + f(y + e^j) \pmod 2$ (where $y + e^j$ denotes componentwise addition modulo 2, or equivalently, flipping the jth coordinate of y).
>
> *Analysis:* Since both y and $y + e^j$ are uniformly distributed (even though they are dependent), the union bound implies that with probability $1 - 2\rho$, $f(y) = x \odot y$ and $f(y + e^j) = x \odot (y + e^j)$. But by the bilinearity of the operation $\odot$, this implies that

$f(y) + f(y + e^j) = x \odot y + x \odot (y + e^j) = 2(x \odot y) + x \odot e^j = x \odot e^j \pmod 2$. Yet, $x \odot e^j = x_j$ and so with probability $1 - 2\rho$, the algorithm outputs the right value. (The success probability can be amplified by repetition.)

This algorithm can be modified to locally compute not just $x_i = x \odot e^j$ but in fact the value $x \odot z$ for every $z \in \{0, 1\}^n$. Thus we can use it to compute not just every bit of the original message x but also every bit of the uncorrupted codeword $\mathsf{WH}(x)$. This property is sometimes called the *self-correction property* of the Walsh-Hadamard code. ∎

19.4.2 Local decoder for Reed-Muller

We now show a local decoder for the Reed-Muller code. It runs in time polynomial in ℓ and d, which, for an appropriate setting of the parameters, is polylogarithmic in the output length of the code:

Theorem 19.19 *For every field $|\mathbb{F}|$ and numbers d, ℓ, there is a $\mathrm{poly}(|\mathbb{F}|, \ell, d)$-time local decoder for the Reed-Muller code with parameters $\mathbb{F}, d, \ell$ handling $(1 - \frac{d}{|\mathbb{F}|})/6$ errors.*

That is, there is a $\mathrm{poly}(|\mathbb{F}|, \ell, d)$-time algorithm D that given random access to a function $f : \mathbb{F}^\ell \to \mathbb{F}$ that agrees with some degree d polynomial P on a $1 - (1 - \frac{d}{|\mathbb{F}|})/6$ fraction of the inputs and $x \in \mathbb{F}^\ell$ outputs $P(x)$ with probability at least $2/3$. ◇

PROOF: Recall that the input to a Reed-Muller code is an ℓ-variable d-degree polynomial P over some field $\mathbb{F}$. When we discussed the code before, we assumed that this polynomial is represented as the list of its coefficients. However, below it will be more convenient for us to assume that the polynomial is represented by a list of its values on its first $\binom{d+\ell}{\ell}$ inputs according to some canonical ordering. Using standard interpolation, we still have a polynomial-time encoding algorithm even given this representation. Thus, it suffices to show an algorithm that, given access to a corrupted version of P, computes $P(x)$ for every $x \in \mathbb{F}^\ell$. We now show such an algorithm.

REED-MULLER LOCAL DECODER for $\rho \le (1 - \frac{d}{|\mathbb{F}|})/6$.

Input: A string $x \in \mathbb{F}^\ell$, random access to a function f such that $\Pr_{x \in \mathbb{F}^\ell}[P(x) \ne f(x)] < \rho$, where $P : \mathbb{F}^\ell \to \mathbb{F}$ is an ℓ-variable degree-d polynomial.

Output: $y \in \mathbb{F}$ (*Goal:* $y = P(x)$.)

Operation:
1. Let L_x be a random line passing through x. That is $L_x = \{x + tz : t \in \mathbb{F}\}$ for a random $z \in \mathbb{F}^\ell$.
2. Query f on all the $|\mathbb{F}|$ points of L_x to obtain a set of points $\{(t, f(x + tz))\}$ for every $t \in \mathbb{F}$.
3. Run the Reed-Solomon decoding algorithm to obtain the univariate polynomial $Q : \mathbb{F} \to \mathbb{F}$ such that $Q(t) = f(x + tz)$ for the largest number of t's (see Figure 19.6).[4]
4. Output $Q(0)$.

---

[4] If ρ is sufficiently small, (e.g., $\rho < 1/(10d)$), then we can use the simpler randomized Reed-Solomon decoding procedure described in Section 19.3.

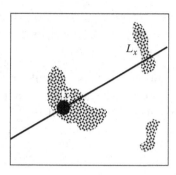

Figure 19.6. Given access to a corrupted version of a polynomial $P : \mathbb{F}^\ell \to \mathbb{F}$, to compute $P(x)$, we pass a random line L_x through x, and use Reed-Solomon decoding to recover the restriction of P to the line L_x.

Analysis: For every d-degree ℓ-variable polynomial P, the univariate polynomial $Q(t) = P(x + tz)$ has degree at most d. Thus to show that the Reed-Solomon decoding works, it suffices to show that with probability at least $2/3$, the number of points on $w \in L_x$ for which $f(w) \neq P(w)$ is less than $(1 - d/|\mathbb{F}|)/2$. Yet, for every $t \neq 0$, the point $x + tz$ where z is chosen at random in $\mathbb{F}^\ell$ is uniformly distributed (independently of x), and so the expected number of points on L_x for which f and P differ is at most $\rho|\mathbb{F}|$. By the Markov inequality, the probability that there will be more than $3\rho|\mathbb{F}| < (1 - d/|\mathbb{F}|)|\mathbb{F}|/2$ such points is at most $2/3$ and hence Reed-Solomon decoding will be successful with probability $2/3$. In this case, we obtain the correct polynomial q that is the restriction of Q to the line L_x and hence $q(0) = P(x)$.

∎

19.4.3 Local decoding of concatenated codes

As the following lemma shows, given two locally decodable ECCs E_1 and E_2, we can locally decode their concatenation $E_1 \circ E_2$.

Lemma 19.20 *Let $E_1 : \{0, 1\}^n \to \Sigma^m$ and $E_2 : \Sigma \to \{0, 1\}^k$ be two ECC's with local decoders of q_1 (resp. q_2) queries with respect to ρ_1 (resp. ρ_2) errors. Then there is an $O(q_1 q_2 \log q_1 \log |\Sigma|)$-query local decoder handling $\rho_1 \rho_2$ errors for the concatenated code $E = E_2 \circ E_1 : \{0, 1\}^n \to \{0, 1\}^{mk}$.* ◇

PROOF: We prove the lemma using the natural algorithm. Namely, we run the decoder for E_1, but answer its queries using the decoder for E_2 (see Figure 19.7).

LOCAL DECODER FOR CONCATENATED CODE: $\rho < \rho_1 \rho_2$

Input: An index $i \in [n]$, random access to a string $y \in \{0, 1\}^{km}$ such that $\Delta(y, E_1 \circ E_2(x)) < \rho_1 \rho_2$ for some $x \in \{0, 1\}^n$.

Output: $b \in \{0, 1\}^n$ (*Goal:* $b = x_i$).

Operation: Simulate the actions of the decoder for E_1, whenever the decoder needs access to the jth symbol of $E_1(x)$, use the decoder of E_2 with $O(q_2 \log q_1 \log |\Sigma|)$ queries applied to the jth block of y to recover all the bits of this symbol with probability at least $1 - 1/(10q_1)$.

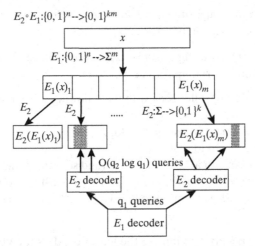

Figure 19.7. To locally decode a concatenated code $E_2 \circ E_1$ we run the decoder for E_1 using the decoder for E_2. The crucial observation is that if y is within $\rho_1 \rho_2$ distance to $E_2 \circ E_1(x)$, then at most a ρ_1 fraction of the blocks in y are of distance more than ρ_2 the corresponding block in $E_2 \circ E_1(x)$.

Analysis: The crucial observation is that at most a ρ_1 fraction of the length k blocks in y can be of distance more than ρ_2 from the corresponding blocks in $E_2 \circ E_1(x)$. Therefore, with probability at least 0.9, all our q_1 answers to the decoder of E_1 are consistent with the answer it would receive when accessing a string that is of distance at most ρ_1 from a codeword of E_1.

■

19.4.4 Putting it all together

We now have the ingredients to prove our second main theorem of this chapter: transformation of a hard-on-the-worst-case function into a function that is "mildly" hard on the average case.

Theorem 19.21 *(Worst-case hardness to mild hardness)*
Let $S : \mathbb{N} \to \mathbb{N}$ and $f \in \mathbf{E}$ such that $\mathsf{H}_{\mathrm{wrs}}(f)(n) \geq S(n)$ for every n. Then there exists a function $g \in \mathbf{E}$ and a constant $c > 0$ such that $\mathsf{H}_{\mathrm{avg}}^{0.99}(g)(n) \geq S(n/c)/n^c$ for every sufficiently large n.

PROOF: For every n, we treat the restriction of f to $\{0, 1\}^n$ as a string $f' \in \{0, 1\}^N$ where $N = 2^n$. We then encode this string f' using a suitable error correcting code $E : \{0, 1\}^N \to \{0, 1\}^{N^C}$ for some constant $C > 1$. We will define the function g on every input $x \in \{0, 1\}^{Cn}$ to output the xth coordinate of $E(f')$.[5] For the function g to satisfy the conclusion of the theorem, all we need is for the code E to satisfy the following properties:

1.   For every $x \in \{0, 1\}^N$, $E(x)$ can be computed in poly(N) time.

---

[5]   By padding with zeros as necessary, we can assume that all the inputs to g are of length that is a multiple of C.

2. There is a local decoding algorithm for E that uses $\text{polylog}(N)$ running time and queries and can handle a 0.01 fraction of errors.

But this can be achieved using a concatenation of a Walsh-Hadamard code with a Reed-Muller code of appropriate parameters:

1. Let RM denote the Reed-Muller code with the following parameters:
    - The field $\mathbb{F}$ is of size $\log^5 N$.
    - The number of variables ℓ is equal to $\log N / \log \log N$.
    - The degree is equal to $\log^2 N$.

    RM takes an input of length at least $(\frac{d}{\ell})^\ell > N$ (and so using padding we can assume its input is $\{0, 1\}^n$). Its output is of size $|\mathbb{F}|^\ell \le \text{poly}(n)$. Its distance is at least $1 - 1/\log N$.
2. Let WH denote the Walsh-Hadamard code from $\{0, 1\}^{\log F} = \{0, 1\}^{5 \log \log N}$ to $\{0, 1\}^{|\mathbb{F}|} = \{0, 1\}^{\log^5 N}$.

Our code will be $\text{WH} \circ \text{RM}$. Combining the local decoders for Walsh-Hadamard and Reed-Muller we get the desired result. ∎

Combining Theorem 19.21 with Yao's XOR Lemma (Theorem 19.2), we get the following corollary.

Corollary 19.22 *Let $S : \mathbb{N} \to \mathbb{N}$ be a monotone and time-constructible function. Then there is some $\epsilon > 0$ such that if there exists $f \in \mathbf{E}$ with $H_{\text{wrs}}(f)(n) \ge S(n)$ for every n then there exists $\hat{f} \in \mathbf{E}$ with $ACH(f)(n) \ge S(\sqrt{n})^\epsilon$.* ◇

PROOF: By Theorem 19.21, under this assumption there exists a function $g \in \mathbf{E}$ with $H_{\text{avg}}^{0.99}(g)(n) \ge S'(n) = S(n)/\text{poly}(n)$, where we can assume $S'(n) \ge \sqrt{S(n)}$ for sufficiently large n (otherwise S is polynomial and the theorem is trivial). Consider the function $g^{\oplus k}$ where $k = c \log S'(n)$ for a sufficiently small constant c. By Yao's XOR Lemma, on inputs of length kn, it cannot be computed with probability better than $1/2 + 2^{-cS'(n)/1000}$ by circuits of size $S'(n)$. Since $S(n) \le 2^n$, $kn < \sqrt{n}$, and hence we get that $H_{\text{avg}}(g^{\oplus k}) \ge S^{c/2000}$. ∎

19.5 LIST DECODING

Corollary 19.22 is extremely surprising in the qualitative sense (transforming worst-case hardness to average-case hardness), but it is still not fully satisfying quantitatively because it loses quite a bit in the circuit size when moving from a worst-case hard to an average-case hard function. In particular, even if we start with a function f that is hard in the worst case for $2^{\Omega(n)}$-sized circuits, we only end up with a function $\hat{f}$ that is hard on the average case for $2^{\Omega(\sqrt{n})}$-sized circuits. This can make a difference in some applications, and in particular it falls short of what we will need to fully derandomize **BPP** under worst-case assumptions in Chapter 20.

Our approach to obtain stronger worst-case to average-case reduction will be to bypass the XOR Lemma, and use error-correcting codes to get directly from worst-case hardness to a function that is hard to compute with probability slightly better than $1/2$. However, this idea seems to run into a fundamental difficulty: If f is worst-case hard, then it seems hard to argue that the encoding of f, *under any error-correcting code*, is hard to compute with probability 0.6. The reason is that any binary error-correcting code has to have distance at most $1/2$ but the decoding algorithms work for at most half the distance and hence cannot recover a string f from $E(f)$ if the latter was corrupted in more than a $1/4$ of its locations (i.e., from a string with less than 0.75 agreement with $E(f)$).

This seems like a real obstacle, and indeed was considered as such in many contexts where ECC's were used, until the realization of the importance of the following insight: "If y is obtained by corrupting $E(x)$ in, say, a 0.4 fraction of the coordinates (where E is some ECC with good enough distance) then, while there may be more than one codeword within distance 0.4 to y, *there can not be too many such codewords*." Formally, we have the following theorem:

Theorem 19.23 (*Johnson bound* [Joh62]) *If* $E : \{0, 1\}^n \rightarrow \{0, 1\}^m$ *is an ECC with distance at least* $1/2 - \epsilon$, *then for every* $x \in \{0, 1\}^m$, *and* $\delta \geq \sqrt{\epsilon}$, *there exist at most* $1/(2\delta^2)$ *vectors* $y_1, \ldots, y_\ell$ *such that* $\Delta(x, y_i) \leq 1/2 - \delta$ *for every* $i \in [\ell]$. ◇

PROOF: Suppose that $x, y_1, \ldots, y_\ell$ satisfy this condition, and define ℓ vectors $z_1, \ldots, z_\ell$ in $\mathbb{R}^m$ as follows: For every $i \in [\ell]$ and $k \in [m]$, set $z_{i,k}$ to equal $+1$ if $y_k = x_k$ and set it to equal -1 otherwise. Under our assumptions, for every $i \in [\ell]$,

$$\sum_{k=1}^m z_{i,k} \geq 2\delta m \tag{19.10}$$

since z_i agrees with x on an $1/2 + \delta$ fraction of its coordinates. Also, for every $i \neq j \in [\ell]$,

$$\langle z_i, z_j \rangle = \sum_{k=1}^m z_{i,k} z_{j,k} \leq 2\epsilon m \leq 2\delta^2 m \tag{19.11}$$

since E is a code of distance at least $1/2 - \epsilon$.

We will show that (19.10) and (19.11) together imply that $\ell \leq 1/(2\delta^2)$. Indeed, set $w = \sum_{i=1}^\ell z_i$. On one hand, by (19.11),

$$\langle w, w \rangle = \sum_{i=1}^\ell \langle z_i, z_i \rangle + \sum_{i \neq j} \langle z_i, z_j \rangle \leq \ell m + \ell^2 2\delta^2 m$$

On the other hand, by (19.10), $\sum_k w_k = \sum_{i,j} z_{i,j} \geq 2\delta m \ell$ and hence $\langle w, w \rangle \geq |\sum_k w_k|^2/m \geq 4\delta^2 m \ell^2$, since for every c, the vector $w \in \mathbb{R}^m$ with minimal two-norm satisfying $\sum_k w_k = c$ is the uniform vector $(c/m, c/m, \ldots, c/m)$. Thus $4\delta^2 m \ell^2 \leq \ell m + 2\ell^2 \delta^2 m$, implying that $\ell \leq 1/(2\delta^2)$. ∎

19.5.1 List decoding the Reed-Solomon code

In many contexts, obtaining a list of candidate messages from a corrupted codeword can be just as good as unique decoding. For example, we may have some outside information on which messages are likely to appear, allowing us to know which of the messages in the list is the correct one. However, to take advantage of this we need an efficient algorithm that computes this list. Such an algorithm was discovered in 1996 by Sudan for the popular and important Reed-Solomon code. It can recover a polynomial size list of candidate codewords given a length m Reed-Solomon codeword that is corrupted in up to a $1 - 2\sqrt{\frac{d}{m}}$ fraction of the coordinates. Note that this tends to 1 as m/d grows, whereas the Berlekamp-Welch algorithm of Section 19.3 (as is the case with any other unique decoding algorithm) cannot handle a fraction of errors that is more than half the distance.

Theorem 19.24 *(List decoding for the Reed-Solomon code [Sud96])*
There is a polynomial-time algorithm that given a set $\{(a_i, b_i)\}_{i=1}^{m}$ of pairs in $\mathbb{F}^2$, returns the list of all degree d polynomials G such that the number of i's for which $g(a_i) = b_i$ is more than $2\sqrt{dm}$.

PROOF: We prove Theorem 19.24 via the following algorithm.

REED-SOLOMON LIST DECODING: $t > 2\sqrt{dm}$.

1. Find a nonzero bivariate polynomial $Q(x, y)$ of degree at most $\sqrt{dm}$ in x and at most $\sqrt{m/d}$ in y such that $Q(b_i, a_i) = 0$ for every $i \in [m]$.
    We can express this condition as m linear equations in the $(\sqrt{dm} + 1)(\sqrt{m/d} + 1) > m$ coefficients of Q. Since these equations are homogeneous (right side equaling zero) and there are more unknowns than equations, this system has a nonzero solution that can be found using gaussian elimination.
2. Factor $Q(x, y)$ using an efficient polynomial factorization algorithm (see [VG99]). For every factor of the form $(P(x) - y)$ check whether $P(x)$ has degree at most d and agrees with $\{(a_i, b_i)\}_{i=1}^{m}$ in at least t places. If so, output P.
    Indeed, if $G(x)$ agrees with $\{(a_i, b_i)\}_{i=1}^{m}$ in more than t places then $(G(x) - y)$ is a factor of $Q(x, y)$. To see this note that $Q(G(x), x)$ is a univariate polynomial of degree at most $\sqrt{dm} + d\sqrt{m/d} = 2\sqrt{dm} < t$ which has at least t zeroes and hence it is identically zero. It follows that $G(x) - y$ divides $Q(x, y)$ (see Exercise 19.16). ∎

19.6 LOCAL LIST DECODING: GETTING TO **BPP = P**

As in Section 19.4, to actually use list decoding for hardness amplification, we need to provide *local* list decoding algorithms for the codes we use. Fortunately, such algorithms are known for the Walsh-Hadamard code, the Reed-Muller code, and their concatenation. The definition of local list decoding below is somewhat subtle, and deserves a careful reading.

Definition 19.25 *(Local List Decoder)* Let $E : \{0, 1\}^n \to \{0, 1\}^m$ be an ECC and let $\rho = 1 - \epsilon$ for $\epsilon > 0$. An algorithm D is called a *local list decoder for E handling ρ errors*, if for every $x \in \{0, 1\}^n$ and $y \in \{0, 1\}^m$ satisfying $\Delta(E(x), y) \leq \rho$, *there exists a number* $i_0 \in [\text{poly}(n/\epsilon)]$ such that for every $j \in [m]$, on inputs i_0, j and with random access to y, D runs for $\text{poly}(\log(m)/\epsilon)$ time and outputs x_j with probability at least $2/3$.   ◇

One can think of the number i_0 as the index of x in the list of poly(n/ϵ) candidate messages output by L. As is the case for Definition 19.16, Definition 19.25 can be easily generalized to codes with non-binary alphabet.

19.6.1 Local list decoding of the Walsh-Hadamard code

It turns out we already encountered a local list decoder for the Walsh-Hadamard code: The proof of the Goldreich-Levin Theorem (Theorem 9.12). It provided an algorithm that given access to a "black box" that computes the function $y \mapsto x \odot y$ (for $x, y \in \{0, 1\}^n$) with probability $1/2 + \epsilon$, computes a list of values $x_1, \ldots, x_{\text{poly}(n/\epsilon)}$ such that $x_{i_0} = x$ for some i_0. In Chapter 9 we used this algorithm to find the correct value of x from that list by checking it against the value $f(x)$ (where f is a one-way permutation). This is a good example showing how we can use outside information to narrow the list of candidates codewords obtained from a list-decoding algorithm.

19.6.2 Local list decoding of the Reed-Muller code

We now present an algorithm for local list decoding of the Reed-Muller code. Recall that the codeword of this code is the list of evaluations of a d-degree ℓ-variable polynomial $P : \mathbb{F}^\ell \to \mathbb{F}$ and the task of the local decoder is to compute $P(x)$ on a given point $x \in \mathbb{F}^\ell$.

Theorem 19.26 (*Reed-Muller local list decoder* [BF90, Lip91, BFNW93, STV99])
The Reed-Muller code has a local list decoder handling $1 - 10\sqrt{d/|\mathbb{F}|}$ errors.

That is, for every $\mathbb{F}, \ell, d$ there is a poly$(|\mathbb{F}|, d, \ell)$-time algorithm D that given random *access to a function $f : \mathbb{F}^\ell \to \mathbb{F}$, an index $i \in \mathbb{F}^{\ell+1}$ and an input $x \in \mathbb{F}^\ell$ satisfies: if f agrees with a degree-d polynomial $P : \mathbb{F}^\ell \to \mathbb{F}$ on $10\sqrt{d/|\mathbb{F}|}$ fraction of the inputs, then there exists $i_0 \in \mathbb{F}^{\ell+1}$ such that $\Pr[D^f(i_0, x) = P(x)] \geq 2/3$ for every x.* ◇

PROOF: To be a valid local list decoder, given the index i_0, the algorithm should output $P(x)$ with high probability for *every* $x \in \mathbb{F}^\ell$. Below we describe a relaxed decoder that is only guaranteed to output the right value for *most* (i.e., a 0.9 fraction) of the x's in $\mathbb{F}^\ell$. One can transform this algorithm to a valid local list decoder by combining it with the Reed-Muller local decoder described in Section 19.4.2. Thus, Theorem 19.26 is proven via the following algorithm.

REED-MULLER LOCAL LIST DECODER for $\rho \leq 1 - 10\sqrt{d/|\mathbb{F}|}$.

Inputs:
- Random access to a function f such that $\Pr_{x \in \mathbb{F}^\ell}[P(x) = f(x)] > 10\sqrt{d/|\mathbb{F}|}$ where $P : \mathbb{F}^\ell \to \mathbb{F}$ is an ℓ-variable d-degree polynomial. We assume that $|\mathbb{F}| > d^4$ and d is sufficiently large (e.g., $d > 1000$ will do). This can always be ensured in our applications.
- An index $i_0 \in [|\mathbb{F}|^{\ell+1}]$, which we interpret as a pair (x_0, y_0) with $x_0 \in \mathbb{F}^\ell$, $y_0 \in \mathbb{F}$,
- A string $x \in \mathbb{F}^\ell$.

Output: $y \in \mathbb{F}$ (*For some pair (x_0, y_0), it should hold that $P(x) = y$ with probability at least 0.9 over the algorithm's coins and x chosen at random from $\mathbb{F}^\ell$.*)

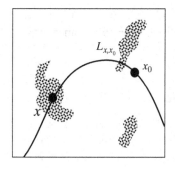

Figure 19.8. Given access to a corrupted version of a polynomial $P : \mathbb{F}^\ell \to \mathbb{F}$ and some index (x_0, y_0), to compute $P(x)$ we pass a random degree-3 curve L_{x,x_0} through x and x_0, and use Reed-Solomon list decoding to recover a list of candidates for the restriction of P to the curve L_{x,x_0}. If only one candidate satisfies that its value on x_0 is y_0, then we use this candidate to compute $P(x)$.

Operation:

1. Let L_{x,x_0} be a random degree 3 curve passing through x, x_0. That is, we find a random degree 3 univariate polynomial $q : \mathbb{F} \to \mathbb{F}^\ell$ such that $q(0) = x$ and $q(r) = x_0$ for some random $r \in \mathbb{F}$, and set $L_{x,x_0} = \{q(t) : t \in \mathbb{F}\}$. (See Figure 19.8.)

2. Query f on all the $|\mathbb{F}|$ points of L_{x,x_0} to obtain the set S of the $|\mathbb{F}|$ pairs $\{(t, f(q(t))) : t \in \mathbb{F})\}$.

3. Run Sudan's Reed-Solomon list decoding algorithm to obtain a list $g_1, \ldots, g_k$ of all degree $3d$ polynomials that have at least $8\sqrt{d|\mathbb{F}|}$ agreement with the pairs in S.

4. If there is a unique i such that $g_i(r) = y_0$ then output $g_i(0)$. Otherwise, halt without outputting anything.

We will show that for every $f : \mathbb{F}^\ell \to \mathbb{F}$ that agrees with an ℓ-variable degree d polynomial on a $10\sqrt{d/|\mathbb{F}|}$ fraction of its input, and every $x \in \mathbb{F}^\ell$, if x_0 is chosen at random from $\mathbb{F}^\ell$ and $y_0 = P(x_0)$, then with probability at least 0.9 (over the choice of x_0 and the algorithm's coins) the above decoder will output $P(x)$. By a standard averaging argument, this implies that there exist a pair (x_0, y_0) such that given this pair, the algorithm outputs $P(x)$ for a 0.9 fraction of the x's in $\mathbb{F}^\ell$.

For every $x \in \mathbb{F}^\ell$, the following fictitious algorithm can be easily seen to have an identical output to the output of our decoder on the inputs x, a random $x_0 \in_R \mathbb{F}^\ell$ and $y_0 = P(x_0)$:

1. Choose a random degree 3 curve L that passes through x. That is, $L = \{q(t) : t \in \mathbb{F}\}$ where $q : \mathbb{F} \to \mathbb{F}^\ell$ is a random degree 3 polynomial satisfying $q(0) = x$.

2. Obtain the list $g_1, \ldots, g_m$ of all univariate polynomials over $\mathbb{F}$ such that for every i, there are at least $6\sqrt{d|\mathbb{F}|}$ values of t such that $g_i(t) = f(q(t))$.

3. Choose a random $r \in \mathbb{F}$. Assume that you are given the value $y_0 = P(q(r))$.

4. If there exists a unique i such that $g_i(r) = y_0$ then output $g_i(0)$. Otherwise, halt without an input.

Yet, this fictitious algorithm will output $P(x)$ with probability at least 0.9. Indeed, since all the points other than x on a random degree 3 curve passing through x are pairwise independent,[6] Chebyshev's inequality implies that with probability at least 0.99, the function f will agree with the polynomial P on at least $8\sqrt{d|\mathbb{F}|}$ points on this curve. (These are easily verified using our discussion of pairwise independence and Chebyshev's inequality in Section A.2.4.) Thus the list $g_1, \ldots, g_m$ we obtain in

---

[6] This can be shown by generalizing the proof of Theorem 8.15 (that obtained pairwise independent functions from random linear functions) using basic facts on polynomials that are reviewed in Section A.6; see also Exercise 11.4.

Step 2. contains the polynomial $g : \mathbb{F} \to \mathbb{F}$ defined as $g(t) = P(q(t))$. We leave it as Exercise 19.15 to show that there cannot be more than $\sqrt{|F|}/4d$ polynomials in this list. Since two $3d$-degree polynomials can agree on at most $3d + 1$ points, with probability at least $1 - \frac{(3d+1)\sqrt{|F|}/4d}{|\mathbb{F}|} > 0.99$, if we choose a random $r \in \mathbb{F}$, then $g(r) \neq g_i(r)$ for every $g_i \neq g$ in this list. Thus with this probability, we will identify the polynomial g and output the value $g(0) = P(x)$. ∎

19.6.3 Local list decoding of concatenated codes

If $E_1 : \{0, 1\}^n \to \Sigma^m$ and $E_2 : \Sigma \to \{0, 1\}^k$ are two codes that are locally list decodable then so is the concatenated code $E_2 \circ E_1 : \{0, 1\}^n \to \{0, 1\}^{mk}$. As in Section 19.4.3, the idea is to simply run the local decoder for E_1 while answering its queries using the decoder of E_2. More concretely, assume that the decoder for E_1 takes an index in the set I_1 and can handle $1 - \epsilon_1$ errors, and that E_2 takes an index in I_2 and can handle $1/2 - \epsilon_2$ errors. Our decoder for $E_2 \circ E_1$ will take a pair of indices $i_1 \in I_1$ and $i_2 \in I_2$ and run the decoder for E_1 with the index i_1 and, whenever this decoder makes a query, answer it using the decoder E_2 with the index i_2. (See Section 19.4.3.) We claim that this decoder can handle $1/2 - \epsilon_1\epsilon_2|I_2|$ number of errors. Indeed, if y agrees with some codeword $E_2 \circ E_1(x)$ on an $\epsilon_1\epsilon_2|I_2|$ fraction of the coordinates, then there are $\epsilon_1|I_2|$ blocks on which it has at least $1/2 + \epsilon_2$ agreement with the blocks this codeword. Thus, by an averaging argument, there exists an index i_2 such that given i_2, the output of the E_2 decoder agrees with $E_1(x)$ on ϵ_1 symbols, implying that there exists an index i_1 such that given (i_1, i_2) and every coordinate j, the combined decoder will output x_j with high probability.

19.6.4 Putting it all together

As promised, we can use local list decoding to transform a function that is merely worst-case hard into a function that cannot be computed with probability significantly better than $1/2$.

Theorem 19.27 *(Worst-case hardness to strong hardness)*
Let $f \in \mathbf{E}$ be such that $\mathsf{H}_{\mathrm{wrs}}(f)(n) \geq S(n)$ for some time-constructible nondecreasing $S : \mathbb{N} \to \mathbb{N}$. Then there exists a function $g \in \mathbf{E}$ and a constant $c > 0$ such that $\mathsf{H}_{\mathrm{avg}}(g)(n) \geq S(n/c)^{1/c}$ for every sufficiently large n.

PROOF SKETCH: As in Section 19.4.4, for every n, we treat the restriction of f to $\{0, 1\}^n$ as an N-bit string for $N = 2^n$ and encode it using the concatenation of a Reed-Muller code with the Walsh-Hadamard code. We obtain a string $g \in \{0, 1\}^{N'}$ and treat it as a function from $\{0, 1\}^{n'}$ to $\{0, 1\}$, where $n' = \lceil \log N' \rceil$. We set the parameters so that $n' = O(n)$, and then show that there is some constant $\epsilon > 0$ so that we can use our local decoders to transform in $S(n)^\epsilon$ time any algorithm computing g on a $1/2 + 1/S(n)^\epsilon$ fraction of the inputs in $\{0, 1\}^{n'}$ into a circuit that computes f perfectly on all inputs in $\{0, 1\}^n$.

To complete the proof, we need to see that this can be achieved by some choice for the parameters of the Reed-Muller code: the field $\mathbb{F}$, the degree d, and number of variables ℓ. We will fix $|\mathbb{F}| = S(n)^\delta$ for some small $\delta > 0$, and $d = \sqrt{|F|}$. We will choose ℓ large enough to ensure that we can indeed encode f as the input to the Reed-Muller code. Since the input length is a tuple of $\binom{d+\ell}{\ell} \geq (d/\ell)^\ell$ field elements, the reader can verify that $\ell = 2 \log N / \log d$ will suffice. (We may assume without loss of generality that $d > (\log N)^3$, since if $S(n) = n^{O(1)}$ the theorem is trivial; similarly we may also assume $S(n) < N$). The output length of the Reed-Muller code will be $|\mathbb{F}|^{\ell}$ elements of $\mathbb{F}$, and each will be encoded by $|\mathbb{F}|$ bits by the Walsh-Hadamard code, for a total of $N' = |\mathbb{F}|^{\ell+1}$ bits. For our setting of parameters, $N' = N^{O(1)}$, and so it indeed holds that $\log N' = O(\log N)$. The running time of the both our Walsh-Hadamard and Reed-Muller decoders is $\text{poly}(|\mathbb{F}|, d, \ell)$ which in our case equals $S(n)^{\delta c}$ for some absolute constant c (independent of δ). We will be able to handle a $1/2 - S(n)^{-\delta/3}$ fraction of errors with a list size of $|\mathbb{F}|^{O(\ell)} = N^{O(1)}$. Thus, by setting δ small enough as a function of ϵ, and by hardwiring the $(O(\log N)$-sized) index of f inside the list, we obtain an $S(n)^{\epsilon} \cdot S'$-sized circuit that computes f perfectly from any S'-sized circuit that computes g on a $1/2 + 1/S(n)^{\epsilon}$ fraction of its inputs. ∎

WHAT HAVE WE LEARNED?

- Yao's XOR Lemma allows us to amplify hardness by transforming a Boolean function with only mild hardness (cannot be computed with say 0.99 success) into a Boolean function with strong hardness (cannot be computed with 0.51 success). The proof of the XOR lemma shows that every mildly hard function has a "hard core" of inputs on which it is very difficult.

- An *error-correcting code* is a function that maps every two strings into a pair of strings that differ on many of their coordinates. An error-correcting code with a *local decoding* algorithm can be used to transform a function hard in the worst case into a function that is mildly hard on the average case.

- A code over the binary alphabet can have distance at most $1/2$. A code with distance δ can be uniquely decoded up to $\delta/2$ errors. *List decoding* allows to a decoder to handle almost a δ fraction of errors, at the expense of returning not a single message but a short list of candidate messages.

- We can transform a function that is merely hard in the worst case to a function that is strongly hard in the average case using the notion of *local list decoding* of error-correcting codes.

CHAPTER NOTES AND HISTORY

Yao's XOR Lemma was first stated and proven by Yao in oral presentations of his paper [Yao82a]. Since then several proofs have been published with the first one by Levin in [Lev87] (see the survey [GNW95]). Russell Impagliazzo's hardcore lemma was proven in [Imp95a]; the proof of Section 19.1.2 is due to Noam Nisan.

The study of error-correcting codes is an extremely beautiful and useful field, and we have barely scratched its surface here. This field was initiated by two roughly concurrent seminal papers of Shannon [Sha48] and Hamming [Ham50]. The lecture notes of Madhu Sudan (available from his home page) provide a good starting point for theoretical computer scientists; see also the survey [Sud01].

Reed-Solomon codes were invented in 1960 by Irving Reed and Gustave Solomon [RS60]. The first efficient decoding algorithm for Reed-Solomon codes was by

Peterson [Pet60]. (Interestingly, this algorithm is one of the first nontrivial polynomial-time algorithms invented, preceding even the formal definition of the class **P**.) The algorithm presented in Section 19.3 is a simplification due to Gemmell and Sudan [GS92] of the Berlekamp-Welch decoder [BW86].

Reed-Muller codes were invented by Muller [Mul54] with the first decoder given by Reed [Ree54]. The first Reed-Muller local decoders were given by Beaver and Feigenbaum [BF90] and Lipton [Lip91], who observed this implies a worst-case to average-case connection for the *permanent* (see also Section 8.6.2). Babai, Fortnow, and Lund [BFL90] observed that by taking multilinear extensions, such connections also hold for **PSPACE** and **EXP**, and Babai et al. [BFNW93] showed that this allows for derandomization from worst-case assumptions. The Reed-Muller local decoding algorithm of Section 19.4.2 is due to Gemmell et al. [GLR+91].

The first list-decoding algorithm for Reed-Solomon codes was given by Sudan [Sud96] and was subsequently improved by Guruswami and Sudan [GS98]. Recently, Parvaresh and Vardy [PV05] showed a list-decoding algorithm handling even more errors for a variant of the Reed-Solomon code, a result that was further improved by Guruswami and Rudra [GR06], achieving an optimal tradeoff between rate and list decoding radius for large alphabets.

The quantitatively strong hardness amplification (Theorem 19.27) was first shown by Impagliazzo and Wigderson [IW97] that gave a *derandomized* version of Yao's XOR Lemma. Our presentation follows the alternative proof by Sudan, Trevisan, and Vadhan [STV99] who were the first to make an explicit connection between error correcting codes and hardness amplification, and also the first to explicitly define local list decoding and use it for hardness amplification. The first local list decoding algorithm for the Walsh-Hadamard code was given by Goldreich and Levin [GL89] (although the result is not explicitly described in these terms there). The Reed-Muller local list decoding algorithm of Section 19.6 is a variant of the algorithm of [STV99].

The question raised in Problem 19.8 is treated in O'Donnell [O'D04], where a hardness amplification lemma is given for **NP**. For a sharper result, see Healy, Vadhan, and Viola [HVV04].

EXERCISES

19.1. Let $X_1, \ldots, X_n$ be independent random variables such that X_i is equal to 1 with probability $1 - \delta$ and equal to 0 with probability δ. Let $X = \sum_{i=1}^{k} X_i$ (mod 2). Prove that $\Pr[X = 1] = 1/2 + (1 - 2\delta)^k/2$.

H539

19.2. Prove that if there exists a δ-density distribution H such that $\Pr_{x \in_R H}[C(x) = f(x)] \leq 1/2 + e$ for every circuit C of size at most S with $S \leq \sqrt{\epsilon^2 \delta 2^n/100}$, then there exists a subset $I \subseteq \{0, 1\}^n$ of size at least $\frac{\delta}{2}2^n$ such that

$$\Pr_{x \in_R I}[C(x) = f(x)] \leq 1/2 + 2\epsilon$$

for every circuit C of size at most S.

H539

19.3. Let H be an δ-density distribution over $\{0, 1\}^n$ (i.e., $\Pr[H = x] \leq 1/(\delta 2^n)$ for every $x \in \{0, 1\}^n$).

   (a) Let G be the distribution defined by $\Pr[G = x] = (2^{-n} - \delta \Pr[H = x])/(1 - \delta)$ for every $x \in \{0, 1\}^n$. Prove that G is indeed a distribution (i.e., all probabilities are nonnegative and sum up to 1).

   (b) Let U be the following distribution: With probability δ pick an element from H and with probability $1 - \delta$ pick an element from G. Prove that U is the uniform distribution.

   H539

19.4. Complete the proof of Impagliazzo's Hardcore Lemma (Lemma 19.3) for general k.

19.5. Prove the hyperplane separation theorem in the following form: If $C, D \subseteq \mathbb{R}^m$ are two disjoint convex set with C closed and D compact (i.e., closed and bounded), then there exists a nonzero vector $\mathbf{z} \in \mathbb{R}^m$ and a number $a \in \mathbb{R}$ such that

$$\mathbf{x} \in C \Rightarrow \langle \mathbf{x}, \mathbf{z} \rangle \geq a$$
$$\mathbf{y} \in D \Rightarrow \langle \mathbf{y}, \mathbf{z} \rangle \leq a$$

   H539

19.6. Prove the Min-Max Theorem (see Note 19.1.2) using the hyperplane separation theorem as stated in Exercise 19.5.

   H539

19.7. ([CG85]) We say that a distribution D over $\{0, 1\}^n$ is K-flat if D is the uniform distribution over a subset of $\{0, 1\}^n$ with size at least K. Prove that for every k, every 2^{-k}-density distribution H is a convex combination of 2^{n-k}-flat distributions. That is, there are N 2^{n-k}-flat distributions $D_1, \ldots, D_N$ and nonnegative numbers $\alpha_1, \ldots, \alpha_N$ such that $\sum_i \alpha_i = 1$ and H is equivalent to the distribution obtained by picking i with probability α_i and then picking a random element from D_i.

   H540

19.8. Suppose we know that **NP** contains a function that is weakly hard for all polynomial-size circuits. Can we use the XOR Lemma to infer the existence of a strongly hard function in **NP**? Why or why not?

19.9. For every $\delta < 1/2$ and sufficiently large n, prove that there exists a function $E : \{0, 1\}^n \to \{0, 1\}^{n/(1-H(\delta))}$ that is an error-correcting code with distance δ, where $H(\delta) = \delta \log(1/\delta) + (1 - \delta) \log(1/(1 - \delta))$.

   H540

19.10. Show that for every $E : \{0, 1\}^n \to \{0, 1\}^m$ that is an error-correcting code of distance $1/2$, $2^n < 10m$. Show if E is an error-correcting code of distance $\delta > 1/2$, then $2^n < 10/(\delta - 1/2)$.

   H540

19.11. Let $E : \{0, 1\}^n \to \{0, 1\}^m$ be an ECC such that there exist two distinct strings $x^1, x^2 \in \{0, 1\}^m$ with $\Delta(E(x^1), E(x^2)) \leq \delta$. Prove that there's no decoder for E handling $\delta/2$ or more errors. That is, show that there is no function $D : \{0, 1\}^m \to \{0, 1\}^n$ such that for every $x \in \{0, 1\}^m$ and y with $\Delta(y, E(x)) \leq \delta/2$, $D(y) = x$.

19.12. Let $E : \{0, 1\}^n \to \{0, 1\}^m$ be a δ-distance ECC. Transform E to a code $E' : \{0, 1, 2, 3\}^{n/2} \to \{0, 1, 2, 3\}^{m/2}$ in the obvious way. Show that E' has distance δ. Show that the opposite direction is not true: Show an example of a δ-distance ECC $E' : \{0, 1, 2, 3\}^{n/2} \to \{0, 1, 2, 3\}^{m/2}$ such that the corresponding binary code has distance 2δ.

19.13. Prove Theorem 19.15 as stated. That is show how to recover a d-degree polynomial G from a sequence of pairs $(a_1, b_1), \ldots, (a_m, b_m)$ agreeing with G in t places whenever $t \geq \frac{m}{2} + \frac{d}{2} + 1$.

19.14. Prove Theorem 19.17.

H540

19.15. Let $f : \mathbb{F} \to \mathbb{F}$ be any function. Suppose integer $d \geq 0$ and number ϵ satisfy $\epsilon > 2\sqrt{\frac{d}{|\mathbb{F}|}}$. Prove that there are at most $2/\epsilon$ degree d polynomials that agree with f on at least an ϵ fraction of its coordinates.

H540

19.16. Prove that if $Q(x, y)$ is a bivariate polynomial over some field $\mathbb{F}$ and $P(x)$ is a univariate polynomial over $\mathbb{F}$ such that $Q(P(x), x)$ is the zero polynomial, then $Q(x, y) = (y - P(x))A(x, y)$ for some polynomial $A(x, y)$.

H540

19.17. *(Linear Codes)* We say that an ECC $E : \{0, 1\}^n \to \{0, 1\}^m$ is *linear* if for every $x, x' \in \{0, 1\}^n$, $E(x + x') = E(x) + E(x')$ where $+$ denotes componentwise addition modulo 2. A linear ECC E can be described by an $m \times n$ matrix A such that (thinking of x as a column vector) $E(x) = Ax$ for every $x \in \{0, 1\}^n$.

(a) Prove that the distance of a linear ECC E is equal to the minimum over all nonzero $x \in \{0, 1\}^n$ of the fraction of 1's in $E(x)$.

(b) Prove that for every $\delta > 0$, there exists a linear ECC $E : \{0, 1\}^n \to \{0, 1\}^{1.1n/(1-H(\delta))}$ with distance δ, where $H(\delta) = \delta \log(1/\delta) + (1-\delta) \log(1/(1-\delta))$.

H540

(c) Prove that for some $\delta > 0$ there is an ECC $E : \{0, 1\}^n \to \{0, 1\}^{\mathrm{poly}(n)}$ of distance δ with polynomial-time encoding and decoding mechanisms. (You need to know about the field $\mathrm{GF}(2^k)$ to solve this, see Appendix A.)

H540

(d) We say that a linear code $E : \{0, 1\}^n \to \{0, 1\}^m$ is ϵ-*biased* if for every non-zero $x \in \{0, 1\}^n$, the fraction of 1's in $E(x)$ is between $1/2 - \epsilon$ and $1/2 + \epsilon$. Prove that for every $\epsilon > 0$, there exists an ϵ-biased linear code $E : \{0, 1\}^n \to \{0, 1\}^{\mathrm{poly}(n/\epsilon)}$ with a polynomial-time encoding algorithm.

19.18. Recall that for every m, there is field $\mathbb{F} = \mathrm{GF}(2^m)$ of 2^m elements such that we can represent each element of $\mathbb{F}$ as a vector in $\mathrm{GF}(2)^m$ with addition in $\mathbb{F}$ corresponding to bitwise XOR (see Appendix A). Thus for every $a \in \mathbb{F}$, the operation $x \mapsto a \times x$ (where $\times$ denotes multiplication in $\mathbb{F}$) is a linear operation in $\mathrm{GF}(2)^m$. Moreover, this operation is efficiently computable given the description of a.

(a) Prove that for every nonzero $x \in F$, if we choose a uniformly in $\mathbb{F}$ then $a \times x$ is distributed uniformly over $\mathbb{F}$.

(b) Prove that for every nonzero $x \in F$, the probability over a random $a \in_R \mathbb{F}$ that $a \times x$ has at most $m/10$ ones in its representation as an m-bit vector is less than $2^{-m/10}$. Conclude that there exists $a \in \mathbb{F}$ such that the function that maps $x \in \{0, 1\}^{m/10}$ to $a \times (x \circ 0^{0.9m})$ (where $\circ$ denotes concatenation) is an error-correcting code with distance at least 0.1.

(c) Show that there exists constants $c, \delta > 0$ such that for every n there is an explicit error-correcting code $E : \{0, 1\}^n \to \{0, 1\}^{cn}$ of distance at least δ.

H540

Derandomization

God does not play dice with the universe.

– Albert Einstein

Anyone who considers arithmetical methods of producing random digits is, of course, in a state of sin.

– John von Neumann, quoted by Knuth, 1981

Randomization is an exciting and powerful paradigm in computer science and, as we saw in Chapter 7, often provides the simplest or most efficient algorithms for many computational problems. In fact, in some areas of computer science, such as distributed algorithms and cryptography, randomization is *proven* to be necessary to achieve certain tasks or achieve them efficiently. Thus it's natural to conjecture (as many scientists initially did) that at least for some problems, randomization is *inherently* necessary: One cannot replace the probabilistic algorithm with a deterministic one without a significant loss of efficiency. One concrete version of this conjecture would be that **BPP** $\not\subseteq$ **P** (see Chapter 7 for definition of **BPP**). Surprisingly, recent research has provided more and more evidence that this is likely to be false. As we will see in this chapter, under very reasonable complexity assumptions, there is in fact a way to *derandomize* (i.e., transform into a deterministic algorithm) *every* probabilistic algorithm of the **BPP** type with only a polynomial loss of efficiency. Thus today most researchers believe that **BPP** = **P**. We note that this need not imply that randomness is useless in every setting—we already saw in Chapter 8 its crucial role in the definition of interactive proofs.

In Section 20.1 we define *pseudorandom generators*, which will serve as our main tool for derandomizing probabilistic algorithms. Their definition is a relaxation of the definition of *secure* pseudorandom generators in Chapter 9. This relaxation will allow us to construct such generators with better parameters and under weaker assumptions than what is possible for secure pseudorandom generators. In Section 20.2 we provide a construction of such pseudorandom generators under the assumptions that there exist explicit functions with high *average-case* circuit complexity. In Chapter 19 we show how to provide a construction that merely requires high *worst-case* circuit complexity.

While the circuit lower bounds we assume are widely believed to be true, they also seem to be very difficult to prove. This raises the question of whether assuming or proving such lower bounds is *necessary* to obtain derandomization. In Section 20.3 we show that it's possible to obtain at least a *partial* derandomization result based only on the assumption that **BPP** $\neq$ **EXP**. Alas, as we show in Section 20.4, full derandomization of **BPP** will require proving circuit lower bounds.

Even though we still cannot prove sufficiently strong circuit lower bounds, just as in cryptography, we can use *conjectured* hard problems for derandomization instead of *provable* hard problems, and to a certain extent end up with a win-win situation: If the conjectured hard problem is truly hard then the derandomization will be successful; and if the derandomization fails then it will lead us to an algorithm for the conjectured hard problem.

EXAMPLE 20.1 *(Polynomial identity testing)*

We explain the notion of derandomization with an example. One algorithm that we would like to derandomize is the one described in Section 7.2.3 for testing if a given polynomial (represented in the form of an arithmetic circuit) is the identically zero polynomial. If P is an n-variable nonzero polynomial of total degree d over a large enough finite field $\mathbb{F}$ ($|\mathbb{F}| > 10d$ will do), then most of the vectors $\mathbf{u} \in \mathbb{F}^n$ will satisfy $P(\mathbf{u}) \neq 0$ (see Lemma 7.5). Therefore, checking whether $P \equiv 0$ can be done by simply choosing a random $\mathbf{u} \in_R \mathbb{F}^n$ and applying p on $\mathbf{u}$. In fact, it is easy to show that there exists a set of m^2-vectors $\mathbf{u}^1, \ldots, \mathbf{u}^{m^2}$ such that for *every* such nonzero polynomial P that can be computed by a size m arithmetic circuit, there exists an $i \in [m^2]$ for which $P(\mathbf{u}^i) \neq 0$.

This suggests a natural approach for a deterministic algorithm: Show a deterministic algorithm that for every $m \in \mathbb{N}$, runs in poly(m) time and outputs a set $\mathbf{u}^1, \ldots, \mathbf{u}^{m^2}$ of vectors satisfying the above property. This shouldn't be too difficult—after all the vast majority of the sets of vectors have this property, so how hard can it be to find a single one? Surprisingly this turns out to be quite hard: Without using complexity assumptions, we do not know how to obtain such a set, and in Section 20.4 we will see that in fact obtaining such a set (or even any other deterministic algorithm for this problem) will imply some nontrivial circuit lower bounds.

20.1 PSEUDORANDOM GENERATORS AND DERANDOMIZATION

The main tool we will use for derandomization is a pseudorandom generator. This is a twist on the definition of a cryptographically *secure* pseudorandom generator we saw in Chapter 9, with the main difference that here we will allow the generator to run in *exponential* time (and in particular allow the generator more time than the distinguisher). Another difference is that we consider *nonuniform* distinguishers—in other words, circuits—rather than Turing machines, as was done in Chapter 9. (This second difference is not an essential one. As mentioned in the notes at the end of Chapter 9, we could have used circuits there as well.)

Definition 20.2 *(Pseudorandom generators)* A distribution R over $\{0, 1\}^m$ is (S, ϵ)-*pseudorandom* (for $S \in \mathbb{N}, \epsilon > 0$) if for every circuit C of size at most S

$$\left| \Pr[C(R) = 1] - \Pr[C(U_m) = 1] \right| < \epsilon$$

where U_m denotes the uniform distribution over $\{0, 1\}^m$.

Let $S : \mathbb{N} \to \mathbb{N}$ be some function. A 2^n-time computable function $G : \{0, 1\}^* \to \{0, 1\}^*$ is an $S(\ell)$-*pseudorandom generator* if $|G(z)| = S(|z|)$ for every $z \in \{0, 1\}^*$ and for every $\ell \in \mathbb{N}$ the distribution $G(U_\ell)$ is $(S(\ell)^3, 1/10)$-pseudorandom.

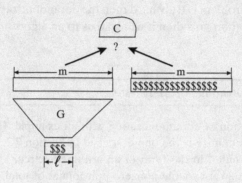

The choices of the constants 3 and $1/10$ in the definition of an $S(\ell)$-pseudorandom generator are arbitrary and made for convenience. To avoid annoying cases, we will restrict our attention to $S(\ell)$-pseudorandom generators for functions $S : \mathbb{N} \to \mathbb{N}$ that are *time-constructible* and *nondecreasing* (i.e., $S(\ell') \geq S(\ell)$ for $\ell' \geq \ell$).

20.1.1 Derandomization using pseudorandom generators

The relation between pseudorandom generators and simulating probabilistic algorithms is rather straightforward.

Lemma 20.3 *Suppose that there exists an $S(\ell)$-pseudorandom generator for a time-constructible nondecreasing $S : \mathbb{N} \to \mathbb{N}$. Then for every polynomial-time computable function $\ell : \mathbb{N} \to \mathbb{N}$, $\mathbf{BPTIME}(S(\ell(n))) \subseteq \mathbf{DTIME}(2^{c\ell(n)})$ for some constant c.* ◇

Before proving Lemma 20.3 it is instructive to see what derandomization results it implies for various values of S. This is observed in the following simple corollary, left as Exercise 20.1.

Corollary 20.4

1. *If there exists a $2^{\epsilon \ell}$-pseudorandom generator for some constant $\epsilon > 0$ then $\mathbf{BPP} = \mathbf{P}$.*
2. *If there exists a 2^{ℓ^ϵ}-pseudorandom generator for some constant $\epsilon > 0$ then $\mathbf{BPP} \subseteq \mathbf{QuasiP} = \mathbf{DTIME}(2^{\mathrm{polylog}(n)})$.*
3. *If for every $c > 1$ there exists an ℓ^c-pseudorandom generator, then $\mathbf{BPP} \subseteq \mathbf{SUBEXP} = \cap_{\epsilon > 0} \mathbf{DTIME}(2^{n^\epsilon})$.*

PROOF OF LEMMA 20.3: A language L is in **BPTIME**$(S(\ell(n)))$ if there is an algorithm A that on input $x \in \{0, 1\}^n$ runs in time $cS(\ell(n))$ for some constant c, and satisfies

$$\Pr_{r \in_R \{0,1\}^m}[A(x,r) = L(x)] \geq 2/3, \tag{20.1}$$

where $m \leq S(\ell(n))$ and we define $L(x) = 1$ if $x \in L$ and $L(x) = 0$ otherwise.

The main idea is that if we replace the truly random string r with the string $G(z)$ produced by picking a random $z \in \{0, 1\}^{\ell(n)}$, then an algorithm such as A that runs in only $S(\ell)$ time cannot detect this switch most of the time, and so the probability $2/3$ in the previous expression does not drop below $2/3 - 0.1 > 0.5$. Thus to derandomize A, we do not need to enumerate over all $r \in \{0, 1\}^m$: It suffices to enumerate over all the strings $G(z)$ for $z \in \{0, 1\}^{\ell(n)}$ and check whether or not the majority of these make A accept. This derandomized algorithm runs in $2^{O(\ell(n))}$ time instead of the trivial 2^m time.

Now we make this formal. On input $x \in \{0, 1\}^n$, our deterministic algorithm B will go over all $z \in \{0, 1\}^{\ell(n)}$, compute $A(x, G(z))$, and output the majority answer.[1] We claim that for n sufficiently large, the fraction of z's such that $A(x, G(z)) = L(x)$ is at least $2/3 - 0.1$. This suffices to prove that $L \in$ **DTIME**$(2^{c\ell(n)})$ as we can "hard-wire" into the algorithm the correct answer for finitely many inputs.

Suppose this is false and there exists an infinite sequence of x's for which $\Pr[A(x, G(z)) = L(x)] < 2/3 - 0.1$. Then there exists a distinguisher for the pseudorandom generator: Just use the Cook-Levin transformation (e.g., as in the proof of Theorem 6.6) to construct a circuit computing the function $r \mapsto A(x, r)$, where x is hard-wired into the circuit. (This "hard-wiring" is the place in the proof where we use nonuniformity.) This circuit has size $O(S(\ell(n)))^2$ which is smaller than $S(\ell(n))^3$ for sufficiently large n. ∎

The proof of Lemma 20.3 shows why it is OK to allow the pseudorandom generator in Definition 20.2 to run in time exponential in its seed length. The reason is that the derandomized algorithm enumerates over all possible seeds of length ℓ, and thus would take exponential (in ℓ) time even if the generator itself were to run in less than $\exp(\ell)$ time. Notice also that allowing the generator $\exp(\ell)$ time means that it has to "fool" distinguishers that run for *less* time than it does. By contrast, the definition of cryptographically *secure pseudorandom generators* (Definition 9.8 in Chapter 9) required the generator to run in some fixed polynomial time, and yet fool arbitrary polynomial-time distinguishers. This difference in these definitions stems from the intended usage. In the cryptographic setting the generator is used by honest users and the distinguisher is the adversary attacking the system—and it is reasonable to assume the attacker can invest more computational resources than those needed for normal/honest use of the system. In derandomization, the generator is used by the derandomized algorithm, and the "distinguisher" is the probabilistic algorithm that is being derandomized. In this case it is reasonable to allow the derandomized algorithm more running time than the original probabilistic algorithm. Of course, allowing the generator to run in exponential time potentially makes it easier to prove their existence compared with secure

---

[1] If $m < S(\ell(n))$ then $A(x, G(z))$ denotes the output of A on input x using the first m bits of $G(z)$ for its random choices.

pseudorandom generators, and this indeed appears to be the case. If we relaxed the definition even further and made no efficiency requirements then showing the existence of such generators becomes almost trivial (see Exercise 20.2), but they no longer seem useful for derandomization.

We will construct pseudorandom generators based on complexity assumptions, using quantitatively stronger assumptions to obtain quantitatively stronger pseudorandom generators (i.e., $S(\ell)$-pseudorandom generators for larger functions S). The strongest (though still reasonable) assumption will yield a $2^{\Omega(\ell)}$-pseudorandom generator, thus implying that **BPP = P**.

20.1.2 Hardness and derandomization

We construct pseudorandom generators under the assumptions that certain explicit functions are hard. In this chapter we use assumptions about *average-case* hardness, but using the results of Chapter 19 we will be able to also construct pseudorandom generators assuming only *worst-case* hardness. Both worst-case and average-case hardness refer to the size of the minimum Boolean circuit computing the function. Recall that we define the *average-case hardness* of a function $f : \{0, 1\}^n \to \{0, 1\}$, denoted by $\mathsf{H}_{\mathsf{avg}}(f)$, to be the largest number S such that $\Pr_{x \in_R \{0,1\}^n}[C(x) = f(x)] < 1/2 + 1/S$ for every Boolean circuit C on n inputs with size at most S (see Definition 19.1). For $f : \{0, 1\}^* \to \{0, 1\}$, we let $\mathsf{H}_{\mathsf{avg}}(f)(n)$ denote the average-case hardness of the restriction of f to $\{0, 1\}^n$.

EXAMPLE 20.5

Here are some examples of functions and their conjectured or proven hardness:
1. If $f : \{0, 1\}^* \to \{0, 1\}$ is a random function (i.e., for every $x \in \{0, 1\}^*$ we choose $f(x)$ using an independent unbiased coin), then with high probability both the worst-case and average-case hardness of f are exponential (see Exercise 20.3). In particular, with probability tending to 1 as n grows, both $\mathsf{H}_{\mathsf{wrs}}(f)(n)$ and $\mathsf{H}_{\mathsf{avg}}(f)(n)$ exceed $2^{0.99n}$.
2. If $f \in \mathbf{BPP}$ then, since $\mathbf{BPP} \subseteq \mathbf{P}_{/\mathbf{poly}}$, both $\mathsf{H}_{\mathsf{wrs}}(f)$ and $\mathsf{H}_{\mathsf{avg}}(f)$ are bounded by some polynomial.
3. It seems reasonable to believe that 3SAT has exponential worst-case hardness; that is, $\mathsf{H}_{\mathsf{wrs}}(3\mathsf{SAT}) \geq 2^{\Omega(n)}$. A weaker assumption is that $\mathbf{NP} \not\subseteq \mathbf{P}_{/\mathbf{poly}}$, in which case $\mathsf{H}_{\mathsf{wrs}}(3\mathsf{SAT})$ is not bounded by any polynomial. The average case complexity of 3SAT for uniformly chosen inputs is currently unclear, and in any case is dependent upon the way we choose to represent formulas as strings.
4. Under widely believed cryptographic assumptions, **NP** contains functions that are hard on the average. If g is a one-way permutation (as defined in Chapter 9) that cannot be inverted with polynomial probability by polynomial-sized circuits, then by Theorem 9.12, the function f that maps the pair $x, r \in \{0, 1\}^n$ to $g^{-1}(x) \odot r$ (where $x \odot r = \sum_{i=1}^{n} x_i r_i \pmod 2$) has super-polynomial *average-case* hardness: $\mathsf{H}_{\mathsf{avg}}(f) \geq n^{\omega(1)}$.

The main theorem of this section uses hard-on-the average functions to construct pseudorandom generators.

Theorem 20.6 *(PRGs from average-case hardness) Let $S : \mathbb{N} \to \mathbb{N}$ be time-constructible and nondecreasing. If there exists $f \in \mathbf{DTIME}(2^{O(n)})$ such that $\mathsf{H}_{\mathsf{avg}}(f)(n) \geq S(n)$ for every n, then there exists an $S(\delta\ell)^{\delta}$-pseudorandom generator for some constant $\delta > 0$.*

Combining this result with Theorem 19.27 we obtain the following theorem that gives even stronger evidence (given the plethora of plausible hard functions mentioned above) for the conjecture that derandomizing probabilistic algorithms is possible.

Theorem 20.7 *(Derandomization under worst-case assumptions) Let $S : \mathbb{N} \to \mathbb{N}$ be time-constructible and nondecreasing. If there exists $f \in \mathbf{DTIME}(2^{O(n)})$ such that $\mathsf{H}_{\mathsf{wrs}}(f)(n) \geq S(n)$ for every n, then there exists an $S(\delta\ell)^{\delta}$-pseudorandom generator for some constant $\delta > 0$. In particular, the following corollaries hold:*

1. *If there exists $f \in \mathbf{E} = \mathbf{DTIME}(2^{O(n)})$ and $\epsilon > 0$ such that $\mathsf{H}_{\mathsf{wrs}}(f) \geq 2^{\epsilon n}$, then $\mathbf{BPP} = \mathbf{P}$.*
2. *If there exists $f \in \mathbf{E} = \mathbf{DTIME}(2^{O(n)})$ and $\epsilon > 0$ such that $\mathsf{H}_{\mathsf{wrs}}(f) \geq 2^{n^{\epsilon}}$, then $\mathbf{BPP} \subseteq \mathbf{QuasiP}$.*
3. *If there exists $f \in \mathbf{E} = \mathbf{DTIME}(2^{O(n)})$ such that $\mathsf{H}_{\mathsf{wrs}}(f) \geq n^{\omega(1)}$, then $\mathbf{BPP} \subseteq \mathbf{SUBEXP}$.*

We can replace $\mathbf{E}$ with $\mathbf{EXP} = \mathbf{DTIME}(2^{\mathrm{poly}(n)})$ in Corollaries 2 and 3 above. Indeed, for every $f \in \mathbf{DTIME}(2^{n^c})$, let g be the function that on input $x \in \{0,1\}^*$ outputs f applied to the first $|x|^{1/c}$ bits of x. Then, g is in $\mathbf{DTIME}(2^n)$ and satisfies $\mathsf{H}_{\mathsf{avg}}(g)(n) \geq \mathsf{H}_{\mathsf{avg}}(f)(n^{1/c})$. Therefore, if there exists $f \in \mathbf{EXP}$ with $\mathsf{H}_{\mathsf{avg}}(f) \geq 2^{n^{\delta}}$, then there exists a constant $\delta' > 0$ and a function $g \in \mathbf{E}$ with $\mathsf{H}_{\mathsf{avg}}(g) \geq 2^{n^{\delta'}}$, and so we can replace $\mathbf{E}$ with $\mathbf{EXP}$ in Corollary 2. A similar observation holds for Corollary 3. Note that $\mathbf{EXP}$ contains many classes we believe to have hard problems, such as $\mathbf{NP}$, $\mathbf{PSPACE}$, $\oplus\mathbf{P}$ and more.

Remark 20.8

Nisan and Wigderson [NW88] were the first to show a pseudorandom generator from average-case hardness, but they did not prove Theorem 20.6 as it is stated above. Rather, Theorem 20.6 was proven by Umans [Uma03] following a long sequence of works including [BFNW93, IW97, ISW99, STV99, SU01]. Nisan and Wigderson only proved that under the same assumptions there exists an $S'(\ell)$-pseudorandom generator, where $S'(\ell) = S(n)^{\delta}$ for some constant $\delta > 0$ and n satisfying $n \geq \delta\sqrt{\ell \log S(n)}$. Note that this bound is still sufficient to derive all three corollaries above. It is this weaker version we prove in this book.

20.2 PROOF OF THEOREM 20.6: NISAN-WIGDERSON CONSTRUCTION

How can we use a hard function to construct a pseudorandom generator? As a warmup we start with two "toy examples." We first show how to use a hard function to construct a pseudorandom generator whose output is only a single bit longer than its input. Then we show how to obtain such a generator whose output is two bits longer than the input. Of course, neither of these suffices to prove Theorem 20.6, but they do give insight into the connection between hardness and randomness.

20.2.1 Two toy examples

Extending the input by one bit using Yao's Theorem
The following lemma uses a hard function to construct a "toy" generator that extends its input by a single bit.

Lemma 20.9 *(One-bit generator) Suppose that there exist $f \in \mathbf{E}$ with $\mathsf{H}_{\mathsf{avg}}(f) \geq n^4$. Then there exists an $S(\ell)$-pseudorandom generator G for $S(\ell) = \ell + 1$.*   ◇

PROOF: The generator G is very simple: for every $z \in \{0, 1\}^\ell$, we set

$$G(z) = z \circ f(z)$$

(where $\circ$ denotes concatenation). G clearly satisfies the output length and efficiency requirements of an $(\ell + 1)$-pseudorandom generator. To prove that its output is $((\ell + 1)^3, 1/10)$-pseudorandom we use Yao's Theorem from Chapter 9 showing that pseudorandomness is implied by unpredictability.[2]

Theorem 20.10 *(Theorem 9.11 restated) Let Y be a distribution over $\{0, 1\}^m$. Suppose that there exist $S > 10n$ and $\epsilon > 0$ such that for every circuit C of size at most $2S$ and $i \in [m]$*

$$\Pr_{r \in_R Y}[C(r_1, \ldots, r_{i-1}) = r_i] \leq \frac{1}{2} + \frac{\epsilon}{m}$$

Then Y is (S, ϵ)-pseudorandom.   ◇

By Theorem 20.10, to prove Lemma 20.9 it suffices to show that there does not exist a circuit C of size $2(\ell + 1)^3 < \ell^4$ and a number $i \in [\ell + 1]$ such that

$$\Pr_{r = G(U_\ell)}[C(r_1, \ldots, r_{i-1}) = r_i] > \frac{1}{2} + \frac{1}{20(\ell + 1)} \tag{20.2}$$

However, for every $i \leq \ell$, the ith bit of $G(z)$ is completely uniform and independent from the first $i - 1$ bits, and hence cannot be predicted with probability larger than $1/2$ by a circuit of any size. For $i = \ell + 1$, Equation (20.2) becomes

$$\Pr_{z \in_R \{0,1\}^\ell}[C(z) = f(z)] > \frac{1}{2} + \frac{1}{20(\ell + 1)} > \frac{1}{2} + \frac{1}{\ell^4},$$

which cannot hold under the assumption that $\mathsf{H}_{\mathsf{avg}}(f) \geq n^4$. ∎

Extending the input by two bits using the averaging principle
We continue to progress in "baby steps" and consider the next natural toy problem: Constructing a pseudorandom generator that extends its input by two bits. This is obtained in the following lemma.

---

[2] Although this theorem was stated and proved in Chapter 9 for the case of *uniform* Turing machines, the proof extends to the case of circuits; see Exercise 20.5.

Lemma 20.11 *(Two-Bit Generator) Suppose that there exists $f \in \mathbf{E}$ with $H_{\mathsf{avg}}(f) \geq n^4$. Then there exists an $(\ell+2)$-pseudorandom generator G.*   ◇

PROOF: The construction is again very natural: for every $z \in \{0, 1\}^\ell$, we set

$$G(z) = z_1 \cdots z_{\ell/2} \circ f(z_1, \ldots, z_{\ell/2}) \circ z_{\ell/2+1} \cdots z_\ell \circ f(z_{\ell/2+1}, \ldots, z_\ell)$$

Again, the efficiency and output length requirements are clearly satisfied. To show $G(U_\ell)$ is $((\ell + 2)^3, 1/10)$-pseudorandom, we again use Theorem 20.10, and so need to prove that there does not exists a circuit C of size $2(\ell + 1)^3$ and $i \in [\ell + 2]$ such that

$$\Pr_{r=G(U_\ell)}[C(r_1, \ldots, r_{i-1}) = r_i] > \frac{1}{2} + \frac{1}{20(\ell + 2)}. \tag{20.3}$$

Once again, (20.3) cannot occur for those indices i in which the ith output of $G(z)$ is truly random, and so the only two cases we need to consider are $i = \ell/2+1$ and $i = \ell+2$. Equation (20.3) cannot hold for $i = \ell/2 + 1$ for the same reason as in Lemma 20.9. For $i = \ell + 2$, Equation (20.3) becomes

$$\Pr_{r,r' \in_R \{0, 1\}^{\ell/2}}[C(r \circ f(r) \circ r') = f(r')] > \frac{1}{2} + \frac{1}{20(\ell + 2)} \tag{20.4}$$

This may seem somewhat problematic to analyze since the input to C contains the bit $f(r)$, which C could not compute on its own (as f is a hard function). Couldn't it be that the input $f(r)$ helps C in predicting the bit $f(r')$? The answer is NO, and the reason is that r' and r are *independent*. Formally, we use the following principle (see Section A.2.2):

> THE AVERAGING PRINCIPLE: If A is some event depending on two independent random variables X, Y, then there exists some x in the range of X such that $\Pr_Y[A(x, Y)] \geq \Pr_{X,Y}[A(X, Y)]$.

Applying this principle here, if (20.4) holds then there exists a string $r \in \{0, 1\}^{\ell/2}$ such that

$$\Pr_{r' \in_R \{0, 1\}^{\ell/2}}[C(r, f(r), r') = f(r')] > \frac{1}{2} + \frac{1}{20(\ell + 2)}$$

(Note that this probability is now only over the choice of r'.) If this is the case, we can "hard-wire" the $\ell/2 + 1$ bits $r \circ f(r)$ (as fixing r to some constant also fixes $f(r)$) to the circuit C and obtain a circuit D of size at most $2(\ell + 2)^3 < (\ell/2)^4$ such that

$$\Pr_{r' \in_R \{0, 1\}^{\ell/2}}[D(r') = f(r')] > \frac{1}{2} + \frac{1}{20(\ell + 2)}$$

contradicting the hardness of f. ■

Beyond two bits

A generator that extends the output by two bits is still useless for our goals. We can generalize the proof of Lemma 20.11 to obtain a generator G that extends its input by k bits setting

$$G(z_1, \ldots, z_\ell) = z^1 \circ f(z^1) \circ z^2 \circ f(z^2) \cdots z^k \circ f(z^k) \tag{20.5}$$

where z^i is the ith block of ℓ/k bits in z. However, no matter how big we set k and no matter how hard the function f is, we cannot get in this way a generator that expands its input by a multiplicative factor larger than two. Note that to prove Theorem 20.6 we need a generator whose output might even be *exponentially larger* than the input! Clearly, we need a new idea.

20.2.2 The NW construction

The new idea is still inspired by the construction (20.5), but instead of taking $z^1, \ldots, z^k$ to be independently chosen strings (or equivalently, disjoint pieces of the input z), we take them to be *partly dependent* (nondisjoint pieces) by using *combinatorial designs*. Doing this will allow us to take k so large that we can drop the actual inputs from the generator's output and use only $f(z^1) \circ f(z^2) \cdots \circ f(z^k)$. The proof of correctness is similar to the above toy examples and uses Yao's technique, except the fixing of the input bits has to be done more carefully because of dependence among the strings.

Definition 20.12 *(NW generator)* Let $\mathcal{I} = \{I_1, \ldots, I_m\}$ be a family of subsets of $[\ell]$ with $|I_j| = n$ for every j, and let $f : \{0, 1\}^n \to \{0, 1\}$. The $(\mathcal{I}, f)$-*NW generator* is the function $\mathsf{NW}_{\mathcal{I}}^f : \{0, 1\}^\ell \to \{0, 1\}^m$ that maps every $z \in \{0, 1\}^\ell$ to

$$\mathsf{NW}_{\mathcal{I}}^f(z) = f(z_{I_1}) \circ f(z_{I_2}) \cdots \circ f(z_{I_m}) \tag{20.6}$$

where for $z \in \{0, 1\}^\ell$ and $I \subseteq [\ell]$, z_I denotes the restriction of z to the coordinates in I.

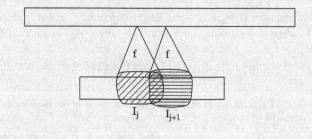

Conditions on the set systems and function
We will see that in order for the generator to produce pseudorandom outputs, the function f must display some *hardness*, and the family of subsets should come from a *combinatorial design*, defined as follows.

Definition 20.13 *(Combinatorial Designs)* Let d, n, ℓ satisfy $\ell > n > d$. A family $\mathcal{I} = \{I_1, \ldots, I_m\}$ of subsets of $[\ell]$ is an (ℓ, n, d)-*design* if $|I_j| = n$ for every j and $|I_j \cap I_k| \leq d$ for every $j \neq k$.   ⬦

The next lemma (whose proof we defer to the end of this section) yields sufficiently efficient constructions of such designs.

Lemma 20.14 *(Construction of Designs) There is an algorithm A that on input $\langle \ell, d, n \rangle$ where $n > d$ and $\ell > 10n^2/d$, runs for $2^{O(\ell)}$ steps and outputs an (ℓ, n, d)-design $\mathcal{I}$ containing $2^{d/10}$ subsets of $[\ell]$.* ◇

The next lemma shows that if f is a hard function and $\mathcal{I}$ is a design with sufficiently good parameters, then $\mathsf{NW}_{\mathcal{I}}^f(U_\ell)$ is indeed a pseudorandom distribution.

Lemma 20.15 *(Pseudorandomness Using the NW Generator) If $\mathcal{I}$ is an (ℓ, n, d)-design with $|\mathcal{I}| = 2^{d/10}$ and $f : \{0,1\}^n \to \{0,1\}$ satisfies $\mathsf{H}_{\mathsf{avg}}(f) > 2^{2d}$, then the distribution $\mathsf{NW}_{\mathcal{I}}^f(U_\ell)$ is $(\mathsf{H}_{\mathsf{avg}}(f)/10, 1/10)$-pseudorandom.* ◇

PROOF: Let $S = \mathsf{H}_{\mathsf{avg}}(f)$. By Yao's Theorem, to show that $\mathsf{NW}_{\mathcal{I}}^f(U_\ell)$ is $(S/10, 1/10)$-pseudorandom it suffices to prove that for every $i \in [2^{d/10}]$, there does *not* exist an $S/2$-sized circuit C such that

$$\Pr_{\substack{Z \sim U_\ell \\ R = \mathsf{NW}_{\mathcal{I}}^f(Z)}} [C(R_1, \ldots, R_{i-1}) = R_i] \geq \frac{1}{2} + \frac{1}{10 \cdot 2^{d/10}} \tag{20.7}$$

For contradiction's sake, assume that (20.7) holds for some circuit C and some i. Plugging in the definition of $\mathsf{NW}_{\mathcal{I}}^f$, (20.7) becomes

$$\Pr_{Z \sim U_\ell} [C(f(Z_{I_1}), \ldots, f(Z_{I_{i-1}})) = f(Z_{I_i})] \geq \frac{1}{2} + \frac{1}{10 \cdot 2^{d/10}} \tag{20.8}$$

Letting Z_1 and Z_2 denote the two independent variables corresponding to the coordinates of Z in I_i and $[\ell] \setminus I_i$ respectively, (20.8) becomes

$$\Pr_{\substack{Z_1 \sim U_n \\ Z_2 \sim U_{\ell-n}}} [C(f_1(Z_1, Z_2), \ldots, f_{i-1}(Z_1, Z_2)) = f(Z_1)] \geq \frac{1}{2} + \frac{1}{10 \cdot 2^{d/10}} \tag{20.9}$$

where for every $j \in [2^{d/10}]$, f_j applies f to the coordinates of Z_1 corresponding to $I_j \cap I_i$ and the coordinates of Z_2 corresponding to $I_j \setminus I_i$. By the averaging principle, if (20.9) holds, then there exists a string $z_2 \in \{0,1\}^{\ell-n}$ such that

$$\Pr_{Z_1 \sim U_n} [C(f_1(Z_1, z_2), \ldots, f_{i-1}(Z_1, z_2)) = f(Z_1)] \geq \frac{1}{2} + \frac{1}{10 \cdot 2^{d/10}} \tag{20.10}$$

We may now appear to be in some trouble: Since all of $f_j(Z_1, z_2)$ for $j \leq i - 1$ do depend upon Z_1, one might worry that they together contain enough information about Z_1 and so a circuit *could potentially* predict $f_i(Z_1)$ after seeing all of them. To prove that this fear is baseless we use the fact that $\mathcal{I}$ is a design and f is a sufficiently hard function.

Since $|I_j \cap I_i| \leq d$ for $j \neq i$, the function $Z_1 \mapsto f_j(Z_1, z_2)$ (for the fixed string z_2) depends at most d coordinates of Z_1 and hence can be trivially computed by a $d2^d$-sized circuit (or even $O(2^d/d)$ sized circuit, see Exercise 6.1). Thus if (20.9) holds, then there exists a circuit B of size $2^{d/10} \cdot d2^d + S/2 < S$ such that

$$\Pr_{Z_1 \sim U_n}[B(Z_1) = f(Z_1)] \geq \frac{1}{2} + \frac{1}{10 \cdot 2^{d/10}} > \frac{1}{2} + \frac{1}{S} \qquad (20.11)$$

But this contradicts the fact that $S = \mathsf{H}_{\mathsf{avg}}(f)$. ∎

The proof of Lemma 20.15 shows that if $\mathsf{NW}^f_{\mathcal{I}}(U_\ell)$ is distinguishable from the uniform distribution $U_{2d/10}$ by some circuit D, then there exists a circuit B (of size polynomial in the size of D and in 2^d) that computes the function f with probability noticeably larger than $1/2$. The construction of this circuit B actually uses the circuit D as a *black-box*, invoking it on some chosen inputs. This property of the NW generator (and other constructions of pseudorandom generators) turned out to be useful in several settings. In particular, Exercise 20.7 uses it to show that under plausible complexity assumptions, the complexity class **AM** (containing all languages with a constant round interactive proof, see Chapter 8) is equal to **NP**. We will also use this property in Chapter 21 to construct *randomness extractors* based on pseudorandom generators.

Putting it all together: Proof of Theorem 20.6 from Lemmas 20.14 and 20.15

As noted in Remark 20.8, we do not prove here Theorem 20.6 as stated but only the weaker statement, that given $f \in \mathbf{DTIME}(2^{O(n)})$ and $S : \mathbb{N} \to \mathbb{N}$ with $\mathsf{H}_{\mathsf{avg}}(f) \geq S$, we can construct an $S'(\ell)$-pseudorandom generator, where $S'(\ell) = S(n)^\epsilon$ for some $\epsilon > 0$ and n satisfying $n \geq \epsilon\sqrt{\ell \log S(n)}$. On input $z \in \{0,1\}^\ell$, our generator will operate as follows:

- Set n to be the largest number such that $\ell > \frac{100n^2}{\log S(n)}$. Thus, $\ell \leq \frac{100(n+1)^2}{\log S(n+1)} \leq \frac{200n^2}{\log S(n)}$, and hence $n \geq \sqrt{\ell \log S(n)/200}$.
- Set $d = \log S(n)/10$.
- Run the algorithm of Lemma 20.14 to obtain an (ℓ, n, d)-design $\mathcal{I} = \{I_1, \ldots, I_{2^{d/5}}\}$.
- Output the first $S(n)^{1/40}$ bits of $\mathsf{NW}^f_{\mathcal{I}}(z)$.

This generator makes $2^{d/5}$ invocations of f, taking a total of $2^{O(n)+d}$ steps. By possibly reducing n by a constant factor, we can ensure the running time is bounded by 2^ℓ. Moreover, since $2^d \leq S(n)^{1/10}$, Lemma 20.15 implies that the distribution $\mathsf{NW}^f(U_\ell)$ is $(S(n)/10, 1/10)$-pseudorandom. ∎

Construction of combinatorial designs

All that is left to complete the proof is to show the construction of combinatorial designs with the required parameters.

PROOF OF LEMMA 20.14: *(Construction of Combinatorial Designs)* On inputs ℓ, d, n with $\ell > 10n^2/d$, our Algorithm A will construct an (ℓ, n, d)-design $\mathcal{I}$ with $2^{d/10}$ sets using the simple greedy strategy:

> Start with $\mathcal{I} = \emptyset$ and after constructing $\mathcal{I} = \{I_1, \ldots, I_m\}$ for $m < 2^{d/10}$, search all subsets of $[\ell]$ and add to $\mathcal{I}$ the first n-sized set I satisfying the following condition (*): $|I \cap I_j| \leq d$ for every $j \in [m]$.

Clearly, A runs in $\mathrm{poly}(m)2^\ell = 2^{O(\ell)}$ time and so we only need to prove it never gets stuck. In other words, it suffices to show that if $\ell = 10n^2/d$ and $\{I_1, \ldots, I_m\}$ is a collection of n-sized subsets of $[\ell]$ for $m < 2^{d/10}$, then there exists an n-sized subset $I \subseteq [\ell]$ satisfying (*). We do so by showing that if we pick I at random by choosing independently every element $x \in [\ell]$ to be in I with probability $2n/\ell$, then

$$\Pr[|I| \geq n] \geq 0.9 \tag{20.12}$$

$$\text{For every } j \in [m], \quad \Pr[|I \cap I_j| \geq d] \leq 0.5 \cdot 2^{-d/10} \tag{20.13}$$

Because the expected size of I is $2n$, while the expected size of the intersection $I \cap I_j$ is $2n^2/\ell < d/5$, both (20.13) and (20.12) follow from the Chernoff bound. Yet, because $m \leq 2^{d/10}$, together these two conditions imply that with probability at least 0.4, the set I will simultaneously satisfy (*) and have size at least n. Since we can always remove elements from I without damaging (*), this completes the proof. ∎

20.3 DERANDOMIZATION UNDER UNIFORM ASSUMPTIONS

Circuit lower bounds are notoriously hard to prove. Despite decades of effort, at the moment we do not know of a single function in **NP** requiring more than $5n$-sized circuits to compute, let alone super-linear or super-polynomial sized circuits. A natural question is whether such lower bounds are *necessary* to achieve derandomization.[3] Note that pseudorandom generators as in Definition 20.2 can be easily shown to imply circuit lower bounds; see Exercise 20.4. However, there could potentially be a different way to show **BPP** = **P** without constructing pseudorandom generators.

The following result shows that to some extent this is possible: One can get a nontrivial derandomization of **BPP** under a *uniform* hardness assumption. Namely, that **BPP** $\neq$ **EXP**.

Theorem 20.16 *(Uniform derandomization* [IW98]*) Suppose that* **BPP** $\neq$ **EXP**. *Then for every* $L \in$ **BPP** *there exists a subexponential (i.e.,* $2^{n^{o(1)}}$ *) time deterministic algorithm A such that for infinitely many n's*

$$\Pr_{x \in_R \{0,1\}^n}[A(x) = L(x)] \geq 1 - 1/n$$

This means that unless randomness is a panacea, and every problem with an exponential-time algorithm (including 3SAT, TQBF, the permanent, etc.) can be solved in probabilistic polynomial time, we can at least partially derandomize **BPP**: Obtain a subexponential deterministic simulation that succeeds well in the average case. In fact, the conclusion of Theorem 20.16 can be considerably strengthened: We can find an algorithm A that will solve L with probability $1 - 1/n$ not only for inputs chosen according to the uniform distribution, but on inputs chosen according to *every* distribution that can be sampled in polynomial time. Thus, while this deterministic simulation may sometimes fail, it is hard to find inputs on which it does!

---

[3] Note that we do not know much better lower bounds for Turing machines either. However, a priori it seems that a result such as **BPP** $\neq$ **EXP** may be easier to prove than circuit lower bounds, and that a natural first step to proving such a result is to get derandomization results without assuming such lower bounds.

PROOF SKETCH OF THEOREM 20.16: We only sketch the proof of Theorem 20.16 here. We start by noting that we may assume in the proof that $\mathbf{EXP} \subseteq \mathbf{P}_{/poly}$, since otherwise there is some problem in $\mathbf{EXP}$ with superpolynomial circuit complexity, and such a problem can be used to build a pseudorandom generator that is strong enough to imply the conclusion of the theorem. (This follows from Theorem 20.7 and Exercise 20.8.) Next, note that if $\mathbf{EXP} \subseteq \mathbf{P}_{/poly}$, then $\mathbf{EXP}$ is contained in the polynomial hierarchy (see Theorem 6.20 and also Lemma 20.18 below). But that implies $\mathbf{EXP} = \mathbf{PH}$ and hence we can conclude from Toda's and Valiant's Theorems (Theorems 17.14 and 17.11) that the *permanent* function perm is $\mathbf{EXP}$-complete under polynomial-time reductions. In addition, the lemma hypothesis implies that perm is not in $\mathbf{BPP}$. This is a crucial point in the proof since perm is a very special function that is downward self-reducible (see Chapter 8).

The next idea is to build a pseudorandom generator G with super-polynomial output size using the permanent as a hard function. We omit the details, but this can be done following the proofs of Theorems 19.27 and 20.6 (one needs to handle the fact that the permanent's output is not a single bit, but this can be handled for example using the Goldreich-Levin Theorem of Chapter 9). Looking at the proof of correctness for this pseudorandom generator G, it can be shown to yield an algorithm T to transform for every n a distinguisher D between G's output) and the uniform distribution into a polynomial-sized circuit C_n that computes perm_n (which this denotes the restriction of the permanent to length n inputs). This algorithm T is similar to the transformation shown in the proof of the standard NW generator (proof of Theorem 20.6): The only reason it is not efficient is that it requires computing the hard function (in this case the permanent) on several randomly chosen inputs, which are then "hard-wired" into the distinguisher.[4]

Suppose for the sake of contradiction that the conclusion of Theorem 20.16 is false. This means that there is a probabilistic algorithm A whose derandomization using G fails with noticeable probability (over the choice of a random input) for all but finitely many input lengths. This implies that not only is there a sequence of polynomial-sized circuits $\{D_n\}$ distinguishing the output of G from the uniform distribution on all but finitely many input lengths, but in fact there is a probabilistic polynomial-time algorithm that on input 1^n will find such a circuit D_n with probability at least $1/n$ (Exercise 20.9). We now make the simplifying assumption that this probabilistic algorithm in facts finds such a distinguisher D_n with high probability, say at least $1 - 1/n^2$.[5] Plugging this into the proof of pseudorandomness for the generator G, this means that there exists a probabilistic polynomial-time algorithm T that can "learn" the permanent function: Given oracle access to perm_n (the restriction of perm to length n inputs) the algorithm T runs in poly(n) time and produces a poly(n)-sized circuit computing perm_n.

But using T we can come up with a probabilistic polynomial-time algorithm for the permanent that doesn't use any oracle! To compute the permanent on length n inputs,

---

[4] The proof of Theorem 20.6 only showed that there exists some inputs that when these inputs and their answers are "hard-wired" into the distinguisher then we get a circuit computing the hard function. However, because the proof used the probabilistic method/averaging argument, it's not hard to show that with good probability random inputs will do.

[5] This gap can be handled using the fact that the permanent is a low-degree polynomial and hence has certain self-correction/self-testing properties, see Sections 8.6.2 and 19.4.2.

we compute inductively the circuits $C_1, \ldots, C_n$. Given the circuit C_{n-1} we can compute the permanent on length n inputs using the permanent's *downward self-reducibility* property (see Section 8.6.2 and the proof of Lemma 20.19 below), and so implement the oracle to T that allows us to build the circuit C_n. Since we assumed **BPP** $\neq$ **EXP**, and under **EXP** $\subseteq$ **P**$_{/\text{poly}}$ the permanent is **EXP**-complete, we get a contradiction. ∎

20.4 DERANDOMIZATION REQUIRES CIRCUIT LOWER BOUNDS

Section 20.3 shows that circuit lower bounds imply derandomization. However, circuit lower bounds have proved tricky, so one might hope that derandomization could somehow be done *without* circuit lower bounds. In this section we show this is not the case: Proving that **BPP** = **P** or even that a specific problem in **BPP** (namely the problem ZEROP of testing whether a given polynomial is identically zero) will imply super-polynomial lower bounds for either Boolean or arithmetic circuits. Depending upon whether you are an optimist or a pessimist, you can view this either as evidence that derandomizing **BPP** is difficult or as a reason to double our efforts to derandomize **BPP** since once we do so we'll get "two for the price of one": Both derandomization and circuit lower bounds.

Recall (Definition 16.7) that we say that a function f defined over the integers is in **AlgP**$_{/\text{poly}}^{\mathbb{Z}}$ (or just **AlgP**$_{/\text{poly}}$ for short) if f can be computed by a polynomial size algebraic circuit whose gates are labeled by $+$, $-$, and $\times$.[6] We let perm denote the problem of computing the permanent of matrices over the integers. Recall also the *Polynomial Identity Testing* (ZEROP) problem in which the input consists of a polynomial represented by an arithmetic circuit computing it and we have to decide if it is the identically zero polynomial (see Example 20.1 and Section 7.2.3). The problem ZEROP is in **coRP** $\subseteq$ **BPP**, and we will show that if it is in **P**, then some super-polynomial circuit lower bounds hold.

Theorem 20.17 (*Derandomization implies lower bounds* [KI03])
If ZEROP $\in$ **P** *then either* **NEXP** $\not\subseteq$ **P**$_{/\text{poly}}$ *or* perm $\notin$ **AlgP**$_{/\text{poly}}$.

Theorem 20.17 is known to be true even if its hypothesis is relaxed to ZEROP $\in$ $\cap_{\delta>0}$**NTIME**(2^{n^δ}). Thus even a derandomization of **BPP** to subexponential nondeterministic time would still imply super-polynomial circuit lower bounds. The proof of Theorem 20.17 relies on many results described earlier in the book. (This is a good example of "third generation" complexity results that use a clever combination of both "classical" results from the 1960s and 1970s and newer results from the 1990s.) Our first ingredient is the following lemma.

Lemma 20.18 ([BFL90],[BFNW93]) **EXP** $\subseteq$ **P**$_{/\text{poly}}$ $\Rightarrow$ **EXP** = **MA**.   ◇

---

[6] The results below extend also to circuits that are allowed to work over the rational or real numbers and use division.

Recall that **MA** is the class of languages that can be proven by a one-round interactive proof between two players Arthur and Merlin (see Definition 8.10).

PROOF OF LEMMA 20.18: Suppose **EXP** $\subseteq$ **P**$_{/\text{poly}}$. By Meyer's Theorem (Theorem 6.20), in this case **EXP** collapses to the second level Σ_2^p of the polynomial hierarchy. Hence under our assumptions $\Sigma_2^p =$ **PH** $=$ **PSPACE** $=$ **IP** $=$ **EXP** $\subseteq$ **P**$_{/\text{poly}}$. Thus every $L \in$ **EXP** has an interactive proof, and furthermore, since our assumption implies that **EXP** = **PSPACE**, we can just use the interactive proof for TQBF, for which the prover is a **PSPACE** machine and (given that we assume **PSPACE** $\subseteq$ **P**$_{/\text{poly}}$) can be replaced by a polynomial size circuit family $\{C_n\}$. Now we see that the interactive proof can actually be carried out in one round: Given an input x of length n, Merlin will send Arthur a polynomial-size circuit C, which is supposed to be circuit C_n for the prover's strategy for L. Then Arthur simulates the interactive proof for L, using C as the prover and tossing coins to simulate the verifier. Note that if the input is not in the language, then *no* prover has a decent chance of convincing the verifier, and in particular this holds for the prover described by C. Thus we have described an **MA** protocol for L implying that **EXP** $\subseteq$ **MA** and hence that **EXP** = **MA**. ∎

Our second lemma connects the complexity of identity testing and the permanent to the power of the class **P**^{perm}.

Lemma 20.19 *If* ZEROP $\in$ **P** *and* perm $\in$ **AlgP**$_{/\text{poly}}$, *then* **P**$^{\text{perm}} \subseteq$ **NP**.   ◇

PROOF OF LEMMA 20.19: Suppose perm has algebraic circuits of size n^c and that ZEROP has a polynomial-time algorithm. Let L be a language that is decided by an n^d-time TM M using queries to a perm-oracle. We construct an **NP** machine N for L.

Suppose x is an input of size n. Clearly, M's computation on x makes queries to perm of size at most $m = n^d$. So N will use nondeterminism as follows: It guesses a sequence of m algebraic circuits $C_1, C_2, \ldots, C_m$ where C_i has size i^c. The hope is that C_i solves perm on $i \times i$ matrices, and N will verify this in poly(m) time. The verification starts by verifying C_1, which is trivial. Inductively, having verified the correctness of $C_1, \ldots, C_{t-1}$, one can verify that C_t is correct using downward self-reducibility, namely, that for a $t \times t$ matrix A,

$$\text{perm}(A) = \sum_{i=1}^{t} a_{1i}\text{perm}(A_{1,i}),$$

where $A_{1,i}$ is the $(t-1) \times (t-1)$ submatrix of A obtained by removing the first row and ith column of A. Thus if circuit C_{t-1} is known to be correct, then the correctness of C_t can be checked by substituting $C_t(A)$ for perm(A) and $C_{t-1}(A_{1,i})$ for perm($A_{1,i}$): This yields an identity involving algebraic circuits with t^2 inputs, which can be verified deterministically in poly(t) time using the algorithm for ZEROP. Proceeding this way N verifies the correctness of $C_1, \ldots, C_m$ and then simulates M^{perm} on input x using these circuits. ∎

The heart of the proof of Theorem 20.17 is the following lemma, which is interesting in its own right.

Lemma 20.20 *([IKW01])* $\mathbf{NEXP} \subseteq \mathbf{P}_{/\text{poly}} \Rightarrow \mathbf{NEXP} = \mathbf{EXP}$. ⬦

PROOF: We prove the contrapositive. That is, we assume that $\mathbf{NEXP} \neq \mathbf{EXP}$ and will prove thsat $\mathbf{NEXP} \not\subseteq \mathbf{P}_{/\text{poly}}$. Let $L \in \mathbf{NEXP} \setminus \mathbf{EXP}$ (such a language exists under our assumption). Since $L \in \mathbf{NEXP}$ there exists a constant $c > 0$ and a relation R such that

$$x \in L \Leftrightarrow \exists y \in \{0, 1\}^{2^{|x|^c}} \text{ s.t. } R(x, y) \text{ holds}$$

where we can test whether $R(x, y)$ holds in, say, time $2^{|x|^{10c}}$.

We now consider the following approach to try to solve L in exponential deterministic time. For every constant $D > 0$, let M_D be the following machine: On input $x \in \{0, 1\}^n$ enumerate over all possible Boolean circuits C of size n^{100D} that take n^c inputs and have a single output. For every such circuit let $\mathsf{tt}(C)$ be the 2^{n^c}-long string that corresponds to the truth table of the function computed by C. If $R(x, \mathsf{tt}(C))$ holds, then halt and output 1. If this does not hold for any of the circuits then output 0. Since M_D runs in time $2^{n^{101D}+n^c}$, under our assumption that $L \notin \mathbf{EXP}$, M_D does not solve L and hence for every D there exists an infinite sequence of inputs $\mathcal{X}_D = \{x_i\}_{i \in \mathbb{N}}$ on which $M_D(x_i)$ outputs 0 even though $x_i \in L$ (note that M_D can only make one-sided errors). This means that for every string x in the sequence $\mathcal{X}_D$ and every y such that $R(x, y)$ holds, the string y represents the truth table of a function on n^c bits that cannot be computed by circuits of size n^{100D}, where $n = |x|$. Using the pseudorandom generator based on worst-case assumptions (Theorem 20.7), we can use such a string y to obtain an ℓ^D-pseudorandom generator. This method is called the "easy witness" method [Kab00] because it shows that unless the input x has a witness/certificate y (i.e., string satisfying $R(x, y) = 1$) that is "easy" in the sense that it can be computed by a small circuit, then any certificate for x can be used for derandomization.

Now, if $\mathbf{NEXP} \subseteq \mathbf{P}_{/\text{poly}}$ then $\mathbf{EXP} \subseteq \mathbf{P}_{/\text{poly}}$ and then by Lemma 20.18 $\mathbf{EXP} \subseteq \mathbf{MA}$. That is, every language in $\mathbf{EXP}$ has a proof system where Merlin proves that an n-bit string is in the language by sending a proof that Arthur then verifies using a probabilistic algorithm of at most n^D steps for some constant D. Yet, if n is the input length of some string in the sequence $\mathcal{X}_D$ and we are given $x \in \mathcal{X}_D$ with $|x| = n$, then we can replace Arthur by nondeterministic $\text{poly}(n^D)2^{n^{10c}}$ time algorithm that does not toss any coins: Arthur will guess a string y such that $R(x, y)$ holds and then use y as a function for a pseudorandom generator to verify Merlin's proof.

This means that there is an absolute constant $c > 0$ such that *every* language in $\mathbf{EXP}$ can be decided on infinitely many inputs by an $\mathbf{NTIME}(2^{n^c})$ time algorithm using n bits of advice, and hence (since we assume $\mathbf{NEXP} \subseteq \mathbf{P}_{/\text{poly}}$) by a size $n^{c'}$ circuit family for an absolute constant c'. But using standard diagonalization we can easily come up with a language in $\mathbf{DTIME}(2^{O(n^{c'})}) \subseteq \mathbf{EXP}$ that cannot be computed by such a circuit family on almost every input. ∎

It might seem that Lemma 20.20 should have an easier proof that goes along the lines of the proof of Lemma 20.18 ($\mathbf{EXP} \subseteq \mathbf{P}_{/\text{poly}} \Rightarrow \mathbf{EXP} = \mathbf{MA}$) but instead of using the interactive proof for TQBF uses the *multiprover* interactive proof system for $\mathbf{NEXP}$. However, we do not know how to implement the provers' strategies for this latter system in $\mathbf{NEXP}$. Intuitively, the problem arises from the fact that a $\mathbf{NEXP}$ statement may have several certificates, and it is not clear how we can ensure all provers use the same one.

We now have all the ingredients for the proof of Theorem 20.17.

PROOF OF THEOREM 20.17: For contradiction's sake, assume that the following are all true:

$$\mathsf{ZEROP} \in \mathbf{P} \tag{20.14}$$

$$\mathbf{NEXP} \subseteq \mathbf{P}_{/\mathbf{poly}} \tag{20.15}$$

$$\mathsf{perm} \in \mathbf{AlgP}_{/\mathbf{poly}} \tag{20.16}$$

Statement (20.15) together with Lemmas 20.18 and 20.20 imply that $\mathbf{NEXP} = \mathbf{EXP} = \mathbf{MA}$. Now recall that $\mathbf{MA} \subseteq \mathbf{PH}$ and that by Toda's Theorem (Theorem 17.14) $\mathbf{PH} \subseteq \mathbf{P^{\#P}}$. Recall also that by Valiant's Theorem (Theorem 17.11) perm is $\mathbf{\#P}$-complete. Thus under our assumptions

$$\mathbf{NEXP} \subseteq \mathbf{P}^{\mathsf{perm}} \tag{20.17}$$

Since we assume that $\mathsf{ZEROP} \in \mathbf{P}$, Lemma 20.19 together with statements (20.16) and (20.17) implies that $\mathbf{NEXP} \subseteq \mathbf{NP}$, contradicting the Nondeterministic Time Hierarchy Theorem (Theorem 3.2). Thus the three statements (20.14), (20.15), and (20.14) cannot be simultaneously true. ∎

WHAT HAVE WE LEARNED?

- Under the assumption of certain circuit lower bounds, there exist pseudorandom generators that can derandomize every probabilistic algorithm.
- In particular, if we make the reasonable assumption that there exists a function in $\mathbf{E}$ with exponentially large average-case circuit complexity, then $\mathbf{BPP} = \mathbf{P}$.
- Proving that $\mathbf{BPP} = \mathbf{P}$ will require proving at least some type of circuit lower bounds.

CHAPTER NOTES AND HISTORY

As mentioned in the notes to Chapter 9, pseudorandom generators were first studied in the context of cryptography, by Shamir [Sha81], Blum-Micali [BM82], and Yao [Yao82a]. In particular Yao was the first to point out their potential uses for derandomizing $\mathbf{BPP}$. He showed that if secure pseudorandom generators exist then $\mathbf{BPP}$ can be partially derandomized, specifically, $\mathbf{BPP} \subseteq \cap_{\epsilon>0}\mathbf{DTIME}(2^{n^{\epsilon}})$. In their seminal paper [NW88], Nisan and Wigderson showed that such derandomization is possible under significantly weaker complexity assumptions, and that under some plausible assumptions it may even be possible to achieve full derandomization of $\mathbf{BPP}$, namely, to show $\mathbf{BPP} = \mathbf{P}$. Since then a large body of work by was devoted to improving the derandomization and weakening the assumptions (see also the notes to Chapter 19). In particular it was shown that *worst-case* hardness assumptions suffice for derandomization (see Chapter 19 and its notes). A central goal of this line of work was achieved by Impagliazzo and Wigderson [IW97], who showed that if **E** has a function with exponential circuit complexity then **BPP** = **P**.

A pseudorandom generator with optimal dependence on the hardness assumptions (Theorem 20.6) was given by Umans [Uma03] (see Remark 20.8). Interestingly, this pseudorandom generator is based directly on *worst-case* (as opposed to *average-case*) hardness (and indeed uses the local-decoding techniques originating from the works on hardness amplification). Umans's construction, which uses the Reed-Muller code described in Chapter 19, is based on a previous paper of Shaltiel and Umans [SU01] that constructed a *hitting set generator* (a relaxation of a pseudorandom generator) with the same parameters. Andreev, Clementi, and Rolim [ACR96] showed that such hitting set generators suffice for the application of derandomizing **BPP** (see [GVW00] for a simpler proof).

Impagliazzo and Wigderson [IW98] gave the first derandomization result based on the *uniform* hardness of a function in **EXP** (i.e., Theorem 20.16), a result that gave hope that perhaps the proof of **BPP** = **P** (or at least **BPP** $\neq$ **EXP**) will not have to wait for progress on circuit lower bounds. Alas, Impagliazzo, Kabanets, and Wigderson [IKW01] showed that derandomizing **MA** (or equivalently, the promise-problem version of **BPP**) would imply lower bounds for **NEXP**, while Kabanets and Impagliazzo [KI03] proved Theorem 20.17. That is, they showed that some circuit lower bounds would follow even from derandomizing **BPP**.

EXERCISES

20.1. Verify Corollary 20.4.

20.2. Show that there exists a number $\epsilon > 0$ and a function $G : \{0, 1\}^* \to \{0, 1\}^*$ that satisfies all of the conditions of a $2^{\epsilon n}$-pseudorandom generator per Definition 20.2, save for the computational efficiency condition.
    H540

20.3. Show by a counting argument (i.e., probabilistic method) that for every large enough n there is a function $f : \{0, 1\}^n \to \{0, 1\}$, such that $\mathsf{H}_{\mathsf{avg}}(f) \geq 2^{n/10}$.

20.4. Prove that if there exists an $S(\ell)$-pseudorandom generator, then there exists a function $f \in \mathbf{DTIME}(2^{O(n)})$ such that $\mathsf{H}_{\mathsf{wrs}}(f)(n) \geq S(n)$.
    H540

20.5. Prove Theorem 20.10.

20.6. Prove that if there exists $f \in \mathbf{E}$ and $\epsilon > 0$ such that $\mathsf{H}_{\mathsf{avg}}(f)(n) \geq 2^{\epsilon n}$ for every $n \in \mathbb{N}$, then **MA** = **NP**.
    H540

20.7. We define an *oracle Boolean circuit* to be a Boolean circuit that have special gates with unbounded fan-in that are marked ORACLE. For a Boolean circuit C and language $O \subseteq \{0, 1\}^*$, we define by $C^O(x)$ the output of C on x, where the operation of the oracle gates when fed input q is to output 1 iff $q \in O$.

   (a) Prove that if every $f \in \mathbf{E}$ can be computed by polynomial-size circuits with oracle to SAT, then the polynomial hierarchy collapses.

(b) For a function $f : \{0, 1\}^* \to \{0, 1\}$ and $O \subseteq \{0, 1\}^*$, define $\mathsf{H}_{\mathsf{avg}}^O(f)$ to be the function that maps every $n \in \mathbb{N}$ to the largest S such that $\Pr_{x \in_R \{0,1\}^n}[C^O(x) = f(x)] \leq 1/2 + 1/S$. Prove that if there exists $f \in \mathbf{E}$ and $\epsilon > 0$ with $\mathsf{H}_{\mathsf{avg}}^{3\mathsf{SAT}}(f) \geq 2^{\epsilon n}$, then $\mathbf{AM} = \mathbf{NP}$.

20.8. Prove that if $\mathbf{EXP} \not\subseteq \mathbf{P}_{/\mathbf{poly}}$, then the conclusions of Theorem 20.16 hold.

H540

20.9. Let $G : \{0, 1\}^* \to \{0, 1\}^*$ be an $S(\ell)$-length candidate pseudorandom generator that *fails* to derandomize a particular **BPP** algorithm A on the average case. That is, letting $L \in \mathbf{BPP}$ be the language such that $\Pr[A(x) = L(x)] \geq 2/3$, it holds that for every sufficiently large n, with probability at least $1/n$ over the choice of $x \in_R \{0, 1\}^n$, $\Pr[A(x; G(U_{\ell(n)})) = L(x)] \leq 1/2$ (we let $\ell(n)$ be such that $S(\ell(n)) = m(n)$ where $m(n)$ denotes the length of random tape used by A on inputs of length n). Prove that there exists a probabilistic polynomial-time algorithm D that on input 1^n outputs a circuit D_n such that with probability at least $1/(2n)$ over the randomness of D,

$$\| \mathrm{E}[D_n(G(U_{\ell(n)}))] - \mathrm{E}[D_n(U_{m(n)})] \| > 0.1$$

H540

20.10. (van Melkebeek 2000, see [IKW01]) Prove that if $\mathbf{NEXP} = \mathbf{MA}$, then $\mathbf{NEXP} \subseteq \mathbf{P}_{/\mathbf{poly}}$.

CHAPTER 21

Pseudorandom constructions:
Expanders and extractors

How difficult could it be to find hay in a haystack?

– Howard Karloff

The probabilistic method is a powerful method to show the existence of objects (e.g., graphs, functions) with certain desirable properties. We have already seen it used in Chapter 6 to show the existence of functions with high-circuit complexity, in Chapter 19 to show the existence of good error-correcting codes, and in several other places in this book. But sometimes the mere *existence* of an object is not enough: We need an *explicit* and *efficient* construction. This chapter provides such constructions for two well-known (and related) families of pseudorandom objects, *expanders* and *extractors*. They are important in computer science because they can often be used to replace (or reduce) the amount of randomness needed in certain settings. This is reminiscent of derandomization, the topic of Chapter 20, and indeed we will see several connections to derandomization throughout the chapter. However, a big difference between Chapter 20 and this one is that all results proven here are *unconditional*, in other words do not rely on unproven assumptions. Another topic that is related to expanders is constructions of error-correcting codes and related hardness-amplification results, which we saw in Chapter 19. For a brief discussion of the many deep and fascinating connections between codes, expanders, pseudorandom generators, and extractors, see the chapter notes.

Expanders are graphs whose connectivity properties (how many edges lie between every two sets A, B of vertices) are similar to those of "random" graphs—in this sense they are "pseudorandom" or "like random." Expanders have found a vast number of applications ranging from fast sorting networks, to counterexamples in metric space theory, to proving the **PCP** Theorem. The study of expanders is closely tied to study of *eigenvalues* of adjacency matrices. In Section 21.1 we lay the groundwork for this study, showing how random walks on graphs can be analyzed in terms of the adjacency matrix's eigenvalues. Then in Section 21.2 we give two equivalent definitions for expander graphs. We also describe their use in randomness-efficient error reduction of probabilistic algorithms. In Section 21.3 we show an explicit construction of expander graphs. Finally, in Section 21.4, we use this construction to show a *deterministic* logspace algorithm for undirected graph connectivity.

Our second example of an explicit construction concerns the following issue: Although randomized algorithms are modeled using a sequence of unbiased and independent coin tosses, real-life randomness sources are imperfect and have correlations and biases. Philosophically speaking, it is unclear if there is even a single source of unbiased random bits in the universe. Therefore researchers have tried to quantify ways in which a source of random bits could be imperfect and still be used to run randomized algorithms.

In Section 21.5 we define *weakly random* sources. This definition encapsulates the minimal notion of "randomness" that still allows an imperfect source to be used in randomized algorithms. We also define *randomness extractors* (or extractors for short)—algorithms that extract unbiased random bits from such a source—and give explicit constructions for them. One philosophical consequence of these results is that the model of randomized polynomial-time Turing machines (and the associated classes like **BPP**) is realistic if and only if weakly random sources exist in the real world.

In Section 21.6 we use extractors to derandomize probabilistic logspace computations, albeit at the cost of some increase in the space requirement. We emphasize that in contrast to the results of Chapters 19 and 20, this derandomization (as well as all the other results of this chapter) is *unconditional* and uses no unproven assumptions.

Both the constructions and analysis of this chapter are somewhat involved. You might wonder why should coming up with explicit construction be so difficult. After all, a proof of existence via the probabilistic method shows not only that an object with the desired property exists but in fact the vast majority of objects have the property. As Karloff said (see quote at the beginning of the chapter), how difficult can it be to find a single one? But perhaps it's not so surprising this task is so difficult: After all, we know that almost all Boolean functions have exponential circuit complexity, but finding even a single one in **NP** with this property will show that $\mathbf{P} \neq \mathbf{NP}$!

21.1 RANDOM WALKS AND EIGENVALUES

In this section we study random walks on graphs. Using elementary linear algebra we relate eigenvalues of the graph's adjacency matrix to the behavior of the random walk on that graph. As a corollary we obtain the proof of correctness for the random-walk space-efficient algorithm for undirected connectivity described in Section 7.7. We restrict ourselves here to *regular* graphs, in which every vertex has the same degree. However, we do allow our graphs to have self-loops and parallel edges. Most of the definitions and results can be suitably generalized to undirected graphs that are not regular.

Some linear algebra.
We will use some basic properties of the linear space $\mathbb{R}^n$. These are covered in Section A.5, but here is a quick review. If $\mathbf{u}, \mathbf{v} \in R^n$ are two vectors, then their *inner product* is defined as $\langle \mathbf{u}, \mathbf{v} \rangle = \sum_{i=1}^{n} \mathbf{u}_i \mathbf{v}_i$. We say that $\mathbf{u}$ and $\mathbf{v}$ are *orthogonal*, denoted by $\mathbf{u} \perp \mathbf{v}$, if $\langle \mathbf{u}, \mathbf{v} \rangle = 0$. The L_2-*norm* of a vector $\mathbf{v} \in \mathbb{R}^n$, denoted by $\|\mathbf{v}\|_2$ is defined as $\sqrt{\langle \mathbf{v}, \mathbf{v} \rangle} = \sqrt{\sum_{i=1}^{n} \mathbf{v}_i^2}$. A vector whose L_2-norm equals 1 is called a *unit vector*. A simple but useful fact is the *Pythagorean Theorem*, that says that if $\mathbf{u}$ and $\mathbf{v}$ are orthogonal

then $\|\mathbf{u} + \mathbf{v}\|_2^2 = \|\mathbf{u}\|_2^2 + \|\mathbf{v}\|_2^2$. The L_1-*norm* of $\mathbf{v}$, denoted by $|\mathbf{v}|_1$ is defined as $\sum_{i=1}^n |\mathbf{v}_i|$. Both these norms satisfy the basic properties (1) $\|\mathbf{v}\| > 0$ with $\|\mathbf{v}\| = 0$ iff $\mathbf{v}$ is the all zero vector, (2) $\|\alpha\mathbf{v}\| = |\alpha|\|\mathbf{v}\|$ for every $\alpha \in \mathbb{R}$, and (3) $\|\mathbf{u} + \mathbf{v}\| \le \|\mathbf{u}\| + \|\mathbf{v}\|$. The relation between these norms is captured in the following claim, whose proof is left as Exercise 21.1.

Claim 21.1 *For every vector* $\mathbf{v} \in \mathbb{R}^n$,

$$|\mathbf{v}|_1 / \sqrt{n} \le \|\mathbf{v}\|_2 \le |\mathbf{v}|_1 \qquad\qquad \diamond$$

21.1.1 Distributions as vectors and the parameter $\lambda(G)$

Let G be a d-regular n-vertex graph, and let $\mathbf{p}$ be some probability distribution over the vertices of G. We can think of $\mathbf{p}$ as a (column) vector in $\mathbb{R}^n$ where $\mathbf{p}_i$ is the probability that vertex i is obtained by the distribution. Note that the L_1-norm of $\mathbf{p}$ is equal to 1. Now let $\mathbf{q}$ represent the distribution of the following random variable: Choose a vertex i in G according to $\mathbf{p}$, then take a random neighbor of i in G. We can easily compute $\mathbf{q}$, since the probability $\mathbf{q}_j$ that j is chosen is equal to the sum over all of j's neighbors i of the probability $\mathbf{p}_i$ that i is chosen times $1/d$ (since vertex i touches d edges, for each edge $\overline{ij}$ the probability that conditioned on i being chosen then the next move will take this edge is $1/d$). Thus $\mathbf{q} = A\mathbf{p}$, where $A = A(G)$ is the matrix such that for every two vertices i, j of G, $A_{i,j}$ is equal to the number of edges between i and j divided by d. (In other words, A is equal to the adjacency matrix of G multiplied by $1/d$.) We call A the *random-walk matrix* of G. Note that A is a symmetric matrix[1] with all its entries between 0 and 1, and the sum of entries in each row and column is exactly one. Such a matrix is called a symmetric *stochastic* matrix.

The relation between the matrix A and random walks on the graph G is straightforward—for every $\ell \in \mathbb{N}$ and $i \in [n]$, the vector $A^\ell \mathbf{e}^i$ (where $\mathbf{e}^i$ is the vector that has 1 in the ith coordinate and zero everywhere else) represents the distribution X_ℓ of the last step in an ℓ-step random walk starting from the ith vertex.

Definition 21.2 *(The parameter $\lambda(G)$)* Denote by $\mathbf{1}$ the vector $(1/n, 1/n, \ldots, 1/n)$ corresponding to the uniform distribution. Denote by $\mathbf{1}^\perp$ the set of vectors perpendicular to $\mathbf{1}$ (i.e., $\mathbf{v} \in \mathbf{1}^\perp$ if $\langle \mathbf{v}, \mathbf{1} \rangle = (1/n) \sum_i \mathbf{v}_i = 0$).

The parameter $\lambda(A)$, denoted also as $\lambda(G)$, is the maximum value of $\|A\mathbf{v}\|_2$ over all vectors $\mathbf{v} \in \mathbf{1}^\perp$ with $\|\mathbf{v}\|_2 = 1$.

Relation to eigenvalues

The value $\lambda(G)$ is called the *second largest eigenvalue* of G. The reason is that since A is a symmetric matrix, we can find an orthogonal basis of eigenvectors $\mathbf{v}^1, \ldots, \mathbf{v}^n$ with corresponding eigenvalues $\lambda_1, \ldots, \lambda_n$ (see Section A.5.3) which we can sort to ensure $|\lambda_1| \ge |\lambda_2| \ge \cdots \ge |\lambda_n|$. Note that $A\mathbf{1} = \mathbf{1}$. Indeed, for every i, $(A\mathbf{1})_i$ is equal to the inner product of the ith row of A and the vector $\mathbf{1}$ which (since the sum of entries in the row

---

[1] A matrix A is *symmetric* if $A_{i,j} = A_{j,i}$ for every i, j. That is, $A = A^\dagger$ where $A^\dagger$ denotes the *transpose* of A (see Section A.5).

is one) is equal to $1/n$. Thus, $\mathbf{1}$ is an *eigenvector* of A with the corresponding eigenvalue equal to 1. One can show that a symmetric stochastic matrix has all eigenvalues with absolute value at most 1 (see Exercise 21.5) and hence we can assume $\lambda_1 = 1$ and $\mathbf{v}^1 = \mathbf{1}$. Also, because $\mathbf{1}^\perp = \mathrm{Span}\{\mathbf{v}^2, \ldots, \mathbf{v}^n\}$, the value λ above will be maximized by (the normalized version of) $\mathbf{v}^2$, and hence $\lambda(G) = |\lambda_2|$. The quantity $1 - \lambda(G)$ is called the *spectral gap* of the graph. We note that some texts define the parameter $\lambda(G)$ using the standard (unnormalized) adjacency matrix (rather than the random-walk matrix), in which case $\lambda(G)$ is a number between 0 and d and the spectral gap is defined to be $d - \lambda(G)$. Knowledge of basic facts about eigenvalues and eigenvectors (all covered in the appendix) can serve as useful background for this chapter, but is not strictly necessary to follow the results and proofs.

One reason that $\lambda(G)$ is an important parameter is the following lemma.

Lemma 21.3 *Let G ba an n-vertex regular graph and $\mathbf{p}$ a probability distribution over G's vertices, then*

$$\|A^\ell \mathbf{p} - \mathbf{1}\|_2 \le \lambda^\ell \qquad \diamond$$

PROOF: By the definition of $\lambda(G)$, $\|A\mathbf{v}\|_2 \le \lambda \|\mathbf{v}\|_2$ for every $\mathbf{v} \perp \mathbf{1}$. Note that if $\mathbf{v} \perp \mathbf{1}$, then $A\mathbf{v} \perp \mathbf{1}$ since $\langle \mathbf{1}, A\mathbf{v} \rangle = \langle A^\dagger \mathbf{1}, \mathbf{v} \rangle = \langle \mathbf{1}, \mathbf{v} \rangle = 0$ (as $A = A^\dagger$ and $A\mathbf{1} = \mathbf{1}$). Thus A maps the subspace $\mathbf{1}^\perp$ to itself. Note that the eigenvectors that are different from $\mathbf{1}$ span this subspace, and A shrinks each of these eigenvectors by at least λ factor in ℓ_2 norm. Hence A must shrink every vector in $\mathbf{1}^\perp$ by at least λ. Thus A^ℓ shrinks every vector in $\mathbf{1}^\perp$ by a factor at least λ^ℓ, and we conclude $\lambda(A^\ell) \le \lambda(A)^\ell$. (In fact, using the eigenvalue definition of λ, it can be shown that $\lambda(A^\ell) = \lambda(A)^\ell$.)

Let $\mathbf{p}$ be some vector. We can break $\mathbf{p}$ into its components in the spaces parallel and orthogonal to $\mathbf{1}$ and express it as $\mathbf{p} = \alpha \mathbf{1} + \mathbf{p}'$ where $\mathbf{p}' \perp \mathbf{1}$ and α is some number. If $\mathbf{p}$ is a probability distribution, then $\alpha = 1$ since the sum of coordinates in $\mathbf{p}'$ is zero. Therefore,

$$A^\ell \mathbf{p} = A^\ell (\mathbf{1} + \mathbf{p}') = \mathbf{1} + A^\ell \mathbf{p}'$$

Since $\mathbf{1}$ and $\mathbf{p}'$ are orthogonal, $\|\mathbf{p}\|_2^2 = \|\mathbf{1}\|_2^2 + \|\mathbf{p}'\|_2^2$ and in particular $\|\mathbf{p}'\|_2 \le \|\mathbf{p}\|_2$. Since $\mathbf{p}$ is a probability vector, $\|\mathbf{p}\|_2 \le |\mathbf{p}|_1 = 1$ (see Claim 21.1). Hence $\|\mathbf{p}'\|_2 \le 1$ and

$$\|A^\ell \mathbf{p} - \mathbf{1}\|_2 = \|A^\ell \mathbf{p}'\|_2 \le \lambda^\ell \qquad (21.1)$$

∎

It turns out that every connected graph has a noticeable spectral gap.

Lemma 21.4 *If G is a regular connected graph with self-loops at each vertex, then $\lambda(G) \le 1 - \frac{1}{12n^2}$.* $\qquad \diamond$

PROOF: Let $\epsilon = \frac{1}{6n^2}$, let $\mathbf{u} \perp \mathbf{1}$ be a unit vector and let $\mathbf{v} = A\mathbf{u}$. We need to prove that $\|\mathbf{v}\|_2 \le 1 - \epsilon/2$ and for this it suffices to prove that $1 - \|\mathbf{v}\|_2^2 \ge \epsilon$. (Indeed, if $\|\mathbf{v}\|_2 > 1 - \epsilon/2$, then $\|\mathbf{v}\|_2^2 > 1 - \epsilon$ and hence $1 - \|\mathbf{v}\|_2^2 < \epsilon$.) Since $\mathbf{u}$ is a unit vector,

$1 - \|\mathbf{v}\|_2^2 = \|\mathbf{u}\|_2^2 - \|\mathbf{v}\|_2^2$. We claim that this is equal to $\sum_{i,j} A_{i,j}(\mathbf{u}_i - \mathbf{v}_j)^2$ where i,j range from 1 to n. Indeed,

$$\sum_{i,j} A_{i,j}(\mathbf{u}_i - \mathbf{v}_j)^2 = \sum_{i,j} A_{i,j}\mathbf{u}_i^2 - 2\sum_{i,j} A_{i,j}\mathbf{u}_i\mathbf{v}_j + \sum_{i,j} A_{i,j}\mathbf{v}_j^2$$

$$= \|\mathbf{u}\|_2^2 - 2\langle A\mathbf{u}, \mathbf{v}\rangle + \|\mathbf{v}\|_2^2 = \|\mathbf{u}\|_2^2 - 2\|\mathbf{v}\|_2^2 + \|\mathbf{v}\|_2^2 = \|\mathbf{u}\|_2^2 - \|\mathbf{v}\|_2^2$$

where these equalities are due to the sum of each row and column in A equalling one, and to $\|\mathbf{v}\|_2^2 = \langle \mathbf{v}, \mathbf{v}\rangle = \langle A\mathbf{u}, \mathbf{v}\rangle = \sum_{i,j} A_{i,j}\mathbf{u}_i\mathbf{v}_j$.

Thus it suffices to show $\sum_{i,j} A_{i,j}(\mathbf{u}_i - \mathbf{v}_j)^2 \geq \epsilon$. Since $\mathbf{u}$ is a unit vector with coordinates summing to zero, there must exist vertices i, j such that $\mathbf{u}_i > 0, \mathbf{u}_j < 0$ and at least one of these coordinates has absolute value $\geq \frac{1}{\sqrt{n}}$, meaning that $\mathbf{u}_i - \mathbf{u}_j \geq \frac{1}{\sqrt{n}}$. Furthermore, because G, is connected, there is a path between i and j containing at most $D + 1$ vertices (where D is the *diameter* of the graph[2] G). By renaming vertices, let's assume that $i = 1, j = D + 1$, and the coordinates $2, 3, \ldots, D$ correspond to the vertices on this path in order. Now, we have

$$\frac{1}{\sqrt{n}} \leq \mathbf{u}_1 - \mathbf{u}_{D+1} = (\mathbf{u}_1 - \mathbf{v}_1) + (\mathbf{v}_1 - \mathbf{u}_2) + \cdots + (\mathbf{v}_D - \mathbf{u}_{D+1})$$

$$\leq \mathbf{u}_1 - \mathbf{u}_{D+1} = |\mathbf{u}_1 - \mathbf{v}_1| + |\mathbf{v}_1 - \mathbf{u}_2| + \cdots + |\mathbf{v}_D - \mathbf{u}_{D+1}|$$

$$\leq \sqrt{(\mathbf{u}_1 - \mathbf{v}_1)^2 + (\mathbf{v}_1 - \mathbf{u}_2)^2 + \cdots + (\mathbf{v}_D - \mathbf{u}_{D+1})^2}\sqrt{2D+1} \qquad (21.2)$$

where the last inequality follows by relating the L_2 and L_1 norms of the vector $(\mathbf{u}_1 - \mathbf{v}_1, \mathbf{v}_1 - \mathbf{u}_2, \ldots, \mathbf{v}_D - \mathbf{u}_{D+1})$ using Claim 21.1. But this means that

$$\sum_{i,j} A_{i,j}(\mathbf{u}_i - \mathbf{v}_j)^2 \geq \frac{1}{dn(2D+1)} \qquad (21.3)$$

since the left-hand side of (21.3) is a sum of nonnegative terms and (21.2) implies that the terms of the form $A_{i,i}(\mathbf{u}_i - \mathbf{v}_i)^2$ and $A_{i,i+1}(\mathbf{v}_i - \mathbf{u}_{i+1})^2$ (for $i = 1, \ldots, D$) contribute at least $\frac{1}{dn(2D+1)}$ to this sum (both $A_{i,i}$ and $A_{i,i+1}$ are at least $1/d$ since they correspond to self-loops and edges of the graph).

Plugging in the trivial bound $D \leq n - 1$ this already shows that $\lambda(G) \leq 1 - \frac{1}{4dn^2}$. To prove the lemma as stated, we use the fact (left as Exercise 21.4) that for every d-regular connected graph, $D \leq 3n/(d+1)$. ∎

The proof can be strengthened to show a similar result for every connected nonbipartite graph (not just those with self-loops at every vertex). Note that this condition is essential: If A is the random-walk matrix of a bipartite graph, then one can find a vector $\mathbf{v}$ such that $A\mathbf{v} = -\mathbf{v}$ (Exercise 21.3).

---

[2] The *diameter* of a graph G is the maximum distance (i.e., length of shortest path) between any pair of vertices in G. Note that the diameter of a connected n-vertex graph is always at most $n - 1$.

21.1.2 Analysis of the randomized algorithm for undirected connectivity

Together, Lemmas 21.3 and 21.4 imply that, at least for regular graphs, if s is connected to t, then a sufficiently long random walk from s will hit t in polynomial time with high probability.

Corollary 21.5 *Let G be a d-regular n-vertex graph with all vertices having a self-loop. Let s be a vertex in G. Let $\ell > 24n^2 \log n$ and let X_ℓ denote the distribution of the vertex of the ℓth step in a random walk from s. Then, for every t connected to s, $\Pr[X_\ell = t] > \frac{1}{2n}$.* ◇

PROOF: By Lemmas 21.3 and 21.4, if we consider the restriction of an n-vertex graph G to the connected component of s, then for every probability vector $\mathbf{p}$ over this component and $\ell \geq 24n^2 \log n$, $\|A^\ell \mathbf{p} - \mathbf{1}\|_2 < (1 - \frac{1}{12n^2})^{24n^2 \log n} < \frac{1}{n^2}$, where $\mathbf{1}$ here is the uniform distribution over this component. But this means that in particular for every coordinate i, $|A^\ell \mathbf{p} - \mathbf{1}|_i < \frac{1}{n^2}$ and hence every element in the connected component appears in $A^\ell \mathbf{p}$ with probability at least $1/n - 1/n^2 \geq 1/(2n)$. ∎

Note that Corollary 21.5 implies that if we repeat the $24n^2 \log n$ walk for $O(n \log n)$ times (or equivalently, if we take a walk of, say, length $100n^3 \log^2 n$), then we will hit *every* vertex t connected to s with high probability.

21.2 EXPANDER GRAPHS

Expander graphs are extremely useful combinatorial objects, which we encounter several times in the book. They can be defined in two equivalent ways. At a high level, these two equivalent definitions can be described as follows:

- *Combinatorial definition:* A constant-degree regular graph G is an *expander* if for every subset S of less than half of G's vertices, a constant fraction of the edges touching S are from S to its complement in G; see Figure 21.1.

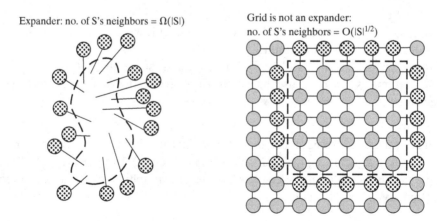

Figure 21.1. In an *edge expander*, every subset S of the vertices that is not too big has at least $\Omega(|S|)$ edges to neighbors outside the set. The grid (and every other planar graph) is not an edge expander as a $k \times k$ square in the grid has only $O(k)$ neighbors outside it.

- *Algebraic expansion:* A constant-degree regular graph G is an *expander* if its parameter $\lambda(G)$ bounded away from 1 by some constant. That is, $\lambda(G) \leq 1 - \epsilon$ for some constant $\epsilon > 0$.

What do we mean by a constant?

By *constant* we refer to a number that is independent of the size of the graph. We will typically talk about graphs that are part of an infinite *family* of graphs, and so by constant we mean a value that is the same for all graphs in the family, regardless of their size. Below we make the definitions more precise, and show their equivalence.

21.2.1 The algebraic definition

The algebraic definition of expanders is as follows.

Definition 21.6 ((n, d, λ)-*expander graphs*) If G is an n-vertex d-regular G with $\lambda(G) \leq \lambda$ for some number $\lambda < 1$, then we say that G is an (n, d, λ)-graph.

A family of graphs $\{G_n\}_{n\in\mathbb{N}}$ is an *expander graph family* if there are some constants $d \in \mathbb{N}$ and $\lambda < 1$ such that for every n, G_n is an (n, d, λ)-graph.

Many texts use simply the name (n, d, λ)-graphs for such graphs. Also, as mentioned above, some texts use *unnormalized* adjacency matrices, and so have λ range between 0 and d. The smallest λ can be for a d-regular n-vertex graph is $(1 - o(1))\frac{2\sqrt{d-1}}{d}$, where $o(1)$ denotes a function tending to 0 as the number of vertices grows. This is called the Alon-Boppana bound and graphs meeting this bound are called *Ramanujan graphs* (see also Exercises 21.9 and 21.10).

Explicit constructions

As we will see in Section 21.2.2, it is not hard to show that expander families exist using the probabilistic method. But this does not yield *explicit* constructions of such graphs, which are often needed for applications. We say that an expander family $\{G_n\}_{n\in\mathbb{N}}$ is *explicit* if there is a polynomial-time algorithm that on input 1^n outputs the adjacency matrix of G_n (or, equivalently, the random-walk matrix). We say that the family is *strongly explicit* if there is a polynomial-time algorithm that on inputs $\langle n, v, i \rangle$ where $v \in [n], i \in [d]$ outputs the (index of the) ith neighbor of v. Note that in the strongly explicit case, the lengths of the algorithm's inputs and outputs are $O(\log n)$ and so it runs in time polylog(n).

Fortunately, several explicit and strongly explicit constructions of expander graphs are known. Some of these constructions are very simple and efficient, but their analysis is highly nontrivial and uses relatively deep mathematics.[3] In Section 21.3 we will see a strongly explicit construction of expanders with elementary analysis. This construction also introduces a tool that we'll use to derandomize the random-walk algorithm for UPATH in Section 21.4.

---

[3] An example is the following 3-regular expander graph: The vertices are the numbers 0 to $p - 1$ for some prime p, and each number x is connected to $x + 1, x - 1$, and x^{-1} modulo p (letting $0^{-1} = 0$). The analysis uses some deep results in mathematics (i.e., Selberg's 3/16 theorem), see Section 11.1.2 in [HLW06].

21.2.2 Combinatorial expansion and existence of expanders

We now describe a combinatorial criterion that is roughly equivalent to Definition 21.6. One advantage of this criterion is that it makes it easy to prove that a nonexplicit expander family exists using the probabilistic method. It is also quite useful in several applications.

Definition 21.7 *(Combinatorial (edge) expansion)* An n-vertex d-regular graph $G = (V, E)$ is called an (n, d, ρ)-*combinatorial edge expander* if for every subset S of vertices satisfying $|S| \leq n/2$,

$$|E(S, \overline{S})| \geq \rho d |S|$$

where $\overline{S}$ denotes the complement of S and for subsets S, T of vertices, $E(S, T)$ denotes the set of edges $\overline{ij}$ with $i \in S$ and $j \in T$.

Note that in this case the bigger ρ is the better the expander. We will often use the shorthand "edge expander" (dropping the prefix "combinatorial"). Also we'll loosely use the term "expander" for any (n, d, ρ)-combinatorial edge expander with ρ a positive constant (independent of n). Using the probabilistic method, one can prove the following theorem. (Exercise 21.11 asks you to prove a slightly weaker version.)

Theorem 21.8 *Existence of expanders Let $\epsilon > 0$ be any constant. Then there exists $d = d(\epsilon)$ and $N \in \mathbb{N}$ such that for every $n > N$ there exists an $(n, d, 1/2 - \epsilon)$ edge expander.* ◇

Theorem 21.8 is tight in the sense that there is no (n, d, ρ) edge expander for $\rho > 1/2$ (Exercise 21.13). The following theorem relates combinatorial expansion with our previous Definition 21.6.

Theorem 21.9 *(Combinatorial vs. algebraic expansion)*
1. *If G is an (n, d, λ)-expander graph, then it is an $(n, d, (1 - \lambda)/2)$ edge expander.*
2. *If G is an (n, d, ρ) edge expander, then its second largest eigenvalue (without taking absolute values) is at most $1 - \frac{\rho^2}{2}$. If furthermore G has all self loops, then it is an $(n, d, 1 - \epsilon)$-expander where $\epsilon = \min\left\{\frac{2}{d}, \frac{\rho^2}{2}\right\}$.*

The condition that G has all the self-loops of Theorem 21.9 is used again to rule out bipartite graphs, which can be very good edge expanders but have one eigenvalue equal to -1 and hence a spectral gap of zero.

21.2.3 Algebraic expansion implies combinatorial expansion

The first part of Theorem 21.9 follows immediately from the following lemma.

Lemma 21.10 *Let G be an* (n, d, λ) *graph, S a subset of G's vertices and T its complement. Then*

$$|E(S,T)| \geq (1 - \lambda) \, \frac{d|S||T|}{|S| + |T|} \qquad \diamond$$

PROOF: Let $\mathbf{x} \in \mathbb{R}^n$ denote the following vector:

$$\mathbf{x}_i = \begin{cases} +|T| & i \in S \\ -|S| & i \in T \end{cases}$$

Note that $\|\mathbf{x}\|_2^2 = |S||T|^2 + |T||S|^2 = |S||T|(|S| + |T|)$ and $\mathbf{x} \perp \mathbf{1}$.

Let $Z = \sum_{i,j} A_{i,j}(x_i - x_j)^2$. On the one hand $Z = \frac{2}{d}|E(S,T)|(|S| + |T|)^2$, since every edge $\overline{ij}$ with $i \in S$ and $j \in T$ appears twice in this sum, each time contributing $\frac{1}{d}(|S| + |T|)^2$ to the total. On the other hand,

$$Z = \sum_{i,j} A_{i,j}x_i^2 - 2\sum A_{i,j}x_ix_j + \sum_{i,j} A_{i,j}x_j^2 = 2\|\mathbf{x}\|_2^2 - 2\langle \mathbf{x}, A\mathbf{x} \rangle$$

(using the fact that A's rows and columns sum up to one). Since $\mathbf{x} \perp \mathbf{1}$ and $\|A\mathbf{x}\|_2 \leq \lambda\|\mathbf{x}\|_2$, we get that

$$\tfrac{1}{d}|E(S,T)|(|S| + |T|)^2 \geq (1 - \lambda)\|x\|_2^2$$

Plugging in $\|x\|_2^2 = |S||T|(|S| + |T|)$ completes the proof. ∎

Algebraic expansion also allows us to obtain an estimate on the number of edges between not-too-small subsets S and T, even if they are not disjoint:

Lemma 21.11 *Expander Mixing Lemma Let $G = (V, E)$ be an (n, d, λ)-expander graph. Let $S, T \subseteq V$, then*

$$\left| |E(S,T)| - \frac{d}{n}|S||T| \right| \leq \lambda d\sqrt{|S||T|} \qquad \diamond$$

The Mixing Lemma gives a good idea of why expanders are "pseudorandom." In a random d-regular graph, we would expect $|E(S,T)|$ to be about $\frac{d}{n}|S||T|$. The lemma says that in an expander $|E(S,T)|$ is close to this expectation for *all* S, T that are sufficiently large. We leave the proof of Lemma 21.11 as Exercise 21.14.

21.2.4 Combinatorial expansion implies algebraic expansion

We now prove the second part of Theorem 21.9. Let $G = (V, E)$ be an n-vertex d-regular graph such that for every subset $S \subseteq V$ with $|S| \leq n/2$, there are $\rho d|S|$ edges between S and $\overline{S} = V \setminus S$, and let A be G's random-walk matrix.

Let λ be the second largest eigenvalue of A (not taking absolute values). We need to prove that $\lambda \leq 1 - \rho^2/2$. By the definition of an eigenvalue there exists a vector $\mathbf{u} \perp \mathbf{1}$

such that $A\mathbf{u} = \lambda\mathbf{u}$. Write $\mathbf{u} = \mathbf{v} + \mathbf{w}$ where $\mathbf{v}$ is equal to $\mathbf{u}$ on the coordinates on which $\mathbf{u}$ is positive and equal to 0 otherwise, and $\mathbf{w}$ is equal to $\mathbf{u}$ on the coordinates on which $\mathbf{u}$ is negative and equal to 0 otherwise. (Since $\mathbf{u} \perp \mathbf{1}$, both $\mathbf{v}$ and $\mathbf{w}$ are nonzero.) We can assume that $\mathbf{v}$ is nonzero on at most $n/2$ of its coordinates (otherwise take $-\mathbf{u}$ instead of $\mathbf{u}$). Let $Z = \sum_{i,j} A_{i,j}|\mathbf{v}_i^2 - \mathbf{v}_j^2|$. Part 2 of the theorem (except for the "furthermore" clause) follows immediately from the following two claims.

Claim 1 $Z \geq 2\rho\|\mathbf{v}\|_2^2.$

Claim 2 $Z \leq \sqrt{8(1-\lambda)}\|\mathbf{v}\|_2^2.$

PROOF OF CLAIM 1: Sort the coordinates of $\mathbf{v}$ so that $\mathbf{v}_1 \geq \mathbf{v}_2 \geq \cdots \geq \mathbf{v}_n$ (with $\mathbf{v}_i = 0$ for $i > n/2$). Then, using $\mathbf{v}_i^2 - \mathbf{v}_j^2 = \sum_{k=i}^{j+1}(\mathbf{v}_k^2 - \mathbf{v}_{k+1}^2)$,

$$Z = \sum_{i,j} A_{i,j}|\mathbf{v}_i^2 - \mathbf{v}_j^2| = 2\sum_{i<j} A_{i,j} \sum_{k=i}^{j-1}(\mathbf{v}_k^2 - \mathbf{v}_{k+1}^2)$$

Note that every term $(\mathbf{v}_k^2 - \mathbf{v}_{k+1}^2)$ appears in this sum once (with a weight of $2/d$) per each edge $\overline{ij}$ such that $i \leq k < j$. Since $\mathbf{v}_k = 0$ for $k > n/2$, this means that

$$Z = \frac{2}{d}\sum_{k=1}^{n/2} |E(\{1..k\}, \{k+1..n\})|(\mathbf{v}_k^2 - \mathbf{v}_{k+1}^2) \geq \frac{2}{d}\sum_{k=1}^{n/2} \rho k(\mathbf{v}_k^2 - \mathbf{v}_{k+1}^2)$$

by G's expansion. But, rearranging the terms (and using the fact that $\mathbf{v}_k = 0$ for $k > n/2$), the last sum is equal to

$$\frac{2}{d}d\rho \sum_{k=1}^{n/2} k\mathbf{v}_k^2 - (k-1)\mathbf{v}_k^2 = 2\sum_{k=1}^{n} \mathbf{v}_k^2 = 2\rho\|\mathbf{v}\|_2^2$$

∎

PROOF OF CLAIM 2: Since $A\mathbf{u} = \lambda\mathbf{u}$ and $\langle \mathbf{v}, \mathbf{w} \rangle = 0$,

$$\langle A\mathbf{v}, \mathbf{v} \rangle + \langle A\mathbf{w}, \mathbf{v} \rangle = \langle A(\mathbf{v} + \mathbf{w}), \mathbf{v} \rangle = \langle A\mathbf{u}, \mathbf{v} \rangle = \langle \lambda(\mathbf{v} + \mathbf{w}), \mathbf{v} \rangle = \lambda\|\mathbf{v}\|_2^2$$

Since $\langle A\mathbf{w}, \mathbf{v} \rangle$ is not positive, $\langle A\mathbf{v}, \mathbf{v} \rangle/\|\mathbf{v}\|_2^2 \geq \lambda$, meaning that

$$1 - \lambda \geq 1 - \frac{\langle A\mathbf{v}, \mathbf{v} \rangle}{\|\mathbf{v}\|_2^2} = \frac{\|\mathbf{v}\|_2^2 - \langle A\mathbf{v}, \mathbf{v} \rangle}{\|\mathbf{v}\|_2^2} = \frac{\sum_{i,j} A_{i,j}(\mathbf{v}_i - \mathbf{v}_j)^2}{2\|\mathbf{v}\|_2^2} \qquad (21.4)$$

where the last equality is due to $\sum_{i,j} A_{i,j}(\mathbf{v}_i - \mathbf{v}_j)^2 = \sum_{i,j} A_{i,j}\mathbf{v}_i^2 - 2\sum_{i,j} A_{i,j}\mathbf{v}_i\mathbf{v}_j + \sum_{i,j} A_{i,j}\mathbf{v}_j^2 = 2\|\mathbf{v}\|_2^2 - 2\langle A\mathbf{v}, \mathbf{v} \rangle$. (We use here the fact that each row and column of A sums to one.)

Multiply both numerator and denominator of the last term in (21.4) by $\sum_{i,j} A_{i,j} \left(\mathbf{v}_i^2 + \mathbf{v}_j^2 \right)$. The new numerator is

$$\left(\sum_{i,j} A_{i,j}(\mathbf{v}_i - \mathbf{v}_j)^2 \right) \left(\sum_{i,j} A_{i,j}(\mathbf{v}_i + \mathbf{v}_j)^2 \right) \geq \left(\sum_{i,j} A_{i,j}(\mathbf{v}_i - \mathbf{v}_j)(\mathbf{v}_i + \mathbf{v}_j) \right)^2$$

using the Cauchy-Schwarz inequality.[4] Hence, using $(a - b)(a + b) = a^2 - b^2$,

$$1 - \lambda \geq \frac{\left(\sum_{i,j} A_{i,j}(\mathbf{v}_i^2 - \mathbf{v}_j^2) \right)^2}{2\|\mathbf{v}\|_2^2 \sum_{i,j} A_{i,j}(\mathbf{v}_i + \mathbf{v}_j)^2} = \frac{z^2}{2\|\mathbf{v}\|_2^2 \left(\sum_{i,j} A_{i,j}\mathbf{v}_i^2 + 2 \sum_{i,j} A_{i,j}\mathbf{v}_i\mathbf{v}_j + \sum_{i,j} A_{i,j}\mathbf{v}_j^2 \right)}$$

$$= \frac{z^2}{2\|\mathbf{v}\|_2^2 \left(2\|\mathbf{v}\|_2^2 + 2\langle A\mathbf{v}, \mathbf{v} \rangle \right)} \geq \frac{z^2}{8\|\mathbf{v}\|_2^4}$$

where the last inequality is due to the fact that A is a symmetric stochastic matrix, and hence $\|A\mathbf{v}\|_2 \leq \|\mathbf{v}\|_2$ for every $\mathbf{v}$, implying that $\langle A\mathbf{v}, \mathbf{v} \rangle \leq \|\mathbf{v}\|_2^2$.

The "furthermore" part is obtained by noticing that adding all the self-loops to a $(d - 1)$-regular graph is equivalent to transforming its random-walk matrix A into the matrix $\frac{d-1}{d} A + \frac{1}{d} I$ where I is the identity matrix. Since A's smallest eigenvalue (not taking absolute values) is at least -1, the new smallest eigenvalue is at least $-\frac{d-1}{d} + \frac{1}{d} = -1 + \frac{2}{d}$. ∎

21.2.5 Error reduction using expanders

Before constructing expanders, let us see one application for them in the area of probabilistic algorithms. Recall that in Section 7.4.1 we saw that we can reduce the error of a probabilistic algorithm from, say, $1/3$ to $2^{-\Omega(k)}$ by executing it k times independently and taking the majority value. If the algorithm utilized m random coins, this procedure will use $m \cdot k$ random coins, and it seems hard to think of a way to save on randomness. Nonetheless, using expanders we can obtain such error reduction using only $m + O(k)$ random coins.

The idea is simple: Take an expander graph G from a strongly explicit family that is an $(M = 2^m, d, 1/10)$-expander graph for some constant d. (Note that we can use graph powering to transform any explicit expander family into an expander family with parameter $\lambda < 1/10$; see also Section 21.3.) Choose a vertex v_1 at random, and take a length $k - 1$ long random walk on G to obtain vertices $v_2, \ldots, v_k$ (note that choosing a random neighbor of a vertex requires $O(\log d) = O(1)$ random bits). Invoke the algorithm k times using $v_1, \ldots, v_k$ for the random coins (we identify the set $[M]$ of vertices with the set $\{0, 1\}^m$ of possible random coins for the algorithm) and output the majority answer.

To keep things simple, we analyze here only the case of algorithms with one-sided error. For example, consider an **RP** algorithm that will never output "accept" if the

---

input is not in the language, and for inputs in the language will output "accept" with probability, say, 2/3 (the case of a **coRP** algorithm is analogous). For such an algorithm the procedure will output "accept" if the algorithm accepts even on a single set of coins v_i. If the input is not in the language, the procedure will never accept. If the input is in the language, then let $\mathcal{B} \subseteq [M]$ denote the "bad" set of coins on which the algorithms rejects. We know that $|\mathcal{B}| \leq \frac{M}{3}$. Plugging in $\beta = 1/3$ and $\lambda = 1/10$ in the following theorem immediately implies that the probability the above procedure will reject an input in the language is bounded by $2^{-\Omega(k)}$.

Theorem 21.12 *(Expander walks)*
Let G be an (n, d, λ) graph, and let $\mathcal{B} \subseteq [n]$ satisfying $|\mathcal{B}| \leq \beta n$ for some $\beta \in (0, 1)$. Let $X_1, \ldots, X_k$ be random variables denoting a $k - 1$-step random walk in G from X_1, where X_1 is chosen uniformly in $[n]$. Then

$$\Pr[\forall_{1 \leq i \leq k} X_i \in B] \leq ((1 - \lambda)\sqrt{\beta} + \lambda)^{k-1}$$

Note that if λ and β are both constants smaller than 1 then so is the expression $(1 - \lambda)\sqrt{\beta} + \lambda$.

PROOF: For $1 \leq i \leq k$, let B_i be the event that $X_i \in \mathcal{B}$. Note that the probability we're trying to bound is

$$\Pr[\wedge_{i=1}^{k} B_i] = \Pr[B_1] \Pr[B_2|B_1] \cdots \Pr[B_k|B_1, \ldots, B_{k-1}] \quad (21.5)$$

Denote by B the linear transformation from $\mathbb{R}^n$ to $\mathbb{R}^n$ that "zeroes out" the coordinates that are not in $\mathcal{B}$. That is, for every $i \in [n]$, $(B\mathbf{u})_i = \mathbf{u}_i$ if $i \in \mathcal{B}$ and $(B\mathbf{u})_i = 0$ otherwise. It's not hard to verify that for every probability vector $\mathbf{p}$ over $[n]$, $B\mathbf{p}$ is a vector whose coordinates sum up to the probability that a vertex i is chosen according to $\mathbf{p}$ is in $\mathcal{B}$. Furthermore, if we normalize the vector $B\mathbf{p}$ to sum up to one, we get the probability vector corresponding to the conditional distribution of p conditioned on the event that the vertex chosen this way is in $\mathcal{B}$.

Thus, if we let $\mathbf{1} = (1/n, \ldots, 1/n)$ denote the uniform distribution over $[n]$ and $\mathbf{p}^i \in \mathbb{R}^N$ be the distribution of X_i conditioned on the events $B_1, \ldots, B_i$, then

$$\mathbf{p}^1 = \frac{1}{\Pr[B_1]} B\mathbf{1}$$

$$\mathbf{p}^2 = \frac{1}{\Pr[B_2|B_1]} \frac{1}{\Pr[B_1]} BAB\mathbf{1}$$

and more generally

$$\mathbf{p}^i = \frac{1}{\Pr[B_i|B_{i-1} \cdots B_1] \cdots \Pr[B_1]} (BA)^{i-1} B\mathbf{1}.$$

Since every probability vector $\mathbf{p}$ satisfies $|\mathbf{p}|_1 = 1$, it follows that the probability on the left-hand side of (21.5) is equal to

$$|(BA)^{k-1} B\mathbf{1}|_1 \quad (21.6)$$

Using the relation between the L_1 and L_2 norms (Claim 21.1), we can bound (21.6) by showing

$$\|(BA)^{k-1}B\mathbf{1}\|_2 \leq \frac{((1-\lambda)\sqrt{\beta}+\lambda)^{k-1}}{\sqrt{n}} \tag{21.7}$$

To prove (21.7), we will use the following definition and lemma.

Definition 21.13 *(Spectral norm)* For every matrix A, the *spectral norm* of A, denoted by $\|A\|$, is defined as the maximum of $\|A\mathbf{v}\|_2$ over all vectors $\mathbf{v}$ satisfying $\|\mathbf{v}\|_2 = 1$. ◇

Exercises 21.5 and 21.6 ask you to prove that the spectral norm of every random-walk matrix is 1, and that for every two n by n matrices A, B, $\|A + B\| \leq \|A\| + \|B\|$ and $\|AB\| \leq \|A\|\|B\|$.

Lemma 21.14 *Let A be a random-walk matrix of an (n, d, λ)-expander graph G. Let J be the random-walk matrix of the n-clique with self-loops (i.e., $J_{i,j} = 1/n$ for every i, j). Then*

$$A = (1-\lambda)J + \lambda C \tag{21.8}$$

where $\|C\| \leq 1$. ◇

Note that for every probability vector $\mathbf{p}$, $J\mathbf{p}$ is the uniform distribution, and so this lemma tells us that in some sense, we can think of a step on a (n, d, λ)-expander graph as going to the uniform distribution with probability $1 - \lambda$, and to a different distribution with probability λ. This is of course completely inaacurate, as a step on a d-regular graph will only go the one of the d neighbors of the current vertex, but we'll see that for the purposes of our analysis, the condition (21.8) will be just as good.[5]

PROOF OF LEMMA 21.14: Indeed, simply define $C = \frac{1}{\lambda}(A - (1-\lambda)J)$. We need to prove $\|C\mathbf{v}\|_2 \leq \|\mathbf{v}\|_2$ for very $\mathbf{v}$. Decompose $\mathbf{v}$ as $\mathbf{v} = \mathbf{u} + \mathbf{w}$ where $\mathbf{u} = \alpha\mathbf{1}$ for some $\alpha \in \mathbb{R}$ and $\mathbf{w} \perp \mathbf{1}$. Since $A\mathbf{1} = \mathbf{1}$ and $J\mathbf{1} = \mathbf{1}$, we get that $C\mathbf{u} = \frac{1}{\lambda}(\mathbf{u} - (1-\lambda)\mathbf{u}) = \mathbf{u}$. Now, let $\mathbf{w}' = A\mathbf{w}$. Then $\|\mathbf{w}'\|_2 \leq \lambda\|\mathbf{w}\|_2$ and, as we saw in the proof of Lemma 21.3, $\mathbf{w}' \perp \mathbf{1}$. In other words, the sum of the coordinates of $\mathbf{w}$ is zero, meaning that $J\mathbf{w} = \mathbf{0}$. We get that $C\mathbf{w} = \frac{1}{\lambda}\mathbf{w}'$. Since $\mathbf{w}' \perp \mathbf{u}$, $\|C\mathbf{v}\|_2^2 = \|\mathbf{u} + \frac{1}{\lambda}\mathbf{w}'\|_2^2 = \|\mathbf{u}\|_2^2 + \|\frac{1}{\lambda}\mathbf{w}'\|_2^2 \leq \|\mathbf{u}\|_2^2 + \|\mathbf{w}\|_2^2 = \|\mathbf{v}\|_2^2$, where we use twice the Pythagorean Theorem that for $\mathbf{u} \perp \mathbf{w}$, $\|\mathbf{u}+\mathbf{w}\|_2^2 = \|\mathbf{u}\|_2^2 + \|\mathbf{w}\|_2^2$. ∎

Returning to the proof of Theorem 21.12, we can write $BA = B((1-\lambda)J + \lambda C)$, and hence $\|BA\| \leq (1-\lambda)\|BJ\| + \lambda\|BC\|$. Since J's output is always a vector of the form $\alpha\mathbf{1}$, and it can be easily verified that $\|B\mathbf{1}\|_2 = \sqrt{\frac{\beta n}{n^2}} = \frac{\sqrt{\beta}}{\sqrt{n}} = \sqrt{\beta}\|\mathbf{1}\|_2$, $\|BJ\| = \sqrt{\beta}$. Also, because B is an operation that merely zeros out some parts of its input, $\|B\| \leq 1$ implying that $\|BC\| \leq 1$. Thus, $\|BA\| \leq (1-\lambda)\sqrt{\beta}+\lambda$. This means that $\|(BA)^{k-1}B\mathbf{1}\|_2 \leq ((1-\lambda)\sqrt{\beta}+\lambda)^{k-1}\frac{\sqrt{\beta}}{\sqrt{n}}$, establishing (21.7). ∎

The success of the error-reduction procedure for *two-sided error* algorithms is obtained by the following theorem, whose proof we omit (but see Exercise 21.12).

---

[5] Algebraically, the reason (21.8) is not equivalent to going to the uniform distribution in each step with probability $1 - \lambda$ is that C is not necessarily a stochastic matrix and may have negative entries.

Theorem 21.15 *(Expander Chernoff Bound)*
Let G be an (n, d, λ)-expander graph and $B \subseteq [n]$ with $|B| = \beta N$. Let $X_1, \ldots, X_k$ be random variables denoting a $(k-1)$-step random walk in G (where X_1 is chosen uniformly). For every $i \in [k]$, define B_i to be 1 if $X_i \in B$ and 0 otherwise. Then, for every $\delta > 0$,

$$\Pr\left[\left|\frac{\sum_{i=1}^{k} B_i}{k} - \beta\right| > \delta\right] < 2e^{-(1-\lambda)\delta^2 k/4}$$

21.3 EXPLICIT CONSTRUCTION OF EXPANDER GRAPHS

We now show a construction of a very explicit expander graph family. The main tools in our construction will be several types of graph products. A *graph product* is an operation that takes two graphs G, G' and outputs a graph H. Typically we're interested in the relation between properties of the graphs G, G' and the properties of the resulting graph H. In this section we will mainly be interested in three parameters—the number of vertices (denoted n), the degree (denoted d), and the second largest eigenvalue of the random-walk matrix (denoted λ)—and study how different products affect these parameters. We then use these products to obtain a construction of a strongly explicit expander graph family. In the next section we will use the same products to show a *deterministic* logspace algorithm for undirected connectivity.

21.3.1 Rotation maps

Thus far we usually represented a graph via its adjacency matrix or, as in this chapter, via its random-walk matrix. If the graph is d-regular we can also represent it via its *rotation map*. If G is an n-vertex degree-d graph this involves giving a number from 1 to d to each neighbor of each vertex, and then letting a rotation map $\hat{G}$ be a function from $[n] \times [d]$ to $[n] \times [d]$ that maps a pair $\langle v, i \rangle$ to $\langle u, j \rangle$ where u is the ith neighbor of v and v is the jth neighbor of u. Clearly, this map is a permutation (i.e., is one-to-one and onto) of $[n] \times [d]$. The reader may wonder why one should not renumber the neighbors at each node so that $\hat{G}(u, i) = (v, i)$ (i.e., v is the ith neighbor of u iff u is the ith neighbor of v). This is indeed possible, but it requires some global computation that will turn out to be too complicated in the scenarios we will be interested in, where the graph is constructed by some space-bounded computation.

Below we will describe graph products, which is usually a way to map two graphs into one. We use whichever graph representation happens to be most natural, but it would be a good exercise for the reader to to work out the equivalent descriptions in the other representations (e.g., in terms of random-walk matrices and rotation maps).

21.3.2 The matrix/path product

G: (n, d, λ)-graph G': (n, d', λ')-graph $G'G$: $(n, dd', \lambda\lambda')$-graph

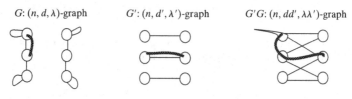

For every two n-vertex graphs G, G' with degrees d, d' and random-walk matrices A, A', the graph $G'G$ is the graph described by the random-walk matrix $A'A$. That is, $G'G$ has an edge (u, v) for every length two-path from u to v where the first step in the path is taken on an edge of G and the second is on an edge of G'. Note that G has n vertices and degree dd'. Typically, we are interested in the case $G = G'$, where it is called *graph squaring*. More generally, we denote by G^k the graph $G \cdot G \cdots G$ (k times). We have already encountered this case in Lemma 21.3, and similar analysis yields the following lemma (whose proof we leave as Exercise 21.8).

Lemma 21.16 *(Matrix product improves expansion)* $\lambda(G'G) \leq \lambda(G')\lambda(G')$.   ◇

Note that one can easily compute the rotation map of $G'G$ using the rotation maps of G and G'.

21.3.3 The tensor product

G: (n, d, λ)-graph G': (n', d', λ')-graph $G \circledR G'$: $(nn', dd', \max\{\lambda, \lambda'\})$-graph

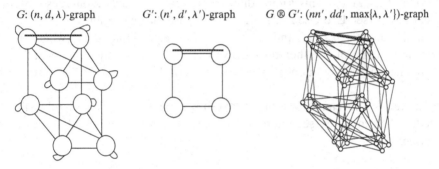

Let G and G' be two graphs with n (resp n') vertices and d (resp. d') degree, and let $\hat{G} : [n] \times [d] \to [n] \times [d]$ and $\hat{G}' : [n'] \times [d'] \to [n'] \times [d']$ denote their respective *rotation maps*. The *tensor product* of G and G', denoted $G \otimes G'$, is the graph over nn' vertices and degree dd' whose rotation map $\widehat{G \otimes G'}$ is the permutation over $([n] \times [n']) \times ([d] \times [d'])$ defined as

$$\widehat{G \otimes G'}(\langle u, v \rangle, \langle i, j \rangle) = \langle u', v' \rangle, \langle i', j' \rangle$$

where $(u', i') = \hat{G}(u, i)$ and $(v', j') = \hat{G}'(v, j)$. That is, the vertex set of $G \otimes G'$ consists of pairs of vertices, one from G and the other from G', and taking the step $\langle i, j \rangle$ on $G \otimes G'$ from the vertex $\langle u, v \rangle$ is akin to taking two independent steps: Move to the pair $\langle u', v' \rangle$ where u' is the ith neighbor of u in G and v' is the jth neighbor of v in G'.

In terms of random-walk matrices, the tensor product is also quite easy to describe. If $A = (a_{i,j})$ is the $n \times n$ random-walk matrix of G and $A' = (a'_{i',j'})$ is the $n' \times n'$ random-walk matrix of G', then the random-walk matrix of $G \otimes G'$, denoted as $A \otimes A'$, will be an $nn' \times nn'$ matrix that in the $\langle i, i' \rangle$th row and the $\langle j, j' \rangle$ column has the value $a_{i,j} \cdot a'_{i',j'}$. That is, $A \otimes A'$ consists of n^2 copies of A', with the (i, j)th copy scaled by $a_{i,j}$:

$$A \otimes A' = \begin{pmatrix} a_{1,1}A' & a_{1,2}A' & \cdots & a_{1,n}A' \\ a_{2,1}A' & a_{2,2}A' & \cdots & a_{2,n}A' \\ \vdots & & & \vdots \\ a_{n,1}A' & a_{n,2}A' & \cdots & a_{n,n}A' \end{pmatrix}$$

The tensor product can also be described in the language of graphs as having a cluster of n' vertices in $G \otimes G'$ for every vertex of G. Now if, u and v are two neighboring vertices in G, we will put a bipartite version of G' between the cluster corresponding to u and the cluster corresponding to v in G. That is, if (i, j) is an edge in G', then there is an edge between the ith vertex in the cluster corresponding to u and the jth vertex in the cluster corresponding to v.

Lemma 21.17 (*Tensor product preserves expansion*) Let $\lambda = \lambda(G)$ and $\lambda' = \lambda(G')$, then $\lambda(G \otimes G') \leq \max\{\lambda, \lambda'\}$. ◇

One intuition for this bound is the following: Taking a T step random walk on the graph $G \otimes G'$ is akin to taking two independent random walks on the graphs G and G'. Hence, if both walks converge to the uniform distribution within T steps, then so will the walk on $G \otimes G'$.

PROOF OF LEMMA 21.17: This is immediate from some basic facts about tensor products and eigenvalues (see Exercise 21.22). If $\lambda_1, \ldots, \lambda_n$ are the eigenvalues of A (where A is the random-walk matrix of G) and $\lambda'_1, \ldots, \lambda'_{n'}$ are the eigenvalues of A' (where A' is the random-walk matrix of G'), then the eigenvalues of $A \otimes A'$ are all numbers of the form $\lambda_i \cdot \lambda'_j$, and hence the largest ones apart from 1 are of the form $1 \cdot \lambda(G')$ or $\lambda(G) \cdot 1$ ∎

We note that one can show that $\lambda(G \otimes G') \leq \lambda(G) + \lambda(G')$ without relying on any knowledge of eigenvalues (see Exercise 21.23). Even this weaker bound suffices for our applications.

21.3.4 The replacement product

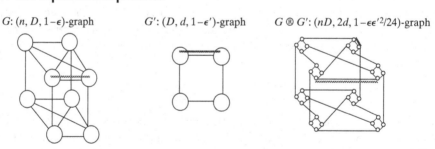

$G: (n, D, 1-\epsilon)$-graph $\qquad$ $G': (D, d, 1-\epsilon')$-graph $\qquad$ $G \circledR G': (nD, 2d, 1-\epsilon\epsilon'^2/24)$-graph

In both the matrix and tensor products, the degree of the resulting graph is larger than the degree of the input graphs. The following product will enable us to reduce the degree of one of the graphs. Let G, G' be two graphs such that G has n vertices and degree D, and G' has D vertices and degree d. The *balanced replacement product* (below we use simply *replacement product* for short) of G and G' is denoted by $G \circledR G'$ is the nD-vertex $2d$-degree graph obtained as follows:

1. For every vertex u of G, the graph $G \circledR G'$ has a copy of G' (including both edges and vertices).
2. If u, v are two neighboring vertices in G, then we place d parallel edges between the ith vertex in the copy of G' corresponding to u and the jth vertex in the copy of G'

corresponding to v, where i is the index of v as a neighbor of u and j is the index of u as a neighbor of v in G. (That is, taking the ith edge out of u leads to v and taking the jth edge out of v leads to u.)

Some texts use the term "replacement product" for the variant of this product that uses only a single edge (as opposed to d parallel edges) in Item 2 above. The addition of parallel edges ensures that a random step from a vertex v in $G \circledR G'$ will move with probability $1/2$ to a neighbor within the same cluster and with probability $1/2$ to a neighbor outside the cluster.

The replacement product also has a simple description in terms of rotation maps: Since $G \circledR G'$ has nD vertices and $2d$ degree, its rotation map $G \hat{\circledR} G'$ can be thought of as a permutation over $([n] \times [D]) \times ([d] \times \{0, 1\})$ that takes four inputs u, v, i, b where $u \in [n]$, $v \in [D]$, $i \in [d]$ and $b \in \{0, 1\}$. If $b = 0$, then it outputs $u, \hat{G}'(v, i), b$, and if $b = 1$, then it outputs $\hat{G}(u, v), i, b$. That is, depending on whether b is equal to 0 or 1, the rotation map either treats v as a vertex of G' or as an edge label of G.

In the language of random-walk matrices the replacement product is described as follows:

$$A \circledR A' = 1/2\hat{A} + 1/2(I_n \otimes A') \tag{21.9}$$

where A, A' denote the random-walk matrices of G and G' respectively, and $\hat{A}$ denotes the permutation matrix corresponding to the rotation map of G. That is, $\hat{A}$ is an $(nD) \times (nD)$ matrix whose (i, j)th column is all zeroes except a single 1 in the (i', j')th place where $(i', j') = \hat{G}(i, j)$.

If $D \gg d$, then the replacement product's degree will be significantly smaller than G's degree. The following lemma shows that this dramatic degree reduction does not cause too much of a deterioration in the graph's expansion.

Lemma 21.18 *(Expansion of replacement product)* *If $\lambda(G) \leq 1 - \epsilon$ and $\lambda(H) \leq 1 - \delta$, then $\lambda(G \circledR H) \leq 1 - \frac{\epsilon \delta^2}{24}$.* ◇

The intuition behind Lemma 21.18 is the following: Think of the input graph G as a good expander whose only drawback is that it has a too high degree D. This means that a k step random walk on G' requires $O(k \log D)$ random bits. However, as we saw in Section 21.2.5, sometimes we can use fewer random bits if we use an expander. So a natural idea is to generate the edge labels for the walk by taking a walk using a smaller expander G' that has D vertices and degree $d \ll D$. The definition of $G \circledR G'$ is motivated by this intuition: A random walk on $G \circledR G'$ is roughly equivalent to using an expander walk on G' to generate labels for a walk on G. In particular, each step a walk over $G \circledR G'$ can be thought of as tossing a coin and then, based on its outcome, either taking a a random step on G', or using the current vertex of G' as an edge label to take a step on G. Another way to gain intuition on the replacement product is to solve Exercise 21.24, that analyzes the *combinatorial* (edge) expansion of the resulting graph as a function of the edge expansion of the input graphs.

PROOF OF LEMMA 21.18: It suffices to show that $\lambda(G \circledR H)^3 \leq 1 - \frac{\epsilon \delta^2}{8}$. Since for every graph F, $\lambda(F^k) = \lambda(F)^k$, we will do so by showing $\lambda((G \circledR H)^3) \leq 1 - \frac{\epsilon \delta^2}{8}$. Let A

be the $n \times n$ random-walk matrix of G (with $\hat{A}$ the $(nD) \times (nD)$ permutation matrix corresponding to the rotation map $\hat{G}$), let B be the $D \times D$ random-walk matrix of H, and let C be the random-walk matrix of $(G \circledR H)^3$. Then, (21.9) implies that

$$C = (1/2\hat{A} + 1/2(I_n \otimes B))^3 \tag{21.10}$$

Now Lemma 21.14 implies that $B = (1 - \delta)B' + \delta J_D$ for some matrix B' with norm at most 1 (where J_D is the $D \times D$ all $1/D$ matrix). We plug this into (21.10), expand all terms, and then collect together all the terms except for the one corresponding to $1/2\delta(I_n \otimes J_D)1/2\hat{A}1/2\delta(I_n \otimes J_D)$. The reader can verify that all terms correspond to matrices of norm at most 1 and hence (21.10) becomes

$$C = (1 - \tfrac{\delta^2}{8})C' + \tfrac{\delta^2}{8}(I_n \otimes J_D)\hat{A}(I_n \otimes J_D) \tag{21.11}$$

where C' is some $(nD) \times (nD)$ matrix of norm at most 1. The lemma will follow from the following claim.

Claim $(I_n \otimes J_D)\hat{A}(I_n \otimes J_D) = A \otimes J_D$.

PROOF: Indeed, the left-hand side is the random-walk matrix of the graph on nD vertices on which a step from a vertex (i,j) corresponds to (1) choosing a random $k \in [D]$, (2) letting i' be the kth neighbor of i in G, (3) choosing j' at random in $[D]$ moving to the vertex (i,k). We can equivalently describe this as going to a random neighbor i' of i in G and choosing j' at random in $[D]$, which is the graph corresponding to the matrix $A \otimes J_D$. ∎

The claim concludes the proof since $\lambda(A \otimes J_D) \leq \max\{\lambda(A), \lambda(J_D)\} = \max\{\lambda(A), 0\}$. The lemma follows by plugging this into (21.11) and using the fact that $\lambda(C') \leq 1$ for every matrix of norm at most 1. ∎

21.3.5 The actual construction

We now use the three graph products described above to show a strongly explicit construction of an expander graph family; that is, we prove the following theorem.

> **Theorem 21.19** *(Explicit construction of expanders)*
> *There exists a strongly explicit (λ, d)-expander family for some constants $d \in \mathbb{N}$ and $\lambda < 1$.*

Note that using the matrix/graph product, Theorem 21.19 can be improved to yield a strongly explicit (λ, d)-expander family for *every* $\lambda > 0$ (albeit at the expense of allowing d to be an arbitrarily large constant depending on λ.

PROOF: We will start by showing something slightly weaker: a very explicit family of graphs $\{G_k\}$ where G_k is not a graph on k vertices but on roughly c^k vertices for some constant c. That is, rather than showing a family of graphs for *every* size n, we will only show a family of graphs that contains a graph of size n for every n that is a power of c. We will then sketch how the construction can be improved to yield a graph family containing a graph of every size n.

The construction is recursive: We start by a finite size graph G_1 (which we can find using brute force search) and construct the graph G_k from the graph G_{k-1}. On a high level the construction is as follows: Each of the three products will serve a different purpose in the construction. The *Tensor product* allows us to take G_{k-1} and increase its number of vertices, at the expense of increasing the degree and possibly some deterioration in the expansion. The *replacement product* allows us to dramatically reduce the degree at the expense of additional deterioration in the expansion. Finally, we use the *Matrix/Path product* to regain the loss in the expansion at the expense of a mild increase in the degree. The actual definition is as follows:

- Let H be a $(D = (2d)^{100}, d, 0.01)$-expander graph, which we can find using brute force search. (We choose d to be a large enough constant that such a graph exists.) We let G_1 be a $((2d)^{100}, 2d, 1/2)$-expander graph and G_2 be a $((2d)^{200}, 2d, 1/2)$-expander graphs (again, such graphs can be easily found via brute force).
- For $k > 2$ define

$$G_k = \left(G_{\lfloor \frac{k-1}{2} \rfloor} \otimes G_{\lceil \frac{k-1}{2} \rceil} \right)^{50} \circledR H.$$

We prove the following claim:

Claim *For every k, G_k is a $((2d)^{100k}, 2d, 1 - 1/50)$-expander graph. Furthermore, there is a poly(k)-time algorithm that given a label of a vertex i in G_k and an index j in $[2d]$ finds the jth neighbor of i in G_k.*

PROOF: We prove the first part by induction. Verify directly that it holds for $k = 1, 2$. For $k > 2$, if we let n_k be the number of vertices of G_k, then $n_k = n_{\lfloor (k-1)/2 \rfloor} n_{\lceil (k-1)/2 \rceil} (2d)^{100}$. By induction we assume $n_{\lfloor (k-1)/2 \rfloor} = (2d)^{100 \lfloor (k-1)/2 \rfloor}$ and $n_{\lceil (k-1)/2 \rceil} = (2d)^{100 \lceil (k-1)/2 \rceil}$ which implies that $n_k = (2d)^{100k}$ (using the fact that $\lfloor (k-1)/2 \rfloor + \lceil (k-1)/2 \rceil = k - 1$). It's also easy to verify that G_k has degree $2d$ for every j: If G has degree $2d$, then $G \otimes G$ has degree $(2d)^2$, $(G \otimes G)^{50}$ has degree $(2d)^{100}$ and $(G \otimes G)^{50}) \circledR H$ has degree $(2d)$. The eigenvalue analysis also follows by induction: If $\lambda(G) \leq 1 - 1/50$ then $\lambda(G \otimes G)^{50} \leq 1/e < 1/2$. Hence, by Lemma 21.18, $\lambda((G \otimes G)^{50} \circledR H) \leq 1 - 1/2(0.99)^2/24 \leq 1 - 1/50$.

To obtain the "furthermore" part, note that there is a natural algorithm to compute the neighborhood function of G_k that makes 100 recursive calls to the neighborhood function of $G_{\lfloor (k-1)/2 \rfloor}$, thus running in time roughly $n^{\log 100}$. ∎

The above construction and analysis yields an expander graph family containing an n vertex graph for every n of the form c^k for some constant c. The proof of Theorem 21.19 is completed by observing that one can transform an (n, d, λ)-expander graph to an (n', cd, λ')-expander graph (where $\lambda' < 1$ is a constant depending on λ, d) for any $n/c \leq n' \leq n$ by joining together into a "mega-vertex" sets of at most c vertices (Exercise 21.16). ∎

Remark 21.20

The quantitative bounds obtained from the proof of Theorem 21.19 are pretty bad, both in terms of the relation between degree and expansion and the running time (in particular the initial brute force search alone will take more than 2^{100} steps). This is partly because for pedagogical reasons we chose to present this construction in its simplest form, without covering various known optimizations. However, even with these optimizations this construction is not the most efficient known.

There are different known constructions of expanders that are highly practical and efficient (e.g., [LPS86, Mar88]). However, their analysis typically uses deep facts in number theory. Also, the replacement product (and its close cousin, the zig-zag product) have found applications beyond the proof of Theorem 21.15. One such application is the deterministic logspace algorithm for undirected connectivity described in the next section. Another application is a construction of combinatorial vertex expanders with a greater expansion of small sets that what is implied by the parameter λ ([CRVW02], see also Exercise 21.15).

21.4 DETERMINISTIC LOGSPACE ALGORITHM FOR UNDIRECTED CONNECTIVITY

This section describes a recent result of Reingold, showing that at least the most famous randomized logspace algorithm, the random walk algorithm for the problem UPATH of s-t-connectivity in undirected graphs (see Chapter 7), can be completely "derandomized."

Theorem 21.21 *(Reingold's Theorem)*
UPATH ∈ **L**.

Reingold describes a set of poly(n) walks starting from s such that if s is connected to t then one of the walks is guaranteed to hit t. The *existence* of such a small set of walks can be shown using the probabilistic method and Corollary 21.5. The point here is that Reingold's enumeration of walks can be carried out deterministically in logspace.

Proof outline
As before we are interested in undirected graphs that may have parallel edges. We restrict our attention to checking connectivity for d-regular graphs for say $d = 4$. This is without loss of generality: If a vertex has degree $d'' < 3$, we add a self-loop of multiplicity to bring the degree up to d, and if the vertex has degree $d' \geq 3$, we can replace it by a cycle of d' vertices, and each of the d' edges that were incident to the old vertex then attach to one of the cycle nodes. Of course, a logspace machine does not have space to store the modified graph, but it can pretend that these modifications have taken place, since it can perform them on the fly whenever it accesses the graph. (To put this more formally, the transformation is implicitly computable in logspace as per Definition 4.16.) In fact, the proof below will perform a series of other local modifications on the graph, each with the property that the logspace algorithm can perform them on the fly.

We start by observing that checking connectivity in *expander* graphs is easy. Specifically, if every connected component in G is an expander, then there is a number $\ell = O(\log n)$ such that if s and t are connected, then they are connected with a path of length at most ℓ. Indeed, Lemma 21.3 implies that in every n-vertex regular graph G, the distribution of the ℓth vertex in a random walk is within $\sqrt{n}\lambda^\ell$ statistical (or L_1)

distance from the uniform distribution. In particular this means that if each connected component H of G is an *expander* graph, having $\lambda(H)$ bounded away from 1, then a random walk of length $\ell = O(\log n)$ from a vertex u in H will reach every vertex of H with positive probability.

The idea behind Reingold's algorithm is to transform the graph G (in an implicitly computable in logspace way) to a graph G' such that every connected component in G becomes an expander in G', but two vertices that were not connected will stay unconnected.

21.4.1 The logspace algorithm for connectivity (proof of Theorem 21.21)

By adding more self-loops we may assume that the input graph G is of degree d^{50} for some constant d that is sufficiently large to ensure the existence of a $(d^{50}, d/2, 0.01)$-expander graph H. Since the size of H is constant, we can store all of it in memory using $O(1)$ bits.[6] Let $G_0 = G$ and for $k \geq 1$, define $G_k = (G_{k-1} ®H)^{50}$, where $®$ denotes the balanced replacement product defined in Section 21.3.4.

If G_{k-1} is an N-vertex graph with degree d^{50}, then $G_{k-1}®H$ is a $d^{50}N$-vertex graph with degree d and thus $G_k = (G_{k-1}®H)^{50}$ is a $d^{50}N$-vertex graph with degree d. Note also that if two vertices were connected (resp., disconnected) in G_{k-1}, then they are still connected (resp., disconnected) in G_k. The key observation is that the graph $G_{10\log n}$ an expander, and therefore an easy instance of UPATH. Specifically, we have the following claim.

Claim *For every $k \geq 0$, every connected component in G_k is an $(d^{50k}n, d^{20}, 1 - \epsilon)$-expander, where $\epsilon = \min\{1/20, 1.5^k/(12n^2)\}$ and n denotes the number of vertices in $G = G_0$.*

PROOF: Indeed, by Lemmas 21.16 and 21.18, for every $\epsilon < 1/20$ and D-degree graph F, if $\lambda(F) \leq 1 - \epsilon$, then $\lambda(F®H) \leq 1 - \epsilon/25$ and hence $\lambda\left((F®H)^{50}\right) \leq 1 - 2\epsilon$. By Lemma 21.4, every connected component of G has expansion parameter at most $1 - \frac{1}{12n^2}$ (note that n is at least as large as the number of vertices in the connect component). ∎

It follows that every connected component in $G_{10\log n}$ is an expansion (with expansion parameter at most $1 - 1/20$), and hence to find whether a pair of vertices s, t are connected in $G_{10\log n}$ we simply need to enumerate over all paths in $G_{10\log n}$ that start at s and have length $\ell = O(\log n)$, and see whether any one of these hits t. The catch is of course that the graph provided to our algorithm is G, not $G_{10\log n}$. A simpler question is whether, given G, our algorithm can perform even a *single* step of a random walk on G_k for $k = 10\log n$. Specifically, given a description of a vertex s in G_k and an index $i \in [d^{20}]$, it has to compute the ith neighbor of s in G_k using only logarithmic space. It is easy to see that if we can perform this single step in logarithmic space, then we can just as easily perform ℓ steps as well by repeating the single step again and again while keeping a counter and reusing the same space to compute each step.

---

[6] We can either use an explicit construction of such a graph or simply find it using an exhaustive search among all graphs of this size.

The graph G_k is equal to $(G_{k-1} ® H)^{50}$ and thus it suffices to show that we can take a single step in the graph $G_{k-1} ® H$ in logspace (we can then repeat the same process for 50 times). Now by the definition of the replacement product, a vertex in $G_{k-1} ® H$ is represented by a pair $\langle u, v \rangle$ where u is a vertex of G_{k-1} and v is a vertex of H. The index of a neighbor of $\langle u, v \rangle$ is represented by a pair $\langle b, i \rangle$ where $b \in \{0, 1\}$ and $i \in [d/2]$. If $b = 0$, then the $\langle b, i \rangle$th neighbor of $\langle u, v \rangle$ is $\langle u, v' \rangle$ where v' is the ith neighbor of v' in H. If $b = 1$, then the $\langle b, i \rangle$th neighbor of $\langle u, v \rangle$ is the pair $\langle u', v' \rangle$ denoting the result of applying G_{k-1}'s rotation map to $\langle u, v \rangle$. (That is, u' is the vth neighbor of u in G_{k-1}, and v' is the index of u as a neighbor of u' in G_{k-1}.) This description already implies an obvious recursive algorithm to compute the rotation map of G_k. Letting s_k denotes the space needed to compute a rotation map of G_k by this algorithm, we see that s_k satisfies the equation $s_k = s_{k-1} + O(1)$, implying that $s_{10 \log n} = O(\log n)$.[7]

21.5 WEAK RANDOM SOURCES AND EXTRACTORS

Suppose, that despite any philosophical difficulties, we are happy with probabilistic algorithms, and see no need to "derandomize" them, especially at the expense of some unproven assumptions. We still need to tackle the fact that real-world sources of randomness and unpredictability rarely, if ever, behave as a sequence of perfectly uncorrelated and unbiased coin tosses. Can we still execute probabilistic algorithms using real-world "weakly random" sources?

21.5.1 Min entropy

For starters, we try to define what we could mean by a weakly random source. Historically speaking, several definitions were proposed, which are recalled in Example 21.23. The following definition (due to D. Zuckerman) encompasses all previous definitions.

Definition 21.22 Let X be a random variable. The *min entropy* of X, denoted by $H_\infty(X)$, is the largest real number k such that $\Pr[X = x] \le 2^{-k}$ for every x in the range of X.

If X is a distribution over $\{0, 1\}^n$ with $H_\infty(X) \ge k$ then it is called an (n, k)-*source*. ◇

It is not hard to see that if X is a random variable over $\{0, 1\}^n$, then $H_\infty(X) \le n$ with $H_\infty(X) = n$ if and only if X is distributed according to the uniform distribution U_n. Our goal in this section is to be able to execute probabilistic algorithms given access to a distribution X with $H_\infty(X)$ as small as possible. It can be shown that min entropy is a *minimal requirement* in the sense that a general simulation of a probabilistic algorithm that uses k random bits requires access to a distribution X that is (close to) having min entropy at least k (see Exercise 21.18).

---

[7] When implementing the algorithm, one needs to take care *not* to make a copy of the input when invoking the recursive procedure but rather have all procedure operate on a globally accessible memory that contains the index k and the vertex and edge labels; otherwise we'd get an $O(\log n \log \log n)$-space algorithm. For more details see the original paper [Rei05] or [Gol08, Section 5.2.4].

EXAMPLE 21.23

We will now see that min entropy is a pretty general notion and can allow us to model many other models of "imperfectly random" sources. Here are some examples for distributions X over $\{0, 1\}^n$.

- (von Neumann's model: biased coins) X is composed of n independent coin tosses, each outputting 1 with probability $\delta < 1/2$ and 0 with probability $1 - \delta$. It is easily checked that[8] $H_\infty(X) = \log(1/(1-\delta))n$.

- (Santha-Vazirani sources) X has the property that for every $i \in [n]$, and every string $x \in \{0, 1\}^{i-1}$, conditioned on $X_1 = x_1, \ldots, X_{i-1} = x_{i-1}$ it holds that both $\Pr[X_i = 0]$ and $\Pr[X_i = 1]$ are between δ and $1 - \delta$. This generalizes von Neumann's model and can model sources such as stock market fluctuations, where current measurements do have some limited dependence on the previous history. It is easily checked that $H_\infty(X) \geq \log(1/(1-\delta))n$.

- (Bit fixing and generalized bit fixing sources) In a *bit-fixing* source, there is a subset $S \subseteq [n]$ with $|S| = k$ such that X's bits in the coordinates given by S are uniformly distributed over $\{0, 1\}^k$, and X's bits in the coordinates given by $[n] \setminus S$ is a fixed string (say the all-zeros string). Then $H_\infty(X) = k$. The same holds if X's projection to $[n] \setminus S$ is a fixed deterministic function of its projection to S, in which case we say that X is a *generalized bit-fixing source*. For example, if the bits in the odd positions of X are independent and uniform and for every even position $2i$, $X_{2i} = X_{2i-1}$, then $H_\infty(X) = \lceil \frac{n}{2} \rceil$. This may model a scenario where we measure some real-world data at too high a rate (think of measuring every second a physical event that changes only every minute).

- (Linear subspaces) If X is the uniform distribution over a linear subspace of $GF(2)^n$ of dimension k, then $H_\infty(X) = k$. (In this case X is actually a generalized bit-fixing source—can you see why?)

- (Uniform over subset) If X is the uniform distribution over a set $S \subseteq \{0, 1\}^n$ with $|S| = 2^k$, then $H_\infty(X) = k$. As we will see, this is a very general case that "essentially captures" all distributions X with $H_\infty(X) = k$.

21.5.2 Statistical distance

Next we formalize what it means to *extract* random—more precisely, almost random—bits from an (n, k) source. We will use the notion of *statistical distance* (see Section A.2.6) to qualify when two distributions are close to one another. Recall that if X and Y are two distributions over some domain Ω, then the *statistical distance* between X and Y, denoted by $\Delta(X, Y)$, is equal to

$$\max_{f:\Omega \to \{0,1\}} |E[f(X)] - E[f(Y)]| \tag{21.12}$$

---

[8] In fact, as n grows X is close to a distribution with min-entropy $H(\delta)n$ where H is the Shannon entropy function defined as $H(\delta) = \delta \log \frac{1}{\delta} + (1 - \delta) \log \frac{1}{1-\delta}$. The same holds for Santha-Vazirani sources defined below. See [DFR+07] for this and more general results of this form.

It is also known that $\Delta(X, Y) = 1/2|\mathbf{x} - \mathbf{y}|_1$, where $\mathbf{x}$ and $\mathbf{y}$ are the vectors in $\mathbb{R}^\Omega$ that represent the distributions X and Y respectively. For any $\epsilon > 0$, we say that two distribution X and Y are ϵ-*close*, denoted $X \approx_\epsilon Y$, if $\Delta(X, Y) \le \epsilon$.

21.5.3 Definition of randomness extractors

We can now define randomness extractors—these are functions that transform an (n, k) source into an almost uniform distribution. The extractor uses a small number of additional truly random bits, called a *seed* and denoted by d in the definition below.

> **Definition 21.24** *(Randomness extractors)* A function $\mathsf{Ext} : \{0, 1\}^n \times \{0, 1\}^d \to \{0, 1\}^m$ is a (k, ϵ) extractor if for any (n, k)-source X, the distribution $\mathsf{Ext}(X, U_d)$ is ϵ-close to U_m. (For every ℓ, U_ℓ denotes the uniform distribution over $\{0, 1\}^\ell$.)

Why an additional input?

Our stated motivation for extractors is to execute probabilistic algorithms without access to perfect unbiased coins. Yet, it seems that an extractor is not sufficient for this task, as we only guarantee that its output is close to uniform if it is given an additional *seed* that is uniformly distributed. We have two answers to this objection. First, note that the requirement of an additional input is necessary: For every function $\mathsf{Ext} : \{0, 1\}^n \to \{0, 1\}^m$ and every $k \le n - 1$, there exists an (n, k)-source X such that the first bit of $\mathsf{Ext}(X)$ is constant (i.e, is equal to some value $b \in \{0, 1\}$ with probability 1), and so has statistical distance at least $1/2$ from the uniform distribution (Exercise 21.17). Second, if the length t of the second input is sufficiently short (e.g., $t = O(\log n)$) then, for the purposes of simulating probabilistic algorithms, we can do without any access to true random coins, by enumerating over all the 2^t possible inputs. Clearly, d has to be somewhat short for the extractor to be nontrivial. The completely trivial case is when $d \ge m$, in which case the extractor can simply ignore its first input and output the seed!

21.5.4 Existence proof for extractors

It turns out that at least if we ignore issues of computational efficiency, very good extractors exist.

Theorem 21.25 *For every $k, n \in \mathbb{N}$ and $\epsilon > 0$, there exists a (k, ϵ)-extractor $\mathsf{Ext} : \{0, 1\}^n \times \{0, 1\}^d \to \{0, 1\}^k$ with $d = \log n + 2\log(1/\epsilon) + O(1)$.*   ◇

PROOF: Call an (n, k) source X *flat* if X is the uniform distribution over a 2^k-sized subset of $\{0, 1\}^n$. In Exercise 19.7 it is shown that every (n, k) source can be expressed as a convex combination of flat (n, k)-sources. Because the statistical distance of a convex combination of distributions $Y_1, \ldots, Y_N$ from a distribution U is at most the maximum of $\Delta(Y_i, X)$ (Exercise 21.19), it suffices to show a function Ext such that $\mathsf{Ext}(X, U_d)$ is close to the uniform distribution when X is an (n, k)-flat source.

     We will prove the existence of such an extractor by the probabilistic method, choosing Ext as a random function from $\{0, 1\}^n \times \{0, 1\}^d \to \{0, 1\}^k$. Let X be an (n, k)-flat source and let f be a function from $\{0, 1\}^k \to \{0, 1\}$. If we choose Ext, at random then the expectation $\mathrm{E}[f(\mathsf{Ext}(X, U_d))]$ is obtained by evaluating f on $2^k \times 2^d$ random points, and hence by the Chernoff bound the probability that this expectation deviates from $\mathrm{E}[f(U_k)]$ by more than ϵ is bounded by $2^{-2^{k+d}/4\epsilon^2}$. This means that if $d > \log n + 2\log(1/e) + 3$, then this probability is bounded by $2^{-2n(2^k)}$. But the number of flat distributions is at most $(2^n)^{2^k}$ and the number of functions from $\{0, 1\}^k \to \{0, 1\}$ is 2^{2^k} and hence the union bound implies that there is a choice of Ext guaranteeing

$$|\mathrm{E}[f(\mathsf{Ext}(X, U_d))] - \mathrm{E}[f(U_k)]| < \epsilon$$

for *every* (n, k)-flat source and function $f : \{0, 1\}^k \to \{0, 1\}$. In other words, $\mathsf{Ext}(X, U_d)$ is ϵ-close to U_k for every (n, k)-flat source and hence for every (n, k)-source. $\blacksquare$

This extractor is optimal in the sense that there is an absolute constant c such that every (k, ϵ) extractor that is nontrivial (has output longer than seed length and $\epsilon < 1/2$) must satisfy $d \geq \log(n - k) + 2\log(1/\epsilon) - c$ [NZ93, RTS97].

21.5.5 Extractors based on hash functions

The nonexplicit extractor of Theorem 21.25 is not very useful: For most applications we need *explicit* extractors—namely extractors computable in polynomial time. One such explicit extractor (though with a long seed length) can be obtained using pairwise independent hash functions.

Recall (Section 8.2.2) that a collection $\mathcal{H}$ of functions from $\{0, 1\}^n$ to $\{0, 1\}^m$ is *pairwise independent* if for every $x \neq x'$ in $\{0, 1\}^n$ and $y, y' \in \{0, 1\}^m$, the probability that $h(x) = y$ and $h(x') = y'$ for a random $h \in_R \mathcal{H}$ is 2^{-2m}. There are known construction of such collections where each function h can be described by a string of length $n + m$ (we abuse notation and call this string also h). Choosing a random function from the collection is done by choosing a random string in $\{0, 1\}^{n+m}$. The next famous lemma shows that with an appropriate setting of parameters, the map $x, h \mapsto h(x) \circ h$ (where $\circ$ denotes concatenation) is an extractor. This is not a superb extractor in terms of parameter values but it is useful in many settings.

Lemma 21.26 *(Leftover hash lemma [BBR88, ILL89]) Let $m = k - 2\log(1/\epsilon)$, then for every (n, k) source X,*

$$\Delta(H(X) \circ H, U_n \circ H) < \epsilon$$

where H denotes a randomly chosen (description of) function in a pairwise independent hash function collection from $\{0, 1\}^n$ to $\{0, 1\}^m$.   ◇

PROOF: We study the *collision probability* of $H(X) \circ H$, where we identify H with U_ℓ where $\ell = n + m$ is the length of description of the hash function. That is, the probability that $h(x) \circ h = h'(x') \circ h'$ for random $h, h' \in_R \mathcal{H}$ and $x, x' \in_R X$. This is bounded by the probability that $h = h'$ (which is equal to $2^{-\ell}$) times the probability that $h(x) = h(x')$. The latter is bounded by 2^{-k} (a bound on the probability that $x = x'$ implies by the fact that X is an (n, k)-source) plus 2^{-m} (the probability that $h(x) = h(x')$

for a random $h \in_R \mathcal{H}$ and $x \neq x'$). Thus the collision probability of $(H(X), H)$ is at most $2^{-\ell}(2^{-k} + 2^{-m}) = 2^{-(\ell+m)} + 2^{-\ell-k}$.

Now, treat this distribution as a probability vector $\mathbf{p} \in \mathbb{R}^{2^{\ell+m}}$. Then the collision probability is precisely the L_2-norm of $\mathbf{p}$ squared. We can write $\mathbf{p} = \mathbf{1} + \mathbf{w}$ where $\mathbf{1}$ is the probability vector corresponding to the distribution $U_n \circ H = U_{n+\ell}$ and $\mathbf{w}$ is orthogonal to $\mathbf{1}$. (For a general vector $\mathbf{p}$ we'd only be able to write $\mathbf{p} = \alpha\mathbf{1} + \mathbf{w}$ for some $\alpha \in \mathbb{R}$, but since $\mathbf{p}$ is a probability vector, it must hold that $\alpha = 1$, as otherwise the entries of the right-hand side will not sum up to one.) Thus by the Pythagorean Theorem $\|\mathbf{p}\|_2^2 = \|\mathbf{u}\|_2^2 + \|\mathbf{w}\|_2^2$, and since $\|\mathbf{u}\|_2^2 = 2^{-\ell-m}$ we get that

$$\|\mathbf{w}\|_2^2 = \|\mathbf{p} - \mathbf{1}\|_2^2 \leq 2^{-\ell-m}$$

Using the relation between the L_1 and L_2 norms (Claim 21.1), we see that

$$\Delta(H(X) \circ H, U_{\ell+m}) = 1/2|\mathbf{p} - \mathbf{1}|_1 \leq 1/2 2^{(m+\ell)/2}\|\mathbf{v} - \mathbf{1}\|_2$$
$$\leq 2^{k/2+\ell/2-\log(1/\epsilon)}2^{-k/2-\ell/2}$$
$$< \epsilon$$

∎

21.5.6 Extractors based on random walks on expanders

We can also construct explicit extractors using expander graphs.

Lemma 21.27 *Let $\epsilon > 0$. For every n and $k \leq n$, there exists an explicit (k, ϵ)-extractor* $\mathsf{Ext} : \{0,1\}^n \times \{0,1\}^t \to \{0,1\}^n$, *where $t = O(n - k + \log 1/\epsilon)$.*   ◇

PROOF: Suppose X is an (n, k)-source and we are given a sample a from it. Let G be a $(2^n, d, 1/2)$-expander graph for some constant d (see Definition 21.6 and Theorem 21.19).

Let z be a truly random seed of length $t = \log d(n/2 - k/2 + \log 1/\epsilon + 1) = O(n - k + \log 1/\epsilon)$. We interpret z as a random walk in G of length $\ell = n/2 - k/2 + \log 1/\epsilon + 1$ starting from the node whose label is a. (That is, we think of z as ℓ labels in $[d]$ specifying the steps taken in the walk.) The output $\mathsf{Ext}(a, z)$ of the extractor is the label of the final node on the walk.

Following the proof of Lemma 21.3 (see Equation (21.1)) we see that, letting $\mathbf{p}$ denote the probability vector corresponding to X and A the random-walk matrix of G,

$$\|A^\ell \mathbf{p} - \mathbf{1}\|_2 \leq 2^{-\ell}\|\mathbf{p} - \mathbf{1}\|_2$$

But since X is an (n, k) source, $\|\mathbf{p}\|_2^2$ (which is equal to the collision probability of X) is at most 2^{-k}, and hence in particular $\|\mathbf{p}-\mathbf{1}\|_2 \leq \|\mathbf{p}\|_2 + \|\mathbf{1}\|_2 \leq 2^{-k/2} + 2^{-n/2} \leq 2^{-k/2+1}$. Thus for our choice of ℓ

$$\|A^\ell \mathbf{p} - \mathbf{1}\|_2 \leq 2^{-n/2+k/2-\log(1/\epsilon)+1}2^{-k/2+1} \leq \epsilon 2^{-n/2}$$

which completes the proof using the relation between the L_1 and L_2 norms. ∎

21.5.7 Extractors from pseudorandom generators

For many years explicit constructions of randomness extractors fell quite a bit behind the parameters achieved by the optimal nonexplicit construction of Theorem 21.25. For example, we did not have explicit extractors that allowed us to run any randomized polynomial time algorithm using $\sim k$ bits using an (n, k) source where $k = n^\epsilon$ for arbitrarily small constant $\epsilon > 0$. (Generally, the smaller k is as a function of n, the harder the problem of constructing extractors; intuitively if $n \gg k$ then it's harder to "distill" the k bits of randomness that are hidden in the n-bit input.) To realize this goal, one should try to design an extractor that uses a seed of $O(\log n)$ bits to extract from an (n, n^ϵ)-source at least a polynomial number of bits (i.e., at least n^δ bits for some $\delta > 0$).[9] In 1999 Trevisan showed how to do this using an improved extractor construction. But more interesting than the result itself was Trevisan's idea: He showed that *pseudorandom generators* such as the ones we've seen in Chapters 20 and 19, when viewed in the right way, are in fact also randomness extractors. This was very surprising, since these pseudorandom generators rely on *hardness assumptions* (such as the existence of a function in **E** with high-circuit complexity). Thus it would seem that these generators will not be useful in the context of randomness extractors, where we are looking for constructions with *unconditional* analysis and are not willing to make any unproven assumptions.

But thinking further, we realize that the abovementioned difference between the two notions arises due to the type of "adversary" or "distinguisher" they have to work against. For a generator, the set of possible adversaries is the class of computationally limited algorithms (i.e., those that can be computed by circuits of some prescribed size). For an extractor, on the other hand, the set of adversaries is the set of all Boolean functions. The reason is that an extractor needs to produce a distribution $\mathcal{D}$ on $\{0, 1\}^m$ whose statistical difference from U_m is at most ϵ, meaning that $\left| \Pr_{x \in \mathcal{D}}[D(x) = 1] - \Pr_{x \in U_m}[D(x) = 1] \right| \leq \epsilon$ for every function $D : \{0, 1\}^m \to \{0, 1\}$.

Trevisan noticed further that while we normally think of a pseudorandom generator G as having only one input, we can think of it as a function that takes two inputs: a short seed and the truth table of a candidate hard function f. While our theorems state that the pseudorandom generator works if f is a hard function, the proofs of these theorems are actually *constructive*: They transform a distinguisher D that distinguishes between the generator's output and a random string into a small circuit A that computes the function f. This circuit A uses the distinguisher D as a *black box*. Therefore we can apply this transformation even when the distinguisher D is an arbitrary function that is not necessarily computable by a small circuit. This is the heart of Trevisan's argument.

Concretely, to make this all work we will need the stronger constructions of pseudorandom generators (e.g., of Theorem 20.7) that start with functions with high *worst-case* complexity. If there is a distinguisher D that distinguishes the output of such a generator from the uniform distribution, then the proof of correctness of the generator gives a way to compute the candidate hard function f on *every* input. Formally, we have the following theorem. (Below G^f refers to the algorithm G using f as a black box.)

---

[9] The work of Ta-Shma [TS96] did come close to this goal, achieving such an extractor with slightly super-logarithmic seed length.

Theorem 21.28 *(Constructive version of Theorem 20.7)*
For every time-constructible function $S : \mathbb{N} \to \mathbb{N}$ (the "security parameter"), there is a constant c and algorithms G and R satisfying the following:

- *On input a function $f : \{0, 1\}^\ell \to \{0, 1\}$ and a string $z \in \{0, 1\}^{c\ell}$, algorithm G runs in $2^{O(\ell)}$ time and outputs a string $G^f(z)$ of length $m = S(\ell)^{1/c}$.*
- *If $D : \{0, 1\}^m \to \{0, 1\}$ is a function such that $\left| E[D(G^f(U_{c\ell}))] - E[D(U_m)] \right| > 1/10$, then there is an advice string a of length at most $S(\ell)^{1/4}$ such that on every input x, $R^D(a, x) = f(x)$ and furthermore R runs in time at most $S(\ell)^{1/4}$.*

The algorithm R mentioned in the theorem is just the reduction that is implicit in the proof of correctness of the pseudorandom generator in Chapter 20.

The following is Trevisan's extractor construction. Let G be as in Theorem 21.28. Let X be an (n, k)-source. Assume without loss of generality that n is a power of 2, and $n = 2^\ell$. Let $S(\ell)$, the "security parameter," stand for k. Given any string f from the source and the seed $z \in \{0, 1\}^{c \log n}$, the extractor interprets f as a function from $\{0, 1\}^\ell$ to $\{0, 1\}$ and outputs

$$\mathsf{Ext}(f, z) = G^f(z) \tag{21.13}$$

Thus given a string of length n and a seed of size $c \log n$, Ext produces $S(\ell)^{1/c} = k^{1/c}$ bits. Let us show that Ext is an extractor.

Claim 21.29 *For every k, n, the function Ext defined in (21.13) is a $(k, 1/5)$-extractor.* ◇

PROOF: Suppose otherwise, that there is a (k, n)-source X and a Boolean function D that distinguishes between $\mathsf{Ext}(X, U_{c\ell})$ and U_m with bias at least $1/5$, where $m = S(\ell)^{1/c}$. Then, with probability at least $1/10$ over $f \in_R X$, function D distinguishes between $G^f(U_{c\ell})$ and U_m with bias at least $1/10$. Let's call an f for which this happens "bad." Note that for every bad f there exists an advice string $a \in \{0, 1\}^{k^{1/4}}$ such that f is computed by the algorithm $x \mapsto R^D(a, x)$. Since R^D is a deterministic algorithm, this means that the number of bad f's is at most the number of choices for a, which is $2^{k^{1/4}}$. But since X is a k-source, it assigns probability not more than 2^{-k} to any particular string. Hence the probability of a random f being bad is at most $2^{k^{1/4}} 2^{-k} \ll 1/10$, and we've arrived at a contradiction to the assumption that D is a good distinguisher. ∎

Remark 21.30
Readers mystified by this construction should try to look inside the generator G to get a better understanding. The extractor Ext turns out to do be very simple. Given a string $f \in \{0, 1\}^n$ from the weak random source, the extractor first applies an error-correcting code (specifically, one that is *list decodable*) to f to get a string $\hat{f} \in \{0, 1\}^{\text{poly}(n)}$. Intuitively speaking, this has the effect of "smearing out" the randomness over the entire string. The extractor then selects a subset of the coordinates of $\hat{f}$ using the construction of the Nisan-Wigderson generator (see Section 20.2.2). That is, treating $\hat{f}$ as a Boolean function on $s = O(\log n)$ bits, we use a seed z of size $t = O(s)$ and output $\hat{f}(z_{I_1}) \circ \cdots \circ$

$\hat{f}(z_{I_m})$, where $I_1, \ldots, I_m$ are s-sized subsets of $[t]$ that form a combinatorial design (see Definition 20.13).

21.6 PSEUDORANDOM GENERATORS FOR SPACE-BOUNDED COMPUTATION

We now show how extractors can be used to obtain a pseudorandom generator for space-bounded randomized computation, which allows randomized logspace computations to be run with $O(\log^2 n)$ random bits. We stress that this generator does not use any unproven assumptions.

The goal here will be to derandomize randomized logspace computations, in other words, classes such as **BPL** and **RL**. Recall from Chapter 4 the notion of a *configuration graph* for a space-bounded TM. If we fix an input of size n for a logspace machine, then the configuration graph has size poly(n). If the logspace machine is randomized, then it uses random coin tosses to make transitions within the configuration graph (i.e., each configuration has two outgoing edges, and each is taken with probability $1/2$). To derandomize this computation, we will replace the random string used by the logspace machine with the output of a "pseudorandom generator" (albeit one tailor-made for fooling logspace computations) and show that the logspace machine cannot "tell the difference" (i.e., the probability it ends up in an accepting state at the end is essentially unchanged).

> **Theorem 21.31** *Nisan's pseudorandom generator* [Nis90]
> *For every d there is a $c > 0$ and a poly(n)-time computable function $g : \{0, 1\}^{c \log^2 n} \to \{0, 1\}^{n^d}$ (the "pseudorandom generator") such that for every space-bounded machine M that has a configuration graph of size $\leq n^d$ on inputs of size n:*
>
> $$\left| \Pr_{r \in \{0,1\}^{n^d}} [M(x, r) = 1] - \Pr_{z \in \{0,1\}^{c \log^2 n}} [M(x, g(z)) = 1] \right| < \frac{1}{10} \qquad (21.14)$$

By trying all possible choices for the $O(\log^2 n)$-bit input for the generator g in Nisan's Theorem, we can simulate every algorithm in **BPL** in $O(\log^2 n)$ space. Note that Savitch's Theorem (Theorem 4.14) also implies that **BPL** $\subseteq$ **SPACE**($\log^2 n$) but it doesn't yield such a pseudorandom generator. In fact Theorem 21.31 can be strengthened to show that **BPL** can be decided using simultaneously polynomial time and space $O(\log^2 n)$, though we will not prove it here. Saks and Zhou [SZ95] improved Nisan's ideas to show that **BPL** $\subseteq$ **SPACE**($\log^{1.5} n$), which leads many experts to conjecture that **BPL** = **L** (i.e., randomness does not help logspace computations at all). Indeed, we've seen in Section 21.4 that the famous random-walk algorithm for undirected connectivity can be derandomized in logspace.

The main intuition behind Nisan's construction—and also the conjecture **BPL** = **L**—is that the logspace machine has one-way access to the random string and only $O(\log n)$ bits of memory. So it can only "remember" $O(\log n)$ of the random bits it has seen. To exploit this we will use the following simple lemma, which shows how to recycle a random string about which only a little information is known.

Lemma 21.32 *(Recycling Lemma) Let $f : \{0, 1\}^n \to \{0, 1\}^s$ be any function and* Ext : $\{0, 1\}^n \times \{0, 1\}^t \to \{0, 1\}^m$ *be a $(k, \epsilon/2)$-extractor, where $k = n - (s + 1) - \log \frac{1}{\epsilon}$. Then*

$$\Delta \left(f(X) \circ U_m, f(X) \circ \mathsf{Ext}(X, U_t) \right) < \epsilon$$

where X is a random variable distributed uniformly in $\{0, 1\}^n$. ◇

To understand why we call it the Recycling Lemma, focus on the case $s \ll n$ and $n = m$. Suppose we use a random string X of length n to produce $f(X)$. Since $f(X)$ has length $s \ll n$, typically each string in $\{0, 1\}^s$ will have many preimages under f. Thus anybody looking at $f(X)$ has only very little information about X. More formally, for every fixed choice of $f(X)$, the set of X that map to this value can be viewed as a weak random source. The lemma says that applying an appropriate extractor (whose random seed z can have length as small as $t = O(s + \log(1/\epsilon))$ if we use Lemma 21.27) on X we can get a new m-bit string $\mathsf{Ext}(X, z)$ that looks essentially random, even to somebody who knows $f(X)$.

PROOF: For $v \in \{0, 1\}^s$ we denote by X_v the random variable that is uniformly distributed over the set $f^{-1}(v)$. Then we can express $\Delta(f(X) \circ W, f(X) \circ \mathsf{Ext}(X, z))$ as

$$\frac{1}{2} \sum_{v,w} \left| \Pr[f(X) = v \wedge W = w] - \Pr_z[f(X) = v \wedge \mathsf{Ext}(X, z) = w] \right|$$

$$= \sum_v \Pr[f(X) = v] \cdot \Delta(W, \mathsf{Ext}(X_v, z)) \tag{21.15}$$

Let $V = \{v : \Pr[f(X) = v] \geq \epsilon/2^{s+1}\}$. If $v \in V$, then we can view X_v as a (n, k)-source, where $k \geq n - (s + 1) - \log \frac{1}{\epsilon}$. Thus by definition of an extractor, $\mathsf{Ext}(X_v, r) \approx_{\epsilon/2} W$ and hence the contributions from $v \in V$ sum to at most $\epsilon/2$. The contributions from $v \notin V$ are upperbounded by $\sum_{v \notin V} \Pr[f(X) = v] \leq 2^s \times \frac{\epsilon}{2^{s+1}} = \epsilon/2$. The lemma follows. ∎

Now we describe how the Recycling Lemma is useful in Nisan's construction. Let M be a logspace machine. Fix an input of size n. Then for some $d \geq 1$ the graph of all configurations of M on this input has $\leq n^d$ configurations and runs in time $L \leq n^d$ (see Figure 21.2). Assume without loss of generality—since unneeded random bits can always be ignored—that M uses 1 random bit at each step. Assume also (by giving M a separate worktape that maintains a time counter) that the configuration graph is leveled: It has L levels, with level i containing configurations obtainable at time i. The first level contains only the start node and the last level contains two nodes, "accept" and "reject"; every other level has $W = n^d$ nodes. Each level i node has two outgoing edges to level $i+1$ nodes and the machine's computation at this node involves using the next bit in the random string to pick one of these two outgoing edges. We sometimes call L the *length* of the configuration graph and W the *width*.

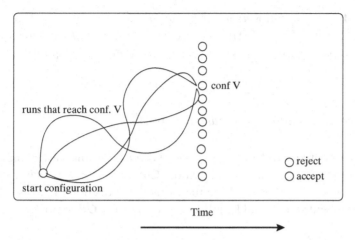

Figure 21.2. Configuration graph for machine M. V is a node/configuration in the middle level. Many different random strings could take the machine from the start configuration to v.

For simplicity we first describe how to reduce the number of random bits by a factor 2. Think of the L steps of the computation as divided in two halves, each consuming $L/2$ random bits. Suppose we use some random string X of length $L/2$ to run the first half, and the machine is now at node v in the middle level. The only information known about X at this point is the index of v, which is a string of length $d \log n$. We may thus view the first half of the branching program as a (deterministic) function that maps $\{0, 1\}^{L/2}$ bits to $\{0, 1\}^{d \log n}$ bits. The Recycling Lemma allows us to use a random seed of length $O(\log n)$ to recycle X to get an almost-random string $\mathsf{Ext}(X, z)$ of length $L/2$, which can be used in the second half of the computation. Thus we can run L steps of computation using $L/2 + O(\log n)$ bits, a saving of almost a factor 2. Using a similar idea recursively, Nisan's generator runs L steps using $O(\log n \log L)$ random bits.

Now we formally define Nisan's generator.

Definition 21.33 *(Nisan's generator)* For some $r > 0$ let $\mathsf{Ext}_k : \{0, 1\}^{kr} \times \{0, 1\}^r \to \{0, 1\}^{kr}$ be an extractor function for each $k \geq 0$. For every integer $k \geq 0$ the associated Nisan generator $G_k : \{0, 1\}^{kr} \to \{0, 1\}^{2^k}$ is defined recursively as (where $|a| = (k - 1)r, |z| = r$)

$$G_k(a \circ z) = \begin{cases} z_1 \ (\text{i.e., first bit of } z) & k = 1 \\ G_{k-1}(a) \circ G_{k-1}(\mathsf{Ext}_{k-1}(a, z)) & k > 1 \end{cases} \qquad \diamond$$

Now we use this generator to prove Theorem 21.31. We only need to show that the probability that the machine goes from the start node to the "accept" node is similar for truly random strings and pseudorandom strings. However, we will prove a stronger statement involving intermediate steps as well.

If nodes u is a node in the configuration graph, and s is a string of length 2^k, then we denote by $f_{u,2^k}(s)$ the node that the machine reaches when started in u and its random string is s. Thus if s comes from some distribution $\mathcal{D}$, we can define a distribution $f_{u,2^k}(\mathcal{D})$ on nodes that are 2^k levels further from u.

Lemma 21.34 *Let* $r = O(\log n)$ *be such that for each* $k \leq d \log n$, $\mathsf{Ext}_k : \{0, 1\}^{kr} \times \{0, 1\}^r \to \{0, 1\}^{kr}$ *is a* $(kr - 2d \log n, \epsilon)$-*extractor. For every machine of the type described in the previous paragraphs, and every node* u *in its configuration graph*

$$\Delta(f_{u,2^k}(U_{2^k}), f_{u,2^k}(G_k(U_{kr}))) \leq 3^k \epsilon \tag{21.16}$$

where U_l *denotes the uniform distribution on* $\{0, 1\}^l$.   ◇

To prove Theorem 21.31 from Lemma 21.34 let $u = u_0$, the start configuration, and $2^k = L$, the length of the entire computation. Choose $3^k \epsilon < 1/10$ (say), which means $\log 1/\epsilon = O(\log L) = O(\log n)$. Using the extractor of Section 21.5.6 as Ext_k, we can let $r = O(\log n)$ and so the seed length $kr = O(r \log L) = O(\log^2 n)$.

PROOF OF LEMMA 21.34: Let ϵ_k denote the maximum value of the left hand side of (21.16) over all machines. The lemma is proved if we can show inductively that $\epsilon_k \leq 2\epsilon_{k-1} + 2\epsilon$. The case $k = 1$ is trivial. At the inductive step, we need to upper bound the distance between two distributions $f_{u,2^k}(\mathcal{D}_1), f_{u,2^k}(\mathcal{D}_4)$, for which we introduce two distributions $\mathcal{D}_2, \mathcal{D}_3$ and use triangle inequality (which holds since $\Delta(\cdot, \cdot)$ is a distance function on distributions):

$$\Delta(f_{u,2^k}(\mathcal{D}_1), f_{u,2^k}(\mathcal{D}_4)) \leq \sum_{i=1}^{3} \Delta(f_{u,2^k}(\mathcal{D}_i), f_{u,2^k}(\mathcal{D}_{i+1})) \tag{21.17}$$

The distributions will be

$$\mathcal{D}_1 = U_{2^k}$$
$$\mathcal{D}_4 = G_k(U_{kr})$$
$$\mathcal{D}_2 = U_{2^{k-1}} \circ G_{k-1}(U_{(k-1)r})$$
$$\mathcal{D}_3 = G_{k-1}(U_{(k-1)r}) \circ G_{k-1}(U'_{(k-1)r}) \qquad (U, U' \text{ are identical but independent})$$

We bound the summands in (21.17) one by one.

Claim 1 $\Delta(f_{u,2^k}(\mathcal{D}_1) - f_{u,2^k}(\mathcal{D}_2)) \leq \epsilon_{k-1}$.

Denote $\Pr[f_{u,2^{k-1}}(U_{2^{k-1}}) = w]$ by $p_{u,w}$ and $\Pr[f_{u,2^{k-1}}(G_{k-1}(U_{(k-1)r})) = w]$ by $q_{u,w}$. According to the inductive assumption,

$$\frac{1}{2} \sum_{w} |p_{u,w} - q_{u,w}| = \Delta(f_{u,2^{k-1}}(U_{2^{k-1}}), f_{u,2^{k-1}}(G_{k-1}(U_{(k-1)r}))) \leq \epsilon_{k-1}$$

Since $\mathcal{D}_1 = U_{2^k}$ may be viewed as two independent copies of $U_{2^{k-1}}$ we have

$$\Delta(f_{u,2^k}(\mathcal{D}_1), f_{u,2^k}(\mathcal{D}_2)) = \sum_{v} \frac{1}{2} \left| \sum_{w} p_{uw} p_{wv} - \sum_{w} p_{uw} q_{wv} \right|$$

where w, v denote nodes 2^{k-1} and 2^k levels respectively from u

$$= \sum_w p_{uw} \frac{1}{2} \sum_v |p_{wv} - q_{wv}|$$

$$\leq \epsilon_{k-1} \quad \left(\text{using inductive hypothesis and } \sum_w p_{uw} = 1 \right)$$

Claim 2 $\Delta(f_{u,2^k}(\mathcal{D}_2), f_{u,2^k}(\mathcal{D}_3)) \leq \epsilon_{k-1}$.

The proof is similar to the previous case and is omitted.

Claim 3 $\Delta(f_{u,2^k}(\mathcal{D}_3), f_{u,2^k}(\mathcal{D}_4)) \leq 2\epsilon$.

We use the Recycling Lemma. Let $g_u : \{0, 1\}^{(k-1)r} \to [1, W]$ be defined as $g_u(a) = f_{u,2^{k-1}}(G_{k-1}(a))$. (To put it in words, apply the Nisan generator to the seed a, and use the result as a random string for the machine, using u as the start node. Output the node you reach after 2^{k-1} steps.) Let $X, Y \in U_{(k-1)r}$ and $z \in U_r$. According to the Recycling Lemma,

$$g_u(X) \circ Y \approx_\epsilon g_u(X) \circ \mathsf{Ext}_{k-1}(X, z)$$

and then Part 5. of Lemma A.21 implies that the equivalence continues to hold if we apply a (deterministic) function to the second string on both sides. Thus

$$g_u(X) \circ g_w(Y) \approx_\epsilon g_u(X) \circ g_w(\mathsf{Ext}_{k-1}(X, z))$$

for all nodes w that are 2^{k-1} levels after u. The left distribution corresponds to $f_{u,2^k}(\mathcal{D}_3)$ (by which we mean that $\Pr[f_{u,2^k}(\mathcal{D}_3) = v] = \sum_w \Pr[g_u(X) = w \wedge g_w(Y) = v]$) and the right one to $f_{u,2^k}(\mathcal{D}_4)$ and the proof is completed. ∎

WHAT HAVE WE LEARNED?

- Often we can easily show that a random object has certain attractive properties, but it's nontrivial to come up with an *explicit* construction of an object with these properties. Yet, once found, such explicit constructions are often extremely useful.
- The behavior of random walks on a graph is tightly related to the eigenvalues of its adjacency matrix (or, equivalently, its normalized version—the random-walk matrix).
- An *expander* graph family is a collection of constant-degree graphs whose second largest eigenvalue is bounded away from 1. Such families can be shown to exist using the probabilistic method, but we also know of *explicit* constructions.
- An ℓ-step random walk on an expander graph is to a certain extend "pseudorandom" and behaves similarly to ℓ randomly chosen vertices under certain measures. This fact has been found useful in a variety of setting, from the randomness efficient error reduction procedure for **BPP** to the logspace algorithm for undirected connectivity.

- Extractors are functions that transform a distribution with a large min-entropy into (close to) the uniform distribution.
- Pseudorandom generators with a "black-box" analysis of their correctness can be used to construct randomness extractors, even though the latter are based on no unproven assumptions or lower bounds.

CHAPTER NOTES AND HISTORY

Expanders were first defined by Bassalygo and Pinsker [BP73], and Pinsker [Pin73] proved their existence using the probabilistic method. They were motivated by the question of finding explicit graphs to replace the random graphs in an error-correcting code construction by Gallager [Gal63]. Margulis [Mar73] gave the first explicit construction of an expander family, although he did not give any bound on the parameter $\lambda(G)$ of graphs G in the family except to prove it is bounded away from 1. Gabber and Galil [GG79] improved Margulis's analysis and gave an explicit bound on $\lambda(G)$, a bound that was later improved by Jimbo and Marouka [JM85]. Lubotzky, Phillips, and Sarnak [LPS86] and Margulis [Mar88] constructed *Ramanujan* graphs that are expander with an optimal dependence between the parameter λ and their degree. The Alon-Boppanna lower bound on the second eigenvalue of a d-regular graph was first stated in [Alo86]; a tight bound on the $o(1)$ error term was given in [Nil04].

The relation between the algebraic (eigenvalue-based) and combinatorial definitions of expanders was developed by Dodziuk, Alon, and Milman, and Alon in the papers [Dod84, AM84, AM85, Alo86]. Sinclair and Jerrum [SJ88] generalized this relation to the case of general reversible Markov chains. All of these results can be viewed as a discrete version of a result by Cheeger [Che70] on compact Riemannian manifolds.

Lemma 21.4 (every connected graph has some spectral gap) is from Alon and Sudakov [AS00a] and is an improved version of a result appearing as Problem 11.29 in Lovász's book [Lov07]. Lemma 21.11 (Expander Mixing Lemma) is from Alon and Chung [AC86] (though there it's stated with $T = V \setminus S$).

Karp, Pippenger, and Sipser [KPS85] were the first to use expanders for derandomization, specifically showing how to use them to reduce the error of an **RP**-algorithm from $1/3$ to $1/\sqrt{k}$ using only $O(k)$ additional random bits. Ajtai, Komlos, and Szemeredi [AKS87] were the first to use random walks on expander graphs for derandomization in their result that every **RL** algorithm using less than $\log^2 n / \log\log n$ random bits can be simulated in deterministic log space. Cohen and Wigderson [CW89] and Impagliazzo-Zuckerman [IZ89] independently showed how to use the [AKS87] analysis to reduce the error of both **RP** and **BPP** algorithms as described in Section 21.2.5 (error reduction from $1/3$ to 2^{-k} using $O(k)$ additional bits). An improved analysis of such walks was given by Gillman [Gil93] who proved the Expander Chernoff Bound (Theorem 21.15). Some additional improvements were given in [Kah97, WX05, Hea06].

The explicit construction of expanders presented in Section 21.3 is due to Reingold, Vadhan, and Wigderson [RVW00], although our presentation follows [RV05, RTV06]. The expansion properties of the replacement product were also analyzed in a particular case of products of two cubes by Gromov [Gro83] and for general graphs (in a somewhat different context) by Martin and Randall [MR00].

Hoory, Linial, and Wigderson [HLW06] give an excellent introduction to expander graphs and their computer science applications. The Alon-Spencer book [AS00b] also contains several results on expanders.

The problem of randomness extraction was first considered in the 1950s by von Neumann [vN51] who wanted to extract randomness from biased (but independent) random coins. This was generlized to Markov chains by Blum [Blu84]. Santha and Vazirani [SV84] studied extraction for the much more general class now known as "Santha Vazirani sources" (see Exercise 21.23), that necessitates adding a seed and allowing the output to have some small statistical distance from the uniform. Vazirani and Vazirani [VV85] showed how to simulate **RP** using a Santha-Vazirani source. Chor and Goldreich [CG85] improved the analysis of [SV84, VV85] and generalized further the class of sources. In particular they introduced the notion of *min-entropy* and studied *block*-sources, where each block has significant min-entropy even conditioned on the previous block. They also studied extraction from several (two or more) independent sources of high min-entropy (i.e., (k, n) sources for $k > n/2$). Zuckerman [Zuc90] put forward the goal of simulating probabilistic algorithms using a single source of high min-entropy and observed this generalizes all models that had been studied to date. (See [SZ94] for an account of various models considered by previous researchers.) Zuckerman also gave the first simulation of probabilistic algorithms from (k, n)-sources assuming $k = \Omega(n)$. We note that extractors were also used implicitly in an early work of Sipser [Sip86] who showed certain conditional derandomization results under the assumption that certain (variants of) extractors exist (though he described them in a different way).

Extractors (albeit with long seed length) were also implicitly constructed and used in cryptography, using pairwise independent hash functions and the *Leftover Hash Lemma* (Lemma 21.26) of Impagliazzo, Levin, and Luby [ILL89] and a related precursor by Bennett, Brassard, and Robert [BBR88]. Nisan [Nis90] then showed that hashing (in particular the [VV85] generator) could be used to obtain provably good pseudorandom generators for logspace. Nisan and Zuckerman [NZ93] first defined extractors. They also gave a new extractor construction and used it to achieve their result that in general the amount of randomness used by a probabilistic algorithm can be reduced from polynomial to linear in the algorithm's space complexity. Since then a long sequence of beautiful works was dedicated to improving the parameters of extractors, on the way discovering many important tools that were used in other areas of theoretical computer science. In particular, Guruswami et al. [GUV07] (slightly improving over Lu et al. [LRVW03]) constructed an extractor that has both seed length and output length within a constant factor of the optimal nonexplicit extractor of Theorem 21.25. See [Sha02] for a good (though slightly outdated) survey on extractor constructions and their applications.

Trevisan's [Tre99] insight about using pseudorandom generators to construct extractors (see Section 21.5.7) has now been greatly extended. It is now understood that three combinatorial objects studied in three different fields are very similar: pseudorandom generators (cryptography and derandomization), extractors (weak random sources) and list-decodable error-correcting codes (coding theory and information theory). Constructions of any one of these objects often gives constructions of the other two. See the survey by Vadhan [Vad07].

Theorem 21.31 is by Nisan [Nis90], who also showed that all of **BPL** can be simulated using polynomial-time and $O(\log^2 n)$ space. The proof we presented is by Impagliazzo, Nisan, and Wigderson [INW94], with the extractor-based viewpoint due to Raz and Reingold [RR99]. Saks and Zhou [SZ95] extended Nisan's techniques to show an $O(\log^{1.5} n)$-space algorithm for every problem in **BPL**.

As perhaps the most important example of an **RL** problem, undirected connectivity has received special attention in the literature. Nisan, Szemeredi, and Wigderson [NSW92] gave the first deterministic algorithm for undirected connectivity using $o(log^2 n)$ space, specifically $O(\log^{1.5} n)$; as mentioned above this result was later generalized to all of **RL** by [SZ95]. Armoni et al. [ATSWZ97] improved the bound for undirected connectivity to $O(\log^{4/3} n)$ space. The deterministic space complexity of undirected connectivity was finally resolved by Reingold [Rei05] who showed that it lies in **L** (Theorem 21.21). Trifonov [Tri05] proved concurrently and independently the slightly weaker result of an $O(\log n \log \log n)$-space algorithm for this problem.

EXERCISES

21.1. Prove Claim 21.1 using the Cauchy-Schwarz Inquality—$|\langle \mathbf{u}, \mathbf{v} \rangle| \leq \|\mathbf{u}\|_2 \|\mathbf{v}\|_2$ for every two vectors $\mathbf{u}, \mathbf{v} \in \mathbb{R}^n$.

21.2. **(a)** Prove Hölder's Inequality (see Section A.5.4): For every p, q with $\frac{1}{p} + \frac{1}{q} = 1$, $\|\mathbf{u}\|_p \|\mathbf{v}\|_q \geq \sum_{i=1}^n |\mathbf{u}_i \mathbf{v}_i|$. Note that the Cauchy-Schwarz Inequality is the special case of Hölder's Inequality with $p = q = 2$.

H540

(b) For a vector $\mathbf{v} \in \mathbb{R}^n$, define $\|\mathbf{v}\|_\infty = \max_{i \in [n]} |\mathbf{v}_i|$. Show that this is a norm and that for every $\mathbf{v}$

$$\|\mathbf{v}\|_\infty = \lim_{p \to \infty} \left(\sum_{i=1}^n |\mathbf{v}_i|^p \right)^{1/p}$$

(c) Prove that $\|\mathbf{v}\|_2 \leq \sqrt{|\mathbf{v}|_1 \|\mathbf{v}\|_\infty}$ for every vector $\mathbf{v} \in \mathbb{R}^n$.

H540

21.3. Prove that if G is an n-vertex bipartite graph then there exists a vector $\mathbf{v} \in \mathbb{R}^n$ such that $A\mathbf{v} = -\mathbf{v}$ where A is the random-walk matrix of G.

21.4. Prove that for every n-vertex d-regular graph G, the diameter of G (maximum over all pairs of distinct vertices i, j in G of the length of the shortest path in G between i and j) is at most $3n/(d + 1)$.

H540

21.5. Recall that the *spectral norm* of a matrix A, denoted $\|A\|$, is defined as the maximum of $\|A\mathbf{v}\|_2$ for every unit vector $\mathbf{v}$. Let A be a symmetric stochastic matrix (i.e., $A = A^\dagger$ and every row and column of A has nonnegative entries summing up to one). Prove that $\|A\| \leq 1$.

H541

21.6. Let A, B be two $n \times n$ matrices.
   (a) Prove that $\|A + B\| \leq \|A\| + \|B\|$.
   (b) Prove that $\|AB\| \leq \|A\|\|B\|$.

21.7. Let A, B be two symmetric stochastic matrices. Prove that $\lambda(A + B) \leq \lambda(A) + \lambda(B)$.

21.8. Prove Lemma 21.16.
   H541

21.9. **(a)** Prove that if a probability distribution X has support of size at most d, its collision probability is at least $1/d$.
   (b) Prove that if G is an (n, d, λ)-graph and X is the distribution over a random neighbor of the first vertex, then the collision probability of X is at most $\lambda^2 + 1/n$.
   (c) Prove that $\lambda \geq \sqrt{\frac{1}{d} - \frac{1}{n}} = \frac{1}{\sqrt{d}} + o(1)$ (where $o(1)$ is a term that tends to 0 with n).

21.10. Recall that the *trace* of a Matrix A, denoted $\mathrm{tr}(A)$, is the sum of the entries along its diagonal.
   (a) Prove that if an $n \times n$ matrix A has eigenvalues $\lambda_1, \ldots, \lambda_n$, then $\mathrm{tr}(A) = \sum_{i=1}^{n} \lambda_i$.
   (b) Prove that if A is a random-walk matrix of an n-vertex graph G, and $k \geq 1$, then $\mathrm{tr}(A^k)$ is equal to n times the probability that a if we select a vertex i uniformly at random and take a k step random walk from i, then we end up back in i.
   (c) Prove that for every d-regular graph G, $k \in \mathbb{N}$ and vertex i of G, the probability that a path of length k from i ends up back in i is at least as large as the corresponding probability in T_d, where T_d is the complete $(d-1)$-ary tree of depth k rooted at i. (That is, every internal vertex has degree d—one parent and $d - 1$ children.)
   (d) Prove that for even k the probability that a path of length k from the root of T_d ends up back at v is at least $2^{k - k \log(d-1)/2 + o(k)}$.
   H541
   (e) Prove that for every n-vertex d-degree graph G, $\lambda(G) \geq \frac{2}{\sqrt{d}}(1 + o(1))$, where $o(1)$ denotes a term, depending on n and d that tends to 0 as n grows.
   H541

21.11. Let an n, d random graph be an n-vertex graph chosen as follows: choose d random permutations $\pi_1, \ldots, \pi_d$ from $[n]$ to $[n]$. Let the the graph G contains an edge (u, v) for every pair u, v such that $v = \pi_i(u)$ for some $1 \leq i \leq d$. Prove that for every n and $d \geq 2$ a random n, d graph is an $(n, 2d, \frac{1}{10})$ edge expander with probability $1 - o(1)$ (i.e., tending to one with n).
   H541

21.12. In this exercise we show how to extend the error-reduction procedure of Section 21.2.5 to two-sided (**BPP**) algorithms.
   (a) Prove that under the conditions of Theorem 21.12, for every subset $I \subseteq [k]$,

$$\Pr[\forall_{i \in I} X_i \in B] \leq ((1 - \lambda)\sqrt{\beta} + \lambda)^{|I|-1}$$

   (b) Conclude that if $|B| < n/100$ and $\lambda < 1/100$, then the probability that there exists a subset $I \subseteq [k]$ such that $|I| > k/10$ and $\forall_{1 \leq i \leq I} X_i \in B$ is at most $2^{-k/100}$.
   (c) Use this to show a procedure that transforms every **BPP** algorithm A that uses m coins and decides a language L with probability 0.99 into an algorithm B that uses $m + O(k)$ coins and decides the language L with probability $1 - 2^{-k}$.

21.13. Prove that for every n-vertex d-regular graph, there exists a subset S of $n/2$ vertices, such that $E(S, \bar{S}) \leq dn/4$. Conclude that there does not exist an (n, d, ρ)-edge expander for $\rho > 1/2$.

H541

21.14. Prove the Expander Mixing Lemma (Lemma 21.11).

H541

21.15. [Tan84] A graph where $|\Gamma(S)| \geq c|S|$ for every not-too-big set S (say, $|S| \leq n/(10d)$) is said to have *vertex expansion* c. This exercise shows that graphs with the minimum possible second eigenvalue $\frac{2}{\sqrt{d}}(1 + o(1))$ have vertex expansion roughly $d/4$. It is known that such graphs have in fact vertex expansion roughly $d/2$ [Kah92], and there are counterexamples showing this is tight. In contrast, random d-regular graphs have vertex expansion $(1 - o(1))d$.

   (a) Prove that if $\mathbf{p}$ is a probability vector, then $\|\mathbf{p}\|_2^2$ is equal to the probability that if i and j are chosen from $\mathbf{p}$, then $i = j$.

   (b) Prove that if $\mathbf{s}$ is the probability vector denoting the uniform distribution over some subset S of vertices of a graph G with random-walk matrix A, then $\|A\mathbf{s}\|_2^2 \geq 1/|\Gamma(S)|$, where $\Gamma(S)$ denotes the set of S's neighbors.

   (c) Prove that if G is an (n, d, λ)-expander graph, and S is a subset of ϵn vertices, then

$$|\Gamma(S)| \geq \frac{|S|}{\lambda^2(1 - \epsilon) + \epsilon}$$

H541

21.16. If G is a graph and S is a subset of G's vertices, then by *contracting* S we mean transforming G into a graph H where all of S's members are replaced by a single vertex s with an edge $\overline{sv}$ in H for every edge $\overline{uv}$ in G where $u \in S$. Let G be an (n, d, ρ)-edge expander, and let H be the $n' = n - (c - 1)k$-vertex cd-degree graph obtained by taking k disjoint c-sized subsets $S_1, \ldots, S_k$ of G's vertices and contracting them, and then adding self loops to the other vertices to ensure that the graph is regular. Prove that H is an $(n', cd, \rho/(2c))$-edge expander. Use this to complete the proof of Theorem 21.19.

H541

21.17. Prove that for every function $\mathsf{Ext} : \{0, 1\}^n \to \{0, 1\}^m$ and there exists an $(n, n - 1)$-source X and a bit $b \in \{0, 1\}$ such that $\Pr[\mathsf{Ext}(X)_1 = b] = 1$ (where $\mathsf{Ext}(X)_1$ denotes the first bit of $\mathsf{Ext}(X)$). Prove that this implies that $\Delta(\mathsf{Ext}(X), U_m) \geq 1/2$.

21.18. **(a)** Show that there is a deterministic poly(n)-time algorithm A that—given an input distributed according to the distribution X with $H_\infty(X) \geq n^{100}$ and black-box access to any function $f : \{0, 1\}^n \to \{0, 1\}$—outputs 1 with probability at least 0.99 if $\mathrm{E}[f(U_n)] \geq 2/3$ and outputs 0 with probability at least 0.99 if $\mathrm{E}[f(U_n)] \leq 1/3$. We call such an algorithm a *function approximator*.

   (b) Show that there is no deterministic polynomial-time function approximator A without getting an additional randomized input (i.e., there is no deterministic function approximator).

H541

   (c) Show that for every probability distribution X, if $\Delta(X, Y) > 1/10$ for every Y with $H_\infty(Y) \geq n/2$, then there is no polynomial-time function approximator that gets X as an input. Conclude that access to a high min entropy distribution is necessary for black-box simulation of **BPP** algorithms.

H541

21.19. Say that a distribution Y is a *convex combination* of distributions $Y_1, \ldots, Y_N$ if there exist some nonnegative numbers $\alpha_1, \ldots, \alpha_N$ summing up to 1 such that Y is the distribution obtained by picking i with probability α_i and sampling an element from Y_i. Prove that if this is the case then for every distribution X,

$$\Delta(X, Y) \le \sum_i \alpha_i \Delta(X, Y_i) \le \max_i \Delta(X, Y_i)$$

H541

21.20. Suppose Boolean function f is (S, ϵ)-hard, and let D be the distribution on m-bit strings defined by picking inputs $x_1, x_2, \ldots, x_m$ uniformly at random and outputting $f(x_1)f(x_2)\cdots f(x_m)$. Show that the statistical distance between D and the uniform distribution is at most ϵm.

21.21. Prove Lemma 21.26.

21.22. Let A be an $n \times n$ matrix with eigenvectors $\mathbf{u}^1, \ldots, \mathbf{u}^n$ and corresponding values $\lambda_1, \ldots, \lambda_n$. Let B be an $m \times m$ matrix with eigenvectors $\mathbf{v}^1, \ldots, \mathbf{v}^m$ and corresponding values $\alpha_1, \ldots, \alpha_m$. Prove that the matrix $A \otimes B$ has eigenvectors $\mathbf{u}^i \otimes \mathbf{v}^j$ and corresponding values $\lambda_i \cdot \alpha_j$.

21.23. Prove that for every two graphs G, G', $\lambda(G \otimes G') \le \lambda(G) + \lambda(G')$ without using the fact that every symmetric matrix is diagonalizable.

H541

21.24. Let G be an n-vertex D-degree graph with ρ-edge expansion for some $\rho > 0$. (That is, for every subset S of G's vertices of size at most $n/2$, the number of edges between S and its complement is at least $\rho d|S|$.) Let G' be a D-vertex d-degree graph with ρ'-edge expansion for some $\rho' > 0$. Prove that $G \circledR G'$ has at least $\rho^2 \rho'/1000$ edge expansion.

H541

CHAPTER 22

Proofs of **PCP** theorems and the Fourier transform technique

The improvements in the constants has many times been obtained by extracting some important property from a previous protocol, using that protocol as a black box and then adding some conceptually new construction. This is more or less what we do in the current paper. ... The long code is universal in that it contains every other binary code as a sub-code. Thus it never hurts to have this code available, but it is still surprising that it is beneficial to have such a wasteful code.
– Johan Håstad, 1997

We saw in Chapter 11 that the **PCP** Theorem implies that computing approximate solutions to many optimization problems is **NP**-hard. This chapter gives a complete proof of the **PCP** Theorem. In Chapter 11 we also mentioned that the **PCP** Theorem does not suffice for proving several other similar results, for which we need stronger (or simply different) "**PCP** Theorems." In this chapter we survey some such results and their proofs. The two main results are Raz's *Parallel Repetition Theorem* (see Section 22.3) and Håstad's Three-Bit **PCP** Theorem (Theorem 22.16). Raz's theorem leads to strong hardness results for the 2CSP problem over large alphabets. Håstad's theorem shows that certificates for **NP** languages can be probabilistically checked by examining only three bits in them. One of the consequences of Håstad's result is that computing a $(7/8 + \epsilon)$-approximation for the MAX-3SAT problem is **NP**-hard for every $\epsilon > 0$. Since we know that 7/8-approximation is in fact possible in polynomial time (see Example 11.2 and Exercise 11.3), this shows (assuming **P** $\neq$ **NP**) that the approximability of MAX-3SAT has an abrupt transition from easy to hard at 7/8. Such a result is called a *threshold* result, and threshold results are now known for a few other problems.

Håstad's result builds on the other results we have studied, including the (standard) **PCP** Theorem, and Raz's theorem. It also uses Håstad's method of analyzing the verifier's acceptance probability using *Fourier transforms*. Such Fourier analysis has also proved useful in other areas in theoretical computer science. We introduce this technique in Section 22.5 by using it to show the correctness of the linearity-testing algorithm of Section 11.5, which completes the proof of the result **NP** $\subseteq$ **PCP**(poly(n), 1) in Section 11.5. We then use Fourier analysis to prove Håstad's Three-Bit **PCP** Theorem.

In Section 22.8 we prove the hardness of approximating the SET-COVER problem. In Section 22.2.3 we prove that computing $n^{-\epsilon}$-approximation to MAX-INDSET in

NP-hard. In Section 22.9 we briefly survey other **PCP** theorems that have been proved, including those that assume the so-called *unique games conjecture*.

22.1 CONSTRAINT SATISFACTION PROBLEMS WITH NONBINARY ALPHABET

In this chapter we will often use the problem $q\mathsf{CSP}_W$, which is defined by extending the definition of $q\mathsf{CSP}$ in Definition 11.11 from binary alphabet to an alphabet of size W.

Definition 22.1 ($q\mathsf{CSP}_W$) For integers $q, W \geq 1$, the $q\mathsf{CSP}_W$ problem is defined analogously to the $q\mathsf{CSP}$ problem of Definition 11.11, except the underlying alphabet is $[W] = \{1, 2, \ldots, W\}$ instead of $\{0, 1\}$. Thus constraints are functions mapping $[W]^q$ to $\{0, 1\}$.

For $\rho < 1$ we define the promise problem $\mathsf{.GAP}q\mathsf{CSP}W\rho$ analogously to the definition of $\rho\text{-}\mathsf{GAP}q\mathsf{CSP}$ for binary alphabet (see Definition 11.13).   ◇

EXAMPLE 22.2

$3\mathsf{SAT}$ is the subcase of $q\mathsf{CSP}_W$ where $q = 3$, $W = 2$, and the constraints are OR's of the involved literals.

   Similarly, the **NP**-complete problem $3\mathsf{COL}$ can be viewed as a subcase of $2\mathsf{CSP}_3$ instances where for each edge (i, j), there is a constraint on the variables u_i, u_j that is satisfied iff $u_i \neq u_j$. The graph is three-colorable iff there is a way to assign a number in $\{0, 1, 2\}$ to each variable such that all constraints are satisfied.

22.2 PROOF OF THE PCP THEOREM

This section proves the **PCP** Theorem. We present Dinur's proof [Din06], which simplifies half of the original proof of [AS92, ALM+92]. Section 22.2.1 gives an outline of the main steps. Section 22.2.2 describes one key step, Dinur's gap amplification technique. Section 22.2.5 describes the other key step, which is from the original proof of the **PCP** Theorem [ALM+92], and its key ideas were presented in the proof of **NP** $\subseteq$ **PCP**$(\text{poly}(n), 1)$ in Section 11.5.

22.2.1 Proof outline for the PCP Theorem

As we have seen, the **PCP** Theorem is equivalent to Theorem 11.14, stating that $\rho\text{-}\mathsf{GAP}q\mathsf{CSP}$ is **NP**-hard for some constants q and $\rho < 1$. Consider the case that $\rho = 1 - \epsilon$ where ϵ is not necessarily a constant but can be a function of m (the number of constraints). Since the number of satisfied constraints is always a whole number, if φ is unsatisfiable, then $\mathsf{val}(\varphi) \leq 1 - 1/m$. Hence, the gap problem $(1 - 1/m)\text{-}\mathsf{GAP3CSP}$ is a generalization of $3\mathsf{SAT}$ and is **NP** hard. The idea behind the proof is to start with this observation, and iteratively show that $(1 - \epsilon)\text{-}\mathsf{GAP}q\mathsf{CSP}$ is **NP**-hard for larger and larger values of ϵ, until ϵ is as large as some absolute constant independent of m. This is formalized in the following definition and lemma.

Definition 22.3 Let f be a function mapping CSP instances to CSP instances. We say that f is a *CL-reduction* (short for *complete linear-blowup reduction*) if it is polynomial-time computable and, for every CSP instance φ, satisfies:

Completeness: If φ is satisfiable then so is $f(\varphi)$.

Linear blowup: If m is the number of constraints in φ, then the new $q\mathsf{CSP}$ instance $f(\varphi)$ has at most Cm constraints and alphabet W, where C and W can depend on the arity and the alphabet size of φ (but not on the number of constraints or variables). ◇

Lemma 22.4 (**PCP** *Main Lemma*) *There exist constants* $q_0 \geq 3$, $\epsilon_0 > 0$, *and a CL-reduction* f *such that for every* $q_0\mathsf{CSP}$*-instance* φ *with binary alphabet, and every* $\epsilon < \epsilon_0$, *the instance* $\psi = f(\varphi)$ *is a* $q_0\mathsf{CSP}$ *(over binary alphabet) satisfying*

$$\mathsf{val}(\varphi) \leq 1 - \epsilon \Rightarrow \mathsf{val}(\psi) \leq 1 - 2\epsilon$$

Lemma 22.4 can be succinctly described as follows:

	Arity	Alphabet	Constraints	Value
Original	q_0	binary	m	$1 - \epsilon$
	$\Downarrow$	$\Downarrow$	$\Downarrow$	$\Downarrow$
Lemma 22.4	q_0	binary	Cm	$1 - 2\epsilon$

This lemma allows us to easily prove the **PCP** Theorem.

Proving Theorem 11.5 from Lemma 22.4

Let $q_0 \geq 3$ be as stated in Lemma 22.4. As already observed, the decision problem $q_0\mathsf{CSP}$ is **NP**-hard. To prove the **PCP** Theorem we give a reduction from this problem to GAP $q_0\mathsf{CSP}$. Let φ be a $q_0\mathsf{CSP}$ instance. Let m be the number of constraints in φ. If φ is satisfiable, then $\mathsf{val}(\varphi) = 1$ and otherwise $\mathsf{val}(\varphi) \leq 1 - 1/m$. We use Lemma 22.4 to amplify this gap. Specifically, apply the function f obtained by Lemma 22.4 to φ a total of $\log m$ times. We get an instance ψ such that if φ is satisfiable, then so is ψ, but if φ is not satisfiable (and so $\mathsf{val}(\varphi) \leq 1 - 1/m$), then $\mathsf{val}(\psi) \leq 1 - \min\{2\epsilon_0, 1 - 2^{\log m}/m\} = 1 - 2\epsilon_0$. Note that the size of ψ is at most $C^{\log m} m$, which is polynomial in m. Thus we have obtained a gap-preserving reduction from L to the $(1 - 2\epsilon_0)$-GAP $q_0\mathsf{CSP}$ problem, and the **PCP** theorem is proved. ∎

The rest of this section proves Lemma 22.4 by combining two transformations: The first transformation amplifies the gap (i.e., fraction of violated constraints) of a given CSP instance, at the expense of increasing the alphabet size. The second transformation reduces back the alphabet to binary, at the expense of a modest reduction in the gap. The transformations are described in the next two lemmas.

Lemma 22.5 (*Gap amplification* [Din06]) *For every* $\ell, q \in \mathbb{N}$, *there exist numbers* $W \in \mathbb{N}, \epsilon_0 > 0$ *and a CL-reduction* $g_{\ell,q}$ *such that for every* $q\mathsf{CSP}$ *instance* φ *with binary alphabet, the instance* $\psi = g_{\ell,q}(\varphi)$ *has arity only 2, uses alphabet of size at most* W *and satisfies*

$$\mathsf{val}(\varphi) \leq 1 - \epsilon \Rightarrow \mathsf{val}(\psi) \leq 1 - \ell\epsilon$$

for every $\epsilon < \epsilon_0$.

Lemma 22.6 *(Alphabet reduction) There exists a constant q_0 and a CL- reduction h such that for every* CSP *instance φ, if φ had arity two over a (possibly nonbinary) alphabet $\{0..W{-}1\}$ then $\psi = h(\varphi)$ has arity q_0 over a binary alphabet and satisfies:*

$$\mathsf{val}(\varphi) \le 1 - \epsilon \Rightarrow \mathsf{val}(h(\varphi)) \le 1 - \epsilon/3$$

Lemmas 22.5 and 22.6 together imply Lemma 22.4 by setting $f(\varphi) = h(g_{6,q_0}(\varphi))$. Indeed, if φ was satisfiable, then $f(\varphi)$ will be also. If $\mathsf{val}(\varphi) \le 1 - \epsilon$, for $\epsilon < \epsilon_0$ (where ϵ_0 the value obtained in Lemma 22.5 for $\ell = 6, q = q_0$) then $\mathsf{val}(g_{6,q_0}(\varphi)) \le 1 - 6\epsilon$ and hence $\mathsf{val}(h(g_{6,q_0}(\varphi))) \le 1 - 2\epsilon$. This composition is described in the following table:

	Arity	Alphabet	Constraints	Value
Original	q_0	binary	m	$1 - \epsilon$
	$\Downarrow$	$\Downarrow$	$\Downarrow$	$\Downarrow$
Lemma 22.5 ($\ell = 6$, $q = q_0$)	2	W	Cm	$1 - 6\epsilon$
	$\Downarrow$	$\Downarrow$	$\Downarrow$	$\Downarrow$
Lemma 22.6	q_0	binary	$C'Cm$	$1 - 2\epsilon$

22.2.2 Dinur's gap amplification: Proof of Lemma 22.5

To prove Lemma 22.5, we need to exhibit a function g that maps a qCSP instance to a 2CSP$_W$ instance over a larger alphabet $\{0..W{-}1\}$ in a way that increases the fraction of violated constraints. In the proof verification viewpoint (Section 11.3), the fraction of violated constraints is merely the soundness parameter. So at first sight, our task merely seems to be reducing the "soundness" parameter of a **PCP** verifier, which as already noted (in the Remarks following Theorem 11.5) can be easily done by repeating the verifier's operation 2 (or more generally, k) times. The problem with this trivial idea is that the CSP instance corresponding to k repeated runs of the verifier is not another 2CSP instance, but an instance of arity $2k$ since the verifier's decision depends upon $2k$ different entries in the proof. In the next chapter, we will see another way of "repeating" the verifier's operation using *parallel repetition*, which does result in 2CSP instances, but greatly increases the size of the CSP instance. By contrast, here we desire a CL-reduction, which means the size must only increase by a constant factor. The key to designing such a CL-reduction is walks in expander graphs, which we describe separately first in Section 22.2.3 since it is of independent interest.

22.2.3 Expanders, walks, and hardness of approximating INDSET

Dinur's proof uses expander graphs, which are described in Chapter 21. Here we recap the facts about expanders used in this chapter, and as illustration we use them to prove a hardness result for MAX-INDSET.

In Chapter 21 we define a parameter $\lambda(G) \in [0, 1]$ for every regular graph G (see Definition 21.2). For every $c \in (0, 1)$, we call a regular graph G satisfying $\lambda(G) \le c$ a *c-expander graph*. If $c < 0.9$, we drop the prefix c and simply call G an *expander graph*. (The choice of the constant 0.9 is arbitrary.) As shown in Chapter 21, for every constant $c \in (0, 1)$ there is a constant d and an algorithm that given input $n \in N$, runs in poly(n) time and outputs the adjacency matrix of an n-vertex d-regular c-expander (see Theorem 21.19).

The main property we need in this chapter is that for every regular graph $G = (V, E)$ and every $S \subseteq V$ with $|S| \leq |V|/2$,

$$\Pr_{(u,v)\in E}[u \in S, v \in S] \leq \frac{|S|}{|V|}\left(\frac{1}{2} + \frac{\lambda(G)}{2}\right) \tag{22.1}$$

(Exercise 22.1) Another property we use is that $\lambda(G^\ell) = \lambda(G)^\ell$ for every $\ell \in \mathbb{N}$, where G^ℓ is obtained by taking the adjacency matrix of G to the ℓth power (i.e., an edge in G^ℓ corresponds to an $(\ell-1)$-step path in G). Thus (22.1) also implies that

$$\Pr_{(u,v)\in E(G^\ell)}[u \in S, v \in S] \leq \frac{|S|}{|V|}\left(\frac{1}{2} + \frac{\lambda(G)^\ell}{2}\right) \tag{22.2}$$

EXAMPLE 22.7

As an application of random walks in expanders, we describe how to prove a stronger version of the hardness of approximation result for INDSET in Theorem 11.15. This is done using the next lemma, which immediately implies (since $m = \text{poly}(n)$) that there is some $\epsilon > 0$ such that computing $n^{-\epsilon}$-approximation to MAX-INDSET is **NP**-hard in graphs of size n. (See Section 22.9.2 for a survey of stronger hardness results for MAX-INDSET.) Below, $\tilde{\alpha}(F)$ denotes the fractional size of the largest independent set in F. It is interesting to note how this lemma gives a more efficient version of the "self-improvement" idea of Theorem 11.15.

Lemma 22.8 *For every $\lambda > 0$, there is a polynomial-time computable reduction f that maps every n-vertex graph F into an m-vertex graph H such that*

$$(\tilde{\alpha}(F) - 2\lambda)^{\log n} \leq \tilde{\alpha}(H) \leq (\tilde{\alpha}(F) + 2\lambda)^{\log n}$$

PROOF: We use random walks to define a more efficient version of the "graph product" used in the proof of Corollary 11.17. Let G be an expander on n nodes that is d-regular (where d is some constant independent of n) and let $\lambda = \lambda(G)$. For notational ease we assume G, F have the same set of vertices. We will map F into a graph H of $nd^{\log n-1}$ vertices in the following way:

- The vertices of H correspond to all the $(\log n-1)$-step paths in the λ-expander G.
- We put an edge between two vertices u, v of H corresponding to the paths $\langle u_1, \ldots, u_{\log n}\rangle$ and $\langle v_1, \ldots, v_{\log n}\rangle$ if there exists an edge in G between two vertices in the set $\{u_1, \ldots, u_{\log n}, v_1, \ldots, v_{\log n}\}$.

It is easily checked that for any independent set in H if we take all vertices of F appearing in the corresponding walks, then that constitutes an independent set in F. From this observation the proof is concluded using Exercise 22.2. ∎

22.2.4 Dinur's gap amplification

We say that a $q\text{CSP}_W$ instance φ is "nice" if it satisfies the following properties:

Property 1: The arity q of φ is 2 (though the alphabet may be nonbinary).

Property 2: Let the *constraint graph* of φ be the graph G with vertex set $[n]$ where for every constraint of φ depending on the variables u_i, u_j, the graph G has the edge (i, j). We allow G to have parallel edges and self-loops. Then G is d-regular for some constant d (independent of the alphabet size), and at every node, half the edges incident to it are self-loops.

Property 3: The constraint graph is an expander. That is, $\lambda(G) \leq 0.9$.

It turns out that when proving Lemma 22.5 we may assume without loss of generality that the CSP instance φ is nice, since there is a relatively simple CL reduction mapping arbitrary qCSP instances to "nice" instances. (See Section 22.A; we note that these CL reductions will actually *lose* a factor depending on q in the soundness gap, but we can regain this factor by choosing a large enough value for t in Lemma 22.9 below.) The rest of the proof consists of a "powering" operation for nice 2CSP instances. This is described in the following lemma.

Lemma 22.9 *(Powering) There is an algorithm that given any* $2CSP_W$ *instance* ψ *satisfying Properties 1 through 3 and an integer* $t \geq 1$ *produces an instance* ψ^t *of* $2CSP$ *such that:*

1. ψ^t *is a* $2CSP_{W'}$-*instance with alphabet size* $W' < W^{d^{5t}}$, *where d denotes the degree of ψ's constraint graph. The instance ψ^t has $d^{t+\sqrt{t}+1}n$ constraints, where n is the number of variables in ψ.*
2. *If ψ is satisfiable, then so is ψ^t.*
3. *For every* $\epsilon < \frac{1}{d\sqrt{t}}$, *if* $\mathsf{val}(\psi) \leq 1 - \epsilon$, *then* $\mathsf{val}(\psi^t) \leq 1 - \epsilon'$ *for* $\epsilon' = \frac{\sqrt{t}}{10^5 dW^4}\epsilon$.
4. *The formula ψ^t is produced from ψ in time-polynomial in m and W^{d^t}.* $\diamond$

PROOF: Let ψ be a $2CSP_W$-instance with n variables and $m = nd$ constraints, and as before let G denote the *constraint graph* of ψ. To prove Lemma 22.9, we first show how we construct the formula ψ^t from ψ. The main idea is a certain "powering" operation on constraint graphs using random walks of a certain length.

Construction of ψ^t

The formula ψ^t will have the same number of variables as ψ. The new variables $\mathbf{y} = y_1, \ldots, y_n$ take values over an alphabet of size $W' = W^{d^{5t}}$, and thus a value of a new variable y_i is a d^{5t}-tuple of values in $\{0..W-1\}$. To avoid confusion in the rest of the proof, we reserve the term "variable" for these new variables, and say "old variables" if we mean the variables of ψ.

We will think of a value of variable y_i as giving a value in $\{0..W-1\}$ to every old variable u_j where j can be reached from i using a path of at most $t + \sqrt{t}$ steps in G (see Figure 22.1). In other words, it gives an assignment for every u_j such that j is in the ball of radius $t + \sqrt{t}$ and center i in G. Since graph G is d-regular, the number of such nodes is at most $d^{t+\sqrt{t}+1}$, which is less than d^{5t}, so this information can indeed be encoded using an alphabet of size W'.

Below, we will often say that an assignment to y_i "claims" a certain value for the old variable u_j. Of course, the assignment to a different variable $y_{i'}$ could claim a different value for u_j; these potential inconsistences make the rest of the proof nontrivial. In fact, the constraints in the $2CSP_{W'}$ instance ψ^t are designed to reveal such consistencies.

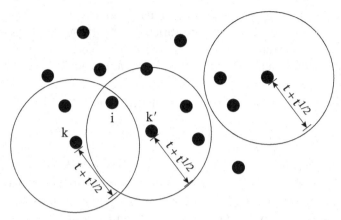

Figure 22.1. The CSP ψ^t consists of n variables taking values in an alphabet of size $W^{d^{5t}}$. An assignment to a new variable y_i encodes an assignment to all old variables of ψ corresponding to nodes that are in a ball of radius $t + \sqrt{t}$ around i in ψ's constraint graph. An assignment $y_1, \ldots, y_n$ to ψ^t may be *inconsistent* in the sense that if j falls in the intersection of two such balls centered at i and i', then y_i and $y_{i'}$ may claim different values for u_j.

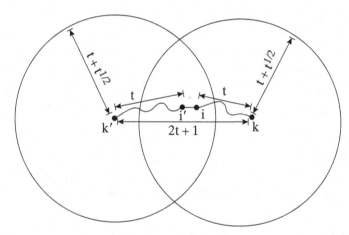

Figure 22.2. ψ^t has one constraint for every path of length $2t + 1$ in ψ's constraint graph, checking that the views of the balls centered on the path's two endpoints are consistent with one another and the constraints of ψ.

For every $(2t + 1)$-step path $p = \langle i_1, \ldots, i_{2t+2} \rangle$ in G, we have one corresponding constraint C_p in ψ^t (see Figure 22.2). The constraint C_p depends on the variables y_{i_1} and $y_{i_{2t+2}}$ (so we do indeed produce an instance of $2\mathsf{CSP}_{W'}$) and outputs FALSE if (and only if) there is some $j \in [2t + 1]$ such that

1. i_j is in the $t + \sqrt{t}$-radius ball around i_1.
2. i_{j+1} is in the $t + \sqrt{t}$-radius ball around i_{2t+2}.
3. If w denotes the value y_{i_1} claims for u_{i_j} and w' denotes the value $y_{i_{2t+2}}$ claims for $u_{i_{j+1}}$, then the pair (w, w') violates the constraint in ψ that depends on u_{i_j} and $u_{i_{j+1}}$.

A few observations are in order. First, the time to produce this $2\mathsf{CSP}_{W'}$ instance is polynomial in m and W^{d^t}, so part 4 of Lemma 22.5 is trivial. Second, for every

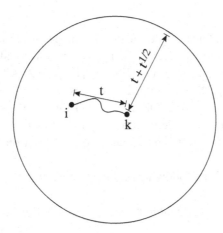

Figure 22.3. An assignment y for ψ^t induces a plurality assignment u for ψ in the following way: u_i gets the most likely value that is claimed for it by y_k, where k is obtained by taking a t-step random walk from i in the constraint graph of ψ.

assignment to the old variables $u_1, u_2, \ldots, u_n$ we can "lift" it to a *canonical* assignment to $y_1, \ldots, y_n$ by simply assigning to each y_i the vector of values assumed by u_j's that lie in a ball of radius $t + \sqrt{t}$ and center i in G. If the assignment to the u_j's was a satisfying assignment for ψ, then this canonical assignment satisfies ψ^t, since it will satisfy all constraints encountered in walks of length $2t + 1$ in G. Thus part 2 of Lemma 22.5 is also trivial. This leaves part 3 of the lemma, the most difficult part. We have to show that if $\mathtt{val}(\psi) \leq 1 - \epsilon$ then every assignment to the y_i's satisfies at most $1 - \epsilon'$ fraction of constraints in ψ^t, where $\epsilon < \frac{1}{d\sqrt{t}}$ and $\epsilon' = \frac{\sqrt{t}}{10^5 dW^4} \epsilon$.

The plurality assignment
To prove part 3 of the lemma, we show how to transform every assignment $\mathbf{y}$, for ψ^t, into an assignment $\mathbf{u}$ for ψ and then argue that if $\mathbf{u}$ violates a "few" (i.e., ϵ fraction) of ψ's constraints then $\mathbf{y}$ violates "many" (i.e., $\epsilon' = \Omega(\sqrt{t}\epsilon)$ fraction) of constraints of ψ^t.

From now on, let us fix some arbitrary assignment $\mathbf{y} = y_1, \ldots, y_n$ to ψ^t's variables. As already noted, the values y_i's may be mutually *inconsistent* and not correspond to any obvious assignment for the old variable u_j's. The following notion is key because it tries to extract a single assignment for the old variables.

For every variable u_i of ψ, we define the random variable Z_i over $\{0, \ldots, W - 1\}$ to be the result of the following process: Starting from the vertex i, take a t step random walk in G to reach a vertex k, and output the value that y_k claims for u_i. We let z_i denote the most likely value of Z_i. If more than one value is most likely, we break ties arbitrarily. We call the assignment $z_1, \ldots, z_n$ the *plurality assignment* (see Figure 22.3). Note that $Z_i = z_i$ with probability at least $1/W$.

Since $\mathtt{val}(\psi) \leq 1 - \epsilon$, *every* assignment for ψ fails to satisfy ϵ fraction of the constraints, and this is therefore also true for the plurality assignment. Hence there exists a set F of $\epsilon m = \epsilon nd/2$ constraints in ψ that are violated by the assignment $\mathbf{z} = z_1, \ldots, z_n$. We will use this set F to show that at least an ϵ' fraction of ψ^t's constraints are violated by the assignment $\mathbf{y}$.

Analysis

The rest of the proof defines events in the following probability space: We pick a $(2t+1)$-step path, denoted $\langle i_1, \ldots, i_{2t+2} \rangle$, in G from among all such paths (in other words, pick a random constraint of ψ^t). For $j \in \{1, 2, \ldots, 2t+1\}$, say that the jth edge in the path, namely (i_j, i_{j+1}), is *truthful* if y_{i_1} claims the plurality value for i_j and $y_{i_{2t+2}}$ claims the plurality value for i_{j+1}. Observe that if the path has an edge that is truthful and also lies in F, then by definition of F the constraint corresponding to that path is unsatisfied. Our goal is to show that at least ϵ' fraction of the paths have such edges.

The proof will follow the following sequence of claims.

Claim 22.10 *For each edge e of G and each $j \in \{1, 2, \ldots, 2t+1\}$,*

$$\Pr[e \text{ is the } j'\text{th edge of the path}] = \frac{1}{|E|} = \frac{2}{nd}$$

PROOF: It is easily checked that in a d-regular graph if we take a random starting point i_1 and pick a random path of length $2t+1$ going of it, then the j'th edge on a random path is also a random edge of G. ∎

The next claim shows that edges that are roughly in the middle of the path (specifically, in the interval of size $\delta\sqrt{t}$ in the middle) are quite likely to be truthful.

Claim 22.11 *Let $\delta < \frac{1}{100W}$. For each edge e of G and each $j \in \{t, t, \ldots, t+\delta\sqrt{t}\}$,*

$$\Pr[j\text{th edge of path is truthful} \mid e \text{ is the } j\text{th edge}] \geq \frac{1}{2W^2}$$

PROOF: The main intuition is that since half the edges of G are self-loops, a random walk of length in $[t - \delta\sqrt{t}, t + \delta\sqrt{t}]$ is statistically very similar to a random walk of length t.

Formally, the lemma is proved by slightly inverting the viewpoint of how the path is picked. By the previous claim, the set of walks of length $2t+1$ that contain $e = (i_j, i_{j+1})$ at the jth step can be generated by concatenating a random walk of length j out of i_j and a random walk of length $2t - j$ out of i_{j+1} (where the two walks are chosen independently). Let i_1 and i_{2t+2} denote the endpoints of these two walks. Then we need to show that

$$\Pr[y_{i_1} \text{ claims plurality value for } i_j \bigwedge y_{i_{2t+2}} \text{ claims plurality value for } i_{j+1}] \geq \frac{1}{2W^2}$$
$$(22.3)$$

Since the plurality assignment was defined using walks of length exactly t, it follows that if j is precisely t, then the expression on the left-hand side in (22.3) is at least $\frac{1}{W} \times \frac{1}{W} = \frac{1}{W^2}$. (This crucially uses that the walks to y_{i_1} and $y_{i_{2t+2}}$ are independently chosen.)

However, here j varies in $\{t, t+1, \ldots, t+\delta\sqrt{t}\}$, so these random walks have lengths between $t - \delta\sqrt{t}$ and $t + \delta\sqrt{t}$. We nevertheless show that the expression cannot be too different from $1/W^2$ for each j.

Since half the edges incident to each vertex are self-loops, we can think of an ℓ-step random walk from a vertex i as follows: (1) throw ℓ coins and let S_ℓ denote the number of the coins that came up "heads" (2) take S_ℓ "real" (non-self-loop) steps on the graph. Recall that S_ℓ, the number of heads in ℓ tosses, is distributed according to the familiar *binomial distribution*.

It can be shown that the distributions S_t and $S_{t+\delta\sqrt{t}}$ are within statistical distance at most 10δ for every δ, t (see Exercise 22.3). In other words,

$$\frac{1}{2}\sum_m \left| \Pr[S_t = m] - \Pr[S_{t+\delta\sqrt{t}} = m] \right| \leq 10\delta$$

It follows that the distribution of the endpoint of a t-step random walk out of e will be *statistically close* to the endpoint of a $(t + \delta\sqrt{t})$-step random walk, and the same is true for the $(t - \delta\sqrt{t})$-step random walk. Thus the expression on the left-hand side of (22.3) is at least

$$\left(\frac{1}{W} - 10\delta\right)\left(\frac{1}{W} - 10\delta\right) \geq \frac{1}{2W^2}$$

which completes the proof. ∎

Now let V be the random variable denoting the number of edges among the middle $\delta\sqrt{t}$ edges that are truthful and in F. Since it is enough for a path to contain one such edge for the corresponding constraint to be violated, our goal is to to show that $\Pr[V > 0] \geq \epsilon'$.

The previous two claims imply that the chance that any particular one of the edges in the interval of size $\delta\sqrt{t}$ is truthful and in F is $\frac{|F|}{|E|} \times \frac{1}{2W^2}$. Hence linearity of expectations implies

$$E[V] \geq \delta\sqrt{t} \times \frac{|F|}{|E|} \times \frac{1}{2W^2} = \frac{\delta\sqrt{t}\epsilon}{2W^2}$$

This shows that $E[V]$ is high, but we are not done since the expectation could be high and yet V could still be 0 for most of the walks. To rule this out, we consider the second moment. This calculation is the only place we use the fact that the contraint graph is an expander.

Claim 22.12 $E[V^2] \leq 30\epsilon\delta\sqrt{t}d.$ ◇

PROOF: Let random variable V' denote the number of edges in the middle interval that are in F. Since V counts the number of edges that are in F *and* are truthful, $V \leq V'$. It suffices to show $E[V'^2] \leq 30\epsilon\delta\sqrt{t}d$. To prove this we use the mixing property of expanders and the fact that F contains ϵ fraction of the edges.

Specifically, for $j \in \{t, t, \ldots, t + \delta\sqrt{t}\}$ let I_j be an indicator random variable that is 1 if the jth edge is in F and 0 otherwise. Then $V' = \sum_{j \in \{t,t,\ldots,t+\delta\sqrt{t}\}} I_j$. Let S be the set of vertices that have at least one end point in F, implying $|S|/n \leq d\epsilon$.

$$E[V'^2] = E[\sum_{jj'} I_j I_{j'}]$$

$$= E[\sum_j I_j^2] + E[\sum_{j \neq j'} I_j I_{j'}]$$

$$= \epsilon\delta\sqrt{t} + E[\sum_{j \neq j'} I_j I_{j'}] \quad \text{(linearity of expectation and Claim 22.10)}$$

$$= \epsilon\delta\sqrt{t} + 2\sum_{j<j'} \Pr[(j\text{th edge is in } F) \wedge (j'\text{th edge is in } F)]$$

$$\leq \epsilon\delta\sqrt{t} + 2\sum_{j<j'} \Pr[(j\text{th vertex of walk lies in } S) \wedge (j'\text{th vertex of walk lies in } S)]$$

$$\leq \epsilon\delta\sqrt{t} + 2\sum_{j<j'} \epsilon d(\epsilon d + (\lambda(G))^{j'-j}) \quad \text{(using (22.2))}$$

$$\leq \epsilon\delta\sqrt{t} + 2\epsilon^2\delta\sqrt{t}d^2 + 2\epsilon\delta\sqrt{t}d\sum_{k\geq 1}(\lambda(G))^k$$

$$\leq \epsilon\delta\sqrt{t} + 2\epsilon^2\delta\sqrt{t}d^2 + 20\epsilon\delta\sqrt{t}d \quad \text{(using } \lambda(G) \leq 0.9)$$

$$\leq 30\epsilon\delta\sqrt{t}d \quad \text{(using } \epsilon < \tfrac{1}{d\sqrt{t}}, \text{ an assumption of Lemma 22.9)}$$

∎

Finally, since $\Pr[V > 0] \geq E[V]^2/E[V^2]$ for any nonnegative random variable (see Exercise 22.4), we conclude that $\Pr[V > 0] \geq \frac{\sqrt{t}}{10^5 dW^4}\epsilon = \epsilon'$, and Lemma 22.9 is proved. ∎

22.2.5 Alphabet reduction: Proof of Lemma 22.6

Interestingly, the main component in the proof of Lemma 22.6 is the exponential-sized **PCP** of Section 11.5 (An alternative proof is explored in Exercise 22.5.)

Let φ be a 2CSP instance as in the statement of Lemma 22.6, with n variables $u_1, u_2, \ldots, u_n$, alphabet $\{0..W-1\}$ and m constraints $C_1, C_2, \ldots, C_m$. Think of each variable as taking values that are bit strings in $\{0, 1\}^{\log W}$. Then if constraint C_s involves variables, say, u_i, u_j, we may think of it as a circuit applied to the bit strings representing u_i, u_j where the constraint is said to be satisfied iff this circuit outputs 1. Say ℓ is an upper bound on the size of this circuit over all constraints. Note that ℓ is at most $2^{2\log W} < W^4$. We will assume without loss of generality that all circuits have the same size.

The idea in alphabet reduction will be to write a small CSP instance for each of these circuits, and replace each old variable by a set of new variables. This technique from [AS92] was called *verifier composition*, and more recently, a variant was called *PCP's of proximity,* and both names stem from the "proof verification" view of **PCP**'s (see Section 11.2). We state the result (a simple corollary of Theorem 11.19) first in the verification viewpoint and then translate into the CSP viewpoint.

Corollary 22.13 (*PCP of proximity*) *There exists a verifier V that given any circuit C with 2k input wires and size ℓ has the following property:*

1. *If $\mathbf{u_1}, \mathbf{u_2}$ are strings of k bits each such that $\mathbf{u_1} \circ \mathbf{u_2}$ is a satisfying assignment for circuit C, then there is a string π_3 of size $2^{\text{poly}(\ell)}$ such that V accepts $\mathsf{WH}(\mathbf{u_1}) \circ \mathsf{WH}(\mathbf{u_2}) \circ \pi_3$ with probability 1.*
2. *For every three bit strings π_1, π_2, π_3, where π_1 and π_2 have size 2^k, if V accepts $\pi_1 \circ \pi_2 \circ \pi_3$ with probability at least $1/2$, then π_1, π_2 are 0.99-close to $\mathsf{WH}(\mathbf{u_1})$, $\mathsf{WH}(\mathbf{u_2})$, respectively, for some k-bit strings $\mathbf{u_1}, \mathbf{u_2}$ where $\mathbf{u_1} \circ \mathbf{u_2}$ is a satisfying assignment for circuit C.*
3. *V runs in poly(ℓ) time, uses poly(ℓ) random bits and examines only O(1) bits in the provided strings.* ◇

Before giving the proof, we describe how it allows us to do alphabet reduction, as promised. First we note that in the CSP viewpoint of Corollary 22.13, (see Table 11.1) the variables are the bits of π_1, π_2, π_3, and V can be represented as a CSP instance of size $2^{\text{poly}(\ell)}$ in these new variables. The arity of the constraints is the number of bits that the verifier reads in the proof, which is *some fixed constant independent of W and ϵ*. The fraction of satisfied constraints is the acceptance probability of the verifier.

Returning to the instance whose alphabet size we want to reduce, we replace each original variable u_i from the alphabet $\{0, \ldots, W-1\}$ by a sequence $U_i = (U_{i,1}, \ldots, U_{i,2^W})$ of 2^W binary-valued variables, which in a valid assignment would be an encoding of u_i using the Walsh-Hadamard code. For each old constraint $C_s(u_i, u_j)$ we apply the constraint satisfaction view of Corollary 22.13, using C_s as the circuit whose assignment is being verified. Thus for each original constraint C_s we have a vector of $2^{\text{poly}(\ell)}$ new binary-valued variables Π_s, which plays the role of π_3 in Corollary 22.13, whereas U_i, U_j play the role of π_1, π_2, respectively. The set of new constraints corresponding to C_s is denoted $\mathcal{C}_s$. As already noted, the arity of the new constraints is some fixed constant independent of W, ϵ.

The overall CSP instance is the union of these constraints $\cup_{s=1}^{m} \mathcal{C}_s$; see Figure 22.4. Clearly, if the old instance was satisfiable, then so is this union. Now we show that if some assignment satisfies more than $1 - \epsilon/3$ fraction of the new constraints, then we can construct an assignment for the original instance that satisfies more than $1 - \epsilon$ fraction of its constraints. This is done by "decoding" the assignment for each each set of new variables U_i by the following rule: if U_i is 0.99-close to some linear function $\mathsf{WH}(a_i)$, then use a_i as the assignment for the old variable u_i, and otherwise use an arbitrary string. Now consider how well we did on any old constraint $C_s(u_i, u_j)$. If the decodings a_i, a_j of U_i, U_j do not satisfy C_s, then Corollary 22.13 implies that at least half the constraints of $\mathcal{C}_s$ were not satisfied anyway. Thus if δ is the fraction of old constraints that are not satisfied, then $\delta/2 \leq \epsilon/3$, implying $\delta < 2\epsilon/3$, and the lemma is proved.

To finish, we prove Corollary 22.13.

PROOF (OF COROLLARY 22.13): The proof uses the reduction from CKT-SAT to QUADEQ (see Section 11.5.2 and Exercise 11.15). This reduction transforms a circuit C with ℓ wires (where "inputs" are considered as wires in the circuit) to an instance of QUADEQ of with ℓ variables and $O(\ell)$ equations where the variables in the QUADEQ instance correspond to values of wires in the circuit. Thus every solution to the QUADEQ instance has ℓ bits, of which the first k bits give a satisfying assignment to the circuit.

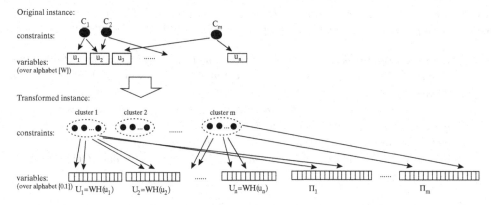

Figure 22.4. The alphabet reduction transformation maps a $2\mathsf{CSP}$ instance φ over alphabet $\{0..W{-}1\}$ into a $q\mathsf{CSP}$ instance ψ over the binary alphabet. Each variable of φ is mapped to a block of binary variables that in the correct assignment will contain the Walsh-Hadamard encoding of this variable. Each constraint C_ℓ of φ depending on variables u_i, u_j is mapped to a cluster of constraints corresponding to all the **PCP** of proximity constraints for C_ℓ. These constraint depend on the encoding of u_i and u_j, and on additional auxiliary variables that in the correct assignment contain the **PCP** of proximity proof that these are indeed encoding of values that make the constraint C_ℓ true.

The verifier expects π_3 to contain whatever our verifier of Theorem 11.19 expects in the proof for this instance of QUADEQ, namely, a linear function f that is $\mathsf{WH}(w)$, and another linear function g that is $\mathsf{WH}(w \otimes w)$, where w satisfies the QUADEQ instance. The verifier checks these functions as described in the proof of Theorem 11.19.

However, in the current setting our verifier is also given strings π_1, π_2, which we think of as functions $\pi_1, \pi_2 : \mathrm{GF}(2)^k \to \mathrm{GF}(2)$. The verifier checks that both are 0.99-close to linear functions, say $\tilde{\pi}_1, \tilde{\pi}_2$. Then to check that $\tilde{f}$ encodes a string whose first $2k$ bits are the same as the string encoded by $\tilde{\pi}_1, \tilde{\pi}_2$, the verifier does the following *concatenation test*, which uses the properties of the Walsh-Hadamard code.

Concatenation test
We are given three linear functions π_1, π_2, f that encode strings of lengths $k, k,$ and ℓ, respectively. Denoting by **u** and **v** the strings encoded by π_1, π_2, respectively (that is, $\pi_1 = \mathsf{WH}(\mathbf{u})$ and $\pi_2 = \mathsf{WH}(\mathbf{v})$), and by w the string encoded by f, we have to check by examining only $O(1)$ bits in these functions that $\mathbf{u} \circ \mathbf{v}$ is the same as the first $2k$ bits of w. By the random subsum principle, the following simple test rejects with probability 1/2 if this is not the case. Pick random $\mathbf{x}, \mathbf{y} \in \{0, 1\}^k$, and denote by $\mathbf{XY} \in \mathrm{GF}(2)^\ell$ the string whose first k bits are $\mathbf{x}$, the next k bits are $\mathbf{y}$ and the remaining bits are all 0. Accept if $f(\mathbf{XY} = \pi_1(\mathbf{x}) + \pi_2(\mathbf{y})$ and else reject. ∎

22.3 HARDNESS OF $2\mathsf{CSP}_W$: TRADEOFF BETWEEN GAP AND ALPHABET SIZE

The problem $2\mathsf{CSP}_W$ often plays a role in proofs of advanced **PCP** theorems. The (standard) **PCP** Theorem implies that there is some constant W and some $\nu < 1$ such that computing ν-approximation to $2\mathsf{CSP}_W$ is **NP**-hard (see Definition 22.1).

Corollary 22.14 *(of **PCP** Theorem) There is some $v < 1$ and some W such that $GAP\,2CSP_W(v)$ is **NP**-hard.*   ◇

For advanced **PCP** theorems we would like to prove the same result for smaller v, without making W too large. (*Note*: If W is allowed to be $\exp(n)$ then the problem is **NP**-hard even for $v = 0$!) At first glance the "gap amplification" of Lemma 22.5 seems relevant, but that doesn't suffice because, first, it cannot lower v below some fixed constant and, second, it greatly increases the alphabet size. The next theorem gives the best tradeoff possible (up to the value of c) between these two parameters. For further constructions of **PCP**s, it is useful to restrict attention to a special subclass of $2CSP$ instances, which have the so-called *projection* property. This means that for each constraint $\varphi_r(y_1, y_2)$ and each value of y_1, there is a *unique* value of y_2 such that $\varphi_r(y_1, y_2) = 1$. Another way to state this is that for each constraint φ_r there is a function $h:[W] \to [W]$ such that the constraint is satisfied by (u, v) iff $h(u) = v$.

A $2CSP$ instance is said to be *regular* if every variable appears in the same number of constraints.

Theorem 22.15 *(Raz [Raz95]) There is a $c > 1$ such that for every $t > 1$, $GAP\,2CSP_W(\epsilon)$ is **NP**-hard for $\epsilon = 2^{-t}, W = 2^{ct}$, and this is true also for $2CSP$ instances that are regular and have the projection property.*   ◇

A weaker version of this theorem, with a somewhat simpler proof, was obtained by Feige and Kilian [FK93]. This weaker version is sufficient for many applications, including for Håstad's 3-bit **PCP** theorem (see Section 22.4).

22.3.1 Idea of Raz's proof: Parallel repetition

Let φ be the $2CSP_W$ instances produced by the reduction of Corollary 22.14. For some $v < 1$ it has the property that either $\mathtt{val}(\varphi) = 1$ or $\mathtt{val}(\varphi) = v < 1$, but deciding which case holds is hard. There is an obvious "powering" idea for trying to lower the gap while maintaining the arity at 2. Let φ^{*t} denote the following instance. Its variables are t-tuples of variables of φ. Its constraints correspond to t-tuples of constraints, in the sense that for every t-tuple of constraints $\varphi_1(y_1, z_1), \varphi_2(y_2, 2), \dots, \varphi_t(y_t, z_t)$ the new instance has a constraint of arity 2 involving the new variables $(y_1, y_2, \dots, y_t)$ and $(z_1, z_2, \dots, z_t)$ and the Boolean function describing this constraint is simply

$$\bigwedge_{i=1}^{t} \varphi_i(y_i, z_i)$$

(To put it in words, the new constraint is satisfied iff all the t constituent constraints are.)

In the verification viewpoint, this new $2CSP$ instance corresponds to running the verifier in parallel t times, hence Raz's Theorem is also called the *Parallel Repetition Theorem*.

It is easy to convert a satisfying assignment for φ into one for φ^{*t} by taking t-tuples of the values. Furthermore, given an assignment for φ that satisfies v fraction of the constraints, it is easy to see that the assignment that forms t-tuples of these values satisfies at least ν^t fraction of the constraints of φ^{*t}. It seemed "obvious" to researchers that no assignment can do better. Then a simple counterexample was found, whereby more than ν^t fraction of constraints in φ^{*t} could be satisfied (see Exercise 22.6). Raz shows, however, that no assignment can satisfy more than ν^{ct} fraction of the constraints of φ^{*t}, where c depends upon the alphabet size W. The proof is quite difficult, though there have been some simplifications (see the chapter notes and the book's Web site).

22.4 HÅSTAD'S 3-BIT PCP THEOREM AND HARDNESS OF MAX-3SAT

In Chapter 11 we showed **NP** = **PCP**$(\log n, 1)$, in other words certificates for membership in **NP** languages can be checked by examining $O(1)$ bits in them. Now we are interested in keeping the number of query bits as low as possible, *while keeping the soundness around* $1/2$. The next theorem shows that the number of query bits can be reduced to three, and furthermore the verifier's decision process consists of simply looking at the parity of these three bits.

Theorem 22.16 *(Håstad's 3-bit* **PCP**[Hås97]*)*
*For every $\delta > 0$ and every language $L \in$ **NP**, there is a **PCP**-verifier V for L making three (binary) queries having completeness parameter $1 - \delta$ and soundness parameter at most $1/2 + \delta$.*
Moreover, the tests used by V are linear. That is, given a proof $\pi \in \{0, 1\}^m$, V chooses a triple $(i_1, i_2, i_3) \in [m]^3$ and $b \in \{0, 1\}$ according to some distribution and accepts iff $\pi_{i_1} + \pi_{i_2} + \pi_{i_3} = b \pmod 2$.

22.4.1 Hardness of approximating MAX-3SAT

We first note that Theorem 22.16 is intimately connected to the hardness of approximating a problem called MAX-E3LIN, which is a subcase of 3CSP$_2$ in which the constraints specify the *parity* of triples of variables. Another way to think of such an instance is that it gives a set of linear equations mod 2 where each equation has at most three variables. We are interested in determining the largest subset of equations that are simultaneously satisfiable. We claim that Theorem 22.16 implies that $(1/2 + \nu)$-approximation to this problem is **NP**-hard for every $\nu > 0$. This is a *threshold result* since the problem has a simple $1/2$-approximation algorithm. (It uses observations similar to those we made in context of MAX-3SAT in Chapter 11; a random assignment satisfies, in the expectation, half of the constraints, and this observation can be turned into a deterministic algorithm that satisfies at least half of the equations.)

To prove our claim about the hardness of MAX-E3LIN, we convert the verifier of Theorem 22.16 into an equivalent CSP by the recipe of Section 11.3. Since the verifier imposes parity constraints on triples of bits in the proof, the equivalent CSP instance is an instance of MAX-E3LIN where either $1 - \delta$ fraction of the constraints are satisfiable, or at most $1/2 + \delta$ are. Since distinguishing between the two cases is **NP**-hard, we conclude that it is **NP**-hard to compute a ρ-approximation to MAX-E3LIN where $\rho = \frac{1/2 + \delta}{1 - \delta}$.

Since $\delta > 0$ is allowed to be arbitrarily small, ρ can be arbitrarily close to $1/2$, and we conclude that $(1/2 + \nu)$-approximation is **NP**-hard for every $\nu > 0$.

Also note that the fact that completeness is strictly less than 1 in Theorem 22.16 is inherent if $\mathbf{P} \neq \mathbf{NP}$, since determining if there is a solution satisfying *all* of the equations (in other words, the satisfiability problem for MAX-E3LIN) is possible in polynomial time using Gaussian elimination

Now we prove a hardness result for MAX-3SAT, which as mentioned earlier, is also a threshold result.

Corollary 22.17 *For every $\epsilon > 0$, computing $(7/8 + \epsilon)$-approximation to* MAX-3SAT *is* **NP**-*hard.*   ◇

PROOF: We reduce MAX-E3LIN to MAX-3SAT. Take the instance of MAX-E3LIN produced by the above reduction, where we are interested in determining whether $(1 - \nu)$ fraction of the equations can be satisfied or at most $1/2 + \nu$ are. Represent each linear constraint by four $3CNF$ clauses in the obvious way. For example, the linear constraint $a+b+c = 0 \pmod 2$ is equivalent to the clauses $(\overline{a} \vee b \vee c), (a \vee \overline{b} \vee c), (a \vee b \vee \overline{c}), (\overline{a} \vee \overline{b} \vee \overline{c})$. If a, b, c satisfy the linear constraint, they satisfy all four clauses and otherwise they satisfy at most three clauses. We conclude that in one case at least $(1 - \epsilon)$ fraction of clauses are simultaneously satisfiable, and in the other case at most $1 - (\frac{1}{2} - \nu) \times \frac{1}{4} = \frac{7}{8} + \frac{\nu}{4}$ fraction are. The ratio between the two cases tends to $7/8$ as ν decreases. Since Theorem 22.16 implies that distinguishing between the two cases is **NP**-hard for every constant ν, the result follows. ∎

22.5 TOOL: THE FOURIER TRANSFORM TECHNIQUE

Theorem 22.16 is proved using Fourier analysis. The continuous Fourier transform is extremely useful in mathematics and engineering. Likewise, the discrete Fourier transform has found many uses in algorithms and complexity, in particular for constructing and analyzing **PCP**s. The Fourier transform technique for **PCP**s involves calculating the maximum acceptance probability of the verifier using Fourier analysis of the functions presented in the proof string. (See Note 22.21 for a broader perspective of uses of discrete Fourier transforms in combinatorial and probabilistic arguments.) It is delicate enough to give "tight" inapproximability results for MAX-INDSET, MAX-3SAT, and many other problems.

To introduce the technique we start with a simple example: analysis of the linearity test over GF(2) (i.e., proof of Theorem 11.21). We then introduce the *Long Code* and show how to test for membership in it. These ideas are then used to prove Håstad's 3-Bit PCP Theorem.

22.5.1 **Fourier transform over** $GF(2)^n$

The Fourier transform over $GF(2)^n$ is a tool to study functions on the Boolean hypercube. In this chapter, it will be useful to use the set $\{+1, -1\} = \{\pm 1\}$ instead of $\{0, 1\}$.

To transform $\{0, 1\}$ to $\{\pm 1\}$, we use the mapping $b \mapsto (-1)^b$ (i.e., $0 \mapsto +1$, $1 \mapsto -1$). Thus we write the hypercube as $\{\pm 1\}^n$ instead of the more usual $[0, 1]^n$. Note this maps the XOR operation (i.e., addition in GF(2)) into the multiplication operation over $\mathbb{R}$.

The set of functions from $\{\pm 1\}^n$ to $\mathbb{R}$ defines a 2^n-*dimensional Hilbert space* (i.e., a vector space with an associated inner product) as follows. Addition and multiplication by a scalar are defined in the natural way: $(f + g)(\mathbf{x}) = f(\mathbf{x}) + g(\mathbf{x})$ and $(\alpha f)(\mathbf{x}) = \alpha f(\mathbf{x})$ for every $f, g : \{\pm 1\}^n \to \mathbb{R}, \alpha \in \mathbb{R}$. We define the inner product of two functions f, g, denoted $\langle f, g \rangle$, to be $E_{\mathbf{x} \in \{\pm 1\}^n}[f(\mathbf{x})g(\mathbf{x})]$. (This is the *expectation inner product*.)

The *standard basis* for this space is the set $\{\mathbf{e_x}\}_{\mathbf{x} \in \{\pm 1\}^n}$, where $\mathbf{e_x}(\mathbf{y})$ is equal to 1 if $\mathbf{y} = \mathbf{x}$, and equal to 0 otherwise. This is an orthogonal basis, and every function $f : \{\pm 1\}^n \to \mathbb{R}$ can be represented in this basis as $f = \sum_{\mathbf{x}} a_{\mathbf{x}} \mathbf{e_x}$. For every $\mathbf{x} \in \{\pm 1\}^n$, the coefficient $a_{\mathbf{x}}$ is equal to $f(\mathbf{x})$.

The *Fourier basis* is an alternative orthonormal basis that contains, for every subset $\alpha \subseteq [n]$, a function χ_α where $\chi_\alpha(\mathbf{x}) = \prod_{i \in \alpha} x_i$. (We define $\chi_\emptyset$ to be the function that is 1 everywhere). This basis is actually the Walsh-Hadamard code (see Section 11.5.1) in disguise: The basis vectors correspond to the *linear* functions over GF(2). To see this, note that every linear function of the form $\mathbf{b} \mapsto \mathbf{a} \odot \mathbf{b}$ (with $\mathbf{a}, \mathbf{b} \in \{0, 1\}^n$) is mapped by our transformation to the function taking $\mathbf{x} \in \{\pm 1\}^n$ to $\prod_{i \text{ s.t. } a_i = 1} x_i$. To check that the Fourier basis is indeed an orthonormal basis for $\mathbb{R}^{2^n}$, note that the random subsum principle implies that for every $\alpha, \beta \subseteq [n]$, $\langle \chi_\alpha, \chi_\beta \rangle = \delta_{\alpha, \beta}$ where $\delta_{\alpha, \beta}$ is equal to 1 iff $\alpha = \beta$ and equal to 0 otherwise.

Remark 22.18

Note that in the $\{-1, 1\}$ view, the basis functions can be viewed as *multilinear polynomials* (i.e., multivariate polynomials whose degree in each variable is 1). Thus the fact that every real-valued function $f : \{-1, 1\}^n$ has a Fourier expansion can also be phrased as "Every such function can be represented by a multilinear polynomial." This is very much in the same spirit as the polynomial representations used in Chapters 8 and 11.

Since the Fourier basis is an orthonormal basis, every function $f : \{\pm 1\}^n \to \mathbb{R}$ can be represented as $f = \sum_{\alpha \subseteq [n]} \hat{f}_\alpha \chi_\alpha$. We call $\hat{f}_\alpha$ the αth *Fourier coefficient* of f. We will often use the following simple lemma:

Lemma 22.19 *Every two functions $f, g : \{\pm 1\}^n \to \mathbb{R}$ satisfy*

1. $\langle f, g \rangle = \sum_\alpha \hat{f}_\alpha \hat{g}_\alpha$
2. *(Parseval's Identity)* $\langle f, f \rangle = \sum_\alpha \hat{f}_\alpha^2$

PROOF: The second property follows from the first. To prove the first we expand

$$\langle f, g \rangle = \langle \sum_\alpha \hat{f}_\alpha \chi_\alpha, \sum_\beta \hat{g}_\beta \chi_\beta \rangle = \sum_{\alpha, \beta} \hat{f}_\alpha \hat{g}_\beta \langle \chi_\alpha, \chi_\beta \rangle = \sum_{\alpha, \beta} \hat{f}_\alpha \hat{g}_\beta \delta_{\alpha, \beta} = \sum_\alpha \hat{f}_\alpha \hat{g}_\alpha$$

∎

EXAMPLE 22.20

Some examples for the Fourier transform of particular functions:

1. The majority function on 3 variables (i.e., the function $MAJ(u_1, u_2, u_3)$ that outputs $+1$ if and only if at least two of its inputs are $+1$, and -1 otherwise) can be expressed as $1/2u_1 + 1/2u_2 + 1/2u_3 - 1/2u_1u_2u_3$. Thus, it has four Fourier coefficients equal to $1/2$ and the rest are equal to zero.

2. If $f(u_1, u_2, \ldots, u_n) = u_i$ (i.e., f is a *coordinate function*, a concept we will see again in context of long codes) then $f = \chi_{\{i\}}$ and so $\hat{f}_{\{i\}} = 1$ and $\hat{f}_\alpha = 0$ for $\alpha \neq \{i\}$.

3. If f is a random Boolean function on n bits, then each $\hat{f}_\alpha$ is a random variable that is a sum of 2^n binomial variables (equally likely to be $1, -1$) and hence looks like a normally distributed variable with standard deviation $2^{n/2}$ and mean 0. Thus with high probability, all 2^n Fourier coefficients have values in $[-\frac{\text{poly}(n)}{2^{n/2}}, \frac{\text{poly}(n)}{2^{n/2}}]$.

22.5.2 The connection to PCPs: High-level view

In the PCP context we are interested in *Boolean-valued* functions (i.e., those from $GF(2)^n$ to $GF(2)$). Under our transformation they turn into functions from $\{\pm 1\}^n$ to $\{\pm 1\}$. Thus we say that $f : \{\pm 1\}^n \to \mathbb{R}$ is *Boolean* if $f(\mathbf{x}) \in \{\pm 1\}$ for every $\mathbf{x} \in \{\pm 1\}^n$. Note that if f is Boolean then $\langle f, f \rangle = E_\mathbf{x}[f(\mathbf{x})^2] = 1$.

On a high level, we use the Fourier transform in the soundness proofs for PCPs to show that if the verifier accepts a proof π with high probability, then π is "close to" being "well-formed" (where the precise meaning of "close-to" and "well-formed" is context dependent). Usually we relate the acceptance probability of the verifier to an expectation of the form $\langle f, g \rangle = E_\mathbf{x}[f(\mathbf{x})g(\mathbf{x})]$, where f and g are Boolean functions arising from the proof. We then use techniques similar to those used to prove Lemma 22.19 to relate this acceptance probability to the Fourier coefficients of f, g, allowing us to argue that if the verifier's test accepts with high probability, then f and g have few relatively large Fourier coefficients. This will provide us with some nontrivial useful information about f and g, since in a "generic" or random function, all the Fourier coefficient are small and roughly equal.

22.5.3 Analysis of the linearity test over $GF(2)$

We will now prove Theorem 11.21, thus completing the proof of the **PCP** Theorem. Recall that the linearity test is provided a function $f : GF(2)^n \to GF(2)$ and has to determine whether f has significant agreement with a linear function. To do this it picks $\mathbf{x}, \mathbf{y} \in GF(2)^n$ randomly and accepts iff $f(\mathbf{x} + \mathbf{y}) = f(\mathbf{x}) + f(\mathbf{y})$.

Now we rephrase this test using $\{\pm 1\}$ instead of $GF(2)$, so linear functions turn into Fourier basis functions. For every two vectors $\mathbf{x}, \mathbf{y} \in \{\pm 1\}^n$, we denote by $\mathbf{xy}$ their componentwise multiplication. That is, $\mathbf{xy} = (x_1y_1, \ldots, x_ny_n)$. Note that for every basis function $\chi_\alpha(\mathbf{xy}) = \chi_\alpha(\mathbf{x})\chi_\alpha(\mathbf{y})$.

For two Boolean functions f, g, their inner product $\langle f, g \rangle$ is equal to the fraction of inputs on which they *agree* minus the fraction of inputs on which they *disagree*. It follows that for every $\epsilon \in [0, 1]$ and functions $f, g : \{\pm 1\}^n \to \{\pm 1\}$, f has agreement $\frac{1}{2} + \frac{\epsilon}{2}$ with g iff $\langle f, g \rangle = \epsilon$. Thus, if f has a large Fourier coefficient, then it has significant agreement with some Fourier basis function, or in the $GF(2)$ worldview, f is close to some linear function. This means that Theorem 11.21 concerning the correctness of the linearity test can be rephrased as follows.

NOTE 22.21 *(Self-Correlated Functions, Isoperimetry, Phase Transitions)*

Although it is surprising to see Fourier transforms used in proofs of PCP theorems, in retrospect this is quite natural. We try to put this in perspective, and refer the reader to the survey of Kalai and Safra [KS06] and the Web-based lecture notes of O'Donnell, Mossell and others for further background on this topic.

Classically, Fourier tranforms are very useful in proving results of the following form: "If a function is correlated with itself in some structured way, then it belongs to some small family of functions." In the PCP setting, the "self-correlation" of a function $f : \{0, 1\}^n \to \{0, 1\}$ means that if we run some designated verifier on f that examines only a few bits in it, then this verifier accepts with reasonable probability. For example, in the linearity test over $GF(2)$, the acceptance probability of the test is $E_{x,y}[I_{x,y}]$ where $I_{x,y}$ is an indicator random variable for the event $f(x)+f(y) = f(x+y)$.

Another classical use of Fourier transforms is study of *isoperimetry*, which is the study of subsets of "minimum surface area." A simple example is the fact that of all connected regions in $\mathbb{R}^2$ with a specified area, the circle has the minimum perimeter. Again, isoperimetry can be viewed as a study of "self-correlation" by thinking of the characteristic function of the set in question and realizing that the "perimeter" of "surface" of the set consists of points in space where taking a small step in some direction causes the value of this function to switch from 1 to 0.

Håstad's "noise" operator of Section 22.7 appears in works of mathematicians Nelson, Bonamie, Beckner, and others on *hypercontractive estimates*, and the general theme is again one of identifying properties of functions based upon their "self-correlation" behavior. One considers the correlation of the function f with the function $T_\rho(f)$ obtained by (roughly speaking) computing at each point the average value of f in a small ball around that point. One can show that the norms of f and $T_\rho(f)$ are related—not used in Håstad's proof but very useful in the **PCP** theorems surveyed in Section 22.9; see also Exercise 22.10 for a small taste.

Fourier transforms and especially hypercontractivity estimates have also proved useful in study of *phase transitions* in random graphs (e.g., see Friedgut [Fri99]). The simplest case is the graph model $G(n, p)$ whereby each possible edge is included in the graph independently with probability p. A *phase transition* is a value of p at which the graph goes from almost never having a certain property to almost always having that property. For example, it is known that there is some constant c such that around $p = c \log n/n$ the probability of the graph being connected suddenly jumps from close to 0 to close to 1. Fourier transforms are useful to study phase transition because a phase transition is as an isoperimetry problem on a "Graph" (with a capital G) where each "Vertex" is an n-vertex graph, and an "Edge" between two "Vertices" means that one of the graphs is obtained by adding a few edges to the graph. Note that adding a few edges corresponds to raising the value of p by a little.

Finally, we mention some interesting uses of Fourier transforms in the results mentioned in Sections 22.9.4 and 22.9.5. These involve isoperimetry on the

---

hypercube $\{0, 1\}^n$. One can study isoperimetry in a graph setting by defining "surface area" of a subset of vertices as the "number of edges leaving the set," or some other notion, and then try to study isoperimetry in such settings. The Fourier transform can be used to prove isoperimetry theorems about hypercube and hypercube-like graphs. The reason is that a subset $S \subseteq \{0, 1\}^n$ is nothing but a Boolean function that is 1 on S and -1 elsewhere. Assuming the graph is D-regular, and $|S| = 2^{n-1}$

$$E_{(x,y): \text{ edge}}[f(x)f(y)] = \frac{1}{2^n D}\left(|E(S,S)| + |\overline{S},\overline{S}| - 2|E(S,\overline{S})|\right),$$

which implies that the fraction of edges of S that leave the set is $1/2 - E[f(x)f(y)]/2$. This kind of expression can be analysed using the Fourier transform; see Exercise 22.11(b).

Theorem 22.22 *Suppose that* $f : \{\pm 1\}^n \to \{\pm 1\}$ *satisfies* $\Pr_{x,y}[f(xy) = f(x)f(y)] \geq \frac{1}{2} + \epsilon$. *Then, there is some* $\alpha \subseteq [n]$ *such* $\hat{f}_\alpha \geq 2\epsilon$. ◇

PROOF: We can rephrase the hypothesis as $E_{x,y}[f(xy)f(x)f(y)] \geq (\frac{1}{2}+\epsilon) - (\frac{1}{2}-\epsilon) = 2\epsilon$. We note that from now on we do not need f to be Boolean, but merely to satisfy $\langle f, f \rangle = 1$.

Expressing f by its Fourier expansion,

$$2\epsilon \leq \mathop{E}_{x,y}[f(xy)f(x)f(y)] = \mathop{E}_{x,y}[(\sum_\alpha \hat{f}_\alpha \chi_\alpha(xy))(\sum_\beta \hat{f}_\beta \chi_\beta(x))(\sum_\gamma \hat{f}_\gamma \chi_\gamma(y))].$$

Since $\chi_\alpha(xy) = \chi_\alpha(x)\chi_\alpha(y)$ this becomes

$$= \mathop{E}_{x,y}[\sum_{\alpha,\beta,\gamma} \hat{f}_\alpha \hat{f}_\beta \hat{f}_\gamma \chi_\alpha(x)\chi_\alpha(y)\chi_\beta(x)\chi_\gamma(y)].$$

Using linearity of expectation,

$$= \sum_{\alpha,\beta,\gamma} \hat{f}_\alpha \hat{f}_\beta \hat{f}_\gamma \mathop{E}_{x,y}[\chi_\alpha(x)\chi_\alpha(y)\chi_\beta(x)\chi_\gamma(y)]$$

$$= \sum_{\alpha,\beta,\gamma} \hat{f}_\alpha \hat{f}_\beta \hat{f}_\gamma \mathop{E}_{x}[\chi_\alpha(x)\chi_\beta(x)]\mathop{E}_{y}[\chi_\alpha(y)\chi_\gamma(y)]$$

(because x, y are independent)

By orthonormality $E_x[\chi_\alpha(x)\chi_\beta(x)] = \delta_{\alpha,\beta}$, so we simplify to

$$= \sum_\alpha \hat{f}_\alpha^3$$

$$\leq (\max_\alpha \hat{f}_\alpha) \times (\sum_\alpha \hat{f}_\alpha^2) = \max_\alpha \hat{f}_\alpha$$

since $\sum_\alpha \hat{f}_\alpha^2 = \langle f, f \rangle = 1$. Hence $\max_\alpha \hat{f}_\alpha \geq 2\epsilon$ and the theorem is proved. ∎

22.6 COORDINATE FUNCTIONS, LONG CODE, AND ITS TESTING

Håstad's 3-Bit PCP Theorem uses a coding method called the *long code*. Let $W \in \mathbb{N}$. We say that $f : \{\pm1\}^W \to \{\pm1\}$ is a *coordinate function* if there is some $w \in [W]$, such that $f(x_1, x_2, \ldots, x_W) = x_w$; in other words, $f = \chi_{\{w\}}$.[1] (Aside: Unlike the previous section, here we use W instead of n for the number of variables; the reason is to be consistent with our use of W for the alphabet size in $2\mathsf{CSP}_W$ in Section 22.7.)

Definition 22.23 *(Long Code)* The *long code* for $[W]$ encodes each $w \in [W]$ by the table of all values of the function $\chi_{\{w\}} : \{\pm1\}^{[W]} \to \{\pm1\}$.   ◇

Note that w, normally written using $\log W$ bits, is being represented using a table of 2^W bits, a doubly exponential blowup! This inefficiency is the reason for calling the code "long."

The problem of testing for membership in the Long Code is defined by analogy to the earlier test for the Walsh-Hadamard code. We are given a function $f : \{\pm1\}^W \to \{\pm1\}$, and wish to determine if f has good agreement with $\chi_{\{w\}}$ for some w, namely, whether $\hat{f}_{\{w\}}$ is significant. Such a test is described in Exercise 22.5, but it is not sufficient for the proof of Håstad's Theorem, which requires a test using only *three* queries. Below we show such a three query test, albeit at the expense of achieving the following weaker guarantee: If the test passes with high probability then f has a good agreement with a function χ_α where $|\alpha|$ is small (but not necessarily equal to 1). This weaker conclusion will be sufficient in the proof of Theorem 22.16.

Let $\rho > 0$ be some arbitrarily small constant. The test picks two uniformly random vectors $\mathbf{x}, \mathbf{y} \in_R \{\pm1\}^W$ and then a vector $\mathbf{z} \in \{\pm1\}^W$ according to the following distribution: for every coordinate $i \in [W]$, with probability $1 - \rho$ we choose $z_i = +1$, and with probability ρ we choose $z_i = -1$. Thus with high probability, about ρ fraction of coordinates in $\mathbf{z}$ are -1 and the other $1 - \rho$ fraction are $+1$. We think of $\mathbf{z}$ as a "noise" vector. The test accepts iff $f(\mathbf{x})f(\mathbf{y}) = f(\mathbf{xyz})$. Note that the test is similar to the linearity test except for the use of the noise vector $\mathbf{z}$.

Suppose $f = \chi_{\{w\}}$. Then since $b \cdot b = 1$ for $b \in \{\pm1\}$,

$$f(\mathbf{x})f(\mathbf{y})f(\mathbf{xyz}) = x_w y_w (x_w y_w z_w) = 1 \cdot z_w$$

Hence the test accepts iff $z_w = 1$, which happens with probability $1 - \rho$. We now prove a certain converse.

Lemma 22.24 *If the test accepts with probability* $1/2 + \delta$, *then* $\sum_\alpha \hat{f}_\alpha^3 (1 - 2\rho)^{|\alpha|} \geq 2\delta$.   ◇

---

[1]   Some texts call such a function a *dictatorship* function, since one variable ("the dictator") completely determines the outcome. The name comes from social choice theory, which studies different election setups. That field has also been usefully approached using Fourier analysis ideas described in Note 22.21.

PROOF: If the test accepts with probability $1/2+\delta$ then $E[f(\mathbf{x})f(\mathbf{y})f(\mathbf{xyz})] = 2\delta$. Replacing f by its Fourier expansion, we have

$$2\delta \leq \mathop{E}_{\mathbf{x},\mathbf{y},\mathbf{z}}\left[\left(\sum_\alpha \hat{f}_\alpha \chi_\alpha(\mathbf{x})\right) \cdot \left(\sum_\beta \hat{f}_\beta \chi_\beta(\mathbf{y})\right) \cdot \left(\sum_\gamma \hat{f}_\gamma \chi_\gamma(\mathbf{xyz})\right)\right]$$

$$= \mathop{E}_{\mathbf{x},\mathbf{y},\mathbf{z}}\left[\sum_{\alpha,\beta,\gamma} \hat{f}_\alpha \hat{f}_\beta \hat{f}_\gamma \chi_\alpha(\mathbf{x})\chi_\beta(\mathbf{y})\chi_\gamma(\mathbf{x})\chi_\gamma(\mathbf{y})\chi_\gamma(\mathbf{z})\right]$$

$$= \sum_{\alpha,\beta,\gamma} \hat{f}_\alpha \hat{f}_\beta \hat{f}_\gamma \mathop{E}_{\mathbf{x},\mathbf{y},\mathbf{z}}\left[\chi_\alpha(\mathbf{x})\chi_\beta(\mathbf{y})\chi_\gamma(\mathbf{x})\chi_\gamma(\mathbf{y})\chi_\gamma(\mathbf{z})\right]$$

Orthonormality implies the expectation is 0 unless $\alpha = \beta = \gamma$, so this is

$$= \sum_\alpha \hat{f}_\alpha^3 \mathop{E}_{\mathbf{z}}[\chi_\alpha(z)]$$

Now $E_{\mathbf{z}}[\chi_\alpha(\mathbf{z})] = E_{\mathbf{z}}\left[\prod_{w\in\alpha} z_w\right]$, which is equal to $\prod_{w\in\alpha} E[z_w] = (1-2\rho)^{|\alpha|}$ because each coordinate of $\mathbf{z}$ is chosen independently. Hence we get that

$$2\delta \leq \sum_\alpha \hat{f}_\alpha^3 (1-2\rho)^{|\alpha|}. \quad \blacksquare$$

The conclusion of Lemma 22.24 is reminiscent of the calculation in the proof of Theorem 22.22, except for the extra factor $(1-2\rho)^{|\alpha|}$. This factor depresses the contribution of $\hat{f}_\alpha$ for large α, allowing us to conclude that the small α's must contribute a lot. This is formalized in the following corollary (which is a simple calculation and left as Exercise 22.8).

Corollary 22.25 *If f passes the long code test with probability $1/2+\delta$, then for $k = \frac{1}{2\rho}\log\frac{1}{\epsilon}$, there exists α with $|\alpha| \leq k$ such that $\hat{f}_\alpha \geq 2\delta - \epsilon$.* ◇

22.7 PROOF OF THEOREM 22.16

We now prove Håstad's Theorem. The starting point is the $2CSP_W$ instance φ given by Theorem 22.15, so we know that φ is either satisfiable, or we can satisfy at most ϵ fraction of the constraints, where ϵ is arbitrarily small. Let W be the alphabet size, n be the number of variables, and m the number of constraints. We think of an assignment as a function π from $[n]$ to $[W]$. Since the 2CSP instance has the *projection* property, we can think of each constraint φ_r as being equivalent to some function $h: [W] \to [W]$, where the constraint is satisfied by assignment π iff $\pi(j) = h(\pi(i))$.

Håstad's verifier uses the Long Code, but expects these encodings to be *bifolded*, a technical property we now define and is motivated by the observation that coordinate functions satisfy $\chi_{\{w\}}(-\mathbf{v}) = -\chi_{\{w\}}(\mathbf{v})$ for every vector $\mathbf{v}$.

Definition 22.26 A function $f: \{\pm 1\}^W \to \{\pm 1\}$ is *bifolded* if for all $\mathbf{v} \in \{\pm 1\}^W$, $f(-\mathbf{v}) = -f(\mathbf{v})$. ◇

(Aside: In mathematics we would call such a function *odd* but the term "folding" is more standard in the **PCP** literature where it has a more general meaning.)

Whenever the **PCP** proof is supposed to contain a codeword of the Long Code, we may assume without loss of generality that the function is bifolded. The reason is that the verifier can identify, for each pair of inputs $\mathbf{v}, -\mathbf{v}$, one designated representative—say the one whose first coordinate is $+1$ – and just define $f(-\mathbf{v})$ to be $-f(\mathbf{v})$. One benefit— though of no consequence in the proof – of this convention is that bifolded functions require only half as many bits to represent. We will use the following fact.

Lemma 22.27 *If $f : \{\pm 1\}^W \to \{\pm 1\}$ is bifolded and $\hat{f}_\alpha \neq 0$ then $|\alpha|$ must be an odd number (and in particular, nonzero).*   ◇

PROOF: By definition,

$$\hat{f}_\alpha = \langle f, \chi_\alpha \rangle = \mathop{\mathrm{E}}_{\mathbf{v}}[f(\mathbf{v}) \prod_{i \in \alpha} \mathbf{v}_i]$$

If $|\alpha|$ is even then $\prod_{i \in \alpha} \mathbf{v}_i = \prod_{i \in \alpha}(-\mathbf{v}_i)$. So if f is bifolded, the contributions corresponding to $\mathbf{v}$ and $-\mathbf{v}$ cancel each other and the entire expectation is 0. ∎

Håstad's verifier

Now we describe Håstad's verifier V_H. It expects the proof $\tilde{\pi}$ to consist of a satisfying assignment to φ where the value of each of the n variables is encoded using the (bifolded) long code. Thus the proof contains $n2^W$ bits (rather, $n2^{W-1}$ if we take the bifolding into account), which V_H treats as n functions $f_1, f_2, \ldots, f_n$ each mapping $\{\pm 1\}^W$ to $\{\pm 1\}$. The verifier V_H randomly picks a constraint, say $\varphi_r(i, j)$, in the $2\mathsf{CSP}_W$ instance. Then V_H tries to check (while reading only three bits!) that functions f_i, f_j encode two values in $[W]$ that would satisfy φ_r, in other words, they encode two values w, u satisfying $h(w) = u$ where $h : [W] \to [W]$ is the function describing constraint φ_r. Now we describe this test, which is reminiscent of the long code test we saw earlier.

THE BASIC HÅSTAD TEST.

> *Given:* Two functions $f, g : \{\pm 1\}^W \to \{\pm 1\}$. A function $h : [W] \to [W]$.
>
> *Goal:* Check if f, g are Long Codes of two values w, u such that $h(w) = u$.
>
> *Test:* For $u \in [W]$ let $h^{-1}(u)$ denote the set $\{w : h(w) = u\}$. Note that the sets $\{h^{-1}(u) : u \in [W]\}$ form a partition of $[W]$. For a string $\mathbf{y} \in \{\pm 1\}^W$ we define $\mathcal{H}^{-1}(\mathbf{y})$ as the string in $\{\pm 1\}^W$ such that for every $w \in [W]$, the wth bit of $\mathcal{H}^{-1}(\mathbf{y})$ is $y_{h(w)}$. In other words, for each $u \in [W]$, the bit y_u appears in $\mathcal{H}^{-1}(\mathbf{y})$ in all coordinates corresponding to $h^{-1}(u)$. V_H chooses uniformly at random $\mathbf{v}, \mathbf{y} \in \{\pm 1\}^W$ and chooses $\mathbf{z} \in \{\pm 1\}^W$ by letting $z_i = +1$ with probability $1 - \rho$ and $z_i = -1$ with probability ρ. It then accepts if
>
> $$f(\mathbf{v})g(\mathbf{y}) = f(\mathcal{H}^{-1}(\mathbf{y})\mathbf{v}\mathbf{z}) \tag{22.4}$$

and rejects otherwise.

Translating back from $\{\pm 1\}$ to $\{0, 1\}$, note that V_H's test is indeed linear, as it accepts iff $\tilde{\pi}[i_1] + \tilde{\pi}[i_2] + \tilde{\pi}[i_3] = b$ for some $i_1, i_2, i_3 \in [n2^W]$ and $b \in \{0, 1\}$. (The bit b can indeed equal 1 because of the way V_H ensures the bifolding property.)

Now since ρ, ϵ can be arbitrarily small the next claim suffices to prove the theorem. (Specifically, making $\rho = \epsilon^{1/3}$ makes the completeness parameter at least $1 - \epsilon^{1/3}$ and the soundness at most $1/2 + \epsilon^{1/3}$.)

Claim 22.28 *(Main) If φ is satisfiable, then there is a proof which V_H accepts with probability $1 - \rho$. If $\mathsf{val}(\varphi) \le \epsilon$, then V_H accepts no proof with probability more than $1/2 + \delta$ where $\delta = \sqrt{\epsilon/\rho}$.*   ◇

The rest of the section is devoted to proving Claim 22.28.

Completeness part; easy

If φ is satisfiable, then take any satisfying assignment $\pi : [n] \to [W]$ and form a proof for V_H containing the bifolded Long Code encodings of the n values. (As already noted, coordinate functions are bifolded.) To show that V_H accepts this proof with probability $1 - \rho$, it suffices to show that the Basic Håstad Test accepts with probability $1 - \rho$ for every constraint.

Suppose f, g are Long Codes of two integers w, u satisfying $h(w) = u$. Then, using the fact that for $x \in \{\pm 1\}$, $x^2 = 1$,

$$f(\mathbf{v})g(\mathbf{y})f(\mathcal{H}^{-1}(\mathbf{y})\mathbf{vz}) = \mathbf{v}_w \mathbf{y}_u (\mathcal{H}^{-1}(\mathbf{y})_w \mathbf{v}_w \mathbf{z}_w)$$

$$= \mathbf{v}_w \mathbf{y}_u (\mathbf{y}_{h(w)} \mathbf{v}_w \mathbf{z}_w) \qquad = \mathbf{z}_w$$

Hence V_H accepts iff $\mathbf{z}_w = 1$, which happens with probability $1 - \rho$.

Soundness of V_H; more difficult

We first show that if the Basic Håstad Test accepts two functions f, g with probability significantly more than $1/2$, then the Fourier transforms of f, g must be correlated. To formalize this we define for $\alpha \subseteq [W]$,

$$h_2(\alpha) = \{u \in [W] : \ |h^{-1}(u) \cap \alpha| \text{ is odd}\} \qquad (22.5)$$

Notice in particular that for *every* $t \in h_2(\alpha)$ there is at least one $w \in \alpha$ such that $h(w) = t$.

In the next lemma δ is allowed to be negative. It is the only place where we use the bifolding property.

Lemma 22.29 *Let $f, g : \{\pm 1\}^W \to \{\pm 1\}$, be bifolded functions and $h : [W] \to [W]$ be such that they pass the Basic Håstad Test (22.4) with probability at least $1/2 + \delta$. Then*

$$\sum_{\alpha \subseteq [W], \alpha \neq \emptyset} \hat{f}_\alpha^2 \hat{g}_{h_2(\alpha)} (1 - 2\rho)^{|\alpha|} \ge 2\delta \qquad (22.6)$$

◇

PROOF: By hypothesis, f, g are such that $E[f(\mathbf{v})f(\mathbf{v}\mathcal{H}^{-1}(\mathbf{y})\mathbf{z})g(\mathbf{y})] \geq 2\delta$. Replacing f, g by their Fourier expansions we get

$$2\delta \leq = \operatorname*{E}_{\mathbf{v},\mathbf{y},\mathbf{z}} \left[\left(\sum_\alpha \hat{f}_\alpha \chi_\alpha(\mathbf{v}) \right) \left(\sum_\beta \hat{g}_\beta \chi_\beta(\mathbf{y}) \right) \left(\sum_\gamma \hat{f}_\gamma \chi_\gamma(\mathbf{v}\mathcal{H}^{-1}(\mathbf{y})\mathbf{z}) \right) \right]$$

$$= \sum_{\alpha,\beta,\gamma} \hat{f}_\alpha \hat{g}_\beta \hat{f}_\gamma \operatorname*{E}_{\mathbf{v},\mathbf{y},\mathbf{z}} \left[\chi_\alpha(\mathbf{v}) \chi_\beta(\mathbf{y}) \chi_\gamma(\mathbf{v}) \chi_\gamma(\mathcal{H}^{-1}(\mathbf{y})) \chi_\gamma(\mathbf{z}) \right]$$

By orthonormality this simplifies to

$$= \sum_{\alpha,\beta} \hat{f}_\alpha^2 \hat{g}_\beta \operatorname*{E}_{\mathbf{y},\mathbf{z}} \left[\chi_\beta(\mathbf{y}) \chi_\alpha(\mathcal{H}^{-1}(\mathbf{y})) \chi_\alpha(\mathbf{z}) \right]$$

$$= \sum_{\alpha,\beta} \hat{f}_\alpha^2 \hat{g}_\beta (1 - 2\rho)^{|\alpha|} \operatorname*{E}_{\mathbf{y}} \left[\chi_\alpha(\mathcal{H}^{-1}(\mathbf{y}) \chi_\beta(\mathbf{y}) \right] \tag{22.7}$$

since $\chi_\alpha(\mathbf{z}) = (1 - 2\rho)^{|\alpha|}$, as noted in our analysis of the Long Code test. Now we have

$$\operatorname*{E}_{\mathbf{y}}[\chi_\alpha(\mathcal{H}^{-1}(\mathbf{y})) \chi_\beta(\mathbf{y})] = \operatorname*{E}_{\mathbf{y}} \left[\prod_{w \in \alpha} \mathcal{H}^{-1}(\mathbf{y})_w \prod_{u \in \beta} \mathbf{y}_u \right]$$

$$= \operatorname*{E}_{\mathbf{y}} \left[\prod_{w \in \alpha} \mathbf{y}_{h(w)} \prod_{u \in \beta} \mathbf{y}_u \right]$$

which is 1 if $h_2(\alpha) = \beta$ and 0 otherwise. Hence (22.7) simplifies to

$$\sum_\alpha \hat{f}_\alpha^2 \hat{g}_{h_2(\alpha)} (1 - 2\rho)^{|\alpha|}$$

Finally we note that since the functions are assumed to be bifolded, the Fourier coefficients $\hat{f}_\emptyset$ and $\hat{g}_\emptyset$ are zero. Thus those terms can be dropped from the summation and the lemma is proved. ■

The following lemma completes the proof of the Claim 22.28 and hence of Håstad's 3-bit PCP Theorem.

Lemma 22.30 *Suppose φ is an instance of* $2\mathsf{CSP}_W$ *such that* $\mathsf{val}(\varphi) < \epsilon$. *If ρ, δ satisfy $\rho\delta^2 > \epsilon$ then verifier V_H accepts any proof with probability at most $1/2 + \delta$.*   ◇

PROOF: Suppose V_H accepts a proof $\tilde{\pi}$ of length $n2^W$ with probability at least $1/2 + \delta$. We give a probabilistic construction of an assignment π to the variables of φ such that the expected fraction of satisfied constraints is at least $\rho\delta^2$, whence it follows by the probabilistic method that a specific assignment π exists that lives up to this expectation. This contradicts the hypothesis if $\rho\delta^2 > \epsilon$.

The distribution from which π is chosen

We can think of $\tilde{\pi}$ as providing, for every $i \in [n]$, a function $f_i : \{\pm 1\}^W \to \{\pm 1\}$. The probabilistic construction of assignment π comes in two steps. We first use f_i to define a distribution $\mathcal{D}_i$ over $[W]$ as follows: Select $\alpha \subseteq [W]$ with probability $\hat{f}_\alpha^2$ where $f = f_i$, and then select w at random from α. This is well-defined because $\sum_\alpha \hat{f}_\alpha^2 = 1$ and (due to bifolding) the Fourier coefficient $f_\emptyset$ corresponding to the empty set is 0. We then pick $\pi[i]$ by drawing a random sample from distribution $\mathcal{D}_i$. Thus the assignment π is a random element of the product distribution $\prod_{i=1}^m \mathcal{D}_i$. We wish to show

$$\underset{\pi}{\mathrm{E}}[\ \underset{r\in[m]}{\mathrm{E}}\ [\pi \text{ satisfies } r\text{th constraint}]] \geq \rho\delta^2 \tag{22.8}$$

The analysis

For every constraint φ_r where $r \in [m]$ denote by $1/2 + \delta_r$ the conditional probability that the Basic Håstad Test accepts $\tilde{\pi}$, conditioned on V_H having picked φ_r. (*Note:* δ_r could be negative.) Then the acceptance probability of V_H is $\mathrm{E}_r[\frac{1}{2} + \delta_r]$ and hence $\mathrm{E}_r[\delta_r] = \delta$. We show that

$$\Pr_\pi[\pi \text{ satisfies } \varphi_r] \geq \rho\delta_r^2, \tag{22.9}$$

whence it follows that the left-hand side of (22.8) is (by linearity of expectation) at least $\rho \mathrm{E}_{r\in[m]}[\delta_r^2]$. Since $E[X^2] \geq E[X]^2$ for any random variable, this in turn is at least $\rho(\mathrm{E}_r[\delta_r])^2 \geq \rho\delta^2$. Thus to finish the proof it only remains to prove (22.9).

Let $\varphi_r(i,j)$ be the rth constraint and let h be the function describing this constraint, so that

$$\pi \text{ satisfies } \varphi_r \qquad \text{iff} \qquad h(\pi[i]) = \pi[j]$$

Let I_r be the indicator random variable for the event $h(\pi[i] = \pi[j])$. From now on we use the shorthand $f = f_i$ and $g = f_j$. What is the chance that a pair of assignments $\pi[i] \in_{\mathrm{R}} D_i$ and $\pi[j] \in_{\mathrm{R}} D_j$ will satisfy $\pi[j] = h(\pi[i])$? Recall that we pick these values by choosing α with probability $\hat{f}_\alpha^2$, β with probability $\hat{g}_\beta^2$, and $\pi[i] \in_{\mathrm{R}} \alpha, \pi[j] \in_{\mathrm{R}} \beta$. Assume that α is picked first. The conditional probability that $\beta = h_2(\alpha)$ is $\hat{g}_{h_2(\alpha)}^2$. If $\beta = h_2(\alpha)$, we claim that the conditional probability of satisfying the constraint is at least $1/|\alpha|$. The reason is that by definition, $h_2(\alpha)$ consists of u such that $|h^{-1}(u) \cap \alpha|$ is odd, and an odd number cannot be 0! Thus regardless of which value $\pi[j] \in h_2(\alpha)$ we pick, there *exists* $w \in \alpha$ with $h(w) = \pi[j]$, and the conditional probability of picking such a w as $\pi[i]$ is at least $1/|\alpha|$. Thus, we have that

$$\sum_\alpha \frac{1}{|\alpha|} \hat{f}_\alpha^2 \hat{g}_{h_2(\alpha)}^2 \leq \underset{D_i,D_j}{\mathrm{E}}[I_r] \tag{22.10}$$

This is similar to (but not quite the same as) the expression in Lemma 22.29, according to which

$$2\delta_r \leq \sum_\alpha \hat{f}_\alpha^2 \hat{g}_{h_2(\alpha)}(1 - 2\rho)^{|\alpha|}$$

However, since one can easily see that $(1 - 2\rho)^{|\alpha|} \leq \dfrac{2}{\sqrt{\rho\,|\alpha|}}$, we have

$$2\delta_r \leq \sum_\alpha \hat{f}_\alpha^2 \, |\hat{g}_{h_2(\alpha)}| \, \frac{2}{\sqrt{\rho\,|\alpha|}}$$

Rearranging,

$$\delta_r \sqrt{\rho} \leq \sum_\alpha \hat{f}_\alpha^2 \left| \hat{g}_{h_2(\alpha)} \right| \frac{1}{\sqrt{|\alpha|}}$$

Applying the Cauchy-Schwarz inequality, $\sum_i a_i b_i \leq (\sum_i a_i^2)^{1/2}(\sum_i b_i^2)^{1/2}$, with $\hat{f}_\alpha \left| \hat{g}_{\pi_2(\alpha)} \right| \frac{1}{\sqrt{|\alpha|}}$ playing the role of the a_i's and $\hat{f}_\alpha$ playing that of the b_i's, we obtain

$$\delta_r \sqrt{\rho} \leq \sum_\alpha \hat{f}_\alpha^2 \left| \hat{g}_{h_2(\alpha)} \right| \frac{1}{\sqrt{|\alpha|}} \leq \left(\sum_\alpha \hat{f}_\alpha^2 \right)^{1/2} \left(\sum_\alpha \hat{f}_\alpha^2 \hat{g}_{h_2(\alpha)}^2 \frac{1}{|\alpha|} \right)^{1/2} \tag{22.11}$$

Since $\sum_\alpha \hat{f}_\alpha^2 = 1$, by squaring (22.11) and combining it with (22.10) we get that for every r,

$$\delta_r^2 \rho \leq \operatorname*{E}_{\mathcal{D}_i, \mathcal{D}_j} [I_r]$$

which proves (22.9) and finishes the proof. ∎

22.8 HARDNESS OF APPROXIMATING SET-COVER

In the SET-COVER problem we are given a ground set $\mathcal{U}$ and a collection of its subsets $S_1, S_2, \ldots, S_n$ whose union is $\mathcal{U}$, and we desire the smallest subcollection I such that $\cup_{i \in I} S_i = \mathcal{U}$. Such a subcollection is called a *set cover* and its *size* is $|I|$. An algorithm is said to ρ-approximate this problem, where $\rho < 1$ if for every instance it finds a set cover of size at most OPT/ρ, where OPT is the size of the smallest set cover.

Theorem 22.31 ([LY94]) *If for any constant $\rho > 0$, there is an algorithm that ρ-approximates* SET-COVER, *then* **P** = **NP**. *Specifically for every $\epsilon, W > 0$ there is a polynomial-time transformation f from* 2CSP$_W$ *instances to instances of* SET-COVER *such that if the* 2CSP$_W$ *instance is regular and satisfies the projection property then*

$$\mathrm{val}(\varphi) = 1 \Rightarrow f(\varphi) \text{ has a set cover of size } N$$

$$\mathrm{val}(\varphi) < \epsilon \Rightarrow f(\varphi) \text{ has no set cover of size} \frac{N}{4\sqrt{\epsilon}}$$

where N depends upon φ. ◇

Actually one can prove a somewhat stronger result; see the note at the end of the proof.

The proof needs the following gadget.

Definition 22.32 ((k, ℓ)-set gadget) A (k, ℓ)-*set gadget* consists of a ground set $\mathcal{B}$ and some of its subsets $C_1, C_2, \ldots, C_\ell$ with the following property: Every collection of at most k sets out of $C_1, \overline{C_1}, C_2, \overline{C_2}, \ldots, C_\ell, \overline{C_\ell}$ that is a set cover for $\mathcal{B}$ must include both C_i and $\overline{C_i}$ for some i. ◇

The following lemma is left as Exercise 22.13.

Lemma 22.33 *There is an algorithm that given any k, ℓ, runs in time* $\mathrm{poly}(m, 2^\ell)$ *and outputs a* (k, ℓ)-*set gadget.*   ◇

We can now prove Theorem 22.31. We give a reduction from $2\mathrm{CSP}_W$, specifically, the instances obtained from Theorem 22.15.

Let φ be an instance of $2\mathrm{CSP}_W$ such that either $\mathrm{val}(\varphi) = 1$ or $\mathrm{val}(\varphi) < \epsilon$ where ϵ is some arbitrarily small constant. Suppose it has n variables and m constraints. Let Γ_i denote the set of constraints in which the ith variable is the first variable, and Δ_i the set of constraints in which it is the second variable.

The construction

Construct a (k, W)-set gadget $(\mathcal{B}; C_1, C_2, \ldots, C_W)$ where $k > 2/\sqrt{\epsilon}$. Since variables take values in $[W]$, we can associate a set C_u with each variable value u.

The instance of SET-COVER is as follows. The ground set is $[m] \times \mathcal{B}$, which we will think of as m copies of $\mathcal{B}$, one for each constraint of φ. The number of subsets is nW; for each variable $i \in [n]$ and value $u \in [W]$ there is a subset $S_{i,u}$ which is the union of the following sets: $\{r\} \times C_u$ for each $r \in \Delta_i$ and $\{r\} \times \mathcal{B} \setminus C_{h(u)}$ for each $r \in \Gamma_i$. The use of complementary sets like this is at the root of how the gadget allows 2CSP (with projection property) to be encoded as SET-COVER.

The analysis

If the $2\mathrm{CSP}_W$ instance is satisfiable then we exhibit a set cover of size n. Let $\pi : [n] \to W$ be any satisfying assignment where $\pi(i)$ is the value of the ith variable. We claim that the collection of n subsets given by $\{S_{i,\pi[i]} : i \in [n]\}$ is a set cover. It suffices to show that their union contains $\{r\} \times \mathcal{B}$ for each constraint r. But this is trivial since if i is the first variable of constraint r and j the second variable, then by definition $S_{j,\pi[j]}$ contains $\{r\} \times C_{\pi[j]}$ and $S_{i,\pi[i]}$ contains $\{r\} \times \mathcal{B} \setminus C_{\pi[j]}$, and thus $S_{i,\pi[i]} \cup S_{j,\pi[j]}$ contains $\{r\} \times \mathcal{B}$.

Conversely, suppose less than ϵ fraction of the constraints in the $2\mathrm{CSP}_W$ instance are simultaneously satisfiable. We claim that every set cover must have at least nT sets, for $T = \frac{1}{4\sqrt{\epsilon}}$. For contradiction's sake suppose a set cover of size less than nT exists. Let us probabilistically construct an assignment for the $2\mathrm{CSP}_W$ instance as follows. For each variable i, say that a value u is *associated* with it if $S_{i,u}$ is in the set cover. We pick a value for i by randomly picking one of the values associated with it. It suffices to prove the following claim since our choice of k ensures that $8T < k$.

Claim *If $8T < k$, then the expected number of constraints satisfied by this assignment is more than* $\frac{m}{16T^2}$.

PROOF: Call a variable *good* if it has less than $4T$ values associated with it. The average number of values associated per variable is less than T, so less than a fourth of the variables have more than $4T$ values associated with them. Thus less than a fourth of the variables are not good.

Since the 2CSP instance is regular, each variable occurs in the same number of clauses. Thus the fraction of constraints containing a variable that is not good is less than $2 \times 1/4 = 1/2$. Thus for more than half of the constraints both variables in them are good. Let r be such a constraint and i, j be the variables in it. Then $\{r\} \times \mathcal{B}$ is covered by the union of $\cup_u S_{i,u}$ and $\cup_v S_{j,v}$ where the unions are over values associated with the variables i, j, respectively. Since $8T < k$, the definition of a (k, W)-set gadget implies that any cover of $\mathcal{B}$ by less than $8T$ sets must contain two sets that are complements of one another. We conclude that there are values u, v associated with i, j, respectively such that $h(u) = v$. Thus when we randomly construct an assignment by picking for each variable one of the values associated with it, these values are picked with probability at least $\frac{1}{4}T \times \frac{1}{4}T = \frac{1}{16}T^2$, and then the rth constraint gets satisfied. The claim (and hence Theorem 22.31) now follows by linearity of expectation. ∎

Remark 22.34

The same proof actually can be used to prove a stronger result: There is a constant $c > 0$ such that if there is an algorithm that α-approximates SET-COVER for $\alpha = c/\log n$, then **NP** $\subseteq$ **DTIME**$(n^{O(\log n)})$. The idea is to use Raz's Parallel Repetition Theorem where the number of repetitions t is superconstant so that the soundness is $1/\log n$. However, the running time of the reduction is $n^{O(t)}$, which is slightly superpolynomial.

22.9 OTHER **PCP** THEOREMS: A SURVEY

As mentioned in the introduction, proving inapproximability results for various problems often requires proving new **PCP** Theorems. We already saw one example, namely, Håstad's Three-Bit **PCP** Theorem. Now we survey some other variants of the **PCP** Theorem that have been proved.

22.9.1 **PCP**'s with subconstant soundness parameter

The way we phrased Theorem 22.15, the soundness is an arbitrary small constant 2^{-t}. From the proof of the theorem it was clear that the reduction used to prove this **NP**-hardness runs in time n^t (since it forms all t-tuples of constraints). Thus if t is larger than a constant, the running time of the reduction is superpolynomial. Nevertheless, several hardness results use superconstant values of t. They end up not showing **NP**-hardness, but instead showing the nonexistence of a good approximation algorithms assuming **NP** does not have say $n^{\log n}$ time deterministic algorithms (this is still a very believable assumption). We mentioned this already in Remark 22.34.

It is still an open problem to prove the **NP**-hardness of 2CSP for a factor ρ that is smaller than any constant. If instead of 2CSP one looks at 3CSP or 4CSP then one can achieve low soundness using larger alphabet size, while keeping the running time polynomial [RS97]. Often these suffice in applications.

22.9.2 Amortized query complexity

Some applications require binary-alphabet **PCP** systems enjoying a tight relation between the number of queries (which can be an arbitrarily large constant) and the soundness parameter. The relevant parameter here turns out to be the *free bit complexity* [FK93, BS94]. This parameter is defined as follows. Suppose the number of queries is q. After the verifier has picked its random string, and picked a sequence of

q addresses, there are 2^q possible sequences of bits that could be contained in those addresses. If the verifier accepts for only t of those sequences, then we say that the free bit parameter is $\log t$ (note that this number need not be an integer). In fact, for proving hardness result for MAX-INDSET and MAX-CLIQUE, it suffices to consider the *amortized free bit complexity* [BGS95]. This parameter is defined as $\lim_{s\to 0} f_s/\log(1/s)$, where f_s is the number of free bits needed by the verifier to ensure the soundness parameter is at most s (with completeness at least say $1/2$). Håstad constructed systems with amortized free bit complexity tending to zero [Hås96]. That is, for every $\epsilon > 0$, he gave a **PCP**-verifier for **NP** that uses $O(\log n)$ random bits and ϵ amortized free bits. The completeness is 1. He then used this **PCP** system to show (borrowing the basic framework from [FGL+91, FK93, BS94, BGS95]) that MAX-INDSET (and so, equivalently, MAX-CLIQUE) is **NP**-hard to $n^{-1+\epsilon}$-approximate for arbitrarily small $\epsilon > 0$.

22.9.3 2-bit tests and powerful Fourier analysis

Recent advances on Håstad's line of work consist of using more powerful ideas from Fourier analysis. The Fourier analysis in Håstad's proof hardly uses the fact that the functions being tested are Boolean. However, papers of Kahn, Kalai, and Linial [KKL88], Friedgut [Fri99], and Bourgain [Bou02] have led to important new insights into the Fourier coefficients of Boolean functions, which in turn have proved useful in analysing **PCP** verifiers. (See also Note 22.21.) The main advantage is for designing verifiers that read only 2 bits in the proof, which arise while proving hardness results for a variety of graph problems such as VERTEX-COVER, MAX-CUT, and SPARSEST-CUT.

These new results follow Håstad's overall idea, namely, to show that if the verifier accepts some provided functions with good probability, then the function has a few large Fourier coefficients (see Corollary 22.25 for example). However, Håstad's analysis (even for the Long Code test in Section 22.6) inherently requires the verifier to query 3 bits in the proof, and we briefly try to explain why. For simplicity we focus on the Long Code test. We did a simple analysis of the Long Code test to arrive at the conclusion of Lemma 22.24:

$$\sum_\alpha \hat{f}_\alpha^3 (1 - 2\rho)^{|\alpha|} \geq 2\delta$$

where $1/2 + \delta$ is the probability that the verifier accepts the function. From this fact, Corollary 22.25 concludes that at least one Fourier coefficient has value at least $c = c(\delta, \rho) > 0$. This is a crucial step because it lets us conclude that f has some (admittedly very weak) connection with some small number of codewords in the Long Code.

One could design an analogous 2-bit test. The first part of the above analysis still goes through but in the conclusion the cubes get replaced by squares:

$$\sum_\alpha \hat{f}_\alpha^2 (1 - 2\rho)^{|\alpha|} \geq 2\delta \tag{22.12}$$

For a non-Boolean function this condition is not enough to let us conclude that some Fourier coefficient of f has value at least $c = c(\delta, \rho) > 0$. However, the following lemma of Bourgain allows such a conclusion if f is Boolean. We say that a function $f : \{0, 1\}^n \to \{0, 1\}$ is a *k-junta* if it depends only on k of the n variables. Note that

Parseval's identity implies that at least one Fourier coefficient of a k-junta is $1/2^{k/2}$. The next lemma implies that if a boolean function f is such that the LHS of (22.12) is at least $1 - \rho^t$ where $t > 1/2$, then f is close to a k-junta for a small k.

Lemma 22.35 ([Bou02]) *For every* $\epsilon, \delta > 0$ *and integer* r *there is a constant* $k = k(r, \epsilon, \delta)$ *such that if*

$$\sum_{\alpha : |\alpha| > r} \hat{f}_\alpha^2 < \frac{1}{r^{1/2+\epsilon}}$$

then f *has agreement* $1 - \delta$ *with a* k-*junta.*   ◇

We suspect that there will be many other uses of fourier analysis in **PCP** constructions.

22.9.4 Unique games and threshold results

Håstad's ideas led to determination of the approximation threshold for several problems. But the status of other problems such as VERTEX-COVER and MAX-CUT remained open. In 2002 Khot [Kho02] proposed a new complexity theoretic conjecture called the *unique games conjecture* (UGC) that is stronger than **P** $\neq$ **NP** but still consistent with current knowledge. This conjecture concerns a special case of $2\mathsf{CSP}_W$ in which the constraint function is a *permutation* on $[W]$. In other words, if the constraint φ_r involves variables i, j, the constraint function h is a bijective mapping from $[W]$ to $[W]$. Then assignment $u_1, u_2, \ldots, u_n$ to the variables satisfies this constraint iff $u_j = h(u_i)$. According to UGC, for every constants $\epsilon, \delta > 0$ there is a domain size $W = W(\epsilon, \delta)$ such that there is no polynomial-time algorithm that given such an instance of $2\mathsf{CSP}_W$ with $\mathsf{val}(\cdot) \geq 1 - \epsilon$ produces an assignment that satisfies δ fraction of constraints.[2]

Khot suggested that current algorithmic techniques seem unable to design such an algorithm (an insight that seems to have been confirmed by lack of progress in the last few years, despite much effort). He also showed that this conjecture implies several strong results about hardness of approximation. The reason in a nutshell is that the Fourier analysis technique of Håstad (fortified with the above-mentioned discoveries regarding Fourier analysis of Boolean functions) can be sharpened if one starts with the instances of $2\mathsf{CSP}_W$ with the uniqueness constraint.

Subsequently, a slew of results have shown optimal or threshold results about hardness of approximation (often using some of the advanced Fourier analysis mentioned above) assuming UGC is true. For instance UGC implies that there is no polynomial-time algorithm that computes a $1/2 + \delta$-approximation to VERTEX-COVER for any $\delta > 0$ [KR08], and similarly no algorithm that computes a 0.878-approximation to MAX-CUT [KKMO05, MOO05]. Both of these lead to threshold results since these ratios are also the ones achieved by the current approximation algorithms.

Thus it is of great interest to prove or disprove the unique games conjecture. Algorithms designers have tried to disprove the conjecture using clever tools from semidefinite programming, and currently the conjecture seems truly on the fine line

---

[2] In fact, Khot phrased the UGC as the even stronger conjecture that solving this problem is **NP**-hard.

between being true and being false. It is known that it will suffice to restrict attention to the further subcase where the constraint function h is linear (i.e., the constraints are linear equations mod W in two variables).

22.9.5 Connection to isoperimetry and metric space embeddings

A *metric space* (X, d) consists of set of points X and a function d mapping pairs of points to nonnegative real numbers satisfying (a) $d(i, j) = 0$ iff $i = j$. (b) $d(i,j) + d(j,k) \geq d(i,k)$ (*triangle inequality*). An *embedding* of space (X, d) into space (Y, d') is a function $f : X \to Y$. Its *distortion* is the maximum over all point pairs $\{i, j\}$ of the quantities $\frac{d'(f(i),f(j))}{d(i,j)}, \frac{d(i,j)}{d'(f(i),f(j))}$. It is of great interest in algorithm design (and in mathematics) to understand the minimum *distortion* required to embed one family of metric spaces into another. One interesting subcase is where the host space (Y, d') is a subset of the ℓ_1 metric space on $\Re^n$ for some n (in other words, distance d' is defined using the ℓ_1 norm). Bourgain showed that every n-point metric space embeds in ℓ_1 with distortion $O(\log n)$. This fact is important in design of algorithms for graph partitioning problems such as SPARSEST-CUT. In that context, a metric called ℓ_2^2 had been identified. Goemans and Linial conjectured that this metric would be embeddable in ℓ_1 with distortion $O(1)$. If the conjecture were true, we would have an $O(1)$-approximation algorithm for SPARSEST-CUT. Khot and Vishnoi [KV05] disproved the conjecture, using a construction of an interesting ℓ_2^2 metric that is inspired by the advanced **PCP** theorems discussed in this chapter. The main idea is that since there is an intimate relationship between ℓ_1 metrics and cuts, one has to construct a graph whose cut structure and isoperimetry properties are tightly controlled. So Khot and Vishnoi use a hypercube-like graph, and use Fourier analysis to show its isoperimetry properties. (See Note 22.21.)

Their work has inspired other results about lower bounds on the distortions of metric embeddings.

22.A TRANSFORMING qCSP INSTANCES INTO "NICE" INSTANCES

We can transform a qCSP-instance φ into a "nice" 2CSP-instance ψ through the following three claims:

Claim 22.36 *There is a CL-reduction mapping any qCSP instance φ into a $2CSP_{2^q}$ instance ψ such that*

$$\mathsf{val}(\varphi) \leq 1 - \epsilon \Rightarrow \mathsf{val}(\psi) \leq 1 - \epsilon/q$$

$\diamond$

PROOF: Given a qCSP-instance φ over n variables $u_1, \ldots, u_n$ with m constraints, we construct the following $2CSP_{2^q}$ formula ψ over the variables $u_1, \ldots, u_n, y_1, \ldots, y_m$. Intuitively, the y_i variables will hold the restriction of the assignment to the q variables used by the ith constraint, and we will add constraints to check consistency: that is to make sure that if the ith constraint depends on the variable u_j then u_j is indeed given a value consistent with y_i. Specifically, for every φ_i of φ that depends on the variables $u_1, \ldots, u_q$, we add q constraints $\{\psi_{i,j}\}_{j \in [q]}$ where $\psi_{i,j}(y_i, u_j)$ is true iff y_i encodes an assignment to

$u_1, \ldots, u_q$ satisfying φ_i and u_j is in $\{0, 1\}$ and agrees with the assignment y_i. Note that the number of constraints in ψ is qm.

Clearly, if φ is satisfiable, then so is ψ. Suppose that $\mathsf{val}(\varphi) \le 1 - \epsilon$ and let $u_1, \ldots, u_k, y_1, \ldots, y_m$ be any assignment to the variables of ψ. There exists a set $S \subseteq [m]$ of size at least ϵm such that the constraint φ_i is violated by the assignment $u_1, \ldots, u_k$. For any $i \in S$ there must be at least one $j \in [q]$ such that the constraint $\psi_{i,j}$ is violated. ∎

Claim 22.37 *There is an absolute constant d and a CL- reduction mapping any* $2\mathsf{CSP}_W$ *instance φ into a* $2\mathsf{CSP}_W$ *instance ψ such that*

$$\mathsf{val}(\varphi) \le 1 - \epsilon \Rightarrow \mathsf{val}(\psi) \le 1 - \epsilon/(100Wd)$$

and the constraint graph of ψ is d-regular. That is, every variable in ψ appears in exactly d constraints.   ◇

PROOF: Let φ be a $2\mathsf{CSP}_W$ instance, and let $\{G_n\}_{n\in\mathbb{N}}$ be an explicit family of d-regular expanders. Our goal is to ensure that each variable appears in φ at most $d + 1$ times (if a variable appears less than that, we can always add artificial constraints that touch only this variable). Suppose that u_i is a variable that appears in k constraints for some $n > 1$. We will change u_i into k variables $y_i^1, \ldots, y_i^k$, and use a different variable of the form y_i^j in the place of u_i in each constraint u_i originally appeared in. We will also add a constraint requiring that y_i^j is equal to $y_i^{j'}$ for every edge (j, j') in the graph G_k. We do this process for every variable in the original instance, until each variable appears in at most d equality constraints and one original constraint. We call the resulting $2\mathsf{CSP}$-instance ψ. Note that if φ has m constraints, then ψ will have at most $m + dm$ constraints.

Clearly, if φ is satisfiable then so is ψ. Suppose that $\mathsf{val}(\varphi) \le 1 - \epsilon$ and let **y** be any assignment to the variables of ψ. We need to show that **y** violates at least $\frac{\epsilon m}{100W}$ of the constraints of ψ. Recall that for each variable u_i that appears k times in φ, the assignment **y** has k variables $y_i^1, \ldots, y_i^k$. We compute an assignment **u** to φ's variables as follows: u_i is assigned the plurality value of $y_i^1, \ldots, y_i^k$. We define t_i to be the number of y_i^j's that *disagree* with this plurality value. Note that $0 \le t_i \le k(1 - 1/W)$ (where W is the alphabet size). If $\sum_{i=1}^n t_i \ge \frac{\epsilon}{4}m$, then we are done. Indeed, by (22.1) (see Section 22.2.3), in this case we will have at least $\sum_{i=1}^n \frac{t_i}{10W} \ge \frac{\epsilon}{40W}m$ equality constraints that are violated.

Suppose now that $\sum_{i=1}^n t_i < \frac{\epsilon}{4}m$. Since $\mathsf{val}(\varphi) \le 1 - \epsilon$, there is a set S of at least ϵm constraints violated in φ by the plurality assignment **u**. All of these constraints are also present in ψ and since we assume $\sum_{i=1}^n t_i < \frac{\epsilon}{4}m$, at most half of them are given a different value by the assignment **y** than the value given by **u**. Thus the assignment **y** violates at least $\frac{\epsilon}{2}m$ constraints in ψ. ∎

Claim 22.38 *There is an absolute constant d and a CL-reduction mapping any* $2\mathsf{CSP}_W$ *instance φ with d'-regular constraint graph for $d \ge d'$ into a* $2\mathsf{CSP}_W$ *instance ψ such that*

$$\mathsf{val}(\varphi) \le 1 - \epsilon \Rightarrow \mathsf{val}(\psi) \le 1 - \epsilon/(10d)$$

and the constraint graph of ψ is a 4d-regular expander, with half the edges coming out of each vertex being self-loops.   ◇

PROOF: There is a constant d and an explicit family $\{G_n\}_{n \in \mathbb{N}}$ of graphs such that for every n, G_n is a d-regular n-vertex 0.1-expander graph (see Section 22.2.3).

Let φ be a 2CSP-instance as in the claim's statement. By adding self-loops, we can assume that the constraint graph has degree d (this can at worst decrease the gap by factor of d). We now add "null" constraints (constraints that always accept) for every edge in the graph G_n. In addition, we add $2d$ null constraints forming self-loops for each vertex. We denote by ψ the resulting instance. Adding these null constraints reduces the fraction of violated constraints by a factor at most four. Moreover, because any regular graph H satisfies $\lambda(H) \leq 1$ and because of λ's subadditivity (see Exercise 21.7), $\lambda(\psi) \leq \frac{3}{4} + \frac{1}{4}\lambda(G_n) \leq 0.9$ where by $\lambda(\psi)$ we denote the parameter λ of ψ's constraint graph. ∎

WHAT HAVE WE LEARNED?

- The PCP Theorem is a reduction that amplifies the gap between YES and NO instances of **NP** problems. Dinur's proof, presented here, obtains this gap amplification by a sequence of many small combinatorial steps. The original proof used algebraic tools and error-correcting codes to obtain the amplification in (almost) one shot.
- The discrete Fourier transform is a powerful technique in analysis of Boolean function. It is particularly useful in analyzing the behavior of functions under perturbation or "noise."
- Some hardness of approximation results follow immediately from the PCP Theorem. But often for strong results more sophisticated reductions or different PCP theorems are needed.

CHAPTER NOTES AND HISTORY

As mentioned in the notes to Chapter 11, the **PCP** Theorem was proved in 1992 in the early versions of the papers [AS92, ALM+92]. The AS-ALMSS proof of the **PCP** Theorem resisted simplification for over a decade. The overall idea of that proof (as indeed in **MIP** = **NEXP**) is similar to the proof of Theorem 11.19. (Indeed, Theorem 11.19 is the only part of the original proof that still survives in our writeup.) However, in addition to using encodings based upon the Walsh-Hadamard code the proof also used encodings based upon low-degree multivariate polynomials. These have associated procedures analogous to the linearity test and local decoding, though the proofs of correctness are a fair bit harder. The proof also drew intuition from the topic of self-testing and self-correcting programs [BLR90, RS92], which was surveyed in Section 8.6. The alphabet reduction in the AS-ALMSS proof was also somewhat more complicated. A draft writeup of the original proof is available on this book's Web-site. (We dropped it from the published version in favor of Dinur's proof but feel it is interesting in its own right and may be useful in future research.)

Dinur's main contribution in simplifying the proof is the gap amplification lemma (Lemma 22.5), which allows one to iteratively improve the soundness parameter of the **PCP** from very close to 1 to being bounded away from 1 by some positive constant. This allows her to use a simpler alphabet reduction. In fact, the alphabet reduction is the only part of the proof that now uses the "proof verification" viewpoint, and one imagines that in a few years this too will be replaced by a purely combinatorial construction. A related open problem is to find a Dinur-style proof of **MIP = NEXP**.

We also note that Dinur's general strategy is somewhat reminiscent of the zig-zag construction of expander graphs and Reingold's deterministic logspace algorithm for undirected connectivity described in Chapter 20, which suggests that more connections are waiting to be made between these different areas of research.

As mentioned in the notes at the end of Chapter 11, Papadimitriou and Yannakakis [PY88] had shown around 1988 that if it is **NP**-hard to ρ-approximate MAX-3SAT for some $\rho < 1$, then it is also **NP**-hard to ρ'-approximate a host of other problems where ρ' depends upon the problem. Thus after the discovery of the **PCP** Theorem, attention turned toward determining the exact approximation threshold for problems; see for example [BS94, BGS95]. Håstad's threshold results for MAX-CLIQUE [Hås96] and MAX-3SAT [Hås97] came a few years later and represented a quantum jump in our understanding.

The issue of parallel repetition comes from the paper of Fortnow, Rompel, and Sipser [FRS88] that erroneously claimed that $\mathsf{val}(\varphi^{*t}) = \mathsf{val}(\varphi)^t$ for every $2\mathsf{CSP}\ \varphi$ and $t \in \mathbb{N}$. However, Fortnow [For89] soon found a counter example (see Exercise 22.6). Papers by Lapidot and Shamir [LS91] and Feige-Lovasz [FL92], which predate Raz's paper, imply hardness results for $2\mathsf{CSP}$, but the running time of the reduction is super-polynomial. Verbitsky [Ver94] and Feige and Kilian [FK93] proved weaker versions of Raz's Theorem (Theorem 22.15). Raz's proof of the parallel repetition is based on an extension of techniques developed by Razborov [Razb90] in the context of communication complexity. The proof is beautiful but quite complex, though recently Holenstein [Hol07] gave some simplifications for Raz's proof; a writeup of this simplified proof is available from this book's Web site.

The hardness result for INDSET in Lemma 22.8 can be improved so that for all $\epsilon > 0$, $n^{-1+\epsilon}$-approximation in **NP**-hard in graphs with n vertices. This result is due to [Hås96], which caps a long line of other work [FGL+91, AS92, ALM+92, BS94, BGS95]. The use of expanders in the reduction of Lemma 22.8 is from [AFWZ95]. Note that a $(1/n)$-approximation is trivial: just output a single vertex, which is always an independent set. Thus this result can be viewed as a *threshold* result.

The hardness of SET-COVER is due to Lund and Yannakakis [LY94], which was also the first paper to implicitly use $2\mathsf{CSP}_W$ with projection property; the importance of this problem was identified in [Aro94, ABSS93], where it was called *label cover* used to prove other results. This problem is now ubiquitous in **PCP** literature.

A threshold result for SET-COVER was shown by Feige [Fei96]: computing $(1 + \delta)/\ln n$ approximation is hard for every $\delta > 0$, whereas we know a simple $(1/\ln n)$-approximation algorithm.

See Arora and Lund [AL95] for a survey circa 1995 of how to prove the basic results about hardness of approximation. See Khot [Kho05] for a more recent survey about the results that use fourier analysis.

EXERCISES

22.1. Prove Equation (22.1).

H542

22.2. Let $G = (V, E)$ be a λ-expander graph for some $\lambda \in (0, 1)$. Let S be a subset of V with $|S| = \beta |V|$ for some $\beta \in (0, 1)$. Let $(X_1, \ldots, X_\ell)$ be a tuple of random variables denoting the vertices of a uniformly chosen $(\ell-1)$-step path in G. Then, prove that

$$(\beta - 2\lambda)^k \leq \Pr[\forall_{i \in [\ell]} X_i \in S] \leq (\beta + 2\lambda)^k$$

H542

22.3. Let S_t be the binomial distribution over t balanced coins. That is, $\Pr[S_t = k] = \binom{t}{k} 2^{-t}$. Prove that for every $\delta < 1$, the statistical distance (see Section A.2.6) of S_t and $S_{t + \delta \sqrt{t}}$ is at most 10δ.

H542

22.4. Prove that for every nonnegative random variable V, $\Pr[V > 0] \geq \mathrm{E}[V]^2 / \mathrm{E}[V^2]$.

H542

22.5. In this problem we explore an alternative approach to the Alphabet Reduction Lemma (Lemma 22.6) using Long Codes instead of Welsh-Hadamard codes. We already saw that the *long-code* for a set $\{0, \ldots, W-1\}$ is the function $\mathsf{LC} : \{0, \ldots, W-1\} \to \{0, 1\}^{2^W}$ such that for every $i \in \{0..W-1\}$ and a function $f : \{0..W-1\} \to \{0, 1\}$, (where we identify f with an index in $[2^w]$) the fth position of $\mathsf{LC}(i)$, denoted by $\mathsf{LC}(i)_f$, is $f(i)$. We say that a function $L : \{0, 1\}^{2^W} \to \{0, 1\}$ is a *long-code codeword* if $L = \mathsf{LC}(i)$ for some $i \in \{0..W-1\}$.

(a) Prove that LC is an error-correcting code with distance half. That is, for every $i \neq j \in \{0..W-1\}$, the fractional Hamming distance of $\mathsf{LC}(i)$ and $\mathsf{LC}(j)$ is half.

(b) Prove that LC is *locally-decodable*. That is, show an algorithm that given random access to a function $L : 2^{\{0,1\}^W} \to \{0, 1\}$ that is $(1-\epsilon)$-close to $\mathsf{LC}(i)$ and $f : \{0..W-1\} \to \{0, 1\}$ outputs $\mathsf{LC}(i)_f$ with probability at least 0.9 while making at most 2 queries to L.

(c) Let $L = \mathsf{LC}(i)$ for some $i \in \{0..W-1\}$. Prove the for every $f : \{0..W-1\} \to \{0, 1\}$, $L(f) = 1 - L(\bar{f})$, where $\bar{f}$ is the negation of f (i.e. , $\bar{f}(i) = 1 - f(i)$ for every $i \in \{0..W-1\}$).

(d) Let T be an algorithm that given random access to a function $L : 2^{\{0,1\}^W} \to \{0, 1\}$, does the following:

  (a) Choose f to be a random function from $\{0..W-1\} \to \{0, 1\}$.

  (b) If $L(f) = 1$ then output TRUE.

  (c) Otherwise, choose $g : \{0..W-1\} \to \{0, 1\}$ as follows: for every $i \in \{0..W-1\}$, if $f(i) = 0$ then set $g(i) = 0$ and otherwise set $g(i)$ to be a random value in $\{0, 1\}$.

  (d) If $L(g) = 0$ then output TRUE; otherwise output FALSE.

Prove that if L is a *long-code* codeword (i.e., $L = \mathsf{LC}(i)$ for some i) then T outputs TRUE with probability one.

Prove that if L is a *linear function* that is nonzero and not a *long-code* codeword then T outputs TRUE with probability at most 0.9.

(e) Prove that LC is *locally testable*. That is, show an algorithm that given random access to a function $L : \{0, 1\}^W \to \{0, 1\}$ outputs TRUE with probability one if L is a *long-code* codeword and outputs FALSE with probability at least $1/2$ if L is not 0.9-close to a *long-code* codeword, while making at most a constant number of queries to L.

H542

(f) Using the test above, give an alternative proof for the Alphabet Reduction Lemma (Lemma 22.6).

H542

22.6. ([For89, Fei91]) Consider the following 2CSP instance φ on an alphabet of size 4 (which we identify with $\{0, 1\}^2$). The instance φ has four variables $x_{0,0}, x_{0,1}, x_{1,0}, x_{1,1}$ and four constraints $C_{0,0}, C_{0,1}, C_{1,0}, C_{1,1}$. The constraint $C_{a,b}$ looks at the variables $x_{0,a}$ and $x_{1,b}$ and outputs TRUE if and only if $x_{0,a} = x_{1,b}$ and $x_{0,a} \in \{0a, 1b\}$.

(a) Prove that $\text{val}(\varphi^{*2}) = \text{val}(\varphi)$, where φ^{*t} denotes the 2CSP over alphabet W^t that is the t-times parallel repeated version of φ as in Section 22.3.1.

H542

(b) Prove that for every t, $\text{val}(\varphi^{*t}) \geq \text{val}(\varphi)^{t/2}$.

22.7. (Solvability of Unique Games) We encountered unique games in Section 22.9.4; it is a special case of 2CSP_W in which the constraint function h is a *permutation* on $[W]$. In other words, if constraint φ_r involves variables i, j, then assignment $u_1, u_2, \ldots, u_n$ to the variables satisfies this constraint iff $u_j = h(u_i)$. Prove that there is a polynomial-time algorithm that given such an instance, finds a satisfying assignment if one exists.

22.8. Prove Corollary 22.25.

22.9. Prove that the **PCP** system resulting from the proof of Claim 22.36 (Chapter 11) satisfies the projection property.

22.10. This question explores the notion of noise-senstivity of Boolean functions, which ties in to the discussion in Note 22.5.3. Let $f : \{\pm 1\}^n \to \{\pm 1\}$ and let $I \subseteq [n]$. Let M_I be the following distribution: We choose $z \in_R M_I$ by for $i \in I$, choose z_i to be $+1$ with probability $1/2$ and -1 with probability $1/2$ (independently of other choices), for $i \notin I$ choose $z_i = +1$. We define the *variation of f on I* to be $\Pr_{\mathbf{x} \in_R \{\pm 1\}^n, \mathbf{z} \in_R M_I}[f(\mathbf{x}) \neq f(\mathbf{xz})]$.

Suppose that the variation of f on I is less than ϵ. Prove that there exists a function $g : \{\pm 1\}^n \to \mathbb{R}$ such that **(1)** g does not depend on the coordinates in I and **(2)** g is 10ϵ-close to f (i.e., $\Pr_{\mathbf{x} \in_R \{\pm 1\}^n}[f(\mathbf{x}) \neq g(\mathbf{x})] < 10\epsilon$). Can you come up with such a g that outputs values in $\{\pm 1\}$ only?

22.11. For $f : \{\pm 1\}^n \to \{\pm 1\}$ and $\mathbf{x} \in \{\pm 1\}^n$ we define $N_f(\mathbf{x})$ to be the number of coordinates i such that if we let y to be $\mathbf{x}$ flipped at the ith coordinate (i.e., $y = \mathbf{xe}^i$ where $\mathbf{e}^i$ has -1 in the ith coordinate and $+1$ everywhere else), then $f(\mathbf{x}) \neq f(\mathbf{y})$. We define the *average sensitivity of f*, denoted by $as(f)$ to be the expectation of $N_f(\mathbf{x})$ for $\mathbf{x} \in_R \{\pm 1\}^n$.

(a) Prove that for every balanced function $f : \{\pm 1\}^n \to \{\pm 1\}$ (i.e., $\Pr[f(\mathbf{x}) = +1] = 1/2$), $as(f) \geq 1$.

(b) Let f be balanced function from $\{\pm 1\}^n$ to $\{\pm 1\}$ with $as(f) = 1$. Prove that f is a coordinate function or its negation (i.e., $f(\mathbf{x}) = x_i$ or $f(\mathbf{x}) = -x_i$ for some $i \in [n]$ and for every $\mathbf{x} \in \{\pm 1\}^n$). (*Restatement using the language of isoperimetry as in Note 22.21: If a subset of half the vertices of the hypercube $\{0, 1\}^n$ has exactly*

2^{n-1} edges leaving it, then there is some i such that this subset is simply the set of vertices where $x_i = 0$ (or $x_i = 1$).)

22.12. ([KM91]) This exercise asks you to give an alternative proof of the Goldreich-Levin Theorem 9.12 using Fourier analysis.

(a) For every function $f : \{\pm 1\}^n \to \mathbb{R}$, denote $\tilde{f}_{\alpha\star} = \sum_{\beta \in \{0,1\}^{n-k}} \hat{f}^2_{\alpha\circ\beta}$, where $\circ$ denotes concatenation and we identify strings in $\{0, 1\}^n$ and subsets of $[n]$ in the obvious way. Prove that

$$\tilde{f}_{0^k\star} = \mathop{E}_{\substack{\mathbf{x},\mathbf{x}' \in_R \{0,1\}^k \\ \mathbf{y} \in_R \{0,1\}^{n-k}}} [f(\mathbf{x} \circ \mathbf{y})f(\mathbf{x}' \circ \mathbf{y})]$$

H542

(b) Prove that for every $\alpha \in \{0, 1\}^k$,

$$\tilde{f}_{\alpha\star} = \mathop{E}_{\substack{\mathbf{x},\mathbf{x}' \in_R \{0,1\}^k \\ \mathbf{y} \in_R \{0,1\}^{n-k}}} [f(\mathbf{x} \circ \mathbf{y})f(\mathbf{x}' \circ \mathbf{y})\chi_\alpha(\mathbf{x})\chi_\alpha(\mathbf{x}')] \tag{22.13}$$

H542

(c) Show an algorithm Estimate that given $\alpha \in \{0, 1\}^k, \epsilon > 0$, and oracle access to $f : \{\pm 1\}^n \to \{\pm 1\}$ runs in time poly$(n, 1/\epsilon)$ and outputs an estimate of f_α within ϵ accuracy with probability $1 - \epsilon$.

H542

(d) Show an algorithm LearnFourier that given $\epsilon > 0$ and oracle access to $f : \{\pm 1\}^n \to \{\pm 1\}$ runs in poly$(n, 1/\epsilon)$ time and outputs a set L of poly$(1/\epsilon)$ strings such that with probability at least 0.9, for every $\alpha \in \{0, 1\}^n$, if $|\hat{f}_\alpha| > \epsilon$ then $\alpha \in L$.

H542

(e) Show that the above algorithm implies Theorem 9.12.

22.13. Prove Lemma 22.33, albeit using a randomized algorithm.

H542

22.14. Derandomize the algorithm of the previous exercise.

H542

22.15. ([ABSS93]) In Problem 11.16 we explored the approximability of the problem of finding the largest feasible subsystem in a system of linear equations over the rationals. Show that there is an $\epsilon > 0$ such that computing an $n^{-\epsilon}$-approximation to this problem is **NP**-hard.

H542

22.16. ([PY88]) Suppose we restrict attention to MAX-3SAT in which each variable appears in at most five clauses. Show that there is still a constant $\rho < 1$ such that computing a ρ-aproximation to this problem is **NP**-hard.

H542

22.17. ([PY88]) In the MAX-CUT problem we are given a graph $G = (V, E)$ and seek to partition the vertices into two sets $S, \bar{S}$ such that we maximize the number of edges $|E(S, \bar{S})|$ between them. Show that there is still a constant $\rho < 1$ such that computing a ρ-aproximation to this problem is **NP**-hard.

CHAPTER 23

Why are circuit lower bounds so difficult?

The main hurdle in proving a lower bound is the existence of an algorithm.

– Steven Rudich

Why have we not been able to prove strong lower bounds for general circuits? Despite the dramatic success in proving lower bounds on restricted circuit classes as described in Chapter 14, we seem utterly at a loss when it comes to showing limitations of general Boolean circuits.

In 1994 Razborov and Rudich [RR94] described what they view as the main technical limitation of current approaches for proving circuit lower bounds. They defined a notion of "natural mathematical proofs" for a circuit lower bound. They pointed out that current lower bound arguments involve such mathematical proofs, and showed that obtaining strong lower bound with such proof techniques would violate a stronger form of the $\mathbf{P} \neq \mathbf{NP}$ conjecture—specifically, the conjecture that strong one-way functions exist that cannot be inverted by algorithms running in subexponential time. Since current evidence suggests that such strong one-way functions do exist (factoring integers, discrete log, etc., as described in Chapter 9), we conclude that current techniques are inherently incapable of proving strong lower bounds on general circuits.

The Razborov-Rudich result may be viewed as a modern analog of the 1970s results on the limits of diagonalization (see Chapter 3). What is particularly striking is that computational complexity (namely, the existence of strong one-way functions) is used here to shed light on a metamathematical question about computational complexity: "Why have we been unable to prove $\mathbf{P} \neq \mathbf{NP}$?" This is a good example of our claim at the start of the book that computational tractability has an intimate connection with issues of mathematical tractability amd proveability.

This chapter is organized as follows. We define natural proofs in Section 23.1, and then in Section 23.2 we discuss why they are indeed "natural." We then prove in Section 23.3 that under widely believed assumptions, such techniques will not be able to prove $\mathbf{NP} \not\subseteq \mathbf{P}_{/poly}$.

Can we design lower bound techniques that circumvent the "natural proof barrier"? We describe an interesting such example in Section 23.4. We end in Section 23.5 with some philosophical musings on the meaning of the natural proof barrier and our personal viewpoint.

23.1 DEFINITION OF NATURAL PROOFS

Let $f : \{0, 1\}^n \rightarrow \{0, 1\}$ be some Boolean function and $c \geq 1$ be some number. Any proof that f does not have n^c-sized circuits can be viewed as exhibiting some property that f has, and which every function with an n^c-sized circuit does not possess. That is, such a proof can be viewed as providing a predicate $\mathcal{P}$ on Boolean functions such that $\mathcal{P}(f) = 1$, but

$$\mathcal{P}(g) = 0 \quad \text{for every } g \in \mathbf{SIZE}(n^c) \tag{23.1}$$

We call the condition (23.1) n^c-*usefulness*. We say such a predicate $\mathcal{P}$ is *natural* if it satisfies in addition the following two conditions:

Constructiveness: There is an $2^{O(n)}$ time algorithm that on input (the truth table of) a function $g : \{0, 1\}^n \rightarrow \{0, 1\}$ outputs $\mathcal{P}(g)$. Note that the truth table has size 2^n, so this algorithm runs in time that is polynomial in its input size.

Largeness: The probability that a random function $g : \{0, 1\}^n \rightarrow \{0, 1\}$ satisfies $\mathcal{P}(g) = 1$ is at least $1/n$.

We will discuss in Section 23.2 the motivation behind these conditions, but for now note that the largeness condition does not contradict the n^c-usefulness condition since only a very small fraction of functions have polynomial-sized circuits (see the proof of Theorem 6.21). The following theorem says that, under reasonable assumptions, natural proofs cannot be used to prove that a function is not in $\mathbf{P}_{/poly}$.

Theorem 23.1 *(Natural proofs [RR94])*
Suppose that subexponentially strong one-way functions exist. Then there exists a constant $c \in \mathbb{N}$ such that there is no n^c-useful natural predicate $\mathcal{P}$.

One-way functions were defined in Chapter 9 (Section 9.2), and by a subexponentially strong one-way function we mean one that resists inverting even by a 2^{n^ϵ}-time adversary for some fixed $\epsilon > 0$. It is widely believed that such one-way functions exist. We defer the proof of Theorem 23.1 to Section 23.3, but we first discuss why such predicates do deserve the name "natural."

EXAMPLE 23.2

To develop some understanding of the definition of natural proofs, let us consider two predicates.

The first is $\mathcal{P}(g) = 1$ iff g is a Boolean function on n bits that has circuit complexity more than $n^{\log n}$. This predicate is n^c-useful for every constant c since $n^c = o(n^{\log n})$. The predicate also satisfies largeness since a random Boolean function satisfies it with probability almost 1 (see the proof of Theorem 6.21). However, we do not know if this predicate is *constructive*, since the trival algorithm for computing it would involve enumerating all circuits of size $n^{\log n}$, which requires $2^{n^{\log n}}$ time.

The second example is $\mathcal{P}'(g) = 1$ iff g correctly solves the decision problem 3SAT on inputs of size n. This function is *constructive*: To compute it, simply enumerate all inputs of size n and verify using a trivial 2^n-time algorithm for 3SAT that g gives the correct answer on all inputs. If 3SAT $\notin$ **SIZE**(n^c) (an open problem, of course), then $\mathcal{P}'$ satisfies n^c-usefulness since it is 0 on all functions in **SIZE**(n^c). However, $\mathcal{P}'$ does not satisfy largeness since it is 1 for only one function.

23.2 WHAT'S SO NATURAL ABOUT NATURAL PROOFS?

Now we recall some of the circuit lower bounds we proved earlier and check that they implicitly involve natural proofs. (This of course is the justification for the name "natural.")

EXAMPLE 23.3 (**AC**^{0})

The result that the parity function is not computable in **AC**^{0} (Section 14.1) involved the following steps: (a) Showing that every **AC**^{0} circuit can be simplified by restricting at most $n - n^\epsilon$ input bits so that it then becomes a constant function and (b) showing that the parity function cannot be made constant by restricting at most $n - n^\epsilon$ of its input bits.

Clearly, we can verify whether the property defined in (a) holds for a function $f : \{0, 1\}^n \to \{0, 1\}$ in $2^{O(n)}$ time—just enumerate all possible choices for the subsets of variables and all ways of setting them to 0/1. Thus, this proof satisfies the "constructiveness" condition. Moreover, it's not hard to show that a random function also cannot be made constant by fixing at most $n - n^\epsilon$ of its input bits (see Exercise 23.2), and so this proof satisfies the "largeness" condition as well.

EXAMPLE 23.4 *(Two-party communication complexity)*

To prove that f has high two-party communication complexity, it suffices to prove that the $n \times n$ matrix $M(f)$ introduced in Chapter 13 (namely, one whose (x, y) entry is $f(x, y)$) has no large subrectangle that is monochromatic. Now imagine the algorithmic complexity of checking this condition, where the input to the algorithm is $M(f)$ (i.e., a string of length 2^{2n}). The statement "$M(f)$ has no $k \times l$ monochromatic rectangle" is a **coNP** statement, and in fact is **coNP**-complete for general f (it's equivalent to the bipartite clique problem). However, the lower bound methods considered in Chapter 13 such as computing the rank or eigenvalues involve polynomial-time computation, which mean that they satisfy the "constructiveness" condition. The lower bound method using discrepancy is actually not a polynomial-time computation, but discrepancy can also be approximated within a factor $O(1)$ in polynomial-time (see the notes of Chapter 13) and hence this proof satisfies the constructiveness condition as well.

Moreover, all of the conditions used in these lower bounds, namely having small second-largest eigenvalue, high rank, or low discrepancy, are satisfied by a random matrix with high probability, and hence all these proofs satisfy the largeness condition as well.

We see that many lower bounds do use natural proofs, and in fact it turns out that all the known "combinatorial" circuit lower bounds are natural (e.g., lower bounds such as the ones in Chapters 12–16 that argue directly about the structure of circuits or protocols). But is there a more general principle at work here? Is there some inherent reason why lower bounds should satisfy the constructiveness and largeness conditions?

23.2.1 Why constructiveness?

Note that there is an old controversy within mathematics about "nonconstructive" proofs, whereby the existence of an object is established (usually by some argument about infinite sets) without giving an explicit algorithm for constructing the object. Most mathematicians today are completely comfortable with nonconstructive proofs.

In the context of natural proofs, we are insisting upon a much stronger form of "constructiveness"—the proof must yield not only a finite algorithm but in fact a polynomial-time algorithm. Many proofs that would be "constructive" for a mathematician would be nonconstructive under our definition. Surprisingly, even with this stricter definition, proofs in combinatorial mathematics are usually constructive, and the same is true of current circuit lower bounds as well.

In fact, circuit lower bounds usually rely upon techniques from combinatorics and in general, combinatorics techniques tend to be constructive in our sense of the word. In a few cases, combinatorial results initially proved "nonconstructively" later turned out to have constructive proofs: a famous example is the Lovàsz Local Lemma (discovered in 1975 [EL75]; algorithmic version discovered in 1991 [Bec91]). The same is true for several circuit lower bounds—Razborov and Rudich found a "naturalized" version of the lower bound for $\mathbf{ACC}^0[q]$ of Section 14.2, and Raz [Raz00] gave a natural proof (presented in Section 13.3) of the lower bound for multiparty communication complexity originally proved nonconstructively by Babai et al. in 1992 [BNS89].

Though nonconstructive techniques do exist is combinatorics—probabilistic method, nullstellensatz, topological arguments, etc.—we have not been able to use them to find better lower bounds for explicit functions. For speculative musings on these topics, please see Section 23.5.

23.2.2 Why largeness?

Why should a lower bound for a specific function, whether it's parity or 3SAT, use a property that holds with good probability for a random function as well? Below, we try to formalize this. The intuition in a nutshell is that every proof that a specific function $f_0 : \{0, 1\}^n \to \{0, 1\}$ does not have a size S circuit, actually implies that at least half of the functions from $\{0, 1\}^n$ to $\{0, 1\}$ do not have a circuit of size $S/2 - 10$. The reason is that if we choose a random $g : \{0, 1\}^n \to \{0, 1\}$, and write $f_0 = (f_0 \oplus g) \oplus g$ (where $g \oplus h$ denotes the function that maps every input x to $g(x) \oplus h(x)$), then we see that if both $(f_0 \oplus g)$ and g have circuits of size $< S/2 - 10$, then f_0 has a circuit of size $< S$. Since both g and $(f_0 \oplus g)$ are uniformly distributed, it follows that a lower bound on the circuit complexity of f_0 implies a lower bound on the complexity of half the functions.

23.2.3 Natural proofs from complexity measures

More generally, a large class of lower bound techniques turns out to yield properties that simultaneously satisfy the constructiveness and largeness properties (i.e., are natural).

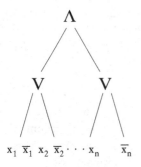

Figure 23.1. A Boolean formula.

For concreteness, let us focus on Boolean formulas (see Figure 23.1), which are Boolean circuits where gates have in-degree 2 and out-degree 1. It is tempting to prove a lower bound using some kind of induction. Suppose we have a function that we believe to be "complicated," in the sense that it requires a large Boolean formula to compute. Since the function computed at the output is "complicated," at least one of the functions on the incoming edges to the output gate should also be "pretty complicated" (after all those two functions can be combined with a single gate to produce a "complicated" function). Now we try to formalize this intuition and point out why one ends up proving a lower bound on the formula complexity of random functions.

The most obvious way to formalize "complicatedness" is as a function μ that maps every Boolean function on $\{0,1\}^n$ to a nonnegative integer. We say that μ is a *formal complexity measure* if it satisfies the following properties: First, the measure is low for trivial functions: $\mu(x_i) \leq 1$ and $\mu(\bar{x}_i) \leq 1$ for all i. Second, we require that

- $\mu(f \wedge g) \leq \mu(f) + \mu(g)$ for all f, g and
- $\mu(f \vee g) \leq \mu(f) + \mu(g)$ for all f, g

For instance, the following function ρ is trivially a formal complexity measure

$$\rho(f) = 1 + \text{the smallest formula size for } f \qquad (23.2)$$

In fact, it is easy to prove the following by induction.

Theorem 23.5 *If μ is any formal complexity measure, then $\mu(f)$ is a lower bound on the formula complexity of f.* $\diamond$

Thus to formalize the inductive approach outlined earlier, it suffices to define a measure μ such that, say, $\mu(3\mathsf{SAT})$ is super-polynomial. For example, one could try "fraction of inputs for which the function agrees with the $3\mathsf{SAT}$ function" or some suitably modified version of this. In general, one imagines that defining a measure that lets us prove a good lower bound for $3\mathsf{SAT}$ would involve some deep observation about the $3\mathsf{SAT}$ function. The next lemma seems to show, however, that even though all we care about is the $3\mathsf{SAT}$ function, our lower bound necessarily must reason about random functions.

Lemma 23.6 *Suppose μ is a formal complexity measure and there exists a function f : $\{0,1\}^n \rightarrow \{0,1\}$ such that $\mu(f) \geq S$ for some large number S. Then for at least $1/4$ of all functions $g : \{0,1\}^n \rightarrow \{0,1\}$, we must have $\mu(g) \geq S/4$.*

PROOF: The proof follows by the same observation as above. For a random function $g : \{0,1\}^n \to \{0,1\}$, we can write $f = h \oplus g$ where $h = f \oplus g$. So $f = (\bar{h} \wedge g) \vee (h \wedge \bar{g})$ and $\mu(f) \leq \mu(g) + \mu(\bar{g}) + \mu(h) + \mu(\bar{h})$. But if more than 3/4 of the functions have measure less than $S/4$, then by the union bound with positive probability all four functions $g, h, \bar{g}, \bar{h}$ will have measure less than $S/4$, implying that $\mu(f) < S$ and contradicting our assumption. ∎

In fact, the following stronger theorem holds.

Theorem 23.7 *If $\mu(f) > S$, then for all $\epsilon > 0$ and for at least $1 - \epsilon$ of all functions g we have that*

$$\mu(g) \geq \Omega \left(\frac{S}{(n + \log(1/\epsilon))^2} \right) \qquad \diamond$$

The idea behind the proof of the theorem is to write f as the Boolean combination of a small number of functions and then proceed similarly as in the proof of the lemma. These results mean that every lower bound that is obtained through a $2^{O(n)}$-time computable formal complexity measure μ will be natural.

23.3 PROOF OF THEOREM 23.1

Now we prove Theorem 23.1. We will use the key fact from Section 9.5.1 that we can build from every pseudorandom generator a *pseudorandom function family*. Recall that this is a family of functions $\{f_s\}_{s \in \{0,1\}^*}$, where for $s \in \{0, 1\}^m$, f_s is a function from $\{0, 1\}^m$ to $\{0, 1\}$. This family has the following two properties: (a) there is a polynomial-time algorithm that given s, x outputs $f_s(x)$ and (b) no polynomial-time algorithm can distinguish with non-negligible probability between oracle access to the function $f_s(\cdot)$ for a randomly chosen $s \in_R \{0, 1\}^m$ and oracle access to a random function from $\{0, 1\}^m$ to $\{0, 1\}$.

Since pseudorandom generators can be based on any one-way function [HILL99], we can obtain such a family from this assumption as well. In fact, one can verify by going over these reductions that if we start from a one-way function that cannot be inverted by 2^{n^ϵ}-time algorithms for some constant $\epsilon > 0$, then we obtain a pseudorandom function family $\{f_s\}_{s \in \{0,1\}^*}$ such that $f_s(\cdot)$ for $s \in_R \{0, 1\}^m$ cannot be distinguished from a random function by $2^{m^{\epsilon'}}$-time algorithms for some constant ϵ'.

What does all this have to do with natural proofs? Suppose $\mathcal{P}$ is a natural property on n-bit functions that is n^c-useful. It is an algorithm (albeit one running in $2^{O(n)}$ time) that (a) outputs 0 on functions with circuit complexity lower than n^c. (b) outputs 1 on a nonnegligible fraction of functions. Thus one can hope that such an algorithm allows us some nonnegligible chance of distinguishing a pseudorandom function from a truly random function, and this is what we show now.

Let $\{f_s\}$ be a 2^{m^ϵ}-secure pseudorandom function collection as described earlier. We use the natural property $\mathcal{P}$ to design an algorithm that distinguishes between a random function from $\{0, 1\}^m$ to $\{0, 1\}$ and f_s (to both of which it has oracle access) with nonnegligible probability.

Given oracle access to an unknown function h (which could either be f_s for some s or a random function), the distinguisher lets n be $m^{\epsilon/2}$ and constructs the truth table of the function g from $\{0, 1\}^n$ to $\{0, 1\}$ defined as $g(x) = h(x0^{m-n})$. Constructing this truth table only requires $2^{O(n)}$ time. Then the distinguisher runs algorithm $\mathcal{P}$ on this function and outputs whatever $\mathcal{P}$ does. Now consider the two cases under consideration. In one case, the provided function h was a random function, and so this new function g is also a random function on $\{0, 1\}^n$. Hence the probability that $\mathcal{P}$ outputs 1 is at least $1/n$. In the other case, the provided function h was f_s for some s. Then function g has circuit complexity at most n^c since the map $s, x \mapsto f_s(x)$ can be computed in poly(m) time, and hence the map $x \mapsto g(x)$ is computable by circuit of size poly$(m) = n^c$ that has s "hard-wired" into it. (To be sure, the distinguisher does not know s or this circuit; we are only asserting that the circuit *exists*.) Hence $\mathcal{P}$ given the truth table for g must output 0.

Thus the distinguisher distinguishes between f_s and a random function with probability at least $1/n$ and furthermore does so in $2^{O(n)}$ time, which is less than 2^{m^ϵ}. Viewed contrapositively, this implies that if the pseudorandom function was subexponentially strong, then the natural property cannot exist. ∎

23.4 AN "UNNATURAL" LOWER BOUND

Can we prove circuit lower bounds using proofs that are not natural? Here we show an interesting example that uses (among other ideas) simple old diagonalization! After presenting the result we comment more on why it is not natural.

To present this result we'll need the notion of a *promise problem*, which is a partially defined Boolean function from $\{0, 1\}^*$ to $\{0, 1\}$. That is, we can think of such a problem as a function $f : \{0, 1\}^* \to \{0, 1, \bot\}$ where $\bot$ represents "undefined". We say that an algorithm A solves a promise problem f, if whenever $f(x) \in \{0, 1\}$ then $A(x) = f(x)$, but we make no requirement on A's output when $f(x) = \bot$. We can generalize the definition of every complexity class to promise problems, and in particular denote by **PromiseMA** the corresponding generalization of the class **MA** defined in Section 8.2. That is, a promise problem f is in **PromiseMA** if there is a probabilistic polynomial-time algorithm A and a polynomial $p(\cdot)$ such that for every $x \in \{0, 1\}^*$, (a) if $f(x) = 1$ then there exists $y \in \{0, 1\}^{p(|x|)}$ such that $\Pr[A(x, y) = 1] \geq 2/3$ and (b) if $f(x) = 0$ then for every $y \in \{0, 1\}^{p(|x|)}$, $\Pr[A(x, y) = 1] \leq 1/3$. We have the following lower bound.

Theorem 23.8 ([San07])
For every $c \in \mathbb{N}$,

$$\textbf{PromiseMA} \not\subseteq \textbf{SIZE}(n^c) \,,$$

where $\textbf{SIZE}(n^c)$ denotes the set of promise problems with n^c-sized circuits.

PROOF: Recall that in the interactive proof for **PSPACE** shown in Section 8.3, the prover algorithm can be implemented itself in polynomial space. This means that if L is a **PSPACE**-complete problem, then there is an interactive proof for L where the prover can prove that a string x is in L using polynomial time and oracle access to the language

L itself. In fact, it turns out that there is a such a language L_0 where on inputs of length n the prover needs only to make queries of length at most n [TV02]. This means that if this language L_0 can be decided by a circuit of size $S(n)$, then the prover can simply send this circuit, which a probabilistic verifier can then use to run the interactive protocol on its own. Therefore, we see that if $L_0 \in$ **SIZE**$(S(n))$ then there's a poly$(S(n))$-time **MA** protocol for L_0. (We saw similar reasoning in Theorem 8.22 and Lemma 20.18.)

Define $S(n)$ to be one plus the size of the smallest circuit that solves L_0 on length-n inputs. Now if $S(n) \leq$ poly(n), this means that **PSPACE** $\subseteq$ **MA**, but in this case **MA** clearly has a language outside of **SIZE**(n^c) for every c (see Exercise 6.5 of Chapter 6). In fact, the same reasoning holds even if there's a constant c such that $S(n) \leq n^c$ infinitely often, and so we may assume that $S(n) = n^{\omega(1)}$. Note that L_0 has a poly$(S(n))$-time **MA** protocol but has no $S(n)$-sized circuit. If only $S(n)$ was time constructible, we could "scale down" this separation by defining the language L_1 to be $\{x01^{S(|x|)^{1/c}-|x|-1} : x \in L_0\}$, implying that L_1 is in **MA** but not in **SIZE**(n^c). Unfortunately, we cannot assume that $S(n)$ is time constructible and hence cannot ensure that L_1 is in **MA**. Nonetheless, we can define the following *promise problem* f_1: It is defined only on inputs of the form $y = x01^{S(|x|)^{1/c}-|x|-1}$ and on such inputs $f_1(y) = L_0(x)$. It's not hard to see that $f_1 \in$ **PromiseMA** $\setminus$ **SIZE**(n^c). ∎

This proof is unnatural because underlying it is the proof that **PSPACE** $\not\subseteq$ **SIZE**(n^c), which uses diagonalization—an inherently unnatural technique that focuses on one very specific function and hence violates the largeness condition. Alternatively, one can also view a diagonalization proof as showing that a function has the property that it disagrees with every small circuit on some input—a property that satisfies largeness but not constructiveness. In fact, Theorem 23.1 shows that there are no natural proofs for Theorem 23.8, unless subexponentially strong one-way functions do not exist. It is also known that this lower bound does not relativize [Aar06]. Unfortunately, "pushing down" these diagonalization/arithmetization-based techniques to obtain a lower bound on a function in **NP** seems very hard.

23.5 A PHILOSOPHICAL VIEW

We think that the natural proof idea and other negative results of this nature are very valuable. When one is stuck on a difficult question, it is useful to try to prove that it can't be solved, or can't be solved with particular methods. This can give additional insight on the question that might otherwise be very hard to obtain. By understanding the obstacles, we know what we'll have to tackle or bypass to solve certain problems, and this has proven to be extremely useful countless times in complexity theory and theoretical computer science at large. In this case, the natural proofs paradigm shows that any complexity class that has a plausible pseudorandom function generator is going to pose a problem to known lower bound techniques. Since even low classes like **NC**^{1} and TC$_0$ contain plausible pseudorandom functions, one gets a fairly good understanding of why the project of proving lower bounds ground to a halt at the class **ACC**^{0}.

However, perhaps natural proofs have been so successful at encompassing known lower bound techniques, that this discouraged researchers from thinking too hard about circuit lower bounds. This need not be the case. There are techniques in combinatorics that do not satisfy either the constructiveness or the largeness properties. Personally, we feel that the constructiveness property may be easier to get around, and one sees this already in the nonnatural proof of the previous section. Looking more broadly at combinatorics, a relevant example is Lovàsz's lower bound of the chromatic number of the Kneser graph [Lov78]. Lower bounding the chromatic number is **coNP**-complete in general. Lovàsz gives a topological proof (using the famous Borsuk-Ulam Fixed-Point Theorem) that determines the chromatic number of the Kneser graph exactly. From his proof one can indeed obtain an algorithm for solving chromatic number on all graphs ([MZ04])—but it runs in **PSPACE** for general graphs! So if this were a circuit lower bound we could call it "nonconstructive." Nevertheless, Lovàsz's reasoning for the particular case of the Kneser graph is not overly complicated because the graph is highly symmetrical. This suggests we should not blindly trust the intuition that "nonconstructive ≡ difficult." We should also remember the lesson learned from the results on limitations of relativizing techniques (Section 3.4). We've seen that one new nonrelativizing technique—arithmetization—allowed us to prove a host of results in Chapters 8, 11, etc., that cannot be proven using relativizing techniques. It may very well be that a single new "unnatural" technique will open the floodgates for a great many lower bounds.

CHAPTER NOTES AND HISTORY

The observation that circuit lower bounds may unwittingly end up reasoning about random functions first appears in Razborov [Razb89]'s result about the limitations of the method of approximation. We did not cover the full spectrum of ideas in the Razborov-Rudich paper [RR94], where it is observed that candidate pseudorandom function generators exist even in the class TC^0, which lies between $\mathbf{ACC}^0$ and $\mathbf{NC}^1$. Thus natural proofs will probably not allow us to separate even TC^0 from **P**. Razborov's observation about submodular measures in Exercise 23.4 is important because many existing approaches for formula complexity use submodular measures; thus they will fail to even prove superlinear lower bounds. The lower bound of Section 23.4 is due to Santhanam [San07]; similar techniques were first used to show hierarchy theorems for probabilistic algorithms with small advice [Bar02, FS04, GST04].

In contrast with our limited optimism, Razborov himself expresses (in the introduction to [Razb03b]) a view that the obstacle posed by the natural proofs observation is very serious. He observes that existing lower bound approaches use weak theories of arithmetic such as bounded arithmetic. He conjectures that any circuit lower bound attempt in such a logical system must be natural (and hence unlikely to work). But there are several theorems even in discrete mathematics use reasoning (e.g., fixed-point theorems like Borsuk-Ulam) that does not seem to be formalizable in bounded arithmetic, which is our reason for optimism. Some researchers are far more pessimistic: They fear that **P** versus **NP** may be independent of mathematics (say, of Zermelo-Fraenkel Set Theory). See Aaronson's survey [Aar03] for more on this issue.

Very recently, Aaronson and Wigderson [AW08] showed a new obstacles for complexity results called algebrization. A complexity class separation $\mathcal{C} \nsubseteq \mathcal{D}$ cannot be solved using "algebrizing techniques" if there is there is an oracle O such that $\mathcal{C}^{\tilde{O}} \subseteq \mathcal{D}^O$, where $\tilde{O}$ denotes the *low-degree extension* of the Boolean function O to a larger field or ring such as the integers. Roughly speaking, algebrizing techniques capture all results such as **IP = PSPACE** and the **PCP** theorems that are proven by arithmetization. In particular, the lower bound of Section 23.4 uses algebrizing techniques, but [AW08] show that one cannot prove even a superlinear lower bound on **NP** using such techniques.

EXERCISES

23.1. Prove Theorem 23.7.

23.2. Prove that a random function $g : \{0, 1\}^n \to \{0, 1\}$ satisfies $\mathcal{P}(g) = 1$ with high probability, where $\mathcal{P}$ is the property, defined in Example 23.3, that for no fixing of $n - n^\epsilon$ of g's turns g into a constant function.

23.3. Prove Wigderson's observation: There is no natural proof that the DISCRETE LOG problem (i.e., given a prime p, and $g, y \in \mathbb{Z}_p^*$, with $g \neq 1$, find $x \in \mathbb{Z}_p^*$ such that $y = g^p$ (mod p)) requires circuits of 2^{n^ϵ} size for some constant $\epsilon > 0$.
H543

23.4. (Razborov [Razb92]) A *submodular* complexity measure is a complexity measure that satisfies $\mu(f \vee g) + \mu(f \wedge g) \le \mu(f) + \mu(g)$ for all functions f, g. Show that for every n-bit function f_n, such a measure satisfies $\mu(f_n) = O(n)$.
H543

23.5. Let L be the language containing all triples $\langle \varphi, P, i \rangle$ such that the ith bit of φ (mod P) is equal to 1, where P is a number and φ is an expression involving constants, the arithmetic operations $+, -, \cdot$ and sum and product quantifiers of the form $\sum_{x_i \in \{0, 1\}}$ or $\prod_{x_i \in \{0, 1\}}$, satisfying the following property: if we sort $x_1, \dots, x_n$ according to their order of appearance in φ, then for every variable x_i there is at most a single $\prod$ quantifier involving x_j (for $j > i$) appearing before the last occurrence of x_i in φ. Show that L is **PSPACE** complete and furthermore, there is an interactive proof for L where the prover algorithm runs in polynomial time using an oracle for L, and when proving that some $x \in \{0, 1\}^n$ is in L it uses queries of length at most n to its oracle.
H543

Mathematical background

This appendix reviews the mathematical notions used in this book. However, most of these are only used in few places, and so the reader might want to only quickly review Sections A.1 and A.2, and come back to the other sections as needed. In particular, apart from probability, the first part of the book essentially requires only comfort with mathematical proofs and some very basic notions of discrete math.

The topics described in this appendix are covered in greater depth in many texts and online sources. Almost all of the mathematical background needed is covered in a good undergraduate "discrete math for computer science" course as currently taught at many computer science departments. Some good sources for this material are the lecture notes by Papadimitriou and Vazirani [PV06], and the book by Rosen [Ros06].

The mathematical tool we use most often is discrete probability. Alon and Spencer [AS00b] is a great resource in this area. Also, the books of Mitzenmacher and Upfal [MU05] and Motwani and Raghavan [MR95] cover probability from a more algorithmic perspective.

Although knowledge of algorithms is not strictly necessary for this book, it would be quite useful. It would be helpful to review either one of the two recent books by Dasgupta et al. [DPV06] and Kleinberg and Tardos [KT06] or the earlier text by Cormen et al. [CLRS01]. This book does not require prior knowledge of computability and automata theory, but some basic familiarity with that theory could be useful: See Sipser's book [Sip96] for an excellent introduction. See Shoup's book [Sho05] for a computer science introduction to algebra and number theory.

Perhaps *the* mathematical prerequisite needed for this book is a certain level of comfort with *mathematical proofs*. The fact that a mathematical proof has to be absolutely convincing does not mean that it has to be overly formal and tedious. It just has to be clearly written, and contain no logical gaps. When you write proofs, try to be clear and concise, rather than using too much formal notation. Of course, to be absolutely convinced that some statement is true, we need to be certain of what that statement means. This is why there is a special emphasis in mathematics (and this book) on very precise *definitions*. Whenever you read a definition, try to make sure you completely understand it, perhaps by working through some simple examples. Oftentimes, understanding the meaning of a mathematical statement is more than half the work to prove that it is true.

A.1 SETS, FUNCTIONS, PAIRS, STRINGS, GRAPHS, LOGIC

Sets. A *set* contains a finite or infinite number of elements, without repetition or respect to order, for example $\{2, 17, 5\}$, $\mathbb{N} = \{1, 2, 3, \ldots\}$ (the set of natural numbers), $[n] = \{1, 2, \ldots, n\}$ (the set of natural numbers from 1 ro n), $\mathbb{R}$ (the set of real numbers). For a finite set A, we denote by $|A|$ the number of elements in A. Some operations on sets are (1) *union*: $A \cup B = \{x : x \in A \text{ or } x \in B\}$, (2) *intersection*: $A \cap B = \{x : x \in A \text{ and } x \in B\}$, and (3) *set difference*: $A \setminus B = \{x : x \in A \text{ and } x \notin B\}$.

Functions. We say that f is a *function* from a set A to B, denoted by $f : A \to B$, if it maps any element of A into an element of B. If B and A are finite, then the number of possible functions from A to B is $|B|^{|A|}$. We say that f is *one-to-one* if for every $x, w \in A$ with $x \neq w$, $f(x) \neq f(w)$. If A, B are finite, the existence of such a function implies that $|A| \leq |B|$. We say that f is *onto* if for every $y \in B$, there exists $x \in A$ such that $f(x) = y$. If A, B are finite, the existence of such a function implies that $|A| \geq |B|$. We say that f is a *permutation* if it is both one-to-one and onto. For finite A, B, the existence of a permutation from A to B implies that $|A| = |B|$.

Pairs and tuples. If A, B are sets, then the $A \times B$ denotes the set of all ordered pairs $\langle a, b \rangle$ with $a \in A, b \in B$. Note that if A, B are finite, then $|A \times B| = |A| \cdot |B|$. We can define similarly $A \times B \times C$ to be the set of ordered triples $\langle a, b, c \rangle$ with $a \in A, b \in B, c \in C$. For $n \in \mathbb{N}$, we denote by A^n the set $A \times A \times \cdots \times A$ (n times). We will often use the set $\{0, 1\}^n$, consisting of all length-n sequences of bits (i.e., length n strings), and the set $\{0, 1\}^* = \cup_{n \geq 0} \{0, 1\}^n$ ($\{0, 1\}^0$ has a single element: a binary string of length zero, which we call the empty word and denote by ε). As mentioned in Section 0.1 we can represent various objects (numbers, graphs, matrices, etc.) as binary strings, and use $\llcorner x \lrcorner$ (not to be confused with the floor operator $\lfloor x \rfloor$) to denote the representation of x. Moreover, we often drop the $\llcorner \lrcorner$ symbols and use x to denote both the object and its representation.

Graphs. A *graph* G consists of a set V of *vertices* (which we often assume is equal to the set $[n] = \{1, \ldots, n\}$ for some $n \in N$) and a set E of *edges*, which consists of unordered pairs (i.e., size two subsets) of elements in V. We denote the edge $\{u, v\}$ of the graph by $\overline{uv}$. For $v \in V$, the *neighbors* of v are all the vertices $u \in V$ such that $\overline{uv} \in E$. In a *directed graph*, the edges consist of *ordered pairs* of vertices, and to stress this we sometimes denote the edge $\langle u, v \rangle$ in a directed graph by $\overrightarrow{uv}$. One can represent an n-vertex graph G by its *adjacency matrix* which is an $n \times n$ matrix A such that $A_{i,j}$ is equal to 1 if the edge $\overrightarrow{ij}$ is present in G ith and is equal to 0 otherwise. One can think of an undirected graph as a directed graph G that satisfies that for every u, v, G contains the edge $\overrightarrow{uv}$ if and only if it contains the edge $\overrightarrow{vu}$. Hence, one can represent an undirected graph by an adjacency matrix that is *symmetric* ($A_{i,j} = A_{j,i}$ for every $i, j \in [n]$).

Boolean operators. A *Boolean variable* is a variable that can be either TRUE or FALSE (we sometimes identify TRUE with 1 and FALSE with 0). We can combine variables via the logical operations AND ($\wedge$), OR ($\vee$), and NOT ($\neg$, sometimes also denoted by an overline), to obtain *Boolean formulas*. For example, the following is a Boolean formula on the variables u_1, u_2, u_3: $(u_1 \wedge \overline{u}_2) \vee \neg(u_3 \wedge \overline{u}_1)$. The definitions of the operations are the usual: $a \wedge b = \text{TRUE}$ if $a = \text{TRUE}$ and $b = \text{TRUE}$ and is equal to FALSE otherwise; $\overline{a} = \neg a = \text{TRUE}$ if $a = \text{FALSE}$ and is equal to FALSE otherwise; $a \vee b = \neg(\overline{a} \vee \overline{b})$. We sometimes use other Boolean operators such as the XOR ($\oplus$) operator, but they can be always replaced with the equivalent expression using $\wedge, \vee, \neg$ (e.g., $a \oplus b = (a \wedge \bar{b}) \vee (\bar{a} \wedge b)$). If φ is a formula in n variables $u_1, \ldots, u_n$, then for any *assignment* of values $u \in \{\text{FALSE}, \text{TRUE}\}^n$ (or equivalently, $\{0, 1\}^n$), we denote by $\varphi(u)$ the value of φ when its variables are assigned the values in u. We say that φ is *satisfiable* if there exists a u such that $\varphi(u) = \text{TRUE}$.

Quantifiers. We will often use the *quantifiers* $\forall$ (for all) and $\exists$ (exists). That is, if φ is a condition that can be TRUE or FALSE depending on the value of a variable x, then we write $\forall_x \varphi(x)$ to denote the statement that φ is TRUE for *every* possible value that can be assigned to x. If A is a set then we write $\forall_{x \in A} \varphi(x)$ to denote the statement that φ is TRUE for every assignment for x from the set A. The quantifier $\exists$ is defined similarly. Formally, we say that $\exists_x \varphi(x)$ holds if and only if $\neg(\forall_x \neg \varphi(x))$ holds.

Big-Oh Notation. We will often use the big-Oh notation (i.e., $O, \Omega, \Theta, o, \omega$) as defined in Section 0.3.

A.2 PROBABILITY THEORY

A *finite probability space* is a finite set $\Omega = \{\omega_1, \ldots, \omega_N\}$ along with a set of numbers $p_1, \ldots, p_N \in [0, 1]$ such that $\sum_{i=1}^{N} p_i = 1$. A random element is selected from this space by choosing ω_i with probability p_i. If x is chosen from the sample space Ω, then we denote this by $x \in_R \Omega$. If no distribution is specified, then we use the uniform distribution over the elements of Ω (i.e., $p_i = \frac{1}{N}$ for every i).

An *event* over the space Ω is a subset $A \subseteq \Omega$ and the *probability* that A occurs, denoted by $\Pr[A]$, is equal to $\sum_{i:\omega_i \in A} p_i$. To give an example, the probability space could be that of all 2^n possible outcomes of n tosses of a fair coin (i.e., $\Omega = \{0, 1\}^n$ and $p_i = 2^{-n}$ for every $i \in [2^n]$) and the event A can be that the number of coins that come up "heads" (or, equivalently, 1) is even. In this case, $\Pr[A] = 1/2$ (exercise). The following simple bound—called the *union bound*—is often used in the book. For every set of events $A_1, A_2, \ldots, A_n$,

$$\Pr[\cup_{i=1}^{n} A_i] \leq \sum_{i=1}^{n} \Pr[A_i] \tag{A.1}$$

Inclusion exclusion principle

The union bound is a special case of a more general principle. Indeed, note that if the sets $A_1, \ldots, A_n$ are not *disjoint* then the probability of $\cup_i A_i$ could be smaller than $\sum_i \Pr[A_i]$ since we are overcounting elements that appear in more than one set. We can correct this by subtracting $\sum_{i<j} \Pr[A_i \cap A_j]$, but then we might be undercounting, since we subtracted elements that appear in at least three sets too many times. Continuing this process we get the following.

Claim A.1 *(Inclusion-exclusion principle) For every $A_1, \ldots, A_n$,*

$$\Pr[\cup_{i=1}^{n} A_i] = \sum_{i=1}^{n} \Pr[A_i] - \sum_{1 \leq i < j \leq n} \Pr[A_i \cap A_j] + \cdots + (-1)^{n-1} \Pr[A_1 \cap \cdots \cap A_n]$$

Moreover, this is an alternating sum, which means that if we take only the first k summands of the right-hand side, then this upper bounds the left-hand side if k is odd, and lower bounds it if k is even.   ◇

We sometimes use the following corollary of this claim, known as the Bonefforni inequality.

Corollary A.2 *For every events $A_1, \ldots, A_n$,*

$$\Pr[\cup_{i=1}^n A_i] \geq \sum_{i=1}^n \Pr[A_i] - \sum_{1 \leq i < j \leq n} \Pr[A_i \cap A_j] \qquad ◇$$

A.2.1 Random variables and expectations

A *random variable* is a mapping from a probability space to $\mathbb{R}$. For example, if Ω is as above (i.e., the set of all possible outcomes of n tosses of a fair coin), then we can denote by X the number of coins that came up heads.

The *expectation* of a random variable X, denoted by $E[X]$, is its weighted average. That is, $E[X] = \sum_{i=1}^N p_i X(\omega_i)$. The following simple claim follows from the definition.

Claim A.3 *(Linearity of expectation) For X, Y random variables over a space Ω, denote by $X + Y$ the random variable that maps ω to $X(\omega) + Y(\omega)$. Then*

$$E[X + Y] = E[X] + E[Y] \qquad ◇$$

This claims implies that the random variable X from the example above has expectation $n/2$. Indeed $X = \sum_{i=1}^n X_i$, where X_i is equal to 1 if the ith coins came up heads and is equal to 0 otherwise. But clearly, $E[X_i] = 1/2$ for every i.

For a real number α and a random variable X, we define αX to be the random variable mapping ω to $\alpha \cdot X(\omega)$. Note that $E[\alpha X] = \alpha E[X]$.

EXAMPLE A.4

Suppose that we choose k random numbers $x_1, \ldots, x_k$ independently in $[n]$. What is the expected number of *collisions*: unordered pairs $\{i, j\}$ such that $x_i = x_j$? For every $i \neq j$, define the random variable $Y_{i,j}$ to equal 1 if $x_i = x_j$ and 0 otherwise. Since for every choice of x_i, the probability that $x_j = x_i$ is $1/n$, we have that $E[Y_{i,j}] = 1/n$. The number of collisions is the sum of $Y_{i,j}$ over all $i \neq j$ in $[k]$. Thus by linearity of expectation the expected number of collisions is

$$\sum_{1 \leq i < j \leq n} E[Y_{i,j}] = \binom{k}{2} \frac{1}{n}$$

This means that we expect at least one collision once $\binom{k}{2} \geq n$, which happens once k is larger than roughly $\sqrt{2n}$. This fact is often known as the *birthday paradox* because it explains the seemingly strange phenomenon that a class of more than 27 or so students is quite likely to have a pair of students sharing the same birthday, even though there are 365 days in the year.

Note that in contrast, if $k \ll \sqrt{n}$ then by the union bound, the probability there will be even one collision is at most $\binom{k}{2}/n \ll 1$.

Notes: (1) We sometimes also consider random variables whose range is not $\mathbb{R}$, but other sets such as $\mathbb{C}$ or $\{0, 1\}^n$. (2) Also, we often identify a random variable X over the sample space Ω with the distribution $X(\omega)$ for $\omega \in_{_R} \Omega$. For example, we may use both $\Pr_{x \in_{_R} X}[x^2 = 1]$ and $\Pr[X^2 = 1]$ to denote the probability that for $\omega \in_{_R} \Omega$, $X(\omega)^2 = 1$.

A.2.2 The averaging argument

The following simple fact can be surprisingly useful:

> *The Averaging Argument*: If $a_1, a_2, \ldots, a_n$ are some numbers whose average is c then some $a_i \geq c$.

Equivalently, we can state this in probabilistic terms as follows:

Lemma A.5 *(The probabilistic method) If X is a random variable which takes values from a finite set and $E[X] = \mu$ then the event "$X \geq \mu$" has nonzero probability.*   ◇

The following two facts are also easy to verify.

Lemma A.6 *If $a_1, a_2, \ldots, a_n \geq 0$ are numbers whose average is c, then the fraction of a_i's that are at least kc is at most $1/k$.*   ◇

Lemma A.7 *(Markov's inequality) Any nonnegative random variable X satisfies*

$$\Pr(X \geq k\, E[X]) \leq \frac{1}{k}$$ ◇

Can we give any meaningful upper bound on the probability that X is much *smaller* than its expectation? Yes, if X is bounded.

Lemma A.8 *If $a_1, a_2, \ldots, a_n$ are numbers in the interval $[0, 1]$ whose average is ρ then at least $\rho/2$ of the a_i's are at least as large as $\rho/2$.*   ◇

PROOF: Let γ be the fraction of i's such that $a_i \geq \rho/2$. Then the average of the a_i's is bounded by $\gamma \cdot 1 + (1 - \gamma)\rho/2$. Hence, $\rho \leq \gamma + \rho/2$, implying $\gamma \geq \rho/2$. ∎

More generally, we have the following.

Lemma A.9 *If $X \in [0, 1]$ and $E[X] = \mu$ then for any $c < 1$ we have*

$$\Pr[X \leq c\mu] \leq \frac{1 - \mu}{1 - c\mu}$$

EXAMPLE A.10

Suppose you took a lot of exams, each scored from 1 to 100. If your average score was 90, then in at least half the exams you scored at least 80.

A.2.3 Conditional probability and independence

If we already know that an event B happened, this reduces the space from Ω to $\Omega \cap B$, where we need to scale the probabilities by $1/\Pr[B]$ so they will sum up to one. Thus, the probability of an event A *conditioned* on an event B, denoted $\Pr[A|B]$, is equal to $\Pr[A \cap B]/\Pr[B]$ (where we always assume that B has positive probability).

We say that two events A, B are *independent* if $\Pr[A \cap B] = \Pr[A]\Pr[B]$. Note that this implies that $\Pr[A|B] = \Pr[A]$ and $\Pr[B|A] = \Pr[B]$. We say that a set of events $A_1, \ldots, A_n$ are *mutually independent* if for every subset $S \subseteq [n]$,

$$\Pr[\cap_{i \in S} A_i] = \prod_{i \in S} \Pr[A_i] \tag{A.2}$$

We say that $A_1, \ldots, A_n$ are *k-wise independent* if (A.2) holds for every $S \subseteq [n]$ with $|S| \le k$.

We say that two random variables X, Y are *independent* if for every $x, y \in \mathbb{R}$, the events $\{X = x\}$ and $\{Y = y\}$ are independent. We generalize similarly the definition of mutual independence and k-wise independence to sets of random variables $X_1, \ldots, X_n$. We have the following claim.

Claim A.11 *If $X_1, \ldots, X_n$ are mutually independent, then*

$$E[X_1 \cdots X_n] = \prod_{i=1}^{n} E[X_i] \qquad \diamond$$

PROOF:

$$E[X_1 \cdots X_n] = \sum_x x \Pr[X_1 \cdots X_n = x]$$

$$= \sum_{x_1, \ldots, x_n} x_1 \cdots x_n \Pr[X_1 = x_1 \text{ and } X_2 = x_2 \cdots \text{ and } X_n = x_n]$$

$$= \text{(by independence)}$$

$$\sum_{x_1, \ldots, x_n} x_1 \cdots x_n \Pr[X_1 = x_1] \cdots \Pr[X_n = x_n]$$

$$= \left(\sum_{x_1} x_1 \Pr[X_1 = x_1] \right) \left(\sum_{x_2} x_2 \Pr[X_2 = x_2] \right) \cdots \left(\sum_{x_n} x_n \Pr[X_n = x_n] \right) = \prod_{i=1}^{n} E[X_i]$$

where the sums above are over all the possible real numbers that can be obtained by applying the random variables or their products to the finite set Ω. ∎

A.2.4 Deviation upper bounds

Under various conditions, one can give better upper bounds on the probability of a random variable "straying too far" from its expectation. These upper bounds are usually derived by clever use of Markov's inequality.

The *variance* of a random variable X is defined to be $\mathrm{Var}[X] = \mathrm{E}[(X - \mathrm{E}(X))^2]$. Note that since it is the expectation of a nonnegative random variable, $\mathrm{Var}[X]$ is always nonnegative. Also, using linearity of expectation, we can derive that $\mathrm{Var}[X] = \mathrm{E}[X^2] - (\mathrm{E}[X])^2$. The *standard deviation* of a variable X is defined to be $\sqrt{\mathrm{Var}[X]}$.

The first bound is Chebyshev's inequality, useful when only the variance is known.

Lemma A.12 *(Chebyshev Inequality) If X is a random variable with standard deviation σ, then for every $k > 0$,*

$$\Pr[|X - E[X]| > k\sigma] \leq 1/k^2$$

$\diamond$

PROOF: Apply Markov's inequality to the random variable $(X - \mathrm{E}[X])^2$, noting that by definition of variance, $E[(X - \mathrm{E}[X])^2] = \sigma^2$. ∎

Chebyshev's inequality is often useful in the case that X is equal to $\sum_{i=1}^{n} X_i$ for pairwise independent random variables $X_1, \ldots, X_n$. This is because of the following claim, that is left as an exercise.

Claim A.13 *If $X_1, \ldots, X_n$ are pairwise independent then*

$$Var(\sum_{i=1}^{n} X_i) = \sum_{i=1}^{n} Var(X_i)$$

$\diamond$

The next inequality has many names and is widely known in theoretical computer science as the *Chernoff bound* (see also Note 7.11). It considers scenarios of the following type. Suppose we toss a fair coin n times. The expected number of heads is $n/2$. How tightly is this number concentrated? Should we be very surprised if after $1,000$ tosses we have 625 heads? The bound we present is slightly more general, since it concerns n different coin tosses of possibly different expectations (the expectation of a coin is the probability of obtaining "heads"; for a fair coin this is $1/2$). These are sometimes known as Poisson trials.

Theorem A.14 *("Chernoff" bounds) Let $X_1, X_2, \ldots, X_n$ be mutually independent random variables over $\{0, 1\}$ (i.e., X_i can be either 0 or 1) and let $\mu = \sum_{i=1}^{n} E[X_i]$. Then for every $\delta > 0$,*

$$\Pr[\sum_{i=1}^{n} X_i \geq (1+\delta)\mu] \leq \left[\frac{e^\delta}{(1+\delta)^{(1+\delta)}} \right]^\mu \tag{A.3}$$

$$\Pr[\sum_{i=1}^{n} X_i \leq (1-\delta)\mu] \leq \left[\frac{e^{-\delta}}{(1-\delta)^{(1-\delta)}} \right]^\mu \tag{A.4}$$

$\diamond$

Often, we will only use the following corollary.

Corollary A.15 *Under the above conditions, for every c > 0,*

$$\Pr\left[\left|\sum_{i=1}^{n} X_i - \mu\right| \geq c\mu\right] \leq 2 \cdot e^{-\min\{c^2/4, c/2\}\mu}$$

In particular this probability is bounded by $2^{-\Omega(\mu)}$ (where the constant in the Ω notation depends on c). ◇

PROOF: Surprisingly, the Chernoff bound is also proved using the Markov inequality. We only prove the first inequality; the second inequality can be proved similarly. We introduce a positive dummy variable t and observe that

$$E[\exp(tX)] = E\left[\exp\left(t\sum_i X_i\right)\right] = E\left[\prod_i \exp(tX_i)\right] = \prod_i E[\exp(tX_i)] \quad (A.5)$$

where $\exp(z)$ denotes e^z and the last equality holds because the X_i r.v.s are independent. Now,

$$E[\exp(tX_i)] = (1 - p_i) + p_i e^t$$

therefore,

$$\prod_i E[\exp(tX_i)] = \prod_i [1 + p_i(e^t - 1)] \leq \prod_i \exp(p_i(e^t - 1))$$

$$= \exp\left(\sum_i p_i(e^t - 1)\right) = \exp(\mu(e^t - 1)) \quad (A.6)$$

as $1 + x \leq e^x$. Finally, apply Markov's inequality to the random variable $\exp(tX)$, viz.

$$\Pr[X \geq (1 + \delta)\mu] = \Pr[\exp(tX) \geq \exp(t(1 + \delta)\mu)] \leq \frac{E[\exp(tX)]}{\exp(t(1 + \delta)\mu)} = \frac{\exp((e^t - 1)\mu)}{\exp(t(1 + \delta)\mu)}$$

using (A.5), (A.6), and the fact that t is positive. Since t is a dummy variable, we can choose any positive value we like for it. Simple calculus shows that the right-hand side is minimized for $t = \ln(1 + \delta)$, and this leads to the theorem statement. ∎

So, if all n coin tosses are fair (Heads has probability ½) then the the probability of seeing N heads where $|N - n/2| > a\sqrt{n}$ is at most $2e^{-a^2/4}$. In particular, the chance of seeing at least 625 heads in 1,000 tosses of an unbiased coin is less than 5.3×10^{-7}.

A.2.5 Some other inequalities

Jensen's inequality

The following inequality, generalizing the inequality $E[X^2] \geq E[X]^2$, is also often useful.

Lemma A.16 *(Jensen's Inequality) A function $f : \mathbb{R} \to \mathbb{R}$ is convex if for every $p \in [0, 1]$ and $x, y \in \mathbb{R}$, $f(px + (1 - p)y) \leq p \cdot f(x) + (1 - p) \cdot f(y)$. For every random variable X and convex function f, $f(E[X]) \leq E[f(X)]$.* ◇

Approximating the binomial coefficient

Of special interest is the *Binomial* random variable B_n denoting the number of coins that come up "heads" when tossing n fair coins. For every k, $\Pr[B_n = k] = 2^{-n}\binom{n}{k}$ where $\binom{n}{k} = \frac{n!}{k!(n-k)!}$ denotes the number of size-k subsets of $[n]$. Clearly, $\binom{n}{k} \leq n^k$, but sometimes we will need a better estimate for $\binom{n}{k}$ and use the following approximation.

Claim A.17 *For every* n, $k < n$, $\left(\frac{n}{k}\right)^k \leq \binom{n}{k} \leq \left(\frac{ne}{k}\right)^k$. ◇

The best approximation can be obtained via Stirling's formula.

Lemma A.18 *(Stirling's Formula) For every* n,

$$\sqrt{2\pi n}\left(\frac{n}{e}\right)^n e^{\frac{1}{12n+1}} < n! < \sqrt{2\pi n}\left(\frac{n}{e}\right)^n e^{\frac{1}{12n}}$$ ◇

It can be proven by taking natural logarithms and approximating $\ln n! = \ln(1 \cdot 2 \cdots n) = \sum_{i=1}^{n} \ln i$ by the integral $\int_1^n \ln x\, dx = n \ln n - n + 1$. It implies the following corollary.

Corollary A.19 *For every* $n \in \mathbb{N}$ *and* $\alpha \in [0,1]$,

$$\binom{n}{\alpha n} = (1 \pm O(n^{-1}))\frac{1}{\sqrt{2\pi n\alpha(1-\alpha)}}2^{H(\alpha)n}$$

where $H(\alpha) = \alpha \log(1/\alpha) + (1-\alpha)\log(1/(1-\alpha))$ *and the constants hidden in the* O *notation are independent of both* n *and* α. ◇

More useful estimates

The following inequalities can be obtained via elementary calculus:

- For every $x \geq 1$, $\left(1 - \frac{1}{x}\right)^x \leq \frac{1}{e} \leq \left(1 - \frac{1}{x+1}\right)^x$.
- For every k, $\sum_{i=1}^{n} i^k = \Theta\left(\frac{n^{k+1}}{k+1}\right)$.
- For every $k > 1$, $\sum_{i=1}^{\infty} i^{-k} < O(1)$.
- For every $c, \epsilon > 0$, $\sum_{i=1}^{\infty} \frac{i^c}{(1+\epsilon)^i} < O(1)$.
- For every n, $\sum_{i=1}^{n} \frac{1}{i} = \ln n \pm O(1)$.

A.2.6 Statistical distance

The following notion of when two distributions are close to one another is often very useful.

Definition A.20 *(Statistical distance)* Let Ω be some finite set. For two random variables X and Y with range Ω, their *statistical distance* (also known as *variation distance*) is defined as $\Delta(X, Y) = \max_{S \subseteq \Omega}\{|\Pr[X \in S] - \Pr[Y \in S]|\}$. ◇

Some texts use the name *total variation distance* for the statistical distance. The next lemma gives some useful properties of this distance.

Lemma A.21 *Let X, Y, Z be any three distributions taking values in the finite set Ω. Then*

1. $\Delta(X, Y) \in [0, 1]$ *where* $\Delta(X, Y) = 0$ *iff X is identical to Y.*
2. *(Triangle Inequality)* $\Delta(X, Z) \leq \Delta(X, Y) + \Delta(Y, Z)$.
3. $\Delta(X, Y) = \frac{1}{2} \sum_{x \in \Omega} |\Pr[X = x] - \Pr[Y = x]|$.
4. $\Delta(X, Y) \geq \epsilon$ *iff there is a Boolean function* $f : \Omega \to \{0, 1\}$ *such that* $|E[f(X)] - E[f(Y)]| \geq \epsilon$.
5. *For every finite set Ω' and function $f : \Omega \to \Omega'$, $\Delta(f(X), f(Y)) \leq \Delta(X, Y)$. (Here $f(X)$ is a distribution on Ω' obtained by taking a sample of X and applying f.)*

Note that Item 3. means that $\Delta(X, Y)$ is equal to the L_1-distance of X and Y divided by 2 (see Section A.5.4). That is, if we think of X as a vector in $\mathbb{R}^\Omega$ where $X_\omega = \Pr[X = \omega]$, and define for every vector $\mathbf{v} \in \mathbb{R}^\Omega$, $|\mathbf{v}|_1 = \sum_{\omega \in \Omega} |\mathbf{v}_\omega|$, then $\Delta(X, Y) = 1/2|X - Y|_1$.

PROOF OF LEMMA A.21: We start with Item 3. For every pairs of distributions X, Y over $\{0, 1\}^n$ let S be the set of strings x such that $\Pr[X = x] > \Pr[X = y]$. Then it is easy to see that this choice of S maximizes the quantity $b(S) = \Pr[X \in S] - \Pr[Y \in S]$ and in fact $b(S) = \Delta(X, Y)$ since if we had a set T with $b(T) < -b(S)$, then the complement $\overline{T}$ of T would satisfy $b(\overline{T}) > b(S)$. But,

$$\sum_{x \in \{0,1\}^n} |\Pr[X = x] - \Pr[Y = x]|$$

$$= \sum_{x \in S} \Pr[X = x] - \Pr[Y = x] + \sum_{x \notin S} \Pr[Y = x] - \Pr[X = x]$$

$$= \Pr[X \in S] - \Pr[Y \in S] + (1 - \Pr[Y \in S]) - (1 - \Pr[X \in S])$$

$$= 2\Pr[X \in S] - 2\Pr[Y \in S]$$

establishing Item 3.

The triangle inequality (Item 2.) follows immediately from Item 3. since $\Delta(X, Y) = 1/2|X - Y|_1$ and the L_1 norm satisfies the triangle inequality. Item 3. also implies Item 1. since $|X - Y|_1 = 0$ iff $X = Y$ and $|X - Y|_1 \leq \|X\| + |Y|_1 = 1 + 1$.

Item 4. is just a rephrasing of the definition of statistical distance, identifying a set $S \subseteq \{0, 1\}^n$ with the function $f : \{0, 1\}^n \to \{0, 1\}$ such that $f(x) = 1$ iff $x \in S$. Item 5. follows from Item 4. noting that if $\Delta(X, Y) \leq \epsilon$ then $|E[g(f(X))] - E[g(f(Y))]| \leq \epsilon$ for every function g. ∎

A.3 NUMBER THEORY AND GROUPS

The *integers* are the set $\mathbb{Z} = \{0, \pm 1, \pm 2, \ldots\}$, while the natural numbers are the subset $\mathbb{N} = \{0, 1, 2, \ldots\}$.[1] A basic fact is that we can *divide* any integer n by an nonzero integer k to obtain ℓ, r such that $n = k\ell + r$ and $r \in \{0, \ldots, n - 1\}$. If $r = 0$, then we say that k *divides* n and denote this by $k|n$. The *factors* of n are the set of positive integers that divide n.

---

[1] Some texts exclude 0 in $\mathbb{N}$; in most cases, this does not make any difference.

The *greatest common divisor* of two integers n, m, denoted by $gcd(n, m)$ is the largest integers d such that $d|n$ and $d|m$. We say that n and m are *coprime* if their greatest common divisor is equal to 1. The following basic facts are not hard to verify:

- If a nonzero integer c divides both n and m then $c|d$.
- The greatest common divisor of n and m is the smallest positive integer d such that there exist integers x, y satisfying $nx + my = d$.
- There is a polynomial-time (i.e., polylog(n, m)-time) algorithm that on input n, m outputs the greatest common divisor d of n, m and the integers x, y satisfying $nx + my = d$. (This algorithm is known as *Euclid's Algorithm*.)

A number $p > 1$ is *prime* if its only factors are 1 and p. The following basic facts are known about prime numbers:

- Every positive integer n can be written uniquely (up to ordering) as a product of prime numbers. This is called the *prime factorization* of n.
- If $gcd(p, a) = 1$ and $p|ab$, then $p|b$. In particular, if a prime p divides $a \cdot b$, then either $p|a$ or $p|b$.

A fundamental question in number theory is how many primes exist. A celebrated result follows.

Theorem A.22 *(The Prime Number Theorem (Hadamard, de la Vallée Poussin 1896))* *For $n > 1$, let $\pi(n)$ denote the number of primes between 1 and n, then*

$$\pi(n) = \frac{n}{\ln n}(1 \pm o(1)) \qquad \diamond$$

The original proofs of the prime number theorem used rather deep mathematical tools, and in fact people have conjectured that this is *inherently* the case. But in 1949 both Erdös and Selberg (independently) found elementary proofs for this theorem. For most computer science applications, the following weaker statement proven by Chebychev suffices.

Theorem A.23 $\pi(n) = \Theta(\frac{n}{\log n})$. $\qquad \diamond$

PROOF: Consider the number $\binom{2n}{n} = \frac{2n!}{n!n!}$. By Stirling's formula, we know that $\log \binom{2n}{n} = (1 - o(1))2n$ and in particular $n \leq \log \binom{2n}{n} \leq 2n$. Also, all the prime factors of $\binom{2n}{n}$ are between 0 and $2n$, and each factor p cannot appear more than $k = \left\lfloor \frac{\log 2n}{\log p} \right\rfloor$ times. Indeed, for every n, the number of times p appears in the factorization of $n!$ is $\sum_i \left\lfloor \frac{n}{p^i} \right\rfloor$, since we get $\left\lfloor \frac{n}{p} \right\rfloor$ times a factor p in the factorizations of $\{1, \ldots, n\}$, $\left\lfloor \frac{n}{p^2} \right\rfloor$ times a factor of the form p^2, etc. Thus the number of times p appears in the factorization of $\binom{2n}{n} = \frac{(2n)!}{n!n!}$ is equal to $\sum_i \left\lfloor \frac{2n}{p^i} \right\rfloor - 2 \left\lfloor \frac{n}{p^i} \right\rfloor$: a sum of at most k elements (since $p^{k+1} > 2n$) each of which is either 0 or 1.

Thus, $\binom{2n}{n} \le \prod_{\substack{1 \le p \le 2n \\ p \text{ prime}}} p^{\left\lfloor \frac{\log 2n}{\log p} \right\rfloor}$. Taking logs we get that

$$n \le \log \binom{2n}{n} \le \sum_{\substack{1 \le p \le 2n \\ p \text{ prime}}} \left\lfloor \frac{\log 2n}{\log p} \right\rfloor \log p \le \sum_{\substack{1 \le p \le 2n \\ p \text{ prime}}} \log 2n = \pi(2n) \log 2n$$

establishing $\pi(n) = \Omega(\frac{n}{\log n})$.

To prove that $\pi(n) = O(\frac{n}{\log n})$, we define the function $\vartheta(n) = \sum_{\substack{1 \le p \le n \\ p \text{ prime}}} \log p$. It suffices to prove that $\vartheta(n) = O(n)$ (exercise!). But since all the primes between $n + 1$ and $2n$ divide $\binom{2n}{n}$ at least once, $\binom{2n}{n} \ge \prod_{\substack{n+1 \le p \le 2n \\ p \text{ prime}}} p$. Taking logs we get

$$2n \ge \log \binom{2n}{n} \ge \sum_{\substack{n+1 \le p \le 2n \\ p \text{ prime}}} \log p = \vartheta(2n) - \vartheta(n)$$

thus getting a recursive equation $\vartheta(2n) \le \vartheta(n) + 2n$, which solves to $\vartheta(n) = O(n)$. ∎

A.3.1 Groups

A *group* is an abstraction that captures some properties of mathematical objects such as the integers, matrices, functions, and more. Formally, a group is a set that has a binary operation, say $\star$, defined on it that is associative and has an inverse. That is, $(G, \star)$ is a group if

1. For every $a, b, c \in G$, $(a \star b) \star c = a \star (b \star c)$.
2. There exists a special element $id \in G$ such that $a \star id = a$ for every $a \in G$, and for every $a \in G$, there exists $b \in G$ such that $a \star b = b \star a = id$. (This element b is called the *inverse* of a, and is often denote as a^{-1} or $-a$.)

Examples for groups are the integers, with addition being the group operation (and zero the identity element), the nonzero real numbers with multiplication being the group operation(and one the identity element), and the set of functions from a domain A to itself, with function composition being the group operation.

Often, it is natural to use additive ($+$) or multiplicative ($\cdot$) notation to denote the group operation rather than $\star$. In these cases we will use ℓa (or respectively a^ℓ) to denote the result of applying the operation to a ℓ times.

A.3.2 Finite groups

A group is *finite* if it has a finite number of elements. We denote by $|G|$ the number of elements of G. Examples for finite groups are the following:

- The group $\mathbb{Z}_n$ of the integers from 0 to $n - 1$ with the operation being addition modulo n. In particular $\mathbb{Z}_2$ is the set $\{0, 1\}$ with the XOR operation.
- The group S_n of the permutations on $[n]$, with the operation being function composition.
- The group $(\mathbb{Z}_2)^n$ of n-bit strings with the operation being bitwise XOR. More generally for every two groups G and H, we can define the group $G \times H$ to be a group whose

elements are pairs $\langle g, h \rangle$ with $g \in G$ and $h \in H$ and with the group operation corresponding to applying the group operations of G and H componentwise. Similarly, we define G^n to be the group $G \times G \times \cdots \times G$ (n times).

- For every n, the group $\mathbb{Z}_n^*$ consists of the set $\{k : 1 \leq k \leq n - 1, \ gcd(k, n) = 1\}$ and the operation of multiplication modulo n. Note that if $gcd(k, n) = 1$, then there exist x, y such that $kx + ny = 1$ or in other words $kx = 1 \pmod{n}$, meaning that x is the inverse of k modulo n. This also means that we can find this inverse in polynomial time using Euclid's algorithm. The size of $\mathbb{Z}_n^*$ is denoted by $\varphi(n)$ and the function φ is known as *Euler's quotient function*. Note that if n is prime then $\varphi(n) = n - 1$. It is known that for every $n > 6$, $\varphi(n) \geq \sqrt{n}$.

A *subgroup* of G is a subset of G that is itself a group (i.e., closed under the group operation and taking inverses). The following result is often quite useful.

Theorem A.24 *If G is a finite group and H is a subgroup of G then $|H|$ divides $|G|$.* ⋄

PROOF: Consider the family of sets of the form $aH = \{ah : h \in H\}$ for all $a \in G$ (we're using here multiplicative notation for the group). It is easy to see that the map $x \mapsto ax$ is one-to-one and hence $|aH| = |H|$ for every a. Hence it will suffice to show that we can partition G into disjoint sets from this family. Yet this family clearly covers G (as $a \in aH$ for every $a \in G$), and hence it suffices to show that for every a, b either $aH = bH$ or aH and bH are disjoint. Indeed, suppose that there exist $x, y \in H$ such that $ax = by$ then for every element $az \in aH$, we have that $az = (byx^{-1})z$ and since $yx^{-1}z \in H$ we get that $az \in bH$. ■

Corollary A.25 *(Fermat's Little Theorem) For every n and $x \in \{1, \ldots, n - 1\}$, $x^{\varphi(n)} = 1 \pmod{n}$. In particular, if n is prime then $x^{n-1} = 1 \pmod{n}$.* ⋄

PROOF: Consider the set $H = \{x^\ell : \ell \in \mathbb{Z}\}$. This is clearly a subgroup of $\mathbb{Z}_n^*$ and hence $|H|$ divides $\varphi(n)$. But the size of H is simply the smallest number k such that $x^k = 1 \pmod{n}$. Indeed, there must be such a number since, because $\mathbb{Z}_n^*$, if we consider the sequence of numbers $1, x, x^2, x^3, \ldots$, then eventually we get i, j such that $x^i = x^j$ for $i < j$, meaning that $x^{i-j} = 1 \pmod{n}$. Thus, the above sequence looks like $1, x, x^2, \ldots, x^{k-1}, 1, x, x^2, \ldots$, meaning that $|H| = k$.

Since $x^{|H|} = 1 \pmod{n}$, obviously taking x to the power $\varphi(n)$ (which is a multiple of $|H|$) yields also 1 modulo n. ■

The *order* of an element x of a group G is the smallest integer k such that x^k is equal to the identity element. The proof above shows that in a finite group G, every element has a finite order and furthermore this order divides the size of G. An element x of G with order $|G|$ is called a *generator* of G, since in this case the subgroup $\{x, x^1, x^2, \ldots\}$ is all of G.[2] If a group G has a generator then we say that G is *cyclic*. An example for a simple cyclic group is the group $\mathbb{Z}_n$ of the numbers $\{0, \ldots, n - 1\}$ with addition modulo

---

[2] A more general definition (that works also for infinite groups) is that x is a generator of G if the subgroup $\{x^\ell : \ell \in \mathbb{Z}\}$ is equal to G.

n, that is generated by the element 1 (and also by any other element that is co-prime to n—exercise).

A.3.3 The Chinese Remainder Theorem

Let $n = pq$ where p, q are coprime. The Chinese Remainder Theorem (CRT) says that the group $\mathbb{Z}_n^*$ (multiplicative group modulo n) is isomorphic to the group $Z_p^* \times \mathbb{Z}_q^*$ (pairs of numbers with multiplication done componentwise modulo p and q, respectively).

Theorem A.26 *If $n = pq$ where p, q coprime then function f that maps x to $\langle x \pmod{p}, x \pmod{q} \rangle$ is one-to-one on $\mathbb{Z}_n^*$. Furthermore f is an isomorphism in the sense that $f(xy) = f(x)f(y)$ (where multiplication on the left-hand side is modulo n and on the right-hand side is componentwise modulo p and q, respectively).* ◇

PROOF: The "furthermore" part can be easily verified, and so we focus on showing that f is one-to-one. We need to show that if $f(x) = f(x')$, then $x = x'$. Since $f(x - x') = f(x) - f(x')$, it suffices to show that if $x = 0 \pmod{p}$ (i.e., $p|x$) and $x = 0 \pmod{q}$ (i.e., $q|x$), then $x = 0 \pmod{n}$ (i.e., $pq|x$). Yet, assume that $p|x$, and write $x = pk$. Then since $gcd(p, q) = 1$ and $q|x$, we know that $q|k$, meaning that $pq|x$. ∎

The Chinese Remainder Theorem can be easily generalized to show that for every $n = p_1 p_2 \cdots p_k$, where all the p_i's are coprime, there is an isomorphism between Z_n^* to $\mathbb{Z}_{p_1}^* \times \cdots \times \mathbb{Z}_{p_k}^*$, meaning that for every n, the group $\mathbb{Z}_n^*$ is isomorphic to a product of groups of the form $\mathbb{Z}_q^*$ for q a prime power (i.e., number of the form p^ℓ for prime p). In fact, it can be generalized even further to show that every Abelian group G is isomorphic to a product $G_1 \times G_2 \times \cdots \times G_k$ where all the G_i's are cyclic. (This can be viewed as a generalization of the CRT because all the groups of the form $\mathbb{Z}_q^*$ for q a power of an odd prime are cyclic, and all groups of the form $\mathbb{Z}_{2^k}^*$ are either cyclic or products of two cyclic groups.)

A.4 FINITE FIELDS

A *field* is a set $\mathbb{F}$ that has an addition ($+$) and multiplication ($\cdot$) operations that behave in the expected way: Satisfy associative, commutative, and distributive laws have both additive and multiplicative inverses and neutral elements 0 and 1 for addition and multiplication, respectively. In other words, $\mathbb{F}$ is a field if it is an Abelian group with the operation $+$ and an identity element 0, and has an additional operation $\cdot$ such that $\mathbb{F} \setminus \{0\}$, and $\cdot$ forms an Abelian group, and furthermore the two operation satisfy the distributive rule $a(b + c) = ab + ac$.

Familiar fields are the real numbers ($\mathbb{R}$), the rational numbers ($\mathbb{Q}$) and the complex numbers ($\mathbb{C}$), but there are also *finite* fields. Recall that for a prime p, the set $\{0, \ldots, p - 1\}$ is an Abelian group with the addition modulo p operation and the set $\{1, \ldots, p - 1\}$ is an Abelian group with the multiplication modulo p operation. Hence $\{0, \ldots, p - 1\}$ form a field with these two operations, which we denote by GF(p).

The simplest example for such a field is the field GF(2) consisting of $\{0, 1\}$ where multiplication is the AND ($\wedge$) operation and addition is the XOR operation.

Every finite field $\mathbb{F}$ has a number ℓ such that for every $x \in F, x+x+\cdots+x$ (ℓ times) is equal to the zero element of $\mathbb{F}$ (exercise). This number ℓ is called the *characteristic* of $\mathbb{F}$. For every prime q, the characteristic of GF(q) is equal to q.

A.4.1 Nonprime fields

One can see that if n is not prime, then the set $\{0, \ldots, n-1\}$ with addition and multiplication modulo n is not a field, as there exist two nonzero elements x, y in this set such that $x \cdot y = n = 0 \pmod{n}$. Nevertheless, there are finite fields of size n for nonprime n. Specifically, for every prime q, and $k \geq 1$, there exists a field of q^k elements, which we denote by GF(q^k). We will very rarely need to use such fields in this book but still provide an outline of their construction below.

For every prime q and k there exists an *irreducible* degree k polynomial P over the field GF(q) (P is irreducible if it cannot be expressed as the product of two polynomials P', P'' of lower degree). We then let GF(q^k) be the set of all $(k-1)$-degree polynomials over GF(q). Each such polynomial can be represented as a vector of its k coefficients. We perform both addition and multiplication modulo the polynomial P. Note that addition corresponds to standard vector addition of k-dimensional vectors over GF(q), and both addition and multiplication can be easily done in poly($n, \log q$) time (we can reduce a polynomial S modulo a polynomial P using a similar algorithm to long division of numbers). It turns out that no matter how we choose the irreducible polynomial P, we will get the same field, up to renaming of the elements. There is a deterministic poly(q, k)-time algorithm to obtain an irreducible polynomial of degree k over GF(q). There are also probabilistic algorithms (and deterministic algorithms whose analysis relies on unproven assumptions) that obtain such a polynomial in poly($\log q, k$) time (see the book [Sho05]).

For us, the most important example of a finite field is GF(2^k), which consists of the set $\{0, 1\}^k$, with addition being component-wise XOR, and multiplication being polynomial multiplication via some irreducible polynomial which we can find in poly(k) time. In fact, we will mostly not even be interested in the multiplicative structure of GF(2^k) and only use the addition operation (i.e., use it as the vector space GF(2)^k, see below).

A.5 BASIC FACTS FROM LINEAR ALGEBRA

For $\mathbb{F}$ a field and $n \in \mathbb{N}$, we denote by $\mathbb{F}^n$ the set of n-length tuples (or *vectors*) of elements of $\mathbb{F}$. If $\mathbf{u}, \mathbf{v} \in \mathbb{F}^n$ and $x \in \mathbb{F}$ then we denote by $\mathbf{u} + \mathbf{v}$ the vector obtained by componentwise addition of $\mathbf{u}$ and $\mathbf{v}$ and by $x\mathbf{u}$ the vector obtained by multiplying each entry of $\mathbf{u}$ by x.

A set of vectors $\mathbf{u}^1, \ldots, \mathbf{u}^k$ in $\mathbb{F}^n$ is *linearly independent* if the only solution to the equation $x_1\mathbf{u}^1 + \cdots + x_k\mathbf{u}^k = \mathbf{0}$ (where $\mathbf{0}$ denotes the all-zero vector) is $x_1 = x_2 = \cdots = x_k = 0$. It can be shown that if $\mathbf{u}^1, \ldots, \mathbf{u}^k$ are linearly independent then $k \leq n$ (exercise). A set of n linearly independent vectors in $\mathbb{F}^n$ is called a *basis* of $\mathbb{F}^n$. It is not hard to see that if $\mathbf{u}^1, \ldots, \mathbf{u}^n$ is a basis of $\mathbb{F}^n$ then every vector $\mathbf{v} \in \mathbb{F}^n$ can be expressed as a linear combination $\mathbf{v} = \sum_i x_i \mathbf{u}^i$ of the vectors $\mathbf{u}^1, \ldots, \mathbf{u}^n$ and furthermore this expression is unique. The *standard basis* of $\mathbb{F}^n$ is the set $\mathbf{e}^1, \ldots, \mathbf{e}^n$, where $\mathbf{e}^i_j$ is equal to 1 if $j = i$ and to 0 otherwise.

A subset $S \subseteq \mathbb{F}^n$ is called a *subspace* if it is closed under addition and scalar multiplication (i.e., $\mathbf{u}, \mathbf{v} \in S$ and $x, y \in \mathbb{F}$ implies that $x\mathbf{u} + y\mathbf{v} \in S$). The *dimension* of S, denoted by $\dim(S)$ is defined to be the maximum number k such that there are k linearly independent vectors in S. Such a set of $\dim(S)$ linearly independent vectors in S is called a *basis*, and one can see that every vector in S can be expressed as a linear combination of the vectors in the basis.

A function $f : \mathbb{F}^n \to \mathbb{F}^m$ is *linear* if $f(\mathbf{u} + \mathbf{v}) = f(\mathbf{u}) + f(\mathbf{v})$. It's not hard to verify that the following hold for every linear function f:

- If $\mathbf{u}^1, \ldots, \mathbf{u}^n$ is a basis for $\mathbb{F}^n$, then for every $\mathbf{v} \in \mathbb{F}^n$, $f(\mathbf{v}) = \sum_i x_i f(\mathbf{u}_i)$ where $x_1, \ldots, x_n$ are the elements such that $\mathbf{v} = \sum x_i \mathbf{u}^i$. Thus, to know f's value at every point, it suffices to know its value on the basis elements.
- The set $Im(f) = \{f(\mathbf{v}) : \mathbf{v} \in \mathbb{F}^n\}$ is a subspace of $\mathbb{F}^m$.
- The set $Ker(f) = \{\mathbf{v} : f(\mathbf{v}) = 0\}$ is a subspace of $\mathbb{F}^n$.
- $\dim(Im(f)) + \dim(Ker(f)) = n$.

A linear function $f : \mathbb{F}^n \to \mathbb{F}^m$ is often described by an $m \times n$ matrix A whose ith column is $f(\mathbf{e}^i)$. The *multiplication* of an $m \times n$ matrix A and an $n \times k$ matrix B is the $n \times k$ matrix $C = AB$ where $C_{i,j} = \sum_{\ell \in [n]} A_{i,\ell} B_{\ell,j}$. One can verify that if A describes a function $f : \mathbb{F}^n \to \mathbb{F}^m$ and B describes a function $g : \mathbb{F}^k \to \mathbb{F}^n$, then C describes the function $h : \mathbb{F}^k \to \mathbb{F}^m$ mapping $\mathbf{v}$ to $f(g(\mathbf{v}))$. It can also be verified that if we identify members of $\mathbb{F}^n$ with $n \times 1$ matrices (i.e., column vectors), then $f(\mathbf{v}) = A\mathbf{v}$.

The *determinant* of an $n \times n$ matrix A, denoted by $\det(A)$ is equal to $\sum_{\sigma \in S_n} (-1)^{sgn(\sigma)} \prod_{i=1}^n A_{i,\sigma(i)}$, where S_n denotes the group of permutations over $[n]$ and $sgn(\sigma)$ is equal to 1 if the number of pairs $\langle i, j \rangle$ such that $i < j$ but $\sigma(i) > \sigma(j)$ is odd, and is equal to 0 otherwise.[3] We have the following two facts:

- $\det(AB) = \det(A)\det(B)$. This can be verified by direct computation.
- If A is an upper triangular matrix (i.e., $A_{i,j} = 0$ whenever $i > j$), then $\det(A) = A_{1,1}A_{2,2}\cdots A_{n,n}$. Indeed, for a permutation σ to give a nonzero contribution to the determinant in this case it must satisfy $\sigma(i) \geq i$ for every i, which means that it is the identity permutation.

Together these two rules give a polynomial-time algorithm to compute the determinant of a matrix A by following the well-known Gaussian elimination algorithm to express A as $E_1 E_2 \cdots E_m D$ where the E_i's are elementary matrices (multiplication by which corresponds to switching two columns, multiplying a column by a field element, or adding one column to another) and the D is upper diagonal. Since the determinant is easy to compute for all these matrices, we can compute the determinant of A as well.

---

[3] It is known that every permutation $\sigma \in S_n$ can be represented as a composition of transpositions, where a transposition is a permutation that only switches between two elements in $[n]$ and leaves the other elements intact (one proof for this statement is the Bubblesort algorithm). If $\tau_1, \ldots, \tau_m$ is a sequence of transpositions such that their composition equals σ, then the *sign* of σ is equal to $(-1)^m$. It can be shown that the sign is well-defined in the sense that it does not depend on the representation of σ as a composition of transpositions.

The following lemma relates the determinant of a matrix to the function it represents.

Lemma A.27 *For a function $f : \mathbb{F}^n \to \mathbb{F}^n$ represented by an $n \times n$ matrix A, the following conditions are equivalent:*

- *The columns of A are a basis for $\mathbb{F}^n$.*
- *f is one-to-one.*
- *$\dim(Im(f)) = n$.*
- *$\dim(Ker(f)) = 0$.*
- *$\det(A) \neq 0$.*
- *There exists $\mathbf{v} \in \mathbb{F}^n$ such that the equation $A\mathbf{x} = \mathbf{v}$ has exactly one solution.*
- *For every $\mathbf{v} \in \mathbb{F}^n$, the equation $A\mathbf{x} = \mathbf{v}$ has exactly one solution.*

Furthermore, if f is one-to-one, then the mapping f^{-1} is linear and is represented by an $n \times n$ matrix A^{-1} whose (i,j)th entry is $\frac{\det(A_{-(i,j)})}{\det(A)}$, where $A_{-(i,j)}$ denotes the $(n-1) \times (n-1)$ matrix obtained by removing the ith row and jth column from A.

A.5.1 Inner product

The vector spaces $\mathbb{R}^n$ and $\mathbb{C}^n$ have an additional structure that is often quite useful.[4] An *inner product* over $\mathbb{C}^n$ to be a function mapping two vectors $\mathbf{u}, \mathbf{v}$ to a complex number $\langle \mathbf{u}, \mathbf{v} \rangle$ satisfying the following conditions:

- $\langle x\mathbf{u} + y\mathbf{w}, \mathbf{v} \rangle = x\langle \mathbf{u}, \mathbf{v} \rangle + y\langle \mathbf{w}, \mathbf{v} \rangle$.
- $\langle \mathbf{v}, \mathbf{u} \rangle = \overline{\langle \mathbf{u}, \mathbf{v} \rangle}$ where $\overline{z}$ denotes complex conjugation (i.e., if $z = a + ib$, then $\overline{z} = a - ib$).
- For every $\mathbf{u}$, $\langle \mathbf{u}, \mathbf{u} \rangle$ is a nonnegative real number with $\langle \mathbf{u}, \mathbf{u} \rangle = 0$ iff $\mathbf{u} = \mathbf{0}$.

The two examples for inner products we will use are the standard inner product mapping $\mathbf{x}, \mathbf{y} \in \mathbb{C}^n$ to $\sum_{i=1}^{n} x_i \overline{y}_i$, and the expectation or normalized inner product mapping $\mathbf{x}, \mathbf{y} \in \mathbb{C}^n$ to $\frac{1}{n} \sum_{i=1}^{n} x_i \overline{y}_i$. We can also define inner products over the space $\mathbb{R}^n$, in which case we drop the conjugation.

If $\langle \mathbf{u}, \mathbf{v} \rangle = 0$ we say that $\mathbf{u}$ and $\mathbf{v}$ are *orthogonal* and denote this by $\mathbf{u} \perp \mathbf{v}$. We have the following result.

Lemma A.28 *If nonzero vectors $\mathbf{u}^1, \ldots, \mathbf{u}^k$ satisfy $\mathbf{u}^i \perp \mathbf{u}^j$ for all $i \neq j$, then they are linearly independent.* ◇

PROOF: Suppose that $\sum_i x_i \mathbf{u}^i = \mathbf{0}$ and consider take an inner product of this vector with itself. We get that

$$0 = \left\langle \sum_i x_i \mathbf{u}^i, \sum_j x_j \mathbf{u}^j \right\rangle = \sum_{i,j} x_i \overline{x}_j \langle \mathbf{u}^i, \mathbf{u}^j \rangle = \sum_i |x_i|^2 \langle \mathbf{u}^i, \mathbf{u}^j \rangle \tag{A.7}$$

---

[4] The reason we restrict ourselves to these fields is that they have characteristic zero, which means that there does not exist a number $k \in \mathbb{N}$ and nonzero $a \in \mathbb{F}$ such that $ka = 0$ (where ka is the result of adding a to itself k times). You can check that if there is such a number for a field $\mathbb{F}$, then there will not be an inner product over $\mathbb{F}^n$.

where the last equality follows from the fact that $\langle \mathbf{u}^i, \mathbf{u}^j \rangle = 0$ for $i \neq j$. But unless all the x_i's are zero, the right-hand side of (A.7) is strictly positive. (Recall that for a complex number $x = a + ib$, $|x| = \sqrt{a^2 + b^2}$ and $|x|^2 = x\bar{x}$.) ∎

A set $\mathbf{u}^1, \ldots, \mathbf{u}^n$ of nonzero vectors in $\mathbb{C}^n$ satisfying $\langle \mathbf{u}^i, \mathbf{u}^j \rangle = 0$ for $i \neq j$ is called an *orthogonal basis* of $\mathbb{C}^n$. If in addition $\langle \mathbf{u}^i, \mathbf{u}^i \rangle = 1$ for all i, then we say this is an *orthonormal basis*. An orthonormal basis consists of n linearly independent vectors and hence as its name implies is a basis of $\mathbb{C}^n$, meaning that every vector $\mathbf{v}$ can be expressed as $\mathbf{v} = \sum_i x_i \mathbf{u}^i$. By taking an inner product of this equality with $\mathbf{u}^i$, one can see that $x_i = \langle \mathbf{v}, \mathbf{u}^i \rangle$.

The following identity (that can be viewed as a generalization of the Pythagorean Theorem) is often useful.

Lemma A.29 *(Parseval's Identity) If $\mathbf{u}^1, \ldots, \mathbf{u}^n$ is an orthonormal basis for $\mathbb{C}^n$, then for every $\mathbf{v}$,*

$$\langle \mathbf{v}, \mathbf{v} \rangle = \sum_{i=1}^{n} |x_i|^2$$

where $x_1, \ldots, x_n$ are the numbers such that $\mathbf{v} = \sum_i x_i \mathbf{u}^i$. ◇

PROOF: As in the proof of Lemma A.28,

$$\langle \mathbf{v}, \mathbf{v} \rangle = \left\langle \sum_i x_i \mathbf{u}^i, \sum_j x_j \mathbf{u}^j \right\rangle = \sum_i |x_i|^2 \langle \mathbf{u}^i, \mathbf{u}^i \rangle . \blacksquare$$

Vector spaces with an inner product are known as *Hilbert spaces*.

A.5.2 Dot product

Even in a field $\mathbb{F}$ that doesn't have an inner product, we can define the *dot product* of two vectors $\mathbf{u}, \mathbf{v} \in \mathbb{F}^n$, denoted by $\mathbf{u} \odot \mathbf{v}$, as $\sum_{i=1}^{n} \mathbf{u}_i \mathbf{v}_i$. For every subspace $S \subseteq \mathbb{F}^n$, we define $S^\perp = \{\mathbf{u} : \mathbf{u} \odot \mathbf{v} = 0 \forall \mathbf{v} \in S\}$. We leave the following simple claim as an exercise.

Claim A.30 $\dim(S) + \dim(S^\perp) = n$. ◇

In particular for every nonzero vector $\mathbf{u} \in \mathbb{F}^n$, the subspace $\mathbf{u}^\perp$ of vectors $\mathbf{v}$ satisfying $\mathbf{u} \odot \mathbf{v} = 0$ has dimension $n - 1$ and hence cardinality $|\mathbb{F}|^{n-1}$. As a corollary we get the following very useful fact.

Claim A.31 *(The random subsum principle) For every nonzero $\mathbf{u} \in GF(2)$ (the field $\{0, 1\}$ with addition and multiplication modulo 2):*

$$\Pr_{\mathbf{v} \in_R GF(2)^n} [\mathbf{u} \odot \mathbf{v} = 0] = 1/2$$

◇

A.5.3 Eigenvectors and eigenvalues

If A is an $n \times n$ complex matrix and $\mathbf{v} \in \mathbb{C}^n$ is a nonzero vector, we say that $\mathbf{v}$ is an *eigenvector* of A if there exists $\lambda \in \mathbb{C}$ such that $A\mathbf{v} = \lambda\mathbf{v}$. The value λ is called an *eigenvalue* of A. We say that A is *diagonalizable* if there is a basis $\mathbf{v}_1, \ldots, \mathbf{v}_n$ of eigenvectors for A. In other words, there is an invertible matrix P such that PAP^{-1} is a diagonal matrix.

Note that A has an eigenvector with eigenvalue λ if and only if the matrix $A - \lambda I$ is noninvertible, where I is the identity matrix. Thus in particular λ is a root of the polynomial $p(x) = \det(A - xI)$. Thus the fundamental Theorem of Algebra (that every complex polynomial has as many roots as the degree) that every square matrix has at least one eigenvector. (A noninvertible matrix has an eigenvector zero.)

For a matrix A, the *conjugate transpose* of A, denoted A^*, is the matrix such that for every i, j, $A^*_{i,j} = \overline{A}_{j,i}$ where - denotes the complex conjugate operation. We say that an $n \times n$ matrix A is *Hermitian* if $A = A^*$. An Hermitian matrix with only real entries is called *symmetric*. That is, a real matrix is symmetric if $A = A^\dagger$ where $\dagger$ is the transpose operation (i.e., $A^\dagger_{i,j} = A_{j,i}$). An equivalent condition (exercise) is that A is Hermitian if and only if

$$\langle A\mathbf{u}, \mathbf{v} \rangle = \langle \mathbf{u}, A\mathbf{v} \rangle \tag{A.8}$$

An important useful fact about Hermitian matrices is the following theorem.

Theorem A.32 *If A is an $n \times n$ Hermitian matrix, then there exists an orthogonal basis of eigenvectors for A.*   ◇

PROOF: We prove this by induction on n. We know that A has one eigenvector $\mathbf{v}$ with eigenvalue λ. Now let $S = \mathbf{v}^\perp$ be the $n - 1$ dimensional space of all vectors orthogonal to $\mathbf{v}$. We claim that for every $\mathbf{u} \in S$, $A\mathbf{u} \in S$. Indeed, if $\langle \mathbf{u}, \mathbf{v} \rangle = 0$, then

$$\langle A\mathbf{u}, \mathbf{v} \rangle = \langle \mathbf{u}, A\mathbf{v} \rangle = \overline{\lambda}\langle \mathbf{u}, \mathbf{v} \rangle = 0$$

Thus the restriction of A to S is an $n - 1$ dimensional linear operator satisfying (A.8) and hence by induction this restriction has an orthogonal basis of eigenvectors $\mathbf{v}^2, \ldots, \mathbf{v}^n$. Adding $\mathbf{v}$ to this set we get an n-dimensional orthogonal basis of eigenvectors for A. ∎

Note that if A is real and symmetric, then all its eigenvalues must be real also (with no imaginary components). Indeed, if $A\mathbf{v} = \lambda\mathbf{v}$, then

$$\lambda\langle \mathbf{v}, \mathbf{v} \rangle = \langle A\mathbf{v}, \mathbf{v} \rangle = \langle \mathbf{v}, A\mathbf{v} \rangle = \overline{\lambda}\langle \mathbf{v}, \mathbf{v} \rangle$$

meaning that for a nonzero $\mathbf{v}$, $\lambda = \overline{\lambda}$. This implies that the eigenvectors, that are obtained by solving a linear equation with real coefficients, are also real.

A.5.4 Norms

A *norm* of a vector in $\mathbb{C}^n$ is a function mapping a vector $\mathbf{v}$ to a real number $\|\mathbf{v}\|$ satisfying:

- For every $\mathbf{v}$, $\|\mathbf{v}\| \geq 0$ with $\|\mathbf{v}\| = 0$ iff $\mathbf{v} = \mathbf{0}$.

- If $x \in \mathbb{C}$, then $\|x\mathbf{v}\| = |x| \|\mathbf{v}\|$.
- (Triangle inequality) For every $\mathbf{u}, \mathbf{v}$, $\|\mathbf{u} + \mathbf{v}\| \leq \|\mathbf{u}\| + \|\mathbf{v}\|$.

For every $\mathbf{v} \in \mathbb{C}^n$ and number $p \geq 1$, the L_p *norm* of $\mathbf{v}$, denoted $\|\mathbf{v}\|_p$, is equal to $\left(\sum_{i=1}^n |\mathbf{v}_i|^p\right)^{1/p}$. One particularly interesting case is $p = 2$, the so-called *Euclidean norm*, in which $\|\mathbf{v}\|_2 = \sqrt{\sum_{i=1}^n |\mathbf{v}_i|^2} = \sqrt{\langle \mathbf{v}, \mathbf{v} \rangle}$. Another interesting case is $p = 1$, where we use the single bar notation and denote $|\mathbf{v}|_1 = \sum_{i=1}^n |\mathbf{v}_i|$. Another case is $p = \infty$, where we denote $\|\mathbf{v}\|_\infty = \lim_{p \to \infty} \|\mathbf{v}\|_p = \max_{i \in [n]} |\mathbf{v}_i|$.

Some relations between the different norms can be derived from the *Hölder inequality*, stating that for every p, q with $\frac{1}{p} + \frac{1}{q} = 1$, $\|\mathbf{u}\|_p \|\mathbf{v}\|_q \geq \sum_{i=1}^n |\mathbf{u}_i \mathbf{v}_i|$. To prove it, note that by simple scaling, it suffices to consider norm one vectors, and so is enough to show that if $\|\mathbf{u}\|_p = \|\mathbf{v}\|_q = 1$ then $\sum_{i=1}^n |\mathbf{u}_i| |\mathbf{v}_i| \leq 1$. But $\sum_{i=1}^n |\mathbf{u}_i| |\mathbf{v}_i| = \sum_{i=1}^n |\mathbf{u}_i|^{p(1/p)} |\mathbf{v}_i|^{q(1/q)} \leq \sum_{i=1}^n \frac{1}{p}|\mathbf{u}_i|^p + \frac{1}{q}|\mathbf{v}_i|^q = \frac{1}{p} + \frac{1}{q} = 1$, where the last inequality uses the fact that for every $a, b > 0$ and $\alpha \in [0, 1]$, $a^\alpha b^{1-\alpha} \leq \alpha a + (1 - \alpha)b$.

The Hölder inequality implies the following relations between the L_2, L_1 and L_∞ norms of every vector (see Exercise 21.2):

$$|\mathbf{v}|_1 / \sqrt{n} \leq \|\mathbf{v}\|_2 \leq \sqrt{|\mathbf{v}|_1 \|\mathbf{v}\|_\infty} \tag{A.9}$$

Vector spaces with a norm are sometimes known as *Banach spaces*.

A.5.5 Metric spaces

For any set Ω and $d : \Omega^2 \to \mathbb{R}$, we say that d is a *metric* on Ω if it satisfies the following conditions:

1. $d(x, y) \geq 0$ for every $x, y \in \Omega$ where $d(x, y) = 0$ if and only if $x = y$.
2. $d(x, y) = d(y, x)$ for every $x, y \in \Omega$.
3. (Triangle inequality) For every $x, y, z \in \Omega$, $d(x, z) \leq d(x, y) + d(y, z)$.

That is, $d(x, y)$ denotes the *distance* between x and y according to some measure. If Ω is a vector space with a norm, then the function $d(x, y) = \|x - y\|$ is a metric over Ω, but there are other examples for metrics that do not come from any norm. For example, for every graph G we can define a metric over the vertex set of G by letting the distance of x and y be the length of the shortest path between them. Various metric spaces and the relations between them have found recently many applications in theoretical computer science, see Chapter 15 of [Mat02] for a good survey.

A.6 POLYNOMIALS

We list some basic facts about univariate polynomials.

Theorem A.33 *A nonzero polynomial of degree d has at most d distinct roots.* ◇

PROOF: Suppose $p(x) = \sum_{i=0}^d c_i x^i$ has $d + 1$ distinct roots $\alpha_1, \ldots, \alpha_{d+1}$ in some field $\mathbb{F}$. Then

$$\sum_{i=0}^d \alpha_j^i \cdot c_i = p(\alpha_j) = 0$$

for $j = 1, \ldots, d+1$. This means that the system $\mathbf{Ay} = \mathbf{0}$ with

$$\mathbf{A} = \begin{pmatrix} 1 & \alpha_1 & \alpha_1^2 & \cdots & \alpha_1^d \\ 1 & \alpha_2 & \alpha_2^2 & \cdots & \alpha_2^d \\ \cdots\cdots\cdots\cdots\cdots\cdots\cdots \\ 1 & \alpha_{d+1} & \alpha_{d+1}^2 & \cdots & \alpha_{d+1}^d \end{pmatrix}$$

has a solution $\mathbf{y} = \mathbf{c}$. The matrix $\mathbf{A}$ is a *Vandermonde* matrix, and it can be shown that

$$\det \mathbf{A} = \prod_{i>j}(\alpha_i - \alpha_j)$$

which is nonzero for distinct α_i. Hence rank$\mathbf{A} = d+1$. The system $\mathbf{Ay} = \mathbf{0}$ has therefore only a trivial solution—a contradiction to $\mathbf{c} \neq \mathbf{0}$. ∎

This theorem has an interesting corollary.

Corollary A.34 *For every finite field* $\mathbb{F}$, *the multiplicative group* $\mathbb{F}^*$ *is cyclic.*   ◇

PROOF: The fact that the polynomial $x^k - 1$ has at most k roots implies that the group $\mathbb{F}^*$ has the property (*) that for every k the number of elements x satisfying $x^k = 1$ is always at most k. We will prove by induction that every group G satisfying (*) is cyclic.
    Let $n = |G|$. We consider three cases:

- n is prime. In this case every element of G has either order 1 or order n. Since the only element with order 1 is the identity element, we see that G has an element of order n—G is cyclic.
- $n = p^c$ for some prime p and $c > 1$. In this case if there is no element of order n, then all the orders must divide p^{c-1}. We get $n = p^c$ elements x such that $x^{p^{c-1}} = 1$, violating (*).
- $n = pq$ for coprime p and q. In this case let H and F be two subgroups of G defined as follows: $H = \{a : a^p = 1\}$ and $F = \{b : b^q = 1\}$. Then $|H| \leq p < n$ and $|F| \leq q < n$ and also as subgroups of G both H and F satisfy (*). Thus by the induction hypothesis both H and F are cyclic and have generators a and b, respectively. We claim that ab generates the entire group G. Indeed, let c be any element in G. Since p, q are coprime, there are x, y such that $xq + yp = 1$ and hence $c = c^{xq+yp}$. But $(c^{xq})^p = 1$ and $(c^{yp})^q = 1$ and hence c is a product of an element of H and an element of F, and hence $c = a^i b^j$ for some $i \in \{0, \ldots, p-1\}$ and $j \in \{0, \ldots, q-1\}$. Thus, to show that $c = (ab)^z$ for some z all we need to do is to find z such that $z = i \pmod{p}$ and $z = j \pmod{q}$, but this can be done using the Chinese Remainder Theorem.

∎

Theorem A.35 *For any set of pairs* $(a_1, b_1), \ldots, (a_{d+1}, b_{d+1})$ *there exists a unique polynomial* $g(x)$ *of degree at most* d *such that* $g(a_i) = b_i$ *for all* $i = 1, 2, \ldots, d+1$.   ◇

PROOF: The requirements are satisfied by *Lagrange Interpolating Polynomial*:

$$\sum_{i=1}^{d+1} b_i \cdot \frac{\prod_{j \neq i}(x - a_j)}{\prod_{j \neq i}(a_i - a_j)}$$

If two polynomials $g_1(x), g_2(x)$ satisfy the requirements then their difference $p(x) = g_1(x) - g_2(x)$ is of degree at most d, and is zero for $x = a_1, \ldots, a_{d+1}$. Thus, from the previous theorem, polynomial $p(x)$ must be zero, and polynomials $g_1(x), g_2(x)$, identical. ∎

The following elementary result is usually attributed to Schwartz and Zippel in the computer science community, though it was certainly known earlier (see, e.g., DeMillo and Lipton [DLne]).

Lemma A.36 *If a polynomial $p(x_1, x_2, \ldots, x_m)$ over $F = GF(q)$ is nonzero and has total degree at most d, then*

$$\Pr[p(a_1 \cdots a_m) \neq 0] \geq 1 - \frac{d}{q}$$

where the probability is over all choices of $a_1 \cdots a_m \in F$.   ◇

PROOF: We use induction on m. If $m = 1$ the statement follows from Theorem A.33. Suppose the statement is true when the number of variables is at most $m - 1$. Then p can be written as

$$p(x_1, x_2, \ldots, x_m) = \sum_{i=0}^{d} x_1^i p_i(x_2, \ldots, x_m)$$

where p_i has total degree at most $d - i$. Since p is nonzero, at least one of p_i is nonzero. Let i be the largest i such that p_i is nonzero. Then by the inductive hypothesis,

$$\Pr_{a_2, a_3, \ldots, a_m}[p_i(a_2, a_3, \ldots, a_m) \neq 0] \geq 1 - \frac{d - i}{q}$$

whenever $p_i(a_2, a_3, \ldots, a_m) \neq 0, p(x_1, a_2, a_3, \ldots, a_m)$ is a nonzero univariate polynomial of degree i, and hence becomes 0 only for at most i values of x_1. Hence

$$\Pr[p(a_1 \cdots a_m) \neq 0] \geq \left(1 - \frac{i}{q}\right)\left(1 - \frac{d - i}{q}\right) \geq 1 - \frac{d}{q}$$

and the induction is completed. ∎

Hints for selected exercises

Chapter 0

0.2   Answers are: (a) n (b) n^2 (c) 2^n (d) $\log n$ (e) n (f) $n \log n$ (g) $n^{\log 3}$ (h) n^2.

Chapter 1

1.1   Follow the grade-school algorithms.

1.5   Use the proof of Claim 1.6.

1.6   show that the universal TM $\mathcal{U}$ obtained by the proof of Theorem 1.9 can be tweaked to be oblivious.

1.12.   **b.** By possibly changing from S to its complement, we may assume that the empty function $\emptyset$ (that is not defined on any input) is in S and that there is some function f that is defined on some input x that is not in S. Use this to show that an algorithm to compute f_S can compute the function HALT_x, which outputs 1 on input α iff M_α halts on input x. Then reduce computing HALT to computing HALT_x thereby deriving Rice's Theorem from Theorem 1.11.

Chapter 2

2.2 $\mathsf{CONNECTED}$ and $\mathsf{2COL}$ are shown to be in **P** in Exercise 1.14 (though $\mathsf{2COL}$ is called $\mathsf{BIPARTITE}$ there). $\mathsf{3COL}$ is shown to be **NP**-complete in Exercise 2.21, and hence it is unlikely that it is in **P**.

2.3   First show that for every rational matrix A, the determinant of A can always be represented using a number of bits that is polynomial in the representation of A. Then use Cramer's rule for expressing the solution of linear equations in terms of determinants.

2.4   Use the previous question.

2.5   The certificate that n is prime is the list of prime factors $q_1, \ldots, q_\ell$ of $n - 1$ along with the corresponding numbers $a_1, \ldots, a_\ell$ and (recursive) primality certificates for $q_1, \ldots, q_\ell$.

2.6   **b.** A simulation in $O(|\alpha| t \log t)$ time can be obtained by a straightforward adaptation of the proof of Theorem 1.9. To do a more efficient simulation, the main idea is to first run a simulation of M without actually reading the contents of the work tapes, but rather simply nondeterministically guessing these contents and writing those guesses down. Then, go over tape by tape and verify that all guesses were consistent.

2.11 Why is this language in **NP**? Is Boolean satisfiability a mathematical statement?

2.13. **a.** Modify the machine M so that it clears up its work tape before outputting a 1 and moves both heads to one end of the tape. Then the final snapshot and head locations are unique.

2.15 Reduce from INDSET.

2.17 For Exactly One 3SAT replace each occurrence of a literal v_i in a clause C by a new variable $z_{i,C}$ and clauses and auxiliary variables ensuring that if v_i is TRUE, then $z_{i,C}$ is allowed to be either TRUE or FALSE, but if v_i is false, then $z_{i,C}$ must be FALSE. The approach for the reduction of Exactly One 3SAT to SUBSET SUM is that given a formula φ, we map it to a SUBSET SUM instance by mapping each possible literal u_i to the number $\sum_{j \in S_i}(2n)^j$ where S_i is the set of clauses that the literal u_i satisfies, and setting the target T to be $\sum_{j=1}^{m}(2n)^j$. An additional trick is required to ensure that the solution to the subset sum instance will not include two literals that correspond to a variable and its negation.

2.19 Reduce from SAT.

2.20 You can express the constraint $x \in \{0, 1\}$ using the equation $x^2 = x$.

2.21 Reduce from 3SAT.

2.22 Reduce from SAT.

2.30 If there is a n^c time reduction from 3SAT to a unary language L, then this reduction can only map size n instances of 3SAT to some string of the form 1^i where $i \le n^c$. Use this observation to obtain a polynomial-time algorithm for SAT using the downward self reducibility argument of Theorem 2.18.

2.31 Start with an exponential-time recursive algorithm for SUBSET SUM, and show that in this case you can make it into a polynomial-time algorithm by storing previously computed values in a table.

Chapter 3

3.6. **a.** To compute $H(n)$ we need to (1) compute $H(i)$ on every $i \le \log n$, (2) simulate at most $\log \log n$ machines on inputs of lengths at most $\log n$ for less than $\log \log n (\log n)^{\log \log n} = o(n)$ steps, and (3) compute SAT on inputs of size at most $\log n$. Thus, if $T(n)$ denotes the time to compute $H(n)$, then $T(n) \le \log n T(\log n) + O(n^2)$, and hence $T(n) = O(n^2)$.

3.6. **b.** If f is the reduction from SAT to SAT_H that runs in time $O(n^i)$, let N be the number such that $H(n) > i$ for $n > N$. The following recursive algorithm A solves SAT in polynomial time: On input a formula φ, if $|\varphi| \le N$, then compute the output using brute force; otherwise compute $x = f(\varphi)$. If x is not of the form $\psi 01^{n^{H(|\psi|)}}$, then output FALSE. Otherwise, output $A(\psi)$.

Chapter 4

4.6 The proof of the Cook-Levin Theorem in Chapter 2 used oblivious TMs. You need to verify that the construction of oblivious TMs implied in Remark 1.7 and Exercise 1.5

is such that the position of the head at any step can be computed in logarithmic space.

4.7 Use the previous exercise.

Chapter 5

5.1 Use the **NP**-completeness of SAT.

5.7 The nontrivial direction **EXP** $\subseteq$ **APSPACE** uses ideas similar to those in the proof of Theorem 5.11.

5.13. **b.** Reduce from Σ_3-3SAT. Also, the collection S produced by your reduction can use the same set multiple times.

Chapter 6

6.1. **a.** Use the equation $f(x_1,\ldots,x_n) = x_n \wedge f(x_1,\ldots,x_{n-1},1) \vee \bar{x}_n \wedge f(x_1,\ldots,x_{n-1},0)$ to build recursively a $O(2^n)$ circuit for f.

6.1. **b.** There are only 2^{2^k} functions on k bits, which means that we can trivially use $2^{2^k} \cdot (k2^{2^k})$ gates to compute every possible such function on $x_1,\ldots,x_k$. But after we have done this, we can use the recursive circuit of the previous item only for $n - k$ levels of the recursion, using up $O(2^{n-k})$ gates. Setting k to equal, say, $\log n - 2$ gives the result.

6.5 Keep in mind the proof of the *existence* of functions with high circuit complexity, and try to show that you can compute, say, the lexicographically smallest such function using a constant number of quantifier alternations.

6.7 Keep the previous problem in mind.

6.9 Show a recursive exponential-time algorithm S that on inputting a n-variable formula φ and a string $v \in \{0, 1\}^n$ outputs 1 iff φ has a satisfying assignment v such that $v > u$ when both are interpreted as the binary representation of a number in $[2^n]$. Use the reduction from SAT to L to prune possibilities in the recursion tree of S.

6.12. **a.** You can use a different processor to compute each entry of AB.

6.12. **b.** Use repeated squaring: $A^{2^k} = (A^{2^{k-1}})^2$.

6.12. **c.** Let A be the adjacency matrix of a graph. What is the meaning of the (i,j)th entry of A^n?

6.13 A formula may be viewed—once we exclude the input nodes—as a directed binary tree, and in a binary tree of size m there is always a node whose removal leaves subtrees of size at most $2m/3$ each.

6.16 First design **NC** circuits for matrix multiplication and then, using fast exponentiation, for computing A^r in poly$(\log n + \log r)$ depth. Then use the fact that the determinant is the product of the eigenvalues, and that trace(A^r) is the sum of the rth power of the eigenvalues. Then use manipulations of the symmetric functions of eigenvalues.

6.19 In your reduction, express the CIRCUIT-EVAL problem as a linear program and use the fact that $x \vee y = 1$ iff $x + y \geq 1$. Be careful; the variables in a linear program are real-valued and not Boolean!

Chapter 7

7.3   Use the binary representation of n and repeated squaring.

7.4   Use the fact that if $B_1, \ldots, B_k$ are k independent events each occurring with probability at most p, then the probability that $\wedge_{i \in [n]} B_i$ occurs is at most p^n.

7.5   Think of the real number ρ as an advice string. How can its bits be recovered?

7.8   Follow the ideas of the proof of the Karp-Lipton Theorem (Theorem 6.19).

7.9   Try to compute the probability that the machine ends up in the accept configuration using either dynamic programming or matrix multiplication.

7.11.   **c.** Consider the infinite random walk starting from u. If $E_u > K$, then by standard bounds (e.g., Chernoff), u appears in less than a $2/K$ fraction of the places in this walk.

7.11.   **d.** Start with the case $k = 1$ (i.e., u and v are connected by an edge), the case of $k > 1$ can be reduced to this using linearity of expectation. Note that the expectation of a random variable X over $\mathbb{N}$ is equal to $\sum_{m \in \mathbb{N}} \Pr[X \geq m]$ and so it suffices to show that the probability that an ℓn^2-step random walk from u does not hit v decays exponentially with ℓ.

Chapter 8

8.1.   **c.** Use **IP = PSPACE**.

8.5   First note that in the current set lower bound protocol we can have the prover choose the hash function. Consider the easier case of constructing a protocol to distinguish between the case $|S| \geq K$ and $|S| \leq \frac{1}{c}K$ where $c > 2$ can even be a function of K. If c is large enough, we can allow the prover to use *several* hash functions $h_1, \ldots, h_i$, and it can be proven that if i is large enough, we'll have $\cup_i h_i(S) = \{0, 1\}^k$. The gap can be increased by considering instead of S the set S^ℓ, that is the ℓ times cartesian product of S.

8.7   Start by showing that **MAM $\subseteq$ AM**, where **MAM** denotes the class of languages that can be proven by a three-message protocol in which the prover sends one message, the verifier sends random coins, and then the prover sends another message (see footnote 2). We can change an **MAM** protocol to an **AM** protocol by having the verifier send its random coins as the first message. This will not harm completeness. Show that if we first use parallel repetition to reduce the soundness error to a low enough value (as a function of the length of the prover's messages) then the new protocol will still be sound.

8.8.   **a.** Show that in this case there is at most a blowup of 2 in the degree due to a product operation.

8.8.   **b.** If ψ is not already of this form and has a fragment of the form $\forall x_j \cdots \forall x_{j'} p(x_i, \ldots)$ where $j' > j > i$ and p is some formula involving x_i and possibly other variables, then we can introduce a new variable y_i and change the formula to the equivalent form $\forall x_j \exists y_i \, s.t. \, (y_i = x_i) AND \cdots \forall x_{j'} p(y_i, \ldots)$. Apply this procedure iteratively from right to left.

8.12   Show how to simulate poly(n) provers using two. In this simulation, one of the provers plays the role of all $m(n)$ provers, and the other prover is asked to simulate one of the provers, chosen randomly from among the $m(n)$ provers. Then repeat this a few times.

Chapter 9

9.2   Can all the distributions of the form $E_{U_n}(x)$ have the same support?

9.4   Define $\mathcal{D}$ to be the following distribution over $\{0, 1\}^{n+10}$: Choose y at random from $E_{U_n}(0^{n+5})$, choose k at random in $\{0, 1\}^n$, and let $x = D_k(y)$. Show a function A such that if we set $x_0 = 0^{n+10}$ and (9.11) fails for every x_1, then for every $x \in \{0, 1\}^{n+10}$, $\Pr[\mathcal{D} = x] > 2^{-n}$. Derive from this a contradiction.

9.6.   **a.** Use padding.

9.7   Show that if $X^2 = Y^2 \pmod{M}$ and $X \neq \pm Y \pmod{M}$, then one can find a factor of M by computing the greatest common denominator (gcd) of M and $X - Y$. Then show that you can find such a pair X, Y using an invertion algorithm.

9.8   For every prime p, generator g of $\mathbb{Z}_p^*$, and $x \in \{0, .., p-1\}$, if we choose $y \in_R \{0, .., p-1\}$ then $g^x g^y \pmod{p}$ is uniformly distributed in $\mathbb{Z}_p^*$.

9.9.   **b.** For the algorithm B use $A(E_{U_n}(0^m))$.

9.9.   **c.** Use the same algorithm B as previously.

9.10   Use the ideas of the proof of Theorem 9.13.

9.13   You need to show that a certain determinant is nonzero.

9.16   Prove this first for the case where the language 3COL is replaced by $L = \{(y, r, b) : \exists x \text{ s.t. } y = f(x), b = r \odot x\}$, where f is a one-way permutation.

Chapter 10

10.2   First prove that Condition 3 holds iff Condition 1 holds iff Condition 4 holds. This follows almost directly from the definition of the inner product and the fact that for all matrices A, B it holds that $(AB)^* = B^* A^*$ and $(A^*)^* = A$. Then prove that Condition 3 implies Condition 2, which follows from the fact that the norm is invariant under a change of basis. Finally, prove that Condition 2 implies Condition 3 by showing that if two orthogonal unit vectors $\mathbf{v}, \mathbf{u}$ are mapped to nonorthogonal unit vectors $\mathbf{v}', \mathbf{u}'$, then the norm of the vector $\mathbf{u} + \mathbf{v}$ is not preserved.

10.5   Add another qubit to the register with the semantic that when this qubit is zero, all amplitudes correspond to the real part of the amplitudes in the original algorithm, and when it is one, the amplitudes correspond to the imaginary part of the amplitudes of the original algorithm.

10.10   Start by solving the case that $x = 2^k$ for some k. Then, show an algorithm for general x by using x's binary expansion.

10.12   Use the fact that if N and A are coprime, then there are whole numbers α, β such that $\alpha N + \beta A = 1$ and multiply this equation by B.

10.15   let $d = \gcd(r, M)$, $r' = r/d$, and $M' = M/d$. Now use the same argument as in the case that M and r are coprime to argue that there exist $\Omega(\frac{r}{d \log r})$ values $x \in \mathbb{Z}_{M'}$ satisfying this condition, and that if x satisfies it, then so does $x + cM$ for every c.

Chapter 11

11.3 Show that a random assignment is expected to satisfy at least a 7/8 fraction of the clauses, and then use Markov's inequality to show that the probability of satisfying at least a $7/8 - 1/(2m)$ fraction (where m is the number of clauses) is at least $1/\text{poly}(m)$.

11.4 Use the method of *conditional expectation*. Given any partial assignment to the variables $u_1, \ldots, u_i$, one can compute in polynomial time the expectation of the fraction of clauses satisfied if the variables $u_{i+1}, \ldots, u_n$ are chosen at random. There is a way to assign values to the variables $u_1, u_2, \ldots$ in order so that the invariant that this expectation is at least 7/8 is always maintained. (Another approach for obtaining a deterministic algorithm is to select the assignment using a three-wise independent sample space; see hint to Exercise 11.14.)

11.8 Use the hypothesis to infer a downward-self-reducibility property for SAT.

11.9 Design a verifier for 3SAT. The trivial idea would be that the proof contains a satisfying assignment and the verifier randomly picks a clause and reads the corresponding three bits in the proof to check if the clause is satisfied. This doesn't work. Why? The better idea is to require the "proof" to contain many copies of the satisfying assignment. The verifiers uses pairwise independence to run the previous test on these copies—which may or may not be the same string.

11.11 The Cook-Levin reduction actually transforms *every* $x \in \{0, 1\}^*$ into a formula almost all of whose clauses are satisfiable since almost all of the clauses are various consistency checks that are satisfied by the transcript of the execution of the corresponding TM M on x and *every* string u, even if $M(x, u) = 0$.

11.12 First show that the problem can be solved exactly using dynamic programming in time $\text{poly}(n, m)$ if all the numbers involved are in the set $[m]$. Then, show one can obtain an approximation algorithm by keeping only the $O(\log(1/\epsilon) + \log n)$ most significant bits of every number.

11.14 As in Exercise 11.4, the randomized algorithm can be derandomized using either the method of conditional expectation or using q-wise independent functions. These can be obtained by generalizing the construction of pairwise independent hash functions from Section 8.2.2 to use a polynomials of degree $q - 1$ over $\text{GF}(2^n)$ instead of linear functions.

11.15 Show you can express satisfiability for SAT formulas using quadratic equations.

11.16 Reduce from MAX-3SAT.

Chapter 12

12.1 Let $x_1, \ldots, x_n$ be such that $f(x_i) \neq f(x_i^i)$. Prove that for every k, there is a set X of at least $n/2^k$ of the x_i's such that the decision tree sees the same answers for its first k queries on every member of X.

12.2 Use induction.

Chapter 13

13.3 Show that there is no one-tape TM M solving PAL such that for every input of the form $x_{n/2} \cdots x_1 0^n x_1 \cdots x_{n/2}$, and every index $i \in [n/2 + 1, \ldots, 3n/2 - 1]$, M travels less than $o(n)$ times between the ith and $i + 1$th cells of its tape. Otherwise by letting

Alice simulate M's execution when its head is in the first i cells, and Bob simulate M when the head is in the rest of the tape, we can design a communication complexity protocol for equality that uses $o(n)$ communication for more than $2^{n/2}/n$ inputs.

13.4 As in the previous question, make this into a communication complexity protocol, where Alice and Bob transmit to one another the contents of the working tape. (This time the input tape is read only.) Create a "buffer zone" of zeroes, forcing the machine to take n steps just to transmit every message between Alice and Bob.

13.5 Arbitrarily number the rectangles in the monochromatic tiling and let $N = \chi(f)$. Define graphs G_R, G_C on $\{1, \ldots, N\}$ where $\{i, j\}$ is an edge in G_R (resp., G_C) iff rectangles i, j share a row (resp., column). Let $deg_R(\cdot)$ and $deg_C(\cdot)$ denote degrees in these graphs. At each step, the row player tries to look for a rectangle i containing his input with $deg_L(i) \leq 3|G_R|/4$ and sends such an index i if it exists. Both players then remove from G_L, G_C all vertices that are not neighbors of i. Similarly, the column player tries to find a column j containing his input such that $deg_C(j) \leq 3|G_C|/4$. We claim if either such i, j can be found, it represents progress—can you see why? Furthermore, can you show they will always find such i, j? It may be helpful to note that in a N-vertex graph with minimum degree at least $N/2 + 1$, each two vertices have a common neighbor.

13.6 First, show that for every two matrices A, B, $\text{rank}(A + B) \leq \text{rank}(A) + \text{rank}(B)$, implying that if $A = \sum_{i=1}^{\ell} \alpha_i B_i$ for rank-1 matrices $B_1, \ldots, B_\ell$, then $\text{rank}(A) \leq \ell$. Then, use the fact that if A has rank at most ℓ, then it has ℓ rows such that all other rows are linear combination of these rows to express A as a sum of ℓ rank-1 matrices $B_1, \ldots, B_\ell$ (the rows of the matrix B_i will be scalar multiples of some row of A).

13.9 Use the fact that $M' = J - 2M$ where J is the all 1's matrix.

13.10 Transform the problem to ± 1 first and compute rank over the reals. Could you prove this by taking rank in GF(2)?

13.11 Lower bound the rank.

13.12 Use the fact that $-1^{a \odot b} - 1^{a' \odot b} - 1^{a \odot b'} - 1^{a' \odot b'} = -1^{(a+a') \odot (b+b')}$.

13.15 Use the *fingerprinting* technique encountered in Section 7.2.3.

13.16 To turn the circuit into a communication protocol, imagine two players, OR and AND. The OR player gets an input such that $f(x) = 0$, and the AND player gets one where $f(y) = 1$. They know that their inputs differ on at least one bit, and use the circuit to figure out which bit this is. They both evaluate the circuit on their inputs. If the top gate is an OR, then the OR player sees both incoming wires as 0, whereas the AND player sees at least one incoming wire with a 1 on it. So the AND player communicates a bit about which wire this was. They continue this way down the tree. To turn a communication protocol into a circuit you have to do something similar and use induction.

13.19 Reduce the task to a communication complexity protocol for disjointness, where Alice sees the first, say, $n/4$ inputs and Bob sees the rest.

Chapter 14

14.1 Each gate in the old circuit gets a twin that computes its negation.

14.3 Start with the trivial representation of f as a CNF that has a clause per each assignment x such that $f(x) = 0$. Then show that each clause C can be replaced with a clause D, which contains at most s of C's literals while still ensuring that if $f(x) = 0$, then $D(x) = 0$ for one of the reduced clauses D.

14.4 Use the equality $\binom{n}{t+k} = \binom{n}{t}\binom{n-t}{k}/\binom{t+k}{t}$ and the estimate $\left(\frac{n}{k}\right)^k \le \binom{n}{k} \le \left(\frac{en}{k}\right)^k$.

14.10 Show that if $I \subseteq [\ell]$ and $x_1 < x_2 < \cdots < x_m$ is an increasing sequence of numbers in $[2^\ell - 1]$ such that for every i, the most significant bit in which x_i and x_{i-1} differ is *not* in I, then the sequence $x'_1, \ldots, x'_m$ is still increasing, where x'_i is obtained from x_i by "zeroing out" all the bits in I. Conclude that $m \le 2^{\ell - |I|}$.

Chapter 15

15.1 Try to mimic the obvious exponential-time algorithm for finding a satisfying assignment for φ.

15.2. **a.** For every j, let $d_j(\mathbf{c})$ be zero if the jth clause $\tilde{C}_j$ in the "stripped" refutation can be derived using the $\mathbf{y}$ variables only. Show (1) that every $d_j(\mathbf{c})$ can be computed by an $O(S^2)$-sized monotone circuit in $\mathbf{c}$ and (2) that we can set $I(\mathbf{c}) = d_S(\mathbf{c})$ in the proof of Theorem 15.4.

15.2. **b.** Use the assignment $z'_i = \neg z_i$ and the function $I' = \neg I$ to reduce to the previous case.

15.4 The difficult part is completeness. A simpler subcase is when the set of axioms include $0 \le X_i \le 1$. In this case, try to prove that the derivation rule with D restricted to the value 2 suffices. As warmup in this case, first try to prove that all resolution proofs can be recast as cutting planes proofs of essentially the same size that only involve $D = 2$.

15.6 For $i \le n + 1, j \le n$, have a variable x_{ij} that is 1 iff i maps to j.

Chapter 16

16.4. **a.** Start by proving this for n's that are powers of k. If $n = k^\ell$, then you can decompose a $k^\ell \times k^\ell$ matrix into k^2 blocks of size $k^{\ell-1}$—use recursion to multiply blocks and the program Π_k to combine the results of the recursion.

16.4. **b.** We don't have a good intuition how to find this program, but since these are just 2×2 matrices, one can do so by trial and error.

16.6. **c.** First use the fact that the determinant of A can be expressed in terms of the determinant of its minors to show that $p(x) = (A_{1,1} - x)\det(M - xI) + \mathbf{r}ADJ(M - xI)\mathbf{c}$, where for every matrix B, $ADJ(B)$ is the matrix whose i, jth entry is equal to $(-1)^{i+j}$ times the determinant of the minor of B with the ith row and jth column removed (i.e., for nonsingular B, $ADJ(B) = \det(B)B^{-1}$). Then use the Caley-Hamilton Theorem (that says that $q_M(M)$ is equal to the zero matrix) to express the coefficients of the matrix-valued polynomial $ADJ(M - xI)$ using the coefficients of q_A and powers of M.

16.8 See Example 16.9.

16.10 First show that it suffices to compute $k!$ where k is the smallest nontrivial factor of n, and in fact it suffices to compute $s!$ where s is a power of 2 larger than k. Then, noting that $\binom{2r}{r} = \frac{(2r)!}{(r!)^2}$, it suffices to compute $\binom{2r}{r}$ for arbitrary r. But this is just one of the terms of $(t^2 + 1)^{2r}$. How large does t need to be before $\binom{2r}{r}$ can be "read out" of $(t^2 + 1)^{2r}$ using an appropriate mod operation?

16.12 The machine's "program" can contain a constant number of arbitrary real numbers.

Chapter 17

17.5 Use hashing and ideas similar to those in the proof of Toda's Theorem, where we also needed to estimate the size of a set of strings. If you find this question difficult, you might want to come back to it after seeing the Goldwasser-Sipser set lower bound protocol of Chapter 8. To make the algorithm deterministic use the ideas of the proof that **BPP** $\subseteq$ **PH** (Theorem 7.15).

17.6 Use the proof of Lemma 17.17.

17.7 Real numbers can be approximated by rationals, so it suffices to prove this in the case where the matrices representing the quantum operations only involve rational numbers.

Chapter 18

18.1 A three-colorable graph better not contain a complete graph on four vertices.

18.2 The probability that a random graph has a independent set of size at least k is at most $\binom{n}{k} 2^{-\binom{k}{2}}$.

18.5 Construct a sampleable distribution $\mathcal{D}$ on CNF formulas such that it's possible to compute the number of satisfying assignments of a formula φ from the probability of φ in $\mathcal{D}$.

18.6 Use the fact that for every nonnegative random variable X and $d \geq 1$, $E[X^d] \geq E[X]^d$.

Chapter 19

19.1 Define $Y_i = (-1)^{X_i}$ and $Y = \prod_{i=1}^{k} Y_i$. Then, use the fact that the expectation of a product of independent random variables is the product of their expectations.

19.2 Choose $x \in \{0, 1\}^n$ to be in I with probability $\delta 2^n \Pr[H = x]$. Prove that (1) $\Pr[|I| \geq \frac{\delta}{2} 2^n] > 1/2$ and (2) for every circuit C, if we define $SUCESS_C(I)$ to be the probability that $C(x) = f(x)$ for a random $x \in I$ then the probability (over the choice of I) that $SUCCESS_C(I) \geq 1/2 + 2\epsilon$ is smaller than $1/22^{-S}$.

19.3. b. It might help to look at G, H, U as 2^n-dimensional vectors of probabilities.

19.5 Take $\mathbf{z}$ to be the shortest vector of the form $\mathbf{x} - \mathbf{y}$ for $\mathbf{x} \in C$ and $\mathbf{y} \in D$ ($\mathbf{z}$ can be shown to exist and be nonzero using the fact that C, D are closed and D is compact, which means that we can restrict attention to the intersection of C with a sufficiently large ball).

19.6 Note that $\max_q \min_p \mathbf{q} A \mathbf{p} > c$ if and only if the convex set $D = \{A\mathbf{p} : \mathbf{p} \in [0, 1]^n \ \sum_i p_i = 1\}$ does not intersect with the convex set $C = \{\mathbf{x} \in \mathbb{R}^m : \forall_{i \in [m]} x_i \leq c\}$. Use the Hyperplane Separating Theorem to show that this implies the existence of a probability vector $\mathbf{q}$ such that $\langle \mathbf{q}, \mathbf{y} \rangle \geq c$ for every $\mathbf{y} \in D$.

19.7 Assume that there is a 2^{-k}-density distribution that is outside of this convex set and use the separating hyperplane theorem to derive a contradiction by rearranging the terms of the distribution according to their inner product with the normal of the hyperplane, and shifting weight until we get a flat distribution.

19.9 Use a greedy strategy, to select the codewords of E one by one, never adding a codeword that is within distance δ to previous ones. When will you get stuck?

19.10 Follow the proof of the Johnson bound and present the problem as asking how many unit vectors in $\mathbb{R}^m$ you can have such that every pair of vectors is pretty far apart.

19.14 See the discussion before the theorem's statement and the proof of Theorem 19.21.

19.15 The first polynomial describes f in an ϵ fraction of points say S_1, the second polynomial describes f in $\epsilon - d/|\mathbb{F}|$ fraction of points S_2 where $S_1 \cap S_2 = \emptyset$, etc.

19.16 Think of $Q(x, y)$ as a univariate polynomial in y with its coefficients being polynomials in x (i.e., elements in the ring $\mathbb{F}[x]$). Then, divide $Q(x, y)$ by $y - P(x)$ to obtain $Q(x, y) = (y - P(x))A(x, y) + R(x, y)$ where the remainder $R(x)$ has y-degree smaller than $(y - P(x))$.

19.17. b. Use the probabilistic method. Show this holds for a random matrix.

19.17. c. Use the concatenation of Reed-Solomon over $GF(2^k)$ with the Walsh-Hadamard code.

19.18. c. Use concatenation of Reed-Solomon code with the binary code obtained in the previous item. Note that we only apply the binary code on inputs of length $O(\log n)$ and hence can allow exponential-time encoding and decoding algorithms.

Chapter 20

20.2 Show that if for every n, a random function mapping n bits to $2^{n/10}$ bits will have desired properties with high probabilities.

20.4 Let G be a pseudorandom generator and consider the following function f: on input $x \in \{0, 1\}^{\ell+1}, f(x) = 1$ iff there exists $z \in \{0, 1\}^{\ell}$ such that $G(z) = x$.

20.6 Use Theorem 20.6.

20.8 Show that the proofs for Theorems 20.6 and 19.27 imply that given a function $f \in \mathbf{EXP}$ with $H_{\mathrm{avg}}(f)$ that is not bounded from above by any polynomial, one can obtain an $S(\ell)$-pseudorandom generator for a function S that is also not bounded from above by any polynomial (and hence for every polynomial $p, S(\ell) > p(\ell)$ for infinitely many ℓ's).

20.9 Use the fact that the algorithm D can with high probability compute a circuit that decides the language L.

Chapter 21

21.2. a. Use the fact that the log function is concave (has negative second derivative) implying that for $a, b > 0, \alpha \log a + (1 - \alpha) \log b \le \log(\alpha a + (1 - \alpha)b)$.

21.2. c. The expression $|\mathbf{v}|_1^2 = \sum_{i,j} |\mathbf{v}_i||\mathbf{v}_j|$ includes all terms occurring in $\|\mathbf{v}\|_2^2$ plus additional nonnegative terms.

21.4 Show that for every shortest path between two vertices, if we pick any third vertex in the path, then the $(d + 1)$-sized neighborhoods of all the picked vertices are disjoint.

21.5 First show that $\|A\|$ is at most say n^2. Then, prove that for every $k \geq 1$, A^k is also stochastic and $\|A^{2k}\mathbf{v}\|_2 \geq \|A^k\mathbf{v}\|_2^2$ using the equality $\langle \mathbf{w}, B\mathbf{z} \rangle = \langle B^\dagger \mathbf{w}, \mathbf{z} \rangle$ and the inequality $\langle \mathbf{w}, \mathbf{z} \rangle \leq \|\mathbf{w}\|_2 \|\mathbf{z}\|_2$.

21.8 Use the fact that if A is a random-walk matrix of a graph and $\mathbf{v} \perp \mathbf{1}$, then $A\mathbf{v} \perp \mathbf{1}$.

21.10. d. Such a path is obtained by taking $k/2$ moves away from the root and $k/2$ moves back. We have $d-1$ choices for every move away from the root, and so this gives us a factor $2^{k \log d/2}$. The choices of when to make the "back moves" give us an additional factor of roughly $\binom{k}{k/2} = 2^{k-o(k)}$. In fact we have to be more careful since we can't make a "back move" when we're already in the root and so have to ensure that we place the moves in a way so that at any point in time we never made more "back moves" than "away moves." This can be ensured by fixing the first t moves to be "away moves" and the last t moves to be "back moves"—for $t = 100 \log k \sqrt{k}$ (which is $o(k)$), this ensures the vast majority of the $\binom{k-2t}{k/2-2t} = 2^{k-o(k)}$ choices for placing the remaining $k/2 - 2t$ "back moves" will not result in an invalid path. Alternatively we can observe that the number of valid paths is exactly the number of length k valid expressions involving only opening and closing parenthesis. If can be shown that this number is equal to $\frac{1}{k/2+1}\binom{k}{k/2}$ (this is known as the $(k/2)$th *Catalan number*).

21.10. e. Use the previous items to show that, $1 + (n-1)\lambda^k \geq n2^{k-k \log d/2-o(k)}$. The bound follows by taking logs of both sides.

21.11 For every set $S \subseteq n$ with $|S| \leq n/2$, try to bound probability that the number of edges between S and $\bar{S}$ deviates strongly from its expectation.

21.13 Use the probabilistic method—choose S to be a random $n/2$-sized subset of the vertices. For every pair of distinct vertices u, v, the probability that $u \in S$ and $v \in \bar{S}$ or vice versa is at most $1/2$ (it would be exactly half if we chose S with replacements). Hence, since there are $dn/2$ edges in the graph, the expected value of in $E(S, \bar{S})$ is at most $dn/4$.

21.14 You can use Lemma 21.14.

21.15. c. Show that if $\mathbf{s}$ is the uniform distribution over S, then $\|A\mathbf{s}\|_2^2 \leq \|A\mathbf{1}\|_2^2 + \lambda^2 \|\mathbf{s} - \mathbf{1}\|_2^2$.

21.16 A subset S of at most $n'/2$ vertices in H corresponds to a subset S' of size at most $(1 - 1/(2c))n$ vertices in G. Use G's expansion to argue about the number of edges between the complement of S' and S.

21.18. b. Show that any deterministic function must query the function an exponential number of times.

21.18. c. Show that under this condition there is a set S of size at most $2^{n/2}$ such that $\Pr[X \in S] \geq 1/20$.

21.19 Represent distributions over an M-element domain as vectors in $\mathbb{R}^m$, and use the triangle inequality for the L_1 norm.

21.23 Use Lemma 21.14.

21.24 Every subset of the replacement product of G and G' can be thought of as n subsets of the individual clusters. Treat differently the subsets that take up more than $1 - \rho/10$ portion of their clusters and those that take up less than that. For the former use the expansion of G, while for the latter use the expansion of G'.

Chapter 22

22.1 Use Lemma 21.10 with $T = V \setminus S$.

22.2 This can be proven using similar techniques to the proof of Theorem 21.12.

22.3 approximate the binomial coefficient using Stirling's formula for approximating factorials.

22.4 Consider the random variable V' defined as V conditioned on $V > 0$, and use the inequality $E[V'^2] \geq E[V']^2$.

22.5. e. Use the test T above combined with linearity testing, self correction, and a simple test to rule out the constant zero function.

22.5. f. To transform a $2CSP_W$ formula φ over n variables into a $qCSP$ ψ over binary alphabet, use 2^W variables $u_j^1, \ldots, u_j^{2^W}$ for each variable u_j of φ. In the correct proof these variables will contain the Long Code encoding of u_j. Then, add a set of 2^{W^2} variables $y_i^1, \ldots, y_i^{2^{W^2}}$ for each constraint φ_i of φ. In the correct proof these variables will contain the long code encoding of the assignment for the constraint φ_i. For every constraint of φ, ψ will contain constraints for testing the Long Code of both the x and y variables involved in the constraint, testing consistency between the x variables and the y variables, and testing that the y variables actually encode a satisfying assignment.

22.6. a. $\mathsf{val}(\varphi) = \mathsf{val}(\varphi^{*2}) = 1/2$.

22.12. a. Express the function f in the Fourier basis, and use the basic properties of the characters and the fact that $\mathbf{x}, \mathbf{x}'$, and $\mathbf{y}$ are independent.

22.12. b. Reduce to the previous case by considering the function $g(\mathbf{x} \circ \mathbf{y}) = f(\mathbf{x} \circ \mathbf{y})\chi_\alpha(\mathbf{x})$.

22.12. c. You can estimate the expectation in (22.13) by evaluating the corresponding functions on randomly chosen inputs.

22.12. d. Think of the full depth-n binary labeled by binary strings of length $\leq n$ (with the root being the empty word and the two children of α being $\alpha 0$ and $\alpha 1$), then by Parseval you can show that at any level of this tree there can be at most $1/\epsilon^2$ strings α such that $\tilde{f}_{\alpha\star} \geq \epsilon$. Use the procedure $\mathsf{Estimate}$ to prune this tree from the root to the leaves, throwing away all branches α for which $\tilde{f}_{\alpha\star} < 10\epsilon$. At the end output the remaining leaves.

22.13 Show that a randomly chosen family of subsets suffices.

22.14 Requires constructions of ϵ-biased random variables, which have not been covered in this book, although they can be obtained from linear error-correcting codes.

22.15 Think of ways to "amplify" the gap of a constant factor in Exercise 11.16. You need to combine equations to get new equations.

22.16 Introduce a bunch of new variables for each variable that occurs in more than five clauses. Design a "gadget" consisting of new clauses that force this bunch of new variables to have the same value in the optimum assignment. You might need to use an expander. This is essentially the same problem as Claim 22.37.

Chapter 23

23.3 If DISCRETE LOG is hard on worst-case inputs with respect to a particular prime p, then it is hard on most inputs with respect to this prime p, and then it can be used to construct pseudorandom functions (assuming p is used as nonuniform advice).

23.4 It suffices to prove this when f_n is a random function. Use induction on the number of variables, and the fact that both f_n and $\overline{f_n}$ are random functions.

23.5 See Exercise 8.8.

Main theorems and definitions

Bibliography

[Aar03] S. Aaronson. Is P versus NP formally independent? *Bulletin of the EATCS*, 81:109–136, 2003.

[Aar05] S. Aaronson. NP-complete problems and physical reality. *SIGACT News*, 36, 2005.

[Aar06] S. Aaronson. Oracles Are Subtle But Not Malicious. *Proceedings of the 21st Annual IEEE Conference on Computational Complexity*, pages 340–354, 2006.

[Aar08] S. Aaronson. The limits of quantum computers. *Scientific American*, pages 62–69, Mar. 2008.

[AB87] N. Alon and R. B. Boppana. The monotone circuit complexity of boolean functions. *Combinatorica*, 7(1):1–22, 1987.

[AB97] D. Aharonov and M. Ben-Or. Fault-tolerant quantum computation with constant error rate. *SIAM J. Comput.*, 38(4):1207–1282, 2008. Prelim version STOC '97.

[ABSS93] S. Arora, L. Babai, J. Stern, and Z. Sweedyk. The hardness of approximate optima in lattices, codes, and systems of linear equations. *J. Comput. Syst. Sci.*, 54(2):317–331, 1997.

[AC86] N. Alon and F. R. K. Chung. Explicit construction of linear sized tolerant networks. *Discrete Mathematics*, 72:15–19, 1988. Prelim version Japan Conf on Graph Theory and Applications '86.

[ACR96] A. E. Andreev, A. E. F. Clementi, and J. D. P. Rolim. A new general derandomization method. *J. ACM*, 45(1):179–213, 1998. Prelim version ICALP '96.

[ACR$^+$07] A. Ambainis, A. M. Childs, B. Reichardt, R. Spalek, and S. Zhang. Any AND-OR formula of size N can be evaluated in time $N^1/2 + o(1)$ on a quantum computer. In *FOCS*, pages 363–372. IEEE, 2007.

[AD97] M. Ajtai and C. Dwork. A public-key cryptosystem with worst-case/average-case equivalence. In *STOC*, pages 284–293. ACM, 1997.

[adH88] F. M. auf der Heide. Fast algorithms for N-dimensional restrictions of hard problems. *J. ACM*, 35(3):740–747, 1988.

[ADH97] L. M. Adleman, J. Demarrais, and M.-D. A. Huang. Quantum computability. *SIAM J. Comput.*, 26(5):1524–1540, 1997.

STOC—ACM Symposium on Theory of Computing; FOCS—IEEE Annual Symposium on Foundations of Computer Science.

[Adl78]   L. Adleman. Two theorems on random polynomial time. In *FOCS*, pages 75–83. IEEE, 1978.

[AFWZ95]   N. Alon, U. Feige, A. Wigderson, and D. Zuckerman. Derandomized graph products. *Computational Complexity*, 5(1):60–75, 1995.

[AG94]   E. Allender and V. Gore. A uniform circuit lower bound for the permanent. *SIAM J. Comput.*, 23(5):1026–1049, 1994.

[AGIK07]   D. Aharonov, D. Gottesman, S. Irani, and J. Kempe. The power of quantum systems on a line. In *FOCS*, pages 373–383. IEEE, 2007.

[AIK04]   B. Applebaum, Y. Ishai, and E. Kushilevitz. Cryptography in NC^0. *SIAM J. Comput.*, 36(4):845–888, 2006. Prelim version FOCS '04.

[AIV93]   S. Arora, R. Impagliazzo, and U. Vazirani. Relativizing versus nonrelativizing techniques: The role of local checkability. Unpublished manuscript, available from the authors' Web pages, 1993.

[Ajt83]   M. Ajtai. Σ_1^1-formulae on finite structures. *Annals of Pure and Applied Logic*, 24:1–48, 1983.

[Ajt88]   M. Ajtai. The complexity of the pigeonhole principle. In *FOCS*, pages 346–355. IEEE, 1988.

[Ajt96]   M. Ajtai. Generating hard instances of lattice problems (extended abstract). In *STOC*, pages 99–108. ACM, 1996.

[AKL+79]   R. Aleliunas, R. M. Karp, L. Lipton, L. Lovász, and C. Rackoff. Random walks, universal traversal sequences, and the complexity of maze problems. In *FOCS*, pages 218–223. IEEE, 29–31 Oct. 1979.

[AKS87]   M. Ajtai, J. Komlos, and E. Szemeredi. Deterministic simulation in LOGSPACE. In *STOC*, pages 132–140. ACM, 1987.

[AKS98]   N. Alon, M. Krivelevich, and B. Sudakov. Finding a large hidden clique in a random graph. *Random Struct. Algorithms*, 13(3–4):457–466, 1998. Prelim version SODA '98.

[AKS04]   M. Agrawal, N. Kayal, and N. Saxena. PRIMES is in P. *Ann. of Math. (2)*, 160(2):781–793, 2004.

[AL95]   S. Arora and C. Lund. Hardness of approximations. In D. S. Hochbaum, editor, *Approximation Algorithms for NP-Hard Problems*, Chapter 10. PWS, 1995.

[ALM+92]   S. Arora, C. Lund, R. Motwani, M. Sudan, and M. Szegedy. Proof verification and the hardness of approximation problems. *J. ACM*, 45(3):501–555, 1998. Prelim version FOCS '92.

[Alo86]   N. Alon. Eigenvalues and expanders. *Combinatorica*, 6(2):83–96, 1986.

[AM84]   N. Alon and V. D. Milman. Eigenvalues, expanders and superconcentrators (extended abstract). In *FOCS*, pages 320–322. IEEE, 24–26 Oct. 1984.

[AM85]   N. Alon and V. D. Milman. λ_1, isoperimetric inequalities for graphs, and superconcentrators. *J. Comb. Theory Series B*, 38:73–88, 1985.

[Amb04]   A. Ambainis. Quantum search algorithms. *SIGACT News*, 35(2):22–35, 2004.

[AMS96]   N. Alon, Y. Matias, and M. Szegedy. The space complexity of approximating the frequency moments. *J. Comput. Syst. Sci.*, 58(1):137–147, 1999. Prelim version STOC '96.

[AN04]   N. Alon and A. Naor. Approximating the cut-norm via grothendieck's inequality. *SIAM J. Comput.*, 35(4):787–803, 2006. Prelim version in STOC '04.

[And85]   A. E. Andreev. On a method for obtaining lower bounds for the complexity of individual monotone functions. *Soviet Math. Dokl.*, 31(3):530–534, 1985.

[AR04]   D. Aharonov and O. Regev. Lattice problems in NP intersect coNP. *J. ACM*, 52:749–765, 2005. Prelim version FOCS '04.

[Aro94]   S. Arora. *Probabilistic Checking of Proofs and Hardness of Approximation Problems*. PhD thesis, UC Berkeley, 1994.

[Aro96]   S. Arora. Polynomial time approximation schemes for euclidean traveling salesman and other geometric problems. *J. ACM*, 45:753–782 1998. Prelim version FOCS '96.

[AS92]   S. Arora and S. Safra. Probabilistic checking of proofs: A new characterization of NP. *J. ACM*, 45(1):70–122, Jan. 1998. Prelim version FOCS '92.

[AS00a]   N. Alon and B. Sudakov. Bipartite subgraphs and the smallest eigenvalue. *Combinatorics, Probability & Computing*, 9(1):1–12, 2000.

[AS00b]   N. Alon and J. Spencer. *The Probabilistic Method*. John Wiley, 2000.

[ATSWZ97]   R. Armoni, A. Ta-Shma, A. Widgerson, and S. Zhou. An $O(\log(n)^{4/3})$ space algorithm for (s,t) connectivity in undirected graphs. *J. ACM*, 47(2):294–311, Mar. 2000. Prelim version STOC '97.

[AUY83]   A. V. Aho, J. D. Ullman, and M. Yannakakis. On notions of information transfer in VLSI circuits. In *STOC*, pages 133–139. ACM, 1983.

[AvDK$^+$04] D. Aharonov, W. van Dam, J. Kempe, Z. Landau, S. Lloyd, and O. Regev. Adiabatic quantum computation is equivalent to standard quantum computation. *SIAM J. Comput.*, 37(1):166–194, 2007. Prelim version FOCS '04.

[AW08]   S. Aaronson and A. Wigderson. Algebrization: A new barrier in complexity theory. In *STOC*, pages 731–740. ACM, 2008.

[Bab85]   L. Babai. Trading group theory for randomness. In *STOC*, pages 421–429. ACM, 1985.

[Bab90]   L. Babai. E-mail and the unexpected power of interaction. In *Proceedings, Fifth Annual Structure in Complexity Theory Conference*, pages 31–91. IEEE, 8–11 July 1990.

[Bab94]   L. Babai. Transparent proofs and limits to approximations. In *First European Congress of Mathematicians*, 1994.

[Bar86]   D. A. Barrington. Bounded-width polynomial-size branching programs recognize exactly those languages in NC^1. *J. Comput. Syst. Sci.*, 38(1):150–164, Feb. 1989. Prelim version STOC '86.

[Bar02]   B. Barak. A probabilistic-time hierarchy theorem for "slightly non-uniform" algorithms. In *RANDOM*, volume 2483 of *Lecture Notes in Computer Science*, pages 194–208. Springer, 2002.

[BB84]   C. H. Bennett and G. Brassard. Quantum cryptography: Public key distribution and coin tossing. *Proceedings of IEEE International Conference on Computers, Systems, and Signal Processing*, 175, 1984.

[BBBV97]   C. H. Bennett, E. Bernstein, G. Brassard, and U. Vazirani. Strengths and weaknesses of quantum computing. *SIAM J. Comput.*, 26(5):1510–1523, Oct. 1997.

[BBC$^+$98] R. Beals, H. Buhrman, R. Cleve, M. Mosca, and R. de Wolf. Quantum lower bounds by polynomials. *J. ACM*, 48(4):778–797, 2001. Prelim version FOCS '98.

[BBR88]   C. H. Bennett, G. Brassard, and J. Robert. Privacy amplification by public discussion. *SIAM J. Comput.*, 17(2):210–229, Apr. 1988.

[BBR92]   D. A. M. Barrington, R. Beigel, and R. Rudich. Representing Boolean functions as polynomials modulo composite numbers. *Computational Complexity*, 4(4):367–382, 1994. Prelim version STOC '92.

[BC06]   M. Braverman and S. Cook. Computing over the reals: Foundations for scientific computing. *Notices of the AMS*, 53(3):318–329, 2006.

[BCC86]   G. Brassard, D. Chaum, and C. Crépeau. Minimum disclosure proofs of knowl-
            edge. *J. Comput. Syst. Sci.*, 37(2):156–189, Oct. 1988. Prelim versions by
            Brassard and Crépeau (CRYPTO '86, FOCS '86) and Chaum (CRYPTO '86).

[BCE$^+$95] P. Beame, S. Cook, J. Edmonds, R. Impagliazzo, and T. Pitassi. The relative
            complexity of *NP* search problems. In *STOC*, pages 303–314. ACM, 1995.

[BCS97]   P. Bürgisser, M. Clausen, and M. A. Shokrollahi. *Algebraic Complexity Theory*.
            Springer Verlag, 1997.

[BCSS97]   L. Blum, F. Cucker, M. Shub, and S. Smale. *Complexity and Real Computation*.
            Springer Verlag, 1997.

[BDCGL89]   S. Ben-David, B. Chor, O. Goldreich, and M. Luby. On the theory of average
            case complexity. *J. Comput. Syst. Sci.*, 44(2):193–219, Apr. 1992. Prelim version
            Structures in Complexity '89.

[BdW02]   H. Buhrman and R. de Wolf. Complexity measures and decision tree complex-
            ity: A survey. *Theoretical Computer Science*, 288:21–43, 2002.

[BE76]   B. Bollobás and P. Erdös. Cliques in random graphs. *Mathematical Proceedings
            of the Cambridge Philosophical Society*, 80(41):419–427, 1976.

[Bec91]   J. Beck. An algorithmic approach to the lovàsz local lemma. *Random Structures
            and Algorithms*, 2(4):367–378, 1991.

[Bel64]   J. S. Bell. On the Einstein-Podolsky-Rosen paradox. *Physics*, 1(3):195–290,
            1964.

[Ben87]   C. H. Bennett. Demons, engines and the second law. *Scientific American*,
            257(5):88–96, 1987.

[Berch]   S. J. Berkowitz. On computing the determinant in small parallel time using a
            small number of processors. *Inf. Process. Lett.*, 18(3):147–150, 1984.

[BF90]   D. Beaver and J. Feigenbaum. Hiding instances in multioracle queries. In *7th
            Annual Symposium on Theoretical Aspects of Computer Science*, volume 415 of
            lncs, pages 37–48. Springer, 22–24 Feb. 1990.

[BFL90]   L. Babai, L. Fortnow, and L. Lund. Non-deterministic exponential time has two-
            prover interactive protocols. *Computational Complexity*, 1:3–40, 1991. Prelim
            version FOCS '90.

[BFLS91]   L. Babai, L. Fortnow, L. A. Levin, and M. Szegedy. Checking computations in
            polylogarithmic time. In *STOC*, pages 21–32. ACM, 1991.

[BFNW93]   L. Babai, L. Fortnow, N. Nisan, and A. Wigderson. BPP has subexponen-
            tial time simulations unless EXPTIME has publishable proofs. *Computational
            Complexity*, 3(4):307–318, 1993.

[BFT98]   H. Buhrman, L. Fortnow, and T. Thierauf. Nonrelativizing separations. In *Pro-
            ceedings of the 13th Annual IEEE Conference on Computational Complexity
            (CCC-98)*, pages 8–12. IEEE, 15–18 June 1998.

[BG94]   M. Bellare and S. Goldwasser. The complexity of decision versus search. *SIAM
            J. Comput.*, 23(1):97–119, 1994.

[BGS75]   T. Baker, J. Gill, and R. Solovay. Relativizations of the $\mathcal{P} =? \mathcal{NP}$ question.
            SIAM J. Comput., 4(4):431–442, 1975.

[BGS95]   M. Bellare, O. Goldreich, and M. Sudan. Free bits, PCPs, and
            nonapproximability-towards tight results. *SIAM J. Comput.*, 27(3):804–915,
            1998.

[BHZ87]   R. B. Boppana, J. Hastad, and S. Zachos. Does co-NP have short interactive
            proofs? *Inf. Process. Lett.*, 25(2):127–132, 1987.

[BK95]   M. Blum and S. Kannan. Designing programs that check their work. *J. ACM*,
            42(1):269–291, 1995.

[BLR90]   M. Blum, M. Luby, and R. Rubinfeld. Self-testing/correcting with applications to numerical problems. *J. Comput. Syst. Sci.*, 47(3):549–595, 1993.

[Blu67]   M. Blum. A machine-independent theory of the complexity of recursive functions. *J. ACM*, 14(2):332–336, 1967.

[Blu84]   M. Blum. Independent unbiased coin flips from a correlated biased source: A finite state Markov chain. In *FOCS*, pages 425–433. IEEE, 24–26 Oct. 1984.

[Blu87]   M. Blum. How to prove a theorem so no one else can claim it. In *Proceedings of the International Congress of Mathematicians*, pages 1444–1451, 1987.

[BLY92]   A. Björner, L. Lovász, and A. C. C. Yao. Linear decision trees: Volume estimates and topological bounds. In *STOC*, pages 170–177. ACM, 1992.

[BM82]   M. Blum and S. Micali. How to generate cryptographically strong sequences of pseudo-random bits. *SIAM J. Comput.*, 13(4):850–864, Nov. 1984. Prelim version FOCS '82.

[BM88]   L. Babai and S. Moran. Arthur-Merlin games: A randomized proof system, and a hierarchy of complexity classes. *J. Comput. Syst. Sci.*, 36(2):254–276, 1988.

[BMMS00]   J. C. Birget, S. Margolis, J. Meakin, and M. Sapir. *Algorithmic Problems in Groups and Semigroups*. Birkhauser, 2000.

[BNS89]   L. Babai, N. Nisan, and M. Szegedy. Multiparty protocols, pseudorandom generators for logspace, and time-space trade-offs. *J. Comput. Syst. Sci.*, 45(2):204–232, 1992. Prelim version STOC '89.

[BO83]   M. Ben-Or. Lower bounds for algebraic computation trees. In *STOC*, pages 80–86. ACM, 1983.

[BOGKW88]   M. Ben-Or, S. Goldwasser, J. Kilian, and A. Wigderson. Multi-prover interactive proofs: How to remove intractability assumptions. In *STOC*, pages 113–131. ACM, 2–4 May 1988.

[Bol01]   B. Bollobás. *Random Graphs*. Cambridge University Press, 2001.

[Bou02]   J. Bourgain. On the distribution of the fourier spectrum of boolean functions. *Israel J. Math.*, 131(1):269–276, 2002.

[BP73]   L. A. Bassalygo and M. S. Pinsker. The complexity of an optimal non-blocking commutation scheme without rezzzorganization. *Problemy Peredaci Informacii*, 9(1):84–87, 1973. Translated into English in *Problems of Information Transmission*, 9:64–66, 1974.

[BPR97]   M. Bonet, T. Pitassi, and R. Raz. Lower bounds for cutting planes proofs with small coefficients. *J. Symbolic Logic*, 62(3):708–728, 1997.

[Bra04]   G. Brassard. Quantum communication complexity: A survey. In *ISMVL*, page 56. IEEE, 2004.

[Bru04]   C. Bruce. *Schrodinger's Rabbits: Entering The Many Worlds Of Quantum*. Joseph Henry Press, 2004.

[BS90]   R. B. Boppana and M. Sipser. The complexity of finite functions. In J. van Leeuwen, editor, *Handbook of Theoretical Computer Science*, volume 1. Elsevier and MIT Press, 1990.

[BS94]   M. Bellare and M. Sudan. Improved non-approximability results. In *STOC*, pages 184–193. ACM, 1994.

[BS96]   E. Bach and J. Shallit. *Algorithmic Number Theory – Efficient Algorithms*, volume I. MIT Press, 1996.

[BS08]   D. Boneh and V. Shoup. *A graduate course in applied cryptography*. 2008. To appear. Prelim drafts available on http://crypto.stanford.edu/ dabo/cryptobook/.

[BSS89]   L. Blum, M. Shub, and S. Smale. On a theory of computation and complexity over the real numbers: NP-completeness, recursive functions and universal machines. *American Mathematical Society*, 21(1):1–46, 1989.

[BT91]   R. Beigel and J. Tarui. On ACC. *Computational Complexity*, 4(4):350–366, 1994. Prelim version FOCS '91.

[Bus90]   S. R. Buss. Axiomatizations and conservations results for fragments of bunded arithmetic. In *Logic and Computation, Contemporary Mathematics* 106, pages 57–84. American Math. Society, 1990.

[BV93]   E. Bernstein and U. Vazirani. Quantum complexity theory. *SIAM J. Comput.*, 26(5):1411–1473, 1997. Prelim version STOC '93.

[BW86]   E. R. Berlekamp and L. Welch. Error correction of algebraic block codes. US Patent Number 4,633,470, 1986.

[BYJKS02]   Z. Bar-Yossef, T. S. Jayram, R. Kumar, and D. Sivakumar. An information statistics approach to data stream and communication complexity. *J. Comput. Syst. Sci.*, 68(4):702–732, 2004. Prelim version FOCS '02.

[CA08]   A. Chattopadhyay and A. Ada. Multiparty communication complexity of disjointness. *ECCC archive*, 2008. Report TR08–002.

[Can96]   R. Canetti. More on BPP and the polynomial-time hierarchy. *Inf. Process. Lett.*, 57(5):237–241, 1996.

[CDR86]   S. Cook, C. Dwork, and R. Reischuk. Upper and lower time bounds for parallel random access machines without simultaneous writes. *SIAM J. Comput.*, 15(1):87–97, 1986.

[CFL83]   A. K. Chandra, M. L. Furst, and R. J. Lipton. Multi-party protocols. In *STOC*, pages 94–99. ACM, 25–27 Apr. 1983.

[CG85]   B. Chor and O. Goldreich. Unbiased bits from sources of weak randomness and probabilistic communication complexity. *SIAM J. Comput.*, 17(2):230–261, 1988. Prelim version FOCS '85.

[Cha94]   B. Chazelle. A spectral approach to lower bounds with applications to geometric searching. *SIAM J. Comput.*, 27(2):545–556, 1998. Prelim version FOCS '94.

[Che70]   J. Cheeger. A lower bound for the smallest eigenvalue of the Laplacian. In *Problems in Analysis (Papers dedicated to Salomon Bochner, 1969)*, pages 195–199. Princeton Univ. Press, 1970.

[CHSH69]   J. F. Clauser, M. A. Horne, A. Shimony, and R. A. Holt. Proposed experiment to test local hidden-variable theories. *Phys. Rev. Lett.*, 23(15):880–884, 1969.

[Chu36]   A. Church. An unsolvable problem of elementary number theory. *Amer. J. Math.*, 58(2):345–363, 1936.

[Chu90]   F. R. K. Chung. Quasi-random classes of hypergraphs. *Random Struct. Algorithms*, 1(4):363–382, 1990.

[Chv73]   V. Chvátal. Edmonds polytopes and a hierarchy of combinatorial problems. *Discrete Mathematics*, 4:305–337, 1973.

[CK00]   P. Crescenzi and V. Kann. A compendium of NP optimization problems. http://www.nada.kth.se/~viggo/problemlist/, 2000. Web site tracking the tractability of many NP problems.

[CLRS01]   T. H. Cormen, C. E. Leiserson, R. L. Rivest, and C. Stein. *Introduction to Algorithms*. MIT Press, 2001.

[Cob64]   A. Cobham. The intrinsic computational difficulty of functions. In *Proceedings of the 1964 International Congress for Logic, Methodology, and Philosophy of Science*, pages 24–30. Elsevier/North-Holland, 1964.

[Coo71]   S. A. Cook. The complexity of theorem proving procedures. In *Proc. 3rd Ann. ACM Symp. Theory of Computing*, pages 151–158. ACM, 1971.

[Coo72]   S. A. Cook. A hierarchy for nondeterministic time complexity. *J. Comput. Syst. Sci.*, 7(4):343–353, 1973. Prelim version STOC '72.

[Coo75]   S. A. Cook. Feasibly constructive proofs and the propositional calculus. In *STOC*, pages 83–97. ACM, 1975.

[CRVW02]   M. Capalbo, O. Reingold, S. Vadhan, and A. Wigderson. Randomness conductors and constant-degree lossless expanders. In *STOC*, pages 659–668. ACM, 19–21 May 2002.

[CS88]   V. Chvátal and E. Szemerédi. Many hard examples for resolution. *J. ACM*, 35(4):759–768, 1988.

[Csa76]   L. Csanky. Fast parallel matrix inversion algorithms. *SIAM J. Comput.*, 5:618–623, 1976.

[CSWY01]   A. Chakrabarti, Y. Shi, A. Wirth, and A. Yao. Informational complexity and the direct sum problem for simultaneous message complexity. In *FOCS*, pages 270–278. IEEE, 14–17 Oct. 2001.

[CT65]   J. W. Cooley and J. W. Tukey. An algorithm for the machine calculation of complex fourier series. *Math. Computing*, 19:297–301, 1965.

[CW77]   J. L. Carter and M. N. Wegman. Universal classes of hash functions. *J. Comput. Syst. Sci.*, 18(2):143–154, 1979. Prelim version STOC '77.

[CW89]   A. Cohen and A. Wigderson. Dispersers, deterministic amplification, and weak random sources. In *FOCS*, pages 14–19. IEEE, 30 Oct.–1 Nov. 1989.

[CW90]   D. Coppersmith and S. Winograd. Matrix multiplication via arithmetic progressions. *J. Symbolic Computation*, 9(3):251–280, 1990.

[Dav65]   M. Davis. *The Undecidable*. Dover Publications, 1965.

[DDN91]   D. Dolev, C. Dwork, and M. Naor. Nonmalleable cryptography. *SIAM J. Comput.*, 30(2):391–437, 2000. Prelim version STOC '91.

[Deu85]   D. Deutsch. Quantum theory, the Church-Turing principle and the universal quantum computer. *Proc. Roy. Soc. Lond. A*, A400:97–117, 1985.

[Deu89]   D. Deutsch. Quantum computational networks. *Proc. Roy. Soc. Lond. A*, A425:73–90, 1989.

[DFR+07]   I. Damgård, S. Fehr, R. Renner, L. Salvail, and C. Schaffner. A tight high-order entropic quantum uncertainty relation with applications. In *Proceedings of 27th CRYPTO*, volume 4622 of *Lecture Notes in Computer Science*, pages 360–378. Springer, 2007.

[DH76]   W. Diffie and M. E. Hellman. New directions in cryptography. *IEEE Transactions on Information Theory*, 22(5):644–654, 1976.

[DHS94]   M. Dietzfelbinger, J. Hromkovic, and G. Schnitger. A comparison of two lower-bound methods for communication complexity. *Theor. Comput. Sci*, 168(1): 39–51, 1996. Prelim version MFCS '94.

[Din06]   I. Dinur. The PCP theorem by gap amplification. *J. ACM*, 54(3), 2007. Prelim version '06.

[DJ92]   D. Deutsch and R. Jozsa. Rapid solution of problems by quantum computation. *Proc. Roy. Soc. Lond. A*, 439:553–558, Oct. 1992.

[DK00]   D. Z. Du and K. I. Ko. *Theory of Computational Complexity*. Wiley, 2000.

[DL93]   P. Dagum and M. Luby. Approximating probabilistic inference in bayesian belief networks is NP-hard. *Artificial Intelligence*, 60(1):141–153, 1993.

[DLne]   R. A. DeMillo and R. J. Lipton. A probabilistic remark on algebraic program testing. *Inf. Process. Lett.*, 7(4):193–195, 1978.

[dLMSS56]   K. de Leeuw, E. F. Moore, C. E. Shannon, and N. Shapiro. Computability by probabilistic machines. In C. E. Shannon and J. McCarthy, editors, *Automata Studies*, pages 183–212. Princeton University Press, 1956. Annals of Mathematics Studies #34.

[Dod84]   J. Dodziuk. Difference equations, isoperimetric inequality and transience of certain random walks. *Trans. Amer. Math. Soc.*, 284(2):787–794, 1984.

[DP60]   M. Davis and H. Putnam. A computing procedure for quantification theory. *JACM*, 7(3):201–215, 1960.

[DPV06]   S. Dasgupta, C. H. Papadimitriou, and U. V. Vazirani. *Algorithms*. McGraw Hill, 2006. Draft available from the authors' Web page.

[DR02]   J. Daemen and V. Rijmen. *The Design of Rijndael: AES—The Advanced Encryption Standard*. Springer, 2002.

[DvM05]   S. Diehl and D. van Melkebeek. Time-space lower bounds for the polynomial hierarchy on randomized machines. *SIAM J. Comput.*, 56:563–594, 2006. Prelim version ICALP '05.

[Edm65]   J. Edmonds. Paths, trees, and flowers. *Canad. J. Math.*, 17:449–467, 1965.

[EL75]   P. Erdős and L. Lovász. Problems and results on 3-chromatic hypergraphs and some related questions. In *Infinite and finite sets (Colloq., Keszthely, 1973; dedicated to P. Erdős on his 60th birthday), Vol. II*, pages 609–627. Colloq. Math. Soc. János Bolyai, Vol. 10. North-Holland, 1975.

[Ell99]   J. H. Ellis. The history of non-secret encryption. *Cryptologia*, 23(3):267–273, 1999.

[EPR35]   A. Einstein, B. Podolsky, and N. Rosen. Can quantum-mechanical description of physical reality be considered complete? *Phys. Rev.*, 47(10):777–780, 1935.

[ER59]   P. Erdos and A. Renyi. On random graphs. *Publ. Math. Debrecen*, 6:290–297, 1959.

[ER60]   P. Erdős and R. Rado. Intersection theorems for systems of sets. *J. Lond. Math. Soc.*, 35:85–90, 1960.

[Fei91]   U. Feige. On the success probability of the two provers in one-round proof systems. In *Proceedings of the 6th Annual Conference on Structure in Complexity Theory, CSCT'91 (Chicago, Illinois, June 30–July 3, 1991)*, pages 116–123. IEEE, 1991.

[Fei95]   U. Feige. A tight upper bound on the cover time for random walks on graphs. *Random Struct. Algorithms*, 6(1):51–54, 1995.

[Fei96]   U. Feige. A threshold of ln for approximating set cover. *J. ACM*, 45(4):634–652, 1998.

[Fey82]   R. Feynman. Simulating physics with computers. *International Journal of Theoretical Physics*, 21(6&7):467–488, 1982.

[FG06]   J. Flum and M. Grohe. *Parametrized Complexity*. Springer, 2006.

[FGG07]   E. Farhi, J. Goldstone, and S. Gutmann. A quantum algorithm for the Hamiltonian NAND tree. *Arxiv preprint quant-ph/0702144*, 2007.

[FGL+91]   U. Feige, S. Goldwasser, L. Lovász, S. Safra, and M. Szegedy. Interactive proofs and the hardness of approximating cliques. *J. ACM*, 43(2):268–292, 1996. Prelim version FOCS '91.

[Fis04]   E. Fischer. The art of uninformed decisions: A primer to property testing. *Current Trends in Theoretical Computer Science: The Challenge of the New Century* (G. Paun, G. Rozenberg, and A. Salomaa, eds.), World Scientific Publishing (2004), Vol. I.

[FK93]   U. Feige and J. Kilian. Two-prover protocols – Low error at affordable rates. *SIAM J. Comput.*, 30(1):324–34, 2000.

[FKO06]   U. Feige, J. H. Kim, and E. Ofek. Witnesses for non-satisfiability of dense random 3CNF formulas. In *FOCS*, pages 497–508. IEEE, 2006.

[FL92]   U. Feige and L. Lovász. Two-prover one-round proof systems: Their power and their problems (extended abstract). In *STOC*, pages 733–744. ACM, 1992.

[FLvMV00]   L. Fortnow, R. Lipton, D. van Melkebeek, and A. Viglas. Time-space lower bounds for satisfiability. *J. ACM*, 52:835–865, 2005. Prelim version CCC '2000.

[FM05]   G. S. Frandsen and P. B. Miltersen. Reviewing bounds on the circuit size of the hardest functions. *Information Processing Letters*, 95(2):354–357, 2005.

[FO04]   U. Feige and E. Ofek. Easily refutable subformulas of large random 3CNF formulas. In *Proceedings of 31st International Colloquium on Automata, Languages and Programming (ICALP)*, volume 3142 of *Lecture Notes in Computer Science*, pages 519–530. Springer, 2004.

[For89]   L. J. Fortnow. *Complexity-Theoretic Aspects of Interactive Proof Systems*. PhD thesis, Massachussets Institute of Technology, 1989.

[For97a]   L. Fortnow. Time-space tradeoffs for satisfiability. *J. Comput. Syst. Sci.*, 60(2):337–353, 2000. Prelim version CCC '97.

[For97b]   L. Fortnow. Counting complexity. In L. Hemaspaandra and A. Selman, editors, *A Complexity Theory Retrospective II*. Springer Verlag, 1997.

[FR98]   A. M. Frieze and B. Reed. Probabilistic analysis of algorithms. In M. Habib, C. McDiarmid, J. Ramirez-Alfonsin, and B. Reed, editors, *Probabilistic Methods for Algorithmic Discrete Mathematics*, volume 16 of *Algorithms and Combinatorics*, pages 36–92. Springer-Verlag, 1998.

[Fri99]   E. Friedgut. Sharp thresholds of graph properties, and the k-sat problem. *J. Amer. Math. Soc.*, 12(4):1017–1054, 1999. With an appendix by Jean Bourgain.

[FRS88]   L. Fortnow, J. Rompel, and M. Sipser. On the power of multi-prover interactive protocols. *Theoretical Computer Science*, 134(2):545–557, 1994.

[FS88]   L. Fortnow and M. Sipser. Are there interactive protocols for coNP-languages? *Inf. Process. Lett.*, 28(5):249–251, 1988.

[FS04]   L. Fortnow and R. Santhanam. Hierarchy theorems for probabilistic polynomial time. In *FOCS*, pages 316–324. IEEE, 2004.

[FSS81]   M. Furst, J. Saxe, and M. Sipser. Parity, circuits, and the polynomial time hierarchy. *Mathematical Systems Theory*, 17:13–27, 1984. Prelim version FOCS '81.

[Gal63]   R. G. Gallager. *Low-Density Parity-Check Codes*. The MIT Press, 1963.

[Gar72]   M. R. Garey. Optimal binary identification procedures. *SIAM J. Appl. Math.*, 23(2):173–186, 1972.

[GG79]   O. Gabber and Z. Galil. Explicit constructions of linear-sized superconcentrators. *J. Comput. Syst. Sci.*, 22(3):407–420, June 1981. Prelim version FOCS '79.

[GG98]   O. Goldreich and S. Goldwasser. On the limits of nonapproximability of lattice problems. *J. Comput. Syst. Sci.*, 60(3):540–563, 2000. Prelim version STOC '98.

[GGH+07]   S. Goldwasser, D. Gutfreund, A. Healy, T. Kaufman, and G. N. Rothblum. Verifying and decoding in constant depth. In *STOC*, pages 440–449. ACM, 2007.

[GGM84]   O. Goldreich, S. Goldwasser, and S. Micali. How to construct random functions. *J. ACM*, 33(4):792–807, 1986. Prelim version FOCS '84.

[Gil74] J. T. Gill. Computational complexity of probabilistic Turing machines. In *STOC*, pages 91–95. ACM, 1974.

[Gil77] J. Gill. Computational complexity of probabilistic Turing machines. *SIAM J. Comput.*, 6(4):675–695, Dec. 1977.

[Gil93] D. Gillman. A chernoff bound for random walks on expander graphs. *SIAM J. Comput.*, 27(4):1203–1220, 1998. Prelim version FOCS '93.

[GJ79] M. R. Garey and D. S. Johnson. *Computers and Intractability: A Guide to the Theory of NP-Completeness*. W. H. Freeman and Company, 1979.

[GK01] A. Goerdt and M. Krivelevich. Efficient recognition of random unsatisfiable k-SAT instances by spectral methods. In *STACS 2001*, pages 294–304. Springer, 2001.

[GL89] O. Goldreich and L. A. Levin. A hard-core predicate for all one-way functions. In *STOC*, pages 25–32. ACM, 15–17 May 1989.

[GLR+91] P. Gemmell, R. Lipton, R. Rubinfeld, M. Sudan, and A. Wigderson. Self-testing/correcting for polynomials and for approximate functions. In *STOC*, pages 32–42. ACM, 1991.

[GM82] S. Goldwasser and S. Micali. Probabilistic encryption. *J. Comput. Syst. Sci.*, 28(2):270–299, 1984. Prelim version STOC '82.

[GMR84] S. Goldwasser, S. Micali, and R. L. Rivest. A digital signature scheme secure against adaptive chosen-message attacks. *SIAM J. Comput.*, 17(2):281–308, 1988. Prelim version CRYPTO '84.

[GMR85] S. Goldwasser, S. Micali, and C. Rackoff. The knowledge complexity of interactive proof systems. *SIAM J. Comput.*, 18(1):186–208, 1989. Prelim version STOC '85.

[GMW86] O. Goldreich, S. Micali, and A. Wigderson. Proofs that yield nothing but their validity or all languages in NP have zero-knowledge proof systems. *J. ACM*, 38(3):691–729, 1991. Prelim version FOCS '86.

[GMW87] O. Goldreich, S. Micali, and A. Wigderson. How to play any mental game— A completeness theorem for protocols with honest majority. In *STOC*, pages 218–229. ACM, 1987.

[GNW95] O. Goldreich, N. Nisan, and A. Wigderson. On yao's XOR-lemma. *Electronic Colloquium on Computational Complexity (ECCC)*, 2(50), 1995.

[Gol97] O. Goldreich. Notes on levin's theory of average-case complexity. *Electronic Colloquium on Computational Complexity (ECCC)*, 4(58), 1997.

[Gol04] O. Goldreich. *Foundations of Cryptography, Volumes 1 and 2*. Cambridge University Press, 2001, 2004.

[Gol08] O. Goldreich. *Computational Complexity: A Conceptual Perspective*. Cambridge Univerity Press, 2008. Online drafts available at http://www.wisdom. weizmann.ac.il/~oded/cc-drafts.html.

[Gom63] R. Gomory. An algorithm for integer solutions to linear programs. In R. L. Graves and P. Wolfe, editors, *Recent advances in mathematical programming*, pages 269–302. McGraw-Hill, 1963.

[Gow01] W. Gowers. A new proof of Szemerédi's theorem. *Geometric And Functional Analysis*, 11(3):465–588, 2001.

[Gow07] W. T. Gowers. Hypergraph regularity and the multidimensional Szemerédi theorem. *Ann. of Math. (2)*, 166(3):897–946, 2007.

[GR06] V. Guruswami and A. Rudra. Explicit capacity-achieving list-decodable codes. In *STOC*, pages 1–10. ACM, 2006.

[Gra66] R. Graham. Bounds for certain multiprocessor anomalies. *Bell Sys. Tech. J.*, 45:1563–1581, 1966.

[Gro83]   M. Gromov. Filling Riemannian manifolds. *J. Differential Geom.*, 18(1):1–147, 1983.

[Gro96]   L. K. Grover. A fast quantum mechanical algorithm for database search. In *STOC*, pages 212–219. ACM, 22–24 May 1996.

[GS87]   S. Goldwasser and M. Sipser. Private coins versus public coins in interactive proof systems. In S. Micali, editor, *Randomness and Computation*. JAI Press, 1987. Extended Abstract in *Proc. 18th ACM Symp. on Theory of Computing*, 1986.

[GS92]   P. Gemmell and M. Sudan. Highly resilient correctors for polynomials. *Information Processing Letters*, 43(4):169–174, 1992.

[GS98]   V. Guruswami and M. Sudan. Improved decoding of reed-solomon and algebraic-geometry codes. *IEEE Transactions on Information Theory*, 45(6):1757–1767, 1999. Prelim version FOCS '98.

[GST04]   O. Goldreich, M. Sudan, and L. Trevisan. From logarithmic advice to single-bit advice. *Electronic Colloquium on Computational Complexity (ECCC)*, 2004. Report TR04–093.

[GUV07]   V. Guruswami, C. Umans, and S. Vadhan. Unbalanced expanders and random-ness extractors from parvaresh-vardy codes. In *Proc. of CCC*, pages 96–108. IEEE, 2007.

[GVW00]   O. Goldreich, S. Vadhan, and A. Wigderson. Simplified derandomization of BPP using a hitting set generator. *Electronic Colloquium on Computational Complexity (ECCC)*, 7(4), 2000.

[Haj90]   P. Hajnal. On the power of randomness in the decision tree model. In *Proceedings, Fifth Annual Structure in Complexity Theory Conference*, pages 66–77. IEEE, 8–11 July 1990.

[Hak85]   A. Haken. The intractability or resolution. *Theoretical Comput. Sci.*, 39:297–308, 1985.

[Ham50]   R. W. Hamming. Error detecting and error correcting codes. *Bell Sys. Tech. J.*, 29(2):147–160, 1950. Reprinted in E. E. Swartzlander, *Computer Arithmetic*, Vol. 2, IEEE Computer Society Press Tutorial, Los Alamitos, CA, 1990.

[Hås86]   J. Håstad. Almost optimal lower bounds for small depth circuits. In *STOC*, pages 6–20. ACM, 28–30 May 1986.

[Hås96]   J. Håstad. Clique is hard to approximate within $n^{1-\epsilon}$. *Acta Math.*, 182(1):105–142, 1999.

[Hås97]   J. Håstad. Some optimal inapproximability results. *J. ACM*, 48(4):798–859, 2001. Prelim version STOC '97.

[Hea06]   A. Healy. Randomness-efficient sampling within NC^1. In *APPROX-RANDOM*, volume 4110 of *Lecture Notes in Computer Science*, pages 398–409. Springer, 2006.

[HILL99]   J. Håstad, R. Impagliazzo, L. A. Levin, and M. Luby. A pseudorandom generator from any one-way function. *SIAM J. Comput.*, 28(4):1364–1396, 1999.

[HLW06]   S. Hoory, N. Linial, and A. Wigderson. Expander graphs and their applications. *Bulletin of the American Mathematical Society*, 43(4):439–561, 2006.

[HMU01]   J. E. Hopcroft, R. Motwani, and J. D. Ullman. *Introduction to Automata Theory, Language, and Computation*. Addison–Wesley, 2nd edition, 2001.

[HO02]   L. A. Hemaspaandra and M. Ogihara. *The Complexity Theory Companion*. Springer-Verlag, 2002.

[Hoc97]   D. S. Hochbaum, editor. *Approximation Algorithms for NP-Hard Problems*. PWS Publishing, 1997.

[Hod83]   A. Hodges. *Alan Turing: The Enigma*. Burnett Books, 1983.

[Hof82]   C. M. Hoffmann. *Group Theoretic Algorithms and Graph Isomorphism*, volume 136 of *Lecture Notes in Computer Science*. Springer, 1982.

[Hoh30]   G. Hoheisel. Primzahlprobleme in der analysis. *Sitzunsberichte der Königlich Preussischen Akademie der Wissenschaften zu Berlin*, 33:3–11, 1930.

[Hol07]   T. Holenstein. Parallel repetition: Simplifications and the no-signaling case. In *STOC*, pages 411–419. ACM, 2007.

[HPV75]   J. Hopcroft, W. Paul, and L. Valiant. On Time Versus Space. *J. ACM*, 24(2):332–337, 1977. Prelim version FOCS '75.

[HR76]   L. Hyafil and R. L. Rivest. Constructing optimal binary decision trees is NP-complete. *Inf. Process. Lett.*, 5(1):15–17, 1976.

[HS65]   J. Hartmanis and R. E. Stearns. On the computational complexity of algorithms. *Transactions of the American Mathematical Society*, 117:285–306, 1965.

[HS66]   F. C. Hennie and R. E. Stearns. Two-tape simulation of multitape Turing machines. *J. ACM*, 13(4):533–546, 1966.

[HVV04]   A. Healy, S. Vadhan, and E. Viola. Using nondeterminism to amplify hardness. In *STOC*, pages 192–201. ACM, 13–15 June 2004.

[IKW01]   R. Impagliazzo, V. Kabanets, and A. Wigderson. In search of an easy witness: exponential time vs. probabilistic polynomial time. *J. Comput. Syst. Sci.*, 65(4):672–694, 2002. Prelim version CCC '01.

[IL90]   R. Impagliazzo and L. A. Levin. No better ways to generate hard NP instances than picking uniformly at random. In *FOCS*, pages 812–823. IEEE, Oct. 1990.

[ILL89]   R. Impagliazzo, L. A. Levin, and L. Luby. Pseudo-random generation from one-way functions. In *STOC*, pages 12–24. ACM, May 1989.

[ILMR05]   K. Iwama, O. Lachish, H. Morizumi, and R. Raz. An explicit lower bound of $5n - o(n)$ for boolean circuits. Manuscript, 2006. Prelim versions by Raz and Lachish (STOC '01), and Iwama and Morizumi (manuscript, 2005).

[Imm88]   N. Immerman. Nondeterministic space is closed under complementation. *SIAM J. Comput.*, 17(5):935–938, 1988.

[Imm99]   N. Immerman. *Descriptive Complexity*. Springer, 1999.

[Imp95a]   R. Impagliazzo. Hard-core distributions for somewhat hard problems. In *FOCS*, pages 538–544. IEEE, 1995.

[Imp95b]   R. Impagliazzo. A personal view of average-case complexity. In *Structure in Complexity Theory Conference*, pages 134–147, 1995.

[Ing37]   A. E. Ingham. On the difference between consecutive primes. *Quarterly Journal of Mathematics (Oxford Series)*, 8:255–266, 1937.

[INW94]   R. Impagliazzo, N. Nisan, and A. Wigderson. Pseudorandomness for network algorithms. In *STOC*, pages 356–364. ACM, 23–25 May 1994.

[IPZ98]   R. Impagliazzo, R. Paturi, and F. Zane. Which problems have strongly exponential complexity? *J. Comput. Syst. Sci.*, 63(4):512–530, 2001. Prelim version FOCS '98.

[ISW99]   R. Impagliazzo, R. Shaltiel, and A. Wigderson. Reducing the seed length in the nisan-wigderson generator. *Combinatorica*, 26(6):647–681, 2006. Prelim versions in FOCS '99 and STOC '00.

[IW97]   R. Impagliazzo and A. Wigderson. $P = BPP$ if E requires exponential circuits: Derandomizing the XOR lemma. In *STOC*, pages 220–229, New York, 1997. ACM.

[IW98]   R. Impagliazzo and A. Wigderson. Randomness vs time: Derandomization under a uniform assumption. *J. Comput. Syst. Sci.*, 63(4):672–688, 2001. Prelim version FOCS '98.

[IZ89]   R. Impagliazzo and D. Zuckerman. How to recycle random bits. In *FOCS*, pages 248–253. IEEE, 30 Oct.–1 Nov. 1989.

[JM85]   S. Jimbo and A. Maruoka. Expanders obtained from affine transformations. *Combinatorica*, 7(4):343–355, 1987. Prelim version STOC '85.

[Joh62]   S. Johnson. A new upper bound for error correcting codes. *IRE Trans. Information Theory*, pages 203–207, 1962.

[Joh74]   D. S. Johnson. Approximation algorithms for combinatorial problems. *J. Comput. Syst. Sci.*, 9(3):256–278, 1974.

[Joh84]   D. S. Johnson. Solving np-hard problems quickly (on average). *J. Algorithms*, 5(2):284–299, 1984.

[JS90]   M. Jerrum and A. Sinclair. Polynomial-time approximation algorithms for the ising model. *SIAM J. Comput.*, 22(5):1087–1116, 1993. Prelim version ICALP '90.

[JSV01]   M. Jerrum, A. Sinclair, and E. Vigoda. A polynomial-time approximation algorithm for the permanent of a matrix with non-negative entries. *J. ACM*, 51(4):671–697, 2004. Prelim version STOC '01.

[JVV86]   M. R. Jerrum, L. G. Valiant, and V. V. Vazirani. Random generation of combinatorial structures from a uniform distribution. *Theor. Comp. Sci.*, 43(2–3):169–188, 1986.

[Kab00]   V. Kabanets. Easiness assumptions and hardness tests: Trading time for zero error. *J. Comput. Syst. Sci.*, 63(2):236–252, 2001. Prelim version CCC '00.

[Kah92]   N. Kahale. Eigenvalues and expansion of regular graphs. *J. ACM*, 42:1091–1106, 1995. Prelim version FOCS '92.

[Kah96]   D. Kahn. *The Codebreakers: The Story of Secret Writing*. Scribner, revised edition, 1996.

[Kah97]   N. Kahale. Large deviation bounds for markov chains. *Combinatorics, Probability and Computing*, 6(04):465–474, 1997.

[Kan81]   R. Kannan. Circuit-size lower bounds and non-reducibility to sparse sets. *Information and Control*, 55(1–3):40–56, 1982. Prelim version FOCS '81.

[Kan83]   R. Kannan. Alternation and the power of nondeterminism. In *STOC*, pages 344–346. ACM, 1983.

[Kar72]   R. M. Karp. Reducibility among combinatorial problems. In R. E. Miller and J. W. Thatcher, editors, *Complexity of Computer Computations*, pages 85–103. Plenum, 1972.

[Kha79]   L. C. Khačiyan. Polynomial algorithm for linear programming. *Soviet Doklady*, 244:1093–1096, 1979. Typed translation.

[Kho02]   S. Khot. On the power of unique 2-prover 1-round games. In *STOC*, pages 767–775. ACM, 2002.

[Kho05]   S. Khot. Guest column: Inapproximability results via long code based PCPs. *SIGACT News*, 36(2):25–42, 2005.

[KI03]   V. Kabanets and R. Impagliazzo. Derandomizing polynomial identity tests means proving circuit lower bounds. In *STOC*, pages 355–364. ACM, 2003.

[Kil88]   J. Kilian. Founding cryptography on oblivious transfer. In *STOC*, pages 20–31. ACM, 2–4 May 1988.

[Kin88]   V. King. An omega($n^5/4$) lower bound on the randomized complexity of graph properties. *Combinatorica*, 11(1):23–32, 1991. Prelim version STOC '88.

[Kit97]   A. Y. Kitaev. Quantum computations: Algorithms and error correction. *RMS: Russian Mathematical Surveys*, 52(6):1191–1249, 1997.

[KKL88]   J. Kahn, G. Kalai, and N. Linial. The influence of variables on boolean functions (extended abstract). In *FOCS*, pages 68–80. IEEE, 1988.

[KKMO05]   S. Khot, G. Kindler, E. Mossel, and R. O'Donnell. Optimal inapproximability results for MAX-CUT and other 2-variable CSPs? *SIAM J. Comput.*, 37(1):319–357, 2007.

[KL80]   R. Karp and R. Lipton. Turing machines that take advice. *L' Ensignement Mathématique*, 28:191–210, 1982.

[KL07]   J. Katz and Y. Lindell. *Introduction to Modern Cryptography*. Chapman and Hall/CRC Press, 2007.

[KM91]   E. Kushilevitz and Y. Mansour. Learning decision trees using the fourier spectrum. *SIAM J. Comput.*, 22(6):1331–1348, 1993. Prelim version STOC '91.

[KN97]   E. Kushilevitz and N. Nisan. *Communication Complexity*. Cambridge University Press, 1997.

[Knu69]   D. E. Knuth. *Art of Computer Programming, Volume II*. Addison Wesley, 1969. Current edition: 1997.

[Knu73]   D. E. Knuth. *The Art of Computer Programming, Vol. 3 : Sorting and Searching*. Series in Computer Science and Information Processing. Addison-Wesley, 1973. Current edition: 1997.

[Koi97]   P. Koiran. Randomized and deterministic algorithms for the dimension of algebraic varieties. In *FOCS*, pages 36–45. IEEE, 1997.

[Koz97]   D. C. Kozen. *Automata and Computability*. Springer-Verlag, 1997.

[Koz06]   D. C. Kozen. *Theory of Computation*. Springer, 2006.

[KPS85]   R. M. Karp, N. Pippenger, and M. Sipser. A time randomness tradeoff. In *AMS Conf. on Probabilistic Computational Complexity*, 1985. This paper gives the first example of deterministic amplification using expander graphs.

[KR81]   R. M. Karp and M. O. Rabin. Efficient randomized pattern-matching algorithms. *IBM J. Res. Dev.*, 31(2):249–260, 1987. Prelim version report TR-31-81, Harvard University, 1981.

[KR08]   S. Khot and O. Regev. Vertex cover might be hard to approximate to within 2-epsilon. *J. Comput. Syst. Sci.*, 74(3):335–349, 2008.

[Kra94]   J. Krajíček. Lower bounds to the size of constant-depth propositional proofs. *J. Symbolic Logic*, 59(1):73–86, 1994.

[Kra95]   J. Krajíček. *Bounded Arithmetic, Propositional Logic and Complexity Theory*. Cambridge University Press, 1995.

[Kra97]   J. Krajíček. Interpolation theorems, lower bounds for proof systems and independence results for bounded arithmetic. *J. Symbolic Logic*, 62(2):457–486, 1997.

[KRW95]   M. Karchmer, R. Raz, and A. Wigderson. Super-logarithmic depth lower bounds via the direct sum in communication complexity. *Computational Complexity*, 5(3/4):191–204, 1995.

[KS99]   A. R. Klivans and R. A. Servedio. Boosting and hard-core set construction. *Machine Learning*, 51(3):217–238, 2003. Prelim version FOCS '99.

[KS06]   G. Kalai and S. Safra. Threshold phenomena and influence. In C. M. A. G. Percus, G. Istrate, editor, *Computational Complexity and Statistical Physics*. Oxford University Press, 2006.

[KSS83]   J. Kahn, M. E. Saks, and D. Sturtevant. A topological approach to evasiveness. *Combinatorica*, 4(4):297–306, 1984. Prelim version FOCS '83.

[KT06]   J. Kleinberg and É. Tardos. *Algorithm Design*. Pearson Studium, 2006.

[Kuc95]   L. Kucera. Expected complexity of graph partitioning problems. *Discrete Applied Mathematics*, 57(2–3):193–212, 1995.

[KUW85]   R. M. Karp, E. Upfal, and A. Wigderson. Constructing a perfect matching is in random NC. *Combinatorica*, 6:35–48, 1986. Prelim version STOC '85.

[KV89]   M. Kearns and L. Valiant. Cryptographic limitations on learning Boolean formulae and finite automata. *J. ACM*, 41(1):67–95, 1994. Prelim version STOC '89.

[KV94]   M. J. Kearns and U. V. Vazirani. *An Introduction to Computational Learning Theory*. MIT Press, 1994.

[KV05]   S. Khot and N. K. Vishnoi. The unique games conjecture, integrality gap for cut problems and embeddability of negative type metrics into l_1. In *FOCS*, pages 53–62. IEEE, 2005.

[KVS02]   A. Y. Kitaev, M. Vyalyi, and A. Shen. *Classical and Quantum Computation*. AMS Press, 2002.

[KW88]   M. Karchmer and A. Wigderson. Monotone circuits for connectivity require super-logarithmic depth. *SIAM J. Discrete Mathematics*, 3(2):255–265, May 1990. Prelim version STOC '88.

[Lad75]   R. E. Ladner. On the structure of polynomial time reducibility. *J. ACM*, 22(1):155–171, 1975.

[Lau83]   C. Lautemann. BPP and the polynomial hierarchy. *Inf. Process. Lett.*, 17(4):215–217, 1983.

[Lea05]   D. Leavitt. *The Man Who Knew too Much: Alan Turing and the Invention of the Computer*. Great Discoveries. W. W. Norton & Co., 2005.

[Lei91]   F. T. Leighton. *Introduction to Parallel Algorithms and Architectures: Array, Trees, Hypercubes*. Morgan Kaufmann, 1991.

[Lev73]   L. A. Levin. Universal sequential search problems. *PINFTRANS: Problems of Information Transmission (translated from Problemy Peredachi Informatsii (Russian))*, 9, 1973.

[Lev86]   L. A. Levin. Average case complete problems. *SIAM J. Comput.*, 15(1):285–286, 1986.

[Lev87]   L. A. Levin. One-way functions and pseudorandom generators. *Combinatorica*, 7(4):357–363, 1987.

[LFKN90] C. Lund, L. Fortnow, H. Karloff, and N. Nisan. Algebraic methods for interactive proof systems. *J. ACM*, 39(4):859–868, 1992. Prelim version FOCS '90.

[Lip90]   R. J. Lipton. Efficient checking of computations. In *7th Annual Symposium on Theoretical Aspects of Computer Science*, volume 415 of *lncs*, pages 207–215. Springer, 22–24 Feb. 1990.

[Lip91]   R. J. Lipton. New directions in testing. In *Distributed Computing and Cryptography*, volume 2 of *DIMACS Series in Discrete Mathematics and Theoretical Computer Science*, pages 191–202. American Mathematics Society, 1991.

[Liv06]   N. Livne. All natural NPC problems have average-case complete versions. In *ECCCTR: Electronic Colloquium on Computational Complexity, technical reports*, 2006.

[LLKS85] E. L. Lawler, J. K. Lenstra, A. H. G. R. Kan, and D. B. Shmoys, editors. *The Traveling Salesman Problem*. John Wiley, 1985.

[LLMP90] A. K. Lenstra, H. W. Lenstra, Jr., M. S. Manasse, and J. M. Pollard. The number field sieve. In *STOC*, pages 564–572. ACM, 14–16 May 1990.

[Llo06]   S. Lloyd. *Programming the Universe: A Quantum Computer Scientist Takes on the Cosmos*. Knopf, 2006.

[Lov78]   L. Lovász. Kneser's conjecture, chromatic number, and homotopy. *J. Combin. Theory Ser. A*, 25:319–324, 1978.

[Lov79]   L. Lovàsz. On determinants, matchings, and random algorithms. In L. Budach, editor, *Fundamentals of Computation Theory FCT '79*, pages 565–574. Akademie-Verlag, 1979.

[Lov07]   L. Lovász. *Combinatorial Problems and Exercises*. AMS Chelsea Publishing, Providence, RI, second edition, 2007. Corrected reprint of 1993 second edition.

[LPS86]   A. Lubotzky, R. Phillips, and P. Sarnak. Ramanujan graphs. *Combinatorica*, 8:261–277, 1988. Prelim version STOC '86.

[LRVW03]   C.-J. Lu, O. Reingold, S. Vadhan, and W. Wigderson. Extractors: optimal up to constant factors. In *STOC*, pages 602–611. ACM, 2003.

[LS88]   L. Lovász and M. E. Saks. Communication complexity and combinatorial lattice theory. *J. Comput. Syst. Sci.*, 47(2):322–349, 1993. Prelim version FOCS '88.

[LS91]   D. Lapidot and A. Shamir. Fully parallelized multi prover protocols for NEXP-time (extended abstract). In *FOCS*, pages 13–18. IEEE, 1991.

[LS07]   T. Lee and A. Shraibman. Disjointness is hard in the multi-party number on the forehead model, 27 Dec. 2007. Comment: 21 pages.

[Lup58]   O. Lupanov. The synthesis of contact circuits. *Dokl. Akad. Nauk SSSR*, 119:23–26, 1958.

[LW06]   M. Luby and A. Wigderson. Pairwise independence and derandomization. *Found. Trends Theor. Comput. Sci.*, 1(4):237–301, 2006.

[LY94]   C. Lund and M. Yannakakis. On the hardness of approximating minimization problems. *J. ACM*, 41(5):960–981, 1994.

[LY02]   L. Lovász and N. E. Young. Lecture notes on evasiveness of graph properties. *CoRR*, cs.CC/0205031, 2002. Informal publication.

[Maa84]   W. Maass. Quadratic lower bounds for deterministic and nondeterministic one-tape turing machines. In *STOC*, pages 401–408. ACM, 1984.

[Mah80]   S. R. Mahaney. Sparse complete sets of *NP*: solution of a conjecture of berman and hartmanis. *J. Comput. Syst. Sci.*, 25(2):130–143, 1982. Prelim version FOCS '80.

[Mar73]   G. A. Margulis. Explicit constructions of concentrators. *Probl. Peredachi Inf.*, 9(4):71–80, 1973. English translation in *Problems of Information Transmission*, 9(4):325–332, 1973.

[Mar88]   G. A. Margulis. Explicit group-theoretical constructions of combinatorial schemes and their application to the design of expanders and concentrators. *Probl. Peredachi Inf.*, 24(1):51–60, 1988. English translation in *Problems of Information Transmission*, 24(1):39–46, 1988.

[Mat76]   D. W. Matula. The largest clique size in a random graph. Technical report, Dept. of Computer Science, Southern Methodist University, 1976.

[Mat02]   J. Matoušek. *Lectures on Discrete Geometry*. Springer, 2002. Online updated chapters available on http://kam.mff.cuni.cz/~matousek/dg.html.

[MG02]   D. Micciancio and S. S. Goldwasser. *Complexity of Lattice Problems: A Cryptographic Perspective*. Kluwer Academic Publishers, 2002.

[MOO05]   E. Mossel, R. O'Donnell, and K. Oleszkiewicz. Noise stability of functions with low influences: invariance and optimality. In *FOCS*, pages 21–30. IEEE, 2005.

[Mor73]   J. Morgenstern. Note on a lower bound on the linear complexity of the fast fourier transform. *J. ACM*, 20(2):305–306, 1973.

[MR95]   R. Motwani and P. Raghavan. *Randomized algorithms*. Cambridge University Press, 1995.

[MR00]   R. Martin and D. Randall. Sampling adsorbing staircase walks using a new markov chain decomposition method. In *FOCS*, pages 492–502. IEEE, 12–14 Nov. 2000.

[MS72]   A. R. Meyer and L. Stockmeyer. The equivalence problem for regular expres-
            sions with squaring requires exponential time. In *FOCS*, pages 125–129. IEEE,
            1972.

[MS82]   K. Mehlhorn and E. M. Schmidt. Las Vegas is better than determinism in VLSI
            and distributed computing (extended abstract). In *STOC*, pages 330–337. ACM,
            5–7 May 1982.

[MU05]   M. Mitzenmacher and E. Upfal. *Probability and Computing: Randomized
            Algorithms and Probabilistic Analysis*. Cambridge University Press, 2005.

[Mul54]   D. Muller. Application of boolean algebra to switching circuit design and to
            error detection. *IRE Trans. Electronic Computation*, EC-3:6–12, 1954.

[MVV87]   K. Mulmuley, U. V. Vazirani, and V. V. Vazirani. Matching is as easy as matrix
            inversion. *Combinatorica*, 7:105–113, 1987.

[MZ04]   J. Matoušek and G. M. Ziegler. Topological lower bounds for the chro-
            matic number: A hierarchy. *Jahresber. Deutsch. Math.-Verein.*, 106(2):71–90,
            2004.

[NC00]   M. Nielsen and I. Chuang. *Quantum Computation and Quantum Information*.
            Cambridge University Press, 2000.

[Nil04]   A. Nilli. Tight estimates for eigenvalues of regular graphs. *Electr. J. Comb.*,
            11(1), 2004.

[Nis89]   N. Nisan. CREW PRAMs and decision trees. *SIAM J. Comput.*, 20(6):999–1007,
            1991. Prelim version STOC '89.

[Nis90]   N. Nisan. Pseudorandom generators for space-bounded computation. *Combi-
            natorica*, 12(4):449–461, 1992. Prelim version STOC '90.

[NS92]   N. Nisan and M. Szegedy. On the degree of Boolean functions as real
            polynomials. *Computational Complexity*, 4(4):301–313, 1994. Prelim version
            STOC '92.

[NSW92]   N. Nisan, E. Szemeredi, and A. Wigderson. Undirected connectivity in
            $O(log^{1.5}n)$ space. In *FOCS*, pages 24–29. IEEE, Oct. 1992.

[NW88]   N. Nisan and A. Wigderson. Hardness vs randomness. *J. Comput. Syst. Sci.*,
            49(2):149–167, 1994. Prelim version FOCS '88.

[NW94]   N. Nisan and A. Wigderson. On rank vs. communication complexity. *Combi-
            natorica*, 15(4):557–565, 1995. Prelim version FOCS '94.

[NZ93]   N. Nisan and D. Zuckerman. Randomness is linear in space. *J. Comput. Syst.
            Sci.*, 52(1):43–52, 1996. Prelim version STOC '93.

[O'D04]   R. O'Donnell. Hardness amplification within NP. *J. Comput. Syst. Sci.*,
            69(1):68–94, 2004.

[Ost54]   A. M. Ostrowski. On two problems in abstract algebra connected with Horner's
            rule. *Studies in Mathematics and Mechanics*. Academic, 1954.

[Pap85]   C. H. Papadimitriou. Games against nature. *J. Comput. System Sci.*, 31(2):288–
            301, 1985.

[Pap90]   C. H. Papadimitriou. On the complexity of the parity argument and other inef-
            ficient proofs of existence. *J. Comput. Syst. Sci.*, 48(3):498–532, 1994. Prelim
            version FOCS '90.

[Pap94]   C. H. Papadimitriou. *Computational Complexity*. Addison-Wesley, 1994.

[Pen89]   R. Penrose. *The Emperor's New Mind*. Oxford University Press, 1989.

[Pen90]   R. Penrose. The Emperor's New Mind. *Bull. Amer. Math. Soc. 23 (1990)*,
            606–616, 1990.

[Pet60]   W. W. Peterson. Encoding and error-correction procedures for bose-chaudhuri
            codes. *IEEE Trans. Information Theory*, 6:459–470, 1960.

[Pin73]   M. S. Pinsker. On the complexity of a concentrator. *Proc. 7th Int. Teletraffic Cong.*, 1973.

[Pol65]   S. L. Pollack. Conversion of limited-entry decision tables to computer programs. *Commun. ACM*, 8(11):677–682, 1965.

[Pra75]   V. R. Pratt. Every prime has a succinct certificate. *SIAM J. Comput.*, 4:214–220, 1975.

[Pre97]   J. Preskill. Fault tolerant quantum computation. *Arxive e-print*, 1997. arXiv:quant-ph/9712048v1.

[Pre98]   J. Preskill. Reliable quantum computers. *Proc. Roy. Soc. A: Mathematical, Physical and Engineering Sciences*, 454(1969):385–410, 1998.

[PS82]   C. H. Papadimitriou and M. Sipser. Communication complexity. *J. Comput. Syst. Sci.*, 28(2):260–269, 1984. Prelim version STOC '82.

[Pud97]   P. Pudlák. Lower bounds for resolution and cutting planes proofs and monotone computations. *J. Symbolic Logic*, 62(3):981–998, 1997.

[PV05]   F. Parvaresh and A. Vardy. Correcting errors beyond the guruswami-sudan radius in polynomial time. In *FOCS*, pages 285–294. IEEE, 2005.

[PV06]   C. Papadimitriou and U. Vazirani. Lecture notes for CS70: Discrete mathematics for computer science, 2006. Available from the authors' home pages.

[PY82]   C. H. Papadimitriou and M. Yannakakis. The complexity of facets (and some facets of complexity). *J. Comput. Syst. Sci.*, 28(2):244–259, 1982.

[PY88]   C. Papadimitriou and M. Yannakakis. Optimization, approximation, and complexity classes. *J. Comput. Syst. Sci.*, 43(3):425–440, 1991. Prelim version STOC '88.

[Rab72]   M. O. Rabin. Proving simultaneous positivity of linear forms. *J. Comput. Syst. Sci.*, 6:639–650, 1972.

[Rab79]   M. O. Rabin. Digitalized signatures and public-key functions as intractable as factorization. Technical Report MIT/LCS/TR-212, Massachusetts Institute of Technology, Jan. 1979.

[Rab80]   M. O. Rabin. A probabilistic algorithm for testing primality. *J. Number Theory*, 12(1):128–138, 1980.

[Raz95]   R. Raz. A parallel repetition theorem. *SIAM J. Comput.*, 27(3):763–803, 1998. Prelim version STOC '95.

[Raz00]   R. Raz. The BNS-chung criterion for multi-party communication complexity. *Computational Complexity*, 9(2):113–122, 2000.

[Raz02]   R. Raz. On the complexity of matrix product. *SIAM J. Comput.*, 32(5):1356–1369, 2003. Prelim version STOC '02.

[Raz04]   R. Raz. Multi-linear formulas for permanent and determinant are of super-polynomial size. In *STOC*, pages 633–641. ACM, 2004.

[Razb85a]   A. A. Razborov. Lower bounds on the monotone complexity of some boolean functions. *Dokl. Akad. Nauk. SSSR*, 281(4):798–801, 1985. Translation in *Soviet Math. Dokl.* 31:354–357.

[Razb85b]   A. A. Razborov. A lower bound on the monotone network complexity of the logical permanent. *Matematicheskie Zametki*, 37(6):887–900, 1985. In Russian. English translation in *Mathematical Notes of the Academy of Sciences of the USSR* 37(6):485–493.

[Razb87]   A. A. Razborov. Lower bounds on the size of bounded depth networks over a complete basis with logical addition (Russian), in Matematicheskie Zametki, 41(4):598–607, 1987. English Translation in *Mathematical Notes of the Academy of Sciences of the USSR*, 41(4):333–338, 1987.

[Razb89]   A. A. Razborov. On the method of approximations. In *STOC*, pages 169–176. ACM, 1989.

[Razb90]   A. A. Razborov. On the distributed complexity of disjointness. *Theoretical Computer Science*, 106(2):385–390, 1992. Prelim version ICALP '90.

[Razb92]   A. A. Razborov. On submodular complexity measures. In M. Paterson, editor, *Boolean Function Complexity*, pages 76–83. London Mathematical Society Lecture Note Series 169. Cambridge University Press, 1992.

[Razb95]   A. A. Razborov. Unprovability of lower bounds on the circuit size in certain fragments of bounded arithmetic. *Izvestiya of the RAN*, 59(1):201–224, 1995.

[Razb98]   A. A. Razborov. Lower bounds for the polynomial calculus. *Computational Complexity*, 7:291–324, 1998.

[Razb01]   A. A. Razborov. Improved resolution lower bounds for the weak pigeonhole principle. Technical Report TR01–055, Electronic Colloquium on Computational Complexity, 2001.

[Razb03a]   A. A. Razborov. Resolution lower bounds for the weak functional pigeonhole principle. *Theoretical Computer Science*, 303(1):233–243, 2003.

[Razb03b]   A. A. Razborov. Pseudorandom generators hard for k-DNF resolution and polynomial calculus resolution, 2003. Unpublished manuscript, available from the author's Web page.

[Razb04a]   A. A. Razborov. Resolution lower bounds for perfect matching principles. *J. Comput. Syst. Sci.*, 69(1):3–27, 2004.

[Razb04b]   A. A. Razborov. Feasible proofs and computations: Partnership and fusion. In *Proceedings of the 31st International Colloquium, Lecture Notes in Computer Science*, 3142, pages 8–14. Springer-Verlag, 2004. Also appeared in Proceedings of the 19th LICS conference.

[Ree54]   I. S. Reed. A class of multiple error-correcting codes and the decoding scheme. *IRE Trans. Information Theory*, PGIT-4:38–49, 1954.

[Reg06]   O. Regev. Lattice-based cryptography. In *Proceedings of 26th CRYPTO, Lecture Notes in Computer Science*, 4117, pages 131–141. Springer, 2006.

[Rei05]   O. Reingold. Undirected ST-connectivity in log-space. In *STOC*, pages 376–385. ACM, 2005.

[Rog87]   H. Rogers Jr. *Theory of Recursive Functions and Effective Computability*. MIT Press, 1987.

[Ros06]   K. H. Rosen. *Discrete Mathematics and Its Applications*. McGraw-Hill, 2006.

[Rot93]   D. Roth. On the hardness of approximate reasoning. *Artificial Intelligence*, 82(1–2):273–302, 1996. Prelim version IJCAI '93.

[RR94]   A. A. Razborov and S. Rudich. Natural proofs. *J. Comput. Syst. Sci.*, 55(1):24–35, 1997. Prelim version STOC '94.

[RR99]   R. Raz and O. Reingold. On recycling the randomness of states in space bounded computation. In *STOC*, pages 159–168. ACM, 1999.

[RS60]   I. S. Reed and G. Solomon. Polynomial codes over certain finite fields. *J. Soc. Industrial Applied Math.*, 8(2):300–304, 1960.

[RS91]   C. Rackoff and D. R. Simon. Non-interactive zero-knowledge proof of knowledge and chosen ciphertext attack. In *Advances in Cryptology – CRYPTO '91*, volume 576 of *Lecture Notes in Computer Science*, pages 433–444. Springer-Verlag, 1992, 11–15 Aug. 1991.

[RS92]   R. Rubinfeld and M. Sudan. Self-testing polynomial functions efficiently and over rational domains. In *SODA*, pages 23–32, 1992.

[RS93]   R. Raz and B. Spieker. On the "log rank"-conjecture in communication complexity. *Combinatorica*, 15(4):567–588, 1995. Prelim version FOCS '93.

[RS95]   A. Russell and R. Sundaram. Symmetric alternation captures BPP. *Computational Complexity*, 7(2):152–162, 1998. Prelim version MIT Tech report, 1995.

[RS97]   R. Raz and S. Safra. A sub-constant error-probability low-degree test. In *STOC*, pages 475–484. ACM, 1997.

[RSA78]   R. L. Rivest, A. Shamir, and L. Adelman. A method for obtaining digital signatures and public-key cryptosystems. *Communications of the ACM*, 21(2):120–126, 1978.

[RTS97]   J. Radhakrishnan and A. Ta-Shma. Bounds for dispersers, extractors, and depth-two superconcentrators. *SIAM J. Discrete Mathematics*, 13(1):2–24, 2000. Prelim version FOCS '97.

[RTV06]   O. Reingold, L. Trevisan, and S. Vadhan. Pseudorandom walks on regular digraphs and the RL vs. L problem. In *STOC*, pages 457–466. ACM, 2006.

[Rub90]   R. Rubinfeld. *A Mathematical Theory of Self-Checking, Self-Testing and Self-Correcting Programs*. PhD thesis, UC Berkeley, 1990.

[RV76]   R. L. Rivest and J. Vuillemin. On recognizing graph properties from adjacency matrices. *Theor. Comput. Sci.*, 3(3):371–384, 1976.

[RV05]   E. Rozenman and S. Vadhan. Derandomized squaring of graphs. In *RANDOM: International Workshop on Randomization and Approximation Techniques in Computer Science*. LNCS, 2005.

[RVW00]   O. Reingold, S. Vadhan, and A. Wigderson. Entropy waves, the zig-zag graph product, and new constant-degree expanders and extractors. In *FOCS*, pages 3–13. IEEE, 2000.

[RW93]   A. A. Razborov and A. Wigderson. $n^{\Omega(\log n)}$ Lower bounds on the size of depth-3 threshold circuits with AND gates at the bottom. *Inform. Process. Lett.*, 45(6):303–307, 1993.

[San07]   R. Santhanam. Circuit lower bounds for Merlin-Arthur classes. STOC pages 275–283. ACM, 2007.

[Sav70]   W. J. Savitch. Relationships between nondeterministic and deterministic tape complexities. *J. Comput. Syst. Sci.*, 4:177–192, 1970.

[Sav72]   J. E. Savage. Computational work and time on finite machines. *J. ACM*, 19(4):660–674, 1972.

[SBR02]   M. V. Sapir, J.-C. Birget, and E. Rips. Isoperimetric and isodiametric functions of groups. *Ann. Math. (2)*, 156(2):345–466, 2002.

[Sch37]   A. Scholz. Aufgabe 253. *Jahresber. DMV*, 1937.

[Sch44]   E. Schroedinger. *What Is Life?* Cambridge University Press, 1944.

[Sch96]   M. Schaefer. Deciding the Vapnik-Cervonenkis dimension is Σ_3^p-complete. *J. Comput. Syst. Sci.*, 58(2):177–182, 1999. Prelim version CCC '96.

[SG76]   S. Sahni and T. Gonzalez. P-complete approximation problems. *J. ACM*, 23(3):555–565, 1976.

[Sha48]   C. E. Shannon. A mathematical theory of communication. *Bell Sys. Tech. J.*, 27(3):379–423, 1948.

[Sha49a] C. E. Shannon. The synthesis of two-terminal switching circuits. *Bell Sys. Tech. J.*, 28(1):59–98, 1949.

[Sha49b] C. E. Shannon. Communication theory of secrecy systems. *Bell Sys. Tech. J.*, 28:656–715, 1949.

[Sha79] A. Shamir. Factoring numbers in O(log n) arithmetic steps. *Inf. Process. Lett.*, 8(1):28–31, 1979.

[Sha81] A. Shamir. On the generation of cryptographically strong pseudorandom sequences. *ACM Trans. Computer Sys.*, 1(1):38–44, 1983. Prelim version presented at Crypto '81 and ICALP '81.

[Sha90] A. Shamir. IP = PSPACE. *J. ACM*, 39(4):869–877, 1992. Prelim version FOCS '90.

[Sha02] R. Shaltiel. Recent developments in explicit constructions of extractors. *Bul. EATCS*, 77:67–95, 2002.

[She92] A. Shen. IP = PSPACE: Simplified proof. *J. ACM*, 39(4):878–880, 1992.

[She07] A. A. Sherstov.The pattern matrix method for lower bounds on quantum communication. Technical Report CS-TR-07-46, The University of Texas at Austin, Department of Computer Sciences, Sept. 6 2007. Thu, 3 Jan 108 21:31:32 GMT.

[Shi03] Y. Shi. Both toffoli and controlled-NOT need little help to universal quantum computing. In *Quantum Information and Computation*, volume 3. Rinton Press, 2003.

[SHL65] R. E. Stearns, J. Hartmanis, and P. M. Lewis. Hierarchies of memory limited computations. In *FOCS*, pages 179–190. IEEE, 1965.

[Sho95] P. W. Shor. Scheme for reducing decoherence in quantum computer memory. *Physical Review A*, 52(4):2493–2496, 1995.

[Sho97] P. W. Shor. Polynomial-time algorithms for prime factorization and discrete logarithms on a quantum computer. *SIAM J. Comput.*, 26(5):1484–1509, 1997.

[Sho05] V. Shoup. *A Computational Introduction to Number Theory and Algebra.* Cambridge University Press, 2005.

[Sim94] D. R. Simon. On the power of quantum computation. *SIAM J. Comput.*, 26(5):1474–1483, 1997. Prelim version FOCS '94.

[Sip83] M. Sipser. A complexity theoretic approach to randomness. In *STOC*, pages 330–335. ACM, 25–27 Apr. 1983.

[Sip86] M. Sipser. Expanders, randomness, or time versus space. *J. Comput. Syst. Sci.*, 36:379–383, 1988. Prelim version CSCT '86.

[Sip92] M. Sipser. The history and status of the P versus NP question. In *STOC*, pages 603–618. ACM, 1992.

[Sip96] M. Sipser. *Introduction to the Theory of Computation.* PWS, 1996.

[SJ88] A. Sinclair and M. Jerrum. Approximate counting, uniform generation and rapidly mixing markov chains. *Inf. Comput.*, 82(1):93–133, 1989. Prelim version International Workshop on Graph-Theoretic Concepts in Computer Science '88.

[SM73] L. J. Stockmeyer and A. R. Meyer. Word problems requiring exponential time. In *STOC*, pages 1–9. ACM, 1973.

[Smo87] R. Smolensky. Algebraic methods in the theory of lower bounds for Boolean circuit complexity. In *STOC*, pages 77–82. ACM, 1987.

[Sni81] M. Snir. Lower bounds on probabilistic linear decision trees. *Theor. Comput. Sci.*, 38(1):69–82, 1985. Prelim version ICALP '81.

[SS71] A. Schönhage and V. Strassen. Schnelle Multiplikation großer Zahlen. *Computing (Arch. Elektron. Rechnen)*, 7:281–292, 1971.

[SS77] R. Solovay and V. Strassen. A fast Monte Carlo test for primality. *SIAM J. Comput.*, 6(1):84–85, 1977.

[ST01]   D. A. Spielman and S.-H. Teng. Smoothed analysis of algorithms: Why the simplex algorithm usually takes polynomial time. *J. ACM*, 51(3):385–463, 2004. Prelim version STOC '01.

[Str69]   V. Strassen. Gaussian elimination is not optimal. *Numer. Math.*, 13:354–356, 1969.

[Str72]   V. Strassen. Berechnung und programm. I. *Act. Inf.*, 1:320–335, 1972. In German.

[Str73]   V. Strassen. Vermeidung von divisionen. *J. reine angew. Math.*, 264:184–202, 1973. In German.

[STV99]   M. Sudan, L. Trevisan, and S. Vadhan. Pseudorandom generators without the XOR lemma. *J. Comput. Syst. Sci.*, 62(2):236–266, 2001. Prelim version STOC '99.

[SU01]   R. Shaltiel and C. Umans. Simple extractors for all min-entropies and a new pseudorandom generator. *J. ACM*, 52(2):172–216, 2005. Prelim version FOCS '01.

[SU02a]   M. Schaefer and C. Umans. Completeness in the polynomial-time hierarchy: Part I. *SIGACTN: SIGACT News (ACM Special Interest Group on Automata and Computability Theory)*, 33, Sept. 2002.

[SU02b]   M. Schaefer and C. Umans. Completeness in the polynomial-time hierarchy: Part II. *SIGACTN: SIGACT News (ACM Special Interest Group on Automata and Computability Theory)*, 33, Dec. 2002.

[Sud96]   M. Sudan. Decoding of reed solomon codes beyond the error-correction bound. *J. Complexity*, 13(1):180–193, 1997. Prelim version FOCS '96.

[Sud01]   M. Sudan. Coding theory: Tutorial & survey. In *FOCS*, pages 36–53. IEEE, 2001.

[SV84]   M. Santha and U. V. Vazirani. Generating quasi-random sequences from semi-random sources. *J. Comput. Syst. Sci.*, 33(1):75–87, 1986. Prelim version FOCS '84.

[SV85]   S. Skyum and L. G. Valiant. A complexity theory based on boolean algebra. *J. ACM*, 32(2):484–502, 1985.

[SW86]   M. Saks and A. Wigderson. Probabilistic boolean decision trees and the complexity of evaluating game trees. In *FOCS*, pages 29–38. IEEE, Oct. 1986.

[SZ94]   A. Srinivasan and D. Zuckerman. Computing with very weak random sources. *SIAM J. Comput.*, 28(4):1433–1459, 1999. Prelim version FOCS '94.

[SZ95]   M. Saks and S. Zhou. $BP_H SPACE(S) \subseteq DSPACE(S^{3/2})$. *J. Comput. Syst. Sci.*, 58(2):376–403, 1999. Prelim version FOCS '95.

[Sze76]   E. Szemerédi. Regular partitions of graphs. *Problèmes combinatoires et théorie des graphes*, Orsay, 1976.

[Sze87]   R. Szelepcsényi. The method of forcing for nondeterministic automata. *Bulletin of the European Association for Theoretical Computer Science*, 33:96–100, Oct. 1987. Technical Contributions.

[Tan84]   R. M. Tanner. Explicit construction of concentrators from generalized n-gons. *SIAM J. Algebraic Discrete Methods*, 5:287–293, 1984.

[Tar88]   É. Tardos. The gap between monotone and non-monotone circuit complexity is exponential. *Combinatorica*, 8(1):141–142, 1988.

[Tod91]   S. Toda. PP is as hard as the polynomial-time hierarchy. *SIAM J. Comput.*, 20(5):865–877, 1991.

[Tra84]   B. A. Trakhtenbrot. A survey of Russian approaches to perebor (brute-force search) algorithms. *Annals of the History of Computing*, 6(4):384–400, 1984. Also contains a good translation of [Lev73].

[Tre99]   L. Trevisan. Extractors and pseudorandom generators. *J. ACM*, 48(4):860–879, 2001. Prelim version STOC '99.

[Tre05]   L. Trevisan. Inapproximability of combinatorial optimization problems. In V. Paschos, editor, *Optimisation Combinatiore*, volume 2. Hermes, 2005. English version available from author's Web page.

[Tri05]   V. Trifonov. An $O(\log n \log \log n)$ space algorithm for undirected st-connectivity. In *STOC*, pages 626–633. ACM, 2005.

[TS96]   A. Ta-Shma. On extracting randomness from weak random sources. In *STOC*, pages 276–285. ACM, May 1996.

[Tur36]   A. M. Turing. On computable numbers, with an application to the entscheidungsproblem. In *Proceedings, London Mathematical Society,*, pages 230–265, 1936. Published as *Proceedings, London Mathematical Society*, volume 2, number 42.

[TV02]   L. Trevisan and S. Vadhan. Pseudorandomness and average-case complexity via uniform reductions. *Computational Complexity, 2002. Proceedings. 17th IEEE Annual Conference on*, pages 103–112, 2002.

[TV06]   T. Tao and V. H. Vu. *Additive Combinatorics*. Cambridge University Press, 2006.

[Uma98]   C. Umans. The minimum equivalent DNF problem and shortest implicants. *J. Comput. Syst. Sci.*, 63(4):597–611, 2001. Prelim version FOCS '98.

[Uma03]   C. Umans. Pseudo-random generators for all hardnesses. *J. Comput. Syst. Sci.*, 67(2):419–440, 2003.

[Urq87]   A. Urquhart. Hard examples for resolution. *J. ACM*, 34(1):209–219, 1987.

[Vad99]   S. P. Vadhan. *A Study of Statistical Zero-Knowledge Proofs*. PhD thesis, Massachusetts Institute of Technology, 1999. Revises version to appear in Springer Series on Information Security and Cryptography, 2009.

[Vad00]   S. Vadhan. On transformation of interactive proofs that preserve the prover's complexity. In *STOC*, pages 200–207. ACM, 2000.

[Vad07]   S. Vadhan. The unified theory of pseudorandomness. *SIGACT News*, 38(2), 2007.

[Val75a]   L. G. Valiant. Graph-theoretic properties in computational complexity. *J. Comput. Syst. Sci.*, 13(3):278–285, 1976. Prelim version STOC '75.

[Val75b]   L. G. Valiant. On non-linear lower bounds in computational complexity. In *STOC*, pages 45–53. ACM, 1975.

[Val79a]   L. G. Valiant. Completeness classes in algebra. In *STOC*, pages 249–261. ACM, 1979.

[Val79b]   L. G. Valiant. The complexity of computing the permanent. *Theoretical Computer Science*, 8(2):189–201, 1979.

[Val79c]   L. G. Valiant. The complexity of enumeration and reliability problems. *SIAM J. Comput.*, 8(3):410–421, 1979.

[Val84]   L. G. Valiant. A theory of the learnable. *Commun. ACM*, 27(11):1134–1142, 1984.

[Vaz01]   V. V. Vazirani. *Approximation Algorithms*. Springer-Verlag, 2001.

[vDMV01]   W. van Dam, M. Mosca, and U. Vazirani. How powerful is adiabatic quantum computation? In *FOCS*, pages 279–287. IEEE, 14–17 Oct. 2001.

[Ver94]   O. Verbitsky. Towards the parallel repetition conjecture. In *Structure in Complexity Theory Conference*, pages 304–307, 1994.

[VG99]   J. Von zur Gathen and J. Gerhard. *Modern Computer Algebra*. Cambridge University Press, 1999.

[vM07]   D. van Melkebeek. *A survey of lower bounds for satisfiability and related Prob-lems. Foundations and Trends in Theoretical Computer Science*, 2(3):197–303, 2007.

[vN45]   J. von Neumann. First draft of a report on the EDVAC. Report for the U.S. Army Ordinance Department, University of Pensylvania, 1945. Reprinted in part in Brian Randell, editor, *The Origins of Digital Computers: Selected Papers*, Springer Verlag, 1982.

[vN51]   J. von Neumann. Various techniques used in connection with random digits. *Applied Math Series*, 12:36–38, 1951.

[VSBR81]   L. G. Valiant, S. Skyum, S. Berkowitz, and C. Rackoff. Fast parallel compu-tation of polynomials using few processors. *SIAM J. Comput.*, 12(4):641–644, 1983. Prelim version Mathematical Foundations of CS '81.

[VV85]   U. V. Vazirani and V. V. Vazirani. Random polynomial time is equal to slightly-random polynomial time. In *FOCS*, pages 417–428. IEEE, 1985.

[VV86]   L. G. Valiant and V. V. Vazirani. NP is as easy as detecting unique solutions. *Theor. Comput. Sci.*, 47(1):85–93, 1986.

[vzG88]   J. von zur Gathen. Algebraic complexity theory. *Annual Reviews Computer Science*, 3:317–347, 1988.

[vzGG99]   J. von zur Gathen and J. Gerhard. *Modern Computer Algebra*. Cambridge University Press, 1999.

[Wat03]   J. Watrous. PSPACE has constant-round quantum interactive proof systems. *Theor. Comput. Sci*, 292(3):575–588, 2003.

[Weg87]   I. Wegener. *The Complexity of Boolean Functions*. Wiley-Teubner Series in Computer Science, 1987. Online version available from http://eccc.hpi-web.de/eccc-local/ECCC-Books/wegener_book_readme.html.

[Wel93]   D. J. A. Welsh. *Complexity: Knots, Colourings and Counting*. Cambridge University Press, 1993.

[Wig06]   A. Wigderson. P, NP and mathematics – A computational complexity perspec-tivy. In *Proceedings of ICM '06*, 2006.

[Wil05]   R. Williams. Better time-space lower bounds for SAT and related problems. In *IEEE Conference on Computational Complexity*, pages 40–49. IEEE, 2005.

[Wil07]   R. Williams. Time-space tradeoffs for counting NP solutions modulo integers. Computational Complexity 17(2):179–219, 2008. Prelim version CCC '07.

[WX05]   A. Wigderson and D. Xiao. A randomness-efficient sampler for matrix-valued functions and applications. In *FOCS*, pages 397–406. IEEE, 2005. See also correction in ECCC TR05–107 Revision 01.

[WZ82]   W. K. Wooters and W. H. Zurek. A single quantum cannot be cloned. *Nature*, 299:802f, 1982.

[Yam97]   P. Yam. Bringing Schroedinger's cat back to life. *Scientific American*, pages 124–129, June 1997.

[Yan88]   M. Yannakakis. Expressing combinatorial optimization problems by linear programs. *J. Comput. Syst. Sci.*, 43(3):441–466, 1991. Prelim version STOC '88.

[Yao79]   A. C. C. Yao. Some complexity questions related to distributive comput-ing(prelim report). In *STOC*, pages 209–213. ACM, 1979.

[Yao82a]   A. C. C. Yao. Theory and applications of trapdoor functions. In *FOCS*, pages 80–91. IEEE, 3–5 Nov. 1982.

[Yao82b]   A. C. C. Yao. Protocols for secure computations. In *FOCS*, pages 160–164. IEEE, 3–5 Nov. 1982.

[Yao85]   A. C. C. Yao. Separating the polynomial-time hierarchy by oracles. In *FOCS*, pages 1–10. IEEE, 1985.

[Yao87]   A. C. C. Yao. Lower bounds to randomized algorithms for graph properties. *J. Comput. Syst. Sci.*, 42(3):267–287, 1991. Prelim version FOCS '87.

[Yao90]   A. C. C. Yao. On ACC and threshold circuits. In *FOCS*, volume II, pages 619–627. IEEE, 22–24 Oct. 1990.

[Yao93]   A. C. C. Yao. Quantum circuit complexity. In *FOCS*, pages 352–361. IEEE, 1993.

[Yao94]   A. C. C. Yao. Decision tree complexity and betti numbers. In *STOC*, pages 615–624. ACM, 1994.

[Zak83]   S. Zak. A Turing machine time hierarchy. *Theoret. Computer Sci.*, 26(3):327–333, 1983.

[Zuc90]   D. Zuckerman. General weak random sources. In *FOCS*, volume II, pages 534–543. IEEE, 22–24 Oct. 1990.

Index

Note: The page numbers in bold indicate the location where the term is defined.

Complexity class index

Printed in the United States
By Bookmasters